46

Parts 166 to 199
Revised as of October 1, 2004

Shipping

Containing a codification of documents of general applicability and future effect

As of October 1, 2004

With Ancillaries

Published by
Office of the Federal Register
National Archives and Records
Administration

A Special Edition of the Federal Register

ProStar *Publications*, Inc.

U.S. Government Printing Office
Washington: 2005

For sale by ProStar *Publications*, Inc.^{SM}
3 Church Circle, Suite 109, Annapolis, MD 21401

Table of Contents

	Page
Explanation	v

Title 46:

    Chapter I—Coast Guard, Department of Homeland Security (Continued) ... 3

Finding Aids:

    Material Approved for Incorporation by Reference ... 529

    Table of CFR Titles and Chapters ... 537

    Alphabetical List of Agencies Appearing in the CFR ... 555

    List of CFR Sections Affected ... 565

Cite this Code: CFR

To cite the regulations in this volume use title, part and section number. Thus, 46 CFR 166.01 *refers to title 46, part 166, section 01.*

Explanation

The Code of Federal Regulations is a codification of the general and permanent rules published in the Federal Register by the Executive departments and agencies of the Federal Government. The Code is divided into 50 titles which represent broad areas subject to Federal regulation. Each title is divided into chapters which usually bear the name of the issuing agency. Each chapter is further subdivided into parts covering specific regulatory areas.

Each volume of the Code is revised at least once each calendar year and issued on a quarterly basis approximately as follows:

Title 1 through Title 16..as of January 1
Title 17 through Title 27..as of April 1
Title 28 through Title 41..as of July 1
Title 42 through Title 50..as of October 1

The appropriate revision date is printed on the cover of each volume.

LEGAL STATUS

The contents of the Federal Register are required to be judicially noticed (44 U.S.C. 1507). The Code of Federal Regulations is prima facie evidence of the text of the original documents (44 U.S.C. 1510).

HOW TO USE THE CODE OF FEDERAL REGULATIONS

The Code of Federal Regulations is kept up to date by the individual issues of the Federal Register. These two publications must be used together to determine the latest version of any given rule.

To determine whether a Code volume has been amended since its revision date (in this case, October 1, 2004), consult the "List of CFR Sections Affected (LSA)," which is issued monthly, and the "Cumulative List of Parts Affected," which appears in the Reader Aids section of the daily Federal Register. These two lists will identify the Federal Register page number of the latest amendment of any given rule.

EFFECTIVE AND EXPIRATION DATES

Each volume of the Code contains amendments published in the Federal Register since the last revision of that volume of the Code. Source citations for the regulations are referred to by volume number and page number of the Federal Register and date of publication. Publication dates and effective dates are usually not the same and care must be exercised by the user in determining the actual effective date. In instances where the effective date is beyond the cut-off date for the Code a note has been inserted to reflect the future effective date. In those instances where a regulation published in the Federal Register states a date certain for expiration, an appropriate note will be inserted following the text.

OMB CONTROL NUMBERS

The Paperwork Reduction Act of 1980 (Pub. L. 96–511) requires Federal agencies to display an OMB control number with their information collection request.

Many agencies have begun publishing numerous OMB control numbers as amendments to existing regulations in the CFR. These OMB numbers are placed as close as possible to the applicable recordkeeping or reporting requirements.

OBSOLETE PROVISIONS

Provisions that become obsolete before the revision date stated on the cover of each volume are not carried. Code users may find the text of provisions in effect on a given date in the past by using the appropriate numerical list of sections affected. For the period before January 1, 2001, consult either the List of CFR Sections Affected, 1949–1963, 1964–1972, 1973–1985, or 1986–2000, published in 11 separate volumes. For the period beginning January 1, 2001, a "List of CFR Sections Affected" is published at the end of each CFR volume.

INCORPORATION BY REFERENCE

What is incorporation by reference? Incorporation by reference was established by statute and allows Federal agencies to meet the requirement to publish regulations in the Federal Register by referring to materials already published elsewhere. For an incorporation to be valid, the Director of the Federal Register must approve it. The legal effect of incorporation by reference is that the material is treated as if it were published in full in the Federal Register (5 U.S.C. 552(a)). This material, like any other properly issued regulation, has the force of law.

What is a proper incorporation by reference? The Director of the Federal Register will approve an incorporation by reference only when the requirements of 1 CFR part 51 are met. Some of the elements on which approval is based are:

(a) The incorporation will substantially reduce the volume of material published in the Federal Register.

(b) The matter incorporated is in fact available to the extent necessary to afford fairness and uniformity in the administrative process.

(c) The incorporating document is drafted and submitted for publication in accordance with 1 CFR part 51.

Properly approved incorporations by reference in this volume are listed in the Finding Aids at the end of this volume.

What if the material incorporated by reference cannot be found? If you have any problem locating or obtaining a copy of material listed in the Finding Aids of this volume as an approved incorporation by reference, please contact the agency that issued the regulation containing that incorporation. If, after contacting the agency, you find the material is not available, please notify the Director of the Federal Register, National Archives and Records Administration, Washington DC 20408, or call (202) 741-6010.

CFR INDEXES AND TABULAR GUIDES

A subject index to the Code of Federal Regulations is contained in a separate volume, revised annually as of January 1, entitled CFR INDEX AND FINDING AIDS. This volume contains the Parallel Table of Statutory Authorities and Agency Rules (Table I). A list of CFR titles, chapters, and parts and an alphabetical list of agencies publishing in the CFR are also included in this volume.

An index to the text of "Title 3—The President" is carried within that volume.

The Federal Register Index is issued monthly in cumulative form. This index is based on a consolidation of the "Contents" entries in the daily Federal Register.

A List of CFR Sections Affected (LSA) is published monthly, keyed to the revision dates of the 50 CFR titles.

REPUBLICATION OF MATERIAL

There are no restrictions on the republication of material appearing in the Code of Federal Regulations.

INQUIRIES

For a legal interpretation or explanation of any regulation in this volume, contact the issuing agency. The issuing agency's name appears at the top of odd-numbered pages.

For inquiries concerning CFR reference assistance, call 202-741-6000 or write to the Director, Office of the Federal Register, National Archives and Records Administration, Washington, DC 20408 or e-mail fedreg.info@nara.gov.

SALES

The Government Printing Office (GPO) processes all sales and distribution of the CFR. For payment by credit card, call toll free, 866-512-1800 or DC area, 202-512-1800, M-F, 8 a.m. to 4 p.m. e.s.t. or fax your order to 202-512-2250, 24 hours a day. For payment by check, write to the Superintendent of Documents, Attn: New Orders, P.O. Box 371954, Pittsburgh, PA 15250-7954. For GPO Customer Service call 202-512-1803.

ELECTRONIC SERVICES

The full text of the Code of Federal Regulations, the LSA (List of CFR Sections Affected), The United States Government Manual, the Federal Register, Public Laws, Public Papers, Weekly Compilation of Presidential Documents and the Privacy Act Compilation are available in electronic format at www.access.gpo.gov/nara ("GPO Access"). For more information, contact Electronic Information Dissemination Services, U.S. Government Printing Office. Phone 202-512-1530, or 888-293-6498 (toll-free). E-mail, gpoaccess@gpo.gov.

The Office of the Federal Register also offers a free service on the National Archives and Records Administration's (NARA) World Wide Web site for public law numbers, Federal Register finding aids, and related information. Connect to NARA's web site at www.archives.gov/federal_register. The NARA site also contains links to GPO Access.

RAYMOND A. MOSLEY,
Director,
Office of the Federal Register.

October 1, 2004.

THIS TITLE

Title 46—SHIPPING is composed of nine volumes. The parts in these volumes are arranged in the following order: Parts 1–40, 41–69, 70–89, 90–139, 140–155, 156–165, 166–199, 200–499 and 500 to End. The first seven volumes containing parts 1–199 comprise chapter I—Coast Guard, DHS. The eighth volume, containing parts 200 to 499, includes chapter II—Maritime Administration, DOT and chapter III—Coast Guard (Great Lakes Pilotage), DHS. The ninth volume, containing part 500 to End, includes chapter IV—Federal Maritime Commission. The contents of these volumes represent all current regulations codified under this title of the CFR as of October 1, 2004.

Subject indexes appear in chapter I, subchapters A—I, I-A, J, K, L, and Q—W following the subchapters.

For this volume, Cheryl E. Sirofchuck was Chief Editor. The Code of Federal Regulations publication program is under the direction of Frances D. McDonald, assisted by Alomha S. Morris.

Would you like to know...

if any changes have been made to the *Code of Federal Regulations* or what documents have been published in the *Federal Register* without reading the *Federal Register* every day? If so, you may wish to subscribe to the *LSA* (List of CFR Sections Affected), the *Federal Register Index,* or both.

LSA
The *LSA* (List of CFR Sections Affected) is designed to lead users of the *Code of Federal Regulations* to amendatory actions published in the *Federal Register.* The *LSA* is issued monthly in cumulative form. Entries indicate the nature of the changes—such as revised, removed, or corrected. $31 per year.

Federal Register Index
The index, covering the contents of the daily *Federal Register,* is issued monthly in cumulative form. Entries are carried primarily under the names of the issuing agencies. Significant subjects are carried as cross-references.
$28 per year.

A finding aid is included in each publication which lists *Federal Register* page numbers with the date of publication in the *Federal Register.*

Superintendent of Documents Subscription Order Form

Order Processing Code: ***5421**

☐ **YES,** send me the following indicated subscriptions for one year:

____ **LSA (List of CFR Sections Affected),** (LCS) for $31 per year.

____ **Federal Register Index** (FRSU) $28 per year.

The total cost of my order is $ _____.
Price is subject to change. International customers please add 25%.

_____
Company or personal name

_____
Street address

_____
City, State, ZIP code

_____
Daytime phone with area code

_____
Purchase order No.   (optional)

(Includes regular shipping and handling.)

For privacy check box below:
☐ Do not make my name available to other mailers

Check method of payment:
☐ Check payable to Superintendent of Documents
☐ GPO Deposit Account ☐☐☐☐☐☐☐–☐
☐ VISA ☐ MasterCard ☐☐☐☐ (expiration date)

Credit card No.   (must be 20 digits)

Thank you for your order!

_____
Authorizing signature   7/00

Mail To: Superintendent of Documents
P.O. Box 371954
Pittsburgh, PA 15250–7954

Fax your orders (202) 512–2250
Phone your orders (202) 512–1800

Title 46—Shipping

(This book contains parts 166 to 199)

	Part
CHAPTER I—Coast Guard, Department of Homeland Security (Continued)	166

CHAPTER I—COAST GUARD, DEPARTMENT OF HOMELAND SECURITY (CONTINUED)

SUBCHAPTER R—NAUTICAL SCHOOLS

Part		Page
166	Designation and approval of nautical school ships	5
167	Public nautical school ships	6
168	Civilian nautical school vessels	28
169	Sailing school vessels	31
	Index	85

SUBCHAPTER S—SUBDIVISION AND STABILITY

170	Stability requirements for all inspected vessels	95
171	Special rules pertaining to vessels carrying passengers	111
172	Special rules pertaining to bulk cargoes	144
173	Special rules pertaining to vessel use	157
174	Special rules pertaining to specific vessel types	168
	Index	183

SUBCHAPTER T—SMALL PASSENGER VESSELS (UNDER 100 GROSS TONS)

175	General provisions	191
176	Inspection and certification	205
177	Construction and arrangement	225
178	Intact stability and seaworthiness	235
179	Subdivision, damage stability, and watertight integrity	242
180	Lifesaving equipment and arrangements	248
181	Fire protection equipment	260
182	Machinery installation	268
183	Electrical installation	288
184	Vessel control and miscellaneous systems and equipment	297
185	Operations	302

Part		Page
186–187	[Reserved]	
	Index	317

SUBCHAPTER U—OCEANOGRAPHIC RESEARCH VESSELS

188	General provisions	330
189	Inspection and certification	344
190	Construction and arrangement	359
191–192	[Reserved]	
193	Fire protection equipment	368
194	Handling, use, and control of explosives and other hazardous materials	381
195	Vessel control and miscellaneous systems and equipment	391
196	Operations	398
	Index	411

SUBCHAPTER V—MARINE OCCUPATIONAL SAFETY AND HEALTH STANDARDS

197	General provisions	422
198	[Reserved]	
	Index	465

SUBCHAPTER W—LIFESAVING APPLIANCES AND ARRANGEMENTS

199	Lifesaving systems for certain inspected vessels	471
	Index	519

SUBCHAPTER R—NAUTICAL SCHOOLS

PART 166—DESIGNATION AND APPROVAL OF NAUTICAL SCHOOL SHIPS

Sec.
166.01 Approval of nautical school ships.
166.05 Course of study for deck students.
166.10 Course of study for engineering students.
166.15 Training for maintenance of discipline; ship sanitation; fire and lifeboat drills.
166.20 Applicants for certificates; when eligible for examination.

AUTHORITY: 46 U.S.C. 2103, 3306, 8105; 46 U.S.C. App. 1295g; Department of Homeland Security Delegation No. 0170.1.

SOURCE: CGFR 52–43, 17 FR 9542, Oct. 18, 1952, unless otherwise noted.

§ 166.01 Approval of nautical school ships.

(a) Under 46 U.S.C. 7315, graduation from a nautical school vessel may be substituted for the service requirements for able seaman and qualified member of the engine department endorsements or merchant mariner's documents.

(b) It has been made to appear to the satisfaction of the Commandant that the school ships operated by the States in which they are located; namely, by the California Maritime Academy, Great Lakes Maritime Academy at Northwestern Michigan College, Maine Maritime Academy, Massachusetts Maritime Academy, New York State Maritime College, and Texas Maritime Academy, and by the United States Merchant Marine Academy, the United States Naval Academy, and the United States Coast Guard Academy, have adopted a course of study for their students complying with the rules prescribed by the Commandant, and a system of instruction adequate to equip the deck and engineering students theoretically and physically in the rudiments of seamanship and navigation necessary to qualify the graduates for the rating of "able seamen" and in all branches of marine engineering necessary to qualify the graduates for the rating of "qualified member of the engine department," respectively.

(c) The school ships operated by the State organizations and the Federal academies named in paragraph (b) of this section are hereby approved and their graduates, if meeting the other qualifications required by law and regulations promulgated thereunder, are entitled to the rating of able seamen or qualified members of the engine department and to be certified as such.

(d) A graduate of any of those school ships, if meeting the other qualifications required by law and regulations promulgated thereunder, is also entitled to the rating of lifeboatman and to be certified as such.

[CGFR 52–43, 17 FR 9542, Oct. 18, 1952, as amended by CGD 72–92R, 38 FR 29320, Oct. 24, 1973; CGD 95–028, 62 FR 51216, Sept. 30, 1997]

§ 166.05 Course of study for deck students.

The course of study for deck students shall include (a) all the instructions in the rudiments of seamanship and navigation necessary to equip the student fully with the theoretical knowledge required for the proper discharge of the duties developing upon able seaman; (b) a thorough practical training in the mechanics of all operations incident to the sailing and management of a vessel insofar as such operations form a part of the duties of able seamen.

§ 166.10 Course of study for engineering students.

The course of study for engineering students shall include (a) all the instruction necessary to fully equip the student with the theoretical knowledge required for the proper discharge of the duties developing upon qualified members of the engine department; (b) a thorough practical training in the mechanics of all operations incident to the sailing and management of a vessel insofar as such operations form a part of the duties of qualified members of the engine department.

§ 166.15 Training for maintenance of discipline; ship sanitation; fire and lifeboat drills.

All students shall be trained to obey all lawful orders emanating from their

§ 166.20

superior officers and schooled in the rules of conduct to be observed in order that proper discipline may be maintained on shipboard. They shall also be instructed in the fundamentals of ship sanitation as prescribed by law and regulations, and shall be given intensive instruction and practical training in all the operations incident to fire and lifeboat drills, both in port and at sea.

§ 166.20 Applicants for certificates; when eligible for examination.

Applicants for certificates as able seamen will be eligible for examination after they have completed a course of study as outlined in §§ 166.05, 166.15, and applicants for certificates as qualified members of the engine department after they have completed a course of study as outlined in §§ 166.10, 166.15.

PART 167—PUBLIC NAUTICAL SCHOOL SHIPS

Subpart 167.01—General Provisions

Sec.
167.01-1 Basis and purpose of part.
167.01-5 Application of regulations.
167.01-7 Ocean or unlimited coastwise vessels on inland and Great Lakes routes.
167.01-8 Inspection of school ships using gross tonnage criterion.
167.01-10 Effective date of regulations.
167.01-15 Specifications for articles or materials.
167.01-20 OMB control numbers assigned pursuant to the Paperwork Reduction Act.

Subpart 167.05—Definitions

167.05-1 Definition of terms.
167.05-5 Approved.
167.05-10 Commandant.
167.05-15 Coast Guard District Commander.
167.05-20 Marine inspector or inspector.
167.05-25 Nautical school ship.
167.05-30 Officer in Charge, Marine Inspection.
167.05-35 Public nautical school.
167.05-40 Underwater survey.

Subpart 167.10—Enforcement and Right of Appeal

167.10-1 Enforcement.
167.10-50 Right of appeal.

Subpart 167.15—Inspections

167.15-1 Inspections required.

167.15-5 Authority of marine inspectors.
167.15-10 Application for annual inspection.
167.15-15 Application for inspection of a new nautical school ship or a conversion of a vessel to a nautical school ship.
167.15-20 Inspections of nautical school ships.
167.15-25 Inspection standards for hulls, boilers and machinery.
167.15-27 Definitions relating to hull examinations.
167.15-28 Inspection of lifesaving appliances and arrangements.
167.15-30 Drydock examination, internal structural examination, and underwater survey intervals.
167.15-33 Underwater Survey in Lieu of Drydocking (UWILD).
167.15-35 Notice and plans required.
167.15-40 Integral fuel oil tank examinations—T/ALL.
167.15-50 Tailshaft examinations.

Subpart 167.20—Hull Requirements, Construction and Arrangement of Nautical School Ships

167.20-1 Construction.
167.20-7 Subdivision and stability.
167.20-10 Means of escape.
167.20-15 Scupper, sanitary and similar discharges.
167.20-17 Bilge pumps, bilge piping and sounding arrangements.
167.20-35 Liquid ballast.

Subpart 167.25—Marine Engineering

167.25-1 Boilers, pressure vessels, piping and appurtenances.
167.25-5 Inspection of boilers, pressure vessels, piping and appurtenances.

Subpart 167.30—Repairs or Alterations

167.30-1 Notice of repairs or alterations required.
167.30-5 Proceeding to another port for repairs.
167.30-10 Special operating requirements.

Subpart 167.35—Lifesaving Equipment

167.35-1 General.

Subpart 167.40—Certain Equipment Requirements

167.40-1 Electrical installations.
167.40-5 Alarm bells.
167.40-7 Voice tubes, telephone, and telegraph systems.
167.40-20 Deep-sea sounding apparatus.
167.40-25 Signaling lamp.
167.40-30 Guards and rails.
167.40-40 Radar.
167.40-45 Magnetic compass and gyrocompass.

Coast Guard, DHS

Subpart 167.43—Work Vests

167.43-1 Application.
167.43-5 Approved types of work vests.
167.43-10 Use.
167.43-15 Shipboard stowage.
167.43-20 Shipboard inspections.
167.43-25 Additional requirements for hybrid work vests.

Subpart 167.45—Special Firefighting and Fire Prevention Requirements

167.45-1 Steam, carbon dioxide, and halon fire extinguishing systems.
167.45-5 Steam fire pumps or their equivalent.
167.45-10 Couplings on fire hose.
167.45-15 Capacity of pipes and hose.
167.45-20 Examination and testing of pumps and fire-extinguishing equipment.
167.45-25 Fire mains and hose connections.
167.45-30 Use of approved fire-fighting equipment.
167.45-40 Fire-fighting equipment on nautical school ships using oil as fuel.
167.45-45 Carbon dioxide fire-extinguishing system requirements.
167.45-50 Foam smothering system requirements.
167.45-60 Emergency breathing apparatus and flame safety lamps.
167.45-65 Portable fire extinguishers in accommodation spaces.
167.45-70 Portable fire extinguishers, general requirements.
167.45-75 Fire extinguishers for emergency powerplants.
167.45-80 Fire axes.

Subpart 167.50—Accommodations

167.50-1 Hospital accommodations.

Subpart 167.55—Special Markings Required

167.55-1 Draft marks and draft indicating systems.
167.55-5 Marking of fire and emergency equipment.

Subpart 167.60—Certificates of Inspection

167.60-1 Issuance by Officer in Charge, Marine Inspection.
167.60-5 Period of time for which valid.
167.60-10 Exhibition of certificate of inspection.
167.60-15 Manning and persons allowed to be carried.

Subpart 167.65—Special Operating Requirements

167.65-1 Emergency training, musters, and drills.
167.65-5 Flashing the rays of a searchlight or other blinding light.
167.65-15 Routing instructions; strict compliance with.
167.65-20 Unnecessary whistling.
167.65-25 Steering gear tests.
167.65-35 Use of auto pilot.
167.65-38 Loading doors.
167.65-40 Draft.
167.65-42 Verification of vessel compliance with applicable stability requirements.
167.65-45 Notice to mariners; aids to navigation.
167.65-50 Posting placards of lifesaving signals.
167.65-60 Examination of boilers and machinery by engineer.
167.65-65 Notice and reporting of casualty and voyage records.
167.65-70 Reports of accidents, repairs, and unsafe boilers and machinery by engineers.

AUTHORITY: 46 U.S.C. 3306, 3307, 6101, 8105; E.O. 12234, 45 FR 58801, 3 CFR, 1980 Comp., p. 277; Department of Homeland Security Delegation No. 0170.1.

SOURCE: CGFR 51-11, 16 FR 3218, Apr. 12, 1951, unless otherwise noted.

Subpart 167.01—General Provisions

§ 167.01-1 Basis and purpose of part.

The rules and regulations in this part are prescribed and apply to public nautical school ships, except vessels of the Navy or Coast Guard. It is the intent of the regulations in this part to provide minimum standards for vessels used as nautical school ships in accordance with the various inspection statutes and to obtain their correct and uniform application. This part is not applicable to civilian nautical school ships.

[CGD 95-028, 62 FR 51216, Sept. 30, 1997]

§ 167.01-5 Application of regulations.

(a) Regulations in this part contain requirements for the design, construction, inspection, lifesaving equipment, firefighting and fire prevention requirements, special operating requirements and number of persons allowed to be carried on nautical school ships.

(b) Vessels owned or chartered by the United States Maritime Administration that may be used by or in connection with any nautical school are not normally considered as merchant vessels of the United States and, therefore, are not documented.

§ 167.01-7

(c) Documented nautical school ships of 500 gross tons or more, on international voyages, shall comply with the standards of the International Convention for Safety of Life at Sea, 1974, for cargo vessels.

[CGFR 51-11, 16 FR 3218, Apr. 12, 1951, as amended by CGFR 69-127, 35 FR 9982, June 17, 1970; CGD 90-008, 55 FR 30663, July 26, 1990]

§ 167.01-7 Ocean or unlimited coastwise vessels on inland and Great Lakes routes.

(a) Vessels inspected and certificated for ocean or unlimited coastwise routes shall be considered suitable for navigation insofar as the provisions of this subchapter are concerned on any inland route, including the Great Lakes.

[CGFR 59-10, 24 FR 3240, Apr. 25, 1959]

§ 167.01-8 Inspection of school ships using gross tonnage criterion.

(a) One of the criteria used for invocation of safety standards is the descriptions of school ships by relative sizes in gross tonnages. When it is determined in accordance with § 70.05-20 of this chapter that a particular school ship has a Bureau of Customs' assigned gross register tonnage which is not indicative of the relative physical size of the vessel, the requirements in this part and the manning shall be that applicable to a vessel of the greater relative size.

[CGFR 60-50, 25 FR 7982, Aug. 18, 1960]

§ 167.01-10 Effective date of regulations.

(a) The regulations in this part shall be in effect on and after July 1, 1951: *Provided*, That amendments, revisions, or additions shall become effective 90 days after the date of publication in the FEDERAL REGISTER unless the Commandant shall fix a different time.

(b) Amendments to regulations in this part will not be retroactive in effect unless specifically made so at the time the amendments are issued.

§ 167.01-15 Specifications for articles or materials.

Articles of equipment or materials used in the equipment or the construction of vessels, which conform to the specifications of the Navy or Coast Guard or their approved equivalent, may be accepted.

§ 167.01-20 OMB control numbers assigned pursuant to the Paperwork Reduction Act.

(a) *Purpose*. This section collects and displays the control numbers assigned to information collection and recordkeeping requirements in this subchapter by the Office of Management and Budget (OMB) pursuant to the Paperwork Reduction Act of 1980 (44 U.S.C. 3501 *et seq.*). The Coast Guard intends that this section comply with the requirements of 44 U.S.C. 3507(f), which requires that agencies display a current control number assigned by the Director of the OMB for each approved agency information collection requirement.

(b) *Display*.

46 CFR part or section where identified or described	Current OMB control No
§ 167.15-35	1625-0032
§ 167.65-38	1625-0064
§ 167.65-42	1625-0064

[CGD 88-072, 53 FR 34298, Sept. 6, 1988, as amended by CGD 89-037, 57 FR 41824, Sept. 11, 1992; USCG-2004-18884, 69 FR 58350, Sept. 30, 2004]

Subpart 167.05—Definitions

§ 167.05-1 Definition of terms.

Certain terms used in the regulations of this part are defined in this subpart.

§ 167.05-5 Approved.

This term means approved by the Commandant unless otherwise stated.

§ 167.05-10 Commandant.

This term means Commandant of the Coast Guard.

§ 167.05-15 Coast Guard District Commander.

This term means an officer of the Coast Guard designated as such by the Commandant to command all Coast Guard activities within the officer's district, which include the inspections, enforcement, and administration of Subtitle II of Title 46, U.S. Code, Title

Coast Guard, DHS

46 and Title 33 U.S. Code, and regulations issued under these statutes.

[CGD 95–028, 62 FR 51216, Sept. 30, 1997]

§ 167.05–20 Marine inspector or inspector.

These terms mean any person from the civilian or military branch of the Coast Guard assigned under the superintendence and direction of an Officer in Charge, Marine Inspection, or any other person as may be designated for the performance of duties with respect to the inspections, enforcement, and administration of Subtitle II of Title 46, U.S. Code, Title 46 and Title 33 U.S. Code, and regulations issued under these statutes.

[CGD 95–028, 62 FR 51217, Sept. 30, 1997]

§ 167.05–25 Nautical school ship.

The term *nautical school ship* means a vessel operated by or in connection with a nautical school or an educational institution under Section 13 of the Coast Guard Authorization Act of 1986.

[CGD 84–069, 61 FR 25311, May 20, 1996]

§ 167.05–30 Officer in Charge, Marine Inspection.

This term means any person from the civilian or military branch of the Coast Guard designated as such by the Commandant and who, under the superintendence and direction of the Coast Guard District Commander, is in charge of an inspection zone for the performance of duties with respect to the inspections, enforcement, and administration of Subtitle II of Title 46, U.S. Code, Title 46 and Title 33 U.S. Code, and regulations issued under these statutes.

[CGD 95–028, 62 FR 51217, Sept. 30, 1997]

§ 167.05–35 Public nautical school.

The term *public nautical school* means any school or branch thereof operated by any State or political subdivision thereof or a school operated by the United States Maritime Administration that offers instruction for the primary purpose of training for service in the merchant marine.

[CGD 84–069, 61 FR 25311, May 20, 1996]

§ 167.05–40 Underwater survey.

Underwater survey means the examination of the vessel's underwater hull including all through-hull fittings and appurtenances, while the vessel is afloat.

[USCG–2000–6858, 67 FR 21082, Apr. 29, 2002]

Subpart 167.10—Enforcement and Right of Appeal

§ 167.10–1 Enforcement.

The Officer in Charge, Marine Inspection, is responsible for the performance of duties within the officer's jurisdiction with respect to inspection of nautical school ships.

[CGD 95–028, 62 FR 51217, Sept. 30, 1997]

§ 167.10–50 Right of appeal.

Any person directly affected by a decision or action taken under this part, by or on behalf of the Coast Guard, may appeal therefrom in accordance with subpart 1.03 of this chapter.

[CGD 88–033, 54 FR 50381, Dec. 6, 1989]

Subpart 167.15—Inspections

§ 167.15–1 Inspections required.

(a) Before a vessel may be used as a nautical school ship, it shall be inspected by the Coast Guard to determine that the hull, boilers, machinery, equipment and appliances comply with the regulations in this part.

(b) Every nautical school ship subject to the regulations in this part shall be inspected annually, or oftener if necessary, by the Coast Guard to determine that the hull, boilers, machinery, equipment and appliances comply with the regulations in this part.

(c) Nautical school ships while laid up and dismantled and out of commission are exempt from any or all inspections required by law or regulations in this part.

§ 167.15–5 Authority of marine inspectors.

Marine inspectors may at any time lawfully inspect any nautical school ship.

§ 167.15-10 Application for annual inspection.

Application in writing for the annual inspection of every nautical school ship required to be inspected by law and the regulations in this part shall be made by the master, owner, or agent to the Officer in Charge, Marine Inspection, at any local Marine Inspection Office, U.S. Coast Guard, where the nautical school ship may be operating. The application shall be on Form CG 3752, Application for Inspection of U.S. Vessel, which requires information on name and type of vessel, nature of employment and route in which to be operated, place where and date when the vessel may be inspected, and that no other application has been made to any Officer in Charge, Marine Inspection, since the issuance of the last valid certificate of inspection.

[CGFR 51–11, 16 FR 3218, Apr. 12, 1951, as amended by CGFR 64–19, 29 FR 7361, June 5, 1964]

§ 167.15-15 Application for inspection of a new nautical school ship or a conversion of a vessel to a nautical school ship.

Prior to the commencement of the construction of a new nautical school ship, or a conversion of a vessel to a nautical school ship, application for the approval of contract plans and specifications and for a certificate of inspection shall be made in writing by the owner or agent to the Officer in Charge, Marine Inspection, at the nearest local Marine Inspection Office, U.S. Coast Guard.

§ 167.15-20 Inspections of nautical school ships.

(a) At each annual inspection, or oftener if deemed necessary, the inspector will inspect the hull, boilers, machinery, equipment, and appliances generally for compliance with the regulations in this subpart and in addition will inspect and test certain specific items as specifically set forth in this part.

(b) To renew a Certificate of Inspection, you must submit an application at least 30 days before the expiration of the vessel's current certificate.

[CGFR 51–11, 16 FR 3218, Apr. 12, 1951, as amended by USCG–1999–4976, 65 FR 6507, Feb. 9, 2000]

§ 167.15-25 Inspection standards for hulls, boilers and machinery.

Except as otherwise provided by law or regulations in this subpart, the following standards shall be accepted as standard by the inspectors:

(a) American Bureau of Shipping "Rules for Building and Classing Steel Vessels" regarding the construction of hulls, boilers and machinery in effect on the date of inspection. These rules may be purchased from the American Bureau of Shipping (ABS), ABS Plaza, 16855 Northchase Drive, Houston, TX 77060.

(b) U. S. Navy Standard Construction Specification in effect on the date of inspection.

(c) U. S. Coast Guard Standard Construction Specification in effect on the date of inspection.

[CGFR 51–11, 16 FR 3218, Apr. 12, 1951, as amended by USCG–1999–6216, 64 FR 53228, Oct. 1, 1999; USCG–2000–7790, 65 FR 58464, Sept. 29, 2000]

§ 167.15-27 Definitions relating to hull examinations.

As used in this part—

(a) *Drydock examination* means hauling out a vessel or placing a vessel in a drydock or slipway for an examination of all accessible parts of the vessel's underwater body and all through-hull fittings, sea chests, sea valves, sea strainers, and valves for the emergency bilge suction.

(b) *Internal structural examination* means an examination of the vessel while afloat or in drydock and consists of a complete examination of the vessel's main strength members, including the major internal framing, the hull plating, voids, and ballast tanks, but not including cargo or fuel oil tanks.

[CGD 84–024, 52 FR 39655, Oct. 23, 1987, as amended at 53 FR 32232, Aug. 24, 1988]

§ 167.15-28 Inspection of lifesaving appliances and arrangements.

The inspection of lifesaving appliances and arrangements must be in accordance with the requirements for special purpose vessels in subchapter W (Lifesaving Appliances and Arrangements) of this chapter.

[CGD 84–069, 61 FR 25311, May 20, 1996]

§ 167.15–30 Drydock examination, internal structural examination, and underwater survey intervals.

(a) Except as provided for in paragraphs (b) through (e) of this section, each vessel must undergo drydock and internal structural examinations as follows:

(1) If your vessel operates in saltwater, it must undergo two drydock examinations and two internal structural examinations within any 5-year period unless it has been approved to undergo an underwater survey (UWILD) under § 167.15–33 of this part. No more than three years may elapse between any two examinations.

(2) If your vessel operated in fresh water at least 50 percent of the time since your last drydocking, it must undergo a dry dock and internal structural examination at intervals not to exceed 5 years unless it has been approved to undergo an underwater survey (UWILD) under § 167.15–33 of this part.

(b) Vessels with wooden hulls must undergo two drydock and two internal structural examinations within any five year period regardless of the type of water in which they operate. No more than three years may elapse between any two examinations.

(c) If, during an internal structural examination damage or deterioration to the hull plating or structural members is discovered, the Officer in Charge, Marine Inspection, may require the vessel to be drydocked or otherwise taken out of service to further assess the extent of the damage and to effect permanent repairs.

(d) Each vessel which has not met with the applicable examination schedules in paragraphs (a) through (c) of this section because it is on a voyage, must undergo the required examinations upon completion of the voyage.

(e) The Commandant (G–MOC) may authorize extensions to the examination intervals specified in paragraphs (a) and (b) of this section.

[CGD 84–024, 52 FR 39655, Oct. 23, 1987, as amended at 53 FR 32232, Aug. 24, 1988; CGD 95–072, 60 FR 50467, Sept. 29, 1995; CGD 96–041, 61 FR 50734, Sept. 27, 1996; USCG–2000–6858, 67 FR 21082, Apr. 29, 2002]

§ 167.15–33 Underwater Survey in Lieu of Drydocking (UWILD).

(a) The Officer in Charge, Marine Inspection (OCMI), may approve an underwater survey instead of a drydock examination at alternating intervals if your vessel is—

(1) Less than 15 years of age;
(2) A steel or aluminum hulled vessel;
(3) Fitted with an effective hull protection system; and
(4) Described in 46 CFR 167.15–30(a)(1) or (2).

(b) For vessels less than 15 years of age, you must submit an application for an underwater survey to the OCMI at least 90 days before your vessel's next required drydock examination. The application must include—

(1) The procedure for carrying out the underwater survey;
(2) The time and place of the underwater survey;
(3) The method used to accurately determine the diver's or remotely operated vehicle's (ROV) location relative to the hull;
(4) The means for examining all through-hull fittings and appurtenances;
(5) The means for taking shaft bearing clearances;
(6) The condition of the vessel, including the anticipated draft of the vessel at the time of survey;
(7) A description of the hull protection system; and
(8) The name and qualifications of any third party examiner.

(c) If your vessel is 15 years old or older, the District Commander, may approve an underwater survey instead of a drydock examination at alternating intervals. You must submit an application for an underwater survey to the OCMI at least 90 days before your vessel's next required drydock examination. You may be allowed this option if—

(1) The vessel is qualified under paragraphs (a)(2) through (4) of this section;

§ 167.15-35

(2) Your application includes the information in paragraphs (b)(1) through (b)(8) of this section; and

(3) During the vessel's drydock examination, preceding the underwater survey, a complete set of hull gaugings was taken and they indicated that the vessel was free from appreciable hull deterioration.

(d) After the drydock examination required in paragraph (c)(3) of this section, the Officer in Charge, Marine Inspection submits a recommendation for future underwater surveys, the results of the hull gauging, and the results of the Coast Guards' drydock examination results to the cognizant District Commander for review.

[USCG-2000-6858, 67 FR 21083, Apr. 29, 2002]

§ 167.15-35 Notice and plans required.

(a) The master, owner, operator, or agent of the vessel shall notify the Officer in Charge, Marine Inspection, whenever the vessel is to be drydocked regardless of the reason for drydocking.

(b) Each vessel, except barges, that holds a Load Line Certificate must have on board a plan showing the vessel's scantlings. This plan must be made available to the Coast Guard marine inspector whenever the vessel undergoes a drydock examination, internal structural examination, underwater survey, or whenever repairs are made to the vessel's hull.

(c) Each barge that holds a Load Line Certificate must have a plan showing the barge's scantlings. The plan need not be maintained on board the barge but must be made available to the Coast Guard marine inspector whenever the barge undergoes a drydock examination, internal structural examination, underwater survey, or whenever repairs are made to the barge's hull.

[CGD 84-024, 52 FR 39655, Oct. 23, 1987; USCG-2000-6858, 67 FR 21083, Apr. 29, 2002]

§ 167.15-40 Integral fuel oil tank examinations—T/ALL.

(a) Each fuel oil tank with at least one side integral to the vessel's hull and located within the hull ("integral fuel oil tank") is subject to inspection as provided in this section. The owner or operator of the vessel shall have the tanks cleaned out and gas freed as necessary to permit internal examination of the tank or tanks designated by the marine inspector. The owner or operator shall arrange for an examination of the fuel tanks of each vessel during an internal structural examination at intervals not to exceed five years.

(b) Integral non-double-bottom fuel oil tanks need not be cleaned out and internally examined if the marine inspector is able to determine by external examination that the general condition of the tanks is satisfactory.

(c) Double-bottom fuel oil tanks on vessels less than 10 years of age need not be cleaned out and internally examined if the marine inspector is able to determine by external examination that the general condition of the tanks is satisfactory.

(d) Double-bottom fuel oil tanks on vessels 10 years of age or older but less than 15 years of age need not be cleaned out and internally examined if the marine inspector is able to determine by internal examination of at least one forward double-bottom fuel oil tank, and by external examination of all other double-bottom fuel oil tanks on the vessel, that the general condition of the tanks is satisfactory.

(e) All double-bottom fuel oil tanks on vessels 15 years of age or older need not be cleaned out and internally examined if the marine inspector is able to determine by internal examination of at least one forward, one amidships, and one aft double-bottom fuel oil tank, and by external examination of all other double-bottom fuel oil tanks on the vessel, that the general condition of the tanks is satisfactory.

[CGD 84-024, 52 FR 39655, Oct. 23, 1987, as amended at 53 FR 32232, Aug. 24, 1988]

§ 167.15-50 Tailshaft examinations.

Tailshaft examinations on nautical school ships must conform with the examination requirements in part 61 of this chapter.

[CGD 84-024, 52 FR 39655, Oct. 23, 1987]

Subpart 167.20—Hull Requirements, Construction and Arrangement of Nautical School Ships

§ 167.20-1 Construction.

Except as otherwise provided by law or regulations in this subpart, the following standards for construction are acceptable.

(a) American Bureau of Shipping "Rules for Building and Classing Steel Vessels" regarding the construction of hulls, boilers and machinery in effect on the date of inspection. These rules may be purchased from the American Bureau of Shipping (ABS), Two World Trade Center—106th Floor, New York, NY 10048.

(b) U. S. Navy Standard Construction Specification in effect on the date of inspection.

(c) U. S. Coast Guard Standard Construction Specification in effect on the date of inspection.

[CGFR 51-11, 16 GR 3218, Apr. 12, 1951, as amended by USCG-1999-6216, 64 FR 53228, Oct. 1, 1999]

§ 167.20-7 Subdivision and stability.

Each vessel must meet the applicable requirements in Subchapter S of this chapter.

[CGD 79-023, 48 FR 51010, Nov. 4, 1983]

§ 167.20-10 Means of escape.

(a) On all nautical school ships where the arrangements will possibly permit, all inclosures where persons may be quartered, or where anyone may be employed, shall be provided with not less than two avenues of escape, so located that if one of such avenues is not available another may be.

§ 167.20-15 Scupper, sanitary and similar discharges.

(a) All scupper, sanitary, and other similar discharges which lead through the ship's hull shall be fitted with efficient means for preventing the ingress of water in the event of a fracture of such pipes. The requirements do not apply to the discharges in the machinery space connected with the main and auxiliary engines, pumps, etc.

§ 167.20-17 Bilge pumps, bilge piping and sounding arrangements.

The number, capacity, and arrangement of bilge pumps and bilge piping shall be in accordance with the requirements for cargo vessels contained in parts 50 to 61 of Subchapter F (Marine Engineering) of this chapter. Sounding pipes shall be fitted in each compartment, except those accessible at all times. The main and secondary drain systems installed in accordance with U.S. Navy or U.S. Coast Guard Construction Specifications shall be accepted as meeting the intent of this section.

[CGFR 52-43, 17 FR 9542, Oct. 18, 1952]

§ 167.20-35 Liquid ballast.

When water ballasting of fuel tanks is necessary, such oily ballast shall not be subsequently discharged overboard within any of the prohibited zones as defined by the Oil Pollution Act, 1961 (33 U.S.C. 1011), except through oily water separators which meet the requirements in 33 CFR 155.330 through 155.380, or directly into sludge barges or shore facilities, or other approved means.

[CGFR 62-17, 27 FR 9046, Sept. 11, 1962, as amended by CGD 95-072, 60 FR 50468, Sept. 29, 1995]

Subpart 167.25—Marine Engineering

§ 167.25-1 Boilers, pressure vessels, piping and appurtenances.

(a) Except as otherwise provided by law or regulations in this subpart, all vessels constructed or reconverted to use as nautical school ships on or after July 1, 1951, shall conform with one of the following standards for boilers, pressure vessels, piping and appurtenances:

(1) Marine engineering regulations in parts 50 to 63, inclusive, of Subchapter F (Marine Engineering) of this chapter.

(2) Navy Standard Construction Specifications in effect at time of construction or conversion.

(3) U.S. Coast Guard Standard Construction Specifications in effect at time of construction or conversion.

§ 167.25-5

(b) The boilers, pressure vessels, and appurtenances shall be inspected initially under the provisions of part 52 of Subchapter F (Marine Engineering) of this chapter. All alterations, replacements or repairs on nautical school ships shall conform to the applicable standards in paragraph (a) of this section insofar as practicable.

[CGFR 51-11, 16 FR 3218, Apr. 12, 1951, as amended by CGFR 68-82, 33 FR 18908, Dec. 18, 1968]

§ 167.25-5 Inspection of boilers, pressure vessels, piping and appurtenances.

The inspection of boilers, pressure vessels, piping and appurtenances shall be in accordance with the applicable regulations in parts 50 to 63, inclusive, of Subchapter F (Marine Engineering) of this chapter, insofar as they relate to tests and inspection of cargo vessels.

[CGFR 68-82, 33 FR 18908, Dec. 18, 1968]

Subpart 167.30—Repairs or Alterations

§ 167.30-1 Notice of repairs or alterations required.

(a) It shall be the duty of the master, owner, or agent to notify the nearest Officer in Charge, Marine Inspection, whenever repairs or alterations are required, or will be made on a nautical school ship.

(b) Whenever a nautical school ship is placed upon the dock, it shall be the duty of the master, owner or agent to report the same to the Officer in Charge, Marine Inspection, so that a thorough inspection may be made by the Coast Guard to determine what is necessary to make such a nautical school ship seaworthy, if the condition or age of the nautical school ship, in the judgment of the Officer in Charge, Marine Inspection, renders such examination necessary.

§ 167.30-5 Proceeding to another port for repairs.

(a) The Officer in Charge, Marine Inspection, may issue a permit to proceed to another port for repairs, if in his judgment it can be done with safety. In the issuance of such a permit the Officer in Charge, Marine Inspection, will state upon its face, the conditions upon which it is granted.

(b) When a nautical school ship obtains a permit from the Officer in Charge, Marine Inspection, to go to another port for repairs, the Officer in Charge, Marine Inspection, shall so notify the Coast Guard District Commander, and state the repairs to be made. The Coast Guard District Commander shall notify the Coast Guard District Commander of the district where such repairs are to be made, furnishing him a copy of the report indicating the repairs ordered.

§ 167.30-10 Special operating requirements.

Inspection and testing required when making alterations, repairs, or other such operations involving riveting, welding, burning, or like fire-producing actions are as follows:

(a) The provisions of "Standard for the Control of Gas Hazards on Vessels to be Repaired", NFPA No. 306, published by National Fire Protection Association, 1 Batterymarch Park, Quincy, MA 02269 shall be used as a guide in conducting the inspections and issuance of certificates required by this section.

(b) Until an inspection has been made to determine that such operation can be undertaken with safety, no alterations, repairs, or other such operations involving riveting, welding, burning, or like fire-producing actions shall be made:

(1) Within or on the boundaries of cargo tanks which have been used to carry combustible liquids or chemicals in bulk; or,

(2) Within spaces adjacent to cargo tanks which have been used to carry Grade D combustible liquid cargo, except where the distance between such cargo tanks and the work to be performed is not less than twenty-five (25) feet;

(3) Within or on the boundaries of fuel tanks; or,

(4) To pipe lines, heating coils, pumps, fittings, or other appurtenances connected to such cargo or fuel tanks.

(c) Such inspections shall be made and evidenced as follows:

(1) In ports or places in the United States or its territories and possessions, the inspection shall be made by a marine chemist certificated by the National Fire Protection Association; however, if the services of such certified marine chemist are not reasonably available, the Officer in Charge, Marine Inspection, upon the recommendation of the vessel owner and his contractor or their representative, shall select a person who, in the case of an individual vessel, shall be authorized to make such inspection. If the inspection indicates that such operations can be undertaken with safety, a certificate setting forth the fact in writing and qualified as may be required, shall be issued by the certified marine chemist or the authorized person before the work is started. Such qualifications shall include any requirements, as may be deemed necessary to maintain, insofar as can reasonably be done, the safe conditions in the spaces certified throughout the operation and shall include such additional tests and certifications as considered required. Such qualifications and requirements shall include precautions necessary to eliminate or minimize hazards that may be present from protective coatings or residues from cargoes.

(2) When not in such a port or place, and a marine chemist or such person authorized by the Officer in Charge, Marine Inspection, is not reasonably available, the inspection shall be made by the senior officer present and a proper entry shall be made in the vessel's logbook.

(d) It shall be the responsibility of the senior officer present to secure copies of certificates issued by the certified marine chemist or such person authorized by the Officer in Charge, Marine Inspection. It shall be the responsibility of the senior officer present, insofar as the persons under his control are concerned, to maintain a safe condition on the vessel by full observance of all qualifications and requirements listed by the marine chemist in the certificate.

[CGFR 64–19, 29 FR 7361, June 5, 1964, as amended by CGD 95–072, 60 FR 50468, Sept. 29, 1995]

Subpart 167.35—Lifesaving Equipment

§ 167.35-1 General.

Lifesaving appliances and arrangements on nautical school ships must be in accordance with the requirements for special purpose vessels in subchapter W (Lifesaving Appliances and Arrangements) of this chapter.

[CGD 84–069, 61 FR 25311, May 20, 1996]

Subpart 167.40—Certain Equipment Requirements

§ 167.40-1 Electrical installations.

(a) Except as otherwise provided by law or regulation in this part, the electrical equipment may be considered acceptable if it complies with the requirements covered by any one of the following:

(1) U.S. Navy Standard Construction Specifications currently in effect.

(2) U. S. Coast Guard electrical engineering requirements in Subchapter J (Electrical Engineering) of this chapter.

(3) Institute of Electrical and Electronic Engineers, Inc. (IEEE) Standard No. 45, 1945 or 1948 Revision. These standards may be purchased from the Institute of Electrical and Electronic Engineers, Inc. (IEEE), IEEE Service Center, 445 Hoes Lane, Piscataway, NJ 08855.

(b) Changes or alterations in the electrical installations of vessels now in service shall be in accordance with standards set forth in paragraph (a) of this section.

(c) Special attention shall be given by the inspectors in the examination of present installation to see that it is of such nature as to preclude any danger of fire, giving particular attention to wiring which is carried through wooden bulkheads, partitions, etc.

[CGFR 51–11, 16 FR 3218, Apr. 12, 1951, as amended by CGFR 52–43, 17 FR 9543, Oct. 18, 1952; USCG–1999–6216, 64 FR 53228, Oct. 1, 1999]

§ 167.40-5 Alarm bells.

All nautical school ships over 100 gross tons shall have all sleeping accommodations, public spaces, and machinery spaces equipped with a sufficient number of alarm bells so located

§ 167.40–7

as to warn all occupants. The system shall operate from a continuous source of electric energy capable of supplying the system for a period of at least 8 hours without being dependent upon the main, auxiliary or emergency generating plants. Each bell shall produce a signal of a tone distinct from that of other bell signals in the vicinity and shall be independently fused, with each of these fuses located above the bulkhead deck. The bells shall be controlled by a manually-operated contact maker located in the pilothouse. The characteristics of the contact maker shall be such that it possesses:

(a) Positive contact;

(b) Watertightness (when located in open spaces subject to weather);

(c) Means whereby its electrically open or closed position can be determined by sense of touch;

(d) Means to affect a make-or-break circuit for signaling; and

(e) Self-maintaining contacts.

§ 167.40–7 Voice tubes, telephone, and telegraph systems.

(a) Each nautical school ship shall be fitted with an efficient means of communication between the pilothouse and engine room. This may be by bell signals with voice tubes, telephone, or telegraph systems.

(b) A voice tube or telephone system between the radio room and the navigating bridge shall be provided when the nautical school ship is equipped with a radio installation.

(c) A voice tube or telephone system between the pilothouse and emergency steering station shall be provided when the nautical school ship is equipped with an emergency steering station.

§ 167.40–20 Deep-sea sounding apparatus.

Nautical school ships shall be equipped with an efficient or electronic deep-sea sounding apparatus. The electronic deep-sea sounding apparatus required shall be installed, kept in working order, and ready for immediate use.

[CGFR 58–10, 23 FR 4686, June 26, 1958, as amended by CGD 75–074, 42 FR 5964, Jan. 31, 1977; CGD 95–027, 61 FR 26010, May 23, 1996]

§ 167.40–25 Signaling lamp.

Nautical school ships of over 150 gross tons shall be equipped with an efficient signaling lamp. This lamp shall be permanently fixed above the bridge and equipped with a Fresnel lens and high-speed bulb, operated by a weatherproof key, fitted with a suitable condenser. The lamp shall be so connected that it can be operated from the normal source of the nautical school ship's current, the emergency source, and other emergency batteries if provided.

§ 167.40–30 Guards and rails.

On nautical school ships all exposed and dangerous places, such as gears and machinery shall be properly protected with covers, guards, or rails, in order that the danger of accidents may be minimized. On nautical school ships equipped with radio (wireless) the lead-ins shall be efficiently incased or insulated to insure the protection of persons from accidental shock. Such lead-ins shall be located so as not to interfere with the launching of lifeboats and life rafts.

§ 167.40–40 Radar.

All mechanically propelled vessels of 1,600 gross tons and over in ocean or coastwise service must be fitted with a marine radar system for surface navigation. Facilities for plotting radar readings must be provided on the bridge.

[CGFR 75–074, 42 FR 5964, Jan. 31, 1977]

§ 167.40–45 Magnetic compass and gyrocompass.

(a) All mechanically propelled vessels in ocean or coastwise service must be fitted with a magnetic compass.

(b) All mechanically propelled vessels of 1,600 gross tons and over in ocean or coastwise service must be fitted with a gyrocompass in addition to the magnetic compass.

(c) Each vessel must have an illuminated repeater for the gyrocompass required under paragraph (b) of this section that is at the main steering stand unless the gyrocompass is illuminated and is at the main steering stand.

[CFD 75–074, 42 FR 5964, Jan. 31, 1977]

Subpart 167.43—Work Vests

SOURCE: CGFR 59-22, 24 FR 4962, June 18, 1959, unless otherwise noted.

§ 167.43-1 Application.

(a) Provisions of this subpart shall apply to all vessels inspected and certificated in accordance with this subchapter.

§ 167.43-5 Approved types of work vests.

(a) Each buoyant work vest carried under the permissive authority of this section must be approved under—
  (1) Subpart 160.053 of this chapter; or
  (2) Subpart 160.077 of this chapter as a commercial hybrid PFD.

[CGD 78-174A, 51 FR 4351, Feb. 4, 1986]

§ 167.43-10 Use.

(a) Approved buoyant work vests are considered to be items of safety apparel and may be carried aboard vessels to be worn by crew members when working near or over the water under favorable working conditions. They shall be used under the supervision and control of designated ship's officers. When carried, such vests shall not be accepted in lieu of any portion of the required number of approved life preservers and shall not be substituted for the approved life preservers required to be worn during drills and emergencies.

§ 167.43-15 Shipboard stowage.

(a) The approved buoyant work vests shall be stowed separately from the regular stowage of approved life preservers.

(b) The locations for the stowage of work vests shall be such as not to be easily confused with that for approved life preservers.

§ 167.43-20 Shipboard inspections.

(a) Each work vest shall be subject to examination by a marine inspector to determine its serviceability. If found to be satisfactory, it may be continued in service, but shall not be stamped by a marine inspector with a Coast Guard stamp. If a work vest is found not to be in a serviceable condition, then such work vest shall be removed from the vessel. If a work vest is beyond repair, it shall be destroyed or mutilated in the presence of a marine inspector so as to prevent its continued use as a work vest.

§ 167.43-25 Additional requirements for hybrid work vests.

(a) In addition to the other requirements in this subpart, commercial hybrid PFD's must be—
  (1) Used, stowed, and maintained in accordance with the procedures set out in the manual required for these devices by § 160.077-29 of this chapter and any limitations(s) marked on them; and
  (2) Of the same or similar design and have the same method of operation as each other hybrid PFD carried on board.

[CGD 78-174A, 51 FR 4351, Feb. 4, 1986]

Subpart 167.45—Special Firefighting and Fire Prevention Requirements

§ 167.45-1 Steam, carbon dioxide, and halon fire extinguishing systems.

(a) *General requirements.* (1) Nautical school ships shall be provided with an inert-gas fire-extinguishing system when required.

(2) All nautical school ships carrying combustible cargo in the holds, between decks, or other closed cargo compartments shall be equipped with means for extinguishing fire in such compartments by the use of any inert-gas fire-extinguishing system approved by the Coast Guard or Navy. However, in specific cases where by reason of the design, such compartments are normally accessible and considered to be part of the working or living quarters, a water sprinkling system may be installed in lieu of an inert-gas fire-extinguishing system. On such vessels contracted for prior to January 1, 1962, a steam smothering system may be accepted in lieu of the inert gas system for the protection of cargo holds, paint lockers, and similar spaces. However, although existing steam smothering systems may be repaired, replaced, or extended, no new systems contracted for on or after January 1, 1962, will be permitted.

§ 167.45-1

(3) Cabinets, boxes, or casings inclosing manifolds or valves shall be distinctly marked in painted letters about 3 inches in height, "Steam Fire Apparatus," or "CO₂ Fire Apparatus," as the case may be.

(4) Steam or gas piping fitted for extinguishing fire shall not be used for any other purpose except that it may be used for fire-detecting purposes.

(5) Pipes for conveying steam from the boilers for the purpose of extinguishing fire shall not be led into the cabins, other living spaces, or working spaces. Pipes for conveying carbon dioxide or other extinguishing vapors for the purpose of extinguishing fire shall not be led into the cabins or other living spaces.

(6) Steam smothering lines shall be tested with at least 50 pounds air pressure with ends of the smothering lines capped, or by blowing steam through the lines, and a survey made for detecting corrosion and defects, using the hammer test or such other means as may be necessary.

(7) At annual inspections, all carbon dioxide (CO₂) cylinders, whether fixed or portable, shall be examined externally and replaced if excessive corrosion is found; and all cylinders shall also be checked by weighing to determine contents and if found to be more than 10 percent under required contents of carbon dioxide, the same shall be recharged.

(8) Carbon dioxide and halon cylinders carried on board nautical school ships must be tested and marked in accordance with the requirements of §§ 147.60 and 147.65 of this chapter.

(9) Regarding the limitations on the use of steam smothering in subparagraph (2) of this paragraph, this does not preclude the introduction of steam into such confined spaces as boiler casings or into tanks for steaming out purposes. Such installations are not to be considered as part of any required fire extinguishing system.

(b) *Steam systems.* (1) As noted in subparagraph (a)(2) of this section, steam smothering systems are not permitted on nautical school ships contracted for on or after January 1, 1962, nor for new installations on vessels contracted for prior to that date. Where steam smothering systems are installed, the provisions of this paragraph shall be met.

(2) Steam for fire-extinguishing systems shall be available at a suitable pressure from the main boilers or a donkey or auxiliary boiler.

(3) The pipe lines shall be led from not more than three stations in easily accessible locations on the weather deck to each cargo hold, cargo 'tween-decks, or other closed cargo compartments, and to each cargo-oil deep tank, lamp locker, oil room, and like compartments, which lamp locker, oil room, and like compartments, shall be wholly and tightly lined with metal. The steam connections to the lamp lockers, oil rooms, and like compartments may be taken from the nearest steam supply line, independent of the extinguishing manifolds. In lamp lockers, oil rooms, and like compartments, adequate means may be provided for ventilation if suitable dampers capable of being operated from outside the spaces are fitted in each vent duct.

(4) Each pipe in the extinguishing manifolds shall be fitted with a shut-off valve plainly and permanently marked to indicate into which compartment it discharges. This requirement also applies to independent extinguishing lines.

(5) Manifold steam supply pipes shall be fitted with master valves at the manifolds, and provision shall be made for draining the manifold and individual lines to protect them against freezing. If the manifolds are located on an open deck, they shall be enclosed in a metal box.

(6) The minimum diameter of any steam fire-extinguishing pipe to a cargo hold, cargo 'tween-decks, other closed cargo compartments, or cargo-oil deep tank shall be one inch, the size and number of pipes to be governed by the size of the compartment. The minimum diameter of any steam fire-extinguishing pipe to a lamp locker, oil room, or like compartments, shall be three-fourths of an inch.

(c) *Inert-gas systems.* (1) When a carbon dioxide (CO₂) smothering system is fitted in the cargo hold, cargo 'tween-decks, or other closed cargo compartments, or cargo-oil deep tanks, the quantity of carbon dioxide shall be sufficient to give a gas saturation of 30

18

Coast Guard, DHS § 167.45-5

percent of the gross volume of the largest cargo hold. The quantity in pounds of carbon dioxide required may be determined approximately by the following formula:

$$W = \frac{L \times B \times D}{30} \quad (1)$$

where:

W=the weight of CO_2 required, in pounds.
L=the length of the hold, in feet.
B=the mean breadth of the hold, in feet.
D=the depth from tank top or flat forming lower boundary to top of uppermost space in which freight may be carried, in feet.

(2) When a carbon dioxide (CO_2) smothering system is fitted in the lamp locker, oil room, or like compartments, the quantity in pounds of carbon dioxide required may be determined by dividing the gross volume of the space by a factor of 22. Lamp lockers, oil rooms, and like compartments, in all classes of vessels, shall be wholly and tightly lined with metal. The whole charge of gas shall be capable of being released simultaneously by operating one valve and control, and all cylinders shall be completely discharged in not more than two minutes.

(3) Pipes used for supplying carbon dioxide to the cargo holds, cargo 'tween-decks, other closed cargo compartments, and cargo-oil deep tanks shall be not less than three-fourths inch inside diameter. Pipes used for supplying carbon dioxide to lamp lockers, oil rooms, and like compartments shall not be less than one-half inch inside diameter.

(4) The control(s) releasing the inert gas shall be located in a position(s) outside the space(s) protected and shall be readily accessible when the vessel is being navigated. All valves shall be permanently marked to indicate into which compartment they discharge. A space which is protected by a carbon dioxide extinguishing system, and is normally accessible to crew while the nautical school ship is being navigated shall be fitted with an approved audible alarm in such space, which will be automatically sounded when the carbon dioxide is admitted to the space.

(5) Provisions shall be made to prevent the admission of air into the lower parts of cargo holds, cargo 'tween-decks, and other closed cargo compartments while the inert-gas system is in operation.

(6) Cylinders, piping, and controls for the inert-gas system shall be protected from damage and shall be securely fastened and supported.

[CGFR 51-11, 16 FR 3218, Apr. 12, 1951, as amended by CGFR 54-46, 19 FR 8708, Dec. 18, 1954; CGFR 61-15, 26 FR 9303, Sept. 30, 1961; CGFR 65-9, 30 FR 11494, Sept. 8, 1965; CGD 84-044, 53 FR 7752, Mar. 10, 1988]

§ 167.45-5 Steam fire pumps or their equivalent.

(a) All nautical school ships shall be equipped with fire pumps.

(b) Nautical school ships of 100 gross tons and under shall be equipped with one hand fire pump with a pump-cylinder capacity not less than 100 cubic inches, or a power-driven pump of equivalent discharge capacity.

(c) Nautical school ships over 100 gross tons shall be equipped with fire pumps and piping as follows:

(1) All nautical school ships shall be provided with powerful pumps available for use as fire pumps. When of less than 1,000 gross tons it shall have 1, and when larger it shall have at least 2 independently driven pumps connected to the fire main. Each pump shall be capable of delivering two powerful jets of water simultaneously from the highest outlets on the fire main at a Pitot tube pressure of approximately 50 pounds per square inch.

(2) On oil-burning nautical school ships, where two pumps are required, they may be located in the same compartment, if the compartment is equipped with an approved fixed carbon dioxide extinguishing system.

(d) Outlets from the fire mains shall be of a sufficient number and so arranged that any part of the living quarters, weather decks and any part of cargo decks, accessible to crew, while the nautical school ship is being navigated, may be reached with a single 50-foot length of hose. Outlets within accommodations and service spaces adjacent thereto shall comply with the above or they may be so arranged that any part may be reached with a single 75-foot length of hose provided a siamese connection is fitted at each outlet. Where the fire main is located on

§ 167.45-10

an exposed deck, branches shall be provided so that the hose connections necessary to comply with the foregoing be distributed on both sides of the nautical school ship. The fire hose shall be connected to the outlet at all times, except on open decks where the location of the fire hydrants is such that no protection is afforded for the hose in heavy weather. The fire hose may be temporarily removed from the hydrant when it will interfere with the handling of cargo.

(e) Outlet openings shall have a diameter of not less than 1½ inches and shall be fitted with suitable hose connections and spanners. The arrangement of the fire hydrant shall be limited to any position from the horizontal to the vertical pointing downward, so that the hose will lead downward or horizontally, in order to minimize the possibility of kinking. In no case will a hydrant arranged in a vertical position with the outlet pointing upward be accepted.

(f) Fire pumps shall be fitted on the discharge side with relief valves set to relieve at 25 pounds higher than the pressure necessary to maintain the requirements of paragraph (c)(1) of this section and a pressure gage to indicate the pressure on the fire main. If the fire pumps operating under shut-off conditions are not capable of producing a pressure exceeding 125 pounds per square inch, the relief valve may be omitted.

(g) Each section of fire hose used after January 1, 1980 must be lined commercial fire hose that conforms to Underwriters' Laboratories, Inc. Standard 19 or Federal Specification ZZ-H-451E. Hose that bears the label of Underwriters' Laboratories, Inc. as lined fire hose is accepted as conforming to this requirement. Each section of replacement fire hose or any section of new fire hose placed aboard a vessel after January 1, 1977 must also conform to the specification required by this paragraph.

(h) Each fire hydrant must have at least one length of firehose. Each firehose on the hydrant must have a combination solid stream and water spray

46 CFR Ch. I (10-1-04 Edition)

firehose nozzle that is approved under subpart 162.027 of this chapter.

[CGFR 51-11, 16 FR 3218, Apr. 12, 1951, as amended by CGFR 60-36, 25 FR 10642, Nov. 5, 1960; CGD 74-60, 41 FR 43152, Sept. 30, 1976; CGD 76-086, 44 FR 2394, Jan. 11, 1979]

§ 167.45-10   Couplings on fire hose.

The couplings on fire hose shall be of brass, copper, or composition material. All hydrants shall be provided with suitable spanners.

§ 167.45-15   Capacity of pipes and hose.

The capacity of the pipes and hose leading from the pumps shall in no case be less than that of the discharge opening of the pump: *Provided, however,* That the pipe and hose shall in no instance be less than 1½ inches in internal diameter.

§ 167.45-20   Examination and testing of pumps and fire-extinguishing equipment.

The inspectors will examine all pumps, hose, and other fire apparatus and will see that the hose is subjected to a pressure of 100 pounds to the square inch at each annual inspection and that the hose couplings are securely fastened.

§ 167.45-25   Fire mains and hose connections.

All pipes used as mains for conducting water from fire pumps on nautical school ships shall be of steel, wrought iron, brass, or copper with wrought iron brass, or composition hose connections.

§ 167.45-30   Use of approved fire-fighting equipment.

Portable fire extinguishers or fire-extinguishing systems which conform to the specifications of the Navy or Coast Guard, or their approved equivalent, may be accepted for use on nautical school ships.

§ 167.45-40   Fire-fighting equipment on nautical school ships using oil as fuel.

Steam-propelled nautical school ships burning oil for fuel shall be fitted with the fire-fighting equipment of the following type and character:

Coast Guard, DHS § 167.45–45

(a) In each boiler room and in each of the machinery spaces of a nautical school ship propelled by steam, in which a part of the fuel-oil installation is situated, 2 or more approved fire extinguishers of the foam type of not less than 9.5 liters (2½ gallons) each or 2 or more approved fire extinguishers of the carbon dioxide type of not less than 33 kilograms (15 pounds) each must be placed where accessible and ready for immediate use. On a nautical school ship of 1,000 gross tons and under, only 1 of the fire extinguishers may be required.

(b) In boiler and machinery spaces, at least 2 fire hydrants must have a firehose of a length that allows each part of the boiler and machinery spaces to be reached by water from a combination solid stream and water spray firehose nozzle.

(c) Each firehose under paragraph (b) of this section must have a combination solid stream and water spray firehose nozzle that meets subpart 162.027 of this chapter. Combination nozzles and low-velocity water spray applicators previously approved under subpart 162.027 of this chapter may remain so long as they are maintained in good condition to the satisfaction of the Officer in Charge, Marine Inspection.

(d) On every steam propelled nautical school ship of over 1,000 gross tons having one boiler room there shall be provided one fire extinguisher of the foam type of at least 40 gallons rated capacity or one carbon dioxide (CO_2) extinguisher of at least 100 pounds. If the nautical school ship has more than one boiler room, an extinguisher of the above type shall be provided in each boiler room. On every steam propelled nautical school ship of 1,000 gross tons and under, foam type fire extinguishers of at least 20 gallons rated capacity or carbon dioxide (CO_2) extinguishers of at least 50 pounds shall be used. Extinguishers fitted shall be equipped with suitable hose and nozzles on reels or other practicable means easy of access, and of sufficient length to reach any part of the boiler room and spaces containing oil-fuel pumping units.

(e) All nautical school ships propelled by internal-combustion engines shall be equipped with the following foam type or carbon dioxide type fire extinguishers in the machinery spaces:

(1) One approved 12-gallon foam-type extinguisher or one approved 35-pound carbon dioxide type extinguisher.

(2) One approved 2½-gallon foam-type, or one approved 15-pound carbon dioxide type extinguisher for each 1,000 B. H. P. of the main engines, or fraction thereof. The total number of fire extinguishers carried shall not be less than two and need not exceed six.

(3) When a donkey boiler fitted to burn oil as fuel is located in the machinery space, there shall be substituted for the 12-gallon foam type or 35-pound carbon dioxide type fire extinguisher required either one 40-gallon foam type or one 100-pound carbon dioxide type fire extinguisher.

(f) In this section any reference to an approved fire extinguisher means either approved by the Coast Guard or the Navy.

[CGFR 51–11, 16 FR 3218, Apr. 12, 1951, as amended by CGD 76–086, 44 FR 2394, Jan. 11, 1979; CGD 95–027, 61 FR 26010, May 23, 1996]

§ 167.45–45 Carbon dioxide fire-extinguishing system requirements.

(a) When a carbon dioxide (CO_2) smothering system is fitted in the boiler room, the quantity of carbon dioxide carried shall be sufficient to give a gas saturation of 25 percent of the gross volume of the largest boiler room from tank top to top of the boilers. Top of the boilers is to be considered as the top of the shell of a Scotch or leg type of boiler, and the top of the casing or drum, whichever is the higher, on water-tube boilers. The quantity of carbon dioxide required may be determined approximately by the following formula:

$$W = \frac{L \times B \times D}{36} \quad (1)$$

where:

W=the weight of CO_2 required in pounds.
L=the length of the boiler room in feet.
B=the breadth of the boiler room in feet.
D=the distance in feet from tank top or flat forming lower boundary to top of boilers.

(b) When a carbon dioxide (CO_2) smothering system is fitted in the machinery space of a nautical school ship

§ 167.45-50

propelled by internal combustion engines, the quantity of carbon dioxide required may be determined approximately by the following formula:

$$W = \frac{L \times B \times D}{22} \quad (2)$$

where:

W=the weight of CO_2 required in pounds.
L=the length of machinery space in feet.
B=breadth of the machinery space in feet.
D=distance in feet from tank top or flat forming lower boundary to the underside of deck forming the batch opening.

(c) The whole charge of gas shall be capable of being released simultaneously by operating one valve and control. All cylinders shall be completely discharged in not more than two minutes. The arrangement of the piping shall be such as to give a general and fairly uniform distribution over the entire area protected. An alarm which shall operate automatically with the operation of the system shall be provided to give a warning in the space when the carbon dioxide is about to be released. Provision shall be made to prevent the admission of air into the lower parts of the boiler or engine room while the system is in operation.

§ 167.45-50 Foam smothering system requirements.

(a) When a foam-type system is fitted, its capacity shall be such as to rapidly discharge over the entire area of the bilge (tank top) of the largest boiler room a volume of foam 6 inches deep in not more than 3 minutes. The arrangement of piping shall be such as to give a uniform distribution over the entire area protected.

(b) The foam-type system may be of a type approved by the Navy or Coast Guard. All containers and valves by which the system is operated shall be easily accessible and so placed that control valves and containers will not readily be cut off from use by an outbreak of fire.

§ 167.45-60 Emergency breathing apparatus and flame safety lamps.

Each nautical-school ship must be equipped with the following devices:

(a) Two pressure-demand, open circuit, self-contained breathing apparatus, approved by the Mine Safety and Health Administration (MSHA) and by the National Institute for Occupational Safety and Health (NIOSH) and having at a minimum a 30-minute air supply, a full face piece, and a spare charge for each. A self-contained compressed-air breathing apparatus previously approved under part 160, subpart 160.011, of this chapter may continue in use as required equipment if it was part of the vessel's equipment on November 23, 1992, and as long as it is maintained in good condition to the satisfaction of the Officer in Charge, Marine Inspection.

(b) One flame safety lamp approved by the Coast Guard or Navy.

[CGD 86-036, 57 FR 48326, Oct. 23, 1992, as amended by CGD 95-028, 62 FR 51217, Sept. 30, 1997]

§ 167.45-65 Portable fire extinguishers in accommodation spaces.

(a) All nautical school ships shall be provided with such number of good and efficient portable fire extinguishers approved by the Navy or Coast Guard as follows:

(1) Nautical school ships less than 150 feet in length shall have at least two fire extinguishers on each passenger deck.

(2) Nautical school ships 150 feet and over in length shall be provided with at least one fire extinguisher for every 150 linear feet of corridor length or fraction thereof in the spaces occupied by passengers and crew.

(3) In all public spaces fire extinguishers shall be located not more than 150 feet apart.

(b) The number of required fire extinguishers is based on the capacity of the ordinary fire extinguisher, which is about 2½ gallons, and no fire extinguisher of larger capacity shall be allowed a greater rating than that of the ordinary fire extinguisher. Fire extinguishers of approved types of less capacity are allowable when their total contents equal the required quantity.

§ 167.45-70 Portable fire extinguishers, general requirements.

(a) Extra charges shall be carried on board for 50 percent of each size and variety of fire extinguishers provided. If 50 percent of each size and variety of fire extinguishers carried gives a fractional result, extra charges shall be provided for the next largest whole number.

(1) The following is an example:

Fire extinguishers carried:	Extra charges required
1	1
2	1
3	2
4	2
5	3

(2) When the portable fire extinguisher is of such variety that it cannot be readily recharged by the vessel's personnel, one spare unit of the same classification shall be carried in lieu of spare charges for all such units of the same size and variety.

(b) Recharges, particularly the acid, used in charging soda-and-acid type of fire extinguishers, shall be packed in such manner that the filling operation (i.e., in recharging the extinguisher) can be performed without subjecting the person doing the recharging to undue risk of acid burns and shall be contained in Crown stopper type of bottle.

(c) [Reserved]

(d) Fire extinguishers shall be located in such places as in the judgment of the Officer in Charge, Marine Inspection, will be most convenient and serviceable in case of emergency and so arranged that they may be easily removed from their fastenings.

(e) Every fire extinguisher provided shall be examined at each annual inspection to determine that it is still in good condition. Soda-and-acid and foam fire extinguishers shall be tested by discharging the contents, cleaning thoroughly, and then refilling. Carbon dioxide fire extinguishers shall be checked by weighing to determine contents and if found to be more than 10 percent under required contents of carbon dioxide shall be recharged. Pump tank fire extinguishers shall be tested by pumping and discharging the contents, cleaning thoroughly, and then refilling or recharging. Cartridge-operated type fire extinguishers shall be checked by examining the extinguishing agents to determine if in still good condition and by examining the pressure cartridge. If the cartridge end is punctured, or it the cartridge is otherwise determined to have leaked or to be in an unsuitable condition, the pressure cartridge shall be rejected and a new one inserted. Stored pressure type extinguishers shall be checked by determining that the pressure gage is in the operating range, and the full charge of extinguishing agent is in the chamber. The hoses and nozzles of all fire extinguishers shall be inspected to see that they are clear and in good condition.

[CGFR 51–11, 16 FR 3218, Apr. 12, 1951, as amended by CGFR 54–46, 19 FR 8708, Dec. 18, 1954; CGFR 59–21, 24 FR 7196; Sept. 5, 1959; CGFR 60–17, 25 FR 2667, Mar. 30, 1960; CGFR 62–17, 27 FR 9047, Sept. 11, 1962]

§ 167.45–75 Fire extinguishers for emergency powerplants.

In compartments where emergency lighting and wireless units are located, two fire extinguishers approved by the Coast Guard or the Navy, of either carbon dioxide or dry chemical type, shall be permanently located at the most accessible points. In addition, two fire extinguishers of the above types, or foam type, shall be permanently located so as to be readily accessible to the emergency fuel tanks containing gasoline, benzine or naphtha.

[CGFR 58–29, 23 FR 6882, Sept. 6, 1958, as amended by CGD 95–028, 62 FR 51217, Sept. 30, 1997]

§ 167.45–80 Fire axes.

(a) All nautical school ships shall be provided with fire axes, as follows:

Gross tons of nautical school ships:	Number of axes
All not over 50 tons	1
All over 50 tons and not over 200 tons	2
All over 200 tons and not over 500 tons	4
All over 500 tons and not over 1,000 tons	6
All over 1,000 tons	8

(b) All fire axes shall be located so as to be readily found in time of need, shall not be used for general purposes, and shall be kept in good condition.

§ 167.50-1

Subpart 167.50—Accommodations

§ 167.50-1 Hospital accommodations.

Each nautical school ship, which makes voyages of more than 3 days' duration between ports and carries 12 or more persons, shall be equipped with a compartment suitably separated from other spaces for hospital purposes, and such compartment shall have at least 1 bunk for every 12 persons allowed to be carried: *Provided,* That not more than 6 bunks shall be required in any case.

Subpart 167.55—Special Markings Required

§ 167.55-1 Draft marks and draft indicating systems.

(a) All vessels must have draft marks plainly and legibly visible upon the stem and upon the sternpost or rudderpost or at any place at the stern of the vessel as may be necessary for easy observance. The bottom of each mark must indicate the draft.

(b) The draft must be taken from the bottom of the keel to the surface of the water at the location of the marks.

(c) In cases where the keel does not extend forward or aft to the location of the draft marks, due to a raked stem or cut away skeg, the draft must be measured from a line projected from the bottom of the keel forward or aft, as the case may be, to the location of the draft marks.

(d) In cases where a vessel may have a skeg or other appendage extending locally below the line of the keel, the draft at the end of the vessel adjacent to such appendage must be measured to a line tangent to the lowest part of such appendage and parallel to the line of the bottom of the keel.

(e) Draft marks must be separated so that the projections of the marks onto a vertical plane are of uniform height equal to the vertical spacing between consecutive marks.

(f) Draft marks must be painted in contrasting color to the hull.

(g) In cases where draft marks are obscured due to operational constraints or by protrusions, the vessel must be fitted with a reliable draft indicating system from which the bow and stern drafts can be determined.

[CGD 89-037, 57 FR 41824, Sept. 11, 1992]

§ 167.55-5 Marking of fire and emergency equipment.

Marking of fire and emergency apparatus, watertight doors, lifeboat embarkation stations and direction signs, stateroom notices, instructions for changing steering gears, etc., shall be carried out as follows:

(a) *General alarm bell switch.* The general alarm bell switch in the pilothouse or fire control station shall be clearly marked with lettering on a brass plate or with a sign in red letters on suitable background: "General Alarm."

(b) *General alarm bells.* General alarm bells shall be marked in not less than ½-inch red letters: "General Alarm—When Bell Rings Go to Your Station."

(c) *Steam, foam or CO_2 fire smothering apparatus.* Steam, foam or CO_2 fire smothering apparatus shall be marked "Steam Fire Apparatus" or "Foam Fire Apparatus" or "CO_2 Fire Apparatus", as appropriate, in not less than 2-inch red letters. The valves of all branch piping leading to the several compartments shall be distinctly marked to indicate the compartments or parts of the nautical school ship to which they lead.

(d) *Fire hose stations.* At each fire hose valve there shall be marked in not less than 2-inch red letters and figures "Fire Station 1," 2, 3, etc.

(e) *Emergency squad equipment.* Lockers or spaces containing equipment for use of the emergency squad shall be marked "Emergency Squad Equipment." Lockers or spaces where oxygen or fresh air breathing apparatus is stowed shall be marked "Oxygen Breathing Apparatus" or "Fresh Air Breathing Apparatus," as appropriate.

(f) *Fire extinguishers.* Each fire extinguisher shall be marked with a number and the location where stowed shall be marked in corresponding numbers in not less than 1-inch figures.

(g) *Watertight doors.* Each watertight door shall be numbered in at least 2-inch letters and figures "W.T.D. 1," 2, 3, etc. The color of the marking shall be in contrast to the background. All watertight door remote hand-closing

Coast Guard, DHS § 167.60-15

stations shall be marked in at least 2-inch letters and figures "W. T. D. 1," 2, 3, etc. The direction of operation of the lever or wheel provided to close or open the door at all watertight door remote hand-closing stations shall be marked. The color of the sign shall contrast with the background.

(h) *Instructions for changing steering gear.* Instructions in at least ½-inch letters and figures shall be posted at each emergency steering station and in the steering engine room, relating in order, the different steps to be taken in changing to the emergency steering gear. Each clutch, gear wheel, level, valve, or switch which is used during the changeover shall be numbered or lettered on a brass plate or painted so that the markings can be recognized at a reasonable distance. The instructions shall indicate each clutch or pin to be "in" or "out" and each valve or switch which is to be "opened" or "closed" in shifting to any means of steering for which the vessel is equipped. Instructions shall be included to line up all steering wheels and rudder amidship before changing gears.

(i) *Rudder orders.* At all steering stations, there shall be installed a suitable notice on the wheel or device or at such other position as to be directly in the helmsman's line of vision, to indicate the direction in which the wheel or device must be turned for "right rudder" and for "left rudder."

(j) *Lifesaving appliances.* Each lifesaving appliance must be marked as required under subchapter W (Lifesaving Appliances and Arrangements) of this chapter.

[CGFR 51-11, 16 FR 3218, Apr. 12, 1951, as amended by CGFR 54-46, 19 FR 8708, Dec. 18, 1954; CGFR 60-36, 25 FR 10642, Nov. 5, 1960; CGD 73-24R, 39 FR 10139, Mar. 18, 1974; CGD 75-040, 40 FR 58454, Dec. 17, 1975; CGD 84-069, 61 FR 25311, May 20, 1996]

Subpart 167.60—Certificates of Inspection

§ 167.60-1 Issuance by Officer in Charge, Marine Inspection.

(a) Every nautical school ship shall be inspected annually and if in the opinion of the Officer in Charge, Marine Inspection, the nautical school ship can be operated safely, he shall issue a certificate of inspection with the following indorsement: "Nautical School Ship" in lieu of the classification "Passenger vessel", "cargo vessel", etc.

(b) When a nautical school ship, in the opinion of the Officer in Charge, Marine Inspection, may be navigated on the waters of any ocean or the Gulf of Mexico more than 20 nautical miles offshore, the route shall be designated on certificate of inspection as "Ocean".

(c) When a nautical school ship, in the opinion of the Officer in Charge, Marine Inspection, may be navigated on the waters of any ocean or the Gulf of Mexico 20 nautical miles or less offshore, the route shall be designated on the certificate of inspection as "Coastwise".

(d) Documented vessels of 500 gross tons or more, certificated for ocean or coastwise service, which do not comply with the requirements of SOLAS 74 for cargo vessels shall have their certificate of inspection endorsed "Domestic Voyages Only."

[CGFR 51-11, 16 FR 3218, Apr. 12, 1951, as amended by CGFR 69-127, 35 FR 9882, June 17, 1970; CGD 90-008, 55 FR 30663, July 26, 1990]

§ 167.60-5 Period of time for which valid.

A certificate of inspection for any period less than one year shall not be issued, but nothing herein shall be construed as preventing the revocation or suspension of a certificate of inspection in case such process is authorized by law.

§ 167.60-10 Exhibition of certificate of inspection.

On every nautical school ship, the original certificate of inspection shall be framed under glass and posted in a conspicuous place.

§ 167.60-15 Manning and persons allowed to be carried.

The Officer in Charge, Marine Inspection, shall specify in the Certificate of Inspection the minimum complement of officers and crew necessary for the safe navigation of the vessel and shall specify the total number of persons allowed to be carried.

[CGD 74-201, 41 FR 19647, May 13, 1976]

Subpart 167.65—Special Operating Requirements

§ 167.65–1 Emergency training, musters, and drills.

Onboard training, musters, and drills must be in accordance with subchapter W (Lifesaving Appliances and Arrangements) of this chapter.

[CGD 84–069, 61 FR 25311, May 20, 1996]

§ 167.65–5 Flashing the rays of a searchlight or other blinding light.

Flashing the rays of a searchlight or other blinding light onto the bridge or into the pilothouse of any vessel under way is prohibited.

§ 167.65–15 Routing instructions; strict compliance with.

All licensed masters, officers, and certificated seamen on nautical school ships must strictly comply with routing instructions issued by competent naval authority.

[CGD 95–027, 61 FR 26010, May 23, 1996]

§ 167.65–20 Unnecessary whistling.

Unnecessary sounding of a nautical school ship's whistle is prohibited within any harbor limits of the United States.

§ 167.65–25 Steering gear tests.

On all nautical school ships making voyages of more than 48 hours' duration, the entire steering gear, the whistle, the means of communication and the signaling appliances between the bridge or pilothouse and engine room shall be examined and tested by an officer of the nautical school ship within a period of not more than 12 hours before leaving port. All nautical school ships making voyages of less than 48 hours' duration shall be so examined and tested at least once in every week. The fact and time of such examination and test shall be recorded in the log book.

§ 167.65–35 Use of auto pilot.

Except as provided in 33 CFR 164.15, when the automatic pilot is used in—

(a) Areas of high traffic density;
(b) Conditions of restricted visibility; and

(c) All other hazardous navigational situations, the master shall ensure that—

(1) It is possible to immediately establish human control of the ship's steering;

(2) A competent person is ready at all times to take over steering control; and

(3) The changeover from automatic to manual steering and vice versa is made by, or under, the supervision of the officer of the watch.

[CFR 75–074, 42 FR 5964, Jan. 17, 1977]

§ 167.65–38 Loading doors.

(a) The master of a vessel fitted with loading doors shall assure that all loading doors are closed watertight and secured during the entire voyage except that—

(1) If a door cannot be opened or closed while the vessel is at a dock, it may be open while the vessel approaches and draws away from the dock, but only as far as necessary to enable the door to be immediately operated.

(2) If needed to operate the vessel, or embark and disembark passengers when the vessel is at anchor in protected waters, loading doors may be open provided that the master determines that the safety of the vessel is not impaired.

(b) For the purposes of this section, "loading doors" include all weathertight ramps, bow visors, and openings used to load personnel, equipment, and stores, in the collision bulkhead, the side shell, and the boundaries of enclosed superstructures that are continuous with the shell of the vessel.

(c) The master shall enter into the log book the time and door location of every closing of the loading doors.

(d) The master shall enter into the log book any opening of the doors in accordance with paragraph (a)(2) of this section setting forth the time of the opening of the doors and the circumstances warranting this action.

[CGD 89–037, 57 FR 41824, Sept. 11, 1992]

§ 167.65–40 Draft.

The master of every nautical school ship over 50 gross tons shall, whenever leaving port, enter the maximum draft of his nautical school ship in the log book.

§ 167.65-42 Verification of vessel compliance with applicable stability requirements.

(a) After loading and prior to departure and at all other times necessary to assure the safety of the vessel, the master shall determine that the vessel complies with all applicable stability requirements in the vessel's trim and stability book, stability letter, Certificate of Inspection, and Load Line Certificate, as the case may be, and then enter an attestation statement of the verification in the log book. The vessel may not depart until it is in compliance with these requirements.

(b) When determining compliance with applicable stability requirements the vessel's draft, trim, and stability must be determined as necessary and any stability calculations made in support of the determination must be retained on board the vessel for the duration of the voyage.

[CGD 89-037, 57 FR 41824, Sept. 11, 1992]

§ 167.65-45 Notice to mariners; aids to navigation.

(a) Officers are required to acquaint themselves with the latest information published by the Coast Guard and the National Imagery and Mapping Agency regarding aids to navigation, and neglect to do so is evidence of neglect of duty. It is desirable that nautical school ships navigating oceans and coastwise and Great Lakes waters shall have available in the pilothouse for convenient reference at all times a file of the applicable Notice to Mariners.

(b) Weekly Notices to Mariners (Great Lakes Edition), published by the Commander, 9th Coast Guard District, contain announcements and information on changes in aids to navigation and other marine information affecting the safety of navigation on the Great Lakes. These notices may be obtained free of charge, by making application to Commander, 9th Coast Guard District.

(c) Weekly Notices to Mariners (Worldwide coverage) are prepared jointly by the National Imagery and Mapping Agency, National Ocean Service, and the U.S. Coast Guard. They include changes in aids to navigation in assembled form for the 1st, 5th, 7th, Greater Antilles Section, 8th, 11th, 13th, 14th, and 17th Coast Guard Districts. Foreign marine information is also included in these notices. These notices are available without charge from the National Imagery and Mapping Agency, U.S. Collector of Customs of the major seaports in the United States and are also on file in the U.S. Consulates where they may be inspected.

(d) As appropriate for the intended voyage, all nautical school ships must carry adequate and up-to-date—
(1) Charts;
(2) Sailing directions;
(3) Coast pilots;
(4) Light lists;
(5) Notices to mariners;
(6) Tide tables;
(7) Current tables; and
(8) All other nautical publications necessary.[1]

[CGFR 66-33, 31 FR 15298, Dec. 6, 1966, as amended by CGFR 75-074, 42 FR 5964, Jan. 31, 1977; CGD 95-028, 62 FR 51217, Sept. 30, 1997; USCG-2001-10224, 66 FR 48621, Sept. 21, 2001]

§ 167.65-50 Posting placards of lifesaving signals.

On all vessels to which this subpart applies there must be readily available to the deck officer of the watch a placard containing instructions for the use of the life saving signals set forth in regulation 16, chapter V, of the International Convention for Safety of Life at Sea, 1974. These signals must be used by vessels or persons in distress when communicating with lifesaving stations and maritime rescue units.

[CGD 95-027, 61 FR 26010, May 23, 1996]

§ 167.65-60 Examination of boilers and machinery by engineer.

It shall be the duty of an engineer when he assumes charge of the boilers and machinery of a nautical school ship to examine the same forthwith and thoroughly, and if he finds any part thereof in bad condition, he shall immediately report the facts to the

---

[1] For United States vessels in one or on the navigable waters of the United States, see 33 CFR 164.33.

§ 167.65-65

master, owner, or agent, and to the Officer in Charge, Marine Inspection, of the district, who shall thereupon investigate the matter and take such actions as may be necessary.

§ 167.65–65 Notice and reporting of casualty and voyage records.

The requirements for providing notice and reporting of marine casualties and for retaining voyage records are contained in part 4 of this chapter.

[CGD 84-099, 52 FR 47536, Dec. 14, 1987]

§ 167.65–70 Reports of accidents, repairs, and unsafe boilers and machinery by engineers.

(a) Before making repairs to a boiler of a nautical school ship the engineer in charge shall report, in writing, the nature of such repairs to the nearest Officer in Charge, Marine Inspection, where such repairs are to be made.

(b) And it shall be the duty of all engineers when an accident occurs to the boilers or machinery in their charge tending to render the further use of such boilers or machinery unsafe until repairs are made, or when, by reason of ordinary wear, such boilers or machinery have become unsafe, to report the same to the Officer in Charge, Marine Inspection, immediately upon the arrival of the nautical school ship at the first port reached subsequent to the accident, or after the discovery of such unsafe condition by said engineer.

PART 168—CIVILIAN NAUTICAL SCHOOL VESSELS

Subpart 168.01—Authority and Purpose

Sec.
168.01-1   Purpose of regulations.

Subpart 168.05—General Requirements

168.05-1   Application of passenger vessel inspection laws.
168.05-5   Application of passenger vessel inspection regulations.
168.05-10   Subdivision and stability.
168.05-15   Right of appeal.

Subpart 168.10—Definitions of Terms Used in This Part

168.10-1   Nautical school vessels.
168.10-5   Civilian nautical school.

Subpart 168.15—Accommodations

168.15-1   Intent.
168.15-5   Location of crew spaces.
168.15-10   Construction.
168.15-15   Size.
168.15-20   Equipment.
168.15-25   Washrooms.
168.15-30   Toilet rooms.
168.15-35   Hospital space.
168.15-40   Lighting.
168.15-45   Heating and cooling.
168.15-50   Ventilation.
168.15-55   Screening.
168.15-60   Inspection.

AUTHORITY: 46 U.S.C. 3305, 3306; Department of Homeland Security Delegation No. 0170.1.

SOURCE: CGFR 52-43, 17 FR 9543, Oct. 18, 1952, unless otherwise noted.

Subpart 168.01—Authority and Purpose

§ 168.01–1 Purpose of regulations.

(a) The purpose of the regulations in this part is to set forth uniform minimum requirements for vessels, whether being navigated or not, which are used by or in connection with any civilian nautical school, except vessels of the Navy or Coast Guard.

Subpart 168.05—General Requirements

§ 168.05–1 Application of passenger vessel inspection laws.

(a) All laws covering the inspection of passenger vessels are hereby made applicable to all vessels or other floating equipment used by or in connection with any civilian nautical school, whether such vessels or other floating equipment are being navigated or not, except vessels of the Navy or Coast Guard.

§ 168.05–5 Application of passenger vessel inspection regulations.

Where the requirements are not covered specifically in this part, all the regulations applying to passenger vessels in subchapters E (Load Lines), F (Marine Engineering), H (Passenger Vessels), J (Electrical Engineering), K (Small Passenger Vessels Carrying More Than 150 Passengers Or With Overnight Accommodations For More Than 49 Passengers), P (Manning), Q

Coast Guard, DHS § 168.15-15

(Specifications), T (Small Passenger Vessels), and W (Lifesaving Appliances and Arrangements) of this chapter are hereby made applicable to all vessels or other floating equipment used by or in connection with any civilian nautical school, whether such vessels or other floating equipment are being navigated or not, except vessels of the Navy or Coast Guard.

[CGD 84-069, 61 FR 25312, May 20, 1996, as amended at 63 FR 52816, Oct. 1, 1998]

§ 168.05-10 Subdivision and stability.

Each vessel must meet the applicable requirements in Subchapter S of this chapter.

[CGD 79-023, 48 FR 51010, Nov. 4, 1983]

§ 168.05-15 Right of appeal.

Any person directly affected by a decision or action taken under this part, by or on behalf of the Coast Guard, may appeal therefrom in accordance with subpart 1.03 of this chapter.

[CGD 88-033, 54 FR 50281, Dec. 6, 1989]

Subpart 168.10—Definitions of Terms Used in This Part

§ 168.10-1 Nautical school vessels.

The term *nautical school vessel* means a vessel operated by or in connection with a nautical school or an educational institution under Section 13 of the Coast Guard Authorization Act of 1986.

[CGD 84-069, 61 FR 25312, May 20, 1996]

§ 168.10-5 Civilian nautical school.

The term *civilian nautical school* means any school or branch thereof operated and conducted in the United States, except State nautical schools and schools operated by the United States or any agency thereof, which offers instruction for the primary purpose of training for service in the merchant marine.

[CGD 84-069, 61 FR 25312, May 20, 1996]

Subpart 168.15— Accommodations

Source: CGD 95-027, 61 FR 26010, May 23, 1996, unless otherwise noted.

§ 168.15-1 Intent.

The accommodations provided for members of the crew, passengers, cadets, students, instructors or any other persons at any time quartered on board a vessel to which this part applies must be securely constructed, properly lighted, heated, drained, ventilated, equipped, located, arranged and insulated from undue noise, heat and odors.

§ 168.15-5 Location of crew spaces.

(a) Quarters must be located so that sufficient fresh air and light are obtainable compatible with accepted practice or good arrangement and construction.

(b) Unless approved by the Commandant, quarters, must not be located forward of the collision bulkhead, nor may such section or sections of any deck head occupied by quarters be below the deepest load line.

§ 168.15-10 Construction.

(a) The accommodations provided must be securely constructed, properly lighted, heated, drained, ventilated, equipped, located, arranged, and insulated from undue noise, heat, and odors.

(b) All accommodations must be constructed and arranged so that they can be kept in a clean, workable, and sanitary condition.

§ 168.15-15 Size.

(a) Sleeping accommodations must be divided into rooms, no one of which may berth more than six persons. The purpose for which each space is to be used and the number of persons it may accommodate, must be marked outside the space.

(b) Each room must be of such size that there is at least 1.8 square meters (20 square feet) of deck area and a volume of at least 4.2 cubic meters (150 cubic feet) for each person accommodated. In measuring sleeping quarters, any furnishings contained therein are not to be deducted from the total volume or from the deck area.

[CGD 95-027, 61 FR 26010, May 23, 1996; 61 FR 35138, July 5, 1996]

§ 168.15-20 Equipment.

(a) Each person shall have a separate berth and not more than 1 berth may be placed above another. The berths must be of metal framework. The overall size of a berth must not be less than 68 centimeters (27 inches) wide by 190 centimeters (75 inches) long. Where 2 tiers of berths are fitted, the bottom of the lower berth must not be less than 30 centimeters (12 inches) above the deck, and the bottom of the upper must not be less than 76 centimeters (30 inches) from both the bottom of the lower and from the deck overhead. The berths must not be obstructed by pipes, ventilating ducts, or other installations.

(b) A metal locker must be provided for each person accommodated in a room.

§ 168.15-25 Washrooms.

(a) There must be provided 1 shower for each 10 persons or fraction thereof and 1 wash basin for each 6 persons or fraction thereof for all persons who do not occupy rooms to which private or semi-private facilities are attached.

(b) All wash basins and showers must be equipped with adequate plumbing, including hot and cold running fresh water.

[CGD 95-027, 61 FR 26010, May 23, 1996; 61 FR 35138, July 5, 1996]

§ 168.15-30 Toilet rooms.

(a) There must be provided 1 toilet for each 10 persons or fraction thereof to be accommodated who do not occupy rooms to which private facilities are attached.

(b) The toilet rooms must be located convenient to the sleeping quarters of the persons to which they are allotted but must not open directly into such quarters except when they are provided as private or semiprivate facilities.

(c) Where more than 1 toilet is located in a space or compartment, each toilet must be separated by partitions.

§ 168.15-35 Hospital space.

(a) Each vessel must be provided with a hospital space. This space must be situated with due regard for the comfort of the sick so that they may receive proper attention in all weather.

(b) The hospital must be suitably separated from other spaces and must be used for the care of the sick and for no other purpose.

(c) The hospital must be fitted with berths in the ratio of 1 berth to every 12 persons, but the number of berths need not exceed 6.

(d) [Reserved]

(e) The hospital must have a toilet, wash basin, and bathtub or shower conveniently located. Other necessary suitable equipment of a sanitary type such as a clothes locker, a table and a seat must be provided.

§ 168.15-40 Lighting.

All quarters, including washrooms, toilet rooms, and hospital spaces, must be adequately lighted.

§ 168.15-45 Heating and cooling.

All quarters must be adequately heated and cooled in a manner suitable to the purpose of the space.

§ 168.15-50 Ventilation.

(a) All quarters must be adequately ventilated in a manner suitable to the purpose of the space and route of the vessel.

(b) When mechanical ventilation is provided for sleeping rooms, washrooms, toilet rooms, hospital spaces, and messrooms, these spaces must be supplied with fresh air equal to at least 10 times the volume of the room each hour.

§ 168.15-55 Screening.

Provision must be made to protect the quarters against the admission of insects.

§ 168.15-60 Inspection.

The Officer in Charge, Marine Inspection, shall inspect the quarters of every such vessel at least once in each month or at such time as the vessel enters an American port and shall satisfy himself that such vessel is in compliance with the regulations in this part.

PART 169—SAILING SCHOOL VESSELS

Subpart 169.100—General Provisions

Sec.
169.101 Purpose.
169.103 Applicability.
169.107 Definitions.
169.109 Equivalents.
169.111 Administrative procedures.
169.112 Special consideration.
169.113 Right of appeal.
169.115 Incorporation by reference.
169.117 OMB control numbers.
169.119 Vessel status.
169.121 Loadlines.

Subpart 169.200—Inspection and Certification

CERTIFICATE OF INSPECTION

169.201 When required.
169.203 Description.
169.205 Obtaining or renewing a Certificate of Inspection.
169.207 Period of validity for a Certificate of Inspection.
169.209 Routes permitted.
169.211 Permit to proceed for repair.
169.213 Permit to carry excursion party.
169.215 Certificate of inspection amendment.
169.217 Posting.

LETTER OF DESIGNATION

169.218 Procedures for designating sailing school vessels.
169.219 Renewal of letter of designation.

INSPECTION FOR CERTIFICATION

169.220 General.
169.221 Initial inspection for certification.
169.222 Scope of inspection for certification.
169.223 Subsequent inspections for certification.

REINSPECTION

169.225 Annual inspection.
169.226 Periodic inspection.
169.227 Certificate of Inspection: Conditions of validity.

DRYDOCKING OR HAULING OUT

169.229 Drydock examination, internal structural examination, and underwater survey intervals.
169.230 Underwater Survey in Lieu of Drydocking (UWILD).
169.231 Definitions relating to hull examinations.
169.233 Notice and plans required.
169.234 Integral fuel oil tank examinations.

REPAIRS AND ALTERATIONS

169.235 Permission required.
169.236 Inspection and testing required.

INSPECTIONS

169.237 Inspection standards.
169.239 Hull.
169.241 Machinery.
169.243 Electrical.
169.245 Lifesaving equipment.
169.247 Firefighting equipment.
169.249 Pressure vessels.
169.251 Steering apparatus.
169.253 Miscellaneous systems and equipment.
169.255 Sanitary inspection.
169.257 Unsafe practices.
169.259 Limitations of inspections.

Subpart 169.300—Construction and Arrangement

PLANS

169.305 Plans required.
169.307 Plans for sister vessels.

HULL STRUCTURE

169.309 Structural standards.
169.311 Fire protection.
169.313 Means of escape.
169.315 Ventilation (other than machinery spaces).

LIVING SPACES

169.317 Accommodations.
169.319 Washrooms and toilets.
169.323 Furniture and furnishings.

RAILS AND GUARDS

169.327 Deck rails.
169.329 Storm rails.
169.331 Guards in hazardous locations.

Subpart 169.400—Watertight Integrity, Subdivision, and Stability

169.401 Applicability.

Subpart 169.500—Lifesaving and Firefighting Equipment

LIFESAVING EQUIPMENT—GENERAL

169.505 Equipment installed but not required.
169.507 Responsibility of master.
169.509 Approval for repairs and alterations.

PRIMARY LIFESAVING EQUIPMENT

169.513 Types of primary equipment.
169.515 Number required.
169.517 Rescue boat.
169.519 Availability.
169.521 Stowage.

Pt. 169

EQUIPMENT FOR PRIMARY LIFESAVING APPARATUS

169.525 General.
169.527 Required equipment for lifeboats.
169.529 Description of lifeboat equipment.
169.535 Required equipment for lifefloats.
169.537 Description of equipment for lifefloats.

PERSONAL FLOTATION DEVICES

169.539 Type required.
169.541 Number required.
169.543 Distribution and stowage.
169.545 Markings.

ADDITIONAL LIFESAVING EQUIPMENT

169.549 Ring lifebuoys and water lights.
169.551 Exposure suits.
169.553 Pyrotechnic distress signals.
169.555 Emergency position indicating radio beacon (EPIRB).
169.556 Work vests.

FIREFIGHTING EQUIPMENT

169.559 Fire pumps.
169.561 Firemain.
169.563 Firehose.
169.564 Fixed extinguishing system, general.
169.565 Fixed carbon dioxide system.
169.567 Portable extinguishers.
169.569 Fire axes.

Subpart 169.600—Machinery and Electrical

169.601 General.

INTERNAL COMBUSTION ENGINE INSTALLATIONS

169.605 General.
169.607 Keel cooler installations.
169.608 Non-integral keel cooler installations.
169.609 Exhaust systems.
169.611 Carburetors.

FUEL SYSTEMS

169.613 Gasoline fuel systems.
169.615 Diesel fuel systems.

STEERING SYSTEMS

169.618 General.
169.619 Reliability.
169.621 Communications.
169.622 Rudder angle indicators.
169.623 Power-driven steering systems.

VENTILATION

169.625 Compartments containing diesel machinery.
169.627 Compartments containing diesel fuel tanks.
169.629 Compartments containing gasoline machinery or fuel tanks.
169.631 Separation of machinery and fuel tank spaces from accommodation spaces.

46 CFR Ch. I (10–1–04 Edition)

PIPING SYSTEMS

169.640 General.
169.642 Vital systems.

BILGE SYSTEMS

169.650 General.
169.652 Bilge piping.
169.654 Bilge pumps.

ELECTRICAL

169.662 Hazardous locations.

ELECTRICAL INSTALLATIONS OPERATING AT POTENTIALS OF LESS THAN 50 VOLTS ON VESSELS OF LESS THAN 100 GROSS TONS

169.664 Applicability.
169.665 Name plates.
169.666 Generators and motors.
169.667 Switchboards.
169.668 Batteries.
169.669 Radiotelephone equipment.
169.670 Circuit breakers.
169.671 Accessories.
169.672 Wiring for power and lighting circuits.
169.673 Installation of wiring for power and lighting circuits.

ELECTRICAL INSTALLATIONS OPERATING AT POTENTIALS OF 50 VOLTS OR MORE ON VESSELS OF LESS THAN 100 GROSS TONS

169.674 Applicability.
169.675 Generators and motors.
169.676 Grounded electrical systems.
169.677 Equipment protection and enclosure.
169.678 Main distribution panels and switchboards.
169.679 Wiring for power and lighting circuits.
169.680 Installation of wiring for power and lighting circuits.
169.681 Disconnect switches and devices.
169.682 Distribution and circuit loads.
169.683 Overcurrent protection, general.
169.684 Overcurrent protection for motors and motor branch circuits.
169.685 Electric heating and cooking equipment.
169.686 Shore power.

ELECTRICAL INSTALLATIONS ON VESSELS OF 100 GROSS TONS AND OVER

169.687 General.
169.688 Power supply.
169.689 Demand loads.
169.690 Lighting branch circuits.
169.691 Navigation lights.
169.692 Remote stop stations.
169.693 Engine order telegraph systems.

Subpart 169.700—Vessel Control, Miscellaneous Systems, and Equipment

169.703 Cooking and heating.
169.705 Mooring equipment.

Coast Guard, DHS § 169.103

169.709 Compass.
169.711 Emergency lighting.
169.713 Engineroom communication system.
169.715 Radio.
169.717 Fireman's outfit.
169.721 Storm sails and halyards (exposed and partially protected waters only).
169.723 Safety belts.
169.725 First aid kit.
169.726 Radar reflector.

Markings

169.730 General alarm bell switch.
169.731 General alarm bells.
169.732 Carbon dioxide alarm.
169.733 Fire extinguishing branch lines.
169.734 Fire extinguishing system controls.
169.735 Fire hose stations.
169.736 Self-contained breathing apparatus.
169.737 Hand portable fire extinguishers.
169.738 Emergency lights.
169.739 Lifeboats.
169.740 Liferafts and lifefloats.
169.741 Personal flotation devices and ring life buoys.
169.743 Portable magazine chests.
169.744 Emergency position indicating radio beacon (EPIRB).
169.745 Escape hatches and emergency exits.
169.746 Fuel shutoff valves.
169.747 Watertight doors and hatches.
169.750 Radio call sign.
169.755 Draft marks and draft indicating systems.

Subpart 169.800—Operations

169.805 Exhibition of licenses.
169.807 Notice of casualty.
169.809 Charts and nautical publications.
169.813 Station bills.
169.815 Emergency signals.
169.817 Master to instruct ship's company.
169.819 Manning of lifeboats and liferafts.
169.821 Patrol person.
169.823 Openings.
169.824 Compliance with provisions of certificate of inspection.
169.825 Wearing of safety belts.

Tests, Drills, and Inspections

169.826 Steering, communications and control.
169.827 Hatches and other openings.
169.829 Emergency lighting and power systems.
169.831 Emergency position indicating radio beacon (EPIRB).
169.833 Fire and boat drills.
169.837 Lifeboats, liferafts, and lifefloats.
169.839 Firefighting equipment.
169.840 Verification of vessel compliance with applicable stability requirements.
169.841 Logbook entries.
169.847 Lookouts.

169.849 Posting placards containing instructions for launching and inflating inflatable liferafts.
169.853 Display of plans.
169.855 Pre-underway training.
169.857 Disclosure of safety standards.

AUTHORITY: 33 U.S.C. 1321(j); 46 U.S.C. 3306, 6101; Pub. L. 103–206, 107 Stat. 2439; E.O. 11735, 38 FR 21243, 3 CFR, 1971–1975 Comp., p. 793; Department of Homeland Security Delegation No. 0170.1; § 169.117 also issued under the authority of 44 U.S.C. 3507.

SOURCE: CGD 83–005, 51 FR 896, Jan. 9, 1986, unless otherwise noted.

Subpart 169.100—General Provisions

§ 169.101 Purpose.

The regulations in this part set forth uniform requirements which are suited to the particular characteristics and specialized operations of sailing school vessels as defined in Title 46, United States Code section 2101(30).

§ 169.103 Applicability.

(a) This subchapter applies to each domestic vessel operating as a sailing school vessel.

(b) This subchapter does not apply to—

(1) Any vessel operating exclusively on inland waters, which are not navigable waters of the United States;

(2) Any vessel while laid up, dismantled, and out of service;

(3) Any vessel with title vested in the United States and which is used for public purposes except vessels of the U.S. Maritime Administration;

(4) Any vessel carrying one or more passengers;

(5) Any vessel operating under the authority of a current valid certificate of inspection issued per the requirements of 46 CFR chapter I, subchapter H or T, 46 CFR parts 70 through 78 and parts 175 through 187, respectively; or

(6) Any foreign vessel.

(c) A vessel which engages in trade or commerce or carries one or more passengers, cannot operate under a certificate of inspection as a sailing school vessel, but must meet the rules and

§ 169.107

regulations governing the service in which it is engaged.

CGD 83–005, 51 FR 896, Jan. 9, 1986, as amended by USCG–1999–5040, 67 FR 34799, May 15, 2002]

§ 169.107 Definitions.

Anniversary date means the day and the month of each year, which corresponds to the date of expiration of the Certificate of Inspection.

Approved means accepted by the Commandant unless otherwise stated.

Coast Guard District Commander means an officer of the Coast Guard designated by the Commandant to command all Coast Guard activities within a district.

Commandant means the Commandant of the Coast Guard or an authorized representative of the Commandant.

Demise charter means a legally binding document for a term of one year or more under which for the period of the charter, the party who leases or charters the vessel, known as the demise or bareboat charterer, assumes legal responsibility for all of the incidents of ownership, including insuring, manning, supplying, repairing, fueling, maintaining and operating the vessel. The term demise or bareboat charterer is synonymous with "owner pro hac vice".

Existing vessel means a sailing school vessel, whose keel was laid prior to (January 9, 1986), which applies for certification as a sailing school vessel prior to (January 9, 1987), and whose initial inspection for certification is completed prior to (January 9, 1988).

Exposed Waters means waters more than 37 kilometers (20 nautical miles) from the mouth of a harbor of safe refuge, or other waters the Officer in Charge, Marine Inspection determines to present special hazards due to weather or other circumstances.

Headquarters means the Office of the Commandant, United States Coast Guard, Washington, DC 20593.

Instructor means any person who is aboard a sailing school vessel for the purpose of providing sailing instruction and is not an officer, operator, or member of the crew required by regulation to be aboard the vessel, and has not paid any consideration, either directly or indirectly for his or her carriage on the vessel.

Length means the mean length. It is the mean or average between length on deck (LOD) and length between perpendiculars (LBP). *Length on deck* (LOD) means the length between the forward-most and after-most points on the weather deck, excluding sheer. *Length between perpendiculars* (LBP) means the horizontal distance between the perpendiculars taken at the forward-most and after-most points on a vessel's waterline corresponding to the deepest operating draft.

Marine Inspector means any person from the civilian or military branch of the Coast Guard assigned by the Officer in Charge, Marine Inspection or any other person designated by the Coast Guard to perform duties with respect to the inspection, enforcement, and administration of vessel safety and navigation laws and regulations.

Master means the senior licensed individual having command of the vessel.

New vessel means a sailing school vessel which is not an existing vessel.

Officer In Charge, Marine Inspection (OCMI) means any person from the civilian or military branch of the Coast Guard designated as such by the Commandant and who, under the direction of the Coast Guard District Commander, is in charge of the inspection zone in which the vessel is located for the performance of duties with respect to the inspections, enforcement, and administration of vessel safety and navigation laws and regulations.

Partially Protected Waters means—

(1) Waters within 37 kilometers (20 nautical miles) of a harbor of safe refuge, unless determined by the OCMI to be exposed waters; and

(2) Those portions of rivers, harbors, lakes, etc. which the OCMI determines not to be sheltered.

Passenger on a sailing school vessel means an individual carried on the vessel except—

(1) The owner or an individual representative of the owner or, in the case of a vessel under charter, an individual charterer or individual representative of the charterer;

(2) The master;

(3) A member of the crew engaged in the business of the vessel, who has not

contributed consideration for carriage, and who is paid for onboard services;

(4) An employee of the owner of the vessel engaged in the business of the owner, except when the vessel is operating under a demise charter;

(5) An employee of the demise charterer of the vessel engaged in the business of the demise charterer; or

(6) A sailing school instructor or sailing school student. *Protected Waters* means sheltered waters presenting no special hazards such as most rivers, harbors, lakes, etc.

Qualified Organization means an educational organization, State, or political subdivision of a State that owns or demise charters, and operates a sailing school vessel for the purpose of providing sailing instruction. The educational organization must satisfy the requirements of section 501(c)(3) of the Internal Revenue Code of 1954 and must be exempt from tax under section 501(a) of such Code, as now or hereafter amended.

Recognized Classification Society means the American Bureau of Shipping or other classification society recognized by the Commandant.

Rules of the Road means the statutory and regulatory rules governing navigation of vessels.

Sailing instruction means teaching, research, and practical experience in operating vessels propelled primarily by sail, and may include any subject related to that operation and the sea, including seamanship, navigation, oceanography, other nautical and marine sciences, and maritime history and literature. In conjunction with any of those subjects, "sailing instruction" also includes instruction in mathematics and language arts skills to a sailing school student with a learning disability.

Sailing School Student means any person who is aboard a sailing school vessel for the purpose of receiving sailing instruction.

Sailing School Vessel means a vessel of less than 500 gross tons, carrying six or more individuals who are sailing school students or sailing school instructors, principally equipped for propulsion by sail even if the vessel has an auxiliary means of propulsion, and owned or demise chartered and operated by a qualified organization during such times as the vessel is operated exclusively for the purposes of sailing instruction.

Ship's Company means the officers and crew of a sailing school vessel, sailing school students, and sailing school instructors.

Watertight means designed and constructed to withstand a static head of water without any leakage, except that *watertight equipment* means enclosed equipment constructed so that a stream of water from a hose (not less than 1 inch in diameter) under head of about 35 feet from a distance of about 10 feet, and for a period of 5 minutes, can be played on the apparatus without leakage.

Weathertight means that water will not penetrate into the unit in any sea condition, except that *weathertight equipment* means equipment constructed or protected so that exposure to a beating rain will not result in the entrance of water.

[CGD 83–005, 51 FR 897, Jan. 9, 1986; 51 FR 3785, Jan. 30, 1986, as amended by USCG–1999–4976, 65 FR 6507, Feb. 9, 2000; USCG–1999–5040, 67 FR 34799, May 15, 2002]

§ 169.109 Equivalents.

Substitutes for a fitting, appliance, apparatus, or equipment, may be accepted by the Commandant if the substituted item is as effective and consistent with the requirements and minimum safety standards specified in this subchapter.

§ 169.111 Administrative procedures.

(a) Upon receipt of a written application for inspection, the Officer in Charge, Marine Inspection assigns a marine inspector to inspect the vessel at a mutually agreed upon time and place.

(b) The owner or a representative shall be present during the inspection.

(c) If during the inspection, the vessel or its equipment is found not to conform to the requirements of law or the regulations in this subchapter, the marine inspector lists all requirements which have not been met and presents the list to the owner or a representative.

(d) In any case where the owner of a vessel or his representative desires further clarification of, or reconsideration

§ 169.112

of any requirement placed against his vessel, he may discuss the matter with the Officer in Charge, Marine Inspection.

§ 169.112 Special consideration.

In applying the provisions of this part, the Officer in Charge, Marine Inspection, may give special consideration to departures from the specific requirements when special circumstances or arrangements warrant such departures and an equivalent level of safety is provided.

§ 169.113 Right of appeal.

Any person directly affected by a decision or action taken under this part, by or on behalf of the Coast Guard, may appeal therefrom in accordance with subpart 1.03 of this chapter.

[CGD 88-033, 54 FR 50381, Dec. 6, 1989]

§ 169.115 Incorporation by reference.

(a) In this subchapter portions or the entire text of certain industrial standards and specifications are referred to as the governing requirements for materials, equipment, tests, or procedures to be followed. These standards and specification requirements specifically referred to in this subchapter are the governing requirements for the subject matters covered unless specifically limited, modified, or replaced by other regulations in this subchapter.

(b) These materials are incorporated by reference into this part with the approval of the Director of the Federal Register. The Office of the Federal Register publishes a table, "Material Approved for Incorporation by Reference," which appears in the Finding Aids section of this volume. In that table is found citations to the particular sections of this part where the material is incorporated with the approval by the Director of the Federal Register. To enforce any edition other than the one listed in paragraph (c) of this section, notice of change must be published in the FEDERAL REGISTER and the material must be made available. All approved material is on file at the Office of the Federal Register, Washington, DC 20408 and at the U.S. Coast Guard, Office of Design and Engineering Standards, Washington DC 20593.

(c) The materials approved for incorporation by reference in this part are:

(1) American Boat and Yacht Council (ABYC), 3069 Solomons Island Road, Edgewater, MD 21037

P-1-73—"Safe Installation of Exhaust Systems for Propulsion and Auxiliary Engines" (1973)

H-24.9 (g) and (h)—"Fuel Strainers and Fuel Filters" (1975)

H-2.5—"Ventilation of Boats Using Gasoline—Design and Construction" (1981)

A-1-78—"Marine LPG—Liquefied Petroleum Gas Systems"

A-3-70—"Recommended Practices and Standards Covering Galley Stoves"

A-22-78—"Marine CNG—Compressed Natural Gas Systems"

(2) National Bureau of Standards, c/o Superintendent of Documents, U.S. Government Printing Office, Washington D.C. 20402

Special Pub. 440 (SD Cat. No. C13.10:490), "Color: Universal Language and Dictionary of Names", 1976

(3) National Fire Protection Association (NFPA), 1 Batterymarch Park, Quincy, MA 02269

302—"Pleasure and Commercial Motor Craft," Chapter 6 (1980)

306—"Control of Gas Hazards on Vessels" (1980)

70—"National Electrical Code," Article 310-8 and Table 310-13 (1980)

(4) Naval Publications and Forms Center, Customer Service Code 1052, 5801 Tabor Ave., Philadelphia, PA 19120

Federal Specification ZZ-H-451 "Hose, Fire, Woven-Jacketed Rubber or Cambric-Lined, with Couplings, F."

(5) Underwriters Laboratories, Inc. (UL), 12 Laboratory Drive, Research Triangle Park, NC 27709-3995

UL 19-78—"Woven Jacketed, Rubber Lined Fire Hose"

[CGD 83-005, 51 FR 896, Jan. 9, 1986, as amended by CGD 95-072, 60 FR 50468, Sept. 29, 1995; CGD 96-041, 61 FR 50734, Sept. 27, 1996; USCG-1999-6216, 64 FR 53228, Oct. 1, 1999]

§ 169.117 OMB control numbers.

(a) *Purpose.* This section collects and displays the control numbers assigned to information collection and recordkeeping requirements in this subchapter by the Office of Management and Budget (OMB) pursuant to the Paperwork Reduction Act of 1980 (44 U.S.C. 3501 *et seq.*). The Coast Guard intends that this section comply with the requirements of 44 U.S.C. 3507(f) which requires that agencies display a current control number assigned by the Director of OMB for each approved agency information collection requirement.

(b) *Display.*

46 CFR part—	OMB control No.
§ 169.111	1625–0002
§ 169.201	1625–0002
§ 169.205	1625–0002, 1625–0014, 1625–0018, 1625–0032, and 1625–0038
§ 169.211	1625–0002
§ 169.213	1625–0002
§ 169.215	1625–0002
§ 169.217	1625–0002
§ 169.218	1625–0002, 1625–0014, 1625–0018, 1625–0032, and 1625–0038
§ 169.219	1625–0002, 1625–0014, 1625–0018, 1625–0032, and 1625–0038
§ 169.233	1625–0032
§ 169.235	1625–0002
§ 169.305	1625–0038, 1625–0064
§ 169.509	1625–0035, 1625–0038
§ 169.807	1625–0001
§ 169.813	1625–0002, 1625–0014, 1625–0018, 1625–0032, and 1625–0038
§ 169.840	1625–0064
§ 169.841	1625–0002, 1625–0014, 1625–0018, 1625–0032, and 1625–0038
§ 169.857	1625–0002, 1625–0014, 1625–0018, 1625–0032, and 1625–0038.

[CGD 83–005, 51 FR 896, Jan. 9, 1986, as amended by CGD 88–072, 53 FR 34298, Sept. 6, 1988; CGD 89–037, 57 FR 41824, Sept. 11, 1992; USCG–2004–18884, 69 FR 58350, Sept. 30, 2004]

§ 169.119 Vessel status.

For the purpose of 46 U.S.C. 11101, 46 App. U.S.C. 291 and 46 App. U.S.C. 883 a sailing school vessel is not deemed a merchant vessel or a vessel engaged in trade or commerce.

§ 169.121 Loadlines.

Sailing school vessels must meet the applicable loadline regulations contained in Subchapter E (Load Lines) of this chapter.

Subpart 169.200—Inspection and Certification

CERTIFICATE OF INSPECTION

§ 169.201 When required.

(a) No sailing school vessel shall be operated without a valid Certificate of Inspection, Form CG–3753.

(b) Except as noted in this subpart, each sailing school vessel inspected and certificated under the provisions of this subchapter must, during the tenure of the certificate, be in full compliance with the terms of the certificate when carrying six or more individuals who are sailing school students or sailing school instructors.

(c) If necessary to prevent delay of the vessel, a temporary Certificate of Inspection, Form CG–854, is issued pending the issuance and delivery of the regular Certificate of Inspection, Form CG–3753. The temporary certificate is carried in the same manner as the regular certificate and is considered the same as the regular certificate of inspection which it represents.

§ 169.203 Description.

The certificate of inspection issued to a vessel describes the vessel, the route which it may travel, the minimum manning requirements, the major lifesaving equipment carried, the minimum fire extinguishing equipment and life preservers required to be carried, the maximum number of sailing school students and instructors and the maximum number of persons which may be carried, the name of the owner and operator, and such conditions of operations as may be determined by the Officer in Charge, Marine Inspection.

§ 169.205 Obtaining or renewing a Certificate of Inspection.

(a) A qualified organization attempting to obtain or renew a certificate of inspection for a vessel must submit to

§ 169.207

the Coast Guard Officer in Charge, Marine Inspection located in or nearest the port at which the inspection is to be made, the following—

(1) An application for inspection on Form CG–3752; and

(2) Evidence that the vessel has been designated as a sailing school vessel or an application for designation, as set forth in § 169.218; and

(3) Information concerning the program's age and physical qualifications for students and instructors and the ratio of students to instructors.

(b) The application for initial inspection of a vessel being newly constructed or converted must be submitted prior to the start of such construction or conversion.

(c) The construction, arrangement and equipment of all vessels must be acceptable to the cognizant Officer in Charge, Marine Inspection, as a prerequisite of the issuance of the initial certificate of inspection. Acceptance will be based on the information, specifications, drawings and calculations available to the Officer in Charge, Marine Inspection, and on the successful completion of an initial inspection for certification.

(d) You must submit a written application for an inspection for certification to the cognizant Officer in Charge, Marine Inspection. To renew a Certificate of Inspection, you must submit an application at least 30 days before the expiration of the vessel's current certificate. Applications are available at any U.S. Coast Guard Marine Safety Office or Marine Inspection Office. When renewing a Certificate of Inspection, you must schedule an inspection for certification within the 3 months before the expiration date of the current Certificate of Inspection.

(e) The condition of the vessel and its equipment must be acceptable to the cognizant Officer in Charge, Marine Inspection, as a prerequisite of the certificate of inspection renewal. Acceptance will be based on the condition of the vessel as found at the inspection for certification.

[CGD 83–005, 51 FR 896, Jan. 9, 1986, as amended by USCG–1999–4976, 65 FR 6507, Feb. 9, 2000]

§ 169.207 Period of validity for a Certificate of Inspection.

(a) A Certificate of Inspection is valid for 5 years.

(b) Certificates of inspection may be revoked, or suspended and withdrawn by the Officer in Charge, Marine Inspection, at any time for noncompliance with the provisions of this subchapter or requirements established thereunder.

[CGD 83–005, 51 FR 896, Jan. 9, 1986, as amended by USCG–1999–4976, 65 FR 6507, Feb. 9, 2000]

§ 169.209 Routes permitted.

(a) The area of operation for each vessel is designated by the Officer in Charge, Marine Inspection and recorded on its Certificate of Inspection. Each area of operation is described on the Certificate of Inspection under the major headings "exposed waters," "partially protected waters," or "protected waters," as applicable. Further limitations imposed or extensions granted are described by reference to bodies of waters, geographical points, distance from geographical points, distances from land, depths of channel, seasonal limitations, etc.

(b) Operation of vessels on routes of lesser severity than those specifically described or designated on the Certificate of Inspection are permitted, unless expressly prohibited on the Certificate of Inspection. The general order of severity is: exposed, partially protected, and protected waters.

§ 169.211 Permit to proceed for repair.

(a) The Officer in Charge, Marine Inspection, may issue a permit to proceed to another port for repair, Form CG–948, to a vessel if in his judgment it can be done with safety even if the Certificate of Inspection of the vessel has expired or is about to expire.

(b) The permit is issued only upon the written application of the master, owner, or agent of the vessel.

(c) The permit states upon its face the conditions under which it is issued and that guests may not be carried when operating under the permit. The permit must be carried in a manner similar to that described in § 169.217(a) for a certificate of inspection.

§ 169.213 Permit to carry excursion party.

(a) A vessel may be permitted to engage in a temporary excursion operation with a greater number of persons and/or on a more extended route than permitted by its certificate of inspection when in the opinion of the Officer in Charge, Marine Inspection, the operation can be undertaken with safety. A "Permit To Carry Excursion Party" Form CG–949, is a prerequisite of such an operation.

(b) Any Officer in Charge, Marine Inspection, having jurisdiction may issue a permit to carry an excursion party upon the written application of the operator, owner or agent of the vessel.

(c) The OCMI will reevaluate the vessel's sailing instruction program to ensure that the permit fits within the scope of the training program and that the vessel continues to meet the definition of a sailing school vessel.

(d) The OCMI may require an inspection prior to the issuance of a permit to carry an excursion party.

(e) The permit states upon its face the conditions under which it is issued, a reminder about the prohibition against carrying passengers, the number of persons the vessel may carry, the crew required, and additional life-saving or safety equipment required, the route for which the permit is granted, and the dates on which the permit is valid.

(f) The permit must be carried with the certificate of inspection. Any vessel operating under a permit to carry an excursion party must be in full compliance with the terms of its certificate of inspection as supplemented by the permit.

§ 169.215 Certificate of inspection amendment.

(a) An amended certificate of inspection may be issued at any time by any Officer in Charge, Marine Inspection. The amended certificate of inspection replaces the original. An amended certificate of inspection may be issued to authorize and record a change in the character of a vessel or in its route, equipment, ownership, operator, etc., from that specified in the current certificate of inspection.

(b) A request for an amended certificate of inspection must be made to the Officer in Charge, Marine Inspection, by the master, operator, owner, or agent of the vessel at any time there is a change in the character of a vessel or in its route, equipment, ownership, operation etc., as specified in its current certificate of inspection.

(c) The OCMI may require an inspection prior to the issuance of an amended certificate of inspection.

§ 169.217 Posting.

The certificate of inspection must be framed under glass or other suitable transparent material and posted in a conspicuous place on the vessel except on open boats where the certificate may be retained in a watertight container, which is secured to the vessel.

LETTER OF DESIGNATION

§ 169.218 Procedures for designating sailing school vessels.

(a) Upon written request by a qualified institution, a determination is made by the OCMI whether the vessel may be designated as a sailing school vessel.

(b) The request should contain sufficient information to allow the OCMI to make this determination. At a minimum the following items must be submitted:

(1) A detailed description of the vessel, including its identification number, owner, and charterer.

(2) A specific operating plan stating precisely the intended use of the vessel and the intended course of instruction for sailing school students.

(3) A copy of the Internal Revenue Service designation as a non-profit, tax-exempt, organization under sections 501(a) and 501(c)(3) of the Internal Revenue Code.

(4) An affidavit certifying that the owner or charterer has financial resources to meet any liability incurred for death or injury to sailing school students or sailing school instructors on voyages aboard the vessel, in an amount not less than $50,000 for each student and instructor.

(5) Any additional information as requested by the Officer in Charge, Marine Inspection.

§ 169.219

(c) If a designation is granted it is indicated on the certificate of inspection and remains valid for the duration of the certificate, provided all operating conditions remain unchanged.

(d) In the event of a change, the institution must advise the OCMI who issued the designation. After reviewing the pertinent information concerning the change, the OCMI shall determine if the vessel is eligible to retain its designation as a sailing school vessel.

§ 169.219 **Renewal of letter of designation.**

At least 60 days prior to the expiration date of the certificate of inspection, a request for renewal must be submitted in the same manner as described in § 169.218. If the request for renewal is submitted to the OCMI who made the initial determination and all operating conditions remain unchanged, the information need not be resubmitted.

INSPECTION FOR CERTIFICATION

§ 169.220 **General.**

(a) An inspection is required before the issuance of a certificate of inspection.

(b) An inspection for certification is not made until after receipt of the information required in § 169.205(a) of this subchapter.

§ 169.221 **Initial inspection for certification.**

(a) The initial inspection includes an inspection of the hull structure, yards, masts, spars, rigging, sails, machinery, and equipment, including unfired pressure vessels.

(b) The initial inspection of a vessel being newly constructed or converted normally consists of a series of inspections during the construction or conversion.

(c) The inspection ensures that the vessel and its equipment comply with the regulations in this subchapter to the extent they are applicable to the vessel being inspected, and are in accordance with approved plans. The inspection also ensures that the materials, workmanship and condition of all parts of the vessel and its machinery and equipment are in all respects satisfactory for the service intended, and that the vessel is in possession of a valid certificate issued by the Federal Communications Commission, if required.

(d) Before construction is started, the owner, operator, or builder must develop plans indicating the proposed arrangement and construction of the vessel. This list of plans to be developed and the required disposition of these plans are set forth in § 169.305.

§ 169.222 **Scope of inspection for certification.**

Items normally included in an Inspection for Certification are:
(a) Structure.
(b) Watertight integrity.
(c) Pressure vessels and appurtenances.
(d) Piping.
(e) Auxiliary machinery.
(f) Steering apparatus.
(g) Electrical installations.
(h) Lifesaving appliances.
(i) Navigation equipment.
(j) Fire detecting and extinguishing systems.
(k) Pollution prevention equipment.
(l) Sanitary conditions.
(m) Fire hazards.
(n) Verification of valid certificates issued by the Federal Communications Commission.
(o) Lights and signals required by navigation rules.
(p) Bilge and ballast systems.
(q) Rigging, yards, masts, spars, and sails.

§ 169.223 **Subsequent inspections for certification.**

An inspection for renewal of a certificate of inspection includes an inspection of the structure, machinery, yards, spars, masts, rigging, sails, and equipment. The inspection ensures that the vessel is in satisfactory condition, fit for the service intended and complies with the applicable regulations in this subchapter.

REINSPECTION

§ 169.225 **Annual inspection.**

(a) Your vessel must undergo an annual inspection within 3 months before or after each anniversary date, except as specified in § 169.226.

Coast Guard, DHS § 169.229

(b) You must contact the cognizant Officer in Charge, Marine Inspection to schedule an inspection at a time and place which he or she approves. No written application is required.

(c) The scope of the annual inspection is the same as the inspection for certification as specified in § 169.222 but in less detail unless the cognizant marine inspector finds deficiencies or determines that a major change has occurred since the last inspection. If deficiencies are found or a major change to the vessel has occurred, the marine inspector will conduct an inspection more detailed in scope to ensure that the vessel is in satisfactory condition and fit for the service for which it is intended. If your vessel passes the annual inspection, the marine inspector will endorse your current Certificate of Inspection.

(d) If the annual inspection reveals deficiencies in your vessel's maintenance, you must make any or all repairs or improvements within the time period specified by the Officer in Charge, Marine Inspection.

(e) Nothing in this subpart limits the marine inspector from conducting such tests or inspections he or she deems necessary to be assured of the vessel's seaworthiness.

[USCG–1999–4976, 65 FR 6507, Feb. 9, 2000]

§ 169.226 Periodic inspection.

(a) Your vessel must undergo a periodic inspection within 3 months before or after the second or third anniversary of the date of your vessel's Certificate of Inspection. This periodic inspection will take the place of an annual inspection.

(b) You must contact the cognizant Officer in Charge, Marine Inspection to schedule an inspection at a time and place which he or she approves. No written application is required.

(c) The scope of the periodic inspection is the same as that for the inspection for certification, as specified in § 169.222. The Officer in Charge, Marine Inspection will insure that the vessel is in satisfactory condition and fit for the service for which it is intended. If your vessel passes the periodic inspection, the marine inspector will endorse your current Certificate of Inspection.

(d) If the periodic inspection reveals deficiencies in your vessel's maintenance, you must make any or all repairs or improvements within the time period specified by the Officer in Charge, Marine Inspection.

(e) Nothing in this subpart limits the marine inspector from conducting such tests or inspections he or she deems necessary to be assured of the vessel's seaworthiness.

[USCG–1999–4976, 65 FR 6507, Feb. 9, 2000]

§ 169.227 Certificate of Inspection: Conditions of validity.

To maintain a valid Certificate of Inspection, you must complete your annual and periodic inspections within the periods specified in §§ 169.225 and 169.226 respectively and your Certificate of Inspection must be endorsed.

[USCG–1999–4976, 65 FR 6507, Feb. 9, 2000]

DRYDOCKING OR HAULING OUT

§ 169.229 Drydock examination, internal structural examination, and underwater survey intervals.

(a) Except as provided for in paragraphs (b) through (e) of this section, each vessel must undergo drydock and internal structural examinations as follows:

(1) If your vessel operates in saltwater, it must undergo two drydock examinations and two internal structural examinations within any 5-year period unless it has been approved to undergo an underwater survey (UWILD) under § 169.230 of this part. No more than 3 years may elapse between any two examinations.

(2) If your vessel operated in fresh water at least 50 percent of the time since your last drydocking, it must undergo a dry dock and internal structural examination at intervals not to exceed 5 years unless it has been approved to undergo an underwater survey (UWILD) under § 169.230 of this part.

(b) Vessels with wooden hulls must undergo two drydock and two internal structural examinations within any five year period regardless of the type of water in which they operate. No more than three years may elapse between any two examinations.

§ 169.230

(c) If, during an internal structural examination damage or deterioration to the hull plating or structural members is discovered, the Officer in Charge, Marine Inspection, may require the vessel to be drydocked or otherwise taken out of service to further assess the extent of the damage and to effect permanent repairs.

(d) Each vessel which has not met with the applicable examination schedules in paragraphs (a) through (c) of this section because it is on a voyage, must undergo the required examinations upon completion of the voyage.

(e) The Commandant (G–MOC) may authorize extensions to the examination intervals specified in paragraphs (a) and (b) of this section.

[CGD 84–024, 52 FR 39656, Oct. 23, 1987, as amended at 53 FR 32232, Aug. 24, 1988; CGD 95–072, 60 FR 50468, Sept. 29, 1995; CGD 96–041, 61 FR 50734, Sept. 27, 1996; USCG–2000–6858, 67 FR 21083, Apr. 29, 2002]

§ 169.230 Underwater Survey in Lieu of Drydocking (UWILD).

(a) The Officer in Charge, Marine Inspection (OCMI), on a case-by-case basis, may approve an underwater survey instead of a drydock examination at alternating intervals if your vessel is—

(1) Less than 15 years of age;
(2) A steel or aluminum hulled vessel;
(3) Fitted with an effective hull protection system; and
(4) Listed in § 169.229(a)(1) or (2) of this part.

(b) For vessels less than 15 years of age, you must submit an application for an underwater survey to the OCMI at least 90 days before your vessel's next required drydock examination. The application must include—

(1) The procedure for carrying out the underwater survey;
(2) The time and place of the underwater survey;
(3) The method used to accurately determine the diver's or remotely operated vehicle's (ROV) location relative to the hull;
(4) The means for examining all through-hull fittings and appurtenances;
(5) The condition of the vessel, including the anticipated draft of the vessel at the time of survey;
(6) A description of the hull protection system; and
(7) The name and qualifications of any third party examiner.

(c) If your vessel is 15 years old or older, the cognizant District Commander, on a case-by-case basis, may approve an underwater survey instead of a drydock examination at alternating intervals. You must submit an application for an underwater survey to the OCMI at least 90 days before your vessel's next required drydock examination. You may be allowed this option if—

(1) The vessel is qualified under paragraphs (a)(2) through (4) of this section;
(2) Your application includes the information in paragraphs (b)(1) through (b)(7) of this section; and
(3) During the vessel's drydock examination, preceding the underwater survey, a complete set of hull gaugings was taken and they indicated that the vessel was free from appreciable hull deterioration.

(d) After the drydock examination required by paragraph (c)(3) of this section, the OCMI submits a recommendation for future underwater surveys, the results of the hull gauging, and the results of the Coast Guards' drydock examination results to the cognizant District Commander, for review.

[USCG–2000–6858, 67 FR 21083, Apr. 29, 2002]

§ 169.231 Definitions relating to hull examinations.

As used in the part—

(a) *Drydock examination* means hauling out a vessel or placing a vessel in a drydock or slipway for an examination of all accessible parts of the vessel's underwater body and all through-hull fittings, sea chests, sea valves, sea strainers, and valves for the emergency bilge suction.

(b) *Underwater survey* means the examination of the vessel's underwater hull including all through-hull fittings and appurtenances, while the vessel is afloat.

(c) *Internal structural examination* means an examination of the vessel while afloat or in drydock and consists of a complete examination of the vessel's main strength members, including the major internal framing, the hull plating, voids, and ballast tanks, but not including cargo or fuel oil tanks.

[CGD 84–024, 52 FR 39656, Oct. 23, 1987, as amended at 53 FR 32232, Aug. 24, 1988; USCG–2000–6858, 67 FR 21084, Apr. 29, 2002]

§ 169.233 Notice and plans required.

(a) The master, owner, operator, or agent of the vessel shall notify the Officer in Charge, Marine Inspection, whenever the vessel is to be drydocked regardless of the reason for drydocking.

(b) Each vessel, except barges, that holds a Load Line Certificate must have on board a plan showing the vessel's scantlings. This plan must be made available to the Coast Guard marine inspector whenever the vessel undergoes a drydock examination or internal structural examination or whenever repairs are made to the vessel's hull.

(c) Each barge that holds a Load Line Certificate must have a plan showing the barge's scantlings. The plan need not be maintained on board the barge but must be made available to the Coast Guard marine inspector whenever the barge undergoes a drydock examination or internal structural examination or whenever repairs are made to the barge's hull.

[CGD 84–024, 52 FR 39656, Oct. 23, 1987]

§ 169.234 Integral fuel oil tank examinations.

(a) Each fuel oil tank with at least one side integral to the vessel's hull and located within the hull ("integral fuel oil tank") is subject to inspection as provided in this section. The owner or operator of the vessel shall have the tanks cleaned out and gas freed as necessary to permit internal examination of the tank or tanks designated by the marine inspector. The owner or operator shall arrange for an examination of the fuel tanks of each vessel during an internal structural examination at intervals not to exceed five years.

(b) Integral non-double-bottom fuel oil tanks need not be cleaned out and internally examined if the marine inspector is able to determine by external examination that the general condition of the tanks is satisfactory.

(c) Double-bottom fuel oil tanks on vessels less than 10 years of age need not be cleaned out and internally examined if the marine inspector is able to determine by external examination that the general condition of the tanks is satisfactory.

(d) All double-bottom fuel oil tanks on vessels 10 years of age or older but less than 15 years of age need not be cleaned out and internally examined if the marine inspector is able to determine by internal examination of at least one forward double-bottom fuel oil tank, and by external examination of all other double-bottom fuel oil tanks on the vessel, that the general condition of the tanks is satisfactory.

(e) All double-bottom fuel oil tanks on vessels 15 years of age or older need not be cleaned out and internally examined if the marine inspector is able to determine by internal examination of at least one forward, one amidships, and one aft double-bottom fuel oil tank, and by external examination of all other double-bottom fuel oil tanks on the vessel, that the general condition of the tanks is satisfactory.

[CGD 84–024, 52 FR 39656, Oct. 23, 1987, as amended at 53 FR 32232, Aug. 24, 1988]

REPAIRS AND ALTERATIONS

§ 169.235 Permission required.

(a) Repairs or alterations to the hull, machinery, or equipment which affects the safety of the vessel may not be made without the knowledge and approval of the Officer in Charge, Marine Inspection.

(b) Drawings, sketches or written specifications describing the alterations in detail must be submitted to the OCMI. Proposed alterations must be approved by the Officer in Charge, Marine Inspection, before work is started.

(c) Drawings are not required for repairs or replacements in kind.

§ 169.236 Inspection and testing required.

(a) The provisions of NFPA 306, "Control of Gas Hazards on Vessels," are used as a guide in conducting the inspections and issuing certificates required by this section.

§ 169.237

(b) Until an inspection has been made to determine that the operations can be undertaken safely, no alterations, repairs, or other operations involving riveting, welding, burning, or other fire-producing actions may be made—

(1) Within or on the boundaries of fuel tanks; or

(2) To pipelines, heating coils, pumps, fittings, or other appurtenances connected to fuel tanks.

(c) Inspections must be conducted as follows:

(1) In ports or places in the United States or its territories and possessions, the inspection must be made by a marine chemist certificated by the National Fire Protection Association; however, if the services of such certified marine chemist are not reasonably available, the Officer in Charge, Marine Inspection, upon the recommendation of the vessel owner and his contractor on their representative, may authorize a person to inspect the particular vessel. If the inspection indicates that the operations can be undertaken with safety, a certificate setting forth this fact in writing must be issued by the certified marine chemist or the authorized person before the work is started. The certificate must include any requirements necessary to reasonably maintain safe conditions in the spaces certified throughout the operation, including any precautions necessary to eliminate or minimize hazards that may be present from protective coatings or residues from cargoes.

(2) When not in a port or place in the United States or its territories and possessions, and when a marine chemist or a person authorized by the Officer in Charge, Marine Inspection, is not reasonably available, the senior officer present shall conduct the inspection and enter the results of the inspection in the vessel's logbook.

(d) It is the responsibility of the senior officer present to secure copies of certificates issued by the certified marine chemist or a person authorized by the Officer in Charge, Marine Inspection. It is the responsibility of the senior officer present, insofar as the persons under his control are concerned, to maintain a safe condition on the vesssel by full observance of all requirements listed by the marine chemist in the certificate.

INSPECTIONS

§ 169.237 Inspection standards.

Vessels are inspected for compliance with the standards required by this subchapter. Items not covered by standards in this subchapter must be in accordance with good marine practice and acceptable to the Officer in Charge, Marine Inspection.

§ 169.239 Hull.

At each inspection for certification and periodic inspection, the vessel must be afloat and ready for the following tests and inspections of the hull structure and its appurtenances:

(a) All accessible parts of the exterior and interior of the hull, the watertight bulkheads, and weather deck are examined. Where the internals of the vessel are completely concealed, sections of the lining or ceiling may be removed or the parts otherwise probed or exposed so that the inspector may be satisfied as to the condition of the hull structure.

(b) All watertight closures in the hull, decks and bulkheads are examined and operated.

(c) The condition of the superstructure, masts, and similar arrangements constructed on the hull is checked. All spars, standing rigging, running rigging, blocks, fittings, and sails, including storm sails are inspected.

(d) All railings and bulwarks and their attachment to the hull structure are inspected. Special attention is paid to ensure that guards or rails are provided in all dangerous places.

(e) All weathertight closures above the weather deck are inspected. The provisions for drainage of sea water from the exposed decks are checked.

[CGD 83–005, 51 FR 896, Jan. 9, 1986, as amended by USCG–1999–4976, 65 FR 6508, Feb. 9, 2000]

§ 169.241 Machinery.

(a) At each inspection for certification and periodic inspection, the marine inspector will examine and test the following items to the extent necessary, to determine that they are in proper operating condition and fit for the service for which they are intended:

(1) *Engine starting system.* Alternate methods of starting are checked.

(2) *Engine control mechanisms.* Mechanisms are operationally tested and visually examined.

(3) *Auxiliary machinery.* All machinery essential to the routine operation of the vessel is checked.

(4) *Fuel systems.* Tanks, tank vents and other appurtenances, piping and pipe fittings are examined. The fuel systems for the auxiliary propulsion engines and all other fuel systems installed are checked. All valves in the fuel lines are tested by operating locally and at remote operating positions.

(5) *Sea valves and bulkhead closure valves.* All overboard discharge and intake valves are checked.

(6) *Bilge and drainage systems.* The means provided for pumping bilges are operationally tested. All suction strainers are examined.

(b) During all inspections special attention is paid to ensure that no fire hazards exist and that guards or protective devices are provided in all hazardous places.

[CGD 83–005, 51 FR 896, Jan. 9, 1986, as amended by USCG–1999–4976, 65 FR 6508, Feb. 9, 2000]

§ 169.243 Electrical.

At each inspection for certification and periodic inspection, the marine inspector will examine and test the following items to the extent necessary, to determine that they are in proper operating condition, in safe electrical condition, and fit for the service for which they are intended:

(a) *Electrical cable.* All cable is examined as far as practicable without undue disturbance of the cable or electrical apparatus.

(b) *Overload or circuit protective devices.* Circuit breakers are tested by manual operation and fuses examined visually. The ratings of fuses are checked to determine suitability for the service intended.

(c) *Rotating machinery.* Rotating electrical machinery essential to the routine operation of the vessel is examined.

(d) *Generators, etc.* All generators, motors, lighting fixtures and circuit interrupting devices located in spaces or areas which may contain flammable vapors are checked.

(e) *Storage batteries.* Batteries are checked for condition and security of stowage.

(f) *Fire detection and alarm system.* Electrical apparatus, which operates as part of or in conjunction with a fire detection or alarm system installed on board the vessel, is operationally tested. The test is applied, in a manner to simulate, as closely as practicable, the actual operation in case of fire.

[CGD 83–005, 51 FR 896, Jan. 9, 1986, as amended by USCG–1999–4976, 65 FR 6508, Feb. 9, 2000]

§ 169.245 Lifesaving equipment.

At each inspection for certification and periodic inspection the following tests and inspections of lifesaving equipment will be conducted:

(a) All air tank buoyant units of all lifesaving appliances are tested for airtightness.

(b) Each lifeboat is lowered to near the water and loaded with its allowed capacity, evenly distributed throughout the length. The total weight used is at least equal to the allowed capacity of the lifeboat considering persons to weigh 75 kg (165 pounds) each. The lifeboat is then lowered into the water until it is afloat and released from the falls.

(c) Each personal flotation device is examined to determine its serviceability. If found to be satisfactory, it is stamped "Passed," together with the date and the port. If found to be unsatisfactory, the personal flotation device must be removed from the vessel's equipment and repaired. If it is beyond repair it must be destroyed in the presence of the Coast Guard inspector.

(d) Each lifeboat winch electrical control apparatus is opened and inspected.

(e) Where gravity davits are installed, it must be demonstrated that the lifeboat can be swung out and lowered from any stopped position by merely releasing the brake on the lifeboat winch. The use of force to start the davits or the lifeboat winch is not permitted.

(f) Inflatable liferaft containers are examined for defects and the inspector verifies that the inflatable liferafts and

§ 169.247

hydraulic releases, if installed, have been serviced at an approved facility in accordance with the provisions of subparts 160.051 and 160.062, respectively, of this chapter.

(g) All other items of lifesaving equipment are examined to determine that they are in suitable condition.

[CGD 83–005, 51 FR 896, Jan. 9, 1986, as amended by USCG–1999–4976, 65 FR 6508, Feb. 9, 2000]

§ 169.247 Firefighting equipment.

(a) At each inspection for certification and periodic inspection and at such other times as considered necessary all fire-extinguishing equipment is inspected to ensure it is in suitable condition. Tests may be necessary to determine the condition of the equipment. The inspector verifies that the tests and inspections required in Tables 169.247 (a)(1) and (a)(2) of this subchapter have been conducted by a qualified servicing facility at least once every twelve months.

(1) Hand portable fire extinguishers and semi-portable fire extinguishing systems are examined for excessive corrosion and general condition.

(2) All parts of the fixed fire-extinguishing systems are examined for excessive corrosion and general condition.

(3) Piping, controls, valves, and alarms on all fire-extinguishing systems are checked to be certain the system is in operating condition.

(4) The fire main system is operated and the pressure checked at the most remote and highest outlets.

(5) Each firehose is subjected to a test pressure equivalent to its maximum service pressure.

TABLE 169.247(a)(1)—PORTABLE EXTINGUISHERS

Type unit	Test
Foam	Discharge. Clean hose and inside of extinguisher thoroughly. Recharge.
Carbon dioxide	Weigh cylinders. Recharge if weight loss exceeds 10 pct of weight of charge. Inspect hose and nozzle to be sure they are clear.

TABLE 169.247(a)(1)—PORTABLE EXTINGUISHERS—Continued

Type unit	Test
Dry chemical (cartridge-operated type).	Examine pressure cartridge and replace if end is punctured or if cartridge is otherwise determined to have leaked or to be in unsuitable condition. Inspect hose and nozzle to see they are clear. Insert charged cartridge. Be sure dry chemical is free-flowing (not caked) and chamber contains full charge.
Dry chemical (stored pressure).	See that pressure gage is in operating range. If not, or if seal is broken, weigh or otherwise determine that full charge of dry chemical is in extinguisher. Recharge if pressure is low or if dry chemical is needed.
HALON 1211 or HALON 1301).	See that pressure gage, if provided, is in operating range. Recharge if pressure is low. Weigh cylinder. Recharge if weight loss exceeds 10 pct of weight of charge. Inspect hose and nozzle to ensure they are clear.

TABLE 169.247(a)(2)—FIXED SYSTEMS

Type system	Test
Carbon dioxide or HALON 1301.	Weigh cylinders. Recharge if weight loss exceeds 10 pct of weight of charge.

[CGD 83–005, 51 FR 896, Jan. 9, 1986, as amended by USCG–1999–4976, 65 FR 6508, Feb. 9, 2000]

§ 169.249 Pressure vessels.

Pressure vessels must meet the requirements of part 54 of this chapter. The inspection procedures for pressure vessels are contained in subpart 61.10 of this chapter.

§ 169.251 Steering apparatus.

At each inspection for certification and periodic inspection the steering apparatus is inspected and operationally tested to determine that its condition is satisfactory and that it is fit for the service intended.

[CGD 83–005, 51 FR 896, Jan. 9, 1986, as amended by USCG–1999–4976, 65 FR 6508, Feb. 9, 2000]

§ 169.253 Miscellaneous systems and equipment.

(a) At each inspection for certification and periodic inspection all items in the ship's outfit, such as

Coast Guard, DHS § 169.307

ground tackle, navigation lights, compass, etc., which are required to be carried by the regulations in this subchapter are examined and tested as necessary to determine that they are fit the service intended.

(b) Approved work vests, where carried, are inspected as provided in § 169.556.

[CGD 83–005, 51 FR 896, Jan. 9, 1986, as amended by USCG–1999–4976, 65 FR 6508, Feb. 9, 2000]

§ 169.255 Sanitary inspection.

At each inspection for certification, periodic inspection, and annual inspection quarters, toilet and washing spaces, galleys, serving pantries, lockers, etc., are examined to determine that they are serviceable and in a sanitary condition.

[CGD 83–005, 51 FR 896, Jan. 9, 1986, as amended by USCG–1999–4976, 65 FR 6508, Feb. 9, 2000]

§ 169.257 Unsafe practices.

(a) At each inspection for certification, periodic inspection, annual inspection, and at every other vessel inspection all observed unsafe practices and hazardous situations must be corrected.

(b) At each inspection for certification, periodic inspection, annual inspection, and at every other vessel inspection the bilges and other spaces are examined to see that there is no accumulation of oil or other matter which might create a fire hazard.

[CGD 83–005, 51 FR 896, Jan. 9, 1986, as amended by USCG–1999–4976, 65 FR 6508, Feb. 9, 2000]

§ 169.259 Limitations of inspections.

The OCMI may require that a vessel and its equipment meet any test or inspection deemed necessary to determine that they are suitable for the service in which they are to be employed.

Subpart 169.300—Construction and Arrangement

PLANS

§ 169.305 Plans required.

(a) Except as provided in paragraphs (b) and (c) of this section the owner or builder shall, before the start of construction or before the initial inspeciton of the vessel, submit to the Officer in Charge, Marine Inspection of the inspection zone where the vessel is to be inspected, at least one copy of each of the following plans:

(1) Midship section.
(2) Outboard profile.
(3) Inboard profile.
(4) Arrangement of decks.
(5) Lifesaving equipment installation and arrangement.
(6) Machinery installation.
(7) Electrical installation.
(8) Fire control plan.
(9) Fuel tanks.
(10) Piping systems.
(11) Hull penetrations and shell connections.
(12) Lines and offsets, curves of form, and capacities of the tanks including size and location on vessel.
(13) Masts, including integration into the ship's structure.
(14) Rigging plan showing sail areas and centers of effort as well as the arrangement, dimensions, and connections of the standing rigging.

(b) For vessels less than 65 feet in length, the owner may submit specifications, sketches, photographs, line drawings or written descriptions in lieu of any of the required drawings provided the required information is adequately detailed and acceptable to the Officer in Charge, Marine Inspection.

(c) The Officer in Charge, Marine Inspection, may waive submission of some or all of the structural plans called for by paragraph (a) of this section for an existing vessel with a history of at least 5 years of safe operation, or if the design and construction of the vessel are essentially similar to a vessel which has a proven record of safe operation in similar service upon similar waters.

§ 169.307 Plans for sister vessels.

Plans are not required for any vessel which is a sister ship to a vessel, provided that—

(a) The approved plans for the original vessels are already on file at any Marine Inspection Office;

(b) The owner of the plans authorizes their use for the new construction;

(c) The regulations have not changed since the original plan approval; and

§ 169.309

(d) There are no major modifications to any of the systems used.

HULL STRUCTURE

§ 169.309 Structural standards.

(a) Compliance with the standards established by a recognized classification society will, in general, be considered satisfactory evidence of the structural adequacy of a vessel.

(b) Masts, posts and other supporting structures are to have adequate strength to withstand the highest loadings imposed by the sail systems during all normal and emergency conditions. Particular attention must be given to the integration of the masts and rigging into the hull structure. The hull structure must be adequately reinforced and stiffened locally to ensure sufficient strength and resistance to plate buckling.

(c) The design, materials, and construction of masts, yards, booms, bowsprits, and standing rigging must be suitable for the intended service. Detailed calculations with respect to the strength of the sail system may be required. Approval by a recognized classification society may be considered satisfactory evidence of the adequacy of the sail system.

(d) When scantlings differ from established standards and it can be demonstrated that a craft approximating the same size, power and displacement has been built to the proposed scantlings and has been in satisfactory service, insofar as structural adequacy is concerned, for a period of a least 5 years, the proposed scantling may be approved. A detailed structural analysis may be required.

(e) Special consideration will be given to the structural requirements of vessels not contemplated by the standards of a recognized classification society and to the use of materials not specially included in these standards.

§ 169.311 Fire protection.

(a) The general construction of the vessel must be designed to minimize fire hazards. Each vessel which carries more than 100 persons or has overnight accommodations for more than 49 persons must meet the requirements of subpart 72.05 of this chapter. Each vessel which is certificated to carry 100 persons or less or had overnight accommodations for less than 50 persons must meet the requirements of § 169.323.

(b) A fire detector, listed by a recognized testing laboratory, must be installed in each unmanned engine space.

(c) Smoke detectors, listed by a recognized testing laboratory, must be installed in each berthing compartment, sail locker, and public area.

(d) Internal combustion engine exhausts, boiler and galley uptakes, and similar sources of ignition must be kept clear of and suitably insulated from any woodwork or other combustible matter.

(e) Lamp, paint, oil lockers and similar compartments must be constructed of metal or wholly lined with metal.

[CGD 83–005, 51 FR 897, Jan. 9, 1986; 51 FR 3785, Jan. 30, 1986]

§ 169.313 Means of escape.

(a) Except as provided by paragraph (f) of this section, there must be at least two means of escape from all areas generally accessible to persons onboard. At least one means of escape must be independent of watertight doors and lead directly to the open deck. Windows and windshields of sufficient size and proper accessibility may be used as one avenue of escape.

(b) The two means of escape must be as widely separated as practical to minimize the possibility of one incident blocking both escapes.

(c) Except as provided by paragraph (d) of this section, a vertical ladder and deck scuttle may not be designated as one of the means of escape.

(d) A vertical ladder and deck scuttle may be used as a second means of escape if—

(1) The primary means of escape is an enclosed stairtower or stairway;

(2) The installation of two stairways is impracticable;

(3) The scuttle is located where it can not be interfered with; and

(4) The scuttle is fitted with a quick-acting release and a hold-back to hold the scuttle in an open position.

(e) The required means of escape must not have locking devices.

(f) Where the length of the compartment is less than 12 feet, one vertical means of escape is acceptable provided that—

(1) There is no source of fire in the space, such as a galley stove, heater, etc., and the vertical escape is remote from the engine or fuel tank space, and

(2) The arrangement is such that the installation of two means of escape does not materially improve the safety of the vessel or those on board.

(g) Dead end corridors or the equivalent, more than 40 feet in length are prohibited.

(h) Each means of escape must be of adequate size to accommodate rapid evacuation.

(i) Each vertical ladder must have rungs that are:

(1) At least 16 inches in length;

(2) Not more than 12 inches apart, uniform for the length of the ladder;

(3) At least 3 inches from the nearest permanent object in back of the ladder; and

(4) Except when unavoidable obstructions are encountered, there must be at least 4½ inches clearance above each rung.

§ 169.315 Ventilation (other than machinery spaces).

(a) All enclosed spaces within the vessel must be properly ventilated in a manner suitable for the purpose of the space.

(b) A means must be provided to close off all vents and ventilators.

(c) Living spaces must be ventilated by a mechanical system unless it can be shown that a natural system will provide adequate ventilation in all ordinary weather conditions. Provided that paragraph (a) of this section is satisfied, a vessel having only a natural ventilation system must satisfy the following: $V/A \geq 1.4$ where V is the total area of the vents in square inches and A is the product in square feet of the vessel's design waterline length times its maximum beam.

LIVING SPACES

§ 169.317 Accommodations.

(a) Quarters must have sufficient fresh air, light and heat. Quarters must not be located forward of the collision bulkhead or farther forward in the vessel than a vertical plane located at 5 percent of the vessel's loadline length abaft the forward side of the stem. The space must not be located totally below the deepest load waterline.

(b) Bulkheads separating accommodations from machinery spaces, paint lockers, storerooms, washrooms, and toilet facilities are to be odorproof.

(c) All quarters are to be properly drained, odorproof and protected from heat and noise.

(d) Each person on board must have a separate berth which is of sufficient size and generally clear of all pipes, ventilation ducts and other installations.

(e) Each bunk must be constructed of wood, fiberglass or metal. If fitted with a mattress, the mattress must be covered with material which has been treated to give it fire resistant properties and which will provide the mattress with a reasonably smooth surface. There must be a minimum vertical distance between bunks of 24 inches.

(f) A means of access must be provided for each berthing arrangement where the upper berth is more than 60 inches above the deck.

(g) The construction and arrangement must allow free and unobstructed access to each berth. Each berth must be immediately adjacent to an aisle leading to a means of escape from the living area.

(h) A properly arranged hammock may be used as a berth.

§ 169.319 Washrooms and toilets.

(a) Sailing school vessels must have one toilet and one washbasin for every 20 persons. Each toilet and washbasin must have adequate plumbing.

(b) Each washroom and toilet room must properly drain and the scupper to the washroom must be of sufficient size and situated in the lowest part of the space.

(c) Each sailing school vessel must meet the applicable requirements of Title 33, Code of Federal Regulations, part 159.

§ 169.323 Furniture and furnishings.

Each sailing school vessel certificated to carry 100 persons or less or having overnight accommodations for

§ 169.327

less than 50 persons must meet the following requirements:

(a) Except as provided by paragraph (b) of this section, all free-standing furniture must be constructed of non-combustible material. Upholstery and padding used in furniture must be of fire resistant materials.

(b) Existing solid wooden furniture may be retained on existing vessels.

(c) Draperies must be fabricated of fire resistant fabrics.

(d) Rugs and carpets must be of wool or other material having equivalent fire resistant qualities.

(e) Trash receptacles must be constructed of non-combustible materials with solid sides and bottoms and have solid noncombustible covers.

RAILS AND GUARDS

§ 169.327 Deck rails.

(a) All rails or lifelines must be at least 30 inches high and permanently supported by stanchions at intervals of not more than 7 feet. Stanchions must be through bolted or welded to the deck.

(b) Rails or lifelines must consist of evenly spaced courses. The spacing between courses must not be greater than 12 inches. The opening below the lowest course must not be more than 9 inches. Lower rail courses are not required where all or part of the space below the upper rail is fitted with a bulwark, chain link fencing, wire mesh, or an equivalent.

(c) Small vessels of the open type and vessels of unusual construction must have rails or equivalent protection as considered necessary by the Officer in Charge, Marine Inspection.

§ 169.329 Storm rails.

Suitable storm rails or hand grabs must be installed where necessary in all passageways, at deckhouse sides, and at ladders and hatches where persons might have normal access.

§ 169.331 Guards in hazardous locations.

Each exposed hazard, such as gears or machinery, must be properly protected with covers, guards, or rails.

Subpart 169.400—Watertight Integrity, Subdivision, and Stability

§ 169.401 Applicability.

Each vessel must meet the applicable requirements in Subchapter S, parts 170–174, of this chapter.

Subpart 169.500—Lifesaving and Firefighting Equipment

LIFESAVING EQUIPMENT—GENERAL

§ 169.505 Equipment installed but not required.

Each item of lifesaving equipment installed on board a vessel must be of an approved type.

§ 169.507 Responsibility of master.

The master or operator shall ensure that the lifeboats, liferafts, davits, falls, personal flotation devices, and other lifesaving appliances are at all times ready for use, and that all equipment required by the regulations in this subchapter is provided, maintained, serviced, and replaced as indicated.

§ 169.509 Approval for repairs and alterations.

No extensive repairs or alterations, except in an emergency, may be made to any item of lifesaving equipment without advance notice to the Officer in Charge, Marine Inspection. Repairs and alterations must be made to the original standard of construction and tested in the manner specified in this subpart and applicable requirements in Subchapter Q of this chapter. Emergency repairs or alterations must be reported as soon as practicable to the nearest Officer in Charge, Marine Inspection.

PRIMARY LIFESAVING EQUIPMENT

§ 169.513 Types of primary equipment.

(a) *Lifeboats.* Each lifeboat must be of a type approved under subpart 160.035 of this chapter. Installation and arrangement of each lifeboat including davits and winches must meet the requirements of part 94 of this chapter.

(b) *Inflatable liferafts.* (1) Each inflatable liferaft must be a SOLAS A inflatable liferaft approved under part 160, subpart 160.151, of this chapter, except that inflatable liferafts on vessels operating on protected or partially protected waters may be SOLAS B inflatable liferafts approved under part 160, subpart 160.151, of this chapter.

(2) Each approved inflatable liferaft on the vessel on September 30, 2002, may be used to meet the requirements of this part as long as it is continued in use on the vessel, and is in good and serviceable condition.

(c) *Life floats.* Each lifefloat must be of a type approved under subpart 160.027 of this subchapter.

[CGD 83–005, 51 FR 896, Jan. 9, 1986, as amended by USCG–2001–11118, 67 FR 58541, Sept. 17, 2002]

§ 169.515 Number required.

(a) Except as provided in paragraph (c) of this section, each vessel must have sufficient lifeboats or inflatable liferafts to accommodate all persons on board.

(b) Each vessel certificated for exposed waters must have additional inflatable liferafts to accommodate 25% of the persons on board or the number of persons accommodated in the largest lifeboat or liferaft, whichever is greater.

(c) Vessels certificated for protected waters only may carry lifefloats of a combined capacity to accommodate all persons on board in lieu of the lifeboats and inflatable liferafts required in paragraph (a) of this section.

§ 169.517 Rescue boat.

All vessels certificated for exposed or partially protected waters service must have a suitable motor rescue boat, except when a motor lifeboat is provided or when, in the opinion of the Officer in Charge, Marine Inspection, the vessel is of such design and operating characteristics that the vessel itself provides a satisfactory man overboard rescue platform.

§ 169.519 Availability.

(a) Each lifeboat, inflatable liferaft, and lifefloat must be kept in good working order and be readily available.

(b) The decks on which lifeboats, liferafts, and lifefloats are carried must be kept clear of obstructions which could interfere with the immediate boarding and launching of the lifesaving appliances.

§ 169.521 Stowage.

(a) *General.* Each lifeboat, inflatable liferaft, and lifefloat must be stowed so that—

(1) It is capable of being launched within 10 minutes or, in the case of vessels having one compartment subdivision, 30 minutes;

(2) It does not impede the launching or handling of other lifesaving appliances;

(3) It does not impede the marshaling of persons at the embarkation stations, or their embarkation; and

(4) It is capable of being put in the water safely and rapidly even under unfavorable conditions of list and trim.

(b) *Lifeboat stowage.* Each lifeboat must be stowed to meet the following requirements:

(1) Each lifeboat must be attached to a separate set of davits.

(2) Lifeboats must not be stowed in the bow of the vessel nor so far aft as to be endangered by the propellers or overhang of the stern.

(3) Lifeboats must be stowed so that it is not necessary to lift them in order to swing out the davits.

(4) Means must be provided for bringing the lifeboats against the ship's side and holding them there so that persons may safely embark, unless the lifeboats are arranged for boarding at the stowage position.

(5) Lifeboats must be fitted with skates or other suitable means to facilitate launching against an adverse list of up to 15 degrees. However, skates may be dispensed with if, in the opinion of the Commandant, the arrangements ensure that the lifeboats can be satisfactorily launched without them.

(6) Means must be provided outside the machinery space to prevent the discharge of water into the lifeboats while they are being lowered.

(c) *Inflatable liferaft stowage.* Inflatable liferafts must be stowed so that they will float free in the event of the vessel sinking. Stowage and launching arrangements must be to the satisfaction of the Officer in Charge, Marine Inspection.

§ 169.525

(d) *Life float stowage.* Each life float must be stowed to meet the requirements of this paragraph.

(1) Each life float must be secured to the vessel by a painter and a float-free link that is—

(i) Certified to meet subpart 160.073 of this chapter;

(ii) Of proper strength for the size of the life float as indicated on its identification tag; and

(iii) Secured to the painter at one end and secured to the vessel on the other end.

(2) The means by which the float-free link is attached to the vessel must—

(i) Have a breaking strength of at least the breaking strength of the painter.

(ii) If synthetic, be of a dark color or of a material certified to be resistant to deterioration from ultraviolet light; and

(iii) If metal, be corrosion resistant.

(3) If the life float does not have a painter attachment fitting, a means for attaching the painter must be provided by a wire or line that—

(i) Encircles the body of the device;

(ii) Will not slip off;

(iii) Has a breaking strength that is at least the breaking strength of the painter; and

(iv) If synthetic, is of a dark color or is of a material certified to be resistant to deterioration from ultraviolet light.

(4) The float-free link described in paragraphs (d)(1) and (d)(2) of this section is not required if the vessel operates solely in waters that have a depth less than the length of the painter.

(5) If the vessel carries more than one life float, the life floats may be grouped and each group secured by a single painter, provided that—

(i) The combined weight of each group of life floats does not exceed 400 pounds;

(ii) Each life float is individually attached to the painter by a line that meets paragraphs (d)(2) and (d)(3) of this section and which is long enough so that each can float without contacting any other life float in the group; and

(iii) The strength of the float-free link and the strength of the painter under paragraphs (d)(1)(ii) and (d)(2) of this section is determined by the combined capacity of the group of life floats.

(6) Each life float, as stowed, must be capable of easy launching. Life floats weighing over 400 pounds must not require lifting before launching.

(7) Life floats must be secured to the vessel only by a painter and lashings that can be easily released or by hydraulic releases. They must not be stowed in more than four tiers. When stowed in tiers, the separate units must be kept apart by spacers.

(8) There must be means to prevent shifting.

(e) *Hydraulic Releases.* Each hydraulic release used in the installation of any inflatable liferaft or life float must meet subpart 160.062 of this chapter.

EQUIPMENT FOR PRIMARY LIFESAVING APPARATUS

§ 169.525 General.

(a) Equipment for primary lifesaving apparatus must kept in good condition.

(b) Lifeboats, inflatable liferafts and lifefloats must be fully equipped before the vessel is navigated and throughout the voyage.

(c) No person may stow in any lifeboat, inflatable liferaft, or lifefloat any article not required by this subpart unless the article is authorized by the OCMI, in good working order, and properly stowed so as not to reduce the seating capacity, the space available to the occupants, or adversely affect the seaworthiness of the livesaving apparatus.

(d) Loose equipment, except boathooks in lifeboats, must be securely attached to the lifesaving appliance to which it belongs.

§ 169.527 Required equipment for lifeboats.

Lifeboats must be equipped in accordance with Table 169.527. This equipment is described in § 169.529.

TABLE 169.527

Letter identification and item	Exposed and partially protected waters	Protected waters
a—Bailer	1	None
b—Bilge pump	1	None
c—Boathooks	2	1
d—Bucket	2	1
e—Compass and mounting	1	None

Coast Guard, DHS § 169.529

TABLE 169.527—Continued

Letter identification and item	Exposed and partially protected waters	Protected waters
f—Ditty bag	1	None
g—Drinking cup	1	None
h—Fire extinguisher (motor-propelled lifeboats only)	2	2
i—First-aid kit	1	None
j—Flashlight	1	None
k—Hatchet	2	1
l—Heaving line	2	None
m—Jackknife	1	None
n—Ladder, lifeboat, gunwale	1	None
o—Lantern	1	1
p—Lifeline	1	1
q—Life preservers	2	2
r—Locker	1	None
s—Mast and sail (oar-propelled lifeboats only)	1	None
t—Matches (boxes)	2	1
u—Mirror, signaling	2	None
v—Oars (units)	1	1
w—Oil, illuminating (quarts)	1	None
x—Oil, storm, (gallons)	1	None
y—Painter	2	1
z—Plug	1	1
aa—Provisions (per person)	2	None
bb—Rowlocks (units)	1	1
cc—Rudder and tiller	1	None
dd—Sea anchor	1	None
ee—Signals, distress, floating orange smoke	2	None
ff—Signals, distress, red hand flare (units)	1	None
gg—Signals, distress, red parachute flare (units)	1	None
hh—Tool kit (motor-propelled lifeboats only)	1	1
ii—Water (quarts per person)	3	None
jj—Whistle, signaling	1	None
kk—Fishing kit	1	None
ll—Cover, protecting	1	None
mm—Signals, lifesaving	1	None

§ 169.529 Description of lifeboat equipment.

(a) *Bailer.* The bailer must have a lanyard attached and must be of sufficient size and suitable for bailing.

(b) *Bilge pump.* Bilge pumps must be approved under subpart 160.044 of this chapter. They must be of the size given in Table 169.529(b) depending upon the capacity of the lifeboat as determined by the six-tenths rule as described in § 160.035–9(b) of this chapter.

TABLE 169.529(b)

Capacity of lifeboat, cubic feet		Bilge pump size
Over—	Not over—	
	330	1
330	700	2
700		3

(c) *Boathooks.* Boathooks must be of the single hook ballpoint type. Boathook handles must be of clear grained white ash, or equivalent, and of a length and diameter as given in Table 169.529(c).

TABLE 169.529(c)

Length of lifeboat, feet		Boathook handles	
Over—	Not over—	Diameter, inches	Length, feet
	23	1.50	8
23	29	1.75	10
29		2	12

(d) *Bucket.* Each bucket must be of heavy gage galvanized iron, or other suitable corrosion-resistant metal, of not less than 2-gallon capacity, and must have a 6-foot lanyard of 12-thread manila or equivalent attached.

(e) *Compass and mounting.* The compass and mounting must be of an approved type.

(f) *Ditty bag.* The ditty bag must consist of a canvas bag or equivalent and must contain a sailmaker's palm, needles, sail twine, marline, and marline spike.

(g) *Drinking cups.* Drinking cups must be enamel coated or plastic, graduated in milliliters or ounces, and provided with lanyards 3 feet in length.

(h) *Fire extinguishers.* Each fire extinguisher must be an approved Type B-C, Size I. One must be attached to each end of the lifeboat.

(i) *First-aid kit.* The first-aid kit must be approved under subpart 160.041 of this chapter.

(j) *Flashlights.* Each flashlight must be approved under § 94.20–15(j) of this chapter. Three spare cells (or one 3-cell battery) and two spare bulbs, stowed in a watertight container, must be provided with each flashlight. Batteries must be replaced yearly during the annual stripping, clearing, and overhaul of the lifeboat.

(k) *Hatchets.* Hatchets must be approved under subpart 160.013 of this chapter. They must be attached to the lifeboat by individual lanyards and be readily available for use, one at each end of the lifeboat.

(l) *Heaving line.* The heaving line must be of adequate strength, 10 fathoms in length, and 1 inch in circumference. It must remain buoyant after being submerged for 24 hours.

§ 169.529

(m) *Jackknife.* The jackknife must be approved under subpart 160.043 of this chapter.

(n) *Ladder, lifeboat gunwale.* The lifeboat gunwale ladder must consist of 3 flat wood steps with cut outs for hand holds. The steps must be spaced 12 inches apart and fastened with 5/8 inch diameter manila rope or equivalent. Each rope end must be tied inside the lifeboat at about amidships with the ladder stowed on top of the side benches and ready for immediate use.

(o) *Lantern.* The lantern must contain sufficient oil to burn for at least 9 hours, and be ready for immediate use. In totally enclosed lifeboats, an interior lighting system may be used in lieu of a lantern.

(p) *Lifeline.* The lifeline must be properly secured to both sides of the lifeboat along its entire length, festooned in bights not longer than 3 feet, with a seine float in each bight. The float may be omitted if the line is of an inherently buoyant material and absorbs little or no water. The lifeline must be of a size and strength not less than 3/8-inch diameter manila. The bights must hang to within 12 inches of the water when the lifeboat is light.

(q) *Life preservers.* Life preservers must be of an approved type. These preservers are in addition to those required by § 169.539 of this chapter.

(r) *Locker.* The locker must be suitable for the storage and preservation of the small items of equipment required under § 169.527.

(s) *Mast and sail.* A unit, consisting of a standing lug sail together with the necessary spars and rigging, must be provided in accordance with Table 169.529(s). The sails must be of good quality canvas, or other material acceptable to the Commandant, colored Indian Orange (Cable No. 70072, Standard Color Card of America). Rigging must consist of galvanized wire rope not less than three-sixteenths inch in diameter. The mast and sail must be protected by a suitable cover.

Coast Guard, DHS §169.529

TABLE 169.529(s)

Standing lug sail

Length of lifeboat, feet		Area, square feet	Luff and head lengths		Leach length		Foot length		Clew to throat		Ounces per square yard	Commercial designation number	Mast [1]			Yard [1]		
Over—	Not over—		Feet	Inches	Feet	Inches	Feet	Inches	Feet	Inches			Length		Diameter, inches	Length		Diameter, inches
													Feet	Inches		Feet	Inches	
17	19	58	5	11	12	1	8	10	10	10	14.35	10	11	2	3	6	11	2
19	21	74	6	8	13	8	10	0	12	2	14.35	10	12	6	3	7	8	2
21	23	93	7	5	15	1	11	2	13	8	14.35	10	13	10	3½	8	5	2½
23	25	113	8	3	16	11	12	4	15	1	14.35	10	15	2	3½	9	3	2½
25	27	135	9	0	18	6	13	6	16	6	14.35	10	16	6	4	10	0	3
27	29	158	9	9	20	0	14	7	17	10	17.50	8	17	10	4	10	9	3
29	31	181	10	5	21	5	15	7	19	1	17.50	8	19	2	4½	11	5	3¼
31 [2]		203	11	0	22	8	16	6	20	3	20.74	6	20	6	4½	12	0	3¼

[1] Mast lengths measured from heel to center of upper halyard sheave. Mast diameters measured at thwart. Mast and yard shall be of clear-grained spruce, fir, or equivalent.
[2] Subject to special consideration.

55

§ 169.529

(t) *Matches.* A box of friction matches in a watertight container, stowed in an equipment locker or secured to the underside of the stern thwart if no locker is fitted, must be provided.

(u) *Mirrors, signaling.* Signaling mirrors must be of an approved type.

(v) *Oars.* A unit, consisting of a complement of rowing oars and steering oar, must be provided for each lifeboat in accordance with Table 169.529(v) except that motor-propelled and hand-propelled lifeboats need only be equipped with four rowing oars and one steering oar. In any case, the emergency lifeboats must be provided with the full complement of oars prescribed by the table. All oars must be buoyant.

TABLE 169.529(v)

| Length of lifeboat (feet) || Number of oars— || Length of oars (feet)— ||
Over—	Not over—	Rowing	Steering	Rowing	Steering
	15	4	1	8	9
15	19	6	1	10	11
19	21	6	1	11	12
21	23	6	1	12	13
23	25	8	1	13	14
25	27	8	1	14	15
27	....	8	1	15	16

(w) *Oil, illuminating.* One quart of illuminating oil must be provided in a metal container if a lantern is carried.

(x) *Oil, storm.* One gallon of vegetable, fish, or animal oil must be provided in a suitable metal container so constructed as to permit a controlled distribution of oil on the water, and so arranged that it can be attached to the sea anchor.

(y) *Painter.* Painters must be of manila rope not less than 2¾ inches in circumference, or equivalent, and of a length not less than 3 times the distance between the deck on which the lifeboat is stowed and the light draft of the vessel. For lifeboats on vessels certificated for exposed or partially protected water service, one of the painters must have a long eye splice and be attached to the thwart with a toggle. The other painter must be attached to the stem.

(z) *Plug.* The automatic drain required in the lifeboat must be provided with a cap or plug attached to the lifeboat by a suitable chain.

(aa) *Provisions.* Approved emergency rations must be provided, consisting of 10,000 kJ (2390 calories) for each person the lifeboat is approved to carry. The provisions must be stowed in lockers or other compartments providing suitable protection.

(bb) *Rowlocks.* A unit, consisting of sufficient rowlocks and rowlock sockets for each oar required by Table 169.529(v) plus 2 additional rowlocks must be provided. The rowlocks must be attached to the lifeboat by separate chains so as to be available for immediate use, except that the 2 additional spare rowlocks must be carried in the equipment locker or stowed near the stern if no locker is fitted. The rowlocks and rowlock sockets must be distributed so as to provide the maximum amount of single banked oars practicable.

(cc) *Rudder and tiller.* The rudder and tiller must be constructed in accordance with § 160.035–3(t) of this chapter.

(dd) *Sea anchor.* The sea anchor must be of an approved type.

(ee) *Signals, distress, floating orange smoke.* The floating orange smoke distress signals must be approved under subpart 160.022 of this chapter. The signals must be replaced no later than the first annual stripping, cleaning, and overhaul of the lifeboat after the date of expiration.

(ff) *Signals, distress, red hand flare.* A unit consists of twelve hand red flare distress signals approved under subpart 160.021 or 160.023 of this chapter and stored in a watertight container. Signals must be replaced no later than the first annual stripping, cleaning, and overhaul of the lifeboat after the date of expiration.

(gg) *Signals, distress, red parachute flare.* A unit consists of twelve parachute red flare distress signals with an approved means of projection approved under subparts 160.024 and 160.028 respectively; or twelve approved hand-held rocket-propelled parachute red flare distress signals approved under subpart 160.036. Flares must be stored in a portable watertight container. Flares must be replaced no later than the first annual stripping, cleaning, and overhaul of the lifeboat after the date of expiration.

(hh) *Tool kit.* The tool kit must consist of at least the following tools in a suitable container:

(1) One 12-ounce ball peen hammer.
(2) One screwdriver with 6-inch blade.
(3) One pair 8-inch slip joint pliers.
(4) One 8-inch adjustable end wrench.

(ii) *Water.* (1) For each person the lifeboat is certified to carry, there must be provided three quarts of drinking water in containers approved under subpart 160.026. Water must be replaced no later than the first annual stripping, cleaning, and overhaul of the lifeboat after date of expiration.

(2) One or more desalting kits, approved under subpart 160.058 of this chapter, may be used as a substitute for one-third of the drinking water required.

(3) The drinking water must be stowed in drinking water tanks, lockers, or other compartments providing suitable protection.

(jj) *Whistle, signaling.* The whistle must be of the ball-type or multi-tone type, of corrosion resistant construction, with a 36-inch lanyard attached, and in good working order.

(kk) *Fishing kit.* The fishing kit must be approved under subpart 160.061 of this chapter.

(ll) *Cover, protecting.* The cover must be of highly visible color and capable of protecting the occupants against exposure.

(mm) *Table of lifesaving signals.* The table of lifesaving signals must be in accordance with the provisions of Chapter V, Regulation 16, of the International Convention for Safety of Life at Sea, 1974, and must be printed on water resistant paper.

[CGD 83–005, 51 FR 896, Jan. 9, 1986, as amended by CGD 95–072, 60 FR 50468, Sept. 29, 1995]

§ 169.535 Required equipment for lifefloats.

Each lifefloat must be equipped in accordance with Table 169.535. The equipment is described in § 169.537.

TABLE 169.535

Letter identification and Item	Number required for each lifefloat	
	Exposed and partially protected water	Protected water
(a) Boathook	1	1
(b) Lifeline	1	1
(c) Paddles	4	4

TABLE 169.535—Continued

Letter identification and Item	Number required for each lifefloat	
	Exposed and partially protected water	Protected water
(d) Painter	1	1
(e) Water light	1	None

§ 169.537 Description of equipment for lifefloats.

(a) *Boathook.* Each boathook must be of the single hook ball point type. Boathook handles must be of clear grained white ash, or equivalent, not less than 6 feet long and 1½ inches in diameter.

(b) *Lifeline and pendants.* The lifeline and pendants must be as furnished by the manufacturer with approved life floats. Replacement lifelines and pendants must meet the requirements in subpart 160.010 of this chapter.

(c) *Paddles.* Paddles must be not less than 5 feet long.

(d) *Painter.* The painter must—

(1) Be at least 30m (100 ft.) long, but not less than 3 times the distance between the deck on which the life float(s) are stowed and the light draft of the vessel,

(2) Have a breaking strength of at least 6.7 KN (1500 lbs.), except that if the capacity of the life float is 50 persons or more, the breaking strength must be at least 13.4 KN (3000 lbs.),

(3) Be of a dark color, if synthetic, or of a type certified to be resistant to deterioration from ultraviolet light, and

(4) Be stowed in such a way it runs freely when the life float floats away from the sinking vessel.

(e) *Water light.* The water light must be approved under subpart 161.010 of this chapter. The water light must be attached to the lifefloat by a 12-thread manila or equivalent synthetic lanyard 3 fathoms in length.

PERSONAL FLOTATION DEVICES

§ 169.539 Type required.

All personal flotation devices (PFDs) must be either—

(a) A Type I approved under subpart 160.055, 160.002, or 160.005 of Subchapter Q (specification) of this chapter; or

(b) a Type V approved specifically for sailing school vessel use under subpart

§ 169.541

160.064 or 160.077 of Subchapter Q of this chapter; or

(c) a Type II approved under subparts 160.047, 160.052, or 160.060 or a Type III approved under subpart 160.064 if the vessel carries exposure suits or Type V exposure PFDs, in accordance with section 169.551.

§ 169.541 Number required.

Each vessel must be provided with an approved adult personal flotation device of an appropriate size for each person carried. In addition, unless the service is such that children are never carried, there must be provided an approved personal flotation device of a suitable size for each child carried.

§ 169.543 Distribution and stowage.

(a) Personal flotation devices must be distributed through the upper part of the vessel in protected places convenient to the persons on board.

(b) If practicable, personal flotation device containers must be designed to allow the PFDs to float free.

(c) Personal flotation devices for children, when provided, must be stowed separately.

(d) Lockers, boxes, and closets in which PFDs are stowed must not be capable of being locked.

§ 169.545 Markings.

(a) Each personal flotation device must be marked with the vessel's name.

(b) Where PFDs are stowed so that they are not readily visible to persons onboard, the containers in which they are stowed must be marked "adult personal flotation devices" or "child personal flotation devices", as appropriate, and with the number contained therein, in at least 1-inch letters and figures.

(c) Each personal flotation device carried on vessels certificated for exposed or partially protected waters service must have a light approved under subpart 161.012 of this chapter. The light must be securely attached to the front shoulder area of the personal flotation device.

(d) Each personal flotation device must have at least 200 sq. cm. (31 sq. in.) of retroreflective material attached on its front side and at least 200 sq. cm. on its back side. If the personal flotation device is reversible, retroreflective material must be applied as described above on both sides.

(e) Retroreflective material required by this section must be Type I material that is approved under subpart 164.018 of this chapter.

ADDITIONAL LIFESAVING EQUIPMENT

§ 169.549 Ring lifebuoys and water lights.

(a)(1) The minimum number of life buoys and the minimum number to which water lights must be attached must be in accordance with the following table:

TABLE 169.549(a)(1)

Length of vessel	Minimum number of buoys	Minimum number of buoys with waterlights attached
Under 100	2	1
100 feet to less than 200 ft	4	2
200 feet to less than 300 ft	6	2
300 feet to less than 400 ft	12	4
400 feet to less than 600 ft	18	9

(2) One lifebuoy on each side of a vessel must have an attached line at least 15 fathoms in length.

(b) All lifebuoys must be placed where they are readily accessible. They must be capable of being readily cast loose.

(c)(1) All ring lifebuoys must be approved under subpart 160.050 or 160.064 of this chapter and be international orange in color.

(2) Each water light must be approved under subpart 161.010 of this chapter.

§ 169.551 Exposure suits.

(a) This section applies to each vessel operating in exposed or partially protected waters service except those—

(1) Operating on routes between 32° N and 32° S in the Atlantic Ocean.

(2) Operating on routes between 35° N and 35° S latitude in all other waters.

(b) Each vessel to which this section applies must have for each person on board an exposure suit approved under subpart 160.171 or a Type V exposure PFD approved under subpart 160.053.

[CGD 83–005, 51 FR 896, Jan. 9, 1986, as amended by CGD 95–072, 60 FR 50468, Sept. 29, 1995]

Coast Guard, DHS

§ 169.559

§ 169.553 Pyrotechnic distress signals.

(a) All pyrotechnic distress signals must be of an approved type.

(b) Replacement must be made no later than the first inspection for certification or reinspection after the date of expiration.

(c) Except as otherwise provided in this section, each vessel must carry the following pyrotechnic distress signals:

(1) 6 hand red flare distress signals, and 6 hand orange smoke distress signals; or,

(2) 12 hand held rocket propelled parachute red flare distress signals.

(d) [Reserved]

(e) All pyrotechnic distress signals must be carried near the helm or in a location considered suitable by the Officer in Charge, Marine Inspection.

(f) All pyrotechnic distress signals must be stowed in a portable watertight container.

§ 169.555 Emergency position indicating radio beacon (EPIRB).

(a) Each vessel certificated for exposed waters must have an approved Class A emergency position indicating radiobeacon (EPIRB), and each vessel certificated for partially protected waters must have an approved Class C emergency position indicating radiobeacon (EPIRB). The required EPIRB must be—

(1) Operational;

(2) Stowed where it is readily accessible for testing and use; and

(3) Stowed in a manner so that it will float free if the vessel sinks.

(b) Each vessel must have an additional Class B EPIRB for every twenty-five persons onboard, for use in the lifeboats and liferafts.

[CGD 83–005, 51 FR 896, Jan. 9, 1986; 51 FR 10632, Mar. 28, 1986]

§ 169.556 Work vests.

(a) Buoyant work vests carried under the permissive authority of this section must be approved under subpart 160.053 of this chapter.

(b) Approved buoyant work vests are items of safety apparel and may be carried aboard vessels to be worn by persons when working near or over the water under favorable working conditions. Work vests are not accepted in lieu of any of the required number of approved personal flotation devices and must not be worn during drills and emergencies.

(c) The approved buoyant work vests must be stowed separately from personal flotation devices, and in locations where they will not be confused with personal flotation devices.

(d) Each work vest is subject to examination by a marine inspector to determine its serviceability. If a work vest is found not to be in a serviceable condition, then it must be repaired or removed from the vessel. If a work vest is beyond repair, it must be destroyed in the presence of the marine inspector.

FIREFIGHTING EQUIPMENT

§ 169.559 Fire pumps.

(a) Each sailing school vessel must be equipped with fire pumps as required in Table 169.559(a).

TABLE 169.559(a)—FIRE PUMPS

Length	Exposed and partially protected water service	Protected water service
65 feet but less than 90 feet	[1]1	0
90 feet but less than 120 feet ...	[2]1	[1]1
120 feet or greater	[3]2	[1]1

[1] May be driven off a propulsion engine and may be used as a bilge pump.
[2] Must be driven by a source of power independent of the propulsion engine and may be used as a bilge pump.
[3] One pump may be driven off a propulsion unit and one pump may be used as a bilge pump. Pumps must be located in separate spaces.

(b) Fire pump capacity must be in accordance with the following:

Vessel length	Minimum capacity
Less than 90 ft	5.5 m^3/hr (25 gpm).
90 feet but less than 120 ft	11.0 m^3/hr (50 gpm).
Greater than 120 ft	14.3 m^3/hr (66.6 gpm).

(c) Each fire pump must be fitted with a pressure gage on the discharge side of the pump.

(d) Each vessel must have a hand operated portable fire pump having a capacity of at least 1.1 m^3/hr (5 gpm). This pump must be equipped with suction and discharge hose suitable for use in firefighting.

§ 169.561 Firemain.

(a) Each vessel required to be provided with a power-driven fire pump must also be provided with a fire main, hydrants, hoses and nozzles.

(b) Fire hydrants must be of sufficient number and located so that any part of the vessel may be reached with an effective stream of water from a single length of hose.

(c) All piping, valves, and fittings must be in accordance with good marine practice and suitable for the purpose intended.

§ 169.563 Firehose.

(a) One length of firehose must be provided for each fire hydrant required.

(b) Vessels less than 90 feet in length must have commercial firehose or equivalent of not over 1½ inch diameter or garden hose of not less than ⅝ inch nominal inside diameter. If garden hose is used, it must be of a good commercial grade constructed of an inner rubber tube, plies of braided cotton reinforcement and an outer rubber cover, or of equivalent material, and must be fitted with a commercial garden hose nozzle of good grade bronze or equivalent metal.

(c) Vessels of 90 feet or greater must have lined commercial firehose that conform to Underwriters' Laboratories, Inc. Standard 19 or Federal Specification ZZ-H-451. The firehose must be fitted with a combination nozzle approved under § 162.027 of this chapter.

(d) Each length of firehose must be a single piece 50 feet long.

(e) Firehose must be connected to the hydrants at all times, except that, on open decks where no protection is afforded to the hose, it may be temporarily removed from the hydrant in heavy weather and stowed in an accessible nearby location.

§ 169.564 Fixed extinguishing system, general.

(a) Fixed carbon dioxide or halogenated extinguishing systems must be installed to protect the following spaces—

(1) The machinery and fuel tank spaces of all vessels, except where machinery and fuel tank spaces are so open to the atmosphere as to make the use of a fixed system ineffective;

(2) The paint and oil rooms and similar hazardous spaces; and

(3) The galley stove area, for vessels greater than 90 feet in length and certificated for exposed or partially protected water service.

(b) Each fixed extinguishing system must be of an approved carbon dioxide or halogenated type and installed to the satisfaction of the Officer in Charge, Marine Inspection.

§ 169.565 Fixed carbon dioxide system.

(a) The number of pounds of carbon dioxide required for each space protected must be equal to the gross volume of the space divided by the appropriate factor in Table 169.565(a).

TABLE 169.565(a)

Gross volume of compartment, cubic feet		Factor
Over—	Not over—	
0	500	15
500	1,600	16
1,600	4,500	18
4,500		20

(b) A separate supply of carbon dioxide is not required for each space protected. The total available supply must be sufficient for the space requiring the greatest amount.

(c) *Controls.* (1) Each control and valve for the operation of the system must be outside the spaces protected and accessible at all times.

(2) Each branch line must be fitted with an approved shutoff valve. Each valve must be kept closed at all times except to operate the particular system.

(3) The arrangements must be such that the entire charge to any space can be introduced into the space by the operation of one valve selecting the space, and one control for releasing the required amount of fire extinguishing agent. The release control must be of an approved type and located adjacent to the branch line shutoff valve.

(4) Complete but simple instructions for the operation of the system must be located in a conspicuous place at or near the releasing control device.

(5) Each control valve to branch lines must be labeled to indicate the space served.

(d) *Piping.* (1) The pipe and fittings for the extinguishing systems must be

Coast Guard, DHS § 169.567

in accordance with the system manufacturer's approved design manual.

(2) Each pipe, valve, and fitting of ferrous materials must be galvanized.

(3) Each dead-end line must extend at least 2 inches beyond the last orifice and must be closed with cap or plug.

(4) Each pipe, valve, and fitting must be securely supported and, where necessary, protected against injury.

(5) Drains and dirt traps must be fitted where necessary to prevent accumulation of dirt or moisture. Each drain and dirt trap must be located in accessible locations but not in accommodation spaces.

(e) *Discharge outlets.* (1) The area of discharge outlets shall be as specified in the manufacturer's approved design manual.

(2) The discharge of the required amount of carbon dioxide must be complete within two minutes.

(f) *Cylinders.* (1) Each cylinder must be securely fastened and supported, and where necessary protected against injury. Cylinders must be located outside the space protected.

(2) Each cylinder must be mounted in an upright position or inclined not more than 30° from the vertical, except that cylinders which are fitted with flexible or bent siphon tubes may be inclined not more than 80° from the vertical.

(3) Each cylinder used for storing extinguishing agent must be approved and marked in accordance with Department of Transportation regulations.

(4) Each cylinder must be mounted so it is readily accessible and capable of easy removal for recharging and inspection. Cylinders must be capable of being weighed in place.

(5) Where subject to moisture, cylinders must be installed so that a space of at least 2 inches is provided between the flooring and the bottom of the cylinders.

(6) Each cylinder storage area must be properly ventilated and the temperature inside must not exceed 130 °F.

(g) Provision must be made by means of plugs, covers, dampers, etc., to prevent the admission of air into the space protected.

(h) Systems must be fitted with a delayed discharge and an alarm bell arranged so the alarm sounds for at least twenty seconds before the carbon dioxide is released into the space.

§ 169.567 Portable extinguishers.

(a) The minimum number of portable fire extinguishers required on each vessel is determined by the Officer in Charge, Marine Inspection, in accordance with Table 169.567(a) and other provisions of this subpart.

TABLE 169.567(a)

Space protected	Total number extinguishers required	Type extinguishers permitted — Medium	Type extinguishers permitted — Minimum size	Coast Guard classification
Living space and open boats.	1 per 1000 cu. ft. of space.	Halon 1211 of 1301	2½ pounds	
		Foam	1¼ gallons	
		Carbon dioxide	4 pounds	B-I.
		Dry chemical	2 pounds	
Propulsion machinery space with fixed CO₂ or halon system.	1	Foam	1¼ gallons	
		Carbon dioxide. 4 pounds B-I..		
		Dry chemical	2 pounds	
		Halon 1211 or 1301	2½ pounds	
Propulsion machinery space without fixed CO₂ or halon system.	2	Foam	2½ gallons	
		Carbon dioxide. 15 pounds B-II..		
		Dry chemical	10 pounds	
		Halon 1211 or 1301	10 pounds	
Galley (without fixed system).	1 per 500 cu. ft	Foam	2½ gallons	

TABLE 169.567(a)—Continued

Space protected	Total number extinguishers required	Type extinguishers permitted		Coast Guard classification
		Medium	Minimum size	
		Carbon dioxide	15 pounds	B–II.
		Dry chemical	10 pounds	
		Halon 1211 or 1301	10 pounds	

(b) The Officer in Charge, Marine Inspection, may permit the use of any approved fire extinguishers, including semiportable extinguishers, which provide equivalent fire protection.

(c) All portable fire extinguishers installed on vessels must be of an approved type.

(d) Portable fire extinguishers must be stowed in a location convenient to the space protected.

(e) Portable fire extinguishers must be installed and located to the satisfaction of the Officer in Charge, Marine Inspection.

(f) Portable fire extinguishers which are required to be protected from freezing must not be located where freezing temperatures may be expected.

(g) Each vessel must carry spare charges for at least 50 percent of each size and variety of hand portable extinguishers required. For units that can not be readily recharged on the vessel, one spare extinguisher for each classification carried onboard must be provided in lieu of spare charges.

[CGD 83–005, 51 FR 897, Jan. 9, 1986; 51 FR 3785, Jan. 30, 1986]

§ 169.569 Fire axes.

(a) Each vessel must carry at least the number of fire axes set forth in Table 169.569(a). The Officer in Charge, Marine Inspection may require additional fire axes necessary for the proper protection of the vessel.

TABLE 169.569(a)

Length		Number of axes
Over	Not over	
	65	0
65	90	1
90	120	2
120	150	3
150	....	4

(b) Fire axes must be stowed so as to be readily available in the event of emergency.

(c) If fire axes are not located in the open or behind glass, they must be placed in marked enclosures containing the fire hose.

Subpart 169.600—Machinery and Electrical

§ 169.601 General.

(a) The regulations in this subpart contain requirements for the design, construction and installation of machinery on sailing school vessels.

(b) Machinery must be suitable in type and design for the purpose intended. Installations of an unusual type and those not addressed by this subpart are subject to the applicable regulations in Subchapter F (Marine Engineering) and Subchapter J (Electrical Engineering) of this chapter.

(c) The use of liquefied inflammable gases, such as propane, methane, butane, etc., as fuel, except for cooking purposes, is prohibited.

INTERNAL COMBUSTION ENGINE INSTALLATIONS

§ 169.605 General.

(a) Generators, starting motors, and other spark producing devices must be mounted as high above the bilges as practicable.

(b) Gages to indicate engine cooling water temperature, exhaust cooling water temperature and engine lubricating oil pressure must be provided and located in plain view.

(c) All electrical components of the engine must be protected in accordance with § 183.410 of Title 33, Code of Federal Regulations to prevent ignition of flammable vapors.

Coast Guard, DHS

§ 169.607 Keel cooler installations.

(a) Except as provided in this section, keel cooler installations must meet the requirements of § 56.50-96 of this chapter.

(b) Approved metallic flexible connections may be located below the deepest load waterline if the system is a closed loop below the waterline and its vent is located above the waterline.

(c) Fillet welds may be used in the attachment of channels and half round pipe sections to the bottom of the vessel.

(d) Short lengths of approved non-metallic flexible hose may be used at machinery connections fixed by hose clamps provided that—

(1) The clamps are of a corrosion resistant material;

(2) The clamps do not depend on spring tension for their holding power; and

(3) Two clamps are used on each end of the hose or one hose clamp is used and the pipe ends are expanded or beaded to provide a positive stop against hose slippage.

§ 169.608 Non-integral keel cooler installations.

(a) Hull penetrations for non-integral keel cooler installations must be made through a cofferdam or at a sea chest.

(b) Non-integral keel coolers must be suitably protected against damage from debris and grounding by recessing the unit into the hull or by the placement of protective guards.

(c) Each non-integral keel cooler hull penetration must be equipped with a shutoff valve.

[CGD 83-005, 51 FR 896, Jan. 9, 1986, as amended by USCG-2000-7790, 65 FR 58464, Sept. 29, 2000]

§ 169.609 Exhaust systems.

Engine exhaust installations and associated cooling sytems must be built in accordance with the requirements of American Boat and Yacht Council, Inc. Standard P-1, "Safe Installation of Exhaust Systems for Propulsion and Auxiliary Machinery" and the following additional requirements:

(a) All exhaust installations with pressures in excess of 15 pounds per square inch gage or employing runs passing through living or working spaces must meet the material specifications of part 56 of Title 46, Code of Federal Regulations.

(b) Horizontal dry exhaust pipes are permitted if they do not pass through living or berthing spaces, terminate above the deepest load waterline, are arranged to prevent entry of cold water from rough seas, and are constucted of corrosion resistant material at the hull penetration.

(c) When the exhaust cooling system is separate from the engine cooling system, a suitable warning device must be provided to indicate a failure of water flow in the exhaust cooling system.

§ 169.611 Carburetors.

(a) This section applies to all vessels having gasoline engines.

(b) Each carburetor other than a down-draft type, must be equipped with integral or externally fitted drip collectors of adequate capacity and arranged so as to permit ready removal of fuel leakage. Externally fitted drip collectors must be covered with flame screens.

(c) All gasoline engines must be equipped with an acceptable means of backfire flame control. Installations of backfire flame arresters bearing basic Approval Nos. 162.015 or 162.041 or engine air and fuel induction systems bearing basic Approval Nos. 162.015 or 165.042 may be continued in use as long as they are serviceable and in good condition. New installations or replacements must meet the applicable requirements of part 58, subpart 58.10 (Internal Combustion Engine Installations) of this chapter.

[CGD 83-005, 51 FR 896, Jan. 9, 1986, as amended by CGD 88-032, 56 FR 35827, July 29, 1991]

FUEL SYSTEMS

§ 169.613 Gasoline fuel systems.

(a) Except as provided in paragraph (b) each gasoline fuel system must meet the requirements of § 56.50-70 of this chapter

(b) Each vessel of 65 feet and under must meet the requirements of §§ 182.15-25, 182.15-30, 182.15-35 and 182.15-40 of this chapter.

§ 169.615

§ 169.615 Diesel fuel systems.

(a) Except as provided in paragraph (b) each diesel fuel system must meet the requirements of § 56.50-75 of this chapter.

(b) Each vessel of 65 feet and under must meet the requirements of §§ 182.20-22, 182.20-25, 182.20-30, 182.20-35 and 182.20-40 of this chapter.

STEERING SYSTEMS

§ 169.618 General.

(a) Each vessel must have an effective steering system.

(b) The steering system must be designed to withstand all anticipated loading while under sail, including shocks to the rudder. Additionally, the steering system on vessels with an auxiliary means of propulsion must not be susceptible to damage or jamming at the vessel's maximum astern speed.

(c) The main steering gear must be capable of moving the rudder from hard-over to hard-over at an average rate of not less than $2\frac{1}{3}°$ per second with the vessel at design service speed (ahead).

§ 169.619 Reliability.

(a) Except where the OCMI judges it impracticable, the steering system must—

(1) Provide continued or restored steering capability in the event of a failure or malfunction of any single steering system component other than the rudder or rudder stock;

(2) Be independent of other systems, including auxiliary propulsion machinery; and

(3) Be operable in the event of localized fire or flooding.

(b) A main and independent auxiliary steering gear must be provided, except when—

(1) A small vessel uses a tiller or direct mechanical linkage as the primary means of controlling the rudder; or

(2) Installation of an auxiliary steering gear is not possible.

NOTE: A partial reduction of normal steering capability as a result of malfunction or failure is acceptable. This reduction should not be below that necessary for the safe navigation of the vessel.

(c) The strength and reliability of any component that is not provided in duplicate must be suitable to the cognizant OCMI. Where redundant or backup equipment or components are provided to meet the requirements of paragraphs (a) and (b) of this section, the following must be provided:

(1) A means to readily transfer from the failed equipment or component to the backup.

(2) Readily available tools or equipment necessary to make the transfer.

(3) Instructions for transfer procedures, posted at the main steering location.

(4) A means to steady the rudder while making the transfer.

§ 169.621 Communications.

A reliable means of voice communications must be provided between the main steering location and each alternate steering location.

§ 169.622 Rudder angle indicators.

Each vessel must have a rudder angle indicator at the main steering location that meets the requirements of § 113.40-10 of this chapter, except where a tiller or direct mechanical linkage is the primary means of controlling the rudder.

§ 169.623 Power-driven steering systems.

(a) Power-driven steering systems must have means to be brought into operation from a dead ship condition, without external aid. The system must automatically resume operation after an electric power outage.

(b) Control of power-driven steering systems from the main steering control location must include, as applicable—

(1) Control of any necessary ancillary device (motor, pump, valve, etc.);

(2) A pilot light to indicate operation of each power unit; and

(3) Visual and audible alarms to indicate loss of power to the control system or power units and overload of electric motors.

(c) Overcurrent protection for steering system electric circuits must meet § 111.93-11 of this chapter, as applicable.

Coast Guard, DHS

§ 169.640

Ventilation

§ 169.625 Compartments containing diesel machinery.

(a) Spaces containing machinery must be fitted with adequate dripproof ventilators, trunks, louvers, etc., to provide sufficient air for proper operation of the propulsion and auxiliary engines.

(b) Air-cooled propulsion and auxiliary engines installed below deck must be fitted with air intake ducts or piping from the weather deck. The ducts or piping must be arranged and supported to safely sustain stresses induced by weight and engine vibration and to minimize transfer of vibration to the supporting structure. Prior to installing ventilation for the engines, plans or sketches showing the machinery arrangement including air intakes, exhaust stack, method of attachment of ventilation ducts to the engine, location of spark arresting mufflers and capacity of ventilation blowers must be submitted to the OCMI for approval.

(c) Spaces containing machinery must be fitted with at least two ducts to furnish natural or mechanical supply and exhaust ventilation. One duct must extend to a point near the bottom of the compartment, and be installed so that the ordinary collection of water in the bilge will not trap the duct. Where forced ventilation is installed, the duct extending to the bottom of the compartment must be the exhaust. The total inlet area and the total outlet area of ventilation ducts must be not less than one square inch for each foot of beam of the vessel. These minimum areas must be increased when such ducts are considered part of the air supply to the engines.

(d) All ducts must be of rigid permanent noncombustible construction, properly fastened, supported, and reasonably gastight from end to end.

(e) All supply ducts for ventilation purposes must be provided with cowls or scoops having a free area not less than twice the required duct area. When the cowls or scoops are screened, the mouth area must be increased to compensate for the area of the screen wire. Dampers are prohibited in supply ducts. Cowls or scoops must be kept open at all times except when weather would endanger the vessel if the openings were not temporarily closed. Supply and exhaust openings must not be located where the natural flow of air is unduly obstructed, or adjacent to possible sources of vapor ignition, and must not be located where exhaust air may be taken into the supply vents.

§ 169.627 Compartments containing diesel fuel tanks.

Unless they are adequately ventilated, enclosed compartments or spaces containing diesel fuel tanks and no machinery must be provided with a gooseneck vent of not less than 2½ inches in diameter. The vent opening must not be located adjacent to possible sources of vapor ignition.

§ 169.629 Compartments containing gasoline machinery or fuel tanks.

Spaces containing gasoline machinery or fuel tanks must have natural supply and mechanical exhaust ventilation meeting the requirements of American Boat and Yacht Council Standard H–2.5, "Design and Construction; Ventilation of Boats Using Gasoline.

§ 169.631 Separation of machinery and fuel tank spaces from accommodation spaces.

(a) Machinery and fuel tank spaces must be separated from accommodation spaces by watertight or vapor tight bulkheads of double diagonal wood, marine plywood, steel plate, or equivalent construction.

(b) On vessels less than 90 feet in length, segregation may be by means of a watertight or vapor tight engine box.

Piping Systems

§ 169.640 General.

(a) Vital piping systems, as defined in § 169.642 of this subpart, must meet the material and pressure design requirements of Subchapter F of this chapter.

(b) Except as provided in this paragraph, nonmetallic piping system materials must meet the applicable requirements of 46 CFR 56.60–25.

(1) Rigid nonmetallic materials are acceptable for use in bilge, ballast, and machinery-connected piping systems on vessels less than 120 feet in length,

§ 169.642

provided that bilge and fire systems do not use the same piping.

(2) Nonmetallic piping is prohibited in fuel systems except where flexible hose is permitted.

(3) Rigid nonmetallic materials may be used in non-vital systems.

§ 169.642 Vital systems.

For the purpose of this part, the following are considered vital systems—

(a) A marine engineering system identified by the OCMI as being crucial to the survival of the vessel or to the protection of the personnel on board; and

(b) On vessels greater than 120 feet in length—

(1) Bilge system;
(2) Ballast system;
(3) Fire protection system;
(4) Fuel oil system; and
(5) Steering and steering control system.

BILGE SYSTEMS

§ 169.650 General.

All vessels must be provided with a satisfactory arrangement for draining any compartment, other than small buoyancy compartments, under all practical conditions. Sluice valves are not permitted in watertight bulkheads except as specified in § 169.652(a).

§ 169.652 Bilge piping.

(a) All vessels of 26 feet in length and over must be provided with individual bilge lines and suction for each compartment except that the space forward of the collision bulkhead may be serviced by a sluice valve or portable bilge pump if the arrangement of the vessel is such that ordinary leakage can be removed this way.

(b) The bilge pipe on vessels 65 feet in length and under must be not less than one inch nominal pipe size. On vessels greater than 65 but less than 120 feet in length the bilge pipe must be not less than one and one-half inches. Piping on vessels of 120 feet or greater or of 100 gross tons or greater must meet the requirements contained in § 56.50–50 of this chapter.

(c) Each bilge suction must be fitted with a suitable strainer having an open area not less than three times the area of the bilge pipe.

(d) Each individual bilge suction line must be led to a central control point or manifold. Each line must be provided with a stop valve at the control point or manifold and a check valve at some accessible point in the bilge line, or a stop-check valve located at the control point or manifold.

(e) Each bilge pipe piercing the collision bulkhead must be fitted with a screw-down valve located on the forward side of the collision bulkhead and operable from above the weather deck.

§ 169.654 Bilge pumps.

(a) Vessels of less than 65 feet in length must have a portable hand bilge pump having a maximum capacity of 5 gpm.

(b) In addition to the requirements of paragraph (a) of this section, vessels of 26 feet but less than 40 feet in length must have a fixed hand bilge pump or fixed power bilge pump having a minimum capacity of 10 gpm. If a fixed hand pump is installed, it must be operable from on deck.

(c) In addition to the requirements of paragraph (a) of this section, vessels of 40 feet but less than 65 feet must have a fixed power bilge pump having a minimum capacity of 25 gpm.

(d) Vessels of 65 feet in length but less than 120 feet and under 100 gross tons must have two fixed power bilge pumps having a combined minimum capacity of 50 gpm.

(e) Vessels of 120 feet or greater and vessels of 100 gross tons and over must have two fixed power pumps meeting the capacity requirements of § 56.50–55(c) of this chapter.

(f) Each power driven bilge must be self priming.

(g) Each fixed bilge pump required by this section must be permanently connnected to the bilge main.

(h) Bilge pumps may also be connected to the firemain provided that the bilge system and firemain system may be operated simultaneously.

ELECTRICAL

§ 169.662 Hazardous locations.

Electrical equipment must not be installed in lockers that are used to store paint, oil, turpentine, or other flammable liquids unless the equipment is explosion-proof or intrinsically safe in accordance with § 111.105-9 or § 111.105-11 of this chapter.

ELECTRICAL INSTALLATIONS OPERATING AT POTENTIALS OF LESS THAN 50 VOLTS ON VESSELS OF LESS THAN 100 GROSS TONS

§ 169.664 Applicability.

The requirements in this subpart apply to electrical installations operating at potentials of less than 50 volts on vessels of less than 100 gross tons.

§ 169.665 Name plates.

Each generator, motor and other major item f power equipment must be provided with a name plate indicating the manufacturer's name, its rating in volts and amperes or in volts and watts and, when intended for connection to a normally grounded supply, the grounding polarity.

§ 169.666 Generators and motors.

(a) Each vessel of more than 65 feet in length having only electrically driven fire and bilge pumps must have two generators. One of these generators must be driven by a means independent of the auxiliary propulsion plant. A generator that is not independent of the auxiliary propulsion plant must meet the requirements of § 111.10-4(c) of this chapter.

(b) Each generator and motor must be in a location that is accessible, adequately ventilated, and as dry as practicable.

(c) Each generator and motor must be mounted as high as practicable above the bilges to avoid damage by splash and to avoid contact with low lying vapors.

(d) Each generator must be protected from overcurrent by a circuit breaker, fuse or an overcurrent relay.

§ 169.667 Switchboards.

(a) Each switchboard must be in as dry a location as praticable, accessible, protected from inadvertent entry, and adequately ventilated. All uninsulated current carrying parts must be mounted on nonabsorbent, noncombustible, high dielectric insulating material.

(b) Each switchboard must be—
(1) Totally enclosed; and
(2) Of the dead front type.

(c) Each ungrounded conductor of a circuit must have at the point of attachment to the power source either—
(1) A Circuit breaker; or
(2) A switch and fuse.

(d) Each switch other than one mounted on a switchboard must be of the enclosed type.

§ 169.668 Batteries.

(a) Each battery must be in a location that allows the gas generated in charging to be easily dissipated by natural or induced ventilation.

(b) Except as provided in paragraph (c) of this section, a battery must not be located in the same compartment with a gasoline tank or gasoline engine.

(c) If compliance with paragraph (b) of this section is not practicable, the battery must be effectively screened by a cage or similar structure to minimize the danger of accidental spark through dropping a metal object across the terminals.

(d) Each battery must be located as high above the bilges as practicable and secured against shifting with motion of the vessel. Each battery and battery connection must be accessible so as to permit removal.

(e) All connections must be made to battery terminals with permanent type connectors. Spring clips or other temporary type clamps may not be used.

(f) Each battery must be located in a tray of lead or other suitable material resistant to deteriorating action by the electrolyte.

(g) Each battery charger intended for connection to a commercial supply voltage must employ a transformer of the isolating type. An ammeter that is readily visible must be included in the battery charger circuit.

(h) A voltage dropping resistor, provided for charging a battery, must be mounted in a ventilated noncombustible enclosure that prevents hazardous temperatures at adjacent combustible materials.

(i) The main supply conductor from the battery must have an emergency switch, located as close as practicable

§ 169.669

to the battery, that opens all ungrounded conductors.

(j) If a storage battery is not in the same compartment and adjacent to the panel or box that distributes power to the various lighting, motor and appliance branch circuits, the storage battery lead must be fused at the battery.

§ 169.669 Radiotelephone equipment.

A separate circuit from the switchboard must be provided for each radiotelephone installation.

§ 169.670 Circuit breakers.

Each circuit breaker must be of the manually reset type designed for—
 (a) Inverse time delay;
 (b) Instantaneous short circuit protection; and
 (c) Repeated opening of the circuit without damage to the circuit breaker.

§ 169.671 Accessories.

Each light, receptacle and switch exposed to the weather must be watertight and must be constructed of corrosion-resistant material.

§ 169.672 Wiring for power and lighting circuits.

(a) Wiring for power and lighting circuits must have copper conductors, of 14 AWG or larger, and—
 (1) Meet Article 310–8 and Table 310–13 of the National Electrical Code;
 (2) Be listed as "50 volt boat cable"; or
 (3) Meet subpart 111.60 of this chapter.

(b) Wiring for power and lighting circuits on new vessels must have stranded conductors.

(c) Conductors must be sized so that—
 (1) They are adequate for the loads carried; and
 (2) The voltage drop at the load terminals is not more than 10 percent.

§ 169.673 Installation of wiring for power and lighting circuits.

(a) Wiring must be run as high as practicable above the bilges.

(b) Wiring, where subject to mechanical damage, must be protected.

(c) A wiring joint or splice must be mechanically secure and made in a junction box or enclosure.

46 CFR Ch. I (10–1–04 Edition)

(d) Unless a splice is made by an insulated pressure wire connector, it must be thoroughly soldered and taped with electrical insulating tape or the soldered joint must be otherwise protected to provide insulation equivalent to that of the conductors joined.

(e) Where ends of stranded conductors are to be clamped under terminal screws, they must be formed and soldered unless fitted with pressure terminal connectors.

(f) Conductors must be protected from overcurrent in accordance with their current-carrying capacities.

(g) Conductors supplying motors and motor operated appliances must be protected by a separate overcurrent device that is responsive to motor current. This device must be rated or set at not more than 125 percent of the motor full-load current rating.

(h) On metallic vessels the enclosures and frames of all major electrical equipment must be permanently grounded to the metal hull of the vessel by the mounting bolts or other means. Cable armor must not be used as the normal grounding means.

(i) On nonmetallic vessels, the enclosures and frames of major electrical equipment must be bonded together to a common ground by a normally non-current carrying conductor.

(j) For grounded systems the negative polarity of the supply source must be grounded to the metal hull or, for nonmetallic vessels, connected to the common ground.

(k) On a nonmetallic vessel, where a ground plate is provided for radio equipment it must be connected to the common ground.

(l) For grounded systems, hull return must not be used except for engine starting purposes.

ELECTRICAL INSTALLATIONS OPERATING AT POTENTIALS OF 50 VOLTS OR MORE ON VESSELS OF LESS THAN 100 GROSS TONS

§ 169.674 Applicability.

The requirements in this subpart apply to electrical installations operating at potentials of 50 volts or more, on vessels of less than 100 gross tons.

§ 169.675 Generators and motors.

(a) Each generator and motor must be fitted with a nameplate of corrosion-resistant material marked with the following information as applicable:

(1) Name of manufacturer.
(2) Manufacturer's type and frame designation.
(3) Output in kilowatts or horsepower rating.
(4) Kind of rating (continuous, intermittent, etc.).
(5) Revolutions per minute at rated load.
(6) Amperes at rated load.
(7) Voltage.
(8) Frequency if applicable.
(9) Number of phases, if applicable.
(10) Type of winding (for direct-current motors).

(b) Each vessel of more than 65 feet in length having only electrically driven fire and bilge pumps must have two generators. One of these generators must be driven by a means independent of the auxiliary propulsion plant. A generator that is not independent of the auxiliary propulsion plant must meet the requirements of § 111.10–4(c) of this chapter.

(c) Each generator and motor must be in a location that is accessible, adequately ventilated, and as dry as practicable.

(d) Each generator and motor must be mounted as high as practicable above the bilges to avoid damage by splash and to avoid contact with low lying vapors.

(e) Each motor for use in a location exposed to the weather must be of the watertight or waterproof type or must be enclosed in a watertight housing. The motor enclosure or housing must be provided with a check valve for drainage or a tapped hole at the lowest part of the frame for attaching a drain pipe or drain plug.

(f) Except as provided in paragraphs (g) and (h) of this section, each generator and motor for use in a machinery space must be designed for an ambient temperature of 50 degrees C. (122 degrees F.).

(g) A generator or motor may be designed for an ambient temperature of 40 degrees C. (104 degrees F.) if the vessel is designed so that the ambient temperature in the machinery space will not exceed 40 degrees C. under normal operating conditions.

(h) A generator or motor designed for 40 degrees C. may be used in a 50 degrees C. ambient location provided it is derated to 80 percent of full load rating, and the rating or setting of the overcurrent device is reduced accordingly. A nameplate specifying the derated capacity must be provided for each motor and generator.

(i) A voltmeter and an ammeter must be provided that can be used for measuring voltage and current of each generator that is in operation. For each alternating-current generator a means for measuring frequency must also be provided. Additional control equipment and measuring instruments must be provided, if needed, to ensure satisfactory operation of each generator.

§ 169.676 Grounded electrical systems.

(a) Except as provided in paragraph (b) of this section, each electrical system must meet subpart 111.05 of this chapter.

(b) Ground detection is not required.

§ 169.677 Equipment protection and enclosure.

(a) Except as provided in this section, all electrical equipment including motors, generators, controllers, distribution panels, consoles, etc., must be at least dripproof and protected.

(b) Equipment mounted on a hinged door of an enclosure must be constructed or shielded so that no live parts of the door mounted equipment will be exposed to accidental contact by a person with the door open and the circuit energized.

(c) Any cabinet, panel, or box containing more than one source of potential in excess of 50 volts must be fitted with a sign warning personnel of this condition and identifying the circuits to be disconnected to remove all the potentials in excess of 50 volts.

(d) Each distribution panelboard must be enclosed.

§ 169.678 Main distribution panels and switchboards.

(a) A distribution panel to which the generator leads are connected, and

§ 169.679

from which the electric leads throughout the vessel directly or indirectly receive their electric power is a switchboard.

(b) Each switchboard must have a driphood or an equivalent means of protecting against falling liquid.

(c) Nonconductive deck materials, mats, or gratings must be provided in front of each switchboard.

(d) If the switchboard is accessible from the rear, nonconductive deck material, mats, or gratings must be provided in the rear of the switchboard.

(e) Metal cases of instruments and secondary windings of instrument transformers must be grounded.

(f) Each switchboard must be placed in a location that is accessible, adequately ventilated, and as dry as practicable. All uninsulated current carrying parts must be mounted on nonabsorbent, noncombustible, high dielectric insulating material.

(g) Each switchboard must be of the dead front type.

(h) Each switchboard must have front and, if accessible from the back, rear non-conducting hand rails except on vessels where the surrounding bulkheads and decks are of an insulating material such as fiberglass or wood.

§ 169.679 Wiring for power and lighting circuits.

Wiring for each power and lighting circuit must meet subpart 111.60 of this chapter.

§ 169.680 Installation of wiring for power and lighting circuits.

(a) Wiring must be run as high as practicable above the bilges.

(b) Each cable installed where particularly susceptible to damage such as locations in way of doors, hatches, etc, must be protected by removable metal coverings, angle irons, pipe, or other equivalent means. All metallic coverings must be electrically continuous and grounded to the metal hull or common ground, and all coverings such as pipe that may trap moisture must be provided with holes for drainage. Where cable protection is carried through a watertight deck or bulkhead, the installation must maintain the watertight integrity of the structure.

46 CFR Ch. I (10-1-04 Edition)

(c) Each cable entering a box or fitting must be protected from abrasion, and must meet the following requirements:

(1) Each opening through which conductors enter must be adequately closed.

(2) Cable armor must be secured to the box or fitting.

(3) In damp or wet locations, each cable entrance must be watertight.

(d) The enclosures of all equipment must be permanently grounded to the metal hull of the vessel by the mounting bolts or other means. Cable armor must not be used as the normal grounding means.

(e) On a nonmetallic vessel, the enclosures must be bonded to a common ground by a normal noncurrent carrying conductor.

(f) On a nonmetallic vessel, where a ground plate is provided for radio equipment it must be connected to the common ground.

(g) Except as provided in paragraph (i) of this section, each armored cable must have a metallic covering that is—

(1) Electrically and mechanically continuous; and

(2) Grounded at each end of the run to—

(i) The metal hull; or

(ii) The common ground required by paragraph (e) of this section on non-metallic vessels.

(h) In lieu of being grounded at each end of the run as required by paragraph (g) of this section, final sub-circuits may be grounded at the supply end only.

(i) All equipment, including switches, fuses, lampholders, etc., must be of a type designed for the proper potential and be so identified.

(j) Except as provided in paragraph (l) of this section, each junction box, connection box, and outlet box, must have an internal depth of at least 1½ inches.

(k) For a box incorporated in a fixture having a volume of not less than 20 cubic inches, the depth may be decreased to not less than 1 inch.

(l) Each conductor, except a fixture wire within a box, must have a free space computed using the volume per conductor given in Table 169.680(l). If a fitting or device such as a cable clamp,

70

Coast Guard, DHS § 169.683

hickey, switch or receptacle is contained in the box, each fitting or device must count as one conductor.

TABLE 169.680(l)

Size of conductor A.W.G.	Free space for each conductor in box, cubic inches
14	2.0
12	2.25
8	2.50
1	3.0

(m) Each junction box, connection box, and outlet box for use in a damp or wet location must be of watertight construction.

(n) Each lighting fixture must be constructed in accordance with the requirements of Subchapter J of this chapter.

(o) A separate circuit from the switchboard must be provided for each radiotelephone installation.

(p) Knife switches must be so placed or designed that gravity or vibration will not tend to close them. Knife switches, unless of the double throw type, must be connected so that the blades are dead when the switch is in the open position.

(q) Circuits must be connected to the fuse end of switches and to the coil end of circuit breakers, except that generator leads or incoming feeders may be connected to either end of circuit breakers.

(r) Receptacle outlets and attachment plugs for the attachment of portable lamps, tools, and similar apparatus supplied as ship's equipment and operating at 100 volts or more, must provide a grounding pole and a grounding conductor in the portable cord to ground the non-current carrying metal parts of the apparatus.

(s) Receptacle outlets of the type providing a grounded pole must be of a configuration that will not permit the dead metal parts of portable apparatus to be connected to a live conductor.

§ 169.681 Disconnect switches and devices.

(a) Externally operable switches or circuit breakers must be provided for motor and controller circuits and must open all ungrounded conductors of the circuit.

(b) If the disconnect means is not within sight of the equipment that the circuit supplies, means must be provided for locking the disconnect device in the "open" position.

(c) For circuits protected by fuses, the disconnect switch required for fuses in § 169.683(b) of this chapter is adequate for disconnecting the circuit from the supply.

(d) The disconnect means may be in the same enclosure with motor controllers.

(e) Disconnect means must be provided to open all conductors of generator and shore power cables.

[CGD 83–005, 51 FR 896, Jan. 9, 1986; 51 FR 10632, Mar. 28, 1986]

§ 169.682 Distribution and circuit loads.

(a) Except as provided in paragraph (b) of this section, the connected load on a lighting branch circuit must not exceed 80 percent of the rating of the overcurrent protective device, computed using the greater of—

(1) The lamp sizes to be installed; or
(2) 50 watts per outlet.

(b) Circuits supplying electrical discharge lamps must be computed using the ballast input current.

(c) The branch circuit cables for motor and lighting loads must be no smaller than No. 14 AWG.

§ 169.683 Overcurrent protection, general.

(a) Overcurrent protection must be provided for each ungrounded conductor for the purpose of opening the electric circuit if the current reaches a value that causes an excessive or dangerous temperature in the conductor or conductor insulation.

(b) Disconnect means must be provided on the supply side of and adjacent to all fuses for the purpose of de-energizing the fuses for inspection and maintenance purposes. All disconnect means must open all ungrounded conductors of the circuit simultaneously.

(c) Each conductor, including a generator lead and shore power cable, must be protected in accordance with its current-carrying capacity.

(d) If the allowable current-carrying capacity of a conductor does not correspond to a standard size fuse, the next larger size or rating may be used

71

§ 169.684

but not exceeding 150 percent of the allowable current-carrying capacity of the conductor.

(e) Plug (screw in type) fuses and fuseholders must not be used in circuits exceeding 125 volts between conductors. The screw shell of plug type fuseholders must be connected to the load of the circuit. Edison base fuses may not be used.

(f) If the allowable current-carrying capacity of the conductor does not correspond to a standard rating of circuit breakers, the next larger rating not exceeding 150 percent of the allowable current-carrying capacity of the conductor may be used.

(g) Lighting branch circuits must be protected against overcurrent either by fuses or circuit breakers rated at not more than 20 amperes.

(h) Each circuit breaker must be of the manually reset type designed for—

(1) Inverse time delay;

(2) Instantaneous short circuit protection; and

(3) Repeated opening of the circuit in which it is to be used without damage to the circuit breaker.

(i) Circuit breakers must indicate whether they are in the open or closed position.

(j) Devices such as instruments, pilot lights, ground detector lights, potential transformers, etc. must be supplied by circuits protected by overcurrent devices.

(k) Each generator must be protected with an overcurrent device set at a value not exceeding 15 percent above the full-load rating for continuous rated machines or the overload rating for special rated machines.

§ 169.684 Overcurrent protection for motors and motor branch circuits.

(a) Except as provided in paragraph (d) of this section, each motor must be provided with running protection against overcurrent. A protective device integral with the motor that is responsive to motor current or to both motor current and temperature may be used.

(b) The motor branch circuit conductors, the motor control apparatus, and the motors must be protected against overcurrent due to short circuits or grounds with overcurrent devices.

(c) The motor branch circuit overcurrent device must be capable of carrying the starting current of the motor.

(d) Each manually started continous duty motor, rated at one horsepower or less, that is within sight from the starter location, is considered as protected against overcurrent by the overcurrent device protecting the conductors of the branch circuit.

§ 169.685 Electric heating and cooking equipment.

(a) Each electric space heater for heating rooms and compartments must be provided with thermal cutouts to prevent overheating. Each heater must be so constructed and installed as to prevent the hanging of towels, clothing, etc., on the heater, and to prevent overheating of heater parts and adjacent bulkheads or decks.

(b) All electric cooking equipment, attachments, and devices, must be of rugged construction and so designed as to permit complete cleaning, maintenance, and repair.

(c) Doors for electric cooking equipment must be provided with heavy duty hinges and locking devices to prevent accidental opening in heavy seas.

(d) Electric cooking equipment must be mounted to prevent dislodgment in heavy seas.

(e) For each grill or similar type cooking equipment, means must be provided to collect grease or fat and to prevent spillage on wiring or the deck.

(f) Where necessary for safety of personnel, grab rails must be provided. Each electric range must be provided with sea rails with suitable barriers to resist accidental movement of cooking pots.

§ 169.686 Shore power.

If a shore power connection is provided it must meet the following requirements:

(a) A shore power connection box or receptacle and a cable connecting this box or receptacle to the main distribution panel must be permanently installed in an accessible location.

(b) The shore power cable must be provided with a disconnect means located on or near the main distribution panel.

Electrical Installations on Vessels of 100 Gross Tons and Over

§ 169.687 General.

Except as provided in this subpart, electrical installations on vessels of 100 gross tons and over must meet the requirements of parts 110-113 of this chapter.

§ 169.688 Power supply.

(a) The requirements of this section apply in lieu of subpart 111.10 of this chapter.

(b) If a generator is used to provide electric power for any vital system listed in § 169.642 of this subchapter, at least two generating sets must be provided. At least one required generating set must be independent of the auxiliary propulsion machinery. A generator that is not independent of the auxiliary propulsion plant must meet the requirements of § 111.10-4(c) of this chapter. With any one generating set stopped, the remaining set(s) must provide the power necessary for each of the following:

(1) Normal at sea load plus starting of the largest vital system load that can be started automatically or started from a space remote from the main distribution panel (switchboard).

(2) All vital systems simultaneously with nonvital loads secured.

(c) The adequacy of ship service generators must be demonstrated to the satisfaction of the OCMI during the initial inspection required by § 169.221 of this subchapter.

§ 169.689 Demand loads.

Demand loads must meet § 111.60-7 of this chapter except that smaller demand loads for motor feeders are acceptable if the cable is protected at or below its current-carrying capacity.

§ 169.690 Lighting branch circuits.

Each lighting branch circuit must meet the requirements of § 111.75-5 of this chapter, except that—

(a) Appliance loads, electric heater loads, and isolated small motor loads may be connected to a lighting distribution panelboard; and

(b) Branch circuits in excess of 30 amperes may be supplied from a lighting distribution panelboard.

§ 169.691 Navigation lights.

Navigation light systems must meet the requirements of § 111.75-17 of this chapter except the requirements of § 111.75-17 (a) and (c).

§ 169.692 Remote stop stations.

In lieu of the remote stopping systems required by subpart 111.103 of this chapter, remote stop stations must be provided as follows:

(a) A propulsion shutdown in the pilothouse for each propulsion unit,

(b) A bilge slop or dirty oil discharge shutdown at the deck discharge,

(c) A ventilation shutdown located outside the space ventilated, and

(d) A shutdown from outside the engineroom for the fuel transfer pump, fuel oil service pump, or any other fuel oil pump.

§ 169.693 Engine order telegraph systems.

An engine order telegraph system is not required.

Subpart 169.700—Vessel Control, Miscellaneous Systems, and Equipment

§ 169.703 Cooking and heating.

(a) Cooking and heating equipment must be suitable for marine use. Cooking installations must meet the requirements of ABYC Standard A-3, "Recommended Practices and Standards Covering Galley Stoves."

(b) The use of gasoline for cooking, heating or lighting is prohibited on all vessels.

(c) The use of liquefied petroleum gas (LPG) or compressed natural gas (CNG) is authorized for cooking purposes only.

(1) The design, installation and testing of each LPG system must meet either ABYC A-1 or Chapter 6 of NFPA 302.

(2) The design, installation, and testing of each CNG system must meet either Chapter 6 of NFPA 302 or ABYC A-22.

(3) The stowage of each cylinder must comply with the requirements for the stowage of cylinders of liquefied or non-liquefied gases used for heating,

cooking, or lighting in part 147 of this chapter.

(4) If the fuel supply line enters an enclosed space on the vessel, a remote shutoff valve must be installed which can be operated from a position adjacent to the appliance. The valve must be a type that will fail closed, and it must be located between the regulator and the point where the fuel supply enters the enclosed portion of the vessel.

(5) If Chapter 6 of NFPA 302 is used as the standard, then the following additional requirements must also be met:

(i) LPG or CNG must be odorized in accordance with ABYC A-1.5.d or A-22.5.b, respectively.

(ii) Ovens must be equipped with a flame failure switch in accordance with ABYC A-1.10.b for LPG or A-22.10.b for CNG.

(iii) The marking and mounting of LPG cylinders must be in accordance with ABYC-1.6.b.

(iv) LPG cylinders must be of the vapor withdrawal type as specified in ABYC A-1.5.b.

(6) If ABYC A-1 or A-22 is used as the standard for an LPG on CNG installation, then pilot lights or glow plugs are prohibited.

(7) If ABYC A-22 is used as the standard for a CNG installation, then the following additional requirements must also be met:

(i) The CNG cylinders, regulating equipment, and safety equipment must meet the installation, stowage, and testing requirements of paragraphs 6-5.11.1, 2, 3; 6-5.11.5; and 6-5.11.8 of NFPA 302.

(ii) The use or stowage of stoves with attached cylinders is prohibited as specified in paragraph 6-5.1 of NFPA 302.

§ 169.705 Mooring equipment.

Each vessel must be fitted with ground tackle and hawsers deemed necessary by the Officer in Charge, Marine Inspection, depending upon the size of the vessel and the waters on which it operates.

§ 169.709 Compass.

(a) Each vessel must be fitted with a magnetic steering compass.

(b) Each vessel certificated for exposed water service must have an emergency compass in addition to the one required in paragraph (a).

§ 169.711 Emergency lighting.

(a) Each vessel must be equipped with a suitable number of portable battery lights.

(b) Each vessel of 100 gross tons and over must satisfy the emergency lighting requirements for a miscellaneous self-propelled vessel as contained in part 112 of this chapter.

(c) Each vessel of less than 100 gross tons that has accommodation spaces located below the main deck must have permanently installed lighting which is connected to a single emergency power source or permanently installed, relay-controlled, battery-operated lanterns. The lighting or lanterns must be fitted along the avenues of escape, in the wheelhouse, and in the engine compartment.

(1) A single emergency power source, if provided, must be independent of the normal power source and must be either a generator or a storage battery.

(d) The emergency power source and batteries for individual, battery-operated, lanterns must have the capacity to supply all connected loads simultaneously for at least 6 hours of continuous operations. If the emergency lighting is provided by battery power, then an automatic battery charger that maintains the battery(s) in a fully charged condition must be provided.

(e) The emergency lighting system must be capable of being fully activated from a single location.

§ 169.713 Engineroom communication system.

An efficient communication system must be provided between the principal steering station and the engineroom on vessels which are not equipped with pilothouse controls if, in the opinion of the Officer in Charge, Marine Inspection, this is necessary for proper operation of the vessel.

§ 169.715 Radio.

(a) Radiotelegraph and radiotelephone installations are required on certain vessels. Details of these requirements and the details of the installations are contained in regulations of the Federal Communications Commission (FCC) in Title 47, Code of Federal Regulations, part 83.

(b) A valid certificate issued by the FCC is evidence that the radio installation is in compliance with the requirements of that agency.

§ 169.717 Fireman's outfit.

(a) Each vessel greater than 120 feet but less than 150 feet in length must carry one fireman's outfit consisting of—

(1) One pressure-demand, open-circuit, self-contained breathing apparatus, approved by the Mine Safety and Health Administration (MSHA) and by the National Institute for Occupational Safety and Health (NIOSH) and having at a minimum a 30-minute air supply and a full facepiece; but a self-contained compressed-air breathing apparatus previously approved by MSHA and NIOSH under part 160, subpart 160.011, of this chapter may continue in use as required equipment if it was part of the vessel's equipment on November 23, 1992, and as long as it is maintained in good condition to the satisfaction of the Officer in Charge, Marine Inspection;

(2) One lifeline with a belt or a suitable harness;

(3) One approved flame safety lamp;

(4) One flashlight listed by an independent testing laboratory as suitable for use in hazardous locations;

(5) One fire ax;

(6) Boots and gloves of rubber or other electrically nonconducting material;

(7) A rigid helmet that provides effective protection against impact; and

(8) Protective clothing.

(b) Each vessel 150 feet or greater must carry two fireman's outfits. The outfits must be stowed in widely separated accessible locations.

(c) Lifelines must be of steel or bronze wire rope. Steel wire rope must be either inherently corrosion resistant or made so by galvanizing or thinning. Each end must be fitted with a hook with keeper having a throat opening which can be readily slipped over a 5/8-inch bolt. The total length of the lifeline is dependent upon the size and arrangement of the vessel, and more than one line may be hooked together to achieve the necessary length. No individual length of lifeline may be less than 50 feet in length. The assembled lifeline must have a minimum breaking strength of 1,500 pounds.

(d) A complete recharge must be carried out for each self-contained breathing apparatus and a complete set of spare batteries and bulb must be carried for each flashlight. The spares must be stowed in the same location as the equipment it is to reactivate.

(e) Protective clothing must be constructed of material that will protect the skin from the heat of fire and burns from scalding steam. The outer surface must be water resistant.

[CGD 83–005, 51 FR 896, Jan. 9, 1986, as amended by CGD 86–036, 57 FR 48326, Oct. 23, 1992]

§ 169.721 Storm sails and halyards (exposed and partially protected waters only).

(a) Unless clearly unsuitable, each vessel must have one storm trysail of appropriate size. It must be sheeted independently of the boom and must have neither headboard nor battens.

(b) Each vessel having headsails must also have one storm head sail of appropriate size and strength.

(c) Each vessel must have at least two halyards, each capable of hoisting a sail.

§ 169.723 Safety belts.

Each vessel must carry a harness type safety belt conforming to Offshore Racing Council (ORC) standards for each person on watch or required to work the vessel in heavy weather.

§ 169.725 First aid kit.

Each vessel must carry an approved first aid kit, constructed and fitted in accordance with subpart 160.041 of this chapter.

§ 169.726 Radar reflector.

Each nonmetallic vessel less than 90 feet in length must exhibit a radar reflector of suitable size and design while underway.

MARKINGS

§ 169.730 General alarm bell switch.

On vessels of 100 gross tons and over there must be a general alarm bell

§ 169.731

switch in the pilothouse, clearly and permanently identified by lettering on a metal plate or with a sign in red letters on a suitable background: "GENERAL ALARM"

§ 169.731 General alarm bells.

On vessels of 100 gross tons and over each general alarm bell must be identified by red lettering at least ½ inch high: "GENERAL ALARM—WHEN BELL RINGS GO TO YOUR STATION."

§ 169.732 Carbon dioxide alarm.

Each carbon dioxide alarm must be conspicuously identified: "WHEN ALARM SOUNDS—VACATE AT ONCE. CARBON DIOXIDE BEING RELEASED."

§ 169.733 Fire extinguishing branch lines.

Each branch line valve of every fire extinguishing system must be plainly and permanently marked indicating the spaces served.

§ 169.734 Fire extinguishing system controls.

Each control cabinet or space containing valves or manifolds for the various fire extinguishing systems must be distinctly marked in conspicuous red letters at least 2 inches high: "CARBON DIOXIDE FIRE EXTINGUISHING SYSTEM," or "HALON FIRE EXTINGUISHING SYSTEM," as appropriate.

§ 169.735 Fire hose stations.

Each fire hydrant must be identified in red letters and figures at least two inches high "FIRE STATION NO. 1," "2," "3," etc. Where the hose is not stowed in the open or readily seen behind glass, this identification must be placed so as to be readily seen from a distance.

§ 169.736 Self-contained breathing apparatus.

Each locker or space containing self-contained breathing apparatus must be marked "SELF-CONTAINED BREATHING APPARATUS."

§ 169.737 Hand portable fire extinguishers.

Each hand portable fire extinguisher must be marked with a number, and the location where it is stowed must be marked with a corresponding number. The marks must be at least ½ inch high. Where only one type and size of hand portable fire extinguisher is carried, the numbering may be omitted.

§ 169.738 Emergency lights.

Each emergency light must be marked with a letter "E" at least ½ inch high.

§ 169.739 Lifeboats.

(a) The name and port of the vessel marked on its stern as required by § 67.15 of this chapter must be plainly marked or painted on each side of the bow of each lifeboat in letters not less than 3 inches high.

(b) Each lifeboat must have its number plainly marked or painted on each side of the bow in figures not less than 3 inches high. The lifeboats on each side of the vessel must be numbered from forward aft, with the odd numbers on the starboard side.

(c) The cubical contents and number of persons allowed to be carried in each lifeboat must be plainly marked or painted on each side of the bow of the lifeboat in letters and numbers not less than 1½ inches high. In addition, the number of persons allowed must be plainly marked or painted on top of at least 2 thwarts in letters and numbers not less than 3 inches high.

(d) Each oar must be conspicuously marked with the vessel's name.

(e) Where mechanical disengaging apparatus is used, the control effecting the release of the lifeboat must be painted bright red and must have thereon in raised letters either the words—"DANGER-LEVER DROPS BOAT", or the words—"DANGER-LEVER RELEASES HOOKS".

(f) The top of thwarts, side benches and footings of lifeboats must be painted or otherwise colored international orange. The area in way of the red mechanical disengaging gear control lever, from the keel to the side bench, must be painted or otherwise colored white, to provide a contrasting background for the lever. This band of white should be approximately 12 inches wide depending on the internal arrangements of the lifeboat.

§ 169.740 Liferafts and lifefloats.

(a) Rigid type liferafts and lifefloats, together with their oars and paddles, must be conspicuously marked with the vessel's name and port of the vessel as marked on its stern as required by § 67.15 of this chapter.

(b) The number of persons allowed on each rigid type liferaft and lifefloat must be conspicuously marked or painted thereon in letters and numbers at least 1½ inches high.

(c) There must be stenciled in a conspicuous place in the immediate vicinity of each inflatable liferaft the following:

INFLATABLE LIFERAFT NO____

_____PERSONS CAPACITY

These markings must not be placed on the inflatable liferaft containers.

§ 169.741 Personal flotation devices and ring life buoys.

Each personal flotation device and ring life buoy must be marked with the vessel's name.

§ 169.743 Portable magazine chests.

Portable magazine chests must be marked in letters at least 3 inches high: "PORTABLE MAGAZINE CHEST—FLAMMABLE—KEEP LIGHTS AND FIRE AWAY."

§ 169.744 Emergency position indicating radio beacon (EPIRB).

Each EPIRB must be marked with the vessel's name.

§ 169.745 Escape hatches and emergency exits.

Each escape hatch and other emergency exit must be marked on both sides using at least 1-inch letters: "EMERGENCY EXIT, KEEP CLEAR", unless the markings are deemed unnecessary by the Officer in Charge, Marine Inspection.

§ 169.746 Fuel shutoff valves.

Each remote fuel shutoff station must be marked in at least 1-inch letters indicating purpose of the valves and direction of operation.

§ 169.747 Watertight doors and hatches.

Each watertight door and watertight hatch must be marked on both sides in at least 1-inch letters: "WATERTIGHT DOOR—CLOSE IN EMERGENCY" or "WATERTIGHT HATCH—CLOSE IN EMERGENCY", unless the markings are deemed unnecessary by the Officer in Charge, Marine Inspection.

§ 169.750 Radio call sign.

Each vessel certificated for exposed or partially protected water service must have its radio call sign permanently displayed or readily available for display upon its deck or cabin top in letters at least 18 inches high.

§ 169.755 Draft marks and draft indicating systems.

(a) All vessels must have draft marks plainly and legibly visible upon the stem and upon the sternpost or rudderpost or at any place at the stern of the vessel as may be necessary for easy observance. The bottom of each mark must indicate the draft.

(b) The draft must be taken from the bottom of the keel to the surface of the water at the location of the marks.

(c) In cases where the keel does not extend forward or aft to the location of the draft marks, due to a raked stem or cut away skeg, the draft must be measured from a line projected from the bottom of the keel forward or aft, as the case may be, to the location of the draft marks.

(d) In cases where a vessel may have a skeg or other appendage extending locally below the line of the keel, the draft at the end of the vessel adjacent to such appendage must be measured to a line tangent to the lowest part of such appendage and parallel to the line of the bottom of the keel.

(e) Draft marks must be separated so that the projections of the marks onto a vertical plane are of uniform height equal to the vertical spacing between consecutive marks.

(f) Draft marks must be painted in contrasting color to the hull.

(g) In cases where draft marks are obscured due to operational constraints

§ 169.805

or by protrusions, the vessel must be fitted with a reliable draft indicating system from which the bow and stern drafts can be determined.

[CGD 89-037, 57 FR 41824, Sept. 11, 1992]

Subpart 169.800—Operations

§ 169.805 Exhibition of licenses.

Licensed personnel on any vessel subject to this subchapter shall have their licenses in their possession and available for examination at all times when the vessel is being operated.

§ 169.807 Notice of casualty.

(a) The owner, agent, master, or person in charge of a vessel involved in a marine casualty shall give notice as soon as possible to the nearest Coast Guard Marine Safety or Marine Inspection Office, whenever the casualty involves any of the following:

(1) Each accidental grounding and each intentional grounding which also meets any of the other reporting criteria or creates a hazard to navigation, the environment or the safety of the vessel;

(2) Loss of main propulsion or primary steering or any associated component or control system which causes a reduction of the maneuvering capabilities of the vessel. Loss means that systems, components, sub-system or control systems do not perform the specified or required function;

(3) An occurrence materially and adversely affecting the vessel's seaworthiness or fitness for service or route, including but not limited to fire, flooding, or failure or damage to fixed fire extinguishing systems, lifesaving equipment, auxiliary power generating equipment, Coast Guard approved equipment or bilge pumping systems;

(4) Loss of life;

(5) Injury causing a person to remain incapacitated for a period in excess of 72 hours; or

(6) An occurrence resulting in damage to property in excess of $25,000.00. Damage includes the cost necessary to restore the property to the service condition which existed prior to the casualty but does not include the cost of salvage, gas freeing, drydocking, or demurrage.

46 CFR Ch. I (10-1-04 Edition)

(b) The notice must include the name and official number of the vessel involved, the name of the vessel's owner or agent, nature, location and circumstances of the casualty, nature and extent of injury to persons, and the damage to property.

(c) In addition to the notice required, the person in charge of the vessel shall report in writing or in person, as soon as possible to the Officer in Charge, Marine Inspection at the port in which the casualty occurred or nearest the port of first arrival. Casualties must be reported on Form CG-2692.

(d) The owner, agent, master, or other person in charge of any vessel involved in a marine casualty shall retain for three years the voyage records of the vessel such as both rough and smooth deck and engineroom logs, navigation charts, navigation work books, compass deviation cards, gyrocompass records, record of draft, aids to mariners, radiograms sent and received, the radio log, and crew, sailing school student, instructor, and guest lists. The owner agent, master, or other officer in charge, shall make these records available to a duly authorized Coast Guard officer or employee for examination upon request.

(e) Whenever a vessel collides or is connected with a collision with a buoy or other aid to navigation under the jurisdiction of the Coast Guard, the person in charge of the vessel shall report the accident to the nearest Officer in Charge, Marine Inspection. A report on Form CG-2692 is not required unless any of the results listed in paragraph (b) of this section occur.

§ 169.809 Charts and nautical publications.

As appropriate for the intended voyage, all vessels must carry adequate and up-to-date—
(a) Charts;
(b) Sailing directions;
(c) Coast pilots;
(d) Light lists;
(e) Notices to mariners;
(f) Tide tables; and
(g) Current tables.

§ 169.813 Station bills.

(a) A station bill (muster list) shall be prepared and signed by the master of the vessel. The master shall ensure that the bill is posted in conspicuous locations throughout the vessel, particularly in the living spaces, before the vessel sails.

(b) The station bill must set forth the special duties and duty station of each member of the ship's company for the various emergencies. The duties must, as far as possible, be comparable with the regular work of the individual. The duties must include at least the following and any other duties necessary for the proper handling of a particular emergency:

(1) The closing of airports, watertight doors, scuppers, sanitary and other discharges which lead through the vessel's hull below the margin line, etc., the stopping of fans and ventilating systems, and the operating of all safety equipment.

(2) The preparing and launching of lifeboats and liferafts.

(3) The extinguishing of fire.

(4) The mustering of guests, if carried, including the following:

(i) Warning the guests.

(ii) Seeing that they are dressed and have put on their personal flotation devices in a proper manner.

(iii) Assembling the guests and directing them to the appointed stations.

(iv) Keeping order in the passageways and stairways and generally controlling the movement of the guests.

(v) Seeing that a supply of blankets is taken to the lifeboats.

§ 169.815 Emergency signals.

(a) The station bill must set forth the various signals used for calling the ship's company to their stations and for giving instructions while at their stations.

(b) On vessels of 100 gross tons and over the following signals must be used.

(1) The first alarm signal must be a continuous blast of the vessel's whistle for a period of not less than 10 seconds supplemented by the continuous ringing of the general alarm bells for not less than 10 seconds.

(2) For dismissal from fire alarm stations, the general alarm must be sounded three times supplemented by three short blasts of the vessel's whistle.

(3) The signal for boat stations or boat drill must be a succession of more than six short blasts, followed by one long blast, of the vessel's whistle supplemented by a comparable signal on the general alarm bells.

(4) For dismissal from boat stations, there must be three short blasts of the whistle.

(c) Where whistle signals are used for handling the lifeboats, they must be as follows:

(1) To lower lifeboats, one short blast.

(2) To stop lowering the lifeboats, two short blasts.

§ 169.817 Master to instruct ship's company.

The master shall conduct drills and give instructions as necessary to insure that all hands are familiar with their duties as specified in the station bill.

§ 169.819 Manning of lifeboats and liferafts.

(a) The provisions of this section shall apply to all vessels equipped with lifeboats and/or liferafts.

(b) The master shall place a licensed deck officer, an able seaman, or a certificated lifeboatman in command of each lifeboat or liferaft. Each lifeboat or liferaft with a prescribed complement of 25 or more persons must have one additional certificated lifeboatman.

(c) The person in charge of each lifeboat or liferaft shall have a list of its assigned occupants, and shall see that the persons under his orders are acquainted with their duties.

§ 169.821 Patrol person.

(a) The master shall designate a member of the ship's company to be a roving patrol person, whenever the vessel is operational.

(b) The roving patrol person shall frequently visit all areas to ensure that safe conditions are being maintained.

§ 169.823 Openings.

(a) Except as provided in paragraph (b) of this section, all watertight doors in subdivision bulkheads, hatches, and openings in the hull must be kept closed during the navigation of the vessel.

§ 169.824

(b) The master may permit hatches or other openings to be uncovered or opened for reasonable purposes such as ship's maintenance, when existing conditions warrant the action and the openings can readily be closed.

§ 169.824 Compliance with provisions of certificate of inspection.

The master or person in charge of the vessel shall see that all of the provisions of the certificate of inspection are strictly adhered to. Nothing in this subpart shall be construed as limiting the master or person in charge of the vessel, on his own responsibility, from diverting from the route prescribed in the certificate of inspection or taking such other steps as he deems necessary and prudent to assist vessels in distress or for other similar emergencies.

§ 169.825 Wearing of safety belts.

The master of each vessel shall ensure that each person wears an approved safety harness when aloft or working topside in heavy weather.

TESTS, DRILLS, AND INSPECTIONS

§ 169.826 Steering, communications and control.

The master shall test the vessel's steering gear, signaling whistle, engine controls, and communications equipment prior to getting underway.

§ 169.827 Hatches and other openings.

The master is responsible for seeing that all hatches, openings in the hull, and watertight doors are properly closed tight.

§ 169.829 Emergency lighting and power systems.

(a) Where fitted, the master shall have the emergency lighting and power systems operated and inspected at least once in each week that the vessel is navigated to ensure that the system is in proper operating condition.

(b) The master shall have the internal combustion engine driven emergency generators operated under load for at least 2 hours at least once in each month that the vessel is navigated.

(c) The master shall have the storage batteries for emergency lighting and power systems tested at least once in each 6-month period that the vessel is navigated to demonstrate the ability of the storage battery to supply the emergency loads for the specified period of time.

(d) The date of each test and the condition and performance of the apparatus must be noted in the official logbook.

§ 169.831 Emergency position indicating radio beacon (EPIRB).

The master shall ensure that—

(a) The EPIRB required in § 169.555 of this subchapter is tested monthly, using the integrated test circuit and output indicator, to determine that it is operative; and

(b) The EPIRB's battery is replaced after the EPIRB is used and before the marked expiration date.

§ 169.833 Fire and boat drills.

(a) When the vessel is operating, the master shall conduct a fire and boat drill each week. The scheduling of drills is at the discretion of the master except that at least one fire and boat drill must be held within 24 hours of leaving a port if more than 25 percent of the ship's company have been replaced at that port.

(b) The fire and boat drill must be conducted as if an actual emergency existed. All persons on board including guests shall report to their respective stations and be prepared to perform the duties specified in the station bill.

(1) Fire pumps must be started and a sufficient number of outlets used to ascertain that the system is in proper working order.

(2) All rescue and safety equipment must be brought from the emergency equipment lockers and the persons designated must demonstrate their ability to use the equipment.

(3) All watertight doors which are in use while the vessel is underway must be operated.

(4) Weather permitting, lifeboat covers and strongbacks must be removed, plugs or caps put in place, boat ladders secured in position, painters led forward and tended, and other life saving equipment prepared for use. The motor

and hand-propelling gear of each lifeboat, where fitted, must be operated for at least 5 minutes.

(5) In port, every lifeboat must be swung out, if practicable. The unobstructed lifeboats must be lowered to the water and the ship's company must be exercised in the use of the oars or other means of propulsion. Although all lifeboats may not be used in a particular drill, care must be taken that all lifeboats are given occasional use to ascertain that all lowering equipment is in proper order and the crew properly trained. The master shall ensure that each lifeboat is lowered to the water at least once every 3 months.

(6) When the vessel in underway, and weather permitting, all lifeboats must be swung out to ascertain that the gear is in proper order.

(7) The person in charge of each lifeboat and liferaft shall have a list of its crew and shall ensure that the persons under his or her command are acquainted with their duties.

(8) Lifeboat equipment must be examined at least once a month to ensure that it is complete.

(9) The master shall ensure that all persons on board fully participate in these drills and that they have been instructed in the proper method of donning and adjusting the personal flotation devices and exposure suits used and informed of the stowage location of these devices.

(c) The master shall have an entry made in the vessel's official logbook relative to each fire and boat drill setting forth the date and hour, length of time of the drill, numbers on the lifeboats swung out and numbers on those lowered, the length of time that motor and hand-propelled lifeboats are operated, the number of lengths of hose used, together with a statement as to the condition of all fire and lifesaving equipment, watertight door mechanisms, valves, etc. An entry must also be made to report the monthly examination of the lifeboat equipment. If in any week the required fire and boat drills are not held or only partial drills are held, an entry must be made stating the circumstances and extend of the drills held.

(d) A copy of these requirements must be framed under glass or other transparent material and posted in a conspicuous place about the vessel.

§ 169.837 **Lifeboats, liferafts, and lifefloats.**

(a) The master or person in charge shall ensure that the lifeboats, rescue boats, liferafts, and lifefloats, are properly maintained at all times, and that all equipment for the vessel required by the regulations in this subchapter is provided, maintained, and replaced as indicated or when necessary and no less frequently than required by paragraph (b) of this section.

(b) The master shall ensure that:

(1) Each lifeboat has been stripped, cleaned and thoroughly overhauled at least once in each year.

(2) The fuel tanks of motor propelled lifeboats have been emptied and fuel changed once every twelve months.

(3) Each lifefloat has been cleaned and thorughly overhauled once every twelve months.

(4) Each inflatable liferaft has been serviced at a facility specifically approved by the Commandant for the particular brand, and in accordance with servicing procedures meeting the requirements of part 160, part 160.151, of this chapter—

(i) No later than the month and year on its servicing sticker affixed under 46 CFR 160.151-57(n), except that servicing may be delayed until the next scheduled inspection of the vessel, provided that the delay does not exceed 5 months; and

(ii) Whenever the container is damaged or the container straps or seals are broken.

[CGD 83-005, 51 FR 896, Jan. 9, 1986, as amended by USCG-2001-11118, 67 FR 58541, Sept. 17, 2002]

§ 169.839 **Firefighting equipment.**

(a) The master or person in charge shall ensure that the vessel's firefighting equipment is at all times ready for use and that all firefighting equipment required by the regulations in this subchapter is provided, maintained, and replaced as indicated.

(b) The master or person in charge shall have performed at least once

§ 169.840

every 12 months the tests and inspections of all hand portable fire extinguishers, semiportable fire extinguishing systems, and fixed fire extinguishing systems on board as described in § 169.247 of this subchapter. The master or person in charge shall keep records of the tests and inspections showing the dates when performed, the number and/or other identification of each unit tested and inspected, and the name(s) of the person(s) and/or company conducting the tests and inspections. These records must be made available to the marine inspectors upon request and must be kept for the period of validity of the vessel's current certificate of inspection. Conducting these tests and inspections does not relieve the master or person in charge of his responsibility to maintain this firefighting equipment in proper condition at all times.

§ 169.840 Verification of vessel compliance with applicable stability requirements.

(a) After loading and prior to departure and at all other times necessary to assure the safety of the vessel, the master shall determine that the vessel complies with all applicable stability requirements in the vessel's trim and stability book, stability letter, Certificate of Inspection, and Load Line Certificate, as the case may be, and then enter an attestation statement of the verification in the log book. The vessel may not depart until it is in compliance with these requirements.

(b) When determining compliance with applicable stability requirements the vessel's draft, trim, and stability must be determined as necessary and any stability calculations made in support of the determination must be retained on board the vessel for the duration of the voyage.

[CGD 89–037, 57 FR 41825, Sept. 11, 1992]

§ 169.841 Logbook entries.

(a) Each vessel subject to the inspection provisions of this subchapter must have an official logbook.

(b) The master shall place all entries required by law or regulation in the logbook.

(c) A Coast Guard form "Official Logbook" may be utilized or the owner may utilize his own format for an official logbook. The logs must be kept available for review by the Coast Guard for a period of one year after the date to which the records refer or for the period of validity of the vessel's current certificate of inspection, whichever is longer.

(d) All tests, drills, inspections and notifications required in this subchapter must be entered in the official logbook.

(e) Prior to getting underway the master shall enter in the logbook the name of each sailing school student, sailing school instructor, and guest onboard, and the fact that each person was notified of the applicable safety standards for sailing school vessels as required by § 169.857 of this chapter.

§ 169.847 Lookouts.

Nothing in this part exonerates any master or officer of the watch from the consequences of any neglect to keep a proper lookout.

§ 169.849 Posting placards containing instructions for launching and inflating inflatable liferafts.

Every vessel equipped with inflatable liferafts must have posted in conspicuous places readily accessible to the ship's company and guests approved placards containing instructions for launching and inflating inflatable liferafts. The number and location of such placards for a particular vessel shall be determined by the Officer in Charge, Marine Inspection.

§ 169.853 Display of plans.

(a) Each vessel of 100 gross tons and over must have permanently exhibited for the guidance of the master, general arrangement plans for each deck showing the fire control stations, the various sections enclosed by fire resisting bulkheads, the sections enclosed by fire retarding bulkheads, together with the particulars of the fire alarms, detecting systems, fire extinguishing appliances, means of access to different compartments, ventilation systems and the position of dampers and remote stops.

(b) Plans must clearly show for each deck the boundaries of the watertight compartments, the openings therein with the means of closure and the position of any controls, and the arrangements for the correction of any list due to flooding.

§ 169.855 Pre-underway training.

Prior to getting underway the master shall ensure that each sailing school student and sailing school instructor, who has not previously been instructed, is instructed in the handling of sails, emergency procedures, nautical terms, location and use of lifesaving and firefighting equipment, and the general layout of the vessel.

§ 169.857 Disclosure of safety standards.

(a) This section applies to all sailing school vessels and all promotional literature or advertisements offering passage or soliciting sailing school students or instructors for voyages on sailing school vessels.

(b) Each item of promotional literature or advertisement that offers passage or solicits students or instructors of voyages onboard a sailing school vessel must contain the following information:

(1) The name of the vessel;

(2) The country of registry;

(3) A statement detailing the role and responsibility of a sailing school student or instructor; and

(4) A statement that the vessel is inspected and certificated as a sailing school vessel and is not required to meet the same safety standards required of a passenger vessel on a comparable route.

(c) Before getting underway the master shall ensure that each sailing school student, sailing school instructor, and guest, who has not previously been notified, is notified of the specialized nature of sailing school vessels and that the applicable safety requirements for these vessels are not the same as those applied to passenger vessels.

INDEX

SUBCHAPTER R—NAUTICAL SCHOOLS

EDITORIAL NOTE: This listing is provided for informational purposes only. It is compiled and kept current by the U.S. Coast Guard, Department of Homeland Security. This index is updated as of October 1, 2003.

Part, subpart, or section

A

Able seamen	166.01(b)
Accessories	169.671
Accidents, reports of	167.65-70
Accommodations	167.50, 168.15, 169.317
Accommodation spaces, portable fire extinguishers	167.45-65
Accommodation spaces, separation of machinery and fuel tank spaces from	169.631
Act, Paperwork Reduction	167.01-20
Additional requirements for hybrid work vests	167.43-25
Administrative procedures	169.111
Aids to navigation	167.65-45
Alarm bells	167.40-5, 169.730, 169.731
Alterations, approval for	169.509
Alterations, required notice of	167.30-1
Amendment, Certificate of Inspection	169.215
American Boat and Yacht Council	169.115(c)
American Bureau of Shipping	167.15-25(a)
American Institute of Electrical Engineers	167.40-1)a)(3)
Appeal, right of	167.10-50, 168.05-15, 169.113
Applicable stability requirements	167.65-42
Applicability	169.103, 169.401, 169.664, 169.674
Application, work vests	167.43-1
Application for annual inspection	167.15-10
Application for inspection for new nautical school ship or a conversion of a vessel to a nautical school ship	167.15-15
Applicants for certificates	166.20
Application of passenger vessel inspection laws	168.05-1
Application of passenger vessel inspection regulations	168.05-5
Application of regulations	167.01-5
Approval for repairs and alterations	169.509
Approval of nautical school ships	166.01
Approved	167.05-5, 169.107(a)
Approved types of work vests	167.43-5
Arrangement of nautical school ships	167.20
Assignment of functions	168.01-5
Authority for regulations	168.01-10
Authority of marine inspectors	167.15-5
Auto pilot, use of	167.65-35
Auxiliary machinery	169.241(a)(3)

85

B

Ballast, liquid	167.20-35
Basis and purpose of part	167.01-1
Batteries	169.668
Bells, general alarm	169.731
Bell, general alarm switch	169.730
Bilge and drainage system	169.241(a)(6)
Bilge piping	167.20-17, 169.652
Bilge pumps	167.20-17, 169.654
Bills, Station	169.813
Blinding light	167.65-5
Boat drills	169.833
Boat, rescue	169.517
Boilers	167.15-25, 167.25-1, 167.65-70
Branch circuits, lighting	169.690
Branch circuits, motors	169.684
Branch lines, fire extinguishing	169.733
Breakers, circuit	169.670
Breathing apparatus, emergency	167.45-60
Buoys, life	169.741
Bureau of Customs	167.01-8

C

Cable armor	169.680(c)(2)
California Maritime Academy	166.01(b)
Capacity of pipes and hoses	167.45-15
Carbon dioxide	167.45-1
Carbon dioxide alarm	169.732
Carbon dioxide fire-extinguishing system requirements	167.45-45
Carburetors	169.611
Carrying of excess steam	167.25-20
Casualty, notice and reporting of	167.65-65, 169.807
Certain equipment requirements	167.40
Certificates of Inspection	167.60
Certificate of Inspection amendment	169.215
Charts	169.809
Circuit breakers	169.670
Circuit loads	169.682
Circuits, installation of wiring for power and lighting	169.673
Circuits, wiring for power and lighting	169.679
Civilian nautical school	168.10-5
Coast Guard	167.01-1, 167.01-15, 167.05-30
Coast Guard District Commander	167.05-15, 169.107(b)
Coastwise vessels	167.01-7
Commandant	166.01(b), 167.05-107(c)
Communications	169.621, 169.713, 169.826
Compartments containing diesel fuel tanks	169.627
Compartments containing gasoline machinery or fuel tanks	169.629
Compartments containing diesel machinery	169.625
Compass	169.709
Compass, gyro	167.40-45
Compass, magnetic	167.40-45
Compliance with applicable stability requirements	167.65-42
Compliance with provisions of Certificate of Inspection	169.824
Construction	167.20-1, 168.15-10
Construction and arrangement of nautical school ships	167.20, 169.300

Subchapter R Index

Control 169.826
Control numbers, OMB 167.01-20
Controls, fire extinguishing system 169.734
Cooking 169.685, 169.703
Cooling, accommodation spaces 168.15-45
Couplings on fire hose 167.45-10
Crew spaces, location of 168.15-5
Customs, Bureau of .... 167.01-8(c)

D

Deck .... 166.01(b)
Deck rails 169.327
Deck students, course of study 166.05
Deep-sea sounding apparatus 167.40-20
Definitions 167.05-1, 167.15-27, 169.107, 169.231
Demand loads 169.689
Department of Transportation Act .... 1678.01-5(a)
Designating sailing school vessels, procedures 169.218
Description, Certificate of Inspection 169.203
Description, lifeboat equipment 169.529
Description, lifefloat equipment 169.537
Disconnect switches and devices 169.681
Diesel fuel systems 169.615
Disclosure of safety standards 169.857
Display of plans 169.853
Distress signals, pyrotechnic 169.553
Distribution and circuit loads 169.682
Distribution and stowage, personal flotation devices 169.543
Distribution panels, main 169.678
Doors, loading 167.65-38
Double-bottom fuel oil tanks 167.15-40
Draft 167.65-40
Draft indicating systems 167.55-1, 169.755
Draft marks 167.55-1, 169.755
Drills 167.65-1
Drydock examination .... 169.231(a)
Drydock examination and internal structural examination intervals 167.15-30, 169.229

E

Effective date of regulations 167.01-10
Electric heating and cooking equipment 169.685
Electrical cable .... 169.243(a)
Electrical, inspections 169.243
Electrical installations 167.40-1
Electrical installations operating at potentials of less than 50 volts on vessels of less than 100 gross tons; applicability 169.664
Electrical installations operating at potentials of 50 volts or more on vessels of less than 100 gross tons; applicability 169.674
Electrical installations on vessels of 100 gross tons and over; general 169.687
Electrical systems, grounded 169.676
Emergency breathing apparatus 167.45-60
Emergency equipment, markings 167.55-5
Emergency exits 169.745
Emergency lighting 169.711, 169.738, 169.829
Emergency Position Indicating Radio Beacon (EPIRB) 169.555, 169.744, 169.831

87

Emergency powerplants, fire extinguishers	167.45-75
Emergency power systems	169.829
Emergency signals	169.815
Emergency training, musters, and drills	167.65-1
Enforcement	167.10-1
Engine control mechanism	169.241(a)(2)
Engine order telegraph systems	169.693
Engine starting system	169.241(a)(1)
Engineering	166.01(b)
Engineering students, course of study	166.10
Engineroom communication system	169.713
Equipment, accommodation	168.15-20
Equipment, fire-fighting	169.247
Equipment installed, but not required	169.505
Equivalents	169.109
Escape hatches	169.745
Escape, means of	167.20-10, 169.313
Examination and testing of pumps and fire extinguishing equipment	167.45-20
Examination of boilers and machinery by engineers	167.65-60
Examinations, integral fuel oil tank	167.15-40
Examinations, tailshafts	167.15-50
Excursion party, permit to carry	169.213
Exhibition of certificate of inspection	167.60-10
Exhaust systems	169.609
Existing vessel	169.107(d)
Exposed waters	169.107(e)
Exposure suits	169.551

F

Fire axes	167.45-80, 169.569
Fire detection and alarm system	169.243(f)
Fire equipment, marking of	167.55-5
Fire extinguishers, portable	167.45-60, 167.45-70, 167.45-75
Fire extinguishing equipment	167.45-20
Fire extinguishers for emergency power plants	167.45-75
Fire extinguishing branch lines	169.733
Fire extinguishing system controls	169.734
Fire extinguishing systems	167.45-1, 167.45-45
Fire-fighting equipment	167.45-30, 169.247, 169.839
Fire-fighting equipment on nautical school ships using oil as fuel	167.45-40
Fire hose	169.563
Fire hose stations	169.735
Fire mains	167.45-25, 169.561
Fire protection	169.311
Fire pumps	169.559
Fireman's outfit	169.717
First aid kit	169.725
Fixed carbon dioxide system	169.565
Fixed extinguishing system, general	169.564
Flame safety lamps	167.45-60
Flashing the rays of a searchlight or other blinding light	167.65-5
Foam smothering system requirements	167.45-50
Form CG-948, Permit to Proceed	169.211(a)
Fresh water operation	167.15-30(a)(2)
Fuel oil tank, double-bottom	167.15-40
Fuel oil tank examinations, integral-T/ALL	167.15-40, 169.234
Fuel shutoff valves	169.746

Subchapter R Index

Fuel systems .... 169.241(a)(4)
Functions, assignment of 168.01-5
Furniture and furnishings 169.323

G

General alarm bell switch 169.730
General alarm bells 169.731
General provisions 169.100
General requirements, portable fire extinguishers 167.45-70
Generators, etc. .... 169.243(d)
Generators and motors 169.666, 169.675
Great Lakes Maritime Academy .... 166.01(b)
Great Lakes routes 167.01-7
Grid cooler installations 169.608
Gross tonnage criterion 167.01-8
Grounded electrical systems 169.676
Guards 167.40-30
Guards in hazardous locations 169.331
Guest .... 169.107(f)
Gyrocompass 167.40-45

H

Halon fire extinguishing systems 167.45-1
Halyards 169.721
Hand portable fire extinguishers 169.737
Hatches 169.747, 169.827
Hazardous locations 169.662
Headquarters .... 169.107(g)
Heating equipment, electric 169.685
Heating, accommodation spaces 168.15-45
Hoses, capacity of 167.45-15
Hose connections 167.45-25
Hospital accommodations 167.50-1, 168.15-35
Hull examination 167.15-27, 169.231
Hulls 167.15-25, 169.239
Hybrid work vests, additional requirements 167.43-25

I

Incorporation by reference 169.115
Inert gas systems .... 167.45-1(c)
Initial inspection for certification 169.221
Inland routes 167.01-7
Inspection, accommodation spaces 168.15-60
Inspection application, annual 167.15-10
Inspection, Certificates of, Issuance by Officer-in-Charge, Marine Inspection 167.60-1
Inspection for Certification, scope of 169.222
Inspection for Certification, subsequent 169.223
Inspection, required 167.15-1
Inspection, sanitary 169.255
Inspection standards 169.237
Inspections, boilers, pressure vessels, piping, and appurtenances 167.25-5
Inspections, lifesaving appliances and arrangements 167.15-28
Inspections, limitations of 169.259
Inspections, nautical school ships 167.01-8, 167.15-20
Inspectors, marine, authority for 167.15-5

89

Installations, electrical 167.40-1
Installation of wiring for power and lighting circuits 169.673, 169.680
Instructions, routing 167.65-15
Instructor .... 169.107(h)
Integral fuel oil tank examinations - T/ALL 167.15-40, 169.234
International Convention for Safety of Life at Sea, 1974 .... 167.01-5(c)
Intent, accommodation spaces 168.15-1
Internal structural examination .... 169.231(b)
Internal structural examination intervals 167.15-30

K

Keel cooler installations 169.607
Knife switches .... 169.680(p)

L

Lakes, Great 167.01-7
Lamp, signaling 167.40-25
Lamp sizes .... 169.682(a)(1)
Lamps, flame safety 167.45-60
Length .... 169.107(i)
Lifeboats 169.739, 169.819, 169.837
Lifeboat drills 166.15
Lifeboatman .... 166.01(d)
Lifefloats 169.740, 169.837
Liferafts 169.740, 169.819, 169.837
Lifesaving and fire fighting equipment 169.500
Lifesaving equipment 169.245
Lifesaving signals 167.65-50
Lighting, accommodation spaces 168.15-40
Limitations of inspections 169.259
Liquid ballast 167.20-35
Loading doors 167.65-38
Loadline certificate .... 167.15-35(c)
Loadlines 169.121
Location of crew spaces 168.15-5
Logbook entries 169.841
Lookouts 169.847

M

Machinery 167.15-25, 167.65-60, 167.65-70, 169.241
Magnetic compass 167.40-45
Main distribution panels and switchboards 169.678
Maine Maritime Academy .... 166.01(b)
Manning and persons allowed to be carried 167.60-15
Manning of lifeboats and liferafts 169.819
Marine engineering .... 166.01(b), 167.25
Marine Inspection, Officer in Charge 167.05-30
Marine inspector or inspector .... 167.05-20, 169.107(j)
Marine inspector, authority of 167.15-5
Mariners 167.65-45
Markings 169.545
Marking of fire and emergency equipment 167.55-5
Massachusetts Maritime Academy .... 166.01(b)
Master .... 169.107(k)
Master to instruct ship's company 169.817
Means of escape 167.20-10

Subchapter R Index

Merchant mariner's document .... 166.01(a)
Mine Safety and Health Administration (MSHA) .... 167.45-60(a)
Miscellaneous systems and equipment 169.253
Mooring equipment 169.705
Musters 167.65-1

N

Name plates 169.665
National Fire Protection Association (NFPA) .... 167.30-10(a)
National Institute for Occupational Safety and Health (NIOSH) .... 167.45-60(a)
Nautical publications 169.809
Nautical school .... 166.01(a), 167.05-35, 168.10-5
Nautical school ship 167.15-15, 167.15-20, 168.10-1
Navigation .... 166.01(b)
Navigation lights 169.691
Navy 167.01-15
New vessel .... 169.107(l)
New York State Maritime Academy .... 166.01(b)
Notice and plans required 167.15-35, 169.233
Notice and reporting of casualties 167.65-65
Notice of casualty 169.807
Notice to mariners 167.65-42
Notice of repairs or alterations required 167.30-1
Number required, personal flotation devices 169.541
Number required, primary lifesaving equipment 169.515

O

Ocean vessels 167.01-7
Officer in Charge, Marine Inspection .... 167.05-30, 169.107(m)
Oil Pollution Act 167.20-35
OMB control numbers 167.01-20, 169.117
Openings 169.823
Operating requirements, special 167.30-10
Overcurrent protection for motors and motor branch circuits 169.684
Overcurrent protection, general 169.683
Overload or circuit protective devices .... 169.243(b)

P

Paperwork Reduction Act 167.01-20
Partially protected waters .... 169.107(n)
Passenger .... 169.107(o)
Passenger vessel inspection laws 168.05-1
Passenger vessel inspection regulations 168.01-5
Patrol person 169.821
Period of validity, Certificate of Inspection 169.207
Periodic inspection 169.226
Permission required for repairs and alterations 169.235
Permit to carry excursion party 169.213
Permit to proceed for repair 169.211
Personal flotation devices and ring life buoys 169.741
Pilot, auto 167.65-35
Piping 167.25-1
Piping, bilge 167.20-17
Pipes, capacity of 167.45-15
Placards, lifesaving signals, posting 167.65-50
Plans for sister vessel 169.307

Plans, required	167.15-35, 169.305
Plug fuses	169.683(e)
Portable fire extinguishers	167.45-65, 167.45-70
Portable magazine chests	169.743
Posting, Certificate of Inspection	169.217
Posting, lifesaving signals placard	167.65-50
Posting placards containing instructions for launching and inflating inflatable liferafts	169.849
Power-driven steering systems	169.623
Powerplants, fire extinguishers for	167.45-75
Pressure vessels	167.25-1, 169.249
Pre-underway training	169.855
Primary lifesaving equipment, types	169.513
Procedures for designating sailing school vessels	169.218
Proceeding to another Port for repairs	167.30-5
Protected waters	169.107(p)
Public nautical school	167.05-35
Publications required	167.65-45(d), 169.809
Pumps, bilge	167.20-17
Pumps, fire	167.45-5, 167.45-20, 169.559
Purpose of regulations	168.01-1, 169.101
Pyrotechnic distress signals	169.553

Q

Qualified Member of the Engine Department	166.01(a),(b)
Qualified organization	169.107(q)

R

Radar	167.40-40
Radar reflector	169.726
Radio	169.715
Radio call sign	169.750
Radiotelephone equipment	169.669
Rails	167.40-30
Receptacle outlets	169.680(r)
Recognized classification society	169.107(r)
Regulations, application of	167.01-5
Regulations, authority for	168.01-10
Regulations, effective date of	167.01-10
Regulations, purpose of	168.01-1
Reliability, steering systems	169.619
Remote stop stations	169.692
Renewal of letter of designation	169.219
Repairs, approval for	169.509
Repairs, required notice of	167.30-1, 167.65-70
Reporting of casualties	167-65-65
Reports of accidents, repairs, and unsafe boilers and machinery by engineers	167.65-70
Required equipment for lifeboats	169.527
Required equipment for lifefloats	169.535
Required equipment for liferafts	169.531
Required inspections	167.15-1
Required notice and plans for inspections	167.15-35
Rescue boat	169.517
Responsibility of master	169.507
Right of appeal	167.10-50, 168.05-15, 169.113
Ring lifebuoys	169.549

Subchapter R Index

Rotating machinery ... 169.243(c)
Routes ... 167.01-7
Routes permitted ... 169.209
Routing instructions ... 167.65-15
Rudder angle indicators ... 169.622
Rules of the Road ... 169.107(s)

S

Safety belts, wearing of ... 169.723, 169.825
Sailing instruction ... 169.107(t)
Sailing school student ... 169.107(u)
Sailing school vessel ... 169.107(v)
Salt water operation ... 167.15-30(a)(1)
Sanitary, discharges ... 167.20-15
Sanitary inspection ... 169.255
Sea valves and bulkhead closure valves ... 169.241(a)(5)
Seamanship ... 166.01(b)
Searchlight ... 167.65-5
Separation of machinery and fuel tank spaces from accommodation spaces ... 169.631
School ships ... 166.01(c), 167.01-8, 167.05-25, 167.15-15
Screening, accommodation spaces ... 168.15-55
Scope of inspection for certification ... 169.222
Scope, reinspection ... 169.227
Scupper, discharges ... 167.20-15
Self-contained breathing apparatus ... 169.736
Shipboard inspections ... 167.43-20
Shipboard stowage ... 167.43-15
Ship sanitation ... 166.15
Ship's company ... 169.107(w)
Shore power ... 169.686
Signals, lifesaving ... 167.65-50
Sister vessels, plans for ... 169.307
Size, accommodation spaces ... 168.15-15
Smothering, foam system ... 167.45-50
Sounding apparatus, deep-sea ... 167.40-20
Sounding arrangements ... 167.20-17
Special consideration ... 169.112
Special operating requirements ... 167.30-10
Specifications for articles or materials ... 167.01-15
Standard for the Control of Gas Hazards on Vessels to be Repaired ... 167.30-10(a)
Stability ... 167.20-7, 167.65-42, 168.05-10, 169.840
Station bills ... 169.813
Steam, carrying excess ... 167.25-20
Steam fire-fighting systems ... 167.45-1
Steam fire pumps ... 167.45-5
Steering ... 169.826
Steering apparatus ... 169.251
Steering gear tests ... 167.65-25
Storage batteries ... 169.243(e)
Storm sails ... 169.721
Stowage, personal flotation devices ... 169.543
Stowage, primary lifesaving equipment ... 169.521
Structural standards ... 169.309
Subdivision ... 167.20-7, 168.05-10
Subsequent inspections for certification ... 169.223
Switchboards ... 169.667

T

Tailshafts, examination of	167.15-50
Tank, integral fuel oil	167.15-40
Telegraph systems	167.40-7
Telephone systems	167.40-7
Terms, definitions of	167.05-1
Texas Maritime Academy	166.01(b)
Toilet rooms, accommodation spaces	168.15-30, 169.319
Tonnage, gross criterion	167.01-8
Training	166.15, 169.855
Tubes, voice	167.40-7

U

Underwriters' Laboratories	167.45-5(g)
United States Coast Guard Academy	166.01(b)
United States Maritime Administration	167.01-5(b)
United States Merchant Marine Academy	166.01(b)
United States Naval Academy	166.01(b)
Unlimited coastwise vessels	167.01-7
Unnecessary whistling	167.65-20
Unsafe boilers	167.65-70
Unsafe practices	169.257
Use of auto pilot	167.65-35
Use, work vests	167.43-10
U.S. Coast Guard Standard Construction Specification	167.15-25(c), 167.20-1(b), 167.25-1(a)(2)
U.S. Naval Oceanographic Office	167.65-45(c)
U.S. Navy Standard Construction Specification	167.15-25(b), 167.20-1(c), 167.25-1(a)(3)

V

Ventilation, accommodation spaces	168.15-50
Ventilation, other than machinery spaces	169.315
Verification of vessel compliance with applicable stability requirements	167.65-42, 169.840
Vessel status	169.119
Vital systems, piping	169.642
Voice tubes	167.40-7
Voyage records	167.65-65

W

Washrooms	168.15-25, 169.319
Waterlights	169.549
Watertight	169.107(x)
Watertight doors and hatches	169.747
Wearing of safety belts	169.825
Weathertight	169.107(y)
Whistling, unnecessary	167.65-20
Wiring for power and lighting circuits	169.672, 169.679
Wooden hull vessels	167.15-30(b)
Work vests, application	167.43-1, 169.556
Work vests, approved types	167.43-5
Work vests, use	167.43-10

SUBCHAPTER S—SUBDIVISION AND STABILITY

PART 170—STABILITY REQUIREMENTS FOR ALL INSPECTED VESSELS

Subpart A—General Provisions

Sec.
170.001 Applicability.
170.003 Right of appeal.
170.005 Vessel alteration or repair.
170.010 Equivalents.
170.015 Incorporation by reference.
170.020 OMB control numbers assigned pursuant to the Paperwork Reduction Act.

Subpart B—Definitions

170.050 General terms.
170.055 Definitions concerning a vessel.

Subpart C—Plan Approval

170.070 Applicability.
170.075 Plans.
170.080 Stability booklet.
170.085 Information required before a stability test.
170.090 Calculations.
170.093 Specific approvals.
170.095 Data submittal for a vessel equipped to lift.
170.100 Addresses for submittal of plans and calculations.

Subpart D—Stability Instructions for Operating Personnel

170.105 Applicability.
170.110 Stability booklet.
170.120 Stability letter.
170.125 Operating information for a vessel engaged in lifting.
170.135 Operating information for a vessel with Type III subdivision.

Subpart E—Weather Criteria

170.160 Specific applicability.
170.170 Calculations required.
170.173 Criterion for vessels of unusual proportion and form.

Subpart F—Determination of Lightweight Displacement and Centers of Gravity

170.174 Specific applicability.
170.175 Stability test: General.
170.180 Plans and information required at the stability test.
170.185 Stability test preparations.
170.190 Stability test procedure modifications.
170.200 Estimated lightweight vertical center of gravity.

Subpart G—Special Installations

170.235 Fixed ballast.
170.245 Form flotation material.

Subpart H—Watertight Bulkhead Doors

170.248 Applicability.
170.250 Types and classes.
170.255 Class 1 doors; permissible locations.
170.260 Class 2 doors; permissible locations.
170.265 Class 3 doors; required locations.
170.270 Door design, operation, installation, and testing.
170.275 Special requirements for cargo space watertight doors.

Subpart I—Free Surface

170.285 Free surface correction for intact stability calculations.
170.290 Free surface correction for damage stability calculations.
170.295 Special considerations for free surface of passive roll stabilization tanks.
170.300 Special consideration for free surface of spoil in hopper dredge hoppers.

AUTHORITY: 43 U.S.C. 1333; 46 U.S.C. 2103, 3306, 3703; E.O. 12234, 45 FR 58801, 3 CFR, 1980 Comp., p. 277; Department of Homeland Security Delegation No. 0170.1.

SOURCE: CGD 79–023, 48 FR 51010, Nov. 4, 1983, unless otherwise noted.

Subpart A—General Provisions

§ 170.001 Applicability.

(a) This subchapter, except where specifically stated otherwise, applies to each vessel contracted for on or after March 11, 1996, that is—

(1) Inspected under another subchapter of this chapter; or

(2) A foreign vessel that must comply with the requirements in Subchapter O of this chapter.

(b) Each vessel contracted for before March 11, 1996 may be constructed in accordance with the regulations in effect at the time. However, any alterations or repairs must be done in accordance with § 170.005.

§ 170.003

(c) Certain regulations in this subchapter apply only to limited categories of vessels. Specific applicability statements are provided at the beginning of those regulations.

[CGD 79–023, 48 FR 51010, Nov. 4, 1983, as amended by CGD 89–037, 57 FR 41825, Sept. 11, 1992; CGD 85–080, 61 FR 943, Jan. 10, 1996]

§ 170.003 Right of appeal.

Any person directly affected by a decision or action taken under this subchapter, by or on behalf of the Coast Guard, may appeal therefrom in accordance with subpart 1.03 of this chapter.

[CGD 88–033, 54 FR 50382, Dec. 6, 1989]

§ 170.005 Vessel alteration or repair.

(a) Alterations and repairs to inspected vessels must be done—

(1) Under the direction of the Officer in Charge, Marine Inspection; and

(2) Except as provided in paragraph (b) of this section, in accordance with the regulations in this subchapter, to the extent practicable.

(b) Minor alterations and repairs may be done in accordance with regulations in effect at the time the vessel was contracted for.

§ 170.010 Equivalents.

Substitutions for fittings, equipment, arrangements, calculations, information, or tests required in this subchapter may be approved by the Commandant, the Commanding Officer, U.S. Coast Guard Marine Safety Center, 400 Seventh St., SW., Washington, DC 20590–0001 or the Officer in Charge, Marine Inspection, if the substitution provides an equivalent level of safety.

[CGD 89–025, 54 FR 19572, May 8, 1989, as amended by CGD 96–041, 61 FR 50734, Sept. 27, 1996]

§ 170.015 Incorporation by reference.

(a) Certain material is incorporated by reference into this part with the approval of the Director of the Federal Register in accordance with 5 U.S.C. 552(a). To enforce any edition other than that specified in paragraph (b) of this section, the Coast Guard must publish notice of change in the FEDERAL REGISTER and make the material available to the public. All approved material is on file at the U.S. Coast Guard, Office of Design and Engineering Standards (G–MSE), 2100 Second Street SW., Washington, DC 20593–0001 and at the National Archives and Records Administration (NARA). For information on the availability of this material at NARA, call 202–741–6030, or go to: *http://www.archives.gov/ federal_register/ code_of_federal_regulations/ ibr_locations.html.* All approved material is available from the sources indicated in paragraph (b) of this section.

(b) The material approved for incorporation by reference in this part and the sections affected are:

American Society for Testing and Materials (ASTM)

100 Barr Harbor Drive, West Conshohocken, PA 19428–2959.

ASTM F 1196–94, Standard Specification for Sliding Watertight Door Assemblies—170.270

ASTM F 1197–89 (1994), Standard Specification for Sliding Watertight Door Control Systems—170.270

Military Specification

Naval Publications and Forms Center, Code 1052, 5801 Tabor Avenue, Philadelphia, PA 19120

MIL–P–21929B, Plastic Material, Cellular Polyurethane, Foam in Place, Rigid, 1970 ....170.245

International Maritime Organization (IMO)

Publications Section, International Maritime Organization, 4 Albert Embankment, London SE1 7SR, United Kingdom

Resolution A.265 (VIII) 170.135

[CGD 88–032, 56 FR 35827, July 29, 1991, as amended by CGD 95–072, 60 FR 50468, Sept. 29, 1995; CGD 96–041, 61 FR 50734, Sept. 27, 1996; CGD 97–057, 62 FR 51049, Sept. 30, 1997; USCG–1999–5151, 64 FR 67186, Dec. 1, 1999; 69 FR 18803, Apr. 9, 2004]

§ 170.020 OMB control numbers assigned pursuant to the Paperwork Reduction Act.

(a) *Purpose.* This section collects and displays the control numbers assigned to information collection and recordkeeping requirements in this subchapter by the Office of Management and Budget (OMB) pursuant to the Paperwork Reduction Act of 1980 (44 U.S.C. 3501 *et seq.*). The Coast Guard intends that this section comply with the

Coast Guard, DHS § 170.055

requirements of 44 U.S.C. 3507(f), which requires that agencies display a current control number assigned by the OMB for each approved agency information collection requirement.

(b) *Display.*

46 CFR part—	Current OMB control No.
§ 170.075	1625–0064
§ 170.080	1625–0064
§ 170.085	1625–0064
§ 170.090	1625–0064
§ 170.095	1625–0064
§ 170.100	1625–0064
§ 170.110	1625–0064
§ 170.120	1625–0064
§ 170.125	1625–0064
§ 170.135	1625–0064
§ 170.180	1625–0064

[CGD 89–037, 57 FR 41825, Sept. 11, 1992, as amended by USCG–2004–18884, 69 FR 58350, Sept. 30, 2004]

Subpart B—Definitions

§ 170.050 General terms.

(a) *Commanding Officer, Marine Safety Center (CO, MSC)* means a district commander described in 33 CFR part 3 whose command includes a merchant marine technical office or an authorized representative of the district commander.

(b) *Commandant* means the Commandant of the Coast Guard or an authorized representative of the Commandant.

(c) *Exposed waters* means waters more than 20 nautical miles (37 kilometers) from the mouth of a harbor of safe refuge and other waters which the Officer in Charge, Marine Inspection determines to present special hazards due to weather or other circumstances.

(d) *Great Lakes* includes both the waters of the Great Lakes and of the St. Lawrence River as far east as a straight line drawn from Cap de Rosiers to West Point, Anticosti Island, and west of a line along the 63rd meridian from Anticosti Island to the north shore of the St. Lawrence River.

(e) *Lakes, Bays, and Sounds* includes the waters of any lake, bay, or sound, except the Great Lakes.

(f) *Oceans* includes the waters of—
(1) Any ocean;
(2) The Gulf of Mexico;
(3) The Caribbean Sea;
(4) The Gulf of Alaska; and

(5) Any other waters designated as "oceans" by the Commandant.

(g) *Officer in Charge Marine Inspection (OCMI)* means an officer of the Coast Guard who commands a Marine Inspection Zone described in 33 CFR part 3 or an authorized representative of that officer.

(h) *Oil* means oil of any kind or in any form, and includes but is not limited to petroleum, fuel oil, sludge, oil refuse, and oil mixed with wastes other than dredged spoil.

(i) *Partially protected waters* means—
(1) Waters within 20 nautical miles (37 kilometers) of the mouth of a harbor of safe refuge, unless determined by the OCMI to be exposed waters; and
(2) Those portions of rivers, harbors, lakes, etc. which the OCMI determines not to be sheltered.

(j) *Protected waters* means sheltered waters presenting no special hazards such as most rivers, harbors, lakes, etc.

(k) *Rivers* means any river, canal, or any other similar body of water designated by the OCMI.

[CGD 79–023, 48 FR 51010, Nov. 4, 1983, as amended by CGD 88–070, 53 FR 34537, Sept. 7, 1988]

§ 170.055 Definitions concerning a vessel.

(a) *Auxiliary sailing vessel* means a vessel capable of being propelled both by mechanical means and by sails.

(b) *Barge* means a vessel not equipped with a means of self-propulsion.

(c) *Beam* or *B* means the maximum width of a vessel from—
(1) Outside of planking to outside of planking on wooden vessels; and
(2) Outside of frame to outside of frame on all other vessels.

(d) *Bulkhead deck* means the uppermost deck to which watertight bulkheads and the watertight shell extend.

(e) *Downflooding* means, except as provided in § 174.035(b), the entry of seawater through any opening into the hull or superstructure of an undamaged vessel due to heel, trim, or submergence of the vessel.

(f) *Documented alterations* means changes to the vessel which are reflected in the approved stability information carried on board the vessel.

(g) *Downflooding angle* means, except as specified by §§ 171.055(f), 172.090(d),

§ 170.055

173.095(e), 174.015(b), and 174.035(b)(2) of this chapter, the static angle from the intersection of the vessel's centerline and waterline in calm water to the first opening that cannot be closed watertight and through which downflooding can occur.

(h) *Draft* means the vertical distance from the molded baseline amidships to the waterline.

(i) *Length* means the distance between fore and aft points on a vessel. The following specific terms are used and correspond to specific fore and aft points:

(1) *Length between perpendiculars (LBP)* means the horizontal distance measured between perpendiculars taken at the forward-most and after-most points on the waterline corresponding to the deepest operating draft. For a small passenger vessel which has underwater projections extending forward of the forward-most point or aft of the after-most point on the deepest waterline of the vessel, the Commanding Officer, U.S. Coast Guard Marine Safety Center, may include the length or a portion of the length of the underwater projections in the value used for the LBP for the purposes of this subchapter. The length or a portion of the length of projections which contribute more than 2 percent of the underwater volume of the vessel is normally added to the actual LBP.

(2) *Length overall (LOA)* means the horizontal distance between the forward-most and after-most points on the hull.

(3) *Length on the waterline (LWL)* means the horizontal distance between the forward-most and after-most points on a vessel's waterline.

(4) *Length on deck (LOD)* means the length between the forward-most and after-most points on a specified deck measured along the deck, excluding sheer.

(5) *Load line length (LLL)* has the same meaning that is provided for the term *length* in § 42.13-15(a) of this chapter.

(6) *Mean length* is the average of the length between perpendiculars (LBP) and the length on deck (LOD).

(j) *Lightweight* means with fixed ballast and with machinery liquids at operating levels but without any cargo,

46 CFR Ch. I (10-1-04 Edition)

stores, consumable liquids, water ballast, or persons and their effects.

(k) *Main transverse watertight bulkhead* means a transverse bulkhead that must be maintained watertight in order for the vessel to meet the damage stability and subdivision requirements in this subchapter.

(l) *Major conversion,* as applied to Great Lakes bulk carriers, means a conversion of an existing vessel that substantially changes the dimensions or carrying capacity of the vessel or changes the the type of vessel or substantially prolongs its life or that otherwise so changes the vessel that it is essentially a new vessel.

(m) *Permeability* is the percentage of the volume of a space that can be occupied by water.

(n) *Sailing vessel* means a vessel propelled only by sails.

(o) *Ship* means a self-propelled vessel.

(p) *Tank vessel* means a vessel that is specially constructed or converted to carry liquid bulk cargo in tanks.

(q) *Tank barge* means a tank vessel not equipped with a means of self-propulsion.

(r) *Tank ship* means a tank vessel propelled by mechanical means or sails.

(s) *Vessel* means any vessel and includes both ships and barges.

(t) *Weather deck* means the uppermost deck exposed to the weather.

(u) *Existing sailing school vessel* means a sailing vessel whose keel was laid prior to (January 9, 1986), which has an application for initial inspection for certification as a sailing school vessel on file with the Coast Guard prior to (January 9, 1987), and whose initial inspection for certification is completed prior to (January 9, 1988).

(v) *New sailing school vessel* means a sailing school vessel which is not an existing sailing school vessel.

(w) *Small passenger vessel* means a vessel of less than 100 gross tons—

(1) Carrying more than 6 passengers, including at least one passenger for hire;

(2) That is chartered with the crew provided or specified by the owner or owner's representative and carrying more than 6 passengers;

(3) That is chartered with no crew provided or specified by the owner or

Coast Guard, DHS § 170.085

owner's representative and carrying more than 12 passengers; or

(4) That is a submersible vessel carrying at least one passenger for hire.

[CGD 79-023, 48 FR 51010, Nov. 4, 1983, as amended by CGD 83-005, 51 FR 923, Jan. 9, 1986; 51 FR 3785, Jan. 30, 1986; CGD 80-159, 51 FR 33059, Sept. 18, 1986; 51 FR 35515, Oct. 6, 1986; CGD 89-037, 57 FR 41825, Sept. 11, 1992; CGD 82-004 and CGD 86-074, 60 FR 57671, Nov. 16, 1995; CGD 85-080, 61 FR 943, Jan. 10, 1996; CGD 82-004 and CGD 86-074, 62 FR 49353, Sept. 19, 1997]

Subpart C—Plan Approval

§ 170.070 Applicability.

(a) Except as provided in paragraph (b) of this section, this subpart applies to each vessel.

(b) This subpart does not apply to any of the following vessels unless the stability of the vessel is questioned by the OCMI:

(1) A passenger vessel that—

(i) Is less than 100 gross tons;

(ii) Is less than 65 feet (19.8 meters) LOD measured over the weather deck; and

(iii) Carries 49 or less passengers.

(2) A deck cargo barge that complies with the requirements in § 174.020 of this chapter.

(3) A tank vessel that only carries a product listed in § 30.25-1 of this chapter and that is less than 150 gross tons.

(4) A tank barge that—

(i) Operates only in rivers or lakes, bays, and sounds service;

(ii) Does not have to meet 33 CFR part 157, subpart B; and

(iii) Only carries a product listed in § 30.25-1 of this chapter.

(5) A sailing school vessel that is an open boat that complies with the requirements in § 173.063(e) of this subchapter.

[CGD 79-023, 48 FR 51010, Nov. 4, 1983, as amended by CGD 83-005, 51 FR 923, Jan. 9, 1986]

§ 170.075 Plans.

(a) Except as provided in paragraph (b) of this section, each applicant for an original certificate of inspection and approval of plans must also submit three copies for plan review being conducted by the Coast Guard Marine Safety Center or four copies for plan review being conducted by the American Bureau of Shipping (ABS) of each of the following plans:

(1) General arrangement plan of decks, holds, and inner bottoms including inboard and outboard profiles.

(2) Lines.

(3) Curves of form.

(4) Capacity plan showing capacities and vertical, longitudinal, and transverse centers of gravity of stowage spaces and tanks.

(5) Tank sounding tables showing—

(i) Capacities, vertical centers of gravity, and longitudinal centers of gravity in graduated intervals; and

(ii) Free surface data for each tank.

(6) Draft mark locations including longitudinal location and vertical reference points.

(b) Each small passenger vessel that is designed to comply with the alternate intact stability requirements in § 178.320 of this subchapter and the simplified method of spacing main transverse watertight bulkheads in § 179.220 of this subchapter does not have to submit the plans required by paragraph (a) of this section.

[CGD 79-023, 48 FR 51010, Nov. 4, 1983, as amended by CGD 85-080, 61 FR 944, Jan. 10, 1996; CGD 95-028, 62 FR 51217, Sept. 30, 1997]

§ 170.080 Stability booklet.

Before issuing an original certificate of inspection, the following number of copies of the stability booklet required by § 170.110 must be submitted for approval; three copies for plan review being conducted by the Coast Guard Marine Safety Center or four copies for plan review being conducted by the ABS.

[CGD 95-028, 62 FR 51217, Sept. 30, 1997]

§ 170.085 Information required before a stability test.

If a stability test is to be performed, a stability test procedure that contains the information prescribed in § 170.185(g) must be submitted to the Coast Guard Marine Safety Center or the ABS at least two weeks before the test.

[CGD 95-028, 62 FR 51217, Sept. 30, 1997]

§ 170.090

§ 170.090 Calculations.

(a) Except as provided in § 170.098, all calculations required by this subchapter must be submitted with the plans required by § 170.075.

(b) If it is necessary to compute and plot any of the following curves as part of the calculations required in this subchapter, these plots must also be submitted:
 (1) Righting arm or moment curves.
 (2) Heeling arm or moment curves.
 (3) Cross curves of stability.
 (4) Floodable length curves.

§ 170.093 Specific approvals.

Certain rules in this subchapter require specific approval of equipment or arrangements by the Commandant, OCMI, or Coast Guard Marine Safety Center. These approval determinations will be made as a part of the plan review process. When plan review is conducted by the ABS, ABS is authorized to make the approval.

[CGD 95–028, 62 FR 51217, Sept. 30, 1997]

§ 170.095 Data submittal for a vessel equipped to lift.

The following data must be submitted with the plans required by § 170.075 if the vessel is engaged in lifting and is required to comply with subpart B of part 173 of this chapter:

(a) A graph of maximum hook load versus maximum crane radius.

(b) A table of crane radius versus the maximum distance above the main deck to which the hook load can be raised.

(c) A table showing maximum vertical and transverse moments at which the crane is to operate.

§ 170.100 Addresses for submittal of plans and calculations.

The plans, information, and calculations required by this subpart must be submitted to one of the following:

(a) The Marine Safety Office in the zone where the vessel is to be built or altered.

(b) Commanding Officer, U.S. Coast Guard Marine Safety Center, 400 Seventh St., SW., Washington, DC 20590–0001.

(c) The American Bureau of Shipping (ABS), Two World Trade Center, 106th Floor, New York, NY 10048.

(d) The American Bureau of Shipping (ABS), ABS Plaza, 16855 North Chase Dr., Houston, TX 77060–6008.

[CGD 95–028, 62 FR 51217, Sept. 30, 1997]

Subpart D—Stability Instructions for Operating Personnel

§ 170.105 Applicability.

(a) Except as provided in paragraph (b) of this section, this subpart applies to each vessel.

(b) This subpart does not apply to any of the following vessels unless the stability of the vessel is questioned by the OCMI:

(1) A deck cargo barge that complies with the requirements in § 174.020 of this chapter.

(2) A tank vessel that only carries a product listed in § 30.25–1 of this chapter and that is less than 150 gross tons.

(3) A tank barge that—
 (i) Operates only in rivers or lakes, bays, and sounds service;
 (ii) Does not have to meet 33 CFR part 157, subpart B; and
 (iii) Only carries a product listed in § 30.25–1 of this chapter.

(4) A sailing school vessel that is an open boat that complies with the requirements in § 173.063(e) of this subchapter.

[CGD 79–023, 48 FR 51010, Nov. 4, 1983, as amended by CGD 83–005, 51 FR 923, Jan. 9, 1986; CGD 85–080, 61 FR 944, Jan. 10, 1996]

§ 170.110 Stability booklet.

(a) Except as provided in paragraph (e) of this section, a stability booklet must be prepared for each vessel, except for mobile offshore drilling units subject to the operating manual requirements of § 109.121 of this chapter.

(b) Each stability booklet must be approved by the Coast Guard Marine Safety Center or the ABS.

(c) Each stability book must contain sufficient information to enable the master to operate the vessel in compliance with applicable regulations in this subchapter. Information on loading restrictions used to determine compliance with applicable intact and damage stability criteria must encompass

Coast Guard, DHS § 170.125

the entire range of operating drafts and the entire range of the operating trims. Information must include an effective procedure for supervision and reporting of the opening and closing of all loading doors, where applicable.

(d) The format of the stability booklet and the information included will vary dependent on the vessel type and operation. Units of measure used in the stability booklet must agree with the units of measure of the draft markings. In developing the stability booklet, consideration must be given to including the following information:

(1) A general description of the vessel, including lightweight data.

(2) Instructions on the use of the booklet.

(3) General arrangement plans showing watertight compartments, closures, vents, downflooding angles, and allowable deck loadings.

(4) Hydrostatic curves or tables.

(5) Capacity plan showing capacities and vertical, longitudinal, and transverse centers of gravity of stowage spaces and tanks.

(6) Tank sounding tables showing capacities, vertical centers of gravity, and longitudinal centers of gravity in graduated intervals and showing free surface data for each tank.

(7) Information on loading restrictions, such as a maximum KG or minimum GM curve that can be used to determine compliance with applicable intact and damage stability criteria.

(8) Examples of loading conditions.

(9) A rapid and simple means for evaluating other loading conditions.

(10) A brief description of the stability calculations done including assumptions.

(11) General precautions for preventing unintentional flooding.

(12) A table of contents and index for the booklet.

(13) Each ship condition which, if damage occurs, may require cross-flooding for survival and information concerning the use of any special cross-flooding fittings.

(14) The amount and location of fixed ballast.

(15) Any other necessary guidance for the safe operation of the vessel under normal and emergency conditions.

(16) For each self-propelled hopper dredge with a working freeboard, the maximum specific gravity allowed for dredge spoil.

(e) A stability booklet is not required if sufficient information to enable the master to operate the vessel in compliance with the applicable regulations in this subchapter can be placed on the Certificate of Inspection, Load Line Certificate, or in the stability letter required in § 170.120.

(f) On board electronic stability computers may be used as an adjunct to the required booklet, but the required booklet must contain all necessary information to allow for the evaluation of the stability of any intact condition that can be evaluated by use of the computer.

[CGD 79–023, 48 FR 51010, Nov. 4, 1983, as amended by CGD 83–071, 52 FR 6979, Mar. 6, 1987; CGD 88–070, 53 FR 34537, Sept. 7, 1988; CGD 76–080, 54 FR 36977, Sept. 6, 1989; CGD 89–037, 57 FR 41825, Sept. 11, 1992; CGD 95–028, 62 FR 51217, Sept. 30, 1997]

§ 170.120 Stability letter.

(a) Except as provided in paragraph (b) of this section, each vessel must have a stability letter issued by the Coast Guard or the ABS before the vessel is placed into service. This letter sets forth conditions of operation.

(b) A stability letter is not required if the information can be placed on the Certificate of Inspection or the Load Line Certificate.

[CGD 79–023, 48 FR 51010, Nov. 4, 1983, as amended by CGD 95–028, 62 FR 51217, Sept. 30, 1997]

§ 170.125 Operating information for a vessel engaged in lifting.

In addition to the information required in § 170.110, the following information must be included in the stability booklet of a vessel that is required to comply with § 173.005 of this subchapter:

(a) *Non-counterballasted vessel.* If a vessel is not counterballasted, stability information setting forth hook load limits corresponding to boom radii based on the intact stability criterion in § 173.020 must be provided.

(b) *Counterballasted vessel.* If a vessel is counterballasted with water, the following information must be provided:

§ 170.135

(1) Instructions on the effect of the free surface of the counterballast water.

(2) Instructions on the amounts of counterballast needed to compensate for hook load heeling moments.

(3) If a vessel has fixed counterballast, a table of draft versus maximum vertical moment of deck cargo and hook load combined.

(4) If a vessel has variable counterballast, a table of draft versus maximum vertical moment of deck cargo and hook load combined for each counterballasted condition.

§ 170.135 Operating information for a vessel with Type III subdivision.

(a) In addition to the information required in § 170.110, the stability booklet of a passenger vessel with Type III subdivision must contain the information required by Regulation 8(b) of IMO Resolution A.265 (VIII).

(b) International Maritime Organization Resolution A.265 (VIII) is incorporated by reference into this part.

(c) As used in IMO Resolution A.265 (VIII), *Administration* means the Commandant, U. S. Coast Guard.

Subpart E—Weather Criteria

§ 170.160 Specific applicability

(a) Except as provided in paragraphs (b) and (c) of this section, this subpart applies to each vessel.

(b) This subpart does not apply to any of the following vessels unless the stability of the vessel is questioned by the OCMI:

(1) A deck cargo barge that complies with the requirements in § 174.020 of this chapter.

(2) A tank vessel that only carries a product listed in § 30.25–1 of this chapter and that is—

(i) Less than 150 gross tons; or

(ii) A tank barge that operates only in river or lakes, bays, and sounds service.

(3) A sailing school vessel that is an open boat that complies with the requirements in § 173.063(e) of this subchapter.

(c) This subpart does not apply to the following vessels:

(1) A tank barge that carries a product listed in Table 151.01–10(b) of this chapter.

(2) A mobile offshore drilling unit.

(3) A vessel that performs the test required by § 171.030(c) of this subchapter.

[CGD 79–023, 48 FR 51010, Nov. 4, 1983, as amended by CGD 83–005, 51 FR 923, Jan. 9, 1986; CGD 85–080, 61 FR 944, Jan. 10, 1996]

§ 170.170 Calculations required.

(a) Each vessel must be shown by design calculations to have a metacentric height (GM) that is equal to or greater than the following in each condition of loading and operation:

$$GM \geq \frac{PAH}{W \tan(T)}$$

Where—

$P = .005 + (L/14,200)^2$ tons/ft² . . . for ocean service, Great Lakes winter service, or service on exposed waters.

$P = .055 + (L/1309)^2$ metric tons/m² . . . for ocean service, Great Lakes winter service, or service on exposed waters.

$P = .0033 + (L/14,200)^2$ tons/ft² . . . for Great Lakes summer service or service on partially protected waters.

$P = .036 + (L/1309)^2$ metric tons/m² . . . for Great lakes summer service or service on partially protected waters.

$P = .0025 + (L/14,200)^2$ tons/ft² . . . for service on protected waters.

$P = .028 + (L/1309)^2$ metric tons/m² . . . for service on protected waters.

L = LBP in feet (meters).

A = projected lateral area in square feet (square meters) of the portion of the vessel and deck cargo above the waterline.

H = the vertical distance in feet (meters) from the center of A to the center of the underwater lateral area or approximately to the one-half draft point.

W = displacement in long (metric) tons.

T = either:

(1) the lesser of either 14 degrees heel or the angle of heel in degrees at which one-half the freeboard to the deck edge is immersed; or

(2) for a sailing vessel, T = the lesser of either 14 degrees or the angle of heel in degrees to the deck edge.

The deck edge is to be taken as the intersection of the sideshell and the uppermost continuous deck below which the sideshell is weathertight.

(b) If approved by the Coast Guard Marine Safety Center or the ABS, a larger value of T may be used for a vessel with a discontinuous weather deck or abnormal sheer.

Coast Guard, DHS § 170.173

(c) When doing the calculations required by paragraph (a) of this section for a sailing vessel or auxiliary sailing vessel, the vessel must be assumed—
(1) To be under bare poles; or
(2) If the vessel has no auxiliary propulsion, to have storm sails set and trimmed flat.

(d) The criterion specified in this section is generally limited in application to flush deck, mechanically powered vessels of ordinary proportions and form that carry cargo below the main deck. On other types of vessels, the Coast Guard Marine Safety Center or the ABS requires calculations in addition to those in paragraph (a) of this section. On a mechanically powered vessel under 328 feet (100 meters) in length, other than a tugboat or a towboat, the requirements in §170.173 are applied.

[CGD 79–023, 48 FR 51010, Nov. 4, 1983; 49 FR 37384, Sept. 24, 1984, as amended by CGD 88–070, 53 FR 34537, Sept. 7, 1988; CGD 85–080, 61 FR 944, Jan. 10, 1996; 61 FR 20556, May 7, 1996; CGD 95–028, 62 FR 51217, Sept. 30, 1997]

§ 170.173 Criterion for vessels of unusual proportion and form.

(a) If required by the Coast Guard Marine Safety Center or the ABS, each mechanically powered vessel less than 328 feet (100 meters) LLL, other than a tugboat or towboat, must be shown by design calculations to comply with—
(1) Paragraph (b) or (c) of this section if the maximum righting arm occurs at an angle of heel less than or equal to 30 degrees; or
(2) Paragraph (b) of this section if the maximum righting arm occurs at an angle of heel greater than 30 degrees.

(b) Each vessel must have—
(1) An initial metacentric height (GM) of at least 0.49 feet (0.15 meters);
(2) A righting arm (GZ) of at least 0.66 feet (0.20 meters) at an angle of heel equal to or greater than 30 degrees;
(3) A maximum righting arm that occurs at an angle of heel not less than 25 degrees;
(4) An area under each righting arm curve of at least 10.3 foot-degrees (3.15 meter-degrees) up to an angle of heel of 30 degrees;
(5) An area under each righting arm curve of at least 16.9 foot-degrees (5.15 meter-degrees) up to an angle of heel of 40 degrees or the downflooding angle, whichever is less; and
(6) An area under each righting arm curve between the angles of 30 degrees and 40 degrees, or between 30 degrees and the downflooding angle if this angle is less than 40 degrees, of not less than 5.6 foot-degrees (1.72 meter-degrees).

(c) Each vessel must have—
(1) An initial metacentric height (GM) of at least 0.49 feet (0.15 meters);
(2) A maximum righting arm that occurs at an angle of heel not less than 15 degrees;
(3) An area under each righting arm curve of at least 16.9 foot-degrees (5.15 meter-degrees) up to an angle of heel of 40 degrees or the downflooding angle, whichever is less;
(4) An area under each righting arm curve between the angles of 30 degrees and 40 degrees, or between 30 degrees and the downflooding angle if this angle is less than 40 degrees, of not less than 5.6 foot-degrees (1.72 meter-degrees); and
(5) An area under each righting arm curve up to the angle of maximum righting arm of not less than the area determined by the following equation:

$A = 10.3 + 0.187 \,(30 - Y)$ foot-degrees

$A = 3.15 + 0.057 \,(30 - Y)$ meter-degrees

where—
A = area in foot-degrees (meter-degrees).
Y = angle of maximum righting arm, degrees.

(d) For the purpose of demonstrating compliance with paragraphs (b) and (c) of this section, at each angle of heel a vessel's righting arm is calculated after the vessel is permitted to trim free until the trimming moment is zero.

(e) For the purpose of demonstrating acceptable stability on the vessels described in §170.170(d) as having unusual proportion and form, compliance with paragraphs (a) through (d) of this section or the following criteria is required:
(1) For partially protected routes, there must be—
(i) Positive righting arms to at least 35 degrees of heel;
(ii) No down flooding point to at least 20 degrees; and

§ 170.174

(iii) At least 15 foot-degrees of energy to the smallest of the following angles:
(A) Angle of maximum righting arm.
(B) Angle of down flooding.
(C) 40 degrees.
(2) For protected routes, there must be—
(i) Positive righting arms to at least 25 degrees of heel;
(ii) No down flooding point to at least 15 degrees; and
(iii) At least 10 foot-degrees of energy to the smallest of the following angles:
(A) Angle of maximum righting arm.
(B) Angle of down flooding.
(C) 40 degrees.

[CGD 79–023, 48 FR 51010, Nov. 4, 1983, as amended by CGD 85–080, 61 FR 944, Jan. 10, 1996; CGD 95–028, 62 FR 51218, Sept. 30, 1997; CGD 85–080, 62 FR 51353, Sept. 30, 1997]

Subpart F—Determination of Lightweight Displacement and Centers of Gravity

§ 170.174 Specific applicability.

This subpart applies to each vessel for which the lightweight displacement and centers of gravity must be determined in order to do the calculations required in this subchapter.

§ 170.175 Stability test: General.

(a) Except as provided in paragraphs (c) and (d) of this section and in § 170.200, the owner of a vessel must conduct a stability test of the vessel and calculate its vertical and longitudinal centers of gravity and its lightweight displacement.

(b) An authorized Coast Guard or ABS representative must be present at each stability test conducted under this section.

(c) The stability test may be dispensed with, or a deadweight survey may be substituted for the stability test, if the Coast Guard or the ABS has a record of, or is provided with, the approved results of a stability test of a sister vessel.

(d) The stability test of a vessel may be dispensed with if the Coast Guard or the ABS determines that an accurate estimate of the vessel's lightweight characteristics can be made and that locating the precise position of the vessel's vertical center of gravity is not necessary to ensure that the vessel has adequate stability in all probable loading conditions.

[CGD 79–023, 48 FR 51010, Nov. 4, 1983, as amended by CGD 95–028, 62 FR 51218, Sept. 30, 1997; USCG–1998–4442, 63 FR 52192, Sept. 30, 1998]

§ 170.180 Plans and information required at the stability test.

The owner of a vessel must provide the following Coast Guard or ABS approved plans and information to the authorized Coast Guard or ABS representative at the time of the stability test:

(a) Lines.
(b) Curves of form.
(c) Capacity plans showing capacities and vertical and longitudinal centers of gravity of stowage spaces and tanks.
(d) Tank sounding tables.
(e) Draft mark locations.
(f) General arrangement plan of decks, holds, and inner bottoms.
(g) Inboard and outboard profiles.
(h) The stability test procedure described in § 170.185(g).

[CGD 79–023, 48 FR 51010, Nov. 4, 1983, as amended by CGD 95–028, 62 FR 51218, Sept. 30, 1997]

§ 170.185 Stability test preparations.

The following preparations must be made before conducting a stability test:

(a) The vessel must be as complete as practicable at the time of the test.

(b) Each tank vessel must be empty and dry, except that a tank may be partially filled or full if the Coast Guard Marine Safety Center or the ABS determines that empty and dry tanks are impracticable and that the effect of filling or partial filling on the location of the center of gravity and on the displacement can be accurately determined.

(c) All dunnage, tools, and other items extraneous to the vessel must be removed.

(d) The water depth at the mooring site must provide ample clearance against grounding.

(e) Each mooring line must be arranged so that it does not interfere with the inclination of the unit during the test.

(f) The draft and axis of rotation selected for testing a mobile offshore drilling unit must be those that result in acceptable accuracy in calculating the center of gravity and displacement of the unit.

(g) The stability test procedure required by §170.085 must include the following:

(1) Identification of the vessel to be tested.

(2) Date and location of the test.

(3) Inclining weight data.

(4) Pendulum locations and lengths.

(5) Approximate draft and trim of the vessel.

(6) Condition of each tank.

(7) Estimated items to be installed, removed, or relocated after the test, including the weight and location of each item.

(8) Schedule of events.

(9) Person or persons responsible for conducting the test.

[CGD 79–023, 48 FR 51010, Nov. 4, 1983, as amended by CGD 88–070, 53 FR 34537, Sept. 7, 1988; CGD 95–028, 62 FR 51218, Sept. 30, 1997]

§ 170.190 Stability test procedure modifications.

The authorized Coast Guard or ABS representative present at a stability test may allow a deviation from the requirements of §§170.180 and 170.185 if the representative determines that the deviation would not decrease the accuracy of the test results.

[CGD 95–028, 62 FR 51218, Sept. 30, 1997]

§ 170.200 Estimated lightweight vertical center of gravity.

(a) Each tank vessel that does not carry a material listed in either Table 1 of part 153 or Table 4 of part 154 of this chapter may comply with this section in lieu of § 170.175 if it—

(1) Is 150 gross tons or greater;

(2) Is of ordinary proportions and form;

(3) Has a flush weather deck, one or more longitudinal bulkheads, and no independent tanks; and

(4) Is designed not to carry cargo above the freeboard deck.

(b) When doing the calculations required by §§170.170 and 172.065, the vertical center of gravity of a tank vessel in the lightweight condition must be assumed to be equal to the following percentage of the molded depth of the vessel measured from the keel amidship:

(1) For a tank ship—70%.

(2) For a tank barge—60%.

(c) As used in this section, *molded depth* has the same meaning that is provided for the term in §42.13–15(e) of this chapter.

[CGD 79–023, 48 FR 51010, Nov. 4, 1983, as amended by CGD 85–080, 61 FR 944, Jan. 10, 1996]

Subpart G—Special Installations

§ 170.235 Fixed ballast.

(a) Fixed ballast, if used, must be—

(1) Installed under the supervision of the OCMI; and

(2) Stowed in a manner that prevents shifting of position.

(b) Fixed ballast may not be removed from a vessel or relocated unless approved by the Coast Guard Marine Safety Center or the ABS. However, ballast may be temporarily moved for vessel examination or repair if done under the supervision of the OCMI.

[CGD 79–023, 48 FR 51010, Nov. 4, 1983, as amended by CGD 88–070, 53 FR 34537, Sept. 7, 1988; CGD 95–028, 62 FR 51218, Sept. 30, 1997]

§ 170.245 Foam flotation material.

(a) Installation of foam must be approved by the OCMI.

(b) If foam is used to comply with §171.070(d), §171.095(c), or §173.063(e) of this subchapter, the following applies:

(1) Foam may be installed only in void spaces that are free of ignition sources.

(2) The foam must comply with MIL–P–21929B including the requirements for fire resistance.

(3) A submergence test must be conducted for a period of at least 7 days to demonstrate whether the foam has adequate strength to withstand a hydrostatic head equivalent to that which would be imposed if the vessel were submerged to its margin line.

(4) The effective buoyancy at the end of the submergence test must be used as the buoyancy credit; however, in no case will a credit greater than 55 lbs per cubic foot (881 kilograms per cubic meter) be allowed.

§ 170.248

(5) The structure enclosing the foam must be strong enough to accommodate the buoyancy of the foam.

(6) Piping and cables must not pass through foamed spaces unless they are within piping and cable trunks accessible from both ends.

(7) Sample specimens must be prepared during installation and the density of the installed foam must be determined.

(8) Foam may be installed adjacent to fuel tanks if the boundary between the tank and space has double continuous fillet welds.

(9) MIL-P-21929B is incorporated by reference into this part.

(10) The results of all tests and calculations must be submitted to the OCMI.

(11) Blocked foam must—

(i) Be used in each area that may be exposed to water; and

(ii) Have a protective cover approved by the OCMI.

[CGD 79-023, 48 FR 51010, Nov. 4, 1983, as amended by CGD 83-005, 51 FR 923, Jan. 9, 1986]

Subpart H—Watertight Bulkhead Doors

§ 170.248 Applicability.

(a) Except as provided in paragraph (b) or paragraph (c) of this section, this subpart applies to vessels with watertight doors in bulkheads that have been made watertight to comply with the flooding or damage stability regulations in this subchapter.

(b) A watertight door on a MODU must comply with § 174.100 of this subchapter.

(c) A watertight door on a self-propelled hopper dredge with a working freeboard must comply with § 174.335 of this subchapter.

[CGD 79-023, 48 FR 51010, Nov. 4, 1983, as amended by CGD 76-080, 54 FR 36977, Sept. 6, 1989]

§ 170.250 Types and classes.

(a) Watertight doors, except doors between cargo spaces, are classed as follows:

(1) Class 1—Hinged door.

(2) Class 2—Sliding door, operated by hand gear only.

(3) Class 3—Sliding door, operated by power and by hand gear.

(b) The following types of watertight doors are not permitted:

(1) A plate door secured only by bolts; and

(2) A door required to be closed by dropping or by the action of dropping weights.

(c) Whenever a door of a particular class is prescribed by these regulations, a door of a class bearing a higher number may be used.

§ 170.255 Class 1 doors; permissible locations.

(a) Except as provided in paragraphs (b) and (c) of this section, Class 1 doors within passenger, crew, and working spaces are permitted only above a deck, the molded line of which, at its lowest point at side, is at least 7 feet (2.14 meters) above the deepest load line.

(b) Class 1 doors are permitted within passenger, crew, and working spaces, wherever located, if—

(1) In the judgment of the OCMI, the door is in a location where it will be closed at all times except when actually in use; and

(2) The vessel is less than 150 gross tons and will not proceed more than 20 nautical miles (37 kilometers) from shore; or

(3) The vessel is in rivers or lakes, bays, and sounds service.

(c) Class 1 doors are permitted in any location on a vessel that—

(1) Is less than 100 gross tons; and

(2) Will operate only in the offshore oil industry trade.

(d) Quick-acting Class 1 doors are permitted in any location on a vessel that operates on the Great Lakes and is required to meet the damage stability standards of subpart H of part 172 of this chapter.

(e) For vessels required to meet the damage stability standards of subpart H of this chapter, when Class 1 doors are installed below a deck the molded line of which at its lowest point at side is less than 7 feet (2.14 meters) above the deepest load line, an indicator light for each door which warns when the door is open must be installed on the bridge.

[CGD 79–023, 48 FR 51010, Nov. 4, 1983, as amended by CGD 80–159, 51 FR 33059, Sept. 18, 1986]

§ 170.260 Class 2 doors; permissible locations.

(a) Except as provided in paragraphs (b) and (c) of this section, a Class 2 door is permitted only if—

(1) Its sill is above the deepest load line; and

(2) It is not a door described in § 170.265(d).

(b) If passenger spaces are located below the bulkhead deck, Class 2 doors with sills below the deepest load line may be used if—

(1) The number of watertight doors located below the deepest load line that are used intermittently during operation of the vessel does not exceed two, and;

(2) The doors provide access to or are within spaces containing machinery.

(c) If no passenger spaces are located below the bulkhead deck, Class 2 doors may be used if the number of watertight doors located below the deepest load line that are used intermittently during operation of the vessel does not exceed five.

(d) In determining whether Class 2 doors are allowed under paragraph (c) of this section, the watertight doors at the entrance to shaft tunnels need not be counted. If Class 2 doors are allowed under paragraph (c) of this section, the doors at the entrance to shaft tunnels may also be Class 2.

§ 170.265 Class 3 doors; required locations.

The following doors must always be Class 3:

(a) Doors in all locations not addressed in §§ 170.255 and 170.260.

(b) Doors between coal bunkers below the bulkhead deck that must be opened at sea.

(c) Doors into trunkways that pass through more than one main transverse watertight bulkhead if the door sills are less than 2.14 meters above the deepest load line.

(d) Doors below a deck, the molded line of which, at its lowest point at side, is less than 2.14 meters (7 feet) above the deepest load line if—

(1) The vessel is engaged on a short international voyage as defined in § 171.010 of this subchapter; and

(2) The vessel is required by § 171.065 of this subchapter to have a factor of subdivision of 0.5 or less.

[CGD 79–023, 48 FR 51010, Nov. 4, 1983, as amended by CGD 85–080, 61 FR 944, Jan. 10, 1996; CGD 96–041, 61 FR 50734, Sept. 27, 1996]

§ 170.270 Door design, operation, installation, and testing.

(a) Each Class 1 door must have a quick action closing device operative from both sides of the door.

(b) Each Class 1 door on a vessel in ocean service must be designed to withstand a head of water equivalent to the depth from the sill of the door to the margin line but in no case less than 10 feet (3.05 meters).

(c) Each Class 2 and Class 3 door must—

(1) Be designed, constructed, tested, and marked in accordance with ASTM F 1196 (incorporated by reference, see § 170.015);

(2) Have controls in accordance with ASTM F 1197 (incorporated by reference, see § 170.015); and

(3) If installed in a subdivision bulkhead, meet Supplemental Requirements Nos. S1 and S3 of ASTM F 1196 (incorporated by reference, see § 170.015), unless the watertight doors are built in accordance with plans previously approved by the Coast Guard, in which case, only Supplemental Requirements Nos. S1 and S3.1.4 of ASTM F 1196 (incorporated by reference, see § 170.015) must be met. In either case, control systems for watertight doors must have power supplies, power sources, installation tests and inspection, and additional remote operating consoles in accordance with Supplemental Requirements Nos. S1 through S4 of ASTM F 1197 (incorporated by reference, see § 170.015).

(d) Installations of sliding watertight door assemblies must be in accordance with the following:

(1) Before a sliding watertight door assembly is installed in a vessel, the bulkhead in the vicinity of the door opening must be stiffened. Such bulkhead stiffeners, or deck reinforcement

§ 170.275

where flush deck door openings are desired, must not be less than 6 inches nor more than 12 inches from the door frame so that an unstiffened diaphragm of bulkhead plating 6 to 12 inches wide is provided completely around the door frame. Where such limits cannot be maintained, alternative installations will be considered by the Marine Safety Center. In determining the scantlings of these bulkhead stiffeners, the door frame should not be considered as contributing to the strength of the bulkhead. Provision must also be made to adequately support the thrust bearings and other equipment that may be mounted on the bulkhead or deck.

(2) Sliding watertight door frames must be either bolted or welded watertight to the bulkhead.

(i) If bolted, a suitable thin heat and fire resistant gasket or suitable compound must be used between the bulkhead and the frame for watertightness. The bulkhead plating must be worked to a plane surface in way of the frame when mounting.

(ii) If welded, caution must be exercised in the welding process so that the door frame is not distorted.

(e) For each watertight door which is in a required subdivision bulkhead, an indicator light must be installed in the pilothouse and at each other vessel operating station from which the door is not visible. The indicator must show whether the door is open or closed.

[CGD 79–023, 48 FR 51010, Nov. 4, 1983, as amended by CGD 88–032, 56 FR 35828, July 29, 1991; CGD 85–080, 61 FR 944, Jan. 10, 1996; USCG–2000–7790, 65 FR 58464, Sept. 29, 2000]

§ 170.275 Special requirements for cargo space watertight doors.

(a) A door between cargo spaces—

(1) Must not be designed for remote operation;

(2) Must be located as high as practicable; and

(3) Must be located as far inboard of the side shell as practicable but in no case closer to the side shell than one-fifth of the beam of the vessel where the beam is measured at right angles to the centerline of the vessel at the level of the deepest load line.

(b) If the door is accessible while the ship is in operation, it must have installed a lock or other device that prevents unauthorized opening.

(c) Before installing a watertight door in a cargo space, approval must be obtained from the Commanding Officer, Marine Safety Center.

[CGD 79–023, 48 FR 51010, Nov. 4, 1983, as amended by CGD 88–070, 53 FR 34537, Sept. 7, 1988]

Subpart I—Free Surface

§ 170.285 Free surface correction for intact stability calculations.

(a) When doing the intact stability calculations required by this subchapter, the virtual increase in the vessel's vertical center of gravity due to liquids in tanks must be determined by calculating—

(1) For each type of consumable liquid, the maximum free surface effect of at least one transverse pair of wing tanks or a single centerline tank; and

(2) The maximum free surface effect of each partially filled tank containing non-consumable liquids.

(b) For the purpose of paragraph (a)(1) of this section, the tank or combination of tanks selected must be those having the greatest free surface effect.

§ 170.290 Free surface correction for damage stability calculations.

(a) When doing the damage stability calculations required by this subchapter, the virtual increase in the vessel's vertical center of gravity due to liquids in tanks must be determined by calculating—

(1) For each type of consumable liquid, the free surface effect of at least one transverse pair of wing tanks or a single centerline tank; and

(2) The free surface effect of each partially filled tank containing other than consumable liquids.

(b) For the purpose of paragraph (a)(1) of this section, the tank or combination of tanks selected must be those having the greatest free surface effect.

(c) When doing the calculations in paragraph (a) of this section, the free surface effect of a liquid in a tank must be determined by—

(1) Assuming the vessel is heeled five degrees from the vertical; or

Coast Guard, DHS § 170.295

(2) Calculating the shift of the center of gravity of the liquid in the tank by the moment of transference method.

§ 170.295 Special consideration for free surface of passive roll stabilization tanks.

(a) The virtual increase in the vertical center of gravity due to a liquid in a roll stabilization tank may be calculated in accordance with paragraph (b) of this section if—

(1) The virtual increase in the vertical center of gravity of the vessel is calculated in accordance with § 170.285(a); and

(2) The slack surface in the roll stabilization tank is reduced during vessel motions because of the shape of the tank or the amount of liquid in the tank.

(b) The virtual rise in the vertical center of gravity calculated in accordance with § 170.285(a) for a stabilization tank may be reduced in accordance with the following equation:

E.F.S.=(K)(F.F.S.)

where—

E.F.S.=the effective free surface.

F.F.S.=the full free surface calculated in accordance with § 170.285(a).

K=the reduction factor calculated in accordance with paragraph (c) of this section.

(c) The factor (K) must be calculated as follows:

(1) Plot (I/d)tan T on Graph 170.295 where—

(i) (I) is the moment of inertia of the free surface in the roll tank;

(ii) (d) is the density of the liquid in the roll tank; and

(iii) (T) is the angle of heel.

(2) Plot the moments of transference of the liquid in the roll tank on Graph 170.295.

(3) Construct a line A on Graph 170.295 so that the area under line A between T = 0 and the angle at which the deck edge is immersed or 28 degrees, whichever is smaller, is equal to the area under the curve of actual moments of transference between the same angles.

(4) The factor (K) is calculated by determining the ratio of the ordinate of line A to the ordinate of the curve of (I/d)tan T, both measured at the angle at which the deck edge is immersed or 28 degrees, whichever is smaller.

GRAPH 170.295

Special Free Surface Correction
for
Stabilization Tanks

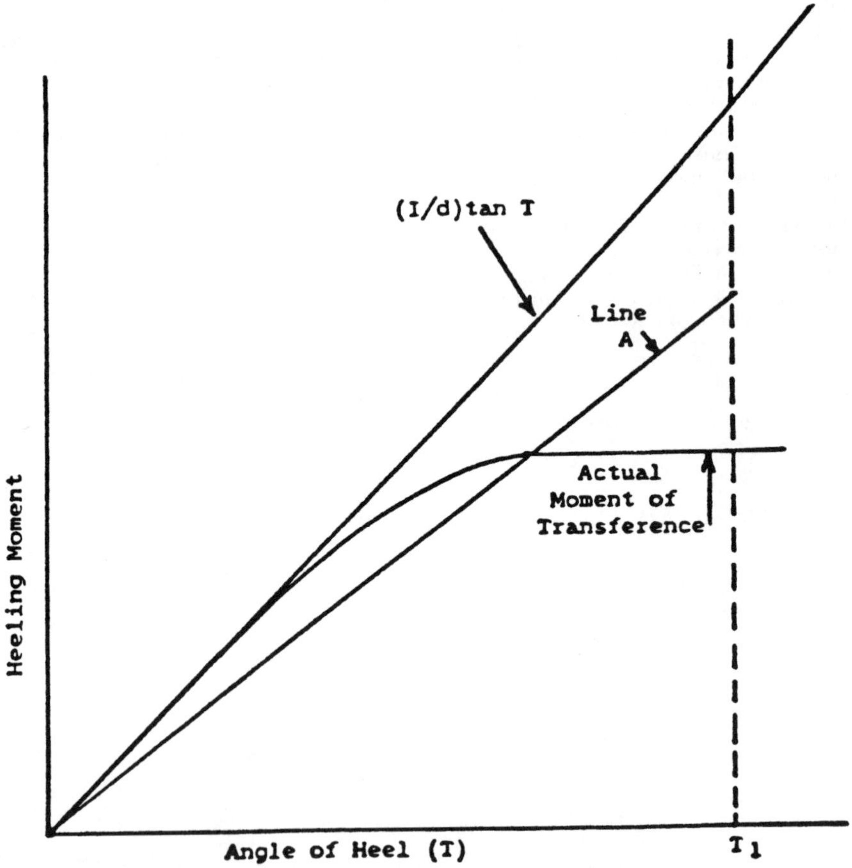
(I/d)tan T
Line
A
Actual
Moment of
Transference
Heeling Moment
Angle of Heel (T)
T_1

T_1 = the angle at which the deck edge is immersed or 28 degrees, whichever is smaller.

§ 170.300 Special consideration for free surface of spoil in hopper dredge hoppers.

The calculations required by this subchapter for each self-propelled hopper dredge must include—

(a) The free surface effect of consumable liquids and the free surface effect of the dredged spoil in the hoppers; and

(b) Either of the following assumptions when performing the calculations required by § 174.310(b) of this chapter:

(1) If the dredged spoil is assumed to be jettisoned, the free surface of the dredged spoil may be disregarded.

(2) If the dredged spoil is not assumed to be jettisoned. the free surface of the dredged spoil must be calculated.

[CGD 76–080, 54 FR 36977, Sept. 6, 1989]

PART 171—SPECIAL RULES PERTAINING TO VESSELS CARRYING PASSENGERS

Subpart A—General

Sec.
171.001 Applicability.
171.010 Definitions.
171.015 Location of margin line.
171.017 One and two compartment standards of flooding.

Subpart B [Reserved]

Subpart C—Large Vessels

171.045 Specific applicability.
171.050 Intact stability requirements for a mechanically propelled or a nonself-propelled vessel.
171.055 Intact stability requirements for a monohull sailing vessel or a monohull auxiliary sailing vessel.
171.057 Intact stability requirements for a sailing catamaran.
171.060 Watertight subdivision: General.
171.065 Subdivision requirements—Type I.
171.066 Calculation of permeability for Type I subdivision.
171.067 Treatment of stepped and recessed bulkheads in Type I subdivision.
171.068 Special considerations for Type I subdivision for vessels on short international voyages.
171.070 Subdivision requirements—Type II.
171.072 Calculation of permeability for Type II subdivision.
171.073 Treatment of stepped and recessed bulkheads in Type II subdivision.
171.075 Subdivision requirements—Type III.
171.080 Damage stability standards for vessels with Type I or Type II subdivision.
171.082 Damage stability standards for vessels with Type III subdivision.

Subpart D—Additional Subdivision Requirements

171.085 Collision bulkhead.
171.090 Aft peak bulkhead.
171.095 Machinery space bulkhead.
171.100 Shaft tunnels and stern tubes.
171.105 Double bottoms.
171.106 Wells in double bottoms.
171.108 Manholes in double bottoms.
171.109 Watertight floors in double bottoms.

Subpart E—Penetrations and Openings in Watertight Bulkheads

171.110 Specific applicability.
171.111 Penetrations and openings in watertight bulkheads in vessels of 100 gross tons or more.
171.112 Watertight door openings.
171.113 Trunks.
171.114 Penetrations and openings in watertight bulkheads in a vessel less than a 100 gross tons.

Subpart F—Openings in the Side of a Vessel Below the Bulkhead or Weather Deck

171.115 Specific applicability.
171.116 Port lights.
171.117 Dead covers.
171.118 Automatic ventilators and side ports.
171.119 Openings below the weather deck in the side of a vessel less than 100 gross tons.

Subpart G—Watertight Integrity Above the Margin Line

171.120 Specific applicability.
171.122 Watertight integrity above the margin line in a vessel of 100 gross tons or more.
171.124 Watertight integrity above the margin line in a vessel less than 100 gross tons.

Subpart H—Drainage of Weather Decks

171.130 Specific applicability.
171.135 Weather deck drainage on a vessel of 100 gross tons or more.
171.140 Drainage of a flush deck vessel.
171.145 Drainage of a vessel with a cockpit.
171.150 Drainage of a vessel with a well deck.
171.155 Drainage of an open boat.

AUTHORITY: 46 U.S.C. 2103, 3306; E.O. 12234, 45 FR 58801, 3 CFR, 1980 Comp., p. 277; Department of Homeland Security Delegation No. 0170.1.

§ 171.001

SOURCE: CGD 79-023, 48 FR 51017, Nov. 4, 1983, unless otherwise noted.

Subpart A—General

§ 171.001 Applicability.

(a) This part applies to passenger vessels inspected under subchapter K or H of this chapter.

(b) Specific sections of this part also apply to nautical school ships, sailing school vessels and oceanographic vessels. The applicable sections are listed in subparts C and D of part 173 of this chapter.

[CGD 79-023, 48 FR 51017, Nov. 4, 1983, as amended by CGD 83-005, 51 FR 923, Jan. 9, 1986; CGD 95-012, 60 FR 48052, Sept. 18, 1995; 60 FR 50120, Sept. 28, 1995; CGD 85-080, 61 FR 944, Jan. 10, 1996]

§ 171.010 Definitions.

(a) *Cockpit* means an exposed recess in the weather deck extending no more than one-half of the vessel's length over deck (LOD) measured over the weather deck.

(b) *Deepest subdivision load line* means the waterline that corresponds to the deepest draft permitted by the applicable subdivision requirements in this part.

(c) *Equivalent plane bulkhead* means a bulkhead that is—

(1) Used in lieu of a recessed or stepped bulkhead when doing the subdivision calculations required in this part; and

(2) Located as shown in Figure 171.010(a).

(d) *Ferry* means a vessel that—

(1) Operates in other than ocean or coastwise service;

(2) Has provisions only for deck passengers or vehicles, or both;

(3) Operates on a short run on a frequent schedule between two points over the most direct water route;

(4) Offers a public service of a type normally attributed to a bridge or tunnel.

(e) *Freeing port* means any direct opening through the vessel's bulwark or hull to quickly drain overboard water which has been shipped on exposed decks.

(f) *Floodable length* means the length of a shell to shell segment of the vessel that, when flooded, will sink and trim the vessel until the margin line is tangent to the waterline.

(g) *Flush deck* means a continuous weather deck located at the uppermost sheer line of the hull.

(h) *International voyage* has the same meaning provided for the term in § 70.05-10 of this chapter.

(i) *Machinery space* means, unless otherwise prescribed by the Commandant for unusual arrangements, the space extending from the molded base line to the margin line and between the main transverse watertight bulkheads bounding the following spaces:

(1) Each space containing main and auxiliary propelling machinery.

(2) Each space containing propulsion boilers.

(3) Each space containing permanent coal bunkers.

(j) *Open boat* means a vessel not protected from entry of water by means of a complete deck, or by a combination of a partial weather deck and superstructure which is seaworthy for the waters upon which the vessel operates.

(k) *Passenger space* means a space which is provided for the accommodation and use of passengers, other than a baggage, store, provision or mail room.

(l) *Recessed bulkhead* means a bulkhead that is recessed as shown by bulkhead B in Figure 171.010(b).

(m) *Small passenger vessel* means a vessel of less than 100 gross tons—

(1) Carrying more than 6 passengers, including at least one passenger for hire;

(2) That is chartered with the crew provided or specified by the owner or owner's representative and carrying more than 6 passengers;

(3) That is chartered with no crew provided or specified by the owner or owner's representative and carrying more than 12 passengers; or

(4) That is a submersible vessel carrying at least one passenger for hire.

(n) *Short international voyage* means an international voyage where—

(1) A vessel is not more than 200 nautical miles (370 kilometers) from a port or place in which the passengers and crew could be placed in safety; and

(2) The total distance between the last port of call in the country in

Coast Guard, DHS

§ 171.010

which the voyage began and the final port of destination does not exceed 600 nautical miles (1111 kilometers).

(o) *Scupper* means a pipe or tube of at least 30 millimeters (1.25 inches) in diameter leading down from a deck or sole and through the hull to drain water overboard.

(p) *Stepped bulkhead* means a bulkhead that is stepped as shown by bulkhead A in Figure 171.010(b).

Figure 171.010(a)

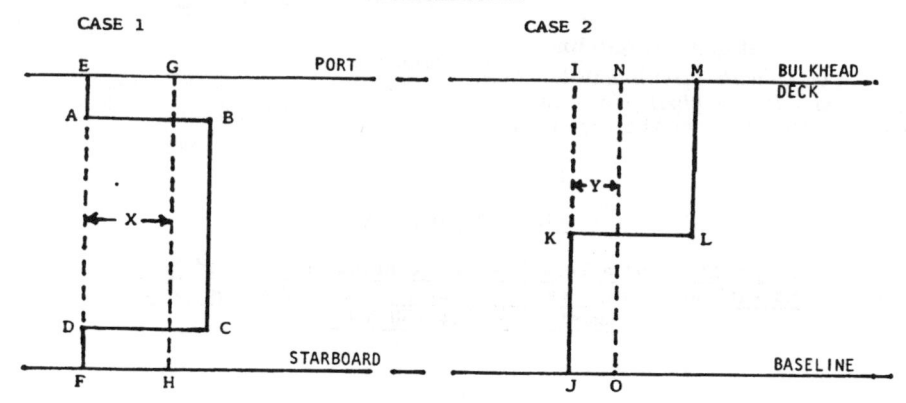

Case 1: X = V/A
where—
X = Distance between EF and the equivalent plane bulkhead GH.
V = Volume of the space directly below ABCD and extending to the shell.
A = Sectional area midway between EF and GH.

Case 2: Y = V/A
where—
Y = Distance between IJ and the equivalent plane bulkhead NO.
V = Volume of the space directly below IKLM and extending to the shell.
A = Sectional area midway between IJ and NO.

Figure 171.010(b)

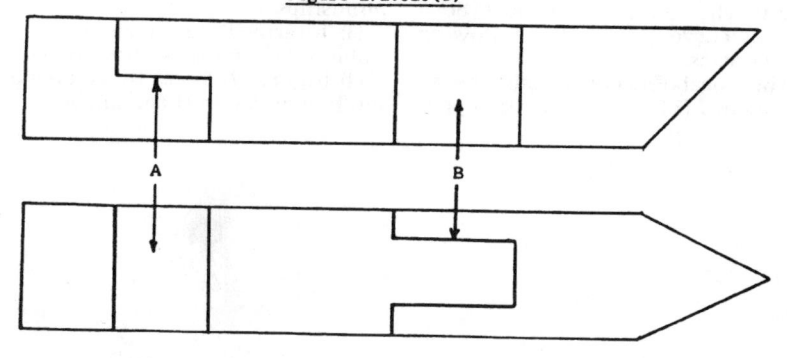

113

§ 171.015

(q) *Well deck* means a weather deck fitted with solid bulwarks that impede the drainage of water over the sides or an exposed recess in the weather deck extending one-half or more of the length of the vessel (LOD) measured over the weather deck.

[CGD 79–023, 48 FR 51017, Nov. 4, 1983, as amended by CGD 85–080, 61 FR 944, Jan. 10, 1996]

§ 171.015 Location of margin line.

(a) *A vessel with a continuous bulkhead deck and sufficient sheer.* If the average value of the sheer at the forward perpendicular (FP) and the after perpendicular (AP) is at least 12 inches (30.5 cm), the margin line must be located no less than 3 inches (7.6 cm) below the upper surface of the bulkhead deck at side as illustrated in Figure 171.015(a).

TABLE 171.015

Average value of sheer at FP and AP in inches (cm)	Required position of margin line below top of deck amidships in inches (cm)
12 (30.5)	3 (7.6)
6 (15.2)	6 (15.2)
0	9 (22.8)

Figure 171.015(a)

Margin Line for a Vessel With a Continuous Bulkhead Deck and With an Average Value of Sheer at the FP and AP of at Least 12 Inches (30.5 cm)

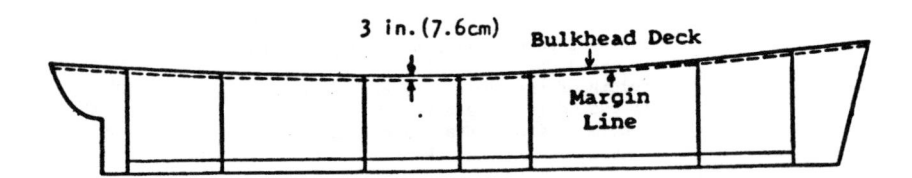

(b) *A vessel with a continuous bulkhead deck and insufficient sheer.* If the average value of the sheer at the forward perpendicular (FP) and the after perpendicular (AP) is less than 12 inches (30.5 cm), the margin line must be a parabolic curve with the following characteristics:

(1) The parabolic curve must be at least 3 inches (7.6 cm) below the upper surface of the bulkhead deck at the FP and AP.

(2) The parabolic curve must be at least the distance given in Table 171.015 below the surface of the bulkhead deck amidships.

(3) Intermediate values not shown in Table 171.015 must be interpolated.

(4) Figure 171.015(b) illustrates a margin line drawn in this manner.

Coast Guard, DHS § 171.015

Figure 171.015(b)

Margin Line for a Vessel With a Continuous Bulkhead Deck and With an Average Value of Sheer at the FP and AP Less Than 12 Inches (30.5 cm)

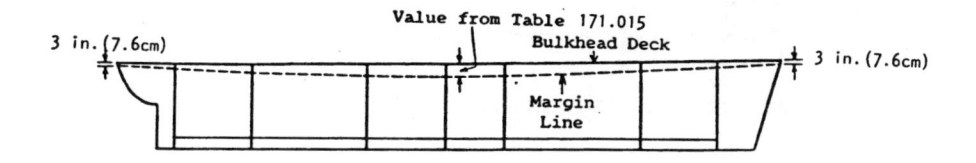

(c) *A vessel with a discontinuous bulkhead deck.* A continuous margin line must be drawn that is no more than 3 inches (7.6 cm) below the upper surface of the bulkhead deck at side as illustrated in Figure 171.015(c).

Figure 171.015(c)

Margin Line for a Vessel With a Discontinuous Bulkhead Deck

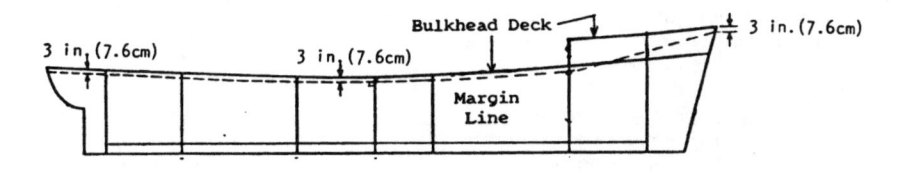

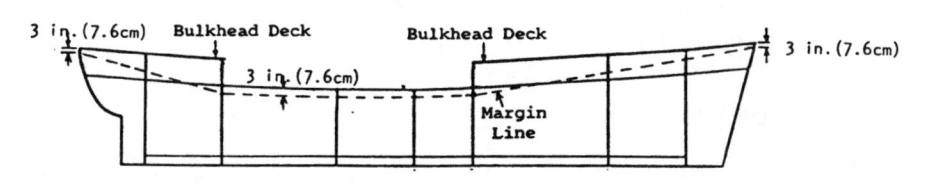

(d) *A vessel with a discontinuous bulkhead deck where the side shell is carried watertight to a higher deck.* A continuous margin line must be drawn as illustrated in Figure 171.015(d).

115

§ 171.017

46 CFR Ch. I (10–1–04 Edition)

Figure 171.015(d)

Margin Line for a Vessel With a Discontinuous
Bulkhead Deck and With Side Shell Watertight to a Higher Deck

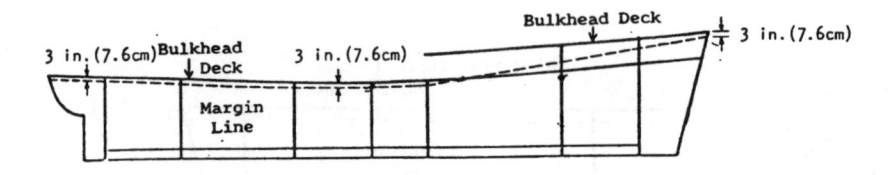

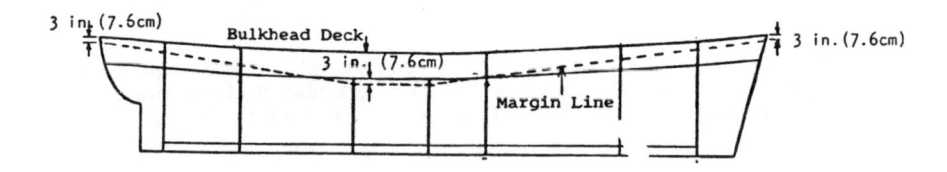

§ 171.017 One and two compartment standards of flooding.

(a) *One compartment standard of flooding.* A vessel is designed to a one compartment standard of flooding if the margin line is not submerged when the total buoyancy between each set of two adjacent main transverse watertight bulkheads is lost.

(b) *Two compartment standard of flooding.* A vessel is designed to a two compartment standard of flooding if the margin line is not submerged when the total buoyancy between each set of three adjacent main transverse watertight bulkheads is lost.

Subpart B [Reserved]

Subpart C—Large Vessels

§ 171.045 Specific applicability.

This subpart applies to each vessel that fits into any one of the following categories:

(a) Greater than 100 gross tons.
(b) Greater than 65 feet (19.8 meters) in length.
(c) Carries more than 12 passengers on an international voyage.
(d) Carries more than 150 passengers.
(e) The stability of which is questioned by the OCMI.

§ 171.050 Intact stability requirements for a mechanically propelled or a nonself-propelled vessel.

Each vessel must be shown by design calculations to have a metacentric height (GM) in feet (meters) in each condition of loading and operation, that is not less than the value given by the following equation:

$$GM = \frac{Nb}{(K)(W)(\tan(T))}$$

where—
N=number of passengers.
W=displacement of the vessel in long (metric) tons.
T=14 degrees or the angle of heel at which the deck edge is first submerged, whichever is less.
b=distance in feet (meters) from the centerline of the vessel to the geometric center of the passenger deck on one side of the centerline.
K=24 passengers/long ton (23.6 passengers/metric ton).

§ 171.055 Intact stability requirements for a monohull sailing vessel or a monohull auxiliary sailing vessel.

(a) Except as specified in paragraph (b) of this section, each monohull sailing vessel and auxiliary sailing vessel must be shown by design calculations to meet the stability requirements in this section.

Coast Guard, DHS § 171.055

(b) Additional or different stability requirements may be needed for a vessel of unusual form, proportion, or rig. The additional requirements, if needed, will be prescribed by the Commandant.

(c) Each vessel must have positive righting arms in each condition of loading and operation from—

(1) 0 to at least 70 degrees of heel for service on protected or partially protected waters; and

(2) 0 to at least 90 degrees of heel for service on exposed waters.

(d) Each vessel must be designed to satisfy the following equations:

(1) For a vessel in service on protected or partially protected waters—

$$\frac{1000(W)HZA}{(A)(H)} \geq X$$

$$\frac{1000(W)HZB}{(A)(H)} \geq Y$$

$$\frac{1000(W)HZC}{(A)(H)} \geq Z$$

where—

X=1.0 long tons/sq. ft. (10.9 metric tons/sq. meter).
Y=1.1 long tons/sq. ft. (12.0 metric tons/sq. meter).
Z=1.25 long tons/sq. ft. (13.7 metric tons/sq. meter).

(2) For a vessel on exposed waters—

$$\frac{1000(W)HZA}{(A)(H)} \geq X$$

$$\frac{1000(W)HZB}{(A)(H)} \geq Y$$

$$\frac{1000(W)HZC}{(A)(H)} \geq Z$$

where—

HZA, HZB, and HZC are calculated in the manner specified in paragraph (e) or (f) of this section.
X=1.5 long tons/sq. ft. (16.4 metric tons/sq. meter).
Y=1.7 long tons/sq. ft. (18.6 metric tons/sq. meter).
Z=1.9 long tons/sq. ft. (20.8 metric tons/sq. meter).
A=the projected lateral area or silhouette in square feet (meters) of the portion of the vessel above the waterline computed with all sail set and trimmed flat. Sail overlap areas need not be included except parachute type spinnakers which are to be added regardless of overlap.
H=the vertical distance in feet (meters) from the center of A to the center of the underwater lateral area or approximately to the one-half draft point.
W=the displacement of the vessel in long (metric) tons.

(e) Except as provided in paragraph (f) of this section, HZA, HZB, and HZC must be determined as follows for each condition of loading and operation:

(1) Plot the righting arm curve on Graphs 171.055 (b), (c), and (d) or (e).

(2) If the angle at which the maximum righting arm occurs is less than 35 degrees, the righting arm curve must be truncated as shown on Graph 171.055(a).

(3) Plot an assumed heeling arm curve on Graph 171.055(b) that satisfies the following conditions:

(i) The assumed heeling arm curve must be defined by the equation—

HZ=HZA cos² (T)

where—

HZ=heeling arm.
HZA=heeling arm at 0 degrees of heel.
T=angle of heel.

(ii) The first intercept shown on Graph 171.055(b) must occur at the angle of heel corresponding to the angle at which deck edge immersion first occurs.

(4) Plot an assumed heeling arm curve on Graph 171.055(c) that satisfies the following conditions:

(i) The assumed heeling arm curve must be defined by the equation—

HZ=HZB cos² (T)

where—

HZ=heeling arm.
HZB=heeling arm at 0 degrees of heel.
T=angle of heel.

§ 171.055

(ii) The area under the assumed heeling arm curve between 0 degrees and the downflooding angle or 60 degrees, whichever is less, must be equal to the area under the righting arm curve between the same limiting angles.

(5) Plot an assumed heeling arm curve on Graph 171.055 (d) or (e) that satisfies the following conditions:

(i) The assumed heeling arm curve must be defined by—

$$\leq HZ = HZC \cos^2 (T)$$

where—
HZ=heeling arm.
HZC=heeling arm at 0 degrees of heel.
T=angle of heel.

(ii) The area under the assumed heeling arm curve between the angles of 0 and 90 degrees must be equal to the area under the righting arm curve between 0 degrees and—

(A) 90 degrees if the righting arms are positive to an angle less than or equal to 90 degrees; or

(B) The largest angle corresponding to a positive righting arm but no more than 120 degrees if the righting arms are positive to an angle greater than 90 degrees.

(6) The values of HZA, HZB, and HZC are read directly from Graphs 171.055 (b), (c), and (d) or (e).

(f) For the purpose of this section, the downflooding angle means the static angle from the intersection of the vessel's centerline and waterline in calm water to the first opening that cannot be rapidly closed watertight.

(g) HZB and, if the righting arms are positive to an angle of 90 degrees or greater, HZC may be computed from the following equation:

$$HZB \text{ (or } HZC) = \frac{I}{((T/2) + 14.3 \sin 2T)}$$

where—
I=the area under the righting arm curve to—
(1) the downflooding angle or 60 degrees, whichever is less, when computing HZB; or
(2) the largest angle corresponding to a positive righting arm or 90 degrees, whichever is greater, but no greater than 120 degrees when computing HZC.
T=the downflooding angle or 60 degrees, whichever is less, when computing HZB or 90 degrees when computing HZC.

Coast Guard, DHS § 171.055

GRAPH 171.055(a)

Truncation of Righting Arm Curve if Maximum Righting
Arm Occurs at an Angle of Heel Less Than 35 Degrees

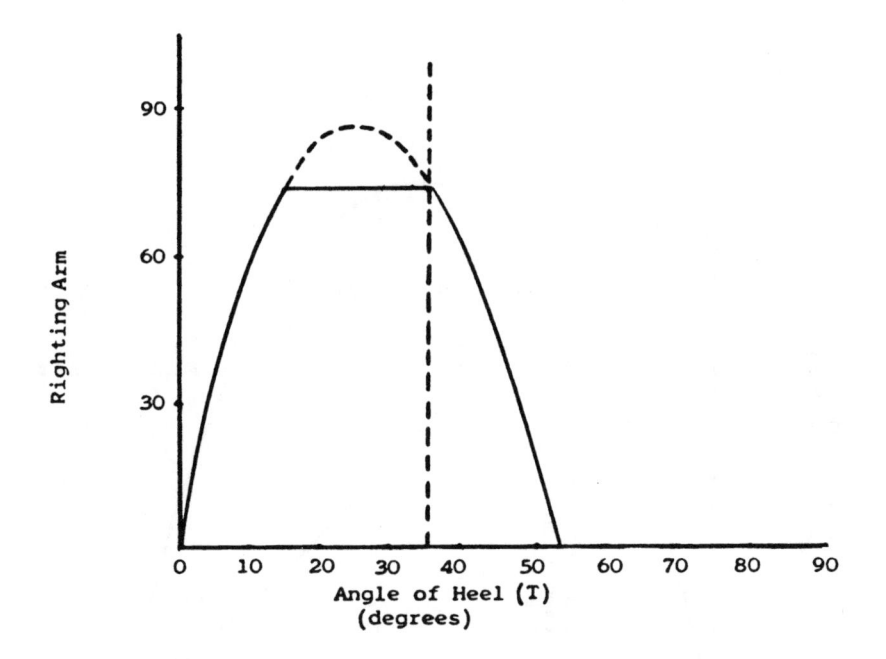

Righting Arm vs. Angle of Heel (T) (degrees)

GRAPH 171.055(b)

First Intercept Occurs at the Angle at Which Deck Edge Immersion First Occurs

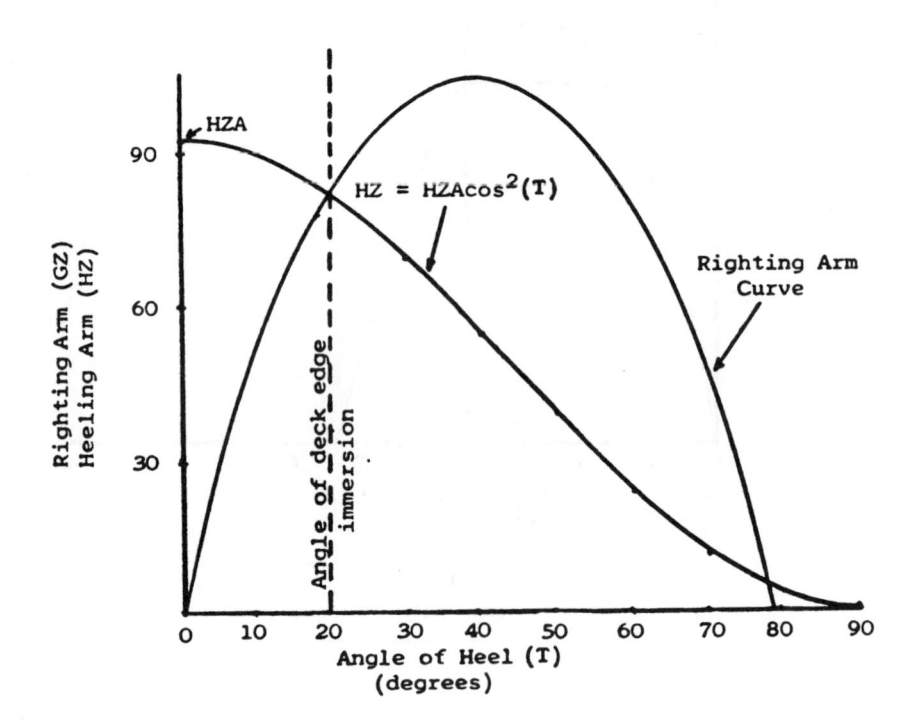

Righting Arm (GZ)
Heeling Arm (HZ)

HZA

$HZ = HZA\cos^2(T)$

Righting Arm Curve

Angle of deck edge immersion

Angle of Heel (T) (degrees)

Coast Guard, DHS § 171.055

GRAPH 171.055(c)

Shaded Areas are Balanced to the Downflooding Angle

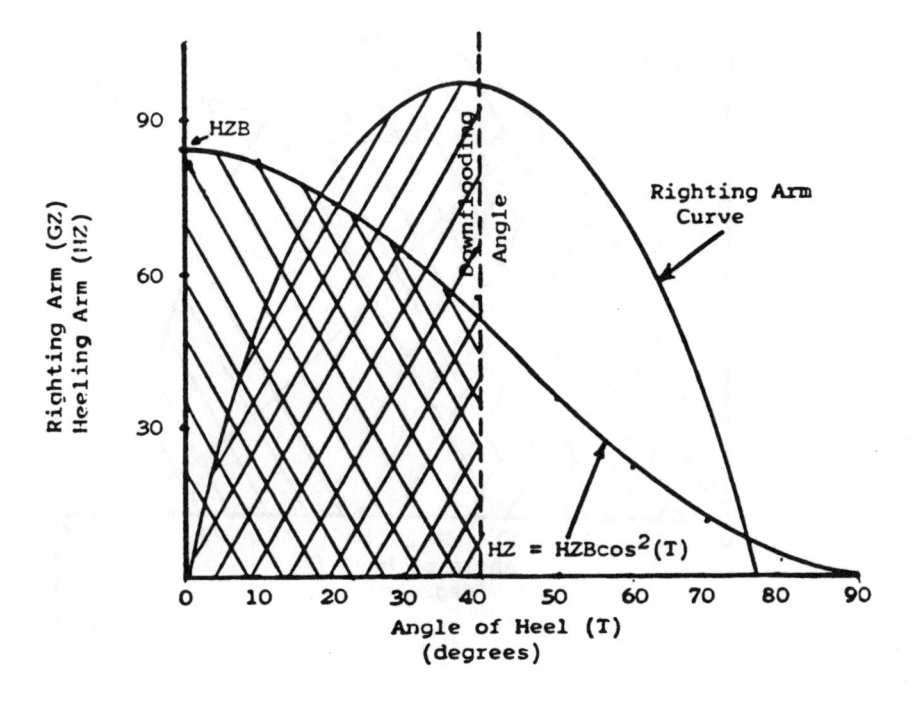

Righting Arm (GZ)
Heeling Arm (HZ)

HZB

Downflooding Angle

Righting Arm Curve

$HZ = HZB\cos^2(T)$

Angle of Heel (T) (degrees)

121

§ 171.055

46 CFR Ch. I (10–1–04 Edition)

GRAPH 171.055(d)

Righting Arm Curve is not Positive to 90 Degrees and Negative Area is Included

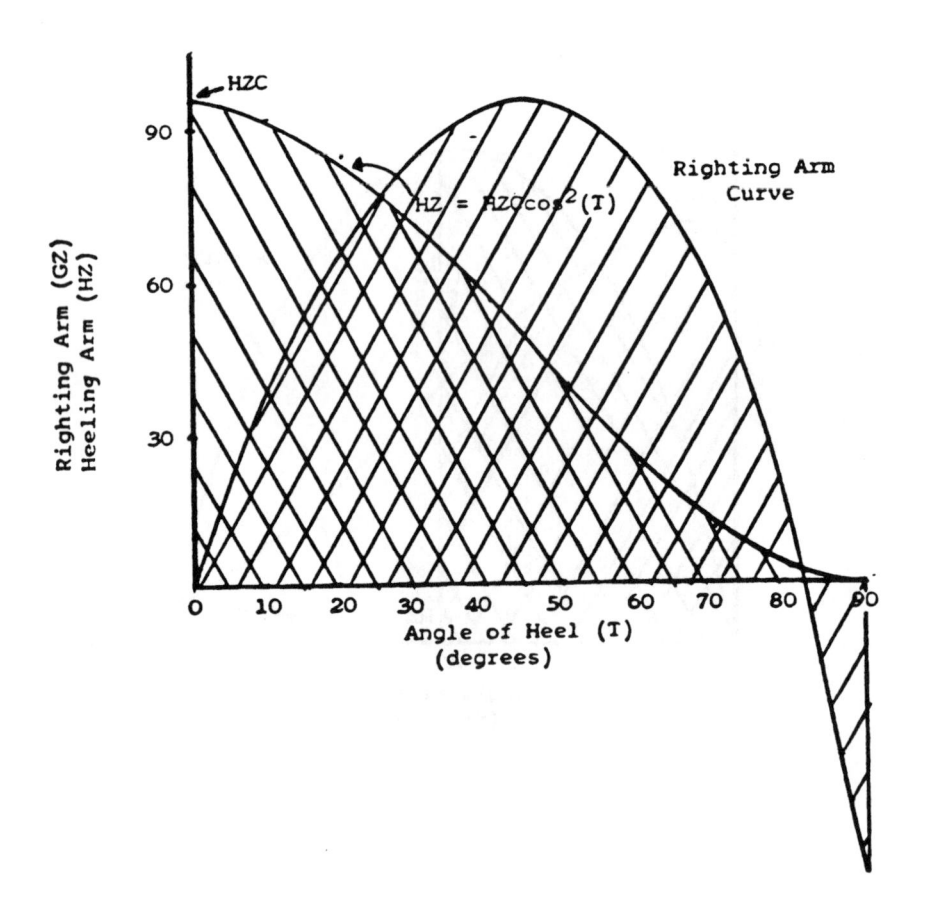

Coast Guard, DHS § 171.057

GRAPH 171.055(e)

Righting Arm Curve is Positive Beyond 90 Degrees

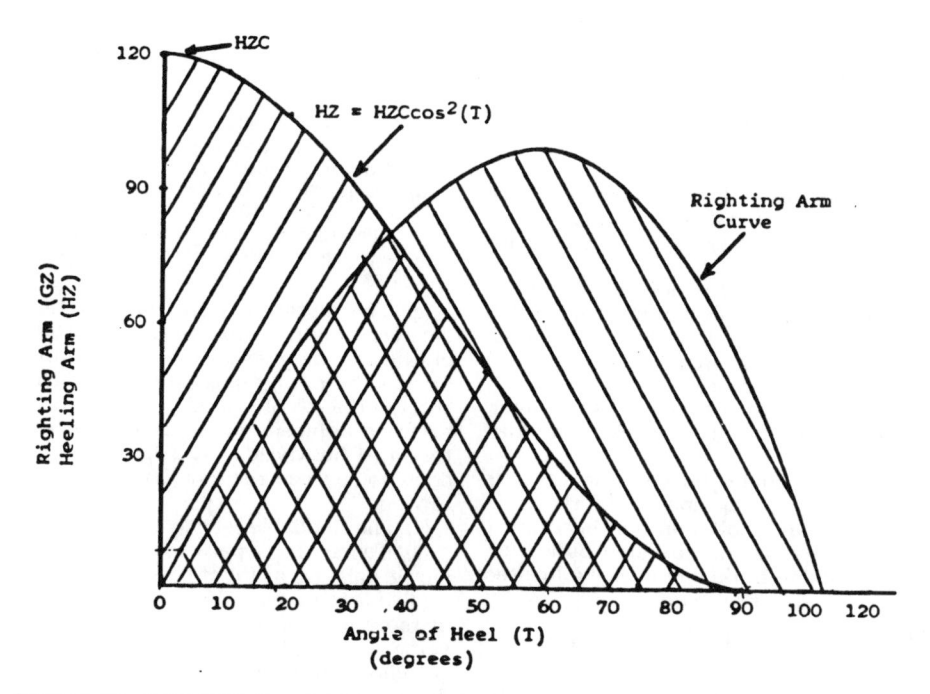

[Graph showing Righting Arm (GZ) / Heeling Arm (HZ) versus Angle of Heel (I) in degrees, with curves labeled HZC, HZ = HZCcos²(I), and Righting Arm Curve]

[CGD 79–023, 48 FR 51017, Nov. 4, 1983, as amended by CGD 83–005, 51, FR 924, Jan. 9, 1986]

§ 171.057 Intact stability requirements for a sailing catamaran.

(a) A sailing vessel that operates on protected waters must be designed to satisfy the following equation:

$$\frac{0.1(W)B}{(As)(Hc)} \geq X$$

Where—

B=the distance between hull centerlines in meters (feet).
As=the maximum sail area in square meters (square feet).
Hc=the height of the center of effort of the sail area above the deck, in meters (feet).
W=the total displacement of the vessel, in kilograms (pounds).
X=4.88 kilograms/square meter (1.0 pounds/square foot).

(b) A sailing vessel that operates on partially protected or exposed waters must be designed to satisfy the following equation:

$$\frac{0.1(W)B}{(As)(Hc)} \geq X$$

Where—

B=the distance between hull centerlines in meters (feet).

123

§ 171.060

As = the maximum sail area in square meters (square feet).
Hc = the height of the center of effort of the sail area above the deck, in meters (feet).
W = the total displacement of the vessel, in kilograms (pounds).
X = 7.32 kilograms/square meter (1.5 pounds/square foot).

[CGD 79–023, 48 FR 51017, Nov. 4, 1983, as amended by CGD 83–005, 51 FR 924, Jan. 9, 1986; CGD 85–080, 61 FR 944, Jan. 10, 1996]

§ 171.060 Watertight subdivision: General.

(a) Each of the following vessels must be shown by design calculations to comply with the requirements in §§ 171.065 through 171.068 for Type I subdivision or § 171.075 for Type III subdivision:

(1) Each vessel 100 gross tons or more on an international voyage: and

(2) Each vessel 150 gross tons or more in ocean service.

(b) Each vessel not described in paragraph (a) of this section must be shown by design calculations to comply with the requirements in §§ 171.070 to 171.073 for Type II subdivision.

(c) Except as allowed in § 171.070(c), each vessel must have a collision bulkhead.

(d) Each double-ended ferry that is required by paragraph (c) of this section to have a collision bulkhead must also have a second collision bulkhead. One collision bulkhead must be located in each end of the vessel.

§ 171.065 Subdivision requirements—Type I.

(a) Except as provided in paragraphs (c) and (f) of this section, the separation between main transverse watertight bulkheads on a vessel, other than one described in paragraph (b) of this section, must not exceed—

(floodable length)×(factor of subdivision)

where—
the factor of subdivision is listed under FS in Table 171.065(a).

(b) The factor of subdivision used to determine compliance with paragraph (a) of this section must be the smaller of 0.5 or the value determined from Table 171.065(a) if—

(1) The vessel is 430 feet (131 meters) or more in LBP; and

(2) The greater of the values of Y as determined by the following equations equals or exceeds the value of X in Table 171.065(b):

$$Y = \frac{(M+2P)}{V}$$

or

$$Y = \frac{(M+2P)}{V + P1 - P}$$

where—

M, V, and P have the same value as listed in Table 171.065(a); and
P1 = the smaller of the following:
  (i) 0.6LN (0.056LN) where—
    N = the total number of passengers; and
    L = LBP in feet (meters).
  (ii) The greater of the following:
    (A) 0.4LN (0.037LN).
    (B) The sum of P and the total volume of passenger spaces above the margin line.

(c) The distance A in Figure 171.065 between main transverse watertight bulkheads may exceed the maximum allowed by paragraphs (a) or (b) of this section if each of the distances B and C between adjacent main transverse watertight bulkheads in Figure 171.065 does not exceed the smaller of the following:

(1) The floodable length.

(2) Twice the separation allowed by paragraphs (a) or (b) of this section.

(d) In each vessel 330 feet (100 meters) or more in LBP, one of the main transverse watertight bulkheads aft of the collision bulkhead must be located at a distance from the forward perpendicular that is not greater than the maximum separation allowed by paragraph (a) or (b) of this section.

(e) The minimum separation between two adjacent main transverse watertight bulkheads must be at least 10 feet (3.05 meters) plus 3 percent of the LBP of the vessel, or 35 feet (10.7 meters), whichever is less.

(f) The maximum separation of bulkheads allowed by paragraphs (a) or (b) of this section may be increased by the amount allowed in paragraph (g) of this section if—

(1) The space between two adjacent main transverse watertight bulkheads contains internal watertight volume; and

Coast Guard, DHS § 171.065

(2) After the assumed side damage specified in paragraph (h) of this section is applied, the internal watertight volume will not be flooded.

(g) For the purpose of paragraph (f) of this section, the allowable increase in separation is as follows:

$$\text{Increase in separation} = \frac{\text{"total volume of allowed local subdivision"}}{\text{"transverse sectional area at center of compartment"}}$$

where—

"total volume of allowed local subdivision" is determined by calculating the unflooded volume on each side of the centerline and multiplying the smaller volume by two.

(h) The assumed extents of side damage are as follows:

(1) *The longitudinal extent of damage* must be assumed to extend over a length equal to the minimum spacing of bulkheads specified in paragraph (e) of this section.

(2) *The transverse extent of damage* must be assumed to penetrate a distance from the shell plating equal to one-fifth the maximum beam of the vessel and at right angles to the centerline at the level of the deepest subdivision load line.

(3) *The vertical extent of damage* must be assumed to extend vertically from the baseline to the margin line.

(i) The maximum separation between the following bulkheads must not exceed the maximum separation between main transverse watertight bulkheads:

(1) The collision bulkhead and the first main transverse watertight bulkhead aft of the collision bulkhead; and

(2) The last main transverse watertight bulkhead and the aftermost point on the bulkhead deck.

(j) The minimum separation between the following bulkheads must not be less than the minimum separation between main transverse watertight bulkheads:

(1) The collision bulkhead and the first main transverse watertight bulkhead aft of the collision bulkhead; and

(2) The last main transverse watertight bulkhead and the aftermost point on the bulkhead deck.

Figure 171.065

Combined Separation of Bulkheads

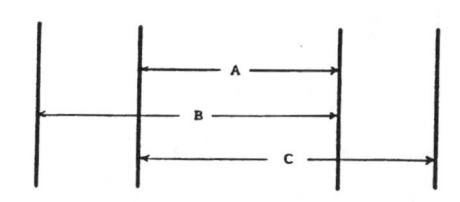

TABLE 171.065(a) (ENGLISH UNITS)

Vessel length (LBP)	Criterion numeral (CN)	FS
Vessel length greater than 392 feet.	CN less than or equal to 23.	A
	CN greater than 23 and less than 123.	F1
	CN greater than or equal to 123.	B
Vessel length greater than or equal to 200 feet and less than or equal to 392 feet.	CN less than or equal to S.	1
	CN greater than S and less than 123.	F2
	CN greater than or equal to 123.	B
Vessel length less than 200 feet.	....	1

Where—

FS=the factor of subdivision.
CN=60((M+2P)/V)+30000(N/L^2)
A=(190/(L−160))+0.18
B=(94/(L−85))+0.18
F1=A−((A−B)(CN−23)/100)
S=(10904−25L)/48
F2=1−((1−B)(CN−S)/(123−S))
L=the length of the vessel (LBP) in feet.
M=the sum of the volume of the machinery space and the volumes of any fuel tanks which are located above the inner bottom forward or aft of the machinery space in cubic feet.
P=the volume of passenger spaces below the margin line.
V=the volume of the vessel below the margin line.
N=the number of passengers that the vessel is to be certificated to carry.

125

§ 171.066

TABLE 171.065(a) (METRIC UNITS)

Vessel length (LBP)	Criterion numeral (CN)	FS
Vessel length greater than 120 meters.	CN lesthan or equal to 23	A
	CN greater than 23 and less than 123.	F1
	CN greater than or equal to 123.	B
Vessel length greater than or equal to 61 meters and less than or equal to 120 meters.	CN less than or equal to S.	1
	CN greater than S and less than 123.	F2
	CN greater than or equal to 123.	B
Vessel length less than 61 meters.	....	1

Where—
FS=the factor of subdivision.
$CN=60((M+2P)/V)+2787(N/L^2)$
$A=(58/(L-49))+0.18$
$B=(29/(L-26))+0.18$
$F1=A-((A-B)(CN-23)/100)$
$S=(3323.5-25L)/14.6$
$F2=1-((1-B)(CN-S)/(123-S))$
L=the length of the vessel (LBP) in meters.
M=the sum of the volume of the machinery space and the volumes of any fuel tanks which are located above the inner bottom forward or aft of the machinery space in cubic meters.
P=the volume of passenger spaces below the margin line.
V=the volume of the vessel below the margin line.
N=the number of passengers that the vessel is to be certificated to carry.

TABLE 171.065(b)—TABLE OF X

Vessel LBP in feet (meters)	X[1]
430 (131)	1.336
440 (134)	1.285
450 (137)	1.230
460 (140)	1.174
470 (143)	1.117
480 (146)	1.060
490 (149)	1.002
500 (152)	0.944
510 (155)	0.885
520 (158)	0.826
530 (162)	0.766
540 (165)	0.706
550 (168)	0.645
554 (169) and up	0.625

[1] Interpolate for intermediate values.

§ 171.066 Calculation of permeability for Type I subdivision.

(a) Except as prescribed in paragraph (b) of this section, the following permeabilities must be used when doing the calculations required to demonstrate compliance with § 171.065(a), (b), and (c):

(1) When doing calculations required to demonstrate compliance with § 171.065(a) and (b), the uniform average permeability given by the formulas in Table 171.066 must be used.

(2) When doing calculations required to demonstrate that compartments on opposite sides of a main transverse watertight bulkhead that bounds the machinery space comply with § 171.065(c), the mean of the uniform average permeabilities determined from Table 171.066 for the two compartments must be used.

(b) If an average permeability can be calculated that is less than that given by the formulas in Table 171.066, the lesser value may be substituted if approved by the Commanding Officer, Marine Safety Center. When determining this lesser value, the following permeabilities must be used:

(1) 95% for passenger, crew, and all other spaces that, in the full load condition, normally contain no cargo, stores, provisions, or mail.

(2) 60% for cargo, stores, provisions, or mail spaces.

(3) 85% for spaces containing machinery.

(4) Values approved by the Commanding Officer, Marine Safety Center for double bottoms, oil fuel, and other tanks.

(c) In the case of unusual arrangements, the Commanding Officer, Marine Safety Center may require a detailed calculation of average permeability for the portions of the vessel forward or aft of the machinery spaces. When doing these calculations, the permeabilities specified in paragraph (b) of this section must be used.

(d) When calculating permeability, the total volume of the 'tween deck spaces between two adjacent main transverse watertight bulkheads that contains any passenger or crew space must be regarded as passenger space volume, except that the volume of any space that is completely enclosed in steel buldheads and is not a crew or passenger space may be excluded.

TABLE 171.066—TABLE OF UNIFORM AVERAGE PERMEABILITIES

Location	Uniform average permeability
Machinery space	10 (a−c) 85+──── v
Volume forward of machinery space	35(a) 63+────

TABLE 171.066—TABLE OF UNIFORM AVERAGE PERMEABILITIES—Continued

Location	Uniform average permeability
	v
Volume aft of machinery space	35(a)
	63+
	v

For each location specified in this table—
  a=volume below the margin line of all spaces that, in the full load condition, normally contain no cargo, baggage, stores, provisions, or mail.
  c=volume below the margin line of the cargo, stores, provisions, or mail spaces within the limits of the machinery space.
  v=total volume below the margin line.

[CGD 79-023, 48 FR 51017, Nov. 4, 1983, as amended by CGD 88-070, 53 FR 34537, Sept. 7, 1988]

§ 171.067 Treatment of stepped and recessed bulkheads in Type I subdivision.

(a) For the purpose of this section—

(1) The main transverse watertight bulkhead immediately forward of a stepped bulkhead is referred to as bulkhead 1; and

(2) The main transverse watertight bulkhead immediately aft of the stepped bulkhead is referred to as bulkhead 3.

(b) If a main transverse watertight bulkhead is stepped, it and bulkheads 1 and 3 must meet one of the following conditions:

(1) The separation between bulkheads 1 and 3 must not exceed the following:

(i) If the factor of subdivision (FS) determined from § 171.065 (a) or (b) is greater than 0.9, the distance between bulkheads 1 and 3 must not exceed the maximum separation calculated to demonstrate compliance with § 171.065.

(ii) If the factor of subdivision is 0.9 or less, the distance between bulkheads 1 and 3 must not exceed 90% of the floodable length or twice the maximum bulkhead separation calculated to demonstrate compliance with § 171.065, whichever is smaller.

(2) Additional watertight bulkheads must be located as shown in Figure 171.067(a) so that distances A, B, C, and D, illustrated in Figure 171.067(a), satisfy the following:

(i) Distances A and B must not exceed the maximum spacing allowed by § 171.065.

(ii) Distances C and D must not be less than the minimum separation prescribed by § 171.065(e).

(3) The distance A, illustrated in Figure 171.067(b), must not exceed the maximum length determined in § 171.065 corresponding to a margin line taken 3 inches (7.6 cm) below the step.

(c) A main transverse bulkhead may not be recessed unless all parts of the recess are inboard from the shell of the vessel a distance A as illustrated in Figure 171.067(c).

(d) Any part of a recess that lies outside the limits defined in paragraph (c) of this section must be treated as a step in accordance with paragraph (b) of this section.

(e) The distance between a main transverse watertight bulkhead and the transverse plane passing through the nearest portion of a recessed bulkhead must be greater than the minimum separation specified by § 171.065(e).

(f) If a main transverse bulkhead is stepped or recessed, equivalent plane bulkheads must be used in the calculations required to demonstrate compliance with § 171.065.

§ 171.067   46 CFR Ch. I (10-1-04 Edition)

Figure 171.067(a)

Additional Subdivision

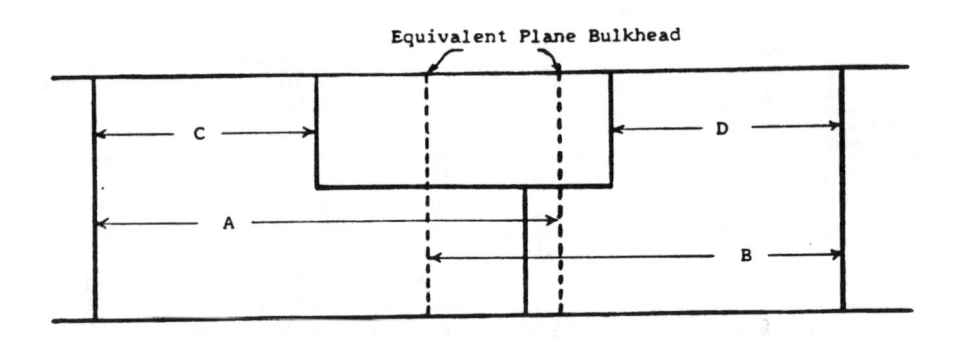

Figure 171.067(b)

Margin Line Below Step

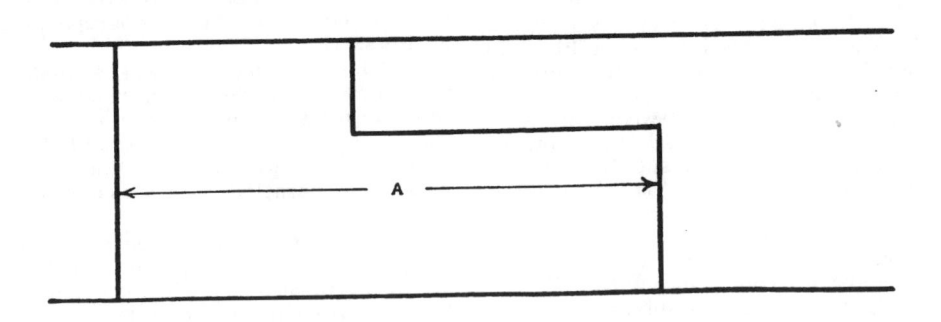

Coast Guard, DHS § 171.068

Figure 171.067(c)

Limits of a Recess

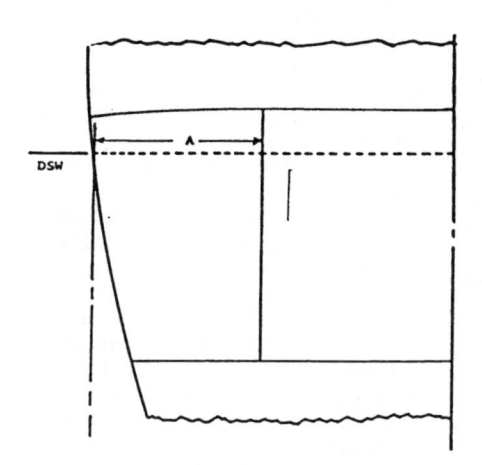

Section Through Recess At ZZ

A = One-fifth the maximum beam measured on the waterline corresponding to the deepest subdivision waterline.

DSW = Deepest subdivision waterline

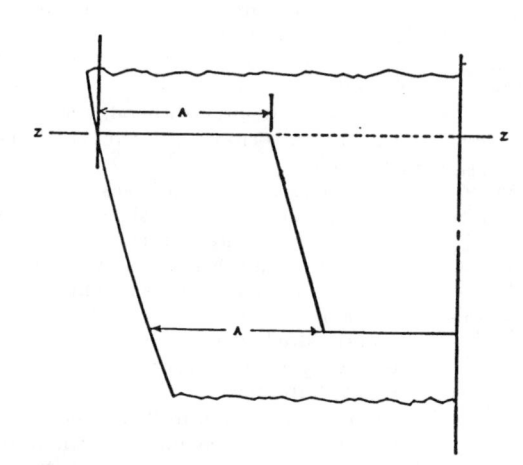

Plan View of Recess at the waterline corresponding to the deepest subdivision waterline

§ 171.068 **Special considerations for Type I subdivision for vessels on short international voyages.**

(a) The calculations done to demonstrate compliance with § 171.065 for a vessel that makes short international voyages and is permitted under § 75.10-10 of this chapter to carry a number of persons on board in excess of the lifeboat capacity must—

(1) Assume the uniform average permeabilities given in Table 171.068 in lieu of those in Table 171.066; and

(2) Use a factor of subdivision (FS) that is the smaller of the following:

(i) The value from Table 171.065(a).

(ii) 0.50.

129

§ 171.070

(b) For a vessel less than 300 feet (91 meters) in length, the Commanding Officer, Marine Safety Center may approve the separation of main transverse watertight bulkheads greater than that permitted by paragraph (a) of this section if—

(1) The shorter separation is impracticable; and

(2) The separation is the smallest that is practicable.

(c) In the case of ships less than 180 feet (55 meters) in length, the Commanding Officer, Marine Safety Center may approve a further relaxation in the bulkhead spacing. However, in no case may the separation be large enough to prevent the vessel from complying with the flooding requirements for Type II subdivision in § 171.070.

TABLE 171.068—TABLE OF UNIFORM AVERAGE PERMEABILITIES

Location	Uniform average permeability
Machinery Space	$\dfrac{10(a-c)}{85+} $ v
Volume Forward of Machinery Space	$\dfrac{35(b)}{95-}$ v
Volume Aft of Machinery Space	$\dfrac{35(b)}{95-}$ v

For each location specified in this table—
a=volume below the margin line of all spaces that, in the full load condition, normally contain no cargo, baggage, stores, provisions, or mail.
b=volume below the margin line and above the tops of floors, inner bottoms, or peak tanks of coal or oil fuel bunkers, chain lockers, fresh water tanks, and of all spaces that, in the full load condition, normally contain stores, baggage, mail, cargo, or provisions. If cargo holds are not occupied by cargo, no part of the cargo space is to be included in this volume.
c=volume below the margin line of the cargo, stores, provisions, or mail spaces within the limits of the machinery space.
v=total volume below the margin line.

[CGD 79–023, 48 FR 51017, Nov. 4, 1983, as amended by CGD 88–070, 53 FR 34537, Sept. 7, 1988]

§ 171.070 Subdivision requirements—Type II.

(a) Each vessel, except a ferry vessel, must be designed so that, while in each condition of loading and operation, it complies with the standard of flooding specified in Table 171.070(a).

(b) Except as provided in paragraph (c), each ferry vessel must be designed so that, while in each condition of loading and operation, it meets the standard of flooding specified in Table 171.070(b).

(c) A ferry vessel described in paragraph (d) of this section need not meet the standard of flooding specified in Table 171.070(b), except that a ferry vessel in Great Lakes service must at least have a collision bulkhead.

(d) Paragraph (c) of this section applies to a ferry vessel that—

(1) Is 150 feet (46 meters) or less in length; and

(2) Has sufficient air tankage, or other internal buoyancy to float the vessel with no part of the margin line submerged when the vessel is completely flooded. If foam is used to comply with this paragraph, it must be installed in accordance with the requirements in § 170.245 of this subchapter.

(e) Except as specified in paragraph (f) of this section, each main transverse watertight bulkhead must be spaced as follows:

(1) If the LBP of the vessel is 143 feet (43.5 meters) or more, each main transverse watertight bulkhead must be at least 10 feet (3 meters) plus 3 percent of the vessel's LBP from—

(i) Every other main transverse watertight bulkhead;

(ii) The collision bulkhead; and

(iii) The aftermost point on the bulkhead deck.

(2) If the LBP of the vessel is less than 143 feet (43.5 meters) and the vessel does not make international voyages, each main transverse watertight bulkhead must be no less than 10 percent of the vessel's LBP or 6 feet (1.8 meters), whichever is greater, from—

(i) Every other main transverse watertight bulkhead;

(ii) The collision bulkhead; and

(iii) The aftermost point on the bulkhead deck.

(f) If a vessel is required by § 171.060 to have a collision bulkhead in each end of the vessel, then each main transverse watertight bulkhead must be no less than the distance specified in paragraph (e) of this section from—

(1) Every other main transverse watertight bulkhead; and

(2) Each collision bulkhead.

Coast Guard, DHS § 171.080

TABLE 171.070(a)—STANDARD OF FLOODING

Passengers carried	Part of vessel	Standard of flooding (compartments)
400 or less	All	1
401 to 600	All of the vessel forward of the first MTWB aft of the collision bulkhead..	2
	All remaining portions of the vessel.	1
601 to 800	All of the vessel forward of the first MTWB that is aft of a point 40% of the vessel's LBP aft of the forward perpendicular.	2
	All remaining portions of the vessel.	1
801 to 1000	All of the vessel forward of the first MTWB that is aft of a point 60% of the vessel's LBP aft of the forward prependicular..	2
	All remaining portions of the vessel.	1
More than 1000	All	2

Where for this table—
"MTWB" means main transverse watertight bulkhead; and "Standard of Flooding" is explained in § 171.017 of this subchapter.

TABLE 171.070(b)—STANDARD OF FLOODING FOR FERRY VESSELS

Vessel length	Part of vessel	Standard of flooding (compartments)
150 feet (46 meters) or less.	All	1
Greater than 150 feet (46 meters) and less than or equal to 200 feet (61 meters).	All of the vessel forward of the first MTWB aft of the collision bulkhead.	2
	All of the vessel aft of the first MTWB forward of the aft peak bulkhead.	2
	All remaining portions of the vessel.	1
Greater than 200 feet (61 meters).	All	2

Where for this table—
"MTWB" means main transverse watertight bulkhead; and "Standard of Flooding" is explained in § 171.017 of this subchapter.

§ 171.072 Calculation of permeability for Type II subdivision.

When doing calcualtions to show compliance with § 171.070, the following uniform average permeabilities must be assumed:

(a) 85 percent in the machinery space.
(b) 60 percent in the following spaces:
(1) Tanks that are normally filled when the vessel is in the full load condition.
(2) Chain lockers.
(3) Cargo spaces.
(4) Stores spaces.
(5) Mail or baggage spaces.
(c) 95 percent in all other spaces.

§ 171.073 Treatment of stepped and recessed bulkheads in Type II subdivision.

(a) A main transverse watertight bulkhead may not be stepped unless additional watertight bulkheads are located as shown in Figure 171.067(a) so that the distances A, B, C, and D illustrated in Figure 171.067(a) comply with the following:
(1) A and B must not exceed the maximum bulkhead spacing that permits compliance with § 171.070; and
(2) C and D must not be less than the minimum spacing specified in § 171.070(e).
(b) A main transverse watertight bulkhead may not be recessed unless all parts of the recess are inboard from the shell of the vessel as illustrated in Figure 171.067(c).
(c) If a main transverse watertight bulkhead is recessed or stepped, an equivalent plane bulkhead must be used in the calculations required by § 171.070.

§ 171.075 Subdivision requirements—Type III.

(a) Each vessel must be shown by design calculations to comply with the requirements of Regulations 1, 2, 3, 4, 6, and 7 of the Annex to Resolution A.265 (VIII) of the International Maritime Organization (IMO).
(b) International Maritime Organization Resolution A.265 (VIII) is incorporated by reference into this part.
(c) As used in IMO Resolution A.265 (VIII), "Administration" means the Commandant, U.S. Coast Guard.

§ 171.080 Damage stability standards for vessels with Type I or Type II subdivision.

(a) *Calculations.* Each vessel with Type I or Type II subdivision must be

§ 171.080

shown by design calculations to meet the survival conditions in paragraph (e), (f), or (g) of this section in each condition of loading and operation assuming the extent and character of damage specified in paragraph (b) of this section.

(b) *Extent and character of damage.* For the purpose of paragraph (a) of this section, design calculations must assume that the damage—

(1) Has the character specified in Table 171.080(a); and

(2) Consists of a penetration having the dimensions specified in Table 171.080(a) except that, if the most disabling penetration would be less than the penetration described in the table, the smaller penetration must be assumed.

(c) *Permeability.* When doing the calculations required in paragraph (a) of this section, the permeability of each space must be calculated in a manner approved by the Commanding Officer, Marine Safety Center or be taken from Table 171.080(c).

(d) *Definitions.* For the purposes of paragraphs (e) and (f) of this section, the following definitions apply:

(1) *New vessel* means a vessel—

(i) For which a building contract is placed on or after April 15, 1996;

(ii) In the absence of a building contract, the keel of which is laid, or which is at a similar stage of construction, on or after April 15, 1996;

(iii) The delivery of which occurs on or after January 1, 1997;

(iv) Application for the reflagging of which is made on or after January 1, 1997; or

(v) That has undergone—

(A) A major conversion for which the conversion contract is placed on or after April 15, 1996;

(B) In the absence of a contract, a major conversion begun on or after April 15, 1996; or

(C) A major conversion completed on or after January 1, 1997.

(2) *Existing vessel* means other than a new vessel.

(3) *Watertight* means capable of preventing the passage of water through the structure in any direction under a head of water for which the surrounding structure is designed.

(4) *Weathertight* means capable of preventing the penetration of water, even boarding seas, into the vessel in any sea condition.

(e) *Damage survival for all existing vessels except those vessels authorized to carry more than 12 passengers on an international voyage requiring a SOLAS Passenger Ship Safety Certificate.* An existing vessel is presumed to survive assumed damage if it meets the following conditions in the final stage of flooding:

(1) On a vessel required to survive assumed damage with a longitudinal extent of 10 feet (3 meters) plus 0.03L, the final angle of equilibrium must not exceed 7 degrees after equalization, except that the final angle may be as large as 15 degrees if—

(i) The vessel is not equipped with equalization or is equipped with fully automatic equalization; and

(ii) The Commanding Officer, Marine Safety Center approves the vessel's range of stability in the damaged condition.

(2) On a vessel required to survive assumed damage with a longitudinal extent of 20 feet (6.1 meters) plus 0.04L, the angle of equilibrium must not exceed 15 degrees after equalization.

(3) The margin line may not be submerged at any point.

(4) The vessel's metacentric height (GM) must be at least 2 inches (5 cm) when the vessel is in the upright position.

(f) *Damage survival for all new vessels except those vessels authorized to carry more than 12 passengers on an international voyage requiring a SOLAS Passenger Ship Safety Certificate.* A new vessel is presumed to survive assumed damage if it is shown by calculations to meet the conditions set forth in paragraphs (f) (1) through (7) of this section in the final stage of flooding and to meet the conditions set forth in paragraphs (f) (8) and (9) of this section in each intermediate stage of flooding. For the purposes of establishing boundaries to determine compliance with the requirements in paragraphs (f) (1) through (9), openings that are fitted with weathertight closures and that are not submerged during any stage of flooding will not be considered downflooding points.

Coast Guard, DHS § 171.080

(1) Each vessel must have positive righting arms for a minimum range beyond the angle of equilibrium as follows:

Vessel service	Required range (degrees)
Exposed waters, oceans, or Great Lakes winter ..	15
Partially protected waters or Great Lakes summer	10
Protected waters	5

(2) No vessel may have any opening through which downflooding can occur within the minimum range specified by paragraph (f)(1) of this section.

(3) Each vessel must have an area under each righting-arm curve of at least 0.015 meter-radians, measured from the angle of equilibrium to the smaller of the following angles:

(i) The angle at which downflooding occurs.

(ii) The angle of vanishing stability.

(4) Except as provided by paragraph (f)(5) of this section, each vessel must have within the positive range the greater of a righting arm (GZ) equal to or greater than 0.10 meter or a GZ as calculated using the formula:

$$GZ(m) = C\left(\frac{\text{Heeling Moment}}{\Delta} + 0.04\right)$$

where—

C=1.00 for vessels on exposed waters, oceans, or Great Lakes winter;
C=0.75 for vessels on partially protected waters or Great Lakes summer;
C=0.50 for vessels on protected waters;
Δ=intact displacement; and
Heeling moment=greatest of the heeling moments as calculated in paragraphs (f)(4)(i) through (iv) of this section.

(i) The passenger heeling moment is calculated using the formula:

Passenger Heeling Moment=0.5 (n w b)

where—

n=number of passengers;
w=passenger weight = 75 kilograms; and
b=distance from the centerline of the vessel to the geometric center on one side of the centerline of the passenger deck used to leave the vessel in case of flooding.

(ii) The heeling moment due to asymmetric escape routes for passengers, if the vessel has asymmetric escape routes for passengers, is calculated assuming that—

(A) Each passenger weighs 75 kilograms;

(B) Each passenger occupies 0.25 square meter of deck area; and

(C) All passengers are distributed, on available deck areas unoccupied by permanently affixed objects, toward one side of the vessel on the decks where passengers would move to escape from the vessel in case of flooding, so that they produce the most adverse heeling moment.

(iii) The heeling moment due to the launching of survival craft is calculated assuming that—

(A) All survival craft, including davit-launched liferafts and rescue boats, fitted on the side to which the vessel heels after sustained damage, are swung out if necessary, fully loaded and ready for lowering;

(B) Persons not in the survival craft swung out and ready for lowering are distributed about the centerline of the vessel so that they do not provide additional heeling or righting moments; and

(C) Survival craft on the side of the vessel opposite that to which the vessel heels remain stowed.

(iv) The heeling moment due to wind pressure is calculated assuming that—

(A) The wind exerts a pressure of 120 Newtons per square meter;

(B) The wind acts on an area equal to the projected lateral area of the vessel above the waterline corresponding to the intact condition; and

(C) The lever arm of the wind is the vertical distance from a point at one-half the mean draft, or the center of area below the waterline, to the center of the lateral area.

(5) Each vessel whose arrangements do not generally allow port or starboard egress may be exempted, by the Commanding Officer, Marine Safety Center, from the transverse passenger heeling moment required by paragraph (f)(4)(i) of this section. Each vessel exempted must have sufficient longitudinal stability to prevent immersion of the deck edge during forward or aft egress.

(6) Each vessel must have an angle of equilibrium that does not exceed—

(i) 7 degrees for flooding of one compartment;

133

§ 171.080

(ii) 12 degrees for flooding of two compartments; or

(iii) A maximum of 15 degrees for flooding of one or two compartments where—

(A) The vessel has positive righting arms for at least 20 degrees beyond the angle of equilibrium; and

(B) The vessel has an area under each righting-arm curve, when the equilibrium angle is between 7 degrees and 15 degrees, in accordance with the formula:

$$A \geq 0.0025(\theta - 1)$$

where—

A=Area required in m-rad under each righting-arm curve measured from the angle of equilibrium to the smaller of either the angle at which downflooding occurs or the angle of vanishing stability.
θ=actual angle of equilibrium in degrees

(7) The margin line of the vessel must not be submerged when the vessel is in equilibrium.

(8) Each vessel must have a maximum angle of equilibrium that does not exceed 15 degrees during intermediate stages of flooding.

(9) Each vessel must have a range of stability and a maximum righting arm during each intermediate stage of flooding as follows:

Vessel service	Required range (degrees)	Required maximum righting arm
Exposed waters, oceans, or Great Lakes winter	7	0.05 m
Partially-protected waters or Great Lakes summer	5	0.035 m
Protected waters	5	0.035 m

Only one breach in the hull and only one free surface need be assumed when meeting the requirements of this paragraph.

(g) *Damage survival for vessels authorized to carry more than 12 passengers on an international voyage requiring a SOLAS Passenger Ship Safety Certificate.* A vessel is presumed to survive assumed damage if it is shown by calculations to comply with the damage stability required for that vessel by the International Convention for the Safety of Life at Sea, 1974, as amended, chapter II-1, part B, regulation 8.

(h) *Equalization.* (1) Equalization systems on vessels of 150 gross tons or more in ocean service must meet the following:

(i) Equalization must be automatic except that the Commanding Officer, Marine Safety Center may approve other means of equalization if—

(A) It is impracticable to make equalization automatic; and

(B) Controls to cross-flooding equipment are located above the bulkhead deck.

(ii) Equalization must be fully accomplished within 15 minutes after damage occurs.

(2) Equalization on vessels under 150 gross tons in ocean service and on all vessels in other than ocean service must meet the follmwing:

(i) Equalization must not depend on the operation of valves.

(ii) Equalization must be fully accomplished within 15 minutes after damage occurs.

(3) The estimated maximum angle mf heel before equalization must be approved by the Commanding Officer, Marine Safety Center.

TABLE 171.080(a)—EXTENT AND CHARACTER OF DAMAGE

Vessel designator [1]	Longitudinal penetration [2]	Transverse penetration [3,4]	Vertical penetration	Character of Damage
Z	10 feet (3 meters) plus).03L or 35 feet (10.7 meters) whichever is less.[5]	B/5	from the baseline upward without limit.	Assumes no damage to any main transverse watertight bulkhead.
Y	10 feet (3 meters) plus)0.03L or 35 feet (10.7 meters) whichever is less.	B/5	From the baseline upward without limit.	Assumes damage to no more than one main transverse watertight bulkhead.
X	10 feet (3 meters) plus)0.03L or 35 feet (10.7 meters) whichever is less.	B/5	from the baseline upward without limit.	Assumes damage to no more than one main transverse watertight bulkhead.
	20 feet (6.1 meters) plus 0.04L	B/5	From the top of the double bottom upward without limit.	Assumes damage to no more than one main transverse watertight bulkhead.

Coast Guard, DHS § 171.085

TABLE 171.080(a)—EXTENT AND CHARACTER OF DAMAGE—Continued

Vessel designator [1]	Longitudinal penetration [2]	Transverse penetration [3,4]	Vertical penetration	Character of Damage
W	20 feet (6.1 meters) plus 0.04L	B/5	From the baseline upward without limit.	Assumes damage to at least two main transverse watertight bulkheads.

([1]) W,X,Y, and Z are determined from Table 171.080(b).
([2]) L=LBP of the vessel in feet (meters).
([3]) B=the beam of the vessel in feet (meters) measured at or below the deepest subdivision load line as defined in 171.010(a) except that, when doing calculations for a vessel that operates only on inland waters or a ferry vessel, B may be taken as the mean of the maximum beam on the bulkhead deck and the maximum beam at the deepest subdivision load line.
([4]) The transverse penetration is applied inboard from the side of the vessel, at right angles to the centerline, at the level of the deepest subdivision load line.
([5]) .1L or 6 feet (1.8 meters) whichever is greater for vessels described in § 171.070(e)(2).

TABLE 171.080(b)

Vessel category	Vessel designator
Vessels with type I subdivision and a factor of subdivision as determined from § 171.065 (a) or (b) of 0.33 or less.	W.
Vessels with type I subdivision and a factor of subdivision as determined from § 171.065 (a) or (b) greater than 0.33 and less than or equal to 0.50.	X.
Vessels with Type II subdivision that are required to meet a two compartment standard of flooding.	Y.
All other vessels	Z.

TABLE 171.080(c)—PERMEABILITY

Spaces and tanks	Permeability (percent
Cargo, coal, stores	60.
Accommodations	95.
Machinery	85.
Tanks	0 or 95.[1]

[1] Whichever value results in the more disabling condition.

[CGD 79-023, 48 FR 51017, Nov. 4, 1983, as amended by CGD 88-070, 53 FR 34537, Sept. 7, 1988; CGD 89-037, 57 FR 41826, Sept. 11, 1992; CGD 94-010, 60 FR 53713, Oct. 17, 1995; CGD 97-057, 62 FR 51049, Sept. 30, 1997]

§ 171.082 **Damage stability standards for vessels with Type III subdivision.**

(a) Each vessel must be shown by design calculations to comply with the requirements of Regulations 1 and 5 of the Annex to Resolution A.265 (VIII) of the International Maritime Organization (IMO).

(b) International Maritime Organization Resolution A.265 (VIII) is incorporated by reference into this part.

(c) As used in IMO Resolution A.265 (VIII), "Administration" means the Commandant, U.S. Coast Guard.

(d) Section 56.50-57 of this chapter contains additional requirements on bilge pumping and piping systems.

Subpart D—Additional Subdivision Requirements

§ 171.085 **Collision bulkhead.**

(a) Paragraphs (b) through (g) of this section apply to each vessel of 100 gross tons or more and paragraphs (h) through (j) of this section apply to each vessel that is less than 100 gross tons.

(b) The portion of the collision bulkhead that is below the bulkhead deck must be watertight.

(c) Each portion of the collision bulkhead must be at least—

(1) 5 percent of the LBP from the forward perpendicular in a motor vessel; and

(2) 5 feet (1.52 meters) from the forward perpendicular in a steam vessel.

(d) The collision bulkhead must be no more than 10 feet (3 meters) plus 5 percent of the LBP from the forward perpendicular.

(e) The collision bulkhead must extend to the deck above the bulkhead deck if the vessel—

(1) Is in ocean service; and

(2) Has a superstructure that extends from a point forward of the collision bulkhead to a point at least 15 percent of the LBP aft of the collision bulkhead.

(f) The collision bulkhead required by paragraph (e) of this section must have the following characteristics:

(1) The portion of the collision bulkhead above the bulkhead deck must be weathertight.

(2) If the portion of the collision bulkhead above the bulkhead deck is

135

§ 171.090

not located directly above the collision bulkhead below the bulkhead deck, then the bulkhead deck between must be weathertight.

(g) Each opening in the collision bulkhead must—
(1) Be located above the bulkhead deck; and
(2) Have a watertight closure.

(h) Each collision bulkhead—
(1) Must extend to the deck above the bulkhead deck if in ocean service as defined in § 170.050(f) of this chapter or to the bulkhead deck if in service on other waters;
(2) May not have watertight doors in it; and
(3) May have penetrations and openings that—
(i) Are located as high and as far inboard as practicable; and
(ii) Except as provided in paragraph (i) of this section, have means to make them watertight.

(i) Each vessel that is not required to comply with a one or two compartment standard of flooding may have an opening that cannot be made watertight in the collision bulkhead below the bulkhead deck if—
(1) The lowest edge of the opening is not more than 12 inches (30.5 centimeters) below the bulkhead deck; and
(2) There are at least 36 inches (92 centimeters) of intact collision bulkhead below the lower edge of the opening.

(j) Each portion of the collision bulkhead must be—
(1) At least 5 percent of the LBP from the forward perpendicular; and
(2) No more than 15 percent of the LBP from the forward perpendicular if the space forward of the collision bulkhead is not subject to damage stability requirements and at any location aft of the location described in paragraph (j)(1) of this section if the space forward of the collision bulkhead is subject to damage stability requirements.

[CGD 79–023, 48 FR 51017, Nov. 4, 1983, as amended by CGD 85–080, 61 FR 945, Jan. 10, 1996]

§ 171.090 Aft peak bulkhead.

(a) Each of the following vessels must have an aft peak bulkhead:
(1) Each vessel 100 gross tons or more on an international voyage.
(2) Each other vessel of more than 150 gross tons.

(b) Except as specified in paragraph (c) of this section, each portion of the aft peak bulkhead below the bulkhead deck must be watertight.

(c) A vessel may have an aft peak bulkhead that does not intersect the bulkhead deck if approved by the Commanding Officer, Marine Safety Center.

[CGD 79–023, 48 FR 51017, Nov. 4, 1983, as amended by CGD 88–070, 53 FR 34537, Sept. 7, 1988]

§ 171.095 Machinery space bulkhead.

(a) This section applies to each vessel of 100 gross tons or more.

(b) Except as provided in paragraph (c) of this section, a vessel required to have Type I or II subdivision must have enough main transverse watertight bulkheads to separate the machinery space from the remainder of the vessel. All portions of these bulkheads must be watertight below the bulkhead deck.

(c) Compliance with paragraph (b) of this section is not required if the vessel has sufficient air tanks or other internal buoyancy to maintain the vessel afloat while in the full load condition when all compartments and all other tanks are flooded. If foam is used to comply with this paragraph, it must be installed in accordance with the requirements in § 170.245 of this subchapter.

§ 171.100 Shaft tunnels and stern tubes.

(a) Stern tubes in each of the following vessels must be enclosed in watertight spaces:
(1) Each vessel of 100 gross tons or more on an international voyage.
(2) Each other vessel over 150 gross tons in ocean or Great Lakes service.
(3) Each vessel under 100 gross tons that carries more than 12 passengers on an international voyage.

(b) The watertight seal in the bulkhead between the stern tube space and the machinery space must be located in a watertight shaft tunnel. The vessel must be designed so that the margin line will not be submerged when the watertight shaft tunnel is flooded.

(c) If a vessel has two or more shaft tunnels, they must be connected by a watertight passageway.

Coast Guard, DHS § 171.105

(d) If a vessel has two or less shaft tunnels, only one door is permitted between them and the machinery space. If a vessel has more then two shaft tunnels, only two doors are permitted between them and the machinery space.

§ 171.105   Double bottoms.

(a) This section applies to each vessel that carries more than 12 passengers on an international voyage and all other vessels that are—

(1) 100 gross tons or more; and

(2) In ocean or Great Lakes service.

(b) Each vessel over 165 feet (50 meters) and under 200 feet (61 meters) in LBP must have a double bottom that extends from the forward end of the machinery space to the fore peak bulkhead.

(c) Each vessel over 200 feet (61 meters) and under 249 feet (76 meters) in LBP must have a double bottom that extends from the fore peak bulkhead to the forward end of the machinery space and a double bottom that extends from the aft peak bulkhead to the aft end of the machinery space.

(d) Each vessel 249 feet (76 meters) in LBP and upward must have a double bottom that extends from the fore to the aft peak bulkhead.

(e) Each double bottom required by this section must be at least the depth at the centerline given by the following equation:

$D=18.0+0.05(L)$ inches

$D=45.7+0.417(L)$ centimeters

where—

D=the depth at the centerline in inches (centimeters).

L=LBP in feet (meters).

(f) The line formed by the intersection of the margin plate and the bilge plating must be above the horizontal plane C, illustrated in Figure 171.105, at all points. The horizontal plane C is defined by point B, located, as shown in Figure 171.105, in the midships section.

Figure 171.105

Lower Limit of the Intersection of Margin Plate and Bilge Plating

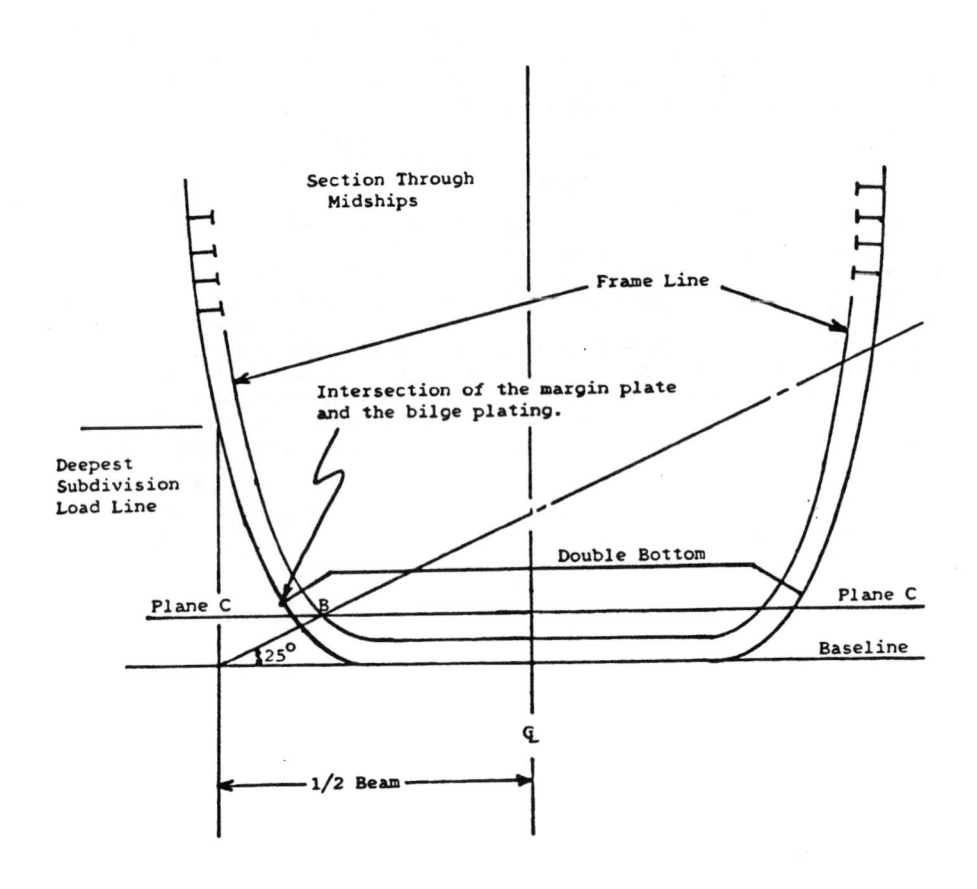

(g) A double bottom is not required in a tank that is integral with the hull of a vessel if—

(1) The tank is used exclusively for the carriage of liquids; and

(2) It is approved by the Commanding Officer, Marine Safety Center.

(h) A double bottom is not required in any part of a vessel where the separation of main transverse watertight bulkheads is governed by a factor of subdivision less than or equal to 0.50 if—

(1) The Commanding Officer, Marine Safety Center approves;

(2) The vessel makes short international voyages; and

(3) The vessel is permitted by §75.10–10 of this chapter to carry a number of passengers in excess of the lifeboat capacity.

[CGD 79–023, 48 FR 51017, Nov 4. 1983, as amended by CGD 88–070, 53 FR 34532, Sept. 7, 1988]

§171.106 Wells in double bottoms.

(a) This section applies to each vessel that has a well installed in a double bottom required by §171.105.

Coast Guard, DHS § 171.112

(b) Except as provided in paragraph (c) of this section—

(1) The depth of a well must be at least 18 inches (45.7 cm) less than the depth of the double bottom at the centerline; and

(2) The well may not extend below the horizontal plane C illustrated in Figure 171.105.

(c) A well may extend to the outer bottom of a double bottom at the after end of a shaft tunnel.

§ 171.108 Manholes in double bottoms.

(a) The number of manholes in the inner bottom of a double bottom required by § 171.105 must be reduced to the minimum required for adequate access.

(b) Each manhole must have a cover that can be—

(1) Made watertight; and

(2) Protected from damage by cargo or coal.

§ 171.109 Watertight floors in double bottoms.

If a vessel is required to have a double bottom, a watertight transverse division must be located in the double bottom under each main transverse watertight bulkhead or as near as practicable to the main transverse watertight bulkhead. If a vessel also has duct keels, the transverse divisions need not extend across them.

Subpart E—Penetrations and Openings in Watertight Bulkheads

§ 171.110 Specific applicability.

(a) Sections 171.111, 171.112, and 171.113 apply to each vessel of 100 gross tons or more.

(b) Section 171.114 applies to each vessel under 100 gross tons.

[CGD 79–023, 48 FR 51017, Nov. 4, 1983, as amended by CGD 85–080, 61 FR 945, Jan. 10, 1996; 62 FR 51353, Sept. 30, 1997]

§ 171.111 Penetrations and openings in watertight bulkheads in vessels of 100 gross tons or more.

(a) Except as provided in paragraph (f) of this section, each opening in a watertight bulkhead must have a means to close it watertight.

(b) Except in a machinery space, the means for closing each opening may not be by bolted portable plates.

(c) If a main transverse watertight bulkhead is penetrated, the penetration must be made watertight. Lead or other heat sensitive materials must not be used in a system that penetrates a main transverse watertight bulkhead if fire damage to this system would reduce the watertight integrity of the bulkhead.

(d) A main transverse watertight bulkhead must not be penetrated by valves or cocks unless they are a part of a piping system.

(e) If a pipe, scupper, or electric cable passes through a main transverse watertight bulkhead, the opening through which it passes must be watertight.

(f) A main transverse watertight bulkhead may not have non-watertight penetrations below the bulkhead deck unless—

(1) The margin line is more than 9 inches (23 centimeters) below the bulkhead deck at the intersection of the margin line and the line formed by the intersection of the plane of the main transverse watertight bulkhead and the shell; and

(2) Making all penetrations watertight is impracticable.

(g) Penetrations approved in accordance with paragraph (f) of this section must comply with the following:

(1) The bottom of the penetration must not be located—

(i) More than 24 inches (61 centimeters) below the bulkhead deck; nor

(ii) Less than 9 inches (23 centimeters) above the margin line.

(2) The penetration must not be located outboard from the centerline more than ¼ of the beam of the vessel measured—

(i) On the bulkhead deck; and

(ii) In the vertical plane of the penetration.

(h) No doors, manholes, or other access openings may be located in a watertight bulkhead that separates two cargo spaces or a cargo space and a permanent or reserve bunker.

§ 171.112 Watertight door openings.

(a) The opening for a watertight door must be located as high in the bulkhead and as far inboard as practicable.

§ 171.113

(b) No more than one door, other than a door to a bunker or shaft alley, may be fitted in a main transverse watertight bulkhead within spaces containing the following:

(1) Main and auxiliary propulsion machinery.
(2) Propulsion boilers.
(3) Permanent bunkers.

§ 171.113 Trunks.

(a) For the purpose of this section, "trunk" means a large enclosed passageway through any deck or bulkhead of a vessel.

(b) Each trunk, other than those specified in paragraph (c) of this section, must have a watertight door at each end except that a trunk may have a watertight door at one end if—

(1) The trunk does not pass through more than one main compartment;
(2) The sides of the trunk are not nearer to the shell than is permitted by § 171.067(c) for the sides of a recess in a bulkhead; and
(3) The vessel complies with the subdivision requirements in this part when the volume of the trunk is included with the volume of the compartment into which it opens.

(c) Each trunk that provides access from a crew accommodation space and that passes through a main transverse watertight bulkhead must comply with the following:

(1) The trunk must be watertight.
(2) The trunk, if used for passage at sea, must have at least one end above the margin line and access to the other end of the trunk must be through a watertight door.
(3) The trunk must not pass through the first main transverse watertight bulkhead aft of the collision bulkhead.

§ 171.114 Penetrations and openings in watertight bulkheads in a vessel less than a 100 gross tons.

(a) Penetrations and openings in watertight bulkheads must—

(1) Be kept as high and as far inboard as practicable; and
(2) Have means to make them watertight.

(b) Watertight bulkheads must not have sluice valves.

(c) Each main traverse watertight bulkhead must extend to the bulkhead deck.

[CGD 85–080, 62 FR 51353, Sept. 30, 1997]

Subpart F—Openings in the Side of a Vessel Below the Bulkhead or Weather Deck

§ 171.115 Specific applicability.

(a) Sections 171.116, 171.117, and 171.118 apply to each vessel of 100 gross tons or more.

(b) Section 171.119 applies to each vessel under 100 gross tons.

[CGD 79–023, 48 FR 51017, Nov. 4, 1983, as amended by CGD 85–080, 61 FR 945, Jan. 10, 1996; 62 FR 51353, Sept. 30, 1997]

§ 171.116 Port lights.

(a) A vessel may have port lights below the bulkhead deck if—

(1) It is greater than 150 gross tons; and
(2) It is in ocean service.

(b) All port lights in a space must be non-opening if the sill of any port light in that space is below a line that—

(1) Is drawn parallel to the line formed by the intersection of the bulkhead deck and the shell of the vessel; and
(2) Has its lowest point 2½ percent of the beam of the vessel above the deepest subdivision load line.

(c) For the purpose of paragraph (b) of this section, the beam of the vessel is measured at or below the deepest subdivision load line.

(d) Except as provided in paragraph (e) of this section, no port light may be located in a space that is used exclusively for the carriage of cargo, stores, or coal.

(e) A port light may be located in a space used alternately for the carriage of cargo or passengers.

(f) Each port light installed below the bulkhead deck must conform to the following requirements:

(1) The design of each port light must be approved by the Commanding Officer, Marine Safety Center.
(2) Each non-opening port light must be watertight.
(3) Each opening port light must be constructed so that it can be secured watertight.

Coast Guard, DHS § 171.119

(4) Each opening port light must be installed with at least one bolt that is secured by a round slotted or recessed nut that requires a special wrench to remove. The nut must be protected by a sleeve or guard to prevent it from being removed with ordinary tools.

[CGD 79–023, 48 FR 51017, Nov. 4, 1983, as amended by CGD 88–070, 53 FR 34537, Sept. 7, 1988]

§ 171.117 Dead covers.

(a) Except as provided in paragraph (b) of this section, each port light with the sill located below the margin line must have a hinged, inside dead cover.

(b) The dead cover on a port light located in an accommodation space for passengers other than steerage passengers may be portable if—

(1) The apparatus for stowing the dead cover is adjacent to its respective port light;

(2) The port light is located above the deck that is immediately above the deepest subdivision load line;

(3) The port light is aft of a point one-eighth of the LBP of the vessel from the forward perpendicular; and

(4) The port light is above a line that—

(i) Is parallel to the line formed by the intersection of the bulkhead deck and the side of the vessel; and

(ii) Has its lowest point at a height of 12 feet (3.66 meters) plus 2½ percent of the beam of the vessel above the deepest subdivision load line.

(c) For the purpose of paragraph (b) of this section, the beam of the vessel is measured at or below the deepest subdivision load line.

(d) Each dead cover must be designed so that—

(1) It can be secured watertight; and

(2) It is not necessary to release any of the special nuts required in § 171.116(f)(4) in order to secure the dead cover.

§ 171.118 Automatic ventilators and side ports.

(a) An automatic ventilator must not be fitted in the side of a vessel below the bulkhead deck unless approved by the Commanding Officer, Marine Safety Center.

(b) The design and construction of each gangway, cargo and coaling port, and similar opening in the side of a vessel must be approved by the Commanding Officer, Marine Safety Center.

(c) In no case may the lowest point of any gangway, cargo and coaling port, or similar opening be below the deepest subdivision load line.

[CGD 79–023, 48 FR 51017, Nov. 4, 1983, as amended by CGD 88–070, 53 FR 34537, Sept. 7, 1988]

§ 171.119 Openings below the weather deck in the side of a vessel less than 100 gross tons.

(a) If a vessel operates on exposed or partially protected waters, an opening port light is not permitted below the weather deck unless—

(1) The sill is at least 30 inches (76.2 centimeters) above the deepest subdivision load line; and

(2) It has an inside, hinged dead cover.

(b) Except for engine exhausts, each inlet or discharge pipe that penetrates the hull below a line drawn parallel to and at least 6 inches (15.2 centimeters) above the deepest subdivision load line must have means to prevent water from entering the vessel if the pipe fractures or otherwise fails.

(c) A positive action valve or cock that is located as close as possible to the hull is an acceptable means for complying with paragraph (b) of this section.

(d) If an inlet or discharge pipe is inaccessible, the means for complying with paragraph (b) of this section must be a shut-off valve that is—

(1) Operable from the weather deck or other accessible location above the bulkhead deck; and

(2) Labeled at the operating point for identity and direction of closing.

(e) Any connecting device or valve in a hull penetration must not be cast iron.

(f) Each plug cock in an inlet or discharge pipe must have a means, other than a cotter pin, to prevent its loosening or removal from the body.

[CGD 85–080, 62 FR 51353, Sept. 30, 1997]

Subpart G—Watertight Integrity Above the Margin Line

§ 171.120 Specific applicability.

Each vessel that is 100 gross tons or more must comply with § 171.122 and each vessel under 100 gross tons must comply with § 171.124.

[CGD 85–080, 62 FR 51354, Sept. 30, 1997]

§ 171.122 Watertight integrity above the margin line in a vessel of 100 gross tons or more.

(a) For the purpose of this section, a partial watertight bulkhead is one in which all portions are not watertight.

(b) Except as provided in paragraph (d) of this section, the bulkhead deck or a deck above it must be weathertight.

(c) Partial watertight bulkheads or web frames must be located in the immediate vicinity of main transverse watertight bulkheads to minimize as much as practicable the entry and spread of water above the bulkhead deck.

(d) If a partial watertight bulkhead or web frame is located on the bulkhead deck in order to comply with paragraph (c) of this section, the joint between it and the shell and bulkhead deck must be watertight.

(e) If a partial watertight bulkhead does not line up with a main transverse watertight bulkhead below the bulkhead deck, the bulkhead deck between them must be watertight.

(f) Each opening in an exposed weather deck must—

(1) Have a coaming that complies with the height requirements in table 171.124(d); and

(2) Have a means for closing it weathertight.

(g) Each port light located between the bulkhead deck and the next deck above the bulkhead deck must have an inside dead cover than can be secured watertight.

[CGD 79–023, 48 FR 51017, Nov. 4, 1983, as amended by CGD 85–080, 61 FR 945, Jan. 10, 1996; 62 FR 51354, Sept. 30, 1997]

§ 171.124 Watertight integrity above the margin line in a vessel less than 100 gross tons.

(a) Each hatch exposed to the weather must be watertight; except that, the following hatches may be weathertight:

(1) Each hatch on a watertight trunk that extends at least 12 inches (30.5 centimeters) above the weather deck.

(2) Each hatch in a cabin top.

(3) Each hatch on a vessel that operates only on protected waters.

(b) Each hatch cover must—

(1) Have securing devices; and

(2) Be attached to the hatch frame or coaming by hinges, captive chains, or to other devices to prevent its loss.

(c) Each hatch that provides access to crew or passenger accommodations must be operable from either side.

(d) Except as provided in paragraph (e) of this section, a weathertight door with permanent watertight coamings that comply with the height requirements in table 171.124(d) must be provided for each opening located in a deck house or companionway that—

(1) Gives access into the hull; and

(2) Is located in—

(i) A cockpit;

(ii) A well; or

(iii) An exposed location on a flush deck vessel.

TABLE 171.124(d)

Route	Height of coaming
Exposed or partially protected	6 inches (15.2 centimeters).
Protected	3 inches (7.6 centimeters).

(e) If an opening in a location specified in paragraph (d) of this section is provided with a Class 1 watertight door, the height of the watertight coaming need only be sufficient to accommodate the door.

[CGD 85–080, 62 FR 51354, Sept. 30, 1997]

Subpart H—Drainage of Weather Decks

§ 171.130 Specific applicability.

(a) Section 171.135 applies to each vessel that is 100 gross tons or more.

Coast Guard, DHS § 171.150

(b) Sections 171.140, 171.145, 171.150, and 171.155 apply to each vessel under 100 gross tons.

[CGD 79–023, 48 FR 51017, Nov. 4, 1983, as amended by CGD 85–080, 61 FR 945, Jan. 10, 1996; 62 FR 51354, Sept. 30, 1997]

§ 171.135 Weather deck drainage on a vessel of 100 gross tons or more.

The weather deck must have freeing ports, open rails, and scuppers, as necessary, to allow rapid clearing of water under all weather conditions.

§ 171.140 Drainage of a flush deck vessel.

(a) Except as provided in paragraph (b) of this section, the weather deck on a flush deck vessel must be watertight and have no obstruction to overboard drainage.

(b) Each vessel with a flush deck may have solid bulwarks in the forward one-third length of the vessel if—

(1) The bulwarks do not form a well enclosed on all sides; and

(2) The foredeck of the vessel has sufficient sheer to ensure drainage aft.

[CGD 85–080, 62 FR 51354, Sept. 30, 1997]

§ 171.145 Drainage of a vessel with a cockpit.

(a) Except as follows, the cockpit must be watertight:

(1) A cockpit may have companionways if they comply with § 171.124(d).

(2) A cockpit may have ventilation openings along its inner periphery if—

(i) The vessel operates only on protected or partially protected waters;

(ii) The ventilation openings are located as high as possible in the side of the cockpit; and

(iii) The height of the ventilation opening does not exceed 2 inches (5 centimeters).

(b) The cockpit must be designed to be self-bailing.

(c) Scuppers installed in a cockpit must be located to allow rapid clearing of water in all probable conditions of list and trim.

(d) Scuppers must have a combined area of at least the area given by either of the following equations:

A=0.1(D) square inches.
A=6.94(D) square centimeters.

Where—

A = the combined area of the scuppers in square inches (square centimeters).
D = the area of the cockpit in square feet (square meters).

(e) The cockpit deck of a vessel that operates on exposed or partially protected waters must be at least 10 inches (24.5 centimeters) above the deepest subdivision load line, unless the vessel complies with—

(1) The intact stability requirements of § 171.150;

(2) The Type II subdivision requirements in §§ 171.070, 171.072, and 171.073; and

(3) The damage stability requirements in § 171.080.

(f) The cockpit deck of all vessels that do not operate on exposed or partially protected waters must be located as high above the deepest subdivision load line as practicable.

[CGD 85–080, 62 FR 51354, Sept. 30, 1997]

§ 171.150 Drainage of a vessel with a well deck.

(a) Each well deck on a vessel must be watertight.

(b) Except as provided in paragraphs (c) and (d) of this section, the area required for freeing ports in the bulwarks that form a well must be determined as follows:

(1) If a vessel operates on exposed or partially protected waters, it must have at least 100 percent of the freeing port area derived from table 171.150.

(2) If a vessel operates only on protected or partially protected waters and complies with the requirements in the following sections for a vessel that operates on exposed waters, it must have at least 50 percent of the freeing port area derived from table 171.150:

(i) The intact stability requirements of § 171.030 or 171.050 and § 171.170.

(ii) The subdivision requirements of § 171.040, 171.043, or 171.070.

(iii) The damage stability requirements of § 171.080.

(3) If a vessel operates only on protected waters, the freeing port area must be at least equal to the scupper area required by § 171.145(d) for a cockpit of the same size.

(c) The freeing ports must be located to allow rapid clearing of water in all probable conditions of list and trim.

143

§ 171.155

(d) If a vessel that operates on exposed or partially protected waters does not have free drainage from the foredeck aft, then the freeing port area must be derived from table 171.150 using the entire bulwark length rather than the bulwark length in the after two-thirds of the vessel as stated in the table.

TABLE 171.150

Height of solid bulwark in inches (centimeters)	Freeing port area [1] [2]
6(15)	2(42.3)
12(30)	4(84.7)
18(46)	8(169.3)
24(61)	12(253.9)
30(76)	16(338.6)
36(91)	20(423.2)

[1] Intermediate values of freeing port area can be obtained by interpolation.
[2] In square inches per foot (square centimeters per meter) of bulwark length in the after 2/3 of the vessel.

[CGD 85–080, 62 FR 51354, Sept. 30, 1997]

§ 171.155 Drainage of an open boat.

The deck within the hull of an open boat must drain to the bilge. Overboard drainage of the deck is not permitted.

[CGD 85–080, 62 FR 51355, Sept. 30, 1997]

PART 172—SPECIAL RULES PERTAINING TO BULK CARGOES

Subpart A—General

Sec.
172.005 Applicability.

Subpart B—Bulk Grain

172.010 Applicability.
172.015 Document of authorization.
172.020 Incorporation by reference.
172.030 Exemptions for certain vessels.
172.040 Certificate of loading.

Subpart C—Special Rules Pertaining to a Barge That Carries a Cargo Regulated Under Subchapter D of This Chapter

172.047 Specific applicability.
172.048 Definitions.
172.050 Damage stability.

Subpart D—Special Rules Pertaining to a Vessel That Carries a Cargo Regulated Under 33 CFR Part 157

172.060 Specific applicability.
172.065 Damage stability.
172.070 Intact stability.

Subpart E—Special Rules Pertaining to a Barge That Carries a Hazardous Liquid Regulated Under Subchapter O of This Chapter

172.080 Specific applicability.
172.085 Hull type.
172.087 Cargo loading assumptions.
172.090 Intact transverse stability.
172.095 Intact longitudinal stability.
172.100 Watertight integrity.
172.103 Damage stability.
172.104 Character of damage.
172.105 Extent of damage.
172.110 Survival conditions.

Subpart F—Special Rules Pertaining to a Ship That Carries a Hazardous Liquid Regulated Under Subchapter O of This Chapter

172.125 Specific applicability.
172.127 Definitions.
172.130 Calculations.
172.133 Character of damage.
172.135 Extent of damage.
172.140 Permeability of spaces.
172.150 Survival conditions.

Subpart G—Special Rules Pertaining to a Ship That Carries a Bulk Liquefied Gas Regulated Under Subchapter O of This Chapter

172.155 Specific applicability.
172.160 Definitions.
172.165 Intact stability calculations.
172.170 Damage stability calculations.
172.175 Character of damage.
172.180 Extent of damage.
172.185 Permeability of spaces.
172.195 Survival conditions.
172.205 Local damage.

Subpart H—Special Rules Pertaining to Great Lakes Dry Bulk Cargo Vessels

172.215 Specific applicability.
172.220 Definitions.
172.225 Calculations.
172.230 Character of damage.
172.235 Extent of damage.
172.240 Permeability of spaces.
172.245 Survival conditions.

AUTHORITY: 46 U.S.C. 3306, 3703, 5115; E.O. 12234, 45 FR 58801, 3 CFR, 1980 Comp., p. 277; Department of Homeland Security Delegation No. 0170.1.

SOURCE: CGD 79–023, 48 FR 51040, Nov. 4, 1983, unless otherwise noted.

Coast Guard, DHS § 172.030

Subpart A—General

§ 172.005 Applicability.

This part applies to each vessel that carries one of the following cargoes in bulk:

(a) Grain.

(b) A cargo listed in Table 30.25-1 of this chapter.

(c) A cargo regulated under 33 CFR part 157.

(d) A cargo listed in Table 151.01-10(b) of this chapter.

(e) A cargo listed in Table I of part 153 of this chapter.

(f) A cargo listed in Table 4 of part 154 of this chapter.

(g) Any dry bulk cargo carried in a new Great Lakes vessel.

[CGD 79–023, 48 FR 51040, Nov. 4, 1983, as amended by CGD 80–159, 51 FR 33059, Sept. 18, 1986]

Subpart B—Bulk Grain

SOURCE: CGD 95–028, 62 FR 51218, Sept. 30, 1997, unless otherwise noted.

§ 172.010 Applicability.

This subpart applies to each vessel that loads grain in bulk, except vessels engaged solely on voyages on rivers, lakes, bays, and sounds or on voyages between Great Lake ports and St. Lawrence River ports as far east as a straight line drawn from Cape de Rosiers to West Point, Anticosti Island and as far east of a line drawn along the 63rd meridian from Anticosti Island to the north shore of the St. Lawrence River.

§ 172.015 Document of authorization.

(a) Except as specified in § 172.030, each vessel that loads grain in bulk must have a Document of Authorization issued in accordance with one of the following:

(1) Section 3 of the International Code for the Safe Carriage of Grain in Bulk if the Document of Authorization is issued on or after January 1, 1994. As used in the Code, the term "Administration" means "U.S. Coast Guard".

(2) Regulation 10 part (a) of the Annex to IMO Assembly resolution A.264(VIII) if the Document of Authorization was issued before January 1, 1994.

(b) The Commandant recognizes the National Cargo Bureau, Inc., 30 Vesey Street, New York, NY 10007–2914, for the purpose of issuing Documents of Authorization in accordance with paragraph (a)(1) of this section.

§ 172.020 Incorporation by reference.

(a) Certain material is incorporated by reference into this part under approval of the Director of the Federal Register under 5 U.S.C. 552(a) and 1 CFR part 51. To enforce any edition other than that specified in paragraph (b) of this section, the Coast Guard must publish notice of change in the FEDERAL REGISTER; and the material must be made available to the public. All approved material is available for inspection at the U.S. Coast Guard, Naval Architecture Division, Office of Design and Engineering Standards, 2100 Second Street SW., Washington, DC 20593–0001, and at the National Archives and Records Administration (NARA). For information on the availability of this material at NARA, call 202–741–6030, or go to: *http://www.archives.gov/federal_register/code_of_federal_regulations/ibr_locations.html*. All approved material is available from the sources indicated in paragraph (b) of this section.

(b) The material approved for incorporation by reference in this part and the sections affected are as follows:

International Maritime Organization (IMO)

Publications Section, 4 Albert Embankment, London, SE1 7SR United Kingdom.

Amendment to Chapter VI of the International Convention for the Safety of Life at Sea, 1960, Resolution A.264(VIII)—172.015

Publication No. 240–E, International Code for the Safe Carriage of Grain in Bulk—172.015

[CGD 95–028, 62 FR 51218, Sept. 30, 1997, as amended by USCG–1998–4442, 63 FR 52192, Sept. 30, 1998; 69 FR 18803, Apr. 9, 2004]

§ 172.030 Exemptions for certain vessels.

(a) Vessels are exempt from 172.015 on voyages between:

(1) United States ports along the East Coast as far south as Cape Henry, VA;

(2) Wilmington, NC and Miami, FL;

145

§ 172.040

(3) United States ports in the Gulf of Mexico;

(4) Puget Sound ports and Canadian west coast ports or Columbia River ports, or both;

(5) San Francisco, Los Angeles, and San Diego, CA.

(b) Vessels exempt by paragraph (a) of this section must comply with the following conditions:

(1) The master is satisfied that the vessel's longitudinal strength is not impaired.

(2) The master ascertains the weather to be encountered on the voyage.

(3) Potential heeling moments are reduced to a minimum by carrying as few slack holds as possible.

(4) Each slack surface must be leveled.

(5) The transverse metacentric height (GM), in meters, of the vessel throughout the voyage, after correction for liquid free surface, has been shown by stability calculations to be in excess of the required GM (GMR), in meters.

(i) The GMR is the sum of the increments of GM (GMI) multiplied by the correction factor, f and r.

Where:

r=(available freeboard) (beam) of the vessel and

f=1 if r is > 0.268 or

f=(0.268 r) if r is < 0.268.

(ii) The GMI for each compartment which has a slack surface of grain, i.e., is not trimmed full, is calculated by the following formula:

GMI=(B3×L×0.0661)(Disp.×SF))

where:

B=breadth of slack grain surface (m)
L=Length of compartment (m)
Disp.=Displacement of vessel (tons)
SF=Stowage factor of grain in compartment (cubic meters/tons)

(c) Vessels which do not have the Document of Authorization required by § 172.015 may carry grain in bulk up to one third of their deadweight tonnage provided the stability complies with the requirements of Section 9 of the International Code for the Safe Carriage of Grain in Bulk.

§ 172.040 Certificate of loading.

(a) Before it sails, each vessel that loads grain in bulk, except vessels engaged solely on voyages on the Great Lakes, rivers, or lakes, bays, and sounds, must have a certificate of loading issued by an organization recognized by the Commandant for that purpose. The certificate of loading may be accepted as prima facie evidence of compliance with the regulations in this subpart.

(b) The Commandant recognizes the National Cargo Bureau, Inc., 30 Vesey Street, New York, NY, 10007–2914, for the purpose of issuing certificates of loading.

Subpart C—Special Rules Pertaining to a Barge That Carries a Cargo Regulated Under Subchapter D of This Chapter

§ 172.047 Specific applicability.

This section applies to each tank barge that carries, in independent tanks described in § 151.15–1(b) of this chapter, a cargo listed in Table 30.25–1 of this chapter that is a—

(a) Liquefied flammable gas; or

(b) Flammable liquid that has a Reid vapor pressure in excess of 25 pounds per square inch (172.4 KPa).

§ 172.048 Definitions.

As used in this subpart—

MARPOL 73/38 means the International Convention for the Prevention of Pollution from Ships, 1973, as modified by the Protocol of 1978 relating to that Convention.

[USCG–2000–7641, 66 FR 55574, Nov. 2, 2001]

§ 172.050 Damage stability.

(a) Each tank barge is assigned a hull type number by the Commandant in accordance with § 32.63–5 of this chapter. The requirements in this section are specified according to the hull type number assigned.

(b) Except as provided in paragraph (c) of this section, each Type I and II barge hull must have a watertight weather deck.

(c) If a Type I or II barge hull has an open hopper, the fully loaded barge must be shown by design calculations to have at least 2 inches (50mm) of positive GM when the hopper space is flooded to the height of the weather deck.

(d) When demonstrating compliance with paragraph (c) of this section, credit may be given for the buoyancy of the immersed portion of cargo tanks if the tank securing devices are shown by design calculations to be strong enough to hold the tanks in place when they are subjected to the buoyant forces resulting from the water in the hopper.

(e) Each tank barge must be shown by design calculations to have at least 2 inches (50 mm) of positive GM in each condition of loading and operation after assuming the damage specified in paragraph (f) of this section is applied in the following locations:

(1) *Type I barge hull not in an integrated tow.* If a Type I hull is required and the barge is not a box barge designed for use in an integrated tow, design calculations must show that the barge hull can survive damage at any location including on the intersection of a transverse and longitudinal watertight bulkhead.

(2) *Type I barge hull in an integrated tow.* If a Type I hull is required and the barge is a box barge designed for operation in an integrated tow, design calculations must show that the barge can survive damage—

(i) To any location on the bottom of the tank barge except on a transverse watertight bulkhead; and

(ii) To any location on the side of the tank barge including on a transverse watertight bulkhead.

(3) *Type II hull.* If a Type II hull is required, design calculations must show that the barge can survive damage to any location except to a transverse watertight bulkhead.

(f) For the purpose of paragraph (e) of this section—

(1) Design calculations must include both side and bottom damage, applied separately; and

(2) Damage must consist of the most disabling penetration up to and including penetrations having the following dimensions:

(i) Side damage must be assumed to be as follows:

(A) Longitudinal extent—6 feet (183 centimeters).

(B) Transverse extent—30 inches (76 centimeters).

(C) Vertical extent—from the baseline upward without limit.

(ii) Bottom damage must be assumed to be 15 inches (38.1 centimeters) from the baseline upward.

Subpart D—Special Rules Pertaining to a Vessel That Carries a Cargo Regulated Under 33 CFR Part 157

§ 172.060 Specific applicability.

This subpart applies to each U.S. tank vessel that is required to comply with 33 CFR 157.21.

[CGD 90–051, 57 FR 36246, Aug. 12, 1992]

§ 172.065 Damage stability.

(a) *Definitions.* As used in this section, *Length* or *L* means load line length (LLL).

(b) *Calculations.* Each tank vessel must be shown by design calculations to meet the survival conditions in paragraph (g) of this section in each condition of loading and operation except as specified in paragraph (c) of this section, assuming the damage specified in paragraph (d) of this section.

(c) *Conditions of loading and operation.* The design calculations required by paragraph (b) of this section need not be done for ballast conditions if the vessel is not carrying oil, other than oily residues, in cargo tanks.

(d) *Character of damage.* (1) If a tank vessel is longer than 738 feet (225 metes) in length, design calculations must show that it can survive damage at any location.

(2) If a tank vessel is longer than 492 feet (150 meters) in length, but not longer than 738 feet (225 meters), design calculations must show that it can survive damage at any location except the transverse bulkheads bounding an aft machinery space. The machinery space is calculated as a single floodable compartment.

(3) If a tank vessel is 492 feet (150 meters) or less in length, design calculations must show that it can survive damage—

(i) At any location between adjacent main transverse watertight bulkheads except for an aft machinery space;

(ii) To a main transverse watertight bulkhead spaced closer than the longitudinal extent of collision penetration

§ 172.065

specified in Table 172.065(a) from another main transverse watertight bulkhead; and

(iii) To a main transverse watertight bulkhead or a transverse watertight bulkhead bounding a side tank or double bottom tank if there is a step or a recess in the transverse bulkhead that is longer than 10 feet (3.05 meters) and that is located within the extent of penetration of assumed damage. The step formed by the after peak bulkhead and after peak tank top is not a step for the purpose of this regulaton.

(e) *Extent of damage.* For the purpose of paragraph (b) of this section—

(1) Design calculations must include both side and bottom damage, applied separately; and

(2) Damage must consist of the penetrations having the dimensions given in Table 172.065(a) except that, if the most disabling penetrations would be less than the penetrations described in this paragraph, the smaller penetration must be assumed.

(f) *Permeability of spaces.* When doing the calculations required in paragraph (b) of this section—

(1) The permeability of a floodable space, other than a machinery space, must be as listed in Table 172.065(b);

(2) Calculations in which a machinery space is treated as a floodable space must be based on an assumed machinery space permeability of 85%, unless the use of an assumed permeability of less than 85% is justified in detail; and

(3) If a cargo tank would be penetrated under the assumed damage, the cargo tank must be assumed to lose all cargo and refill with salt water, or fresh water if the vessel operates solely on the Great Lakes, up to the level of the tank vessel's final equilibrium waterline.

(g) *Survival conditions.* A vessel is presumed to survive assumed damage if it meets the following conditions in the final stage of flooding:

(1) *Final waterline.* The final waterline, in the final condition of sinkage, heel, and trim, must be below the lower edge of an opening through which progressive flooding may take place, such as an air pipe, or an opening that is closed by means of a weathertight door or hatch cover. This opening does not include an opening closed by a—

(i) Watertight manhole cover;

(ii) Flush scuttle;

(iii) Small watertight cargo tank hatch cover that maintains the high integrity of the deck;

(iv) Class 1 door in a watertight bulkhead within the superstructure;

(v) Remotely operated sliding watertight door; or

(vi) Side scuttle of the non-opening type.

(2) *Heel angle.* The maximum angle of heel must not exceed 25 degrees, except that this angle may be increased to 30 degrees if no deck edge immersion occurs.

(3) *Range of stability.* Through an angle of 20 degrees beyond its position of equilibrium after flooding, a tank vessel must meet the following conditions:

(i) The righting arm curve must be positive.

(ii) The maximum righting arm must be at least 3.94 inches (10 cm).

(iii) Each submerged opening must be weathertight.

(4) *Progressive flooding.* Pipes, ducts or tunnels within the assumed extent of damage must be either—

(i) Equipped with arrangements such as stop check valves to prevent progressive flooding to other spaces with which they connect; or

(ii) Assumed in the design calculations required in paragraph (b) of this section to permit progressive flooding to the spaces with which they connect.

(h) *Buoyancy of superstructure.* For the purpose of paragraph (b) of this section, the buoyancy of any superstructure directly above the side damage is to be disregarded. The unflooded parts of superstructures beyond the extent of damage may be taken into consideration if they are separated from the damaged space by watertight bulkheads and no progressive flooding of these intact spaces takes place.

TABLE 172.065(a)—EXTENT OF DAMAGE

COLLISION PENETRATION

Longitudinal extent	$0.495L^{2/3}$ or 47.6 feet (($1/3$)$L^{2/3}$ 14.5m) whichever is shorter.
Transverse extent [1]	B/5 or 37.74 feet (11.5m) which is shorter.

Coast Guard, DHS

TABLE 172.065(a)—EXTENT OF DAMAGE—Continued

Vertical extent	From the baseline upward without limit.
GROUNDING PENETRATION AT THE FORWARD END BUT EXCLUDING ANY DAMAGE AFT OF A POINT 0.3L AFT OF THE FORWARD PERPENDICULAR	
Longitudinal extent	0.495L $^{2/3}$ or 47.6 feet (($^{1}\!/\!_{3}$)L $^{2/3}$ or 14.5m) whichever is shorter.
Transverse extent	B/6 or 32.81 feet (10m) whichever is shorter but not less than 16.41 feet (5m).
Vertical extent from the baseline.	B/15 or 19.7 feet (6m) whichever is shorter.
GROUNDING PENETRATION AT ANY OTHER LONGITUDINAL POSITION	
Longitudinal extent	L/10 or 16.41 feet (5m) whichever is shorter.
Transverse extent	16.41 feet (5m).
Vertical extent from the baseline.	B/15 or 19.7 feet (6m) whichever is shorter.
GROUNDING PENETRATION FOR RAKING DAMAGE	
For tank vessels of 20,000 DWT and above, the following assumed bottom raking damage must supplement the damage assumptions:.	
Longitudinal extent	For vessels of 75,000 DWT and above, 0.6L measured from the forward perpendicular.
	For vessels of less than 75,000 DWT, 0.4L measured from the forward perpendicular.
Transverse extent	B/3 anywhere in the bottom.
Vertical extent	Breach of the outer hull.

[1] Damage applied inboard from the vessel's side at right angles to the centerline at the level of the summer load line assigned under Subchapter E of this chapter.

TABLE 172.065(b)—PERMEABILITY

Spaces and tanks	Permeability (percent)
Storeroom spaces	60.
Accommodation spaces	95.
Voids	95.
Consumable liquid tanks	95 or 0.[1]
Other liquid tanks	95 or 0.[2]

[1] Whichever results in the more disabling condition.
[2] If tanks are partially filled, the permeability must be determined from the actual density and amount of liquid carried.

[CGD 79–023, 48 FR 51040, Nov. 4, 1983, as amended by USCG–2000–7641, 66 FR 55574, Nov. 2, 2001]

§ 172.070 Intact stability.

All tank vessels of 5,000 DWT and above contracted after the effective date of this rulemaking must comply with the intact stability requirements of Regulation 25A, annex I of MARPOL 73/78.

[USCG–2000–7641, 66 FR 55575, Nov. 2, 2001]

Subpart E—Special Rules Pertaining to a Barge That Carries a Hazardous Liquid Regulated Under Subchapter O of This Chapter

§ 172.080 Specific applicability.

This subpart applies to each tank barge that carries a cargo listed in Table 151.01–10(b) of this chapter.

§ 172.085 Hull type.

If a cargo listed in Table 151.05 of part 151 of this chapter is to be carried, the tank barge must be at least the hull type specified in Table 151.05 of this chapter for that cargo.

§ 172.087 Cargo loading assumptions.

(a) The calculations required in this subpart must be done for cargo weights and densities up to and including the maximum that is to be endorsed on the Certificate of Inspection in accordance with § 151.04–1(c) of this chapter.

(b) For each condition of loading and operation, each cargo tank must be assumed to have its maximum free surface.

§ 172.090 Intact transverse stability.

(a) Except as provided in paragraph (b) of this section, each tank barge must be shown by design calculations to have a righting arm curve with the following characteristics:

(1) If the tank barge is in river service, the area under the righting arm curve must be at least 5 foot-degrees (1.52 meter-degrees) up to the smallest of the following angles:

(i) The angle of maximum righting arm.

(ii) The downflooding angle.

(2) If the tank barge is in lakes, bays and sounds or Great Lakes summer service, the area under the righting arm curve must be at least 10 foot-degrees (3.05 meter-degrees) up to the smallest of the following angles:

(i) The angle of maximum righting arm.

(ii) The downflooding angle.

(3) If the tank barge is in ocean or Great Lakes winter service, the area under the righting arm curve must be

§ 172.095

at least 15 foot-degrees (4.57 meter-degrees) up to the smallest of the following angles:

(i) The angle of maximum righting arm.

(ii) The downflooding angle.

(b) If the vertical center of gravity of the cargo is below the weather deck at the side of the tank barge amidships, it must be shown by design calculations that the barge has at least the following metacentric height (GM) in feet (meters) in each condition of loading and operation:

$$GM = \frac{(K)(B)}{f_e}$$

where—
K=0.3 for river service.
K=0.4 for lakes, bays and sounds and Great Lakes summer service.
K=0.5 for ocean and Great Lakes winter service.
B=beam in feet (meters).
fe=effective freeboard in feet (meters).

(c) The effective freeboard is given by—

fe=f + fa ; or
fe=d, whichever is less.

where—
f=the freeboard to the deck edge amidships in feet (meters).
fa=(1.25)(a/L)((2b/B)−1)(h); or
fa=h, whichever is less.

where—
a=trunk length in feet (meters).
L=LOA in feet (meters)
b=breadth of a watertight trunk in feet (meters).
B=beam of the barge in feet (meters).
h=height of a watertight trunk in feet (meters).
d=draft of the barge in feet (meters).

(d) For the purpose of this section, downflooding angle means the static angle from the intersection of the vessel's centerline and waterline in calm water to the first opening that does not close watertight automatically.

§ 172.095 Intact longitudinal stability.

Each tank barge must be shown by design calculations to have a longitudinal metacentric height (GM) in feet (meters) in each condition of loading and operation, at least equal to the following:

$$GM = \frac{0.02(L)^2}{d}$$

where—
L=LOA in feet (meters)
d=draft in feet (meters).

§ 172.100 Watertight integrity.

(a) Except as provided in paragraph (b) of this section, each Type I or II hopper barge hull must have a weathertight weather deck.

(b) If a Type I or II barge hull has an open hopper, the fully loaded barge must be shown by design calculations to have at least 2 inches (50 mm) of positive GM when the hopper space is flooded to the height of the weather deck.

(c) When doing the calculations required by this section, credit may be given for the buoyancy of the immersed portion of cargo tanks if the tank securing devices are shown by design calculations to be strong enough to hold the tanks in place when they are subjected to the buoyant forces resulting from the water in the hopper.

§ 172.103 Damage stability.

Each tank barge must be shown by design calculations to meet the survival conditions in § 172.110 assuming the damage specified in § 172.104 to the hull type specified in Table 151.05 of part 151 of this chapter.

§ 172.104 Character of damage.

(a) *Type I barge hull not in an integrated tow.* If a Type I hull is required and the barge is not a box barge designed for use in an integrated tow, design calculations must show that the barge can survive damage at any location including the intersection of a transverse and a longitudinal bulkhead.

(b) *Type I barge hull in an integrated tow.* If a Type I barge hull is required and the barge is a box barge designed for operation in an integrated tow, design calculations must show that the barge can survive damage—

(1) At any location on the bottom of the tank barge except on a transverse watertight bulkhead; and

Coast Guard, DHS § 172.130

(2) At any location on the side of the tank barge including on a transverse watertight bulkhead.

(c) *Type II barge hull.* If a Type II hull is required, design calculations must show that a barge can survive damage at any location except on a transverse watertight bulkhead.

§ 172.105 Extent of damage.

For the purpose of § 172.103, design calculations must include both side and bottom damage, applied separately. Damage must consist of the most disabling penetration up to and including penetrations having the following dimensions:

(a) Side damage must be assumed to be as follows:

(1) Longitudinal extent—6 feet (183 centimeters).

(2) Transverse extent—30 inches (76 centimeters).

(3) Vertical extent—from the baseline upward without limit.

(b) Bottom damage must be assumed to be 15 inches (38 centimeters) from the baseline upward.

§ 172.110 Survival conditions.

(a) Paragraphs (c) and (d) of this section apply to a hopper barge and paragraphs (e) through (i) apply to all other tank barges.

(b) A barge is presumed to survive assumed damage if it meets the following conditions in the final stage of flooding:

(c) A hopper barge must not heel or trim beyond the angle at which—

(1) The deck edge is first submerged; or

(2) If the barge has a coaming that is at least 36 inches (91.5 centimeters) in height, the intersection of the deck and the coaming is first submerged, except as provided in paragraph (d) of this section.

(d) A hopper barge must not heel beyond the angle at which the deck edge is first submerged by more than "fa" as defined in § 172.090(c).

(e) Except as provided in paragraphs (h) and (i) of this section, each tank barge must not heel beyond the angle at which—

(1) The deck edge is first submerged; or

(2) If the barge has one or more watertight trunks, the deck edge is first submerged by more than "fa" as defined in § 172.090(c).

(f) Except as provided in paragraphs (h) and (i) of this section, a tank barge must not trim beyond the angle at which—

(1) The deck edge is first submerged; or

(2) If the barge has one or more watertight trunks, the intersection of the deck and the trunk is first submerged.

(g) If a tank barge experiences simultaneous heel and trim, the trim requirements in paragraph (f) of this section apply only at the centerline.

(h) Except as provided in paragraph (i) of this section, in no case may any part of the actual cargo tank top be underwater in the final condition of equilibrium.

(i) If a barge has a "step-down" in hull depth on either or both ends and all cargo tank openings are located on the higher deck level, the deck edge and tank top in the stepped-down area may be submerged.

Subpart F—Special Rules Pertaining to a Ship That Carries a Hazardous Liquid Regulated Under Subchapter O of This Chapter

§ 172.125 Specific applicability.

This subpart applies to each tankship that carries a cargo listed in Table I of part 153 of this chapter, except that it does not apply to a tankship whose cargo tanks are clean and gas free.

§ 172.127 Definitions.

Length or L means load line length (LLL).

§ 172.130 Calculations.

(a) Except as provided in § 153.7 of this chapter, each tankship must be shown by design calculations to meet the survival conditions in § 172.150 in each condition of loading and operation assuming the damage specified in § 172.133 for the hull type prescribed in part 153 of this chapter.

(b) If a cargo listed in Table I of part 153 of this chapter is to be carried, the vessel must be at least the hull type

§ 172.133

specified in part 153 of this chapter for that cargo.

[CGD 79–023, 48 FR 51040, Nov. 4, 1983, as amended by CGD 81–101, 52 FR 7799, Mar. 12, 1987]

§ 172.133 Character of damage.

(a) If a type I hull is required, design calculations must show that the vessel can survive damage at any location.

(b) Except as provided in § 153.7 of this chapter, if a type II hull is required, design calculations must show that a vessel—

(1) Longer than 492 feet (150 meters) in length can survive damage at any location; and

(2) Except as specified in paragraph (d) of this section, 492 feet (150 meters) or less in length can survive damage at any location.

(c) If a Type III hull is required, design calculations must show that a vessel—

(1) Except as specified in paragraph (d) of this section, 410 feet (125 meters) in length or longer can survive damage at any location; and

(2) Less than 410 feet (125 meters) in length can survive damage at any location except to an aft machinery space.

(d) A vessel described in paragraph (b)(2) or (c)(1) of this section need not be designed to survive damage to a main transverse watertight bulkhead bounding an aft machinery space. Except as provided in § 153.7 of this chapter, the machinery space must be calculated as a single floodable compartment.

[CGD 79–023, 48 FR 51040, Nov. 4, 1983, as amended by CGD 81–101, 52 FR 7799, Mar. 12, 1987]

§ 172.135 Extent of damage.

For the purpose of § 172.133—

(a) Design calculations must include both side and bottom damage, applied separately; and

(b) Damage must consist of the penetrations having the dimensions given in Table 172.135 except that, if the most disabling penetrations would be less than the penetrations given in Table 172.135, the smaller penetration must be assumed.

TABLE 172.135—EXTENT OF DAMAGE

COLLISION PENETRATION

Longitudinal extent	0.495L$^{2/3}$ or 47.6 feet (($^{1}/_{3}$)L$^{2/3}$ or 14.5m) whichever is shorter.
Transverse extent [1]	B/5 or 37.74 feet (11.5m) [2] whichever is shorter.
Vertical extent	From the baseline upward without limit.

GROUNDING PENETRATION AT THE FORWARD END BUT EXCLUDING ANY DAMAGE AFT OF A POINT 0.3L AFT OF THE FORWARD PERPENDICULAR

Longitudinal extent	L/10.
Transverse extent	B/6 or 32.81 feet (10m) whichever is shorter.
Vertical extent from the baseline upward.	B/15 or 19.7 feet (6m) whichever is shorter.

GROUNDING PENETRATION AT ANY OTHER LONGITUDINAL POSITION

Longitudinal extent	L/10 or 16.41 feet (5m) whichever is shorter.
Transverse extent	16.41 feet (5m).
Vertical extent from the baseline upward.	B/15 or 19.7 feet (6m) whichever is shorter.

[1] Damage applied inboard from the vessel's side at right angles to the centerline at the level of the summer load line assigned under Subchapter E of this chapter.
[2] B is measured amidships.

§ 172.140 Permeability of spaces.

(a) When doing the calculations required in § 172.130, the permeability of a floodable space other than a machinery space must be as listed in Table 172.060(b).

(b) Calculations in which a machinery space is treated as a floodable space must be based on an assumed machinery space permeability of 0.85, unless the use of an assumed permeability of less than 0.85 is justified in detail.

(c) If a cargo tank would be penetrated under the assumed damage, the cargo tank must be assumed to lose all cargo and refill with salt water up to the level of the tankship's final equilibrium waterline.

§ 172.150 Survival conditions.

A tankship is presumed to survive assumed damage if it meets the following conditions in the final stage of flooding:

(a) *Final waterline.* The final waterline, in the final condition of sinkage, heel, and trim, must be below the lower edge of openings such as air pipes and openings closed by weathertight doors or hatch covers. The following types of openings may be submerged when the tankship is at the final waterline:

(1) Openings covered by watertight manhole covers or watertight flush scuttles.

Coast Guard, DHS

§ 172.170

(2) Small watertight cargo tank hatch covers.

(3) A Class 1 door in a watertight bulkhead within the superstructure.

(4) Remotely operated sliding watertight doors.

(5) Side scuttles of the non-opening type.

(b) *Heel angle.* (1) Except as described in paragraph (b)(2) of this section, the maximum angle of heel must not exceed 15 degrees (17 degrees if no part of the freeboard deck is immersed).

(2) The Commanding Officer, Marine Safety Center will consider on a case by case basis each vessel 492 feet (150 meters) or less in length having a final heel angle greater than 17 degrees but less than 25 degrees.

(c) *Range of stability.* Through an angle of 20 degrees beyond its position of equilibrium after flooding, a tankship must meet the following conditions:

(1) The righting arm curve must be positive.

(2) The maximum righting arm must be at least 3.95 inches (10 cm).

(3) Each submerged opening must be weathertight.

(d) *Progressive flooding.* Pipes, ducts or tunnels within the assumed extent of damage must be either—

(1) Equipped with arrangements such as stop check valves to prevent progressive flooding to other spaces with which they connect; or

(2) Assumed in the design calculations required by §172.130 to flood the spaces with which they connect.

(e) *Buoyancy of superstructure.* The buoyancy of any superstructure directly above the side damage is to be disregarded. The unflooded parts of superstructures beyond the extent of damage may be taken into consideration if they are separated from the damaged space by watertight bulkheads and no progressive flooding of these intact spaces takes place.

(f) *Metacentric height.* After flooding, the tankship's metacentric height must be at least 2 inches (50mm) when the ship is in the upright position.

(g) *Equalization arrangements.* Flooding equalization arrangements requiring mechanical operation such as valves or cross-flooding lines may not be assumed to reduce the angle of heel.

Spaces joined by ducts of large cross sectional area are treated as common spaces.

(h) *Intermediate stages of flooding.* If an intermediate stage of flooding is more critical than the final stage, the tankship must be shown by design calculations to meet the requirements in this section in the intermediate stage.

[CGD 79–023, 48 FR 51040, Nov. 4, 1983, as amended by CGD 88–070, 53 FR 34537, Sept. 7, 1988]

Subpart G—Special Rules Pertaining to a Ship That Carries a Bulk Liquefied Gas Regulated Under Subchapter O of This Chapter

§ 172.155 Specific applicability.

This subpart applies to each tankship that has on board a bulk liquefied gas listed in Table 4 of part 154 of this chapter as cargo, cargo residue, or vapor.

§ 172.160 Definitions.

As used in this subpart—

(a) *Length* or *L* means the load line length (LLL).

(b) *MARVS* means the Maximum Allowable Relief Valve Setting of a cargo tank.

§ 172.165 Intact stability calculations.

(a) Design calculations must show that 2 inches (50mm) of positive metacentric height can be maintained by each tankship when it is being loaded and unloaded.

(b) For the purpose of demonstrating compliance with the requirements of paragraph (a) of this section, the effects of the addition of water ballast may be considered.

§ 172.170 Damage stability calculations.

(a) Each tankship must be shown by design calculations to meet the survival conditions in §172.195 in each condition of loading and operation assuming the damage specified in §172.175 for the hull type specified in Table 4 of part 154 of this chapter.

(b) If a cargo listed in Table 4 of part 154 of this chapter is to be carried, the vessel must be at least the ship type

§ 172.175

specified in Table 4 of part 154 of this chapter for the cargo.

§ 172.175 Character of damage.

(a) If a type IG hull is required, design calculations must show that the vessel can survive damage at any location.

(b) If a type IIG hull is required, design calculations must show that a vessel—

(1) Longer than 492 feet (150 meters) in length can survive damage at any location; and

(2) 492 feet (150 meters) or less in length can survive damage at any location except the transverse bulkheads bounding an aft machinery space. The machinery space is calculated as a single floodable compartment.

(c) If a vessel has independent tanks type C with a MARVS of 100 psi (689 kPa) gauge or greater, is 492 feet (150 meters) or less in length, and Table 4 of part 154 of this chapter allows a type IIPG hull, design calculations must show that the vessel can survive damage at any location, except as prescribed in paragraph (e) of this section.

(d) If a type IIIG hull is required, except as specified in paragraph (e) of this section, design calculations must show that a vessel—

(1) 410 feet (125 meters) in length or longer can survive damage at any location; and

(2) Less than 410 feet (125 meters) in length can survive damage at any location, except in the main machinery space.

(e) The calculations in paragraphs (c) and (d) of this section need not assume damage to a transverse bulkhead unless it is spaced closer than the longitudinal extent of collision penetration specified in Table 172.180 from another transverse bulkhead.

(f) If a main transverse watertight bulkhead or transverse watertight bulkhead bounding a side tank or double bottom tank has a step or a recess that is longer than 10 feet (3.05 meters) located within the extent of penetration of assumed damage, the vessel must be shown by design calculations to survive damage to this bulkhead. The step formed by the after peak bulkhead and after peak tank top is not a step for the purpose of this regulation.

§ 172.180 Extent of damage.

For the purpose of § 172.170—

(a) Design calculations must include both side and bottom damage, applied separately; and

(b) Damage must consist of the penetrations having the dimensions given in Table 172.180 except that, if the most disabling penetrations would be less than the penetrations given in Table 172.180, the smaller penetration must be assumed.

TABLE 172.180—EXTENT OF DAMAGE

COLLISION PENETRATION

Longitudinal extent	0.495$L^{2/3}$ or 47.6 feet ((1/3)$L^{2/3}$ or 14.5m) whichever is shorter.
Transverse extent [1]	B/5 or 37.74 feet (11.5m) [2] whichever is shorter.
Vertical extent	From the baseline upward without limit.

GROUNDING PENETRATION AT THE FORWARD END BUT EXCLUDING ANY DAMAGE AFT OF A POINT 0.3L AFT OF THE FORWARD PERPENDICULAR

Longitudinal extent	0.495$L^{2/3}$ or 47.6 feet ((1/3)$L^{2/3}$ or 14.5m) whichever is shorter.
Transverse extent	B/6 or 32.81 feet (10m) whichever is shorter.
Vertical extent from the molded line of the shell at the centerline.	B/15 or 6.6 feet (2m) whichever is shorter.

GROUNDING PENETRATION AT ANY OTHER LONGITUDINAL POSITION

Longitudinal extent	L/10 or 16.41 feet (5m) whichever is shorter.
Transverse extent	B/6 or 16.41 feet (5m) whichever is shorter.
Vertical extent from the molded line of the shell at the centerline.	B/15 or 6.6 feet (2m) whichever is shorter.

[1] Damage applied inboard from the vessel's side at right angles to the centerline at the level of the summer load line assigned under Subchapter E of this chapter.
[2] B is measured amidships.

§ 172.185 Permeability of spaces.

(a) When doing the calculations required in § 172.170, the permeability of a floodable space other than a machinery space must be as listed in Table 172.060(b).

(b) Calculations in which a machinery space is treated as a floodable space must be based on an assumed machinery space permeability of 85%, unless use of an assumed permeability of less than 85% is justified in detail.

(c) If a cargo tank would be penetrated under the assumed damage, the cargo tank must be assumed to lose all cargo and refill with salt water up to the level of the tankship's final equilibrium waterline.

§ 172.195 Survival conditions.

A vessel is presumed to survive assumed damage if it meets the following conditions in the final stage of flooding:

(a) *Final waterline.* The final waterline, in the final condition of sinkage, heel, and trim, must be below the lower edge of an opening through which progressive flooding may take place, such as an air pipe, or an opening that is closed by means of a weathertight door or hatch cover. This opening does not include an opening closed by a—

(1) Watertight manhole cover;
(2) Flush scuttle;
(3) Small watertight cargo tank hatch cover that maintains the high integrity of the deck;
(4) A Class 1 door in a watertight bulkhead within the superstructure;
(5) Remotely operated sliding watertight door; or
(6) A side scuttle of the non-opening type.

(b) *Heel angle.* The maximum angle of heel must not exceed 30 degrees.

(c) *Range of stability.* Through an angle of 20 degrees beyond its position of equilibrium after flooding, a tankship must meet the following conditions:

(1) The righting arm curve must be positive.
(2) The maximum righting arm must be at least 3.94 inches (10 cm).
(3) Each submerged opening must be weathertight.

(d) *Progressive flooding.* If pipes, ducts, or tunnels are within the assumed extent of damage, arrangements must be made to prevent progressive flooding to a space that is not assumed to be flooded in the damaged stability calculations.

(e) *Buoyancy of superstructure.* The buoyancy of any superstructure directly above the side damage is to be disregarded. The unflooded parts of superstructures beyond the extent of damage may be taken into consideration if they are separated from the damaged space by watertight bulkheads and no progressive flooding of these intact spaces takes place.

(f) *Metacentric height.* After flooding, the tank ship's metacentric height must be at least 2 inches (50 mm) when the vessel is in the upright position.

(g) *Equalization arrangements.* Equalization arrangements requiring mechanical aids such as valves or cross-flooding lines may not be considered for reducing the angle of heel. Spaces joined by ducts of large cross-sectional area are treated as common spaces.

(h) *Intermediate stages of flooding.* If an intermediate stage of flooding is more critical than the final stage, the tank vessel must be shown by design calculations to meet the requirements in this section in the intermediate stage.

§ 172.205 Local damage.

(a) Each tankship must be shown by design calculations to meet the survival conditions in paragraph (b) of this section in each condition of loading and operation assuming that local damage extending 30 inches (76 cm) normal to the hull shell is applied at any location in the cargo length:

(b) The vessel is presumed to survive assumed local damage if it does not heel beyond the smaller of the following angles in the final stage of flooding:

(1) 30 degrees.
(2) The angle at which restoration of propulsion and steering, and use of the ballast system is precluded.

Subpart H—Special Rules Pertaining to Great Lakes Dry Bulk Cargo Vessels

SOURCE: CGD 80-159, 51 FR 33059, Sept. 18, 1986, unless otherwise noted.

§ 172.215 Specific applicability.

This subpart applies to each new Great Lakes vessel of 1600 gross tons or more carrying dry cargo in bulk.

§ 172.220 Definitions.

(a) As used in this subpart *Length (L)*, *Breadth (B)*, and *Molded Depth (D)* are as defined in § 45.3 of this chapter.

(b) As used in this part *new Great Lakes Vessel* means a vessel operating solely within the limits of the Great

§ 172.225

Lakes as defined in this subchapter that:

(1) Was contracted for on or after November 17, 1986, or delivered on or after November 17, 1988.

(2) Has undergone a major conversion under a contract made on or after November 17, 1986, or completed a major conversion on or after November 17, 1987.

[CGD 80-159, 51 FR 33059, Sept. 18, 1986]

§ 172.225 Calculations.

(a) Each vessel must be shown by design calculations to meet the survival conditions in § 172.245 in each condition of loading and operation, assuming the damage specified in § 172.230.

(b) When doing the calculations required by paragraph (a) of this section, the virtual increase in the vertical center of gravity due to a liquid in a space must be determined by calculating either—

(1) The free surface effect of the liquid with the vessel assumed heeled five degrees from the vertical; or

(2) The shift of the center of gravity of the liquid by the moment of transference method.

(c) In calculating the free surface effect of consumable liquids, it must be assumed that, for each type of liquid, at least one transverse pair of wing tanks or a single centerline tank has a free surface. The tank or combination of tanks selected must be those having the greatest free surface effect.

(d) When doing the calculations required by paragraph (a) of this section, the buoyancy of any superstructure directly above the side damage must not be considered. The unflooded parts of superstructures beyond the extent of damage may be considered if they are separated from the damaged space by watertight bulkheads and no progressive flooding of these intact spaces takes place.

§ 172.230 Character of damage.

(a) Design calculations must show that each vessel can survive damage—

(1) To any location between adjacent main transverse watertight bulkheads;

(2) To any location between a main transverse bulkhead and a partial transverse bulkhead in way of a side wing tank;

(3) To a main or wing tank transverse watertight bulkhead spaced closer than the longitudinal extent of collision penetration specified in Table 172.235 to another main transverse watertight bulkhead; and

(4) To a main transverse watertight bulkhead or a transverse watertight bulkhead bounding a side tank or double bottom tank if there is a step or a recess in the transverse bulkhead that is longer than 10 feet (3.05 meters) and that is located within the extent of penetration of assumed damage. The step formed by the after peak bulkhead and after peak tank top is not a step for the purpose of this paragraph.

§ 172.235 Extent of damage.

For the purpose of the calculations required in § 172.225—

(a) Design calculations must include both side and bottom damage, applied separately; and

(b) Damage must consist of the penetrations having the dimensions given in Table 172.235 except that, if the most disabling penetrations would be less than the penetrations described in this paragraph, the smaller penetration must be assumed.

TABLE 172.235—EXTENT OF DAMAGE

Collision Penetration	
Longitudinal extent	0.495 $L^{2/3}$ or 47.6 feet. (1/3 $L^{2/3}$ or 14.5 m), whichever is less.
Transverse extent	4 feet 2 inches (1.25 m).[1]
Vertical extent	From the baseline upward without limit.

Grounding Penetration Forward of a Point 0.3L Aft of the Forward Perpendicular	
Longitudinal	0.495 $L^{2/3}$ or 47.6 feet. (1/3 $L^{2/3}$ or 14.5 m), whichever is less.
Transverse	B/6 or 32.8 feet (10 m), whichever is less, but not less than 16.4 feet (5 m).[1]
Vertical extent	0.75 m from the baseline.

Grounding Penetration at Any Other Longitudinal Position	
Longitudinal extent	L/10 or 16.4 feet (5 m), whichever is less.
Transverse	4 feet 2 inches (1.25 m).
Vertical extent	2 feet 6 inches (0.75 m) from the baseline.

[1] Damage applied inboard from the vessel's side at right angles to the centerline at the level of the summer load line assigned under Subchapter E of this chapter.

§ 172.240 Permeability of spaces.

When doing the calculations required in § 172.225,

(a) The permeability of a floodable space, other than a machinery or cargo space, must be assumed as listed in Table 172.240;

(b) Calculations in which a machinery space is treated as a floodable space must be based on an assumed machinery space permeability of 85% unless the use of an assumed permeability of less than 85% is justified in detail; and

(c) Calculations in which a cargo space that is completely filled is considered flooded must be based on an assumed cargo space permeability of 60% unless the use of an assumed permeability of less than 60% is justified in detail. If the cargo space is not completely filled, a cargo space permeability of 95% must be assumed unless the use of an assumed permeability of less than 95% is justified in detail.

TABLE 172.240—PERMEABILITY

Spaces and tanks	Permeability (percent)
Storeroom spaces	60
Accommodations spaces	95
Voids	95
Consumable liquid tanks	[1] 95 or 0
Other liquid tanks	[2] 95 or 0
Cargo (completely filled)	60
Cargo (empty)	95
Machinery	85

[1] Whichever results in the more disabling condition.
[2] If tanks are partially filled, the permeability must be determined from the actual density and amount of liquid carried.

§ 172.245 Survival conditions.

A vessel is presumed to survive assumed damage if it meets the following conditions in the final stage of flooding:

(a) *Final waterline.* The final waterline, in the final condition of sinkage, heel, and trim must be below the lower edge of an opening through which progressive flooding may take place, such as an air pipe, or an opening that is closed by means of a weathertight door or hatch cover. This opening does not include an opening closed by a:

(1) Watertight manhole cover;
(2) Flush scuttle;
(3) Small watertight cargo tank hatch cover that maintains the high integrity of the deck;
(4) Class 1 door in a watertight bulkhead;
(5) Remotely operated sliding watertight door;
(6) Side scuttle of the nonopening type;
(7) Retractable inflatable seal; or
(8) Guillotine door.

(b) *Heel angle.* The maximum angle of heel must not exceed 15 degrees, except that this angle may be increased to 17 degrees if no deck edge immersion occurs.

(c) *Range of stability.* Through an angle of 20 degrees beyond its position of equilibrium after flooding, a vessel must meet the following conditions:

(1) The righting arm curve must be positive.
(2) The maximum righting arm must be at least 4 inches (10 cm).
(3) Each submerged opening must be weathertight.

(d) *Metacentric height.* After flooding, the metacentric height must be at least 2 inches (50 mm) when the vessel is in the equilibrium position.

(e) *Progressive flooding.* In the design calculations required by § 172.225, progressive flooding between spaces connected by pipes, ducts or tunnels must be assumed unless:

(1) Pipes within the assumed extent of damage are equipped with arrangements such as stop check valves to prevent progressive flooding to other spaces with which they connect; and,

(2) Progressive flooding through ducts or tunnels is protected against by:

(i) Retractable inflatable seals to cargo hopper gates; or
(ii) Guillotine doors in bulkheads in way of the conveyor belt.

PART 173—SPECIAL RULES PERTAINING TO VESSEL USE

Subpart A—General

Sec.
173.001 Applicability.

Subpart B—Lifting

173.005 Specific applicability.
173.007 Location of the hook load.
173.010 Definitions.
173.020 Intact stability standards: Counterballasted and non-counterballasted vessels.

§ 173.001

173.025 Additional intact stability standards: Counterballasted vessels.

Subpart C—School Ships

173.050 Specific applicability.
173.051 Public nautical school ships.
173.052 Civilian nautical school ships.
173.053 Sailing school vessels.
173.054 Watertight subdivision and damage stability standards for new sailing school vessels.
173.055 Watertight subdivision and damage stability standards for existing sailing school vessels.
173.056 Collision and other watertight bulkheads.
173.057 Permitted locations for Class I watertight doors.
173.058 Double bottom requirements.
173.059 Penetrations and openings in watertight bulkheads.
173.060 Openings in the side of a vessel below the bulkhead or weather deck.
173.061 Watertight integrity above the margin line.
173.062 Drainage of weather deck.
173.063 Intact stability requirements.

Subpart D—Oceanographic Research

173.070 Specific applicability.
173.075 Subdivision requirements.
173.080 Damage stability requirements.
173.085 General subdivision requirements.

Subpart E—Towing

173.090 General.
173.095 Towline pull criterion.

AUTHORITY: 43 U.S.C. 1333; 46 U.S.C. 2113, 3306, 5115; E.O. 12234, 45 FR 58801, 3 CFR, 1980 Comp., p. 277; Department of Homeland Security Delegation No. 0170.1.

SOURCE: CGD 79-023, 48 FR 51045, Nov. 4, 1983, unless otherwise noted.

Subpart A—General

§ 173.001 Applicability.

Each vessel that is engaged in one of the following activities must comply with the applicable provisions of this part:
(a) Lifting.
(b) Training (schoolship).
(c) Oceanographic research.
(d) Towing.

Subpart B—Lifting

§ 173.005 Specific applicability.

This subpart applies to each vessel that—

(a) Is equipped to lift cargo or other objects; and
(b) Has a maximum heeling moment due to hook load greater than or equal to—

$(0.67)(W)(GM)(F/B)$ in meter-metric tons (foot-long tons), where—
W=displacement of the vessel with the hook load included in metric (long) tons.
GM=metacentric height with hook load included in meters (feet).
F=freeboard to the deck edge amidships in meters (feet).
B=beam in meters (feet).

[CGD 79-023, 48 FR 51045, Nov. 4, 1983, as amended by CGD 85-080, 61 FR 945, Jan. 10, 1996]

§ 173.007 Location of the hook load.

When doing the calculations required in this subpart, the hook load must be considered to be located at the head of the crane.

§ 173.010 Definitions.

As used in this part—
(a) *Hook load* means the weight of the object lifted by the crane.
(b) *Crane radius* means the distance illustrated in Figure 173.010.

Figure 173.010

Crane Radius

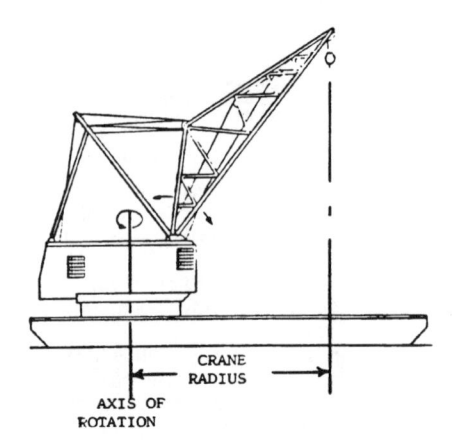

§ 173.020 Intact stability standards: Counterballasted and non-counterballasted vessels.

(a) Except as provided in paragraph (c) of this section, each vessel that is not equipped to counter-ballast while

Coast Guard, DHS § 173.025

lifting must be shown by design calculations to comply with this section in each condition of loading and operation and at each combination of hook load and crane radius.

(b) Each vessel must have a righting arm curve with the following characteristics:

(1) If the vessel operates in protected or partially protected waters, the area under the righting arm curve up to the smallest of the following angles must be at least 10 foot-degrees (3.05 meter-degrees):

(i) The angle corresponding to the maximum righting arm.

(ii) The downflooding angle.

(iii) 40 degrees.

(2) If the vessel operates in exposed waters, the area under the righting arm curve up to the smallest of the following angles must be at least 15 foot-degrees (4.57 meter-degrees):

(i) The angle corresponding to the maximum righting arm.

(ii) The downflooding angle.

(iii) 40 degrees.

(c) If the vessel's hull proportions fall within all three of the following limits, in lieu of complying with paragraph (b) of this section, the vessel owner may demonstrate in the presence of the OCMI that the vessel will not heel beyond the limits specified in paragraph (d) of this section:

(1) Beam to depth—3.40 to 4.75.
(2) Length to beam—3.20 to 4.50.
(3) Draft to depth—0.60 to 0.85.

(d) For the purpose of paragraph (c) of this section, the following limits of heel apply with the vessel at its deepest operating draft:

(1) Protected and partially protected waters and Great Lakes in summer—heel to main deck immersion or bilge emergence, whichever occurs first.

(2) Exposed waters and Great Lakes in winter—heel permitted to one-half of the freeboard or one-half of the draft, whichever occurs first.

[CGD 79-023, 48 FR 51045, Nov. 4, 1983, as amended by CGD 85-080, 61 FR 945, Jan. 10, 1996]

§ 173.025 Additional intact stability standards: Counterballasted vessels.

(a) Each vessel equipped to counterballast while lifting must be shown by design calculations to be able to withstand the sudden loss of the hook load, in each condition of loading and operation and at each combination of hook load and crane radius.

(b) When doing the calculations required by this section, the hook load and counterballast heeling arms and vessel righting arms, as plotted on graph 173.025, must define areas that satisfy the following equation:

Area II > Area I + K

Where—

(1) K=0 for operation on protected waters and 7 foot-degrees (2.13 meter-degrees) for operation on partially protected and exposed waters.

(2) Areas I and II are shown on graph 173.025.

(c) Each heeling arm curve must be defined by—

HA=HAO cos (T)

Where—
HA=heeling arm.
HAO=heeling arm at 0 degrees of heel.
T=angle of heel.

§ 173.050

GRAPH 173.025

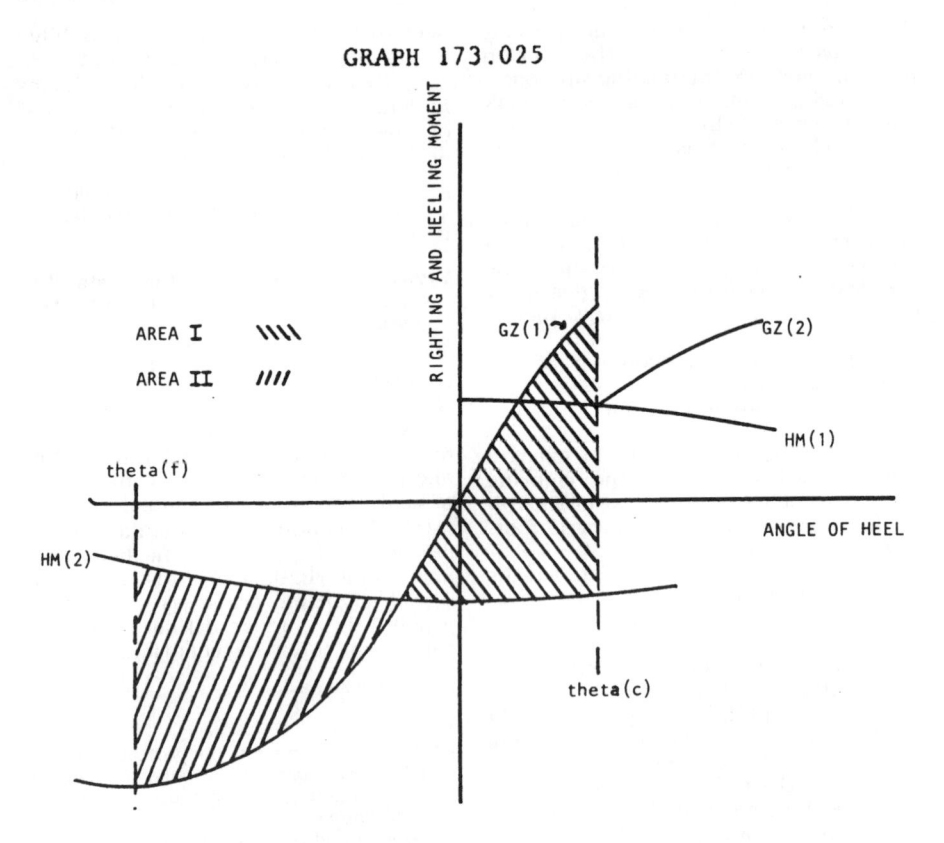

Where—

GZ(1) is the righting arm curve at the displacement corresponding to the vessel without hooking load.

GZ(2) is the righting arm curve at the displacement corresponding to the vessel with hook load.

HA(1) is the heeling arm curve due to the combined heeling moments of the hook load and the counterballast at the displacement with hook load.

HA(2) is the heeling arm due to the counterballast at the displacement without hook load.

Theta(c) is the angle of static equilibrium due to the combined hook load and counterballast heeling moments.

Theta(f) is the downflooding angle on the counterballasted side of the vessel.

[CGD 79–023, 48 FR 51045, Nov. 4, 1983, as amended by CGD 85–080, 61 FR 945, Jan. 10, 1996]

Subpart C—School Ships

§ 173.050 Specific applicability.

Each nautical school ship, inspected under Subchapter R of this chapter, must comply with this subpart.

§ 173.051 Public nautical school ships.

Each public nautical school ship must comply with—

(a) Section 171.070(a) of this subchapter as a passenger vessel carrying 400 or less passengers;

(b) Section 171.070(e) of this subchapter;

(c) Section 171.072 of this subchapter; and

(d) Section 171.073 of this subchapter.

[CGD 79–023, 48 FR 51045, Nov. 4, 1983. Redesignated by CGD 83–005, 51 FR 924, Jan. 9, 1986]

§ 173.052 Civilian nautical school ships.

Each civilian nautical school ship must comply with part 171 of this subchapter as though it were a passenger vessel. In addition to regular passengers, for the purpose of complying with part 171, the following will also count as passengers;
(a) A student.
(b) A cadet.
(c) An instructor who is not also a member of the crew.

[CGD 79–023, 48 FR 51045, Nov. 4, 1983. Redesignated by CGD 83–005, 51 FR 924, Jan. 9, 1986]

§ 173.053 Sailing school vessels.

(a) In addition to the requirements in §§ 173.054 through 173.063, each sailing school vessel must comply with the provisions of subpart A of part 171 of this subchapter.

(b) In addition to regular passengers, for the purpose of complying with §§ 171.070 through 171.073 and § 171.080, the following will also be counted as passengers:
(1) Sailing school students.
(2) Sailing school instructors.
(3) Guests.

[CGD 83–005, 51 FR 924, Jan. 9, 1986]

§ 173.054 Watertight subdivision and damage stability standards for new sailing school vessels.

(a) Each new sailing school vessel which has a mean length greater than 75 feet (22.8 meters) *or* which carries more than 30 persons must comply with—
(1) Section 179.210(a) of this chapter;
(2) Sections 171.070 through 171.073; and
(3) Section 171.080 for Type II subdivision and damage stability.

(b) Each new sailing school vessel which has a mean length of 75 feet (22.8 meters) or less and carries more than 30 persons must comply with either—
(1) Section 179.210(a) of this chapter and § 179.220 of this chapter; or
(2) Section 171.040(a)(1), §§ 171.070 through 171.073, and § 171.080.

(c) Each new sailing school vessel which does not carry more than 30 persons must have a collision bulkhead unless it has a mean length less than 40 feet (12.2 meters) and is certificated for protected or partially protected waters service only.

[CGD 83–005, 51 FR 924, Jan. 9, 1986, as amended by CGD 85–080, 61 FR 946, Jan. 10, 1996]

§ 173.055 Watertight subdivision and damage stability standards for existing sailing school vessels.

(a) Except as provided in paragraph (c) of this section, an existing sailing school vessel which carries more than 49 persons must be fitted with a collision bulkhead and any additional bulkheads necessary to provide one compartment subdivision.

(b) Except as provided in paragraph (c) of this section, an existing sailing school vessel which has a mean length greater than 65 feet (19.8 meters), must be fitted with additional transverse watertight bulkheads necessary to provide one compartment subdivision, when the following Subdivision Numerals are exceeded:
(1) For vessels to be operated on Exposed Waters:

L × N > 4000

(2) For vessels to be operated on Partially Protected Waters:

L × N > 4500

(3) For vessels to be operated on Protected Waters:

L × N > 5000

where L is the mean length and N is the number of persons on board

(c) An existing sailing school vessel which is required to meet a one compartment subdivision standard and has a mean length of 90 feet (27.4 meters) or less may, instead of one compartment subdivision, be fitted with a collision bulkhead and sufficient air tankage or other internal buoyancy to maintain the fully-loaded vessel afloat with positive stability in the flooded condition.

(d) Except as provided in paragraph (e) of this section, an existing sailing school vessel which has a mean length greater than 65 feet (19.8 meters) must be fitted with a collision bulkhead.

(e) On an existing sailing school vessel, operating on protected waters, which has a mean length of 90 feet (27.4 meters) or less with no other requirement for subdivision, the collision bulkhead may be omitted.

§ 173.056

(f) An existing sailing school vessel, operating on exposed waters, which has a mean length of 65 feet (19.8 meters) or less and is carrying more than 15 persons, must be fitted with a collision bulkhead.

[CGD 83–005, 51 FR 924, Jan. 9, 1986]

§ 173.056 Collision and other watertight bulkheads.

(a) Collision bulkheads required by this section must comply with the requirements in § 171.085 of this subchapter.

(b) Each sailing school vessel required to meet paragraph (a) of § 173.054 must comply with the machinery space bulkhead requirements in § 171.095 of this subchapter.

[CGD 83–005, 51 FR 924, Jan. 9, 1986]

§ 173.057 Permitted locations for Class I watertight doors.

(a) Class I doors are permitted in any location on a sailing school vessel which has a mean length of 125 feet (38.1 meters) or less.

(b) Class I doors fitted in accordance with § 170.270 of this subchapter shall additionally be marked in two-inch letters "RECLOSE AFTER USE", and be provided with a remote position indicator at the main navigating station of the vessel.

[CGD 83–005, 51 FR 924, Jan. 9, 1986]

§ 173.058 Double bottom requirements.

Each new sailing school vessel which has a mean length greater than 165 feet (50.3 meters) and is certificated for exposed water service must comply with the double bottom requirements in §§ 171.105 through 171.109, inclusive, of this subchapter.

[CGD 83–005, 51 FR 924, Jan. 9, 1986]

§ 173.059 Penetrations and openings in watertight bulkheads.

Penetrations and openings in watertight bulkheads must comply with the requirements in subpart E of part 171 of this subchapter or §§ 179.320, 179.330, and 179.340 in subchapter T of this chapter.

[CGD 83–005, 51 FR 924, Jan. 9, 1986, as amended by CGD 85–080, 61 FR 946, Jan. 10, 1996]

§ 173.060 Openings in the side of a vessel below the bulkhead or weather deck.

(a) Openings in the side of a vessel below the bulkhead or weather deck must comply with the requirements in subpart F of part 171 of this subchapter or § 179.350 in subchapter T of this chapter.

(b) In addition to the requirements in paragraph (a) of this section, each sailing school vessel which has a mean length greater than 90 feet must comply with the requirements in § 56.50–95 of Subchapter F of this chapter.

[CGD 83–005, 51 FR 924, Jan. 9, 1986, as amended by CGD 85–080, 61 FR 945, Jan. 10, 1996]

§ 173.061 Watertight integrity above the margin line.

The watertight integrity of each sailing school vessel above the margin line must comply with the requirements in subpart G of part 171 of this subchapter or § 179.360 in subchapter T of this chapter.

[CGD 83–005, 51 FR 925, Jan. 9, 1986, as amended by CGD 85–080, 61 FR 946, Jan. 10, 1996; 61 FR 20556, May 7, 1996]

§ 173.062 Drainage of weather deck.

The weather deck of each sailing school vessel must be provided with drainage in accordance with the requirements in subpart H of part 171 of this subchapter or subpart D of part 178 in subchapter T of this chapter.

[CGD 83–005, 51 FR 925, Jan. 9, 1986, as amended by CGD 85–080, 61 FR 946, Jan. 10, 1996]

§ 173.063 Intact stability requirements.

(a) Except as provided in this section, each sailing school vessel must meet the intact stability requirements in §§ 170.170, 171.050, and 171.055 of this chapter.

(b) In applying the requirements in §§ 170.170 and 171.050 of this subchapter, the value of "T" is equal to the angle of heel at which the deck edge is immersed or ⅓ of the downflooding angle, whichever is less.

(c) In applying the requirements of § 171.055(d) (1) and (2) of this subchapter—

(1) The value "X" is equal to 0.6 long tons/square foot (9.8 metric tons/square meter).

Coast Guard, DHS § 173.063

(2) For a vessel in service on protected or partially protected waters, values "Y" and "Z" are determined from graphs 173.063 (a) and (b) and multiplied by the multiplier in graph 173.063(e).

(3) For a vessel in service on exposed waters, "Y" and "Z" are determined from graphs 173.063 (c) and (d) and multiplied by the multiplier from graph 173.063(e).

(4) To convert required numerals to units of "metric tons/square meter," multiply by 10.94.

(d) Each vessel of the open boat type that is required to comply with the requirements in §§ 178.300 and 178.310 of this chapter, may instead comply with the requirements in paragraph (e) of this section.

(e) In lieu of complying with the requirements of paragraph (b) of this section, an open boat may be provided with sufficient air tankage or other internal buoyancy to maintain the vessel afloat when the vessel is completely flooded or capsized. If foam is used to comply with this paragraph, it must be installed in accordance with the requirements in § 170.245 of this subchapter.

(f) A sailing school catamaran must meet the intact stability requirements in § 171.057.

163

§ 173.063 46 CFR Ch. I (10–1–04 Edition)

GRAPH 173.063(a)

PROTECTED OR PARTIALLY PROTECTED

Y $\frac{\text{TONS}}{\text{SQ FT}}$

vs. DOWNFLOODING ANGLE

GRAPH 173.063(b)

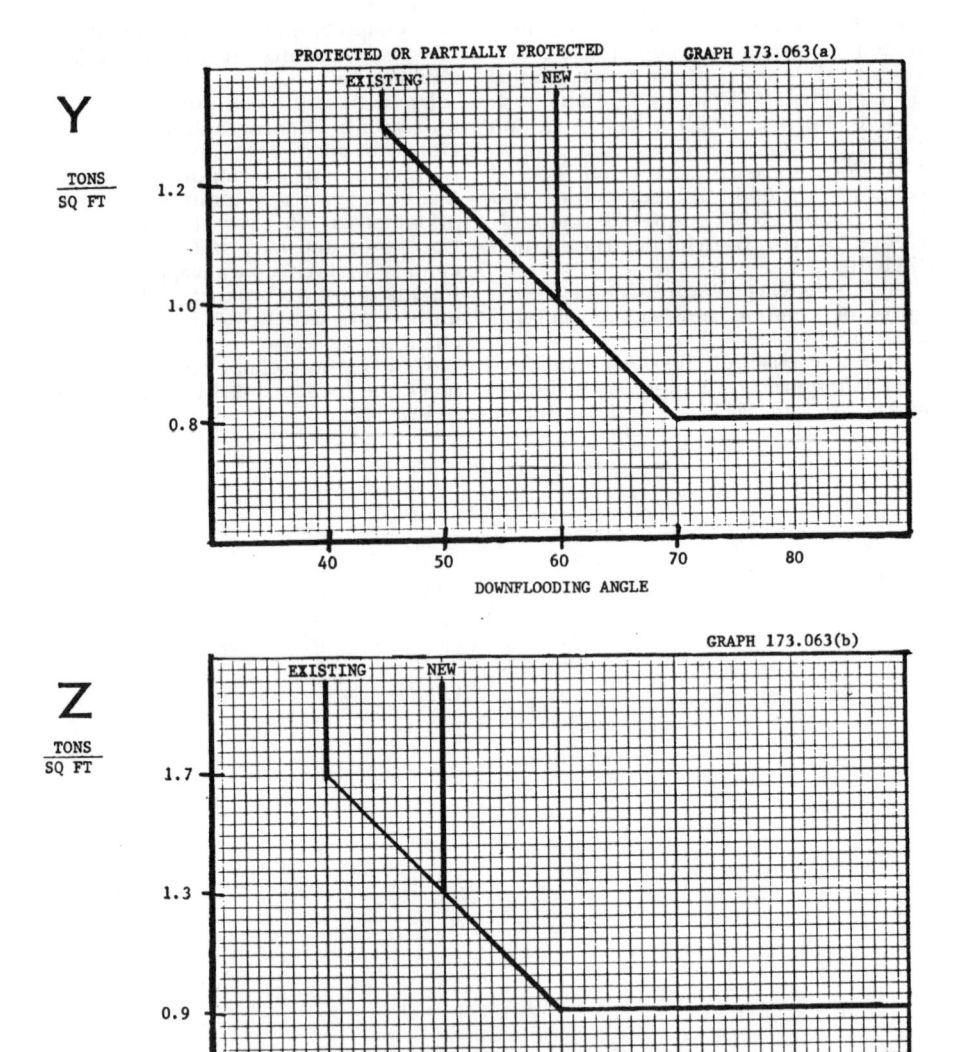

Z $\frac{\text{TONS}}{\text{SQ FT}}$

vs. RANGE OF STABILITY

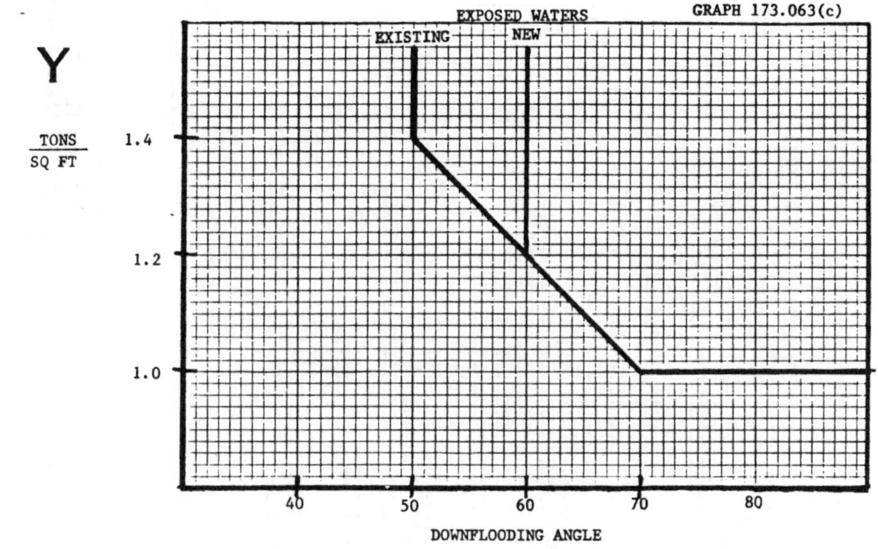
EXPOSED WATERS
GRAPH 173.063(c)
Y
TONS / SQ FT
EXISTING
NEW
1.4
1.2
1.0
40
50
60
70
80
DOWNFLOODING ANGLE

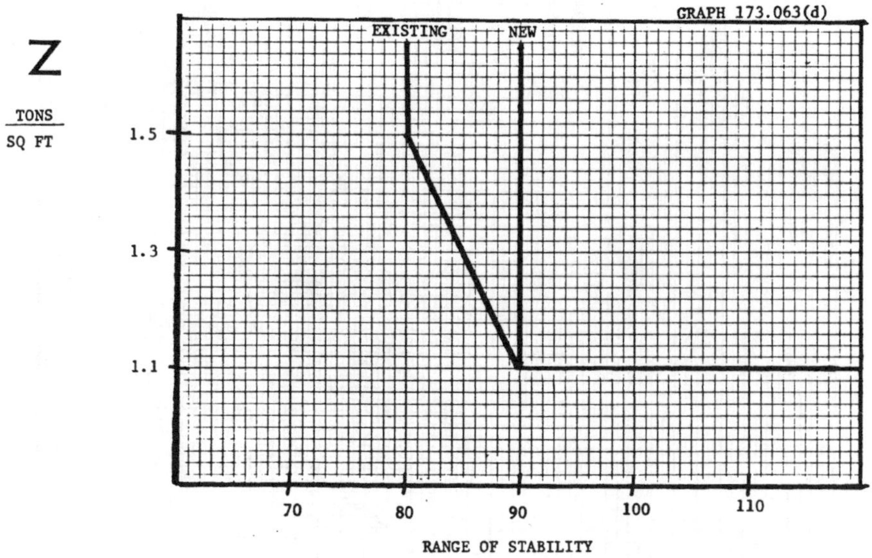
GRAPH 173.063(d)
Z
TONS / SQ FT
EXISTING
NEW
1.5
1.3
1.1
70
80
90
100
110
RANGE OF STABILITY

§ 173.063

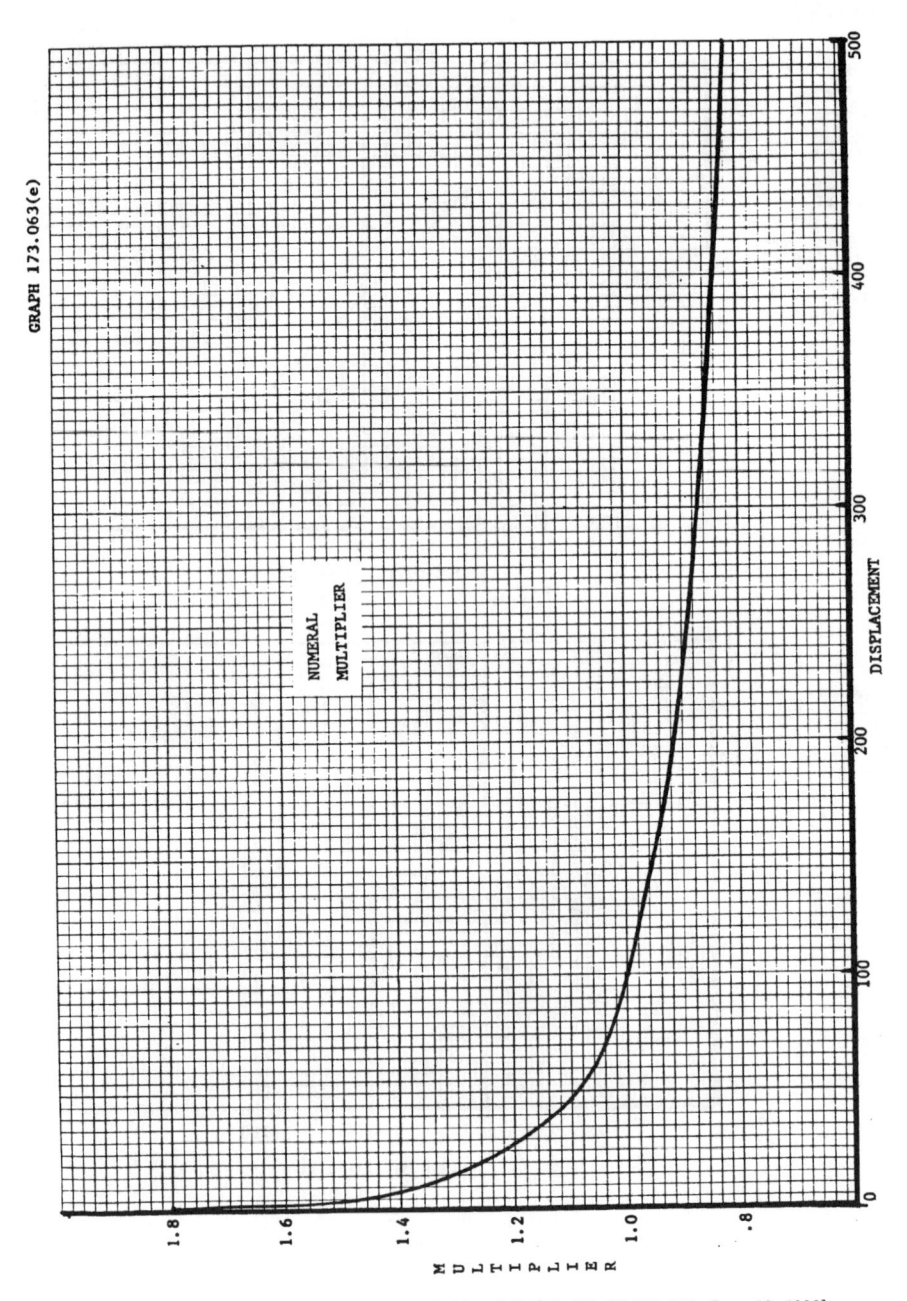

GRAPH 173.063(e)

NUMERAL MULTIPLIER

DISPLACEMENT

[CGD 83–005, 51 FR 925, Jan. 9, 1986, as amended by CGD 85–080, 61 FR 946, Jan. 10, 1996]

Subpart D—Oceanographic Research

§ 173.070 Specific applicability.

Each oceanographic vessel, inspected under Subchapter U of this chapter, except a barge that is less than 300 gross tons, must comply with this subpart.

§ 173.075 Subdivision requirements.

(a) Each oceanographic vessel must comply with the subdivision requirements in §§ 171.070, 171.072, and 171.073 of this subchapter as if it were a passenger vessel carrying 400 or less passengers.

(b) Each vessel must have a collision bulkhead.

§ 173.080 Damage stability requirements.

Each oceanographic vessel must comply with § 171.080 of this subchapter as a category Z vessel.

§ 173.085 General subdivision requirements.

Each oceanographic vessel must comply with the following:

(a) Section 171.085(c)(1), (d) and (g) of this subchapter.

(b) Section 171.105 (a) through (g) of this subchapter except that a reduction or elimination of the required inner bottom is allowed if—

(1) The inner bottom would interfere with the mission of the vessel; and

(2) As a result of other design features, the ability of the vessel to withstand side and bottom damage is not reduced.

(c) Section 171.106 of this subchapter.
(d) Section 171.108 of this subchapter.
(e) Section 171.109 of this subchapter.
(f) Section 171.111 of this subchapter.
(g) Section 171.113 of this subchapter.

(h) The collision bulkhead must not be penetrated by more than one pipe that carries liquid to or from the forepeak tank. This pipe must have a screwdown valve that is—

(1) Operative from above the bulkhead deck; and

(2) Attached to the bulkhead inside the forepeak tank.

(i) Section 171.116 (b), (c), and (e) of this subchapter.

(j) Section 171.117(c) of this subchapter.

(k) Each port light in a space located below the freeboard deck, as defined in § 42.13–15(i) of this chapter, or in a space within an enclosed superstructure must be fitted with a hinged inside dead cover.

(l) Section 171.118 (b) and (c) of this subchapter.

(m) Section 171.122 (a) through (d) and (f) of this subchapter.

(n) Section 171.135 of this subchapter.

(o) A ventilation duct or forced draft duct may not penetrate a main transverse watertight bulkhead unless—

(1) The penetration is watertight;

(2) The penetration is located as near the vessel's centerline as possible; and

(3) The bottom of the duct is not more than—

(i) 18 inches (45.7 cm) below the bulkhead deck; and

(ii) 4 feet (121.9 cm) above the final waterline after damage determined in § 173.080.

Subpart E—Towing

§ 173.090 General.

This subpart applies to each vessel that is equipped for towing.

§ 173.095 Towline pull criterion.

(a) In each towing condition, each vessel must be shown by design calculations to meet the requirements of either paragraph (b) or (c) of this section.

(b) The vessel's metacentric height (GM) must be equal to or greater than the following:

$$GM = \frac{(N)(P \times D)^2{}_3(s)(h)}{K\Delta(f/B)}$$

where—

N=number of propellers.
P=shaft power per shaft in horsepower (kilowatts).
D=propeller diameter in feet (meters).
s=that fraction of the propeller circle cylinder which would be intercepted by the rudder if turned to 45 degrees from the vessel's centerline.
h=vertical distance from propeller shaft centerline at rudder to towing bitts in feet (meters).
Δ=displacement in long tons (metric tons).
f=minimum freeboard along the length of the vessel in feet (meters).
B=molded beam in feet (meters).

K=38 in English units.
K=13.93 in metric units.

(c) When a heeling arm curve, calculated in accordance with paragraph (d) of this section, is plotted against the vessel's righting arm curve—
  (1) Equilibrium must be reached before the downflooding angle; and
  (2) The residual righting energy must be at least 2 foot-degrees (.61 meter-degrees) up to the smallest of the following angles:
    (i) The angle of maximum righting arm.
    (ii) The downflooding angle.
    (iii) 40 degrees.

(d) The heeling arm curve specified in paragraph (c) of this section must be calculated by the following equation:

$$HA = \frac{2(N)(P \times D)^2 (s)(h)(\cos\theta)}{K\Delta}^3$$

where—
HA=heeling arm.
θ=angle of heel.
N, P, D, K, s, h, and Δ are as defined in paragraph (b) of this section.

(e) For the purpose of this section, downflooding angle means the static angle from the intersection of the vessel's centerline and waterline in calm water to the first opening that does not close watertight automatically.

(f) For the purpose of this section, at each angle of heel, a vessel's righting arm may be calculated considering either—
  (1) The vessel is permitted to trim free until the trimming moment is zero; or
  (2) The vessel does not trim as it heels.

PART 174—SPECIAL RULES PERTAINING TO SPECIFIC VESSEL TYPES

Subpart A—General

Sec.
174.005 Applicability.
174.007 Incorporation by reference.

Subpart B—Special Rules Pertaining to Deck Cargo Barges

174.010 Specific applicability.
174.015 Intact stability.
174.020 Alternate intact stability criterion.

Subpart C—Special Rules Pertaining to Mobile Offshore Drilling Units

174.030 Specific applicability.
174.035 Definitions.
174.040 Stability requirements: general.
174.045 Intact stability requirements.
174.050 Stability on bottom.
174.055 Calculation of wind heeling moment (Hm).
174.065 Damage stability requirements.
174.070 General damage stability assumptions.
174.075 Compartments assumed flooded: general.
174.080 Flooding on self-elevating and surface type units.
174.085 Flooding on column stabilized units.
174.090 Permeability of spaces.
174.100 Appliances for watertight and weathertight integrity.

Subpart D [Reserved]

Subpart E—Special Rules Pertaining to Tugboats and Towboats

174.140 Specific applicability.
174.145 Intact stability requirements.

Subpart F [Reserved]

Subpart G—Special Rules Pertaining to Offshore Supply Vessels

174.180 Applicability.
174.185 Intact stability.
174.190 Collision bulkhead.
174.195 Bulkheads in machinery spaces.
174.200 Damaged stability in machinery spaces for all OSVs.
174.205 Additional damaged stability for OSVs carrying more than 16 offshore workers.
174.207 Damaged stability criteria.
174.210 Watertight doors in watertight bulkheads.
174.215 Drainage of weather deck.
174.220 Hatches and coamings.
174.225 Hull penetrations and shell connections.

Subpart H—Special Rules Pertaining to Liftboats

174.240 Applicability.
174.245 General.
174.250 Unrestricted service.
174.255 Restricted service.
174.260 Freeboard.

Subpart I—Hopper Dredges With Working Freeboard Assignments

174.300 Specific applicability.

Coast Guard, DHS § 174.015

174.305 Definitions.

CALCULATIONS

174.310 General.
174.315 Extent and character of damage.
174.320 Damage survival.
174.325 Equalization.
174.330 Jettisoning of spoil.

DESIGN

174.335 Watertight doors.
174.340 Collision bulkhead.

Subpart J—Special Rules Pertaining to Dry Cargo Ships

174.350 Specific applicability.
174.355 Definitions.
174.360 Calculations.

AUTHORITY: 42 U.S.C. 9118, 9119, 9153; 43 U.S.C. 1333; 46 U.S.C. 3306, 3703; E.O. 12234, 45 FR 58801, 3 CFR, 1980 Comp., p. 277; Department of Homeland Security Delegation No. 0170.1.

SOURCE: CGD 79–023, 48 FR 51048, Nov. 4, 1983, unless otherwise noted.

Subpart A—General

§ 174.005 Applicability.

Each of the following vessels must comply with the applicable provisions of this part:

(a) Deck cargo barge.
(b) Mobile offshore drilling unit (MODU) inspected under subchapter IA of this chapter.
(c) Tugboat and towboat inspected under subchapter I of this chapter.
(d) Self-propelled hopper dredge having an assigned working freeboard.
(e) Oceangoing ships of 500 gross tons or over, as calculated by the International Convention on Tonnage Measurement of Ships, 1969, designed primarily for the carriage of dry cargoes, including roll-on/roll-off ships.
(f) Offshore supply vessel inspected under subchapter L of this chapter.
(g) Liftboat inspected under subchapter L of this chapter.

[CGD 95–012, 60 FR 48052, Sept. 18, 1995; 60 FR 50120, Sept. 28, 1995, as amended by CGD 82–004 and CGD 86–074, 60 FR 57671, Nov. 16, 1995; CGD 82–004 and CGD 86–074, 62 FR 49353, Sept. 19, 1997]

§ 174.007 Incorporation by reference.

(a) Certain material is incorporated by reference into this part with the approval of the Director of the Federal Register in accordance with 5 U.S.C. 552(a). To enforce any edition other than that specified in paragraph (b) of this section, the Coast Guard must publish notice of change in the FEDERAL REGISTER and make the material available to the public. All approved material is on file at the U.S. Coast Guard, Office of Design and Engineering Standards (G–MSE), 2100 Second Street SW., Washington, DC 20593–0001 and at the National Archives and Records Administration (NARA). For information on the availability of this material at NARA, call 202–741–6030, or go to: *http://www.archives.gov/federal_register/code_of_federal_regulations/ibr_locations.html.* All approved material is available from the sources indicated in paragraph (b) of this section.

(b) The material approved for incorporation by reference in this part and the sections affected are:

American Society for Testing and Materials (ASTM)

100 Barr Harbor Drive, West Conshohocken, PA 19428–2959.

ASTM F 1196–94, Standard Specification for Sliding Watertight Door Assemblies—174.100
ASTM F 1197–89 (1994), Standard Specification for Sliding Watertight Door Control Systems—174.100

[CGD 88–032, 56 FR 35828, July 29, 1991, as amended by CGD 95–072, 60 FR 50468, Sept. 29, 1995; CGD 96–041, 61 FR 50734, Sept. 27, 1996; CGD 97–057, 62 FR 51049, Sept. 30, 1997; USCG–1999–5151, 64 FR 67186, Dec. 1, 1999; 69 FR 18803, Apr. 9, 2004]

Subpart B—Special Rules Pertaining to Deck Cargo Barges

§ 174.010 Specific applicability.

Each barge that carries cargo above the weather deck must comply with this subpart.

§ 174.015 Intact stability.

(a) Except as provided in § 174.020, in each condition of loading and operation, each barge must be shown by design calculations to have an area under the righting arm curve up to the angle of maximum righting arm, the downflooding angle, or 40 degrees, whichever angle is smallest, equal to or greater than—

§ 174.020

(1) 15 foot-degrees (4.57 meter-degrees) for ocean and Great Lakes winter service; and

(2) 10 foot-degrees (3.05 meter-degrees) for lakes, bays, sounds, and Great Lakes summer service.

(b) For the purpose of this section, downflooding angle means the static angle from the intersection of the vessel's centerline and waterline in calm water to the first opening that does not close watertight automatically.

§ 174.020 Alternate intact stability criterion.

A barge need not comply with § 174.015 and subparts C and E of part 170 of this chapter if it has the following characteristics:

(a) The weather deck is watertight.

(b) The barge's hull proportions fall within any one of the ratios in categories (A) through (D) in Table 174.020.

(c) The maximum cargo height is 30 feet (9.25 meters) or a value equal to the depth of the barge amidships, whichever is less.

TABLE 174.020

Category	Beam/depth ratio	Draft/depth ratio
A	3.00 to 3.74	Equal to or less than 0.70.
B	3.75 to 3.99	Equal to or less than 0.72.
C	4.00 to 4.49	Equal to or less than 0.76.
D	4.50 to 6.00	Equal to or less than 0.80.

Subpart C—Special Rules Pertaining to Mobile Offshore Drilling Units

§ 174.030 Specific applicability.

Each mobile offshore drilling unit (MODU) inspected under Subchapter IA of this chapter must comply with this subpart.

§ 174.035 Definitions.

(a) For the purpose of this subpart the following terms have the same definitions as given in Subchapter IA of this chapter:

(1) *Column stabilized unit.*
(2) *Mobile offshore drilling unit.*
(3) *Self-elevating unit.*
(4) *Surface type unit.*

(b) For the purpose of this subpart—

(1) *Downflooding* means the entry of seawater through any opening that cannot be rapidly closed watertight, into the hull, superstructure, or columns of an undamaged unit due to heel, trim, or submergence of the unit.

(2) *Downflooding angle* means the static angle from the intersection of the unit's centerline and waterline in calm water to the first opening through which downflooding can occur when subjected to a wind heeling moment (Hm) calculated in accordance with § 174.055.

(3) *Normal operating condition* means a condition of a unit when loaded or arranged for drilling, field transit, or ocean transit.

(4) *Severe storm condition* means a condition of a unit when loaded or arranged to withstand the passage of a severe storm.

§ 174.040 Stability requirements: general.

Each unit must be designed to have at least 2 inches (50mm) of positive metacentric height in the upright equilibrium position for the full range of drafts, whether at the operating draft for navigation, towing, or drilling afloat, or at a temporary draft when changing drafts.

§ 174.045 Intact stability requirements.

(a) Each unit must be designed so that the wind heeling moments (Hm) and righting moments calculated for each of its normal operating conditions and severe storm conditions, when plotted on GRAPH 174.045, define areas that satisfy the equation:

Area(A)≥(K)×(Area (B))

where—

(1) K=1.4 except that if the unit is a column stabilized unit K=1.3;
(2) Area (A) is the area on GRAPH 174.045 under the righting moment curve between 0 and the second intercept angle or the angle of heel at which downflooding would occur, whichever angle is less; and
(3) Area (B) is the area on GRAPH 174.045 under the wind heeling moment curve between 0 and the second intercept angle or the angle of heel at which downflooding of the unit would occur whichever angle is less.

(b) Each righting moment on graph § 174.045 must be positive for all angles

Coast Guard, DHS § 174.050

greater than 0 and less than the second intercept angle.

(c) For the purposes of this section, openings fitted with the weathertight closing appliances specified in § 174.100(b) are not considered as openings through which downflooding could occur if they can be rapidly closed and would not be submerged below the units' waterline prior to the first intercept angle, except that ventilation intakes and outlets for machinery spaces, crew spaces, and other spaces where ventilation is normally required are considered as openings through which downflooding could occur regardless of location.

(d) Each unit must be designed so that it can be changed from each of its normal operating conditions to a severe storm condition within a minimum period of time consistent with the operating manual required in § 109.121 of this chapter.

GRAPH 174.045

Intact Stability Curves for a Given Normal Operating or Severe Storm Mode

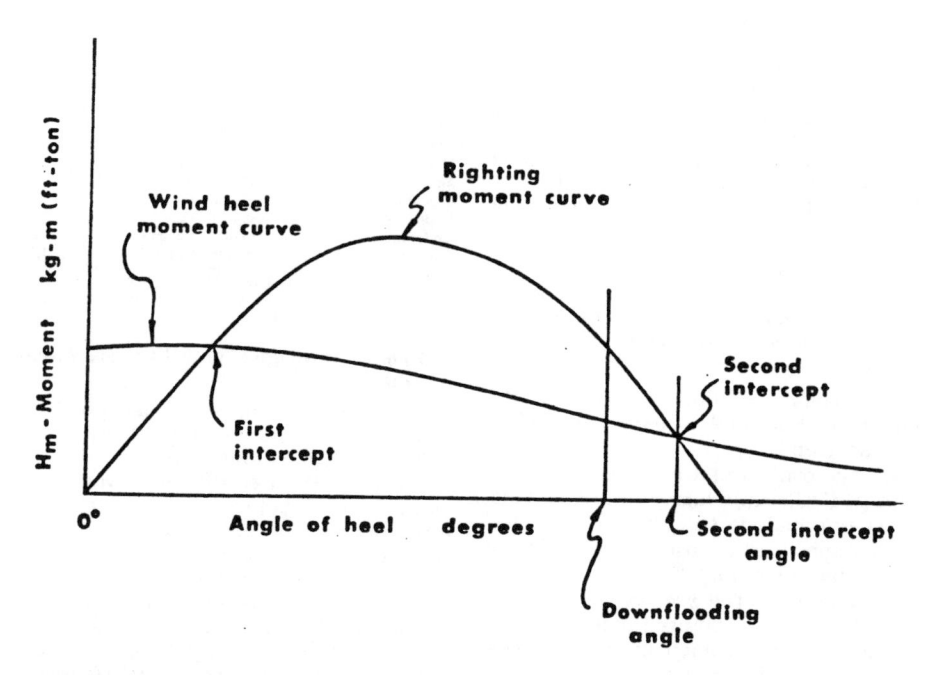

[CGD 79-023, 48 FR 51048, Nov. 4, 1983, as amended by CGD 83-071, 52 FR 6979, Mar. 6, 1987]

§ 174.050 Stability on bottom.

Each bottom bearing unit must be designed so that, while supported on the sea bottom with footings or a mat, it continually exerts a downward force on each footing or the mat when subjected to the forces of wave and current

§ 174.055 Calculation of wind heeling moment (Hm).

(a) The wind heeling moment (Hm) of a unit in a given normal operating condition or severe storm condition is the sum of the individual wind heeling moments (H) calculated for each of the exposed surfaces on the unit; i.e., $Hm = \Sigma H$.

(b) Each wind heeling moment (H) must be calculated using the equation:

$$H = k(v)^2 (Ch)(Cs)(A)(h)$$

where—

(1) H=wind heeling moment for an exposed surface on the unit in foot-pounds (kilogram-meters);
(2) $k = 0.00338$ lb./(ft.^{2}-knots^2) (0.0623 (kg-sec^2)/m^4);
(3) v=wind velocity of—
   (i) 70 knots (36 meters per second) for normal operating conditions.
   (ii) 100 knots (51.5 meters per second) for severe storm conditions.
   (iii) 50 knots (25.8 meters per second) for damage conditions.
(4) A=projected area in square feet (squrae meters) of an exposed surface on the unit;
(5) Ch=height coefficient for "A" from Table 174.055(a);
(6) Cs=shape coefficient for "A" from Table 174.055(b); and
(7) h=the vertical distance in feet (meters) from the center of lateral resistance of the underwater hull to the center of wind pressure on "A".

(c) When calculating "A" in the equation described in paragraph (b) of this section—
(1) The projected area of each column or leg; if the unit has columns or legs, must not include shielding allowances;
(2) Each area exposed as a result of heel must be included;
(3) The projected area of a cluster of deck houses may be used instead of the projected area of each individual deck house in the cluster; and
(4) The projected area of open truss work may be calculated by taking 30% of the projected areas of both the front and back sides of the open truss work rather than by determining the projected area of each structural member of the truss work.

and to wind blowing at the velocities described in § 174.055(b)(3).

TABLE 174.055(a)—Ch VALUES

Feet		Meters		Ch.
Over	Not exceeding	Over	Not exceeding	
0	50	0.0	15.3	1.00
50	100	15.3	30.5	1.10
100	150	30.5	46.0	1.20
150	200	46.0	61.0	1.30
200	250	61.0	76.0	1.37
250	300	76.0	91.5	1.43
300	350	91.5	106.5	1.48
350	400	106.5	2.0	1.52
400	450	122.0	137.0	1.56
450	500	137.0	152.5	1.60
500	550	152.5	167.5	1.63
550	600	167.5	183.0	1.67
600	650	183.0	198.0	1.70
650	700	198.0	213.5	1.72
700	750	213.5	228.5	1.75
750	800	228.5	244.0	1.77
800	850	244.0	256.0	1.79
Above 850		Above 256		1.80

NOTE: The "Ch" value in this table, used in the equation described in section § 174.055(b), corresponds to the value of the vertical distance in feet (meters) from the water surface at the design draft of the unit to the center of area of the "A" value used in the equation.

TABLE 174.055(b)—Cs VALUES

Shape	Cs.
Cylindrical shapes	0.5
Hull (surface type)	1.0
Deckhouse	1.0
Cluster of deckhouses	1.1
Isolated structural shapes (cranes, angles, channels, beams, etc.)	1.5
Under deck areas (smooth surfaces)	1.0
Under deck areas (exposed beams and girders)	1.3
Rig derrick (each face and open truss works)	1.25

NOTE: The "Cs" value in this table, used in the equation described in § 174.055(b), corresponds to the shape of the projected "A" in the equation.

§ 174.065 Damage stability requirements.

(a) Each unit must be designed so that, while in each of its normal operating conditions and severe storm conditions, its final equilibrium waterline would remain below the lowest edge of any opening through which additional flooding could occur if the unit were subjected simultaneously to—
(1) Damage causing flooding described in §§ 174.075 through 174.085; and
(2) A wind heeling moment calculated in accordance with § 174.055(b) using a wind velocity of 50 knots (25.8 meters per second).

(b) Each unit must have a means to close off each pipe, ventilation system, and trunk in each compartment described in § 174.080 or § 174.085 if any portion of the pipe, ventilation system, or

§ 174.070 General damage stability assumptions.

trunk is within 5 feet (1.5 meters) of the hull.

For the purpose of determining compliance with § 174.065, the assumptions are made that during flooding and the resulting change in the unit's waterline—

(a) The unit is not anchored or moored; and

(b) No compartment on the unit is ballasted or pumped out to compensate for the flooding described in §§ 174.075 through 174.085.

§ 174.075 Compartments assumed flooded: general.

The individual flooding of each of the compartments described in §§ 174.080 and 174.085 must be assumed for the purpose of determining compliance with § 174.065 (a). Simultaneous flooding of more than one compartment must be assumed only when indicated in §§ 174.080 and 174.085.

§ 174.080 Flooding on self-elevating and surface type units.

(a) On a surface type unit or self-elevating unit, all compartments within 5 feet (1.5 meters) of the hull of the unit between two adjacent main watertight bulkheads, the bottom shell, and the uppermost continuous deck or first superstructure deck where superstructures are fitted must be assumed to be subject to simultaneous flooding.

(b) On the mat of a self-elevating unit, all compartments of the mat must be assumed to be subject to individual flooding.

§ 174.085 Flooding on column stabilized units.

(a) Watertight compartments that are outboard of, or traversed by, a plane which connects the vertical centerlines of the columns on the periphery of the unit, and within 5 feet (1.5 meters) of an outer surface of a column or footing on the periphery of the unit, must be assumed to be subject to flooding as follows:

(1) When a column is subdivided into watertight compartments by horizontal watertight flats, all compartments in the column within 5 feet (1.5 meters) of the unit's waterline before damage causing flooding must be assumed to be subject to simultaneous flooding.

(2) When a column is subdivided into watertight compartments by vertical watertight bulkheads, each two adjacent compartments must be assumed subject to simultaneous flooding if the distance between the vertical watertight bulkheads, measured at the column periphery, is equal to or less than one-eighth of the column perimeter at the draft under consideration.

(3) When a column is subdivided into watertight compartments by horizontal watertight flats and vertical watertight bulkheads, those compartments that are within the bounds described in paragraph (a)(2) of this section and within 5 feet (1.5 meters) of the unit's waterline before damage causing flooding must be assumed to be subject to simultaneous flooding.

(b) Each compartment in a footing must be assumed to be subject to individual flooding when any part of the compartment is within 5 feet (1.5 meters) of the unit's waterline before damage causing flooding.

§ 174.090 Permeability of spaces.

When doing the calculations required in § 174.065—

(a) The permeability of a floodable space, other than a machinery space, must be as listed in Table 174.090; and

(b) Calculations in which a machinery space is treated as a floodable space must be based on an assumed machinery space permeability of 85%, unless the use of an assumed permeability of less than 85% is justified in detail.

TABLE 174.090—PERMEABILITY

Spaces and tanks	Permeability (percent)
Storeroom spaces	60.
Accommodation spaces	95.
Voids	95.
Consumable liquid tanks	95 or 0.[1]
Other liquid tanks	95 or 0.[2]

[1] Whichever results in the more disabling condition.
[2] If tanks are partially filled, the permeability must be determined from the actual density and amount of liquid carried.

§ 174.100 Appliances for watertight and weathertight integrity.

(a) Appliances to insure watertight integrity include watertight doors,

§ 174.100

hatches, scuttles, bolted manhole covers, or other watertight closures for openings in watertight decks and bulkheads.

(b) Appliances to insure weathertight integrity include weathertight doors and hatches, closures for air pipes, ventilators, ventilation intakes and outlets, and closures for other openings in deckhouses and superstructures.

(c) Each internal opening equipped with appliances to insure watertight integrity that is used intermittently during operation of the unit while afloat must meet the following:

(1) Each door, hatch, and scuttle must—

(i) Be remotely controlled from a normally manned control station, and be operable locally from both sides of the bulkhead; or

(ii) If there is no means of remote control there must be an alarm system that signals whether the appliance is open or closed both locally at each appliance and in a normally manned control station.

(2) Each closing appliance must remain watertight under the design water pressure of the watertight boundary of which it is a part.

(d) Each external opening fitted with an appliance to insure weathertight integrity must be located so that it would not be submerged below the final equilibrium waterline if the unit is subjected simultaneously to—

(1) Damage causing flooding described in §§ 174.075 through 174.085; and

(2) A wind heeling moment calculated in accordance with § 174.055 using a wind velocity of 50 knots (25.8 meters per second).

(e) If a unit is equipped with sliding watertight doors, each sliding watertight door must—

(1) Be designed, constructed, tested, and marked in accordance with ASTM F 1196 (incorporated by reference, see § 174.007);

(2) Have controls in accordance with ASTM F 1197 (incorporated by reference, see § 174.007), except that a remote manual means of closure, as specified in paragraphs 7.1 and 7.5.1, and a remote mechanical indicator, as specified in paragraph 7.5.2, will not be required; and

(3) If installed in a subdivision bulkhead, meet Supplemental Requirements Nos. S1 and S3 of ASTM F 1196 (incorporated by reference, see § 174.007), unless the watertight doors are built in accordance with plans previously approved by the Coast Guard, in which case, only Supplemental Requirements Nos. S1 and S3.1.4 of ASTM F 1196 (incorporated by reference, see § 174.007) must be met. In either case, control systems for watertight doors must have power supplies, power sources, installation tests and inspection, and additional remote operating consoles in accordance with Supplemental Requirements Nos. S1 through S4 of ASTM F 1197 (incorporated by reference, see § 174.007).

(f) Installations of sliding watertight door assemblies must be in accordance with the following:

(1) Before a sliding watertight door assembly is installed in a vessel, the bulkhead in the vicinity of the door opening must be stiffened. Such bulkhead stiffeners, or deck reinforcement where flush deck door openings are desired, must not be less than 6 inches nor more than 12 inches from the door frame so that an unstiffened diaphragm of bulkhead plating 6 to 12 inches wide is provided completely around the door frame. Where such limits cannot be maintained, alternative installations will be considered by the Marine Safety Center. In determining the scantlings of these bulkhead stiffeners, the door frame should not be considered as contributing to the strength of the bulkhead. Provision must also be made to adequately support the thrust bearings and other equipment that may be mounted on the bulkhead or deck.

(2) Sliding watertight door frames must be either bolted or welded watertight to the bulkhead.

(i) If bolted, a suitable thin heat and fire resistant gasket or suitable compound must be used between the bulkhead and the frame for watertightness. The bulkhead plating shall be worked to a plane surface in way of the frame when mounting.

(ii) If welded, caution must be exercised in the welding process so that the door frame is not distorted.

[CGD 79–023, 48 FR 51048, Nov. 4, 1983, as amended by CGD 88–032, 56 FR 35828, July 29, 1991; USCG–2000–7790, 65 FR 58464, Sept. 29, 2000]

Subpart D [Reserved]

Subpart E—Special Rules Pertaining to Tugboats and Towboats

§ 174.140 Specific applicability.

Each tugboat and towboat inspected under subchapter I of this chapter must comply with this subpart.

§ 174.145 Intact stability requirements.

(a) In each condition of loading and operation, each vessel must be shown by design calculations to meet the requirements of paragraphs (b) through (e) of this section.

(b) The area under each righting arm curve must be at least 16.9 foot-degrees (5.15 meter-degrees) up to the smallest of the following angles:

(1) The angle of maximum righting arm.

(2) The downflooding angle.

(3) 40 degrees.

(c) The area under each righting arm curve must be at least 5.6 foot-degrees (1.72 meter-degrees) between the angles of 30 degrees and 40 degrees, or between 30 degrees and the downflooding angle if this angle is less than 40 degrees.

(d) The maximum righting arm shall occur at a heel of at least 25 degrees.

(e) The righting arm curve must be positive to at least 60 degrees.

(f) For the purpose of this section, at each angle of heel, a vessel's righting arm may be calculated considering either—

(1) The vessel is permitted to trim free until the trimming moment is zero; or

(2) The vessel does not trim as it heels.

Subpart F [Reserved]

Subpart G—Special Rules Pertaining to Offshore Supply Vessels

SOURCE: CGD 82–004 and CGD 86–074, 62 FR 49353, Sept. 19, 1997, unless otherwise noted.

§ 174.180 Applicability.

Each offshore supply vessel (OSV), except a liftboat inspected under subchapter L of this chapter, must comply with this subpart.

§ 174.185 Intact stability.

(a) Each OSV must be shown by design calculations to meet, under each condition of loading and operation, the minimal requirements for metacentric height (GM) in § 170.170 of this chapter, and in either § 170.173 of this chapter or paragraphs (b) through (e) of this section.

(b) The area under each righting arm curve must be at least 0.08 meter-radians (15 foot-degrees) up to the smallest of the following angles:

(1) The angle of maximum righting arm;

(2) The downflooding angle; or

(3) 40 degrees.

(c) The downflooding angle must not be less than 20 degrees.

(d) The righting arm curve must be positive to at least 40 degrees.

(e) The freeboard at the stern must be equal to the freeboard calculated to comply with subchapter E of this chapter or to the value taken from Table 174.185, whichever is less.

(f) For paragraphs (b) and (d) of this section, at each angle of heel an OSV's righting arm may be calculated considering either—

(1) The vessel is permitted to trim free until the trimming moment is zero; or

(2) The vessel does not trim as it heels.

(g) For the purpose of paragraphs (b) and (d) of this section, the method of calculating righting arms chosen must be the same for all calculations.

§ 174.190

TABLE 174.185—MINIMAL FREEBOARD AT THE STERN

LBP in meters (feet)	Freeboard at stern in millimeters (inches)
Less than 20 (65)	300 (12)
20 (65) but less than 30 (100)	380 (15)
30 (100) but less than 40 (130)	400 (18)
40 (130) but less than 50 (155)	500 (20)
50 (155) but less than 60 (190)	560 (22)
60 (190) but less than 70 (230)	610 (24)
70 (230) and greater	660 (26)

§ 174.190 Collision bulkhead.

(a) Each OSV must have a collision bulkhead in compliance with §§ 171.085(c)(1), (d), (e)(2), and (f) of this chapter.

(b) Penetration of the collision bulkhead by piping must be minimal, and, where fitted, piping must meet the requirements of §§ 56.50–1(b)(1) and (c) and 128.230 of this chapter.

§ 174.195 Bulkheads in machinery spaces.

(a) The bulkhead in each machinery space of each OSV must be watertight to the bulkhead deck.

(b) Each penetration of, and each opening in, a bulkhead in a machinery space must—

(1) Be kept as high and as far inboard as practicable; and

(2) Except as provided by § 174.210 of this subpart and by paragraph (c) of this section, have means to make it watertight.

(c) No penetration of a bulkhead in a machinery space by a ventilation duct need have means to make the bulkhead watertight if—

(1) Every part of the duct is at least 760 millimeter (30 inches) from the side of the OSV; and

(2) The duct is continuously watertight from the penetration to the main deck.

(d) Each penetration of a bulkhead in a machinery space by piping must meet the design requirements for material and pressure in subchapter F of this chapter.

§ 174.200 Damaged stability in machinery spaces for all OSVs.

Each OSV must be shown by design calculations to comply, under each afloat condition of loading and operation, with § 174.207 of this subpart in case of damage between any two watertight bulkheads in each machinery space.

§ 174.205 Additional damaged stability for OSVs carrying more than 16 offshore workers.

(a) *Calculations.* Each OSV carrying more than 16 offshore workers must be shown by design calculations to comply, under each afloat condition of loading and operation, with § 174.207 of this subpart in case of the damage specified by paragraph (b) of this section.

(b) *Character of damage.* For paragraph (a) of this section, design calculations must show that the OSV can survive damage at any place other than either the collision bulkhead or a transverse watertight bulkhead unless—

(1) The transverse watertight bulkhead is closer than the longitudinal extent of damage, specified by Table 174.207(a), to the adjacent transverse watertight bulkhead; or

(2) The transverse watertight bulkhead has a step or a recess, which must be assumed damaged, if it is both more than 3 meters (10 feet) in length and located within the transverse extent of damage specified by Table 174.207(a) of this section.

§ 174.207 Damaged stability criteria.

(a) *Extent of damage.* Damage must consist of penetrations having the dimensions specified by table 174.207(a) of this section, except that, if the most disabling penetrations are smaller than the penetrations specified by the table, damage must consist of the smaller penetrations.

(b) *Permeability of spaces.* The permeability of a floodable space must be as specified by Table 174.207(b) of this section.

(c) *Survival conditions.* An OSV is presumed to survive assumed damage if it meets the following conditions in the final stage of flooding:

(1) *Final waterline.* The final waterline, in the final stage of sinkage, heel, and trim, must be below the lower edge of an opening through which progressive flooding may take place, such as an air pipe, a tonnage opening, an

opening closed by a weathertight door or hatch-cover, or a tank vent fitted with a ball check-valve. This opening does not include an opening closed by a—

(i) Watertight manhole-cover;
(ii) Flush scuttle;
(iii) Small hatch-cover for a watertight cargo-tank that maintains the high integrity of the deck;
(iv) Watertight door in compliance with § 174.210 of this subpart; or
(v) Side scuttle of the non-opening type.

(2) *Angle of heel.* The angle of heel must not exceed 15 degrees.

(3) *Range of stability.* Through an angle of 20 degrees beyond its position of equilibrium after flooding, an OSV must meet the following conditions:

(i) The righting arm curve must be positive.
(ii) The righting arm must be at least 100 millimeters (4 inches).
(iii) Each submerged opening must be weathertight. (A tank vent fitted with a ball check-valve is weathertight.)

(4) *Progressive flooding.* Piping, ducts, or tunnels within the assumed extent of damage must be either—

(i) Equipped with arrangements, such as stop check-valves, to prevent progressive flooding of the spaces with which they connect; or
(ii) Assumed in the calculations required by paragraph (a) of this section to permit progressive flooding of the spaces with which they connect.

(d) *Buoyancy of superstructure.* For paragraph (a) of this section, the buoyancy of any superstructure directly above the side damage must be considered in the most unfavorable condition.

TABLE 174.207(a)—EXTENT OF DAMAGE

	Collision Penetration
Longitudinal extent (vessels with LBP not greater than 45 meters [143 feet]).	.1L or 1.8 meters (6 feet):, whichever is greater in length.
Longitudinal extent (vessels with LBP greater than 45 meters [143 feet]).	3 meters (10 feet) + .03L.
Transverse extent*	760 millimeters (30 inches).

TABLE 174.207(a)—EXTENT OF DAMAGE—Continued

Vertical extent.	From baseline upward without limit.

*The transverse penetration applies inboard from the side of the vessel, at right angles to the centerline, at the level of the deepest load waterline.

TABLE 174.207(b)—PERMEABILITY OF SPACES

Spaces and tanks	Permeability
Storerooms	60 percent.
Accommodations	95 percent.
Machinery	85 percent.
Voids and passageways	95 percent.
Dry-bulk tanks	0 (*) or 95 percent.
Consumable-liquid tanks	0 (*) or 95 percent.
Other liquid tanks	0 (*) 0 (**) or 95 percent.

*Whichever results in the more disabling condition.
**If tanks are partly filled, the permeability must be determined from the actual density and amount of liquid carried.

§ 174.210 Watertight doors in watertight bulkheads.

(a) This section applies to each vessel with watertight doors in bulkheads made watertight in compliance with this chapter.

(b) Except as provided by paragraph (c) of this section, each watertight door must comply with subpart H of part 170 of this chapter.

(c) A Class-1 door may be installed at any place if—

(1) The door has a quick-acting closing-device operative from both sides of the door;
(2) The door is designed to withstand a head of water equivalent to the depth from the sill of the door to the bulkhead deck or 3 meters (10 feet), whichever is greater; and
(3) The vessel's pilothouse contains a visual indicator showing whether the door is open or closed.

(d) Each watertight door must be marked in compliance with § 131.893 of this chapter.

(e) If a Class-1 door is installed, the vessel's stability letter will require the master to ensure that the door is always closed except when being used for access.

§ 174.215 Drainage of weather deck.

The weather deck must have open rails to allow rapid clearing of water, or must have freeing ports in compliance with § 42.15–70 of this chapter.

§ 174.220 Hatches and coamings.

(a) Each hatch exposed to the weather must be watertight, except that the following hatches may be only weathertight:

(1) Each hatch on a watertight trunk that extends at least 430 millimeters (17 inches) above the weather deck.

(2) Each hatch in a cabin top.

(b) Each hatch cover must—

(1) Have securing-devices; and

(2) Be attached to the hatch frame or coaming by hinges, captive chains, or other devices to prevent its loss.

(c) Each hatch that provides access to quarters or to accommodation spaces for crew members or offshore workers must be capable of being opened and closed from either side.

(d) Except as provided by paragraph (e) of this section, a weathertight door with a permanent watertight coaming at least 380 millimeters (15 inches) high must be installed for each opening in a deckhouse or companionway that—

(1) Gives access into the hull; and

(2) Is in an exposed place.

(e) If an opening in a deckhouse or companionway has a Class-1 watertight door installed, the height of the watertight coaming need only accommodate the door.

§ 174.225 Hull penetrations and shell connections.

Each overboard discharge and shell connection except an engine exhaust must comply with §§ 56.50–95 and 128.230 of this chapter.

Subpart H—Special Rules Pertaining to Liftboats

SOURCE: CGD 82–004 and CGD 86–074, 62 FR 49355, Sept. 19, 1997, unless otherwise noted.

§ 174.240 Applicability.

Each liftboat inspected under subchapter L of this chapter must comply with this subpart.

§ 174.245 General.

Each liftboat must comply with §§ 174.210 through 174.225.

§ 174.250 Unrestricted service.

Each liftboat not limited to restricted service must comply with subpart C of this part in each condition of loading and operation.

§ 174.255 Restricted service.

This section applies to each liftboat unable to comply with § 174.250 and limited to restricted service as defined by § 125.160 of this chapter.

(a) *Intact stability.* (1) Each liftboat must be shown by design calculations to meet, under each condition of loading and operation afloat, the following requirements:

(i) Those imposed by § 174.045, given a "K" value of at least 1.4.

(ii) A range of positive stability of at least 10 degrees extending from the angle of the first intercept of the curves of righting moment and wind heeling moment, either to the angle of the second intercept of those curves or to the angle of heel at which downflooding would occur, whichever angle is less.

(iii) A residual righting energy of at least 0.003 meter radians (5 foot-degrees) between the angle of the first intercept of the curves of righting moment and wind heeling moment, either to the angle of the second intercept of those curves or to the angle of heel at which downflooding would occur, whichever angle is less.

(2) For this section, each wind heeling moment must be calculated as prescribed by § 174.055 of this part using winds of 60 knots for normal conditions of operation afloat and of 70 knots for severe-storm conditions of operation afloat.

(3) For paragraph (a)(1) of this section, the initial metacentric height must be at least 300 millimeters (1 foot) for each leg position encountered while afloat including the full range of leg positions encountered while jacking.

(b) *Damaged stability.* (1) Each liftboat must be designed so that, while it is in each of its normal operating conditions, its final equilibrium waterline will remain below the lowest edge of any opening through which additional flooding can occur if the liftboat is subjected simultaneously to—

(i) Damage causing flooding described by paragraph (b)(4) of this section; and

(ii) A wind heeling moment calculated in compliance with § 174.055(b) using a wind speed of 50 knots.

(2) Each liftboat must have a means of closing off each pipe, ventilation system, and trunk in each compartment described by paragraph (b)(4) of this section if any part of the pipe, ventilation system, or trunk is within 760 millimeters (30 inches) of the hull.

(3) For compliance with paragraph (b)(1) of this section, no compartment on the liftboat may be ballasted or pumped out to compensate for the flooding described by paragraph (b)(4) of this section.

(4) For compliance with paragraph (b)(1) of this section, each compartment within 760 millimeters (30 inches) of the hull, excluding the bottom of the liftboat, between two adjacent main watertight bulkheads and the uppermost continuous deck or first superstructure deck where superstructures are fitted must be assumed subject to simultaneous flooding.

(5) In the calculations required by paragraph (b)(1) of this section, the permeability of a floodable space must be as listed by Table 174.205(d).

(c) *On-bottom stability.* Each liftboat must be shown by design calculations to exert a continuous downward force on each footing when the vessel is supported on the bottom with footings and is subjected to the forces of waves, currents, and winds of 70 knots under normal conditions of operation, and winds of 100 knots under severe-storm conditions of operation when elevated in a safe place, if this place is other than a harbor of safe refuge. The waves and currents must be appropriate for the winds and place.

§ 174.260 **Freeboard.**

(a) Each liftboat not required to obtain and maintain a loadline in compliance with subchapter E of this chapter must place markings on each side of the vessel amidships. These markings must each consist of a horizontal line 460 millimeters (18 inches) in length and 25 millimeters (1 inch) in height. The upper edges of the markings must be at a distance equal to the authorized freeboard measured vertically below the intersection of the continuation outwards of the upper surface of the weather deck and the outer surface of the shell. This distance must be at least 610 millimeters (24 inches).

(b) The markings required by paragraph (a) of this section may not be submerged in any condition of loading or operation.

Subpart I—Hopper Dredges With Working Freeboard Assignments

SOURCE: CGD 76–080, 54 FR 36977, Sept. 6, 1989, unless otherwise noted.

§ 174.300 **Specific applicability.**

This subpart applies to each self-propelled hopper dredge for which a working freeboard assignment is being sought under part 44, subpart C, of this chapter.

§ 174.305 **Definitions.**

Hopper dredge has the same meaning as contained in § 44.310 of this chapter.

Length has the same meaning as contained in § 42.13–15(a) of this chapter.

Working freeboard has the same meaning as contained in § 44.310 of this chapter.

CALCULATIONS

§ 174.310 **General.**

(a) Each hopper dredge under this subpart must be shown by design calculations based on the assumptions under paragraphs (b), (c), (d), and (e) of this section, that it meets—

(1) The requirements in §§ 170.170, 170.173, and 170.300 of this chapter in each condition of loading and operation; and

(2) The survival conditions of § 174.320 in each condition of loading and operation assuming the character and extent of damage specified in § 174.315.

(b) The calculations required by paragraph (a) of this section must assume:

(1) The hoppers are full of seawater;

(2) The permeability of flooded spaces is as provided by Table 174.310;

(3) The equalization provisions of § 174.325; and

(4) The jettisoning provisions of § 174.330.

(c) The calculations required by this section must take into account a sufficient number of loading conditions to

§ 174.315

identify the condition in which the vessel is least stable, including, but not limited to, the most severe loading condition, and the:

(1) Specific gravity of the dredge spoil, from 1.02 up to and including the maximum required by paragraph (e)(1) of this section; and

(2) Draft, up to and including the draft corresponding to the working freeboard for the full range of trim.

(d) The calculations required by this section for a dredge with open hoppers may include spillage of spoil from the hopper resulting from changing the angle of heel and trim.

(e) The following assumptions must be made when doing the calculations required by this section:

(1) Dredged spoil in the hopper is a homogeneous liquid with a maximum specific gravity for the areas of operation.

(2) When calculating the vessel's righting arm, it is assumed at each angle of heel that the vessel trims free and the trimming moment is zero.

TABLE 174.310—PERMEABILITY OF FLOODABLE SPACES

Spaces and tanks	Permeability
Storerooms	0.60
Accommodation spaces	0.95
Consumable liquid tanks	0.00 or 0.95—whichever results in the more disabling condition.
Machinery space	0.85—unless otherwise supported by calculations.
Cargo tanks	Determined from the actual density and amount of liquid carried in the tank.

§ 174.315 Extent and character of damage.

(a) The calculations required by § 174.310 must show that the dredge can survive damage at any location along the length of the vessel including at a transverse bulkhead in accordance with paragraph (b) of this section.

(b) The calculations required by paragraph (a) of this section must assume the most disabling side penetration with the damage collision penetration provided by Table 174.315, except that if the most disabling damage collision penetrations would be less than those provided by Table 174.315, the smaller damage collision penetration must be assumed.

TABLE 174.315—EXTENT OF DAMAGE COLLISION PENETRATION

Longitudinal extent	$0.495L^{2/3}$ or 47.6 feet. $[(1/3)(L)^{2/3}]$ or 14.5 meters] whichever is less.
Transverse extent [1]	B/5 or 37.7 feet. (11.5 meters), whichever is less.
Vertical extent	From the base line upward without limit.

[1] Damage applied inboard from the vessel's side at a right angle to the centerline at the draft corresponding to the working freeboard assigned under subchapter E of this chapter.

§ 174.320 Damage survival.

A hopper dredge survives assumed damage if it meets the following conditions:

(a) The maximum angle of heel in each stage of flooding must not exceed 30 degrees or the angle of downflooding whichever is less.

(b) The final waterline, taking into account sinkage, heel, and trim, must be below the lowest edge of each opening through which progressive flooding may take place.

(c) The righting arm curve calculated after damage must:

(1) Have a minimum positive range of 20 degrees beyond the angle of equilibrium; and

(2) Reach a height of at least 4 inches (100mm) within the 20 degree positive range.

(d) Each opening within, or partially within, the 20 degree range beyond the angle of equilibrium must be weathertight.

(e) After flooding or equalization as allowed by § 174.325, the hopper dredge's metacentric height must be at least 2 inches (50mm) when the dredge is in an upright position.

§ 174.325 Equalization.

When doing the calculations required by § 174.310 of this subpart—

(a) Equalization arrangements requiring mechanical aids, such as valves, may not be assumed to be effective in reducing the angle of heel; and

(b) Spaces joined by ducts may be assumed to be common spaces only if equalization takes place within 15 minutes after flooding begins.

Coast Guard, DHS

§ 174.355

§ 174.330 Jettisoning of spoil.

(a) When doing the calculations required by § 174.310 for a hopper dredge with bottom doors, it may be assumed that the spoil is jettisoned immediately after damage and that the bottom doors remain open if:

(1) The bottom doors are designed so that they may be fully opened from:

(i) The closed position within two minutes even if the main power source is lost or the bottom door actuating mechanism is damaged; and

(ii) The navigating bridge;

(2) The discharge area through the bottom doors is equal to or greater than 30 percent of the maximum cross sectional area of the hopper measured in a plane parallel to the waterline; and

(3) Asymmetrical jettisoning of the spoil is impossible.

(b) When doing the calculations required by § 174.310 for a hopper dredge with a split hull, it may be assumed that the spoil is jettisoned immediately after damage if—

(1) The hull is designed so that—

(i) The complete separation is effected within two minutes even if the main power source is lost or the actuating means is damaged; and

(ii) The actuating means can be operated from the navigating bridge;

(2) It is shown to the Commanding Officer, Marine Safety Center, either by calculations or by operational tests, that the hulls can separate sufficiently to allow the dredged material to dump without bridging; and

(3) Asymmetrical jettisoning of the spoil is impossible.

Design

§ 174.335 Watertight doors.

(a) Each hopper dredge must have sliding watertight doors (Class 3) approved under § 170.270 of this chapter if the sill for the door is—

(1) Installed below the bulkhead deck; and

(2) Less than 24 inches above the final waterline as shown by the calculations required by § 174.310 in each damage condition up to and including the maximum amount of assumed damage.

(b) Each hopper dredge must have sliding watertight doors (Class 3) approved under § 170.270 of this chapter, or quick acting hinged watertight doors (Class 1) approved under the same subpart if the sill of the watertight door is—

(1) Installed below the bulkhead deck; and

(2) Greater than 24 inches above the final waterline as shown by the calculations required by § 174.310 in each damage condition up to and including the maximum amount of assumed damage.

[CGD 76-080, 54 FR 36977, Sept. 6, 1989, as amended by CGD 95-072, 60 FR 50468, Sept. 29, 1995]

§ 174.340 Collision bulkhead.

Each hopper dredge must have a collision bulkhead that is located not less than 5 percent of the length abaft of the forward perpendicular.

Subpart J—Special Rules Pertaining to Dry Cargo Ships

Source: CGD 87-094, 58 FR 17320, Apr. 1, 1993, unless otherwise noted.

§ 174.350 Specific applicability.

This subpart applies to each new ship of 500 gross tons or over, as calculated by the International Convention on Tonnage Measurement of Ships, 1969, designed primarily for the carriage of dry cargoes, including roll-on/roll-off ships and integrated tug and barges (ITBs) when operating as a combined unit.

§ 174.355 Definitions.

New ship means a ship:

(1) For which the building contract is placed on or after February 1, 1992; or

(2) In the absence of a building contract, the keel of which is laid or which is at a similar stage of construction on or after August 1, 1992; or

(3) The delivery of which is on or after February 1, 1997; or

(4) For which application for reflagging is made on or after February 1, 1997; or

(5) Which has undergone a major conversion:

(i) For which the contract is placed on or after February 1, 1992; or

§ 174.360

(ii) In the absence of a contract, the construction work of which is begun on or after August 1, 1992; or

(iii) Which is completed on or after February 1, 1997.

§ 174.360 Calculations.

Each ship to which this subpart applies, must meet the minimum standard of subdivision and damage stability required for that ship by the International Convention for the Safety of Life at Sea, 1974, as amended, chapter II–1, part B–1. Compliance with the applicable requirements must be demonstrated by calculations and reflected in information on loading restrictions, such as a maximum height of the center of gravity (KG) or minimum metacentric height (GM) curve that is part of the stability information required by § 170.110 of this chapter and Regulation 25–8 of The International Convention for the Safety of Life at Sea, 1974, as amended, chapter II–1, part B–1.

INDEX

SUBCHAPTER S—SUBDIVISION AND STABILITY

EDITORIAL NOTE: This listing is provided for informational purposes only. It is compiled and kept current by the U.S. Coast Guard, Department of Homeland Security. This index is updated as of October 1, 2003.

Part, Subpart, or Section

A

Addresses:
  Material incorporated by reference 170.015
  Merchant marine technical offices 170.100
Aft peak bulkhead, passenger vessels 171.090
Alterations .... 170.001(b), 170.005
Auxiliary sailing vessels:
  Defined .... 170.055(a)
  Large passenger vessels 171.045
  Small passenger vessels 170.055, 171.010
  Weather criterion for 170.160

B

Ballast, fixed. (See Fixed ballast)
Barges:
  Deck cargo .... Part 174, Subpart B
  Definitions .... 170.055 (b) and (q)
  Large passenger 171.045
  Oceanographic research 173.070
  Tank. (See Tank barges)
  Weather criterion for 170.160
Bulk cargo vessels, special requirements for .... Part 172
Buoyancy:
  Air tanks .... 171.070(d), 171.095(c)
  Foam flotation material 170.245
  Internal .... 171.070(d), 171.095(c)
  Standards of flooding 171.017

C

Calculations:
  Samples of, in stability booklet .... 170.110(d)
  Stability text results .... 170.175(a)
  Submittal of 170.090
Catamarans 171.057
Center of gravity:
  Determination of .... Part 170, Subpart F
  Estimated position on tank vessels 170.200
  In stability booklet .... 170.110(d)
  Subchapter O barges .... 172.090(b)
  Tanks .... 170.075(a)(5)

183

Virtual increase of .... Part 170, Subpart I
Collision bulkhead:
  Oceanographic research vessels 173.075, 173.085
  Passenger vessels 171.060, 171.065, 171.070, 171.085
Consumable liquids: Effect on stability calculations 170.285, 170.290
Cranes:
  Data required 170.095
  Requirements for vessels with .... Part 173, Subpart B
Cross curves, required .... 170.090(b)(3)
Cross-flooding:
  Liquefied gas carriers, system standards .... 172.195(g)
  Passenger vessels, system standards .... 171.080(e)
  Subchapter O tankships, system standards .... 172.150(g)

D

Damage stability calculations:
  Liquefied gas carriers, local damage 172.205
  Liquefied gas carriers, major damage 172.170
  MODU's, standards for 174.065
  Nautical school ships, standards for 173.055, 173.080
  Oceanographic research vessels, standards for 173.080
  Passenger vessels:
    Cockpits .... 171.145(e)(3)
    Types I and II 171.080
    Type III 171.082
    Well decks .... 171.150(b)(2)
  Subchapter D tank barges carrying cargoes other than oil 172.050
  Subchapter O barges, standards for 172.103
  Subchapter O tankships, standards for 172.133
Dangerous cargoes .... Part 172, Subparts E and F
Dead covers:
  Oceanographic research vessels, required .... 173.085(k)
  Passenger vessels, required .... 171.117, 171.119(a)(2), 171.122(g)
Deadweight surveys .... 170.175(c)
Deck cargo barges. (See Barges)
Definitions:
  Concerning a vessel 170.055
  General terms 170.050
  Pertaining to lifting 173.010
  Pertaining to liquefied gas carriers 172.160
  Pertaining to MODU's 174.035
  Pertaining to passenger vessels 171.010
  Pertaining to Subchapter O tankships 172.127
Discontinuous bulkhead deck, passenger vessels .... 171.015(c)
Discontinuous weather deck .... 170.170(b)
Double bottoms, passenger vessels:
  Manholes in 171.108
  Permeability of .... 171.066(b)(4)
  Required 171.105
  Watertight floors in 171.109
  Wells in 171.106
Downflooding:
  Angle .... 170.055(g)
  Deck cargo barges 174.015
  Defined (except MODU's) .... 170.055(e)
  Lifting vessels .... 173.020(b)
  Liquefied gas carriers 172.195
  Mobile offshore drilling units (MODU's):

Subchapter S Index

    Considered 174.045
    Defined .... 174.035(b)
    Oil tankers .... 170.055(p)
    Sailing passenger vessels 171.055
    Subchapter O barges 172.090
    Subchapter O tankships 172.150
    Tugboats and towboats 174.145
    Vessels of unusual proportion and form 170.173
    Vessels which tow 173.095
Draft marks .... 170.075(a)(6), 170.180(e)
Drainage of weather decks .... Part 171, Subpart H
Deck cargo barges .... Part 174, Subpart B

E

Equalization. (See Cross-flooding)
Equivalent plane bulkhead, passenger vessels:
    Defined .... 171.010(c)
    Required:
        Type I subdivision .... 171.067(f)
        Type II subdivision .... 171.073(c)
Equivalents 170.010
Estimated lightweight vertical center of gravity 170.200
Existing vessels .... 170.001(b)

F

Ferry:
    Collision bulkheads .... 171.060(d)
    Defined .... 171.010(d)
Fixed ballast .... 170.110(d)(14), 170.235
Floodable length:
    Curves required .... 170.090(b)(4)
    Defined .... 171.010(f)
    Passenger vessels:
        Standards, Type I 171.065
        Standards, Type II 171.070
        Standards, Type III 171.075
Floors, watertight—in double bottoms 171.109
Foam flotation .... 170.245, 171.070(d), 171.095(c)
Foreign vessels .... 170.001(a)(2)
Freeboard: Allowable heeling limits, general .... 170.170(a)
Freeing ports:
    Minimum Area 171.150
    Required 171.135
Free surface:
    Instructions concerning:
        Counterballasting .... 170.125(b)(1)
        Stability booklet .... 170.110(d)(6)
        Subchapter O tank barges, assumption .... 172.087(b)
        Treatment of, general .... Part 170, Subpart I

G

Grain in bulk .... Part 172, Subpart B
"Grandfathering" .... 170.001(b)

H

Hazardous liquids	Part 172, Subparts E, F
Hopper barges:	
Subchapter D cargoes other than oil	172.050
Subchapter O cargoes	172.100, 172.110
Hydrostatic curves (curves of form), required	170.075(a)(3)

I

Inclining experiments. (See Stability test)	
Incorporation by reference:	
General	170.015
IMO Resolution A.265(VIII)	170.135, 171.075, 171.082
MIL-P-21929B	170.245(b)(9)
Intact stability:	
Deck cargo barges	174.015, 174.020
Large passenger vessels:	
Catamarans	171.057
Passenger heel	171.050
Sailing	171.055
Lifting vessels	173.020, 173.025
Liquefied gas carriers	172.165
Mobile offshore drilling units (MODU's)	174.045
Passenger vessels:	
Cockpits	171.145(e)(1)
Well decks	171.150(b)(2)
Subchapter O barges	172.090, 172.095
Tugboats and Towboats	174.145
Vessels of unusual proportion and form	170.170(d), 170.173
Weather Criterion	170.160, 170.170
International voyage:	
Passenger vessels:	
Aft peak bulkhead required	171.090(a)
Defined	171.010(h)
Double bottoms required for	171.105(a)
Shaft tunnels	171.100(a)
Special considerations	171.068
Standards	171.045
Subdivision requirements	170.265(d)(1)
Watertight door requirements	170.265(d)(1)

L

Large Passenger vessels	Part 171, Subpart C
Lifting:	
Data submittal requirements	170.095
Operating information requirements	170.125
Standards	Part 173, Subpart B
Lightweight:	
Defined	170.055(j)
Information required, stability booklet	170.110(d)(1)
Determination of	Part 170, Subpart F
Lines drawing required	170.075(a)(2), 170.180(a)
Liquefied flammable gas, barges	Part 172, Subpart C
Liquefied gas carriers	Part 172, Subpart G
LNG Carriers. (See Liquefied gas carriers)	
Load line:	
Certificate stability information on	170.110(e), 170.120(b)

Subchapter S Index

Length, defined...170.055(h)(5)
Locks required:
  Cargo space watertight doors ....170.275(b)
  Port lights below the bulkhead deck..171.116(f)(4)

M

Machinery space bulkhead, passenger vessels 171.095
Main transverse watertight bulkhead ....170.055(k)
Manholes, passenger vessels:
  Double bottoms...171.108
  Prohibited locations..171.111(h)
Margin line:
  Passenger vessels:
    Air tankage or internal buoyancy ....171.070(d)(2)
    Dead covers required on port lights, below..................................171.117(a)
    Location of...171.015
    Location of openings ....171.111(f), (g)
    Openings in trunks...171.113(c)(2)
    Stepped bulkheads ....171.067(b)(3)
    Submergence of..171.017, 171.080(d)(3), 171.100(b)
    Volume below ....Tables 171.065(a), 171.066, 171.068
    Volume of passenger spaces above ....171.065(b)
    Watertight integrity above ....Part 171, Subpart G
Test head:
  Form flotation material ....170.245(b)(3)
  Watertight doors...170.270(b)
Military specifications, MIL-P-21929B...170.015(b), 170.245(b)
Mobile offshore drilling units (MODU's):
  Stability information required...170.110(a)
  Standards for ....174.005(b), Part 174, Subpart C

N

Nautical school ships, standards ....171.001(b), 173.001(b), Part 173, Subpart C

O

Oceanographic vessel, standards ....171.001(b), 173.001(c), Part 173, Subpart D
Oil in bulk, standards for vessels carrying ....172.005(c), Part 172, Subpart D
Openings:
  Closed by weathertight covers:
    Liquefied gas carriers..172.195
    Mobile offshore drilling units ....174.045(c)
    Oil tankers ....172.065(g)
    Subchapter O tankships 172.150
  Downflooding through:
    General ....170.055(e), (f)
    Mobile offshore drilling units ....174.035(b), 174.065(a)
    Subchapter O barges ....172.090(d)
    Sailing passenger vessels ....171.055(e)
  Mobile offshore drilling units:
    Closures for 174.100
    Watertight, closed automatically ....174.015(b)
    Watertight, closed rapidly 174.045
  Passenger vessels:
    Cockpit openings..171.145(a)(2)
    Collision bulkhead 171.085
    Special consideration, exposed weather decks ....171.122(f)

Vessel sides ....Part 171, Subpart F
Watertight bulkheads ....Part 171, Subpart E
Watertight, closed automatically:
  Mobile offshore drilling units ....174.015(b)
  Towing vessels ....173.095(e)

P

Passenger vessels, standards ....Part 171
Penetrations (See Openings)
Permeability
  Calculation of, Type I subdivision 171.066
  Damage stability:
    Liquefied gas carriers 172.185
    Mobile offshore drilling units 174.090
    Oil tankers ....172.065(f)
    Passenger vessels ....171.080(c)
    Subchapter O tankships 172.140
  Defined ....170.055(m)
  Uniform average permeability:
    Type I subdivision ....Table 171.068
    Type II subdivision 171.072
Plans:
  Approval:
    General ....Part 170, Subpart C, 170.180
    Required 170.075
    Specific 170.093
  Submittal of 170.100, 170.180
Port lights 171.116

R

Repairs:
  General ....170.001(b), 170.005
  In way of fixed ballast ....170.235(b)
Roll stabilization tanks 170.295
Rudders, towline pull criterion 173.095

S

Sailing vessels:
  Defined ....170.055(a), (1)
  Intact stability standards:
    Catamarans 171.057
    Large passenger vessels 171.055
    Weather criterion 170.160
School ships (See Nautical school ships)
Shaft power, towline pull criterion 173.095
Shaft tunnels:
  On passenger vessels ....171.100, 171.106(c)
  Watertight doors in ....170.260(d)
Short international voyages, vessels on:
  Class 3 doors ....170.265(d)(1)
  Defined ....171.010(n)
  Double bottoms not required ....171.105(h)(2)
  Special considerations 171.068
Side ports, passenger vessels 171.118
Sister vessel, stability test dispensed with ....170.175(c)

Subchapter S Index

Small passenger vessels, standards .... Part 171
Stability booklets:
  Contents of 170.110
  Lifting vessels, additional information 170.125
  Submission and approval required 170.080
  Vessels with Type III subdivision, additional information 170.135
Stability letters:
  In lieu of stability booklet .... 170.110(e)
  Required 170.120
Stability test:
  General 170.175
  Information required before test 170.085
  Plans and information required at test 170.180
  Preparations for test 170.185
  Test procedure, modification of 170.190
Stern tubes, passenger vessels 171.100
Subdivision:
  Oceanographic vessels 173.075, 173.085
  Passenger vessels:
    Additional requirements .... Part 171, Subpart D
    Calculations:
      Type I 171.065, 171.066, 171.067, 171.068
      Type II 171.070, 171.072, 171.073
      Type III 171.075
  Requirements, large passenger vessels 171.060
  Trunks, effect of .... 171.113(b)(3)
Subdivision load line (draft), passenger vessels:
  Cockpits .... 171.145(e), (f)
  Dead cover locations .... 171.117(b)
  Deepest, defined .... 171.010(b)
  Openings in hull, small passenger vessels .... 171.119(a)
  Port light locations .... 171.116(b)(2)
  Transverse damage extent, relationship to .... 171.065(h)(2), Table 171.080(a)
  Ventilators and side port locations .... 171.118(c)
Superstructures:
  Buoyancy of:
    Liquefied gas carriers .... 172.195(e)
    Oil tankers .... 172.065(h)
    Subchapter O tankships 172.150
  Integrity of, mobile offshore drilling units .... 174.100(b)
  Points of downflooding in:
    General .... 170.055(e)
    Mobile offshore drilling units .... 174.035(b)(1)
  Port lights in, oceanographic vessels .... 173.085(k)

T

Tank barge:
  Assumed center of gravity for .... 170.200(b)(2)
  Carrying oil in bulk .... Part 172, Subpart D
  Carrying Subchapter D cargoes other than oil .... Part 172, Subpart C
  Carrying Subchapter O cargoes .... Part 172, Subpart E
  Defined .... 170.055(q)
Tank vessel:
  Assumed center of gravity 170.200
  Defined .... 170.055(p)
  Standards for .... Part 172, Subparts C, D, E, F, G
Tests:

Foam flotation material 170.245
Stability .... 170.085, Part 170, Subpart F
Watertight doors 170.270
Towboats. (See Towing)
Towing, standards for ... 173.001(d), Part 173, Subpart E, 174.005(d), Part 174, Subpart E
Towline pull criterion 173.095
Tugboats. (See Towing)

U

Unusual proportion and form, vessels of 170.173

V

Ventilators, automatic—passenger vessels 171.118

W

Watertight bulkheads:
  Doors, standards for .... 171.122, 171.124, Part 170, Subpart H
  Liquefied gas carriers 172.175, 172.195
  Mobile offshore drilling units 174.080, 174.085
  Oceanographic vessels, ducts through .... 173.085(o)
  Oil tankers 172.065
  Passenger vessels:
    Above weatherdeck 171.122
    Large passenger vessels, requirements 171.065, 171.067, 171.068, 171.070, 171.073
    Machinery space 171.095
    Penetrations of .... Part 171, Subpart E
    Watertight floors 171.109
  Subchapter D barges not carrying oil 172.050
  Subchapter O barges 172.104
  Subchapter O tankships .... 172.133(d), 172.150
Watertight doors. (See Watertight bulkheads)
Weather criterion .... Part 170, Subpart E
Wind heeling moment: MODU's .... 174.035(b)(2), 174.045, 174.055, 174.065(a)(2), 174.100(d)(2)

SUBCHAPTER T—SMALL PASSENGER VESSELS (UNDER 100 GROSS TONS)

PART 175—GENERAL PROVISIONS

Sec.
175.100 Purpose.
175.110 General applicability.
175.112 Specific applicability for individual parts.
175.115 Applicability to offshore supply vessels.
175.118 Vessels operating under an exemption afforded in the Passenger Vessel Safety Act of 1993 (PVSA).
175.120 Vessels on an international voyage.
175.122 Load lines.
175.200 Gross tonnage as criterion for requirements.
175.400 Definitions of terms used in this subchapter.
175.540 Equivalents.
175.550 Special consideration.
175.560 Appeals.
175.600 Incorporation by reference.
175.800 Approved equipment and material.
175.900 OMB control numbers.

AUTHORITY: 46 U.S.C. 2103, 3205, 3306, 3703; Pub. L 103–206, 107 Stat. 2439; 49 U.S.C. App. 1804; Department of Homeland Security Delegation No. 0170.1; 175.900 also issued under authority of 44 U.S.C. 3507.

SOURCE: CGD 85–080, 61 FR 947, Jan. 10, 1996, unless otherwise noted.

§ 175.100 Purpose.

The purpose of this subchapter is to implement applicable sections of Subtitle II of Title 46, United States Code, which require the inspection and certification of small passenger vessels.

§ 175.110 General applicability.

(a) Except as in paragraph (b) of this section, this subchapter applies to each vessel of less than 100 gross tons that carries 150 or less passengers, or has overnight accommodations for 49 or less passengers, and that—

(1) Carries more than six passengers, including at least one for hire;

(2) Is chartered with a crew provided or specified by the owner or the owner's representative and is carrying more than six passengers;

(3) Is chartered with no crew provided or specified by the owner or the owner's representative and is carrying more than 12 passengers; or

(4) If a submersible vessel, carries at least one passenger for hire.

NOTE TO § 175.110: For a vessel of less than 100 gross tons that carries more than 150 passengers or has overnight accommodations for more than 49 passengers, see subchapter K of this chapter.

(b) This subchapter does not apply to:

(1) A vessel operating exclusively on inland waters that are not navigable waters of the United States;

(2) An oceanographic research vessel;

(3) A boat forming part of a vessel's lifesaving equipment and that is not used for carrying passengers except in emergencies or during emergency drills;

(4) A vessel of a foreign country that is a party to the International Convention for the Safety of Life at Sea, 1974, as amended (SOLAS), to which the United States Government is currently a party, and that has on board a current valid SOLAS Passenger Ship Safety Certificate; or

(5) A vessel of a foreign country, whose government has inspection laws approximating those of the United States and that by its laws accords similar privileges to vessels of the United States, which has on board a current valid certificate of inspection, permitting the carrying of passengers, issued by its government.

[CGD 85–080, 61 FR 947, Jan. 10, 1996; 61 FR 20557, May 7, 1996, as amended at 62 FR 51355, Sept. 30, 1997]

§ 175.112 Specific applicability for individual parts.

At the beginning of certain parts of this subchapter, a more specific application is given for all or particular portions of that part. This application sets forth the type, size, service, or age of a vessel to which certain portions of that part apply or particular dates by which an existing vessel must comply with certain portions of that part.

§ 175.115 Applicability to offshore supply vessels.

(a) Existing OSVs of more than 15 but less than 100 gross tons are subject to

§ 175.118

inspection under this subchapter. New OSVs of more than 15 but less than 100 gross tons are subject to inspection under subchapter L of this chapter.

(b) Each existing OSV permitted grandfathering under paragraph (a) of this section must complete construction and have a Certificate of Inspection by March 16, 1998.

[CGD 82–004 and CGD 86–074, 62 FR 49355, Sept. 19, 1997]

§ 175.118 Vessels operating under an exemption afforded in the Passenger Vessel Safety Act of 1993 (PVSA).

(a) The Passenger Vessel Safety Act of 1993 (PVSA) contained an allowance for the exemption of certain passenger vessels that are—

(1) At least 100 gross tons but less than 300 gross tons; or

(2) Former public vessels of at least 100 gross tons but less than 500 gross tons.

(b) The owner or operator of a vessel must have applied for an exemption under PVSA by June 21, 1994, and then brought the vessel into compliance with the interim guidance in Navigation and Inspection Circular (NVIC) 7–94 not later than December 21, 1996. The PVSA exemption is valid for the service life of the vessel, as long as the vessel remains certified for passenger service. If the Certificate of Inspection (COI) is surrendered or otherwise becomes invalid (not including a term while the vessel is out of service but undergoing an inspection for recertification), the owner or operator must meet the appropriate inspection regulations to obtain a new COI without the PVSA exemption.

(c) Except where the provisions of subchapter H of this chapter apply, the owner or operator must ensure that the vessel meets the requirements of this subchapter, meets any requirements the OCMI deems applicable, and meets any specific additions or exceptions as follows:

(1) If a vessel does not meet the intact stability requirements of subchapter S of this chapter, the vessel's route(s) will be limited to an area within 20 nautical miles from a harbor of safe refuge, provided the vessel has a history of safe operation on those waters. The OCMI may further restrict the vessel's routes if the vessel's service history, condition, or other factors affect its seaworthiness or safety.

(2) The vessel may not carry more than 150 passengers, and not more than 49 passengers in overnight accommodations.

(3) The owner or operator must crew the vessel under the requirements of this subchapter. All officers must be licensed for the appropriate vessel tonnage. The OCMI may require a licensed engineer for those vessels of at least 200 gross tons. Vessels carrying more than 50 passengers must have an additional deckhand, and all deckhands on vessels carrying more than 50 passengers must be adequately trained. The crew members on a vessel of at least 200 gross tons, except those operated exclusively on lakes and rivers, are required to hold merchant mariner documents and 50 percent of the unlicensed deck crew must be rated as at least an able seaman.

(4) The vessel owner or operator must comply with the lifesaving arrangements located in part 180 of this chapter, except that inflatable liferafts are required for primary lifesaving. A rescue boat or suitable rescue arrangement must be provided to the satisfaction of the OCMI.

(5) The vessel owner or operator must comply with the fire protection requirements located in part 181 of this chapter. When a vessel fails to meet the fire protection and structural fire protection requirements of this subchapter, the vessel owner or operator must meet equivalent requirements to the satisfaction of the cognizant OCMI or submit plans for approval from the Coast Guard Marine Safety Center.

(6) At a minimum, the owner or operator must outfit the vessel with portable fire extinguishers per 46 CFR 76.50. In addition, the vessel must meet any additional requirements of the OCMI, even if they exceed the requirements in 46 CFR 76.50.

(7) In addition to the means-of-escape requirements of 46 CFR 177.500, the vessel owner or operator must also meet the requirements for means of escape found in 46 CFR 78.47–40.

(d) The OCMI conducts an inspection and may issue a COI if the vessel meets these requirements. The COI's condition of operation must contain the following endorsement: "This vessel is operating under an exemption afforded in The Passenger Vessel Safety Act of 1993 and as such is limited to domestic voyages and a maximum _____ of passengers and may be subject to additional regulations and restrictions as provided for in Sections 511 and 512 of the Act."

[USCG–1999–5040, 67 FR 34799, May 15, 2002]

§ 175.120 Vessels on an international voyage.

A mechanically propelled vessel that carries more than 12 passengers on an international voyage must comply with the applicable requirements of SOLAS, as well as this subchapter.

§ 175.122 Load lines.

A vessel of 24 meters (79 feet) in length or more, the keel of which was laid or that was at a similar stage of construction on or after July 21, 1968, and that is on a voyage other than a domestic voyage is subject to load line assignment, certification, and marking under suchapter E (Load Lines) of this chapter.

§ 175.200 Gross tonnage as criterion for requirements.

(a) The regulations in this subchapter take into account a vessel's length, passenger capacity, construction, equipment, intended service, and operating area. The criterion for application of this subchapter is the gross tonnage of the vessel. When the Commandant determines that the gross tonnage of a particular vessel, which is attained by exemptions, reductions, or other devices in the basic gross tonnage formulation, will circumvent or be incompatible with the application of specific regulations for a vessel of such physical size, the Commandant will prescribe the regulations to be made applicable to the vessel.

(b) When the Commandant determines that the gross tonnage is not a valid criterion for the use of certain regulations based on the relative size of the vessel, the owner will be informed of the determination and of the regulations applicable to the vessel. The vessel must be brought into compliance with all additional requirements before a Certificate of Inspection is issued.

§ 175.400 Definitions of terms used in this subchapter.

The following terms are used in this subchapter:

Accommodation space means a space (including a space that contains a microwave oven or other low heat appliance with a maximum heating element temperature of less than 121 °C (250 °F)) used as a:

(1) Public space;
(2) Hall;
(3) Dining room and mess room;
(4) Lounge or cafe;
(5) Public sales room;
(6) Overnight accommodation space;
(7) Barber shop or beauty parlor;
(8) Office of conference room;
(9) Washroom or toilet space;
(10) Medical treatment room or dispensary; or
(11) Game or hobby room.

Adequate hull protection system means a method of protecting the vessel's hull from corrosion. It includes, as a minimum, either hull coatings and a cathodic protection (CP) system consisting of sacrificial anodes, or an impressed current CP system.

Alternative Hull Examination (AHE) Program means a program in which an eligible vessel may receive an initial and subsequent credit hull examination through a combination of underwater surveys, internal examinations and annual hull condition assessment.

Anniversary date means the day and the month of each year, which corresponds to the date of expiration of the Certificate of Inspection.

Approval series means the first six digits of a number assigned by the Coast Guard to approved equipment. Where approval is based on a subpart of subchapter Q of this chapter, the approval series corresponds to the number of the subpart. A listing of approved equipment, including all of the approval series, is published periodically by the Coast Guard in Equipment Lists (COMDTINST M16714.3 series), available from the Superintendent of Documents.

Beam or *B* means the maximum width of a vessel from:

§ 175.400

(1) Outside of planking to outside of planking on wooden vessels; and

(2) Outside of frame to outside of frame on all other vessels.

Bulbous bow means a design of bow in which the forward underwater frames ahead of the forward perpendicular are swelled out at the forefoot into a bulbous formation.

Bulkhead deck means the uppermost deck to which watertight bulkheads and the watertight shell extend.

Cable means single or multiple insulated conductors with an outer protective jacket.

Cargo space means a:

(1) Cargo hold;

(2) Refrigerated cargo space;

(3) A trunk leading to or from a space listed above: or

(4) A vehicle space.

Coast Guard District Commander or *District Commander* means an officer of the Coast Guard designated as such by the Commandant to command Coast Guard activities within a district.

Coastwise means a route that is not more than 20 nautical miles offshore on any of the following waters:

(1) Any ocean;

(2) The Gulf of Mexico;

(3) The Caribbean Sea;

(4) The Bering Sea;

(5) The Gulf of Alaska; or

(6) Such other similar waters as may be designated by a Coast Guard District Commander.

Cockpit vessel means a vessel with an exposed recess in the weather deck extending not more than one-half of the length of the vessel measured over the weather deck.

Cold water means water where the monthly mean low water temperature is normally 15 degrees Celsius (59 degrees Fahrenheit) or less.

Commandant means the Commandant of the Coast Guard or an authorized Headquarters staff officer designated in § 1.01 of this chapter.;

Consideration means an economic benefit, inducement, right, or profit including pecuniary payment accruing to an individual, person, or entity, but not including a voluntary sharing of the actual expenses of the voyage, by monetary contribution or donation of fuel, food, beverage, or other supplies.

Corrosion-resistant material or *corrosion-resistant* means made of one of the following materials in a grade suitable for its intended use in a marine environment:

(1) Silver;

(2) Copper;

(3) Brass;

(4) Bronze;

(5) Aluminum alloys with a copper content of no more than 0.4 percent;

(6) Cooper-nickel;

(7) Plastics;

(8) Stainless steel;

(9) Nickel-copper; or

(10) A material, which when tested in accordance with ASTM B 117 (incorporated by reference, see § 175.600) for 200 hours, does not show pitting, cracking, or other deterioration.

Crew accommodation space means an accommodation space designated for the use of crew members and that passengers are normally not allowed to occupy.;

Custom engineered means, when referring to a fixed gas fire extinguishing system, a system that is designed for a specific space requiring individual calculations for the extinguishing agent volume, flow rate, piping, and similar factors for the space.

Dead cover means a metal cover to close or protect a port light to avoid glass breakage in case of heavy weather.

Distribution panel means an electrical panel that receives energy from the switchboard and distributes the energy to energy consuming devices or other panels.;

Draft means the vertical distance from the molded baseline of a vessel amidships to the waterline.;

Dripproof means enclosed equipment so constructed or protected that falling drops of liquid or solid particles striking the enclosure at any angle from 0 to 15 degrees downward from the vertical do not interfere with the operation of the equipment. A National Electrical Manufacturers Association type 1 enclosure with a dripshield is considered to be dripproof.

Drydock examination means hauling out a vessel or placing a vessel in a drydock or slipway for an examination of all accessible parts of the vessel's underwater body and all through-hull fittings and appurtenances.

Embarkation station means the place on the vessel from which a survival craft is boarded.

Enclosed space means a compartment that is not exposed to the atmosphere when all access and ventilation closures are secured.

Existing OSV means an OSV that was contracted for, or the keel of which was laid, before March 15, 1996.

Existing vessel means a vessel that is not a new vessel.

Exposed waters is a term used in connection with stability criteria and means:

(1) Waters, except the Great Lakes, more than 20 nautical miles from a harbor of safe refuge;

(2) Those portions of the Great Lakes more than 20 nautical miles from a harbor of safe refuge from October 1 of one year through April 15 of the next year (winter season); and

(3) Those waters less than 20 nautical miles from a harbor of safe refuge that the cognizant Officer in Charge, Marine Inspection, determines are not partially protected waters or protected waters because they present special hazards due to weather or other circumstances.

Ferry means a vessel that:

(1) Operates in other than ocean or coastwide service;

(2) Has provisions only for deck passengers or vehicles, or both;

(3) Operates on a short run on a frequent schedule between two points over the most direct water route; and

(4) Offers a public service of a type normally attributed to a bridge or tunnel.

Fiber reinforced plastic means plastics reinforced with fibers or strands of some other material.

Flash point means the temperature at which a liquid gives off a flammable vapor when heated using the Pensky-Martens Closed Cup Tester method in accordance with ASTM D-93.

Float-free launching or arrangement means that method of launching a survival craft whereby the survival craft is automatically released from a sinking vessel and is ready for use.

Flush deck vessel means a vessel with a continuous weather deck located at the uppermost sheer line of the hull.

Freeing port means any direct opening through the vessel's bulwark or hull to quickly drain overboard water that has been shipped on exposed decks.

Galley means a space containing appliances with cooking surfaces that may exceed 121° C (250° F), such as ovens, griddles, and deep fat fryers.

Great Lakes means a route on the waters of any of the Great Lakes, except that for the purposes of parts 178 and 179 of this subchapter, "Great Lakes" means both the waters of the Great Lakes and of the St. Lawrence River as far east as a straight line drawn from Cap de Rosiers to West Point, Anticosti Island, and west of a line along the 63rd meridian from Anticosti Island to the north shore of the St. Lawrence River.

Gross tonnage and *gross tons* is an indicator of a vessel's approximate volume as determined in accordance with part 69 (Measurement of Vessels) of this chapter and recorded on the vessel's Tonnage Certificate (formerly Certificate of Admeasurement).

Harbor of safe refuge means a port, inlet, or other body of water normally sheltered from heavy seas by land and in which a vessel can navigate and safely moor. The suitability of a location as a harbor of safe refuge shall be determined by the cognizant Officer in Charge, Marine Inspection, and varies for each vessel, dependent on the vessel's size, maneuverability, and mooring gear.

Hazardous condition means any condition that could adversely affect the safety of any vessel, bridge, structure or shore area or the environmental quality of any port, harbor, or navigable water of the United States. This condition could include but is not limited to, fire, explosion, grounding, leaking, damage, illness of a person on board, or a manning shortage.

High seas means all waters that are neither territorial seas (the waters in a belt 3 nautical miles wide, that is adjacent to the coast and seaward of the territorial sea baseline) nor internal waters of the United States or of any foreign country.

High speed craft means a craft that is operable on or above the water and has

§ 175.400

characteristics so different from those of conventional displacement ships, to which the existing international conventions, particularly SOLAS, apply, that alternative measures should be used to achieve an equivalent level of safety. In order to be considered a high speed craft, the craft must be capable of a maximum speed equal to or exceeding $V = 3.7 \times displ^{.1667}$ h, where "V" is the maximum speed and "displ" is the vessel displacement corresponding to the design waterline in cubic meters.

Independent laboratory means a laboratory accepted under part 159, Subpart 159.010 of this chapter.

Inflatable survival craft or "inflatable life jacket" means one that depends upon nonrigid, gas-filled chambers for buoyancy, and which is normally kept uninflated until ready to use.

Internal structural examination means an examination of the vessel while afloat or in drydock and consists of a complete examination of the vessel's main strength members, including the major internal framing, the hull plating, voids, and ballast tanks, but not including cargo, sewage, or fuel oil tanks.

International voyage means a voyage between a country to which SOLAS applies and a port outside that country. A country, as used in this definition, includes every territory for the international relations of which a contracting government to the convention is responsible or for which the United Nations is the administering authority. For the U.S., the term "territory" includes the Commonwealth of Puerto Rico, all possessions of the United States, and all lands held by the United States under a protectorate or mandate. For the purposes of this subchapter, vessels are not considered as being on an "international voyage" when solely navigating the Great Lakes and the St. Lawrence River as far east as a straight line drawn from Cap des Rosiers to West Point, Anticosti Island and, on the north side of Anticosti Island, the 63rd meridian.

Lakes, bays, and sounds means a route on any of the following waters:

(1) A lake other than the Great Lakes;

(2) A bay;

(3) A sound; or

(4) Such other similar waters as may be designated by a Coast Guard District Commander.

Launching appliance means a device for transferring a survival craft or rescue boat from its stowed position safely to the water. For a launching appliance using a davit, the term includes the davit, winch, and falls.

Length when used in terms of the vessel's length (excluding bow sprits, bumpkins, rudders, outboard motor brackets, handles, and other similar fittings, attachments, and extensions), means:

(1) The length listed on the vessel's Certificate of Documentation issued under the provisions of part 67 (Documentation of Vessels) of this chapter or Certificate of Number issued under the provisions of 33 CFR part 173, subpart B (Numbering); or

(2) For a vessel that does not have a Certificate of Documentation or a Certificate of Number, the "registered length" as defined in § 69.53 in subchapter G of this chapter or, for a vessel that is less than 24 meters (79 feet) in overall length and is measured using simplified admeasurement, the registered length as defined in § 69.203 in subchapter G of this chapter; or

(3) For the purposes of part 179 in subchapter S, the "length" of a vessel with a bulbous bow means the larger of the length as defined in the first paragraph of this definition or the straight line horizontal measurement from the forwardmost tip of the bulbous bow to the aftermost part of the vessel measured parallel to the centerline.

Length between perpendiculars or *LBP* means the horizontal distance measured between perpendiculars taken at the forwardmost and aftermost points on the waterline corresponding to the deepest operating draft.

Limited coastwise means a route that is not more than 20 nautical miles from a harbor of safe refuge.

Machinery space means a space including a trunk, alleyway, stairway, or duct to such a space, that contains:

(1) Propulsion machinery of any type;

(2) Steam or internal combustion machinery;

(3) Oil transfer equipment;

(4) Electrical motors of more than 10 hp;
(5) Refrigeration equipment;
(6) One or more oil-fired boilers or heaters; or
(7) Electrical generating machinery.

Main transverse watertight bulkhead means a transverse bulkhead that must be maintained watertight in order for the vessel to meet the damage stability and subdivision requirements of this subchapter.

Major conversion means a conversion of a vessel that, as determined by the Commandant:
(1) Substantially changes the dimensions or carrying capacity of the vessel;
(2) Changes the type of vessel;
(3) Substantially prolongs the life of the vessel; or
(4) Otherwise so changes the vessel that it is essentially a new vessel.

Marine inspector or *inspector* means any civilian employee or military member of the Coast Guard assigned by an Officer in Charge, Marine Inspection, or the Commandant to perform duties with respect to the inspection, enforcement, and administration of vessel safety and navigation laws and regulations.

Master means the individual having command of the vessel and who is the holder of a valid license that authorized the individual to serve as master of a small passenger vessel.

Means of escape means a continuous and unobstructed way of exit travel from any point in a vessel to an embarkation station. A means of escape can be both vertical and horizontal, and include doorways, passageways, stairtowers, stairways, and public spaces. Cargo spaces, machinery spaces, rest rooms, hazardous areas determined by the cognizant Officer in Charge Marine Inspection, escalators, and elevators must not be any part of the means of escape.

New OSV means an OSV—
(1) That was contracted for, or the keel of which was laid, on or after March 15, 1996; or
(2) That underwent a major conversion initiated on or after March 15, 1996.

New vessel means a vessel:
(1) The initial construction of which began on or after March 11, 1996;
(2) Which was issued an initial Certificate of Inspection on or after September 11, 1996;
(3) Which underwent a major conversion that was initiated on or after March 11, 1996; or
(4) Which underwent a major conversion that was completed and for which an amended Certificate of Inspection was issued on or after September 11, 1996.

Noncombustible material means any material approved in accordance with § 164.009 in subchapter Q, of this chapter or other standard specified by the Commandant.

Non-self-propelled vessel means a vessel that does not have installed means of propulsion, including propulsive machinery, masts, spars, or sails.

Oceans means a route that is more than 20 nautical miles offshore on any of the following waters:
(1) Any ocean;
(2) The Gulf of Mexico;
(3) The Caribbean Sea;
(4) The Bering Sea;
(5) The Gulf of Alaska; or
(6) Such other similar waters as may be designated by a Coast Guard District Commander.

Officer In Charge, Marine Inspection, or *OCMI* means an officer of the Coast Guard designated as such by the Commandant and who, under the direction of the Coast Guard District Commander, is in charge of a marine inspection zone, described in part 1 of this chapter, for the performance of duties with respect to the inspection, enforcement, and administration of vessel safety and navigation laws and regulations. The "cognizant OCMI" is the OCMI that has immediate jurisdiction over a vessel for the purpose of performing the duties previously described.

Offshore supply vessel (OSV) means a vessel that—
(1) Is propelled by machinery other than steam;
(2) Is of above 15 gross tons and of less than 500 gross tons (as measured under the Standard, Dual, or Simplified Measurement System under part 69, subpart C, D, or E, of this chapter), or is less than 6,000 gross tons (as

§ 175.400

measured under the Convention Measurement System under part 69, subpart B, of this chapter); and

(3) Regularly carries goods, supplies, or equipment in support of exploration, exploitation, or production of offshore mineral or energy resources.

Open boat means a vessel not protected from entry of water by means of a complete weathertight deck, or by a combination of a partial weathertight deck and superstructure that is structurally suitable for the waters upon which the vessel operates.

Open deck means a deck that is permanently open to the weather on one or more sides and, if covered, any spot on the overhead is less than 4.5 meters (15 feet) from the nearest opening to the weather.

Open to the atmosphere means a compartment that has at least 9,375 square millimeters (15 square inches) of open area directly exposed to the atmosphere for each cubic meter (35 ft^3) of net compartment volume.

Operating station means the principal steering station on the vessel from which the individual on duty normally navigates the vessel.

Overnight accommodations or *overnight accommodation space* means an accommodation space for use by passengers or by crew members, which has one or more berths, including beds or bunks, for passengers or crew members to rest for extended periods. Staterooms, cabins, and berthing areas are normally overnight accommodation spaces. Overnight accommodations do not include spaces that contain only seats, including reclining seats.

Partially enclosed space means a compartment that is neither open to the atmosphere nor an enclosed space.

Partially protected waters is a term used in connection with stability criteria and means:

(1) Waters not more than 20 nautical miles from the mouth of a harbor of safe refuge, unless determined by the cognizant OCMI to be exposed waters;

(2) Those portions of rivers, estuaries, harbors, lakes, and similar waters that the cognizant OCMI determines not to be protected waters; and

(3) Waters of the Great Lakes from April 16 through September 30 of the same year (summer season).

Passenger means an individual carried on a vessel, except:

(1) The owner or an individual representative of the owner, or in the case of a vessel under charter, an individual charterer or individual representative of the charterer;

(2) The master; or

(3) A member of the crew engaged in the business of the vessel who has not contributed consideration for carriage and who is paid for on board services.

Passenger accommodation space means an accommodation space designated for the use of passengers.

Passenger for hire means a passenger for whom consideration is contributed as a condition of carriage on the vessel, whether directly or indirectly flowing to the owner, charterer, operator, agent, or any other person having an interest in the vessel.

Pilothouse control means that controls to start and stop the engines and control the direction and speed of the propeller of the vessel are located at the operating station.

Piping system includes piping, fittings, and appurtenances as described in § 56.07-5 in subchapter F of this chapter.

Port light means a hinged glass window, generally circular, in a vessel's side or deckhouse for light and ventilation.

Protected waters is a term used in connection with stability criteria and means sheltered waters presenting no special hazards such as most rivers, harbors, and lakes, and that is not determined to be exposed waters or partially protected waters by the cognizant OCMI.

Pre-engineered means, when referring to a fixed gas fire extinguishing system, a system that is designed and tested to be suitable for installation without modification as a complete unit in a space of a set volume, regardless of the specific design of the vessel on which it is installed.

Remotely operated vehicle (ROV) team, at a minimum, consist of an ROV operator, a non-destructive testing inspector, an ROV tender or mechanic, and a team supervisor who is considered by the Officer in Charge, Marine Inspection (OCMI), have the appropriate training and experience to perform the

Coast Guard, DHS § 175.400

survey and to safely operate the ROV in an effective manor. The team must also have a hull-positioning technician present. This position may be assigned to a team member already responsible for another team duty.

Rivers means a route on any of the following waters:

(1) A river;

(2) A canal; or

(3) Such other similar waters as may be designated by a Coast Guard District Commander.

Sailing vessel means a vessel principally equipped for propulsion by sail even if the vessel has an auxiliary means of propulsion.

Scantlings means the dimensions of all structural parts such as frames, girders, and plating, used in building a vessel.

Scupper means a pipe or tube of at least 30 millimeters (1.25 inches) in diameter leading down from a deck or sole and through the hull to drain water overboard.

Self-bailing cockpit means a cockpit, with watertight sides and floor (sole), which is designed to free itself of water by gravity drainage through scuppers.

Shallow water is an ascertained water depth at which the uppermost deck(s) of a sunken vessel remain above the water's surface. The determination of the water's depth is made by the Officer in Charge, Marine Inspection (OCMI) who considers the vessel's stability (passenger heeling moment), the contour of the hull, the composition of the river bottom, and any other factors that would tend to prevent a vessel from resting an even keel.

Ship's service loads means services necessary for maintaining the vessel in normal operational and habitable conditions. These loads include, but are not limited to, safety, lighting, ventilation, navigational, and communications loads.

Short international voyage means an international voyage where:

(1) The vessel is not more than 200 nautical miles from a port or place in which the passengers and crew could be placed in safety; and

(2) The total distance between the last port of call in the country in which the voyage began and the final port of destination does not exceed 600 nautical miles.

Stairway means an inclined means of escape between two decks.

Steel or equivalent material means steel or any noncombustible material that, by itself or due to insulation provided, has structural and integrity properties equivalent to steel at the end of the standard fire test.

Submersible vessel means a vessel that is capable of operating below the surface of the water.

Survival craft means a lifeboat, rigid liferaft, inflatable liferaft, life float, inflatable buoyant apparatus, buoyant apparatus, or a small boat carried aboard a vessel in accordance with § 180.200(b) of this subchapter.

Switchboard means an electrical panel that receives power from a generator, battery, or other electrical power source and distributes power directly or indirectly to all equipment supplied by the generating plant.

Third party examiner means an entity:

(1) With a thorough knowledge of diving operations, including diving limitations as related to diver safety and diver supervision;

(2) Having a familiarity with, but not limited to, the following—

(i) The camera used during the AHE; and

(ii) The NDT equipment used during the AHE, including the effect of water clarity, and marine growth in relation to the quality of the readings obtained;

(3) Having a familiarity with the communications equipment used during the AHE;

(4) Possessing the knowledge of vessel structures, design features, nomenclature, and the applicable AHE regulations; and

(5) Able to present the Officer in Charge, Marine Inspection, with evidence of formal training, demonstrated ability, past acceptance, or a combination of these.

Trunk means a vertical shaft or duct for the passage of pipes, wires, or other devices except that for the purposes of part 179 of this chapter, "trunk" means a large enclosed passageway through any deck or bulkhead of a vessel.

Underwater Survey in Lieu of Drydocking (UWILD) means a program

§ 175.540

in which an eligible vessel may alternate between an underwater survey and the required drydock examinations.

Vehicle space means a space not on an open deck, for the carriage of motor vehicles with fuel in their tanks, into and from which such vehicles can be driven and to which passengers have access.

Vessel includes every description of watercraft or other artificial contrivance, used or capable of being used as a means of transportation on water.

Vessel of the United States means a vessel documented or numbered under the laws of the United States, the states of the United States, Guam, Puerto Rico, the Virgin Islands, American Samoa, the District of Columbia, the Northern Mariana Islands, and any other territory or possession of the United States.

Warm water means water where the monthly mean low water temperature is normally more than 15 degrees Celsius (59 degrees Fahrenheit).

Watertight means designed and constructed to withstand a static head of water without any leakage, except that "watertight" for the purposes of electrical equipment means enclosed so that water does not enter the equipment when a stream of water from a hose with a nozzle one inch in diameter that delivers at least 246 liters (65 gallons) per minute is sprayed on the enclosure from any direction from a distance of ten feet for five minutes.

Weather deck means a deck that is partially or completely exposed to the weather from above or from at least two sides, except that for the purposes of parts 178 and 179 of this chapter, "weather deck" means the uppermost deck exposed to the weather to which a weathertight sideshell extends.

Weathertight means that water will not penetrate in any sea condition, except that "weathertight equipment" means equipment constructed or protected so that exposure to a beating rain will not result in the entrance of water.

Well deck vessel means a vessel with a weather deck fitted with solid bulwarks that impede the drainage of water over the sides or a vessel with an exposed recess in the weather deck extending more than one-half of the length of the vessel measured over the weather deck.

Wire means an individual insulated conductor without an outer protective jacket.

Wood vessel means, for the purposes of subdivision and lifesaving equipment requirements in this subchapter, a traditionally-built, plank-on-frame vessel, where mechanical fasteners (screws, nails, trunnels) are used to maintain hull integrity.

Work space means a space, not normally occupied by a passenger, in which a crew member performs work and includes, but is not limited to, a galley, operating station, or machinery space.

[CGD 85–080, 61 FR 947, Jan. 10, 1996; 61 FR 20557, May 7, 1996, as amended by CGD 82–004 and CGD 86–074, 62 FR 49356, Sept. 19, 1997; CGD 97–057, 62 FR 51049, Sept. 30, 1997; CGD 85–080, 62 FR 51355, Sept. 30, 1997; 62 FR 64306, Dec. 5, 1997; 63 FR 65739, Dec. 15, 1997; USCG–1999–4976, 65 FR 6508, Feb. 9, 2000; USCG–2000–7790, 65 FR 58464, Sept. 29, 2000; USCG–2000–6858, 67 FR 21084, Apr. 29, 2002; USCG–1999–5040, 67 FR 34800, May 15, 2002; 69 FR 47384, Aug. 5, 2004; USCG–2004–18884, 69 FR 58351, Sept. 30, 2004]

§ 175.540 Equivalents.

(a) The Commandant may approve any arrangement, fitting, appliance, apparatus, equipment, calculation, information, or test, which provides a level of safety equivalent to that established by specific provisions of this subchapter. Requests for approval must be submitted to the Marine Safety Center via the cognizant OCMI. If necessary, the Marine Safety Center may require engineering evaluations and tests to demonstrate the equivalence of the substitute.

(b) The Commandant may accept compliance by a high speed craft with the provisions of the International Maritime Organization (IMO) "Code of Safety for High Speed Craft" as an equivalent to compliance with applicable requirements of this subchapter. Requests for a determination of equivalency for a particular vessel must be submitted to the Marine Safety Center via the cognizant OCMI.

(c) The Commandant may approve a novel lifesaving appliance or arrangement as an equivalent if it has performance characteristics at least equivalent to the appliance or arrangement required under this part, and:

(1) Is evaluated and tested under IMO Resolution A. 520(13), "Code of Practice for the Evaluation, Testing and Acceptance of Prototype Novel Life-Saving Appliances and Arrangements"; or

(2) Has successfully undergone an evaluation and tests that are substantially equivalent to those recommendations.

(d) The Commandant may accept alternative compliance arrangements in lieu of specific provisions of the International Safety Management (ISM) Code (IMO Resolution A.741(18)) for the purpose of determining that an equivalent safety management system is in place on board a vessel. The Commandant will consider the size and corporate structure of a vessel's company when determining the acceptability of an equivalent system. Requests for determination of equivalency must be submitted to Commandant (G–MOC) via the cognizant OCMI.

[CGD 85–080, 61 FR 947, Jan. 10, 1996; 61 FR 24464, May 15, 1996, as amended by CGD 95–073, 62 FR 67515, Dec. 24, 1997]

§ 175.550 Special consideration.

In applying the provisions of this subchapter, the OCMI may give special consideration to authorizing departures from the specific requirements when unusual circumstances or arrangements warrant such departures and an equivalent level of safety is provided. The OCMI of each marine inspection zone in which the vessel operates must approve any special consideration granted to a vessel.

§ 175.560 Appeals.

Any person directly affected by a decision or action taken under this subchapter, by or on behalf of the Coast Guard, may appeal therefrom in accordance with § 1.03 in subchapter A of this chapter.

§ 175.600 Incorporation by reference.

(a) Certain material is incorporated by reference into this subchapter with the approval of the Director of the Federal Register in accordance with Title 5 United States Code (U.S.C.) 552(a) and Title 1 Code of Federal Regulations (CFR) Part 51. To enforce any edition other than that specified in paragraph (b) of this section, the Coast Guard must publish a notice of change in the Federal Register and make the material available to the public. All approved material is on file at the U.S. Coast Guard, Office of Operating and Environmental Standards (G–MSO), 2100 Second Street SW., Washington, DC 20593–0001 and at the National Archives and Records Administration (NARA). For information on the availability of this material at NARA, call 202–741–6030, or go to: *http:// www.archives.gov/federal_register/ code_of_federal_regulations/ ibr_locations.html*. All approved material is available from the sources indicated in paragraph (b) of this section.

(b) The material approved for incorporation by reference in this subchapter and the sections affected are:

American Boat and Yacht Council (ABYC), 3069 Solomons Island Rd., Edgewater, MD 21037

A–1–93—Marine Liquefied Petroleum Gas (LPG) Systems.	184.240
A–3–93—Galley Stoves	184.200
A–7–70—Boat Heating Systems	184.200
A–16–89—Electric Navigation Lights	183.130
A–22–93—Marine Compressed Natural Gas (CNG) Systems.	184.240
E–8–94—Alternating Current (AC) Electrical Systems on Boats.	183.130
E–9–90—Direct Current (DC) Electrical Systems on Boats.	183.130
H–2–89—Ventilation of Boats Using Gasoline	182.130; 182.460
H–22–86—DC Electric Bilge Pumps Operating Under 50 Volts.	182.130; 182.500

§ 175.600

H–24–93—Gasoline Fuel Systems	182.130; 182.440; 182.445; 182.450; 182.455
H–25–94—Portable Gasoline Fuel Systems for Flammable Liquids.	182.130; 182.458
H–32–87—Ventilation of Boats Using Diesel Fuel	182.130; 182.465; 182.470
H–33–89—Diesel Fuel Systems	182.130; 182.440; 182.445; 182.450; 182.455
P–1–93—Installation of Exhaust Systems for Propulsion and Auxiliary Engines.	177.405; 177.410; 182.130; 182.425; 182.430
P–4–89—Marine Inboard Engines	182.130; 182.420

American Bureau of Shipping (ABS), ABS Plaza, 16855 Northchase Drive, Houston, TX 77060

Guide for High Speed Craft, 1997	177.300
Rules for Building and Classing Aluminum Vessels, 1975.	177.300
Rules for Building and Classing Reinforced Plastic Vessels, 1978.	177.300
Rules for Building and Classing Steel Vessels, 1995 ..	182.410; 183.360
Rules for Building and Classing Steel Vessels Under 61 Meters (200 feet) in Length, 1983.	177.300
Rules for Building and Classing Steel Vessels for Service on Rivers and Intracoastal Waterways, 1995.	177.300

American National Standards Institute (ANSI), 11 West 42nd Street, New York, NY 10036

A 17.1–1984, including supplements A 17.1a and b–1985—Safety Code for Elevators and Escalators.	183.540
B 31.1–1986—Code for Pressure Piping, Power Piping	182.710
Z 26.1–1977, including 1980 supplement—Safety Glazing Materials For Glazing Motor Vehicles Operating on Land Highways.	177.1030

American Society for Testing and Materials (ASTM), 100 Barr Harbor Drive, West Conshohocken, PA 19428–2959.

ASTM B 96–93, Standard Specification for Copper-Silicon Alloy Plate, Sheet, Strip, and Rolled Bar for General Purposes and Pressure Vessels.	182.440
ASTM B 117–97, Standard Practice for Operating Salt Spray (Fog) Apparatus.	175.400
ASTM B 122/B 122M–95, Standard Specification for Copper-Nickel-Tin Alloy, Copper-Nickel-Zinc Alloy (Nickel Silver), and Copper-Nickel Alloy Plate, Sheet, Strip and Rolled Bar.	182.440
ASTM B 127–98, Standard Specification for Nickel-Copper Alloy (UNS NO4400) Plate, Sheet, and Strip.	182.440
ASTM B 152–97a, Standard Specification for Copper Sheet, Strip, Plate, and Rolled Bar.	182.440
ASTM B 209–96, Standard Specification for Aluminum and Aluminum-Alloy Sheet and Plate.	182.440
ASTM D 93–97, Standard Test Methods for Flash Point by Pensky-Martens Closed Cup Tester.	175.400
ASTM D 635–97, Standard test Method for Rate of Burning and or Extent and Time of Burning of Self-Supporting Plastics in a Horizontal Position.	182.440
ASTM D 2863–95, Standard Method for Measuring the Minimum Oxygen Concentration to Support Candle-Like Combustion of Plastics (Oxygen Index).	182.440

Coast Guard, DHS § 175.600

ASTM E 84-98, Standard Test Method for Surface Burning Characteristics of Building Materials.	177.410

Institute of Electrical and Electronics Engineers, Inc. (IEEE), IEEE Service Center, 445 Hoes Lane, Piscataway, NJ 08854

Standard 45-1977—Recommended Practice for Electrical Installations on Shipboard.	183.340

International Maritime Organization (IMO), International Maritime Organization, Publications Section, 4 Albert Embankment, London SE1 7SR, United Kingdom

Code of Practice for the Evaluation, Testing and Acceptance of Prototype Novel Life-Saving Appliances and Arrangements—Resolution A.520(13), dated 17 November 1983.	175.540(c)
Use and Fitting of Retro-Reflective Materials on Life-Saving Appliances—Resolution A.658(16), dated 20 November 1989.	185.604
Fire Test Procedures For Ignitability of Bedding Components, Resolution A.688(17), dated 06 November 1991.	177.405
Symbols Related to Life-Saving Appliances and Arrangements, Resolution A.760(18), dated 17 November 1993.	185.604(g)

Lloyd's Register of Shipping, 17 Battery Place, Suite 1013, New York, NY 10004

Rules and Regulations for the Classification of Yachts and Small Craft, as amended through 1983.	177.300

National Fire Protection Association (NFPA), 1 Batterymarch Park, Quincy, MA 02269-9101

NFPA 10-1994—Portable Fire Extinguishers	176.810
NFPA 17-1994—Dry Chemical Extinguishing Systems.	181.425
NFPA 17A-1994—Wet Chemical Extinguishing Systems.	181.425

NFPA 70-1996—National Electrical Code (NEC)

Section 250-95	183.370
Section 310-13	183.340
Section 310-15	183.340
Article 430	183.320
Article 445	183.320
NFPA 302-1994—Pleasure and Commercial Motor Craft, Chapter 6.	184.200; 184.240
NFPA 306-1993—Control of Gas Hazards on Vessels	176.710
NFPA 1963-1989—Fire Hose Connections	181.320

Naval Publications and Forms Center, Customer Service Code 1052, 5801 Tabor Ave., Philadelphia, PA 19120

Military Specification MIL-P-21929C (1991)—Plastic Material, Cellular Polyurethane, Foam-in-Place, Rigid (2 and 4 pounds per cubic foot).	179.240
Military Specification MIL-R-21607E(SH) (1990) Resins, Polyester, Low Pressure Laminating, Fire Retardant.	177.410

Society of Automotive Engineers (SAE), 400 Commonwealth Drive, Warrendale, PA 15096-0001

SAE J-1475—Hydraulic Hose Fittings For Marine Applications, 1984.	182.720

§ 175.800

SAE J-1928—Devices Providing Backfire Flame Control for Gasoline Engines in Marine Applications, August 1989.	182.415
SAE J-1942—Hose and Hose Assemblies for Marine Applications, 1992.	182.720

Underwriters Laboratories Inc. (UL), 12 Laboratory Drive, Research Triangle Park, NC 27709

UL 19-1992—Lined Fire Hose and Hose Assemblies	181.320
UL 174-1989, as amended through June 23, 1994—Household Electric Storage Tank Heaters.	182.320
UL 217-1993—Single and Multiple Station Smoke Detectors.	181.450
UL 486A-1992—Wire Connectors and Soldering Lugs For Use With Copper Conductors.	183.340
UL 489-1995—Molded—Case Circuit Breakers and Circuit Breaker Enclosures.	183.380
UL 595-1991—Marine Type Electric Lighting Fixtures.	183.410
UL 710-1990, as amended through September 16, 1993—Exhaust Hoods For Commercial Cooking Equipment.	181.425
UL 1058-1989, as amended through April 19, 1994—Halogenated Agent Extinguishing System Units.	181.410
UL 1102-1992—Non integral Marine Fuel Tanks	182.440
UL 1110-1988, as amended through May 16, 1994—Marine Combustible Gas Indicators.	182.480
UL 1111-1988—Marine Carburetor Flame Arresters ...	182.415
UL 1453-1988, as amended through June 7, 1994—Electric Booster and Commercial Storage Tank Water Heaters.	182.320
UL 1570-1995—Fluorescent Lighting Fixtures	183.410
UL 1571-1995—Incandescent Lighting Fixtures	183.410
UL 1572-1995—High Intensity Discharge Lighting Fixtures.	183.410
UL 1573-1995—Stage and Studio Lighting Units	183.410
UL 1574-1995—Track Lighting Systems	183.410

[CGD 85-080, 61 FR 947, Jan. 10, 1996, as amended by CGD 96-041, 61 FR 50734, Sept. 27, 1996; CGD 97-057, 62 FR 51049, Sept. 30, 1997; CGD 85-080, 62 FR 51355, Sept. 30, 1997; USCG-1999-5151, 64 FR 67186, Dec. 1, 1999; USCG-2000-7790, 65 FR 58465, Sept. 29, 2000; 69 FR 18803, Apr. 9, 2004]

§ 175.800 Approved equipment and material.

(a) Equipment and material that is required by this subchapter to be approved or of an approved type, must have been manufactured and approved in accordance with the design and testing requirements in subchapter Q (Equipment, Construction, and Materials: Specifications and Approval) of this chapter or as otherwise specified by the Commandant.

(b) Coast Guard publication COMDTINST M16714.3 (Series) "Equipment Lists, Items Approved, Certificated or Accepted under Marine Inspection and Navigation Laws" lists approved equipment by type and manufacturer. COMDTINST M16714.3 (Series) may be obtained from New Orders, Superintendent of Documents, P.O. Box 371954, Pittsburgh, PA 15250-7954.

[CGD 85-080, 61 FR 947, Jan. 10, 1996, as amended at 62 FR 51355, Sept. 30, 1997]

§ 175.900 OMB control numbers.

(a) *Purpose.* This section lists the control numbers assigned to information collection and recordkeeping requirements in this subchapter by the Office of Management and Budget (OMB) pursuant to the Paperwork Reduction Act of 1980 (44 U.S.C. 3501 *et.*

Coast Guard, DHS

seq.). The Coast Guard intends that this section comply with the requirements of 44 U.S.C. 3507(f) which requires that agencies display a current control number assigned by the Director of OMB for each approved agency information collection requirement.

(b) *Display.*

46 CFR Section where identified	Current OMB Control Number
176.105(a)	1625–0057
176.202	1625–0057
176.204	1625–0057
176.302	1625–0057
176.306	1625–0057
176.310	1625–0057
176.500(a)	1625–0057
176.612	1625–0057
176.700	1625–0057
176.704	1625–0057
176.710	1625–0057
176.810(b)	1625–0057
176.920(c)	1625–0057
176.930	1625–0057
177.202	1625–0057
177.315	1625–0057
177.330	1625–0057
177.335	1625–0057
177.340	1625–0057
178.210	1625–0057
178.220	1625–0057
178.230	1625–0057
181.610	1625–0057
182.460(e)	1625–0057
182.610(f)	1625–0057
183.220(d)	1625–0057
183.320 (d) and (e)	1625–0057
184.420	1625–0057
184.506	1625–0057
185.202	1625–0001
185.206	1625–0001
185.208	1625–0057
185.220	1625–0057
185.230	1625–0057
185.280	1625–0057
185.340(c)	1625–0057
185.402	1625–0057
185.420	1625–0057
185.502	1625–0057
185.503	1625–0057
185.504	1625–0057
185.506	1625–0057
185.510	1625–0057
185.514	1625–0057
185.516	1625–0057
185.518	1625–0057
185.520	1625–0057
185.524	1625–0057
185.602	1625–0057
185.604	1625–0057
185.606	1625–0057
185.608	1625–0057
185.610	1625–0057
185.612	1625–0057
185.702	1625–0057
185.704(c)	1625–0057
185.728(c)	1625–0057

[CGD 85–080, 61 FR 947, Jan. 10, 1996, as amended by USCG–2004–18884, 69 FR 58351, Sept. 30, 2004]

PART 176—INSPECTION AND CERTIFICATION

Subpart A—Certificate of Inspection

Sec.
176.100 When required.
176.103 Description.
176.105 How to obtain or renew.
176.107 Period of validity for a Certificate of Inspection.
176.110 Routes permitted.
176.112 Total persons permitted.
176.113 Passengers permitted.
176.114 Alternative requirements for a vessel operating as other than a small passenger vessel.
176.120 Certificate of Inspection amendment.

Subpart B—Special Permits and Certificates

176.202 Permit to proceed.
176.204 Permit to carry excursion party.

Subpart C—Posting of Certificates, Permits, and Stability Letters

176.302 Certificates and permits.
176.306 Stability letter.
176.310 Certification Expiration Date Stickers.

Subpart D—Inspection for Certification

176.400 General.
176.402 Initial inspection for certification.
176.404 Subsequent inspections for certification.

Subpart E—Reinspection

176.500 When required.
176.502 Certificate of Inspection: Conditions of validity.

Subpart F—Hull and Tailshaft Examinations

176.600 Drydock examination, internal structural examination, and underwater survey intervals.
176.610 Scope of drydock and internal structural examinations.
176.615 Underwater Survey in Lieu of Drydocking (UWILD).
176.620 Description of the Alternative Hull Examination (AHE) Program for certain passenger vessels.
176.625 Eligibility requirements for the Alternative Hull Examination (AHE) Program for certain passenger vessels.
176.630 The Alternative Hull Examination (AHE) Program application.
176.635 Preliminary examination requirements.
176.640 Pre-survey meeting.

§ 176.100

176.645 AHE Procedure.
176.650 Alternative Hull Examination Program options: Divers or underwater ROV.
176.655 Hull examination reports.
176.660 Continued participation in the Alternative Hull Examination (AHE) Program.
176.665 Notice and plans required.
176.670 Tailshaft examinations.
176.675 Extension of examination intervals.

Subpart G—Repairs and Alterations

176.700 Permission for repairs and alterations.
176.702 Installation tests and inspections.
176.704 Breaking of safety valve seals.
176.710 Inspection and testing prior to hot work.

Subpart H—Material Inspections

176.800 Inspection standards.
176.801 Notice of inspection deficiencies and requirements.
176.802 Hull.
176.804 Machinery.
176.806 Electrical.
176.808 Lifesaving.
176.810 Fire protection.
176.812 Pressure vessels and boilers.
176.814 Steering systems.
176.816 Miscellaneous systems and equipment.
176.818 Sanitary inspection.
176.830 Unsafe practices.
176.840 Additional tests and inspections.

Subpart I—International Convention for Safety of Life at Sea, 1974, as Amended (SOLAS)

176.900 Applicability.
176.910 Passenger Ship Safety Certificate.
176.920 Exemptions.
176.925 Safety Management Certificate.
176.930 Equivalents.

AUTHORITY: 33 U.S.C. 1321(j); 46 U.S.C. 2103, 3205, 3306, 3307; 49 U.S.C. App. 1804; E.O. 11735, 38 FR 21243, 3 CFR, 1971–1975 Comp., p. 743; E.O. 12234, 45 FR 58801, 3 CFR, 1980 Comp., p. 277; Department of Homeland Security Delegation No. 0170.

SOURCE: CGD 85–080, 61 FR 953, Jan. 10, 1996, unless otherwise noted.

Subpart A—Certificate of Inspection

§ 176.100 When required.

(a) A vessel to which this subchapter applies may not be operated without having on board a valid U.S. Coast Guard Certificate of Inspection.

(b) Except as noted in § 176.114 of this part, each vessel inspected and certificated under the provisions of this subchapter must, when any passengers are aboard during the tenure of the certificate, be in full compliance with the terms of the certificate.

(c) If necessary to prevent delay of the vessel, a temporary Certificate of Inspection may be issued pending the issuance and delivery of the regular Certificate of Inspection. The temporary certificate must be carried in the same manner as the regular certificate and is considered the same as the regular Certificate of Inspection that it represents.

(d) A vessel on a foreign voyage between a port in the United States and a port in a foreign country, whose Certificate of Inspection expires during the voyage, may lawfully complete the voyage without a valid Certificate of Inspection provided the voyage is completed within 30 days of expiration and the certificate did not expire within 15 days of sailing on the foreign voyage from a U.S. port.

[CGD 85–080, 61 FR 953, Jan. 10, 1996; 61 FR 20557, May 7, 1996]

§ 176.103 Description.

The Certificate of Inspection issued to a vessel describes the vessel, the route(s) that it may travel, the minimum manning requirements, the survival and rescue craft carried, the minimum fire extinguishing equipment and lifejackets required to be carried, the maximum number of passengers and total persons that may be carried, the number of passengers the vessel may carry in overnight accommodation spaces, the name of the owner and managing operator, any equivalencies accepted or authorized by the Commandant or any Officer in Charge, Marine Inspection (OCMI) in accordance with §§ 175.540 or 175.550 of this chapter, and such other conditions of operations as may be determined by the cognizant OCMI.

§ 176.105 How to obtain or renew.

(a) A Certificate of Inspection is obtained or renewed by making application on Form CG 3752, "Application for Inspection of U.S. Vessel," to the Coast Guard OCMI of the marine inspection

Coast Guard, DHS § 176.112

zone in which the inspection is to be made. Form CG-3752 may be obtained at any U.S. Coast Guard Marine Safety Office or Marine Inspection Office.

(b) The application for initial inspection of a vessel being newly constructed or converted must be submitted prior to the start of the construction or conversion.

(c) The construction, arrangement, and equipment of each vessel must be acceptable to the cognizant OCMI as a prerequisite of the issuance of the initial Certificate of Inspection. Acceptance is based on the information, specifications, drawings and calculations available to the OCMI, and on the successful completion of an initial inspection for certification.

(d) A Certificate of Inspection is renewed by the issuance of a new Certification of Inspection.

(e) The condition of the vessel and its equipment must be acceptable to the cognizant OCMI as a prerequisite to the Certificate of Inspection renewal. Acceptance is based on the condition of the vessel as found at the periodic inspection for certification.

[CGD 85–080, 61 FR 953, Jan. 10, 1996; 61 FR 20557, May 7, 1996]

§ 176.107 Period of validity for a Certificate of Inspection.

(a) A Certificate of Inspection is valid for 1 year for vessels carrying more than 12 passengers on international voyages.

(b) A Certificate of Inspection is valid for 5 years for all other vessels.

(c) A Certificate of Inspection may be suspended and withdrawn or revoked by the cognizant OCMI at any time for noncompliance with the requirements of this subchapter.

[USCG–1999–4976, 65 FR 6508, Feb. 9, 2000]

§ 176.110 Routes permitted.

(a) The area of operation for each vessel and any necessary operational limits are determined by the cognizant OCMI, and recorded on the vessel's Certificate of Inspection. Each area of operation, referred to as a route, is described on the Certificate of Inspection under the major headings "Oceans," "Coastwise," "Limited Coastwise," "Great Lakes," "Lakes, Bays, and Sounds," or "Rivers," as applicable. Further limitations imposed or extensions granted are described by reference to bodies of waters, geographical points, distance from geographical points, distances from land, depths of channel, seasonal limitations, and similar factors.

(b) Operation of a vessel on a route of lesser severity than those specifically described or designated on the Certificate of Inspection is permitted unless expressly prohibited on the Certificate of Inspection. The general order of severity of routes is: oceans, coastwise, limited coastwise, Great Lakes, lakes, bays, and sounds, and rivers. The cognizant OCMI may prohibit a vessel from operating on a route of lesser severity than the primary route a vessel is authorized to operate on if local conditions necessitate such a restriction.

(c) Non-self-propelled vessels are prohibited from operating on an oceans, coastwise, limited coastwise, or Great Lakes route unless the Commandant approves such a route.

(d) When designating a permitted route or imposing any operational limits on a vessel, the OCMI may consider:

(1) Requirements of this subchapter for which compliance is based on the route of the vessel;

(2) The performance capabilities of the vessel based on design, scantlings, stability, subdivision, propulsion, speed, operating modes, maneuverability, and other characteristics; and

(3) The suitability of the vessel for nighttime operations and use in all weather conditions.

[CGD 85–080, 61 FR 953, Jan. 10, 1996; 61 FR 20557, May 7, 1996]

§ 176.112 Total persons permitted.

The cognizant OCMI determines the total number of persons permitted to be carried on a vessel. In determining the total number of persons permitted to be carried, the OCMI may consider stability restrictions and subdivision requirements of the vessel, the vessel's route, general arrangement, means of escape, lifesaving equipment, the minimum manning requirements, and the maximum number of passengers permitted in accordance with § 176.113.

§ 176.113 Passengers permitted.

(a) The maximum number of passengers permitted must be not more than that allowed by the requirements of this section, except as authorized by the OCMI under paragraph (d) of this section.

(b) The maximum number of passengers permitted on any vessel may be the greatest number permitted by the length of rail criterion, deck area criterion, or fixed seating criterion described in this paragraph or a combination of these criteria as allowed by paragraph (c) of this section.

(1) *Length of rail criterion.* One passenger may be permitted for each 760 millimeters (30 inches) of rail space available to the passengers at the periphery of each deck. The following rail space may not be used in determining the maximum number of passengers permitted:

(i) Rail space in congested areas unsafe for passengers, such as near anchor handling equipment or line handling gear, in the way of sail booms, running rigging, or paddle wheels, or along pulpits;

(ii) Rail space on stairways; and

(iii) Rail space where persons standing in the space would block the vision of the licensed individual operating the vessel.

(2) *Deck area criterion.* One passenger may be permitted for each 0.9 square meters (10 square feet) of deck area available for the passengers' use. In computing such deck area, the areas occupied by the following must be excluded:

(i) Areas for which the number of persons permitted is determined using the fixed seating criteria;

(ii) Obstructions, including stairway and elevator enclosures, elevated stages, bars, and cashier stands, but not including slot machines, tables, or other room furnishings;

(iii) Toilets and washrooms;

(iv) Spaces occupied by and necessary for handling lifesaving equipment, anchor handling equipment or line handling gear, or in the way of sail booms or running rigging;

(v) Spaces below deck that are unsuitable for passengers or that would not normally be used by passengers;

(vi) Interior passageways less than 840 millimeters (34 inches) wide and passageways on open deck, less than 710 millimeters (28 inches) wide;

(vii) Bow pulpits, swimming platforms and areas that do not have a solid deck, such as netting on multi-hull vessels;

(viii) Deck areas in way of paddle wheels; and

(ix) Aisle area provided in accordance with § 177.820(d) in this subchapter.

(3) *Fixed seating criterion.* One passenger may be permitted for each 455 millimeter (18 inches) of width of fixed seating provided by § 177.820 of this subchapter. Each sleeping berth in overnight accommodation spaces shall be counted as only one seat.

(c) Different passenger capacity criteria may be used on each deck of a vessel and added together to determine the total passenger capacity of that vessel. Where seats are provided on part of a deck and not on another, the number of passengers permitted on a vessel may be the sum of the number permitted by the seating criterion for the space having seats and the number permitted by the deck area criterion for the space having no seats. The length of rail criterion may not be combined with either the deck area criterion or the fixed seating criterion when determining the maximum number of passengers permitted on an individual deck.

(d) For a vessel operating on short runs on protected waters such as a ferry, the cognizant OCMI may give special consideration to increases in passenger allowances.

§ 176.114 Alternative requirements for a vessel operating as other than a small passenger vessel.

(a) When authorized by the cognizant OCMI by an endorsement of the vessel's Certificate of Inspection, a small passenger vessel carrying six or less passengers, or operating as a commercial fishing vessel or other uninspected vessel, or carrying less than twelve passengers and operating as a recreational vessel, need not meet requirements of:

(1) Subparts C, D, and E, of part 180 of this chapter if the vessel is in satisfactory compliance with the lifesaving equipment regulations for an

Coast Guard, DHS § 176.204

uninspected vessel or recreational vessel in a similar service;

(2) Subpart C of part 177, and parts 178 and 179 of this chapter if the vessel is in satisfactory compliance with applicable regulations for an uninspected vessel or recreational vessel in a similar service or if the owner of the vessel otherwise establishes to the satisfaction of the cognizant OCMI that the vessel is seaworthy for the intended service; and

(3) Sections 184.404 and 184.410 of this chapter providing the vessel is in satisfactory compliance with applicable regulations for an uninspected or recreational vessel in a similar service.

(b) A vessel operating under the alternative regulations of paragraph (a) of this section must:

(1) Not alter the arrangement of the vessel nor remove any equipment required by the certificate for the intended operation, without the consent of the cognizant OCMI;

(2) Comply with the minimum manning specified on the Certificate of Inspection, which may include reduced manning depending on the number of passengers and operation of the vessel;

(3) When carrying from one to six passengers, except for a vessel being operated as a recreational vessel, make the announcement required by § 185.506(a) of this chapter before getting underway; and

(4) If a vessel of more than 15 gross tons, not carry freight for hire.

(c) The endorsement issued under paragraph (a) of this section must indicate the route, maximum number of passengers, and the manning required to operate under the provisions of this section.

[CGD 85–080, 61 FR 953, Jan. 10, 1996, as amended by CGD 97–057, 62 FR 51049, Sept. 30, 1997]

§ 176.120 Certificate of Inspection amendment.

(a) An amended Certificate of Inspection may be issued at any time by any OCMI. The amended Certificate of Inspection replaces the original, but the expiration date remains the same as that of the original. An amended Certificate of Inspection may be issued to authorize and record a change in the dimensions, gross tonnage, owner, managing operator, manning, persons permitted, route permitted, conditions of operations, or equipment of a vessel, from that specified in the current Certificate of Inspection.

(b) A request for an amended Certificate of Inspection must be made to the cognizant OCMI by the owner or managing operator of the vessel at any time there is a change in the character of a vessel or in its route, equipment, ownership, operation, or similar factors specified in its current Certificate of Inspection.

(c) The OCMI may require an inspection prior to the issuance of an amended Certificate of Inspection.

Subpart B—Special Permits and Certificates

§ 176.202 Permit to proceed.

(a) When a vessel is not in compliance with its Certificate of Inspection or fails to comply with a regulation of this subchapter, the cognizant OCMI may permit the vessel to proceed to another port for repair, if in the judgment of the OCMI, the trip can be completed safely, even if the Certificate of Inspection of the vessel has expired or is about to expire.

(b) Form CG–948, "Permit to Proceed to another Port for Repairs," may be issued by the cognizant OCMI to the owner, managing operator, or the master of the vessel stating the conditions under which the vessel may proceed to another port. The permit may be issued only upon the written application of the owner, managing operator, or master, and after the vessel's Certificate of Inspection is turned over tot he OCMI.

(c) A vessel may not carry passengers when operating in accordance with a permit to proceed, unless the cognizant OCMI determines that it is safe to do so.

§ 176.204 Permit to carry excursion party.

(a) The cognizant OCMI may permit a vessel to engage in a temporary excursion operation with a greater number of persons or on a more extended route, or both, than permitted by its Certificate of Inspection when, in the opinion of the OCMI, the operation can be undertaken safely.

§ 176.302

(b) Upon the written application of the owner or managing operator of the vessel, the cognizant OCMI may issue a Form CG-949, "Permit To Carry Excursion Party," to indicate his or her permission to carry an excursion party. The OCMI will indicate on the permit the conditions under which it is issued, the number of persons the vessel may carry, the crew required, any additional lifesaving or safety equipment required, the route for which the permit is granted, and the dates on which the permit is valid.

(c) The number of passengers normally permitted on an excursion vessel shall be governed by § 176.113.

(d) The OCMI will not normally waive the applicable minimum safety standards when issuing an excursion permit. In particular, a vessel that is being issued an excursion permit will normally be required to meet the minimum stability, survival craft, life jacket, fire safety, and manning standards applicable to a vessel in the service for which the excursion permit is requested.

(e) The permit acts as a temporary, limited duration supplement to the vessel's Certificate of Inspection and must be carried with the Certificate of Inspection. A vessel operating under a permit to carry an excursion party must be in full compliance with the terms of its Certificate of Inspection as supplemented by the permit.

(f) The OCMI may require an inspection prior to the issuance of a permit to carry an excursion party.

Subpart C—Posting of Certificates, Permits, and Stability Letters

§ 176.302 Certificates and permits.

The Certificate of Inspection and any SOLAS Certificates must be posted under glass or other suitable transparent material, such that all pages are visible, in a conspicuous place on the vessel where observation by passengers is likely. If posting is impracticable, such as in an open boat, the certificates must be kept on board in a weathertight container readily available for use by the crew and display to passengers and others on request.

[CGD 85-080, 61 FR 953, Jan. 10, 1996, as amended by CGD 97-057, 62 FR 51049, Sept. 30, 1997]

§ 176.306 Stability letter.

When, in accordance with § 178.210 of this chapter, a vessel must be provided with a stability letter, the stability letter must be posted under glass or other suitable transparent material, such that all pages are visible, at the operating station of the vessel. If posting is impracticable, the stability letter must be kept on board in a weathertight container readily available for use by the crew and display to passengers and others on request.

[CGD 85-080, 61 FR 953, Jan. 10, 1996, as amended by CGD 97-057, 62 FR 51049, Sept. 30, 1997]

§ 176.310 Certification Expiration Date Stickers.

(a) A Certification Expiration Date Sticker indicates the date upon which the vessel's Certificate of Inspection expires and is provided by the cognizant OCMI in the number required, upon issuance or renewal of the Certificate of Inspection.

(b) A vessel that is issued a Certificate of Inspection under the provisions of this subchapter must be not be operated without a valid Certification Expiration Date Sticker affixed to the vessel on a place that is:

(1) A glass or other smooth surface from which the sticker may be removed without damage to the vessel;

(2) Readily visible to each passenger prior to boarding the vessel and to patrolling Coast Guard law enforcement personnel; and

(3) Acceptable to the Coast Guard marine inspector.

(c) The Coast Guard marine inspector may require the placement of more than one sticker in order to insure compliance with paragraph (b)(2) of this section.

[CGD 85-080, 61 FR 953, Jan. 10, 1996; 61 FR 20557, May 7, 1996]

Subpart D—Inspection for Certification

§ 176.400 General.

(a) An inspection is required before the issuance of a Certificate of Inspection. Such an inspection for certification is not made until after receipt of the application for inspection required by § 176.105.

(b) Upon receipt of a written application for inspection, the cognizant OCMI assigns a marine inspector to inspect the vessel for compliance with this subchapter at a time and place mutually agreed upon by the OCMI and the owner, managing operator, or representative thereof.

(c) The owner, managing operator, or a representative thereof shall be present during the inspection.

[CGD 85–080, 61 FR 953, Jan. 10, 1996; 61 FR 20557, May 7, 1996, as amended at 62 FR 51356, Sept. 30, 1997]

§ 176.402 Initial inspection for certification.

(a) Before construction or conversion of a vessel intended for small passenger vessel service, the owner of the vessel shall submit plans, manuals, and calculations indicating the proposed arrangement, construction, and operations of the vessel, to the cognizant OCMI for approval, except when submitted to the Marine Safety Center (MSC) as allowed by part 177 of this subchapter. The plan, manuals, and calculations required to be submitted and the disposition of these plans are set forth in part 177, Subpart B of this chapter.

(b) The initial inspection is conducted to determine that the vessel and its equipment comply with applicable regulations and that the vessel was built or converted in accordance with approved plans, manuals, and calculations. Additionally, during the inspection, the materials, workmanship, and condition of all parts of the vessel and its machinery and equipment may be checked to determine if the vessel is satisfactory in all respects for the service intended.

(c) The owner or managing operator of a vessel shall ensure that the vessel complies with the laws and regulations applicable to the vessel and that the vessel is otherwise satisfactory for the intended service. The initial inspection may include an inspection of the following items:

(1) The arrangement, installation, materials, and scantlings of the structure including the hull and superstructure, yards, masts, spars, rigging, sails, piping, main and auxiliary machinery, pressure vessels, steering apparatus, electrical installation, fire resistant construction materials, life saving appliances, fire detecting and extinguishing equipment, pollution prevention equipment, and all other equipment;

(2) Sanitary conditions and fire hazards; and

(3) Certificates and operating manuals, including certificates issued by the FCC.

(d) During an initial inspection for certification the owner or managing operator shall conduct all tests and make the vessel available for all applicable inspections discussed in this paragraph, and in Subpart H of this part, to the satisfaction of the cognizant OCMI, including the following:

(1) The installation of each rescue boat, liferaft, inflatable buoyant apparatus, and launching appliance as listed on its Certificate of Approval (Form CGHQ–10030).

(2) The operation of each rescue boat and survival craft launching appliance required by part 180 of this chapter.

(3) Machinery, fuel tanks, and pressure vessels as required by part 182 of this chapter.

(4) A stability test or a simplified stability test when required by § 170.175 of this chapter or § 178.320 of this chapter.

(5) Watertight bulkheads as required by part 179 of this chapter.

(6) Firefighting systems as required by part 181 of this chapter.

(7) The operation of all smoke and fire detecting systems, and fire alarms and sensors.

§ 176.404 Subsequent inspections for certification.

(a) An inspection for renewal of a Certificate of Inspection is conducted

§ 176.500

to determine if the vessel is in satisfactory condition, fit for the service intended, and complies with all applicable regulations. It normally includes inspection and testing of the structure, machinery, equipment, and on a sailing vessel, rigging and sails. The owner or operator must conduct all tests as required by the OCMI, and make the vessel available for all specific inspections and drills required by subpart H of this part. In addition, the OCMI may require the vessel to get underway.

(b) You must submit your written application for renewal of a Certificate of Inspection to the OCMI at least 30 days prior to the expiration date of the Certificate of Inspection, as required in § 176.105 of this part.

[CGD 85–080, 61 FR 953, Jan. 10, 1996; 61 FR 20557, May 7, 1996; USCG–1999–4976, 65 FR 6508, Feb. 9, 2000; USCG–2003–14749, 68 FR 39315, July 1, 2003]

Subpart E—Reinspection

§ 176.500 When required.

(a) Vessels carrying more than 12 passengers on international voyages must undergo an inspection for certification each year as specified in § 176.404.

(b) All other vessels must undergo an inspection for certification as specified in § 176.404 and annual inspection as specified in paragraph (b)(1) of this section.

(1) *Annual inspection.* Your vessel must undergo an annual inspection within the 3 months before or after each anniversary date.

(i) You must contact the cognizant OCMI to schedule an inspection at a time and place which he or she approves. No written application is required.

(ii) The scope of the annual inspection is the same as the inspection for certification but in less detail unless the cognizant marine inspector finds deficiencies or determines that a major change has occurred since the last inspection. If deficiencies are found or a major change to the vessel has occurred, the marine inspector will conduct an inspection more detailed in scope to ensure that the vessel is in satisfactory condition and fit for the service for which it is intended. If your vessel passes the annual inspection, the marine inspector will endorse your current Certificate of Inspection.

(iii) If the annual inspection reveals deficiencies in your vessel's maintenance, you must make any or all repairs or improvements within the time period specified by the OCMI.

(iv) Nothing in this subpart limits the marine inspector from conducting such tests or inspections he or she deems necessary to be assured of the vessel's seaworthiness.

(2) [Reserved]

[USCG–1999–4976, 65 FR 6508, Feb. 9, 2000]

§ 176.502 Certificate of Inspection: Conditions of validity.

To maintain a valid Certificate of Inspection, you must complete your annual inspection within the periods specified in § 176.500(b)(1) and your Certificate of Inspection must be endorsed.

[USCG–1999–4976, 65 FR 6508, Feb. 9, 2000]

Subpart F—Hull and Tailshaft Examinations

§ 176.600 Drydock and internal structural examination intervals.

(a) The owner or managing operator shall make a vessel available for drydock examinations, internal structural examinations, and underwater surveys (UWILD) required by this section.

(b) If your vessel is operated on international voyages subject to SOLAS requirements, it must undergo a drydock examination once every 12 months unless it has been approved to undergo an underwater survey (UWILD) per § 176.615 of this part. If the vessel becomes due for a drydock examination or an internal structural examination during the voyage, it may lawfully complete the voyage prior to the examination if it undergoes the required examination upon completion of the voyage to the United States but not later than 30 days after the examination was due. If the vessel is due for an examination within 15 days of sailing on an international voyage from the United States port, it must undergo the required examination before sailing.

(c) If your vessel is not operated on international voyages and does not meet the conditions in paragraph (d) of this section, it must undergo a drydock and internal structural examination as follows unless it has been approved to undergo an underwater survey (UWILD) per §176.615 of this part:

(1) A vessel that is exposed to salt water more than three months in any 12 month period since the last examination must undergo a drydock examination and an internal structural at least once every two years; and

(2) A vessel that is exposed to salt water not more than three months in any 12 month period since the last examination must undergo a drydock examination and an internal structural examination at least once every five years.

(d) Whenever damage or deterioration to hull plating or structural members that may affect the seaworthiness of a vessel is discovered or suspected, the cognizant OCMI may conduct an internal structural examination in any affected space including fuel tanks, and may require the vessel to be drydocked or taken out of service to assess the extent of the damage, and to effect permanent repairs. The OCMI may also decrease the drydock examination intervals to monitor the vessel's structural condition.

(e) For a vessel that is eligible per §115.625, and if the owner opts for an alternate hull examination with the underwater survey portion conducted exclusively by divers, the vessel must undergo two alternate hull exams and two internal structural exams within any five-year period. If a vessel completes a satisfactory alternate hull exam, with the underwater survey portion conducted predominantly by an approved underwater remotely operated vehicle (ROV), the vessel must undergo one alternate hull and one internal structural exam, within any five-year period. The vessel may undergo a drydock exam to satisfy any of the required alternate hull exams.

[CGD 85-080, 61 FR 953, Jan. 10, 1996, as amended at 62 FR 51356, Sept. 30, 1997; USCG-2000-6858, 67 FR 21084, Apr. 29, 2002]

§176.610 Scope of drydock and internal structural examinations.

(a) A drydock examination conducted in compliance with §176.600 must be conducted while the vessel is hauled out of the water or placed in a drydock or slipway. During the examination all accessible parts of the vessel's underwater body and all through hull fittings, including the hull plating and planking, appendages, propellers, shafts, bearings, rudders, sea chests, sea valves, and sea strainers shall be made available for examination. Sea chests, sea valves, and sea strainers must be opened for examination. On wooden vessels, fastenings may be required to be pulled for examination.

(b) An internal structural examination conducted in compliance with §176.600 may be conducted while the vessel is afloat or out of the water and consists of a complete examination of the vessel's main strength members, including the major internal framing, the hull plating and planking, voids, and ballast, cargo, and fuel oil tanks. Where the internal framing, plating, or planking of the vessel is concealed, sections of the lining, ceiling or insulation may be removed or the parts otherwise probed or exposed so that the inspector may be satisfied as to the condition of the hull structure. Fuel oil tanks need not be cleaned out and internally examined if the marine inspector is able to determine by external examination that the general condition of the tanks is satisfactory.

§176.615 Underwater Survey in Lieu of Drydocking (UWILD).

(a) The Officer in Charge, Marine Inspection (OCMI), may approve an underwater survey instead of a drydock examination at alternating intervals if your vessel is—

(1) Less than 15 years of age;

(2) A steel or aluminum hulled vessel;

(3) Fitted with an effective hull protection system; and

(4) Described in §176.600(b) or (c) of this part.

(b) For vessels less than 15 years of age, you must submit an application for an underwater survey to the OCMI at least 90 days before your vessel's next required drydock examination. The application must include—

(1) The procedure for carrying out the underwater survey;

(2) The time and place of the underwater survey;

§ 176.620

(3) The method used to accurately determine the diver's or remotely operated vehicle's (ROV) location relative to the hull;

(4) The means for examining all through-hull fittings and appurtenances;

(5) The condition of the vessel, including the anticipated draft of the vessel at the time of survey;

(6) A description of the hull protection system; and

(7) The name and qualifications of any third party examiner.

(c) If your vessel is 15 years old or older, the cognizant District Commander, may approve an underwater survey instead of a drydock examination at alternating intervals (UWILD). You must submit an application for an underwater survey to the OCMI at least 90 days before your vessel's next required drydock examination. You may be allowed this option if—

(1) The vessel is qualified under paragraphs (a)(2) through (4) of this section;

(2) Your application includes the information in paragraphs (b)(1) through (b)(7) of this section; and

(3) During the vessel's drydock examination, preceding the underwater survey, a complete set of hull gaugings was taken and they indicated that the vessel was free from appreciable hull deterioration.

(d) After the drydock examination required by paragraph (c)(3) of this section, the OCMI submits a recommendation for future underwater surveys, the results of the hull gauging, and the results of the Coast Guards' drydock examination results to the cognizant District Commander for review.

[USCG–2000–6858, 67 FR 21084, Apr. 29, 2002]

§ 176.620 Description of the Alternative Hull Examination (AHE) Program for certain passenger vessels.

The Alternative Hull Examination (AHE) Program provides you with an alternative to a drydock examination by allowing your vessel's hull to be examined while it remains afloat. If completed using only divers, this program has four steps: the application process, the preliminary examination, the presurvey meeting, and the hull examination. If the vessel is already participating in the program, or if a remotely operated vehicle (ROV) is used during the program, the preliminary exam step may be omitted. Once you complete these steps, the Officer in Charge, Marine Inspection (OCMI), will evaluate the results and accept the examination as a credit hull exam if the vessel is in satisfactory condition. If only divers are used for the underwater survey portion of the examination process, you may receive credit for a period of time such that subsequent AHEs would be conducted at intervals of twice in every five years, with no more than three years between any two AHEs. The OCMI may waive an underwater survey in accordance with § 176.655(d) provided that the interval does not exceed five years between any two underwater surveys. If an underwater ROV is used as the predominate method to examine the vessel's underwater hull plating, you may receive credit up to five years. At the end of this period, you may apply for further participation under the AHE Program.

NOTE TO § 176.620: The expected hull coverage when using an ROV must be at least 80 percent.

[USCG–2000–6858, 69 FR 47384, Aug. 5, 2004]

§ 176.625 Eligibility requirements for the Alternative Hull Examination (AHE) Program for certain passenger vessels.

(a) Your vessel may be eligible for the AHE Program if—

(1) It is constructed of steel or aluminum;

(2) It has an effective hull protection system;

(3) It has operated exclusively in fresh water since its last drydock examination;

(4) It operates in rivers or protected lakes; and

(5) It operates exclusively in shallow water or within 0.5 nautical miles from shore.

(b) In addition to the requirements in paragraph (a), the Officer in Charge, Marine Inspection (OCMI) will evaluate the following information when determining your vessel's eligibility for the AHE Program:

(1) The overall condition of the vessel, based on its inspection history.

(2) The vessel's history of hull casualties and hull-related deficiencies.

Coast Guard, DHS § 176.640

(3) The AHE Program application, as described in § 176.630 of this part.

(c) When reviewing a vessel's eligibility for the AHE program, the OCMI may modify the standards given by paragraph (a)(5) of this section where it is considered safe and reasonable to do so. In making this determination, the OCMI will consider the vessel's overall condition, its history of safe operation, and any other factors that serve to mitigate overall safety risks.

[USCG–2000–6858, 67 FR 21085, Apr. 29, 2002]

§ 176.630 The Alternative Hull Examination (AHE) Program application.

If your vessel meets the eligibility criteria in § 176.625 of this part, you may apply to the AHE Program. You must submit an application at least 90 days before the requested hull examination date to the Officer in Charge, Marine Inspection (OCMI) who will oversee the survey. The application must include—

(a) The proposed time and place for conducting the hull examination;

(b) The name of the participating diving contractor and underwater remotely operated vehicle (ROV) company accepted by the OCMI under § 176.650 of this part;

(c) The name and qualifications of the third party examiner. This person must be familiar with the inspection procedures and his or her responsibilities under this program. The OCMI has the discretionary authority to accept or deny use of a particular third party examiner;

(d) A signed statement from your vessel's master, chief engineer, or the person in charge stating the vessel meets the eligibility criteria of § 176.625 of this part and a description of the vessel's overall condition, level of maintenance, known or suspected damage, underwater body cleanliness (if known), and the anticipated draft of the vessel at the time of the examination;

(e) Plans or drawings that illustrate the external details of the hull below the sheer strake;

(f) A detailed plan for conducting the hull examination in accordance with §§ 176.645 and 176.650 of this part, which must address all safety concerns related to the removal of sea valves during the inspection; and

(g) A preventative maintenance plan for your vessel's hull, its related systems and equipment.

[USCG–2000–6858, 67 FR 21085, Apr. 29, 2002, as amended at 69 FR 47384, Aug. 5, 2004]

§ 176.635 Preliminary examination requirements.

(a) If you exclusively use divers to examine the underwater hull plating, you must arrange to have a preliminary examination conducted by a third party examiner, with the assistance of qualified divers. The purpose of the preliminary examination is to assess the overall condition of the vessel's hull and identify any specific concerns to be addressed during the underwater hull examination.

(b) The preliminary examination is required only upon the vessel's entry or reentry into the AHE program.

(c) If you use an underwater remotely operated vehicle (ROV) as the predominate means to examine your vessel's hull plating, a preliminary examination and the participation of a third party examiner will not be necessary.

[USCG–2000–6858, 67 FR 21085, Apr. 29, 2002]

§ 176.640 Pre-survey meeting.

(a) In advance of each AHE, you must conduct a pre-survey meeting to discuss the details of the AHE procedure with the Officer in Charge, Marine Inspection (OCMI). If you exclusively use divers to examine the underwater hull plating, the third party examiner must attend the meeting and you must present the results of the preliminary examination. If you use an underwater remotely operated vehicle (ROV) as the predominate means to examine the vessel's hull plating, then the pre-survey meeting must be attended by a representative of the ROV operating company who is qualified to discuss the ROV's capabilities and limitations related to your vessel's hull design and configuration.

(b) A vessel owner, operator, or designated agent must request this meeting in writing at least 30 days in advance of the examination date.

§ 176.645

(c) The pre-survey meeting may be conducted by teleconference, if agreed to in advance by the OCMI.

[USCG–2000–6858, 67 FR 21086, Apr. 29, 2002, as amended at 69 FR 47384, Aug. 5, 2004]

§ 176.645 AHE Procedure.

(a) To complete the underwater survey you must—

(1) Perform a general examination of the underwater hull plating and a detailed examination of all hull welds, propellers, tailshafts, rudders, and other hull appurtenances;

(2) Examine all sea chests;

(3) Remove and inspect all sea valves in the presence of a marine inspector once every five years;

(4) Remove all passengers from the vessel when the sea valves are being examined, if required by the Officer in Charge, Marine Inspection (OCMI);

(5) Allow access to all internal areas of the hull for examination, except internal tanks that carry fuel (unless damage or deterioration is discovered or suspect), sewage, or potable water. Internal sewage and potable water tanks may be examined visually or by non-destructive testing to the satisfaction of the attending marine inspector; and

(6) Meet the requirements in § 176.650 of this part.

(b) A marine inspector may examine any other areas deemed necessary by the OCMI.

(c) If the AHE reveals significant deterioration or damage to the vessel's hull plating or structural members, the OCMI must be immediately notified. The OCMI may require the vessel be drydocked or otherwise taken out of service to further assess the extent of damage or to effect permanent repairs if the assessment or repairs cannot be completed to the satisfaction of the OCMI while the vessel is waterborne.

[USCG–2000–6858, 67 FR 21086, Apr. 29, 2002, as amended at 69 FR 47384, Aug. 5, 2004]

§ 176.650 Alternative Hull Examination Program options: Divers or underwater ROV.

To complete the underwater survey portion of the AHE, you may use divers or an underwater remotely operated vehicle (ROV).

(a) If you use divers to conduct the underwater survey, you must—

(1) Locate the vessel so the divers can work safely under the vessel's keel and around both sides. The water velocity must be safe for dive operations;

(2) Provide permanent hull markings, a temporary grid system of wires or cables spaced not more than 10 feet apart and tagged at one-foot intervals, or any other acoustic or electronic positioning system approved by the OCMI to identify the diver's location with respect to the hull, within one foot of accuracy;

(3) Take ultrasonic thickness gaugings at a minimum of 5 points on each plate, evenly spaced;

(4) Take hull plating thickness gaugings along transverse belts at the bow, stern, and midships, as a minimum. Plating thickness gaugings must also be taken along a longitudinal belt at the wind and water strake. Individual gaugings along the transverse and longitudinal belts must be spaced no more than 3 feet apart;

(5) Ensure the third party examiner observes the entire underwater examination process;

(6) Record the entire underwater survey with audio and video recording equipment and ensure that communications between divers and the third party examiner are recorded; and

(7) Use appropriate equipment, such as a clear box, if underwater visibility is poor, to provide the camera with a clear view of the hull.

(b) You may use an underwater ROV to conduct the underwater survey. The underwater ROV operating team, survey process and equipment, quality assurance methods, and the content and format of the survey report must be accepted by the Officer in Charge, Marine Inspection (OCMI) prior to the survey. If you choose this option, you must—

(1) Locate the vessel to ensure that the underwater ROV can operate effectively under the vessel's keel and around both sides; and

(2) Employ divers to examine any sections of the hull and appurtenances that the underwater ROV cannot access or is otherwise unable to evaluate.

(3) If the OCMI determines that the data obtained by the ROV, including

non-destructive testing results, readability of the results, and positioning standards, will not integrate into the data obtained by the divers, then a third party examiner must be present during the divers portion of the examination.

[USCG–2000–6858, 67 FR 21086, Apr. 29, 2002, as amended at 69 FR 47384, Aug. 5, 2004]

§ 176.655 Hull examination reports.

(a) If you use only divers for the underwater survey portion of the Alternative Hull Examination (AHE), you must provide the Officer in Charge, Marine Inspection (OCMI), with a written hull examination report. This report must include thickness gauging results, bearing clearances, a copy of the audio and video recordings, and any other information that will help the OCMI evaluate your vessel for a credit hull exam. The third party examiner must sign the report and confirm the validity of its contents.

(b) If you use an underwater remotely operated vehicle (ROV) as the predominate means to examine the vessel's underwater hull plating, you must provide the OCMI with a report in a format that is acceptable to the OCMI, per §176.650(b) of this part.

(c) The OCMI will evaluate the hull examination report and grant a credit hull exam if satisfied with the condition of the vessel. If approved and you exclusively use divers to examine the hull plating, you will receive a credit hull exam of up to 36 months. (Underwater examinations are required twice every 5 years.) If approved and you use an underwater ROV as the predominate means to examine the hull plating, you will receive a credit hull exam of up to 60 months (5 years).

(d) At least 60 days prior to each scheduled underwater exam, the owner may request a waiver from the OCMI if:

(1) A satisfactory exam has been completed within the last three years;

(2) The conditions during the last exam allowed at least 80 percent of the bottom surface to be viewed and recorded; and

(3) The results of the last exam indicated that an extended interval is safe and reasonable.

[USCG–2000–6858, 67 FR 21086, Apr. 29, 2002, as amended at 69 FR 47384, Aug. 5, 2004]

§ 176.660 Continued participation in the Alternative Hull Examination (AHE) Program.

(a) To continue to participate in the AHE Program, vessel operators must conduct an annual hull condition assessment. At a minimum, vessel operators must conduct an internal examination and take random hull gaugings internally during the hull condition assessment, unless waived by the Officer in Charge, Marine Inspection (OCMI). If the annual hull assessment reveals significant damage or corrosion, where temporary repairs have been made, or where other critical areas of concern have been identified, the OCMI may require an expanded examination to include an underwater hull examination using divers. If an underwater examination is required, the examination must focus on areas at higher risk of damage or corrosion and must include a representative sampling of hull gaugings.

(b) If an underwater survey is required for the annual hull condition assessment, the OCMI may require the presence of a third party examiner and a written hull examination report must be submitted to the OCMI. This report must include thickness gauging results, a copy of the audio and video recordings and any other information that will help the OCMI evaluate your vessel for continued participation in the AHE program. The third party examiner must sign the report and confirm the validity of its contents.

(c) You must submit your preventive maintenance reports or checklists on an annual basis to the OCMI. These reports or checklists must conform to the plans you submitted in your application under § 176.630 of this part, which the OCMI approved.

(d) Prior to each scheduled annual hull condition assessment—

(1) The owner may submit to the OCMI a plan for conducting the assessment, or a request for a waiver of this

§ 176.665

requirement, no fewer than 30 days before the scheduled assessment; and

(2) The OCMI may reduce the scope or extend the interval of the assessment if the operational, casualty, and deficiency history of the vessel, along with a recommendation of the vessel's master, indicates that it is warranted.

[USCG-2000-6858, 67 FR 21086, Apr. 29, 2002, as amended at 69 FR 47384, Aug. 5, 2004]

§ 176.665 Notice and plans required.

(a) The owner or managing operator shall notify the cognizant OCMI as far in advance as possible whenever a vessel is to be hauled out or placed in a drydock or slipway in compliance with § 176.605 or to undergo repairs or alterations affecting the safety of the vessel, together with the nature of any repairs or alterations contemplated. Hull repairs or alternations that affect the safety of the vessel include but are not limited to the replacement, repair, or refastening of planking, plating, or structural members including the repair of cracks.

(b) Whenever a vessel is hauled out or placed in a drydock or slipway in excess of the requirements of this subpart for the purpose of maintenance, including, but not limited to, changing a propeller, painting, or cleaning the hull, no report need be made to the cognizant OCMI.

(c) The owner or managing operator of each vessel that holds a Load Line Certificate shall make plans showing the vessel's scantlings available to the Coast Guard marine inspector whenever the vessel undergoes a drydock examination, internal structural examination, or an underwater survey or whenever repairs or alterations affecting the safety or seaworthiness of the vessel are made to the vessel's hull.

[CGD 85-080, 61 FR 953, Jan. 10, 1996, as amended at 62 FR 51356, Sept. 30, 1997. Redesignated and amended by USCG-2000-6858, 67 FR 21084, 21087, Apr. 29, 2002]

§ 176.670 Tailshaft examinations.

(a) The marine inspector may require any part or all of the propeller shafting to be drawn for examination of the shafting and stern bearing of a vessel whenever the condition of the shafting and bearings are in question.

(b) The marine inspector may conduct a visual examination and may require nondestructive testing of the propeller shafting whenever the condition of shafting is in question.

[CGD 85-080, 61 FR 953, Jan. 10, 1996. Redesignated by USCG-2000-6858, 67 FR 21084, Apr. 29, 2002]

§ 176.675 Extension of examination intervals.

The intervals between drydock examinations and internal structural examinations specified in § 176.605 of this part may be extended by the cognizant OCMI or Commandant.

[CGD 85-080, 61 FR 953, Jan. 10, 1996. Redesignated and amended by USCG-2000-6858, 67 FR 21084, 21087, Apr. 29, 2002]

Subpart G—Repairs and Alterations

§ 176.700 Permission for repairs and alterations.

(a) Repairs or alterations to the hull, machinery, or equipment that affect the safety of the vessel must not be made without the approval of the cognizant OCMI, except during an emergency. When repairs are made during an emergency, the owner, managing operator, or master shall notify the OCMI as soon as practicable after such repairs or alternations are made. Repairs or alterations that affect the safety of the vessel include, but are not limited to: replacement, repair, or refastening of deck or hull planking, plating, and structural members; repair of plate or frame cracks; damage repair or replacement, other than replacement in kind, of electrical wiring, fuel lines, tanks, boilers and other pressure vessels, and steering, propulsion and power supply systems; alterations affecting stability; and repair or alteration of lifesaving, fire detecting, or fire extinguishing equipment.

(b) The owner or managing operator shall submit drawings, sketches, or written specifications describing the details of any proposed alterations to the cognizant OCMI. Proposed alterations must be approved by the OCMI before work is started.

Coast Guard, DHS § 176.800

(c) Drawings are not required to be submitted for repairs or replacements in kind.

(d) The OCMI may require an inspection and testing whenever a repair or alteration is undertaken.

§ 176.702 Installation tests and inspections.

Whenever a launching appliance, survival craft, rescue boat, fixed gas fire extinguishing system, machinery, fuel tank, or pressure vessel is installed aboard a vessel after completion of the initial inspection for certification of the vessel, as replacement equipment or as a new installation, the owner or managing operator shall conduct the tests and make the vessel ready for the inspections required by § 176.402(d) to the satisfaction of the cognizant OCMI.

§ 176.704 Breaking of safety valve seals.

The owner, managing operator, or master shall notify the cognizant OCMI as soon as practicable after the seal on a boiler safety valve on a vessel is broken.

§ 176.710 Inspection and testing prior to hot work.

(a) An inspection for flammable or combustible gases must be conducted by a certified marine chemist or other person authorized by the cognizant OCMI in accordance with the provisions of National Fire Protection Association (NFPA) 306, "Control of Gas Hazards on Vessels," before alterations, repairs, or other operations involving riveting, welding, burning, or other fire producing actions may be made aboard a vessel:

(1) Within or on the boundaries of fuel tanks; or

(2) To pipelines, heating coils, pumps, fittings, or other appurtenances connected to fuel tanks.

(b) An inspection required by paragraph (a) of this section must be conducted as required by this paragraph.

(1) In ports or places in the United States or its territories and possessions, the inspection must be conducted by a marine chemist certificated by the NFPA. However, if the services of a certified marine chemist are not reasonably available, the cognizant OCMI, upon the recommendation of the vessel owner or managing operator, may authorize another person to inspect the vessel. If the inspection indicates that the operations can be undertaken safely, a certificate setting forth this fact in writing must be issued by the certified marine chemist or the authorized person before the work is started. The certificate must include any requirements necessary to reasonably maintain safe conditions in the spaces certified throughout the operation, including any precautions necessary to eliminate or minimize hazards that may be present from protective coatings or residues from cargoes.

(2) When not in a port or place in the United States or its territories and possessions, and when a marine chemist or a person authorized by the cognizant OCMI is not reasonably available, the master shall conduct the inspection and enter the results in the inspection in the vessel's logbook.

(c) The owner, managing operator, or master shall obtain a copy of certificates issued by the certified marine chemist or the other person authorized by the cognizant OCMI, and shall ensure that all conditions on the certificates are observed and that the vessel is maintained in a safe condition. The owner, managing operator, or master shall maintain a safe condition on the vessel by requiring full observance, by persons under his or her control, of all requirements listed in the certificate.

Subpart H—Material Inspections

§ 176.800 Inspection standards.

(a) A vessel is inspected for compliance with the standards required by this subchapter. Machinery, equipment, materials, and arrangements not covered by standards in this subchapter may be inspected in accordance with standards acceptable to the cognizant OCMI as good marine practice.

(b) In the application of inspection standards due consideration must be given to the hazards involved in the operation permitted by a vessel's Certificate of Inspection. Thus, the standards may vary in accordance with the vessel's area of operation or any other operational restrictions or limitations.

§ 176.801

(c) The published standards of classification societies and other recognized safety associations may be used as guides in the inspection of vessels when such standards do not conflict with the requirements of this subchapter.

§ 176.801 Notice of inspection deficiencies and requirements.

(a) If during the inspection of a vessel, the vessel or its equipment is found not to conform to the requirements of law or the regulations in this subchapter, the marine inspector will point out deficiencies observed and discuss all requirements with the owner, managing operator, or a representative thereof. Normally, the marine inspector will list all such requirements that have not been completed and present the list to the owner, managing operator, or a representative thereof. However, when a deficiency presents a serious safety hazard to the vessel or its passengers or crew, and exists through negligence or willful noncompliance, the marine inspector may issue a Report of Violation (ROV) to the owner, managing operator, or a representative thereof.

(b) In any case where further clarification of or reconsideration of any requirement placed against the vessel is desired, the owner, managing operator, or a representative thereof, may discuss the matter with the cognizant OCMI.

[CGD 85–080, 61 FR 953, Jan. 10, 1996, as amended by CGD 97–057, 62 FR 51049, Sept. 30, 1997]

§ 176.802 Hull.

(a) At each initial and subsequent inspection for certification of a vessel, the owner or managing operator shall be prepared to conduct tests and have the vessel ready for inspections of the hull structure and its appurtenances, including the following:

(1) Inspection of all accessible parts of the exterior and interior of the hull, the watertight bulkheads, and weather decks;

(2) Inspection and operation of all watertight closures in the hull, decks, and bulkheads including through hull fittings and sea valves;

(3) Inspection of the condition of the superstructure, masts, and similar arrangements constructed on the hull, and on a sailing vessel all spars, standing rigging, running rigging, blocks, fittings, and sails;

(4) Inspection of all railings and bulwarks and their attachment to the hull structure;

(5) Inspection to ensure that guards or rails are provided in dangerous places;

(6) Inspection and operation of all weathertight closures above the weather deck and the provisions for drainage of sea water from the exposed decks; and

(7) Inspection of all interior spaces to ensure that they are adequately ventilated and drained, and that means of escape are adequate and properly maintained.

(b) The vessel must be afloat for at least a portion of the inspection as required by the marine inspector.

(c) When required by the marine inspector, a portion of the inspection must be conducted while the vessel is underway so that the hull and internal structure can be observed.

[CGD 85–080, 61 FR 953, Jan. 10, 1996; 61 FR 20557, May 7, 1996, as amended at 62 FR 51356, Sept. 30, 1997]

§ 176.804 Machinery.

At each initial and subsequent inspection for certification of a vessel, the owner or managing operator shall be prepared to conduct tests and have the vessel ready for inspections of machinery, fuel, and piping systems, including the following:

(a) Operation of the main propulsion machinery both ahead and astern;

(b) Operational test and inspection of engine control mechanisms including primary and alternate means of starting machinery;

(c) Inspection of all machinery essential to the routine operation of the vessel including generators and cooling systems;

(d) External inspection of fuel tanks and inspection of tank vents, piping, and pipe fittings;

(e) Inspection of all fuel system;

(f) Operational test of all valves in fuel lines by operating locally and at remote operating positions;

Coast Guard, DHS § 176.808

(g) Operational test of all overboard discharge and intake valves and watertight bulkhead pipe penetration valves;

(h) Operational test of the means provided for pumping bilges; and

(i) Test of machinery alarms including bilge high level alarms.

§ 176.806 Electrical.

At each initial and subsequent inspection for certification of a vessel, the owner or managing operator shall be prepared to conduct tests and have the vessel ready for inspection of electrical equipment and systems, including the following:

(a) Inspection of all cable as far as practicable without undue disturbance of the cable or electrical apparatus;

(b) Test of circuit breakers by manual operation;

(c) Inspection of fuses including ensuring the ratings of fuses are suitable for the service intended;

(d) Inspection of rotating electrical machinery essential to the routine operation of the vessel;

(e) Inspection of all generators, motors, lighting fixtures and circuit interrupting devices located in spaces or areas that may contain flammable vapors;

(f) Inspection of batteries for condition and security of stowage;

(g) Operational test of electrical apparatus, which operates as part of or in conjunction with a fire detection or alarms system installed on board the vessel, by simulating, as closely as practicable, the actual operation in case of fire; and

(h) Operational test of all emergency electrical systems.

§ 176.808 Lifesaving

(a) At each initial and subsequent inspection for certification of a vessel, the owner or managing operator shall be prepared to conduct tests and have the vessel ready for inspection of lifesaving equipment and systems, including the following:

(1) Tests of each rescue boat and each rescue boat launching appliance and survival craft launching appliance in accordance with § 185.520 of this chapter;

(2) Inspection of each lifejacket, work vest, and marine buoyant device;

(3) If used, inspection of the passenger safety orientation cards or pamphlets allowed by § 185.506(b)(2) of this chapter;

(4) Inspection of each inflatable liferaft, inflatable buoyant apparatus, and inflatable lifejacket to determine that it has been serviced as required by § 185.730 of this chapter; and

(5) Inspection of each hydrostatic release unit to determine that it is in compliance with the servicing and usage requirements of § 185.740 of this chapter.

(b) Each item of lifesaving equipment determined by the marine inspector to not be in serviceable condition must be repaired or replaced.

(c) Each item of lifesaving equipment with an expiration date on it must be replaced if the expiration date has passed.

(d) The owner or managing operator shall destroy, in the presence of the marine inspector, each lifejacket, other personal floatation device, and other lifesaving device found to be defective and incapable of repair.

(e) At each initial and subsequent inspection for certification of a vessel, the vessel must be equipped with an adult size lifejacket for each person authorized. The vessel must also be equipped with child size lifejackets equal to at least:

(1) 10 percent of the maximum number of passengers permitted to be carried unless children are prohibited from being carried aboard the vessel; or

(2) 5 percent of the maximum number of passengers permitted to be carried if all extended size lifejackets are provided.

(f) Lifejackets, work vests, and marine buoyant devices may be marked with the date and marine inspection zone to indicate that they have been inspected and found to be in serviceable condition by a marine inspector.

(g) At each initial and subsequent inspection for certification, the marine inspector may require that an abandon ship or man overboard drill be held under simulated emergency conditions specified by the inspector.

[CGD 85–080, 61 FR 953, Jan. 10, 1996, as amended at 62 FR 51356, Sept. 30, 1997]

§ 176.810 Fire protection.

(a) At each initial and subsequent inspection for certification, the owner or managing operator shall be prepared to conduct tests and have the vessel ready for inspection of its fire protection equipment, including the following:

(1) Inspection of each hand portable fire extinguisher, semiportable fire extinguisher, and fixed gas fire extinguishing system to check for excessive corrosion and general condition;

(2) Inspection of piping, controls, and valves, and the inspection and testing of alarms and ventilation shutdowns, for each fixed gas fire extinguishing system and detecting system to determine that the system is in operating condition;

(3) Operation of the fire main system and checking of the pressure at the most remote and highest outlets;

(4) Testing of each fire hose to a test pressure equivalent to its maximum service pressure;

(5) Checking of each cylinder containing compressed gas to ensure it has been tested and marked in accordance with § 147.60 in subchapter N of this chapter;

(6) Testing or renewal of flexible connections and discharge hoses on semiportable extinguishers and fixed gas extinguishing systems in accordance with § 147.65 in subchapter N of this chapter; and

(7) Inspection and testing of all smoke and fire detection systems, including sensors and alarms.

(b) The owner, managing operator, or a qualified servicing facility as applicable shall conduct the following inspections and tests:

(1) For portable fire extinguishers, the inspections, maintenance procedures, and hydrostatic pressure tests required by Chapter 4 of NFPA 10, "Portable Fire Extinguishers," with the frequency specified by NFPA 10. In addition, carbon dioxide and Halon portable fire extinguishers must be refilled when the net content weight loss exceeds that specified for fixed systems by Table 176.810(b). The owner or managing operator shall provide satisfactory evidence of the required servicing to the marine inspector. If any of the equipment or records have not been properly maintained, a qualified servicing facility must be required to perform the required inspections, maintenance procedures, and hydrostatic pressure tests. A tag issued by a qualified servicing organization, and attached to each extinguisher, may be accepted as evidence that the necessary maintenance procedures have been conducted.

(2) For semiportable and fixed gas fire extinguishing systems, the inspections and tests required by Table 176.810(b), in addition to the tests required by §§ 147.60 and 147.65 in subchapter N of this chapter. The owner or managing operator shall provide satisfactory evidence of the required servicing to the marine inspector. If any of the equipment or records have not been properly maintained, a qualified servicing facility may be required to perform the required inspections, maintenance procedures, and hydrostatic pressure tests.

TABLE 176.810(b)—SEMIPORTABLE AND FIXED FIRE EXTINGUISHING SYSTEMS

Type System	Test
Carbon dioxide	Weigh cylinders. Recharge if weight loss exceeds 10% of weight of charge. Test time delays, alarms, and ventilation shutdowns with carbon dioxide, nitrogen, or other nonflammable gas as stated in the system manufacturer's instruction manual. Inspect hoses and nozzles to be sure they are clean.
Halon	Weigh cylinders. Recharge if weight loss exceeds 5% of weight of charge. If the system has a pressure gauge, also recharge if pressure loss (adjusted for temperature) exceeds 10%. Test time delays, alarms and ventilation shutdowns with carbon dioxide, nitrogen, or other nonflammable gas as stated in the system manufacturer's instruction manual. Inspect hoses and nozzles to be sure they are clean.
Dry Chemical (cartridge operated)	Examine pressure cartridge and replace if end is punctured or if determined to have leaked or to be in unsuitable condition. Inspect hose and nozzle to see if they are clear. Insert charged cartridge. Ensure dry chemical is free flowing (not caked) and extinguisher contains full charge.

Coast Guard, DHS § 176.840

TABLE 176.810(b)—SEMIPORTABLE AND FIXED FIRE EXTINGUISHING SYSTEMS—Continued

Type System	Test
Dry chemical (stored pressure)	See that pressure gauge is in operating range. If not, or if the seal is broken, weigh or otherwise determined that extinguisher is fully charged with dry chemical. Recharge if pressure is low or if dry chemical is needed.
Foam (stored pressure)	See that pressure gauge, if so equipped, is in the operating range. If not, or if the seal is broken, weigh or otherwise determine that extinguisher is fully charged with foam. Recharge if pressure is low or if foam is needed. Replace premixed agent every 3 years.
Clean Agents (Halon replacements)	(To be developed)

(c) The owner, managing operator, or master shall destroy, in the presence of the marine inspector, each fire hose found to be defective and incapable of repair.

(d) At each initial and subsequent inspection for certification, the marine inspector may require that a fire drill be held under simulated emergency conditions to be specified by the inspector.

[CGD 85–080, 61 FR 953, Jan. 10, 1996; 61 FR 20557, May 7, 1996, as amended at 62 FR 51356, Sept. 30, 1997]

§ 176.812 **Pressure vessels and boilers.**

(a) Pressure vessels must be tested and inspected in accordance with part 61, subpart 61.10, of this chapter.

(b) Periodic inspection and testing requirements for boilers are contained in § 61.05 in subchapter F of this chapter.

[CGD 85–080, 61 FR 953, Jan. 10, 1996, as amended at 62 FR 51356, Sept. 30, 1997; USCG–1999–4976, 65 FR 6508, Feb. 9, 2000]

§ 176.814 **Steering systems.**

At each initial and subsequent inspection for certification the owner or managing operator shall be prepared to test the steering systems of the vessel and make them available for inspection to the extent necessary to determine that they are in suitable condition and fit for the service intended. Servo-type power systems, such as orbital systems, must be tested and capable of smooth operation by a single person in the manual mode, with hydraulic pumps secured.

§ 176.816 **MIscellaneous systems and equipment.**

At each initial and subsequent inspection for certification the owner or managing operator shall be prepared to test and make available for inspection all items in the ship's outfit, such as ground tackle, navigation lights and equipment, markings, and placards, which are required to be carried by the regulations in this subchapter, as necessary to determine that they are fit for the service intended.

§ 176.818 **Sanitary inspection.**

At each inspection for certification and at every other vessel inspection, quarters, toilet and washing spaces, galleys, serving pantries, lockers, and similar spaces may be examined to determine that they are serviceable and in a sanitary condition.

§ 176.830 **Unsafe practices.**

(a) At each inspection for certification and at every other vessel inspection all observed unsafe practices, fire hazards, and other hazardous situations must be corrected and all required guards and protective devices must be in satisfactory condition.

(b) At each inspection for certification and at every other vessel inspection the bilges and other spaces may be examined to see that there is no excessive accumulation of oil, trash, debris, or other matter that might create a fire hazard, clog bilge pumping systems, or block emergency escapes.

§ 176.840 **Additional tests and inspections.**

The cognizant OCMI may require that a vessel and its equipment undergo any additional test or inspection deemed reasonable and necessary to determine that the vessel and its equipment are suitable for the service in which they are to be employed.

Subpart I—International Convention for Safety of Life at Sea, 1974, as Amended (SOLAS)

§ 176.900 Applicability.

(a) Except as otherwise provided in this subpart, a mechanically propelled vessel of the United States, which carries more than 12 passengers on an international voyage must be in compliance with the applicable requirements of the International Convention for Safety of Life at Sea, 1974, as Amended (SOLAS), to which the United States Government is currently a party.

(b) SOLAS does not apply to a vessel solely navigating the Great Lakes and the St. Lawrence River as far east as a straight line drawn from Cap des Rosiers to West Point, Anticosti Island and, on the north side of Anticosti Island, the 63rd Meridian.

§ 176.910 Passenger Ship Safety Certificate.

(a) A vessel, which carries more than 12 passengers on an international voyage must have a valid SOLAS Passenger Ship Safety Certificate. The Commandant issues the original SOLAS Passenger Ship Safety Certificate after receiving notification from the cognizant OCMI that the vessel complies with the applicable SOLAS regulations. Subsequent SOLAS Passenger Ship Safety Certificates are issued by the cognizant OCMI unless any changes to the vessel or its operations have occurred which changes the information on the certificate, in which case the Commandant will reissue the certificate.

(b) The route specified on the Certificate of Inspection and the SOLAS Passenger Ship Safety Certificate must agree.

(c) A SOLAS Passenger Ship Safety Certificate is issued for a period of not more than 12 months.

(d) The SOLAS Passenger Ship Safety Certificate may be withdrawn, revoked, or suspended at any time when the vessel is not in compliance with applicable SOLAS requirements.

§ 176.920 Exemptions.

(a) In accordance with Chapter I (General Provisions) Regulation 4, of SOLAS, the Commandant may exempt a vessel, which is not normally engaged on an international voyage but that in exceptional circumstances is required to undertake a single international voyage from any of the requirements of the regulations of SOLAS provided that the vessel complies with safety requirements that are adequate, in the Commandant's opinion, for the voyage that is to be undertaken.

(b) In accordance with Chapter II–1 (Construction—Subdivision and Stability, Machinery and Electrical Installations) Regulation 1, Chapter II–2 (Construction—Fire Protection, Fire Detection and Fire Extinction) Regulation 1, and Chapter III (Life Saving Appliances and Arrangements) Regulation 2 of SOLAS, the Commandant may exempt a vessel that does not proceed more than 20 miles from the nearest land from any of the specific requirements of Chapters II–1, II–2, and III of SOLAS if the Commandant determines that the sheltered nature and conditions of the voyage are such as to render the application of such requirements unreasonable or unnecessary.

(c) The Commandant may exempt a vessel from requirements of the regulations of SOLAS in accordance with paragraphs (a) and (b) of this section upon a written request from the owner or managing operator submitted to the Commandant via the cognizant OCMI.

(d) When the Commandant grants an exemption to a vessel in accordance with this section, the Commandant will issue the original SOLAS Exemption Certificate describing the exemption. Subsequent SOLAS Exemption Certificates are issued by the cognizant OCMI unless any changes to the vessel or its operations have occurred that changes the information on the SOLAS Exemption or Passenger Ship Safety Certificates, in which case the Commandant will reissue the certificate. A SOLAS Exemption Certificate is not valid for longer than the period of the SOLAS Passenger Ship Safety Certificate to which it refers.

[CGD 85–080, 61 FR 953, Jan. 10, 1996; 61 FR 20557, May 7, 1996]

Coast Guard, DHS

§ 176.925 Safety Management Certificate.

(a) All vessels that carry more than 12 passengers on an international voyage must have a valid Safety Management Certificate and a copy of their company's valid Document of Compliance certificate on board.

(b) All such vessels must meet the applicable requirements of 33 CFR part 96.

(c) A Safety Management Certificate is issued for a period of not more than 60 months.

[CGD 95–073, 62 FR 67515, Dec. 24, 1997]

§ 176.930 Equivalents.

As outlined in Chapter I (General Provisions) Regulation 5, of SOLAS, the Commandant may accept an equivalent to a particular fitting, material, apparatus, or any particular provision required by SOLAS regulations if satisfied that such equivalent is at least as effective as that required by the regulations. An owner or managing operator of a vessel may submit a request for the acceptance of an equivalent following the procedures in § 175.540 of this chapter. The Commandant will indicate the acceptance of an equivalent on the vessel's SOLAS Passenger Ship Safety Certificate or Safety Management Certificate, as appropriate.

[CGD 95–073, 62 FR 67515, Dec. 24, 1997]

PART 177—CONSTRUCTION AND ARRANGEMENT

Subpart A—General Provisions

Sec.
177.100 General requirement.
177.115 Applicability to existing vessels.

Subpart B—Plans

177.202 Plans and information required.
177.210 Plans for sister vessels.

Subpart C—Hull Structure

177.300 Structural design.
177.310 Satisfactory service as a design basis.
177.315 Vessels of not more than 19.8 meters (65 feet) in length carrying not more than 12 passengers.
177.330 Sailing vessels.

177.340 Alternate design considerations.

Subpart D—Fire Protection

177.405 General arrangement and outfitting.
177.410 Structural fire protection.

Subpart E—Escape Requirements

177.500 Means of escape.

Subpart F—Ventilation

177.600 Ventilation of enclosed and partially enclosed spaces.
177.620 Ventilation of machinery and fuel tank spaces.

Subpart G—Crew Spaces

177.700 General requirements.
177.710 Overnight accommodations.

Subpart H—Passenger Accommodations

177.800 General requirements.
177.810 Overnight accommodations.
177.820 Seating.

Subpart I—Rails and Guards

177.900 Deck rails.
177.920 Storm rails.
177.940 Guards in vehicle spaces.
177.960 Guards for exposed hazards.
177.970 Protection against hot piping.

Subpart J—Window Construction and Visibility

177.1010 Safety glazing materials.
177.1020 Strength.
177.1030 Operating station visibility.

AUTHORITY: 46 U.S.C. 2103, 3306; E.O. 12234, 45 FR 58801, 3 CFR, 1980 Comp., p. 277; Department of Homeland Security Delegation No. 0170.1.

SOURCE: CGD 85–080, 61 FR 961, Jan. 10, 1996, unless otherwise noted.

Subpart A—General Provisions

§ 177.100 General requirement.

The construction and arrangement of a vessel must allow the safe operation of the vessel in accordance with the terms of its Certificate of Inspection giving consideration to provisions for a seaworthy hull, protection against fire, means of escape in case of a sudden unexpected casualty, guards and rails in

§ 177.115

hazardous places, ventilation of enclosed spaces, and necessary facilities for passengers and crew.

[CGD 85–080, 61 FR 961, Jan. 10, 1996, as amended by CGD 97–057, 62 FR 51050, Sept. 30, 1997]

§ 177.115 Applicability to existing vessels.

(a) Except as otherwise required by paragraph (b) of this section, an existing vessel must comply with the construction and arrangement regulations that were applicable to the vessel on March 10, 1996, or, as an alternative, the vessel may comply with the regulations in this part.

(b) Alterations, or modifications made to the structure or arrangements of an existing vessel, that are a major conversion, on or after March 11, 1996, must comply with the regulations of this part. Repairs or maintenance conducted on an existing vessel, resulting in no significant changes to the original structure or arrangement of the vessel, must comply with the regulations applicable to the vessel on March 10, 1996, or, as an alternative, with the regulations in this part. However, when outfit items such as furnishings and mattresses are renewed, they must comply with the regulations in this part.

Subpart B—Plans

§ 177.202 Plans and information required.

(a) Except as provided in paragraph (c) of this section and § 177.210 of this part, the owner of a vessel requesting initial inspection for certification shall, prior to the start of construction unless otherwise allowed by the cognizant Officer in Charge, Marine Inspection (OCMI), submit for approval to the cognizant OCMI, at least two copies of the following plans:

(1) Outboard profile;
(2) Inboard profile; and
(3) Arrangement of decks.

(b) In addition, the owner shall, prior to receiving a Certificate of Inspection, submit for approval to the cognizant OCMI, at least two copies of the following plans, manuals, analyses, and calculations that are applicable to the vessel as determined by the OCMI:

(1) Midship section;
(2) Survival craft embarkation stations;
(3) Machinery installation, including but not limited to:
 (i) Propulsion and propulsion control, including shaft details;
 (ii) Steering and steering control, including rudder details;
 (iii) Ventilation diagrams; and
 (iv) Engine exhaust diagram;
(4) Electrical installation including, but not limited to:
 (i) Elementary one-line diagram of the power system;
 (ii) Cable lists;
 (iii) Bills of materials;
 (iv) Type and size of generators and prime movers;
 (v) Type and size of generator cables, bus-tie cables, feeders, and branch circuit cables;
 (vi) Power, lighting, and interior communication panelboards with number of circuits and rating of energy consuming devices;
 (vii) Type of capacity of storage batteries;
 (viii) Rating of circuit breakers and switches, interrupting capacity of circuit breakers, and rating and setting of overcurrent devices; and
 (ix) Electrical plant load analysis.
(5) Lifesaving equipment locations and installation;
(6) Fire protection equipment installation including, but not limited to:
 (i) Fire main system plans and calculations;
 (ii) Fixed gas fire extinguishing system plans and calculations;
 (iii) Fire detecting system and smoke detecting system plans;
 (iv) Sprinkler system diagram and calculations; and
 (v) Portable fire extinguisher types, sizes and locations;
(7) Fuel tanks;
(8) Piping systems including: bilge, ballast, hydraulic, sanitary, compressed air, combustible and flammable liquids, vents, soundings, and overflows;
(9) Hull penetrations and shell connections;
(10) Marine sanitation device model number, approval number, connecting wiring and piping; and

Coast Guard, DHS § 177.300

(11) Lines and offsets, curves of form, cross curves of stability, and tank capacities including size and location on vessel; and

(12) On sailing vessels:

(i) Masts, including integration into the ship's structure; and

(ii) Rigging plan showing sail areas and centers of effort as well as the arrangement, dimensions, and connections of the standing rigging.

(c) For a vessel of not more than 19.8 meters (65 feet) in length, the owner may submit specifications, sketches, photographs, line drawings or written descriptions instead of any of the required drawings, provided the required information is adequately detailed and acceptable to the cognizant OCMI.

(d) An owner may submit any plans, manuals, or calculations, required to be submitted to the OCMI under this part, to the Commanding Officer, U.S. Coast Guard Marine Safety Center (MSC), 400 Seventh Street, SW., Washington, DC 20590-0001. Three copies of all documents are required to be submitted for Marine Safety Center plan approval.

(e) For a vessel, the construction of which was begun prior to approval of the plans and information required by paragraphs (a) and (b) of this section, the cognizant OCMI may require any additional plans and information, manufacturers' certifications of construction, testing including reasonable destructive testing, and inspections, which the OCMI determines are necessary to verify that the vessel complies with the requirements of this subchapter.

[CGD 85-080, 61 FR 961, Jan. 10, 1996, as amended by USCG-2004-18884, 69 FR 58351, Sept. 30, 2004]

§ 177.210 **Plans for sister vessels.**

(a) Plans are not required for a vessel that is a sister vessel, provided:

(1) Approved plans for the original vessel are on file at the Marine Safety Center or in the files of the cognizant OCMI;

(2) The owner of the plans authorizes their use for the new construction of the sister vessel;

(3) The regulations used for the original plan approval have not changed since the original approval; and

(4) There are no major modifications to any of the systems to be used.

(b) If approved plans for the original vessel are not on file at the MSC or with the cognizant OCMI, the vessel owner shall submit plans as described in § 177.202 of this part.

Subpart C—Hull Structure

§ 177.300 **Structural design.**

Except as otherwise allowed by this subpart, a vessel must comply with the structural design requirements of one of the standards listed below for the hull material of the vessel.

(a) Wooden hull vessels—Rules and Regulations for the Classification of Yachts and Small Craft, Lloyd's Register of Shipping (Lloyd's);

(b) Steel hull vessels:

(1) Rules and Regulations for the Classification of Yachts and Small Craft, Lloyd's; or

(2) Rules for Building and Classing Steel Vessels Under 61 Meters (200 Ft) in Length, American Bureau of Shipping (ABS);

(c) Fiber reinforced plastic vessels:

(1) Rules and Regulations for the Classification of Yachts and Small Craft, Lloyd's; or

(2) Rules for Building and Classing Reinforced Plastic Vessels, ABS; or

(3) ABS Guide for High Speed Craft;

(d) Aluminum hull vessels:

(1) Rules and Regulations for the Classification of Yachts and Small Craft, Lloyd's; or

(i) For a vessel of more than 30.5 meters (100 feet) in length—Rules for Building and Classing Aluminum Vessels, ABS; or

(ii) For a vessel of not more than 30.5 meters (100 feet) in length—Rules for Building and Classing Steel Vessels Under 61 Meters (200 Feet) in Length, ABS, with the appropriate conversions from the ABS Rules for Building and Classing Aluminum Vessels; or

(2) ABS Guide for High Speed Craft;

(e) Steel hull vessels operating in protected waters—Rules for Building and Classing Steel Vessels for Service on Rivers and Intracoastal Waterways, ABS.

[CGD 85-080, 61 FR 961, Jan. 10, 1996, as amended at 62 FR 51356, Sept. 30, 1997]

§ 177.310 Satisfactory service as a design basis.

When scantlings for the hull, deckhouse, and frames of the vessel differ from those specified by the standards listed in § 177.300 of this part, and the owner can demonstrate that the vessel, or another vessel approximating the same size, power, and displacement, has been built to such scantlings and has been in satisfactory service insofar as structural adequacy is concerned for a period of at least 5 years, such scantlings may be approved by the cognizant OCMI instead of the scantlings required by the applicable standards specified in § 177.300 of this part.

§ 177.315 Vessels of not more than 19.8 meters (65 feet) in length carrying not more than 12 passengers.

The scantlings for a vessel of not more than 19.8 meters (65 feet) in length carrying not more than 12 passengers that do not meet the standards in §§ 177.300 or 177.310 may be approved by the cognizant OCMI if the builder of the vessel establishes to the satisfaction of the OCMI that the design and construction of the vessel is adequate for the intended service.

§ 177.330 Sailing vessels.

The design, materials, and construction of masts, posts, yards, booms, bowsprits, and standing rigging on a sailing vessel must be suitable for the intended service. The hull structure must be adequately reinforced to ensure sufficient strength and resistance to plate buckling. The cognizant OCMI may require the owner to submit detailed calculations on the strength of the mast, post, yards, booms, bowsprits, and standing rigging to the Marine Safety Center for evaluation.

§ 177.340 Alternate design considerations.

When the structure of vessel is of novel design, unusual form, or special materials, which cannot be reviewed or approved in accordance with §§ 177.300, 177.310 or 177.315, the structure may be approved by the Commanding Officer, Marine Safety Center, when it can be shown by systematic analysis based on engineering principles that the structure provides adequate safety and strength. The owner shall submit detailed plans, material component specifications, and design criteria, including the expected operating environment, resulting loads on the vessel, and design limitations for such vessel, to the Marine Safety Center.

Subpart D—Fire Protection

§ 177.405 General arrangement and outfitting.

(a) *Fire hazards to be minimized.* The general construction of the vessel must be such as to minimize fire hazards insofar as it is reasonable and practicable.

(b) *Combustibles insulated from heated surfaces.* Internal combustion engine exhausts, boiler and galley uptakes, and similar sources of ignition must be kept clear of and suitably insulated from combustible material. Dry exhaust systems for internal combustion engines on wooden or fiber reinforced plastic vessels must be installed in accordance with American Boat and Yacht Council (ABYC) Standard P-1 "Installation of Exhaust Systems for Propulsion and Auxiliary Engines."

(c) *Separation of machinery and fuel tank spaces from accommodation spaces.* Machinery and fuel tank spaces must be separated from accommodation spaces by boundaries that prevent the passage of vapors.

(d) *Paint and flammable liquid lockers.* Paint and flammable liquid lockers must be constructed of steel or equivalent material, or wholly lined with steel or equivalent material.

(e) *Vapor barriers.* Vapor barriers must be provided where insulation of any type is used in spaces where flammable and combustible liquids or vapors are present, such as machinery spaces and paint lockers.

(f) *Waste receptacles.* Unless other means are provided to ensure that a potential waste receptacle fire would be limited to the receptacle, waste receptacles must be constructed of noncombustible materials with no openings in the sides or bottom.

(g) *Mattresses.* All mattresses must comply with either:

(1) The U.S. Department of Commerce "Standard for Mattress Flammability" (FF 4-72.16), 16 CFR Part

1632, Subpart A and not contain polyurethane foam; or

(2) International Maritime Organization Resolution A.688(17) "Fire Test Procedures For Ignitability of Bedding Components." Mattresses that are tested to this standard may contain polyurethane foam.

§ 177.410 Structural fire protection.

(a) *Cooking areas.* Vertical or horizontal surfaces within 910 millimeters (3 feet) of cooking appliances must have an American Society for Testing and Materials (ASTM) E–84 "Surface Burning Characteristics of Building Materials" flame spread rating of not more than 75. Curtains, draperies, or free hanging fabrics must not be fitted within 910 millimeters (3 feet) of cooking or heating appliances.

(b) *Composite materials.* When the hull, bulkheads, decks, deckhouse, or superstructure of a vessel is partially or completely constructed of a composite material, including fiber reinforced plastic, the resin used must be fire retardant as accepted by the Commandant as meeting MIL-R-21607. Resin systems that have not been accepted as meeting MIL-R-21607 may be accepted as fire retardant if they have an ASTM E–84 flame spread rating of not more than 100 when tested in laminate form. The laminate submitted for testing the resin system to ASTM E–84 must meet the following requirements:

(1) The test specimen laminate total thickness must be between 3.2 and 6.4 millimeters (⅛ to ¼ inch).

(2) The test specimen laminate must be reinforced with glass fiber of any form and must have a minimum resin content of 40 percent by weight.

(3) Tests must be performed by an independent laboratory.

(4) Test results must include, at a minimum, the resin manufacturer's name and address, the manufacturer's designation (part number) for the resin system including any additives used, the test laboratory's name and address, the test specimen laminate schedule, and the flame spread index resulting from the ASTM E–84 test.

(5) Specific laminate schedules, regardless of resin type, that have an ASTM E–84 flame spread rating of not more than 100 may be considered as equivalent to the requirement in this section to use a fire retardant resin. Requests for qualifying a specific laminate schedule as fire retardant for use in a particular vessel may be submitted for consideration to the Commanding Officer, U.S. Coast Guard Marine Safety Center, 400 Seventh Street, SW., Washington, DC 20590–0001.

(c) *Use of general purpose resin.* General purpose resins may be used instead of fire retardant resins if the following additional requirements are met:

(1) *Cooking and heating appliances.* Galleys must be surrounded by B–15 Class fire boundaries. This may not apply to concession stands that are not considered high fire hazards areas (galleys) as long as they do not contain medium to high heat appliances such as deep fat fryers, flat plate griddles, and open ranges with heating surfaces exceeding 121 ° C(250 ° F). Open flame systems for cooking and heating are not allowed.

(2) *Sources of ignition.* Electrical equipment and switch boards must be protected from fuel or water sources. Fuel lines and hoses must be located as far as practical from heat sources. Internal combustion engine exhausts, boiler and galley uptakes, and similar sources of ignition must be kept clear of and suitability insulated from any woodwork or other combustible matter. Internal combustion engine dry exhaust systems must be installed in accordance with ABYC Standard P–1.

(3) *Fire detection and extinguishing systems.* Fire detection and extinguishing systems must be installed in compliance with §§ 181.400 through 181.420 of this chapter. Additionally, all fiber reinforced plastic (FRP) vessels constructed with general purpose resins must be fitted with a smoke activated fire detection system of an approved type, installed in accordance with § 76.27 in subchapter H of this chapter, in all accommodation spaces, all service spaces, and in isolated spaces such as voids and storage lockers that contain an ignition source such as electric equipment or piping for a dry exhaust system.

(4) *Machinery space boundaries.* Boundaries that separate machinery spaces from accommodation spaces, service spaces, and control spaces must

§ 177.500

be lined with noncombustible panels or insulation approved in accordance with § 164.009 in subchapter Q of this chapter, or other standard specified by the Commandant.

(5) *Furnishings.* Furniture and furnishings must comply with § 116.423 in subchapter K of this chapter.

(d) *Limitations on the use of general purpose resin*—(1) *Overnight accommodations.* Vessels with overnight passenger accommodations for more than 12 persons must not be constructed with general purpose resin.

(2) *Gasoline fuel systems.* Vessels with engines powered by gasoline or other fuels having a flash point of 43.3° C (110° F) or lower must not be constructed with general purpose resin, except for vessels powered by outboard engines with portable fuel tanks stored in an open area aft, if, as determined by the cognizant OCMI, the arrangement does not produce an unreasonable hazard.

(3) *Cargo.* Vessels carrying or intended to carry hazardous combustible or flammable cargo must not be constructed with general purpose resin.

[CGD 85–080, 61 FR 961, Jan. 10, 1996; 61 FR 24464, May 15, 1996, as amended at 62 FR 51356, Sept. 30, 1997; USCG–1999–6216, 64 FR 53228, Oct. 1, 1999]

Subpart E—Escape Requirements

§ 177.500 Means of escape.

(a) Except as otherwise provided in this section, each space accessible to passengers or used by the crew on a regular basis, must have at least two means of escape, one of which must not be a watertight door.

(b) The two required means of escape must be widely separated and, if possible, at opposite ends or sides of the space to minimize the possibility of one incident blocking both escapes.

(c) Subject to the restrictions of this section, means of escape may include normal exits and emergency exits, passageways, stairways, ladders, deck scuttles, and windows.

(d) The number and dimensions of the means of escape from each space must be sufficient for rapid evacuation in an emergency for the number of persons served. In determining the number of persons served, a space must be considered to contain at least the number of persons as follows:

(1) Passenger overnight accommodation spaces: Designed capacity;

(2) Accommodation spaces having fixed seating for passengers: Maximum seating capacity;

(3) Public spaces, including spaces such as casinos, restaurants, club rooms, and cinemas, and public accommodation spaces as defined in § 175.400 of this subchapter, except overnight accommodation spaces: One person may be permitted for each 0.9 square meters (10 square feet) of deck area. In computing such deck area, the following areas must be excluded:

(i) Areas for which the number of persons permitted is determined using the fixed seating criterion;

(ii) Obstructions, including stairway and elevator enclosures, elevated stages, bars, and cashier stands, but not including slot machines, tables, or other room furnishings;

(iii) Toilets and washrooms;

(iv) Interior passageways less than 860 millimeters (34 inches) wide and passageways on open deck less than 710 millimeters (28 inches) wide;

(v) Spaces necessary for handling lifesaving equipment, anchor handling equipment, or line handling gear, or in way of sail booms or running rigging; and

(vi) Bow pulpits, swimming platforms, and areas that do not have a solid deck, such as netting on multi hull vessels;

(4) Crew overnight accommodation spaces: Two-thirds designed capacity; and

(5) Work spaces: Occupancy under normal operating conditions.

(e) The dimensions of a means of escape must be such as to allow easy movement of persons when wearing life jackets. There must be no protrusions in means of escape that could cause injury, ensnare clothing, or damage life jackets.

(f) The minimum clear opening of a door or passageway used as a means of escape must not be less than 810 millimeters (32 inches) in width, however, doors or passageways used solely by crew members must have a clear opening not less than 710 millimeters (28 inches). The sum of the width of all

Coast Guard, DHS § 177.600

doors and passageways used as means of escape from a space must not be less than 8.4 millimeters (0.333 inches) multiplied by the number of passengers for which the space is designed.

(g) A dead end passageway, or the equivalent, of more than 6.1 meters (20 feet) in length is prohibited.

(h) Each door, hatch, or scuttle, used as a means of escape, must be capable of being opened by one person, from either side, in both light and dark conditions. The method of opening a means of escape must be obvious, rapid, and of adequate strength. Handles and securing devices must be permanently installed and not capable of being easily removed. A door, hatch or scuttle must open towards the expected direction of escape from the space served.

(i) A means of escape which is not readily apparent to a person from both inside and outside the space must be adequately marked in accordance with § 185.606 of this chapter.

(j) A ladder leading to a deck scuttle may not be used as a means of escape except:

(1) On a vessel of not more than 19.8 meters (65 feet) in length, a vertical ladder and a deck scuttle may be used as not more than one of the means of escape from passenger accommodation space; or

(2) As not more than one of the means of escape from any crew accommodation space or work space.

(k) Each ladder used as a means of escape must be mounted at least 180 millimeters (7 inches) from the nearest permanent object in back of the ladder. Rungs must be:

(1) At least 405 millimeters (16 inches) in width; and

(2) Not more than 305 millimeters (12 inches) apart, and uniformly spaced for the length of the ladder with at least 114 millimeters (4.5 inches) clearance above each rung.

(l) When a deck scuttle serves as a means of escape, it must not be less than 455 millimeters (18 inches) in diameter and must be fitted with a quick acting release and a holdback device to hold the scuttle in an open position.

(m) Footholds, handholds, ladders, and similar means provided to aid escape, must be suitable for use in emergency conditions, of rigid construction, and permanently fixed in position, unless they can be folded, yet brought into immediate service in an emergency.

(n) On a vessel of not more than 19.8 meters (65 feet) in length, a window or windshield of sufficient size and proper accessibility may be used as one of the required means of escape from an enclosed space, provided it:

(1) Does not lead directly overboard;

(2) Can be opened or is designed to be kicked or pushed out; and

(3) Is suitably marked.

(o) Only one means of escape is required from a space where:

(1) The space has a deck area less than 30 square meters (322 square feet);

(2) There is no stove, heater, or other source of fire in the space;

(3) The means of escape is located as far as possible from a machinery space or fuel tank; and

(4) If an accommodation space, the single means of escape does not include a deck scuttle or a ladder.

(p) Alternative means of escape from spaces may be provided if acceptable to the cognizant OCMI.

[CGD 85-080, 61 FR 961, Jan. 10, 1996; 62 FR 64306, Dec. 5, 1997]

Subpart F—Ventilation

§ 177.600 Ventilation of enclosed and partially enclosed spaces.

(a) An enclosed or partially enclosed space within a vessel must be adequately ventilated in a manner suitable for the purpose of the space.

(b) A power ventilation system must be capable of being shut down from the pilot house.

(c) An enclosed passenger or crew accommodation space and any other space occupied by a crew member on a regular basis must be ventilated by a power ventilation system unless natural ventilation in all ordinary weather conditions is satisfactory to the OCMI.

(d) An exhaust duct over a frying vat or a grill must be of at least 11 U.S. Standard Gauge steel.

(e) Combustibles and other foreign materials are not allowed within ventilation ducts. However, metal piping and electrical wiring installed in a

§ 177.620

metal protective enclosure may be installed within ventilation ducts, provided that the piping or the wiring does not interfere with the operation of fire dampers. Electrical wiring and piping may not be installed in an exhaust duct over a frying vat or grill.

[CGD 85–080, 61 FR 961, Jan. 10, 1996, as amended at 62 FR 51356, Sept. 30, 1997]

§ 177.620 **Ventilation of machinery and fuel tank spaces.**

In addition to the requirements of this subpart, ventilation systems for spaces containing machinery or fuel tanks must comply with the requirements of part 182 of this chapter.

Subpart G—Crew Spaces

§ 177.700 **General requirements.**

(a) A crew accommodation space and a work space must be of sufficient size, adequate construction, and with suitable equipment to provide for the safe operation of the vessel and the protection and accommodation of the crew in a manner practicable for the size, facilities, service, route, speed, and modes of operation of the vessel.

(b) The deck above a crew accommodation space must be located above the deepest load waterline.

§ 177.710 **Overnight accommodations.**

Overnight accommodations must be provided for all crew members if the vessel is operated more than 12 hours in a 24 hour period, unless the crew is put ashore and the vessel is provided with a new crew.

[CGD 85–080, 61 FR 961, Jan. 10, 1996, as amended by CGD 97–057, 62 FR 51050, Sept. 30, 1997]

Subpart H—Passenger Accommodations

§ 177.800 **General requirements.**

(a) All passenger accommodations must be arranged and equipped to provide for the safety of the passengers in consideration of the route, modes of operation, and speed of the vessel.

(b) The height of ceilings in a passenger accommodation space, including aisles and passageways, must be at least 1,880 millimeters (74 inches), but may be reduced at the sides of a space to allow the camber, wiring, ventilation ducts, and piping.

(c) A passenger accommodation space must be maintained to minimize fire and safety hazards and to preserve sanitary conditions. Aisles must be kept clear of obstructions.

(d) A passenger accommodation space must not contain:

(1) Electrical generation equipment or transformers, high temperature parts, pipelines, rotating assemblies, or any other item that could injure a passenger, unless such an item is adequately shielded or isolated; and

(2) A control for operating the vessel, unless the control is so protected and located that operation of the vessel by a crew member will not be impeded by a passenger during normal or emergency operations.

(e) The deck above a passenger accommodation space must be located above the deepest load waterline.

(f) A variation from a requirement of this subpart may be authorized by the cognizant OCMI for an unusual arrangement or design provided there is no significant reduction of space, accessibility, safety, or sanitation.

§ 177.810 **Overnight accommodations.**

(a) A berth must be provided for each passenger authorized to be carried in overnight accommodation spaces. Each berth must measure at least 1,880 millimeters (74 inches) by 610 millimeters (24 inches) and have at least 610 millimeters (24 inches) of clear space above.

(b) Berths must not be located more than three high and must be constructed of wood, fiber reinforced plastic, or metal. A berth located more than 1520 millimeters (60 inches) above the deck must be fitted with a suitable aid for access.

(c) The construction and arrangement of berths and other furniture must allow free and unobstructed access to each berth. Each berth must be immediately adjacent to an aisle leading to a means of escape from the accommodation space. An aisle alongside a berth must be at least 610 millimeters (24 inches) wide. An aisle joining two or more aisles in an overnight accommodation space must be at least 1,060 millimeters (42 inches) wide.

[CGD 85–080, 61 FR 961, Jan. 10, 1996, as amended by CGD 97–057, 62 FR 51050, Sept. 30, 1997]

§ 177.820 Seating.

(a) A seat must be provided for each passenger permitted in a space for which the fixed seating criterion in § 176.113(b)(3) of this subchapter has been used to determine the number of passengers permitted.

(b) A seat must be constructed to minimize the possibility of injury and avoid trapping occupants.

(c) Installation of seats must provide for ready escape.

(d) Seats, including fixed, temporary, or portable seats, must be arranged as follows:

(1) An aisle of not more than 3.8 meters (15 feet) in overall length must be not less than 610 millimeters (24 inches) in width.

(2) An aisle of more than 3.8 meters (15 feet) in overall length must be not less than 760 millimeters (30 inches) in width.

(3) Where seats are in rows, the distance from seat front to seat front must be not less than 760 millimeters (30 inches) and the seats must be secured to a deck or bulkhead.

(4) Seats used to determine the number of passengers permitted, in accordance with § 176.113(b)(3) of this chapter, must be secured to the deck, bulkhead, or bulwark.

Subpart I—Rails and Guards

§ 177.900 Deck rails.

(a) Except as otherwise provided in this section, rails or equivalent protection must be installed near the periphery of all decks of a vessel accessible to passengers or crew. Equivalent protection may include lifelines, wire rope, chains, and bulwarks, which provide strength and support equivalent to fixed rails. Deck rails must include a top rail with the minimum height required by this section, and lower courses or equivalent protection as required by this section.

(b) Deck rails must be designed and constructed to withstand a point load of 91 kilograms (200 pounds) applied at any point in any direction, and a uniform load of 74 kilograms per meter (50 pounds per foot) applied to the top rail in any direction. The point and uniform loads do not need to be applied simultaneously.

(c) Where space limitations make deck rails impractical for areas designed for crew use only, such as at narrow catwalks in way of deckhouse sides, hand grabs may be substituted.

(d) The height of top rails required by paragraph (a) of this section must be as follows:

(1) Rails on passenger decks of a ferry or a vessel engaged in excursion trips, including but not limited to sightseeing trips, dinner and party cruises, and overnight cruises, must be at least 1,000 millimeters (39.5 inches) high.

(2) Rails on a vessel subject to the 1966 International Convention on Load Lines must be at least 1,000 millimeters (39.5 inches) high.

(3) All other rails must be at least 910 millimeters (36 inches) high.

(4) While engaged in big game angling, the minimum rail height may be reduced to not less than 760 millimeters (30 inches) in way of a person using specialized angling techniques or equipment, such as when using a pedestal mounted fixed fighting chair on a low freeboard vessel, if it can be shown that a higher rail would interfere with the fishing operation and the lower rail would not significantly reduce safety. A rail complying with the requirements of paragraphs (d)(1), (2), or (3) of this section as applicable must be installed when big game angling is not being conducted.

(e) Where the principal business of the vessel requires the discharge of persons or cargo in a seaway, such as on pilot boats and dive boats, the cognizant OCMI may accept alternatives to the rails required in paragraphs (d)(1), (2), and (3) of this section for those areas of a deck where passengers or cargo are discharged and for which removable rails, lifelines, or chains would hinder discharge operations.

(f) A sailing vessel, an open boat, or any other vessel not specifically covered elsewhere in this section, must have rails of a minimum height or equivalent protection as considered

§ 177.920

necessary by the cognizant OCMI, based on the vessel's operation, route, and seating arrangement.

(g) Rail courses or the equivalent must be installed between a top rail required by paragraph (a) of this section, and the deck so that no open space exists that is more than 305 millimeters (12 inches) high except:

(1) On passenger decks of a ferry or of a vessel on an excursion trip the following must be installed:

(i) Bulwarks;

(ii) Chain link fencing or wire mesh that has openings of not more than 4 inches in diameter; or

(iii) Bars, slats, rail courses, or an equivalent spaced at intervals of not more than 100 millimeters (4 inches).

(2) On a vessel subject to the 1966 International Convention on Load Lines, rail courses, or an equivalent, must be installed so that there is not an open space higher than 230 millimeters (9 inches) from the deck to the first rail course or equivalent.

(h) Rails must be permanently installed except that the following rails may be removable;

(1) Rails in way of embarkation stations and boarding locations;

(2) Rails over 760 millimeters (30 inches) high in way of fishing seats addressed by paragraph (d)(4) of this section; and

(3) Rails on a vessel when the service of the vessel is routinely changed, as determined by the cognizant OCMI, and the required top rail height varies depending on the service of the vessel at a particular time.

§ 177.920 Storm rails.

Suitable storm rails or hand grabs must be installed where necessary in passageways, at deckhouse sides, and at ladders and hatches.

§ 177.940 Guards in vehicle spaces.

On a vessel authorized to carry one or more vehicles, suitable chains, cables, or other barriers must be installed at the end of each vehicle runway. In addition, temporary rails or equivalent protection must be installed in way of each vehicle ramp, in compliance with § 177.900, when the vessel is underway.

§ 177.960 Guards for exposed hazards.

An exposed hazard, such as gears or rotating machinery, must be properly protected by a cover, guard, or rail.

§ 177.970 Protection against hot piping.

Piping, including valves, pipe fittings and flanges, conveying vapor, gas, or liquid, the temperature of which exceeds 65.5° C (150° F), must be suitably insulated where necessary to prevent injuries.

Subpart J—Window Construction and Visibility

§ 177.1010 Safety glazing materials.

Glass and other glazing material used in windows accessible to passengers and crew must be of material that will not break into dangerous fragments if fractured.

[CGD 85–080, 61 FR 961, Jan. 10, 1996; 61 FR 20557, May 7, 1996]

§ 177.1020 Strength.

Each window, port hole, and its means of attachment to the hull or deck house, must be capable of withstanding the maximum load from wave and wind conditions expected due to its location on the vessel and the authorized route of the vessel.

§ 177.1030 Operating station visibility.

(a) Windows and other openings at the operating station must be of sufficient size and properly located to provide an adequate view for safe navigation in all operating conditions.

(b) Glass or other glazing material used in windows at the operating station must have a light transmission of not less than 70 percent according to Test 2 of American National Standards Institute (ANSI) Z 26.1 "Safety Glazing Materials For Motor Vehicles Operating on Land Highways," and must comply with Test 15 of ANSI Z 26.1 for Class I Optical Deviation.

Coast Guard, DHS § 178.230

PART 178—INTACT STABILITY AND SEAWORTHINESS

Subpart A—General Provisions

Sec.
178.115 Applicability to existing vessels.

Subpart B—Stability Instructions for Operating Personnel

178.210 Stability information.
178.220 Stability booklet.
178.230 Stability letter or Certificate of Inspection stability details.

Subpart C—Intact Stability Standards

178.310 Applicability based on length and passenger capacity.
178.320 Intact stability requirements.
178.325 Intact stability requirements for a sailing vessel.
178.330 Simplified stability proof test.
178.340 Stability standards for pontoon vessels on protected waters.

Subpart D—Drainage of Weather Decks

178.410 Drainage of flush deck vessels.
178.420 Drainage of cockpit vessels.
178.430 Drainage of well deck vessels.
178.440 Drainage of open boats.
178.450 Calculation of drainage area for cockpit and well deck vessels.

Subpart E—Special Installations

178.510 Ballast.

AUTHORITY: 43 U.S.C. 1333; 46 U.S.C. 2103, 3306, 3703; E.O. 12234, 45 FR 58801, 3 CFR, 1980 Comp., p. 277; Department of Homeland Security Delegation No. 0170.1.

SOURCE: CGD 85–080, 61 FR 966, Jan. 10, 1996, unless otherwise noted.

Subpart A—General Provisions

§ 178.115 Applicability to existing vessels.

An existing vessel must comply with the intact stability and seaworthiness regulations which were applicable to the vessel on March 10, 1996, or, as an alternative, the vessel may comply with the regulations in this part.

Subpart B—Stability Instructions for Operating Personnel

§ 178.210 Stability information.

(a) Stability information (stability details indicated on the Certificate of Inspection, a stability letter, or a stability booklet) is required on certain vessels by paragraphs (b) or (c) of this section. Enough stability information, including stability calculations and assumptions made to use them, must be provided to allow the master to be able to determine operating guidelines, loading restrictions, and ensure compliance with the applicable intact and damage stability regulations of this chapter.

(b) A vessel which, under § 178.310, must comply with requirements in subchapter S of this chapter, must have stability details on the vessel's Certificate of Inspection, a stability letter issued by the cognizant Officer in Charge, Marine Inspection (OCMI) or the Commanding Officer, Marine Safety Center, or an approved stability booklet. The form in which the stability information must be contained (i.e., stability details on the Certificate of Inspection, a stability letter, or a stability booklet) will be determined by the Commanding Officer, Marine Safety Center.

(c) When necessary for safe operation, the cognizant OCMI may place specific stability restrictions in a stability letter or on the Certificate of Inspection of a vessel of not more than 19.8 meters (65 feet) in length, which, under § 178.310 of this part, must comply with the requirements of § 178.320 of this part.

§ 178.220 Stability booklet.

When the Commanding Officer, Marine Safety Center determines, in accordance with § 178.210(b), that a vessel must have a stability booklet, the owner or operator must prepare the booklet in accordance with subchapter S of this chapter, and submit it to the Commanding Officer, Marine Safety Center.

§ 178.230 Stability letter or Certificate of Inspection stability details.

(a) When the cognizant OCMI or the Commanding Officer, Marine Safety Center determines, in accordance with § 178.210, that a vessel must have stability details indicated on its Certificate of Inspection or a stability letter, the owner or operator must submit the

235

§ 178.310

information listed in paragraph (b) of this section:

(1) If § 178.210(c) is applicable, to the OCMI for approval; or

(2) If § 178.210(b) is applicable, to the Commanding Officer, Marine Safety Center for approval.

(b) The following applicable information, and the necessary calculations used to determine that information, must be submitted as required by paragraph (a) of this section:

(1) Allowable number of passengers and crew on each deck;

(2) Deepest waterline drafts or freeboard;

(3) Location of watertight bulkheads and openings in watertight bulkheads;

(4) Explanation of the vessel's subdivision and specific identification of the vessel's subdivision bulkheads;

(5) Location of openings through watertight bulkheads, such as watertight doors, which must be closed to limit flooding in an emergency;

(6) Location, type and amount of fixed ballast;

(7) Location and details of foam flotation material; and

(8) Maximum weight of portable equipment permitted on the vessel including diving equipment.

Subpart C—Intact Stability Standards

§ 178.310 Applicability based on length and passenger capacity.

(a) A vessel of not more than 19.8 meters (65 feet) in length must meet the applicable requirements of § 178.320 or 178.325, or of §§ 170.170, 170.173, and 171.050 in subchapter S of this chapter, if:

(1) Carrying not more than 150 passengers on a domestic voyage;

(2) Carrying not more than 12 passengers on an international voyage; or

(3) It has not more than one deck above the bulkhead deck, exclusive of a pilot house.

(b) The following vessels must meet the appropriate requirements of §§ 170.170, 170.173, 171.050, 171.055, and 171.057 in subchapter S of this chapter:

(1) A vessel of more than 19.8 meters (65 feet) in length;

(2) A vessel carrying more than 12 passengers on an international voyage; and

(3) A vessel with more than 1 deck above the bulkhead deck exclusive of a pilot house.

[CGD 85–080, 61 FR 966, Jan. 10, 1996, as amended at 62 FR 51356, Sept. 30, 1997]

§ 178.320 Intact stability requirements.

(a) A vessel, except a pontoon vessel operating on protected waters, must undergo a simplified stability proof test in accordance with § 178.330 of this part in the presence of a Coast Guard marine inspector.

(b) A pontoon vessel operating on protected waters must undergo a simplified stability proof test in accordance with § 178.340 of this part in the presence of a Coast Guard marine inspector.

(c) The cognizant OCMI may dispense with the simplified stability proof test in § 178.330 for a vessel carrying not more than 49 passengers where it can be established that, due to the form, arrangement, construction, number of decks, route, and operating restrictions of the vessel, the vessel's stability can be safely determined without such a test. Vessels which carry deck cargo must undergo a simplified stability proof test.

(d) A vessel whose stability is questioned by the cognizant OCMI must be shown by design calculations to meet the applicable stability criteria of §§ 170.170, 170.173, and 171.050 in subchapter S of this chapter in each condition of loading and operation.

(e) A simplified stability proof test in accordance with § 178.330 is conducted to determine if a vessel, as built and operated, has a minimum level of initial stability. Failure of the simplified test does not necessarily mean that the vessel lacks stability for the intended route, service, and operating condition, but that calculations or other methods must be used to evaluate the stability of the vessel.

[CGD 85–080, 61 FR 966, Jan. 10, 1996; 61 FR 20557, May 7, 1996]

§ 178.325 Intact stability requirements for a sailing vessel.

(a) Except as provided in paragraphs (b), (c) and (e) of this section, each sailing vessel must undergo a simplified stability proof test in accordance with § 178.330 of this part in the presence of a Coast Guard marine inspector.

(b) Each of the following sailing vessels must meet the intact stability standards of §§ 170.170 and 171.055 in subchapter S of this chapter:

(1) A vessel to be operated on exposed waters;

(2) A vessel to be operated during non-daylight hours;

(3) A vessel of unusual type, rig, or hull form, including vessels without a weathertight deck, such as open boats;

(4) A vessel that carries more than 49 passengers;

(5) A sailing school vessel that carries a combined total of six or more sailing school students or instructors;

(6) A vessel on which downflooding occurs at angles of 60° or less; and

(7) A vessel which has a cockpit longer than Length Over Deck (LOD)/5.

(c) A catamaran must meet the intact stability requirements of § 171.057 in subchapter S of this chapter while under sail as well as the intact stability requirements of § 170.170 in subchapter S of this chapter or § 178.320 under barepoles (if an auxiliary sailing vessel) and with storm sails set and trimmed flat (if a sailing vessel).

(d) A sailing vessel that is not listed in paragraph (b) or (c) of this section and operates on partially protected waters must be equipped with a self-bailing cockpit.

(e) The cognizant OCMI may perform operational tests to determine whether the vessel has adequate stability and satisfactory handling characteristics under sail for protected waters or partially protected waters, in lieu of conducting a simplified stability proof test.

(f) Commanding Officer, Marine Safety Center, may prescribe additional or different stability requirements for a broad, shallow draft vessel with little or no ballast outside the hull.

§ 178.330 Simplified stability proof test.

(a) A vessel must be in the condition specified in this paragraph when a simplified stability proof test is performed.

(1) The construction of the vessel must be complete in all respects.

(2) Ballast, if necessary, must be in compliance with § 178.510 and must be on board and in place.

(3) Each fuel and water tank must be approximately three-quarters full.

(4) A weight equal to the total weight of all passengers, crew, and other loads permitted on the vessel must be on board and distributed so as to provide normal operating trim and to simulate the vertical center of gravity causing the least stable condition that is likely to occur in service. Unless otherwise specified, weight and vertical center of gravity is assumed to be as follows:

(i) The weight of primary lifesaving equipment should be simulated at its normal location, if not on board at the time of the test;

(ii) The weight of one person is considered to be 72.6 kilograms (160 pounds) except the weight of one person is considered to be 63.5 kilograms (140 pounds) if the vessel operates exclusively on protected waters and the passenger load consists of men, women, and children;

(iii) The vertical center for the simulated weight of passengers, crew, and other loads must be at least 760 millimeters (2.5 feet) above the deck; and

(iv) If the vessel carries passengers on diving excursions, the total weight of diving gear must be included in the loaded condition as follows:

(A) The total weight of individual diving gear for each passenger carried is assumed to be 36 kilograms (80 pounds), which includes the weight of scuba tanks, harness, regulator, weight belt, wet suit, mask, and other personal diving equipment; and

(B) The weight of any air compressors carried.

(v) On vessels having one upper deck above the main deck available to passengers, the weight distribution must not be less severe than the following:

Total Test Weight (W) = ____

Passenger Capacity of Upper Deck: ____

§ 178.330

Weight on Upper Deck = (# of Passengers on Upper Deck) × (Wt per Passenger) × 1.33''
Weight on Main Deck = Total Test Weight − Weight on Upper Deck

(5) All non-return closures on cockpit scuppers or on weather deck drains must be kept open during the test.

(b) A vessel must not exceed the limitations in paragraph (f) of this section, when subjected to the greater of the following heeling moments:

$M_p = (W)(B_p)/6$; or
$M_w = (P)(A)(H)$

where:

M_p = passenger heeling moment in kilogram-meters (foot-pounds);
W = the total passenger weight using 72.5 kilograms (160 pounds) per passenger, or, if the vessel operates exclusively on protected waters and the passenger load consists of men, women, and children, 63.5 kilograms (140 pounds) per passenger may be used;
B_p = the maximum transverse distance in meters (feet) of a deck that is accessible to passengers;
M_w = wind heeling moment in kilogram-meters (foot-pounds);
P = wind pressure of:
  (1) 36.6 kilograms/square meter (7.5 pounds/square foot) for operation on protected waters;
  (2) 48.8 kilogram/square meter (10.0 pounds/square foot) for operation on partially protected waters; or
  (3) 73.3 kilograms/square meter (15.0 pounds/square foot) for operation on exposed waters;
A = area, in square meters (square feet), of the projected lateral surface of the vessel above the waterline (including each projected area of the hull, superstructure and area bounded by railings and structural canopies). For sailing vessels this is the bare poles area, or, if the vessel has no auxiliary power, with storm sails set; and
H = height, in meters (feet), of the center of area (A) above the waterline, measured up from the waterline.

(c) For sailing vessels the heeling moment used for this test must be the greater of the following:

(1) Passenger heeling moment from paragraph (b) of this section.

(2) Wind heeling moment from paragraph (b) of this section.

(3) Wind heeling moment calculated from the wind heeling moment equation in paragraph (b) of this section, where:

M_w = wind heeling moment in kilogram-meters (foot-pounds);
P=4.9 kilograms/square meter (1.0 pounds/square foot) for both protected and partially protected waters.
A=the windage area of the vessel in square meters (square feet) with all sails set and trimmed flat;
H=height, in meters (feet), of the center of effort of area (A) above the waterline, measured up from the waterline; and

(d) A vessel must not exceed the following limits of heel:

(1) On a flush deck vessel, not more than one-half of the freeboard may be immersed.

(2) On a well deck vessel, not more than one-half of the freeboard may be immersed, except that, on a well deck vessel that operates on protected waters and has non-return scuppers or freeing ports, the full freeboard may be immersed if the full freeboard is not more than one-quarter of the distance from the waterline to the gunwale.

(3) On a cockpit vessel, the maximum allowable immersion is calculated from the following equation:

(i) On exposed waters—

$i = f(2L - 1.5L')/4L$

(ii) On protected or partially protected waters—

$i = f(2L - L')/4L$

where:

i=maximum allowable immersion in meters (feet);
f=freeboard in meters (feet);
L=length of the weather deck, in meters (feet); and
L'=length of cockpit in meters (feet).

(4) On an open boat, not more than one quarter of the freeboard may be immersed.

(5) On a flush deck sailing vessel, the full freeboard may be immersed.

(6) In no case may the angle of heel exceed 14 degrees.

(e) The limits of heel must be measured at:

(1) The point of minimum freeboard; or

(2) At a point three-quarters of the vessel's length from the bow if the point of minimum freeboard is aft of this point.

(f) When demonstrating compliance with paragraph (d) of this section, the freeboard must be measured as follows:

Coast Guard, DHS § 178.340

(1) For a flush deck or well deck vessel, the freeboard must be measured to the top of the weatherdeck at the side of the vessel; and

(2) For a cockpit vessel or for an open boat, the freeboard must be measured to the top of the gunwale.

(g) A ferry must also be tested in a manner acceptable to the cognizant OCMI to determine whether the trim or heel during loading or unloading will submerge the deck edge. A ferry passes this test if, with the total number of passengers and the maximum vehicle weight permitted on board, the deck edge is not submerged during loading or unloading of the vessel.

[CGD 85–080, 61 FR 966, Jan. 10, 1996; 61 FR 20557, May 7, 1996, as amended at 62 FR 51356, Sept. 30, 1997; 62 FR 64306, Dec. 5, 1997]

§ 178.340 Stability standards for pontoon vessels on protected waters.

(a) The portion of the deck accessible to passengers on a pontoon vessel must not extend beyond the outboard edge of either pontoon, nor beyond the forward or aft ends of the pontoons.

(b) A pontoon vessel that has more than 2 pontoons or has decks higher than 150 milimeters (6 inches) above the pontoons must meet a stability standard acceptable to the Commanding Officer, Marine Safety Center.

(c) A pontoon vessel must be in the condition described in § 178.330(a) of this part when the simplified stability proof test is performed, except that the simulated load of passengers, crew, and other weights is initially centered on the vessel so that trim and heel are minimized.

(d) A pontoon vessel has the minimum acceptable level of initial stability if it meets the following:

(1) With the simulated load located at the extreme outboard position of the deck on the side with the least initial freeboard, the remaining exposed cross sectional area of the pontoon on that side must be equal to or greater than the cross sectional area submerged due to the load shift, as indicated in Figure 178.340(d)(1); and

FIGURE 178.340(d)(1)

TRANSVERSE STABILITY STANDARD

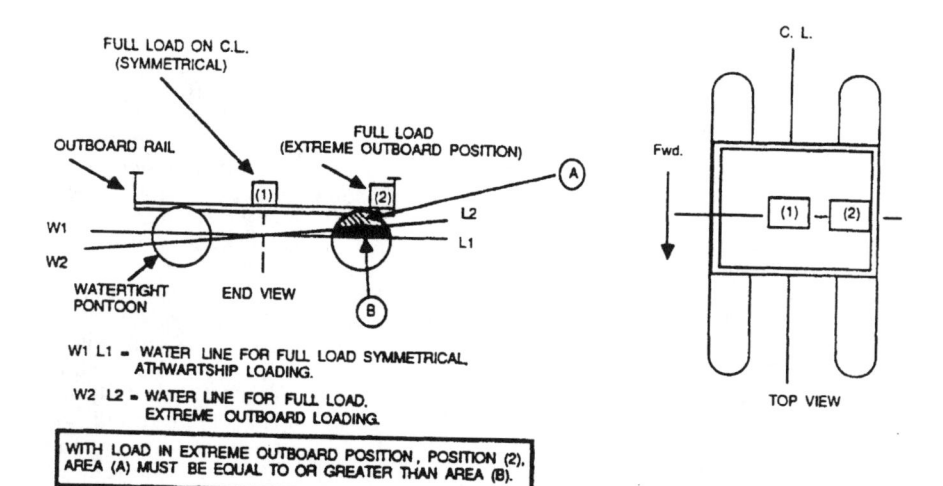

W1 L1 = WATER LINE FOR FULL LOAD SYMMETRICAL ATHWARTSHIP LOADING.

W2 L2 = WATER LINE FOR FULL LOAD. EXTREME OUTBOARD LOADING.

WITH LOAD IN EXTREME OUTBOARD POSITION, POSITION (2), AREA (A) MUST BE EQUAL TO OR GREATER THAN AREA (B).

§ 178.410

(2) With the simulated load located on the centerline at the extreme fore or aft end of the deck, whichever position is further from the initial position of the load, the top of the pontoon must not be submerged at any location, as indicated in Figure 178.340(d)(2).

FIGURE 178.340(d)(2)

LONGITUDINAL STABILITY STANDARD

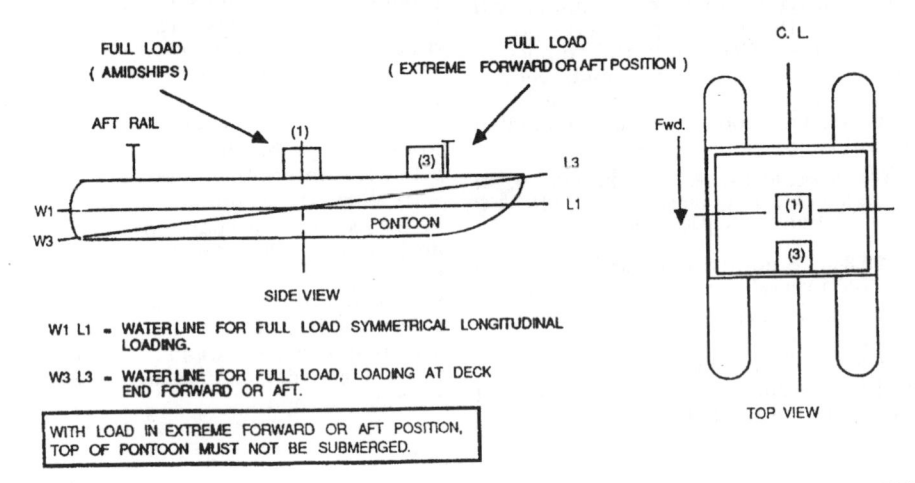

W1 L1 = WATERLINE FOR FULL LOAD SYMMETRICAL LONGITUDINAL LOADING.

W3 L3 = WATERLINE FOR FULL LOAD, LOADING AT DECK END FORWARD OR AFT.

WITH LOAD IN EXTREME FORWARD OR AFT POSITION, TOP OF PONTOON MUST NOT BE SUBMERGED.

[CGD 85–080, 61 FR 966, Jan. 10, 1996, as amended by CGD 97–057, 62 FR 51050, Sept. 30, 1997]

Subpart D—Drainage of Weather Decks

§ 178.410 Drainage of flush deck vessels.

(a) Except as provided in paragraph (b) of this section, the weather deck on a flush deck vessel must be watertight and have no obstruction to overboard drainage.

(b) Each flush deck vessel may have solid bulwarks in the forward one-third length of the vessel if:

(1) The bulwarks do not form a well enclosed on all sides; and

(2) The foredeck of the vessel has sufficient sheer to ensure drainage aft.

[CGD 85–080, 61 FR 966, Jan. 10, 1996, as amended at 62 FR 51357, Sept. 30, 1997]

§ 178.420 Drainage of cockpit vessels.

(a) Except as follows, the cockpit on a cockpit vessel may be watertight:

(1) A cockpit may have companionways if the companionway openings have watertight doors, or weathertight doors and coamings which meet § 179.360 of this subchapter.

(2) A cockpit may have ventilation openings along its inner periphery if the vessel operates only on protected or partially protected waters.

(b) The cockpit deck of a cockpit vessel that operates on exposed or partially protected waters must be at least 255 millimeters (10 inches) above the deepest load waterline unless the vessel complies with:

(1) The intact stability requirements of §§ 170.170, 170.173, 171.050, 171.055, and 171.057 in subchapter S of this chapter;

(2) The Type II subdivision requirements in §§ 171.070, 171.072, and 171.073 in subchapter S of this chapter; and

(3) The damage stability requirements in § 171.080 in subchapter S of this chapter.

(c) The cockpit deck of a cockpit vessel that does not operate on exposed or

Coast Guard, DHS § 178.510

partially protected waters must be located as high above the deepest load waterline as practicable.

(d) The cockpit must be self-bailing. Scuppers or freeing ports for the cockpit deck of a cockpit vessel must:

(1) Be located to allow rapid clearing of water in all probable conditions of list and trim;

(2) Have a combined drainage area of at least the area required by § 178.450 of this part; and

(3) If the deck is less than 255 millimeters (10 inches) above the deepest load waterline of the vessel, be fitted with non-return devices.

§ 178.430 Drainage of well deck vessels.

(a) The weather deck on a well deck vessel must be watertight.

(b) The area required on a well deck vessel for drainage of well formed by the bulwarks shall be determined by § 178.450.

(c) The freeing ports or scuppers on a well deck vessel must be located to allow rapid clearing of water in all probable conditions of list and trim.

(d) The deck of well deck vessel that operates on exposed or partially protected waters must be at least 255 millimeters (10 inches) above the deepest load waterline unless the vessel complies with:

(1) The intact stability requirements of §§ 170.170, 170.173, 171.050, 171.055, and 171.057 in subchapter S of this chapter;

(2) The Type II subdivision requirements in §§ 171.070, 171.072, and 171.073 in subchapter S of this chapter; and

(3) The damage stability requirements in § 171.080 in subchapter S of this chapter.

§ 178.440 Drainage of open boats.

The deck within the hull of an open boat must drain to the bilge. Overboard drainage of the deck is not permitted.

§ 178.450 Calculation of drainage area for cockpit and well deck vessels.

(a) The drainage area required on a vessel must be computed using the following formula:

For protected waters required drainage = $.1 \times$ Basic Drainage

For partially protected waters required drainage = $.5 \times$ Basis Drainage

For exposed waters required drainage = Basic Drainage

where:

Basic Drainage area in centimeters^2 = $4389.12 \times$ [(Recess Volume × Recess Ratio) + (Weather Deck Volume × Weather Deck Ratio)]; or

Basic Drainage area in inch^2 = (Recess Volume × Recess Ratio) + (Weather Deck Volume × Weather Deck Ratio)

Recess Volume = $(B_R \times D_R) - V_R$

B_R=average height in centimeters (feet) of the bulwark above the well deck or cockpit deck;

D_R=total deck area of the cockpit or well deck in the after ⅔ of the vessel length (LOD) measured in centimeters^2 (feet^2).

V_R=volume of any weather tight structure below the bulwark of the well deck or cockpit deck.

Recess Ratio = L_R / L_C

L_R=the length of the recess in the after ⅔ vessel length (LOD).
L_C=⅔ vessel length (LOD).

Weather Deck Volume = $(B_D \times D_D) - V_S$

B_D=average height in centimeters (feet) of the bulwark above the weather deck;
D_D=total deck area of the weather deck adjacent to bulwarks but not in way of the cockpit or well deck in the after ⅔ of the vessel length (LOD) measured in centimenters^2 (feet^2).
V_S=volume of any weather tight superstructure below the bulwark on the weather deck located within D_D.

Weather Deck Ratio = L_D / L_C

L_D=the length of the weather deck bulwark in the after ⅔ of the vessel length (LOD).
L_C=⅔ vessel length (LOD).

(b) Vessels with bulwarks in the forward part of the vessel shall not form a well with the deckhouse which retains water.

[CGD 85–080, 61 FR 966, Jan. 10, 1996; 61 FR 20557, May 7, 1996]

Subpart E—Special Installations

§ 178.510 Ballast.

(a) Any solid fixed ballast used to comply with the requirements of parts 170, 171, 178, and 179 of this chapter must be:

(1) Stowed in a manner that prevents shifting of the ballast; and

(2) Installed to the satisfaction of the cognizant OCMI.

(b) Solid fixed ballast may not be located forward of the collision bulkhead unless the installation and arrangement of the ballast and the collision bulkhead minimizes the risk of the ballast penetrating the bulkhead in a collision.

(c) Solid fixed ballast may not be removed from a vessel or relocated unless approved by the cognizant OCMI except that ballast may be temporarily moved for a vessel examination or repair if it is replaced to the satisfaction of the OCMI.

(d) Water ballast, either as an active system or permanent, must be approved by the Commanding Officer, Marine Safety Center.

PART 179—SUBDIVISION, DAMAGE STABILITY, AND WATERTIGHT INTEGRITY

Subpart A—General Provisions

Sec.
179.115 Applicability to existing vessels.

Subpart B—Subdivision and Damage Stability Requirements

179.210 Collision bulkhead.
179.212 Watertight bulkheads for subdivision.
179.220 Location of watertight bulkheads for subdivision.
179.230 Damage stability requirements.
179.240 Foam flotation material.

Subpart C—Watertight Integrity Requirements

179.310 Collision bulkheads.
179.320 Watertight bulkheads.
179.330 Watertight doors.
179.340 Trunks.
179.350 Openings in the side of a vessel below the bulkhead or weather deck.
179.360 Watertight integrity.

AUTHORITY: 43 U.S.C. 1333; 46 U.S.C. 2103, 3306, 3703; E.O. 12234, 45 FR 58801, 3 CFR, 1980 Comp., p. 277; Department of Homeland Security Delegation No. 0170.1.

SOURCE: CGD 85–080, 61 FR 971, Jan. 10, 1996, unless otherwise noted.

Subpart A—General Provisions

§179.115 Applicability to existing vessels.

An existing vessel must comply with the subdivision, damage stability, and watertight integrity regulations which were applicable to the vessel on March 10, 1996, or, as an alternative, the vessel may comply with the regulations in this part.

Subpart B—Subdivision and Damage Stability Requirements

§179.210 Collision bulkhead.

(a) A vessel of more than 19.8 meters (65 feet) in length must have a collision bulkhead.

(b) A vessel of not more than 19.8 meters (65 feet) in length must have a collision bulkhead if it:

(1) Carries more than 49 passengers;

(2) Operates on exposed waters;

(3) Is of more than 12.2 meters (40 feet) in length and operates on partially protected waters; or

(4) Is constructed of wood on or after March 11, 2001, and operates in cold water.

(c) A double-ended ferry required to have a collision bulkhead must have a collision bulkhead at each end of the vessel.

§179.212 Watertight bulkheads for subdivision.

(a) A vessel of not more than 19.8 meters (65 feet) in length must comply with §179.220 of this part if it:

(1) Carries more than 49 passengers; or

(2) Is constructed of wood on or after March 11, 2001, and operates in cold water.

As an alternative, the above vessels may comply with the intact stability requirements of §§170.170, 170.173, 171.050 and 171.055 of this chapter, and comply with the Type II subdivision requirements of §§171.070 through 171.073 in subchapter S of this chapter.

(b) A vessel of more than 19.8 meters (65 feet) in length must comply with the Type II subdivision requirements of §§171.070 through 171.073 in subchapter S of this chapter.

(c) A vessel that carries more than 12 passengers on an international voyage

Coast Guard, DHS § 179.220

must meet the Type II subdivision requirements of §§ 171.070 through 171.073 in subchapter S of this chapter.

§ 179.220 Location of watertight bulkheads for subdivision.

(a) The maximum distance between adjacent main transverse watertight bulkheads on a vessel, required by § 179.212(a) of this part to comply with this section, must not be more than the smaller of the following:

(1) One third of the length of the bulkhead deck; or

(2) The distance given by the following equation:

$$d = \frac{(F)(f)(L)}{D}$$

where:

d=the maximum length of the bulkhead deck in meters (feet) between adjacent main transverse watertight bulkheads;
F=the floodable length factor from Table 179.220(a);
f=the effective freeboard in meters (feet) calculated for each pair of adjacent bulkheads in accordance with paragraph (b) of this section;
L=Length Over Deck in meters (feet) measured over the bulkhead deck; and
D=the depth in meters (feet), measured amidships at a point one-quarter of the maximum beam out from the centerline, from the inside of the bottom planking or plating to the level of the top of the bulkhead deck at side as shown in Figure 179.220(a).

TABLE 179.220(a)—TABLE OF FLOODABLE LENGTH FACTORS

(d/L) × 100	F
0–15	0.33
20	0.34
25	0.36
30	0.38
35	0.43
40	0.48
45	0.54
50	0.61
55	0.63
60	0.58
65	0.53
70	0.48
75	0.44
80	0.40
85	0.37
90–100	0.34

NOTE 1: Where: d=distance in meters (feet) from the midpoint of the compartment to the forward-most point on the bulkhead deck excluding sheer; and L=length over deck in meters (feet) measured over the bulkhead deck.

NOTE 2: Intermediate values of floodable length factor may be obtained by interpolation.

Figure 179.220(a)

Transverse Location for Measuring Depth (D)

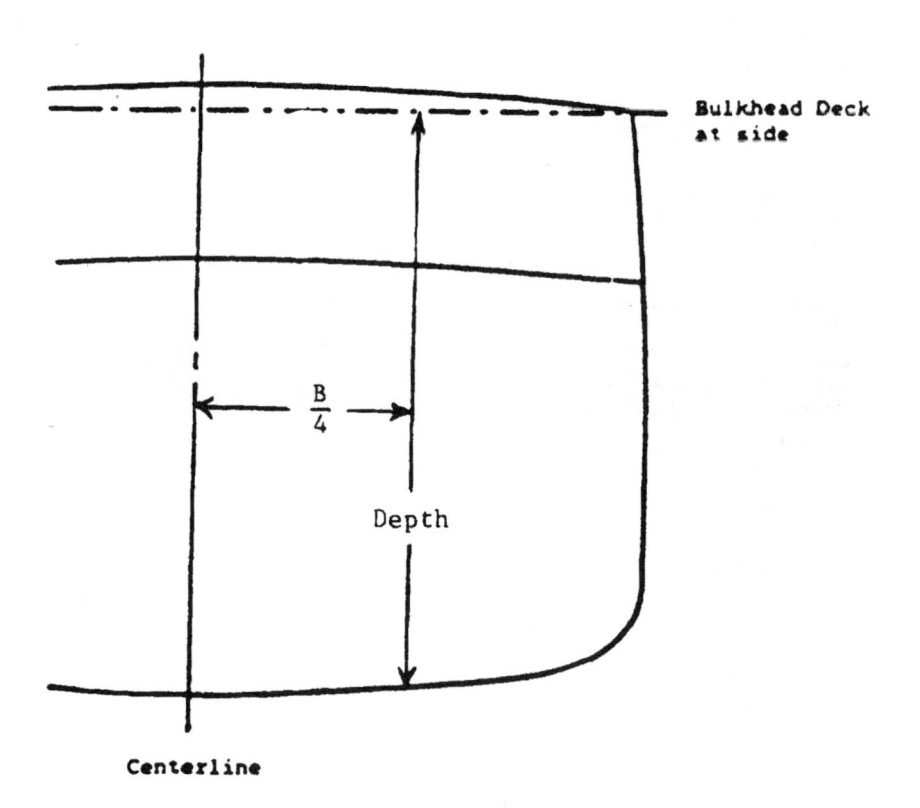

Centerline

Bulkhead Deck at side

$\frac{B}{4}$

Depth

(b) The effective freeboard for each compartment is calculated by the following equation:

f=(a+b)/2

where:
f=the effective freeboard in meters (feet).
a=the freeboard in meters (feet) measured:
 (1) At the forward main transverse watertight bulkhead; and
 (2) From the deepest waterline to:

(i) The top of the bulkhead deck on a flush deck vessel; or
(ii) If a vessel has a stepped bulkhead deck, the line shown in Figure 179.220(b); or
(iii) If a vessel has an opening port light below the bulkhead deck, the line shown in Figure 179.220(c).

b=the freeboard in meters (feet) measured:
 (1) At the aft main transverse watertight bulkhead; and
 (2) From the deepest waterline to:

Coast Guard, DHS § 179.220

(i) The top of the bulkhead deck on a flush deck vessel; or

(ii) If a vessel has a stepped bulkhead deck, the line shown in Figure 1 to §179.220(b); or

Figure 1 to § 179.220(b)

Freeboard Measurement - Vessel with Stepped Bulkhead Deck

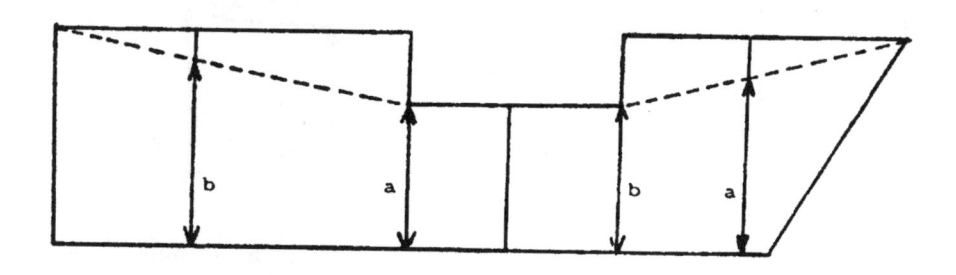

(a and b shown for two sample compartments)

Figure 2 to § 179.220(b)

Freeboard Measurement – Vessel with Stepped Bulkhead Deck and a Port Light Below the Bulkhead Deck

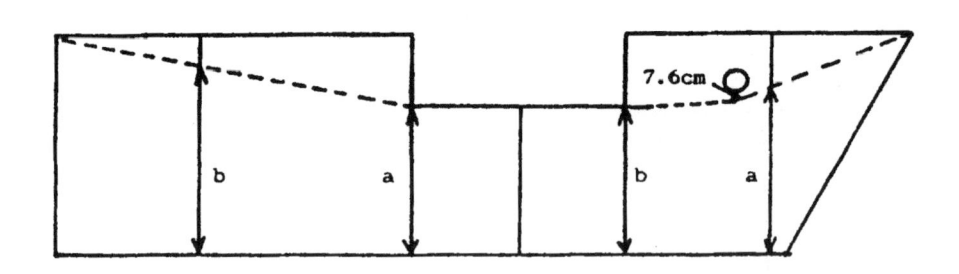

(iii) if a vessel has an opening port light below the bulkhead deck, the line shown in Figure 2 to § 179.220(b).

[CGD 85–080, 61 FR 971, Jan. 10, 1996; 61 FR 20557, May 7, 1996]

§ 179.230 Damage stability requirements.

A vessel which, in accordance with § 179.212, must meet the requirements of §§ 171.070 through 171.073 in subchapter S of this chapter for Type II subdivision, shall also meet the damage stability requirements of § 171.080 in subchapter S of this chapter.

[CGD 85–080, 61 FR 971, Jan. 10, 1996, as amended at 62 FR 51357, Sept. 30, 1997]

§ 179.240 Foam flotation material.

(a) Foam may only be installed as flotation material on a vessel when approved by the cognizant OCMI.

(b) If foam is installed as flotation material on a vessel, the owner shall ensure that the following tests are conducted and requirements are met, to the satisfaction of the cognizant OCMI:

(1) All foam must comply with MIL-P-21929C. The fire resistance test is not required.

(2) Foam may be installed only in void spaces that are free of ignition sources, unless the foam complies with the requirements of 33 CFR 183.114;

(3) Foam may be installed adjacent to fuel tanks only if the boundary between the tank and the space has double continuous fillet welds;

(4) The structure enclosing the foam must be strong enough to accommodate the buoyancy of the foam;

(5) Piping and cables must not pass through foamed spaces unless they are within piping and cable ways accessible from both ends;

(6) Blocked foam must:

(i) Be used in each area that may be exposed to water; and

(ii) Have a protective cover, approved by the cognizant OCMI, to protect it from damage;

(7) A water submergence test must be conducted on the foam for a period of at least 7 days to demonstrate to the satisfaction of the cognizant OCMI that the foam has adequate strength to withstand a hydrostatic head equivalent to that which would be imposed if the vessel were submerged to its bulkhead deck;

Coast Guard, DHS § 179.330

(8) The effective buoyancy of the foam must be determined at the end of the submergence test required by paragraph (b)(7) of this section. The effective buoyancy or 881 kilograms per cubic meter (55 pounds per cubic foot), whichever is less, must be used in determining the location of watertight bulkheads for subdivision required by § 179.212; and

(9) The owner or operator must obtain sample foam specimens during installation of the foam and determine the density of the installed foam.

[CGD 85–080, 61 FR 971, Jan. 10, 1996, as amended at 62 FR 51357, Sept. 30, 1997]

Subpart C—Watertight Integrity Requirements

§ 179.310 Collision bulkheads.

(a) Each collision bulkhead required by § 179.210, must be constructed in accordance with § 179.320, except that a collision bulkhead:

(1) Must extend to the weather deck or to one deck above the bulkhead deck, whichever is lower, for service on oceans or coastwise routes; and

(2) Must not be fitted with any type of penetration or opening except penetrations may be made if they are located as high and as far inboard as practicable and they have a means to make them watertight.

(b) The forward collision bulkhead required to be on a vessel by § 179.210 must be:

(1) Located at least 5 percent but not more than 15 percent of the length between perpendiculars (LBP) aft of the forward perpendicular, or for vessels with bulbous bows extending forward of the forward perpendicular and contributing more than 2 percent of the underwater volume of the vessel, located at least 5 percent but not more than 15 percent of the LBP aft of the mid-length of such extension; and

(2) Installed in a single plane, with no recess or step, up to the bulkhead deck;

(c) The after collision bulkhead on a double-ended ferry of more than 19.8 meters (65 feet) in length must be:

(1) At least 5 percent but not more than 15 percent of the LBP forward of the after perpendicular; and

(2) Installed in a single plane, with no recess or step, at least up to the bulkhead deck.

§ 179.320 Watertight bulkheads.

(a) Each watertight bulkhead must be of sufficient strength to be capable of remaining watertight with a head of water to the top of the bulkhead.

(b) Each watertight bulkhead must extend to the bulkhead deck and be installed in one plane without steps or recesses insofar as is reasonable and practicable. Any steps or recesses permitted must comply with the applicable subdivision requirements in this subchapter.

(c) The number of penetrations in a watertight bulkhead must be minimized. A penetration in a watertight bulkhead must be as high and as far inboard in the bulkhead as practicable, and made watertight.

(d) Sluice valves are not permitted in watertight bulkheads.

§ 179.330 Watertight doors.

(a) Hinged watertight doors are not permitted in bulkheads required by §§ 179.210 or 179.212 unless the vessel will not proceed more than 20 nautical miles from shore and:

(1) The door separates a machinery space from an accommodation space and, in the judgment of the cognizant OCMI, the door will be kept closed except when a person is passing through the door; or

(2) The Commandant determines that, due to the arrangements of the vessel, the door will be kept closed except when a person is passing through the door.

(b) A hinged watertight bulkhead door must be fitted with a quick action closing devise operable from both sides of the door and indicator lights at the operating station showing whether the door is open or closed.

(c) Sliding watertight doors must meet the requirements of part 170, subpart H in subchapter S of this chapter.

(d) No more than one watertight door may be fitted in a watertight bulkhead, and it must be located as high and as far inboard as practicable.

§ 179.340 Trunks.

Where a trunk (i.e., an enclosed passageway through a deck or bulkhead) is installed, it must comply with the requirements of § 179.360(a)(1) and with the requirements of § 171.113 in subchapter S of this chapter.

§ 179.350 Openings in the side of a vessel below the bulkhead or weather deck.

(a) On a vessel operating on exposed or partially protected waters, an opening port light is not permitted below the weather deck unless the sill of the port light is at least 760 millimeters (30 inches) above the deepest load waterline.

(b) A port light must have an inside, hinged dead cover regardless of whether the port light is or is not capable of being opened.

(c) Except for engine exhausts, each inlet or discharge pipe that penetrates the hull below a line drawn parallel to and at least 150 millimeters (6 inches) above the deepest load waterline must have means to prevent water from entering the vessel if the pipe fractures or otherwise fails.

(d) A positive action valve or cock that is located as close as possible to the hull is an acceptable means for complying with paragraph (c) of this section.

(e) If an inlet or discharge pipe is inaccessible, the means for complying with paragraph (c) of this section must be a shut-off valve that is:

(1) Operable from the weather deck or any other accessible location above the bulkhead deck; and

(2) Labeled at the operating point for identity and direction of closing.

(f) Any connecting device or valve in a hull penetration must not be cast iron.

(g) Each plug cock in an inlet or discharge pipe must have a means, other than a cotter pin, to prevent its loosening or removal from the body.

§ 179.360 Watertight integrity.

(a) A hatch exposed to the weather must be watertight, except that the following hatches may be weathertight:

(1) A hatch on a watertight trunk that extends at least 305 millimeters (12 inches) above the weather deck;

(2) A hatch in a cabin top; and

(3) A hatch on a vessel that operates only on protected waters.

(b) A hatch cover must:

(1) Have securing devices; and

(2) Be attached to the hatch frame or coaming by hinges, captive chains, or other devices of substantial strength to prevent its loss.

(c) A hatch cover that provides access to accommodation spaces must be operable from either side.

(d) A weathertight door must be provided for each opening located in a deck house or companionway. Permanent watertight coamings must be provided as follows:

(1) On a vessel on an exposed or partially protected route, a watertight coaming with a height of at least 150 millimeters (6 inches) must be provided under each weathertight door in a cockpit or a well, or on the main deck of a flush deck vessel.

(2) On a vessel on a protected route, a watertight coaming with a height of at least 75 millimeters (3 inches) must be provided under each weathertight door in a cockpit or a well.

(3) The height of the watertight coaming for a hinged watertight door need only be sufficient to accommodate the door.

PART 180—LIFESAVING EQUIPMENT AND ARRANGEMENTS

Subpart A—General Provisions

Sec.
180.10 Applicability to vessels on an international voyage.
180.15 Applicability to existing vessels.
180.25 Additional requirements.

Subpart B—Emergency Communications

180.64 Emergency Position Indicating Radiobeacons (EPIRB).
180.68 Distress flares and smoke signals.

Subpart C—Ring Life Buoys and Life Jackets

180.70 Ring life buoys.
180.71 Life jackets.
180.72 Personal flotation devices carried in addition to life jackets.
180.75 Life jacket lights.

Coast Guard, DHS

§ 180.15

180.78 Stowage of life jackets.

Subpart D—Survival Craft Arrangements and Equipment

180.130 Stowage of survival craft.
180.137 Stowage of life floats and buoyant apparatus.
180.150 Survival craft embarkation arrangements.
180.175 Survival craft equipment.

Subpart E—Number and Type of Survival Craft

180.200 Survival craft—general.
180.202 Survival craft—vessels operating on oceans routes.
180.204 Survival craft—vessels operating on coastwise routes.
180.205 Survival craft—vessels operating on limited coastwise routes.
180.206 Survival craft—vessels operating on Great Lakes routes.
180.207 Survival craft—vessels operating on lakes, bays, and sounds routes.
180.208 Survival craft—vessels operating on rivers routes.
180.210 Rescue boats.

AUTHORITY: 46 U.S.C. 2104, 3306; E.O. 12234, 45 FR 58801, 3 CFR, 1980 Comp., p. 277; Department of Homeland Security Delegation No. 0170.1.

SOURCE: CGD 85–080, 61 FR 975, Jan. 10, 1996, unless otherwise noted.

Subpart A—General Provisions

§ 180.10 Applicability to vessels on an international voyage.

A vessel on an international voyage subject to the International Convention for the Safety of Life at Sea, 1974, (SOLAS) must meet the requirements in subchapter W of this chapter for passenger vessels in the same service, instead of the requirements of this part.

[CGD 85–080, 62 FR 51357, Sept. 30, 1997]

§ 180.15 Applicability to existing vessels.

An existing vessel must comply with the requirements of this part except as otherwise specified by this section.

(a) Before March 11, 2001, or 10 years after the vessel's keel was laid or the vessel was at a similar stage of construction, whichever is later, an existing vessel may comply with the requirements in effect for the vessel prior to March 11, 1996, for the number and type of survival craft, stowage arrangements, and launching appliances for survival craft.

(b) On or before March 11, 2001, or 10 years after the vessel's keel was laid or the vessel was at a similar stage of construction, whichever is later, an existing vessel must:

(1) Be equipped with the number of survival craft required for its route under §§ 180.202, 180.204, 180.205, 180.206, 180.207, or 180.208, as applicable; and

(2) Comply with the stowage and launching appliance requirements for survival craft in §§ 180.130 through 180.150, inclusive.

(c) A vessel that meets the following requirements shall be considered in compliance with the subdivision requirements contained in §§ 180.202, 180.204, 180.205, 180.206, 180.207 and 180.208:

(1) The vessel was constructed before March 11, 2001.

(2) The vessel is of not more than 19.8 meters (65 feet) in length and carries not more than 49 passengers;

(3) The vessel meets the standards for collision bulkheads in § 179.310 of this chapter; and

(4) The vessel meets the standards for one-compartment subdivision in §§ 179.220 and 179.320 of this chapter, at least in way of the engine room and lazarette.

(d) Each inflatable liferaft, inflatable buoyant apparatus, life float, and buoyant apparatus on the vessel on March 11, 1996, may be used to meet the requirements of this part for these survival craft as long as the survival craft is continued in use on the vessel, and is in good and serviceable condition.

(e) New installations of lifesaving equipment on an existing vessel, which are completed to the satisfaction of the cognizant Officer in Charge, Marine Inspection, (OCMI) on or after March 11, 1996, must comply with the regulations in this part. Replacement of existing lifesaving equipment installed before March 11, 1996, must meet the requirements of paragraph (a) of this section.

(f) A combination flare and smoke distress signal approved in accordance with § 160.023 in subchapter Q of this chapter may be used on an existing vessel until the expiration date of the distress signal but no later than March

§ 180.25

11, 1999, as one of the distress signals required by § 180.68.

(g) Until February 1, 1999, a Coast Guard approved 121.5/243 MHz Class A Emergency Position Indicating Radiobeacon (EPIRB) may be used to meet the requirement for an EPIRB under § 180.64, if the EPIRB:

(1) Is operable;

(2) Is installed to automatically float-free and activate;

(3) Was manufactured on or after October 1, 1988; and

(4) Was installed on the vessel on or before March 11, 1996.

(h) Until February 1, 1999, a Federal Communications Commission (FCC) Type Accepted VHF-FM Class C EPIRB may be used to meet the requirement for an EPIRB on a vessel operating on a Great Lakes route under § 180.64, if the EPIRB:

(1) Is operable; and

(2) Was installed on the vessel on or before March 11, 1996.

(i) Until March 11, 1997, an existing vessel on a limited coastwise route, need not comply with § 180.64.

(j) An existing vessel need not comply with § 180.78(a)(4).

(k) An existing vessel must comply with § 180.210 or may comply with the regulations for rescue boats that were in effect for the vessel prior to March 11, 1996.

[CGD 85-080, 61 FR 975, Jan. 10, 1996; 61 FR 24464, May 15, 1996]

§ 180.25 Additional requirements.

(a) Each item of lifesaving equipment carried on board a vessel but not required under this part, must be approved by the Commandant.

(b) The cognizant Officer in Charge, Marine Inspection (OCMI) may require a vessel to carry specialized or additional lifesaving equipment if:

(1) The OCMI determines the conditions of the voyage render the requirements of this part inadequate; or

(2) The vessel is operated in Arctic, Antarctic, or other severe conditions not covered under this part.

Subpart B—Emergency Communications

§ 180.64 Emergency Position Indicating Radiobeacons (EPIRB).

Each vessel that operates on the high seas, or that operates beyond three miles from the coastline of the Great Lakes, must have on board a FCC Type Accepted Category 1, 406 MHz EPIRB, installed to automatically float free and activate.

§ 180.68 Distress flares and smoke signals.

(a) *Oceans, coastwise, limited coastwise, and Great Lakes routes.* A vessel on an oceans, coastwise, limited coastwise, or Great Lakes route must carry—

(1) Six hand red flare distress signals approved in accordance with § 160.021 in subchapter Q of this chapter, or other standard specified by the Commandant; and

(2) Six hand orange smoke distress signals approved in accordance with § 160.037 in subchapter Q of this chapter, or other standard specified by the Commandant.

(b) *Lakes, bays, and sounds, and rivers routes.* A vessel on a lakes, bays, and sounds, or rivers route must carry:

(1) Three hand red flare distress signals approved in accordance with § 160.021 in subchapter Q of this chapter, or other standard specified by the Commandant; and

(2) Three hand orange smoke distress signals approved in accordance with § 160.037 in subchapter Q of this chapter, or other standard specified by the Commandant.

(c) *Substitutions.* (1) A rocket parachute flare approved in accordance with § 160.036 in subchapter Q of this chapter, or other standard specified by the Commandant may be substituted for any of the hand red flare distress signals required under paragraph (a) or (b) of this section.

(2) One of the following may be substituted for any of the hand orange smoke distress signals required under paragraph (a) or (b) of this section:

(i) A rocket parachute flare approved in accordance with §160.036 in subchapter Q of this chapter, or other standard specified by the Commandant.

(ii) A hand red flare distress signal approved in accordance with §160.021 in subchapter Q of this chapter, or other standard specified by the Commandant.

(iii) A floating orange smoke distress signal approved in accordance with §160.022 in subchapter Q of this chapter, or other standard specified by the Commandant.

(d) *Exemption for vessels on short runs.* A vessel operating on short runs limited to approximately 30 minutes away from the dock is not required to carry distress flares and smoke signals under this section.

(e) *Stowage.* Each flare carried to meet this section must be stowed in one of the following:

(1) A portable watertight container marked as required by §185.614 of this chapter, carried at the operating station; or

(2) A pyrotechnic locker secured above the freeboard deck, away from heat, in the vicinity of the operating station.

[CGD 85-080, 61 FR 975, Jan. 10, 1996; 61 FR 20557, May 7, 1996, as amended at 62 FR 51357, Sept. 30, 1997]

Subpart C—Ring Life Buoys and Life Jackets

§ 180.70 Ring life buoys.

(a) A vessel must have one or more ring life buoys as follows:

(1) A vessel of not more than 7.9 meters (26 feet) in length must carry a minimum of one life buoy of not less than 510 millimeters (20 inches) in diameter;

(2) A vessel of more than 7.9 meters (26 feet) in length, but not more than 19.8 meters (65 feet), must carry a minimum of one life buoy of not less than 610 millimeters (24 inches) in diameter; and

(3) A vessel of more than 19.8 meters (65 feet) in length must carry a minimum of three life buoys of not less than 610 millimeters (24 inches) in diameter.

(b) Each ring life buoy on a vessel must:

(1) Be approved in accordance with §160.050 in subchapter Q of this chapter, or other standard specified by the Commandant;

(2) Be readily accessible;

(3) Be stowed in a way that it can be rapidly cast loose;

(4) Not be permanently secured in any way; and

(5) If on a vessel on an oceans or coastwise route, be orange in color.

(c) At least one ring life buoy must be fitted with a lifeline. If more than one ring life buoy is carried, at least one must not have a lifeline attached. Each lifeline on a ring life buoy must:

(1) Be buoyant;

(2) Be of at least 18.3 meters (60 feet) in length;

(3) Be non-kinking;

(4) Have a diameter of at least 7.9 millimeters (5/16 inch);

(5) Have a breaking strength of at least 5 kilonewtons (1,124 pounds); and

(6) Be of a dark color if synthetic, or of a type certified to be resistant to deterioration from ultraviolet light.

(d) A vessel must carry one floating waterlight, unless it is limited to daytime operation, in which case no floating waterlight is required.

(1) Each floating waterlight must be approved in accordance with §161.010 in subchapter Q of this chapter, or other standard specified by the Commandant.

(2) Each ring life buoy with a floating waterlight must have a lanyard of at least 910 millimeters (3 feet) in length, but not more than 1,830 millimeters (6 feet), securing the waterlight around the body of the ring life buoy.

(3) Each floating waterlight installed after March 11, 1997, on a vessel carrying only one ring buoy, must be attached to the lanyard with a corrosion-resistant clip. The clip must have a strength of at least 22.7 kilograms (50 pounds), and allow the waterlight to be quickly disconnected from the ring life buoy.

[CGD 85-080, 61 FR 975, Jan. 10, 1996; 61 FR 20557, May 7, 1996, as amended by CGD 97-057, 62 FR 51050, Sept. 30, 1997; CGD 85-080, 62 FR 51357, Sept. 30, 1997]

§ 180.71 Life jackets.

(a) An adult life jacket must be provided for each person carried on board a vessel.

§ 180.72

(b) In addition, a number of child size life jackets equal to at least 10% of the number of persons permitted on board must be provided, or such greater number as necessary to provide a life jacket for each person being carried that is smaller than the lower size limit of the adult life jackets provided to meet this section, except that:

(1) Child-size life jackets are not required if the vessel's Certificate of Inspection is endorsed for the carriage of adults only; or

(2) When all "extended size" life preservers (those with a lower size limit for persons of 1,195 millimeters (47 inches) in height or weighing 20.4 kilograms (45 pounds)) are carried on board, a minimum of only 5% additional child size devices need be carried.

(c) Except as allowed by paragraph (d) of this section, each life jacket must be approved in accordance with either §§ 160.002, 160.005, or 160.055 in subchapter Q of this chapter, or other standard specified by the Commandant.

(d) Cork and balsa wood life jackets previously approved in accordance with §§ 106.003, or 160.004 in subchapter Q of this section, on board an existing vessel prior to March 11, 1996, may continue to be used to meet the requirements of this section until March 11, 1999, provided the life jackets are maintained in good and serviceable condition.

(e) Each life jacket carried on board the vessel must be marked in accordance with § 185.604 of this chapter.

[CGD 85-080, 61 FR 975, Jan. 10, 1996; 61 FR 24464, May 15, 1996, as ammended by CGD 97-057, 62 FR 51050, Sept. 30, 1997; CGD 85-080, 62 FR 51357, Sept. 30, 1997]

§ 180.72 Personal flotation devices carried in addition to life jackets.

(a) Equipment carried under this section is not acceptable in lieu of any portion of the required number of approved life jackets and must not be substituted for the approved life jackets required to be worn during drills and emergencies.

(b) Wearable marine buoyant devices that include "ski vests," "boating vests," and "fishing vests," approved in accordance with § 160.064 in subchapter Q of this chapter, or other

46 CFR Ch. I (10-1-04 Edition)

standard specified by the Commandant, may be carried as additional equipment.

(c) Buoyant work vests approved in accordance with § 160.053 in subchapter Q of this chapter, or other standard specified by the Commandant, may be carried as additional equipment for use of persons working near or over the water.

(d) Commercial hybrid personal flotation devices (PFD) approved in accordance with § 160.077 of this chapter, or other standard specified by the Commandant, may be carried as additional equipment for use of persons working near or over the water. Each commercial hybrid PFD must be:

(1) Used, stowed, and maintained in accordance with the procedures set out in the manual required for these devices under § 160.077-29 in subchapter Q of this chapter and any limitation(s) marked on them; and

(2) Of the same or similar design and have the same method of operation as each other hybrid PFD carried on board.

§ 180.75 Life jacket lights.

(a) Each life jacket carried on a vessel on oceans, coastwise, or Great Lakes route, must have a life jacket light approved in accordance with § 161.012 in subchapter Q of this chapter, or other standard specified by the Commandant. Each life jacket light must be securely attached to the front shoulder area of the life jacket.

(b) Notwithstanding the requirements of paragraph (a) of this section, life jacket lights are not required for life jackets on:

(1) Ferries; and

(2) Vessels with Certificates of Inspection endorsed only for routes that do not extend more than 20 miles from a harbor of safe refuge.

§ 180.78 Stowage of life jackets.

(a) *General.* Unless otherwise stated in this section, life jackets must be stored in convenient places distributed throughout accommodation spaces.

(1) Each stowage container for life jackets must not be capable of being locked. If practicable, the container must be designed to allow the life jackets to float free.

252

Coast Guard, DHS § 180.137

(2) Each life jacket kept in a stowage container must be readily available.

(3) Each life jacket stowed overhead must be supported in a manner that allows quick release for distribution.

(4) If life jackets are stowed more than 2,130 millimeters (7 feet) above the deck, a means for quick release must be provided and must be capable of operation by a person standing on the deck.

(5) Each child size life jacket must be stowed in a location that is appropriately marked and separated from adult life jackets so the child size life jackets are not mistaken for adult life jackets.

(b) *Additional personal flotation devices.* The stowage locations of the personal flotation devices carried in addition to life jackets under §180.72, must be separate from the life jackets, and such as not to be easily confused with that of the life jackets.

Subpart D—Survival Craft Arrangements and Equipment

§ 180.130 Stowage of survival craft.

(a) Each survival craft must be:

(1) Secured to the vessel by a painter with a float-free link permanently attached to the vessel except that a float-free link is not required if the vessel operates only on waters not as deep as the length of the painter;

(2) Stowed so that when the vessel sinks the survival craft floats free and, if inflatable, inflates automatically;

(3) Stowed in a position that is readily accessible to crew members for launching, or else provided with a remotely operated device that releases the survival craft into launching position or into the water;

(4) Stowed in a way that permits manual release from its securing arrangements;

(5) Ready for immediate use so that crew members can carry out preparations for embarkation and launching in less than 5 minutes;

(6) Provided with means to prevent shifting;

(7) Stowed in a way that neither the survival craft nor its stowage arrangements will interfere with the embarkation and operation of any other survival craft at any other launching station;

(8) Stowed in a way that any protective covers will not interfere with launching and embarkation;

(9) Fully equipped as required under this part; and

(10) Stowed, as far as practicable, in a position sheltered from breaking seas and protected from damage by fire.

(b) A hydrostatic release unit when used in a float-free arrangement must be approved under approval series 160.062 or 160.162 or other standard specified by the Commandant.

(c) A mechanical, manually operated device to assist in launching a survival craft must be provided if:

(1) The survival craft weights more than 90.7 kilograms (200 pounds); and

(2) The survival craft requires lifting more than 300 vertical millimeters (one vertical foot) to be launched.

[CGD 85–080, 61 FR 975, Jan. 10, 1996, as amended at 62 FR 51357, Sept. 30, 1997; 62 FR 64306, Dec. 5, 1997]

§ 180.137 Stowage of life floats and buoyant apparatus.

(a) In addition to meeting §180.130, each life float and buoyant apparatus must be stowed as required under this section.

(b) The float-free link required by §180.130(a)(1) must be:

(1) Certified to meet §160.073 in subchapter Q of this chapter, or other standard specified by the Commandant;

(2) Of proper strength for the size of the life float or buoyant apparatus as indicated on its identification tag; and

(3) Secured to the painter at one end and to the vessel on the other end.

(c) The means used to attach the float-free link to the vessel must:

(1) Have a breaking strength of at least the breaking strength of the painter;

(2) If synthetic, be of a dark color or of a type certified to be resistant to deterioration from ultraviolet light; and

(3) If metal, be corrosion resistant.

(d) If the life float or buoyant apparatus does not have a painter attachment fitting, a means for attaching the painter must be provided by a wire or line that:

(1) Encircles the body of the device;

(2) Will not slip off;

§ 180.150

(3) Has a breaking strength that is at least the strength of the painter; and

(4) If synthetic, is of a dark color or is of a type certified to be resistant to deterioration from ultraviolet light.

(e) If the vessel carries more than one life float or buoyant apparatus in a group with each group secured by a single painter:

(1) The combined weight of each group of life floats and buoyant apparatus must not exceed 181 kilograms (400 pounds);

(2) Each group of life floats and buoyant apparatus is considered a single survival craft for the purposes of § 180.130(c);

(3) Each life float and buoyant apparatus must be individually attached to the painter by a line meeting §§ 180.175(e)(3)(ii), (iii), and (iv) and long enough that each life float or buoyant apparatus can float without contacting any other life float or buoyant apparatus in the group; and

(4) The strength of the float-free link under paragraph (b)(2) of this section and the strength of the painter under § 180.175(e)(3)(ii) must be determined by the combined capacity of the group of life floats and buoyant apparatus.

(f) Life floats and buoyant apparatus must not be stowed in tiers more than 1,220 millimeters (4 feet) high. When stowed in tiers, the separate units must be kept apart by spacers.

[CGD 85-080, 61 FR 975, Jan. 10, 1996; 61 FR 20557, May 7, 1996]

§ 180.150 Survival craft embarkation arrangements.

(a) A launching appliance approved under approval series 160.163 or a marine evacuation system approved under approval series 160.175 must be provided for each inflatable liferaft and inflatable buoyant apparatus when either—

(1) The embarkation station for the survival craft is on a deck more than 4.5 meters (15 feet) above the waterline; or

(2) The inflatable liferaft and inflatable buoyant apparatus is boarded prior to being placed in the water.

(b) An embarkation ladder, approved in accordance with § 160.017 in subchapter Q of this chapter, or other standard specified by the Commandant, must be at each embarkation station if the distance from the deck on which an embarkation station is located to the vessel's lightest operating waterline is more than 3,050 millimeters (10 feet).

[CGD 85-080, 61 FR 975, Jan. 10, 1996, as amended by CGD 97-057, 62 FR 51050, Sept. 30, 1997; CGD 85-080, 62 FR 51357, Sept. 30, 1997]

§ 180.175 Survival craft equipment.

(a) *General.* Each item of survival craft equipment must be of good quality, and efficient for the purpose it is intended to serve. Unless otherwise stated in this section, each item of equipment carried, whether required under this section or not, must be secured by lashings, stored in lockers, compartments, brackets, or have equivalent mounting or storage arrangements that do not:

(1) Reduce survival craft capacity;

(2) Reduce space available to the occupants;

(3) Interfere with launching, recovery, or rescue operations; or

(4) Adversely affect seaworthiness of the survival craft.

(b) *Inflatable liferafts.* Each inflatable liferaft must have one of the following equipment packs as shown by the markings on its container:

(1) Safety of Life at Sea (SOLAS) B Pack; or

(2) SOLAS A Pack.

(c) *Inflatable buoyant apparatus.* Each inflatable buoyant apparatus must be equipped in accordance with the manufacturer's approved servicing manual.

(d) *Life floats.* Each life float must be fitted with a lifeline, pendants, two paddles, a painter, and a light.

(e) *Buoyant apparatus.* Each buoyant apparatus must be fitted with a lifeline, pendants, a painter, and a light.

(f) *Equipment specifications for life floats and buoyant apparatus.* The equipment required for lifefloats and buoyant apparatus must meet the following specifications:

(1) *Lifeline and pendants.* The lifeline and pendants must be as furnished by the manufacturer with the approved life float or buoyant apparatus. Replacement lifelines and pendants must meet the requirements in Subpart 160.010 of this chapter.

(2) *Paddle.* Each paddle must be of at least 1,220 millimeters (4 feet) in

Coast Guard, DHS § 180.200

length, lashed to the life float to which it belongs and buoyant.

(3) *Painter.* The painter must:

(i) Be of at least 30.5 meters (100 feet) in length, but not less than 3 times the distance between the deck where the life float or buoyant apparatus it serves is stowed and the lowest load waterline of the vessel;

(ii) Have a breaking strength of at least 680 kilograms (1,500 pounds), except that if the capacity of the life float or buoyant apparatus is 50 persons or more, the breaking strength must be at least 1,360 kilograms (3,000 pounds);

(iii) Be of a dark color if synthetic, or of a type certified to be resistant to deterioration from ultraviolet light; and

(iv) Be stowed in such a way that it runs out freely when the life float or buoyant apparatus floats away from a sinking vessel.

(4) *Light.* The light must be a floating waterlight approved under approval series 161.010 or other standard specified by the Commandant. The floating waterlight must be attached around the body of the life float or buoyant apparatus by a 10 mm (3/8 inch) lanyard, resistant to deterioration from ultraviolet light, and at least 5.5 meters (18 feet) in length.

(g) *Other survival craft.* If survival craft other than inflatable liferafts, life floats, inflatable buoyant apparatus, and buoyant apparatus are carried on the vessel, such as lifeboats or rigid liferafts, they must be installed, arranged, and equipped as required under subchapter H (Passenger Vessels) of this chapter for passenger vessels on the same route.

[CGD 85–080, 61 FR 975, Jan. 10, 1996, as amended at 62 FR 51357, Sept. 30, 1997]

Subpart E—Number and Type of Survival Craft

§ 180.200 Survival craft—general.

(a) Each survival craft required on a vessel by this part must meet one of the following:

(1) For an inflatable liferaft—Approved under approval series 160.151 or other standard specified by the Commandant, with the applicable equipment pack, as determined by the cognizant OCMI. Each inflatable liferaft required on a vessel by this part must have a capacity of 6 persons or more. Inflatable liferafts may be substituted for inflatable buoyant apparatus or life floats required under this section;

(2) For a life float—Approved under approval series 160.027 or other standard specified by the Commandant. Buoyant apparatus may be used to meet requirements for life floats if the buoyant apparatus was installed on board the vessel on or before March 11, 1996, and if the buoyant apparatus remains in good and serviceable condition;

(3) For an inflatable buoyant apparatus—Approved under approval series 160.010 or other standard specified by the Commandant. Inflatable buoyant apparatus may be substituted for life floats required under this section.

(4) For a buoyant apparatus—Approved under approval series 160.010 or other standard specified by the Commandant. An existing buoyant apparatus may not be used to satisfy the requirements for life floats on existing vessels wishing to upgrade the total number of passengers carried on an oceans route.

(b) If the vessel carries a small boat or boats, the capacity of these boats may be counted toward life float capacity required by this part. Such boats must meet the requirements for safe loading and flotation in 33 CFR part 183, and must meet the stowage, launching, and equipment requirements in this part for the survival craft they replace.

(c) A summary of survival craft requirements is provided in Table 180.200(c).

TABLE 180.200(c)

Route	Survival craft requirements
Oceans	(a) cold water [1]—100% IBA—§ 180.202(a)(1).
	(i) w/subdivision [2]—100% LF—§ 180.202(a)(2).

255

§ 180.202   46 CFR Ch. I (10-1-04 Edition)

TABLE 180.200(c)—Continued

Route	Survival craft requirements

Coastwise	(b) warm water[3]—67% IBA[4]—§ 180.202(b).
	(a) wood vsls in cold water.
	  (i) 67% IBA—§ 180.204(a)(1).
	  (ii) w/subdivision—100% LF—§ 180.204(a)(2).
	(b) nonwood and vsls operating in warm water.
	  (i) 100% LF—§ 180.204 (b) and (c).
	(c) within three miles of shore.
	  (i) w/o subdivision—100% LF—§ 180.204(d)(1).
	  (ii) w/subdivision—50% LF—§ 180.204(d)(2).
	  (iii) w/float free 406 MHz EPIRB—50% LF—§ 180.204(d)(3).

Limited Coastwise (Not more than 20 miles from a harbor of safe refuge).	(a) wood vsls in cold water.
	  (i) 67% IBA—§ 180.205(a)(1).
	  (ii) w/subdivision—100% LF—§ 180.205(a)(2).
	(b) nonwood vessels in cold water—100% LF—§ 180.205(b).
	(c) within three miles of shore—§ 180.205(d).
	  (A) w/o subdivision—100% LF.
	  (B) w/subdivision—50% LF.
	  (C) w/float free 406 MHz EPIRB—50% LF.
	(d) vessels operating in warm water.
	  (i) 50% LF—§ 180.205(c).
	  (ii) within three miles of shore.
	    (A) w/o subdivision—50% LF—§ 180.205(e)(1).
	    (B) w/subdivision—NONE—§ 180.205(e)(2).
	    (C) w/float free 406 MHz EPIRB—NONE— § 180.205(e)(3).

Great Lakes	(a) same as Limited Coastwise (a) & (b)—§ 180.206(a). (b) within one mile of shore—NONE[5]—§ 180.206(b).

Lakes, Bays, & Sounds[6,7]	(a) wood vsls in cold water.
	  (i) 100% LF—§ 180.207(a)(1).
	  (ii) w/subdivision—50% LF—§ 180.207(a)(2).
	(b) nonwood—50% LF—§ 180.207(b).
	(c) within 1 mile of shore—NONE—§ 180.207(e).
	(d) warm water—NONE—§ 180.207(c).

RIVERS[7,8]	(a) cold water.
	  (i) w/o subdivision—50% LF—§ 180.208(a)(1).
	  (ii) w/subdivision—NONE—§ 180.208(a)(2).
	  (iii) within one mile of shore—NONE—§ 180.208(d).
	(b) warm water—NONE—§ 180.208(b)

Abbreviations used:
ILR=Inflatable liferaft
IBA=Inflatable Buoyant Apparatus
LF=Life Float. As allowed by § 180.15(d) any buoyant apparatus in use on an existing vessel on March 11, 1996, may be used to meet the requirements for LF as long as the buoyant apparatus is in good and serviceable condition.
Footnotes:
[1] Cold water means the cognizant OCMI has determined the monthly mean low temperature of the water is ≤ 15 °C (59 °F).
[2] Vessels ≤ 65 ft carrying ≤ 49 passengers built before March 11, 2001, may meet the collision bulkhead standards in § 179.310 and one-compartment subdivision subdivision standards in §§ 179.220 and 179.320 at least in way of the engine room and lazarette in lieu of the subdivision requirements contained in this part.
[3] Warm water means the cognizant OCMI has determined the monthly mean low temperature of the water is > 15° C (59° F).
[4] Vessels operating in warm water may substitute 100% LF in lieu of 67% IBA—§ 180.202(d).
[5] OCMI may reduce primary lifesaving for seasonal or ferry type operations on the Great Lakes—§ 180.206(b).
[6] Shallow water exception—§ 180.207(e).
[7] OCMI may reduce survival craft requirements based upon the route, communications schedule and participation in VTS—§ 180.207(f) and § 180.208(e).
[8] Shallow water exception—§ 180.208(e)C.

[CGD 85-080, 61 FR 975, Jan. 10, 1996, as amended at 62 FR 51357, Sept. 30, 1997]

§ 180.202 Survival craft—vessels operating on oceans routes.

(a) Each vessel certificated to operate on an oceans route in cold water must either:

(1) Be provided with inflatable buoyant apparatus of an aggregate capacity that will accommodate at least 100% of the total number of persons permitted on board; or

(2) Meet either the standards for collision bulkheads in §§ 179.310 in this chapter or 171.085 in subchapter S of this chapter, and the standards for subdivision in §§ 179.220 and 179.320 of this chapter, or the standards for subdivision and damaged stability in §§ 171.070 through 171.073 and 171.080 in subchapter S of this chapter, as appropriate, and be provided with life floats

of an aggregate capacity that will accommodate at least 100% of the total number of persons permitted on board.

(b) Each vessel certificated to operate on an oceans route in warm water must either:

(1) Be provided with inflatable buoyant apparatus of an aggregate capacity that will accommodate at least 67% of the total number of persons permitted on board; or

(2) Be provided with life floats of an aggregate capacity that will accommodate at least 100% of the total number of persons permitted on board.

§ 180.204 Survival craft—vessels operating on coastwise routes.

(a) Except as allowed by paragraph (c) of this section, each vessel constructed of wood certificated to operate on a coastwise route in cold water must either:

(1) Be provided with inflatable buoyant apparatus of an aggregate capacity that will accommodate at least 67% of the total number of persons permitted on board; or

(2) Meet either the standards for collision bulkheads in §§ 179.310 of this chapter or 171.085 in subchapter S of this chapter and the standards for subdivision in §§ 179.220 and 179.320 of this chapter, or the standards for subdivision and damaged stability in §§ 171.070 through 171.073 and 171.080 in subchapter S of this chapter, as appropriate, and be provided with life floats of an aggregate capacity that will accommodate at least 100% of the total number of persons permitted on board.

(b) Each vessel constructed of a material other than wood certificated to operate on a coastwise route in cold water must be provided with life floats of an aggregate capacity that will accommodate at least 100% of the total number of persons permitted on board.

(c) Except as allowed by paragraph (d) of this section, each vessel certificated to operate on a coastwise route in warm water must be provided with life floats of an aggregate capacity that will accommodate at least 100% of the total number of persons permitted on board.

(d) Each vessel certificated to operate on a coastwise route within three miles of land must either:

(1) Be provided with life floats of an aggregate capacity that will accommodate at least 100% of the total number of persons permitted on board; or

(2) Meet either the standards for collision bulkheads in §§ 179.310 of this subchapter or 171.085 in subchapter S of this chapter, and the standards for subdivision in §§ 179.220 and 179.320 of this chapter, or the standards for subdivision and damaged stability in §§ 171.070 through 171.073 and 171.080 in subchapter S of this chapter, as appropriate, and be provided with life floats of an aggregate capacity that will accommodate at least 50% of the total number of persons permitted on board.

(3) Have on board a FCC Type Accepted Category 1 406 MHz EPIRB, installed to automatically float free and activate, and be provided with life floats of an aggregate capacity that will accommodate at least 50% of the total number of persons permitted on board.

[CGD 85–080, 61 FR 975, Jan. 10, 1996; 61 FR 20557, May 7, 1996]

§ 180.205 Survival craft—vessels operating on limited coastwise routes.

(a) Except as allowed by paragraph (d) of this section, each vessel constructed of wood certificated to operate on a limited coastwise route in cold water must either:

(1) Be provided with inflatable buoyant apparatus of an aggregate capacity that will accommodate at least 67% of the total number of persons permitted on board; or

(2) Meet either the standards for collision bulkheads in §§ 179.310 of this chapter or 171.085 in subchapter S of this chapter, and the standards for subdivision in §§ 179.220 and 179.320 of this chapter, or the standards for subdivision and damaged stability in §§ 171.070 through 171.073 and 171.080 in subchapter S of this chapter, as appropriate, and be provided with life floats of an aggregate capacity that will accommodate at least 100% of the total number of persons permitted on board.

(b) Except as allowed by paragraph (d) of this section, each vessel constructed of a material other than wood certificated to operate on a limited coastwise route in cold water must be provided with life floats of an aggregate capacity that will accommodate

§ 180.206

at least 100% of the total number of persons permitted on board.

(c) Except as allowed by paragraph (e) of this section, each vessel certificated to operate on a limited coastwise route in warm water must be provided with life floats of an aggregate capacity that will accommodate at least 50% of the total number of persons permitted on board.

(d) Each vessel certificated to operate on a limited coastwise route within three miles of land in cold water must be provided with the survival craft required by § 180.204(d).

(e) Each vessel certificated to operate on a limited coastwise route within three miles of land in warm water must either:

(1) Be provided with life floats of an aggregate capacity that will accommodate at least 50% of the total number of persons permitted on board; or

(2) Meet either the standards for collision bulkheads in §§ 179.310 of this chapter or 171.085 in subchapter S of this chapter, and the standards for subdivision in §§ 179.220 and 179.320 of this chapter, or the standards for subdivision and damaged stability in §§ 171.070 through 171.073 and 171.080 in subchapter S of this chapter, as appropriate, and not be required to carry survival craft; or

(3) Have on board a FCC Type Accepted Category 1 406 MHz EPIRB, installed to automatically float free and activate, and not be required to carry survival craft.

§ 180.206 Survival craft—vessels operating on Great Lakes routes.

(a) Except as allowed by paragraph (b) of this section, each vessel certificated to operate on a Great Lakes route must be provided with the survival craft required by § 180.205 (a) through (e), as appropriate.

(b) Each vessel certificated to operate on a Great Lakes route within one mile of land is not required to carry survival craft if the OCMI determines that it is safe to do so, taking into consideration the vessel's scope of operation, hazards of the route, and availability of assistance.

[CGD 85–080, 61 FR 975, Jan. 10, 1996, as amended at 62 FR 51357, Sept. 30, 1997]

§ 180.207 Survival craft—vessels operating on lakes, bays, and sounds routes.

(a) Except as allowed by paragraphs (d), (e) and (f) of this section, each vessel constructed of wood certificated to operate on a lakes, bays, and sounds route in cold water must either:

(1) Be provided with life floats of an aggregate capacity that will accommodate at least 100% of the total number of persons permitted on board; or

(2) Meet either the standards for collision bulkheads in §§ 179.310 of this chapter or 171.085 in subchapter S of this chapter, and the standards for subdivision in §§ 179.220 and 179.320 of this chapter, or the standards for subdivision and damaged stability in §§ 171.070 through 171.073 and 171.080 in subchapter S of this chapter, as appropriate, and be provided with life floats of an aggregate capacity that will accommodate at least 50% of the total number of persons permitted on board.

(b) Except as allowed by paragraphs (e) and (f) of this section, each vessel constructed of a material other than wood certificated to operate on a lakes, bays, and sounds route in cold water must be provided with life floats of an aggregate capacity that will accommodate at least 50% of the total number of persons permitted on board.

(c) A vessel certificated to operate on a lakes, bays, and sounds route in warm water is not required to carry survival craft.

(d) A vessel certificated to operate on lakes, bays, and sounds route within one mile of land is not required to carry survival craft.

(e) For a vessel certificated to operate on a lakes, bays, and sounds route in shallow water where the vessel can not sink deep enough to submerge the topmost passenger deck or where survivors can wade ashore, the cognizant OCMI may waive a requirement for life floats, if the OCMI determines that it is safe to do so, taking into consideration the vessel's scope of operation, hazards of the route, and availability of assistance.

(f) Each vessel operating with a set schedule on a specific route that does not take it more than 20 nautical miles from a harbor of safe refuge, and that

Coast Guard, DHS § 180.210

maintains a 15 minute radio communications schedule with an operations base, or participates in a Vessel Traffic Service (VTS), may be granted a reduction in the survival craft requirements of this section if the cognizant OCMI is satisfied that a sufficient level of safety exists.

[CGD 85–080, 61 FR 975, Jan. 10, 1996; 61 FR 24464, May 15, 1996, as amended by CGD 97–057, 62 FR 51050, Sept. 30, 1997]

§ 180.208 Survival craft—vessels operating on rivers routes.

(a) Except as allowed by paragraphs (c), (d) and (e) of this section, each vessel certificated to operate on a rivers route in cold water must either:

(1) Be provided with life floats of an aggregate capacity that will accommodate at least 50% of the total number of persons permitted on board; or

(2) Meet either the standards for collision bulkheads in §§ 179.310 of this chapter or 171.085 in subchapter S of this chapter, and the standards for subdivision in §§ 179.220 and 179.320 of this chapter, or the standards for subdivision and damaged stability in §§ 171.070 through 171.073 and 171.080 in subchapter S of this chapter, as appropriate, and not be required to carry survival craft.

(b) A vessel certificated to operate on a rivers route in warm water is not required to carry survival craft.

(c) A vessel certificated to operate on a rivers route within one mile of land is not required to carry survival craft.

(d) For a vessel certificated to operate on a rivers route in shallow water where the vessel can not sink deep enough to submerge the topmost passenger deck or where survivors can wade ashore, the cognizant OCMI may waive a requirement for life floats, if the OCMI determines that it is safe to do so, taking into consideration the vessel's scope of operation, hazards of the route, and availability of assistance.

(e) Each vessel operating with a set schedule on a specific route that maintains a 15 minute radio communications schedule with an operations base, or participates in a Vessel Traffic Service (VTS), may be granted a reduction in the survival craft requirement of this section if the cognizant OCMI is satisfied that a sufficient level of safety exists.

[CGD 85–080, 61 FR 975, Jan. 10, 1996, as amended by CGD 97–057, 62 FR 51050, Sept. 30, 1997]

§ 180.210 Rescue boats.

(a) A vessel of more than 19.8 meters (65 feet) in length must carry at least one rescue boat unless the cognizant OCMI determines that:

(1) The vessel is sufficiently maneuverable, arranged, and equipped to allow the crew to recover a helpless person from the water;

(2) Recovery of a helpless person can be observed from the operating station; and

(3) The vessel does not regularly engage in operations that restrict its maneuverability.

(b) A vessel of not more than 19.8 meters (65 feet) in length is not required to carry a rescue boat unless:

(1) The vessel carries passengers on an open or partially enclosed deck; and

(2) The cognizant OCMI determines that the vessel is designed, arranged, or involved in operations so that the vessel itself cannot serve as an adequate rescue craft.

(c) In general, a rescue boat must be a small, lightweight boat with built-in buoyancy and capable of being readily launched and easily maneuvered. In addition, it must be of adequate proportion to permit taking an unconscious person on board without capsizing.

(d) On a vessel of more than 19.8 meters (65 feet) in length operating on protected waters, a rescue boat approved under approval series 160.056 is acceptable in meeting the intent of this section. On a vessel of more than 19.8 meters operating on exposed or partially protected waters, a rescue boat approved under approval series 160.156 is acceptable in meeting the intent of this section. On a vessel of not more than 19.8 meters (65 feet) in length, a required rescue boat must be acceptable to the cognizant OCMI.

[CGD 85–080, 61 FR 975, Jan. 10, 1996, as amended at 62 FR 51357, Sept. 30, 1997; 62 FR 64306, Dec. 5, 1997]

PART 181—FIRE PROTECTION EQUIPMENT

Subpart A—General Provisions

Sec.
181.115 Applicability to existing vessels.
181.120 Equipment installed but not required.

Subpart B [Reserved]

Subpart C—Fire Main System

181.300 Fire pumps.
181.310 Fire main and hydrants.
181.320 Fire hoses and nozzles.

Subpart D—Fixed Fire Extinguishing and Detecting Systems

181.400 Where required.
181.410 Fixed gas fire extinguishing systems.
181.420 Pre-engineered fixed gas fire extinguishing systems.
181.425 Galley hood fire extinguishing systems.
181.450 Independent modular smoke detecting units.

Subpart E—Portable Fire Extinguishers

181.500 Required number, type, and location.
181.520 Installation and location.

Subpart F—Additional Equipment

181.600 Fire axe.
181.610 Fire bucket.

AUTHORITY: 46 U.S.C. 2103, 3306; E.O. 12234, 45 FR 58801, 3 CFR, 1980 Comp., p. 277; Department of Homeland Security Delegation No. 0170.1.

SOURCE: CGD 85–080, 61 FR 982, Jan. 10, 1996, unless otherwise noted.

Subpart A—General Provisions

§ 181.115 **Applicability to existing vessels.**

(a) Except as otherwise required by paragraphs (b) and (c) of this section, an existing vessel must comply with the fire protection equipment regulations applicable to the vessel on March 10, 1996, or, as an alternative, the vessel may comply with the regulations in this part.

(b) An existing vessel with a hull, or a machinery space boundary bulkhead or deck, composed of wood or fiber reinforced plastic, or sheathed on the interior in fiber reinforced plastic, must comply with the requirements of § 181.400 of this part on or before March 11, 1999.

(c) New installations of fire protection equipment on an existing vessel, which are completed to the satisfaction of the cognizant Officer in Charge, Marine Inspection (OCMI) on or after March 11, 1996, must comply with the regulations of this part. Replacement of existing equipment installed on the vessel prior to March 11, 1996, need not comply with the regulations in this part.

§ 181.120 **Equipment installed but not required.**

Fire extinguishing and detecting equipment installed on a vessel in excess of the requirements of §§ 181.400 and 181.500 must be designed, constructed, installed and maintained in accordance with a recognized industry standard acceptable to the Commandant.

Subpart B [Reserved]

Subpart C—Fire Main System

§ 181.300 **Fire pumps.**

(a) A self priming, power driven fire pump must be installed on each vessel:
(i) Of not more than 19.8 meters (65 feet) in length which is a ferry vessel;
(ii) Of not more than 19.8 meters (65 feet) in length that carries more than 49 passengers; or
(iii) Of more than 19.8 meters (65 feet) in length.

(b) On a vessel of not more than 19.8 meters (65 feet) in length carrying more than 49 passengers, and on a vessel of more than 19.8 meters (65 feet) in length, the minimum capacity of the fire pump must be 189 liters (50 gallons) per minute at a pressure of not less than 414 kPa (60 psi) at the pump outlet. The pump outlet must be fitted with a pressure gauge.

(c) On a ferry vessel of not more than 19.8 meters (65 feet) in length carrying not more than 49 passengers, the minimum capacity of the fire pump must be 38 liters (10 gallons) per minute. The fire pump must be capable of projecting a hose stream from the highest hydrant, through the hose and nozzle required by §181.320 of this part, a distance of 7.6 meters (25 feet).

(d) A fire pump may be driven by a propulsion engine. A fire pump must be permanently connected to the fire main and may be connected to the bilge system to meet the requirements of §182.520 of this chapter.

(e) A fire pump must be capable of both remote operation from the operating station and local operations at the pump.

[CGD 85–080, 61 FR 982, Jan. 10, 1996, as amended at 62 FR 51358, Sept. 30, 1997]

§181.310 Fire main and hydrants.

(a) A vessel that has a power driven fire pump must have a sufficient number of fire hydrants to reach any part of the vessel using a single length of fire hose.

(b) Piping, valves, and fittings in a fire main system must comply with subpart G, part 182, of this chapter.

(c) Each fire hydrant must have a valve installed to allow the fire hose to be removed while the fire main is under pressure.

[CGD 85–080, 61 FR 982, Jan. 10, 1996, as amended at 62 FR 51358, Sept. 30, 1997]

§181.320 Fire hoses and nozzles.

(a) A fire hose with a nozzle must be attached to each fire hydrant at all times. For fire hydrants located on open decks or cargo decks, where no protection is provided, hoses may be temporarily removed during heavy weather or cargo handling operations, respectively. Hoses so removed must be stored in nearby accessible locations.

(b) On a vessel of not more than 19.8 meters (65 feet) in length carrying more than 49 passengers, and on a vessel of more than 19.8 meters (65 feet) in length, each hose must:

(1) Be lined commercial fire hose that conforms to Underwriters Laboratory (UL) 19 "Lined Fire Hose and Hose Assemblies," or hose that is listed and labeled by an independent laboratory recognized by the Commandant as being equivalent in performance;.

(2) Be 15.25 meters (50 feet) in length and 40 millimeters (1.5 inches) in diameter; and

(3) Have fittings of brass or other suitable corrosion-resistant material that comply with National Fire Protection Association (NFPA) 1963 "Standard for Fire Hose Connections," or other standard specified by the Commandant.

(c) Each fire hose on a vessel of not more than 19.8 meters (65 feet) in length carrying not more than 49 passengers must:

(1) Comply with paragraphs (b)(1) and (b)(3) of this section or be garden type hose of not less than 16 millimeters (0.625 inches) nominal inside diameter;

(2) Be of one piece not less than 7.6 meters (25 feet) and not more than 15.25 meters (50 feet) in length; and

(3) If of the garden type, be of a good commercial grade constructed of an inner rubber tube, plies of braided fabric reinforcement, and an outer cover of rubber or equivalent material, and of sufficient strength to withstand the maximum pressure that can be produced by the fire pump. All fittings on the hose must be of suitable corrosion-resistant material.

(d) Each nozzle must be of corrosion-resistant material and be capable of being changed between a solid stream and a spray pattern. A nozzle on a vessel of not more than 19.8 meters (65 feet) in length carrying more than 49 passengers, and on a vessel of more than 19.8 meters (65 feet) in length, must:

(1) Be of a type approved in accordance with approval series 162.027; or

(2) Be of a type recognized by the Commandant as being equivalent in performance.

[CGD 85–080, 61 FR 982, Jan. 10, 1996; 61 FR 20557, May 7, 1996; 61 FR 24464, May 15, 1996, as amended at 62 FR 51358, Sept. 30, 1997]

Subpart D—Fixed Fire Extinguishing and Detecting Systems

§181.400 Where required.

(a) The following spaces must be equipped with a fixed gas fire extinguishing system, in compliance with §181.410, or other fixed fire extinguishing system specifically approved by the Commandant, except as otherwise allowed by paragraph (b) of this section:

§ 181.400

(1) A space containing propulsion machinery;

(2) A space containing an internal combustion engine of more than 37.3 kW (50 hp);

(3) A space containing an oil fired boiler;

(4) A space containing machinery powered by gasoline or other fuels having a flash point of 43.3° C (110° F) or lower;

(5) A space containing a fuel tank for gasoline or any other fuel having a flash point of 43.3° C (110° F) or lower;

(6) A space containing combustible cargo or ship's stores inaccessible during the voyage (in these types of spaces only carbon dioxide, and not Halon, systems will be allowed);

(7) A paint locker; and

(8) A storeroom containing flammable liquids (including liquors of 80 proof or higher where liquor is packaged in individual containers of 9.5 liters (2.5 gallons) capacity or greater).

(b) Alternative system types and exceptions to the requirements of paragraph (a) of this section are:

(1) A fixed gas fire extinguishing system, which is capable of automatic discharge upon heat detection, may only be installed in a normally unoccupied space with a gross volume of not more than 170 cubic meters (6,000 cubic feet);

(2) A pre-engineered fixed gas fire extinguishing system must be in compliance with § 181.420 of this part and may only be installed in a normally unoccupied machinery space, a paint locker, or a storeroom containing flammable liquids (including liquors of 80 proof or higher where liquor is packaged in individual containers of 9.5 liters (2.5 gallons) capacity or greater), with a gross volume of not more than 57 cubic meters (2,000 cubic feet);

(3) A B-II portable fire extinguisher installed outside the space may be substituted for a fixed gas fire extinguishing system in a storeroom containing flammable liquids (including liquors of 80 proof or higher where liquor is packaged in individual containers of 9.5 liters (2.5 gallons) or a paint locker, with a volume of not more that 5.7 cubic meters (200 cubic feet);

(4) A space which is so open to the atmosphere that a fixed gas fire extinguishing system would be ineffective, as determined by the cognizant OCMI, is not required to have a fixed gas fire extinguishing system; and

(5) Where the amount of carbon dioxide gas required in a fixed fire extinguishing system can be supplied by one portable extinguisher or a semiportable extinguisher, such an extinguisher may be used subject to the following:

(i) The cylinder shall be installed in a fixed position outside the space protected;

(ii) The applicator shall be installed in a fixed position so as to discharge into the space protected; and

(iii) Controls shall be installed in an accessible location outside the space protected.

(c) The following spaces must be equipped with a fire detecting system of an approved type that is installed in accordance with § 76.27 in subchapter H of this chapter, except when a fixed gas fire extinguishing system that is capable of automatic discharge upon heat detection is installed or when the space is manned:

(1) A space containing propulsion machinery;

(2) A space containing an internal combustion engine of more than 50 hp;

(3) A space containing an oil fired boiler;

(4) A space containing machinery powered by gasoline or any other fuels having a flash point of 43.3° C (110° F) or lower; and

(5) A space containing a fuel tank for gasoline or any other fuel having a flash point of 43.3° C (110° F) or lower.

(d) All griddles, broilers, and deep fat fryers must be fitted with a grease extraction hood in compliance with § 181.425.

(e) Each overnight accommodation space on a vessel with overnight accommodations for passengers must be fitted with an independent modular smoke detecting and alarm unit in compliance with § 181.450.

(f) An enclosed vehicle space must be fitted with an automatic sprinkler system that meets the requirements of § 76.25 in subchapter H of this chapter; and

Coast Guard, DHS § 181.410

(1) A fire detecting system of an approved type that is installed in accordance with § 76.27 in subchapter H of this chapter; or

(2) A smoke detecting system of an approved type that is installed in accordance with § 76.33 in subchapter H of this chapter.

(g) A partially enclosed vehicle space must be fitted with a manual sprinkler system that meets the requirements of § 76.23 in subchapter H of this chapter.

[CGD 85–080, 61 FR 982, Jan. 10, 1996, as amended at 62 FR 51358, Sept. 30, 1997; USCG–1999–6216, 64 FR 53228, Oct. 1, 1999]

§ 181.410 Fixed gas fire extinguishing systems.

(a) *General.* (1) A fixed gas fire extinguishing system aboard a vessel must be approved by the Commandant, and be custom engineered to meet the requirements of this section unless the system meets the requirements of § 181.420.

(2) System components must be listed and labeled by an independent laboratory. A component from a different system, even if from the same manufacturer, must not be used unless included in the approval of the installed system.

(3) System design and installation must be in accordance with the Marine Design, Installation, Operation, and Maintenance Manual approved for the system by the Commandant.

(4) A fixed gas fire extinguishing system may protect more than one space. The quantity of extinguishing agent must be at least sufficient for the space requiring the greatest quantity as determined by the requirements of paragraphs (f)(4) and (g)(2) of this section.

(b) *Controls.* (1) Controls and valves for operation of fixed gas fire extinguishing system must be:

(i) Located outside the space protected by the system; and

(ii) Not located in a space that might be inaccessible in the event of fire in the space protected by the system.

(2) Except for a normally unoccupied space of less than 170 cubic meters (6000 cubic feet), release of an extinguishing agent into a space must require two distinct operations.

(3) A system must have local manual controls at the storage cylinders capable of releasing the extinguishing agent. In addition, a normally manned space must have remote controls for releasing the extinguishing agent at the primary exit from the space.

(4) Remote controls must be located in a breakglass enclosure to preclude accidental discharge.

(5) Valves and controls must be of an approved type and protected from damage or accidental activation. A pull cable used to activate the system controls must be enclosed in conduit.

(6) A system protecting more than one space must have a manifold with a normally closed stop valve for each space protected.

(7) A gas actuated valve or device must be capable of manual override at the valve or device.

(8) A system, that has more than one storage cylinder for the extinguishing agent and that relies on pilot cylinders to activate the primary storage cylinders, must have at least two pilot cylinders. Local manual controls, in compliance with paragraph (b)(3) of this section, must be provided to operate the pilot cylinders but are not required for the primary storage cylinders.

(9) A system protecting a manned space must be fitted with an approved time delay and alarm arranged to require the alarm to sound for at least 20 seconds or the time necessary to escape from the space, whichever is greater, before the agent is released into the space. Alarms must be conspicuously and centrally located. The alarm must be powered by the extinguishing agent.

(10) A device must be provided to automatically shut down power ventilation serving the protected space and engines that draw intake air from the protected space prior to release of the extinguishing agent into the space.

(11) Controls and storage cylinders must not be in a locked space unless the key is in a breakglass type box conspicuously located adjacent to the space.

(c) *Storage space.* (1) Except as provided in paragraph (c)(2) of this section, a storage cylinder for a fixed gas extinguishing system must be:

(i) Located outside the space protected by the system; and

263

§ 181.410

(ii) Not located in a space that might be inaccessible in the event of a fire in the space protected by the system.

(2) A normally unoccupied space of less than 170 cubic meters (6,000 cubic feet) may have the storage cylinders located within the space protected. When the storage cylinders are located in the space:

(i) The system must be capable of automatic operation by a heat actuator within the space; and

(ii) Have manual controls in compliance with paragraph (b) of this section except for paragraph (b)(3).

(3) A space containing a storage cylinder must be maintained at a temperature within the range from $-30°$ C ($-20°$ F) to $55°$ C ($130°$ F) or at another temperature as listed by the independent laboratory and stated in the manufacturer's approved manual.

(4) A storage cylinder must be securely fastened, supported, and protected against damage.

(5) A storage cylinder must be accessible and capable of easy removal for recharging and inspection. Provisions must be available for weighing each storage cylinder in place.

(6) Where subject to moisture, a storage cylinder must be installed to provide a space of at least 51 millimeters (2 inches) between the deck and the bottom of the storage cylinder.

(7) A Halon 1301 storage cylinder must be stowed in an upright position unless otherwise listed by the independent laboratory. A carbon dioxide cylinder may be inclined not more than 30° from the vertical, unless fitted with flexible or bent siphon tubes, in which case they may be inclined not more than 80° from the vertical.

(8) Where a check valve is not fitted on an independent storage cylinder discharge, a plug or cap must be provided for closing the outlet resulting from storage cylinder removal.

(9) Each storage cylinder must meet the requirements of § 147.60 in subchapter N of this chapter, or other standard specified by the Commandant.

(10) A storage cylinder space must have doors that open outwards or be fitted with kickout panels installed in each door.

(d) *Piping.* (1) A pipe, valve, or fitting of ferrous material must be protected inside and outside against corrosion unless otherwise approved by the Commandant. Aluminum or other low melting material must not be used for a component of a fixed gas fire extinguishing system except as specifically approved by the Commandant.

(2) A distribution line must extend at least 51 millimeters (2 inches) beyond the last orifice and be closed with a cap or plug.

(3) Piping, valves, and fittings must be securely supported, and where necessary, protected against damage.

(4) Drains and dirt traps must be fitted where necessary to prevent the accumulation of dirt or moisture and located in accessible locations.

(5) Piping must be used for no other purpose except that it may be incorporated with the fire detecting system.

(6) Piping passing through accommodation spaces must not be fitted with drains or other openings within such spaces.

(7) Installation test requirements for carbon dioxide systems. The distribution piping of a carbon dioxide fixed gas extinguishing system must be tested as required by this paragraph, upon completion of the piping installation, using only carbon dioxide, compressed air, or nitrogen gas.

(i) Piping between a storage cylinder and a stop valve in the manifold must be subjected to a pressure of 6,894 kPa (1,000 psi), except as permitted in paragraph (d)(7)(iii) of this section. Without additional gas being introduced to the system, the pressure drop must not exceed 2,068 kPa (300 psi) after two minutes.

(ii) A distribution line to a space protected by the system must be subjected to a test similar to that described in paragraph (d)(7)(i) of this section except the pressure used must be 4,136 kPa (600 psi). For the purpose of this test, the distribution piping must be capped within the space protected at the first joint between the nozzles and the storage cylinders.

(iii) A small independent system protecting a space such as a paint locker may be tested by blowing out the piping with air at a pressure of not less than 689 kPa (100 psi) instead of the tests prescribed in the paragraphs (d)(7)(i) and (d)(7)(ii) of this section.

Coast Guard, DHS § 181.410

(8) *Installation test requirements for Halon 1301 systems.* The distribution piping of a Halon 1301 fixed gas extinguishing system must be tested, as required by this paragraph, upon completion of the piping installation, using only carbon dioxide, compressed air, or nitrogen.

(i) When pressurizing the piping, pressure must be increased in small increments. Each joint must be subjected to a soap bubble leak test, and all joints must be leak free.

(ii) Piping between the storage cylinders and the manifold stop valve must be subjected to a leak test conducted at a pressure of 4,136 kPa (600 psi). Without additional gas being added to the system, there must be no loss of pressure over a two minute period after thermal equilibrium is reached.

(iii) Distribution piping between the manifold stop valve and the first nozzle in the system must be capped and pneumatically tested for a period of 10 minutes at 1,034 kPa (150 psi). At the end of 10 minutes, the pressure drop must not exceed 10% of the test pressure.

(e) *Pressure relief.* When required by the cognizant OCMI, spaces that are protected by a fixed gas fire extinguishing system and that are relatively air tight, such as refrigeration spaces, paint lockers, etc., must be provided with suitable means for relieving excessive pressure within the space when the agent is released.

(f) *Specific requirements for carbon dioxide systems.* A custom engineered fixed gas fire extinguishing system, which uses carbon dioxide as the extinguishing agent, must meet the requirements of this paragraph.

(1) Piping, valves, and fittings must have a bursting pressure of not less than 41,360 kPa (6,000 psi). Piping, in nominal sizes of not more than 19 millimeters (0.75 inches), must be at least Schedule 40 (standard weight), and in nominal sizes of over 19 millimeters (0.75 inches), must be at least Schedule 80 (extra heavy).

(2) A pressure relief valve or equivalent set to relieve at between 16,550 and 19,300 kPa (2,400 and 2,800 psi) must be installed in the distribution manifold to protect the piping from over-pressurization.

(3) Nozzles must be approved by the Commandant.

(4) When installed in a machinery space, paint locker, a space containing flammable liquid stores, or a space with a fuel tank, a fixed carbon dioxide system must meet the following requirements.

(i) The quantity of carbon dioxide in kilograms (pounds) that the system must be capable of providing to a space must not be less than the gross volume of the space divided by the appropriate factor given in Table 181.410(f)(4)(i). If fuel can drain from a space being protected to an adjacent space or if the spaces are not entirely separate, the volume of both spaces must be used to determine the quantity of carbon dioxide to be provided. The carbon dioxide must be arranged to discharge into both such spaces simultaneously.

TABLE 181.410(f)(4)(i)

Factor	Gross volume of space in cubic meters (feet)	
	Over	Not Over
0.94 (15)		14 (500)
1.0 (16)	14 (500)	45 (1,600)
1.1 (18)	45 (1,600)	125 (4,500)
1.2 (20)	125 (4,500)	1400 (50,000)
1.4 (22)	1400 (50,000)	

(ii) The minimum size of a branch line to a space must be as noted in Table 181.410(f)(4)(ii).

TABLE 181.410(f)(4)(ii)

Maximum quantity of carbon dioxide required kg (lbs)	Minimum nominal pipe size mm (inches)
45.4 (100)	12.7 (0.5)
102 (225)	19 (0.75)
136 (300)	25 (1.0)
272 (600)	30 (1.25)
454 (1000)	40 (1.5)
1111 (2450)	50 (2.0)
1134 (2,500)	65 (2.5)
2018 (4,450)	75 (3.0)
3220 (7,100)	90 (3.5)
4739 (10,450)	100 (4.0)
6802 (15,000)	113 (4.5)

(iii) Distribution piping within a space must be proportioned from the distribution line to give proper supply to the outlets without throttling.

§ 181.420

(iv) The number, type, and location of discharge outlets must provide uniform distribution of carbon dioxide throughout a space.

(v) The total area of all discharge outlets must not exceed 85 percent nor be less than 35 percent of the nominal cylinder outlet area or the area of the supply pipe, whichever is smaller. The nominal cylinder outlet area in square millimeters (inches) is determined by multiplying the factor 0.015 (0.0022 if using square inches) by the total capacity in kilograms (pounds) of all carbon dioxide cylinders in the system, except in no case must the outlet area be of less than 71 square millimeters (0.110 square inches if using pounds).

(vi) The discharge of at least 85 percent of the required amount of carbon dioxide must be completed within two minutes.

(5) When installed in an enclosed ventilation system for rotating electrical propulsion equipment a fixed carbon dioxide extinguishing system must meet the following requirements.

(i) The quantity of carbon dioxide in kilograms (pounds) must be sufficient for initial and delayed discharges as required by this paragraph. The initial discharge must be equal to the gross volume of the system divided by 160 (10 if using pounds) for ventilation systems having a volume of less than 57 cubic meters (2,000 cubic feet), or divided by 192 (12 if using pounds) for ventilation systems having a volume of at least 57 cubic meters (2,000 cubic feet). In addition, there must be sufficient carbon dioxide available to permit delayed discharges to maintain at least a 25 percent concentration until the equipment can be stopped. If the initial discharge achieves this concentration, a delayed discharge is not required.

(ii) The piping sizes for the initial discharge must be in accordance with Table 181.410(f)(4)(ii) and the discharge of the required amount must be completed within two minutes.

(iii) Piping for the delayed discharge must not be less than 12.7 millimeters (0.5 inches) nominal pipe size, and need not meet specific requirement for discharge rate.

46 CFR Ch. I (10–1–04 Edition)

(iv) Piping for the delayed discharge may be incorporated with the initial discharge piping.

(6) When installed in a cargo space a fixed carbon dioxide extinguishing system must meet the following requirements.

(i) The number of kilograms (pounds) of carbon dioxide required for each space in cubic meters (feet) must be equal to the gross volume of the space in cubic meters (feet) divided by 480 (30 if using pounds).

(ii) System piping must be of at least 19 millimeters (0.75 inches).

(iii) No specific discharge rate is required.

(g) *Specific requirements for Halon 1301 systems.* (1) A custom engineering fixed gas fire extinguishing system, which uses Halon 1301, must comply with the applicable sections of UL Standard 1058 "Halogenated Agent Extinguishing System Units," and the requirements of this paragraph.

(2) The Halon 1301 quantity and discharge requirements of UL 1058 apply, with the exception that the Halon 1301 design concentration must be 6 percent at the lowest ambient temperature expected in the space. If the lowest temperature is not known, a temperature of −18° C (0° F) must be assumed.

(3) Each storage cylinder in a system must have the same pressure and volume.

(4) Computer programs used in designing systems must have been approved by an independent laboratory.

NOTE TO § 181.410(g): As of Jan. 1, 1994, the United States banned the production of Halon. The Environmental Protection Agency placed significant restrictions on the servicing and maintenance of systems containing Halon. Vessels operating on an international voyage, subject to SOLAS requirements, are prohibited from installing fixed gas fire extinguishing systems containing Halon.

[CGD 85–080, 61 FR 982, Jan. 10, 1996; 61 FR 20557, May 7, 1996, as amended at 62 FR 51358, Sept. 30, 1997; USCG–2000–7790, 65 FR 58465, Sept. 29, 2000]

§ 181.420 Pre-engineered fixed gas fire extinguishing systems.

(a) A pre-engineered fixed gas fire extinguishing system must:

(1) Be approved by the Commandant;

Coast Guard, DHS

§ 181.500

(2) Be capable of manual actuation from outside the space in addition to automatic actuation by a heat detector;

(3) Automatically shut down all power ventilation systems and all engines that draw intake air from within the protected space; and

(4) Be installed in accordance with the manufacturer's instructions.

(b) A vessel on which a pre-engineered fixed gas fire extinguishing system is installed must have the following equipment at the operating station:

(1) A light to indicate discharge;

(2) An audible alarm that sounds upon discharge; and

(3) A means to reset devices used to automatically shut down ventilation systems and engines as required by paragraph (a)(3) of this section.

(c) Only one pre-engineered fixed gas fire extinguishing system is allowed to be installed in each space protected by such a system.

§ 181.425 Galley hood fire extinguishing systems.

(a) A grease extraction hood required by § 181.400 must meet UL 710 "Exhaust Hoods for Commercial Cooking Equipment," or other standard specified by the Commandant.

(b) A grease extraction hood must be equipped with a dry or wet chemical fire extinguishing system meeting the applicable sections of NFPA 17 "Dry Chemical Extinguishing Systems," 17A "Wet Chemical Extinguishing Systems," or other standard specified by the Commandant, and must be listed by an independent laboratory recognized by the Commandant.

§ 181.450 Independent modular smoke detecting units.

(a) An independent modular smoke detecting unit must:

(1) Meet UL Standard 217 and be listed as a "Single Station Smoke detector—Also suitable for use in Recreational Vehicles," or other standard specified by the Commandant;

(2) Contain an independent power source; and

(3) Alarm on low power.

(b) [Reserved]

Subpart E—Portable Fire Extinguishers

§ 181.500 Required number, type, and location.

(a) Each portable fire extinguisher on a vessel must be of an approved type. The minimum number of portable fire extinguishers required on a vessel must be acceptable to the cognizant OCMI, but must be not less than the minimum number required by Table 181.500(a) and other provisions of this section.

TABLE 181.500(a)

Space protected	Minimum No. required	Type extinguisher permitted		
		CG class	Medium	Min size
Operating Station	1	B–I, C–I	Halon	1.1 kg (2.5 lb).
			CO2	1.8kg (4 lb).
Machinery Space	1	B–II, C–II located just outside exit.	Dry Chemical	0.9 kg (2 lb).
			CO2	6.8 kg (15 lb).
Open Vehicle Deck	1 for every 10 vehicles.	B–II	Dry chemical	4.5 kg (10 lb).
			Foam	9.5 L (2.5 gal).
Accomodation Space	1 for each 232.3 square meters (2,500 square feet) or fraction thereof.	A–II	Halon	4.5 kg (10 lb).
			CO2	6.8 kg (15 lb).
			Dry Chemical	4.5 kg (10 lb).
			Foam	9.5 L (2.5 gal).
			Dry Chemical	4.5 kg (10 lb).
Galley, Pantry, Concession Stand.	1	A–II, B–II	Foam	9.5 L (2.5 gal).
			Dry Chemical	4.5 kg (10 lb).

§ 181.520

(b) A vehicle deck without a fixed sprinkler system and exposed to weather must have one B–II portable fire extinguisher for every five vehicles, located near an entrance to the space.

(c) The cognizant OCMI may permit the use of a larger portable fire extinguisher, or a semiportable fire extinguisher, in lieu of those required by this section.

(d) The frame or support of each B–V fire extinguisher permitted by paragraph (c) of this section must be welded or otherwise permanently attached to a bulkhead or deck.

[CGD 85–080, 61 FR 982, Jan. 10, 1996; 61 FR 24464, May 15, 1996, as amended at 62 FR 51358, Sept. 30, 1997]

§ 181.520 Installation and location.

Portable fire extinguishers must be located so that they are clearly visible and readily accessible from the space being protected. The installation and location must be to the satisfaction of the Officer in Charge, Marine Inspection.

Subpart F—Additional Equipment

§ 181.600 Fire axe.

A vessel of more than 19.8 meters (65 feet) in length must have at least one fire axe located in or adjacent to the primary operating station.

§ 181.610 Fire bucket.

A vessel not required to have a power driven fire pump by § 181.300 must have at least three 9.5 liter (2½ gallon) buckets, with an attached lanyard satisfactory to the cognizant OCMI, placed so as to be easily available during an emergency. The words "FIRE BUCKET" must be stenciled in a contrasting color on each bucket.

[CGD 85–080, 61 FR 982, Jan. 10, 1996, as amended at 62 FR 51358, Sept. 30, 1997]

PART 182—MACHINERY INSTALLATION

Subpart A—General Provisions

Sec.
182.100 Intent.
182.115 Applicability to existing vessels.
182.130 Alternative standards.

Subpart B—Propulsion Machinery

182.200 General.
182.220 Installations.

Subpart C—Auxiliary Machinery

182.310 Installations.
182.320 Water heaters.
182.330 Pressure vessels.

Subpart D—Specific Machinery Requirements

182.400 Applicability.
182.405 Fuel restrictions.
182.410 General requirements.
182.415 Carburetors.
182.420 Engine cooling.
182.422 Integral and non-integral keel cooler installations.
182.425 Engine exhaust cooling.
182.430 Engine exhaust pipe installation.
182.435 Integral fuel tanks.
182.440 Independent fuel tanks.
182.445 Fill and sounding pipes for fuel tanks.
182.450 Vent pipes for fuel tanks.
182.455 Fuel piping.
182.458 Portable fuel systems.
182.460 Ventilation of spaces containing machinery powered by, or fuel tanks for, gasoline.
182.465 Ventilation of spaces containing diesel machinery.
182.470 Ventilation of spaces containing diesel fuel tanks.
182.480 Flammable vapor detection systems.

Subpart E—Bilge and Ballast Systems

182.500 General.
182.510 Bilge piping system.
182.520 Bilge pumps.
182.530 Bilge high level alarms.
182.540 Ballast systems.

Subpart F—Steering Systems

182.600 General.
182.610 Main steering gear.
182.620 Auxiliary means of steering.

Subpart G—Piping Systems

182.700 General.
182.710 Piping for vital systems.
182.715 Piping subject to more than 1,034 kPa (150 psig) in non-vital systems.
182.720 Nonmetallic piping materials.
182.730 Nonferrous metallic piping materials.

AUTHORITY: 46 U.S.C. 3306; E.O. 12234, 45 FR 58801, 3 CFR, 1980 Comp., p. 277; Department of Homeland Security Delegation No. 0170.1.

SOURCE: CGD 85–080, 61 FR 986, Jan. 10, 1996, unless otherwise noted.

Subpart A—General Provisions

§ 182.100 Intent.

This part contains requirements for the design, construction, installation, and operation of propulsion and auxiliary machinery, piping and pressure systems, steering apparatus, and associated safety systems. Machinery and equipment installed on each vessel must be suitable for the vessel and its operation and for the purpose intended. All machinery and equipment must be installed and maintained in such a manner as to afford adequate protection from causing fire, explosion, machinery failure, and personnel injury.

§ 182.115 Applicability to existing vessels.

(a) Except as otherwise required by paragraphs (b), (c) and (d) of this section, an existing vessel must comply with the regulations on machinery, bilge and ballast system equipment, steering apparatus, and piping systems or components that were applicable to the vessel on March 10, 1996 or, as an alternative, the vessel may comply with the regulations in this part.

(b) New installations of machinery, bilge and ballast system equipment, steering equipment, and piping systems or components on an existing vessel, which are completed to the satisfaction of the cognizant Officer in Charge, Marine Inspection (OCMI) on or after March 11, 1996, must comply with the regulations of this part. Replacement of existing equipment installed on the vessel prior to March 11, 1996, need not comply with the regulations in this part.

(c) An existing vessel equipped with machinery powered by gasoline or other fuels having a flash point of 43.3° C (110° F) or lower must comply with the requirements of § 182.410(c) on or before March 11, 1999.

(d) On or before March 11, 1999, an existing vessel must comply with the bilge high level alarm requirements in § 182.530.

§ 182.130 Alternative standards.

A vessel of not more than 19.8 meters (65 feet) in length carrying not more than 12 passengers propelled by gasoline or diesel internal combustion engines, other than a High Speed Craft, may comply with the following American Boat and Yacht Council (ABYC) Projects or 33 CFR subchapter S (Boating Safety), where indicated in this part, in lieu of complying with those requirements:

(a) H–2—"Ventilation of Boats Using Gasoline", or 33 CFR 183, subpart K, "Ventilation";

(b) H–22—"DC Electric Bilge Pumps Operating Under 50 Volts";

(c) H–24—"Gasoline Fuel Systems", or 33 CFR 183, subpart J—"Fuel System";

(d) H–25—"Portable Gasoline Fuel Systems for Flammable Liquids";

(e) H–32—"Ventilation of Boats Using Diesel Fuel";

(f) H–33—"Diesel Fuel Systems";

(g) P–1—"Installation of Exhaust Systems for Propulsion and Auxiliary Engines"; and

(h) P–4—"Marine Inboard Engines".

Subpart B—Propulsion Machinery

§ 182.200 General.

(a) Propulsion machinery must be suitable in type and design for propulsion requirements of the hull in which it is installed and capable of operating at constant marine load under such requirements without exceeding its designed limitations.

(b) All engines must have at least two means for stopping the engine(s) under any operating conditions. The fuel oil shutoff required at the engine by § 182.455(b)(4) will satisfy one means of stopping the engine.

§ 182.220 Installations.

(a) Except as otherwise provided in this section, propulsion machinery installations must comply with the provisions of this part.

(b) The requirements for machinery and boilers for steam and electrically propelled vessels are contained in applicable regulations in subchapter F (Marine Engineering) and subchapter J (Electrical Engineering) of this chapter.

(c) Propulsion machinery of an unusual type for small passenger vessels must be given separate consideration and is subject to such requirements as determined necessary by the cognizant

§ 182.310

OCMI. These unusual types of propulsion machinery include:
(1) Gas turbine machinery installations;
(2) Air screws;
(3) Hydraulic jets; and
(4) Machinery installations using lift devices.

Subpart C—Auxiliary Machinery

§ 182.310 Installations.

(a) Auxiliary machinery of the internal combustion piston type must comply with the provisions of this part.

(b) Auxiliary machinery of the steam or gas turbine type will be given separate consideration and must meet the applicable requirements of subchapter F (Marine Engineering) of this chapter as determined necessary by the cognizant OCMI.

(c) Auxiliary boilers and heating boilers and their associated piping and fittings will be given separate consideration and must meet the applicable requirements of subchapter F (Marine Engineering) of this chapter as determined necessary by the cognizant OCMI, except that heating boilers must be tested or examined every three years.

§ 182.320 Water heaters.

(a) A water heater must meet the requirements of parts 53 and 63 of this chapter if rated at not more than 689 kPa (100 psig) and 121° C (250° F), except that an electric water heater is also acceptable if it:

(1) Has a capacity of not more than 454 liters (120 gallons);
(2) Has a heat input of not more than 58.6 kilowatts (200,000 Btu per hour);
(3) Is listed by Underwriters Laboratories (UL) under UL 174, "Household Electric Storage Tank Water Heaters," UL 1453, "Electric Booster and Commercial Storage Tank Water Heaters," or other standard specified by the Commandant; and
(4) Is protected by a pressure-temperature relief device.

(b) A water heater must meet the requirements of parts 52 and 63 of this chapter if rated at more than 689 kPa (100 psig) or 121° C (250° F).

(c) A water heater must be installed and secured from rolling by straps or other devices to the satisfaction of the cognizant OCMI.

[CGD 85–080, 61 FR 986, Jan. 10, 1996; 61 FR 20557, May 7, 1996, as amended at 62 FR 51358, Sept. 30, 1997]

§ 182.330 Pressure vessels.

All unfired pressure vessels must be installed to the satisfaction of the cognizant OCMI. The design, construction, and original testing of such unfired pressure vessels must meet the applicable requirements of subchapter F (Marine Engineering) of this chapter.

Subpart D—Specific Machinery Requirements

§ 182.400 Applicability.

(a) This subpart applies to all propulsion and auxiliary machinery installations of the internal combustion piston type.

(b) Requirements of this subpart that are only applicable to engines that use gasoline or other fuels having a flashpoint of 43.3° C (110° F) or lower are specifically designated in each section.

(c) Requirements of this subpart that are only applicable to engines that use diesel fuel or other fuels having a flashpoint of more than 43.3° C (110° F) are specifically designated in each section.

(d) Where no specific gasoline, diesel, or other fuel designation exists, the requirements of this subpart are applicable to all types of fuels and machinery.

§ 182.405 Fuel restrictions.

The use of alternative fuels, other than diesel fuel or gasoline, as fuel for an internal combustion engine will be reviewed on a case-by-case basis by the Commandant.

[CGD 85–080, 61 FR 986, Jan. 10, 1996, as amended by CGD 97–057, 62 FR 51050, Sept. 30, 1997]

§ 182.410 General requirements.

(a) Starting motors, generators, and any spark producing device must be mounted as high above the bilges as practicable. Electrical equipment in spaces, compartments, or enclosures that contain machinery powered by, or fuel tanks for, gasoline or other fuels having a flashpoint of 43.3° C (110° F) or lower must be explosion-proof, intrinsically safe, or ignition protected for use in a gasoline atmosphere as required by § 183.530 of this chapter.

(b) Gauges to indicate engine revolutions per minute (RPM), jacket water discharge temperature, and lubricating oil pressure must be provided for all propulsion engines installed in the vessel. The gauges must be readily visible at the operating station.

(c) An enclosed space containing machinery powered by gasoline or other fuels having a flash point of 43.3° C (110° F) or lower must be equipped with a flammable vapor detection device in compliance with § 182.480.

(d) In systems and applications where flexible hoses are permitted to be clamped:

(1) Double hose clamping is required where practicable;

(2) The clamps must be of a corrosion resistant metallic material;

(3) The clamps must not depend on spring tension for their holding power; and

(4) Two clamps must be used on each end of the hose, or one hose clamp can be used if the pipe ends are expanded or beaded to provide a positive stop against hose slippage.

§ 182.415   Carburetors.

(a) All carburetors except the downdraft type must be equipped with integral or externally fitted drip collectors of adequate capacity and arranged so as to permit ready removal of fuel leakage. Externally fitted drip collectors, must be covered with flame screens. Drip collectors, where practicable, should automatically drain back to engine air intakes.

(b) All gasoline engines installed in a vessel, except outboard engines, must be equipped with an acceptable means of backfire flame control. Installation of backfire flame arresters bearing basic Approval Numbers 162.015 or 162.041 or engine air and fuel induction systems bearing basic Approval Numbers 162.042 or 162.043 may be continued in use as long as they are serviceable and in good condition. New installations or replacements must meet the applicable requirements of this section.

(c) The following are acceptable means of backfire flame control for gasoline engines:

(1) A backfire flame arrester complying with Society of Automotive Engineers (SAE) J-1928, "Devices Providing Backfire Flame Control for Gasoline Engines in Marine Applications," or UL 1111, "Marine Carburetor Flame Arrestors," and marked accordingly. The flame arrester must be suitably secured to the air intake with a flametight connection.

(2) An engine air and fuel induction system that provides adequate protection from propagation of backfire flame to the atmosphere equivalent to that provided by an acceptable backfire flame arrester. A gasoline engine utilizing an air and fuel induction system, and operated without an approved backfire flame arrester, must either include a reed valve assembly or be installed in accordance with SAE J-1928, or other standard specified by the Commandant.

(3) An arrangement of the carburetor or engine air induction system that will disperse any flames caused by engine backfire. The flames must be dispersed to the atmosphere outside the vessel in such a manner that the flames will not endanger the vessel, persons on board, or nearby vessels and structures. Flame dispersion may be achieved by attachments to the carburetor or location of the engine air induction system. All attachments must be of metallic construction with flametight connections and firmly secured to withstand vibration, shock, and engine backfire. Such installations do not require formal approval and labeling but must comply with this subpart.

(4) An engine air induction system on a vessel with an integrated engine-vessel design must be approved, marked, and tested under § 162.043 in subchapter Q of this chapter, or other standard specified by the Commandant.

§ 182.420   Engine cooling.

(a) Except as otherwise provided in paragraphs (b), (c), (d), and (e) of this section, all engines must be water cooled and meet the requirements of this paragraph.

§ 182.422

(1) The engine head, block, and exhaust manifold must be water-jacketed and cooled by water from a pump that operates whenever the engine is operating.

(2) A suitable hull strainer must be installed in the circulating raw water intake line of an engine cooling water system.

(3) A closed fresh water system may be used to cool the engine.

(b) An engine water cooling system on a vessel of not more than 19.8 meters (65 feet) in length carrying not more than 12 passengers, may comply with the requirements of ABYC Project P-4, "Marine Inboard Engines," instead of the requirements of paragraph (a) of this section.

(c) On a vessel of not more than 19.8 meters (65 feet) in length carrying not more than 12 passengers, a propulsion gasoline engine may be air cooled when in compliance with the requirements of ABYC Project P-4.

(d) An auxiliary gasoline engine may be air cooled when:

(1) It has a self-contained fuel system and it is installed on an open deck; or

(2) On a vessel of not more than 19.8 meters (65 feet) in length carrying not more than 12 passengers, it is in compliance with the requirements of ABYC P-4.

(e) A propulsion or auxiliary diesel engine may be air cooled or employ an air cooled jacket water radiator when:

(1) Installed on an open deck and sufficient ventilation for machinery cooling is available;

(2) Installed in an enclosed or partially enclosed space for which ventilation for machinery cooling is provided, which complies with the requirement of § 182.465(b), and other necessary safeguards are taken so as not to endanger the vessel; or

(3) Installed on a vessel of not more than 19.8 meters (65 feet) in length carrying not more than 12 passengers, in compliance with the requirements of ABYC Project P-4.

§ 182.422 Integral and non-integral keel cooler installations.

(a) A keel cooler installation used for engine cooling must be designed to prevent flooding.

(b) Except as provided in paragraph (e), a shutoff valve must be located where the cooler piping penetrates the shell, as near the shell as practicable, except where the penetration is forward of the collision bulkhead.

(c) The thickness of the inlet and discharge connections, outboard of the shutoff valves required by paragraph (b) of this section, must be at least Schedule 80.

(d) Short lengths of approved non-metallic flexible hose, fixed by two hose clamps at each end of the hose, may be used at machinery connections for a keel cooler installation.

(e) Shutoff valves are not required for integral keel coolers. A keel cooler is considered integral to the hull if the following conditions are satisfied:

(1) The cooler structure is fabricated from material of the same thickness and quality as the hull;

(2) The flexible connections are located well above the deepest subdivision draft;

(3) The end of the structure is faired to the hull with a slope no greater than 4 to 1; and

(4) Full penetration welds are employed in the fabrication of the structure and its attachment to the hull.

[CGD 85-080, 61 FR 986, Jan. 10, 1996, as amended by USCG-2000-7790, 65 FR 58465, Sept. 29, 2000]

§ 182.425 Engine exhaust cooling.

(a) Except as otherwise provided in this paragraph, all engine exhaust pipes must be water cooled.

(1) Vertical dry exhaust pipes are permissible if installed in compliance with §§ 177.405(b) and 177.970 of this chapter.

(2) Horizontal dry exhaust pipes are permitted only if:

(i) They do not pass through living or berthing spaces;

(ii) They terminate above the deepest load waterline;

(iii) They are so arranged as to prevent entry of cold water from rough or boarding seas;

(iv) They are constructed of corrosion resisting material at the hull penetration; and

(v) They are installed in compliance with §§ 177.405(b) and 177.970 of this chapter.

Coast Guard, DHS

§ 182.430

(b) The exhaust pipe cooling water system must comply with the requirements of this paragraph.

(1) Water for cooling the exhaust pipe must be obtained from the engine cooling water system or a separate engine driven pump.

(2) Water for cooling the exhaust pipe, other than a vertical exhaust, must be injected into the exhaust system as near to the engine manifold as practicable. The water must pass through the entire length of the exhaust pipe.

(3) The part of the exhaust system between the point of cooling water injection and the engine manifold must be water-jacketed or effectively insulated and protected in compliance with §§ 177.405(b) and 177.970 of this chapter.

(4) Vertical exhaust pipes must be water-jacketed or suitably insulated as required by § 182.430(g).

(5) When the exhaust cooling water system is separate from the engine cooling water system, a suitable warning device, visual or audible, must be installed at the operating station to indicate any reduction in normal water flow in the exhaust cooling system.

(6) A suitable hull strainer must be installed in the circulating raw water intake line for the exhaust cooling system.

(c) Engine exhaust cooling system built in accordance with the requirements of ABYC Project P-1, "Installation of Exhaust Systems for Propulsion and Auxiliary Machinery," will be considered as meeting the requirements of this section.

[CGD 85-080, 61 FR 986, Jan. 10, 1996; 61 FR 20557, May 7, 1996]

§ 182.430 Engine exhaust pipe installation.

(a) The design of all exhaust systems must ensure minimum risk of injury to personnel. Protection must be provided in compliance with § 177.970 of this chapter at such locations where persons or equipment might come in contact with an exhaust pipe.

(b) Exhaust gas must not leak from the piping or any connections. The piping must be properly supported by noncombustible hangers or blocks.

(c) The exhaust piping must be so arranged as to prevent backflow of water from reaching engine exhaust ports under normal conditions.

(d) Pipes used for wet exhaust lines must be Schedule 80 or corrosion-resistant material and adequately protected from mechanical damage.

(e) Where flexibility is necessary, a section of flexible metallic hose may be used. Nonmetallic hose may be used for wet exhaust systems provided it is especially adapted to resist the action of oil, acid, and heat, has a wall thickness sufficient to prevent collapsing or panting, and is double clamped where practicable.

(f) Where an exhaust pipe passes through a watertight bulkhead, the watertight integrity of the bulkhead must be maintained. Noncombustible packing must be used in bulkhead penetration glands for dry exhaust systems. A wet exhaust pipe may be welded to a steel or equivalent bulkhead in way of a penetration and a fiberglass wet exhaust pipe may be fiberglassed to a fiberglass reinforced plastic bulkhead if suitable arrangements are provided to relieve the stresses resulting from the expansion of the exhaust piping.

(g) A dry exhaust pipe must:

(1) If it passes through a combustible bulkhead or partition, be kept clear of, and suitably insulated or shielded from, combustible material.

(2) Be provided with noncombustible hangers and blocks for support.

(h) An exhaust pipe discharge terminating in a transom must be located as far outboard as practicable so that exhaust gases cannot reenter the vessel.

(i) Arrangements must be made to provide access to allow complete inspection of the exhaust piping throughout its length.

(j) An exhaust installation subject to pressures in excess of 105 kPa (15 psig) gauge or having exhaust pipes passing through living or working spaces must meet the material requirements of part 56 of subchapter F (Marine Engineering) of this chapter.

(k) Engine exhaust installations built in accordance with the requirements of ABYC Project P-1, will be considered as meeting the requirements of this section.

[CGD 85-080, 61 FR 986, Jan. 10, 1996; 61 FR 20557, May 7, 1996; 61 FR 24464, May 15, 1996, as amended at 62 FR 51358, Sept. 30, 1997]

§ 182.435   Integral fuel tanks.

(a) Gasoline fuel tanks must be independent of the hull.

(b) Diesel fuel tanks may not be built integral with the hull of a vessel unless the hull is made of:

(1) Steel;

(2) Aluminum; or

(3) Fiber reinforced plastic when:

(i) Sandwich construction is not used; or

(ii) Sandwich construction is used with only a core material of closed cell polyvinyl chloride or equivalent.

(c) During the initial inspection for certification of a vessel, integral fuel tanks must withstand a hydrostatic pressure test of 35 kPa (5 psig), or the maximum pressure head to which they may be subjected in service, whichever is greater. A standpipe of 3.5 meters (11.5 feet) in height attached to the tank may be filled with water to accomplish the 35 kPa (5 psig) test.

[CGD 85–080, 61 FR 986, Jan. 10, 1996, as amended at 62 FR 51358, Sept. 30, 1997]

§ 182.440   Independent fuel tanks.

(a) *Materials and construction.* Independent fuel tanks must be designed and constructed of materials in compliance with the requirements of this paragraph.

(1) The material used and the minimum thickness allowed must be as indicated in Table 182.440(a)(1), except that other materials that provide equivalent safety may be approved for use under paragraph (a)(3) of this section. Tanks having a capacity of more than 570 liters (150 gallons) must be designed to withstand the maximum head to which they may be subjected in service, but in no case may the thickness be less than that specified in Table 182.440(a)(1).

TABLE 182.440(a)(1)

Material	ASTM specification (latest edition) [see also § 175.600 of this chapter]	Thickness in millimeters (inches) and [gage number][1] vs. tank capacities for:		
		4 to 300 liter (1 to 80 gal) tanks	More than 300 liter (80 gal) and not more than 570 liter (150 gal) tanks	Over 570 liter (150 gal)[2] tanks
Nickel-cooper	B127, hot rolled sheet or plate	0.94 (0.037) [USSG 20][3]	1.27 (0.050) [USSG 18]	2.72 (0.107) [USSG 12]
Copper-nickel[4]	B122, UNS alloy C71500	1.14 (0.045) [AWG 17]	1.45 (0.057) [AWG 15]	3.25 (0.128) [AWG 8]
Copper[4]	B152, UNS alloy C11000	1.45 (0.057) [AWG 15]	2.06 (0.081) [AWG 12]	4.62 (0.182) [AWG 5]
Copper-silicon[4]	B 96, alloys C65100 and C65500	1.29 (0.051) [AWG 16]	1.63 (0.064) [AWG 14]	3.66 (0.144) [AWG 7]
Steel or iron[5,6]	*****	1.90 (0.0747) [MSG 14]	2.66 (0.1046) [MSG 12]	4.55 (0.1793) [MSG 7]
Aluminum[7]	B209, alloy 5052, 5083, 5086	6.35 (0.250) [USSG 3]	6.35 (0.250) [USSG 3]	6.35 (0.250) [USSG 3]
Fiber reinforced plastic	*****	As required[8]	As required[8]	As required[8]

[1] The gage numbers used in this table may be found in many standard engineering reference books. The letters "USSG" stand for "U.S. Standard Gage," which was established by the act of March 3, 1892 (15 U.S.C. 206), for sheet and plate iron and steel. The letters "AWG" stand for "American Wire Gage" (or Brown and Sharpe Gage) for nonferrous sheet thicknesses. The letters "MSG" stand for "Manufacturers' Standard Gage" for sheet steel thickness.
[2] Tanks over 1514 liters (400 gallons) shall be designed with a factor of safety of four on the ultimate strength of the material used with a design head of not less than 1220 millimeters (4 feet) of liquid above the top of the tank.
[3] Nickel-copper not less than 0.79 millimeter (0.031 inch) [USSG 22] may be used for tanks up to 114-liter (30-gallon) capacity.
[4] Acceptable only for gasoline service.
[5] Gasoline fuel tanks constructed of iron or steel, which are less than 5 millimeter (0.1875) inch) thick, shall be galvanized inside and outside by the hot dip process. Tanks intended for use with diesel oil shall not be internally galvanized.
[6] Stainless steel tanks are not included in this category.
[7] Anodic to most common metals. Avoid dissimilar metal contact with tank body.
[8] The requirements of § 182.440(a)(2) apply.

§ 182.440

(2) Fiber reinforced plastic may be used for diesel fuel tanks under the following provisions:

(i) The materials must be fire retardant. Flammability of the material must be determined by the standard test methods in America Society for Testing and Materials (ASTM) D635, "Rate of Burning and/or Extent and Time of Burning of Self-supporting Plastics in a Horizontal Position," and ASTM D2863, "Measuring the Minimum Oxygen Concentration to Support Candle-like Combustion of Plastics (Oxygen Index)," or other standard specified by the Commandant. The results of these tests must show that the average extent of burning is less than 10 millimeters (0.394 inches), the average time of burning is less than 50 seconds, and the limiting oxygen index is greater than 21.

(ii) Tanks must meet UL 1102, "Non integral Marine Fuel Tanks," or other standard specified by the Commandant. Testing may be accomplished by an independent laboratory or by the fabricator to the satisfaction of the OCMI.

(iii) Tanks must be designed to withstand the maximum heat to which they may be subjected to in service.

(iv) Installation of nozzles, flanges or other fittings for pipe connections to the tanks must be acceptable to the cognizant OCMI.

(v) Baffle plates, if installed, must be of the same material and not less than the minimum thickness of the tank walls. Limber holes at the bottom and air holes at the top of all baffles must be provided. Baffle plates must be installed at the time the tests required by UL Standard 1102, or other standard specified by the Commandant, are conducted.

(3) Materials other than those listed in Table 182.440(a)(1) must be approved by the Commandant. An independent tank using material approved by the Commandant under this paragraph must meet the testing requirements of UL Standard 1102, or other standard specified by the Commandant. Testing may be accomplished by an independent laboratory or by the fabricator to the satisfaction of the OCMI.

(4) Tanks with flanged-up top edges that may trap and hold moisture are prohibited.

(5) Openings for fill pipes, vent pipes, and machinery fuel supply pipes, and openings for fuel level gauges, where used, must be on the topmost surfaces of tanks. Tanks may not have any openings in bottoms, sides, or ends, except for:

(i) An opening fitted with a threaded plug or cap installed for tank cleaning purposes; and

(ii) In a diesel fuel tank, openings for supply piping and tubular gauge glasses.

(6) All tank joints must be welded or brazed. Lap joints may not be used.

(7) Nozzles, flanges, or other fittings for pipe connections to a metal tank must be welded or brazed to the tank. Tank openings in way of pipe connections must be properly reinforced where necessary. Where fuel level gauges are used on a metal tank, the flanges to which gauge fittings are attached must be welded or brazed to the tank. No tubular gauge glasses may be fitted to gasoline fuel tanks. Tubular gauge glasses, if fitted to diesel fuel tanks, must be of heat resistant materials, adequately protected from mechanical damage, and provided at the tank connections with devices that will automatically close in the event of rupture of the gauge or gauge lines.

(8) A metal tank exceeding 760 millimeters (30 inches) in any horizontal dimension must:

(i) Be fitted with vertical baffle plates, which meet subparagraph (a)(9) of this section, at intervals not exceeding 760 millimeters (30 inches) to provide strength and to control the excessive surge of fuel; or

(ii) The owner shall submit calculations to the cognizant OCMI demonstrating the structural adequacy of the tank in a fully loaded static condition and in a worst case dynamic (sloshing) condition.

(9) Baffle plates, where required in metal tanks, must be of the same material and not less than the minimum thickness required in the tank walls and must be connected to the tank walls by welding or brazing. Limber holes at the bottom and air holes at the top of all baffles must be provided.

(10) Iron or steel diesel fuel tanks must not be galvanized on the interior. Galvanizing, paint, or other suitable

coating must be used to protect the outside of iron and steel diesel fuel tanks and the inside and outside of iron and steel gasoline fuel tanks.

(b) *Location and installation.* Independent fuel tanks must be located and installed in compliance with the requirements of this paragraph.

(1) Fuel tanks must be located in, or as close as practicable to, machinery spaces.

(2) Fuel tanks and fittings must be so installed as to permit examination, testing, or removal for cleaning with minimum disturbance to the hull structure.

(3) Fuel tanks must be adequately supported and braced to prevent movement. The supports and braces must be insulated from contact with the tank surfaces with a nonabrasive and nonabsorbent material.

(4) All fuel tanks must be electrically bonded to a common ground.

(c) *Tests.* Independent fuel tanks must be tested in compliance with the requirements of this part prior to being used to carry fuel.

(1) Prior to installation, tanks vented to the atmosphere must be hydrostatically tested to, and must withstand, a pressure of 35 kPa (5 psig) or 1½ times the maximum pressure head to which they may be subjected in service, whichever is greater. A standpipe of 3.5 meters (11.5 feet) in height attached to the tank may be filled with water to accomplish the 35 kPa (5 psig) test. Permanent deformation of the tank will not be cause for rejection unless accompanied by leakage.

(2) After installation of the fuel tank on a vessel, the complete installation must be tested in the presence of a marine inspector, or individual specified by the cognizant OCMI, to a heat not less than that to which the tank may be subjected in service. Fuel may be used as the testing medium.

(3) All tanks not vented to the atmosphere must be constructed and tested in accordance with § 182.330 of this part.

(d) *Alternative procedures.* A vessel of not more than 19.8 meters (65 feet) in length carrying not more than 12 passengers, with independent gasoline fuel tanks built in accordance with ABYC Project H–24, or 33 CFR 183, subpart J, or with independent diesel fuel tanks built in accordance with ABYC Project H–33, will be considered as meeting the requirements of this section. However, tanks must not be fabricated from any material not listed in Table 182.440(a)(1) without approval by the Commandant under paragraph (a)(3) of this section.

[CGD 85–080, 61 FR 986, Jan. 10, 1996, as amended by USCG–1999–5151, 64 FR 67186, Dec. 1, 1999]

§ 182.445 Fill and sounding pipes for fuel tanks.

(a) Fill pipes for fuel tanks must be not less than 40 millimeters (1.5 inches) nominal pipe size.

(b) There must be a means of accurately determining the amount of fuel in each fuel tank either by sounding, through a separate sounding pipe or a fill pipe, or by an installed marine type fuel gauge.

(c) Where sounding pipes are used, their openings must be at least as high as the opening of the fill pipe and they must be kept closed at all times except during sounding.

(d) Fill pipes and sounding pipes must be so arranged that overflow of liquid or vapor cannot escape to the inside of the vessel.

(e) Fill pipes and sounding pipes must run as directly as possible, preferably in a straight line, from the deck connection to the top of the tank. Such pipes must terminate on the weather deck and must be fitted with shutoff valves, watertight deck plates, or screw caps, suitably marked for identification. Gasoline fill pipes and sounding pipes must extend to within one-half of their diameter from the bottom of the tank. Diesel fill pipes and sounding pipes may terminate at the top of the tank.

(f) A vessel of not more than 19.8 meters (65 feet) carrying not more than 12 passengers, with a gasoline fuel system built in accordance with ABYC Project H–24, or 33 CFR 183, subpart J, or with a diesel fuel system built in accordance with ABYC Project H–33, will be considered as meeting the requirements of this section.

(g) Where a flexible fill pipe section is necessary, suitable flexible tubing or hose having high resistance to salt

§ 182.450

water, petroleum oils, heat and vibration, may be used. Such hose must overlap metallic pipe ends at the least 1½ times the pipe diameter and must be secured at each end by clamps. The flexible section must be accessible and as near the upper end of the fill pipe as practicable. When the flexible section is a nonconductor of electricity, the metallic sections of the fill pipe separated thereby must be joined by a conductor for protection against generation of a static charge when filling with fuel.

§ 182.450 Vent pipes for fuel tanks.

(a) Each unpressurized fuel tank must be fitted with a vent pipe connected to the highest point of the tank.

(b) The net cross sectional area of the vent pipe for a gasoline fuel tank must not be less than that of 19 millimeters (0.75 inches) outer diameter (O.D.) tubing (0.9 millimeter (0.035 Inch) wall thickness, 20 gauge), except that, where the tank is filled under pressure, the net cross sectional area of the vent pipe must be not less than that of the fill pipe.

(c) The minimum net cross sectional area of the vent pipe for diesel fuel tanks must be as follows:

(1) Not less than the cross sectional area of 16 millimeters (0.625 inches) outer diameter (O.D.) tubing (0.9 millimeter (0.035-inch) wall thickness, 20 gauge), if the fill pipe terminates at the top of the tank;

(2) Not less than the cross sectional area of 19 millimeters (0.75 inches) O.D. tubing (0.9 millimeter (0.035-inch) wall thickness, 20 gauge), if the fill pipe extends into the tank; and

(3) Not less than the cross sectional area of the fill pipe if the tank is filled under pressure.

(d) The discharge ends of fuel tank vent pipes must terminate on the hull exterior as high above the waterline as practicable and remote from any hull openings, or they must terminate in U-bends as high above the weather deck as practicable and as far as practicable from openings into any enclosed spaces. Vent pipes terminating on the hull exterior must be installed or equipped to prevent the accidental contamination of the fuel by water under normal operating conditions.

46 CFR Ch. I (10–1–04 Edition)

(e) The discharge ends of fuel tank vent pipes must be fitted with removable flame screens or flame arresters. The flame screens must consist of a single screen of corrosion resistant wire of at least 30x30 mesh. The flame screens or flame arresters must be of such size and design as to prevent reduction in the net cross sectional area of the vent pipe and permit cleaning or renewal of the flame screens or arrester elements.

(f) A vessel of not more than 19.8 meters (65 feet) in length carrying not more than 12 passengers, with fuel gasoline tank vents built in accordance with ABYC Project H–24, or 33 CFR 183, subpart J, or with diesel fuel tank vents built in accordance with ABYC Project H–33, will be considered as meeting the requirements of this section.

(g) Where a flexible vent pipe section is necessary, suitable flexible tubing or hose having high resistance to salt water, petroleum oils, heat and vibration, may be used. Such hose must overlap metallic pipe ends at least 1½ times the pipe diameter and must be secured at each end by clamps. The flexible section must be accessible and as near the upper end of the vent pipe as practicable.

(h) Fuel tank vent pipes shall be installed to gradient upward to prevent fuel from being trapped in the line.

§ 182.455 Fuel piping.

(a) *Materials and workmanship.* The materials and construction of fuel lines, including pipe, tube, and hose, must comply with the requirements of this paragraph.

(1) Fuel lines must be annealed tubing of copper, nickel-copper, or copper-nickel having a minimum wall thickness of 0.9 millimeters (0.035 inch) except that:

(i) Diesel fuel piping of other materials, such as seamless steel pipe or tubing, which provide equivalent safety may be used;

(ii) Diesel fuel piping of aluminum is acceptable on aluminum hull vessels provided it is a minimum of Schedule 80 wall thickness; and

(iii) when used, flexible hose must meet the requirements of § 182.720(e) of this part.

Coast Guard, DHS § 182.455

(2) Tubing connections and fittings must be of nonferrous drawn or forged metal of the flared type except that flareless fittings of the non-bite type may be used when the tubing system is of nickel-copper or copper-nickel. When making tube connections, the tubing must be cut square and flared by suitable tools. Tube ends must be annealed before flaring.

(3) Cocks are prohibited except for the solid bottom type with tapered plugs and union bonnets.

(4) Valves for gasoline fuel must be of a suitable nonferrous type.

(b) *Installation.* The installation of fuel lines, including pipe, tube, and hose, must comply with the requirements of this paragraph.

(1) Gasoline fuel lines must be connected at the top of the fuel tank and run at or above the level of the tank top to a point as close to the engine connection as practicable, except that lines below the level of the tank top are permitted if equipped with anti-siphon protection.

(2) Diesel fuel lines may be connected to the fuel tank at or near the bottom of the tank.

(3) Fuel lines must be accessible, protected from mechanical injury, and effectively secured against excessive movement and vibration by the use of soft nonferrous metal straps which have no sharp edges and are insulated to protect against corrosion. Where passing through bulkheads, fuel lines must be protected by close fitting ferrules or stuffing boxes. All fuel lines and fittings must be accessible for inspection.

(4) Shutoff valves, installed so as to close against the fuel flow, must be fitted in the fuel supply lines, one at the tank connection and one at the engine end of the fuel line to stop fuel flow when servicing accessories. The shutoff valve at the tank must be manually operable from outside the compartment in which the valve is located, preferably from an accessible position on the weather deck. If the handle to the shutoff valve at the tank is located inside the machinery space, it must be located so that the operator does not have to reach more than 300 millimeters (12 inches) into the machinery space and the valve handle must be shielded from flames by the same material the hull is constructed of, or some noncombustible material. Electric solenoid valves must not be used, unless used in addition to the manual valve.

(5) A loop of copper tubing or a short length of flexible hose must be installed in the fuel supply line at or near the engines. The flexible hose must meet the requirements of § 182.720(e).

(6) A suitable metal marine type strainer, meeting the requirements of the engine manufacturer, must be fitted in the fuel supply line in the engine compartment. Strainers must be leak free. Strainers must be the type of opening on top for cleaning screens. A drip pan fitted with flame screen must be installed under gasoline strainers. Fuel filter and strainer bowls must be highly resistant to shattering due to mechanical impact and resistant to failure due to thermal shock. Fuel filters fitted with bowls of other than steel construction must be approved by the Commandant and be protected from mechanical damage. Approval of bowls of other than steel construction will specify if a flame shield is required.

(7) All accessories installed in the fuel line must be independently supported.

(8) Outlets in gasoline fuel lines that would permit drawing fuel below deck, for any purpose, are prohibited.

(9) Valves for removing water or impurities from diesel fuel in water traps or stainers are permitted. These valves must be provided with caps or plugs to prevent fuel leakage.

(c) *Alternative procedures.* A vessel of not more than 19.8 meters (65 feet) carrying no more than 12 passengers, with machinery powered by gasoline and a fuel system built in accordance with ABYC Project H–24, or 33 CFR 183, subpart J, or with machinery powered by diesel fuel and a fuel system built in accordance with ABYC Project H–33, will be considered as meeting the requirements of this section.

[CGD 85–080, 61 FR 986, Jan. 10, 1996, as amended by USCG–2001–10224, 66 FR 48621, Sept. 21, 2001; USCG–2004–18884, 69 FR 58351, Sept. 30, 2004]

§ 182.458 Portable fuel systems.

(a) Portable fuel systems, including portable tanks and related fuel lines and accessories, are prohibited except where used for portable dewatering pumps or outboard motor installations.

(b) The design, construction and stowage of portable tanks and related fuel lines and accessories must meet the requirements of ABYC Project H–25, "Portable Gasoline Fuel systems for Flammable Liquids," or other standard specified by the Commandant.

[CGD 85–080, 61 FR 986, Jan. 10, 1996, as amended by CGD 97–057, 62 FR 51050, Sept. 30, 1997; CGD 85–080, 62 FR 51358, Sept. 30, 1997]

§ 182.460 Ventilation of spaces containing machinery powered by, or fuel tanks for, gasoline.

(a) A space containing machinery powered by, or fuel tanks for, gasoline must have a ventilation system that complies with this section and consists of:

(1) For an enclosed space:

(i) At least two natural ventilation supply ducts located at one end of the space and that extend to the lowest part of the space or to the bilge on each side of the space; and

(ii) A mechanical exhaust system consisting of at least two ventilation exhaust ducts located at the end of the space opposite from where the supply ducts are fitted, which extend to the lowest part of the bilge of the space on each side of the space, and which are led to one or more powered exhaust blowers; and

(2) For a partially enclosed space, at least one ventilation duct installed in the forward part of the space and one ventilation duct installed in the after part of the space, or as otherwise required by the cognizant OCMI. Ducts for partially enclosed spaces must have cowls or scoops as required by paragraph (i) of this section.

(b) A mechanical exhaust system required by paragraph (a)(1)(ii) of this section must be such as to assure the air changes as noted in Table 182.460(b) depending upon the size of the space.

TABLE 182.460(b)

Size of space in cubic meters (feet)		Minutes per air change
Over	Not over	
0	14 (500)	2
14 (500)	28.50 (1000)	3
28.50 (1000)	43 (1500)	4
43 (1500)		5

(c) An exhaust blower motor may not be installed in a duct, and if mounted in any space required to be ventilated by this section, must be located as high above the bilge as practicable. Blower blades must be nonsparking with reference to their housings.

(d) Where a fixed gas fire extinguishing system is installed in a space, all powered exhaust blowers for the space must automatically shut down upon release of the extinguishing agent.

(e) Exhaust blower switches must be located outside of any space required to be ventilated by this section, and must be of the type interlocked with the starting switch and the ignition switch so that the blowers are started before the engine starter motor circuit or the engine ignition is energized. A red warning sign at the switch must state that the blowers must be operated prior to starting the engines for the time sufficient to insure at least one complete change of air in the space served.

(f) The area of the ventilation ducts must be sufficient to limit the air velocity to a maximum of 10 meters per second (2,000 feet per minute). A duct may be of any shape, provided that in no case will one cross sectional dimension exceed twice the other.

(g) A duct must be so installed that ordinary collection of water in the bilge will not block vapor flow.

(h) A duct must be of rigid permanent construction, which does not allow any appreciable vapor flow except through normal openings, and made of the same material as the hull or of noncombustible material. The duct must lead as directly as possible from its intake opening to its terminus and be securely fastened and supported.

(i) A supply duct must be provided at its intake opening with a cowl or scoop having a free area not less than twice the required duct area. When the cowl or scoop is screened, the mouth area must be increased to compensate for the area of the screen wire. A cowl or scoop must be kept open at all times except when the weather is such as to endanger the vessel if the openings are not temporarily closed.

(j) Dampers may not be fitted in a supply duct.

(k) A duct opening may not be located where the natural flow of air is unduly obstructed, adjacent to possible sources of vapor ignition, or where exhaust air may be taken into a supply duct.

(l) Provision must be made for closing all supply duct cowls or scoops and exhaust duct discharge openings for a space protected by a fixed gas extinguishing system. All closure devices must be readily available and mounted in the vicinity of the vent.

(m) A vessel of not more than 19.8 meters (65 feet) in length carrying not more than 12 passengers, with ventilation installations in accordance with ABYC Project H-2, "Ventilation of Boats Using Gasoline," or 33 CFR 183, subpart K, "Ventilation," will be considered as meeting the requirements of this section.

[CGD 85-080, 61 FR 986, Jan. 10, 1996, as amended by CGD 97-057, 62 FR 51050, Sept. 30, 1997]

§ 182.465 Ventilation of spaces containing diesel machinery.

(a) A space containing diesel machinery must be fitted with adequate means such as dripproof ventilators, ducts, or louvers, to provide sufficient air for proper operation of main engines and auxiliary engines.

(b) Air-cooled propulsion and auxiliary diesel engines installed below deck, as permitted by § 182.420, must be fitted with air supply ducts or piping from the weather deck. The ducts or piping must be so arranged and supported to be capable of safely sustaining stresses induced by weight and engine vibration and to minimize transfer of vibration to the supporting structure. Prior to installation of ventilation system for such engines, plans or sketches showing machinery arrangement including air supplies, exhaust stack, method of attachment of ventilation ducts to the engine, location of spark arresting mufflers and capacity of ventilation blowers must be submitted to the cognizant OCMI for approval.

(c) A space containing diesel machinery must be fitted with at least two ducts to furnish natural or powered supply and exhaust ventilation. The total inlet area and the total outlet area of each ventilation duct may not be less than one square inch for each foot of beam of the vessel. These minimum areas must be increased as necessary when the ducts are considered as part of the air supply to the engines.

(d) A duct must be of rigid permanent construction, which does not allow any appreciable vapor flow except through normal openings, and made of the same material as the hull or of noncombustible material. The duct must lead as directly as possible from its intake opening to its terminus and be securely fastened and supported.

(e) A supply duct must be provided with a cowl or scoop having a free area not less than twice the required duct area. When the cowl or scoop is screened, the mouth area must be increased to compensate for the area of the screen wire. A cowl or scoop must be kept open at all times except when the weather is such as to endanger the vessel if the openings are not temporarily closed.

(f) Dampers may not be fitted in a supply duct.

(g) A duct opening may not be located where the natural flow of air is unduly obstructed, adjacent to possible sources of vapor ignition, or where exhaust air may be taken into a supply duct.

(h) provision must be made for closing all supply duct cowls or scoops and exhaust duct discharge openings for a space protected by a fixed gas extinguishing system. All closure devices must be readily available and mounted in the vicinity of the vent.

(i) A vessel of not more than 19.8 meters (65 feet) in length carrying not more than 12 passengers, with ventilation installations in accordance with ABYC Project H-32, "Ventilation of Boats Using Diesel Fuel," will be considered as meeting the requirements of this section.

§ 182.470

§ 182.470 Ventilation of spaces containing diesel fuel tanks.

(a) Unless provided with ventilation that complies with § 182.465, a space containing a diesel fuel tank and no machinery must meet the requirements of this section.

(1) A space of 14 cubic meters (500 cubic feet) or more in volume must have a gooseneck vent of not less than 65 millimeters (2.5 inches) in diameter.

(2) A space of less than 14 cubic meters (500 cubic feet) in volume must have a gooseneck vent of not less than 40 millimeters (1.5 inches) in diameter.

(b) Vent openings may not be located adjacent to possible sources of vapor ignition.

(c) A vessel of not more than 19.8 meters (65 feet) in length carrying not more than 12 passengers, with ventilation installations in accordance with ABYC Project H–32, "Ventilation of Boats Using Diesel Fuel," will be considered as meeting the requirements of this section.

§ 182.480 Flammable vapor detection systems.

(a) A flammable vapor detection system required by § 182.410(c) must meet UL Standard 1110, "Marine Combustible Gas Indicators," or be approved by an independent laboratory.

(b) Procedures for checking the proper operation of a flammable vapor detection system must be posted at the primary operating station. The system must be self-monitoring and include a ground fault indication alarm.

(c) A flammable vapor detection system must be operational for 30 seconds prior to engine startup and continue sensing the entire time the engine is running.

(d) A flammable vapor detection system must provide a visual and audible alarm at the operating station.

(e) A sensor must be located above the expected bilge water level in the following locations:

(1) The lowest part of a machinery space;

(2) The lowest part of a space containing a fuel tank when separate from the machinery space; and

(3) Any other location when required by the cognizant OCMI.

46 CFR Ch. I (10–1–04 Edition)

(f) A flammable vapor detection system must be installed so as to permit calibration in a vapor free atmosphere.

(g) Electrical connections, wiring, and components for a flammable vapor detection system must comply with part 183 of this chapter.

(h) An operation and maintenance manual for the flammable vapor detection system must be kept onboard.

Subpart E—Bilge and Ballast Systems

§ 182.500 General.

(a) A vessel must be provided with a satisfactory arrangement for draining any watertight compartment, other than small buoyancy compartments, under all practicable conditions. Sluice valves are not permitted in watertight bulkheads.

(b) A vessel of not more than 19.8 meters (65 feet) in length carrying not more than 12 passengers may meet the requirements of ABYC Project H–22, "DC Electric Bilge Pumps Operating Under 50 Volts," in lieu of the requirements of this subpart, provided that each watertight compartment, other than small buoyancy compartments and the compartment forward of the collision bulkhead, is provided with a means for dewatering.

(c) Special consideration may be given to vessels, such as high speed craft, which have a high degree of subdivision and utilize numerous small buoyancy compartments. Where the probability of flooding of the space is limited to external hull damage, compartment drainage may be omitted provided it can be shown by stability calculations, submitted to the cognizant OCMI, that the safety of the vessel will not be impaired.

§ 182.510 Bilge piping system.

(a) A vessel of at least 7.9 meters (26 feet) in length must be provided with individual bilge lines and bilge suctions for each watertight compartment, except that the space forward of the collision bulkhead need not be fitted with a bilge suction line when the arrangement of the vessel is such that ordinary leakage may be removed from this compartment by the use of a hand portable bilge pump or other

Coast Guard, DHS § 182.520

equipment, and such equipment is provided.

(b) A bilge pipe in a vessel of not more than 19.8 meters (65 feet) in length must be not less than 25 millimeters (1 inch) nominal pipe size. A bilge pipe in a vessel of more than 19.8 meters (65 feet) in length must be not less than 40 millimeters (1.5 inches) nominal pipe size. A bilge suction must be fitted with a suitable strainer having an open area not less than three times the area of the bilge pipe.

(c) Except when individual pumps are provided for separate spaces, individual bilge suction lines must be led to a central control point or manifold and provided with a stop valve at the control point or manifold and a check valve at some accessible point in the bilge line. A stop-check valve located at a control point or manifold will meet the requirements for both a stop valve and a check valve.

(d) A bilge pipe piercing the collision bulkhead must be fitted with a screw-down valve located on the forward side of the collision bulkhead and operable from the weather deck, or, if it is readily accessible under service conditions, a screw-down valve without a reach rod may be fitted to the bilge line on the after side of the collision bulkhead.

§ 182.520 Bilge pumps.

(a) A vessel must be provided with bilge pumps in accordance with Table 182.520(a). A second power pump is an acceptable alternative to a hand pump if it is supplied by a source of power independent of the first power bilge pump. Individual power pumps used for separate spaces are to be controlled from a central control point and must have a light or other visual means at the control point to indicate operation.

TABLE 182.520(a)

Number of passengers	Length of vessel	Bilge pumps required	Min. capacity required per pump ltrs/min (gal/min)
Any number	More than 19.8 m (65 ft) ..	2 fixed power pumps	190 LPM (50 GPM).
More than 49 passengers and all ferry vessels.	Not more than 19.8 m (65 ft).	1 fixed power pump and ...	95 LPM (25 GPM).
Not more than 49 passengers (Other than ferry vessels).	7.9 m, 26 feet up to 19.8 m (65 ft).	1 portable hand pump .... 1 fixed power pump and 1 portable hand pump or. 1 fixed hand pump and .... 1 portable hand pump	38 LPM (10 GPM). 38 LPM (10 GPM). 38 LPM (10 GPM). 19 LPM (5 GPM).
	Less than 7.9 m (26 ft)	1 portable hand pump	19 LPM (5 GPM).

(b) A portable hand bilge pump must be:

(1) Capable of pumping water, but not necessarily simultaneously, from all watertight compartments; and

(2) Provided with suitable suction hose capable of reaching the bilge of each watertight compartment and discharging overboard.

(c) Each fixed power bilge pump must be self priming. It may be driven off the main engine or other source of power. It must be permanently connected to the bilge manifold and may also be connected to the fire main. If of sufficient capacity, a power bilge pump may also serve as a fire pump.

(d) Where two fixed power bilge pumps are installed, they must be driven by different sources of power. If one pump is driven off the main engine in a single propulsion engine installation, the other must be independently driven. In a twin propulsion engine installation, each pump may be driven off a different propulsion engine.

(e) A submersible electric bilge pump may be used as a power bilge pump required by Table 182.520(a) only on a vessel of not more than 19.8 meters (65 feet) in length carrying not more than 49 passengers, other than a ferry, provided that:

(1) The pump is listed by Underwriters' Laboratories Inc. or another independent laboratory;

(2) The pump is used to dewater not more than one watertight compartment;

§ 182.530

(3) The pump is permanently mounted;

(4) The pump is equipped with a strainer that can be readily inspected and cleaned without removal;

(5) The pump discharge line is suitably supported;

(6) The opening in the hull for the pump discharge is placed as high above the waterline as possible;

(7) A positive shutoff valve is installed at the hull penetration; and

(8) The capacity of the electrical system, including wiring, and size and number of batteries, is designed to allow all bilge pumps to be operated simultaneously.

(f) A flexible tube or hose may be used instead of fixed pipe for the discharge line of a submersible electric bilge pump provided the hose or tube does not penetrate any required watertight bulkheads and is:

(1) Of good quality and of substantial construction, suitable for the intended use; and

(2) Highly resistant to salt water, petroleum oil, heat, and vibration.

(g) If a fixed hand pump is used to comply with Table 182.520(a), it must be permanently connected to the bilge system.

(h) On a vessel of not more than 19.8 meters (65 feet) in length, a power driven fire pump required by § 181.300 of this chapter may serve as a fixed power bilge pump required by this subpart, provided it has the minimum flow rate required by Table 182.520(a).

(i) On a vessel of more than 19.8 meters (65 feet) in length, a power driven fire pump required by § 181.300 of this subchapter may serve as one of the two fixed power bilge pumps required by this subpart, provided:

(1) The bilge and fire pump systems are interconnected;

(2) The dedicated bilge pump is capable of pumping the bilges at the same time the fire/bilge pump charges the firemain; and

(3) Stop valves and check valves are installed in the piping to isolate the systems during simultaneous operation and prevent possible flooding through the bilge system.

(j) A catamaran vessel must be equipped with bilge pumps for each hull, as if each hull is a separate vessel, in accordance with Table 182.520(a), except where:

(1) One dedicated pump is located in each hull;

(2) Each dedicated pump is driven by an independent source of power; and

(3) The bilge system is permanently cross connected between hulls.

[CGD 85–080, 61 FR 986, Jan. 10, 1996; 61 FR 20557, May 7, 1996, as amended by CGD 97–057, 62 FR 51050, Sept. 30, 1997; CGD 85–080, 62 FR 51358, Sept. 30, 1997]

§ 182.530 Bilge high level alarms.

(a) On a vessel of at least 7.9 meters (26 feet) in length, a visual and audible alarm must be provided at the operating station to indicate a high water level in each of the following normally unmanned spaces:

(1) A space with a through-hull fitting below the deepest load waterline, such as a lazarette;

(2) A machinery space bilge, bilge well, shaft alley bilge, or other spaces subject to flooding from sea water piping within the space; and

(3) A space with a non-watertight closure, such as a space with a non-watertight hatch on the main deck.

(b) Vessels constructed of wood must, in addition to paragraph (a), provide bilge level alarms in all watertight compartments except small buoyancy chambers.

(c) A visual indicator must be provided at the operating station to indicate when any automatic bilge pump is operating.

§ 182.540 Ballast systems.

(a) Ballast piping must not be installed in any compartment integral with the hull of a wooden vessel. Where the carriage of liquid ballast in such a vessel is necessary, suitable ballast tanks, structurally independent of the hull, must be provided.

(b) Solid and water ballast must comply with the requirements of part 178 of this subchapter.

Subpart F—Steering Systems

§ 182.600 General.

A self-propelled vessel must comply with the provisions of this subpart.

§ 182.610 Main steering gear.

(a) A vessel must be provided with a main steering gear that is:

(1) Of adequate strength and capable of steering the vessel at all service speeds;

(2) Designed to operate at maximum astern speed without being damaged or jammed; and

(3) Capable of moving the rudder from 35 degrees on one side to 30 degrees on the other side in not more than 28 seconds with the vessel moving ahead at maximum service speed.

(b) Control of the main steering gear, including control of any necessary associated devices (motor, pump, valve, etc.), must be provided from the operating station.

(c) The main steering gear must be designed so that transfer from the main steering gear or control to the auxiliary means of steering required by § 182.620 can be achieved rapidly. Any tools or equipment necessary to make the transfer must be readily available.

(d) The operating station must be arranged to permit the person steering to have the best possible all around vision.

(e) Strong and effective rudder stops must be provided to prevent jamming and damage to the rudder and its fittings. These stops may be structural or internal to the main steering gear.

(f) In addition to meeting the requirements of paragraphs (a) through (e) of this section, a vessel with a power driven main steering gear must be provided with the following:

(1) A disconnect switch located in the steering compartment, and instantaneous short circuit protection for electrical power and control circuits sized and located in accordance with § 58.25-55(d) of this chapter. Overload protection is prohibited;

(2) An independent rudder angle indicator at the operating station;

(3) An arrangement that automatically resumes operation, without reset, when power is restored after a power failure;

(4) A manual means to center and steady the rudder(s) in an emergency; and

(5) A limit switch to stop the steering gear before its reaches the rudder stops required by paragraph (e) of this section.

(g) In addition to meeting the requirements of paragraphs (a) through (f) of this section, a vessel more than 19.8 meters (65 feet) in length with a power driven main steering gear must be provided with the following:

(1) A visual means, located at the operating station, to indicate operation of the power units; and

(2) Instructions for transfer procedures from the main steering gear or control to the auxiliary means of steering required by § 182.620, posted at the location where the transfer is carried out.

[CGD 85–080, 61 FR 986, Jan. 10, 1996, as amended at 62 FR 51358, Sept. 30, 1997]

§ 182.620 Auxiliary means of steering.

(a) Except as provided in paragraph (c) of this section, a vessel must be provided with an auxiliary means of steering that is:

(1) Of adequate strength;

(2) Capable of moving the rudder from 15 degrees on one side to 15 degrees on the other side in not more than 60 seconds with the vessel at one-half its maximum service speed ahead, or 7 knots, whichever is greater; and

(3) Controlled from a location that permits safe maneuvering of the vessel and does not expose the person operating the auxiliary means of steering to personnel hazards during normal or heavy weather operation.

(b) A suitable hand tiller may be acceptable as the auxiliary means of steering where satisfactory to the cognizant OCMI.

(c) An auxiliary means of steering need not be provided if:

(1) The main steering gear and its controls are provided in duplicate;

(2) Multiple screw propulsion, with independent pilothouse control for each screw, is provided, and the vessel is capable of being steered using pilothouse control;

(3) No regular rudder is fitted and steering action is obtained by a change of setting of the propelling unit; or

(4) Where a rudder and hand tiller are the main steering gear.

[CGD 85–080, 61 FR 986, Jan. 10, 1996, as amended by CGD 97–057, 62 FR 51050, Sept. 30, 1997]

Subpart G—Piping Systems

§ 182.700 General.

Materials used in piping systems must meet the requirements of this subpart and be otherwise acceptable to the cognizant OCMI.

§ 182.710 Piping for vital systems.

(a) Vital systems are those systems that are vital to a vessel's survivability and safety. For the purpose of this part the following are vital systems:

(1) Fuel system;
(2) Fire main;
(3) CO_2 and Halon systems;
(4) Bilge system;
(5) Steering system;
(6) Propulsion system and its necessary auxiliaries and controls;
(7) Ship's service and emergency electrical generation system and its necessary auxiliaries; and
(8) A marine engineering system identified by the cognizant OCMI as being crucial to the survival of the vessel or to the protection of the personnel on board.

(b) For the purpose of this part, a system not identified in paragraph (a) of this section is a non-vital system.

(c) Piping used in a vital system must:

(1) Be composed of ferrous materials except when:

(i) Nonmetallic piping materials are permitted by § 182.720; or

(ii) Nonferrous metallic piping materials are permitted by § 182.730; and

(2) If subject to a pressure of more than 1,034 kPa (150 psig), be designed, fabricated, and inspected in accordance with the principles of American National Standards Institute (ANSI) B 31.1, "Code for Pressure Piping, Power Piping," or other standard specified by the Commandant.

§ 182.715 Piping subject to more than 1,034 kPa (150 psig) in non-vital systems.

Piping subject to more than 1,034 kPa (150 psig) in a non-vital system must be designed, fabricated, and inspected in accordance with the principles of ANSI B 31.1, or other industry standard acceptable to the Commandant.

§ 182.720 Nonmetallic piping materials.

(a) Rigid nonmetallic materials (plastic) may be used only in non-vital systems and in accordance with paragraphs (c) and (d) of this section.

(b) Flexible nonmetallic materials (hose) may be used in vital and non-vital systems where permitted by paragraph (e) of this section.

(c) Nonmetallic piping must not be used in gasoline or diesel fuel systems. Flexible nonmetallic materials (hose) may be used where permitted by paragraph (e) of this section.

(d) Where rigid nonmetallic material (plastic) is permitted for use in piping systems by this section, the following restrictions apply:

(1) Penetrations of required watertight decks and bulkheads by any rigid plastic pipe are prohibited unless the following requirements are met:

(i) Each penetration must be accomplished using an acceptable metallic through deck or through bulkhead fitting that is welded or otherwise attached to the bulkhead or deck by an accepted method; and

(ii) One or more metallic shutoff valves must be installed adjacent to the fitting in one of the following ways:

(A) Only one metallic shutoff valve must be installed if it is operable from above the bulkhead deck;

(B) If two metallic shutoff valves are installed, one on either side of the bulkhead, they need not be operable from above the bulkhead deck provided immediate access to both is possible; or

(C) Where both plastic and metallic materials are used in piping that penetrates a bulkhead, and the two materials exist entirely on opposite sides of the bulkhead, a metallic shutoff valve must be installed at the bulkhead in the metallic part of the system, with the valve being capable of operation from above the bulkhead deck, or locally if immediate access is possible;

(2) Protection from mechanical damage must be specifically considered and all protective covering or shields must be installed to the satisfaction of the cognizant OCMI;

(3) Through hull fittings and shutoff valves must be metallic. In the case of nonmetallic hulls, materials that will

afford an equal degree of safety and heat resistivity as that afforded by the hull may be approved; and

(4) The material specification must show that the rigid nonmetallic material possesses characteristics adequate for its intended service and environment and must be approved for use by the cognizant OCMI.

(e) Where flexible nonmetallic hose is permitted for use in piping systems by this section, it must meet SAE Standard J–1942, "Hose and Hose Assemblies for Marine Applications," or be specifically approved by the Commandant. The following restrictions apply:

(1) Flexible nonmetallic hose must be complete with factory-assembled end fittings requiring no further adjustment of the fittings on the hose, or field attachable type fittings may be used. Hose end fittings must comply with SAE J–1475, "Hydraulic Hose Fittings For Marine Applications."Field attachable fittings must be installed following the manufacturer's recommended practice. If special equipment is required, such as crimping machines, it must be of the type and design specified by the manufacturer. If field attachable type fittings are used, each hose assembly must be individually hydrostatically tested to twice the maximum operating pressure of the system;

(2) Flexible nonmetallic hose may be used in non-vital water and pneumatic systems, subject to the limitations of paragraph (d)(1) through (d)(4) of this section. Unreinforced hoses are limited to a maximum service pressure of 349 kPa (50 psig), reinforced hoses are limited to a maximum service pressure of 1,034 kPa (150 psig); and

(3) Flexible nonmetallic hose may be used in lube oil, fuel oil and fluid power systems, subject to the following requirements:

(i) Flexible hose may only be used at a pressure not to exceed the manufacturer's rating and must have a high resistance to saltwater, petroleum oils, and vibration;

(ii) Flexible hose runs must be visible, easily accessible, protected from mechanical damage, and must not penetrate watertight decks or bulkheads;

(iii) Flexible hose must be fabricated with an inner tube and a cover of synthetic rubber or other suitable material reinforced with wire braid;

(iv) Flexible hose used for alcohol-gasoline blend fuels must meet the permeability requirements specified in 33 CFR part 183, subpart J; and

(v) For the purpose of flexibility only, flexible hose installed in lengths of not more than 760 millimeters (30 inches) and subject to pressures of not more than 35 kPa (5 psig), may meet the following requirements:

(A) Suitable compression type connection fittings may be accepted;

(B) Flexible hose designed for use with hose clamps may be installed with two clamps, at both ends of the hose, which:

(*1*) Do not rely on the spring tension of the clamp for compressive force; and

(*2*) Are installed beyond the bead or flare or over the serrations of the mating spud, pipe, or hose fitting; and

(C) USCG Type A1, A2, B1, or B2 flexible hose may be accepted in accordance with 33 CFR part 183, subpart J.

[CGD 85–080, 61 FR 986, Jan. 10, 1996, as amended at 62 FR 51358, Sept. 30, 1997]

§ 182.730 Nonferrous metallic piping materials.

(a) Nonferrous metallic piping materials are acceptable for use in the following:

(1) Non-vital systems;

(2) Aluminum fuel piping, if of a minimum of Schedule 80 wall thickness on an aluminum hulled vessel;

(3) Aluminum bilge, ballast, and firemain piping on an aluminum hulled vessel;

(4) If acceptable to the cognizant OCMI, nonferrous metallic piping with a melting temperature above 927° C (1,700° F) may be used in vital systems that are deemed to be galvanically compatible; and

(5) Other uses specifically accepted by the cognizant OCMI.

(b) Where nonferrous metallic material is permitted for use in piping systems by this subpart, the restrictions in this paragraph apply:

(1) Provisions must be made to protect piping systems using aluminum alloys in high risk fire areas due to the low melting point of aluminum alloys;

(2) Provisions must be made to prevent or mitigate the effect of galvanic corrosion due to the relative solution potentials of copper, aluminum, and alloys of copper and aluminum, which are used in conjunction with each other, steel, or other metals and their alloys;

(3) A suitable thread compound must be used in making up threaded joints in aluminum pipe to prevent seizing. Pipe in the annealed temper must not be threaded;

(4) The use of aluminum alloys with a copper content exceeding 0.6 percent is prohibited; and

(5) The use of cast aluminum alloys in hydraulic fluid power systems must be in accordance with the requirements of § 58.30–15(f) in subchapter F of this chapter.

PART 183—ELECTRICAL INSTALLATION

Subpart A—General Provisions

Sec.
183.100 Intent.
183.115 Applicability to existing vessels.
183.130 Alternative standards.

Subpart B—General Requirements

183.200 General design, installation, and maintenance requirements.
183.210 Protection from wet and corrosive environments.
183.220 General safety provisions.

Subpart C—Power Sources and Distribution Systems

183.310 Power sources.
183.320 Generators and motors.
183.322 Multiple generators.
183.324 Dual voltage generators.
183.330 Distribution panels and switchboards.
183.340 Cable and wiring requirements.
183.350 Batteries—general.
183.352 Battery categories.
183.354 Battery installations.
183.360 Semiconductor rectifier systems.
183.370 General grounding requirements.
183.372 Equipment and conductor grounding.
183.376 Grounded distribution systems (neutral grounded).
183.378 Ungrounded systems.
183.380 Overcurrent protection.
183.390 Shore power.
183.392 Radiotelephone installations.

Subpart D—Lighting Systems

183.410 Lighting fixtures.
183.420 Navigation lights.
183.430 Portable lights.
183.432 Emergency lighting.

Subpart E—Miscellaneous Systems and Requirements

183.520 Lifeboat winches.
183.530 Hazardous areas.
183.540 Elevators.
183.550 General alarm systems.

AUTHORITY: 46 U.S.C. 2103, 3306; E.O. 12234, 45 FR 58801, 3 CFR, 1980 Comp., p. 277; Department of Homeland Security Delegation No. 0170.1.

SOURCE: CGD 85–080, 61 FR 997, Jan. 10, 1996, unless otherwise noted.

Subpart A—General Provisions

§ 183.100 Intent.

This part contains requirements for the design, construction, installation, and operation of electrical equipment and systems including power sources, lighting, motors, miscellaneous equipment, and safety systems.

§ 183.115 Applicability to existing vessels.

(a) Except as otherwise required by paragraphs (b) and (c) of this section, an existing vessel must comply with the regulations on electrical installations, equipment, and material that were applicable to the vessel on March 10, 1996, or, as an alternative, the vessel may comply with the regulations in this part.

(b) An existing vessel must comply with the requirements of §§ 183.420 and 183.430.

(c) New installations of electrical equipment and material, and the repair or replacement of wire and cable, on an existing vessel, which are completed to the satisfaction of the cognizant Officer in Charge, Marine Inspection (OCMI) on or after March 11, 1996, must comply with this part. Replacement of existing equipment, not including wire or cable, installed on the vessel prior to March 11, 1996 need not comply with the regulations in this part.

§ 183.130 Alternative standards.

(a) A vessel, other than a high speed craft, of not more than 19.8 meters (65 feet) in length carrying not more than 12 passengers, may comply with the following requirements instead of complying with the requirements of this part in their entirety:

(1) Section 183.420; and

(2) The following American Boat and Yacht Council (ABYC) Projects where applicable:

(i) E-8, "Alternating Current (AC) Electrical Systems on Boats;"

(ii) E-9, "Direct Current (DC) Electrical Systems on Boats;" and

(iii) A-16, "Electrical Navigation Lights."

(b) A vessel with an electrical installation operating at less than 50 volts may meet the requirements in 33 CFR 183.430 instead of those in § 183.340 of this part.

[CGD 85-080, 61 FR 997, Jan. 10, 1996; 61 FR 20557, May 7, 1996, as amended by CGD 97-057, 62 FR 51050, Sept. 30, 1997]

Subpart B—General Requirements

§ 183.200 General design, installation, and maintenance requirements.

Electrical equipment on a vessel must be installed and maintained to:

(a) Provide services necessary for safety under normal and emergency conditions;

(b) Protect passengers, crew, other persons, and the vessel from electrical hazards, including fire, caused by or originating in electrical equipment, and electrical shock;

(c) Minimize accidental personnel contact with energized parts; and

(d) Prevent electrical ignition of flammable vapors.

§ 183.210 Protection from wet and corrosive environments.

(a) Electrical equipment used in the following locations must be dripproof:

(1) A machinery space;

(2) A location normally exposed to splashing, water washdown, or other wet conditions within a galley, a laundry, or a public washroom or toilet room that has a bath or shower; or

(3) Another space with a similar moisture level.

(b) Electrical equipment exposed to the weather must be watertight.

(c) Electrical equipment exposed to corrosive environments must be of suitable construction and corrosion-resistant.

§ 183.220 General safety provisions.

(a) Electrical equipment and installations must be suitable for the roll, pitch, and vibration of the vessel underway.

(b) All equipment, including switches, fuses, lampholders, etc., must be suitable for the voltage and current utilized.

(c) Receptacle outlets of the type providing a grounded pole or a specific direct current polarity must be of a configuration that will not permit improper connection.

(d) All electrical equipment and circuits must be clearly marked and identified.

(e) Any cabinet, panel, box, or other enclosure containing more than one source of power must be fitted with a sign warning persons of this condition and identifying the circuits to be disconnected.

Subpart C—Power Sources and Distribution Systems

§ 183.310 Power sources.

(a)(1) Each vessel that relies on electricity to power the following loads must be arranged so that the loads can be energized from two sources of electricity:

(i) The vital systems listed in § 182.710 of this chapter;

(ii) Interior lighting except for decorative lights;

(iii) Communication systems including a public address system required under § 184.610 of this chapter; and

(iv) Navigation equipment and lights.

(2) A vessel with batteries of adequate capacity to supply the loads specified in paragraph (a)(1) of this section for three hours, and a generator or alternator driven by a propulsion engine, complies with the requirement in paragraph (a)(1) of this section.

(b) Where a ship service generator driven by a propulsion engine is used as a source of electrical power, a vessel speed change, throttle movement or

§ 183.320

change in direction of the propeller shaft rotation must not interrupt power to any of the loads specified in paragraph (a)(1) of this section.

§ 183.320 **Generators and motors.**

(a) Each generator and motor must be:

(1) In a location that is accessible, adequately ventilated, and as dry as practicable; and

(2) Mounted above the bilges to avoid damage by splash and to avoid contact with low lying vapors.

(b) Each generator and motor must be designed for an ambient temperature of 50° C (122° F) except that:

(1) If the ambient temperature in the space where a generator or motor will be located will not exceed 40° C (104° F) under normal operating conditions, the generator or motor may be designed for an ambient temperature of 40° C (104° F); and

(2) A generator or motor designed for 40° C (104° F) may be used in 50° C (122° F) ambient locations provided the generator or motor is derated to 80 percent of the full load rating, and the rating or setting of the overcurrent devices is reduced accordingly.

(c) A voltmeter and an ammeter, which can be used for measuring voltage and current of a generator that is in operation, must be provided for a generator rated at 50 volts or more. For each alternating current generator, a means for measuring frequency must also be provided.

(d) Each generator must have a nameplate attached to it containing the information required by Article 445 of the National Electric Code (NEC) (National Fire Protection Association (NFPA) 70), and for a generator derated in accordance with paragraph (b)(2) of this section, the derated capacity.

(e) Each motor must have a nameplate attached to it containing the information required by Article 430 of the NEC (NFPA 70), and for a motor derated in accordance with paragraph (b)(2) of this section, the derated capacity.

(f) Each generator must be protected by an overcurrent device set value not exceeding 115 percent of the generator full load rating.

§ 183.322 **Multiple generators.**

When a vessel is equipped with two or more generators to supply ship's service power, the following requirements must be met:

(a) Each generator must have an independent prime mover; and

(b) The generator circuit breakers must be interlocked to prevent the generators from being simultaneously connected to the switchboard, except for the circuit breakers of a generator operated in parallel with another generator when the installation meets §§ 111.12–11(f) and 111.30–25(d) in subchapter J of this chapter.

§ 183.324 **Dual voltage generators.**

(a) A dual voltage generator installed on a vessel shall be of the grounded type, where:

(1) The neutral of a dual voltage system must be solidly connected at the switchboard's neutral bus; and

(2) The neutral bus shall be connected to ground.

(b) The neutral of a dual voltage system must be accessible for checking the insulation resistance of the generator to ground before the generator is connected to the bus.

(c) Ground detection must be provided that:

(1) For an alternating current system, meets § 111.05–27 in subchapter J of this chapter; and

(2) For a direct current system, meets § 111.05–29 in subchapter J of this chapter.

§ 183.330 **Distribution panels and switchboards.**

(a) Each distribution panel and switchboard must be in as dry a location as practicable, adequately ventilated, and protected from falling debris and dripping or splashing water.

(b) Each distribution panel or switchboard must be totally enclosed and of the dead front type.

(c) Each switchboard must be fitted with a dripshield.

(d) Distribution panels and switchboards that are accessible from the rear must be constructed to prevent a person from accidentally contacting energized parts.

(e) Working space must be provided around all main distribution panels

Coast Guard, DHS § 183.340

and switchboards of at least 610 millimeters (24 inches) in front of the switchboard, and at least 455 millimeters (18 inches) behind the switchboard. Rear access is prohibited when the working space behind the switchboard is less than 455 millimeters (18 inches).

(f) Nonconducting mats or grating must be provided on the deck in front of each switchboard and, if accessible from the rear, on the deck in the rear of the switchboard.

(g) All uninsulated current carrying parts must be mounted on noncombustible, nonabsorbent, high dielectric insulating material.

(h) Equipment mounted on a hinged door of an enclosure must be constructed or shielded so that a person will not accidentally contact energized parts of the door mounted equipment when the door is open and the circuit energized.

(i) In the design of a control, interlock, or indicator circuit, the disconnect device and its connections, including each terminal block for terminating the vessel's wiring, must not have any electrically unshielded or uninsulated surfaces.

(j) Switchboards and distribution panels must be sized in accordance with § 111.30-19(a) in subchapter J of this chapter.

[CGD 85-080, 61 FR 997, Jan. 10, 1996, as amended by CGD 97-057, 62 FR 51050, Sept. 30, 1997]

§ 183.340 Cable and wiring requirements.

(a) If individual wires, rather than cable, are used in systems greater than 50 volts, the wire must be in conduit.

(b) All cable and wire must:

(1) Have stranded copper conductors with sufficient current carrying capacity for the circuit in which they are used;

(2) Be installed in a manner to avoid or reduce interference with radio reception and compass indication;

(3) Be protected from the weather;

(4) Be installed with metal supports spaced not more than 610 millimeters (24 inches) apart, and in such a manner as to avoid chafing and other damage. The use of plastic tie wraps must be limited to bundling or retention of multiple cable installations, and not used as a means of support, except that on vessels of not more than 19.8 meters (65 feet) in length, installations in accordance with paragraph 14.h of ABYC E–8, and paragraph 15.h of ABYC E–9, are acceptable as meeting the requirements of this section;

(5) Not be installed with sharp bends;

(6) Be protected by metal coverings or other suitable means if in areas subject to mechanical abuse. Horizontal pipes used for protection shall have 6 millimeter (.25 inch) holes for drainage every 1,520 millimeters (5 feet);

(7) Be suitable for low temperature and high humidity if installed in refrigerated compartments;

(8) Not be located in a tank unless the cable provides power to equipment in the tank; and

(9) Have sheathing or wire insulation compatible with the fluid in a tank when installed as allowed by paragraph (b)(8) of this section.

(c) Conductors in power and lighting circuits must be No. 14 American Wire Gauge (AWG) or larger. Conductors in control and indicator circuits must be No. 22 AWG or larger.

(d) Cable and wire for power and lighting circuits must:

(1) Meet Section 310–13 of the NEC (NFPA 70), except that asbestos insulated cable and dry location cables cannot be used;

(2) Be listed by Underwriters Laboratories (UL), as UL Boat or UL Marine cable; or

(3) Meet § 111.60–1 in subchapter J of this chapter for cable, and § 111.60–11 in subchapter J of this chapter for wire.

(e) Cable or wire serving vital systems listed in § 182.710 of this chapter or emergency loads must be routed as far as practicable from high risk fire areas, such as galleys, laundries, and machinery spaces.

(f) Cable or wire serving duplicated equipment must be separated so that a casualty that affects one cable does not affect the other.

(g) Each connection to a conductor or terminal part of a conductor must be made within an enclosure and have either:

(1) A pressure type connector on each conductor;

(2) A solder lug on each conductor;

§ 183.340

(3) A splice made with a pressure type connector to a flexible lead or conductor; or

(4) A splice that is soldered, brazed, or welded to a flexible lead or conductor.

(h) A connector or lug of the set screw type must not be used with a stranded conductor smaller than No. 14 AWG except if there is a nonrotating follower that travels with the set screw and makes pressure contact with the conductor.

(i) Each pressure type wire connector and lug must meet UL 486A, "Electric Wire Connectors and Soldering Lugs for Use With Copper Conductors," or other standard specified by the Commandant. The use of twist-on type wire nuts is permitted under the following conditions:

(1) The connections must be made within an enclosure and the insulated cap of the connector must be secured to prevent loosening due to vibration; and

(2) Twist-on type connectors may not be used for making joints in cables, facilitating a conductor splice, or extending the length of a circuit.

(j) Each terminal block must have 6–32 terminal screws or larger.

(k) Wire connectors utilized in conjunction with screw type terminal blocks must be of the captive type such as the ring or the flanged spade type.

(l) A cable must not be spliced in a hazardous location.

(m) A cable may be spliced in a location, other than a hazardous location, under the following conditions:

(1) A cable installed in a subassembly may be spliced to a cable installed in another subassembly;

(2) For a vessel receiving alterations, a cable may be spliced to extend a circuit;

(3) A cable having a large size or exceptional length may be spliced to facilitate its installation; and

(4) A cable may be spliced to replace a damaged section of the cable if, before replacing the damaged section, the insulation resistance of the remainder of the cable is measured, and it is determined that the condition of the insulation is unimpaired.

(n) All material in a cable splice must be chemically compatible with all other material in the splice and with the materials in the cable.

(o) Ampacities of wires must meet Section 310–15 of the NEC (NFPA 70), or other standard specified by the Commandant. Ampacities of cable must meet table A6 of Institute of Electrical and Electronic Engineers (IEEE) Standard 45, "Recommended Practice for Electrical Installations on Shipboard," or other standard specified by the Commandant. Ampacities for Navy cable must meet NAVSEA Design Data Sheet (DDS) 304–2 "Electrical Cable, Ratings and Characteristics" as appropriate.

(p) Conductors for direct current systems must be sized so that the voltage drop at the load terminals does not exceed 10 percent. Table 183.340(p) indicates the size of conductor required for corresponding lengths and steady state (stable) values to obtain not more than this voltage drop at the load terminals of a two conductor circuit.

TABLE 183.340(p)—CONDUCTOR SIZES FOR AMPERES—LENGTHS

Total current on circuit, amperes	Length of conductor in meters (feet) from source of current to most distant fixture									
	3.1(10)	4.5(15)	6.1(20)	7.6(25)	9.2(30)	10.7(35)	12.2(40)	13.7(45)	15.2(50)	16.8(55)	18.3(60)
12-volts, 2 wire—10 percent drop wire sizes (A.W.G.)										
5	14	14	14	14	14	14	14	14	12	12	12
10	14	14	14	12	12	12	10	10	10	10	8
15	14	14	12	10	10	10	8	8	8	8	8
20	12	12	10	10	8	8	8	8	6	6	6
25	10	10	10	8	8	8	6	6	6	6	4

Other values can be computed by means of the following formula:

$$cm = \frac{K \times I \times L (\times 2 \text{ for two-wire circuit})}{E}$$

Coast Guard, DHS § 183.360

Where:

cm = Circular-mil area of conductor
K = 3.28 ohms/mil-meter (metric)
  = 10.75 ohm/mil-foot (english)
  (a constant representing the resistance of copper).
I = Load current, in amperes.
L = length of conductor from center of distribution, in meters (feet).
E = Voltage drop at load, in volts.

(q) If used, each armored cable metallic covering must:

(1) Be electrically continuous; and

(2) Be grounded at each end of the run to:

(i) The metallic hull; or

(ii) The common ground plate on nonmetallic vessels; and

(3) Have final sub-circuits grounded at the supply end only.

(r) A portable or temporary electric cord or cable must be constructed and used in compliance with the requirements of § 111.60–13 in subchapter J of this chapter for a flexible electric cord or cable.

[CGD 85–080, 61 FR 997, Jan. 10, 1996; 61 FR 20557, May 7, 1996, as amended by CGD 97–057, 62 FR 51050, Sept. 30, 1997; CGD 85–080, 62 FR 51358, Sept. 30, 1997]

§ 183.350 Batteries—general.

(a) Where provisions are made for charging batteries, there must be natural or induced ventilation sufficient to dissipate the gases generated.

(b) Each battery must be located as high above the bilge as practicable, secured to protect against shifting with the roll and pitch of the vessel, and free from exposure to water splash or spray.

(c) Batteries must be accessible for maintenance and removal.

(d) Connections must be made to battery terminals with permanent type connectors. Spring clips or other temporary type clamps are prohibited.

(e) Batteries must be mounted in trays lined with, or constructed of, a material that is resistant to damage by the electrolyte.

(f) Battery chargers must have an ammeter connected in the charging circuit.

(g) If the batteries are not adjacent to a distribution panel or switchboard that distributes power to the lighting, motor, and appliance circuits, the battery lead must have a fuse in series as close as practicable to the battery.

(h) Batteries used for engine starting are to be located as close as possible to the engine or engines served.

[CGD 85–080, 61 FR 997, Jan. 10, 1996; 61 FR 20557, May 7, 1996]

§ 183.352 Battery categories.

This section applies to batteries installed to meet the requirements of § 183.310 for secondary sources of power to vital loads, or sources of power to final emergency loads.

(a) *Large.* A large battery installation is one connected to a battery charger having an output of more than 2 kilowatts (kw), computed from the highest possible charging current and the rated voltage of the battery installation.

(b) *Small.* A small battery installation is one connected to a battery charger having an output of 2 kw or less, computed as above.

[CGD 85–080, 61 FR 997, Jan. 10, 1996, as amended by CGD 97–057, 62 FR 51050, Sept. 30, 1997]

§ 183.354 Battery installations.

(a) *Large batteries.* Each large battery installation must be located in a locker, room or enclosed box solely dedicated to the storage of batteries. Ventilation must be provided in accordance with § 111.15–10 in subchapter J of this chapter. Electrical equipment located within the battery enclosure must be approved by an independent laboratory for Class I, Division 1, Group B hazardous locations and meet § 111.105 in subchapter J of this chapter.

(b) *Small batteries.* Each small battery installation must be located in a well ventilated space and protected from falling objects. A small battery installation must not be in a closet, storeroom or similar space.

§ 183.360 Semiconductor rectifier systems.

(a) Each semiconductor rectifier system must have an adequate heat removal system that prevents overheating.

(b) Where a semiconductor rectifier system is used in a propulsion system or in other vital systems it must:

(1) Have a current limiting circuit;

293

§ 183.370

(2) Have external overcurrent protection; and

(3) Meet Sections 35.84.2 and 35.84.4 of the American Bureau of Shipping (ABS), "Rules for Building and Classing Steel Vessels," or other standard specified by the Commandant.

§ 183.370 General grounding requirements.

(a) A vessel's hull must not carry current as a conductor except for the following systems:

(1) Impressed current cathodic protection systems; or

(2) Battery systems for engine starting.

(b) Receptacle outlets and attachment plugs for portable lamps, tools, and similar apparatus operating at 100 volts or more, must have a grounding pole and a grounding conductor in the portable cord.

(c) Each nonmetallic mast and top mast must have a lightning ground conductor.

§ 183.372 Equipment and conductor grounding.

(a) All metallic enclosures and frames of electrical equipment must be permanently grounded to the hull on a metallic vessel. On a nonmetallic vessel, the enclosures and frames of electrical equipment must be bonded together to a common ground by a normally non-current carrying conductor. Metallic cases of instruments and secondary windings of instrument transformers must be grounded.

(b) On a nonmetallic vessel, where a ground plate is provided for radio equipment, it must be connected to the common ground.

(c) Equipment grounding conductors must be sized in accordance with Section 250-95 of the NEC (NFPA 70), or other standard specified by the Commandant.

(d) Each insulated grounding conductor of a cable must be identified by one of the following means:

(1) A green braid or green insulation;

(2) Stripping the insulation from the entire exposed length of the grounding conductor; or

(3) Marking the exposed insulation of the grounding conductor with green tape or green adhesive labels.

46 CFR Ch. I (10-1-04 Edition)

(e) Cable armor must not be used to ground electrical equipment or systems.

§ 183.376 Grounded distribution systems (neutral grounded).

(a) If a grounded distribution system is provided, there must be only one connection to ground, regardless of the number of power sources. This ground connection must be at the switchboard or at the common ground plate, which must be accessible.

(b) Each propulsion, power, lighting, or distribution system having a neutral bus or conductor must have the neutral grounded.

(c) The neutral of each grounded generation and distribution system must be grounded at the generator switchboard and have the ground connection accessible for checking insulation resistance of the generator to ground before the generator is connected to the bus, except the neutral of an emergency power generation system must be grounded with:

(1) No direct ground connection at the emergency switchboard;

(2) The neutral bus permanently connected to the neutral bus on the main switchboard; and

(3) No switch, circuit breaker, or fuse in the neutral conductor of the bus-tie feeder connecting the emergency switchboard to the main switchboard.

(d) On a metallic vessel, a grounded alternating current system must be grounded to the hull. On a nonmetallic vessel, the neutral must be connected to the common ground, except that aluminum grounding conductors must not be used.

§ 183.378 Ungrounded systems.

Each ungrounded system must be provided with a suitably sensitive ground detection system located at the respective switchboard that provides continuous indication of circuit status to ground with a provision to momentarily remove the indicating device from the reference ground.

[CGD 85-080, 62 FR 51358, Sept. 30, 1997]

§ 183.380 Overcurrent protection.

(a) Overcurrent protection must be provided for each ungrounded conductor for the purpose of opening the electric circuit if the current reaches a value that causes an excessive or dangerous temperature in the conductor or conductor insulation.

(b) The grounded conductor of a circuit must not be disconnected by a switch or circuit breaker, unless the ungrounded conductors are simultaneously disconnected.

(c) A conductor of a control, interlock, or indicator circuit, such as a conductor for an instrument, pilot light, ground detector light, or potential transformer, must be protected by an overcurrent device.

(d) Conductors must be protected in accordance with their current carrying capacities. If the allowable current carrying capacity does not correspond to a standard device size, the next larger overcurrent device may be used provided it does not exceed 150 percent of the conductor current carrying capacity.

(e) Steering gear control system circuits must be protected against short circuit.

(f) Each steering gear feeder circuit must be protected by a circuit breaker that meets the requirements of § 58.25-55 in subchapter F of this chapter.

(g) Each lighting branch circuit must be protected against overcurrent either by fuses or circuit breakers rated at not more than 30 amperes.

(h) Overcurrent devices capable of carrying the starting current of the motor must be installed to protect motors, motor conductors, and control apparatus against:

(1) Overcurrent due to short circuits or ground faults; and

(2) Overload due to motor running overcurrent, in accordance with § 111.70-1 in subchapter J of this chapter. A protective device integral with the motor, which is responsive to both motor current and temperature, may be used.

(i) An emergency switch must be provided in the normally ungrounded main supply conductor from a battery. The switch must be accessible and located as close to the battery as practicable.

(j) Disconnect means must be provided on the supply side of and adjacent to all fuses for the purpose of de-energizing the fuses for inspection and maintenance purposes.

(k) If the disconnect means is not within sight of the equipment that the circuit supplies, means must be provided for locking the disconnect device in the open position.

(l) Fuses must be of the cartridge type only and be listed by Underwriters Laboratories or another independent laboratory recognized by the Commandant.

(m) Each circuit breaker must meet UL 489, "Molded—Case Circuit Breakers and Circuit Breaker Enclosures," or other standard specified by the Commandant, and be of the manually reset type designed for:

(1) Inverse time delay;

(2) Instantaneous short circuit protection; and

(3) Switching duty if the breaker is used as a switch.

(n) Each circuit breaker must indicate whether it is in the open or closed position.

[CGD 85–080, 61 FR 997, Jan. 10, 1996, as amended by CGD 97–057, 62 FR 51050, Sept. 30, 1997; USCG–2002–13058, 67 FR 61279, Sept. 30, 2002]

§ 183.390 Shore power.

A vessel with an electrical system operating at more than 50 volts, which is provided with a means to connect to shore power, must meet the following:

(a) A shore power connection box or receptacle must be permanently installed at a convenient location;

(b) A cable connecting the shore power connection box or receptacle to the switchboard or main distribution panel must be permanently installed;

(c) A circuit breaker must be provided at the switchboard or main distribution panel for the shore power connection; and

(d) The circuit breaker, required by paragraph (c) of this section, must be interlocked with the vessel's power sources so that shore power and the vessel's power sources may not be operated simultaneously.

§ 183.392 Radiotelephone installations.

A separate circuit, with overcurrent protection at the main distribution panel, must be provided for each radiotelephone installation.

Subpart D—Lighting Systems

§ 183.410 Lighting fixtures.

(a) Each lighting fixture globe, lens, or diffuser must have a guard or be made of high strength material, except in an accommodation space, radio room, galley, or similar space where it is not subject to damage.

(b) A lighting fixture may not be used as a connection box for a circuit other than the branch circuit supplying the fixture.

(c) A lighting fixture must be installed as follows:

(1) Each fixture must comply with § 183.200.

(2) Each lighting fixture and lampholder must be fixed. A fixture must not be supported by the screw shell of a lampholder.

(3) Each pendant type lighting fixture must be suspended by and supplied through a threaded, rigid conduit stem.

(4) Each table lamp, desk lamp, floor lamp, or similar equipment must be secured in place so that it cannot be displaced by the roll or pitch of the vessel.

(d) An exterior lighting fixture in an electrical system operating at more than 50 volts must comply with the requirements of UL 595, "Marine Type Electric Lighting Fixtures," or other standard specified by the Commandant. A lighting fixture in an accommodation space, radio room, galley or similar interior space may comply with, UL 1570, "Fluorescent Lighting Fixtures," UL 1571, "Incandescent Lighting Fixtures," UL 1572, "High Intensity Discharge Lighting Fixtures," UL 1573, "Stage and Studio Lighting Units," or UL 1574, "Track Lighting Systems," as long as the general marine requirements of UL 595 are satisfied.

§ 183.420 Navigation lights.

All vessels must have navigation lights that are in compliance with the applicable sections of the International and Inland Navigation Rules, except that a vessel of more than 19.8 meters (65 feet) in length must also have navigation lights that meet UL 1104, "Standards for Marine Navigation Lights," or other standard specified by the Commandant.

§ 183.430 Portable lights

Each vessel must be equipped with at least two operable portable battery lights. One of these lights must be located at the operating station and the other at the access to the propulsion machinery space.

§ 183.432 Emergency lighting.

(a) Each vessel must have adequate emergency lighting fitted along the line of escape to the main deck from all passenger and crew accommodation spaces located below the main deck.

(b) The emergency lighting required by paragraph (a) of this section must automatically actuate upon failure of the main lighting system. If a vessel is not equipped with a single source of power for emergency lighting, it must have individual battery powered lights that:

(1) Are automatically actuated upon loss of normal power;

(2) Are not readily portable;

(3) Are connected to an automatic battery charger; and

(4) Have sufficient capacity for a minimum of 2 hours of continuous operation.

[CGD 85–080, 61 FR 997, Jan. 10, 1996, as amended at 62 FR 51358, Sept. 30, 1997]

Subpart E—Miscellaneous Systems and Requirements

§ 183.520 Lifeboat winches.

Each electric power operated lifeboat winch must meet, 111.95 in subchapter J and § 160.015 in subchapter Q of this chapter, or other standard specified by the Commandant.

§ 183.530 Hazardous areas.

(a) Electrical equipment in spaces containing machinery powered by, or fuel tanks for, gasoline or other fuels having a flashpoint of 43.3° C (110° F) or lower must be explosion-proof or ignition-protected, or be part of an intrinsically safe system.

(b) Electrical equipment in lockers used to store paint, oil, turpentine, or other flammable liquids must be explosion-proof or be part of an intrinsically safe system.

(c) Explosion-proof equipment and intrinsically safe systems must meet the

Coast Guard, DHS

requirements of §111.105 in subchapter J of this chapter.

[CGD 85–080, 61 FR 997, Jan. 10, 1996; 61 FR 24465, May 15, 1996]

§183.540 Elevators.

Each elevator on a vessel must meet the requirements of American National Standards Institute (ANSI) A17.1, "Safety Code for Elevators, and Escalators," or other standard specified by the Commandant.

§183.550 General alarm systems.

All vessels with overnight accommodations must be equipped with a general alarm system. The public address system required by §184.610 of this chapter may be used to sound the general alarm signal.

PART 184—VESSEL CONTROL AND MISCELLANEOUS SYSTEMS AND EQUIPMENT

Subpart A—General Provisions

Sec.
184.100 General requirement.
184.115 Applicability to existing vessels.

Subpart B—Cooking and Heating

184.200 General.
184.202 Restrictions.
184.210 Heating equipment.
184.220 Cooking equipment.
184.240 Gas systems.

Subpart C—Mooring and Towing Equipment

184.300 Ground tackle and mooring lines.

Subpart D—Navigation Equipment

184.402 Compasses.
184.404 Radars.
184.410 Electronic position fixing devices.
184.420 Charts and nautical publications.

Subpart E—Radio

184.502 Requirements of the Federal Communications Commission.
184.506 Emergency broadcast placard.
184.510 Recommended emergency broadcast instructions.

Subpart F—Control and Internal Communications Systems

184.602 Internal communications systems.
184.610 Public address systems.

§ 184.200

184.620 Propulsion engine control systems.

Subpart G—Miscellaneous

184.702 Pollution prevention equipment and procedures.
184.704 Marine sanitation devices.
184.710 First-aid kits.

AUTHORITY: 46 U.S.C. 2103, 3306; E.O. 12234, 45 FR 58801, 3 CFR, 1980 Comp., p. 277; Department of Homeland Security Delegation No. 0170.1.

SOURCE: CGD 85–080, 61 FR 1002, Jan. 10, 1996, unless otherwise noted.

Subpart A—General Provisions

§184.100 General requirement.

(a) Vessel control systems and other miscellaneous systems and equipment required by this part must be suitable for the purposes intended.

(b) The cognizant Officer in Charge, Marine Inspection (OCMI) may require navigation, control, or communications equipment, in excess of the equipment specifically required by this part, on a vessel that is of a novel design, operates at high speeds in restricted or high traffic areas, operates in a dynamically supported mode, or operates on extended routes or in remote locations.

§184.115 Applicability to existing vessels.

(a) An existing vessel need not comply with §§184.402(c), 184.404, 184.410, and 184.602 unless the cognizant OCMI specifically requires compliance due to the route or service of the vessel.

(b) An existing vessel need not comply with the requirements of §184.610 until March 11, 2001, or 10 years after its keel was laid or the vessel was at a similar stage of construction, whichever is later.

(c) An existing vessel need not comply with the requirements of §184.710 until March 11, 1997.

Subpart B—Cooking and Heating

§184.200 General.

Cooking and heating equipment must be suitable for marine use. Equipment designed and installed in accordance with American Boat and Yacht Council (ABYC) A–3, "Galley Stoves," and A–7,

§ 184.202

"Boat Heating Systems," or with National Fire Protection Association (NFPA) 302, "Pleasure and Commercial Motor Craft," complies with this requirement, except as restricted by § 184.202 of this part.

§ 184.202 Restrictions.

(a) The use of gasoline for cooking, heating, or lighting is prohibited on all vessels.

(b) Fireplaces or other space heating equipment with open flames are prohibited from being used on all vessels.

(c) Vessels permitted to use liquefied and non-liquefied gases as cooking fuels by 46 CFR part 147 must meet the requirements in § 184.240 of this part. The use of these fuels for cooking, heating, and lighting on ferry vessels is prohibited by part 147 in subchapter N of this chapter.

§ 184.210 Heating equipment.

(a) Each heater must be so constructed and installed as to prevent contact with combustible materials such as towels and clothing.

(b) Each electric space heater must be provided with a thermal cutout to prevent overheating.

(c) Each heater element of an electric space heater must be of an enclosed type, and the element case or jacket must be made of a corrosion resistant material.

§ 184.220 Cooking equipment.

(a) Doors on a cooking appliance must be provided with hinges and locking devices to prevent accidental opening in heavy seas.

(b) A cooking appliance must be installed to prevent movement in heavy seas.

(c) For a grill or similar type of cooking appliance, means must be provided to collect grease or fat and to prevent its spillage on wiring or the deck.

(d) Grab rails must be installed on a cooking appliance when determined by the cognizant OCMI to be necessary for safety.

(e) Sea rails, with suitable barriers to prevent accidental movement of cooking pots, must be installed on a cooking range.

(f) Electric connections for a cooking appliance must be dripproof.

[CGD 85–080, 61 FR 1002, Jan. 10, 1996, as amended at 62 FR 51358, Sept. 30, 1997]

§ 184.240 Gas systems.

Cooking systems using liquefied petroleum gas (LPG) and compressed natural gas (CNG) must meet the following requirements:

(a) The design, installation and testing of each LPG system must meet ABYC A-1, "Marine Liquefied Petroleum Gas (LPG) Systems," Chapter 6 of NFPA 302, or other standard specified by the Commandant.

(b) The design, installation and testing of each CNG system must meet ABYC A-22, "Marine Compressed Natural Gas (CNG) Systems," Chapter 6 of NFPA 302, or other standard specified by the Commandant.

(c) Cooking systems using Chapter 6 of NFPA 302 as the standard must meet the following additional requirements:

(1) The storage or use of CNG containers within the accommodation area, machinery spaces, bilges, or other enclosed spaces is prohibited;

(2) LPG or CNG must be odorized in accordance with ABYC A-1 appendix 4 or A-22 appendix 4, respectively;

(3) The marking and mounting of LPG cylinders must be in accordance with ABYC A-1 appendix 7; and

(4) LPG cylinders must be of the vapor withdrawal type as specified in ABYC A-1 section 1.7.

(d) Continuous pilot lights or automatic glow plugs are prohibited for an LGP or CNG installation using ABYC A-1 or A-22 as the standard.

(e) CNG installation using ABYC A-22 as the standard must meet the following additional requirements:

(1) The storage or use of CNG containers within the accommodation area, machinery spaces, bilges, or other enclosed spaces is prohibited;

(2) CNG cylinders, regulating equipment, and safety equipment must meet the installation, stowage, and testing requirements of paragraph 6-5.12 of NFPA 302.

(3) The use or stowage of stoves with attached CNG cylinders is prohibited as specified in paragraph 6-5.1 of NFPA 302.

Coast Guard, DHS § 184.420

(f) If the fuel supply line of an LPG or CNG system enters an enclosed space on the vessel, a remote shutoff valve must be installed that can be operated from a position adjacent to the appliance. The valve must be located between the fuel tank and the point where the fuel supply line enters the enclosed portion of the vessel. A power operated valve installed to meet this requirement must be of a type that will fail closed.

(g) The following variances from ABYC A–1 section 1.12 are allowed for CNG:

(1) The storage locker or housing access opening need not be in the top.

(2) The locker or housing need not be above the waterline.

(h) The following variances from NFPA 302 are allowed:

(1) The storage locker or housing for CNG tank installations need not be above the waterline as required by paragraph 6–5.12.1.1(a);

(2) Ignition protection need not be provided as required by paragraph 6–5.4.

NOTE TO § 184.240: The ABYC and NFPA standards referenced in this section require the posting of placards containing safety precautions for gas cooking systems.

[CGD 85–080, 61 FR 1002, Jan. 10, 1996, as amended by USCG–2000–7790, 65 FR 58465, Sept. 29, 2000]

Subpart C—Mooring and Towing Equipment

§ 184.300 Ground tackle and mooring lines.

A vessel must be fitted with ground tackle and mooring lines necessary for the vessel to be safely anchored or moored. The ground tackle and mooring lines provided must be satisfactory for the size of the vessel, the waters on which the vessel operates, subject to the approval of the cognizant OCMI.

Subpart D—Navigation Equipment

§ 184.402 Compasses.

(a) Except as otherwise provided in this section every vessel must be fitted with a suitable magnetic compass designed for marine use, to be mounted at the primary operating station.

(b) The following vessels need not be fitted with a compass:

(1) A vessel on a rivers route;

(2) A non-self propelled vessel; and

(3) A vessel operating on short restricted routes on lakes, bays, and sounds.

(c) Except on a vessel limited to daytime operations, the compass must be illuminated.

§ 184.404 Radars.

(a) A vessel must be fitted with a Federal Communications Commission (FCC) type accepted general marine radar system for surface navigation with a radar screen mounted at the primary operating station if:

(1) The vessel is self-propelled;

(2) The vessel has an oceans, coastwise, limited coastwise, or Great Lakes route; and

(3) The vessel carries more than 49 passengers.

(b) A ferry that carries more than 49 passengers on a rivers route not within one mile of land must be fitted with a FCC Type Accepted general marine radar system for surface navigation with a radar screen mounted at the primary operating station.

(c) The radar and its installation must be suitable for the intended speed and route of the vessel.

(d) A vessel operated on a short restricted route need not be fitted with a radar if the cognizant OCMI determines that a radar is not necessary due to the vessel's route and local weather conditions.

§ 184.410 Electronic position fixing devices.

A vessel on an oceans route must be equipped with an electronic position fixing device, capable of providing accurate fixes for the area in which the vessel operates, to the satisfaction of the cognizant OCMI.

[CGD 85–080, 61 FR 1002, Jan. 10, 1996, as amended at 62 FR 51358, Sept. 30, 1997]

§ 184.420 Charts and nautical publications.

(a) As appropriate for the intended voyage, a vessel must carry adequate and up-to-date:

(1) Charts of large enough scale to make safe navigation possible;

§ 184.502

(2) U.S. Coast Pilot or similar publication;
(3) Coast Guard Light List;
(4) Tide tables; and
(5) Current tables, or a river current publication issued by the U.S. Army Corps of Engineers or a river authority.

(b) Extracts from the publications listed above for the areas to be transited may be provided instead of the complete publication.

[CGD 85–080, 61 FR 1002, Jan. 10, 1996, as amended at 62 FR 51358, Sept. 30, 1997]

Subpart E—Radio

§ 184.502 Requirements of the Federal Communications Commission.

A vessel must comply with the applicable requirements for any radio and Electronic Position Indicating Radiobeacon (EPIRB) installations, including the requirements for a station license and installation certificates to be issued by the Federal Communications Commission, as set forth in 47 CFR part 80.

§ 184.506 Emergency broadcast placard.

A durable placard must be posted next to all radiotelephone installations with the emergency broadcast instructions and information, specific to the individual vessel.

[CGD 85–080, 61 FR 1002, Jan. 10, 1996, as amended at 62 FR 51358, Sept. 30, 1997]

§ 184.510 Recommended emergency broadcast instructions.

The following emergency broadcast instructions, when placed on a placard, will satisfy the requirement contained in § 184.506 for an emergency broadcast placard:

(a) Emergency Broadcast Instructions.
(1) Make sure your radiotelephone is on.
(2) Select 156.8 MHz (channel 16 VHF) or 2182 kHz. (Channel 16 VHF and 2182 kHz on SSB are for emergency and calling purposes only.)
(3) Press microphone button and, speaking slowly—clearly—calmly, say:
(i) "MAYDAY—MAYDAY—MAYDAY" for situations involving Immediate Danger to Life and Property; or
(ii) "PAN—PAN—PAN" for urgent situations where there is No Immediate Danger to Life or Property.
(4) Say: "THIS IS (INSERT VESSEL'S NAME), (INSERT VESSEL'S NAME), (INSERT VESSEL'S NAME), (INSERT VESSEL'S CALL SIGN), OVER."
(5) Release the microphone button briefly and listen for acknowledgment. If no one answers, repeat steps 3 & 4.
(6) If there is no acknowledgment, or if the Coast Guard or another vessel responds, say: "MAYDAY" OR "PAN", (INSERT VESSEL'S NAME)."
(7) DESCRIBE YOUR POSITION using latitude and longitude coordinates, LORAN coordinates, or range and bearing from a known point.
(8) STATE THE NATURE OF THE DISTRESS.
(9) GIVE NUMBER OF PERSONS ABOARD AND THE NATURE OF ANY INJURIES.
(10) ESTIMATE THE PRESENT SEAWORTHINESS OF YOUR VESSEL.
(11) BRIEFLY DESCRIBE YOUR VESSEL: (INSERT LENGTH, COLOR, HULL TYPE, TRIM, MASTS, POWER, ANY ADDITIONAL DISTINGUISHING FEATURES).
(12) Say: "I WILL BE LISTENING ON CHANNEL 16/2182."
(13) End message by saying: "THIS IS (INSERT VESSEL'S NAME & CALL SIGN)."
(14) If your situation permits, stand by the radio to await further communications with the Coast Guard or another vessel. If no answer, repeat, then try another channel.

(b) [Reserved]

Subpart F—Control and Internal Communications Systems

§ 184.602 Internal communications systems.

(a) A vessel equipped with pilothouse control must have a fixed means of two-way communications from the operating station to the location where the means of controlling the propulsion machinery, required by § 184.620(a) of this part, is located. Twin screw vessels with pilothouse control for both engines are not required to have a fixed communications system.

(b) A vessel equipped with auxiliary means of steering, required by §182.620 of this subchapter, must have a fixed means of two-way communications from the operating station to the location where the auxiliary means of steering is controlled.

(c) When the propulsion machinery of a vessel cannot be controlled from the operating station, an efficient communications system must be provided between the operating station and the propulsion machinery space.

(d) When the locations addressed in paragraphs (a), (b), and (c) of this section are sufficiently close together, direct voice communications satisfactory to the cognizant OCMI is acceptable instead of the required fixed means of communications.

(e) The OCMI may accept hand held portable radios as satisfying the communications system requirement of this section.

§184.610 Public address systems.

(a) Except as noted in paragraphs (d) and (e) below, each vessel must be equipped with a public address system.

(b) On a vessel of more than 19.8 meters (65 feet) in length, the public address system must be a fixed installation and be audible during normal operating conditions throughout the accommodation spaces and all other spaces normally manned by crew members.

(c) A vessel with more than one passenger deck and a vessel with overnight accommodations must have the public address system operable from the operating station.

(d) On a vessel of not more than 19.8 meters (65 feet) in length, a battery powered bullhorn may serve as the public address system if audible throughout the accommodation spaces of the vessel during normal operating conditions. The bullhorn's batteries are to be continually maintained at a fully charged level by use of a battery charger or other means acceptable to the cognizant OCMI.

(e) On a vessel of not more than 19.8 meters (65 feet) in length carrying not more than 49 passengers, a public address system is not required if a public announcement made from operating station without amplification can be heard throughout the accommodation spaces of the vessel during normal operating conditions, to the satisfaction of the cognizant OCMI.

§184.620 Propulsion engine control systems.

(a) A vessel must have two independent means of controlling each propulsion engine. Control must be provided for the engine speed, direction of shaft rotation, and engine shutdown.

(1) One of the means may be the ability to readily disconnect the remote engine control linkage to permit local operation.

(2) A multiple engine vessel with independent remote propulsion control for each engine need not have a second means of controlling each engine.

(b) In addition to the requirements of paragraph (a), a vessel must have a reliable means for shutting down a propulsion engine, at the main pilothouse control station, which is independent of the engine's speed control.

(c) A propulsion engine control system, including pilothouse control, must be designed so that a loss of power to the control system does not result in an increase in shaft speed or propeller pitch.

Subpart G—Miscellaneous

§184.702 Pollution prevention equipment and procedures.

A vessel must comply with the applicable design, equipment, personnel, procedures, and record requirements of 33 CFR parts 151, 155, and 156.

§184.704 Marine sanitation devices.

A vessel with installed toilet facilities must have a marine sanitation device that complies with 33 CFR part 159.

§184.710 First-aid kits.

A vessel must carry either a first-aid kit approved under approval series 160.041 or a kit with equivalent contents and instructions. For equivalent kits, the contents must be stowed in a suitable, watertight container that is marked "First-Aid Kit". A first-aid kit must be easily visible and readily available to the crew.

[CGD 85-080, 62 FR 51359, Sept. 30, 1997]

PART 185—OPERATIONS

Subpart A—General Provisions

Sec.
185.100 General requirement.
185.115 Applicability to existing vessels.

Subpart B—Marine Casualties and Voyage Records

185.202 Notice of casualty.
185.203 Notice of hazardous conditions.
185.206 Written report of marine casualty.
185.208 Accidents to machinery.
185.210 Alcohol or drug use by individuals directly involved in casualties.
185.212 Mandatory chemical testing following serious marine incidents.
185.220 Records of a voyage resulting in a marine casualty.
185.230 Report of accident to aid to navigation.
185.260 Reports of potential vessel casualty.
185.280 Official Logbook for foreign voyages.

Subpart C—Miscellaneous Operating Requirements

185.304 Navigation underway.
185.315 Verification of vessel compliance with applicable stability requirements.
185.320 Steering gear, controls, and communication system tests.
185.330 Hatches and other openings.
185.335 Loading doors.
185.340 Vessels carrying vehicles.
185.350 Fueling of vessels using fuel having a flash point of 43.3° C (110° F) or lower (such as gasoline).
185.352 Ventilation of gasoline machinery spaces.
185.356 Carriage of hazardous materials.
185.360 Use of auto pilot.

Subpart D—Crew Requirements

185.402 Licenses.
185.410 Watchmen.
185.420 Crew training.

Subpart E—Preparations for Emergencies

185.502 Crew and passenger list.
185.503 Voyage plan.
185.504 Passenger count.
185.506 Passenger safety orientation.
185.508 Wearing of life jackets.
185.510 Emergency instructions.
185.512 Recommended emergency instructions format.
185.514 Station bill.
185.516 Life jacket placards.
185.518 Inflatable survival craft placards.
185.520 Abandon ship and man overboard drills and training.
185.524 Fire fighting drills and training.
185.530 Responsibilities of licensed individuals.

Subpart F—Markings Required

185.602 Hull markings.
185.604 Lifesaving equipment markings.
185.606 Escape hatches and emergency exits.
185.608 Fuel shutoff valves.
185.610 Watertight doors and watertight hatches.
185.612 Fire protection equipment.
185.614 Portable watertight containers for distress flares and smoke signals.

Subpart G—Operational Readiness, Maintenance, and Inspection of Lifesaving Equipment

185.700 Operational readiness.
185.702 Maintenance.
185.704 Maintenance of falls.
185.720 Weekly maintenance and inspections.
185.722 Monthly inspections.
185.724 Quarterly inspections.
185.726 Annual inspections.
185.728 Testing and servicing of Emergency Position Indicating Radiobeacons (EPIRB).
185.730 Servicing of inflatable liferafts, inflatable buoyant apparatus, inflatable life jackets, and inflated rescue boats.
185.740 Periodic servicing of hydrostatic release units.

Subpart H—Penalties

185.900 Penalty for violations.
185.910 Suspension and revocation.

AUTHORITY: 46 U.S.C. 2103, 3306, 6101; E.O. 12234, 45 FR 58801, 3 CFR, 1980 Comp., p. 277; Department of Homeland Security Delegation No. 0170.1.

SOURCE: CGD 85-080, 61 FR 1005, Jan. 10, 1996, unless otherwise noted.

Subpart A—General Provisions

§ 185.100 General requirement.

A vessel must be operated in accordance with applicable laws and regulations and in such a manner as to afford adequate precaution against hazards that might endanger the vessel and the persons being transported.

§ 185.115 Applicability to existing vessels.

(a) An existing vessel need not comply with the hull marking requirements in § 185.602(c) until completion of a vessel's first drydock required by § 176.600 of this subchapter, which occurs after March 11, 1996.

(b) An existing vessel need not comply with the marking requirement in §§ 185.604 and 185.610, where the size and contents of the markings required by these sections vary from the size and contents of required markings on lifesaving equipment, watertight doors, and watertight hatches on the vessel prior to March 11, 1996, until the existing markings are no longer legible as determined by the cognizant Officer in Charge, Marine Inspection (OCMI).

(c) An existing vessel need not comply with the requirements of §§ 185.514, 185.516, and 185.604(i) until completion of the first inspection for certification that occurs after March 11, 1996.

[CGD 85–080, 61 FR 1005, Jan. 10, 1996; 61 FR 24465, May 15, 1996]

Subpart B—Marine Casualties and Voyage Records

§ 185.202 Notice of casualty.

(a) Immediately after the addressing of resultant safety concerns, the owner, agent, master, or person in charge of a vessel involved in a marine casualty shall notify the nearest Marine Safety Office, Marine Inspection Office, or Coast Guard Group Office whenever a vessel is involved in a marine casualty consisting of:

(1) An unintended grounding, or an unintended strike of (allision with) a bridge;

(2) An intended grounding, or an intended strike of a bridge, that creates a hazard to navigation, the environment, or the safety of a vessel, or that meets any criterion of paragraphs (a)(3) through (a)(7) of this section;

(3) Loss of main propulsion or primary steering, or any associated component or control system, that reduces the maneuverability of the vessel;

(4) An occurrence materially and adversely affecting the vessel's seaworthiness or fitness for service or route, including but not limited to fire, flooding, failure of or damage to fixed fire extinguishing systems, lifesaving equipment, auxiliary power generating equipment, or bilge pumping systems;

(5) Loss of life;

(6) Injury that requires professional medical treatment (treatment beyond first aid) and, if the person is engaged or employed on board a vessel in commercial service, which renders the individual unfit to perform his or her routine duties; or

(7) An occurrence not meeting any of the above criteria but causing property damage in excess of $25,000. This damage includes the cost of labor and material to restore the property to its condition before the occurrence, but does not include the cost of salvage, cleaning, gas freeing, drydocking, or demurrage.

(b) A vessel is excluded from the requirements of paragraphs (a)(5) and (a)(6) of this section with respect to the death or injury of shipyard or harbor workers when such accidents are not the result of either a vessel casualty (e.g., collision) or a vessel equipment casualty (e.g., cargo boom failure) and are subject to the reporting requirements of the Occupational Safety and Health Administration (OSHA) in 29 Code of Federal Regulations (CFR) part 1904.

(c) Notice given as required by § 185.203 satisfies the requirement of this section if the marine casualty involves a hazardous condition.

§ 185.203 Notice of hazardous conditions.

Whenever there is a hazardous condition, as defined by § 175.400 of this subchapter, on board the vessel, the owner, master, agent, or person in charge shall immediately notify the Captain of the Port of the port of place of destination and the Captain of the Port of the port or place in which the vessel is located of the hazardous condition.

§ 185.206 Written report of marine casualty.

(a) The owner, master, agent, or person in charge shall, within five days, file a written report of any marine casualty. This written report is in addition to the immediate notice required

§ 185.208

by 185.202. This written report must be delivered to a Coast Guard Marine Safety Office, or Marine Inspection Office. It must be provided on Form CG–2692 (Report of Marine Accident, Injury, or Death), Supplemented as necessary by appended Forms CG–2692A (Barge Addendum) and CG–2692B (Report of Required Chemical Drug and Alcohol Testing Following a Serious Marine Incident).

(b) If filed without delay after the occurrence of the marine casualty, the notice required by paragraph (a) of this section suffices as the notice required by § 185.202.

§ 185.208 Accidents to machinery.

The owner, managing operator, or master shall report damage to a boiler, unfired pressure vessel, or machinery that renders further use of the item unsafe until repairs are made, to the OCMI at the port in which the casualty occurred or nearest the port of first arrival, as soon as practicable after the damage occurs.

§ 185.210 Alcohol or drug use by individuals directly involved in casualties.

(a) For each marine casualty required to be reported by § 185.202, the owner, agent, master, or person in charge of the vessel shall determine whether there is any evidence of alcohol or drug use by individuals directly involved in the casualty.

(b) The owner, agent, master, or person in charge of the vessel shall include in the written report, Form CG 2692, submitted for the casualty information that:

(1) Identifies those individuals for whom evidence of drug or alcohol use, or evidence of intoxication, has been obtained; and

(2) Specifies the method used to obtain such evidence, such as personal observation of the individual, or by chemical testing of the individual.

(c) An entry must be made in the Official Logbook if carried, pertaining to those individuals for whom evidence of intoxication is obtained. The individual shall be informed of this entry and the entry shall be witnessed by a second person.

(d) If an individual directly involved in a casualty refuses to submit to, or cooperate in, the administration of a timely chemical test, when directed by a Coast Guard commissioned, warrant, or petty officer, or any other law enforcement officer authorized to obtain a chemical test under Federal, state, or local law, or by the owner, agent, master, or person in change, this fact must be noted in the Official Logbook, if carried, and in the written report (Form CG 2692), and will be admissible as evidence in any administrative proceeding.

[CGD 85–080, 61 FR 1005, Jan. 10, 1996, as amended by CGD 97–057, 62 FR 51050, Sept. 30, 1997]

§ 185.212 Mandatory chemical testing following serious marine incidents.

A marine employer whose vessel is involved in a casualty or incident that is, or is likely to become, a serious marine incident as defined in § 4.03–2 of subchapter A of this chapter shall comply with the requirements of § 4.06 in subchapter A of this chapter.

§ 185.220 Records of a voyage resulting in a marine casualty.

The owner, agent, master, or person in charge of any vessel involved in a marine casualty for which a report is required under § 185.202 of this part shall retain all voyage records maintained by the vessel, including rough and smooth deck and engine room logs, bell books, navigation charts, navigation work books, compass deviation cards, gyrocompass records, stowage plans, records of draft, aids to mariners, night order books, radiograms sent and received, radio logs, crew and passenger lists and counts, articles of shipment, official logs, and other material that might be of assistance in investigating and determining the cause of the casualty. The owner, agent, master, other officer, or person responsible for the custody thereof, shall make these records available upon request, to a duly authorized investigating officer, administrative law judge, officer or employee of the Coast Guard.

[CGD 85–080, 61 FR 1005, Jan. 10, 1996, as amended by CGD 97–057, 62 FR 51050, Sept. 30, 1997]

§ 185.230 Report of accident to aid to navigation.

Whenever a vessel collides with a buoy, or other aid to navigation under the jurisdiction of the Coast Guard, or is connected with any such collision, the person in charge of such vessel shall report the accident to the nearest OCMI. No report on Form CG 2692 is required unless otherwise required under 185.202.

§ 185.260 Reports of potential vessel casualty.

(a) An owner, charterer, managing operator, or agent of a vessel shall immediately notify either of the following Coast Guard offices if there is reason to believe the vessel is lost or imperiled:

(1) The Coast Guard district rescue coordination center (RCC) cognizant over the area in which the vessel was last operating; or

(2) The Coast Guard search and rescue authority nearest to where the vessel was last operating.

(b) Reasons for belief that a vessel is in distress include, but are not limited to, lack of communication with or nonappearance of the vessel.

(c) The owner, charterer, managing operator, or agent notifying the Coast Guard under paragraph (a) of this section, shall provide the name and identification number of the vessel, a description of the vessel, the names or number of individuals on board, and other information that may be requested by the Coast Guard.

§ 185.280 Official Logbook for foreign voyages.

(a) Every vessel on a voyage from a port in the United States to a foreign port except to a port in Canada, or vice versa, must have an Official Logbook.

(b) The master shall make or have made in the Official Logbook the following entries:

(1) Each legal conviction of a seaman of the vessel and the punishment inflicted;

(2) Each offense committed by a seaman of the vessel for which it is intended to prosecute or to enforce under a forfeiture, together with statements about reading the entry and the reply made to the charge as required by 46 U.S.C. 11502;

(3) A statement of the conduct, character, and qualifications of each seaman of the vessel or a statement that the master declines to give an opinion about that conduct, character, and qualifications;

(4) Each illness of or injury to a seaman of the vessel, the nature of the illness or injury, and the medical treatment;

(5) Each death on board, with the cause of death, and if a seaman, the information required by 46 U.S.C. 10702:

(i) The wages due to a seaman who dies during the voyage and the gross amount of all deductions to be made from the wages;

(ii) The sale of the property of a seaman who dies during the voyage, including a statement of each article sold and the amount received for the property;

(6) Each birth on board, with the sex of the infant and the name of the parents;

(7) Each marriage on board, with the names and ages of the parties;

(8) The name of each seaman who ceases to be a crew member (except by death), with the place, time, manner, and the cause why the seaman ceased to be a crew member;

(9) When a marine casualty occurs, a statement about the casualty and the circumstances under which it occurred, made immediately after the casualty when practicable to do so.

Subpart C—Miscellaneous Operating Requirements

§ 185.304 Navigation underway.

(a) The movement of vessel shall be under the direction and control of the master or a licensed mate at all times. The master shall operate the vessel keeping the safety of the passengers and crew foremost in mind by directing the vessel in order to prevent a casualty. Special attention should be paid to:

(1) The current(s) velocity and direction of the transiting area;

(2) Tidal state;

(3) Prevailing visibility and weather conditions;

(4) Density of marine traffic;

§ 185.315

(5) Potential damage caused by own wake;

(6) The danger of each closing visual or radar contact;

(7) Vessel's handling characteristics; and

(8) Magnetic variation and deviation errors of the compass.

(b) [Reserved]

[CGD 85-080, 61 FR 1005, Jan. 10, 1996, as amended at 62 FR 51359, Sept. 30, 1997]

§ 185.315 Verification of vessel compliance with applicable stability requirements.

After loading and prior to departure and at all other times necessary to assure the safety of the vessel, the master shall determine that the vessel complies with all applicable stability requirements in the vessel's trim and stability book, stability letter, Certificate of Inspection, and Load Line Certificate, as the case may be. The vessel may not depart until it is in compliance with these requirements.

§ 185.320 Steering gear, controls, and communication system tests.

The master of a vessel shall have examined and tested the steering gear, signaling whistle, propulsion controls, and communication systems of the vessel prior to getting underway for a voyage, except that such examination and testing need not be conducted more than once in any 24 hour period.

§ 185.330 Hatches and other openings.

(a) Except when operating on lakes, bays, and sounds, or rivers routes in calm weather, all hatches and openings in the hull, except loading doors, of a vessel must be kept tightly closed except when being used.

(b) All watertight doors in subdivision bulkheads must be kept tightly closed during the navigation of the vessel except when being used for transit between compartments.

§ 185.335 Loading doors.

(a) Except as allowed by paragraph (b) of this section, the master of a vessel fitted with loading doors shall assure that all loading doors are closed and secured during the entire voyage.

(b) Loading doors, other than bow visors, may be opened when operating in protected or partially protected waters, provided the master of the vessel determines that the safety of the vessel is not impaired.

(c) For the purpose of this section, "loading doors" include all weathertight ramps, bow visors, and openings used to load personnel, equipment, and stores, in the collision bulkhead, the side shell, and the boundaries of enclosed superstructures that are continuous with the shell of the vessel.

[CGD 85-080, 61 FR 1005, Jan. 10, 1996, as amended at 62 FR 51359, Sept. 30, 1997]

§ 185.340 Vessels carrying vehicles.

(a) Automobiles or other vehicles must be stowed in such a manner as to permit both passengers and crew to get out and away from the vehicles freely in the event of fire or other disaster. The decks, where necessary, must be distinctly marked with painted lines to indicate the vehicle runways and the aisle spaces.

(b) The master shall take any necessary precautions to see that automobiles or other vehicles have their motors turned off and their emergency brakes set when the vessel is underway, and that the motors are not started until the vessel is secured to the landing. In addition, a vehicle at each end of a line of vehicles or next to a loading ramp must have its wheels securely blocked, while the vessel is being navigated.

(c) The master shall have appropriate "NO SMOKING" signs posted and shall take all necessary precautions to prevent smoking or carrying of lighted or smoldering pipes, cigars, cigarettes, or similar items in the deck area assigned to automobiles or other vehicles.

(d) The master shall, prior to getting underway, ensure that vehicles are properly distributed consistent with the guidance in the vessel's stability letter and Certificate of Inspection, if applicable.

§ 185.350 Fueling of vessels using fuel having a flash point of 43.3 °C (110 °F) or lower (such as gasoline).

A vessel must not take on fuel having a flash point of 43.3 °C (110 °F) or lower when passengers are on board.

§ 185.352 Ventilation of gasoline machinery spaces.

The mechanical exhaust for the ventilation of a gasoline machinery space, required by § 182.460(a)(1)(ii) of this chapter, must be operated prior to starting gasoline engines for the time sufficient to insure at least one complete change of air in the space served.

§ 185.356 Carriage of hazardous materials.

A vessel that transports a hazardous material, listed in 49 CFR 172.101, in commerce shall ensure the material is handled and transported in accordance with 49 CFR parts 171 and 176.

[CGD 85–080, 61 FR 1005, Jan. 10, 1996, as amended at 62 FR 51359, Sept. 30, 1997]

§ 185.360 Use of auto pilot.

Whenever an automatic pilot is used the master shall ensure that:

(a) It is possible to immediately establish manual control of the vessel's steering;

(b) A competent person is ready at all times to take over steering control; and

(c) The changeover from automatic to manual steering and vice versa is made by, or under the supervision of, the master or the mate on watch.

Subpart D—Crew Requirements

§ 185.402 Licenses.

Each licensed individual employed upon any vessel subject to the provisions of this subchapter shall have his or her license on board and available for examination at all times when the vessel is operating.

§ 185.410 Watchmen.

The owner, charterer, master, or managing operator of a vessel carrying overnight passengers shall have a suitable number of watchmen patrol throughout the vessel during the nighttime, whether or not the vessel is underway, to guard against, and give alarm in case of, a fire, man overboard, or other dangerous situation.

[CGD 85–080, 61 FR 1005, Jan. 10, 1996, as amended at 62 FR 51359, Sept. 30, 1997]

§ 185.420 Crew training.

(a) The owner, charterer, master or managing operator shall instruct each crew member, upon first being employed and prior to getting underway for the first time on a particular vessel and at least once every three months, as to the duties that the crew member is expected to perform in an emergency including, but not limited to, the emergency instructions listed on the emergency instruction placard required by § 185.510 of this part and, when applicable, the duties listed in the station bill required by § 185.514 of this part.

(b) Training conducted on a sister vessel may be considered equivalent to the initial and quarterly training requirements contained in paragraph (a) of this section.

(c) Crew training shall be logged or otherwise documented for review by the Coast Guard upon request. The training entry shall include the following information.

(1) Date of the training; and

(2) General description of the training topics.

[CGD 85–080, 61 FR 1005, Jan. 10, 1996, as amended at 62 FR 51359, Sept. 30, 1997]

Subpart E—Preparations for Emergencies

§ 185.502 Crew and passenger list.

(a) The owner, charterer, managing operator, or master of the following vessels must keep a correct list of the names of all persons that embark on and disembark from the vessel:

(1) A vessel making a coastwise or oceans voyage where:

(i) Passengers embark or disembark from the vessel to another vessel or port other than at the port of origin; or

(ii) Passengers are carried overnight;

(2) A vessel making a voyage of more than 300 miles on the Great Lakes, except from a Canadian to a United States port; and

(3) A vessel arriving from a foreign port, except at a United States Great Lakes port from a Canadian Great Lakes port.

(b) The master of a vessel required to prepare a crew and passenger list by paragraph (a) of this section shall see

§ 185.503

that the list is prepared prior to departing on a voyage. The list must be communicated verbally or in writing ashore at the vessel's normal berthing location or with a representative of the owner or managing operator of the vessel. The crew and passenger list shall be available to the Coast Guard upon request.

§ 185.503 Voyage plan.

(a) The master of the following vessels shall prepare a voyage plan:

(1) A vessel making an oceans or coastwise voyage;

(2) A vessel making a voyage of more than 300 miles on the Great Lakes, except from a Canadian to a United States port;

(3) A vessel, with overnight accommodations for passengers, making an overnight voyage; and

(4) A vessel arriving from a foreign port, except at a United States Great Lakes port from a Canadian Great Lakes port.

(b) The voyage plan required by paragraph (a) of this section must be prepared prior to departing on a voyage and communicated verbally or in writing, ashore at the vessel's normal berthing location or with a representative of the owner or managing operator of the vessel. The voyage plan shall be available to the Coast Guard upon request.

§ 185.504 Passenger count.

The master of a vessel, except a vessel listed in § 185.502(a) of this part, shall keep a correct, written count of all passengers that embark on and disembark from the vessel. Prior to departing on a voyage, the passenger count must be communicated verbally or in writing, and available ashore at the vessel's normal berthing location or with a representative of the owner or managing operator of the vessel. The passenger count shall be available to the Coast Guard upon request.

§ 185.506 Passenger safety orientation.

(a) Except as allowed by paragraphs (b) and (c) of this section, before getting underway on a voyage or as soon as practicable thereafter, the master of a vessel shall ensure that suitable public announcements are made informing all passengers of the following:

(1) The location of emergency exits, survival craft embarkation areas, and ring life buoys;

(2) The stowage location(s) of life jackets;

(3) Either:

(i) The proper method of donning and adjusting life jackets of the type(s) carried on the vessel including a demonstration of the proper donning of a lifejacket, or

(ii) That passengers may contact a crew member for a demonstration as appropriate, prior to beginning an oceans or coastwise voyage;

(4) The location of the instruction placards for life jackets and other lifesaving devices;

(5) That all passengers will be required to don life jackets when possible hazardous conditions exist, as directed by the master; and

(6) If the vessel is operating with reduced manning or equipment requirements in § 176.114 of this chapter.

(b) As an alternative to an announcement that complies with paragraph (a) of this section, the master or other designated person may—

(1) Prior to getting underway, deliver to each passenger or, on a vessel that does not carry vehicles and that has seats for each passenger, place near each seat, a card or pamphlet that has the information listed in paragraphs (a)(1) through (a)(6) of this section; and

(2) Make an abbreviated announcement consisting of:

(i) A statement that passengers should follow the instructions of the crew in an emergency;

(ii) The location of life jackets; and

(iii) That further information concerning emergency procedures including the donning of life jackets, location of other emergency equipment, and emergency evacuation procedures are located on the card or pamphlet that was given to each passenger or is located near each seat.

(c) Ferries operating on short runs of less than 15 minutes may substitute bulkhead placards or signs for the announcement required in paragraphs (a) and (b) of this section if the OCMI determines that the announcements are

Coast Guard, DHS § 185.512

not practical due to the vessel's unique operation.

(d) The master of a vessel shall ensure that a passenger, who boards the vessel on a voyage after the initial public announcement has been made as required by paragraphs (a) or (b) of this section, is also informed of the required safety information.

(e) On a vessel on a voyage of more than 24 hours duration, passengers shall be requested to don life jackets and go to the appropriate embarkation station during the safety orientation. If only a small number of passengers embark at a port after the original muster has been held, these passengers must be given the passenger safety orientation required by paragraphs (a) or (b) of this section if another muster is not held.

[CGD 85–080, 61 FR 1005, Jan. 10, 1996; 61 FR 20557, May 7, 1996, as amended by CGD 97–057, 62 FR 51050, Sept. 30, 1997; CGD 85–080, 62 FR 51359, Sept. 30, 1997]

§ 185.508 Wearing of life jackets.

(a) The master of a vessel shall require passengers to don life jackets when possible hazardous conditions exist, including, but not limited to:

(1) When transiting hazardous bars and inlets;

(2) During severe weather;

(3) In event of flooding, fire, or other events that may possibly call for evacuation; and

(4) When the vessel is being towed, except a non-self-propelled vessel under normal operating conditions.

(b) The master or crew shall assist each passenger in obtaining a life jacket and donning it, as necessary.

§ 185.510 Emergency instructions.

(a) The master and crew of a vessel will be familiar with the content of and have mounted at the operating station, emergency instructions containing the actions to be taken in the event of fire, heavy weather, or man overboard conditions.

(b) Except when in the judgment of the cognizant OCMI the operation of a vessel does not present one of the hazards listed, the emergency instruction placard should contain at least the applicable portions of the "Emergency Instructions" listed in § 185.512. The emergency instructions must be designed to address the particular equipment, arrangement, and operation of each individual vessel.

(c) If the cognizant OCMI determines that there is no suitable mounting surface aboard the vessel, the emergency instructions need not be posted but must be carried aboard the vessel and be available to the crew for familiarization.

§ 185.512 Recommended emergency instructions format.

An emergency instruction placard containing the following information will satisfy the requirements of § 185.510.

(a) *Emergency instructions*—(1) *Rough weather at sea, crossing hazardous bars, or flooding.* (i) Close all watertight and weathertight doors, hatches, and airports to prevent taking water aboard or further flooding in the vessel.

(ii) Keep bilges dry to prevent loss of stability due to water in bilges. Use power driven bilge pump, hand pump, and buckets to dewater.

(iii) Align fire pumps to use as bilge pump if possible.

(iv) Check all intake and discharge lines, which penetrate the hull, for leakage.

(v) Passengers must remain seated and evenly distributed.

(vi) Passengers must don life jackets if the going becomes very rough, the vessel is about to cross a hazardous bar, or when otherwise instructed by the master.

(vii) Never abandon the vessel unless actually forced to do so.

(viii) If assistance is needed follow the procedures on the emergency broadcast placard posted by the radiotelephone.

(ix) Prepare survival craft (life floats, (inflatable) rafts, (inflatable) buoyant apparatus, boats) for launching.

(2) *Man overboard.* (i) Throw a ring buoy overboard as close to the person as possible.

(ii) Post a lookout to keep the person overboard in sight.

(iii) Launch rescue boat and maneuver to pick up person in the water, or maneuver the vessel to pick up the person in the water.

§ 185.514

(iv) Have crew member put on life jacket, attach a safety line to him or her, and have him or her stand by jump into the water to assist the person overboard if necessary.

(v) If person is not immediately located, notify Coast Guard and other vessels in vicinity by radiotelephone.

(vi) Continue search until released by Coast Guard.

(3) *Fire.* (i) Cut off air supply to fire—close items such as hatches, ports, doors, ventilators, and louvers, and shut off ventilation system.

(ii) Cut off electrical system supplying affected compartment if possible.

(iii) If safe, immediately use portable fire extinguishers at base of flames for flammable liquid or grease fires or water for fires in ordinary combustible materials. Do not use water on electrical fires.

(iv) If fire is in machinery spaces, shut off fuel supply and ventilation and activate fixed extinguishing system if installed.

(v) Maneuver vessel to minimize effect of wind on fire.

(vi) If unable to control fire, immediately notify the Coast Guard and other craft in the vicinity by radiotelephone.

(vii) Move passengers away from fire, have them put on life jackets, and if necessary, prepare to abandon the vessel.

(b) [Reserved]

§ 185.514 Station bill.

(a) A station bill must be posted by the master on a vessel of more than 19.8 meters (65 feet) in length having a Certificate of Inspection requiring more than four crew members at any one time, including the master.

(b) The station bill required by paragraph (a) of this section must set forth the special duties and duty station of each crew member for various emergencies. The duties must, as far as possible, be comparable with the regular work of the individual. The duties must include at least the following and any other duties necessary for the proper handling of a particular emergency:

(1) The closing of hatches, airports, watertight doors, vents, scuppers, and valves for intake and discharge lines that penetrate the hull, the stopping of fans and ventilating systems, and the operating of all safety equipment;

(2) The preparing and launching of survival craft and rescue boats;

(3) The extinguishing of fire; and

(4) The mustering of passengers including the following:

(i) Warning the passengers;

(ii) Assembling the passengers and directing them to their appointed stations; and

(iii) Keeping order in the passageways and stairways and generally controlling the movement of the passengers.

(c) The station bill must be posted at the operating station and in a conspicuous location in each crew accommodation space.

§ 185.516 Life jacket placards.

(a) Placards containing instructions for the donning and use of the life jackets aboard the vessel must be posted in conspicuous places that are regularly accessible and visible to the crew and passengers.

(b) If the cognizant OCMI determines that there is no suitable mounting surface aboard the vessel, the life jacket placards need not be posted but must be carried aboard the vessel and be available to the crew and passengers for familiarization.

§ 185.518 Inflatable survival craft placards.

(a) Every vessel equipped with an inflatable survival craft must have approved placards or other cards containing instructions for launching and inflating inflatable survival craft for the information of persons on board posted in conspicuous places by each inflatable survival craft.

(b) Under the requirement in § 160.051–6(c)(1) of this chapter, the manufacturer of approved inflatable liferafts is required to provide approved placards containing such instructions with each liferaft. Similar placards must be used for other inflatable survival craft.

[CGD 85–080, 61 FR 1005, Jan. 10, 1996, as amended by CGD 97–057, 62 FR 51050, Sept. 30, 1997; CGD 85–080, 62 FR 51359, Sept. 30, 1997]

§ 185.520 Abandon ship and man overboard drills and training.

(a) The master shall conduct sufficient drills and give sufficient instructions to make sure that all crew members are familiar with their duties during emergencies that necessitate abandoning ship or the recovery of persons who have fallen overboard.

(b) Each abandon ship drill must include:

(1) Summoning the crew to report to assigned stations and prepare for assigned duties;

(2) Summoning passengers on a vessel on an overnight voyage to muster stations or embarkation stations and ensuring that they are made aware of how the order to abandon ship will be given;

(3) Checking that life jackets are correctly donned;

(4) Operation of any davits used for launching liferafts; and

(5) Instruction on the automatic and manual deployment of survival craft.

(c) Each abandon ship drill must, as far as practicable, be conducted as if there were an actual emergency.

(d) Each rescue boat required in accordance with § 180.210 of this chapter must be launched with its assigned crew aboard and maneuvered in the water as if during an actual man overboard situation:

(1) Once each month, if reasonable and practicable; but

(2) At least once within a 3 month period before the vessel gets underway with passengers.

(e) Onboard training in the use of davit launched liferafts must take place at intervals of not more than 3 months on a vessel with a davit launched liferaft.

(f) Abandon ship and man overboard drills and training shall be logged or otherwise documented for review by the Coast Guard upon request. The drill entry shall include the following information:

(1) Date of the drill and training; and

(2) General description of the drill scenario and training topics.

§ 185.524 Fire fighting drills and training.

(a) The master shall conduct sufficient fire drills to make sure that each crew member is familiar with his or her duties in case of a fire.

(b) Each fire drill must include:

(1) Summoning passengers on a vessel on an overnight voyage to muster or embarkation stations;

(2) Summoning the crew to report to assigned stations and to prepare for and demonstrate assigned duties; and

(3) Instruction in the use and location of fire alarms, extinguishers, and any other fire fighting equipment on board.

(c) Each fire drill must, as far as practicable, be conducted as if there were an actual emergency.

(d) Fire fighting drills and training shall be logged or otherwise documented for review by the Coast Guard upon request. The drill entry shall include the following information:

(1) Date of the drill and training; and

(2) General description of the drill scenario and training topics.

[CGD 85–080, 61 FR 1005, Jan. 10, 1996, as amended at 62 FR 51359, Sept. 30, 1997]

§ 185.530 Responsibilities of licensed individuals.

Nothing in the emergency instructions or a station bill required by this subpart exempts any licensed individual from the exercise of good judgment in an emergency situation.

Subpart F—Markings Required

§ 185.602 Hull markings.

(a) Each vessel must be marked as required by part 67, subpart I, of this chapter.

(b) Paragraphs (c) through (g) of this section apply to each vessel that fits into any one of the following categories:

(1) A vessel of more than 19.8 meters (65 feet) in length.

(2) A vessel authorized to carry more than 12 passengers on an international voyage.

(3) A vessel with more than 1 deck above the bulkhead deck exclusive of a pilot house.

(c) Each vessel that complies with the stability requirements of §§ 170.170, 170.173, 171.050, 171.055, and 171.057 of this chapter, or in accordance with § 178.310 of this chapter, must—

§ 185.604

(1) Have permanent draft marks at each end of the vessel; or

(2) Have permanent loading marks placed on each side of the vessel forward and aft to indicate the maximum allowable trim and amidships to indicate the maximum allowable draft.

(d) A loading mark required by paragraph (c)(2) of this section must be a horizontal line of at least 205 millimeters (8 inches) in length and 25 millimeters (1 inch) in height, with its upper edge passing through the point of maximum draft. The loading mark must be painted in a contrasting color to the sideshell paint.

(e) On a vessel that has a load line, the amidships marks required by paragraph (c)(2) of this section must be those required by the International Convention on Load Lines, 1966.

(f) In cases where draft marks are obscured due to operational constraints or by protrusions, the vessel must be fitted with a reliable draft indicating system from which the bow and stern drafts can be determined.

(g) On a vessel on which the number of passengers permitted on upper decks is limited by stability criteria, as indicated by the vessel's stability letter, the maximum number of passengers allowed on an upper deck must be indicated by a durable marking of at least 25 millimeters (1 inch) numbers and letters at the entranceway to that deck.

[CGD 85–080, 62 FR 51359, Sept. 30, 1997]

§ 185.604 Lifesaving equipment markings.

(a) The name of a vessel must be marked or painted in clearly legible letters and numbers:

(1) On each side of the bow of each rescue boat; and

(2) On each life float and buoyant apparatus.

(b) Each life jacket, immersion suit, and ring life buoy must be marked in clearly legible block capital letters with the vessel's name. The marking is not required on a life jacket carried to meet a temporary need for additional life jackets, if the life jacket has the name of another vessel or company marked on it. For an immersion suit, the name of the person to whom the immersion suit is assigned is an acceptable alternative to the name of the vessel.

(c) The name of the vessel must be marked or painted in clearly legible letters on each Emergency Position Indicating Radiobeacon (EPIRB), except on an EPIRB in an inflatable liferaft.

(d) The number of persons capacity must be marked or painted in clearly legible letters and numbers on each side of the bow of each rescue boat.

(e) The number of persons capacity must be marked or painted in clearly legible letters and numbers on each life float and buoyant apparatus. This number must:

(1) Be the number of persons the device is equipped for; and

(2) Not be greater than the number of persons the device is approved for as shown on its nameplate.

(f) The number and identification of the items stowed inside, and their sizes, must be marked in clearly legible letters and numbers on each container for life jackets and immersion suits. Identification of the items may be in words, or the appropriate symbols in International Maritime Organization (IMO) Resolution A.760(18), "Symbols Related to Life-Saving Appliances and Arrangements." Letters and numbers must be at least 50 millimeters (2 inches) high. Symbols must be at least 100 mm (4 inches) square.

(g) The name of the vessel must be marked or painted in clearly legible letters on each life float paddle.

(h) Each life jacket must be marked with Type I retroreflective material approved in accordance with § 164.018 in subchapter Q of this chapter, or other standard specified by the Commandant. The arrangement of the retroreflective material applied after March 11, 1996, must be as specified by IMO Resolution A.658(16), "Use and Fitting Of Retro-Reflective Materials on Life-Saving Appliances."

(i) Each rescue boat and ring life buoy must be marked with Type II retroreflective material approved in accordance with § 164.018 in subchapter Q of this chapter, or other standard specified by the Commandant. The arrangement of the retroreflective material applied after March 11, 1996, must be as specified by IMO Resolution A.658(16).

[CGD 85–080, 61 FR 1005, Jan. 10, 1996, as amended at 62 FR 51359, Sept. 30, 1997; 62 FR 64306, Dec. 5, 1997]

§ 185.606 Escape hatches and emergency exits.

All escape hatches and other emergency exits used as means of escape must be marked on both sides in clearly legible letters at least 50 millimeters (2 inches) high: "EMERGENCY EXIT, KEEP CLEAR", unless such markings are deemed unnecessary by the cognizant OCMI.

§ 185.608 Fuel shutoff valves.

Remote fuel shutoff stations must be marked in clearly legible letters at least 25 millimeters (1 inch) high indicating purpose of the valve and direction of operation.

§ 185.610 Watertight doors and watertight hatches.

Watertight doors and watertight hatches must be marked on both sides in clearly legible letters at least 25 millimeters (1 inch) high: "WATERTIGHT DOOR—KEEP CLOSED" or "WATERTIGHT HATCH—KEEP CLOSED", unless such markings are deemed unnecessary by the cognizant OCMI.

§ 185.612 Fire protection equipment.

(a) Complete but simple instructions for the operation of a fixed gas fire extinguishing system must be located in a conspicuous place at or near each pull box and stop valve control and in the space where the extinguishing agent cylinders are stored. If the storage cylinders are separate from the protected space, the instructions must also include a schematic diagram of the system and instructions detailing alternate methods of releasing the extinguishing agent should the local manual release or stop valve controls fail to operate. Each control valve to a distribution line must be marked to indicate the space served.

(b) An alarm for a fixed gas fire extinguishing system must be clearly and conspicuously marked "WHEN ALARM SOUNDS-VACATE AT ONCE. CARBON DIOXIDE BEING RELEASED". Where a different extinguishing agent is installed, that agent shall be marked in place of "carbon dioxide."

(c) Each distribution line valve of a fixed gas fire extinguishing system and the fire main, must be plainly, conspicuously, and permanently marked indicating the space served.

(d) An alarm for an automatic sprinkler system must be conspicuously marked in clearly legible letters "SPRINKLER ALARM".

(e) An alarm bell for a smoke detecting system must be conspicuously marked in clearly legible letters "SMOKE DETECTION ALARM".

(f) A control cabinet or space containing valves, manifolds, or controls for any fixed gas fire extinguishing system must be conspicuously marked in clearly legible letters "CARBON DIOXIDE FIRE EXTINGUISHING APPARATUS", or as otherwise required by the cognizant OCMI. Where a different extinguishing agent is installed, that agent shall be marked in place of "carbon dioxide."

§ 185.614 Portable watertight containers for distress flares and smoke signals.

Portable watertight containers for distress flares and smoke signals shall be of a bright color, and containers shall be clearly marked in legible contrasting letters at least 12.7 millimeters (0.5 inches) high: "DISTRESS SIGNALS".

[CGD 85–080, 61 FR 1005, Jan. 10, 1996; 61 FR 24465, May 15, 1996]

Subpart G—Operational Readiness, Maintenance, and Inspection of Lifesaving Equipment

§ 185.700 Operational readiness.

(a) Each launching appliance and each survival craft and rescue boat on a vessel must be in good working order and ready for immediate use before the vessel leaves port and at all times when the vessel is underway.

(b) Each deck where survival craft or rescue boats are stowed or boarded must be kept clear of obstructions that would interfere with the boarding and

§ 185.702

launching of the survival craft or rescue boat.

§ 185.702 Maintenance.

(a) The manufacturer's instructions for onboard maintenance of survival craft, rescue boats, and launching appliances, manufactured on or after March 11, 1996, must be onboard a vessel of more than 19.8 meters (65 feet) in length and readily available for a vessel of not more than 19.8 meters (65 feet) in length. The instructions must also be readily available at each inspection for certification and reinspection.

(b) The owner or managing operator shall make sure that maintenance is carried out in accordance with the instructions required under paragraph (a) of this section.

(c) The cognizant OCMI may accept, instead of the instructions required under paragraph (a) of this section, a shipboard planned maintenance program that includes the items listed in that paragraph.

(d) The inspection and maintenance of the equipment listed in paragraph (a) of this section shall be logged or otherwise documented for review by the Coast Guard upon request.

§ 185.704 Maintenance of falls.

(a) Each fall used in a launching appliance on a vessel must be turned end for end at intervals of not more than 30 months.

(b) Each fall must be renewed when necessary due to deterioration or at intervals of not more than 5 years, whichever is earlier.

(c) Each fall must have a corrosion resistant tag with the following permanently marked on it:

(1) The date the new fall was installed; and

(2) If the fall has been turned end for end, the date it was turned.

§ 185.720 Weekly maintenance and inspections.

The following tests and inspections must be carried out weekly on a vessel:

(a) Each survival craft, rescue boat, and launching appliance must be visually inspected to ensure its readiness for use;

(b) Each rescue boat engine must be run ahead and astern for not less than 3 minutes, unless the ambient temperature is below the minimum temperature required for starting the engine; and

(c) Each battery for rescue boat engine starting must be brought up to full charge at least once each week if:

(1) The battery is of a type that requires recharging; and

(2) The battery is not connected to a device that keeps it continuously charged.

§ 185.722 Monthly inspections.

Each survival craft, rescue boat, and launching appliance on a vessel must be inspected monthly, using the manufacturers instructions to make sure it is complete and in good order.

§ 185.724 Quarterly inspections.

(a) Each winch control apparatus of a launching appliance on a vessel, including motor controllers, emergency switches, master switches, and limit switches, must be examined once in each 3 months.

(b) The examination required by paragraph (a) of this section must include the removal of drain plugs and the opening of drain valves to make sure that enclosures are free of water.

§ 185.726 Annual inspections.

(a) Each rescue boat must be stripped, cleaned, and thoroughly inspected, and any necessary repairs made at least once each year, including emptying and cleaning of each fuel tank, and refilling it with fresh fuel.

(b) Each davit, winch, fall and other launching appliance must be thoroughly inspected, and any necessary repairs made, at least once each year.

(c) Each item of lifesaving equipment with an expiration date must be replaced during the annual inspection and repair if the expiration date has passed.

(d) Each battery used in an item of lifesaving equipment, except inflatable survival craft equipment, must be replaced during the annual inspection if the expiration date of the battery has passed. The expiration date of the battery may be marked on the battery or the owner or managing operator may have a record of the expiration date from the manufacturer of a battery marked with a serial number.

(e) Except for a storage battery used in a rescue boat, each battery without an expiration date indicated on it or for which the owner or managing operator does not have a record of the expiration date, used in an item of lifesaving equipment, must be replaced during the annual inspection.

§ 185.728 Testing and servicing of Emergency Position Indicating Radiobeacons (EPIRB).

The master of the vessel shall ensure that:

(a) Each EPIRB, other than an EPIRB in an inflatable liferaft, must be tested monthly, using the integrated test circuit and output indicator, to determine that it is operative;

(b) The EPIRB's battery is replaced after it is used, or before the date required by FCC regulations in 47 CFR part 80, whichever comes sooner; and

(c) The EPIRB test required by paragraph (a) shall be logged or otherwise documented, as applicable.

[CGD 85–080, 61 FR 1005, Jan. 10, 1996, as amended by CGD 97–057, 62 FR 51050, Sept. 30, 1997]

§ 185.730 Servicing of inflatable liferafts, inflatable buoyant apparatus, inflatable life jackets, and inflated rescue boats.

(a) An inflatable liferaft or inflatable buoyant apparatus must be serviced at a facility specifically approved by the Commandant for the particular brand, and in accordance with servicing procedures meeting the requirements of part 160, subpart 160.151, of this chapter—

(1) No later than the month and year on its servicing sticker affixed under 46 CFR 160.151-57(n), except that servicing may be delayed until the next scheduled inspection of the vessel, provided that the delay does not exceed 5 months; and

(2) Whenever the container is damaged or the container straps or seals are broken.

(b) Each inflatable lifejacket and hybrid inflatable lifejacket or work vest must be serviced:

(1) Within 12 months of its initial packing; and

(2) Within 12 months of each subsequent servicing, except that servicing may be delayed until the next scheduled inspection of the vessel, provided that the delay does not exceed 5 months.

(c) Each inflatable life jacket must be serviced in accordance with the servicing procedure under § 160.176 in subchapter Q of this chapter, or other standard specified by the Commandant.

(d) Each hybrid inflatable life jacket or work vest must be serviced in accordance with the servicing procedure under § 160.077 in subchapter Q of this chapter, or other standard specified by the Commandant.

(e) Repair and maintenance of inflated rescue boats must be in accordance with the manufacturer's instructions. All repairs must be made at a servicing facility approved by the Commandant, except for emergency repairs carried out on board the vessel.

[CGD 85–080, 61 FR 1005, Jan. 10, 1996, as amended at 62 FR 51359, Sept. 30, 1997; USCG–2001–11118, 67 FR 58542, Sept. 17, 2002]

§ 185.740 Periodic servicing of hydrostatic release units.

(a) Each hydrostatic release unit, other than a disposable unit, must be serviced:

(1) Within 12 months of its manufacture and within 12 months of each subsequent servicing, except when servicing is delayed until the next scheduled inspection of the vessel, provided that the delay does not exceed 5 months; and

(2) In accordance with the repair and testing procedures under § 160.062 in subchapter Q of this chapter, or other standard specified by the Commandant.

(b) Each disposable hydrostatic release unit must be marked with an expiration date of two years after the date on which the unit is installed.

Subpart H—Penalties

§ 185.900 Penalty for violations.

Violation of the provisions of this subchapter will subject the violator to the applicable penalty provisions of Subtitle II of Title 46, United States Code.

§ 185.910 **Suspension and revocation.**

An individual holding a license, certificate of registry, or merchant mariner's document who commits an act of misconduct, negligence, or incompetence, or who violates or fails to comply with this subchapter or any other law or regulation intending to promote marine safety, is subject to proceedings under the provisions of 46 U.S.C. 7703 and part 5 of this chapter with respect to suspension or revocation of a license, certificate, or document.

PARTS 186—187 [RESERVED]

INDEX

SUBCHAPTER T—SMALL PASSENGER VESSELS (UNDER 100 GROSS TONS)

EDITORIAL NOTE: This listing is provided for informational purposes only. It is compiled and kept current by the U.S. Coast Guard, Department of Homeland Security. This index is updated as of October 1, 2003.

Part, subpart, or section

A

Abandon ship and man overboard drills and training 185.520
Accidents to machines 185.208
Accommodation space, definition 175.400
Accommodations, crew 177.700, 177.710
Accommodations, passenger 177.800, 177.810, 177.820
Additional requirements (Lifesaving) 180.25
Alcohol or drug use by individuals 185.210
Alterations and repairs 176.700, 176.702
Alternative requirements for a vessel operating as other than a small
    passenger vessel 176.114
Alternative standards (Electrical) 183.130
Alternative standards (Machinery) 182.130
American Boat and Yacht Council, Inc. (ABYC) 175.600
American Bureau of Shipping (ABS) 175.600
American National Standards Institute (ANSI) 175.600
American Society for Testing and Materials (ASTM) 175.600
Appeals, right of 175.560
Applicability of regulations (general) 175.110
Applicability to existing vessels 175.112, 177.115, 178.115, 179.115, 180.15, 181.115,
    182.115, 183.115, 184.115, 185.115
Approved equipment and material 175.800
Auto pilot 185.360
Auxiliary machinery 182.310
Auxiliary means of steering 182.620

B

Ballast systems 178.510, 182.540
Batteries 183.350, 183.352, 183.354
Bilge high level alarms 182.530
Bilge piping system 182.510
Bilge pumps 182.520
Boilers, auxiliary; installation 182.310
Boilers, inspection 176.812
Boilers, propulsion 182.220
Bulbous bow, definition 175.400
Bulkhead, collision .... 179.210, 179.310, 182.510(d), 185.335(c)
Bulkhead deck 179.220
Bulkhead deck, definition 175.400
Bulkheads, watertight:
    Exhaust piping passage through .... 182.430 (g)
    For subdivision .... 179.212, 179.220, 180.15(c)

Penetrations by nonmetallic pipe systems .... 182.720(d)(1)
Watertight integrity 179.320
Buoyant apparatus:
    Equipment for 180.175
    General 180.200
    Stowage 180.137
    Use on existing vessel .... 180.15(d)

C

Cable, definition 175.400
Cable and wiring 183.340
Carbon dioxide extinguishing system (Fixed):
    Amount of CO_2 gas required .... 181.410(f)
    Closure of openings .... 182.460(l), 182.465(h)
    Controls .... 181.410(b), 185.612
    Cylinders .... 181.410(c)
    Discharge outlets .... 181.410(f)
    Piping .... 181.410(d)
    Servicing 176.810
    Where required 181.400
Carburetors 182.415
Cargo space, definition 175.400
Carriage of passengers for hire, definition 175.400
Casualty, notice of 185.202
Certificate of inspection:
    Amendment 176.120
    Application for 176.105
    Compliance with provisions of 176.310
    Conditions of validity 176.502
    Description 176.103
    How to obtain or renew 176.105
    Passengers permitted 176.113
    Period of validity 176.107
    Permit to carry excursion party 176.204
    Permit to proceed 176.202
    Posting 176.302
    Routes permitted 176.110
    Subsequent inspections for 176.404
    Total persons permitted 176.112
    When required 176.100
Certificates, International Convention for Safety of Life at Sea, 1974, as amended (SOLAS):
    Duration .... 176.910(c)
    Exemption Certificate 176.920
    Passenger Ship Safety Certificate 176.910
Certification expiration date stickers 176.310
Charts 184.420
Circuit breakers 183.380
Classification societies, recognized: Adoption of standards 175.600, 177.300
Coast Guard District Commander, definition 175.400
Coast Pilot 184.420
Coastwise, definition 175.400
Cockpit vessel, definition 175.400
Cold water, definition 175.400
Collision bulkhead .... 179.210, 179.310, 182.510(d), 185.335(c)
Commandant, definition 175.400
Communication system:

Subchapter T Index

Engineroom .... 184.602(c)
Internal 184.602
Public address 184.610
Testing of 185.320
Compass 184.402
Compressed natural gas (CNG) 184.240
Consideration, definition 175.400
Construction and arrangement:
    Alternate design considerations 177.340
    Applicability to existing vessels 177.115
    Collision bulkhead 179.210, 179.310
    Crew accommodations 177.700, 177.710
    Deck rails 177.900
    Guards for exposed hazards 177.960
    Hull structure 177.300, 177.310, 177.315
    Means of escape 177.500
    Passenger accommodation 177.800, 177.810
    Plans 177.202
    Plans for sister vessels 177.210
    Sailing Vessels 177.330
    Seating 177.820
    Storm rails 177.920
    Structural design 177.300
    Vehicles, guards, rails, etc., for runways on vessels 177.960
    Ventilation for enclosed spaces 177.600
    Ventilation of machinery and fuel tank spaces 177.620
Cooking and heating:
    Equipment 184.220
    Gas systems 184.240
    General 184.200
    Restrictions 184.202
    Structural fire protection 177.410
Corrosion-resistant material, definition 175.400
Crew accommodation space, definition 175.400
Crew accommodations 177.700, 177.710
Crew and passenger list 185.502
Crew training 185.420
Current tables 184.420
Custom engineered, definition 175.400
Cylinders:
    Fire extinguishing equipment 176.810
    Fixed fire extinguishing systems:
        Controls .... 181.410(b)
        Installation .... 181.410(d)
        Storage room, location on instructions .... 181.410(c)

D

Dead cover, definition 175.400
Deck area criterion .... 176.113(b)(2)
Deck rails 177.900
Definition of terms used 175.400
Diesel:
    Engine cooling 182.420
    Engine exhaust cooling 182.425
    Engine exhaust pipe installation 182.430
    Fuel supply piping 182.455
    Ventilation of machinery spaces 182.465

Ventilation of fuel tank spaces	182.470
Discharge outlets (Carbon dioxide)	181.410(f)
Distress signals	180.68, 185.614
Distribution panel, definition	175.400
Doors, loading	185.335
Draft, definition	175.400

Drainage of weather decks:
Calculation of drainage area	178.450
Cockpit vessels	178.420
Flush deck vessels	178.410
Open boats	178.440
Well deck vessels	178.430

Drills and training:
Abandon ship and man overboard	185.520
Fire fighting	185.524
Dripproof, definition	175.400

Dry-docking or hauling out:
Extension of interval	176.670
Notice of	176.612
Scope of dry-dock examination	176.610
When required	176.600

E

Electrical installation:
Alternative standards	183.130
Applicability to existing vessels	183.115
Batteries	183.350, 183.352, 183.354
Cable and wiring requirements	183.340
Cooking equipment	184.220
Circuit breakers	183.380
Disconnect switches and devices	183.380
Distribution panels and switchboards	183.330
Dual voltage generators	183.324
Enclosures	183.220(e)
Equipment and conductor grounding	183.372
General design, installation, and maintenance requirements	183.200
General grounding requirements	183.370
General safety provisions	183.220
Generators and motors	183.320, 183.322
Grounded distribution systems	183.376
Heating equipment	184.210
Name plates	183.320(d)
Overcurrent protection	183.380
Protection from wet and corrosive environments	183.210
Shore power	183.390
Radiotelephone installations	183.392

Electrical material inspection	176.806
Electronic position fixing devices	184.410
Elevators	183.540
Embarkation station, definition	175.400
Emergency broadcast placards	184.506
Emergency instructions	185.510, 185.512
Emergency lighting	183.432
Emergency Position Indicating Radiobeacon (EPIRB)	180.64
Testing and maintenance	185.728
Enclosed space, definition	175.400
Engineroom communication system	184.602(c)

Subchapter T Index

Equivalents..175.540
Escape, means of..177.500
Exemption Certificate ....176.920(d)
Exhaust cooling 182.425
Exhaust pipe installations..182.430
Existing vessel, definition 175.400
Existing waters, definition 175.400

F

Federal Communications Commission (FCC) 184.502
Ferries carrying vehicles...177.940
Ferry, definition 177.400
Fiber reinforced plastic, definition..177.400
Fire axe..181.600
Fire bucket 181.610
Fire extinguishers, portable:
    Installation and location...181.520
    Required number, type, and location..181.500
Fire extinguishing equipment 176.810
Fire extinguishing system, fixed:
    Amount of CO_2 gas required ....181.410(f)
    Closure of openings...182.460(l), 182.465(h)
    Controls...181.410(b), 185.612
    Cylinders..181.410(c)
    Discharge outlets ....181.410(f)
    Piping..181.410(d)
    Pre-engineered..181.420
    Type required..181.410
    Where required...181.400
Fire main system:
    Fire hoses and nozzles..181.320
    Fire main and hydrants..181.310
    Fire pumps...181.300
Fire protection equipment, general:
    Applicability to existing vessels..181.115
    Approved type..175.800
    Installed but not required..181.120
    Inspection requirements..176.810
    Structural fire protection...177.410
Fire pumps...181.300
First aid kits 184.710
Fixed seating criterion...176.113
Flammable vapor detection systems 182.480
Flash point, definition...175.400
Float-free, definition..175.400
Flush deck vessel, definition..175.400
Foam flotation material...179.240
Freeing port, definition...175.400
Fueling operations..185.350
Fuel piping...182.455
Fuel restrictions..182.405
Fuel shutoff valves:
    Marking..185.608
    Where required ....182.455(b)(4)
Fuel systems (Portable)..182.458
Fuel tanks:
    Fill and sounding pipes..182.455

Independent	182.440
Integral	182.435
Vent pipes	182.450
Fuses	183.380(l)

G

Galley, definition	175.400
Galley hood fire extinguishing systems	181.425
Gasoline engines:	
Alternative standards	182.130
Applicability	182.400
Carburetors	182.415
Engine cooling	182.420
Engine exhaust cooling	182.425
Engine exhaust pipe installation	182.430
Ventilation of machinery or fuel tank spaces	182.460
Gasoline fuel supply piping	182.455
Gauges, propulsion engines	182.410(b)
General alarm systems	183.550
Generators and motors	183.320, 183.322
Great Lakes, definition	175.400
Gross tonnage, definition	175.400
Gross tonnage as criterion for requirements	175.200
Grounded distribution system	183.376
Guards for exposed hazards	177.960
Guards in vehicle spaces	177.940

H

Halon:	
Fixed fire extinguishing system	181.410(g), 181.420
Portable extinguishers	176.810
Harbor of safe refuge, definition	175.400
Hatches:	
Closure of	185.512
Escape	177.500, 185.606
Installation of storm rails or hand grabs	177.920
Watertight	179.360, 185.610
Hauling out, dry-docking	176.600
Hazardous areas	183.530
Hazardous condition, definition	175.400
Heaters, water	182.320
Heating and cooking:	
Equipment	184.210, 184.220
Gas systems	184.240
General	184.200
Restrictions	184.202
Structural fire protection	177.410
High seas, definition	175.400
High Speed Craft	175.540
High Speed Craft, definition	175.400
Hose:	
Fire	181.320
Flexible	182.410(d)
Fuel	182.720(b), 182.720(e)
Hot work	176.710
Hull inspection	176.802
Hull markings	185.602

Subchapter T Index

Hull structural design..177.300
Hydrants, fire 181.310
Hydrostatic release units..185.740

I

Incorporation by reference 175.600
Independent laboratory, definition...175.400
Independent modular smoke detecting units..181.450
Inflatable buoyant apparatus:
    Embarkation arrangements...180.150
    Equipment 180.175
    Inspection 176.808
    Placards..185.518
    Servicing...185.730
    Stowage 180.130
    Where required...180.200
Inflatable survival craft, definition 175.400
Inspection of vessels:
    Additional tests and inspections 176.840
    Annual 185.726
    Assignment of marine inspector..176.400(b)
    Electrical 176.806
    Fire extinguishing equipment 176.810
    Hull..176.802
    Initial inspection for certification 176.402
    Inspection standards...176.800
    Lifesaving equipment 176.808
    Machinery...176.804
    Miscellaneous systems and equipment 176.816
    Monthly 185.722
    Notice of deficiencies and requirements...176.801
    Pressure vessels and boilers...176.812
    Quarterly..185.724
    Reinspection 176.500, 176.502
    Renewal of certificate...176.404
    Repairs and alterations 176.700
    Sanitary inspection 176.818
    Special consideration 175.550
    Steering systems 176.814
    Unsafe practices...176.830
    Weekly and maintenance..185.720
Intact stability standard:
    Applicability...178.310
    Requirements...178.320
    Requirements for a sailing vessel 178.325
    Simplified proof test..178.330
    Standard for pontoon vessels on protected waters 178.340
International Convention for Safety of Life at Sea, 1974 (SOLAS): Applicability 176.900
International voyage, definition..175.400
International voyages:
    Applicability...180.10
    Hull markings on vessels 185.602
    Passengers 176.900
    Survival craft...180.10

K

Keel and grid cooler installation 182.422

L

Ladders .... 177.500(j)
Lakes, bays and sounds, definition 175.400
Launching appliance, definition 175.400
Length, definition 175.400
Length between perpendiculars (LBP), definition 175.400
Length of rail criterion 176.113
Licenses:
    Exhibition of 185.402
    Suspension or revocation of 185.910
Lifeboat winches 183.520
Life floats, equipment for 180.175
Life floats, general 180.200
Life jacket lights 180.75
Life jacket placards 185.516
Life jackets 180.71
Life jackets, inspection of .... 176.808(e)
Life jackets, stowage of 180.78
Life jackets, wearing of 185.508
Lifeline .... 180.70(c), 180.175(e)
Liferafts:
    Embarkation arrangements 180.150
    Equipment 180.175
    Inspection 176.808
    Placards 185.518
    Servicing 185.730
    Stowage 180.130
    Where required 180.200
Lifesaving equipment:
    Applicability to existing vessels 180.15
    Approved 175.800
    For vessels in Great Lakes service 180.206
    For vessels in lakes, bays, and sounds service 180.207
    For vessels in ocean service 180.202
    For vessels in coastwise service 180.204
    For vessels in limited coastwise service 180.205
    For vessels in river service 180.208
    Inspection of 176.808
    Installed but not required 180.25
    Life jackets, number required 180.71
    Life jackets, type required 180.71
    Marking .... 185.604(b)
    Personal flotation devices carried in addition to life jackets 180.72
    Pyrotechnic distress signals 180.68
    Rescue boats 180.210
    Ring life buoys and water lights 180.70
    Stowage of life floats and buoyant apparatus 180.137
    Stowage of life jackets 180.78
    Stowage of survival craft 180.130
    Substitutions 180.200
Light lists 184.420
Lighting, emergency 183.432
Lighting, fixtures 183.410

Subchapter T Index

Lighting, portable..183.430
Limited coastwise, definition 175.400
Liquefied petroleum gas (LPG) 184.240
Load Line Certificate 176.612
Load lines 175.122
Loading doors 185.335

M

Machinery, material inspection..176.804
Machinery installation:
    Applicability to existing vessels..182.115
    Auxiliary machinery...182.310
    Machinery requirements, specific:
        Engine cooling 182.420
        Exhaust cooling 182.425
        Exhaust pipe installation..182.430
        Fuel tanks, independent..182.440
        Fuel tanks, integral 182.435
        Pipes, filling and sounding 182.445
        Pipes, vent...182.450
        Piping, fuel..182.455
        Portable fuel systems...182.458
        Ventilation of compartments...182.460, 182.465, 182.470
    Machinery using gasoline as fuel:
        Applicability 182.400
        Carburetors 182.415
        Flammable vapor detectors 182.480
        Fueling...185.350
        Ventilation of compartments...182.460, 185.352
Machinery spaces, definition 175.400
Main transverse watertight bulkhead, definition 175.400
Maintenance of falls 185.704
Major conversion, definition..175.400
Mandatory chemical testing following serious marine incidents...................185.212
Marine inspector or inspector, definition 175.400
Marine sanitation devices..184.704
Marking required:
    Escape hatches and emergency exits 185.606
    Fire protection equipment..185.612
    Fuel shutoff valves 185.608
    Hull markings..185.602
    Lifesaving gear 185.604
    Portable watertight container for distress flares and smoke signals 185.614
    Watertight doors and watertight hatches..185.610
Master:
    Definition 175.400
    Duties:
        Accidents to machinery 185.208
        Alcohol or drug use by individuals directly involved in casualties 185.210
        Closure of loading doors..185.335
        Designation of watchman..185.410
        Drills...185.520(a), 185.524(a)
        Emergency instructions, preparation and posting................................185.510
        Navigation underway 185.304
        Notice of casualty 185.202

Notice of hazardous conditions 185.203
Permission for repairs and alterations 176.700
Securing of hatches 185.330
Testing of:
  Communications systems 185.320
  Emergency position indicating radiobeacon (EPIRB) .... 185.726(d), 185.728
  Propulsion controls 185.320
  Signaling whistle 185.320
  Steering gear 185.320
Use of auto pilot 185.360
Verification of compliance with applicable stability requirements
.... 185.315
Vessels carrying vehicles 185.340
Written report of marine casualty 185.206
Exclusion as passenger 175.400
Prohibition from operation of vessel without certification of expiration date sticker affixed 176.310
Mate: Changeover from automatic to manual steering and vice versa 185.360
Means of escape, definition 175.400
Mooring equipment 184.300
Motors and generators (50 volts or more) 183.320, 183.322
Motors and generators (less than 50 volts) 183.320, 183.322

N

Name plates, electrical equipment .... 183.320(d)
National Electrical Code 175.600, 183.340, 183.372
National Fire Protection Association (NFPA) 175.600, 184.200, 184.240
Nautical publications 184.420
Navigation lights 183.420
Noncombustible material, definition 175.400
Non-self-propelled vessel, definition 175.400
Notice of casualty 185.202

O

Oceans, definition 175.400
Officer in Charge, Marine Inspection (OCMI), definition 175.400
Officers' licenses, exhibition of 185.402
Officers' responsibilities in emergencies 185.530
Oil pollution prevention equipment and procedures 184.702
OMB control numbers 175.900
Open boat, definition 175.400
Open deck, definition 175.400
Open to the atmosphere, definition 175.400
Openings in the side of a vessel below bulkhead or weather deck 179.350
Operating station, definition 175.400
Operating station visibility 177.1030
Outlets, discharge .... 181.410(f)
Overnight accommodations (space), definition 175.400

P

Paddle 180.175
Painter 180.175
Partially enclosed space, definition 175.400
Partially protected waters, definition 175.400
Passenger accommodation space, definition 175.400

Subchapter T Index

Passenger, accommodations 177.810
Passenger count 185.504
Passenger, definition 175.400
Passenger for hire, definition 175.400
Passenger safety orientation 185.506
Passenger Ship Safety Certificate .... 176.910 (a) and (b)
Passengers, number permitted 176.113
Penalties 185.900, 185.910
Permit to carry excursion party 176.204
Permit to proceed to another port for repair 176.202, 176.302
Pilothouse control, definition 175.400
Piping:
   Bilge 182.510
   Diesel engine cooling 182.420, 182.425
   Diesel engine exhaust installation 182.430
   Diesel fuel supply 182.455
   Filling and sounding pipes for diesel fuel tanks 182.445
   Filling and sounding pipes for gasoline fuel tanks 182.445
   Fixed gas fire extinguishing system 181.410
   Gasoline engine exhaust installation 182.425, 182.430
   Gasoline fuel supply 182.455
   Vent pipes for diesel fuel tanks 182.450
   Vent pipes for gasoline fuel tanks 182.450
Piping materials, nonferrous metallic 182.730
Piping materials, nonmetallic 182.700
   General 182.700, 182.720
   Non-vital systems 182.715, 182.720
   Vital systems 182.710, 182.720
Piping system, definition 175.400
Plans, submission for approval 177.202
Port light, definition 175.400
Posting:
   Certificate of inspection 176.302
   Convention certificates 176.302
   Placards containing instructions for launching and inflating inflatable
      life rafts 185.518
   Stability letters 176.306
Pre-engineered, definition 175.400
Prescription of regulations by Commandant in this subchapter 175.200
Pressure vessels 176.812, 182.330
Propulsion engine control system 184.620
Propulsion machinery 182.200, 182.220
Protected waters, definition 175.400
Public address system 184.610
Pumps:
   Bilge 182.520
   Fire, hand 181.610
   Fire, power 181.300
Pyrotechnic distress signals 180.68

R

Radar 184.404
Radio 184.502
Radio-phone equipment (less than 50 volts) 183.392
Rafts 180.200
Rails and guards 177.900, 177.920, 177.940
Records, retaining of voyage 185.220, 185.280

Reinspection 176.500, 176.502
Repairs and alterations 176.700
Report of Violation (ROV) 176.801
Reporting of casualty 185.206, 185.260
Rescue boat 180.210
Responsibilities of officers in emergencies 185.530
Restrictions, cooking and heating 184.200, 184.202, 184.210, 184.240
Right of appeal 175.560
Ring life buoys 180.70
Rivers, definition 175.400

S

Safety glazing materials 177.1010
Safety valve seals 176.704
Sailing vessel, definition 175.400
Sanitary inspection 176.818
Scantlings, definition 175.400
Scupper, definition 175.400
Seating, fixed 176.113, 177.820
Self-bailing cockpit, definition 175.400
Semiconductor rectifier systems 183.360
Ship's service loads, definition 175.400
Shore power (50 volts or more) 183.390
Short international voyage, definition 175.400
Signaling whistle tests 185.320
Smoke detecting units 181.450
Special consideration 175.550
Specific applicability or individual parts 175.112
Sprinkling system, manual .... 181.400(g)
Stability letter 176.306, 178.230
Stability requirements, verification of vessel compliance with 185.315
Stairway, definition 175.400
Standards, industrial; adoption of 175.600, 176.800
Steel or equivalent material, definition 175.400
Steering apparatus 176.814, 182.610
Steering gear tests 185.320
Storm rails 177.920
Structural standards 177.300, 177.330
Survival craft, definition 175.400
Survival craft embarkation arrangements 180.150
Survival craft equipment 180.175
Suspension and revocation 185.910
Switchboard, definition 175.400
Switchboards (less than 50 volts) 183.330

T

Tailshaft examinations 176.630
Tank fuel:
  Diesel 182.435, 182.440
  Gasoline 182.440
Tests:
  Communication systems 185.320
  Controls 185.320
  Emergency position indicating radiobeacon (EPIRB) ...... 185.726(d), 185.728
  Signaling whistle 185.320
  Steering gear 185.320
Tide tables 184.420

Subchapter T Index

Toilet space 175.400
Trunk, definition 175.400
Trunks 179.340

U

Underwriters' Laboratory, Inc. (UL) 175.600, 183.340, 183.410

V

Vehicle space, definition 175.400
Ventilation:
    Compartments containing diesel fuel tanks 177.620, 182.470
    Compartments containing diesel machinery 177.620, 182.465
    Compartments containing gasoline machinery or fuel tanks 177.600, 182.460, 185.352
    Spaces other than machinery spaces 177.600
Verification of vessel compliance with applicable stability requirements 185.315
Vessel:
    Control systems .... Part 184
    Definition 175.400
    Of the United States, definition 175.400
    On an international voyage 175.120
    Subject to the requirements of International Convention for Safety of Life at Sea, 1974, (SOLAS) 176.900, 176.920
Voyages, international:
    Hull markings on vessels 185.602
    Survival craft 180.10
    Passengers 176.900
Voyages, retaining of records of 185.220

W

Warm water, definition 175.400
Watchmen, duties of 185.410
Waterlights .... 180.70, 180.175(e)
Watertight, definition 175.400
Watertight bulkheads/doors 179.320, 179.330
Watertight doors and watertight hatches, markings on 185.610
Watertight integrity 179.360
Weather deck, definition 175.400
Weathertight, definition 175.400
Well deck vessel, definition 175.400
Winches, lifeboat 183.520
Wire, definition 175.400
Wiring, size, insulation, etc. for lighting and power wiring (less than 50 volts) 183.340
Wiring installation:
    Conductors 183.340, 183.370
    Grounding 183.340, 183.370
    Lighting and power (less than 50 volts) 183.340, 183.370
    Methods and material (50 volts or more) 183.340, 183.410
    Wiring joints and splices 183.340, 183.370
Work space, definition 175.400
Work vests 180.72

SUBCHAPTER U—OCEANOGRAPHIC RESEARCH VESSELS

PART 188—GENERAL PROVISIONS

Subpart 188.01—Authority and Purpose

Sec.
188.01-1   Purpose of regulations.
188.01-3   Scope of regulations.
188.01-7   Right of appeal.
188.01-15 OMB control numbers assigned pursuant to the Paperwork Reduction Act.

Subpart 188.05—Application

188.05-1   Vessels subject to requirements of this subchapter.
188.05-2   Exemptions from inspection laws for oceanographic research vessels and terms and conditions which apply in lieu thereof.
188.05-3   New vessels and existing vessels for the purpose of application of regulations in this subchapter.
188.05-5   Specific application noted in text.
188.05-7   Ocean or unlimited coastwise vessels on inland and Great Lakes routes.
188.05-10 Application to vessels on an international voyage.
188.05-33 Scientific personnel—interpretive rulings.
188.05-35 Load lines—interpretive ruling.

Subpart 188.10—Definitions of Terms Used in This Subchapter

188.10-1   Anniversary date.
188.10-2   Approved.
188.10-3   Approved container.
188.10-5   Barge.
188.10-6   Captain of the Port.
188.10-7   Chemical stores.
188.10-9   Chemical storeroom.
188.10-11 Chemistry laboratory.
188.10-13 Coast Guard District Commander.
188.10-15 Coastwise.
188.10-17 Combustible liquid.
188.10-19 Commandant.
188.10-21 Compressed gas.
188.10-23 Corrosive liquids.
188.10-25 Explosive.
188.10-27 Flammable liquid.
188.10-31 Great Lakes.
188.10-33 Headquarters.
188.10-35 International voyage.
188.10-37 Label.
188.10-39 Lakes, bays, and sounds.
188.10-41 Liquefied compressed gas.
188.10-43 Liquefied flammable gas.
188.10-45 Marine inspector or inspector.
188.10-49 Numbered vessel.
188.10-51 Ocean.
188.10-53 Oceanographic research vessel.
188.10-55 Officer in Charge, Marine Inspection.
188.10-56 Pilot boarding equipment and point of access.
188.10-57 Portable tank.
188.10-59 Recognized classification society.
188.10-61 Rivers.
188.10-65 Seagoing barge.
188.10-67 Scientific equipment.
188.10-69 Scientific laboratory.
188.10-71 Scientific personnel.
188.10-73 Ships' stores and supplies.
188.10-75 Undocumented vessel.
188.10-77 Vessel.

Subpart 188.15—Equivalents

188.15-1   Conditions under which equivalents may be used.
188.15-5   Design of vessels.

Subpart 188.20—General Marine Engineering Requirements

188.20-1   Marine engineering details.

Subpart 188.25—General Electrical Engineering Requirements

188.25-1   Electrical engineering details.

Subpart 188.27—Lifesaving Appliances and Arrangements

188.27-1   Lifesaving appliances and arrangements.

Subpart 188.35—American Bureau of Shipping's Standards

188.35-1   Standards to be used.
188.35-5   Where obtainable.

AUTHORITY: 46 U.S.C. 2113, 3306; Pub. L 103–206, 107 Stat. 2439; 49 U.S.C. 5103, 5106; E.O. 12234, 45 FR 58801, 3 CFR, 1980 Comp., p. 277; Department of Homeland Security Delegation No. 0170.1.

SOURCE: CGFR 67–83, 33 FR 1113, Jan. 27, 1968, unless otherwise noted.

Subpart 188.01—Authority and Purpose

§ 188.01-1 Purpose of regulations.

The purpose of the regulations in this subchapter is to set forth uniform minimum requirements for oceanographic research vessels designated in accordance with § 3.10-1 of this title and subject to Coast Guard inspection requirements. The regulations are necessary to carry out the provisions of applicable laws governing inspection and certification of oceanographic research vessels and have the force of law.

[CGD 95–028, 62 FR 51219, Sept. 30, 1997]

§ 188.01–3 Scope of regulations.

The regulations in this subchapter contain requirements for materials, design, construction, equipment, lifesaving appliances and procedures, fire protection, and fire prevention procedures, inspection and certification, and special operational requirements for oceanographic research vessels, including the handling, use, and control of explosives and other dangerous articles or substances.

[CGFR 67–83, 33 FR 1113, Jan. 27, 1968, as amended by CGD 77–081, 46 FR 56204, Nov. 16, 1981; CGD 95–028, 62 FR 51219, Sept. 30, 1997]

§ 188.01–7 Right of appeal.

Any person directly affected by a decision or action taken under this subchapter, by or on behalf of the Coast Guard, may appeal therefrom in accordance with subchapter 1.03 of this chapter.

[CGD 88–033, 54 FR 50382, Dec. 6, 1989]

§ 188.01–15 OMB control numbers assigned pursuant to the Paperwork Reduction Act.

(a) *Purpose.* This section collects and displays the control numbers assigned to information collection and recordkeeping requirements in this subchapter by the Office of Management and Budget (OMB) pursuant to the Paperwork Reduction Act of 1980 (44 U.S.C. 3501 *et seq.*). The Coast Guard intends that this section comply with the requirements of 44 U.S.C. 3507(f), which requires that agencies display a current control number assigned by the Director of the OMB for each approved agency information collection requirement.

(b) *Display.*

46 CFR part or section where identified or described	Current OMB control No.
§ 189.40–3	1625–0032
§ 189.40–5	1625–0032
§ 196.15–7	1625–0064
§ 196.15–18	1625–0064

[CGD 88–072, 53 FR 34298, Sept. 6, 1988, as amended by CGD 89–037, 57 FR 41828, Sept. 11, 1992; USCG–2004–18884, 69 FR 58351, Sept. 30, 2004]

Subpart 188.05—Application

§ 188.05–1 Vessels subject to requirements of this subchapter.

(a) This subchapter is applicable to all U.S.-flag vessels indicated in Column 6 of Table 188.05–1(a) to the extent prescribed by applicable laws and the regulations in this subchapter, except as follows:

(1) Any foreign vessel.

(2) Any vessel operating exclusively on inland waters which are not navigable waters of the United States.

(3) Any vessel while laid up and dismantled and out of commission.

(4) With the exception of vessels of the U.S. Maritime Administration, any vessel with title vested in the United States and which is used for public purposes.

§ 188.05-1

Table 188.05-1(a)

Method of propulsion, qualified by size or other limitation.[1]	Vessels inspected and certificated under—			Vessels subject to the provisions of—		
	Subchapter D—Tank Vessels.[2]	Subchapter H—Passenger Vessels[2,3,4] and [5] or Subchapter K or T—Small Passenger Vessels.[2,3, and 4]	Subchapter I—Cargo and Miscellaneous Vessels.[2 and 5]	Subchapter C—Uninspected Vessels.[2,3,6,7, and 8]	Subchapter U—Oceanographic Vessels.[2,3,6,7, and 9]	Subchapter O—Certain Bulk and Dangerous Cargoes.[10]
Column 1	Column 2	Column 3	Column 4	Column 5	Column 6	Column 7

(1) Motor, all vessels except seagoing motor vessels ≥ 300 gross tons.	All vessels carrying combustible or flammable liquid cargo in bulk.[5]	i) All vessels carrying more than 12 passengers on an international voyage, except recreational vessels not engaged in trade.[5]
		ii) All vessels < 100 gross tons that—
		  A) Carry more than 6 passengers-for-hire whether chartered or not, or
		  B) Carry more than 6 passengers when chartered with the crew provided, or
		  C) Carry more than 12 passengers when chartered with no crew provided, or
		  D) Carry at least 1 passenger-for-hire and is a submersible vessel.[7]
		iii) All vessels ≥ 100 gross tons that—
		  A) Carry more than 12 passengers-for-hire whether chartered or not, or
		  B) Carry more than 12 passengers when chartered with the crew provided, or
		  C) Carry more than 12 passengers when chartered with no crew provided, or
		  D) Carry at least 1 passenger-for-hire and is a submersible vessel.[7]
		iv) These regulations do not apply to—
		  A) Recreational vessels not engaged in trade.
		  B) Documented cargo or tank vessels issued a permit to carry 16 or fewer persons in addition to the crew.
		  C) Fishing vessels, not engaged in ocean or coastwise service, may carry persons on the legitimate business of the vessel[6] in addition to the crew, as restricted by the definition of passenger.[7]
			All vessels > 15 gross tons carrying freight-for-hire, except those covered by columns 2 and 3, and all vessels when carrying dangerous cargoes when required by 46 CFR part 98.	All vessels not covered by columns 2, 3, 4, and 6.	None.	All vessels carrying cargoes in bulk that are listed in part 153, table 1, or part 154, table 4, or unlisted cargoes that would otherwise be subject to these parts.[12]

332

Coast Guard, DHS § 188.05–1

Table 188.05-1(a) (continued)

Method of propulsion, qualified by size or other limitation.[1]	Vessels inspected and certificated under—			Vessels subject to the provisions of—			
	Subchapter D—Tank Vessels.[2]	Subchapter H—Passenger Vessels[2,3,4,] and [5] or Subchapter K or T—Small Passenger Vessels.[2,3, and 4]	Subchapter I—Cargo and Miscellaneous Vessels.[2 and 5]	Subchapter C—Uninspected Vessels.[2,3,6,7, and 8]	Subchapter U—Oceanographic Vessels.[2,3,6,7, and 9]	Subchapter O—Certain Bulk and Dangerous Cargoes.[10]
Column 1	Column 2	Column 3	Column 4	Column 5	Column 6	Column 7
(2) Motor, seagoing motor vessels ≥ 300 gross tons.	All vessels carrying combustible or flammable liquid cargo in bulk.[3]	i) All vessels carrying more than 12 passengers on an international voyage, except recreational vessels not engaged in trade.[7] ii) These regulations do not apply to— A) Recreational vessels not engaged in trade. B) Documented cargo or tank vessels issued a permit to carry 16 or fewer persons in addition to the crew. C) Fishing vessels, not engaged in ocean or coastwise service, may carry persons on the legitimate business of the vessel[6] in addition to the crew, as restricted by the definition of passenger.[7]	All vessels, including recreational vessels not engaged in trade. This does not include vessels covered by columns 2 and 3, and vessels engaged in the fishing industry.	All vessels not covered by columns 2, 3, 4, 6, and 7.	All vessels engaged in oceanographic research.	All vessels carrying cargoes in bulk that are listed in part 153, table 1, or part 154, table 4, or unlisted cargoes that would otherwise be subject to these parts.[12]
(3) Non-self-propelled, vessels < 100 gross tons.	All vessels carrying combustible or flammable liquid cargo in bulk.[5]	i) All vessels that— A) Carry more than 6 passengers-for-hire whether chartered or not, or B) Carry more than 6 passengers when chartered with the crew provided, or C) Carry more than 12 passengers when chartered with no crew provided, or D) Carry at least 1 passenger-for-hire and is a submersible vessel.[7] E) Carry more than 12 passengers on an international voyage.[7]	All seagoing barges except those covered by columns 2 and 3.	All barges carrying passengers or passengers-for-hire, except those covered by column 3.	None.	All tank barges carrying cargoes listed in Table 151.05 of this chapter or unlisted cargoes that would otherwise be subject to part 151.[1, 11, and 12]
(4) Non-self-propelled, vessels ≥ 100 gross tons.	All vessels carrying combustible or flammable liquid cargo in bulk.[5]	ii) All vessels that— A) Carry more than 12 passengers-for-hire whether chartered or not, or B) Carry more than 6 passengers when chartered with the crew provided, or C) Carry more than 12 passengers when chartered with no crew provided, or D) Carry at least 1 passenger-for-hire and is a submersible vessel, or E) Carry more than 12 passengers on an international voyage.[7]	All seagoing barges except those covered by columns 2 and 3.	All barges carrying passengers or passengers-for-hire, except those covered by columns 3 and 6.	All seagoing barges engaged in oceanographic research.	All tank barges carrying cargoes listed in Table 151.05 of this chapter or unlisted cargoes that would otherwise be subject to part 151.[1, 11, and 12]

333

§ 188.05-1   46 CFR Ch. I (10–1–04 Edition)

Table 188.05-1(a) (continued)

Method of propulsion, qualified by size or other limitation.[1]	Vessels inspected and certificated under—			Vessels subject to the provisions of—		
	Subchapter D—Tank Vessels.[2]	Subchapter H—Passenger Vessels[2,3,4] and [5] or Subchapter K or T—Small Passenger Vessels.[2,3, and 4]	Subchapter I—Cargo and Miscellaneous Vessels.[2 and 5]	Subchapter C—Uninspected Vessels.[2,3,6, 7, and 8]	Subchapter U—Oceanographic Vessels.[2,3, 6,7, and 9]	Subchapter O—Certain Bulk and Dangerous Cargoes.[10]
Column 1	Column 2	Column 3	Column 4	Column 5	Column 6	Column 7

(5) Sail,[13] vessels ≤700 gross tons.	All vessels carrying combustible or flammable liquid cargo in bulk.[5]	i) All vessels carrying more than 12 passengers on an international voyage, except recreational vessels not engaged in trade.[7]
		ii) All vessels < 100 gross tons that—
		  A) Carry more than 6 passengers-for-hire whether chartered or not, or
		  B) Carry more than 6 passengers when chartered with the crew provided, or
		  C) Carry more than 12 passengers when chartered with no crew provided, or
		  D) Carry at least 1 passenger-for-hire and is a submersible vessel.[7]
		iii) All vessels ≥ 100 gross tons that—
		  A) Carry more than 12 passengers-for-hire whether chartered or not, or
		  B) Carry more than 12 passengers when chartered with the crew provided, or
		  C) Carry more than 12 passengers when chartered with no crew provided, or
		  D) Carry at least 1 passenger-for-hire and is a submersible vessel.[7]
		iv) These regulations do not apply to—
		  A) Recreational vessels not engaged in trade.
		  B) Documented cargo or tank vessels issued a permit to carry 16 or fewer persons in addition to the crew.
		  C) Fishing vessels, not engaged in ocean or coastwise service, may carry persons on the legitimate business of the vessel[6] in addition to the crew, as restricted by the definition of passenger.[7]
			Those vessels carrying dangerous cargoes when required by 46 CFR part 98.	All vessels not covered by columns 2, 3, 4, and 6.	None.	All vessels carrying cargoes in bulk that are listed in part 153, table 1, or part 154, table 4, or unlisted cargoes that would otherwise be subject to these parts.[12]

(6) Sail,[13] vessels >700 gross tons.	All vessels carrying combustible or flammable liquid cargo in bulk.[5]	i) All vessels carrying passengers or passengers-for-hire, except recreational vessels.[7]	Those vessels carrying dangerous cargoes when required by 46 CFR part 98.	None.	None.	All vessels carrying cargoes in bulk that are listed in part 153, table 1, or part 154, table 4, or unlisted cargoes that would otherwise be subject to these parts.[12]

334

Coast Guard, DHS § 188.05-1

Table 188.05-1(a) (continued)

Method of propulsion, qualified by size or other limitation.[1]	Vessels inspected and certified under—		Vessels subject to the provisions of—		
	Subchapter D—Tank Vessels.[2]	Subchapter H—Passenger Vessels.[2,3,4, and 5] or Subchapter K or T—Small Passenger Vessels.[2,3, and 4]	Subchapter I—Cargo and Miscellaneous Vessels.[2 and 5]	Subchapter C—Uninspected Vessels.[2,3,6,7, and 8]	Subchapter U—Oceanographic Vessels.[2,3,6,7, and 9]	Subchapter O—Certain Bulk and Dangerous Cargoes.[10]
Column 1	Column 2	Column 3	Column 4	Column 5	Column 6	Column 7

(7) Steam, vessels ≤ 19.8 meters (65 feet) in length.	All vessels carrying combustible or flammable liquid cargo in bulk.[5]	i) All vessels carrying more than 12 passengers on an international voyage, except recreational vessels not engaged in trade.[7]
		 ii) All vessels < 100 gross tons that—
		   A) Carry more than 6 passengers-for-hire whether chartered or not, or
		   B) Carry more than 6 passengers when chartered with no crew provided, or
		   C) Carry more than 12 passengers when chartered with no crew provided, or
		   D) Carry at least 1 passenger-for-hire and is a submersible vessel.[7]
		 iii) All vessels ≥ 100 gross tons that—
		   A) Carry more than 12 passengers-for-hire whether chartered or not, or
		   B) Carry more than 12 passengers when chartered with no crew provided, or
		   C) Carry more than 12 passengers when chartered with no crew provided, or
		   D) Carry at least 1 passenger-for-hire and is a submersible vessel.[7]
		 iv) These regulations do not apply to—
		   A) Recreational vessels not engaged in trade.
		   B) Documented cargo or tank vessels issued a permit to carry 16 or fewer persons in addition to the crew.
		   C) Fishing vessels, not engaged in ocean or coastwise service, may carry persons on the legitimate business of the vessel[5] in addition to the crew, as restricted by the definition of passenger.[7]
			All tugboats and towboats. All vessels carrying dangerous cargoes when required by 46 CFR Part 98.	All vessels not covered by columns 2, 3, 4, and 6.	None.	All vessels carrying cargoes in bulk that are listed in part 153, table 1, or part 154, table 4, or unlisted cargoes that would otherwise be subject to these parts.[12]

335

§ 188.05–1

Table 188.05-1(a) (continued)

Method of propulsion, qualified by size or other limitation.[1]	Vessels inspected and certificated under—			Vessels subject to the provisions of—			
	Subchapter D—Tank Vessels.[2]	Subchapter H—Passenger Vessels[2,3,4, and 5] or Subchapter K or T—Small Passenger Vessels.[2,3, and 4]	Subchapter I—Cargo and Miscellaneous Vessels.[2 and 5]	Subchapter C—Uninspected Vessels.[2,3,6,7, and 8]	Subchapter U—Oceanographic Vessels.[2,3,6,7, and 9]	Subchapter O—Certain Bulk and Dangerous Cargoes.[10]
Column 1	Column 2	Column 3	Column 4	Column 5	Column 6	Column 7

(8) Steam, vessels > 19.8 meters (65 feet) in length.	All vessels carrying combustible or flammable liquid cargo in bulk.[5]	i) All vessels carrying more than 12 passengers on an international voyage, except recreational vessels not engaged in trade.
		ii) All vessels < 100 gross tons that—
		  A) Carry more than 6 passengers-for-hire whether chartered or not, or
		  B) Carry more than 6 passengers when chartered with the crew provided, or
		  C) Carry more than 12 passengers when chartered with no crew provided, or
		  D) Carry at least 1 passenger-for-hire and is a submersible vessel.[7]
		iii) All vessels ≥ 100 gross tons that—
		  A) Carry more than 12 passengers-for-hire whether chartered or not, or
		  B) Carry more than 12 passengers when chartered with the crew provided, or
		  C) Carry more than 12 passengers when chartered with no crew provided, or
		  D) Carry at least 1 passenger-for-hire and is a submersible vessel.[7]
		iv) These regulations do not apply to—
		  A) Recreational vessels not engaged in trade.
		  B) Documented cargo or tank vessels issued a permit to carry 16 or fewer persons in addition to the crew.
		  C) Fishing vessels, not engaged in ocean or coastwise service, may carry persons on the legitimate business of the vessel[6] in addition to the crew, as restricted by the definition of passenger.[7]
			All vessels not covered by columns 2, 3, 6, and 7.	None.	All vessels engaged in oceanographic research.	All vessels carrying cargoes in bulk that are listed in part 153, table 1, or part 154, table 4, or unlisted cargoes that would otherwise be subject to these parts.[12]

Coast Guard, DHS § 188.05-1

Key to symbols used in this table: ≤ is less than or equal to, ≥ is greater than or equal to, > is greater than, < is less than, and ≥ is greater than or equal to.

Footnotes:

1 Where length is used in this table, it means the length measured from end to end over the deck, excluding sheer. This expression means a straight line measurement of the overall length from the foremost part of the vessel to the aftermost part of the vessel, measured parallel to the centerline.

2 Subchapters E (Load Lines), F (Marine Engineering), J (Electrical Engineering), N (Dangerous Cargoes), S (Subdivision and Stability), and W (Lifesaving Appliances and Arrangements) of this chapter may also be applicable under certain conditions. The provisions of 49 CFR parts 171-179 apply whenever packaged hazardous materials are on board vessels (including motorboats), except when specifically exempted by law.

3 Public nautical schoolships, other than vessels of the Navy and Coast Guard, must meet the requirements of part 167 of subchapter R (Nautical Schools) of this chapter, Civilian nautical schoolships, as defined by 46 U.S.C. 1331, must meet the requirements of subchapter H (Passenger Vessels) and part 168 of subchapter R (Nautical Schools) of this chapter.

4 Subchapter H (Passenger Vessels) of this chapter covers only those vessels of 100 gross tons or more, subchapter T (Small Passenger Vessels) of this chapter covers only those vessels of less than 100 gross tons, and subchapter K (Small Passenger Vessels) of this chapter covers only those vessels less than 100 gross tons carrying more than 150 passengers or overnight accommodations for more than 49 passengers.

5 Vessels covered by subchapter H (Passenger Vessels) or I (Cargo and Miscellaneous Vessels) of this chapter, where the principal purpose or use of the vessel is not for the carriage of liquid cargo, may be granted a permit to carry a limited amount of flammable or combustible liquid cargo in bulk. The portion of the vessel used for the carriage of the flammable or combustible liquid cargo must meet the requirements of subchapter D (Tank Vessels) in addition to the requirements of subchapter H (Passenger Vessels) or I (Cargo and Miscellaneous Vessels) of this chapter.

6 Any vessel on an international voyage is subject to the requirements of the International Convention for Safety of Life at Sea, 1974 (SOLAS).

7 The terms "passenger(s)" and "passenger(s)-for-hire" are as defined in 46 U.S.C. 2101(21)(21a). On oceanographic vessels, scientific personnel onboard shall not be deemed to be passengers nor seamen, but for calculations of lifesaving equipment, etc., must be counted as persons.

8 Boilers and machinery are subject to examination on vessels over 40 feet in length.

9 Under 46 U.S.C. 441 and oceanographic research vessel "* * * being employed exclusively in instruction in oceanography or limnology, or both, or exclusively in oceanographic research, * * *." Under 46 U.S.C. 443, "an oceanographic research vessel shall not be deemed to be engaged in trade or commerce." If or when an oceanographic vessel engages in trade or commerce, such vessel cannot operate under its certificate of inspection as an oceanographic vessel, but shall be inspected and certificated for the service in which engaged, and the scientific personnel aboard then become persons employed in the business of the vessel.

10 Bulk dangerous cargoes are cargoes specified in table 151.01-10(b); in table 1 of part 153, and in table 4 of part 154 of this chapter.

11 For manned tankbarges, see § 151.01-10(c) of this chapter.

12. See § 151.01-15, 153.900(d), or 154.30 of this chapter as appropriate.

13. Sail vessel means a vessel with no auxiliary machinery on board. If the vessel has auxiliary machinery, refer to motor vessels.

[CGFR 67-83, 33 FR 1113, Jan. 27, 1968, as amended at 42 FR 49027, Sept. 26, 1977; 43 FR 968, Jan. 5, 1978; CGD 77-081, 46 FR 56204, Nov. 16, 1981; CGD 86-033, 53 FR 36026, Sept. 16, 1988; CGD 86-033, 53 FR 46871, Nov. 21, 1988; CGD 90-008, 55 FR 30664, July 26, 1990; USCG-1999-5040, 67 FR 34800, May 15, 2002]

§ 188.05-2 Exemptions from inspection laws for oceanographic research vessels and terms and conditions which apply in lieu thereof.

(a) The oceanographic research vessel shall comply with 49 CFR parts 171–179 whenever applicable, except to the extent as specifically provided otherwise in this subchapter.

(b) In order not to inhibit the mission of vessels subject to this subchapter, the Coast Guard will not require plan approval of design nor inspection of scientific equipment except to the extent specifically provided otherwise in this subchapter. However, it is the responsibility of the owner to have incorporated into the design and to maintain such equipment to applicable safety standards.

[CGFR 67–83, 33 FR 1113, Jan. 27, 1968, as amended by CGD 77–081, 46 FR 56204, Nov. 16, 1981; CGD 86–033, 53 FR 36026, Sept. 16, 1988; CGD 95–028, 62 FR 51219, Sept. 30, 1997]

§ 188.05-3 New vessels and existing vessels for the purpose of application of regulations in this subchapter.

(a) *New vessels.* In this application of the regulations in this subchapter, a new vessel is meant to be one, the construction of which is contracted for on or after March 1, 1968, or the major alteration of a vessel is contracted for on or after March 1, 1968, or the conversion of any vessel not previously inspected and certificated by the Coast Guard which is contracted for on or after March 1, 1968.

(b) *Existing vessels.* In the application of the regulations in this subchapter an existing vessel is meant to be one which is holding a valid certificate of inspection as an oceanographic research vessel on March 1, 1968.

(c) *Other vessels.* When it is desired to have a vessel, which has been used in trade or for recreational purposes, initially inspected and certificated as an oceanographic research vessel on or after March 1, 1968, such vessel shall be subject to all the requirements governing a vessel contracted for on or after March 1, 1968. However, if such vessel has a current certificate of inspection as a passenger, tank, cargo, or miscellaneous vessel, the Commandant may authorize its inspection and certification under this subchapter as a vessel contracted for prior to March 1, 1968, subject to those requirements necessitated by change in service.

[CGFR 67–83, 33 FR 1113, Jan. 27, 1968, as amended by CGD 77–081, 46 FR 56204, Nov. 16, 1981]

§ 188.05-5 Specific application noted in text.

(a) At the beginning of the various parts, subparts, and sections, a more specific application is generally given for the particular portion of the text involved. This application sets forth the types, sizes, or services or vessels to which the text pertains, and in many cases limits the application of the text to vessels contracted for before or after a specific date. As used in this subchapter, the term "vessels contracted for" includes not only the contracting for the construction of a vessel, but also the contracting for a material alteration to a vessel, the contracting for the conversion of a vessel to an oceanographic research vessel, and the changing of area of operation of a vessel if such change increases or modifies the general requirements for the vessel or increases the hazards to which it might be subjected.

[CGFR 67–83, 33 FR 1113, Jan. 27, 1968, as amended by CGD 77–081, 46 FR 56204, Nov. 16, 1981]

§ 188.05-7 Ocean or unlimited coastwise vessels on inland and Great Lakes routes.

(a) Vessels inspected and certificated for ocean or unlimited coastwise routes shall be considered suitable for navigation insofar as the provisions of this subchapter are concerned on any inland routes, including the Great Lakes.

§ 188.05-10 Application to vessels on an international voyage.

(a) Except as provided in paragraphs (b), (c), and (d) of this section, the regulations in this subchapter that apply to a vessel on an "international voyage" apply to a vessel that—

(1) Is mechanically propelled and of at least 500 gross tons; and

(2) Is engaged on a voyage—

(i) From a country to which the International Convention for Safety of Life at Sea, 1974, (SOLAS 74) applies, to a port outside that country or the reverse;

(ii) From any territory, including the Commonwealth of Puerto Rico, all possessions of the United States, and all lands held by the United States under a protectorate or mandate, whose international relations are the responsibility of a contracting SOLAS 74 government, or which is administered by the United Nations, to a port outside that territory or the reverse; or

(iii) Between the contiguous states of the United States and the states of Hawaii or Alaska or between the states of Hawaii and Alaska.

(b) The regulations that apply to a vessel on an "international voyage" in this subchapter do not apply to a vessel that—

(1) Solely navigates the Great Lakes and the St. Lawrence River as far east as a straight line drawn from Cap des Rosiers to West Point, Anticosti Island and, on the north side of Anticosti Island, the 63rd Meridian; or

(2) Is numbered in accordance with 46 U.S.C. Chapter 123.

(c) The Commandant or his authorized representative may exempt any vessel on an international voyage from the requirements of this subchapter if the vessel—

(1) Makes a single international voyage in exceptional circumstances; and

(2) Meets safety requirements prescribed for the voyage by the Commandant.

(d) The Commandant or his authorized representative may exempt any vessel from the construction requirements of this subchapter if the vessel does not proceed more than 20 nautical miles from the nearest land in the course of its voyage.

[CGD 72–131R, 38 FR 29320, Oct. 24, 1973, as amended by CGD 80–123, 45 FR 64586, Sept. 30, 1980; CGD 90–008, 55 FR 30664, July 26, 1990; CGD 84–069, 61 FR 25312, May 20, 1996; CGD 95–028, 62 FR 51219, Sept. 30, 1997]

§ 188.05-33 Scientific personnel—interpretive rulings.

(a) Scientific personnel on oceanographic research vessels are not considered to be seamen or passengers, but are considered as "persons" when requirements are based on total persons on board.

(b) Scientific personnel on such vessels shall not be required to possess seamen's documents nor shall they be required to sign shipping articles.

[CGFR 67–83, 33 FR 1113, Jan. 27, 1968, as amended by CGD 77–081, 46 FR 56204, Nov. 16, 1981]

§ 188.05-35 Load lines—interpretive ruling.

(a) Certificated vessels shall be subject to the applicable provisions of the Load Line Acts, and regulations in Subchapter E (Load Lines) of this chapter.

Subpart 188.10—Definition of Terms Used in This Subchapter

§ 188.10-1 Anniversary date.

The term *anniversary date* means the day and the month of each year, which corresponds to the date of expiration of the Certificate of Inspection.

[USCG–1999–4976, 65 FR 6509, Feb. 9, 2000]

§ 188.10-2 Approved.

This term means approved by the Commandant unless otherwise stated.

[CGFR 67–83, 33 FR 1113, Jan. 27, 1968. Redesignated by USCG–1999–4976, 65 FR 6509, Feb. 9, 2000]

§ 188.10-3 Approved container.

This term means a container which is properly labeled, marked and approved by DOT for the commodity which it contains.

[CGFR 67–83, 33 FR 1113, Jan. 27, 1968, as amended by CGD 86–033, 53 FR 36026, Sept. 16, 1988]

§ 188.10-5 Barge.

This term means any non-self-propelled vessel.

§ 188.10-6 Captain of the Port.

This term means an officer of the Coast Guard designated as such by the Commandant and who, under the superintendence and direction of the Coast Guard District Commander, gives immediate direction to Coast Guard law enforcement activities within his assigned area. In addition, the

§ 188.10-7

District Commander shall be the Captain of the Port with respect to remaining areas in his district not assigned to officers designated by the Commandant as Captain of the Port.

§ 188.10-7 Chemical stores.

This term means those chemicals intended for use in the performance of the vessel's scientific activities and is further defined in § 194.05-3.

§ 188.10-9 Chemical storeroom.

This term refers to any compartment specifically constructed or modified for the stowage of chemical stores and so designated and identified.

§ 188.10-11 Chemistry laboratory.

This term includes any space in which experiments are conducted or chemicals are used for scientific purposes in conjunction with the research mission of the vessel, and is so identified.

§ 188.10-13 Coast Guard District Commander.

This term means an officer of the Coast Guard designated as such by the Commandant to command all Coast Guard activities within the officer's district, which include the inspections, enforcement, and administration of Subtitle II of Title 46, U.S. Code, Title 46 and Title 33 U.S. Code, and regulations issued under these statutes.

[CGD 95-028, 62 FR 51219, Sept. 30, 1997]

§ 188.10-15 Coastwise.

Under this designation shall be included all vessels normally navigating the waters of any ocean or the Gulf of Mexico 20 nautical miles or less offshore.

§ 188.10-17 Combustible liquid.

This term includes any liquid whose flashpoint, as determined by an open cup tester, is above 80° F.

§ 188.10-19 Commandant.

This term means the Commandant of the Coast Guard.

§ 188.10-21 Compressed gas.

This term includes any material or mixture having in the container an absolute pressure exceeding 40 p.s.i. at 70° F.; or regardless of the pressure at 70° F., having an absolute pressure exceeding 104 p.s.i. at 130° F.; or any liquid flammable material having a vapor pressure exceeding 40 p.s.i. absolute at 100° F. as determined by the Reid method covered by the American Society for Testing Materials Method of Test for Vapor Pressure of Petroleum Products (D-323). Compressed gases are discussed in more detail in 49 CFR parts 171-179.

[CGFR 67-83, 33 FR 1113, Jan. 27, 1968, as amended by CGD 86-033, 53 FR 36026, Sept. 16, 1988]

§ 188.10-23 Corrosive liquids.

(a) This term includes those acids, alkaline caustic liquids, and other corrosive liquids which, when in contact with living tissues, will cause severe damage of such tissues, by chemical action; or in case of leakage, will materially damage or destroy other freight by chemical action, or are liable to cause fire when in contact with organic matter or with certain chemicals.

(b) A corrosive substance may be:

(1) Solid, such as iodine; or,

(2) Liquid, such as acids, or caustic soda solution; or,

(3) Gaseous, such as chlorine or sulfur dioxide.

§ 188.10-25 Explosive.

This term means a chemical compound or mixture, the primary purpose of which is to function by explosion; i.e., with substantially instantaneous release of gas and heat. Explosives are discussed in more detail in 49 CFR parts 171-179.

[CGFR 67-83, 33 FR 1113, Jan. 27, 1968, as amended by CGD 86-033, 53 FR 36026, Sept. 16, 1988]

§ 188.10-27 Flammable liquid.

This term includes any liquid whose flashpoint, as determined by an open cup tester, is 80° F. or below.

§ 188.10-31 Great Lakes.

Under this designation shall be included all vessels navigating the Great Lakes.

§ 188.10-33 Headquarters.

This term means the Office of the Commandant, U.S. Coast Guard, Washington, DC 20593-0001.

[CGFR 67-83, 33 FR 1113, Jan. 27, 1968, as amended by CGD 88-070, 53 FR 34538, Sept. 7, 1988]

§ 188.10-35 International voyage.

(a) This section describes those voyages which are considered to be "international voyages" for the purposes of this subchapter.

(b) Except as provided in paragraph (c) of this section, the term "international voyage" as used in this subchapter shall have the same meaning as that contained in Regulation 2(d), Chapter I of the International Convention for Safety of Life at Sea, 1974, i.e., *International voyage* means a voyage from a country to which the present convention applies to a port outside such country, or conversely."

(c) The International Convention for Safety of Life at Sea, 1974, does not apply to vessels "solely navigating the Great Lakes of North America and the River St. Lawrence as far east as a straight line drawn from Cap de Rosiers to West Point, Anticosti Island and, on the north side of Anticosti Island, the 63d Meridian." Accordingly, such vessels shall not be considered as being on an "international voyage" for the purpose of this subchapter.

(d) In addition, although voyages between the continental United States and Hawaii or Alaska, and voyages between Hawaii and Alaska are not "international voyages" under the provisions of the International Convention for Safety of Life at Sea, 1974, such voyages are similar in nature and shall be considered as "international voyages" for the purposes of this subchapter.

[CGFR 67-83, 33 FR 1113, Jan. 27, 1968, as amended by CGD 80-123, 45 FR 64586, Sept. 30, 1980; CDG 90-008, 55 FR 30664, July 26, 1990]

§ 188.10-37 Label.

This term means the label required by 49 CFR part 172 to be affixed to containers of explosives or other hazardous materials.

[CGD 86-033, 53 FR 36026, Sept. 16, 1988]

§ 188.10-39 Lakes, bays, and sounds.

Under this designation shall be included all vessels navigating the waters of any of the lakes, bays, or sounds, other than the waters of the Great Lakes.

§ 188.10-41 Liquefied compressed gas.

This term means a gas which, under the charged pressure, is partially liquid at a temperature of 70° F.

§ 188.10-43 Liquefied flammable gas.

This term means any flammable gas having a Reid vapor pressure exceeding 40 p.s.i. which has been liquefied.

§ 188.10-45 Marine inspector or inspector.

These terms mean any person from the civilian or military branch of the Coast Guard assigned under the superintendence and direction of an Officer in Charge, Marine Inspection, or any other person as may be designated for the performance of duties with respect to the inspections, enforcement, and administration of Subtitle II of Title 46, U.S. Code, Title 46 and Title 33 U.S. Code, and regulations issued under these statutes.

[CGD 95-028, 62 FR 51219, Sept. 30, 1997]

§ 188.10-49 Numbered vessel.

This term means a vessel which is numbered under the provisions of 46 U.S.C. Chapter 123.

[CGD 95-028, 62 FR 51219, Sept. 30, 1997]

§ 188.10-51 Ocean.

Under this designation shall be included all vessels navigating the waters of any ocean, or the Gulf of Mexico more than 20 nautical miles offshore.

§ 188.10-53 Oceanographic research vessel.

The term *oceanographic research vessel* means a vessel that the Secretary finds is being employed only in instruction in oceanography or limnology, or both, or only in oceanographic or limnological research, including those studies about the sea such as seismic, gravity meter, and magnetic exploration and other marine geophysical or

§ 188.10-55

geological surveys, atmospheric research, and biological research.

[CGD 84-069, 61 FR 25312, May 20, 1996]

§ 188.10-55 Officer in Charge, Marine Inspection.

This term means any person from the civilian or military branch of the Coast Guard designated as such by the Commandant and who, under the superintendence and direction of the Coast Guard District Commander, is in charge of an inspection zone for the performance of duties with respect to the inspections, enforcement, and administration of Subtitle II of Title 46, U.S. Code, Title 46 and Title 33 U.S. Code, and regulations issued under these statutes.

[CGD 95-028, 62 FR 51219, Sept. 30, 1997]

§ 188.10-56 Pilot boarding equipment and point of access.

(a) *Pilot boarding equipment* means a pilot ladder, accomodation ladder, pilot hoist, or combination of them as required by this subchapter.

(b) *Point of access* means the place on deck of a vessel where a person steps onto or off of pilot boarding equipment.

[CGD 79-032, 49 FR 25455, June 21, 1984]

§ 188.10-57 Portable tank.

This phrase means a container having a capacity greater than 110 gallons, which is independent of the vessel's structure.

§ 188.10-59 Recognized classification society.

This term means the American Bureau of Shipping or other classification society recognized by the Commandant.

§ 188.10-61 Rivers.

Under this designation shall be included all vessels whose navigation is restricted to rivers and/or canals exclusively, and to such other waters as may be so designated by the Coast Guard District Commander.

§ 188.10-65 Seagoing barge.

A seagoing barge is a nonself-propelled vessel of at least 100 gross tons making voyages beyond the Boundary Line (as defined in 46 CFR part 7).

[CGD 95-028, 62 FR 51219, Sept. 30, 1997]

§ 188.10-67 Scientific equipment.

This term means equipment installed or carried on board an oceanographic research vessel and not normally required for the operation of a vessel or its machinery or for the navigation of the vessel, and which is used primarily in the gathering of scientific data or samples or in processing, analyzing, preserving, or storing such data or samples.

[CGFR 67-83, 33 FR 1113, Jan. 27, 1968, as amended by CGD 77-081, 46 FR 56204, Nov. 16, 1981]

§ 188.10-69 Scientific laboratory.

This term means those spaces on board an oceanographic research vessel used primarily for scientific experimentation or research, and are so identified.

§ 188.10-71 Scientific personnel.

This term means those persons who are aboard an oceanographic research vessel solely for the purpose of engaging in scientific research, or in instructing, or receiving instruction, in oceanography or limnology, and shall not be considered seamen under the provisions of Title 46, United States Code.

[CGFR 67-83, 33 FR 1113, Jan. 27, 1968, as amended by CGD 77-081, 46 FR 56204, Nov. 16, 1981; CGD 97-057, 62 FR 51050, Sept. 30, 1997]

§ 188.10-73 Ships' stores and supplies.

This term means any article or substance which is used on board a vessel subject to the appropriate portions of part 147 of Subchapter N (Dangerous Cargoes) of this chapter for the upkeep and maintenance of the vessel; or for the safety or comfort of the vessel, its passengers or crew; or for the operation or navigation of the vessel (except fuel for its own machinery).

[CGFR 67-83, 33 FR 1113, Jan. 27, 1968, as amended by CGD 86-033, 53 FR 36026, Sept. 16, 1988]

§ 188.10-75 Undocumented vessel.

This term means any vessel which is not required to have, and does not

Coast Guard, DHS

have, a valid marine document issued by the U.S. Coast Guard.

§ 188.10-77 Vessel.

Where the word "vessel" is used in this subchapter, it shall be considered to include all inspected and certificated oceanographic research vessels as listed in Column 7 of Table 188.05-1(a).

[CGFR 67-83, 33 FR 1113, Jan. 27, 1968, as amended by CGD 77-081, 46 FR 56204, Nov. 16, 1981]

Subpart 188.15—Equivalents

§ 188.15-1 Conditions under which equivalents may be used.

(a) Where in this subchapter it is provided that a particular fitting, material, appliance, apparatus, or equipment, or type thereof, shall be fitted or carried in a vessel, or that any particular provision shall be made or arrangement shall be adopted, the Commandant may accept in substitution therefor any other fitting, material, apparatus, or equipment, or type thereof, or any other arrangement: *Provided,* That he shall have been satisfied by suitable trials that the fitting, material, appliance, apparatus, or equipment, or type thereof, or the provision or arrangement is at least as effective as that specified in this subchapter.

(b) In any case where it is shown to the satisfaction of the Commandant that the use of any particular equipment, apparatus, or arrangement not specifically required by law is unreasonable or impracticable, the Commandant may permit the use of alternate equipment, apparatus, or arrangement to such an extent and upon such conditions as will insure, to his satisfaction, a degree of safety consistent with the minimum standards set forth in this subchapter.

§ 188.15-5 Design of vessels.

(a) In order not to inhibit design and application the Commandant may accept vessels of unusual, unique, special, or exotic design, both new and for conversion, after it is shown to his satisfaction that such a vessel is at least as safe as any vessel which meets the standards required by this subchapter.

Subpart 188.20—General Marine Engineering Requirements

§ 188.20-1 Marine engineering details.

(a) The marine engineering details shall be in accordance with Subchapter F (Marine Engineering) of this chapter.

Subpart 188.25—General Electrical Engineering Requirements

§ 188.25-1 Electrical engineering details.

(a) The electrical engineering details shall be in accordance with subchapter J (Electrical Engineering) of this chapter.

Subpart 188.27—Lifesaving Appliances and Arrangements

§ 188.27-1 Lifesaving appliances and arrangements.

All lifesaving appliances and arrangements shall be in accordance with the requirements for special purpose vessels in subchapter W (Lifesaving Appliances and Arrangements) of this chapter.

[CGD 84-069, 61 FR 25312, May 20, 1996]

Subpart 188.35—American Bureau of Shipping's Standards

§ 188.35-1 Standards to be used.

(a) Where in this subchapter an item, or method of construction, or testing is required to meet the standards established by the American Bureau of Shipping, the current standards in effect at the time of construction of the vessel, or otherwise as applicable, shall be used.

(b) The current standards of other recognized classification societies may also be accepted upon approval by the Commandant.

§ 188.35-5 Where obtainable.

(a) The standards established by the American Bureau of Shipping are usually published annually and may be purchased from the American Bureau of Shipping, ABS Plaza, 16855 Northchase Drive, Houston, TX 77060.

Pt. 189

(b) These standards may also be examined at the Office of the Commandant (G–MOC), U.S. Coast Guard, Washington, DC 20593–0001, or at the Office of any Coast Guard District Commander or Officer in Charge, Marine Inspection.

[CGFR 67–83, 33 FR 1113, Jan. 27, 1968, as amended by CGD 88–070, 53 FR 34538, Sept. 7, 1988; 53 FR 37570, Sept. 27, 1988; 53 FR 44011, Nov. 1, 1988; CGD 95–072, 60 FR 50469, Sept. 29, 1995; CGD 96–041, 61 FR 50735, Sept. 27, 1996; USCG–2000–7790, 65 FR 58465, Sept. 29, 2000]

PART 189—INSPECTION AND CERTIFICATION

Subpart 189.01—Certificate of Inspection

Sec.
189.01–1 When required.
189.01–5 Posting.
189.01–10 Period of validity for a Certificate of Inspection.
189.01–15 Temporary certificate.

Subpart 189.05—Permit to Proceed to Another Port for Repair

189.05–1 When issued.
189.05–5 To whom issued.
189.05–10 Conditions of permit.
189.05–15 Posting.

Subpart 189.15—Inspection of Vessels

189.15–1 Standards in inspection of hulls, boilers, and machinery.

Subpart 189.20—Initial Inspection

189.20–1 Prerequisite of certificate of inspection.
189.20–5 When made.
189.20–10 Plans.
189.20–15 Scope of inspection.
189.20–20 Specific tests and inspections.
189.20–25 Chemical and explosive hazards.

Subpart 189.25—Inspection for Certification

189.25–1 Prerequisite of reissuance of certificate of inspection.
189.25–5 Application for a Certificate of Inspection.
189.25–10 Scope of inspection.
189.25–15 Lifesaving equipment.
189.25–20 Fire-extinguishing equipment.
189.25–25 Hull equipment.
189.25–30 Electrical engineering equipment.
189.25–35 Marine engineering equipment.
189.25–38 Pollution prevention.
189.25–40 Sanitary inspection.
189.25–45 Fire hazards.
189.25–47 Chemical and explosive hazards.

46 CFR Ch. I (10–1–04 Edition)

189.25–50 Inspector not limited.

Subpart 189.27—Annual and Periodic Inspections

189.27–1 Annual inspection.
189.27–5 Periodic inspection.
189.27–10 Certificate of Inspection: Conditions of validity.

Subpart 189.30—Inspection After Accident

189.30–1 General or partial survey.

Subpart 189.33—Sanitary Inspections

189.33–1 When made.

Subpart 189.35—Weight Handling Gear

189.35–1 Application.
189.35–3 Intent.
189.35–5 Tests.
189.35–7 Examinations.
189.35–9 Plans.
189.35–11 Special cases.
189.35–13 Master's responsibility.
189.35–15 Major installations.
189.35–90 Weight handling gear manufactured prior to March 1, 1968.

Subpart 189.40—Drydocking

189.40–1 Definitions relating to hull examinations.
189.40–3 Drydock examination, internal structural examination, cargo tank internal examination, and underwater survey intervals.
189.40–5 Notice and plans required.

Subpart 189.43—Integral Fuel Oil Tank Examinations

189.43–1 When required.

Subpart 189.45—Repairs and Alterations

189.45–1 Notice required.
189.45–5 Inspection required.

Subpart 189.50—Special Operating Requirements

189.50–1 Inspection and testing required when making alterations, repairs, or other such operations involving riveting, welding, burning, or like fire-producing actions.

Subpart 189.55—Plan Approval

189.55–1 General.
189.55–5 Plans and specifications required for new construction.
189.55–10 Plans required for alterations of existing vessels.
189.55–15 Procedure for submittal of plans.

344

Coast Guard, DHS

§ 189.05-1

189.55-20 Number of plans required.

Subpart 189.60—Certificates Under International Convention for Safety of Life at Sea, 1974

189.60-1 Application.
189.60-5 Cargo Ship Safety Construction Certificate.
189.60-10 Cargo Ship Safety Equipment Certificate.
189.60-15 Cargo Ship Safety Radio Certificate.
189.60-25 Exemption Certificate.
189.60-30 Safety Management Certificate.
189.60-35 Availability of Certificates.
189.60-40 Duration of Convention certificates.
189.60-45 American Bureau of Shipping.

AUTHORITY: 33 U.S.C. 1321(j); 46 U.S.C. 2113, 3306, 3307; E.O. 12234, 45 FR 58801, 3 CFR, 1980 Comp., p. 277; E.O. 12777, 56 FR 54757, 3 CFR, 1991 Comp., p. 351; Department of Homeland Security Delegation No. 0170.1.

SOURCE: CGFR 67-83, 33 FR 1118, Jan. 27, 1968, unless otherwise noted.

Subpart 189.01—Certificate of Inspection

§ 189.01-1 When required.

(a) Except as noted in this subpart or subpart 189.05 of this part, no vessel subject to inspection and certification shall be operated without a valid certificate of inspection.

§ 189.01-5 Posting.

(a) The original certificate of inspection shall, in general, be framed under glass or other transparent material and posted in a conspicuous place where it will be most likely to be observed. On other vessels such as barges, where the framing of the certificate under glass would be impracticable, the original certificate of inspection shall be kept on board to be shown on demand.

§ 189.01-10 Period of validity for a Certificate of Inspection.

(a) A Certificate of Inspection is valid for 5 years. Application may be made by the master, owner, or agent for inspection and issuance of a new certificate of inspection at any time during the period of validity of the current certificate.

(b) Certificates of inspection may be revoked or suspended by the Coast Guard where such process is authorized by law. This may occur if the vessel does not meet the requirements of law or regulations in this chapter or if there is a failure to maintain the safety requirements requisite to the issuance of a certificate of inspection.

(c)(1) In the case of the following vessels, modification of the period of validity of the certificate of inspection will be permitted as set forth in this paragraph:

(i) Non-self-propelled vessels of 100 gross tons and over proceeding on the high seas or ocean for the sole purpose of changing place of employment.

(ii) Non-self-propelled vessels of 100 gross tons and over making rare or infrequent voyages on the high seas or ocean and returning to the port of departure.

(2) The certificate of inspection may be issued for a specific period of time to cover a described situation or for one voyage only but not to exceed 5 years. The certificate of inspection will include the conditions under which the vessel must operate. Unless the vessel is in compliance with this subchapter insofar as it applies to seagoing barges of 100 gross tons and over, such vessel shall not carry any person on board while underway, and the certificate of inspection will be endorsed as an unmanned seagoing barge.

[CGFR 67-83, 33 FR 1118, Jan. 27, 1968, as amended by CGFR 68-82, 33 FR 18911, Dec. 18, 1968; CGD 95-012, 60 FR 48052, Sept. 18, 1995; 60 FR 50120, Sept. 28, 1995; USCG-1999-4976, 65 FR 6509, Feb. 9, 2000]

§ 189.01-15 Temporary certificate.

(a) If necessary to prevent delay of the vessel, a temporary certificate of inspection, Form CG-854, shall be issued pending the issuance and delivery of the regular certificate of inspection. Such temporary certificate shall be carried in the same manner as the regular certificate and shall in all ways be considered the same as the regular certificate of inspection which it represents.

Subpart 189.05—Permit to Proceed to Another Port for Repair

§ 189.05-1 When issued.

(a) The Officer in Charge, Marine Inspection, may issue a permit to proceed

§ 189.05-5

to another port for repair, Form CG-948, to a vessel, if in his judgment it can be done with safety, even if the certificate of inspection of the vessel has expired or is about to expire.

§ 189.05-5 To whom issued.

(a) Such permit will only be issued upon the written application of the master, owner, or agent of the vessel.

§ 189.05-10 Conditions of permit.

(a) The permit will state upon its face the conditions under which it is issued.

§ 189.05-15 Posting.

(a) The permit shall be carried in a manner similar to that described in § 189.01-5 for a certificate of inspection.

Subpart 189.15—Inspection of Vessels

§ 189.15-1 Standards in inspection of hulls, boilers, and machinery.

In the inspection of hulls, boilers, and machinery of vessels, the standards established by the American Bureau of Shipping, see part 188, subpart 188.35 of this chapter, respecting material and construction of hulls, boilers, and machinery, and certificate of classification referring thereto, except where otherwise provided for by the rules and regulations in this subchapter, subchapter E (Load Lines), subchapter F (Marine Engineering), subchapter J (Electrical Engineering), and subchapter W (Lifesaving Appliances and Arrangements) of this chapter shall be accepted as standard by the inspectors.

[CGD 84-069, 61 FR 25312, May 20, 1996]

Subpart 189.20—Initial Inspection

§ 189.20-1 Prerequisite of certificate of inspection.

(a) The initial inspection is a prerequisite of the issuance of the original certificate of inspection.

§ 189.20-5 When made.

(a) The initial inspection will only be made upon the written application of the owner or builder of the vessel to the Officer in Charge, Marine Inspection, on Form CG-3752, Application for Inspection of U.S. Vessel, at or nearest the port where the vessel is located.

§ 189.20-10 Plans.

(a) Before application for inspection is made, and before construction is started, the owner or builder shall have plans approved by the Commandant indicating the proposed arrangement and construction of the vessel.

(b) The procedure for submitting plans and the list of plans to be supplied is set forth in subpart 189.55 of this part.

§ 189.20-15 Scope of inspection.

(a) The initial inspection, which may consist of a series of inspections during the construction of a vessel, shall include a complete inspection of the structure, machinery, and equipment, except scientific equipment which does not affect the safety of the vessel or personnel, but including the outside of the vessel's bottom, and the inside and outside of the boilers and unfired pressure vessels. The inspection shall be such as to insure that the arrangements, materials, and scantlings of the structure, boilers and other pressure vessels and their appurtenances, piping, main and auxiliary machinery, electrical installations, lifesaving appliances, fire detecting and extinguishing equipment, pilot boarding equipment, pollution prevention equipment, and other equipment fully comply with the applicable regulations for such vessel and are in accordance with approved plans, and determine that the vessel is in possession of a valid certificate issued by the Federal Communications Commission, if any. The inspection shall be such as to ensure that the workmanship of all parts of the vessel and its equipment is in all respects satisfactory and that the vessel is provided with lights, means of making sound signals, and distress signals as required by applicable statutes and regulations.

(b) When equipment other than scientific equipment is installed which is not required by the applicable regulations in this subchapter, that equipment shall be inspected and tested as may be required for such equipment by the Officer in Charge, Marine Inspection, to assure safety.

(1) The electrical or pressure connections to the ship's supply shall be designed to marine standards and shall be free of personnel hazards.

(2) Scientific equipment will not be inspected but will be examined for external hazards associated with connection to the vessel, dangerous moving parts, extremes in temperature and shock.

[CGFR 67–83, 33 FR 1118, Jan. 27, 1968, as amended by CGFR 68–82, 33 FR 18911, Dec. 18, 1968; CGD 71–161R, 37 FR 28263, Dec. 21, 1972; CGD 82–036, 48 FR 654, Jan. 6, 1983; CGD 79–032, 49 FR 25455, June 21, 1984; CGD 95–012, 60 FR 48052, Sept. 18, 1995; 60 FR 50120, Sept. 28, 1995]

§ 189.20–20 Specific tests and inspections.

The applicable tests and inspections as set forth in subpart 189.25 of this part shall be made at this time. In addition, the following specific tests and inspections shall be made by the marine inspector.

(a) For inspection procedures of lifesaving appliances and arrangements, see subchapter W (Lifesaving Appliances and Arrangements) of this chapter.

(b) Installation of carbon dioxide extinguishing piping. See § 193.15–15 of this subchapter.

(c) Marine engineering equipment and systems. See Subchapter F (Marine Engineering) of this chapter.

(d) Electrical engineering equipment and systems. See Subchapter J (Electrical Engineering) of this chapter.

[CGFR 67–83, 33 FR 1118, Jan. 27, 1968, as amended by CGD 84–069, 61 FR 25312, May 20, 1996]

§ 189.20–25 Chemical and explosive hazards.

(a) If installed, the marine inspector shall examine the laboratories, storerooms, magazines, vans, and chests to insure that hazards are minimized.

Subpart 189.25—Inspection for Certification

§ 189.25–1 Prerequisite of reissuance of certificate of inspection.

(a) An inspection for certification is a prerequisite of the reissuance of a certificate of inspection.

§ 189.25–5 Application for a Certificate of Inspection.

You must submit a written application for an inspection for certification to the cognizant OCMI. To renew a Certificate of Inspection, you must submit an application at least 30 days before the expiration of the tank vessel's current certificate. You must use Form CG–3752, Application for Inspection of U.S. Vessel, and submit it to the OCMI at, or nearest to, the port where the vessel is located. When renewing a Certificate of Inspection, you must schedule an inspection for certification within the 3 months before the expiration date of the current Certificate of Inspection.

[USCG–1999–4976, 65 FR 6509, Feb. 9, 2000]

§ 189.25–10 Scope of inspection.

(a) The inspection for certification shall include an inspection of the structure, boilers, and other pressure vessels, machinery, and equipment. The inspection shall be such as to insure that the vessel, as regards the structure, boilers, and other pressure vessels and their appurtenances, piping, main and auxilliary machinery, electrical installations, life-saving appliances, fire detecting and extinguishing equipment, pilot boarding equipment, pollution prevention equipment, and other equipment, is in satisfactory condition and fit for the service for which it is intended, and that it complies with the applicable regulations for such vessel, and determine that the vessel is in possession of a valid certificate issued by the Federal Communications Commission, if required. The lights, means of making sound signals, and distress signals carried by the vessel shall also be subject to the above-mentioned inspection for the purpose of ensuring that they comply with the requirements of the applicable statutes and regulations.

§ 189.25-15

(b) When equipment other than scientific equipment is installed which is not required by the applicable regulations in this subchapter, that equipment shall be inspected and tested as may be required for such equipment by the Officer in Charge, Marine Inspection, to assure safety.

(1) Scientific equipment and their electrical or pressure connection to the ship's supply and laboratories may be checked to ascertain that they are maintained free of hazards.

[CGFR 67-83, 33 FR 1118, Jan. 27, 1968, as amended by CGFR 68-82, 33 FR 18911, Dec. 18, 1968; CGD 71-161R, 37 FR 28263, Dec. 21, 1972; CGD 82-036, 48 FR 655, Jan. 6, 1983; CGD 79-032, 49 FR 25455, June 21, 1984; CGD 95-012, 60 FR 48052, Sept. 18, 1995; 60 FR 50120, Sept. 28, 1995]

§ 189.25-15 Lifesaving equipment.

For inspection procedures of lifesaving appliances and arrangements, see subchapter W (Lifesaving Appliances and Arrangements) of this chapter.

[CGD 84-069, 61 FR 25312, May 20, 1996]

§ 189.25-20 Fire-extinguishing equipment.

(a) At each inspection for certification, periodic inspection, and at such other times as considered necessary the inspector shall determine that all fire-extinguishing equipment is in suitable condition and he may require such tests as are considered necessary to determine the condition of the equipment. The inspector shall determine if the tests and inspections required by § 196.15-60 of this subchapter have been conducted. At each inspection for certification and periodic inspection the inspector shall conduct the following tests and inspections of fire-extinguishing equipment:

(1) All hand portable fire extinguishers and semiportable fire-extinguishing systems shall be checked as noted in Table 189.25-20(a)(1). In addition, the hand portable fire-extinguishers and semiportable fire-extinguishing systems shall be examined for excessive corrosion and general condition.

TABLE 189.25-20(a)(1)

Type unit	Test
Soda acid	Discharge. Clean hose and inside of extinguisher thoroughly. Recharge.
Foam	Discharge. Clean hose and inside of extinguisher thoroughly. Recharge.
Pump tank (water or antifreeze).	Discharge. Clean hose and inside of extinguisher thoroughly. Recharge with clean water or antifreeze.
Cartridge operated (water, antifreeze, or loaded stream).	Examine pressure cartridge and replace if end is punctured or if cartridge is otherwise determined to have leaked or to be in unsuitable condition. Remove liquid. Clean hose and inside of extinguisher thoroughly. Recharge with water, solution, or antifreeze. Insert charged cartridge.
Carbon dioxide	Weigh cylinders. Recharge if weight loss exceeds 10 percent of weight of charge. Inspect hose and nozzle to be sure they are clear.[1]
Dry chemical (cartridge-operated type).	Examine pressure cartridge and replace if end is punctured or if cartridge is otherwise determined to have leaked or to be in unsuitable condition. Inspect hose and nozzle to see they are clear. Insert charged cartridge. Be sure dry chemical is free-flowing (not caked) and chamber contains full charge.
Dry chemical (stored pressure type).	See that pressure gage is in operating range. If not, or if seal is broken, weigh or otherwise determine that full charge of dry chemical is in extinguisher. Recharge if pressure is low or if dry chemical is needed.
Vaporizing liquid[2]	

[1] Cylinders must be tested and marked and all flexible connections and discharge hoses of semiportable carbon dioxide and halon extinguishers must be tested or renewed as required in §§ 147.60 and 147.65 of this chapter.

[2] Vaporizing-liquid type fire extinguishers containing carbon tetrachloride or chlorobromomethane or other toxic vaporizing liquids are not permitted.

(2) Fixed fire-extinguishing systems shall be checked as noted in Table 189.25-20(a)(2). In addition, all parts of the fixed fire-extinguishing systems shall be examined for excessive corrosion and general conditions.

TABLE 189.25-20(a)(2)

Type system	Test
Foam	Systems utilizing a soda solution shall have such solution replaced. In all cases, ascertain that powder is not caked.
Carbon dioxide	Weigh cylinders. Recharge if weight loss exceeds 10 percent of weight of charge.[1]

[1] Cylinders must be tested and marked and all flexible connections on fixed carbon dioxide and halon systems must be tested or renewed as required in §§ 147.60 and 147.65 of this chapter.

(3) On all fire-extinguishing systems all piping, controls, valves, and alarms

shall be checked to ascertain that the system is in operating condition.

(4) The fire main system shall be operated and the pressure checked at the outlets having the greatest pressure drop between the fire pumps and the nozzles which may not always be the most remote and highest outlets. All firehoses shall be subjected to a test pressure equivalent to the maximum pressure to which they may be subjected in service, but not less than 100 p.s.i.

[CGFR 67-83, 33 FR 1118, Jan. 27, 1968, as amended by CGD 78-154, 44 FR 13492, Mar. 12, 1979; CGD 84-044, 53 FR 7752, Mar. 10, 1988; USCG-1999-4976, 65 FR 6509, Feb. 9, 2000]

§ 189.25-25 Hull equipment.

(a) At each inspection for certification and periodic inspection the inspector shall conduct the following tests and inspections of hull equipment:

(1) All watertight doors shall be operated locally by manual power and also by hydraulic or electric power if so fitted. Where remote control is fitted, the doors shall also be operated by the remote control apparatus.

(2) The remote controls of all valves shall be operated.

(3) An examination of installed weight, handling gear and related shipboard records shall be made to ascertain the condition and suitability of the equipment for the service intended. In conducting this examination the marine inspector shall be guided by the provisions of subpart 189.35. Current valid certificates and registers, issued by a recognized nonprofit organization or association approved by the Commandant, may be accepted as prima facie evidence of the condition and suitability of the weight handling gear. Weight handling gear certificates and registers will not be issued by the Coast Guard.

[CGFR 67-83, 33 FR 1118, Jan. 27, 1968, as amended by USCG-1999-4976, 65 FR 6509, Feb. 9, 2000]

§ 189.25-30 Electrical engineering equipment.

(a) For inspection procedures of Electrical Engineering equipment and systems, see Subchapter J (Electrical Engineering) of this chapter.

§ 189.25-35 Marine engineering equipment.

(a) For inspection procedures of Marine Engineering equipment and systems, see Subchapter F (Marine Engineering) of this chapter.

§ 189.25-38 Pollution prevention.

At each inspection for certification and periodic inspection, the inspector shall examine the vessel to determine that it meets the vessel design and equipment requirements for pollution prevention in 33 CFR part 155, subpart B.

[CGD 71-161R, 37 FR 28263, Dec. 21, 1972; USCG-1999-4976, 65 FR 6509, Feb. 9, 2000]

§ 189.25-40 Sanitary inspection.

(a) At each inspection for certification and periodic inspection, the quarters, toilets, and washing spaces, galleys, serving pantries, lockers, etc., shall be examined by the marine inspector to be assured that they are in a sanitary condition.

[CGFR 67-83, 33 FR 1118, Jan. 27, 1968, as amended by USCG-1999-4976, 65 FR 6509, Feb. 9, 2000]

§ 189.25-45 Fire hazards.

At each inspection for certification and periodic inspection, the inspector shall examine the tank tops and bilges in the machinery spaces to see that there is no accumulation of oil which might create a fire hazard.

[CGFR 67-83, 33 FR 1118, Jan. 27, 1968, as amended by USCG-1999-4976, 65 FR 6509, Feb. 9, 2000]

§ 189.25-47 Chemical and explosive hazards.

(a) The marine inspector shall inspect every chemistry laboratory, scientific laboratory, and chemical storeroom during each inspection for certification and periodic inspection.

(b) Magazines, vans, and chests shall be inspected during each inspection for certification and periodic inspection.

[CGFR 67-83, 33 FR 1118, Jan. 27, 1968, as amended by USCG-1999-4976, 65 FR 6509, Feb. 9, 2000; 65 FR 11904, Mar. 7, 2000]

§ 189.25–50 Inspector not limited.

(a) Nothing in this subpart shall be construed as limiting the inspector from making such tests or inspections as he deems necessary to be assured of the safety and seaworthiness of the vessel.

Subpart 189.27—Annual and Periodic Inspections

§ 189.27–1 Annual inspection.

(a) Your vessel must undergo an annual inspection within the 3 months before or after each anniversary date, except as specified in § 189.27–5.

(b) You must contact the cognizant OCMI to schedule an inspection at a time and place which he or she approves. No written application is required.

(c) The scope of the annual inspection is the same as the inspection for certification, as specified in § 189.25–10, but in less detail unless the cognizant marine inspector finds deficiencies or determines that a major change has occurred since the last inspection. If deficiencies are found or a major change to the vessel has occurred, the marine inspector will conduct an inspection more detailed in scope to ensure that the vessel is in satisfactory condition and fit for the service for which it is intended. If your vessel passes the annual inspection, the marine inspector will endorse your current Certificate of Inspection.

(d) If the annual inspection reveals deficiencies in your vessel's maintenance, you must make any or all repairs or improvements within the time period specified by the OCMI.

(e) Nothing in this subpart limits the marine inspector from conducting such tests or inspections he or she deems necessary to be assured of the vessel's seaworthiness.

[USCG–1999–4976, 65 FR 6509, Feb. 9, 2000]

§ 189.27–5 Periodic inspection.

(a) Your vessel must undergo a periodic inspection within 3 months before or after the second or third anniversary of the date of your vessel's Certificate of Inspection. This periodic inspection will take the place of an annual inspection.

(b) You must contact the cognizant OCMI to schedule an inspection at a time and place which he or she approves. No written application is required.

(c) The scope of the periodic inspection is the same as that for the inspection for certification, as specified in § 189.25–10. The OCMI will insure that the vessel is in satisfactory condition and fit for the service for which it is intended. If your vessel passes the periodic inspection, the marine inspector will endorse your current Certificate of Inspection.

(d) If the periodic inspection reveals deficiencies in your vessel's maintenance, you must make any or all repairs or improvements within the time period specified by the OCMI.

(e) Nothing in this subpart limits the marine inspector from conducting such tests or inspections he or she deems necessary to be assured of the vessel's seaworthiness.

[USCG–1999–4976, 65 FR 6509, Feb. 9, 2000]

§ 189.27–10 Certificate of Inspection: Conditions of validity.

To maintain a valid Certificate of Inspection, you must complete your annual and periodic inspections within the periods specified in §§ 189.27–1 and 189.27–5 respectively, and your Certificate of Inspection must be endorsed.

[USCG–1999–4976, 65 FR 6509, Feb. 9, 2000]

Subpart 189.30—Inspection After Accident

§ 189.30–1 General or partial survey.

(a) A survey, either general or partial, according to the circumstances, shall be made every time an accident occurs or a defect is discovered which affects the safety of the vessel or the efficacy or completeness of its lifesaving appliances, firefighting or other equipment, or whenever any important repairs or renewals are made. The survey shall be such as to insure that the necessary repairs or renewals have been effectively made, that the material and the workmanship of such repairs or renewals are in all respects satisfactory, and that the vessel complies in all respects with the regulations in this subchapter.

Coast Guard, DHS

§ 189.35-9

Subpart 189.33—Sanitary Inspections

§ 189.33-1 When made.

(a) An inspection of quarters, toilet and washing spaces, serving pantries, galleys, etc., shall be made at least once in every month. If the route of the vessel is such that it is away from a U.S. port for more than 1 month, an inspection shall be conducted at least once every trip.

Subpart 189.35—Weight Handling Gear

§ 189.35-1 Application.

(a) The requirements of this subpart shall apply to all weight handling gear installed on oceanographic research vessels except weight handling gear designated to handle primary life-saving equipment. Weight handling gear designated for this use shall meet the applicable portions of Subchapter I (Cargo and Miscellaneous Vessels) of this chapter.

(b) Weight handling gear placed under the inspection and testing required for cargo gear by the classification society or cargo gear bureaus recognized in Subchapter I (Cargo and Miscellaneous Vessels) of this chapter may be considered as having met the intent of this subpart.

§ 189.35-3 Intent.

(a) In recognition of the special nature of oceanographic research vessel operations, it is intended that maximum flexibility be given to the owner or operator in complying with the safety requirements for weight handling gear in this subpart. The primary interest of the Coast Guard shall extend to hazards associated with the connections to the vessel, dangerous moving parts, extremes in temperature and shock hazards.

§ 189.35-5 Tests.

(a) An installation load test and safety assessment shall be conducted by the owner or operator. Section 189.35-13 may be used as a guide for the safety assessment. It shall be the responsibility of the owner or operator to notify the Officer in Charge, Marine Inspection, of the time and place of the installation tests when occurring in a port of the United States to permit a marine inspector to witness the tests if desired. Subsequent owner or operator conducted tests may be required at the time of the vessel's inspection periods if a visual examination or review of the equipment record reveals evidence of an unsafe condition. Tests should normally consist of exercising the equipment as a unit with a proof load 25 percent in excess of the equipment's normal working load, however manufacturer's design limitations should not be exceeded. Consideration shall be given to the plans of loading when conducting these tests. Braking, safety and limiting devices shall be tested whenever feasible.

§ 189.35-7 Examinations.

(a) Examination of weight handling gear will normally consist of a visual examination with access covers removed. Suitability of the equipment for the service intended will be emphasized. Disassembly of the equipment will be required only when there is evidence of a deficiency or an unsafe condition. Non-destructive tests, such as radiography, ultrasonic, electronic, or other methods may be used if appropriate, however will not be required.

§ 189.35-9 Plans.

(a) Plans will not normally be required, however depending on the use of the weight handling gear, submission of plans or other technical information may be required by the Officer in Charge, Marine Inspection. Unless an unsafe condition is in evidence, vessel operations will not be delayed while plans or other technical information are under review. Plans, when required, shall normally include:

(1) One line electrical diagrams showing appropriate overload protection as currently required by subchapter J (Electrical Engineering) of this chapter.

(2) Plans showing hydraulic or pneumatic equipment.

(3) Stress and/or arrangement diagrams with supporting design calculations as appropriate to the specific equipment in question.

§ 189.35-11

(b) When weight handling gear is built to a recognized code or specification, plans or other technical data will not normally be required. Purchase specification or vendor's information may be accepted in lieu of design calculations if sufficiently definitive of materials, design (safety) factors and operating limitations.

(c) Design information, when required, will be evaluated against the following minimum design criteria:

(1) Wet Weight Handling Gear: Wet gear shall be considered to consist of gear used to lower equipment, apparatus or objects beneath the surface of the water or for trailing objects, where the wire rope or cable is payed out beneath the surface and becomes part of the line pull at the head sheave or winch drum. Wet gear shall be designed, as a minimum, to withstand and operate in excess of the breaking strength of the strongest section or wire to be used in any condition of loading. The safety factor for all metal structural parts shall be a minimum of 1.5; i.e., the yield strength of the material shall be at least 1.5 times the calculated stresses resulting from application of a load equal to the nominal breaking strength of the strongest section or wire rope to be used. Suitable assumptions for the actual loading conditions shall be used in the design of wet gear. The lead of the wire rope from the head sheave or winch drum shall be considered to vary from the vertical and in azimuth in a manner to represent the most adverse loading condition.

(2) Other weight handling gear will be evaluated on the basis of the standards of a recognized organization or association recognized by the Commandant under § 31.10-6.

(3) Hydraulic or pneumatic systems will be evaluated on the basis of Subchapter F (Marine Engineering) of this chapter.

[CGFR 67-83, 33 FR 1118, Jan. 27, 1968, as amended by CGFR 69-116, 35 FR 6863, Apr. 30, 1970; CGD 95-028, 62 FR 51219, Sept. 30, 1997]

§ 189.35-11 Special cases.

(a) If the above safety requirements defeat the purpose of any particular piece of weight handling gear, consideration will be given to a relaxation of the requirements.

§ 189.35-13 Master's responsibility.

(a) The master of the vessel shall ensure the following:

(1) The gear is properly installed and secure.

(2) Suitable safety guards are installed in way of rotating machinery, hazardous cable runs and at other appropriate locations.

(3) Operating limitations are posted in an appropriate manner.

(4) Only qualified operators are permitted to operate the weight handling gear. The master shall designate the operators.

(5) A minimum number of persons are allowed in the immediate area.

(6) The installation does not violate the approved trim and stability information.

(7) A suitable permanent record is maintained on the equipment as appropriate showing such items as inspections, tests, important repairs and casualties experienced. This record shall be made available to the Officer in Charge, Marine Inspection, upon request.

(b) Prior to a vessel's departure, an entry shall also be made in the official logbook that the ship's weight handling gear is in compliance with the applicable requirements in this subchapter.

§ 189.35-15 Major installations.

(a) Where the installation of weight handling gear requires modifications to the vessel's structure or affects the stability in a manner which cannot be assessed by the information contained in the approved trim and stability information, appropriate plans and information shall be submitted for approval. The installation shall then be inspected by the Officer in Charge, Marine Inspection for conformance with the approved installation plans and information.

§ 189.35-90 Weight handling gear manufactured prior to March 1, 1968.

(a) Weight handling gear manufactured prior to March 1, 1968, will be accepted on the basis of appropriate tests and examinations should plans or other technical information not be available.

Subpart 189.40—Drydocking

§ 189.40-1 Definitions relating to hull examinations.

As used in this part—

(a) *Drydock examination* means hauling out a vessel or placing a vessel in a drydock or slipway for an examination of all accessible parts of the vessel's underwater body and all through-hull fittings.

(b) *Internal structural examination* means an examination of the vessel while afloat or in drydock and consists of a complete examination of the vessel's main strength members, including the major internal framing, the hull plating, voids, and ballast tanks, but not including cargo or fuel oil tanks.

(c) *Underwater survey* means the examination, while the vessel is afloat, of all accessible parts of the vessel's underwater body and all through-hull fittings.

[CGD 84-024, 52 FR 39656, Oct. 23, 1987, as amended at 53 FR 32232, Aug. 24, 1988; CGD 95-028, 62 FR 51220, Sept. 30, 1997]

§ 189.40-3 Drydock examination, internal structural examination, cargo tank internal examination, and underwater survey intervals.

(a) Except as provided for in paragraphs (b) through (g) of this section, each vessel must undergo drydock and internal structural examinations as follows:

(1) Vessels that operate in salt water must undergo two drydock and two internal structural examinations within any five year period. No more than three years may elapse between any two examinations.

(2) Vessels that operate in fresh water at least six months in every 12 month period since the last drydock examination must undergo drydock and internal structural examinations at intervals not to exceed five years.

(b) Vessels with wooden hulls must undergo two drydock and two internal structural examinations within any five year period regardless of the type of water in which they operate. No more than three years may elapse between any two examinations.

(c) If, during an internal structural examination or underwater survey, damage or deterioration to the hull plating or structural members is discovered, the Officer in Charge, Marine Inspection, may require the vessel to be drydocked or otherwise taken out of service to further assess the extent of the damage and to effect permanent repairs.

(d) Each vessel under paragraph (a) of this section that is less than 15 years of age may be considered for an underwater survey instead of alternate drydock examinations, provided the vessel is fitted with an effective hull protection system. Vessel owners or operators must apply to the Officer in Charge, Marine Inspection, for approval of underwater surveys instead of alternate drydock examinations for each vessel. The application must include the following information:

(1) The procedure to be followed in carrying out the underwater survey.

(2) The location where the underwater survey will be accomplished.

(3) The method to be used to accurately determine the diver location relative to the hull.

(4) The means that will be provided for examining through-hull fittings.

(5) The means that will be provided for taking shaft bearing clearances.

(6) The condition of the vessel, including the anticipated draft of the vessel at the time of the survey.

(7) A description of the hull protection system.

(e) Vessels otherwise qualifying under paragraph (d) of this section, that are 15 years of age or older, may be considered for continued participation in or entry into the underwater survey program on a case-by-case basis if—

(1) Before the vessel's next scheduled drydocking, the owner or operator submits a request for participation or continued participation to Commandant (G-MOC);

(2) During the vessel's next drydocking after the request is submitted, no appreciable hull deterioration is indicated as a result of a complete set of hull gaugings; and

(3) The results of the hull gauging and the results of the Coast Guard drydock examination together with the

§ 189.40-5

recommendation of the Officer in Charge, Marine Inspection, are submitted to Commandant (G–MOC) for final approval.

(f) Each vessel which has not met with the applicable examination schedules in paragraph (a) through (e) of this section because it is on a voyage, must undergo the required examinations upon completion of the voyage.

(g) The Commandant (G–MOC) may authorize extensions to the examination intervals specified in paragraphs (a) and (b) of this section.

[CGD 84–024, 52 FR 39656, Oct. 23, 1987, as amended at 53 FR 32232, Aug. 24, 1988; CGD 95–072, 60 FR 50469, Sept. 29, 1995; CGD 96–041, 61 FR 50735, Sept. 27, 1996; CGD 95–028, 62 FR 51220, Sept. 30, 1997]

§ 189.40–5 Notice and plans required.

(a) The master, owner, operator, or agent of the vessel shall notify the Officer in Charge, Marine Inspection, whenever the vessel is to be drydocked regardless of the reason for drydocking.

(b) Each vessel, except barges, that holds a Load Line Certificate must have on board a plan showing the vessel's scantlings. This plan must be made available to the Coast Guard marine inspector whenever the vessel undergoes a drydock examination, internal structural examination, or underwater survey or whenever repairs are made to the vessel's hull.

(c) Each barge that holds a Load Line Certificate must have a plan showing the barge's scantlings. The plan need not be maintained on board the barge but must be made available to the Coast Guard marine inspector whenever the barge undergoes a drydock examination, internal structural examination, or underwater survey or whenever repairs are made to the barge's hull.

[CGD 84–024, 52 FR 39657, Oct. 23, 1987]

Subpart 189.43—Integral Fuel Oil Tank Examinations

§ 189.43–1 When required.

(a) Each fuel oil tank with at least one side integral to the vessel's hull and located within the hull ("integral fuel oil tank") is subject to inspection as provided in this section. The owner or operator of the vessel shall have the tanks cleaned out and gas freed as necessary to permit internal examination of the tank or tanks designated by the marine inspector. The owner or operator shall arrange for an examination of the fuel tanks of each vessel during an internal structural examination at intervals not to exceed five years.

(b) Integral non-double-bottom fuel oil tanks need not be cleaned out and internally examined if the marine inspector is able to determine by external examination that the general condition of the tanks is satisfactory.

(c) Double-bottom fuel oil tanks on vessels less than 10 years of age need not be cleaned out and internally examined if the marine inspector is able to determine by external examination that the general condition of the tanks is satisfactory.

(d) All double-bottom fuel oil tanks on vessels 10 years of age or older but less than 15 years of age need not be cleaned out and internally examined if the marine inspector is able to determine by internal examination of at least one forward double-bottom fuel oil tank, and by external examination of all other double-bottom fuel oil tanks on the vessel, that the general condition of the tanks is satisfactory.

(e) All double-bottom fuel oil tanks on vessels 15 years of age or older need not be cleaned out and internally examined if the marine inspector is able to determine by internal examination of at least one forward, one amidships, and one aft double-bottom fuel oil tank, and by external examination of all other double-bottom fuel oil tanks on the vessel, that the general condition of the tanks is satisfactory.

[CGD 84–024, 52 FR 39657, Oct. 23, 1987, as amended at 53 FR 32232, Aug. 24, 1988]

Subpart 189.45—Repairs and Alterations

§ 189.45–1 Notice required.

(a) No repairs or alterations affecting the stability or safety of the vessel with regard to the hull, machinery, and equipment shall be made without the knowledge of the Officer in Charge, Marine Inspection.

(b) Drawings of alterations shall be approved before work is started unless deemed unnecessary by the Officer in Charge, Marine Inspection.

(c) Drawings will not be required for repairs in kind.

(d) Notice is not required for repairs or alterations to scientific equipment where the stability or safety of the vessel with regard to the hull and machinery or equipment is not affected.

§ 189.45-5 Inspection required.

(a) An inspection, either general or partial depending upon the circumstances, shall be made whenever any important repairs or alterations are undertaken.

Subpart 189.50—Special Operating Requirements

§ 189.50-1 Inspection and testing required when making alterations, repairs, or other such operations involving riveting, welding, burning, or like fire-producing actions.

(a) The provisions of "Standard for the Control of Gas Hazards on Vessels To Be Repaired," NFPA No. 306, published by National Fire Protection Association, 1 Batterymarch Park, Quincy, MA 02269, shall be used as a guide in conducting the inspections and issuance of certificates required by this section.

(b) Until an inspection has been made to determine that such operation can be undertaken with safety, no alterations, repairs, or other such operations involving riveting, burning, welding, or like fire-producing actions shall be made:

(1) Within or on the boundaries of tanks which have been used to carry combustible liquids or chemicals; or,

(2) Within spaces adjacent to tanks which have been used to carry Grade D combustible liquids, except where the distance between such tanks and the work to be performed is not less than twenty-five (25) feet; or,

(3) Within or on the boundaries of fuel tanks; or,

(4) Within or on the boundaries of tanks carrying Grade B or Grade C flammable liquids or within spaces adjacent to such tanks; or,

(5) To pipelines, heat coils, pumps, fittings, or other appurtenances connected to such fuel tanks.

(c) Such inspections shall be made and evidenced as follows:

(1) In ports or places in the United States or its territories and possessions the inspection shall be made by a marine chemist certificated by the National Fire Protection Association; however, if the services of such certified marine chemist are not reasonably available, the Officer in Charge, Marine Inspection, upon the recommendation of the vessel owner and his contractor or their representative shall select a person who, in the case of an individual vessel, shall be authorized to make such inspection. If the inspection indicates that such operations can be undertaken with safety, a certificate setting forth the fact in writing and qualified as may be required, shall be issued by the certified marine chemist or the authorized person before the work is started. Such qualifications shall include any requirements as may be deemed necessary to maintain, insofar as can reasonably be done, the safe conditions in the spaces certified throughout the operation and shall include such additional tests and certifications as considered required. Such qualifications and requirements shall include precautions necessary to eliminate or minimize hazards that may be present from protective coatings or residues from cargoes.

(2) When not in such a port or place, and a marine chemist or such person authorized by the Officer in Charge, Marine Inspection, is not reasonably available, the inspection shall be made by the senior officer in the crew present and a proper entry shall be made in the vessel's logbook.

(d) It shall be the responsibility of the senior officer present to secure copies of certificates issued by the certified marine chemist or such person authorized by the Officer in Charge, Marine Inspection. It shall be the responsibility of the senior officer in the crew present, insofar as the persons under his control are concerned, to maintain a safe condition on the vessel by full observance of all qualifications

§ 189.55-1

and requirements listed by the marine chemist in the certificate.

[CGFR 67-83, 33 FR 1118, Jan. 27, 1968, as amended by CGD 95-072, 60 FR 50469, Sept. 29, 1995]

Subpart 189.55—Plan Approval

§ 189.55-1 General.

(a) The following list of required plans in § 189.55-5 is general in character, but includes all plans which normally show construction and safety features coming under the cognizance of the Coast Guard. In the case of a particular vessel, all of the plans enumerated may not be applicable and it is intended that only those plans and specifications be submitted as will clearly show the vessel's arrangements, construction and required equipment.

(b) In the following list of required plans in § 189.55-5, the items which must be approved by the American Bureau of Shipping for vessels classed by that organization are indicated by an asterisk. When prints bearing record of such approval by the American Bureau of Shipping are forwarded to the Coast Guard they will in general be accepted as satisfactory except insofar as the law or the Coast Guard regulations contain requirements which are not covered by the American Bureau of Shipping.

§ 189.55-5 Plans and specifications required for new construction.

(a) *General.* (1) Specifications.

(2) General arrangement plan of decks, holds, inner bottoms, etc., and including inboard and outboard profile.

(b) *Hull structure.*[1] (1) *Inner bottom plating and framing.

(2) *Midship section.

(3) *Shell plating and framing.

(4) *Stem, stern frame, and rudder.

(5) *Structural deck plans for strength decks.

(6) *Pillars and girders.

(7) *Watertight and oiltight bulkheads.

(8) *Foundations for main machinery and boilers.

---
[1] The asterisk (*) indicates items which may require approval by the American Bureau of Shipping for vessels classed by that society.

46 CFR Ch. I (10-1-04 Edition)

(9) *Arrangement of ports, doors, and airports in shell plating.

(10) *Hatch coamings and covers in weather and watertight decks.

(11) *Details of hinged subdivision watertight doors and operating gear.

(12) *Scuppers and drains penetrating shell plating.

(13) Weight handling gear when required by the Officer in Charge, Marine Inspection, as provided for by § 189.35-9.

(c) *Subdivision and stability.* Plans required by part 170 of this chapter.

(d) *Fire control.* (1) General arrangement plans showing for each deck the control stations, the various fire sections enclosed by fire resisting bulkheads, the arrangement of the alarm and extinguishing systems, the fire extinguishers, means of access to different compartments and decks and the ventilation system including location of ventilation shutdowns, positions of dampers and the number identifying each system.

(2) Ventilation diagram including dampers and other fire control features.

(3) Details of alarm systems.

(4) Details of extinguishing systems, including fire mains, carbon dioxide, foam and sprinkling systems.

(e) *Marine engineering.* For plans required for marine engineering equipment and systems. See Subchapter F (Marine Engineering) of this chapter.

(f) *Electrical engineering.* For plans required for electrical engineering, equipment, and systems, see Subchapter J (Electrical Engineering) of this chapter.

(g) *Lifesaving equipment.* These plans are to show the location and arrangement of embarkation decks, all overboard discharges and projections in way of launching lifeboats, weights of lifeboats fully equipped and loaded, working loads of davits and winches, types and sizes of falls, the manufacturer's name and identification for all equipment, and all other relevant and necessary information.

(1) Arrangement of lifeboats.

(2) Arrangement of davits.

(3) Location and stowage of liferafts and buoyant apparatus.

(h) *Accommodations for crewmembers and scientific personnel.* Arrangement

356

plans showing accommodations, ventilation, escapes, hospitals, and sanitary facilities for all crewmembers and scientific personnel.

(i) *Magazines and magazine vans.* (1) All plans relating to the arrangement, construction, ventilation, and fire protection system for magazines and magazine vans. (The plans required for magazines and magazine vans to be installed or carried on a vessel after the vessel is in operation, are set forth in subpart 195.11 of this subchapter.)

(2) Ventilation and sprinkler system calculations for magazines and magazine vans.

(j) For vessels of 100 meters (328 feet) or more in length contracted for on or after September 7, 1990, a plan must be included which shows how visibility from the navigation bridge will meet the standards contained in § 190.02–15 of this subchapter.

[CGFR 67–83, 33 FR 1118, Jan. 27, 1968, as amended by CGD 79–023, 48 FR 51052, Nov. 4, 1983; CGD 85–099, 55 FR 32249, Aug. 8, 1990; CGD 88–032, 56 FR 35829, July 29, 1991; 56 FR 46354, Sept. 11, 1991; 56 FR 50754, Oct. 8, 1991]

§ 189.55–10 **Plans required for alterations of existing vessels.**

(a) In the event of alterations involving the safety of the vessel, the applicable plans shall be submitted for approval covering the proposed work except as modified by § 189.45–1.

§ 189.55–15 **Procedure for submittal of plans.**

(a) As the relative location of shipyards, design offices, and Coast Guard offices vary throughout the country, no specific routing will be required in the submittal of plans. In general, one of the following procedures would apply, but in a particular case, if a more expeditious procedure can be used, there will be no objection to its adoption.

(1) The plans may be submitted to the Officer in Charge, Marine Inspection, in the district in which the vessel is to be built. This procedure will be most expeditious in the case of those offices where personnel and facilities are available for examination and approval of plans locally.

(2) The plans may be submitted directly to the Commanding Officer, Marine Safety Center, 400 Seventh Street SW., Washington, DC 20590–0001. In this case, the plans will be returned directly to the submitter, with a copy of the action being forwarded to the interested Officer in Charge, Marine Inspection.

(3) In the case of classed vessels, upon specific request by the submitter, the American Bureau of Shipping will arrange to forward the necessary plans to the Coast Guard indicating its action thereon. In this case, the plans will be returned as noted in paragraph (a)(2) of this section.

[CGFR 67–83, 33 FR 1118, Jan. 27, 1968, as amended by CGD 82–063b, 48 FR 4783, Feb. 3, 1983; CGD 85–048b, 51 FR 15498, Apr. 24, 1986; CGD 88–070, 53 FR 34538, Sept. 7, 1988; CGD 89–025, 54 FR 19572, May 8, 1989; CGD 95–072, 60 FR 50469, Sept. 29, 1995; 60 FR 54106, Oct. 19, 1995; CGD 96–041, 61 FR 50735, Sept. 27, 1996; USCG–2002–13058, 67 FR 61276, Sept. 30, 2002]

§ 189.55–20 **Number of plans required.**

(a) Three copies of each plan are normally required so that one can be returned to the submitter. If the submitter desires additional approved plans, a suitable number should be submitted to permit the required distribution.

[CGFR 67–83, 33 FR 1118, Jan. 27, 1968, as amended by CGFR 69–116, 35 FR 6862 Apr. 30, 1970]

Subpart 189.60—Certificates Under International Convention for Safety of Life at Sea, 1974

§ 189.60–1 **Application.**

The provisions of this subpart shall apply to all oceanographic research vessels on an international voyage. (See § 188.05–10 of this subchapter.)

[CGD 95–012, 60 FR 48052, Sept. 18, 1995; 60 FR 50120, Sept. 28, 1995]

§ 189.60–5 **Cargo Ship Safety Construction Certificate.**

(a) All vessels on an international voyage are required to have a Cargo Ship Safety Construction Certificate. This certificate shall be issued by the U.S. Coast Guard or the American Bureau of Shipping to certain vessels on behalf of the United States of America as provided in Regulation 12, Chapter I,

§ 189.60-10

of the International Convention for Safety of Life at Sea, 1974.

(b) All such vessels shall meet the applicable requirements of this chapter for vessels on an international voyage.

[CGFR 67-83, 33 FR 1118, Jan. 27, 1968, as amended by CGD 90-008, 55 FR 30665, July 26, 1990]

§ 189.60-10 Cargo Ship Safety Equipment Certificate.

(a) All vessels on an international voyage are required to have a Cargo Ship Safety Equipment Certificate.

(b) All such vessels shall meet the applicable requirements of this chapter for vessels on an international voyage.

§ 189.60-15 Cargo Ship Safety Radio Certificate.

Every vessel equipped with a radio installation on an international voyage must have a Cargo Ship Safety Radio Certificate. Each radio installation must meet the requirements of the Federal Communication Commission and the International Convention for Safety of Life at Sea.

[USCG-1999-4976, 65 FR 6510, Feb. 9, 2000]

§ 189.60-25 Exemption Certificate.

(a) A vessel may be exempted by the Commandant from complying with certain requirements of the Convention under his administration upon request made in writing to him and transmitted via the Officer in Charge, Marine Inspection.

(b) When an exemption is granted to a vessel by the Commandant under and in accordance with the Convention, an Exemption Certificate describing such exemption shall be issued through the appropriate Officer in Charge, Marine Inspection, in addition to other required certificates.

§ 189.60-30 Safety Management Certificate.

All vessels to which 33 CFR part 96 applies on an international voyage must have a valid Safety Management Certificate and a copy of their company's valid Document of Compliance certificate on board.

[CGD 95-073, 62 FR 67515, Dec. 24, 1997]

46 CFR Ch. I (10-1-04 Edition)

§ 189.60-35 Availability of Certificates.

The Convention certificates must be on board the vessel and readily available for examination at all times.

[USCG-1999-4976, 65 FR 6510, Feb. 9, 2000]

§ 189.60-40 Duration of Convention certificates.

(a) The following certificates are valid for a period of not more than 60 months (5 years).

(1) A Cargo Ship Safety Construction Certificate.

(2) A Cargo Ship Safety Equipment Certificate.

(3) A Safety Management Certificate.

(4) A Cargo Ship Safety Radio Certificate.

(b) An Exemption certificate must not be valid for longer than the period of the certificate to which it refers.

(c) A Convention certificate may be withdrawn, revoked, or suspended at any time when it is determined that the vessel is no longer in compliance with applicable requirements. (See § 2.01-70 of this chapter for procedures governing appeals.)

[USCG-1999-4976, 65 FR 6510, Feb. 9, 2000]

§ 189.60-45 American Bureau of Shipping.

(a) The American Bureau of Shipping, with its home office at ABS Plaza, 16855 Northchase Drive, Houston, TX 77060, is hereby designated as an organization duly authorized to issue the "Cargo Ship Safety Construction Certificate" to certain oceanographic research vessels on behalf of the United States of America as provided in Regulation 12, Chapter I, of the International Convention for Safety of Life at Sea, 1974, and Executive Order 12234 and the certificate shall be subject to the requirements in this subpart. The American Bureau of Shipping is authorized to place the official seal of the United States of America on the certificate. This designation and delegation to the American Bureau of Shipping shall be in effect until terminated by proper authority and notice of cancellation is published in the FEDERAL REGISTER.

(b) At the option of the owner or agent of a vessel on an international voyage and on direct application to the

Coast Guard, DHS

American Bureau of Shipping, the Bureau may issue to such vessel a Cargo Ship Safety Construction Certificate, having a period of validity of not more than 60 months after ascertaining that the vessel:

(1) Has met the applicable requirements of the Convention; and

(2) Is currently classed by the Bureau and classification requirements have been dealt with to the satisfaction of the Bureau.

(c) When the Bureau determines that a vessel to which it has issued a Cargo Ship Safety Construction Certificate no longer complies with the Bureau's applicable requirements for classification, the Bureau shall immediately furnish to the Coast Guard all relevant information, which will be used by the Coast Guard to determine whether or not to withdraw, revoke or suspend the Cargo Ship Safety Construction Certificate.

[CGFR 67–83, 33 FR 1118, Jan. 27, 1968, as amended by CGD 77–081, 46 FR 56204, Nov. 16, 1981; CGD 90–008, 55 FR 30665, July 26, 1990; CGD 96–041, 61 FR 50735, Sept. 27, 1996; USCG–2000–7790, 65 FR 58465, Sept. 29, 2000]

PART 190—CONSTRUCTION AND ARRANGEMENT

Subpart 190.01—Hull Structure

Sec.
190.01–1 Application.
190.01–5 Vessels subject to load line.
190.01–10 Structural standards.
190.01–15 Special consideration.
190.01–90 Vessels contracted for prior to March 1, 1968.

Subpart 190.02—Navigation Bridge Visibility

190.02–1 Navigation bridge visibility

Subpart 190.03—Subdivision and Stability

190.03–1 General.

Subpart 190.05—General Fire Protection

190.05–1 Application.
190.05–3 Fire hazards to be minimized.
190.05–5 Woodwork insulated from heated surfaces.
190.05–10 Chemical storeroom and lamp room construction.
190.05–15 Segregation of spaces containing the emergency source of electric power.

Pt. 190

190.05–20 Segregation of chemical laboratories and chemical storerooms.

Subpart 190.07—Structural Fire Protection

190.07–1 Application.
190.07–5 Definitions.
190.07–10 Construction.
190.07–90 Vessels contracted for prior to March 1, 1968.

Subpart 190.10—Means of Escape

190.10–1 Application.
190.10–5 Two means required.
190.10–10 Location.
190.10–15 Vertical ladders not accepted.
190.10–20 No means for locking doors.
190.10–25 Stairway size.
190.10–30 Dead end corridors.
190.10–35 Public spaces.
190.10–40 Access to lifeboats.
190.10–45 Weather deck communications.
190.10–90 Vessels contracted for prior to March 1, 1968.

Subpart 190.15—Ventilation

190.15–1 Application.
190.15–5 Vessels using fuel having a flashpoint of 110 °F. or lower.
190.15–10 Ventilation for closed spaces.
190.15–15 Ventilation for living spaces and quarters.
190.15–90 Vessels contracted for prior to March 1, 1968.

Subpart 190.20—Accommodations for Officers, Crew, and Scientific Personnel

190.20–1 Application.
190.20–5 Intent.
190.20–10 Location of crew spaces.
190.20–15 Construction.
190.20–20 Sleeping accommodations.
190.20–25 Washrooms and toilet rooms.
190.20–30 Messrooms.
190.20–35 Hospital space.
190.20–40 Other spaces.
190.20–45 Lighting.
190.20–50 Heating and cooling.
190.20–55 Insect screens.
190.20–90 Vessels contracted for prior to March 1, 1968.

Subpart 190.25—Rails and Guards

190.25–1 Application.
190.25–5 Where rails required.
190.25–10 Storm rails.
190.25–15 Guards in dangerous places.
190.25–90 Vessels contracted for prior to July 1, 1969.

AUTHORITY: 46 U.S.C. 2113, 3306; E.O. 12234, 45 FR 58801, 3 CFR, 1980 Comp., p. 277; Department of Homeland Security Delegation No. 0170.1.

§ 190.01-1

SOURCE: CGFR 67-83, 33 FR 1125, Jan. 27, 1968, unless otherwise noted.

Subpart 190.01—Hull Structure

§ 190.01-1 Application.

(a) The provisions of this subpart, with the exception of § 190.01-90, shall apply to all vessels contracted for on or after March 1, 1968.

(b) Vessels contracted for prior to March 1, 1968, shall meet the requirements of § 190.01-90.

§ 190.01-5 Vessels subject to load line.

(a) For vessels assigned a load line, see Subchapter E (Load Lines) of this chapter for special requirements as to strength, closure of openings, etc.

§ 190.01-10 Structural standards.

(a) In general, compliance with the standards established by the American Bureau of Shipping, see subpart 188.35 of this subchapter, will be considered as satisfactory evidence of the structural efficiency of the vessel. However, in special cases, a detailed analysis of the entire structure or some integral part may be made by the Coast Guard to determine the structural requirements.

§ 190.01-15 Special consideration.

(a) Special consideration will be given to the structural requirements for small vessels or vessels of an unusual design not contemplated by the rules of the American Bureau of Shipping.

§ 190.01-90 Vessels contracted for prior to March 1, 1968.

(a) Existing structure previously approved will be considered satisfactory so long as it is maintained in good condition to the satisfaction of the Officer in Charge, Marine Inspection. Minor repairs and alterations may be made to the same standards as the original construction.

(b) Conversions, major alterations, new installations, and replacements, shall meet the applicable specifications in this subpart for new vessels.

Subpart 190.02—Navigation Bridge Visibility

§ 190.02-1 Navigation bridge visibility.

Each oceanographic research vessel which is 100 meters (328 feet) or more in length and contracted for on or after September 7, 1990, must meet the following requirements:

(a) The field of vision from the navigation bridge, whether the vessel is in a laden or unladen condition, must be such that:

(1) From the conning position, the view of the sea surface is not obscured forward of the bow by more than the lesser of two ship lengths or 500 meters (1640 feet) from dead ahead to 10 degrees on either side of the vessel. Within this arc of visibility any blind sector caused by cargo, cargo gear, or other permanent obstruction must not exceed 5 degrees.

(2) From the conning position, the horizontal field of vision extends over an arc from at least 22.5 degrees abaft the beam on one side of the vessel, through dead ahead, to at least 22.5 degrees abaft the beam on the other side of the vessel. Blind sectors forward of the beam caused by cargo, cargo gear, or other permanent obstruction must not exceed 10 degrees each, nor total more than 20 degrees, including any blind sector within the arc of visibility described in paragraph (a)(1) of this section.

(3) From each bridge wing, the field of vision extends over an arc from at least 45 degrees on the opposite bow, through dead ahead, to at least dead astern.

(4) From the main steering position, the field of vision extends over an arc from dead ahead to at least 60 degrees on either side of the vessel.

(5) From each bridge wing, the respective side of the vessel is visible forward and aft.

(b) Windows fitted on the navigation bridge must be arranged so that:

(1) Framing between windows is kept to a minimum and is not installed immediately in front of any work station.

(2) Front windows are inclined from the vertical plane, top out, at an angle of not less than 10 degrees and not more than 25 degrees.

Coast Guard, DHS

(3) The height of the lower edge of the front windows is limited to prevent any obstruction of the forward view previously described in this section.

(4) The height of the upper edge of the front windows allows a forward view of the horizon at the conning position, for a person with a height of eye of 1.8 meters (71 inches), when the vessel is at a forward pitch angle of 20 degrees.

(c) Polarized or tinted windows must not be fitted.

[CGD 85–099, 55 FR 32249, Aug. 8, 1990]

Subpart 190.03—Subdivision and Stability

§ 190.03-1 General.

Each vessel must comply with the applicable requirements in Subchapter S of this chapter.

[CGD 79–023, 48 FR 51053, Nov. 4, 1983]

Subpart 190.05—General Fire Protection

§ 190.05-1 Application.

(a) The provisions of this subpart shall apply to all vessels, except as noted otherwise in this subpart.

(b) Non-self-propelled vessels of less than 300 gross tons shall not be subject to the provisions of this subpart.

§ 190.05-3 Fire hazards to be minimized.

(a) The general construction of the vessel shall be such as to minimize fire hazards.

§ 190.05-5 Woodwork insulated from heated surfaces.

(a) Internal combustion engine exhausts, boiler, and galley uptakes, and similar sources of ignition shall be kept clear of and suitably insulated from any woodwork or other combustible matter.

§ 190.05-10 Chemical storeroom and lamp room construction.

(a) Chemical storerooms, lamp, paint, and oil lockers and similar compartments shall be constructed of steel or shall be wholly lined with metal.

§ 190.07-1

§ 190.05-15 Segregation of spaces containing the emergency source of electric power.

(a) When a compartment containing the emergency source of electric power, or vital components thereof, adjoins a space containing either the ship's service generators or machinery necessary for the operation of the ship's service generators, all common bulkheads and/or decks shall be protected by approved "structural insulation" or other approved material. This protection shall be such as to be capable of preventing an excessive temperature rise in the space containing the emergency source of electric power, or vital components thereof, for a period of at least 1 hour in the event of fire in the adjoining space. Bulkheads or decks meeting Class A-60 requirements, as defined by § 72.05-10 of Subchapter H (Passenger Vessels) of this chapter, will be considered as meeting the requirements of this paragraph.

§ 190.05-20 Segregation of chemical laboratories and chemical storerooms.

(a) The provisions of this section shall apply to all vessels contracted for on or after March 1, 1968.

(b) Chemical storerooms shall not be located in horizontal proximity to nor below accommodation or safety areas.

(c) Chemical storerooms shall not be located adjacent to the collision bulkhead, nor boundary divisions of the boilerroom, engineroom, galley, or other high fire hazard area.

(d) Chemical laboratories shall not be located adjacent to nor immediately below safety areas. Wherever possible they shall be similarly separated from accomodation spaces and high fire hazard areas such as the galley.

Subpart 190.07—Structural Fire Protection

§ 190.07-1 Application.

(a) The provisions of this subpart, with the exception of § 190.07-90, shall apply to all vessels of 4,000 gross tons and over carrying not more than 150 persons and contracted for on or after March 1, 1968.

(b) The provisions of this subpart, with the exception of § 190.07-90, shall

§ 190.07-5

apply to all vessels of 300 gross tons and over, but less than 4,000 gross tons, carrying in excess of 16 persons in the scientific party but not more than 150 persons and contracted for on or after March 1, 1968.

(c) Vessels contracted for prior to March 1, 1968, shall meet the requirements of § 190.07-90.

(d) Those vessels which carry more than 150 persons shall meet the requirements in §§ 72.05-5 through 72.05-60 of Subchapter H (Passenger Vessels) of this chapter.

§ 190.07-5 Definitions.

(a) *Standard fire tests.* A *standard fire test* is one which develops in the test furnace a series of time temperature relationships as follows:

    5 minutes—1,000° F.
    10 minutes—1,300° F.
    30 minutes—1,550° F.
    60 minutes—1,700° F.

(b) *A Class divisions.* Bulkheads or decks of the *A* Class shall be composed of steel or equivalent metal construction, suitably stiffened and made intact with the main structure of the vessel; such as shell, structural bulkheads, and decks. They shall be so constructed, that if subjected to the standard fire test, they would be capable of preventing the passage of flame and smoke for 1 hour.

(c) *B Class bulkheads.* Bulkheads of the *B* Class shall be constructed with approved incombustible materials and made intact from deck to deck and to shell or other boundaries. They shall be so constructed that, if subjected to the standard fire test, they would be capable of preventing the passage of flame for one-half hour.

(d) *C Class divisions.* Bulkheads or decks of the *C* Class shall be constructed of approved incombustible materials, but need meet no requirements relative to the passage of flame.

(e) *Steel or other equivalent metal.* Where the term *steel or other equivalent metal* is used in this subpart, it is intended to require a material which, by itself or due to insulation provided, has structural and integrity qualities equivalent to steel at the end of the applicable fire exposure.

(f) *Approved material.* Where in this subpart approved materials are required, they refer to materials approved under the applicable subparts of part 164 of Subchapter Q (Specifications) of this chapter, as follows:

Deck coverings	164.006
Structural insulation	164.007
Bulkhead panels	164.008
Incombustible materials	164.009
Interior finish	164.012

[CGFR 67-83, 33 FR 1125, Jan. 27, 1968, as amended by CGD 74-155, 41 FR 17910, Apr. 29, 1976]

§ 190.07-10 Construction.

(a) The hull, superstructure, structural bulkheads, decks, and deckhouses shall be constructed of steel. Alternately, the Commandant may permit the use of other suitable material in special cases, having in mind the risk of fire.

(b) The boundary bulkheads of general laboratory areas, chemical storerooms, galleys, paint and lamp lockers and emergency generator rooms shall be of "A" class construction.

(1) Permanently installed divisional bulkheads between laboratories spaces within a general laboratory area may be of B or C class construction.

(2) Temporary divisional bulkheads between laboratory spaces within a general laboratory area may be constructed of combustible materials when they are necessary to facilitate a specific scientific mission.

(c) The boundary bulkheads and decks separating the accomodations and control stations from hold and machinery spaces, galleys, main pantries, laboratories, and storerooms, other than small service lockers, shall be of "A" Class construction.

(1) The boundary bulkheads and decks separating general laboratory areas of 500 square feet or less from accommodations and control stations shall be of "A-15" Class construction as defined by § 72.05-10 of Subchapter H (Passenger Vessels) of this chapter.

(2) The boundary bulkheads and decks separating general laboratory areas of over 500 square feet from accommodations and control stations shall be of "A-30" Class construction as defined by § 72.05-10 of Subchapter H (Passenger Vessels) of this chapter.

Coast Guard, DHS § 190.10-5

(d) Within the accommodation and service areas the following conditions shall apply:

(1) Corridor bulkheads in accommodation spaces shall be of the "A" or "B" Class intact from deck to deck. Stateroom doors in such bulkheads may have a louver in the lower half.

(2) Elevator, dumbwaiter, stairtower, and other trunks shall be of "A" Class construction.

(3) Bulkheads not already specified to be of "A" or "B" Class construction may be of "A", "B", or "C" Class construction.

(4) The integrity of any deck in way of a stairway, shall be maintained by means of "A" or "B" class bulkheads and doors at one level. The integrity of a stairtower shall be maintained by "A" class doors at every level. The door shall be of the self-closing type. Holdback hooks will not be permitted. However, magnetic holdbacks operated from the bridge or other suitable remote control positions are acceptable.

(5) Interior stairs, including stringers and treads, shall be of steel.

(6) Except for washrooms and toilet spaces, deck coverings within accommodation spaces shall be of an approved type. However, overlays for leveling or finishing purposes which do not meet the requirements for an approved deck covering may be used in thicknesses not exceeding three-eights of an inch.

(7) Ceilings, linings, and insulation, including pipe and duct laggings, shall be approved incombustible materials.

(8) Any sheathing, furring, or holding pieces incidental to the securing of any bulkhead, ceiling, lining, or insulation shall be of approved incombustible materials.

(9) Bulkheads, linings, and ceiling may have a combustible veneer within a room not to exceed two twenty-eighths of an inch in thickness. However, combustible veneers, trim, decorations, etc., shall not be used in corridors or hidden spaces. This is not intended to preclude the use of an approved interior finish or a reasonable number of coats of paint.

(e) Nitrocellulose or other highly flammable or noxious fume-producing paints or lacquers shall not be used.

(f) The provisions of paragraphs (d) (1) through (9) of this section apply to control spaces on vessels whose initial Application for Inspection is submitted to an Officer in Charge, Marine Inspection on or after June 15, 1987.

[CGFR 67-83, 33 FR 1125, Jan. 27, 1968, as amended by CGD 84-073, 52 FR 18364, May 15, 1987; 52 FR 22751, June 15, 1987]

§ 190.07-90 Vessels contracted for prior to March 1, 1968.

(a) Existing structure arrangements and materials previously approved will be considered satisfactory so long as they are maintained in good condition to the satisfaction of the Officer in Charge, Marine Inspection. Minor repairs and alterations may be made to the same standards as the original construction.

(b) Conversions, major alterations, new installations, and replacements shall comply with the applicable specifications and requirements in this subpart for new vessels.

Subpart 190.10—Means of Escape

§ 190.10-1 Application.

(a) The provisions of this subpart, with the exception of § 190.10-90, shall apply to all vessels other than non-self-propelled vessels of less than 300 gross tons, contracted for on or after March 1, 1968.

(b) Vessels contracted for prior to March 1, 1968, shall meet the requirements of § 190.10-90.

(c) Non-self-propelled vessels of less than 300 gross tons shall not be subject to the provisions of this subpart.

§ 190.10-5 Two means required.

(a) There shall be at least two means of escape from all general areas where the crew or scientific personnel may be quartered or normally employed. At least one of these two means of escape shall be independent of watertight doors and hatches, except for quick acting watertight doors giving final access to weather decks.

§ 190.10-10 Location.

(a) The two means of escape shall be as remote as practicable so as to minimize the possibility of one incident blocking both escapes.

§ 190.10-15 Vertical ladders not accepted.

(a) Vertical ladders and deck scuttles shall not in general be considered satisfactory as one of the required means of escape. However, where it is demonstrated that the installation of a stairway would be impracticable, a vertical ladder may be used as the second means of escape.

§ 190.10-20 No means for locking doors.

(a) No means shall be provided for locking door giving access to either of the two required means of escape except that crash doors or locking devices, capable of being easily forced in an emergency, may be employed provided a permanent and conspicuous notice to this effect is attached to both sides of the door. This paragraph shall not apply to outside doors to deckhouses where such doors are locked by key only and such key is under the control of one of the vessel's officers.

§ 190.10-25 Stairway size.

(a) Stairways shall be of sufficient width having in mind the number of persons having access to such stairs for escape purposes.

(b) All interior stairways, other than those within the machinery spaces, shall have minimum width of 28 inches. The angle of inclination with the horizontal of such stairways shall not exceed 50°.

(c) Special consideration for relief may be given if it is shown to be unreasonable or impracticable to meet the requirements in this section.

§ 190.10-30 Dead end corridors.

(a) Dead end corridors, or the equivalent, more than 40 feet in length shall not be permitted.

§ 190.10-35 Public spaces.

(a) In all cases, public spaces having a deck area of over 300 square feet shall have at least two exits. Where practicable, these exits shall give egress to different corridors, rooms, or spaces to minimize the possibility of one incident blocking both exits.

§ 190.10-40 Access to lifeboats.

(a) The stairways, corridors, and doors shall be so arranged as to permit a ready and direct access to the various lifeboat and liferaft embarkation areas.

§ 190.10-45 Weather deck communications.

(a) Vertical communication shall be provided between the various weather decks by means of permanent inclined ladders.

§ 190.10-90 Vessels contracted for prior to March 1, 1968.

(a) Existing arrangements previously approved will be considered satisfactory so long as they are maintained in good condition to the satisfaction of the Officer in Charge, Marine Inspection. Minor repairs and alterations may be made to the same standards as the original design: *Provided,* That in no case will a greater departure from the standards of §§ 190.10-5 through 190.10-45 be permitted than presently exists. Nothing in this paragraph shall be construed as exempting any vessel from having two means of escape from all main compartments where persons on board may be quartered or normally employed.

Subpart 190.15—Ventilation

§ 190.15-1 Application.

(a) The provisions of this subpart, with the exception of § 190.15-90, shall apply to all vessels other than non-self-propelled vessels of less than 300 gross tons, contracted for on or after March 1, 1968.

(b) Vessels contracted for prior to March 1, 1968, shall meet the requirements of § 190.15-90.

(c) Non-self-propelled vessels of less than 300 gross tons shall not be subject to the provisions of this subpart.

§ 190.15-5 Vessels using fuel having a flashpoint of 110 °F. or lower.

(a) Spaces containing machinery which uses, or tanks which contain,

Coast Guard, DHS

§ 190.15-15

fuel having a flashpoint of 110° F. or lower shall have natural supply and mechanical exhaust ventilation as required by this section.

(b) The mechanical exhaust system shall be such as to assure the air changes as noted in Table 190.15-5(b) depending on the size of the space.

TABLE 190.15-5(b)

Size of space, cubic feet		Minute per air change
Over	Not over	
	500	2
500	1000	3
1000	1500	4
1500		5

(c) Exhaust blower motors, unless of a totally enclosed, explosion-proof type, shall be located outside of the ducts and outside of the compartment required to be ventilated. Exhaust blower motors if mounted in any compartment shall be located as high above the bilge as practicable. Blower blades shall be nonsparking with reference to their housings.

(d) Exhaust blower switches shall be located outside of any space required to be ventilated by this section, and shall be of the type interlocked with the ignition switch so that the blowers are started before the engine ignition is switched on. A red warning sign at the switch shall state that the blowers shall be operated prior to starting the engines for a sufficient time to insure at least one complete change of air in the compartments.

(e) The area of the ducts shall be such as to limit the air velocity to a maximum of 2,000 feet per minute. Ducts may be of any shape: *Provided,* That in no case shall one cross section dimension exceed twice the other.

(f) At least two inlet ducts shall be located at one end of the compartment and they shall extend to the lowest part of the compartment or bilge on each side. Similar exhaust ducts shall be led to the mechanical exhaust system from the lowest part of the compartment or bilge on each side of the compartment at the end opposite from that at which the inlet ducts are fitted. These ducts shall be so installed that ordinary collection of water in the bilge will not close off the ducts.

(g) All ducts shall be of steel construction and reasonably gastight from end to end. The ducts shall lead as direct as possible and be properly fastened and supported.

(h) All supply ducts shall be provided with cowls or scoops having a free area not less than twice the required duct area. When the cowls or scoops are screened, the mouth area shall be increased to compensate for the area of the screen wire. Dampers shall not be fitted in the supply ducts. Cowls or scoops shall be kept open at all times except when the stress of weather is such as to endanger the vessel if the openings are not temporarily closed. Supply and exhaust openings shall not be located where the natural flow of air is unduly obstructed, or adjacent to possible sources of vapor ignition, nor shall they be so located that exhaust air may be taken into the supply vents.

(i) Provision shall be made for closing all cowls or scoops when the fixed carbon dioxide system is operated.

§ 190.15-10 Ventilation for closed spaces.

(a) All enclosed spaces within the vessel shall be properly vented or ventilated. Means shall be provided to close off all vents and ventilators.

(b) Means shall be provided for stopping all fans in ventilation systems serving the chemical laboratories, scientific laboratories, chemical storerooms, and machinery spaces and for closing all doorways, ventilators, and annular spaces around funnels and other openings to such spaces, from outside these spaces, in case of fire.

(c) See §§ 194.15-5 and 194.20-5 of this subchapter for ventilation of chemical laboratories, scientific laboratories, and storerooms.

§ 190.15-15 Ventilation for living spaces and quarters.

(a) All living spaces shall be adequately ventilated in a manner suitable to the purpose of the space.

(b) All spaces used as quarters for crewmembers and scientific personnel shall be ventilated by a mechanical system unless it can be shown that a natural system will provide adequate ventilation. By a natural system is meant those spaces so located that the

§ 190.15-90

windows, ports, skylights, etc., and doors to passageways can be kept open and thereby provide adequate ventilation under all ordinary conditions of weather.

§ 190.15-90 Vessels contracted for prior to March 1, 1968.

(a) Existing arrangements previously approved will be considered satisfactory so long as they are maintained in good condition to the satisfaction of the Officer in Charge, Marine Inspection. Minor repairs and alterations may be made to the same standards as the original design: *Provided,* That in no case will a greater departure from the standards of §§ 190.15-5 through 190.15-15 be permitted than presently exists.

Subpart 190.20—Accomodations for Officers, Crew, and Scientific Personnel

SOURCE: CGD 95-027, 61 FR 26011, May 23, 1996, unless otherwise noted.

§ 190.20-1 Application.

(a) Except as noted below, the provisions of this subpart apply to all vessels contracted for on or after March 1, 1968.

(b) Vessels contracted for prior to March 1, 1968, must meet the requirements of § 190.20-90.

§ 190.20-5 Intent.

(a) The accommodations provided for officers, crew, and scientific personnel on all vessels must be securely constructed, properly lighted, heated, drained, ventilated, equipped, located, arranged, and, where practicable, shall be insulated from undue noise, heat, and odors.

(b) Provided the intent of this subpart is met, consideration may be given by the Officer in Charge, Marine Inspection to relax the requirements relating to the size and separation of accommodations for scientific personnel.

§ 190.20-10 Location of crew spaces.

(a) Crew quarters must not be located farther forward in the vessel than a vertical plane located at 5 percent of the vessel's length abaft the forward side of the stem at the designated summer load water line. However, for vessels in other than ocean or coastwise service, this distance need not exceed 8.5 meters (28 feet). For purpose of this paragraph, the vessel's length shall be as defined in § 43.15-1 of subchapter E (Load Lines) of this chapter. Unless approved by the Commandant, no section of the deck head of the crew spaces may be below the deepest load line.

(b) There must be no direct communication, except through solid, close fitted doors or hatches between crew spaces and chain lockers, or machinery spaces.

§ 190.20-15 Construction.

All crew spaces are to be constructed and arranged in a manner suitable to the purpose for which they are intended and so they can be kept in a clean, workable and sanitary condition.

§ 190.20-20 Sleeping accommodations.

(a) Where practicable, each licensed officer must be provided with a separate stateroom.

(b) Sleeping accommodations for the crew must be divided into rooms, no one of which must berth more than 4 persons.

(c) Each room must be of such size that there are at least 2.78 square meters (30 square feet) of deck area and a volume of at least 5.8 cubic meters (210 cubic feet) for each person accommodated. The clear head room must be not less than 190 centimeters (75 inches). In measuring sleeping accommodations any furnishings contained therein for the use of the occupants are not to be deducted from the total volume or from the deck area.

(d) Each person shall have a separate berth and not more than one berth may be placed above another. The berth must be composed of materials not likely to corrode. The overall size of a berth must not be less than 68 centimeters (27 inches) wide by 190 centimeters (75 inches) long, except by special permission of the Commandant. Where two tiers of berths are fitted, the bottom of the lower berth must not be less than 30 centimeters (12 inches) above the deck. The berths must not be obstructed by pipes, ventilating ducts, or other installations.

(e) A locker must be provided for each person accommodated in a room.

§ 190.20-25 Washrooms and toilet rooms.

(a) There must be provided at least 1 toilet, 1 washbasin, and 1 shower or bathtub for each 8 members or portion thereof in the crew to be accommodated who do not occupy rooms to which private or semi-private facilities are attached.

(b) The toilet rooms and washrooms must be located convenient to the sleeping quarters of the crew to which they are allotted but must not open directly into such quarters except when they are provided as private or semi-private facilities.

(c) All washbasins, showers, and bathtubs must be equipped with adequate plumbing, including hot and cold running water. All toilets must be installed with adequate plumbing for flushing. Where more than 1 toilet is located in a space or compartment, each toilet must be separated by partitions.

§ 190.20-30 Messrooms.

(a) Messrooms must be located as near to the galley as is practicable except where the messroom is equipped with a steam table.

(b) Each messroom must seat the number of persons expected to eat in the messroom at one time.

§ 190.20-35 Hospital space.

(a) Except as specifically modified by paragraph (f) of this section, each vessel which in the ordinary course of its trade makes voyages of more than 3 days duration between ports and which carries a crew of 12 or more, must be provided with a hospital space. This space must be situated with regard to the comfort of the sick so that they may receive proper attention in all weather.

(b) The hospital must be suitably separated from other spaces and must be used for the care of the sick and for no other purpose.

(c) The hospital must be fitted with berths in the ratio of 1 berth to every 12 members of the crew or portion thereof who are not berthed in single occupancy rooms, but the number of berths need not exceed 6. Where all single occupancy rooms are provided, the requirement for a separate hospital may be withdrawn, provided that 1 stateroom is fitted with a bunk accessible from both sides.

(d) [Reserved]

(e) The hospital must have a toilet, washbasin, and bathtub or shower conveniently situated. Other necessary suitable equipment such as a clothes locker, a table and a seat must be provided.

(f) On vessels in which the crew is berthed in single occupancy rooms, a hospital space will not be required, provided that 1 room must be designated and fitted with use as a treatment or isolation room. This room must meet the following standards:

(1) The room must be available for immediate medical use; and

(2) A washbasin with hot and cold running water must be installed either in or immediately adjacent to the space and other required sanitary facilities must be conveniently located.

§ 190.20-40 Other spaces.

Each vessel shall have—

(a) Sufficient facilities where the crew may wash and dry their own clothes, including at least 1 sink supplied with hot and cold fresh water;

(b) Recreation spaces; and

(c) A space or spaces of adequate size on the open deck to which the crew has access when off duty.

§ 190.20-45 Lighting.

Each berth must have a light.

§ 190.20-50 Heating and cooling.

(a) All manned spaces must be adequately heated and cooled in a manner suitable to the purpose of the space.

(b) Radiators and other heating apparatus must be so placed and shielded, where necessary, to avoid risk of fire, danger or discomfort to the occupants. Pipes leading to radiators or heating apparatus must be insulated where those pipes create a hazard to persons occupying the space.

§ 190.20-55

§ 190.20-55 Insect screens.

Provisions must be made to protect the crew quarters against the admission of insects.

§ 190.20-90 Vessels contracted for prior to March 1, 1968.

Existing structures, arrangements, materials, and facilities previously approved will be considered satisfactory so long as they are maintained in good condition to the satisfaction of the Officer in Charge, Marine Inspection. Minor repairs and alterations may be made to the same standards as the original construction, provided that in no case will a greater departure from the standards of §§ 190.20-5 through 190.20-55 be permitted than presently exists.

Subpart 190.25—Rails and Guards

§ 190.25-1 Application.

(a) The provisions of this subpart with the exception of § 190.25-90, apply to all vessels contracted for on or after July 1, 1969.

(b) Vessels contracted for prior to July 1, 1969 shall meet the requirements of § 190.25-90.

[CGFR 69-72, 34 FR 17503, Oct. 29, 1969]

§ 190.25-5 Where rails required.

(a) All vessels shall have efficient guard rails or bulwarks on decks and bridges. The height of rails or bulwarks shall be at least 39½ inches from the deck. At exposed peripheries of the freeboard and superstructure decks, the rails shall be in at least three courses, including the top. The opening below the lowest course shall not be more than 9 inches. The courses shall not be more than 15 inches apart. In the case of ships with rounded gunwales the guard rail supports shall be placed in the flat of the deck. On other decks and bridges the rails shall be in at least two courses, including the top, approximately evenly spaced. If it can be shown to the satisfaction of the Officer in Charge, Marine Inspection, that the installation of rails of such height will be unreasonable and impracticable, having regard to the business of the vessel, rails of a lesser height or in some cases grab rails may

be accepted and inboard rails may be eliminated if the deck is not generally accessible.

(b) Where it can be shown to the satisfaction of the Commandant that a vessel is engaged exclusively in voyages of a sheltered nature, the provisions of paragraph (a) of this section may be relaxed.

[CGFR 69-72, 34 FR 17503, Oct. 29, 1969]

§ 190.25-10 Storm rails.

(a) On vessels in ocean and coastwise service, suitable storm rails shall be installed in all passageways and at the deckhouse sides where persons on board might have normal access. Storm rails shall be installed on both sides of passageways which are 6 feet or more in width.

§ 190.25-15 Guards in dangerous places.

(a) Suitable hand covers, guards, or rails shall be installed in way of all exposed and dangerous places such as gears, machinery, etc.

§ 190.25-90 Vessels contracted for prior to July 1, 1969.

(a) Existing structures, arrangements, materials, and facilities previously approved will be considered satisfactory so long as they are maintained in good condition to the satisfaction of the Officer in Charge, Marine Inspection. Minor repairs and alterations may be made to the same standards as the original construction: *Provided,* That in no case will a greater departure from the standards of §§ 190.25-5 through 190.25-15 be permitted than presently exists.

[CGFR 67-83, 33 FR 1125, Jan. 27, 1968, as amended by CGFR 69-72, 34 FR 17503, Oct. 29, 1969]

PARTS 191-192 [RESERVED]

PART 193—FIRE PROTECTION EQUIPMENT

Subpart 193.01—Application

Sec.
193.01-1 General.
193.01-3 Incorporation by reference.
193.01-5 Equipment installed but not required.

Coast Guard, DHS

Subpart 193.05—Fire Detecting and Extinguishing Equipment, Where Required

193.05-1 Fire detecting, manual alarm, and supervised patrol systems.
193.05-5 Fire main system.
193.05-10 Fixed fire extinguishing systems.
193.05-15 Hand portable fire extinguishers and semiportable fire extinguishing systems.

Subpart 193.10—Fire Main System, Details

193.10-1 Application.
193.10-5 Fire pumps.
193.10-10 Fire hydrants and hose.
193.10-15 Piping.
193.10-90 Installations contracted for prior to March 1, 1968.

Subpart 193.15—Carbon Dioxide Extinguishing Systems, Details

193.15-1 Application.
193.15-5 Quantity, pipe sizes, and discharge rates.
193.15-10 Controls.
193.15-15 Piping.
193.15-20 Carbon dioxide storage.
193.15-25 Discharge outlets.
193.15-30 Alarms.
193.15-35 Enclosure openings.
193.15-40 Pressure relief.
193.15-90 Installations contracted for prior to March 1, 1968.

Subpart 193.30—Automatic Sprinkler Systems

193.30-1 Application.

Subpart 193.50—Hand Portable Fire Extinguishers and Semiportable Fire Extinguishing Systems, Arrangements and Details

193.50-1 Application.
193.50-5 Classification.
193.50-10 Location.
193.50-15 Spare charges.
193.50-20 Semiportable fire extinguishers.
193.50-90 Vessels contracted for prior to March 1, 1968.

Subpart 193.60—Fire Axes

193.60-1 Application.
193.60-5 Number required.
193.60-10 Location.

AUTHORITY: 46 U.S.C. 2213, 3102, 3306; E.O. 12234, 45 FR 58801, 3 CFR, 1980 Comp., p. 277; Department of Homeland Security Delegation No. 0170.1.

§ 193.01-3

SOURCE: CGFR 67-83, 33 FR 1145, Jan. 27, 1968, unless otherwise noted.

Subpart 193.01—Application

§ 193.01-1 General.

(a) The provisions of this part shall apply to all vessels other than non-self-propelled vessels of less than 300 gross tons.

(b) Non-self-propelled vessels of less than 300 gross tons shall not be subject to the provisions of this part, except as provided otherwise by §§ 193.01-5 and 193.50-1.

§ 193.01-3 Incorporation by reference.

(a) Certain material is incorporated by reference into this part with the approval of the Director of the Federal Register in accordance with 5 U.S.C. 552(a). To enforce any edition other than that specified in paragraph (b) of this section, the Coast Guard must publish notice of change in the FEDERAL REGISTER and make the material available to the public. All approved material is on file at the U.S. Coast Guard, Office of Design and Engineering Standards (G-MSE), 2100 Second Street SW., Washington, DC 20593-0001 and at the National Archives and Records Administration (NARA). For information on the availability of this material at NARA, call 202-741-6030, or go to: http://www.archives.gov/federal_register/code_of_federal_regulations/ibr_locations.html. All approved material is available from the sources indicated in paragraph (b) of this section.

(b) The material approved for incorporation by reference in this part and the sections affected are:

American Society for Testing and Materials (ASTM)

100 Barr Harbor Drive, West Conshohocken, PA 19428-2959.

ASTM F 1121-87 (1993), Standard Specification for International Shore Connections for Marine Fire Applications—193.10-10

National Fire Protection Association (NFPA)

1 Batterymarch Park, Quincy, MA 02269-9101.

369

§ 193.01–5

NFPA 13-1996, Standard for the Installation of Sprinkler Systems—193.30-1

[CGD 88-032, 56 FR 35829, July 29, 1991, as amended by CGD 95-072, 60 FR 50469, Sept. 29, 1995; CGD 96-041, 61 FR 50735, Sept. 27, 1996; CGD 97-057, 62 FR 51051, Sept. 30, 1997; CGD 95-028, 62 FR 51220, Sept. 30, 1997; USCG-1999-6216, 64 FR 53229, Oct. 1, 1999; USCG-1999-5151, 64 FR 67186, Dec. 1, 1999; 69 FR 18803, Apr. 9, 2004]

§ 193.01–5 Equipment installed but not required.

(a) On all vessels, including non-self-propelled vessels of less than 300 gross tons, where fire detecting or extinguishing systems or equipment are not required, but are installed, the system or equipment and its installation shall meet the requirements of this part.

Subpart 193.05—Fire Detecting and Extinguishing Equipment, Where Required

§ 193.05–1 Fire detecting, manual alarm, and supervised patrol systems.

(a) Fire detecting, manual alarm, and supervised patrol systems are not required, but if installed, the systems shall meet the applicable requirements of part 76 of Subchapter H (Passenger Vessels) of this chapter.

§ 193.05–5 Fire main system.

(a) Fire pumps, hydrants, hose, and nozzles shall be installed on all manned vessels.

(b) Except as provided for in § 193.10–10(e), the fire main must be a pressurized or a remotely controlled system.

(c) The arrangements and details of the fire main system shall be as set forth in subpart 193.10.

[CGFR 67-83, 33 FR 1145, Jan. 27, 1968, as amended by CGD 75-031, 40 FR 48349, Oct. 15, 1975]

§ 193.05–10 Fixed fire extinguishing systems.

(a) Approved fire extinguishing systems shall be installed in those locations delineated in this section.

(b) A fixed carbon dioxide or other approved system shall be installed in all lamp and paint lockers, oil rooms, and similar spaces.

(c) Fire extinguishing systems shall be provided for internal combustion engine installations in accordance with the following:

(1) Enclosed spaces containing gasoline engines shall have fixed carbon dioxide systems.

(2) If a fire extinguishing system is installed to protect an internal combustion or gas turbine installation, the system shall be of the carbon dioxide type.

(3) On vessels of 1,000 gross tons and over, a fixed carbon dioxide system shall be installed in all spaces containing internal combustion or gas turbine main propulsion machinery, auxiliaries with an aggregate power of 1,000 b. hp. or greater, or their fuel oil units, including purifiers, valves, and manifolds.

(d) A fixed carbon dioxide system shall be installed in all chemical storerooms.

(e) On vessels of 1,000 gross tons and over, a fixed carbon dioxide, or foam system shall be installed in all spaces containing oil fired boilers, either main or auxiliary, or their fuel oil units, valves, or manifolds in the line between the settling tanks and the boilers. The arrangement and details of the foam system shall be as set forth in part 95 of Subchapter I (Cargo and Miscellaneous Vessels) of this chapter.

(f) Where an enclosed ventilating system is installed for electric propulsion motors or generators, a fixed carbon dioxide extinguishing system shall be installed in such system.

(g) The arrangements and details of the fixed carbon dioxide extinguishing systems shall be as set forth in subpart 193.15.

(h) Additional specific requirements for fire extinguishing systems for spaces containing explosives and other dangerous articles or substances are in part 194 of this subchapter.

§ 193.05–15 Hand portable fire extinguishers and semiportable fire extinguishing systems.

(a) Approved hand portable fire extinguishers and semiportable fire extinguishing systems shall be installed on all manned vessels as set forth in subpart 193.50.

Subpart 193.10—Fire Main System, Details

§ 193.10-1 Application.

(a) The provisions of this subpart, with the exception of § 193.10-90, shall apply to all vessels contracted for on or after March 1, 1968.

(b) Vessels contracted for prior to March 1, 1968, shall meet the requirements of § 193.10-90.

§ 193.10-5 Fire pumps.

(a) Vessels shall be equipped with independently driven fire pumps in accordance with Table 193.10-5(a).

TABLE 193.10-5(a)

Gross tons		Minimum number of pumps	Hose and hydrant size, inches	Nozzle orifice size, inches	Length of hose, feet
Over	Not over				
	100	[1]1	[1]1½	[1]½	50
100	1,000	1	1½	⅝	50
1,000	1,500	2	1½	⅝	50
1,500		2	[2]2½	[2]⅞	[2]50

[1] On vessels of 65 feet in length or less, ¾-inch hose of good commercial grade together with a commercial garden hose nozzle may be used. The pump may be hand operated and the length of hose shall be sufficient to assure coverage of all parts of the vessel.

[2] 75 feet of 1½-inch hose and ⅝-inch nozzle may be used where specified by § 193.10-10(b) for interior locations and 50 feet 1½-inch hose may be used in exterior locations on vessels in other than ocean or coastwise services.

(b) On vessels of 1,000 gross tons and over on an international voyage, each required fire pump, while delivering water through the fire main system at a pressure corresponding to that required by paragraph (c) of this section, shall have a minimum capacity of at least two-thirds of that required for an independent bilge pump. However, in no case shall the capacity of each fire pump be less than that otherwise required by this section.

(c) Each pump must be capable of delivering water simultaneously from the outlets having the greatest pressure drop from the five pumps to the nozzles which may not always be the two highest outlets, at a Pitot tube pressure of not less than 50 p.s.i. Where 1½-inch hose is permitted in lieu of 2½-inch hose by footnote 2 of Table 193.10-5(a), the pump capacity shall be determined on the same basis as if 2½-inch hose had been permitted. Where ¾-inch hose is permitted by Table 193.10-5(a), the Pitot tube pressure may not be less than 35 p.s.i.

(d) Fire pumps shall be fitted on the discharge side with relief valves set to relieve at 25 p.s.i. in excess of the pressure necessary to maintain the requirements of paragraph (c) of this section or 125 p.s.i., whichever is greater. Relief valves may be omitted if the pumps, operating under shutoff conditions, are not capable of developing a pressure exceeding this amount.

(e) Fire pumps shall be fitted with a pressure gage on the discharge side of the pumps.

(f) Fire pumps may be used for other purposes provided at least one of the required pumps is kept available for use on the fire system at all times. In no case shall a pump having connection to an oil line be used as a fire pump. Branch lines connected to the fire main for purposes other than fire and deck wash shall be so arranged that adequate water can be made continuously available for firefighting purposes.

(g) The total area of the pipes leading from a pump shall not be less than the discharge area of the pump.

(h) On vessels with oil fired boilers, either main or auxiliary, or with internal combustion propulsion machinery, where 2 fire pumps are required, they shall be located in separate spaces, and the arrangement, pumps, sea connections, and sources of power shall be such as to insure that a fire in any one space will not put all of the fire pumps out of operation. However, where it is shown to the satisfaction of the Commandant that it is unreasonable or impracticable to meet this requirement due to the size or arrangement of the vessel, or for other reasons, the installation of a total flooding carbon dioxide system may be accepted as an alternate method of extinguishing any fire which would affect the powering and operation for the required fire pumps.

(i) Except as provided for in § 193.10-10(e), a sufficient number of hose streams for fire fighting purposes must be immediately available from the fire main at all times by either of the following methods:

(1) *Maintenance of water pressure.* (i) Water pressure must be maintained on

§ 193.10-10

the fire main at all times by the continuous operation of:

(A) One of the fire pumps; or

(B) Another suitable pump capable of supplying one hose stream at a Pitot tube pressure of not less than 50 p.s.i. (35 p.s.i. for ¾-inch hose); or,

(C) A pressure tank capable of supplying one hose stream at a Pitot tube pressure of not less than 50 p.s.i. (35 p.s.i. for ¾-inch hose) for five minutes.

(ii) An audible alarm must be installed to sound in a continuously manned space if the pressure in the fire main drops to less than that necessary to maintain the minimum Pitot tube pressures specified in § 193.10-5(i)(1)(i).

(2) *Remote control of fire pumps.* (i) At least one fire pump must be capable of remote activation and control.

(ii) If the fire pump is in a continuously manned machinery space, the controls for operating it and the controls for all necessary valves must be located on the manned operating platform in that space.

(iii) If the fire pump is in an unmanned machinery space, the controls for its operation and the controls for all necessary valves must be located in:

(A) The fire control station, if any; or,

(B) The bridge, if there is no fire control station; or,

(C) A readily accessible space acceptable to the Officer in Charge, Marine Inspection.

[CGFR 67-83, 33 FR 1145, Jan. 27, 1968, as amended by CGD 75-031, 40 FR 48349, Oct. 15, 1975; CGD 95-028, 62 FR 51220, Sept. 30, 1997]

§ 193.10-10 Fire hydrants and hose.

(a) The size of fire hydrants, hose, and nozzles and the length of hose required shall be as noted in Table 193.10-5(a).

(b) In lieu of the 2½-inch hose and hydrants specified in Table 193.10-5(a), on vessels over 1,500 gross tons, the hydrants in interior locations may have siamese connections for 1½-inch hose. In these cases the hose shall be 75 feet in length, and only one hose will be required at each fire station; however, if all such stations can be satisfactorily served with 50-foot lengths, 50-foot hose may be used.

(c) On vessels of 500 gross tons and over there must be at least one shore connection to the fire main available to each side of the vessel in an accessible location. Suitable cutout valves and check valves must be provided for furnishing the vessel's shore connections with couplings mating those on the shore fire lines. Vessels of 500 gross tons and over on an international voyage, must be provided with at least one international shore connection complying with ASTM F 1121 (incorporated by reference, see § 193.01-3). Facilities must be available enabling an international shore connection to be used on either side of the vessel.

(d) Fire hydrants must be of sufficient number and so located that any part of the vessel, other than main machinery spaces, may be reached with at least 2 streams of water from separate outlets, at least one of which must be from a single length of hose. In main machinery spaces, all portions of such spaces must be capable of being reached by at least 2 streams of water, each of which must be from a single length of hose from separate outlets; however, this requirement need not apply to shaft alleys containing no assigned space for the stowage of combustibles. Fire hydrants must be numbered as required by § 196.37-15 of this subchapter.

(e) All parts of the fire main located on exposed decks shall either be protected against freezing or be fitted with cutout valves and drain valves so that the entire exposed parts of such piping may be shut off and drained in freezing weather. Except when closed to prevent freezing, such valves shall be sealed open.

(f) The outlet at the fire hydrant shall be limited to any position from the horizontal to the vertical pointing downward, so that the hose will lead horizontally or downward to minimize the possibility of kinking.

(g) Each fire hydrant shall be provided with a single length of hose with nozzle attached and a spanner. A suitable hose rack or other device shall be provided for the proper stowage of the hose. If the hose is not stowed in the open or behind glass so as to be readily seen, the enclosures shall be marked in accordance with § 196.37-15 of this subchapter.

(h) Fire hose shall be connected to the outlets at all times. However, at open decks where no protection is afforded to the hose in heavy weather, the hose may be temporarily removed from the hydrant and stowed in an accessible nearby location.

(i) Each fire hydrant must have at least 1 length of firehose. Each firehose must have a combination solid stream and water spray nozzle that is approved under subpart 162.027 of this subchapter, except 19 millimeters (3/4 inch) hose may have a garden hose nozzle that is bronze or metal with strength and corrosion resistance equivalent to bronze. Combination solid stream and water spray nozzles previously approved under subpart 162.027 of this chapter may be retained so long as they are maintained in good condition to the satisfaction of the Officer in Charge, Marine Inspection.

(j) When the firehose nozzle in the below locations was previously approved under subpart 162.027 of this chapter, a low-velocity water spray applicator, also previously approved under subpart 162.027, of this chapter must be installed as follows:

(1) At least 1 length of firehose on each fire hydrant outside and in the immediate vicinity of each laboratory;

(2) Each firehose in each propulsion machinery space containing oil-fired boiler, internal combustion machinery, or oil fuel unit on a vessel of 1000 gross tons or more—the length of each applicator must be 1.2 meters (4 feet).

(k) Fixed brackets, hooks, or other means for stowing an applicator must be next to each fire hydrant that has an applicator under paragraph (j) of this section.

(l) Firehose shall not be used for any other purpose than fire extinguishing, drills, and testing.

(m) Fire hydrants, nozzles, and other fittings shall have threads to accommodate the hose connections noted in this paragraph. Firehose and couplings shall be as follows:

(1) Couplings shall be of brass, bronze, or other equivalent metal. National Standard firehose coupling threads shall be used for the 1½-inch and 2½-inch sizes, i.e., 9 threads per inch for 1½-inch hose and 7½ threads per inch for 2½-inch hose.

(2) Unlined hose shall not be used in the machinery spaces.

(3) Where ¾-inch hose is permitted by Table 193.10–5(a), the hose and couplings shall be of good commercial grade.

(4) Each section of fire hose used after January 1, 1980 must be lined commercial fire hose that conforms to Underwriters' Laboratories, Inc. Standard 19 or Federal Specification ZZ-H-451E. Hose that bears the label of Underwriters' Laboratories, Inc. as lined fire hose is accepted as conforming to this requirement. Each section of replacement fire hose or any section of new fire hose placed aboard a vessel after January 1, 1977 must also conform to the specification required by this paragraph.

[CGFR 67–83, 33 FR 1145, Jan. 27, 1968, as amended by CGD 74–60, 41 FR 43152, Sept. 30, 1976; CGD 76–086, 44 FR 2394, Jan. 11, 1979; CGD 88–032, 56 FR 35830, July 29, 1991; CGD 95–027, 61 FR 26012, May 23, 1996; USCG–2000–7790, 65 FR 58465, Sept. 29, 2000]

§ 193.10–15 Piping.

(a) All piping, valves, and fittings, shall meet the applicable requirements of Subchapter F (Marine Engineering) of this chapter.

(b) All distribution cut-off valves shall be marked as required by § 196.37–10 of this subchapter.

(c) For vessels on an international voyage, the diameter of the fire main shall be sufficient for the effective distribution of the maximum required discharge from two fire pumps operating simultaneously. This requirement is in addition to § 193.10–5(c). The discharge of this quantity of water through hoses and nozzles at a sufficient number of adjacent hydrants must be at a minimum Pitot tube pressure of 50 pounds per square inch.

[CGFR 67–83, 33 FR 1145, Jan. 27, 1968, as amended by CGD 75–031, 40 FR 48349, Oct. 15, 1975]

§ 193.10–90 Installations contracted for prior to March 1, 1968.

Installations contracted for prior to March 1, 1968, must meet the following requirements:

(a) Except as specifically modified by this paragraph, vessels must comply with the requirements of §§ 193.10–5

§ 193.15-1

through 193.10-15 insofar as the number and general type of equipment is concerned.

(b) Existing equipment, except firehose nozzles and low-velocity water spray applicators, previously approved but not meeting the applicable requirements of §§ 193.10-5 through 193.10-15, may be continued in service so long as they are maintained in good condition to the satisfaction of the Officer in Charge, Marine Inspection. Minor repairs, alterations, and replacements may be permitted to the same standards as the original installations. However, all new installations or major replacements must meet the applicable requirements in this subpart for new installations.

(c) Vessels must comply with the general requirements of § 193.10-5 (c) through (g), § 193.10-10 (d) through (m), and § 193.10-15 insofar as is reasonable and practicable.

(d) Each firehose nozzle must meet § 193.10-10(i), and each low-velocity water spray applicator must meet § 193.10-10(j).

[CGD 95-027, 61 FR 26013, May 23, 1996]

Subpart 193.15—Carbon Dioxide Extinguishing Systems, Details

§ 193.15-1 Application.

(a) The provisions of this subpart shall apply to all new installations contracted for on or after March 1, 1968.

(b) Installations contracted for prior to March 1, 1968, shall meet the requirements of § 193.15-90.

(c) The requirements of this subpart are based on a "high pressure system," i.e., one in which the carbon dioxide is stored in liquid form at atmospheric temperature. Details for "low pressure systems," i.e., those in which the carbon dioxide is stored in liquid form at a continuously controlled low temperature, may be specifically approved by the Commandant where it is demonstrated that a comparable degree of safety and fire extinguishing ability is achieved.

§ 193.15-5 Quantity, pipe sizes, and discharge rates.

(a) *General.* The amount of carbon dioxide required for each space shall be as determined by paragraphs (b) through (d) of this section.

(b) *Total available supply.* A separate supply of carbon dioxide need not be provided for each space protected. The total available supply shall be at least sufficient for the space requiring the greatest amount.

(c) *Enclosed ventilation systems for rotating electrical propulsion equipment.* (1) The number of pounds of carbon dioxide required for the initial charge shall be equal to the gross volume of the system divided by 10 for systems having a volume of less than 2,000 cubic feet, and divided by 12 for systems having a volume of 2,000 cubic feet or more.

(2) In addition to the amount required by paragraph (c)(1) of this section there shall be sufficient carbon dioxide available to permit delayed discharges of such quantity as to maintain at least a 25-percent concentration until the equipment can be stopped. If the initial discharge is such as to achieve this concentration until the equipment is stopped, no delayed discharge need be provided.

(3) The piping for the delayed discharge shall not be less than ½-inch standard pipe, and no specific discharge rate need be applied to such systems. On small systems, this pipe may be incorporated with the initial discharge piping.

(4) The piping for the initial charge shall be in accordance with Table 193.15-5(d)(4), and the discharge of the required amount shall be completed within 2 minutes.

(d) *Machinery spaces, paint lockers, tanks, chemical storerooms, and similar spaces.* (1) Except as provided in paragraph (d)(3) of this section, the number of pounds of carbon dioxide required for each space shall be equal to the gross volume of the space divided by the appropriate factor noted in Table 193.15-5(d)(1). If fuel can drain from the compartment being protected to an adjacent compartment, or if the compartments are not entirely separate, the requirements for both compartments

Coast Guard, DHS § 193.15-10

shall be used to determine the amount of carbon dioxide to be provided. The carbon dioxide shall be arranged to discharge into both such compartments simultaneously.

TABLE 193.15–5(d)(1)
[Gross volume of compartment, cubic feet]

Over	Not over	Factor
	500	15
500	1,600	16
1,600	4,500	18
4,500	50,000	20
50,000		22

(2) For the purpose of the requirements of this paragraph, the volume of the machinery space shall be taken as exclusive of the normal machinery casing unless the boiler, internal combustion machinery, or fuel oil installations extend into such space, in which case the volume shall be taken to the top of the casing or the next material reduction in casing area, whichever is lower. "Normal machinery casing" and "material reduction in casing area" shall be defined as follows:

(i) By "normal machinery casing" shall be meant a casing the area of which is not more than 40 percent of the maximum area of the machinery space.

(ii) By "material reduction in casing area" shall be meant a reduction to at least 40 percent of the casing area.

(3) For vessels on an international voyage contracted for on or after May 26, 1965, the amount of carbon dioxide required for a space containing propulsion boilers or internal combustion propulsion machinery shall be as given by paragraphs (d)(1) and (2) of this section or by dividing the entire volume, including the casing, by a factor of 25, whichever is the larger.

(4) Branch lines to the various spaces shall be as noted in Table 193.15–5(d)(4).

TABLE 193.15–5(d)(4)

Maximum quantity of carbon dioxide required, pounds	Minimum pipe size, inches
100	½
225	¾
300	1
600	1¼
1,000	1½
2,450	2
2,500	2½
4,450	3

TABLE 193.15–5(d)(4)—Continued

Maximum quantity of carbon dioxide required, pounds	Minimum pipe size, inches
7,100	3½
10,450	4
15,000	4½

(5) Distribution piping within the space shall be proportioned from the supply line to give proper distribution to the outlets without throttling.

(6) The number, type, and location of discharge outlets shall be such as to give a uniform distribution throughout the space.

(7) The total area of all discharge outlets shall not exceed 85 percent nor be less than 35 percent of the normal cylinder outlet area or the area of the supply pipe, whichever is smaller. The nominal cylinder outlet area in square inches shall be determined by multiplying the factor 0.0022 by the number of pounds of carbon dioxide required, except that in no case shall this outlet area be less than 0.110 square inch.

(8) The discharge of at least 85 percent of the required amount of carbon dioxide shall be complete within 2 minutes.

§ 193.15-10 Controls.

(a) Except as noted in § 193.15-20(b), all controls and valves for the operation of the system shall be outside the space protected and shall not be located in any space that might be cut off or made inaccessible in the event of fire in any of the spaces protected.

(b) If the same cylinders are used to protect more than one hazard, a manifold with normally closed stop valves shall be used to direct the carbon dioxide into the proper space. If cylinders are used to protect only one hazard, a normally closed stop valve shall be installed between the cylinders and the hazard except for systems of the type indicated in § 193.15–5(d) which contain not more than 300 pounds of carbon dioxide.

(c) One of the stations controlling the system for the main machinery space and the chemical storerooms shall be located as convenient as practicable to one of the main escapes from these spaces. All control stations and the individual valves and controls shall

§ 193.15-15

be marked as required by §§ 196.37-10 and 196.37-13 of this subchapter.

(d) Systems of the type indicated in § 193.15-5(d) shall be actuated by one control operating the valve to the space and a separate control releasing at least the required amount of carbon dioxide. These two controls shall be located in a box or other enclosure clearly identified for the particular space. Those systems installed without a stop valve shall be operated by one control releasing at least the required amount of carbon dioxide.

(e) Where provisions are made for the simultaneous release of a given amount of carbon dioxide by operation of a remote control, provisions shall also be made for manual control at the cylinders. Where gas pressure from pilot cylinders is used as a means for releasing the remaining cylinders, not less than two pilot cylinders shall be used for systems consisting of more than two cylinders. Each of the pilot cylinders shall be capable of manual control at the cylinder, but the remaining cylinders need not be capable of individual manual control.

(f) Systems of the type indicated in § 193.15-5(d), other than systems for tanks, which are of more than 300 pounds of carbon dioxide, shall be fitted with an approved delayed discharge so arranged that the alarm will be sounded for at least 20 seconds before the carbon dioxide is released into the space. Such systems of not more than 300 pounds of carbon dioxide shall also have a similar delayed discharge, except for those systems for tanks and for spaces which have a suitable horizontal escape.

(g) All distribution valves and controls shall be of an approved type. All controls shall be suitably protected.

(h) Complete but simple instructions for the operation of the systems must be located in a conspicuous place at or near all pull boxes, stop valve controls and in the CO_2 cylinder storage room. On systems in which the CO_2 cylinders are not within the protected space, these instructions must also include a schematic diagram of the system and instructions detailing alternate methods of discharging the system should the manual release or stop valve controls fail to operate. Each control valve to branch lines must be marked to indicate the related space served.

(i) If the space or enclosure containing the carbon dioxide supply for controls is to be locked, a key to the space or enclosure shall be in a break-glass-type box conspicuously located adjacent to the opening.

[CGFR 67-83, 33 FR 1145, Jan. 27, 1968, as amended by CGD 74-100R, 40 FR 6209, Feb. 10, 1975]

§ 193.15-15 Piping.

(a) The piping, valves, and fittings shall have a bursting pressure of not less than 6,000 pounds per square inch.

(b) All piping, in nominal sizes not over ¾ inch shall be at least Schedule 40 (standard weight) and in nominal sizes over ¾ inch, shall be at least Schedule 80 (extra heavy).

(c) All piping valves, and fittings of ferrous materials shall be protected inside and outside against corrosion unless specifically approved otherwise by the Commandant.

(d) A pressure relief valve or equivalent set to relieve between 2,400 and 2,800 pounds per square inch shall be installed in the distribution manifold or such other location as to protect the piping in the event that all branch line shutoff valves are closed.

(e) All dead-end lines shall extend at least 2 inches beyond the last orifice and shall be closed with cap or plug.

(f) All piping, valves, and fittings shall be securely supported, and where necessary, protected against injury.

(g) Drains and dirt traps shall be fitted where necessary to prevent the accumulation of dirt or moisture. Drains and dirt traps shall be located in accessible locations where possible.

(h) Piping shall be used for no other purpose except that it may be incorporated with the fire-detecting system.

(i) Piping passing through living quarters shall not be fitted with drains or other openings within such spaces.

(j) Installation test requirements are:

(1) Upon completion of the piping installation, and before the cylinders are connected, a pressure test shall be applied as set forth in this paragraph. Only carbon dioxide or other inert gas shall be used for this test.

(2) The piping from the cylinders to the stop valves in the manifold shall be

Coast Guard, DHS §193.15-35

subjected to a pressure of 1,000 pounds per square inch. With no additional gas being introduced to the system, it shall be demonstrated that the leakage of the system is such as not to permit a pressure drop of more than 150 pounds per square inch per minute for a 2-minute period.

(3) The individual branch lines to the various spaces protected shall be subjected to a test similar to that described in the preceding subparagraph with the exception that the pressure used shall be 600 pounds per square inch in lieu of 1,000 pounds per square inch. For the purpose of this test, the distribution piping shall be capped within the space protected at the first joint ahead of the nozzles.

(4) In lieu of the tests prescribed in the preceding paragraphs in this paragraph, small independent systems protecting spaces such as emergency generator rooms, lamp lockers, chemical storerooms, etc., may be tested by blowing out the piping with air at a pressure of at least 100 pounds per square inch.

§193.15-20 Carbon dioxide storage.

(a) Except as provided in paragraph (b) of this section, the cylinders shall be located outside the spaces protected, and shall not be located in any space that might be cut off or made inaccessible in the event of a fire in any of the spaces protected.

(b) Systems of the type indicated in §193.15-5(d), consisting of not more than 300 pounds of carbon dioxide, may have cylinders located within the space protected. If the cylinder stowage is within the space protected, the system shall be arranged in an approved manner to be automatically operated by a heat actuator within the space in addition to the regular remote and local controls.

(c) The space containing the cylinders shall be properly ventilated and designed to preclude an anticipated ambient temperature in excess of 130° F.

(d) Cylinders shall be securely fastened and supported, and where necessary, protected against injury.

(e) Cylinders shall be so mounted as to be readily accessible and capable of easy removal for recharging and inspection. Provisions shall be available for weighing the cylinders.

(f) Where subject to moisture, cylinders shall be so installed as to provide a space of at least 2 inches between the flooring and the bottom of the cylinders.

(g) Cylinders shall be mounted in an upright position or inclined not more than 30 degrees from the vertical. However, cylinders which are fitted with flexible or bent siphon tubes may be inclined not more than 80 degrees from the vertical.

(h) Where check valves are not fitted on each independent cylinder discharge, plugs or caps shall be provided for closing outlets when cylinders are removed for inspection or refilling.

(i) All cylinders used for storing carbon dioxide must be fabricated, tested, and marked in accordance with the requirements of §§147.60 and 147.65 of this chapter.

[CGFR 67-83, 33 FR 1145, Jan. 27, 1968, as amended by CGD 84-044, 53 FR 7753, Mar. 10, 1988]

§193.15-25 Discharge outlets.

(a) Discharge outlets shall be of an approved type.

§193.15-30 Alarms.

(a) Space normally accessible to persons on board while the vessel is being navigated which are protected by a carbon dioxide extinguishing system and are required to be fitted with a delayed discharge system other than paint and lamp lockers and similar small spaces, shall be fitted with an approved audible alarm which will be automatically sounded when the carbon dioxide is admitted to the space. The alarm shall be conspicuously and centrally located and shall be marked as required by §196.37-9 of this subchapter. Such alarms shall be so arranged as to sound during the 20-second delay period prior to the discharge of carbon dioxide into the space, and the alarm shall depend on no source of power other than the carbon dioxide.

§193.15-35 Enclosure openings.

(a) Where mechanical ventilation is provided for spaces which are protected by carbon dioxide extinguishing systems provisions shall be made so that

§ 193.15-40

the ventilation system is automatically shut down with the operation of the system to that space.

(b) Where natural ventilation is provided for spaces protected by a carbon dioxide extinguishing system, provisions shall be made for easily and effectively closing off the ventilation.

(c) Means shall be provided for closing all other openings to the space protected from outside such space. In this respect, relatively tight doors, shutters, or dampers shall be provided for openings in the lower portion of the space. The construction shall be such that openings in the upper portion of the space can be closed off either by permanently installed means or by the use of canvas or other material which is normally carried by the vessel.

§ 193.15-40 Pressure relief.

(a) Where necessary, relatively tight compartments such as refrigeration spaces, paint lockers, etc., shall be provided with suitable means for relieving excessive pressure accumulating within the compartment when the carbon dioxide is injected.

§ 193.15-90 Installations contracted for prior to March 1, 1968.

(a) Installations contracted for prior to March 1, 1968, shall meet the following requirements:

(1) Existing arrangements, materials, and facilities previously approved shall be considered satisfactory so long as they meet the minimum requirements of this paragraph and they are maintained in good condition to the satisfaction of the Officer in Charge, Marine Inspection. Minor repairs, alterations, and replacements may be permitted to the same standards as the original installations. However, all new installations or major replacements shall meet the applicable requirements in this subpart for new installations.

(2) The details of the systems shall be in general agreement with §§ 193.15-5 through 193.15-40 insofar as is reasonable and practicable, with the exception of § 193.15-5(d) (1), (2), and (4), covering machinery spaces, etc., which systems may be installed in accordance with paragraphs (a) (3) through (6) of this section.

(3) In boilerrooms, the bilges shall be protected by a system discharging principally below the floorplates. Perforated pipe may be used in lieu of discharge nozzles for such systems. The number of pounds of carbon dioxide shall be equal to the gross volume of the boilerroom taken to the top of the boilers divided by 36. In the event of an elevated boilerroom which drains to the machinery space, the system shall be installed in the engineroom bilge and the gross volume shall be taken to the flat on which the boilers are installed.

(4) In machinery spaces where main propulsion internal combustion machinery is installed, the number of pounds of carbon dioxide required shall be equal to the gross volume of the space taken to the under side of the deck forming the hatch opening divided by 22.

(5) In miscellaneous spaces other than cargo or main machinery spaces the number of pounds of carbon dioxide required shall be equal to the gross volume of the space divided by 22.

(6) Branch lines to the various spaces other than cargo and similar spaces shall be as noted in Table 193.15-90(a)(6). This table is based on cylinders having discharge outlets and siphon tubes of ⅜-inch diameter.

TABLE 193.15-90(a)(6)

| Number of cylinders ||Nominal pipe size, inches|
Over	Not over	
	2	½—standard.
2	4	¾—standard.
4	6	1—extra heavy.
6	12	1¼—extra heavy.
12	16	1½—extra heavy.
16	27	2—extra heavy.
27	39	2½—extra heavy.
39	60	3—extra heavy.
60	80	3½—extra heavy.
80	104	4—extra heavy.
104	165	5—extra heavy.

Subpart 193.30—Automatic Sprinkler Systems

§ 193.30-1 Application.

Automatic sprinkling systems shall comply with NFPA 13–1996.

[CGD 95–028, 62 FR 51220, Sept. 30, 1997]

Subpart 193.50—Hand Portable Fire Extinguishers and Semiportable Fire Extinguishing Systems, Arrangements and Details

§ 193.50-1 Application.

(a) The provisions of this subpart, with the exception of § 193.50-90, shall apply to all vessels, including non-self-propelled vessels of less than 300 gross tons, contracted for on or after March 1, 1968.

(b) All vessels other than unmanned barges contracted for prior to March 1, 1968, shall meet the requirements of § 193.50-90.

(c) All unmanned barges are exempted from the requirements in this subpart. However, if such barges carry on board hand portable fire extinguishers and semiportable fire extinguishing systems, then such equipment shall be in accordance with this subpart for manned barges.

§ 193.50-5 Classification.

(a) Hand portable fire extinguishers and semiportable fire extinguishing systems shall be classified by a combination letter and number symbol. The letter indicating the type of fire which the unit could be expected to extinguish and the number indicating the relative size of the unit.

(b) The types of fire will be designated as follows:

(1) "A" for fires in ordinary combustible materials where the quenching and cooling effects of quantities of water, or solutions containing large percentages of water, are of first importance.

(2) "B" for fires in flammable liquids, greases, etc., where a blanketing effect is essential.

(3) "C" for fires in electrical equipment where the use of nonconducting extinguishing agent is of first importance.

(c) The number designations for size will start with "I" for the smallest to "V" for the largest. Sizes I and II are considered hand portable fire extinguishers and sizes III, IV, and V are considered semiportable fire extinguishing systems which shall be fitted with suitable hose and nozzle or other practicable means so that all portions of the space concerned may be covered. Examples of size graduations for some of the typical hand portable and semiportable fire extinguishing systems are set forth in Table 193.50-5(c).

TABLE 193.50-5(c)

Classification		Soda-acid and water, gals.	Foam, gals.	Carbon dioxide, lbs.	Dry chemical, lbs.
Type	Size				
A	II	2½	2½		
B	I		1¼	4	2
B	II		2½	15	10
B	III		12	35	20
B	IV		20	50	30
B	V		40	100	50
C	I			4	2
C	II			15	10

(d) All hand portable fire extinguishers and semiportable fire extinguishing systems shall have permanently attached thereto a metallic nameplate giving the name of the item, the rated capacity in gallons, quarts, or pounds, the name and address of the person or firm for whom approved, and the identifying mark of the actual manufacturer.

(e) Vaporizing liquid type fire extinguishers containing carbon tetrachloride or chlorobromomethane or other toxic vaporizing liquids shall not be permitted.

§ 193.50-10 Location.

(a) Approved hand portable fire extinguishers and semiportable fire extinguishing systems shall be installed in accordance with Table 193.50-10(a). The location of the equipment shall be to the satisfaction of the Officer in Charge, Marine Inspection. Nothing in this paragraph shall be construed as limiting the Officer in Charge, Marine Inspection, from requiring such additional equipment as he deems necessary for the proper protection of the vessel.

(b) Semiportable fire extinguishing systems shall be located in the open so as to be readily seen.

(c) If hand portable fire extinguishers are not located in the open or behind glass so that they may be readily seen, they may be placed in enclosures together with the firehose, provided such

§ 193.50-15

enclosures are marked as required by § 196.37-15 of this subchapter.

TABLE 193.50-10(a)—HAND PORTABLE FIRE EXTINGUISHER AND SEMIPORTABLE FIRE EXTINGUISHING SYSTEMS

Space	Classification (see § 193.50-5)	Quantity and location
Safety Areas[1]		
Wheelhouse or fire control room		None required.
Stairway and elevator enclosures		Do.
Communicating corridors	A-II	1 in each main corridor not more than 150 feet apart. (May be located in stairways.)
Lifeboat embarkation and lowering stations		None required.
Radio room	C-I[2]	2 in vicinity of exit.[2]
Accommodations[1]		
Staterooms, toilet spaces, public spaces, offices, lockers, isolated storerooms, and pantries open decks, etc.		None required.
Service spaces		
Galleys	B-II or C-II	1 for each 2,500 square feet or fraction thereof suitable for hazards involved.
Machinery spaces		
Paint and lamp rooms	B-II	1 outside space in vicinity of exit.
Accessible baggage, mail, and specie rooms, and storerooms.	A-II	1 for each 2,500 square feet or fraction thereof located in vicinity of exits, either inside or outside the spaces.
Carpenter shop and similar spaces	A-II	1 outside the space in vicinity of exit.
Coal-fired boilers: Bunker and boiler space		None required.
Oil-fired boilers: Spaces containing oil-fired boilers, either main or auxiliary, or their fuel-oil units.	B-II B-V B-V	2 required.[3] 1 required.[4]
Internal combustion or gas turbine propelling machinery spaces.	B-II	1 for each 1,000 brake horsepower, but not less than 2 nor more than 6.[5]
	B-III	1 required.[6,7]
Electric propulsive motors or generators of open type.	C-II	1 for each propulsion motor or generator unit.
Enclosed ventilating systems for motors and generators of electric propelling machinery.		None required.
Auxiliary spaces:		
Internal combustion gas turbine	B-II	1 outside the space in vicinity of exit.[7]
Electric emergency motors or generators	C-II	1 outside the space in vicinity of exit.[8]
Steam		None required.
Trunks to machinery spaces		Do.
Fuel tanks		Do.
Scientific spaces		
Chemistry laboratory or scientific laboratory	C-II	1 dry chemical and 1 carbon dioxide for each 300 square feet or fraction thereof, with one (1) of each kind located in the vicinity of the exit.
Chemical storeroom	C-II	Same as for the chemistry laboratory.

[1] Two B-I hand portable fire extinguishers may be substituted for 1 B-II.
[2] For vessels on an international voyage, substitute 1 C-II in vicinity of exit.
[3] Vessels of less than 1,000 gross tons require 1.
[4] Vessels of less than 1,000 gross tons may substitute 1 B-IV.
[5] Only 1 required for motorboats.
[6] If oil burning donkey boiler fitted in space, the B-V previously required for the protection of the boiler may be substituted. Not required where a fixed carbon dioxide system is installed.
[7] Not required on vessels of less than 300 gross tons if fuel has a flash-point higher than 110° F.
[8] Not required on vessels of less than 300 gross tons.

(d) Hand portable fire extinguishers and their stations shall be numbered in accordance with § 196.37-15 of this subchapter.

(e) Hand portable or semiportable extinguishers, which are required on their nameplates to be protected from freezing, shall not be located where freezing temperatures may be expected.

§ 193.50-15 Spare charges.

(a) For all vessels spare charges shall be carried for at least 50 percent of each size and each variety, i.e., foam, soda-acid, carbon dioxide, etc., of hand portable fire extinguishers required by §193.50–10(a). However, if the unit is of such variety that it cannot be readily recharged by the vessel's personnel, one spare unit of the same classification shall be carried in lieu of spare charges for all such units of the same size and variety.

(b) Spare charges shall be so packaged as to minimize the hazards to personnel while recharging the units. Acid shall be contained in a Crown stopper type of bottle.

§193.50–20 Semiportable fire extinguishers.

(a) The frame or support of each size III, IV, and V fire extinguisher required by Table 193.50–10(a) must be welded or otherwise permanently attached to a bulkhead or deck.

(b) If an approved size III, IV, or V fire extinguisher has wheels and is not required by Table 193.50–10(a), it must be securely stowed when not in use to prevent it from rolling out of control under heavy sea conditions.

[CGD 77–039, 44 FR 34133, June 14, 1979]

§193.50–90 Vessels contracted for prior to March 1, 1968.

(a) Vessels contracted for prior to March 1, 1968, shall meet the following requirements:

(1) Except as specifically modified by this paragraph, the requirements of §§193.50–5 through 193.50–15 shall be complied with insofar as the number and general type of equipment is concerned.

(2) Existing installations previously approved, but not meeting the applicable requirements of §§193.50–5 through 193.50–15 may be continued in service so long as they are maintained in good condition to the satisfaction of the Officer in Charge, Marine Inspection, and they are in general agreement with the degree of safety prescribed by Table 193.50–10(a). Minor modifications may be made to the same standard as the original installation: *Provided*, That in no case will a greater departure from the standards of Table 193.50–10(a) be permitted than presently exists.

(3) All new equipment and installations shall meet the applicable requirements in this subpart for new vessels.

Subpart 193.60—Fire Axes

§193.60–1 Application.

(a) The provisions of this subpart shall apply to all vessels other than unmanned barges.

(b) Unmanned barges are exempted from the requirements in this subpart. However, if such barges carry on board fire axes, then such equipment shall be in accordance with this subpart for manned barges.

§193.60–5 Number required.

(a) All vessels shall carry at least the minimum number of fire axes as set forth in Table 193.60–5(a). Nothing in this paragraph shall be construed as limiting the Officer in Charge, Marine Inspection, from requiring such additional fire axes as he deems necessary for the proper protection of the vessel.

TABLE 193.60–5(a)

Gross tons		Number of axes
Over	Not over	
....	50	1
50	200	2
200	500	4
500	1,000	6
1,000	....	8

§193.60–10 Location.

(a) Fire axes shall be distributed throughout the spaces available to persons on board so as to be most readily available in the event of emergency.

(b) If fire axes are not located in the open, or behind glass, so that they may be readily seen, they may be placed in enclosures together with the firehose, provided such enclosures are marked as required by §196.37–15 of this subchapter.

PART 194—HANDLING, USE, AND CONTROL OF EXPLOSIVES AND OTHER HAZARDOUS MATERIALS

Subpart 194.01—Application

Sec.
194.01–1 General.

Subpart 194.05—Stowage and Marking

194.05–1 General.
194.05–3 Chemical stores.

§ 194.01-1

194.05-5 Chemicals in the chemistry laboratory.
194.05-7 Explosives—Detail requirements.
194.05-9 Flammable liquid chemical stores—Detail requirements.
194.05-11 Flammable solids and oxidizing materials—Detail requirements.
194.05-13 Corrosive liquids as chemical stores—Detail requirements.
194.05-15 Compressed gases as chemical stores—Detail requirements.
194.05-17 Poisonous articles as chemical stores—Detail requirements.
194.05-19 Combustible liquids as chemical stores—Detail requirements.
194.05-21 Other regulated materials.

Subpart 194.10—Magazines

194.10-1 Application.
194.10-5 Type and location.
194.10-10 Integral magazine construction.
194.10-15 Magazine van construction.
194.10-20 Magazine chest construction.
194.10-25 Ventilation.
194.10-30 Magazine sprinklers.
194.10-35 Labeling.

Subpart 194.15—Chemistry Laboratory and Scientific Laboratory

194.15-1 General.
194.15-3 Responsibility.
194.15-5 Ventilation.
194.15-7 Fire protection.
194.15-9 Storage.
194.15-11 Flushing systems.
194.15-15 Chemicals other than compressed gases.
194.15-17 Compressed gases other than inert gases.
194.15-19 Electrical.

Subpart 194.20—Chemical Stores and/or Storerooms

194.20-1 General.
194.20-3 Responsibility.
194.20-5 Ventilation.
194.20-7 Fire protection.
194.20-9 Storage.
194.20-11 Flushing systems.
194.20-15 Chemical stores other than compressed gases.
194.20-17 Compressed gases.
194.20-19 Piping and electrical requirements.

Subpart 194.90—Vessels Contracted for Prior to March 1, 1968

194.90-1 Requirements.

AUTHORITY: 46 U.S.C. 2103, 2113, 3306; 49 U.S.C. App. 1804; E.O. 12234, 45 FR 58801, 3 CFR, 1980 Comp., p. 277; Department of Homeland Security Delegation No. 0170.1.

46 CFR Ch. I (10-1-04 Edition)

SOURCE: CGFR 67-83, 33 FR 1151, Jan. 27, 1968, unless otherwise noted.

Subpart 194.01—Application

§ 194.01-1 General.

(a) The provisions of this part, with the exception of subpart 194.90, shall apply to all vessels other than non-self-propelled vessels of less than 300 gross tons contracted for on or after March 1, 1968.

(b) Non-self-propelled vessels of less than 300 gross tons shall not be subject to the provisions of this part except as provided otherwise by paragraph (c) of this section.

(c) Non-self-propelled vessels of less than 300 gross tons shall be governed by the applicable portions of 49 CFR parts 171–179, and the applicable portions of 33 CFR parts 6 and 121 to 126, inclusively. Alternately, the owner, at his option, may comply with the provisions of this part.

(d) Vessels contracted for prior to March 1, 1968, shall meet the requirements of subpart 194.90.

[CGFR 67-83, 33 FR 1151, Jan. 27, 1968, as amended by CGD 86-033, 53 FR 36026, Sept. 16, 1988]

Subpart 194.05—Stowage and Marking

§ 194.05-1 General.

(a) The master shall be held responsible for and shall require the proper handling, stowage, and marking of all chemical stores and reagents.

(b) Chemical stores shall be stowed in a chemical storeroom in approved drums, barrels, or other packages, properly marked and labeled, as prescribed by 49 CFR part 172 for those specific commodities, except that those chemical stores excluded from the storeroom by §§ 194.20-15 and 194.20-17, and those chemical stores not desired to be located in a chemical storeroom, shall be stored in accordance with the appropriate provisions of 49 CFR part 176 insofar as such regulations apply to cargo vessels.

(c) Ships' stores shall be regulated in accordance with the appropriate provisions of part 147 of Subchapter N (Dangerous Cargoes) of this chapter.

[CGFR 67-83, 33 FR 1151, Jan. 27, 1968, as amended by CGD 86-033, 53 FR 36027, Sept. 16, 1988]

§ 194.05-3 Chemical stores.

(a) Chemical stores are those chemicals which possess one or more of the following properties and shall be classed, marked and labeled in accordance with 49 CFR part 172:

(1) Explosives.
(2) Flammable liquids.
(3) Flammable solids.
(4) Oxidizing materials.
(5) Corrosive materials.
(6) Compressed gasses.
(7) Poisons.
(8) Combustible liquids.
(9) Other Regulated Materials (DOT Hazard Class "ORM").

(b) Substances for use in the chemistry laboratory, or to be stored in the chemical storeroom and generally covered under paragraph (a) of this section but not specifically listed by name in 49 CFR 172.101 must be approved by the Commandant (G-MSO) prior to being carried on board a vessel.

[CGD 86-033, 53 FR 36027, Sept. 16, 1988, as amended by CGD 97-057, 62 FR 51051, Sept. 30, 1997]

§ 194.05-5 Chemicals in the chemistry laboratory.

(a) Small working quantities of chemical stores in the chemistry laboratory which have been removed from the approved shipping container need not be marked or labeled as required by 49 CFR part 172. Reagent containers in the laboratory shall be marked to show at least the following:

(1) Common chemical name.
(2) Hazards, if any; e.g., flammable, poison, etc.

(b) In the interest of facilitating scientific activities, no restrictions are intended which will limit the variety of chemical stores which may be used in the chemical laboratory. With the knowledge and approval of the master, the laboratory supervisor may be responsible for stowage and use of materials within the laboratory and chemical storeroom.

(c) Reagent containers shall be properly secured against shifting and spillage. Insofar as practical all reagents shall be stowed in suitable, unbreakable containers.

[CGFR 67-83, 33 FR 1151, Jan. 27, 1968, as amended by CGD 86-033, 53 FR 36027, Sept. 16, 1988]

§ 194.05-7 Explosives—Detail requirements.

(a) Except as otherwise provided by this part, Division 1.1 and 1.2 (explosive) materials (as defined in 49 CFR 173.50) and blasting-caps must be carried in magazines specifically fitted for that purpose as described by subpart 194.10 of this part.

(b) Class 1 (explosive) materials (as defined in 49 CFR 173.50) must be identified by their appropriate DOT classification.

(c)(1) Compatibility of magazine stowage shall be in accordance with 49 CFR 176.144.

(2) Magazine chests, magazine vans, and deck stowage areas shall be separated by a distance of at least 25 feet if their contents are incompatible with each other. Reduction of this distance to allow for special configurations will be permitted only if specifically approved by the Commandant.

(d) On-deck stowage of unfused depth-charges or other unfused-case-type Class 1 (explosive) materials (as defined in 49 CFR 173.50) is authorized as follows:

(1) Stowage shall be in a location reasonably protected from the full force of boarding seas.

(2) Stowage shall be protected from direct exposure to the sun by overhead decks, awnings, or tarpaulins. Decks shall be constructed of incombustible materials; awnings and tarpaulins shall be fire-resistant and/or flame proof fabric.

(3) Items shall be properly secured by using existing vessel structures such as bulwarks, hatch coamings, shelter deck and poop bulkheads as part boundaries and effectively closing in the items by fitting angle bar closing means secured by bolting to clips or other parts of the ship's structure. Lashing of deck stowage is permitted provided eye pads or

§ 194.05-9

other suitable means are fitted to secure such lashings and provided the individual items are of such a configuration as to prevent slippage of the lashings. Shoring and dunnage may be used as necessary to further facilitate the security of the stowage.

(4) Stowage area shall be selected so as to provide for safe access to all internal spaces and to all parts of the deck required to be used in navigation and working of the vessel. Stowage shall not be on or under the bridge, or navigating deck, or within a distance, in a horizontal plane, of 25 feet of an operating or embarkation point of any lifeboat or raft. Reduction of this distance to allow for special configurations will be permitted only if specifically approved by the Commandant.

[CGFR 67-83, 33 FR 1151, Jan. 27, 1968, as amended by CGD 86-033, 53 FR 36027, Sept. 16, 1988; CGD 92-050, 59 FR 39966, Aug. 5, 1994; CGD 97-057, 62 FR 51051, Sept. 30, 1997]

§ 194.05-9 Flammable liquid chemical stores—Detail requirements.

(a) Flammable liquids as chemical stores and reagents are governed by subparts 194.15 and 194.20.

(b) Other flammable liquids are regulated by the appropriate portions of 49 CFR parts 172, 173, and 176 or part 147 of Subchapter N (Dangerous Cargoes) of this chapter.

[CGFR 67-83, 33 FR 1151, Jan. 27, 1968, as amended by CGD 86-033, 53 FR 36027, Sept. 16, 1988; 53 FR 46872, Nov. 21, 1988]

§ 194.05-11 Flammable solids and oxidizing materials—Detail requirements.

(a) Flammable solids and oxidizing materials used as chemical stores and reagents are governed by subparts 194.15 and 194.20.

(b) Oxidizing materials used as blasting agents are regulated by the appropriate portions of 49 CFR parts 172, 173, and 176.

[CGFR 67-83, 33 FR 1151, Jan. 27, 1968, as amended by CGD 86-033, 53 FR 36027, Sept. 16, 1988; 53 FR 46872, Nov. 21, 1988]

§ 194.05-13 Corrosive liquids as chemical stores—Detail requirements.

(a) Corrosive liquids as chemical stores and reagents are governed by subparts 194.15 and 194.20.

46 CFR Ch. I (10-1-04 Edition)

(b) Other corrosive liquids are regulated by the appropriate portions of 49 CFR parts 172, 173, and 176 or part 147 of Subchapter N (Dangerous Cargoes) of this chapter.

[CGFR 67-83, 33 FR 1151, Jan. 27, 1968, as amended by CGD 86-033, 53 FR 36027, Sept. 16, 1988]

§ 194.05-15 Compressed gases as chemical stores—Detail requirements.

(a) Compressed gases as chemical stores and reagents are governed by subparts 194.15 and 194.20.

(b) Other compressed gases are regulated in accordance with the appropriate portions of 49 CFR parts 172, 173, and 176 or part 147 of Subchapter N (Dangerous Cargoes) of this chapter.

[CGFR 67-83, 33 FR 1151, Jan. 27, 1968, as amended by CGD 86-033, 53 FR 36027, Sept. 16, 1988]

§ 194.05-17 Poisonous articles as chemical stores—Detail requirements.

(a) Poisonous articles as chemical stores and reagents shall be governed by subparts 194.15 and 194.20.

(b) Other poisonous articles shall be regulated by the appropriate portions of 49 CFR parts 172, 173, and 176 or part 147 of Subchapter N (Dangerous Cargoes) of this chapter.

[CGFR 67-83, 33 FR 1151, Jan. 27, 1968, as amended by CGD 86-033, 53 FR 36027, Sept. 16, 1988]

§ 194.05-19 Combustible liquids as chemical stores—Detail requirements.

(a) Combustible liquid chemical stores and reagents shall be governed by subparts 194.15 and 194.20.

(b) Other combustible liquids shall be regulated by the appropriate portions of 49 CFR parts 172, 173, and 176 or part 147 of Subchapter N (Dangerous Cargoes) of this chapter.

[CGFR 67-83, 33 FR 1151, Jan. 27, 1968, as amended by CGD 86-033, 53 FR 36027, Sept. 16, 1988]

§ 194.05-21 Other regulated materials.

(a) Other Regulated Materials (DOT Hazard Class "ORM") as chemical stores and reagents shall be governed by appropriate portions of subparts 194.15 and 194.20 of this part.

Coast Guard, DHS § 194.10-10

(b) Other Regulated Materials (DOT Hazard Class "ORM") which are not chemical stores and reagents shall be regulated by the appropriate portions of 49 CFR parts 172, 173, and 176.

[CGD 86–033, 53 FR 36027, Sept. 16, 1988]

Subpart 194.10—Magazines

§ 194.10-1 Application.

(a) The provisions of this subpart apply to the construction of integral magazines, magazine vans, and magazine chests.

(b) Loading, loading procedures, shipper's requirements, and other features not related to the construction of magazines shall be in accordance with the applicable provisions of 49 CFR parts 173 and 176 and 33 CFR part 6 and parts 121 to 126, inclusive.

[CGFR 67–83, 33 FR 1151, Jan. 27, 1968, as amended by CGD 86–033, 53 FR 36027, Sept. 16, 1988]

§ 194.10-5 Type and location.

(a) *Integral magazines.* (1) Magazines shall be of permanent construction located below the freeboard deck and where practicable below the waterline.

(2) Magazines shall not be located in horizontal proximity to or below accommodation spaces.

(3) Magazines shall not be located adjacent to the collision bulkhead, nor in bearing with a bulkhead forming the boilerroom, engineroom, gallery, or other high fire hazard area boundary. If it is necessary to construct the magazine in proximity to these areas, a cofferdam space of at least 2 feet shall be provided between the bulkhead or deck involved and the magazine. Such a cofferdam shall be provided with suitable ventilation and shall not be used for storage purposes.

(b) *Magazine vans.* (1) Magazine vans may be installed on deck in a location protected from boarding seas. The location selected shall not impair access to accommodations or other spaces necessary to the safe working and navigation of the vessel and shall not be within 15 feet of ventilation terminals emitting warm air or hazardous vapors, such as from galleys and pumprooms, or within 10 feet of any unshielded radio apparatus or antenna lead.

(2) Magazine vans may be installed below decks in holds provided the hold location meets the location requirements for integral magazines. The cofferdam requirement of paragraph (a)(3) of this section is considered as fulfilled if the van is of steel construction. Holds so utilized shall not be used for stowage of other hazardous materials covered by 49 CFR parts 171–179. The stowage of other explosives or oxidizing materials in the same hold is permitted in accordance with the requirements of 49 CFR part 176.

(c) *Magazine chests.* (1) Magazine chests shall be located on the weather decks in a position suitable for jettisoning the contents.

(2) Magazine chests shall be set off at least 4 inches from decks and deckhouse.

(3) Magazine chests shall not be located within 15 feet of ventilation terminals emitting warm air or hazardous vapors, such as from galleys and pumprooms.

(4) Magazine chests intended for the stowage of blasting caps, detonators, or boosters, in addition to the requirements in this paragraph, shall not be stowed within 10 feet of any unshielded radio apparatus or antenna leads.

[CGFR 67–83, 33 FR 1151, Jan. 27, 1968, as amended by CGD 86–033, 53 FR 36027, Sept. 16, 1988]

§ 194.10-10 Integral magazine construction.

(a) Magazines shall be of permanent watertight construction. Bulkheads and decks, including the deck overhead, which are common with storerooms or workshops shall be of A–15 construction as defined by § 72.05–10 of Subchapter H (Passenger Vessels) of this chapter. Flush construction shall be employed where practicable.

(b) Where the shell or unsheathed weather decks form boundaries of the magazine spaces suitable approved incombustible thermal insulation shall be provided to prevent condensation of moisture.

(c) Where a tank top forms the magazine deck it shall be insulated with an approved deck covering to prevent condensation of moisture. Tank top manholes shall not be installed in magazines.

385

§ 194.10-15

(d) Light fixtures shall be of an approved type equipped with globes and guards. Control of the lighting system shall be from a location external to the magazine. An indicator light shall be provided at the switch location to indicate when the lighting circuits are energized. Other electrical equipment and wiring shall not be installed within or pass through the magazine. Electrical cables enclosed in a watertight trunk are permitted.

(e) Piping, other than fresh or salt water service and drainage system, shall not be routed through magazines except as required for the magazines themselves. Other piping systems enclosed in a watertight trunk are permitted.

(f) Access doors for the magazine, or magazine groups, shall be of substantial watertight construction and be provided with means whereby they may be securely locked.

(g) Racks, stanchions, battens, and other devices shall be installed to provide rigid and safe stowage of explosives in their approved shipping containers with a minimum of dunnage.

(h) Decks shall be covered with a permanent nonslip nonspark covering.

§ 194.10-15 Magazine van construction.

(a) Vans shall be of substantial metal construction. Their interior shall be insulated with an approved incombustible insulation to the standards required for A-15 divisional bulkheads as prescribed in part 72 of Subchapter H (Passenger Vessels) of this chapter. The interior shall be lined flush with incombustible materials.

(b) Lighting fixtures, if installed, shall be of an approved type equipped with globes and guards. All electrical installations shall meet the applicable requirements of Subchapter J (Electrical Engineering) of this chapter. The electrical terminals for connections to the ship's electrical system shall be of watertight construction and bear a label plate denoting the power requirement of the van.

(c) Access doors and ventilation closures shall be of watertight construction. Doors shall be provided with means whereby they may be securely locked.

46 CFR Ch. I (10-1-04 Edition)

(d) Vans shall be provided with suitable pads and clips for securing to the deck and for installation of wire rope sway braces.

(e) Vans shall bear a label plate stating light weight, gross weight and weight of explosives. Gross weight shall not exceed 250 pounds per square foot of deck area.

§ 194.10-20 Magazine chest construction.

(a) Magazine chests shall be of watertight metal construction with flush interior. The body and lid shall have a minimum thickness of 1/8 inch.

(b) Permanent sun shields shall be provided for sides and top including the lid. These shall have a minimum thickness of 1/8-inch aluminum or 16-gage steel. Side shields shall be offset from the body a distance of 1 inch. The top shield shall be offset a distance of 1½ inches. Sun shields may be omitted when chests are installed "on deck protected," shielded from direct exposure to the sun.

(c) Chests shall be limited to a gross capacity of 100 cubic feet.

(d) Chests shall be secured to the vessel's structure by means of permanently installed foundation clips or bolts or a combination thereof. Lashings will not be acceptable.

(e) Chests shall be provided with substantial hasps and staples for locking purposes.

§ 194.10-25 Ventilation.

(a) *Integral magazines.* (1) All integral magazines shall be provided with natural or mechanical ventilation. Design calculations shall be submitted demonstrating that the system has sufficient capacity to maintain the magazine temperature below 100° F. with 88° F. weather air. Mechanical cooling may be used where ventilation requirements exceed 1,500 cubic feet per minute.

(2) Ventilation systems shall be of watertight construction and shall serve no other space. Weather cowls shall be provided with a double layer of wire screen of not less than 1/8-inch mesh. Metal watertight closures shall be provided for use when the ventilation system is not in operation. A 2-inch IPS

Coast Guard, DHS § 194.10-35

bypass with check valve shall be provided in parallel with at least one of the ventilation closures to prevent pressure buildup.

(b) *Magazine vans.* (1) All magazine vans shall be provided with natural ventilation sufficient to maintain the inside air temperature below 130° F. with an assumed outside temperature of 115° F.

(2) Ventilation supply weather openings shall be located at least 6 feet above the deck. Exhaust terminals shall be located in the van overhead. Louvers or weather cowls with a double layer of wire screen of not less than ⅛-inch mesh shall be provided for protection of weather openings.

§ 194.10-30 Magazine sprinklers.

(a) *Sprinkler system required.* (1) A manual control, hydraulic control, or automatic sprinkler system shall be installed in each magazine or magazine group. The control valve shall generally be in accordance with Specification MIL-V-17501 insofar as materials and test fittings are concerned. All systems shall be remotely operable from a control station on the freeboard deck and manually operable at the control valve location.

(2) Where automatic systems are installed sprinkler heads shall be of the open head design so as to permit either manual or automatic operation.

(3) Sprinkler systems shall be designed in accordance with the requirements of part 76 of Subchapter H (Passenger Vessels) of this chapter. Minimum total system capacity shall be based on 0.8 gallon per minute per square foot of overhead area.

(4) The normally required fire pumps may be used for magazine sprinkling purposes. However, the use of the magazine sprinkling system shall not interfere with the simultaneous use of the fire main system.

(b) *Magazine vans.* (1) A manual control sprinkler system shall be installed in each magazine van. The system shall be connected to the nearest fire main outlet by jumper hose. The hose shall be protected from physical damage by a grating or similar arrangement. The fire station valve shall serve as the sprinkler control valve.

(2) Sprinkler systems shall be designed in accordance with the requirements of part 76 of Subchapter H (Passenger Vessels) of this chapter, except that the system capacity shall be sufficient to provide a coverage of 0.4 gallon per minute per square foot of overhead area.

[CGFR 67-83, 33 FR 1151, Jan. 27, 1968, as amended by CGD 82-063b, 48 FR 4783, Feb. 3, 1983]

§ 194.10-35 Labeling.

(a) Labeling shall be in 3-inch block type lettering. Letters shall be red or white, whichever provides the better contrast against the background. On small chests the labeling size may be reduced to that consistent with the size of the chest so that the inscription may be placed in its entirety on the side or top.

(b) The access door to magazines and magazine vans shall bear the inscription:

MAGAZINE

KEEP OPEN LIGHTS AND FIRE AWAY

KEEP DOOR CLOSED

REMOVE MATCHES AND LIGHTERS PRIOR TO ENTERING

(c) Magazine chests shall be marked in a conspicuous location, preferably the top, with the inscription:

MAGAZINE CHEST

KEEP OPEN LIGHTS AND FIRE AWAY

(d) Magazine chests used for blasting caps, detonators, or boosters shall be marked in a conspicuous location with the inscription as appropriate:

BLASTING CAP LOCKER

or

DETONATOR LOCKER

or

BOOSTER LOCKER

KEEP OPEN LIGHTS AND FIRE AWAY

(e) Magazine van, unless specifically approved as a portable magazine under provisions of 49 CFR 176.137 shall bear the additional statements on each side:

§ 194.15-1

MAGAZINE

WARNING

DO NOT LIFT WITH CONTENTS

(f) Control locations for magazine sprinkler systems, in addition to the operating instructions required by § 76.20-20 of Subchapter H (Passenger Vessels) of this chapter shall bear the inscription:

MAGAZINE SPRINKLER CONTROL

[CGFR 67-83, 33 FR 1151, Jan. 27, 1968, as amended by CGD 86-033, 53 FR 36027, Sept. 16, 1988; CGD 97-057, 62 FR 51051, Sept. 30, 1997]

Subpart 194.15—Chemistry Laboratory and Scientific Laboratory

§ 194.15-1 General.

(a) Chemical and scientific laboratories shall be considered service areas, and as such shall be subject to the applicable requirements of § 190.07-10(d).

(1) Incombustible materials shall be used, insofar as is reasonable and practicable, for permanently installed laboratory furnishings and equipment, such as desks, file and storage cabinets, waste paper baskets, work benches, chair frames, etc. Working surfaces where chemical stores are used shall be of incombustible material.

(2) Combustible materials may be used for other working surfaces and for temporary furnishings and equipment installed to facilitate a specific scientific mission.

(b) Storage of all equipment, materials, etc., and cleanliness shall be consistent with sound laboratory practices. All items shall be securely stowed.

(c) Provision shall be made for rapid removal of chemical spills and protection of the deck. In areas where chemicals will commonly be used, the deck shall be covered with a nonskid masonry or other suitably resistant material so fashioned that spillage will be contained and easily removed.

(d) The access doors to the laboratory shall bear the inscription "Chemical Laboratory", or "Scientific Laboratory", in lettering meeting requirements of § 194.10-35(a).

§ 194.15-3 Responsibility.

(a) With the knowledge and approval of the master, the senior member of the scientific party embarked may supervise the safety and operation of the chemical laboratory.

(b) The laboratory supervisor shall:

(1) Maintain the highest standards of safe working conditions.

(2) Provide safeguards against hazardous undertakings.

(3) Educate personnel working in the laboratory spaces to be alert for hazards.

§ 194.15-5 Ventilation.

(a) Operations, reactions or experiments which produce toxic, noxious or corrosive vapors shall be conducted under a suitably installed fume hood. The fume hood shall be equipped with an independent power exhaust ventilation system which terminates so as to prevent fumes from entering other portions of the vessel. The exhaust system of the fume hood shall be compatible with the ventilation system of the laboratory to prevent fumes from backing-up within the fume hood system. The terminals shall be equipped with acceptable flame screens.

(b) Chemical laboratories shall be equipped with power ventilation system of the exhaust type serving the entire laboratory for use in the event of spills or other emergencies. The system shall have a capacity sufficient to effect a complete change of air in not more than 4 minutes based upon the volume of the compartment.

(1) Power ventilation units shall have nonsparking impellers and shall not produce a source of vapor ignition in either the compartment or the ventilation system associated with the compartment.

(2) The power ventilation system shall be interlocked with any other ventilation or air-conditioning system serving the laboratory in a manner to prevent the circulation of vapors to other spaces.

(3) This ventilation system shall be independent of any other ventilation system in the vessel. It shall serve no other space. It shall be of watertight construction.

(4) Ventilation exhaust outlets shall terminate more than 6 feet from any

Coast Guard, DHS

§ 194.20–1

opening to the interior part of the vessel and from any possible source of vapor ignition.

(5) The control for the power ventilation system shall be conveniently located and marked in a manner to clearly identify the purpose of the control.

(c) Ventilation of air conditioning systems serving the chemical laboratory shall be designed so that air cannot be recirculated into an accommodation space.

§ 194.15–7 Fire protection.

(a) If a fixed or semiportable firefighting system is installed, it shall meet the applicable requirements in part 193 of this subchapter. Other firefighting systems will be given special consideration by the Commandant.

(b) Portable fire extinguishers are required in accordance with Table 193.50–10(a) of this subchapter.

§ 194.15–9 Storage.

(a) Chemical stores mentioned in § 194.05–3 may be stored in small working quantities in the laboratory provided their containers are labeled in accordance with § 194.05–5(a).

(b) Chemical stores in greater than small laboratory working quantities shall be stored in approved containers in the chemical storeroom as prescribed in § 194.05–1(b).

(c) All material stored in any laboratory shall be securely stowed for sea with due consideration for chemical compatibility and safety standards.

§ 194.15–11 Flushing systems.

(a) Working spaces in which chemical stores are used shall be equipped with a fresh water supply shower.

(b) There shall be a provision for flushing away chemical spills.

§ 194.15–15 Chemicals other than compressed gases.

Chemicals, including those listed in 49 CFR part 172, may be stored in small working quantities in the chemical laboratory.

[CGD 86–033, 53 FR 36027, Sept. 16, 1988]

§ 194.15–17 Compressed gases other than inert gases.

(a) When, in consideration for a particular operation, compressed gases are needed within the laboratory, the cylinders may be temporarily installed in the laboratory, provided no more than one (1) cylinder of each gas is in the laboratory simultaneously. When transporting compressed gas cylinders to, from, or within the vessel, the cylinder valves shall be capped or otherwise protected in accordance with 49 CFR 173.301(g).

(b) Cylinders temporarily installed in the laboratory shall be securely stowed for sea. Appropriate safety signs shall be displayed and safety precautions observed.

(c) Oxygen and acetylene cylinders for use in ship's maintenance shall not be stored in the laboratory.

(d) Systems providing gas for bunsen burners or similar semipermanent/permanent installations shall be installed in accordance with subpart 195.03 of part 195.

[CGFR 67–83, 33 FR 1151, Jan. 27, 1968, as amended by CGD 86–033, 53 FR 36027, Sept. 16, 1988]

§ 194.15–19 Electrical.

(a) All electrical equipment located within 18 inches of the deck of the chemical laboratory shall be in accordance with the applicable requirements of Subchapter J (Electrical Engineering) of this chapter for Class I, Division 2, hazardous locations. Electrical equipment located 18 inches or more above the deck may be of a type suitable for wet or dry locations in accordance with Subchapter J.

Subpart 194.20—Chemical Stores and/or Storerooms

§ 194.20–1 General.

(a) The chemical storerooms shall be considered to be service areas and as such shall be subject to the applicable requirements of § 190.07–10(d).

(1) Installed equipment, such as shelves and cabinets, shall be constructed of incombustible materials.

(2) The access doors to the storeroom shall bear the inscription "Chemical Storeroom."

(b) Storage and cleanliness shall be consistent with good chemical stowage practices.

§ 194.20-3

(c) The deck of the chemical storeroom shall be of a nonskid material suitably resistant to chemical spills. Provision shall be made for the containment and removal of chemical spills.

(d) Chemical reactions and experiments shall not be conducted in the chemical storeroom.

(e) A storeroom, when used as a chemical storeroom, shall be exclusively for the stowage of chemical stores.

(f) All doors shall open in the direction of escape.

(g) Movement of chemical stores to, or from, the storeroom shall be accomplished utilizing suitable, portable containers. In no event shall piping systems, or similar arrangements, be permitted for transfer of chemical stores between the storeroom and the area in which the chemical stores are to be used.

§ 194.20-3 Responsibility.

(a) With the knowledge and approval of the master the senior member of the scientific party embarked may supervise the safety and operation of the chemical storerooms.

(b) The chemical storeroom supervisor shall:

(1) Maintain the highest standards of safe working conditions.

(2) Provide safeguards against hazardous undertakings.

(3) Educate personnel working in, and near, the storeroom to be alert for hazards.

§ 194.20-5 Ventilation.

(a) Chemical storerooms shall be equipped with a power ventilation system of exhaust type. The system shall have a capacity sufficient to effect a complete change of air in not more than 4 minutes based upon the volume of the compartment.

(1) Power ventilation units shall have nonsparking impellers and shall not produce a source of vapor ignition in either the compartment or the ventilation system associated with the compartment.

(2) This ventilation system shall be independent of any other ventilation system. It shall serve no other space in the vessel. It shall be of watertight construction.

(3) Inlets to exhaust ducts shall be provided and located at points where concentration of vapors may be expected. Ventilation exhaust outlets shall terminate more than 6 feet from any opening to the interior part of the vessel and from any possible source of vapor ignition. Terminals shall be fitted with acceptable flame screens.

(4) The control for the power ventilation system shall be conveniently located and marked in a manner to clearly identify the purpose of the control.

(b) Provisions shall be made so that the chemical storeroom will be ventilated before it is entered. An Indicator shall be provided outside the space to show that ventilation is being provided. In addition, the storeroom shall be marked "Danger—Ventilate Before Entering."

§ 194.20-7 Fire protection.

(a) Each chemical storeroom shall be protected by a fixed automatic carbon dioxide extinguishing system installed in accordance with subpart 193.15 of part 193 of this subchapter.

(b) Portable fire extinguishers are required in accordance with Table 193.50-10(a) of this subchapter.

§ 194.20-9 Storage.

(a) Chemical stores shall be stored in the chemical storeroom as prescribed in § 194.05-1(b).

(b) All items stored in the storeroom shall be secured against shifting and with due consideration for chemical compatibility and safety standards.

(1) Items shall not be stowed on the deck.

(2) Shelving shall be so constructed as to provide a clear space of at least 4 inches between the bottom shelf and the deck.

§ 194.20-11 Flushing systems.

(a) Provision shall be made for flushing away chemical spills.

(b) If a drainage system is installed, it shall be separate from any other drainage system.

§ 194.20-15 Chemical stores other than compressed gases.

(a) Flammable liquids are excluded from the storeroom unless contained in properly marked and labeled metal safety cans not in excess of 5 gallons of each kind. Refer to subpart 194.05 for applicable requirements governing quantities greater than 5 gallons.

(b) Combustible liquids in approved portable drums, barrels or containers not in excess of 55 gallons of each kind may be stored in the storeroom. Refer to subpart 194.05 for applicable requirements governing quantities greater than 55 gallons.

(c) Containers when used for dispensing flammable and combustible liquids shall be equipped with automatic closing valves.

(d) Poisons listed in 49 CFR part 172 may be stored in approved containers in the chemical storeroom.

(e) Explosives and oxidizing materials not for use in the chemical laboratory shall not be stored in the chemical storeroom.

(f) Chemical stores specifically mentioned in 49 CFR part 172 may be carried in the chemical storeroom.

[CGFR 67-83, 33 FR 1151, Jan. 27, 1968, as amended by CGD 86-033, 53 FR 36027, Sept. 16, 1988]

§ 194.20-17 Compressed gases.

(a) Nonflammable compressed gases (excluding oxygen) may be securely stowed in the storeroom: *Provided,* That no more than eight (8) cylinders total are stowed simultaneously in the same chemical storeroom.

(b) Flammable compressed gases and oxygen shall be stowed in accordance with 49 CFR part 176, subpart H.

(c) Compressed gas cylinders shall have valve protection in accordance with 49 CFR 173.301(g) and shall be safely stowed in a vertical position in suitable racks.

[CGFR 67-83, 33 FR 1151, Jan. 27, 1968, as amended by CGD 86-033, 53 FR 36027, Sept. 16, 1988]

§ 194.20-19 Piping and electrical requirements.

(a) Piping, electrical equipment, and wiring shall not be installed within or pass through a chemical storeroom except as required for the chemical storeroom itself.

(b) The electrical installation shall be in accordance with the applicable requirements of Subchapter J (Electrical Engineering) of this chapter for Class I, Division 1, Group C hazardous locations.

Subpart 194.90—Vessels Contracted for Prior to March 1, 1968

§ 194.90-1 Requirements.

(a) Vessels contracted for prior to March 1, 1968, shall meet the following requirements:

(1) Existing arrangements, materials, and facilities previously approved but not meeting the applicable requirements of subparts 194.05 through 194.20 may be continued in service so long as they are maintained in good condition to the satisfaction of the Officer in Charge, Marine Inspection. Minor repairs, alterations, and replacements may be permitted to the same standards as the original design: *Provided,* That in no case will a greater departure from the standards of subparts 194.05 through 194.20 be permitted than presently exists.

(2) All new installations, major alterations, and major replacements shall meet the applicable requirements in this part for new vessels.

(3) The general requirements of subparts 194.05 through 194.20 shall apply unless in the opinion of the Officer in Charge, Marine Inspection, it is unreasonable or impracticable, or the arrangement or construction of the vessel makes it unnecessary.

PART 195—VESSEL CONTROL AND MISCELLANEOUS SYSTEMS AND EQUIPMENT

Subpart 195.01—Application

Sec.
195.01-1 General.
195.01-3 Incorporation by reference.

Subpart 195.03—Marine Engineering Systems

195.03-1 Installation and details.

§ 195.01-1   46 CFR Ch. I (10-1-04 Edition)

Subpart 195.05—Electrical Engineering and Interior Communications Systems

195.05-1 Installation and details.

Subpart 195.06—Lifesaving Appliances and Arrangements

195.06-1 Lifesaving appliances and arrangements.

Subpart 195.07—Anchors, Chains, and Hawsers

195.07-1 Application.
195.07-5 Ocean, coastwise, or Great Lakes service.
195.07-10 Lakes, bays, and sounds, or river service.
195.07-90 Vessels contracted for prior to March 1, 1968.

Subpart 195.09—Scientific Equipment

195.09-1 Application.
195.09-5 General.

Subpart 195.11—Portable Vans and Tanks

195.11-1 Application.
195.11-5 Scope.
195.11-10 Design and construction of portable vans.
195.11-15 Plan approval and inspection.
195.11-20 Marking and label plate.
195.11-25 Loading and stowage.
195.11-30 Portable tanks.

Subpart 195.17—Radar

195.17-1 When required.

Subpart 195.19—Magnetic Compass and Gyrocompass

195.19-1 When required.

Subpart 195.27—Sounding Equipment

195.27-1 When required.

Subpart 195.30—Protection From Refrigerants

195.30-1 Application.
195.30-5 General.
195.30-15 Self-contained breathing apparatus.
195.30-90 Vessels contracted for before November 23, 1992.

Subpart 195.35—Fireman's Outfit

195.35-1 Application.
195.35-5 General.
195.35-10 Fireman's outfit.
195.35-15 Stowage.
195.35-20 Spare charges.

195.35-90 Vessels contracted for before November 23, 1992.

Subpart 195.40—Pilot Boarding Equipment

195.40-1 Pilot boarding equipment.

AUTHORITY: 46 U.S.C. 2113, 3306, 3307; 49 U.S.C. App. 1804; E.O. 12234, 45 FR 58801, 3 CFR, 1980 Comp., p. 277; Department of Homeland Security Delegation No. 0170.1.

SOURCE: CGFR 67-83, 33 FR 1156, Jan. 27, 1968, unless otherwise noted.

Subpart 195.01—Application

§ 195.01-1 General.

(a) The provisions of this part shall apply to all vessels except as specifically noted in this part.

§ 195.01-3 Incorporation by reference.

(a) Certain materials are incorporated by reference into this part with the approval of the Director of the Federal Register in accordance with 5 U.S.C. 552(a). To enforce any edition other than the one listed in paragraph (b) of this section, notice of the change must be published in the FEDERAL REGISTER and the material made available to the public. All approved material is on file at the Office of the Federal Register, Washington, DC 20408, and at the U.S. Coast Guard, Office of Design and Engineering Standards, 2100 Second Street SW., Washington, DC 20593-0001, and is available from the address indicated in paragraph (b).

(b) The material approved for incorporation by reference in this part, and the sections affected is:

American Society for Testing and Materials (ASTM)

100 Barr Harbor Drive, West Conshohocken, PA 19428-2959.
ASTM F 1014-92, Standard Specification for Flashlights on Vessels—195.35-5

[CGD 82-042, 53 FR 17706, May 18, 1988, as amended by CGD 96-041, 61 FR 50735, Sept. 27, 1996; CGD 97-057, 62 FR 51051, Sept. 30, 1997; USCG-1999-5151, 64 FR 67187, Dec. 1, 1999]

Subpart 195.03—Marine Engineering Systems

§ 195.03-1 Installation and details.

(a) The installation of all systems of a marine engineering nature, together

Coast Guard, DHS § 195.07-10

with the details of design, construction, and installation, shall be in accordance with the requirements of Subchapter F (Marine Engineering) of this chapter. Systems of this type include the following:

Steering Systems.
Bilge and Ballast Systems.
Tank Vent and Sounding Systems.
Overboard Discharges and Shell Connections.
Pipe and Pressure Systems.
Liquefied Petroleum Gas Systems.

Subpart 195.05—Electrical Engineering and Interior Communications Systems

§ 195.05-1 Installation and details.

(a) The installation of all systems of an electrical engineering or interior communication nature, together with the details of design, construction, and installation shall be in accordance with the requirements of Subchapter J (Electrical Engineering) of this chapter. Systems of this type include the following:

Ship's Service Generating Systems.
Ship's Service Power Distribution Systems.
Ship's Lighting Systems.
Electric Propulsion and Propulsion Control Systems.
Emergency Lighting and Power Systems.
Electric Lifeboat Winch Systems.
Electric Steering Gear and Steering Control Systems.
Fire Detecting and Alarm Systems.
Sound Powered Telephone and Voice Tube Systems.
Engine Order Telegraph Systems.
Rudder Angle Indicator Systems.
Refrigerated Spaces Alarm Systems.
Navigation Lights Systems.
Daylight Signaling Lights.
Miscellaneous Machinery Alarms and Controls.
General Alarm Systems.

Subpart 195.06—Lifesaving Appliances and Arrangements

§ 195.06-1 Lifesaving appliances and arrangements.

All lifesaving appliances and arrangements shall be in accordance with the requirements for special purpose vessels in subchapter W (Lifesaving Appliances and Arrangements) of this chapter.

[CGD 84-069, 61 FR 25312, May 20, 1996]

Subpart 195.07—Anchors, Chains, and Hawsers

§ 195.07-1 Application.

(a) The provisions of this subpart, with the exception of § 195.07-90, shall apply to all vessels other than unmanned barges, contracted for on or after March 1, 1968.

(b) Vessels other than unmanned barges contracted for prior to March 1, 1968 shall meet the requirements of § 195.07-90.

§ 195.07-5 Ocean, coastwise, or Great Lakes service.

(a) Vessels in ocean, coastwise, or Great Lakes service shall be fitted with anchors, chains, and hawsers which shall be in general agreement with the standards established by the American Bureau of Shipping, see subpart 188.35 of part 188 of this subchapter.

(b) In addition to the provisions of paragraph (a) of this section, the following requirements and alternatives also apply:

(1) The American Bureau of Shipping rules relating to anchor equipment are mandatory, not a guide.

(2) Vessels under 200 feet (61 meters) in length and with an American Bureau of Shipping equipment number of less than 150 may be equipped with either:

(i) One anchor of the tabular weight and one-half the tabulated length of anchor chain listed in the applicable standard, or

(ii) Two anchors of one-half the tabular weight with the total length of anchor chain listed in the applicable standard provided both anchors are in a position that allows for ready use at all times and the windlass is capable of heaving in either anchor.

(c) Standards of other recognized classification societies may be used, in lieu of those established by the American Bureau of Shipping, upon approval by the Commandant.

[CGFR 67-83, 33 FR 1156, Jan. 27, 1968, as amended by CGD 87-013, 53 FR 20624, June 6, 1988]

§ 195.07-10 Lakes, bays, and sounds, or river service.

(a) Vessels in lakes, bays, and sounds, or river service shall be fitted with such ground tackle and hawsers as

§ 195.07–90

deemed necessary by the Officer in Charge, Marine Inspection, depending upon the size of the vessel and the waters on which it operates.

§ 195.07–90 Vessels contracted for prior to March 1, 1968.

(a) Vessels contracted for prior to March 1, 1968, shall meet the following requirements:

(1) Existing arrangements, materials, installations, and facilities previously accepted or approved shall be considered satisfactory for the same service so long as they are maintained in good condition to the satisfaction of the Officer in Charge, Marine Inspection. If the service of the vessel is changed, the suitability of the equipment will be established by the Officer in Charge, Marine Inspection.

(2) Minor repairs, alterations and replacements may be permitted to the same standards as the original installations. However, all new installations, major alterations, or major replacements shall meet the applicable requirements in this subpart for new vessels.

Subpart 195.09—Scientific Equipment

§ 195.09–1 Application.

(a) The provisions of this subpart shall apply to all vessels.

§ 195.09–5 General.

(a) All scientific equipment shall be designed to good commercial standards for such appliances, where applicable. Their electrical and pressure connections to the ship's supply shall be designed to marine standards.

(b) It shall be the responsibility of the owner to assure that the scientific equipment and their electrical or pressure connections to the ship's supply are maintained in such a manner as to be free of personnel hazards which may be caused by shock, temperature extremes, and moving parts.

Subpart 195.11—Portable Vans and Tanks

§ 195.11–1 Application.

(a) The provisions of this subpart shall apply to all vessels.

§ 195.11–5 Scope.

(a) The provisions in this subpart contain requirements for the design, construction, and stowage of portable vans, or tanks, which may be carried on board vessels. As used in this subpart, portable vans and tanks, are intended to include those temporary structures which may be carried aboard a vessel for a limited period of time and which are not permanently attached to the vessel.

(b) Special consideration may be given to the approval of portable structures which have been used for other purposes prior to proposed use on these vessels.

(c) As used in this subpart, portable vans, magazines, chests, etc., are intended to include those temporary structures which may be carried aboard a vessel for a limited period of time and which are not permanently attached to the vessel. The use, arrangement, and handling of such portable structures shall be approved by the Officer in Charge, Marine Inspection, prior to placement on board the vessel.

§ 195.11–10 Design and construction of portable vans.

(a) The design and material selection shall incorporate consideration of forces and environmental conditions to which the structure, attachments, and attachment points will be exposed.

(b) Steel, aluminum or other substantial material suitable for a marine environment may be used for construction of the basic van box.

(c) Accommodation vans are those intended to provide increased accommodation and related spaces of a temporary nature aboard a vessel. They shall, insofar as is reasonable and practicable, meet the applicable requirements of this subchapter for means of

Coast Guard, DHS

escape, arrangement, interior construction, and electrical installations.

(d) Power vans are those outfitted with electrical power generating machinery or batteries providing electrical power for other vans or to scientific equipment. They shall insofar as is reasonable and practicable meet the applicable requirements of this subchapter for pressure piping, electrical, fire extinguishing and ventilation systems.

(e) Vans for the use or storage of chemical stores as defined in § 194.05-3 of this subchapter shall be constructed and outfitted in accordance with the applicable requirements of this subchapter.

(f) Vans containing scientific equipment are considered as within the definition of § 188.10-67 of this subchapter.

§ 195.11-15 Plan approval and inspection.

(a) Accommodation, power and chemical stores vans are subject to normal plan submission procedures of subpart 189.55 and to initial construction inspection. They must be inspected at each inspection for certification and periodic inspection.

(b) Vans which have not undergone plan review and initial inspection may be accepted on a single voyage basis by the OCMI provided that they are in good condition and are free of hazards to personnel.

[CGFR 67-83, 33 FR 1156, Jan. 27, 1968, as amended by USCG-1999-4976, 65 FR 6510, Feb. 9, 2000]

§ 195.11-20 Marking and label plate.

(a) All vans shall be provided with a label plate stating light weight, gross weight, and power requirements where applicable.

(b) For vans subject to inspection label plates shall provide space for the date of initial inspection, the marine inspector's initials, and stamp. Space shall also be provided for the reinspection stamping.

§ 195.11-25 Loading and stowage.

(a) Vans required to be inspected and bearing a current inspection stamp may be accepted for loading and stowage by the master of the vessel who shall insure that the van is in good condition.

(1) Vans containing scientific equipment and nonhazardous stores may be accepted by the master of the vessel subject to his inspection to determine that electrical and pressure connections are in good condition and adequate for the service intended.

(b) The master shall insure that all vans are securely stowed and attached to the vessel to prevent shifting in a seaway. Portable vans to be occupied during the vessel's operation shall be securely attached to the vessel by welding, bolting, or equivalent means.

(c) Vans shall be located with due regard to access and to prevent recirculation of the discharge from the exhaust systems of the vessel.

(d) The loading of vans shall be in accordance with the stability requirements of the vessel.

(e) Prior to a vessel's departure, an entry shall be made in the official logbook for each portable van placed on board that such van and its stowage are in compliance with the applicable requirements in this subchapter.

§ 195.11-30 Portable tanks.

(a) All portable tanks, whether hazardous or nonhazardous commodities, shall be loaded and stowed in accordance with the stability requirements of the vessel.

(b) Portable tanks for flammable or combustible liquids in bulk (see § 188.05-30(b) of this subchapter) shall not be carried on vessels.

(c) Portable tanks containing other hazardous materials shall be in accordance with the requirements of 49 CFR parts 171-179.

[CGFR 67-83, 33 FR 1156, Jan. 27, 1968, as amended by CGD 86-033, 53 FR 36027, Sept. 16, 1988]

Subpart 195.17—Radar

§ 195.17-1 When required.

All mechanically propelled vessels of 1,600 gross tons and over in ocean or coastwise service must be fitted with a marine radar system for surface navigation. Facilities for plotting radar

§ 195.19-1

readings must be provided on the bridge.

[CGD 75-074, 42 FR 5965, Jan. 31, 1977]

Subpart 195.19—Magnetic Compass and Gyrocompass

§ 195.19-1 When required.

(a) All mechanically propelled vessels in ocean or coastwise service must be fitted with a magnetic compass.

(b) All mechanically propelled vessels of 1,600 gross tons and over in ocean or coastwise service must be fitted with a gyrocompass in addition to the magnetic compass.

(c) Each vessel must have an illuminated repeater for the gyrocompass required under paragraph (b) that is at the main steering stand unless the gyrocompass is illuminated and is at the main steering stand.

[CGD 75-074, 42 FR 5965, Jan. 31, 1977]

Subpart 195.27—Sounding Equipment

§ 195.27-1 When required.

(a) All mechanically propelled vessels of 500 gross tons and over shall be fitted with an efficient electronic deep-sea sounding apparatus and another independent means of obtaining deep-sea soundings, which may be a deep-sea hand lead.

[CGFR 67-83, 33 FR 1156, Jan. 27, 1968, as amended by CGD 75-074, 42 FR 5965, Jan. 31, 1977]

Subpart 195.30—Protection From Refrigerants

SOURCE: CGD 86-036, 57 FR 48327, Oct. 23, 1992, unless otherwise noted.

§ 195.30-1 Application.

(a) This subpart, except § 195.30-90, applies to each vessel that is contracted for on or after November 23, 1992, and is equipped with any refrigeration unit using—

(1) Ammonia to refrigerate any space with a volume of more than 20 cubic feet; or

(2) Fluorocarbons to refrigerate any space with a volume of more than 1000 cubic feet.

(b) Each vessel that is contracted for before November 23, 1992, must satisfy § 195.30-90 if it is equipped with any refrigeration unit using—

(1) Ammonia to refrigerate any space with a volume of more than 20 cubic feet, or

(2) Fluorocarbons to refrigerate any space with a volume of more than 1000 cubic feet.

§ 195.30-5 General.

(a) Each self-contained breathing apparatus must be of the pressure-demand, open-circuit type, approved by the Mine Safety and Health Administration (MSHA) and by the National Institute for Occupational Safety and Health (NIOSH), and have at a minimum a 30-minute air supply, a full facepiece, and a spare charge.

(b) All equipment shall be maintained in an operative condition, and it shall be the responsibility of the master and chief engineer to ascertain that a sufficient number of the crew are familiar with the operation of the equipment.

§ 195.30-15 Self-contained breathing apparatus.

(a) Each vessel must have a self-contained breathing apparatus for use as protection against gas leaking from a refrigeration unit.

(b) The self-contained breathing apparatus required by paragraph (a) of this section may be one of those required by § 195.35-10.

§ 195.30-90 Vessels contracted for before November 23, 1992.

Vessels contracted for before November 23, 1992, must meet the following requirements:

(a) Each vessel must satisfy §§ 195.30-5 through 195.30-15 concerning the number of items and method of stowage of equipment.

(b) Items of equipment previously approved, but not meeting the applicable specifications set forth in § 195.30-5, may continue in service as long as they are maintained in good condition to the satisfaction of the Officer in Charge, Marine Inspection; but each item in an installation or a replacement must meet all applicable specifications.

(c) Each respirator must either satisfy §195.30–5(a) or be a self-contained compressed-air breathing apparatus previously approved by MSHA and NIOSH under part 160, subpart 160.011, of this chapter.

[CGD 86–036, 57 FR 48327, Oct. 23, 1992, as amended by CGD 95–028, 62 FR 51220, Sept. 30, 1997]

Subpart 195.35—Fireman's Outfit

§195.35–1 Application.

(a) This subpart, except §195.35–90, applies to each vessel, other than an unmanned barge, contracted for on or after November 23, 1992.

(b) Each vessel, other than an unmanned barge, contracted for before November 23, 1992, must satisfy §195.35–90.

(c) All unmanned barges are exempt from the requirements in this subpart. However, if any unmanned barge carries a fireman's outfit, the outfit must meet the requirements in this subpart for such outfits aboard manned barges.

[CGD 86–036, 57 FR 48327, Oct. 23, 1992]

§195.35–5 General.

(a) All flame safety lamps shall be of an approved type, constructed in accordance with subpart 160.016 of part 160 of Subchapter Q (Specifications) of this chapter.

(b) Each self-contained breathing apparatus must be of the pressure-demand, open-circuit type, approved by the Mine Safety and Health Administration (MSHA) and by the National Institute for Occupational Safety and Health (NIOSH), and have at a minimum a 30-minute air supply and a full facepiece.

(c) Flashlights shall be Type II or Type III, constructed and marked in accordance with ASTM F 1014 (incorporated by reference, see §195.01–3).

(d) All lifelines shall be of steel or bronze wire rope. Steel wire rope shall be either inherently corrosion-resistant, or made so by galvanizing or tinning. Each end shall be fitted with a hook with keeper having throat opening which can be readily slipped over a ⅝-inch bolt. The total length of the lifeline shall be dependent upon the size and arrangement of the vessel, and more than one line may be hooked together to achieve the necessary length. No individual length of lifeline may be less than 50 feet in length. The assembled lifeline shall have a minimum breaking strength of 1,500 pounds.

(e) All equipment shall be maintained in an operative condition, and it shall be the responsibility of the master and chief engineer to ascertain that a sufficient number of the crew are familiar with the operation of the equipment.

(f) Boots and gloves shall be of rubber or other electrically nonconducting material.

(g) The helmet shall provide effective protection against impact.

(h) Protective clothing shall be of material that will protect the skin from the heat of fire and burns from scalding steam. The outer surface shall be water resistant.

[CGFR 67–83, 33 FR 1156, Jan. 27, 1968, as amended by CGFR 69–72, 34 FR 17504, Oct. 29, 1969; CGD 82–042, 53 FR 17706, May 18, 1988; CGD 86–036, 57 FR 48327, Oct. 23, 1992; USCG–1999–5151, 64 FR 67187, Dec. 1, 1999]

§195.35–10 Fireman's outfit.

(a) Each fireman's outfit must consist of one self-contained breathing apparatus, one lifeline with a belt or a suitable harness, one flashlight, one flame safety lamp, one rigid helmet, boots and gloves, protective clothing, and one fire ax.

(b) Every vessel shall carry at least two fireman's outfits. The fireman's outfits must be stored in widely separated, accessible locations.

[CGFR 69–72, 34 FR 17504, Oct. 29, 1969, as amended by CGD 75–074, 42 FR 5965, Jan. 31, 1977; CGD 86–036, 57 FR 48327, Oct. 23, 1992]

§195.35–15 Stowage.

(a) Equipment shall be stowed in a convenient, accessible location as determined by the master, for use in case of emergency.

§195.35–20 Spare charges.

(a) A complete recharge shall be carried for each self-contained breathing apparatus, and a complete set of spare batteries shall be carried for each flashlight. The spares shall be stowed in the same location as the equipment it is to reactivate.

§ 195.35-90 Vessels contracted for before November 23, 1992.

Vessels contracted for before November 23, 1992, must meet the following requirements:

(a) Each vessel must satisfy §§ 195.35-5 through 195.35-20 concerning the number of items and method of stowage of equipment.

(b) Items of equipment previously approved, but not meeting the applicable specifications set forth in § 195.35-5, may continue in service as long as they are maintained in good condition to the satisfaction of the Officer in Charge, Marine Inspection; but each item in an installation or a replacement must meet all applicable specifications.

(c) Each respirator must either satisfy § 195.35-5(b) or be a self-contained compressed-air breathing apparatus previously approved by MSHA and NIOSH under part 160, subpart 160.011, of this chapter.

[CGD 86-036, 57 FR 48327, Oct. 23, 1992, as amended by CGD 95-028, 62 FR 51220, Sept. 30, 1997]

Subpart 195.40—Pilot Boarding Equipment

§ 195.40-1 Pilot boarding equipment.

(a) This section applies to each vessel that normally embarks or disembarks a pilot from a pilot boat or other vessel.

(b) Each vessel must have suitable pilot boarding equipment available for use on each side of the vessel. If a vessel has only one set of equipment, the equipment must be capable of being easily transferred to and rigged for use on either side of the vessel.

(c) Pilot boarding equipment must be capable of resting firmly against the vessel's side and be secured so that it is clear from overboard discharges.

(d) Each vessel must have lighting positioned to provide adequate illumination for the pilot boarding equipment and each point of access.

(e) Each vessel must have a point of access that has—

(1) A gateway in the rails or bulwark with adequate handholds; or

(2) Two handhold stanchions and a bulwark ladder that is securely attached to the bulwark rail and deck.

(f) The pilot boarding equipment required by paragraph (b) of this section must include at least one pilot ladder approved under subpart 163.003 of this chapter. Each pilot ladder must be of a single length and capable of extending from the point of access to the water's edge during each condition of loading and trim, with an adverse list of 15°.

(g) Whenever the distance from the water's edge to the point of access is more than 30 feet, access from a pilot ladder to the vessel must be by way of an accommodation ladder or equally safe and convenient means.

(h) Pilot hoists, if used, must be approved under subpart 163.002 of this chapter.

[CGD 79-032, 49 FR 25455, June 21, 1984]

PART 196—OPERATIONS

Subpart 196.01—Application

Sec.
196.01-1 General.

Subpart 196.05—Notice to Mariners and Aids to Navigation

196.05-1 Duty of officers.
196.05-5 Charts and nautical publications.

Subpart 196.07—Notice and Reporting of Casualty and Voyage Records

196.07-1 Notice and reporting of casualty and voyage records.

Subpart 196.12—Stability Letter

196.12-1 Posting.

Subpart 196.13—Station Bills

196.13-1 Muster lists, emergency signals, and manning.

Subpart 196.15—Test, Drills, and Inspections

196.15-1 Application.
196.15-3 Steering gear, whistle, and means of communication.
196.15-5 Drafts.
196.15-7 Verification of vessel compliance with applicable stability requirements.
196.15-10 Sanitation.
196.15-15 Examination of boilers and machinery.
196.15-18 Loading doors.

Coast Guard, DHS

Pt. 196

196.15-20 Hatches and other openings.
196.15-30 Emergency lighting and power systems.
196.15-35 Emergency training, musters, and drills.
196.15-55 Requirements for fuel oil.
196.15-60 Firefighting equipment, general.

Subpart 196.19—Maneuvering Characteristics

196.19-1 Data required.

Subpart 196.20—Whistling

196.20-1 Unnecessary whistling prohibited.

Subpart 196.25—Searchlights

196.25-1 Improper use prohibited.

Subpart 196.27—Lookouts

196.27-1 Master's and officer's responsibility.

Subpart 196.30—Reports of Accidents, Repairs, and Unsafe Equipment

196.30-1 Repairs to boilers and pressure vessels.
196.30-5 Accidents to machinery.
196.30-10 Notice required before repair.
196.30-20 Breaking of safety valve seal.

Subpart 196.33—Communication Between Deckhouses

196.33-1 When required.

Subpart 196.34—Work Vests

196.34-1 Application.
196.34-5 Approved types of work vests.
196.34-10 Use.
196.34-15 Shipboard stowage.
196.34-20 Shipboard inspections.
196.34-25 Additional requirements for hybrid work vests.

Subpart 196.35—Logbook Entries

196.35-1 Application.
196.35-3 Logbooks and records.
196.35-5 Actions required to be logged.

Subpart 196.36—Display of Plans

196.36-1 When required.

Subpart 196.37—Markings for Fire and Emergency Equipment, etc.

196.37-1 Application.
196.37-3 General.
196.37-5 General alarm bell contact makers.
196.37-7 General alarm bells.
196.37-9 Carbon dioxide alarm.

196.37-10 Fire extinguishing system branch lines.
196.37-13 Fire extinguishing system controls.
196.37-15 Firehose stations.
196.37-20 Self-contained breathing apparatus and gas masks.
196.37-23 Hand portable fire extinguishers.
196.37-25 Emergency lights.
196.37-33 Instructions for changing steering gear.
196.37-35 Rudder orders.
196.37-37 Markings for lifesaving appliances, instructions to passengers, and stowage locations.
196.37-47 Portable magazine chests.

Subpart 196.40—Markings on Vessels

196.40-1 Application.
196.40-5 Hull markings.
196.40-10 Draft marks and draft indicating systems.
196.40-15 Load line marks.

Subpart 196.43—Placard of Lifesaving Signals

196.43-1 Application.
196.43-5 Availability.

Subpart 196.45—Carrying of Excess Steam

196.45-1 Master and chief engineer responsible.

Subpart 196.50—Compliance With Provisions of Certificate of Inspection

196.50-1 Master or person in charge responsible.

Subpart 196.53—Exhibition of License

196.53-1 Licensed officers.

Subpart 196.80—Explosive Handling Plan

196.80-1 Master's responsibility.

Subpart 196.85—Magazine Control

196.85-1 Magazine operation and control.

Subpart 196.95—Pilot Boarding Operations

196.95-1 Pilot boarding operations.

AUTHORITY: 33 U.S.C. 1321(j); 46 U.S.C. 2213, 3306, 5115, 6101; E.O. 12777, 56 FR 54757, 3 CFR, 1991 Comp., p. 351; E.O. 12234, 45 FR 58801, 3 CFR, 1980 Comp., p. 277; Department of Homeland Security Delegation No. 0170.1.

SOURCE: CGFR 67-83, 33 FR 1158, Jan. 27, 1968, unless otherwise noted.

Subpart 196.01—Application

§ 196.01-1 General.

(a) The provisions of this part shall apply to all vessels except as specifically noted in this part.

Subpart 196.05—Notice to Mariners and Aids to Navigation

§ 196.05-1 Duty of officers.

(a) Licensed deck officers are required to acquaint themselves with the latest information published by the Coast Guard and the National Imagery and Mapping Agency regarding aids to navigation. Neglect to do so is evidence of neglect of duty. It is desirable that all vessels have available in the pilothouse for convenient reference at all times a file of the applicable Notice to Mariners.

(b) Weekly Notices to Mariners (Great Lakes Edition) as published by the Commander, 9th Coast Guard District, contains announcements and information on changes in aids to navigation and other marine information affecting the safety of navigation on the Great Lakes. These notices may be obtained free of charge, by making application to Commander, 9th Coast Guard District.

(c) Weekly Notices to Mariners (worldwide coverage) are prepared jointly by the National Imagery and Mapping Agency, National Ocean Service, and the U.S. Coast Guard. They include changes in aids to navigation in assembled form for the 1st, 5th, 7th, Greater Antilles Section, 8th, 11th, 13th, 14th, and 17th Coast Guard Districts. Foreign marine information is also included in these notices. These notices are available without charge from the National Imagery and Mapping Agency, U.S. Collector of Customs of the major seaports in the United States and are also on file in the U.S. Consulates where they may be inspected.

[CGFR 67-83, 33 FR 1158, Jan. 27, 1968, as amended by CGFR 68-32, 33 FR 5729, Apr. 12, 1968; CGD 95-028, 62 FR 51220, Sept. 30, 1997; USCG-2001-10224, 66 FR 48621, Sept. 21, 2001]

§ 196.05-5 Charts and nautical publications.

As appropriate for the intended voyage, all vessels except barges, and vessels operating exclusively on rivers, must carry adequate and up-to-date—

(a) Charts;
(b) Sailing directions;
(c) Coast pilots;
(d) Light lists;
(e) Notices to mariners;
(f) Tide tables;
(g) Current tables; and
(h) All other nautical publications necessary.[1]

[CGD 75-074, 42 FR 5965, Jan. 31, 1977]

Subpart 196.07—Notice and Reporting of Casualty and Voyage Records

§ 196.07-1 Notice and reporting of casualty and voyage records.

The requirements for providing notice and reporting of marine casualties and for retaining voyage records are contained in part 4 of this chapter.

[CGD 84-099, 52 FR 47536, Dec. 14, 1987]

Subpart 196.12—Stability Letter

§ 196.12-1 Posting.

If a stability letter is issued in accordance with the requirements in § 170.120 of this chapter, it must be posted under glass or other suitable transparent material in the pilothouse of the vessel.

[CGD 79-023, 48 FR 51053, Nov. 4, 1983]

Subpart 196.13—Station Bills

§ 196.13-1 Muster lists, emergency signals, and manning.

The requirements for muster lists, emergency signals, and manning must be in accordance with subchapter W (Lifesaving Appliances and Arrangements) of this chapter.

[CGD 84-069, 61 FR 25313, May 20, 1996]

---

[1] For United States vessels in or on the navigable waters of the United States, see 33 CFR 164.33.

Subpart 196.15—Test, Drills, and Inspections

§ 196.15-1 Application.

(a) The provisions of this subpart shall apply to all vessels.

§ 196.15-3 Steering gear, whistle, and means of communication.

(a) On all vessels making a voyage of more than 48 hours duration, the entire steering gear, the whistle, and the means of communication between the bridge or pilothouse and engineroom shall be examined and tested by an officer of the vessel within a period of not more than 12 hours prior to departure. On all other vessels similar examinations and tests shall be made at least once in every week.

(b) The date of the test and the condition of the equipment shall be noted in the official logbook.

§ 196.15-5 Drafts.

(a) The master of every vessel on an ocean, coastwise, or Great Lakes voyage shall enter the drafts of the vessel, forward and aft, in the official logbook when leaving port.

(b) On vessels subject to the requirements of Subchapter E (Load Lines) of this chapter at the time of departure from port on an ocean, coastwise, or Great Lakes voyage, the master shall insert in the official logbook a statement of the position of the loadline mark, port, and starboard, in relation to the surface of the water in which the vessel is then floating.

(1) When an allowance for draft is made for density of the water in which the vessel is floating, this density is to be noted in the official logbook.

§ 196.15-7 Verification of vessel compliance with applicable stability requirements.

(a) After loading and prior to departure and at all other times necessary to assure the safety of the vessel, the master shall determine that the vessel complies with all applicable stability requirements in the vessel's trim and stability book, stability letter, Certificate of Inspection, and Load Line Certificate, as the case may be, and then enter an attestation statement of the verification in the log book. The vessel may not depart until it is in compliance with these requirements.

(b) When determining compliance with applicable stability requirements the vessel's draft, trim, and stability must be determined as necessary and any stability calculations made in support of the determination must be retained on board the vessel for the duration of the voyage.

[CGD 89-037, 57 FR 41828, Sept. 11, 1992]

§ 196.15-10 Sanitation.

(a) It shall be the duty of the master and chief engineer to see that the vessel, and, in particular, the quarters are in a clean and sanitary condition. The chief engineer shall be responsible only for the sanitary condition of the engineering department.

§ 196.15-15 Examination of boilers and machinery.

(a) It shall be the duty of the chief engineer when he assumes charge of the boilers and machinery of a vessel to examine them thoroughly. If any parts thereof are in unsatisfactory condition, or if the safety-valve seals are broken, the fact shall immediately be reported to the master, owner, or agent, and the Officer in Charge, Marine Inspection.

§ 196.15-18 Loading doors.

(a) The master of a vessel fitted with loading doors shall assure that all loading doors are closed watertight and secured during the entire voyage except that—

(1) If a door cannot be opened or closed while the vessel is at a dock, it may be open while the vessel approaches and draws away from the dock, but only as far as necessary to enable the door to be immediately operated.

(2) If needed to operate the vessel, or embark and disembark passengers when the vessel is at anchor in protected waters, loading doors may be open provided that the master determines that the safety of the vessel is not impaired.

(b) For the purposes of this section, "loading doors" include all weathertight ramps, bow visors, and openings used to load personnel, equipment,

§ 196.15-20

cargo, and stores, in the collision bulkhead, the side shell, and the boundaries of enclosed superstructures that are continuous with the shell of the vessel.

(c) The master shall enter into the log book the time and door location of every closing of the loading doors.

(d) The master shall enter into the log book any opening of the doors in accordance with paragraph (a)(2) of this section setting forth the time of the opening of the doors and the circumstances warranting this action.

[CGD 89-037, 57 FR 41828, Sept. 11, 1992]

§ 196.15-20 Hatches and other openings.

(a) It shall be the responsibility of the master to assure himself that all exposed hatches and other openings in the hull of his vessel are closed, made properly watertight by the use of tarpaulins, gaskets or similar devices, and in all respects properly secured for sea before leaving protected waters.

(b) The openings to which this section applies are as follows:

(1) Exposed hatches.

(2) Gangway and other ports fitted below the freeboard deck.

(3) Port lights that are not accessible during navigation, including the dead lights for such port lights.

(c) The master at his discretion may permit hatches or other openings to remain uncovered or open, or to be uncovered or opened for reasonable purposes such as ship's maintenance while the vessel is being navigated: *Provided*, That in his opinion existing conditions warrant such action.

(d) In the event the master employs the discretionary provisions of this section after leaving port he shall cause appropriate entries to be made in the official log or equivalent thereof setting forth the time of uncovering, opening, closing or covering of the hatches or other openings to which this section applies and the circumstances warranting the action taken.

(e) The discretionary provisions of this section shall not relieve the master of his responsibility for the safety of his vessel, equipment or persons on board.

§ 196.15-30 Emergency lighting and power systems.

(a) Where fitted, it shall be the duty of the master to see that the emergency lighting and power systems are operated and inspected at least once in each week that the vessel is navigated to be assured that the system is in proper operating condition.

(b) Internal combustion engine driven emergency generators shall be operated under load for at least 2 hours, at least once in each month that the vessel is navigated.

(c) Storage batteries for emergency lighting and power systems shall be tested at least once in each 6-month period that the vessel is navigated to demonstrate the ability of the storage battery to supply the emergency loads for the specified period of time.

(d) The date of the tests and the condition and performance of the apparatus shall be noted in the official logbook.

§ 196.15-35 Emergency training, musters, and drills.

Onboard training, musters, and drills must be in accordance with subchapter W (Lifesaving Appliances and Arrangements) of this chapter.

[CGD 84-069, 61 FR 25313, May 20, 1996]

§ 196.15-55 Requirements for fuel oil.

(a) It shall be the duty of the chief engineer to cause an entry in the log to be made of each supply of fuel oil received on board, stating the quantity received, the name of the vendor, the name of the oil producer, and the flashpoint (closed cup test) for which it is certified by the producer.

(b) It shall be the further duty of the chief engineer to cause to be drawn and sealed and suitably labeled at the time the supply is received on board, a half-pint sample of each lot of fuel oil. These samples shall be preserved until the particular supply of oil is exhausted.

§ 196.15-60 Firefighting equipment, general.

(a) It shall be the duty of the owner, master, or person in charge to see that the vessel's firefighting equipment is at all times ready for use and that all

Coast Guard, DHS § 196.19-1

such equipment required by the regulations in this subchapter is provided, maintained, and replaced as indicated.

(b) It shall be the duty of the owner, master, or person in charge to require and have performed at least once in every 12 months the tests and inspections of all hand portable fire extinguishers, semiportable fire extinguishing systems, and fixed fire extinguishing systems on board as described in Tables 189.25-20(a)(1) and 189.25-20(a)(2) in § 189.25-20(a) of this subchapter. The owner, master, or person in charge shall keep records of such tests and inspections showing the dates when performed, the number and/or other identification of each unit tested and inspected, and the name(s) of the person(s) and/or company conducting the tests and inspections. Such records shall be made available to the marine inspector upon request and shall be kept for the period of validity of the vessel's current certificate of inspection. Where practicable these records should be kept in or with the vessel's logbook. The conduct of these tests and inspections does not relieve the owner, master, or person in charge of his responsibility to maintain this firefighting equipment in proper condition at all times.

Subpart 196.19—Maneuvering Characteristics

§ 196.19-1 Data required.

For each ocean and coastwise vessel of 1,600 gross tons or over, the following apply:

(a) The following maneuvering information must be prominently displayed in the pilothouse on a fact sheet:

(1) For full and half speed, a turning circle diagram to port and starboard that shows the time and the distance of advance and transfer required to alter the course 90 degrees with maximum rudder angle and constant power settings.

(2) The time and distance to stop the vessel from full and half speed while maintaining approximately the initial heading with minimum application of rudder.

(3) For each vessel with a fixed propeller, a table of shaft revolutions per minute for a representative range of speeds.

(4) For each vessel with a controlable pitch propeller a table of control settings for a representative range of speeds.

(5) For each vessel that is fitted with an auxiliary device to assist in maneuvering, such as a bow thruster, a table of vessel speeds at which the auxiliary device is effective in maneuvering the vessel.

(b) The maneuvering information must be provided in the normal load and normal light condition with normal trim for a particular condition of loading assuming the following—

(1) Calm weather—wind 10 knots or less, calm sea;

(2) No current;

(3) Deep water conditions—water depth twice the vessel's draft or greater; and

(4) Clean hull.

(c) At the bottom of the fact sheet, the following statement must appear:

WARNING

The response of the (name of the vessel) may be different from those listed above if any of the following conditions, upon which the maneuvering information is based, are varied:

(1) Calm weather—wind 10 knots or less, calm sea;

(2) No current;

(3) Water depth twice the vessel's draft or greater.

(4) Clean hull; and

(5) Intermediate drafts or unusual trim.

(d) The information on the fact sheet must be:

(1) Verified six months after the vessel is placed in service; or

(2) Modified six months after the vessel is placed into service and verified within three months thereafter.

(e) The information that appears on the fact sheet may be obtained from:

(1) Trial trip observations;

(2) Model tests;

(3) Analytical calculations;

(4) Simulations;

(5) Information established from another vessel of similar hull form, power, rudder and propeller; or

(6) Any combination of the above.

The accuracy of the information in the fact sheet required is that attainable by ordinary shipboard navigation equipment.

§ 196.20–1

(f) The requirements for information for fact sheets for specialized craft such as semi-submersibles, hydrofoils, hovercraft and other vessels of unusual design will be specified on a case by case basis.

[CGD 73–78, 40 FR 2689, Jan. 15, 1975]

Subpart 196.20—Whistling

§ 196.20–1 Unnecessary whistling prohibited.

(a) The unnecessary sounding of the vessel's whistle is prohibited within any harbor limits of the United States.

Subpart 196.25—Searchlights

§ 196.25–1 Improper use prohibited.

(a) No person shall flash or cause to be flashed the rays of a searchlight or other blinding light onto the bridge or into the pilothouse of any vessel underway.

Subpart 196.27—Lookouts

§ 196.27–1 Master's and officer's responsibility.

(a) Nothing in this part shall exonerate any master or officer in command from the consequences of any neglect to keep a proper lookout or the neglect of any precaution which may be required by the ordinary practice of seamen or by the special circumstances of the case.

Subpart 196.30—Reports of Accidents, Repairs, and Unsafe Equipment

§ 196.30–1 Repairs to boilers and pressure vessels.

(a) Before making any repairs to boilers or unfired pressure vessels, the Chief Engineer shall submit a report covering the nature of the repairs to the Officer in Charge, Marine Inspection, at or nearest to the U.S. port where the repairs are to be made.

§ 196.30–5 Accidents to machinery.

(a) In the event of an accident to a boiler, unfired pressure vessel, or machinery tending to render the further use of the item unsafe until repairs are made, or if by ordinary wear such items become unsafe, a report shall be made by the Chief Engineer immediately to the Officer in Charge, Marine Inspection, or if at sea, immediately upon arrival at port.

§ 196.30–10 Notice required before repair.

(a) No repairs or alterations, except in an emergency, shall be made to any lifesaving or fire detecting or extinguishing equipment without advance notice to the Officer in Charge, Marine Inspection. When emergency repairs or alterations have been made, notice shall be given to the Officer in Charge, Marine Inspection, as soon as practicable.

§ 196.30–20 Breaking of safety valve seal.

(a) If at any time it is necessary to break the seal on a safety valve for any purpose, the Chief Engineer shall advise the Officer in Charge, Marine Inspection, at the next port of call, giving the reason for breaking the seal and requesting that the valve be examined and adjusted by an inspector.

Subpart 196.33—Communication Between Deckhouses

§ 196.33–1 When required.

On all vessels navigating in other than protected waters, where the distance between deckhouses is more than 46 meters (150 feet) a fixed means of facilitating communication between both ends of the vessel, such as a raised fore and aft bridge or side tunnels, must be provided. Previously approved arrangements may be retained so long as they are maintained in good condition to the satisfaction of the Officer in Charge, Marine Inspection.

[CGD 95–027, 61 FR 26013, May 23, 1996]

Subpart 196.34—Work Vests

§ 196.34–1 Application.

(a) Provisions of this subpart shall apply to all vessels.

§ 196.34-5 Approved types of work vests.

(a) Each buoyant work vest carried under the permissive authority of this section must be approved under—

(1) Subpart 160.053 of this chapter; or
(2) Subpart 160.077 of this chapter as a commercial hybrid PFD.

[CGD 78-174A, 51 FR 4352, Feb. 4, 1986]

§ 196.34-10 Use.

(a) Approved buoyant work vests are considered to be items of safety apparel and may be carried aboard vessels to be worn by crew members when working near or over the water under favorable working conditions. They shall be used under the supervision and control of designated ship's officers. When carried, such vests shall not be accepted in lieu of any portion of the required number of approved life preservers and shall not be substituted for the approved life preservers required to be worn during drills and emergencies.

§ 196.34-15 Shipboard stowage.

(a) The approved buoyant work vests shall be stowed separately from the regular stowage of approved life preservers.

(b) The locations for the stowage of work vests shall be such as not to be easily confused with that for approved life preservers.

§ 196.34-20 Shipboard inspections.

(a) Each work vest shall be subject to examination by a marine inspector to determine its serviceability. If found to be satisfactory, it may be continued in service, but shall not be stamped by a marine inspector with a Coast Guard stamp. If a work vest is found not to be in a serviceable condition, then such work vest shall be removed from the vessel. If a work vest is beyond repair, it shall be destroyed or mutilated in the presence of a marine inspector so as to prevent its continued use as a work vest.

§ 196.34-25 Additional requirements for hybrid work vests.

(a) In addition to the other requirements in this subpart, commercial hybrid PFD's must be—

(1) Used, stowed, and maintained in accordance with the procedures set out in the manual required for these devices by § 160.077-29 of this chapter and any limitations(s) marked on them; and

(2) Of the same or similar design and have the same method of operation as each other hybrid PFD carried on board.

[CGD 78-174A, 51 FR 4352, Feb. 4, 1986]

Subpart 196.35—Logbook Entries

§ 196.35-1 Application.

(a) Except as specifically noted, the provisions of this subpart shall apply to all manned vessels.

§ 196.35-3 Logbooks and records.

(a) The master or person in charge of an oceanographic research vessel that is required by 46 U.S.C. 11301 to have an official logbook may maintain the logbook on form CG-706 or in the owner's format for an official logbook. Such logs must be kept available for a review for a period of 1 year after the date to which the records refer, or for the period of validity of the vessel's current certificate of inspection, whichever is longer. When the voyage is completed, the master or person in charge shall file the logbook with the Officer in Charge, Marine Inspection.

(b) The master or person in charge of a vessel that is not required by 46 U.S.C. 11301 to have a official logbook, shall maintain, on aboard, an unofficial logbook or record in any form desired for the purposes of making entries therein as required by law or regulations in this subchapter. Such logs or records are not filed with the Officer in Charge, Marine Inspection, but must be kept available for review by a marine inspector for a period of 1 year after the date to which the records refer. Separate records of tests and inspections of fire fighting equipment must be maintained with the vessel's logs for the period of validity of the vessel's certificate of inspection.

[CGD 95-027, 61 FR 26013, May 23, 1996]

§ 196.35-5 Actions required to be logged.

The actions and observations noted in this section shall be entered in the official logbook. This section contains no requirements which are not made in other portions of this subchapter, the items being merely grouped together for convenience.

(a) Onboard training, musters, and drills: held in accordance with subchapter W (Lifesaving Appliances and Arrangements) of this chapter.

(b) Steering gear, whistle, and means of communication. Prior to departure. See § 196.15-3.

(c) Drafts and load line marks. Prior to leaving port, ocean, coastwise, and Great Lakes service only. See § 196.15-5.

(d) Verification of vessel compliance with applicable stability requirements. After loading and prior to departure and at all other times necessary to assure the safety of the vessel. See § 196.15-7.

(e) Loading doors. Where applicable, every closing and any opening when not docked. See § 196.15-18.

(f) Emergency lighting and power systems. Weekly and semiannually. See § 196.15-30.

(g) Fuel oil data: Upon receipt of fuel oil on board. See § 196.15-55.

(h) Hatches and other openings. All openings and closings required by § 196.15-20.

(i) Magazines and magazine chests. Maximum and minimum temperatures as required by § 196.85-1(b).

(j) Portable vans, prior to departure. See § 195.11-25(e) of this subchapter.

(k) Weight handling gear, prior to departure. See § 189.35-13(b) of this subchapter.

[CGFR 67-83, 33 FR 1158, Jan. 27, 1988, as amended by CGD 89-037, 57 FR 41828, Sept. 11, 1992; CGD 84-069, 61 FR 25313, May 20, 1996]

Subpart 196.36—Display of Plans

§ 196.36-1 When required.

(a) All manned vessels shall have permanently exhibited for the guidance of the officer in charge of the vessel, general arrangement plans showing for each deck the various fire retardant bulkheads together with particulars of the fire-detecting, manual alarm and fire extinguishing systems, fire doors, means of ingress to the different compartments, the ventilating systems including the positions of the dampers, the location of the remote means of stopping the fans, and the identification of the fans serving each section.

Subpart 196.37—Markings for Fire and Emergency Equipment, etc.

§ 196.37-1 Application.

(a) The provisions of this subpart shall apply to all vessels.

§ 196.37-3 General.

(a) It is the intent of this subpart to provide such markings as are necessary for the guidance of the persons on board in case of an emergency. In any specific case, and particularly on small vessels, where it can be shown to the satisfaction of the Officer in Charge, Marine Inspection, that the prescribed markings are unnecessary for the guidance of the persons on board in case of emergency, such markings may be modified or omitted.

(b) In addition to English, notices, directional signs, etc., shall be printed in languages appropriate to the service of the vessel.

(c) Where in this subpart red letters are specified, letters of a contrasting color on a red background will be accepted.

§ 196.37-5 General alarm bell contact makers.

(a) Each general alarm contact maker must be marked in accordance with requirements in Subpchapter J (Electrical Engineering Regulations) of this chapter.

[CGD 74-125a, 47 FR 15279, Apr. 8, 1982]

CROSS REFERENCE: See also § 113.25-20 of Subchapter J (Electrical Engineering) of this chapter.

§ 196.37-7 General alarm bells.

(a) All general alarm bells shall be identified by red lettering at least ½ inch high: "GENERAL ALARM—WHEN BELL RINGS GO TO YOUR STATION."

Coast Guard, DHS

§ 196.37-9 Carbon dioxide alarm.

(a) All carbon dioxide alarms shall be conspicuously identified: "WHEN ALARM SOUNDS—VACATE AT ONCE. CARBON DIOXIDE BEING RELEASED."

§ 196.37-10 Fire extinguishing system branch lines.

(a) The branch line valves of all fire extinguishing systems shall be plainly and permanently marked indicating the spaces served.

§ 196.37-13 Fire extinguishing system controls.

(a) The control cabinets or spaces containing valves or manifolds for the various fire extinguishing systems shall be distinctly marked in conspicuous red letters at least 2 inches high: "CARBON DIOXIDE FIRE APPARATUS," or "FOAM FIRE APPARATUS," etc., as the case may be.

§ 196.37-15 Firehose stations.

(a) Each fire hydrant shall be identified in red letters and figures at least 2 inches high "FIRE STATION NO. 1", "2", "3", etc. Where the hose is not stowed in the open or behind glass so as to be readily seen, this identification shall be so placed as to be readily seen from a distance.

§ 196.37-20 Self-contained breathing apparatus and gas masks.

(a) Lockers or spaces containing self-contained breathing apparatus shall be marked "SELF-CONTAINED BREATHING APPARATUS".

§ 196.37-23 Hand portable fire extinguishers.

(a) Each hand portable fire extinguisher shall be marked with a number and the location where stowed shall be marked with a corresponding number at least ½ inch high. Where only one type and size of hand portable fire extinguisher is carried, the numbering may be omitted.

§ 196.37-25 Emergency lights.

(a) All emergency lights shall be marked with a letter "E" at least ½ inch high.

§ 196.37-33 Instructions for changing steering gear.

(a) Instructions in at least ½ inch letters and figures shall be posted in the steering engineroom, relating in order, the different steps to be taken in changing to the emergency steering gear. Each clutch, gear, wheel, lever, valve, or switch which is used during the changeover shall be numbered or lettered on a metal plate or painted so that the markings can be recognized at a reasonable distance. The instructions shall indicate each clutch or pin to be "in" or "out" and each valve or switch which is to be "opened" or "closed" in shifting to any means of steering for which the vessel is equipped. Instructions shall be included to line up all steering wheels and rudder amidship before changing gears.

§ 196.37-35 Rudder orders.

(a) At all steering stations, there shall be installed a suitable notice on the wheel or device or in such other position as to be directly in the helmsman's line of vision, to indicate the direction in which the wheel or device must be turned for "right rudder" and for "left rudder".

§ 196.37-37 Markings for lifesaving appliances, instructions to passengers, and stowage locations.

Lifesaving appliances, instructions to passengers, and stowage locations must be marked in accordance with subchapter W (Lifesaving Appliances and Arrangements) of this chapter.

[CGD 84-069, 61 FR 25313, May 20, 1996]

§ 196.37-47 Portable magazine chests.

(a) Portable magazine chests shall be marked in letters at least 3 inches high:

§ 196.40-1

PORTABLE MAGAZINE CHEST

— FLAMMABLE —

KEEP LIGHTS AND FIRE AWAY.

Subpart 196.40—Markings on Vessels

§ 196.40-1 Application.

(a) The provisions of this subpart shall apply to all vessels except as specifically noted.

§ 196.40-5 Hull markings.

Vessels shall be marked as required by parts 67 and 69 of this chapter.

[CGD 72-104R, 37 FR 14233, July 18, 1972; 37 FR 18537, Sept. 13, 1972]

§ 196.40-10 Draft marks and draft indicating systems.

(a) All vessels must have draft marks plainly and legibly visible upon the stem and upon the sternpost or rudderpost or at any place at the stern of the vessel as may be necessary for easy observance. The bottom of each mark must indicate the draft.

(b) The draft must be taken from the bottom of the keel to the surface of the water at the location of the marks.

(c) In cases where the keel does not extend forward or aft to the location of the draft marks, due to raked stem, or cutaway skeg, the datum line from which the draft shall be taken shall be obtained by projecting the line of the bottom of keel forward, or aft, as the case may be, to the location of the draft marks.

(d) In cases where a vessel may have a skeg or other appendage extending locally below the line of the keel, the draft at the end of the vessel adjacent to such appendage shall be measured to a line tangent to the lowest part of such appendage and parallel to the line of the bottom of the keel.

(e) Draft marks must be separated so that the projections of the marks onto a vertical plane are of uniform height equal to the vertical spacing between consecutive marks.

(f) Draft marks must be painted in contrasting color to the hull.

(g) In cases where draft marks are obscured due to operational constraints or by protrusions, the vessel must be fitted with a reliable draft indicating system from which the bow and stern drafts can be determined.

[CGFR 67-83, 33 FR 1158, Jan. 27, 1988, as amended by CGD 89-037, 57 FR 41828, Sept. 11, 1992]

§ 196.40-15 Load line marks.

(a) Vessels assigned a load line shall have the deck line and the load line marks permanently marked or embossed as required by Subchapter E (Load Lines) of this chapter.

Subpart 196.43—Placard of Lifesaving Signals

SOURCE: CGD 95-027, 61 FR 26013, May 23, 1996, unless otherwise noted.

§ 196.43-1 Application.

The provisions of this subpart apply to all vessels on an international voyage, and all other vessels of 150 gross tons or over in ocean, coastwise, or Great Lakes service.

§ 196.43-5 Availability.

On all vessels to which this subpart applies there must be readily available to the deck officer of the watch a placard containing instructions for the use of the lifesaving signals set forth in regulation 16, chapter V, of the International Convention for Safety of Life at Sea, 1974. These signals must be used by vessels or persons in distress when communicating with lifesaving stations and maritime rescue units.

Subpart 196.45—Carrying of Excess Steam

§ 196.45-1 Master and chief engineer responsible.

(a) It shall be the duty of the master and the engineer in charge of the boilers of any vessel to require that a steam pressure is not carried in excess of that allowed by the certificate of inspection and to require that the safety valves, once set and sealed by the inspector, are in no way tampered with or made inoperative except as provided in § 196.30-20.

Subpart 196.50—Compliance With Provisions of Certificate of Inspection

§ 196.50-1 Master or person in charge responsible.

(a) It shall be the duty of the master or other person in charge of the vessel to see that all of the provisions of the certificate of inspection are strictly adhered to. Nothing in this subpart shall be construed as limiting the master or other person in charge of the vessel, at his own responsibility, from diverting from the route prescribed in the certificate of inspection or taking such other steps as he deems necessary and prudent to assist vessels in distress or for other similar emergencies.

Subpart 196.53—Exhibition of License

§ 196.53-1 Licensed officers.

All licensed officers on a vessel shall have their licenses conspicuously displayed.

[CGD 95-028, 62 FR 51220, Sept. 30, 1997]

Subpart 196.80—Explosive Handling Plan

§ 196.80-1 Master's responsibility.

(a) It shall be the responsibility of the master to have prepared, signed, and prominently posted in conspicuous locations, operating procedures, plans, and safety precautions for all operations involving the use of explosives.

(b) The operating procedures referred to in paragraph (a) of this section include and set forth the special duties and stations of appropriate qualified persons for various operations involving the use of explosives. Assignment of such persons shall be commensurate with their experience and training.

(c) A copy of the operating procedures, plans and safety precautions required by paragraph (a) of this section and all subsequent changes or revisions shall be forwarded to the Officer in Charge, Marine Inspection, issuing the certificate of inspection for review.

Subpart 196.85—Magazine Control

§ 196.85-1 Magazine operation and control.

(a) Keys to magazine spaces and magazine chests shall be kept in the sole control or custody of the Master or one delegated qualified person at all times. Test fittings for magazine sprinkler systems shall be kept in a locked cabinet under the custody of the Master.

(b) Whenever explosives are stored in magazines and magazine chests they shall be inspected daily. Magazine inspection results and corrective action, when taken, shall be noted in the ship's log daily. Maximum and minimum temperatures for the previous 24-hour period shall be recorded in the ship's log along with general magazine condition and corrective action taken when necessary.

(c) The magazine sprinkler controls shall be tested monthly. Test results and all corrective actions taken shall be recorded in the ship's log.

(d) The Master shall limit access to the magazines, or the contents thereof, to persons who can document 3 months on board ship training in the use of explosives. This shall not be construed as prohibiting access to the Master or others designated by the Master.

Subpart 196.95—Pilot Boarding Operations

§ 196.95-1 Pilot boarding operations.

(a) The master shall ensure that pilot boarding equipment is maintained as follows:

(1) The equipment must be kept clean and in good working order.

(2) Each damaged step or spreader step on a pilot ladder must be replaced in kind with an approved replacement step or spreader step, prior to further use of the ladder. The replacement step or spreader step must be secured by the method used in the original construction of the ladder, and in accordance with manufacturer instructions.

(b) The master shall ensure compliance with the following during pilot boarding operations:

(1) Only approved pilot boarding equipment may be used.

(2) The pilot boarding equipment must rest firmly against the hull of the

§ 196.95-1

vessel and be clear of overboard discharges.

(3) Two man ropes, a safety line and an approved lifebuoy with an approved water light must be at the point of access and be immediately available for use during boarding operations.

(4) Rigging of the equipment and embarkation/debarkation of a pilot must be supervised in person by a deck officer.

(5) Both the equipment over the side and the point of access must be adequately lit during the night operations.

(6) If a pilot hoist is used, a pilot ladder must be kept on deck adjacent to the hoist and available for immediate use.

[CGD 79-032, 49 FR 25455, June 21, 1984]

INDEX

SUBCHAPTER U—OCEANOGRAPHIC RESEARCH VESSELS

EDITORIAL NOTE: This listing is provided for informational purposes only. It is compiled and kept current by the U.S. Coast Guard, Department of Homeland Security. This index is updated as of October 1, 2003.

Part, subpart, or section

A

Accidents, reports of	196.30
Accidents to machinery	196.30-5
Access to lifeboats	190.10-40
Accommodations for Officers, Crew, and Scientific Personnel	190.20
Accommodations, sleeping	190.20-20
Actions required to be logged	196.35-5
Additional requirements, for hybrid workvests	196.34-25
Aids to navigation	196.05
Alarm, carbon dioxide	196.37-9
Alarm bell, general	196.37-5, 196.37-7
Alarms	193.15-30
Alaska	188.05-10(a)(2)(iii)
American Bureau of Shipping	188.10.59, 189.60-45
American Bureau of Shipping, address	188.35-5(a)
American Bureau of Shipping's Standards	188.35
American Society of Testing Materials	188.10-21
Ammonia, refrigerant	195.30-1(a)(1), (b)(1)
Anchors	195.07
Anchors, vessels contracted for prior to March 1, 1968	195.07-90
Anticosti Island	188.05-10(b)(1)
Appeal, right of	188.01-7
Application to vessels on an international voyage	188.05-10
Approved	188.10-1
Approved container	188.10-3
Approved types of work vests	196.34-5
Arrangement of hull structure	190.01
Assignment of functions	188.01-5
Authority and purpose	188.01
Automatic sprinkler systems	193.30
Availability, placard of lifesaving signals	196.43-5

B

Barge	188.10-5
Barge, seagoing	188.10-65
Barges, unmanned	193.50-1(b)(c)
Bays	188.10-39, 195.07-10
Bells, general alarm	196.37-5, 196.37-7
Bills, station	196.13
Boarding, operations, pilot	196.95.1
Boiler, examination of	196.15-15
Boilers	189.15-1

411

Boilers, repairs to 196.30-1
Boots .... 195.35-5(f)
Boundary line 188.10-65
Breaking of safety valve 196.30-20
Breathing apparatus, self-contained 195.30-15
Burning 189.50-1

C

Cap des Rosiers .... 188.05-10(b)(1)
Captain of the Port 188.10-6
Carbon dioxide alarm 196.37-9
Carbon dioxide cylinders, storage 193.15-20
Carbon dioxide extinguishing systems, branch lines .... Table 193.15-5
Carbon dioxide extinguishing systems, details 193.15
Carbon dioxide extinguishing systems, enclosure openings 193.15-35
Carbon dioxide extinguishing systems, installations contracted for prior
  to March 1, 1968 .... 193.15-90
Carbon dioxide extinguishing systems, pressure relief 193.15-40
Carbon dioxide extinguishing systems, quantity, pipe sizes, and dis-
  charge rates 193.15-5
Carbon dioxide storage 193.15-20
Carbon dioxide, total available supply .... 193.15-5(b)
Cargo Ship Safety Construction Certificate 189.60-5
Cargo Ship Safety Equipment Certificate 189.60-10
Cargo Ship Safety Radiotelegraphy Certificate 189.60-15
Cargo Ship Safety Radiotelephony Certificate 189.60-20
Casualty, records 196.07-1
Certificate, exemption 189.60-25
Certificate of Inspection 189.01, 196.50
Certificate of Inspection, prerequisite of 189.20-1
  Application 189.25-5
Certificate of Inspection, temporary 189.01-15
Certificates under International Convention for Safety of Life at Sea,
  1974 .... 189.60-60
Chains 195.07
Chains, vessels contracted for prior to March 1, 1968 .... 195.07-90
Charges, spare; fire extinguishers 193.50-15
Charges, spare; fireman's outfit 195.35
Charts 196.05-5
Chemical and explosive hazards 189.20-25, 189.25-47
Chemical laboratory, segregation of 19.05-20
Chemical stores 188.10-7, 194.05-3
Chemical storeroom 188.10-9, 190.05-10
Chemical storeroom and lamproom construction 190.05-10
Chemical storeroom, segregation of 190.05-20
Chemical stores and/or storerooms 194.20
Chemicals in the chemistry laboratory 194.05-5
Chemicals other than compressed gases 194.15-15
Chemistry laboratory 188.10-11, 194.15
Chief engineer 196.45-1
Classification, fire extinguishers 193.50-5
Classification society, recognized 188.10-59
Coast Guard .... 188.01-1, et al
Coast Guard Headquarters, address .... 188.35-5(b)
Coast Guard District Commander 188.10-13
Coastwise 188.10-15, 195.07-5
Combustible liquid 188.10-17

Subchapter U Index

Combustible liquids as chemical stores, detail requirements 194.05-19
Commandant... 188.01-5(b), 188.10-19
Communications, between deck houses... 196.33
Communications, interior 195.05
Communications, means of.. 196.15-3
Communications, weather deck 190.10-45
Compass, magnetic; when required 195.19
Compressed gas... 188.10-21, 194.20-17
Compressed gases as chemical stores, detail requirements 194.05-15
Compressed gases other than inert gases 194.15-17
Conditions of Permit.. 189.05-10
Conditions under which equivalents may be used 188.15-1
Construction.. 190.07-10, 190.20-15
Construction and arrangement, hull structure 190.01
Construction, portable vans.. 195.11-10
Control systems 195.01
Controls, carbon dioxide extinguishing systems...................................... 193.15-10
Cooling.. 190.20-50
Corrosive liquids 188.10-23
Corrosive liquids as chemical stores, detail requirements........................ 194.05-13
Crew spaces, location of 190.20-10

D

Data required, maneuvering characteristics 196.19-1
Dead end corridors 190.10-30
Dead end lines, piping .... 193.15-15(e)
Deckhouses, communications between.. 196.33-1
Deficiencies in maintenance 189.27-10
Definitions of terms 188.10, 190.07-5
Definitions relating to hull examinations... 189.40-1
Department of Transportation 188.01-5
Design and construction of portable van 195.11-10
Design of vessels.. 188.15-5
Discharge outlets 193.15-25
Display of plans... 196.36
Documents, seaman's... 188.05-33(b)
Doors, no means for locking 190.10-20
Double-bottom fuel oil tanks 189.43-1
Drain and dirt traps, piping .... 193.15-15(g)
Draft indicating system 196.40-10
Draft marks 196.40-10
Drafts... 196.15-5
Drills.. 196.15-1, 196.15-35
Drydocking .... 189.40(a)
Drydock examination, internal structural examination, cargo tank internal examination and underwater survey intervals 189.40-3
Duration of certificates 189.60-40
Duty of officers 196.05-1

E

Electrical 194.15-19
Electrical engineering, interior communications systems......................... 195.05-1
Electrical engineering details 188.25-1
Electrical engineering equipment... 189.25-30
Emergency equipment, markings for 196.37
Emergency lighting and power systems.. 196.15-30
Emergency lights 196.37-25

Emergency signals	196.13-1
Emergency source of electrical power, segregation of spaces containing	190.05-15
Emergency training, musters, and drills	196.15-35
Enclosure openings	193.15-35
Engineering details, electrical	188.25-1
Engineering details, marine	188.20-1
Engineering, electrical equipment	189.25-30
Engineering systems, marine	195.03
Equipment installed, but not required	193.01-5
Equivalents	188.15
Escape, means of	190.10-10
Examinations	189.35-7
Examination, boilers and machinery	196.15-15
Excess steam, carrying of	196.45
Exemption, certificate	189.60-25
Exemptions from inspection laws for oceanographic research vessels and terms and conditions which apply in lieu thereof	188.05-2
Exhibition of license	196.53
Existing vessels	188.05-3(b)
Explosive	188.10-25
Explosives—detail requirements	194.05-7
Explosive handling plan	196.80
Explosive hazards	189.20-25, 189.25-47

F

Federal Communications Commission	189.20-15(a), 189.25-10(a)
Field of vision	190.02-1(a)
Fire axes	193.60
Fire axes, location	193.60-10
Fire axes, number required	193.60-5
Fire equipment, markings for	196.37
Fire extinguishers, application	193.50-1
Fire extinguishers, classification	193.50-5
Fire extinguishers, hand portable	193.05-15, 193.50, 196.37-23
Fire extinguishers, location	193.50-10
Fire extinguishers, semiportable	193.05-15, 193.50-20
Fire extinguishers, size graduations	Table 193.50-5(c)
Fire extinguishers, spare charges	193.50-15
Fire extinguishers, vessels contracted for prior to March 1, 1968	193.50-90
Fire extinguishing equipment	189.25-20
Fire extinguishing system branch lines	196.37-10
Fire extinguishing system controls	196.37-13
Fire detecting and extinguishing equipment, where required	193.05
Fire detecting, manual alarm, and supervised patrol systems	193.05-1
Firefighting equipment, general	196.15-60
Fire hazards	189.25-45, 190.05-3
Fire hose	193.10-10
Fire hose stations	196.37-15
Fire hydrants	193.10-10
Fire main, piping	193.10-15
Fire main system	193.05-5, 193.10
Fire main system, installations contracted for prior to March 1, 1968	193.10-90
Fireman's outfit	195.35-10
Fireman's outfit, general	195.35-5
Fireman's outfit, stowage	195.35-15

Subchapter U Index

Fireman's outfit, spare charges 195.35-20
Fireman's outfit, vessels contracted for prior to March 1, 1968
Fire Protection Equipment .... Part 193
Fire protection, labs and chemical stores 194.15-7, 194.20-7
Fire protection, general 190.05
Fire protection, structural 190.07
Fire pumps .... 193.10-5, Table 193.10-5(a)
Fire pumps, maintenance of water pressure .... 193.10-5(i)(1)
Fire pumps, remote control .... 193.10-5(i)(2)
Fixed fire extinguishing systems 193.05-10
Fixed fire extinguishing systems, inspection of .... Table 189.25-20(a)(2)
Flammable liquid 188.10-27
Flammable liquid chemical stores, detail requirements 194.05-9
Flammable solids and oxidizing materials, detail requirements 194.05-11
Flashlights .... 195.35-5(c)
Fluorocarbons, refrigerant .... 195.30-1(a)(2), (b)(2)
Flushing systems 194.20-11
Foreign vessel .... 188.05-1(a)(1)
Fuel oil, requirements for 196.15-55
Fuel oil tanks examinations, integral 189.43

G

Galley uptakes .... 190.05-5(a)
Gas, liquefied compressed 188.10-41
Gas, liquefied flammable 188.10-43
Gas masks 196.37-20
General alarm bell contact makers 196.37-5
General alarm bells 196.37-7
General electrical engineering requirements 188.25
General fire protection 190.05, 193.01-1
General marine engineering requirements 188.20
General or partial survey 189.30-1
General subdivision and stability 190.03
Gloves .... 195.35-5(f)
Great Lakes 188.05-7, 188.10-31, 195.07-5
Guards 190.25, 190.25-15
Gulf of Mexico 188.10-51
Gyrocompass 195.19

H

Hand portable fire extinguishers 193.05-15, 193.50, 196.37-23
Hand portable fire extinguishers, inspection of .... Table 189.25-20(a)(1)
Hatches and other openings 196.15-20
Hawaii .... 188.05-10(a)(2)(iii)
Hawsers 195.07
Hawsers, vessels contracted for prior to March 1, 1968 .... 195.07-90
Hazards, chemical and explosive 189.25-45, 189.25-47
Hazards, fire 189.25-45
Headquarters 188.10-33
Heating and cooling 190.20-50
Helmet .... 195.35-5(g)
Hose, fire 193.10-10
Hospital space 190.20-35
Hull equipment 189.25-25
Hull examinations, definitions relating to 189.40-1
Hull markings 196.40-5
Hull structure 190.01

415

Hulls, standards of inspection 189.15-1
Hybrid work vests 196.34-25
Hydrants, fire 193.10-10
Hydraulic systems .... 189.35-9(c)(3)

I

Illuminated repeater, gyrocompass .... 195.19-1(c)
Improper use, searchlight 196.25-1
Incorporation by reference 190.01-3, 193.01-3
Initial inspection 189.20
Insect screens 190.20-55
Inspection after accident 189.30
Inspection and testing required when making alterations, repairs, or other such operations involving riveting, welding, burning, or like fire-producing actions 189.50-1
Inspection for Certification 189.25
Inspection of vessels 189.15
Inspection, portable vans and tanks 195.11-15
Inspection required, repairs and alternations 189.45-5
Inspections 196.15-1
Inspector 188.10-45
Inspector not limited 189.25-50, 189.27-15
Installation and details, electrical engineering and interior communications systems 195.05
Installation and details, marine engineering systems 195.03-1
Instructions for changing steering gear 196.37-33
Instructions to passengers, lifesaving appliances 196.37-37
Integral fuel oil tank examinations 189.43
Integral magazine construction 194.10-10
Intent 189.35-3, 190.20-5
Interior communications systems 195.05-1
Internal combustion engine exhausts .... 190.05-5(a)
Internal examination, cargo tanks 189.40-3
Internal structural examination .... 189.40-3(b)
International Convention for Safety of Life at Sea 1974 .... 188.05-10(a)(2)(i)
International voyage, application to vessels 188.05-10

K

Keys, magazine spaces .... 196.85-1(a)

L

Label plate, portable vans and tanks 195.11-20
Labeling 194.10-35
Laboratory, scientific 188.10-69
Ladders, vertical not accepted 190.10-15
Lakes, bays, and sounds 188.10-39, 195.07-10
Lamp room construction 190.05-10
License, exhibition of 196.53
Licensed officers 196.53-1
Lifeboats, access to 190.10-40
Lifelines .... 195.35-5(d)
Lifesaving appliances, markings for 196.37-37
Lifesaving appliances and arrangements 188.27-1, 195.06-1
Lifesaving equipment 189.25-15
Liquefied compressed gas 188.10-41
Liquefied flammable gas 188.10-43

Subchapter U Index

Load line marks 196.40-15
Load line, vessel subject to 190.01-5
Load lines—interpretive ruling 188.05-35
Loading and stowage 195.11-25
Loading doors 196.15-18
Location, fire axes 193.60-10
Location, means of escape 190.10-10
Location, portable fire extinguishers 193.50-10
Logbook entries 196.35
Logbooks 196.35-3
Lookouts 196.27

M

Machinery, accidents to 196.30-5
Machinery, examination of 196.15-15
Machinery, standards of inspection 189.15-1
Magazine chest construction 194.10-20
Magazine control 196.85-1
Magazine spaces, keys for .... 196.85-1(a)
Magazine sprinklers 194.10-30
Magazine van construction 194.10-15
Magazines, limited access .... 196.85(d)
Magazines, type and locations 194.10-5
Magnetic compass, when required 195.19-1
Maintenance deficiencies 189.27-10
Major installations 189.35-15
Maneuvering characteristics (including "Warning") 196.19
Manning 196.13-1
Marine Inspection, Officer in Charge 188.10-55
Marine engineering equipment 189.25-35
Marine engineering systems 195.03
Marine inspector or inspector 188.10-45
Maritime Administration, U.S. .... 188.05(a)(4)
Markings, fire and emergency equipment, etc. 196.37, 196.37-37
Markings on vessels 196.40
Mariners, Notice to 169.05
Marking, portable vans and tanks 195.11-20
Master's responsibility 189.35-13, 196.27-1, 196.45, 196.80-1
Means of escape 190.10
Means of escape, two required 190.10-5
Mechanical exhaust system .... Table 190.15-5(b)
Mechanically propelled vessels .... 188.05-10(a)(1), 195.19-1(b), 195.27-1(a)
Messrooms 190.20-30
Method of propulsion (Motor, Non-self-propelled, Sail, and Steam) ..... Table 188.05-1(a)
Mine Safety and Health Administration (MSHA) .... 195.30-5(a)
Miscellaneous systems 195.01-1
Muster lists 196.13-1
Musters 196.15-35

N

National Institute for Occupational Safety and Health (NIOSH) .... 195.30-5(a)
Nautical publications 196.05-5
Navigation bridge visibility 190.02-1
New vessels .... 188.05-3(a)
New vessels and existing vessels for the purpose of application or regulations in this subchapter 188.05-3

417

Nitrocellulose .... 190.07-10(e)
No means for locking doors, means of escape 190.10-20
Non-self-propelled vessels 194.01-1
Notice and plans required, drydocking 189.40-5
Notice and reporting of casualty and voyage records 196.07-1
Notice required, repairs and alterations 189.45-1, 196.30-10
Notice to Mariners 196.05
Number of plans required, plan approval 189.55-20
Number required, fire axes 193.60-5
Numbered vessel 188.10-49

O

Ocean 188.10-51, 195.07-5
Ocean or unlimited coastwise vessels on inland and Great Lakes routes 188.05-7
Oceanographic research vessel 188.10-53
Officer in Charge, Marine Inspection 188.10-55
Officers, duty of 196.05-1
OMB control numbers assigned pursuant to the Paperwork Reduction Act 188.01-15
Orders, rudder 196.37-35
Other Regulated Materials (ORM) 194.05-21
Other spaces 190.20-40
Other vessels .... 188.05-3(c)
Outfit, fireman's 195.35

P

Passengers, lifesaving appliance instructions 196.37-37
Permit, conditions of 189.05-10
Permit to proceed to another Port for repairs 189.05
Permit to proceed to another Port for repairs to whom issued 189.05-5
Personnel, scientific 188.10-71
Pilot boarding equipment and point of access 188.10-56
Pilot boarding operations 196.95
Piping and electrical requirements 194.20-19
Piping, carbon dioxide system 193.15-15
Piping, dead end lines .... 193.15-15(e)
Piping, drain and dirt traps .... 193.15-15(g)
Piping, fire main system 193.10-15
Placard of lifesaving signals 196.43
Plan approval 189.55, 195.11-15
Plan, explosive handling 196.80
Plans, display of 196.36
Plans and specifications required for new construction 189.55-5
Plans, initial inspection 189.20-10
Plans, required 189.40-5
Plans, required for alterations of existing vessels 189.55-10
Plans, weight handling gear 189.35-9
Pneumatic systems .... 189.35-9(c)(3)
Point of access, pilot boarding equipment .... 188.10-56(b)
Poisonous articles as chemical stores, detail requirements 194.05-17
Pollution prevention 189.25-38
Portable fire extinguishers 196.37-23
Portable magazine chests 196.37-47
Portable tanks 188.10-57, 195.11-30
Portable tanks—interpretive rulings 188.05-30
Posting 189.05-15

Subchapter U Index

Posting of Convention certificates..189.60-35
Posting, stability letter..196.12-1
Power systems, emergency..196.15-30
Prerequisite of reissuance of certificate of inspection...............................189.25-1
Pressure vessels..196.30-1
Procedure for submittal of plans...189.55-1
Puerto Rico, Commonwealth of..188.05-10(a)(2)(ii)
Pumps, fire..193.10-5, Table 193.10-5(a)
Public spaces..190.10-35
Publications, nautical..196.05-5
Purpose of regulations..188.01-1

R

Radar, when required..195.17-1
Rails..190.25
Rails, application..190.25-1
Rails, storm..190.25-10
Rails, where required..190.25-5
Reagent containers...194.05-5(c)
Recognized classification society..188.10-59
Records...196.35-3
Records, casualty...196.07-1
Records, voyage...196.07-1
Refrigerants, general..195.30-5
Refrigerants, vessels contracted for prior to March 1, 1968..............195.30-90
Reid vapor pressure..188.10-43
Reinspection...189.27, 189.27-1
Remote controls...189.25-25(a)(2)
Repairs..189.50-1, 196.30-1
Repairs and alterations...189.45
Reporting, casualty and voyage records..196.07-1
Requirements, vessels contracted for prior to March 1, 1968............194.90-1
Reports of accidents, repairs, and unsafe equipment........................196.30
Responsibility, chemical stores and/or storerooms...........................194.20-3
Right of appeal...188.01-7
Rivers...188.10-61, 195.07-10
Riveting...189.50-1
Rudder orders..196.37-35

S

Safety valve seal..196.30-20
Sanitary inspection..189.25-40, 189.33-1
Sanitation...196.15-10
Seagoing barge..188.10-65
Seaman's documents...188.05-33(b)
Scientific equipment...188.10-67
Scientific laboratory...188.10-69, 194.20
Scientific personnel—interpretive rulings..188.05-33
Scope of inspection...189.20-15, 189.25-10
Scope of regulations..188.01-3
Scope of reinspection...189.27-5
Seagoing barge...188.10-65
Searchlights..196.25
Segregation of chemical laboratories and chemical storerooms......190.05-20
Segregation of spaces containing the emergency source of electrical power...190.05-15
Self-contained breathing apparatus.................................195.30-15, 196.37-20

Semiportable fire extinguishers 193.05-15, 193.50-20
Ship's stores and supplies 188.10-73
Shipboard inspections 196.34-20
Shipboard stowage 196.34-15
Shipping articles .... 188.05-33(b)
Signals, emergency 196.13-1
Signals, lifesaving 196.43-1
Size or other limitations .... Table 188.05-1(a)
Sleeping accommodations 190.20-20
SOLAS 74 .... 188.05-10(a)(2)(i)
Sounding equipment, when required 195.27-1
Sounds 188.10-39, 195.07-10
Spare charges, fire extinguishers 193.50-15
Special cases, weight handling gear 189.35-11
Special consideration, hull structure 190.01-15
Special operating requirements 189.50
Specific application noted in text 188.05-5
Specific tests and inspections 189.20-20
Sprinkler systems, automatic 193.30
St. Lawrence River .... 188.05-10(b)(1)
Stability 190.03
Stability letter, posting 196.12
Stability requirements 196.15-7
Stairway size 190.10-25
Standard fire tests' .... 190.07-5(a)
Standards in inspection of hulls, boilers, and machinery 189.15-1
Standards to be used 188.35-1
Station Bills 196.13
Steering gear 196.15-3
Storage, chemical laboratory and scientific laboratory 194.15-9
Storage, chemical stores and/or storerooms 194.20-9
Storm rails 190.25-10
Stowage, fireman's outfit 195.35-15
Stowage locations, lifesaving appliances 196.37-37
Structural fire protection 190.07
Subdivision and stability 190.03
Survey intervals, underwater 189.40-3
Survey, general or partial 189.30-1
Systems:
  Electrical engineering 195.05-1
  Interior communications 195.05-1
  Marine engineering 195.03-1

T

Tanks, cargo 189.40-3
Tanks, portable 188.05-30, 188.10-57, 195.11
Temporary certificate 189.01-15
Tests 189.35-5, 196.15-1
Toilet rooms 190.20-25
Two required, means of escape 190.10-5
Type and location, magazines 194.10-5

U

Underwater survey .... 189.40(c)
Underwater survey intervals 189.40-3
Undocumented vessel 188.10-75
United Nations .... 188.05-10(a)(2)(ii)

Subchapter U Index

Unlimited coastwise vessels 188.05-7
United States .... 188.05-10(a)(2)(iii)
Use, work vests 196.34-10
U.S. Coast Guard Headquarters, address .... 188.35-5(b)
U.S. Maritime Administration .... 188.05-(a)(4)
U.S. Naval Oceanographic Office, address .... 196.05-1(c)

V

Ventilation 190.15, 194.10-25, 194.15-5, 194.20-5
Ventilation for closed spaces 190.15-10
Ventilation for living spaces and quarters 190.15-15
Verification of vessel compliance with applicable stability requirements 196.15-7
Vessel 188.10-77
Vessel design 188.15-5
Vessels contracted for prior to March 1, 1968 ...... 190.01-90, 190.07-90, 190.10-90, 190.15-90, 190.20-90, 190.25-90, 193.50-90
Vessels inspected and certificated under subchapters:
  Subchapter D: Tank Vessels .... Table 188.05-1(a)
  Subchapter H: Passenger Vessels .... Table 188.05-1(a)
  Subchapter I: Cargo and Miscellaneous Vessels .... Table 188.05-1(a)
  Subchapter T: Small Passenger Vessels .... Table 188.05-1(a)
Vessels, markings on 196.40
Vessels subject to load line 190.01-5
Vessels subject to the provisions of subchapters:
  Subchapter C: Uninspected Vessels .... Table 188.05-1(a)
  Subchapter O: Certain Bulk Dangerous Cargoes .... Table 188.05-1(a)
  Subchapter U: Oceanographic Research Vessels .... Table 188.05-1(a)
Vessels subject to the requirements of this subchapter 188.05-1
Vessels using fuel having a flashpoint of 110 °F or lower 190.15-5
Vests, work 196.34
Visibility, navigation bridge 190.02-1
Voyage records 196.07-1

W

Washrooms 190.20-25
Weather deck communications 190.10-45
Weekly Notice to Mariners .... 196.05-1(b)(c)
Welding 189.50-1
West Point .... 188.05-10(b)(1)
Wet Weight Handling Gear .... 189.35-9(c)(1)
Where obtainable, American Bureau of Shipping's Standards 188.35-5
Whistle 196.15-3
Whistling, unnecessary prohibited 196.20-1
Wooden hull vessels .... 189.40-3(b)
Woodwork insulated from heated surfaces 190.05-5
Work vests 196.34

SUBCHAPTER V—MARINE OCCUPATIONAL SAFETY AND HEALTH STANDARDS

PART 197—GENERAL PROVISIONS

Subpart A [Reserved]

Subpart B—Commercial Diving Operations

GENERAL

Sec.
197.200 Purpose of subpart.
197.202 Applicability.
197.203 Right of appeal.
197.204 Definitions.
197.205 Availability of standards.
197.206 Substitutes for required equipment, materials, apparatus, arrangements, procedures, or tests.
197.208 Designation of person-in-charge.
197.210 Designation of diving supervisor.

EQUIPMENT

197.300 Applicability.
197.310 Air compressor system.
197.312 Breathing supply hoses.
197.314 First aid and treatment equipment.
197.318 Gages and timekeeping devices.
197.320 Diving ladder and stage.
197.322 Surface-supplied helmets and masks.
197.324 Diver's safety harness.
197.326 Oxygen safety.
197.328 PVHO—General.
197.330 PVHO—Closed bells.
197.332 PVHO—Decompression chambers.
197.334 Open diving bells.
197.336 Pressure piping.
197.338 Compressed gas cylinders.
197.340 Breathing gas supply.
197.342 Buoyancy-changing devices.
197.344 Inflatable flotation devices.
197.346 Diver's equipment.

OPERATIONS

197.400 Applicability.
197.402 Responsibilities of the person-in-charge.
197.404 Responsibilities of the diving supervisor.
197.410 Dive procedures.
197.420 Operations manual.

SPECIFIC DIVING MODE PROCEDURES

197.430 SCUBA diving.
197.432 Surface-supplied air diving.
197.434 Surface-supplied mixed gas diving.
197.436 Liveboating.

PERIODIC TESTS AND INSPECTIONS OF DIVING EQUIPMENT

197.450 Breathing gas tests.
197.452 Oxygen cleaning.
197.454 First aid and treatment equipment.
197.456 Breathing supply hoses.
197.458 Gages and timekeeping devices.
197.460 Diving equipment.
197.462 Pressure vessels and pressure piping.

RECORDS

197.480 Logbooks.
197.482 Logbook entries.
197.484 Notice of casualty.
197.486 Written report of casualty.
197.488 Retention of records after casualty.

Subpart C—Benzene

197.501 Applicability.
197.505 Definitions.
197.510 Incorporation by reference.
197.515 Permissible exposure limits (PELs).
197.520 Performance standard.
197.525 Responsibility of the person in charge.
197.530 Persons other than employees.
197.535 Regulated areas.
197.540 Determination of personal exposure.
197.545 Program to reduce personal exposure.
197.550 Respiratory protection.
197.555 Personal protective clothing and equipment.
197.560 Medical surveillance.
197.565 Notifying personnel of benzene hazards.
197.570 Recordkeeping.
197.575 Observation of monitoring.
197.580 Appendices.

APPENDIX A TO SUBPART C TO PART 197—SAMPLE SUBSTANCE SAFETY DATA SHEET, BENZENE

APPENDIX B TO SUBPART C TO PART 197—SUBSTANCE TECHNICAL GUIDELINES, BENZENE

APPENDIX C TO SUBPART C TO PART 197—MEDICAL SURVEILLANCE GUIDELINES FOR BENZENE

APPENDIX D TO SUBPART C TO PART 197—SAMPLING AND ANALYTICAL METHODS FOR BENZENE MONITORING—MEASUREMENT PROCEDURES

APPENDIX E TO SUBPART C TO PART 197—RESPIRATOR FIT TESTS

APPENDIX F TO SUBPART C TO PART 197—SAMPLE WORKER CERTIFICATION FORM

APPENDIX A TO PART 197—AIR NO-DECOMPRESSION LIMITS

AUTHORITY: 33 U.S.C. 1509; 43 U.S.C. 1333; 46 U.S.C. 3306, 3703, 6101; Department of Homeland Security Delegation No. 0170.1.

SOURCE: CGD 76–009, 43 FR 53683, Nov. 16, 1978, unless otherwise noted.

Subpart A [Reserved]

Coast Guard, DHS § 197.204

Subpart B—Commercial Diving Operations

GENERAL

§ 197.200 Purpose of subpart.

This subpart prescribes rules for the design, construction, and use of equipment, and inspection, operation, and safety and health standards for commercial diving operations taking place from vessels and facilities under Coast Guard jurisdiction.

§ 197.202 Applicability.

(a) This subpart applies to commercial diving operations taking place at any deepwater port or the safety zone thereof as defined in 33 CFR part 150; from any artificial island, installation, or other device on the Outer Continental Shelf and the waters adjacent thereto as defined in 33 CFR part 147 or otherwise related to activities on the Outer Continental Shelf; and from all vessels required to have a certificate of inspection issued by the Coast Guard including mobile offshore drilling units regardless of their geographic location, or from any vessel connected with a deepwater port or within the deepwater port safety zone, or from any vessel engaged in activities related to the Outer Continental Shelf; except that this subpart does not apply to any diving operation—

(1) Performed solely for marine scientific research and development purposes by educational institutions;

(2) Performed solely for research and development for the advancement of diving equipment and technology; or

(3) Performed solely for search and rescue or related public safety purposes by or under the control of a governmental agency.

(b) Diving operations may deviate from the requirements of this subpart to the extent necessary to prevent or minimize a situation which is likely to cause death, injury, or major environmental damage. The circumstances leading to the situation, the deviations made, and the corrective action taken, if appropriate, to reduce the possibility of recurrence shall be recorded by the diving supervisor in the logbook as required by § 197.482(c).

§ 197.203 Right of appeal.

Any person directly affected by a decision or action taken under this subchapter, by or on behalf of the Coast Guard, may appeal therefrom in accordance with subpart 1.03 of this chapter.

[CGD 88–033, 54 FR 50382, Dec. 6, 1989]

§ 197.204 Definitions.

As used in this subpart:

ACFM means actual cubic feet per minute.

ANSI Code1 means the B31.1 American National Standards Institute "Code for Pressure Piping, Power Piping."

ASME Code means the American Society of Mechanical Engineers "Boiler and Pressure Vessel Code."

ASME PVHO–1 means the ANSI/ASME standard "Safety Standard for Pressure Vessels for Human Occupancy."

ATA means a measure of pressure expressed in terms of atmosphere absolute (includes barometric pressure).

Bell means a compartment either at ambient pressure (open bell) or pressurized (closed bell) that allows the diver to be transported to and from the underwater work site, allows the diver access to the surrounding environment, and is capable of being used as a refuge during diving operations.

Bottom time means the total elapsed time measured in minutes from the time the diver leaves the surface in descent to the time to the next whole minute that the diver begins ascent.

Breathing gas/breathing mixture means the mixed-gas, oxygen, or air as appropriate supplied to the diver for breathing.

Bursting pressure means the pressure at which a pressure containment device would fail structurally.

Commercial diver means a diver engaged in underwater work for hire excluding sport and recreational diving and the instruction thereof.

Commercial diving operation means all activities in support of a commercial diver.

Cylinder means a pressure vessel for the storage of gases under pressure.

Decompression chamber means a pressure vessel for human occupancy such

423

§ 197.204

as a surface decompression chamber, closed bell, or deep diving system especially equipped to recompress, decompress, and treat divers.

Decompression sickness means a condition caused by the formation of gas or gas bubbles in the blood or body tissue as a result of pressure reduction.

Decompression table means a profile or set of profiles of ascent rates and breathing mixtures designed to reduce the pressure on a diver safely to atmospheric pressure after the diver has been exposed to a specific depth and bottom time.

Depth means the maximum pressure expressed in feet of seawater attained by a diver and is used to express the depth of a dive.

Dive location means that portion of a vessel or facility from which a diving operation is conducted.

Dive team means the divers and diver support personnel involved in a diving operation, including the diving supervisor.

Diver means a person working beneath the surface, exposed to hyperbaric conditions, and using underwater breathing apparatus.

Diver-carried reserve breathing gas means a supply of air or mixed-gas, as appropriate, carried by the diver in addition to the primary or secondary breathing gas supplied to the diver.

Diving installation means all of the equipment used in support of a commercial diving operation.

Diving mode means a type of diving requiring SCUBA, surface-supplied air, or surface-supplied mixed-gas equipment, with related procedures and techniques.

Diving stage means a suspended platform constructed to carry one or more divers and used for putting divers into the water and bringing them to the surface when in-water decompression or a heavy-weight diving outfit is used.

Diving supervisor means the person having complete responsibility for the safety of a commercial diving operation including the responsibility for the safety and health of all diving personnel in accordance with this subpart.

Facility means a deepwater port, or an artificial island, installation, or other device on the Outer Continental Shelf subject to Coast Guard jurisdiction.

Fsw means feet of seawater (or equivalent static pressure head).

Gas embolism means a condition caused by expanding gases, which have been taken into and retained in the lungs while breathing under pressure, being forced into the bloodstream or other tissues during ascent or decompression.

Heavy-weight diving outfit means diver-worn surface-supplied deep-sea dress.

Hyperbaric conditions means pressure conditions in excess of surface atmospheric pressure.

Injurious corrosion means an advanced state of corrosion which may impair the structural integrity or safe operation of the equipment.

Liveboating means the support of a surfaced-supplied diver from a vessel underway.

Maximum working pressure means the maximum pressure to which a pressure containment device can be exposed under operating conditions (usually the pressure setting of the pressure relief device).

No-decompression limits means the air depth and bottom time limits of appendix A.

Pressure vessel means a container capable of withstanding an internal maximum working pressure over 15 psig.

Psi(g) means pounds per square inch (gage).

PVHO means pressure vessel for human occupancy but does not include pressure vessels for human occupancy that may be subjected to external pressures in excess of 15 psig but can only be subjected to maximum internal pressures of 15 psig or less (i.e., submersibles, or one atmosphere observation bells).

Saturation diving means saturating a diver's tissues with the inert gas in the breathing mixture to allow an extension of bottom time without additional decompression.

SCUBA diving means a diving mode in which the diver is supplied with a compressed breathing mixture from diver carried equipment.

Standby diver means a diver at the dive location available to assist a diver in the water.

Coast Guard, DHS

Surface-supplied air diving means a diving mode in which the diver is supplied from the dive location or bell with compressed breathing air including oxygen or oxygen enriched air if supplied for treatment.

Surface-supplied mixed-gas diving means a diving mode in which the diver is supplied from the dive location or bell with a compressed breathing mixture other than air.

Timekeeping device means a device for measuring the time of a dive in minutes.

Treatment table means a depth, time, and breathing gas profile designed to treat a diver for decompression sickness.

Umbilical means the hose bundle between a dive location and a diver or bell, or between a diver and a bell, that supplies the diver or bell with a lifeline, breathing gas, communications, power, and heat as appropriate to the diving mode or conditions.

Vessel means any waterborne craft including mobile offshore drilling units required to have a Certificate of Inspection issued by the Coast Guard or any waterborne craft connected with a deepwater port or within the deepwater port safety zone, or any waterborne craft engaged in activities related to the Outer Continental Shelf.

Volume tank means a pressure vessel connected to the outlet of a compressor and used as an air reservoir.

Working pressure means the pressure to which a pressure containment device is exposed at any particular instant during normal operating conditions.

§ 197.205 Availability of standards.

(a) Several standards have been incorporated by reference in this subchapter. The incorporation by reference has been approved by the Director of the Federal Register under the provisions of 1 CFR part 51.

(b) The standards are available from the appropriate organizations whose addresses are listed below:

(1) American National Standards Institute, 11 West 42nd Street, New York, NY 10036.

(2) American Society of Mechanical Engineers, United Engineering Center, 345 East 47th Street, New York, NY 10017.

[CGD 76–009, 43 FR 53683, Nov. 16, 1978, as amended by CGD 96–041, 61 FR 50735, Sept. 27, 1996]

§ 197.206 Substitutes for required equipment, materials, apparatus, arrangements, procedures, or tests.

(a) The Coast Guard may accept substitutes for equipment, materials, apparatus, arrangements, procedures, or tests required in this subpart if the substitute provides an equivalent level of safety.

(b) In any case where it is shown to the satisfaction of the Commandant that the use of any particular equipment, material, apparatus, arrangement, procedure, or test is unreasonable or impracticable, the Commandant may permit the use of alternate equipment, material, apparatus, arrangement, procedure, or test to such an extent and upon such condition as will insure, to his satisfaction, a degree of safety consistent with the minimum standards set forth in this subpart.

§ 197.208 Designation of person-in-charge.

(a) The owner or agent of a vessel or facility without a designated master shall designate, in writing, an individual to be the person-in-charge of the vessel or facility.

(b) Where a master is designated, the master is the person-in-charge.

§ 197.210 Designation of diving supervisor.

The name of the diving supervisor for each commercial diving operation shall be—

(a) Designated in writing; and

(b) Given to the person-in-charge prior to the commencement of any commercial diving operation.

EQUIPMENT

§ 197.300 Applicability.

(a) Each diving installation used on each vessel or facility subject to this subpart must meet the requirements of this subpart.

§ 197.310

(b) In addition to the requirements of this subpart, equipment which is permanently installed on vessels and is part of the diving installation must meet Subchapters F and J of this chapter.

(c) All repairs and modifications to pressure vessels used for commercial diving operations must be made in accordance with the requirements of section VIII, division 1 or division 2 of the ASME Code, ASME PVHO-1, part 54 of this chapter, or 49 CFR 173.34, as applicable.

(d) All repairs and modifications to pressure piping used for commercial diving operations must be made in accordance with the requirements of the ANSI Code or part 56 of this chapter, as applicable.

§ 197.310 Air compressor system.

A compressor used to supply breathing air to a diver must have—

(a) A volume tank that is—

(1) Built and stamped in accordance with section VIII, division 1 of the ASME Code with—

(i) A check valve on the inlet side;

(ii) A pressure gage;

(iii) A relief valve; and

(iv) A drain valve; and

(2) Tested after every repair, modification, or alteration to the pressure boundaries as required by § 197.462;

(b) Intakes that are located away from areas containing exhaust fumes of internal combustion engines or other hazardous contaminants;

(c) An efficient filtration system; and

(d) Slow-opening shut-off valves when the maximum allowable working pressure of the system exceeds 500 psig.

§ 197.312 Breathing supply hoses.

(a) Each breathing supply hose must—

(1) Have a maximum working pressure that is equal to or exceeds—

(i) The maximum working pressure of the section of the breathing supply system in which used; and

(ii) The pressure equivalent of the maximum depth of the dive relative to the supply source plus 100 psig;

(2) Have a bursting pressure of four times its maximum working pressure;

(3) Have connectors that—

(i) Are made of corrosion-resistant material;

(ii) Are resistant to accidental disengagement; and

(iii) Have a maximum working pressure that is at least equal to the maximum working pressure of the hose to which they are attached; and

(4) Resist kinking by—

(i) Being made of kink-resistant materials; or

(ii) Having exterior support.

(b) Each umbilical must—

(1) Meet the requirements of paragraph (a) of this section; and

(2) Be marked from the diver or open bell end in 10-foot intervals to 100 feet and in 50-foot intervals thereafter.

§ 197.314 First aid and treatment equipment.

(a) Each dive location must have—

(1) A medical kit approved by a physician that consists of—

(i) Basic first aid supplies; and

(ii) Any additional supplies necessary to treat minor trauma and illnesses resulting from hyperbaric exposure;

(2) A copy of an American Red Cross Standard First Aid handbook;

(3) A bag-type manual resuscitator with transparent mask and tubing; and

(4) A capability to remove an injured diver from the water.

(b) Each diving installation must have a two-way communications system to obtain emergency assistance except when the vessel or facility ship-to-shore, two-way communications system is readily available.

(c) Each dive location supporting mixed-gas dives, dives deeper than 130 fsw, or dives outside the no-decompression limits must meet the requirements of paragraph (a) of this section and have—

(1) A decompression chamber;

(2) Decompression and treatment tables;

(3) A supply of breathing gases sufficient to treat for decompression sickness;

(4) The medical kit required by paragraph (a)(1) of this section that is—

(i) Capable of being carried into the decompression chamber; and

(ii) Suitable for use under hyperbaric conditions; and

Coast Guard, DHS § 197.328

(5) A capability to assist an injured diver into the decompression chamber.

§ 197.318 Gages and timekeeping devices.

(a) A gage indicating diver depth must be at each dive location for surface-supplied dives.

(b) A timekeeping device must be at each dive location.

§ 197.320 Diving ladder and stage.

(a) Each diving ladder must—
(1) Be capable of supporting the weight of at least two divers;
(2) Extend 3 feet below the water surface;
(3) Be firmly in place;
(4) Be available at the dive location for a diver to enter or exit the water unless a diving stage or bell is provided; and
(5) Be—(i) Made of corrosion-resistant material; or
(ii) Protected against and maintained free from injurious corrosion.

(b) Each diving stage must—
(1) Be capable of supporting the weight of at least two divers;
(2) Have an open-grating platform;
(3) Be available for a diver to enter or exit the water from the dive location and for in-water decompression if the diver is—
(i) Wearing a heavy-weight diving outfit; or
(ii) Diving outside the no-decompression limits, except when a bell is provided; and
(4) Be—(i) Made of corrosion-resistant material; or
(ii) Protected against and maintained free from injurious corrosion.

§ 197.322 Surface-supplied helmets and masks.

(a) Each surface-supplied helmet or mask must have—
(1) A nonreturn valve at the attachment point between helmet or mask and umbilical that closes readily and positively;
(2) An exhaust valve; and
(3) A two-way voice communication system between the diver and the dive location or bell.

(b) Each surface-supplied air helmet or mask must—

(1) Ventilate at least 4.5 ACFM at any depth at which it is operated; or
(2) Be able to maintain the diver's inspired carbon dioxide partial pressure below 0.02 ATA when the diver is producing carbon dioxide at the rate of 1.6 standard liters per minute.

§ 197.324 Diver's safety harness.

Each safety harness used in surface-supplied diving must have—
(a) A positive buckling device; and
(b) An attachment point for the umbilical life line that—
(1) Distributes the pulling force of the umbilical over the diver's body; and
(2) Prevents strain on the mask or helmet.

§ 197.326 Oxygen safety.

(a) Equipment used with oxygen or oxygen mixtures greater than 40 percent by volume must be designed for such use.

(b) Oxygen systems with pressures greater than 125 psig must have slow-opening shut-off valves except pressure boundary shut-off valves may be ball valves.

§ 197.328 PVHO—General.

(a) Each PVHO, contracted for or purchased after February 1, 1979, must be built and stamped in accordance with ASME PVHO-1.

(b) Each PVHO, contracted for or constructed before February 1, 1979, and not Coast Guard approved, must be submitted to the Coast Guard for approval prior to February 1, 1984.

(c) To be approved under paragraph (b), a PVHO must be—
(1) Constructed in accordance with part 54 of this chapter; or—
(2) Be built in accordance with section VIII, division 1 or division 2 of the ASME Code; and—
(i) Have the plans approved in accordance with § 54.01–18 of this chapter;
(ii) Pass the radiographic and other survey tests of welded joints required by section VIII, division 1 or division 2, as appropriate, of the ASME Code; and
(iii) Pass—(A) The hydrostatic test described in § 54.10–10 of this chapter; or

§ 197.330

(B) The pneumatic test described in § 54.10–15 of this chapter and such additional tests as the Officer-in-Charge, Marine Inspection (OCMI) may require.

(d) Each PVHO must—

(1) Have a shut-off valve located within 1 foot of the pressure boundary on all piping penetrating the pressure boundary;

(2) Have a check valve located within 1 foot of the pressure boundary on all piping exclusively carrying fluids into the PVHO;

(3) Have the pressure relief device required by ASME PVHO-1;

(4) Have a built-in breathing system with at least one mask per occupant stored inside each separately pressurized compartment;

(5) Have a two-way voice communications system allowing communications between an occupant in one pressurized compartment of the PVHO and—

(i) The diving supervisor at the dive location;

(ii) Any divers being supported from the same PVHO; and

(iii) Occupants of other separately pressurized compartments of the same PVHO;

(6) If designed to mechanically couple to another PVHO, have a two-way communications system allowing communications between occupants of each PVHO when mechanically coupled;

(7) Have a pressure gage in the interior of each compartment that is—

(i) Designed for human occupancy; and

(ii) Capable of having the compartment pressure controlled from inside the PVHO;

(8) Have viewports that allow observation of occupants from the outside;

(9) Have viewports that meet the requirements of ASME PVHO-1 except those PVHO's approved under paragraph (b) of this section which have nonacrylic viewports;

(10) Have means of illumination sufficient to allow an occupant to—

(i) Read gages; and

(ii) Operate the installed systems within each compartment;

(11) Be designed and equipped to minimize sources of combustible materials and ignition;

(12) Have a protective device on the inlet side of PVHO exhaust lines;

(13) Have a means of extinguishing a fire in the interior;

(14) Have a means of maintaining the oxygen content of the interior atmosphere below 25 percent surface equivalent by volume when pressurized with air as the breathing mixture;

(15) Have a means of maintaining the interior atmosphere below 2 percent surface equivalent carbon dioxide by volume;

(16) Have a means of overriding and controlling from the exterior all interior breathing and pressure supply controls;

(17) Have a speech unscrambler when used with mixed-gas;

(18) Have interior electrical systems that are designed for the environment in which they will operate to minimize the risk of fire, electrical shock to personnel, and galvanic action of the PVHO; and

(19) Be tested after every repair, modification, or alteration to the pressure boundaries as required by § 197.462.

§ 197.330 PVHO—Closed bells.

(a) Except as provided in paragraph (b) of this section, each closed bell must meet the requirements of § 197.328 and—

(1) Have underwater breathing apparatus for each occupant stored inside each separately pressurized compartment;

(2) Have an umbilical;

(3) Have lifting equipment attached to the closed bell capable of returning the occupied closed bell when fully flooded to the dive location;

(4) Be capable of recompressing on the surface to the maximum design diving depth;

(5) Be constructed and equipped as required by § 197.332;

(6) Have an emergency locating device designed to assist personnel on the surface in acquiring and maintaining contact with the submerged PVHO if the umbilical to the surface is severed;

(7) Have a capability to remove an injured diver from the water; and

(8) Have a life support capability for the intact closed bell and its occupants for—

(i) Twelve hours after an accident severing the umbilical to the surface when the umbilical to the surface is

Coast Guard, DHS § 197.338

the only installed means of retrieving the closed bell; or

(ii) A period of time, at least equal to 1 hour plus twice the time required to retrieve the bell from its designed operating depth and attach an auxiliary lifesupport system, after an accident severing the umbilical to the surface when the umbilical is one of the two independent installed means of retrieving the closed bell, each meeting the requirements of paragraph (a)(3) of this section.

(b) A closed bell that does not meet the requirements of paragraphs (a)(3), (a)(4), and (a)(5) of this section, must be capable of attachment to another PVHO that—

(1) Allows the transfer of personnel and diver's equipment under pressure from the closed bell to the PVHO;

(2) Meets the requirements of paragraph (a)(3) of this section;

(3) Is capable of attachment to a decompression chamber meeting the requirements of paragraphs (a)(4) and (a)(5) of this section; and

(4) Allows the transfer of personnel and diver's equipment under pressure from the PVHO to the decompression chamber.

§ 197.332 PVHO—Decompression chambers.

Each decompression chamber must—

(a) Meet the requirements of § 197.328;

(b) Have internal dimensions sufficient to accommodate a diver lying in a horizontal position and another person tending the diver;

(c) Have a capability for ingress and egress of personnel and equipment while the occupants are under pressure;

(d) Have a means of operating all installed man-way locking devices, except disabled shipping dogs, from both sides of a closed hatch;

(e) Have interior illumination sufficient to allow visual observation, diagnosis, and medical treatment of an occupant.

(f) Have one bunk for each two occupants;

(g) Have a capability that allows bunks to be seen over their entire lengths from the exterior;

(h) Have a minimum pressure capability of—

(1) 6 ATA, when used for diving to 300 fsw; or

(2) The maximum depth of the dive, when used for diving operations deeper than 300 fsw, unless a closed bell meeting the requirements of § 197.330(a) (3), (4), and (5) is used;

(i) Have a minimum pressurization rate of 2 ATA per minute to 60 fsw and at least 1 ATA per minute thereafter;

(j) Have a decompression rate of 1 ATA per minute to 33 fsw;

(k) Have an external pressure gage for each pressurized compartment;

(l) Have a capability to supply breathing mixtures at the maximum rate required by each occupant doing heavy work; and

(m) Have a sound-powered headset or telephone as a backup to the communications system required by § 197.328(c) (5) and (6), except when that communications system is a sound-powered system.

§ 197.334 Open diving bells.

Each open diving bell must—

(a) Have an upper section that provides an envelope capable of maintaining a bubble of breathing mixture available to a diver standing on the lower section of the platform with his body through the open bottom and his head in the bubble;

(b) Have lifting equipment capable of returning the occupied open bell to the dive location;

(c) Have an umbilical; and

(d) Be—(1) Made of corrosion-resisting material; or

(2) Protected against and maintained free from injurious corrosion.

§ 197.336 Pressure piping.

Piping systems that are not an integral part of the vessel or facility, carrying fluids under pressures exceeding 15 psig must—

(a) Meet the ANSI Code;

(b) Have the point of connection to the integral piping system of the vessel or facility clearly marked; and

(c) Be tested after every repair, modification, or alteration to the pressure boundaries as set forth in § 197.462.

§ 197.338 Compressed gas cylinders.

Each compressed gas cylinder must—

(a) Be stored in a ventilated area;

§ 197.340

(b) Be protected from excessive heat;
(c) Be prevented from falling;
(d) Be tested after any repair, modification, or alteration to the pressure boundaries as set forth in § 197.462; and
(e) Meet the requirements of—
(1) Part 54 of this chapter; or
(2) 49 CFR 173.34 and 49 CFR part 178, subpart C.

§ 197.340 Breathing gas supply.

(a) A primary breathing gas supply for surface-supplied diving must be sufficient to support the following for the duration of the planned dive:
(1) The diver.
(2) The standby diver.
(3) The decompression chamber, when required by § 197.432(e)(2) or by § 197.434(a) for the duration of the dive and for one hour after completion of the planned dive.
(4) A decompression chamber when provided but not required by this subpart.
(5) A closed bell when provided or required by § 197.434(d).
(6) An open bell when provided or required by § 197.432(e)(4) or by § 197.434(c).

(b) A secondary breathing gas supply for surface-supplied diving must be sufficient to support the following:
(1) The diver while returning to the surface.
(2) The diver during decompression.
(3) The standby diver.
(4) The decompression chamber when required by § 197.432(e)(2) or by § 197.434(a) for the duration of the dive and one hour after the completion of the planned dive.
(5) The closed bell while returning the diver to the surface.
(6) The open bell while returning the diver to the surface.

(c) A diver-carried reserve breathing gas supply for surface-supplied diving must be sufficient to allow the diver to—
(1) Reach the surface.
(2) Reach another source of breathing gas; or
(3) Be reached by a standby diver equipped with another source of breathing gas for the diver.

(d) A primary breathing gas supply for SCUBA diving must be sufficient to support the diver for the duration of the planned dive through his return to the dive location or planned pick-up point.

(e) A diver-carried reserve breathing gas supply for SCUBA diving must be sufficient to allow the diver to return to the dive location or planned pick-up point from the greatest depth of the planned dive.

(f) Oxygen used for breathing mixtures must—
(1) Meet the requirements of Federal Specification BB-O-925a; and
(2) Be type 1 (gaseous) grade A or B.

(g) Nitrogen used for breathing mixtures must—
(1) Meet the requirements of Federal Specification BB-N-411c;
(2) Be type 1 (gaseous);
(3) Be class 1 (oil free); and
(4) Be grade A, B, or C.

(h) Helium used for breathing mixtures must be grades A, B, or C produced by the Federal Government, or equivalent.

(i) Compressed air used for breathing mixtures must—
(1) Be 20 to 22 percent oxygen by volume;
(2) Have no objectionable odor; and
(3) Have no more than—
(i) 1,000 parts per million of carbon dioxide;
(ii) 20 parts per million carbon monoxide;
(iii) 5 milligrams per cubic meter of solid and liquid particulates including oil; and
(iv) 25 parts per million of hydrocarbons (includes methane and all other hydrocarbons expressed as methane).

§ 197.342 Buoyancy-changing devices.

(a) A dry suit or other buoyancy-changing device not directly connected to the exhaust valve of the helmet or mask must have an independent exhaust valve.

(b) When used for SCUBA diving, a buoyancy-changing device must have an inflation source separate from the breathing gas supply.

§ 197.344 Inflatable floatation devices.

An inflatable floatation device for SCUBA diving must—
(a) Be capable of maintaining the diver at the surface in a faceup position;

(b) Have a manually activated inflation device;
(c) Have an oral inflation device;
(d) Have an over-pressure relief device; and
(e) Have a manually operated exhaust valve.

§ 197.346 Diver's equipment.

(a) Each diver using SCUBA must have—
(1) Self-contained underwater breathing equipment including—
(i) A primary breathing gas supply with a cylinder pressure gage readable by the diver during the dive; and
(ii) A diver-carried reserve breathing gas supply provided by—
(A) A manual reserve (J valve); or
(B) An independent reserve cylinder connected and ready for use;
(2) A face mask;
(3) An inflatable floatation device;
(4) A weight belt capable of quick release;
(5) A knife;
(6) Swim fins or shoes;
(7) A diving wristwatch; and
(8) A depth gage.
(b) Each diver using a heavyweight diving outfit must—
(1) Have a helmet group consisting of helmet, breastplate, and associated valves and connections;
(2) Have a diving dress group consisting of a basic dress that encloses the body (except for head and hands) in a tough, waterproof cover, gloves, shoes, weight assembly, and knife;
(3) Have a hose group consisting of the breathing gas hose and fittings, the control valve, the lifeline, communications cable, and a pneumofathometer; and
(4) Be provided with a helmet cushion and weighted shoes.
(c) Each surface-supplied dive operation using a heavyweight diving outfit must have an extra breathing gas hose with attaching tools available to the standby diver.
(d) Each diver using a lightweight diving outfit must have—
(1) A safety harness;
(2) A weight assembly capable of quick release;
(3) A mask group consisting of a lightweight mask and associated valves and connections;
(4) A diving dress group consisting of wet or dry diving dress, gloves, shoes or fins, and knife; and
(5) A hose group consisting of the breathing gas hose and fittings, the control valve, the lifeline, communications cable, and a pneumofathometer (if the breaking strength of the communications cable is at least equal to that required for the lifeline, the communications cable can serve as the lifeline).
(e) Each surface-supplied air dive operation within the no-decompression limits and to depths of 130 fsw or less must have a primary breathing gas supply at the dive location.
(f) Each surface-supplied dive operation outside the no-compression limits, deeper than 130 fsw, or using mixed-gas as a breathing mixture must have at the dive location—
(1) A primary breathing gas supply; and
(2) A secondary breathing gas supply.
(g) Each diver diving outside the no-decompression limits, deeper than 130 fsw, or using mixed-gas must have a diver-carried reserve breathing gas supply except when using a heavyweight diving outfit or when diving in a physically confining area.

OPERATIONS

§ 197.400 Applicability.

Diving operations may only be conducted from a vessel or facility subject to the subpart if the regulations in this subpart are met.

§ 197.402 Responsibilities of the person-in-charge.

(a) The person-in-charge shall—
(1) Be fully cognizant of the provisions of this subpart;
(2) Prior to permitting any commercial diving operation to commence, have—
(i) The designation of the diving supervisor for each diving operation as required by § 197.210;
(ii) A report on—
(A) The nature and planned times of the planned diving operation; and
(B) The planned involvement of the vessel or facility, its equipment, and its personnel in the diving operation.

§ 197.404

(b) Prior to permitting any commerical diving operation involving liveboating to commence, the person-in-charge shall insure that—

(1) A means of rapid communications with the diving supervisor while the diver is entering, in, or leaving the water is established; and

(2) A boat and crew for diver pickup in the event of an emergency is provided.

(c) The person-in-charge shall insure that a boat and crew for SCUBA diver pickup is provided when SCUBA divers are not line-tended from the dive location.

(d) The person-in-charge shall coordinate the activities on and of the vessel or facility with the diving supervisor.

(e) The person-in-charge shall insure that the vessel or facility equipment and personnel are kept clear of the dive location except after coordinating with the diving supervisor.

§ 197.404 Responsibilities of the diving supervisor.

(a) The diving supervisor shall—

(1) Be fully cognizant of the provisions of this subpart;

(2) Be fully cognizant of the provisions of the operations manual required by § 197.420;

(3) Insure that diving operations conducted from a vessel or facility subject to this subpart meet the regulations in this subpart;

(4) Prior to the commencement of any commercial diving operation, provide the report required by § 197.402 to the person-in-charge;

(5) Coordinate with the person-in-charge any changes that are made to the report required by § 197.402; and

(6) Promptly notify the person-in-charge of any diving related casualty, accident, or injury.

(b) The diving supervisor is in charge of the planning and execution of the diving operation including the responsibility for the safety and health of the dive team.

§ 197.410 Dive procedures.

(a) The diving supervisor shall insure that—

(1) Before commencing diving operations, dive team members are briefed on—

46 CFR Ch. I (10-1-04 Edition)

(i) The tasks to be undertaken;

(ii) Any unusual hazards or environmental conditions likely to affect the safety of the diving operation; and

(iii) Any modifications to the operations manual or procedures including safety procedures necessitated by the specific diving operation;

(2) The breathing gas supply systems, masks, helmets, thermal protection, when provided, and bell lifting equipment, when a bell is provided or required, are inspected prior to each diving operation;

(3) Each diver is instructed to report any physical problems or physiological effects including aches, pains, current illnesses, or symptoms of decompression sickness prior to each dive;

(4) A depth, bottom time profile, including any breathing mixture changes, is maintained at the dive location for each diver during the dive, except that SCUBA divers shall maintain their own profiles;

(5) A two-way voice communication system is used between—

(i) Each surface-supplied diver and a dive team member at the dive location or bell (when provided); and

(ii) The bell (when provided) and the dive location;

(6) A two-way communication system is available at the dive location to obtain emergency assistance;

(7) After the completion of each dive—

(i) The physical condition of the diver is checked by—

(A) Visual observation; and

(B) Questioning the diver about his physical well-being;

(ii) The diver is instructed to report any physical problems or adverse physiological effects including aches, pains, current illnesses, or symptoms of decompression sickness or gas embolism;

(iii) The diver is advised of the location of an operational decompression chamber; and

(iv) The diver is alerted to the potential hazards of flying after diving;

(8) For any dive outside the no-decompression limits, deeper than 130 fsw, or using mixed-gas as a breathing mixture—

(i) A depth, time, decompression profile including breathing mixture

432

changes is maintained for each diver at the dive location;

(ii) The diver is instructed to remain awake and in the vicinity of the dive location decompression chamber for at least one hour after the completion of a dive, decompression, or treatment; and

(iii) A dive team member, other than the diver, is trained and available to operate the decompression chamber; and

(9) When decompression sickness or gas embolism is suspected or symptoms are evident, a report is completed containing—

(i) The investigation for each incident including—

(A) The dive and decompression profiles;

(B) The composition, depth, and time of breathing mixture changes;

(C) A description of the symptoms including depth and time of onset; and

(D) A description and results of the treatment;

(ii) The evaluation for each incident based on—

(A) The investigation;

(B) Consideration of the past performance of the decompression table used; and

(C) Individual susceptibility; and

(iii) The corrective action taken, if necessary, to reduce the probability of recurrence.

(b) The diving supervisor shall ensure that the working interval of a dive is terminated when he so directs or when—

(1) A diver requests termination;

(2) A diver fails to respond correctly to communications or signals from a dive team member;

(3) Communications are lost and can not be quickly reestablished between—

(i) The diver and a dive team member at the dive location; or

(ii) The person-in-charge and the diving supervisor during liveboating operations; or

(4) A diver begins to use his diver-carried reserve breathing gas supply.

§ 197.420 Operations manual.

(a) The diving supervisor shall—

(1) Provide an operations manual to the person-in-charge prior to commencement of any diving operation; and

(2) Make an operations manual available at the dive location to all members of the dive team.

(b) The operations manual must be modified in writing when adaptation is required because of—

(1) The configuration or operation of the vessel or facility; or

(2) The specific diving operation as planned.

(c) The operations manual must provide for the safety and health of the divers.

(d) The operations manual must contain the following:

(1) Safety procedures and checklists for each diving mode used.

(2) Assignments and responsibilities of each dive team member for each diving mode used.

(3) Equipment procedures and checklists for each diving mode used.

(4) Emergency procedures for—

(i) Fire;

(ii) Equipment failure;

(iii) Adverse environmental conditions including, but not limited to, weather and sea state;

(iv) Medical illness; and

(v) Treatment of injury.

(5) Procedures dealing with the use of—

(i) Hand-held power tools;

(ii) Welding and burning equipment; and

(iii) Explosives.

SPECIFIC DIVING MODE PROCEDURES

§ 197.430 SCUBA diving.

The diving supervisor shall insure that—

(a) SCUBA diving is not conducted—

(1) Outside the no-decompression limits;

(2) At depths greater than 130 fsw;

(3) Against currents greater than one (1) knot unless line-tended; and

(4) If a diver cannot directly ascend to the surface unless line-tended;

(b) The SCUBA diver has the equipment required by § 197.346(a);

(c) A standby diver is available while a diver is in the water;

(d) A diver is line-tended from the surface or accompanied by another diver in the water in continuous visual contact during the diving operation;

§ 197.432

(e) When a diver is in a physically confining space, another diver is stationed at the underwater point of entry and is line-tending the diver; and

(f) A boat is available for diver pickup when the divers are not line-tended from the dive location.

§ 197.432 Surface-supplied air diving.

The diving supervisor shall insure that—

(a) Surface-supplied air diving is conducted at depths less than 190 fsw, except that dives with bottom times of 30 minutes or less may be conducted to depths of 220 fsw;

(b) Each diving operation has a primary breathing gas supply;

(c) Each diver is continuously tended while in the water;

(d) When a diver is in a physically confining space, another diver is stationed at the underwater point of entry and is line-tending the diver;

(e) For dives deeper than 130 fsw or outside the no-decompression limits—

(1) Each diving operation has a secondary breathing gas supply;

(2) A decompression chamber is ready for use at the dive location;

(3) A diving stage is used except when a bell is provided;

(4) A bell is used for dives with an in-water decompression time greater than 120 minutes, except when the diver is using a heavy-weight diving outfit or is diving in a physically confining space;

(5) A separate dive team member tends each diver in the water;

(6) A standby diver is available while a diver is in the water; and

(7) Each diver has a diver-carried reserve breathing gas supply except when using a heavy-weight diving outfit or when diving in a physically confining space; and

(f) The surface-supplied air diver has the equipment required by § 197.346 (b) or (d).

§ 197.434 Surface-supplied mixed-gas diving.

The diving supervisor shall insure that—

(a) When mixed-gas diving is conducted, a decompression chamber or a closed bell meeting the requirements of § 197.332 is ready for use at the dive location;

(b) A diving stage is used except when a bell is provided;

(c) A bell is used for dives deeper than 220 fsw or when the dive involves in-water decompression times greater than 120 minutes, except when the diver is using a heavy-weight diving outfit or is diving in a physically confining space;

(d) A closed bell is used for dives at depths greater than 300 fsw, except when diving is conducted in a physically confining space;

(e) A separate dive team member tends each diver in the water;

(f) A standby diver is available during all nonsaturation dives;

(g) When saturation diving is conducted—

(1) A standby diver is available when the closed bell leaves the dive location until the divers are in saturation; and

(2) A member of the dive team at the dive location is a diver able to assist in the recovery of the closed bell or its occupants, if required;

(h) When closed bell operations are conducted, a diver is available in the closed bell to assist a diver in the water;

(i) When a diver is in a physically confining space, another diver is stationed at the underwater point of entry and is line-tending the diver;

(j) Each diving operation has a primary and secondary breathing gas supply meeting the requirements of § 197.340; and

(k) The surface-supplied mixed-gas diver has the equipment required by § 197.346 (b) or (d).

§ 197.436 Liveboating.

(a) During liveboating operations, the person-in-charge shall insure that—

(1) Diving is not conducted in seas that impede station-keeping ability of the vessel;

(2) Liveboating operations are not conducted—

(i) From 1 hour after sunset to 1 hour before sunrise; or

(ii) During periods of restricted visibility;

(3) The propellers of the vessel are stopped before the diver enters or exits the water; and

Coast Guard, DHS

§ 197.456

(4) A boat is ready to be launched with crew in the event of an emergency.

(b) As used in paragraph (a)(2)(ii) of this section, *restricted visibility* means any condition in which vessel navigational visibility is restricted by fog, mist, falling snow, heavy rainstorms, sandstorms or any other similar causes.

(c) During liveboating operations, the diving supervisor shall insure that—

(1) Diving is not conducted at depths greater than 220 fsw;

(2) Diving is not conducted in seas that impede diver mobility or work function;

(3) A means is used to prevent the diver's hose from entangling in the propellers of the vessel;

(4) Each diver carries a reserve breathing gas supply;

(5) A standby diver is available while a diver is in the water;

(6) Diving is not conducted with in-water decompression times greater than 120 minutes; and

(7) The person-in-charge is notified before a diver enters or exits the water.

PERIODIC TESTS AND INSPECTIONS OF DIVING EQUIPMENT

§ 197.450 Breathing gas tests.

The diving supervisor shall insure that—

(a) The output of each air compressor is tested and meets the requirements of § 197.340 for quality and quantity by means of samples taken at the connection point to the distribution system—

(1) Every 6 months; and

(2) After every repair or modification.

(b) Purchased supplies of breathing mixtures supplied to a diver are checked before being placed on line for—

(1) Certification that the supply meets the requirements of § 197.340; and

(2) Noxious or offensive odor and oxygen percentage;

(c) Each breathing supply system is checked, prior to commencement of diving operations, at the umbilical or underwater breathing apparatus connection point for the diver, for noxious or offensive odor and presence of oil mist; and

(d) Each breathing supply system, supplying mixed-gas to a diver, is checked, prior to commencement of diving operations, at the umbilical or underwater breathing apparatus connection point for the diver, for percentage of oxygen.

§ 197.452 Oxygen cleaning.

The diving supervisor shall ensure that equipment used with oxygen or oxygen mixtures greater than 40 percent by volume is cleaned of flammable materials—

(a) Before being placed into service; and

(b) After any repair, alteration, modification, or suspected contamination.

§ 197.454 First aid and treatment equipment.

The diving supervisor shall ensure that medical kits are checked monthly to insure that all required supplies are present.

§ 197.456 Breathing supply hoses.

(a) The diving supervisor shall insure that—

(1) Each breathing supply hose is pressure tested prior to being placed into initial service and every 24 months thereafter to 1.5 times its maximum working pressure;

(2) Each breathing supply hose assembly, prior to being placed into initial service and after any repair, modification, or alteration, is tensile tested by—

(i) Subjecting each hose-to-fitting connection to a 200 pound axial load; and

(ii) Passing a visual examination for evidence of separation, slippage, or other damage to the assembly;

(3) Each breathing supply hose is periodically checked for—

(i) Damage which is likely to affect pressure integrity; and

(ii) Contamination which is likely to affect the purity of the breathing mixture delivered to the diver; and

(4) The open ends of each breathing supply hose are taped, capped, or plugged when not in use.

(b) To meet the requirements of paragraph (a)(3) of this section, each breathing supply hose must be—

§ 197.458

(1) Carefully inspected before being shipped to the dive location;
(2) Visually checked during daily operation; and
(3) Checked for noxious or offensive odor before each diving operation.

§ 197.458 Gages and timekeeping devices.

The diving supervisor shall insure that—

(a) Each depth gage and timekeeping device is tested or calibrated against a master reference gage or time-keeping device every 6 months;

(b) A depth gage is tested when a discrepancy exists in a depth gage reading greater than 2 percent of full scale between any two gages of similar range and calibration;

(c) A timekeeping device is tested when a discrepancy exists in a timekeeping device reading greater than one-quarter of a minute in a 4-hour period between any two timekeeping devices; and

(d) Each depth gage and timekeeping device is inspected before diving operations are begun.

§ 197.460 Diving equipment.

The diving supervisor shall insure that the diving equipment designated for use in a dive under § 197.346 is inspected before each dive.

§ 197.462 Pressure vessels and pressure piping.

(a) The diving supervisor shall ensure that each pressure vessel, including each volume tank, cylinder and PVHO, and each pressure piping system is examined and tested as required by this section and after any repair, modification or alteration to determine that they are in satisfactory condition and fit for the service intended.

(b) Pressure vessels and pressure piping shall be examined annually for mechanical damage or deterioration. Any defect that may impair the safety of the pressure vessel or piping shall be repaired and pressure tested to the satisfaction of the Officer in Charge, Marine Inspection.

(c) The following tests shall be conducted at least every three years:

(1) All piping permanently installed on a PVHO shall be pressure tested.

(2) PVHOs subject to internal pressure shall be leak tested at the maximum allowable working pressure using the breathing mixture normally used in service.

(3) Equivalent nondestructive testing may be conducted in lieu of pressure testing. Proposals to use nondestructive testing in lieu of pressure testing shall be submitted to the Officer in Charge, Marine Inspection.

(d) Unless otherwise noted, pressure tests conducted in accordance with this section shall be either hydrostatic tests or pneumatic tests.

(1) When a hydrostatic test is conducted on a pressure vessel, the test pressure shall be no less than 1.25 times the maximum allowable working pressure.

(2) When a pneumatic test is conducted on a pressure vessel, the test pressure shall be the maximum allowable working pressure stamped on the nameplate.

(3) When a pneumatic test is conducted on piping, the test pressure shall be no less than 90 percent of the setting of the relief device.

(4) Pressure tests shall be conducted only after suitable precautions are taken to protect personnel and equipment.

(5) When pressure tests are conducted on pressure vessels or pressure piping, the test pressure shall be maintained for a period of time sufficient to allow examination of all joints, connections and high stress areas.

[CGD 95–028, 62 FR 51220, Sept. 30, 1997]

RECORDS

§ 197.480 Logbooks.

(a) The person-in-charge of a vessel or facility, that is required by 46 U.S.C. 11301 to have an official logbook, shall maintain the logbook on form CG–706.

(b) The person-in-charge of a vessel or facility not required by 46 U.S.C. 11301 to have an official logbook, shall maintain, on board, a logbook for making the entries required by this subpart.

(c) The diving supervisor conducting commercial diving operations from a

Coast Guard, DHS § 197.482

vessel or facility subject to this subpart shall maintain a logbook for making the entries required by this subpart.

[CGD 76–009, 43 FR 53683, Nov. 16, 1978, as amended by CGD 95–028, 62 FR 51220, Sept. 30, 1997]

§ 197.482 Logbook entries.

(a) The person-in-charge shall insure that the following information is recorded in the logbook for each commercial diving operation:

(1) Date, time, and location at the start and completion of dive operations.

(2) Approximate underwater and surface conditions (weather, visibility, temperatures, and currents).

(3) Name of the diving supervisor.

(4) General nature of work performed.

(b) The diving supervisor shall insure that the following information is recorded in the logbook for each commercial diving operation:

(1) Date, time, and location at the start and completion of each dive operation.

(2) Approximate underwater and surface conditions (weather, visibility, temperatures, and currents).

(3) Names of dive team members including diving supervisor.

(4) General nature of work performed.

(5) Repetitive dive designation or elapsed time since last hyperbaric exposure if less than 24 hours for each diver.

(6) Diving modes used.

(7) Maximum depth and bottom time for each diver.

(8) Name of person-in-charge.

(9) For each dive outside the no-decompression limits, deeper than 130 fsw, or using mixed-gas, the breathing gases and decompression table designations used.

(10) When decompression sickness or gas embolism is suspected or symptoms are evident—

(i) The name of the diver; and

(ii) A description and results of treatment.

(11) For each fatality or any diving related injury or illness that results in incapacitation of more than 72 hours or requires any dive team member to be hospitalized for more than 24 hours—

(i) The date;

(ii) Time;

(iii) Circumstances; and

(iv) Extent of any injury or illness.

(c) The diving supervisor shall insure that the following is recorded in the logbook for each diving operation deviating from the requirements of this subpart:

(1) A description of the circumstances leading to the situation.

(2) The deviations made.

(3) The corrective action taken, if appropriate, to reduce the possibility of recurrence.

(d) The diving supervisor shall insure that a record of the following is maintained:

(1) The date and results of each check of the medical kits.

(2) The date and results of each test of the air compressor.

(3) The date and results of each check of breathing mixtures.

(4) The date and results of each check of each breathing supply system.

(5) The date, equipment cleaned, general cleaning procedure, and names of persons cleaning the diving equipment for oxygen service.

(6) The date and results of each test of the breathing supply hoses and system.

(7) The date and results of each inspection of the breathing gas supply system.

(8) The date and results of each test of depth gages and timekeeping devices.

(9) The date and results of each test and inspection of each PVHO.

(10) The date and results of each inspection of the diving equipment.

(11) The date and results of each test and inspection of pressure piping.

(12) The date and results of each test and inspection of volume tanks and cylinders.

(e) The diving supervisor shall insure that a notation concerning the location of the information required under paragraph (d) is made in the logbook.

NOTE: 46 U.S.C. 11301 requires that certain entries be made in an official logbook in addition to the entries required by this section; and 46 U.S.C. 11302 prescribes the manner of making those entries.

[CGD 76–009, 43 FR 53683, Nov. 16, 1978, as amended by USCG–1999–6216, 64 FR 53229, Oct. 1, 1999]

§ 197.484 Notice of casualty.

(a) In addition to the requirements of subpart 4.05 of this chapter and 33 CFR 146.30, the person-in-charge shall notify the Officer-in-Charge, Marine Inspection, as soon as possible after a diving casualty occurs, if the casualty involves any of the following:

(1) Loss of life.

(2) Diving-related injury to any person causing incapacitation for more than 72 hours.

(3) Diving-related injury to any person requiring hospitalization for more than 24 hours.

(b) The notice required by this section must contain the following:

(1) Name and official number (if applicable) of the vessel or facility.

(2) Name of the owner or agent of the vessel or facility.

(3) Name of the person-in-charge.

(4) Name of the diving supervisor.

(5) Description of the casualty including presumed cause.

(6) Nature and extent of the injury to persons.

(c) The notice required by this section is not required if the written report required by § 197.486 is submitted within 5 days of the casualty.

[CGD 76–009, 43 FR 53683, Nov. 16, 1978, as amended by CGD 95–072, 60 FR 50469, Sept. 29, 1995]

§ 197.486 Written report of casualty.

The person-in-charge of a vessel or facility for which a notice of casualty was made under § 197.484 shall submit a report to the Officer-in-Charge, Marine Inspection, as soon as possible after the casualty occurs, as follows:

(a) On Form CG–2692, when the diving installation is on a vessel.

(b) Using a written report, in narrative form, when the diving installation is on a facility. The written report must contain the information required by § 197.484.

(c) The report required by this section must be accompanied by a copy of the report required by § 197.410(a)(9) when decompression sickness is involved.

(d) The report required by this section must include information relating to alcohol or drug involvement as required by § 4.05–12 of this chapter.

(The reporting requirement in paragraph (a) was approved by OMB under control number 2115–0003)

[CGD 76–009, 43 FR 53683, Nov. 16, 1978, as amended by CGD 82–023, 47 FR 35748, Aug. 16, 1982; 48 FR 43328, Sept. 23, 1983; CGD 84–099, 52 FR 47536, Dec. 14, 1987]

§ 197.488 Retention of records after casualty.

(a) The owner, agent, or person-in-charge of a vessel or facility for which a report of casualty is made under § 197.484 shall retain all records onboard that are maintained on the vessel or facility and those records required by this subpart for 6 months after the report of a casualty is made or until advised by the Officer-in-Charge, Marine Inspection, that records need not be retained onboard.

(b) The records required by paragraph (a) of this section to be retained on board include, but are not limited to, the following:

(1) All logbooks required by § 197.480.

(2) All reports required by § 197.402(a)(2)(ii), § 197.404(a)(4), § 197.410(a)(9).

(c) The owner, agent, person-in-charge, or diving supervisor shall, upon request, make the records described in this section available for examination by any Coast Guard official authorized to investigate the casualty.

Subpart C—Benzene

Source: CGD 88–040, 56 FR 52135, Oct. 17, 1991, unless otherwise noted.

§ 197.501 Applicability.

(a) Except for vessels satisfying paragraph (b) of this section, this subpart applies to all Coast Guard inspected vessels, including tank ships and barges, that are carrying benzene or benzene containing liquids in bulk as cargo.

(b) This subpart does not apply to vessels that are carrying only liquid cargoes containing less than 0.5% benzene by volume.

Coast Guard, DHS § 197.510

(c) This subpart does not apply to vessels of foreign registry.

[CGD 88–040, 56 FR 52135, Oct. 17, 1991; 56 FR 65006, Dec. 13, 1991]

§ 197.505 Definitions.

As used in this subpart—

Action level means an airborne concentration of benzene of 0.5 parts of benzene per million parts of air calculated as an eight hour time-weighted average, generated from vessels regulated by this subpart.

Authorized person means a person specifically authorized by the person in charge of the vessel to enter a regulated area.

Benzene means liquefied or gaseous benzene (C_6H_6; Chemical Abstracts Service Registry No. 71–43–2) and includes benzene contained in liquid mixtures and the benzene vapors released by these mixtures. The term does not include trace amounts of unreacted benzene contained in solid materials.

Breathing zone means the area within one foot of a person's mouth and nose.

Employee means an individual who is on board a vessel by reason of that individual's employment and who is employed directly by the owner, charterer, managing operator, or agent of that vessel.

Employer means the owner, charterer, managing operator, or agent of a vessel.

Emergency means an occurrence, such as an equipment failure, a container rupture, or a control equipment failure, which results or may result in an unexpected release of benzene.

Operations involving benzene means any operation that could subject a worker to benzene exposures above the PEL, including cargo transfer operations involving connecting or disconnecting liquid or vapor hoses; cargo tank gauging and sampling; and cargo tank gas freeing, venting, and cleaning.

Performance standard means the standard in § 197.520.

Person in charge means—

(1) For a self propelled vessel, the master or licensed operator of the vessel; and

(2) For an unmanned barge,

(i) The licensed operator of the vessel for barge tows;

(ii) Where there is no licensed operator, the tankerman who signs the declaration of inspection for a cargo transfer for an operation involving benzene; or

(iii) Where there is no licensed operator or tankerman, the individual in charge of the vessel when it is moored at a fleet, terminal, or other place.

Permissible exposure limits or *PELs* mean the exposure limits specified in § 197.515.

Personal exposure means the concentration of airborne benzene to which a person would be exposed if that person were not using a properly fitted respirator in compliance with § 197.550 and the personal protective clothing and equipment in compliance with § 197.555.

Regulated area means an area designated in compliance with § 197.535.

Short-term exposure limit or *STEL* means an airborne concentration of five parts of benzene per million parts of air (five ppm), as averaged over any 15 minute period.

Time-weighted average exposure limit or *TWA* means an airborne concentration of one part of benzene per million parts of air (one ppm), as averaged over an eight-hour period. This eight hour period covers the time, up to eight hours, that the employee works in any 24 hour period. If the exposure period is less than eight hours within the 24 hour period, the difference between eight hours and the time of exposure (that is, the unexposed time) is averaged into the TWA. If the exposure period exceeds eight hours in any 24 hour period, sum the products of each exposure level multiplied by the time at that exposure level. The TWA is the value of that sum divided by eight hours.

Vapor control or recovery system means a system of piping and equipment used to collect vapors by transporting the vapors from a tank being loaded to a tank being unloaded or by collecting the vapors and containing them, recovering them, dispersing them in a location remote from personnel, or destroying them.

§ 197.510 Incorporation by reference.

(a) Certain materials are incorporated by reference into this subpart with the approval of the Director of the

§ 197.515

Federal Register in accordance with 5 U.S.C. 522(a) and 1 CFR part 51. To enforce any edition other than the one listed in paragraph (b) of this section, notice of the change must be published in the FEDERAL REGISTER and the material made available to the public. All approved material is on file at U.S. Coast Guard, Office of Operating and Environmental Standards (G-MSO), 2100 Second Street, SW., Washington, DC 20593-0001 and at the National Archives and Records Administration (NARA). For information on the availability of this material at NARA, call 202-741-6030, or go to: *http://www.archives.gov/federal_register/code_of_federal_regulations/ibr_locations.html*. All approved material is available from the sources indicated in paragraph (b) of this section.

(b) The material approved for incorporation by reference in this subpart and the sections affected are as follows:

American National Standards Institute (ANSI)

11 West 42nd Street, New York, NY 10036

ANSI Z 88.2—1980—Practices for Respiratory Protection ....§ 197.550

[CGD 88-040, 56 FR 52135, Oct. 17, 1991, as amended by CGD 95-072, 60 FR 50469, Sept. 29, 1995; CGD 96-041, 61 FR 50735, Sept. 27, 1996; 61 FR 52497, Oct. 7, 1996; 69 FR 18803, Apr. 9, 2004]

§ 197.515 Permissible exposure limits (PELs).

The permissible exposure limits (PELs) for personal exposure are as follows:

(a) The time-weighted average exposure limit (TWA).

(b) The short-term exposure limit (STEL). Exposures at the STEL must not be repeated more than four times a day. There must be at least 60 minutes between successive exposures at the STEL.

§ 197.520 Performance standard.

No person may be subjected to a personal exposure in excess of the permissible exposure limits unless respiratory protection is used.

§ 197.525 Responsibility of the person in charge.

Unless otherwise specified, the person in charge shall ensure that the performance standard and other requirements of this subpart are complied with on that person's vessel.

§ 197.530 Persons other than employees.

(a) Before a nonemployee (other than Federal, state, and local government personnel) engages in a benzene operation on a vessel in which the person is likely to be exposed to benzene in excess of the PELs, that person must certify that—

(1) That person has had, within the previous 12 months, at least one medical examination in compliance with § 197.560 or 29 CFR 1910.1028;

(2) The physician who performed or who supervised the latest medical examination in compliance with paragraph (a)(1) of this section did not recommend that that person be excluded from areas where personal exposure may exceed the action level;

(3) All respirators and personal protective clothing and equipment that will be used by that person while on the vessel meet the requirements of § 197.550(b) and § 197.555(c) or of 29 CFR 1910.1028; and

(4) All respirators that will be used by that person while on the vessel have been fitted and fit tested in accordance with § 197.550 (c) and (d) or with 29 CFR 1910.1028.

NOTE: The employer need not furnish the required respirators and personal protective clothing and equipment to nonemployees.

(b) The certification required by paragraph (a) of this section must be in writing, list the items in paragraphs (a)(1) through (a)(4) of this section, reference 46 CFR 197.530, state the date of the certification, and be signed by the person making the certification. A sample certification form is contained in appendix F of this subpart.

(c) Before the nonemployee making the certification engages in a benzene operation on a vessel, that person or a representative of the entity which employs that person must show a copy of the certification to the person in charge of the vessel and the person in charge must examine the certification to ensure compliance with the requirements of this section.

§ 197.535 Regulated areas.

(a) Based on the employer's evaluation of the environmental monitoring, whenever the airborne concentration of benzene within an area exceeds or reasonably can be expected to exceed the permissible exposure limits, the person in charge shall mark the area as a regulated area.

(b) The person in charge shall restrict access to regulated areas to authorized persons wearing an appropriate respirator in compliance with § 197.550 and the personal protective clothing and equipment in compliance with § 197.555. The person in charge shall not allow any person to enter a regulated area without another individual in the vicinity to perform rescue or call for help. The second individual must maintain communication with the one entering the regulated area or keep that individual in sight. Also, the second individual must be located at the point of access during confined space entry.

(c) The boundaries of regulated areas must be indicated by barricades, other devices, or by painted areas on the vessel. A sign bearing the following legend in letters at least three inches high (except for the words "DANGER—BENZENE", which must be printed in letters at least 50 percent larger than the other words) must be posted at each access to the regulated areas:

DANGER—BENZENE

REGULATED AREA

CANCER CAUSING AGENT

FLAMMABLE—NO SMOKING

AUTHORIZED PERSONNEL ONLY

RESPIRATOR REQUIRED

§ 197.540 Determination of personal exposure.

(a) *General.* (1) The employer shall ensure that one or more persons in each type of operation conducted on the vessel which involves the handling of or potential exposure to benzene are monitored. The monitoring must be conducted so as to determine the representative personal exposure of all persons engaged in each particular operation involving benzene. Monitoring one vessel of a class is sufficient for all vessels of that class provided the procedures, equipment, work practices, cargo, and control equipment are substantially the same.

(2) For long duration operations, such as cargo loading or tank entry, the persons monitored must be monitored to determine the representative TWA for all persons engaged in the operation. The monitoring must be based on breathing zone air samples taken for the duration of the operation or for eight hours, whichever is less.

(3) For short duration operations, such as tank gauging or hose connection and disconnection, the persons monitored must be monitored to determine the representative short term exposure level for all persons engaged in the operation. The monitoring must be based on 15 minute breathing zone air samples. Brief period measuring devices may be used to determine whether monitoring for the short term exposure level is needed.

(4) If cargoes with different benzene concentrations are being carried on the vessel, an operation involving the lower concentration cargoes need not be monitored if the same type of operation involving the highest concentration cargo is monitored and found to be below the action level.

(5) Initial monitoring must be conducted during weather conditions typical in the geographic area and during the time of day the operation is normally conducted. If the benzene level is above half the action level for the operation, additional monitoring must be conducted under those weather conditions that will maximize benzene exposure, such as low wind, stable air, and high temperature.

(6) The monitoring method used must be accurate to a confidence level of 95 percent to within plus or minus 25 percent for airborne concentrations of benzene equal to or greater than 0.5 ppm.

(b) *Initial exposure monitoring.* When benzene is first loaded as a cargo on board a vessel, an initial monitoring of each type of operation must be conducted to determine accurately the representative personal exposure of persons involved in the operation.

§ 197.545

(c) *Periodic exposure monitoring.* The monitoring must be repeated each July or August if benzene containing cargoes are carried during those months; monitoring must be conducted under those weather conditions that will maximize benzene exposure, such as low wind, stable air, and high temperature. If benzene containing cargoes are not carried during those months, monitoring must be conducted at the time of carriage nearest those months; monitoring must be conducted under those weather conditions that will maximize benzene exposure, such as low wind, stable air, and high temperature.

(d) *Additional exposure monitoring.* (1) Monitoring in compliance with paragraphs (b) and (c) of this section must be repeated for the operation when there has been a change in the procedure, equipment, or work practices of the operation which may increase personal exposure or whenever the employer or person in charge has any reason to suspect that personal exposure has increased.

(2) Whenever emergencies occur that may increase personal exposure, operations affected by the emergency must be monitored using area or personal sampling after the spill is cleaned up or the leak, rupture, or other breakdown is repaired to determine when personal exposure has returned to the level that existed before the emergency. There must be monitoring equipment aboard each ship.

(3) For those cases in which the benzene exposure can vary significantly over the year, the personnel exposure reduction plan can reflect this variation in time if both initial and periodic exposure monitoring are conducted at those times. There must be sufficient monitoring to quantitatively justify differences in the exposure reduction program over the course of the year. The exposure monitoring must be conducted under those weather conditions that will maximize benzene exposure, such as low wind, stable air, and high temperature.

(4) The Coast Guard may require additional monitoring upon reasonable belief that the PEL's are being exceeded.

(e) *Notification of exposure monitoring results.* (1) Within 60 working days after the receipt of the results of monitoring in compliance with this section, each person involved in the operation monitored must be given written notice of the results, either by separate letter or by notice posted in a location accessible to all persons involved.

(2) If the results indicate that the PELs were exceeded, the written notice required by paragraph (e)(1) of this section must state, or refer to a document available to the persons involved which states, the corrective action to be taken to reduce the personal exposure to or below the PELs.

[CGD 88–040, 56 FR 52135, Oct. 17, 1991; 56 FR 65006, Dec. 13, 1991; CGD 95–028, 62 FR 51221, Sept. 30, 1997]

§ 197.545 Program to reduce personal exposure.

(a) When personal exposure for an operation is over the applicable PEL as determined in compliance with § 197.540, the employer shall develop and implement, within 60 working days of the date of that determination, a written program detailing the corrective actions that will be taken to reduce personal exposure to or below the PEL's. The written program must include a timeframe for implementing the corrective actions to be taken.

(b) Corrective actions in compliance with paragraph (a) of this section may include, but are not limited to, one or more of the following:

(1) Engineering controls (e.g. vapor control or recovery systems, closed loading systems, or controlled venting systems);

(2) Revised work practices; or

(3) Respirators in compliance with § 197.550 and personal protective clothing and equipment in compliance with § 197.555.

(c) Whenever the exposure monitoring data show a significant increase in personnel exposure, the program must be revised to reflect the new data.

(d) Each person involved in the operation must be notified that a written program detailing corrective actions is available upon request.

(e) A copy of the written program must be furnished upon request to the Coast Guard.

§ 197.550 Respiratory protection.

(a) *General.* When the use of respirators in compliance with this section and the personal protective clothing and equipment in compliance with § 197.555 is chosen as the method or one of the methods in compliance with § 197.545 to be used in meeting the performance standard, the respirators used must be selected and fitted according to this section.

(b) *Respirator selection.* (1) The respirator must be approved by the Mine Safety and Health Administration (MSHA) in compliance with 30 CFR part 11. When filter elements are used, they must include MSHA approval for organic vapors or benzene.

(2) The employer shall provide affected employees with the appropriate respirators without charge and ensure that the respirators are used properly. Any employee determined by the testing physician as being unable to wear negative pressure respirators, who continues to be subject to exposure over the PEL, must be given the option of wearing a respirator with less breathing resistance, such as a powered air-purifying respirator or a supplied air respirator.

(3) Electrically powered respiratory protective equipment must meet the electrical engineering requirements in subchapter J of this chapter and the electrical equipment requirements in part 151, table 151.05, and part 153, table 1, of this chapter.

(4) The type of respirator provided must be a type specified in table 197.550(b) of this section that is appropriate for the exposure.

TABLE 197.550(b)—RESPIRATORY PROTECTION FOR BENZENE

Airborne concentration of benzene or condition of use	Respirator type
Up to 10 times the TWA	(1) Half-mask air-purifying respirator with organic vapor cartridges.
Up to 50 times the TWA	(1) Full facepiece respirator with organic vapor cartridges. (2) Full facepiece gas mask with chin style canister.[1]
Up to 100 times the TWA	(1) Full facepiece powered air purifying respirator with organic vapor canister.[1]
Up to 1,000 times the TWA	(1) Supplied air respirator with full facepiece in positive-pressure mode.

TABLE 197.550(b)—RESPIRATORY PROTECTION FOR BENZENE—Continued

Airborne concentration of benzene or condition of use	Respirator type
More than 1,000 times the TWA or unknown concentration.	(1) Self-contained breathing apparatus with full facepiece in positive pressure mode. (2) Full facepiece positive-pressure supplied-air respirator with auxiliary self-contained air supply.
Escape	(1) Any organic vapor gas mask. (2) Any self-contained breathing apparatus with full facepiece
Fire fighting	(1) Full facepiece self-contained breathing apparatus in positive pressure mode.

[1] Canisters for non-powered air purifying respirators must have a minimum service life of four hours when tested at 150 ppm benzene, at a flow rate of 64 liters/minute at 25°C and 85% relative humidity. Canisters for powered air-purifying respirators must have a flow rate of 115 liters/minute (for tight fitting respirators) or 170 liters/minute (for loose fitting respirators).

(c) *Respirator fit testing.* (1) Before the person is permitted to use a respirator selected and fitted in compliance with this section, the person must undergo an Initial Fit Test (IFT) and either a Qualitative Fit Test (QLFT) or a Quantitative Fit Test (QNFT), in compliance with Appendix E of this subpart, using the respirator fitted. If a negative pressure respirator is used, the QLFT or QNFT must be repeated at least once a year thereafter.

(2) The objective of the tests is to identify for the person a respirator which minimizes the chance of leakage.

(3) The person conducting the tests required by paragraph (c)(1) of this section must understand the purpose of these tests and how to perform them.

(4) The person conducting the tests required by paragraph (c)(1) of this section must certify the results by signing the test report.

(d) *Respirator fitting.* (1) Employees who are being fitted for respirators must be trained in the methods for properly fitting a respirator and informed of the factors which may affect a proper fit, such as beards, sideburns, dentures, eyeglasses, and goggles, and that an unobstructed sealing surface is critical in fitting a respirator. (See appendix E of this subpart).

(2) For employees requiring eye glasses, corrective lenses should be

§ 197.555

fitted to the respirator faceplate. As a temporary measure, glasses with short temple bars may be taped to the wearer's head. Contact lenses other than soft lenses or gas permeable lenses must not be worn with respirators.

(e) *Respirator use.* Persons wearing a respirator in a regulated area must be permitted to leave the regulated area to wash their face and respirator facepiece, as necessary, in order to prevent skin irritation associated with respirator use or, if an air-purifying respirator is used, to change the filter elements whenever the person wearing the respirator detects a change in breathing resistance or a chemical vapor breakthrough.

(f) *Respirator inspection.* Respirators must be inspected in accordance with ANSI Z88.2—1980, section 8.

(g) *Respirator maintenance.* (1) Respirators must be maintained in accordance with ANSI Z88.2—1980, section 8.

(2) During respirator cleaning, the rubber or elastomer parts of the respirator must be stretched and manipulated with a massaging action to keep the parts pliable and flexible and to keep the parts from taking a set during storage.

(3) The air purifying element of air-purifying respirators must be replaced when the employee detects breakthrough or after a period not to exceed eight hours, which ever comes first. The element must also be replaced at the start of each shift. An air purifying element with an end of useful life indicator approved by MSHA or NIOSH for benzene may be used until the indicator indicates end of useful life even if this exceeds eight hours.

(h) *Respirator storage.* Respirators must be stored in accordance with ANSI Z88.2—1980, section 8.

§ 197.555 Personal protective clothing and equipment.

(a) When the use of respirators in compliance with § 197.550 and the personal protective clothing and equipment in compliance with this section is chosen as the method or one of the methods required by § 197.545 to be used in meeting the performance standard, the clothing and equipment must meet the requirements of this section.

46 CFR Ch. I (10–1–04 Edition)

(b) The employer shall provide employees with the necessary personal protective clothing and equipment without charge and shall ensure that the clothing and equipment are worn or used properly.

(c) Employees must be provided with coveralls or a large apron, boots, gloves, and, if necessary, tight-fitting eye goggles to limit dermal exposure to, and prevent eye contact with, liquid benzene.

§ 197.560 Medical surveillance.

(a) *General.* (1) The employer must provide, and the employees must submit to, the medical surveillance examinations for employees, as required by this section.

(2) All medical surveillance procedures in compliance with this section, other than the pulmonary function test of paragraph (b)(5)(v) of this section and all laboratory tests, must be performed by, or under the supervision of, a licensed physician.

(3) The pulmonary function test of paragraph (b)(5)(v) of this section must be administered by a licensed physician or by a person who has completed a training course in spirometry sponsored by a governmental, academic, or professional institution.

(4) All laboratory tests must be conducted by a laboratory accredited by an accrediting organization acceptable to the Commandant.

(b) *Initial medical examination.* (1) Within March 14, 1992 the employer shall make available to the employees listed in paragraph (b)(2)(i) of this section an initial medical examination. Within six months all initial medical examinations must be completed, including those for the employees listed in paragraph (b)(2)(ii), and each employee notified of the results of that employee's examination.

(2) The initial medical examination must be made available to the following employees before they are permitted to enter or continue working in a workplace in which they will be or may be exposed to benzene:

(i) Employees who were exposed to more than 10 ppm of benzene as an eight-hour TWA on at least 30 calendar days during the year before January 15, 1992 and who were employed by their

444

present employer during each of the 30 days.

(ii) Employees, other than employees defined in paragraph (b)(2)(i) of this section, who may reasonably be expected to be exposed to benzene at or above the action level on at least 30 calendar days, or at a level above a PEL on at least 10 calendar days, during the coming year.

(3) Exposure to benzene, as referred to in paragraph (b)(2) of this section, means any exposure to benzene, whether or not at the time of the exposure, the employee was or will be wearing an appropriate respirator in compliance with §197.550 and the personal protective clothing and equipment in compliance with §197.555.

(4) An initial medical examination is not required if the employer or employee has adequate records showing that the employee has had, within one year, an examination meeting the requirements of paragraph (b)(5) of this section.

(5) The initial medical examination must include at least the following elements:

(i) A detailed occupational history which includes a history of past work exposure to benzene or any other hematological toxin, a family history of blood dyscrasias including hematological neoplasms, a history of blood dyscrasias including genetic hemoglobin abnormalities, bleeding abnormalities, and abnormal functions of formed blood elements, a history of renal or liver dysfunction, a history of medicinal drugs routinely taken, a history of previous exposure to ionizing radiation, and a history of exposure to marrow toxins outside of the employee's current work situation. The employee must provide to the examining physician as complete an occupational history as possible for the period prior to the current employment.

(ii) A complete physical examination.

(iii) A complete blood count, including a leukocyte count, with differential, quantitative thrombocyte count, hematocrit, hemoglobin, erythrocyte count. and erythrocyte indices (MCV, MCH, MCHC). The results of these tests must be reviewed by the examining physician.

(iv) As determined necessary by the examining physician, additional tests based on alterations to the components of the blood or other signs which may be related to benzene exposure.

(v) For employees required to wear respirators for at least 30 days a year, a pulmonary function test.

(c) *Periodic medical examinations.* (1) The employer shall ensure that no one performs a benzene operation exceeding the level criteria of paragraph (b)(2) of this section without having undergone an initial medical examination and periodic medical examinations yearly thereafter. Also, those who in the previous year have performed benzene operations exceeding the level criteria of paragraph (b)(2) of this section shall undergo a periodic medical examination even if they will not perform benzene operations in the current year. Periodic examinations must include, at least, the following elements:

(i) A brief history regarding new exposure to potential marrow toxins, changes in medicinal drug use, and the appearance of physical signs relating to blood disorders.

(ii) A complete blood count, including a leukocyte count with differential, quantitative thrombocyte count, hematocrit, hemoglobin, erythrocyte count, and erythrocyte indices (MCV, MCH, MCHC). The results of these tests must be reviewed by the examining physician.

(iii) As determined necessary by the examining physician, additional tests based on alterations to the components of the blood or other signs which may be related to benzene exposure.

(2) If the employee develops signs and symptoms commonly associated with toxic exposure to benzene, the employee must be provided with an additional medical examination which includes those elements considered appropriate by the examining physician.

(3) For employees required to use respirators for at least 30 days a year, a pulmonary function test must be performed, and specific evaluation of the cardiopulmonary system must be made, at least every three years.

(d) *Additional examinations and referrals.* (1) If the results of the complete blood count laboratory test required

§ 197.560

for the initial or periodic medical examination indicate that any of the following abnormal conditions exist, the blood count must be retaken within four weeks:

(i) The hemoglobin or the hematocrit falls below the normal limit (outside the 95% confidence interval (C.I.)), as determined by the laboratory, or the hemoglobin or hematocrit shows a persistent downward trend from the employee's pre-exposure norms, if these findings can not be explained by other medical reasons.

(ii) The thrombocyte count varies more than 20 percent below the employee's most recent values or falls outside the normal limit (95% C.I.), as determined by the laboratory.

(iii) The leukocyte count is below 4,000 per cubic millimeter or there is an abnormal differential count.

(2) If the abnormal conditions persist, the employee must be referred by the examining physician to a hematologist or an internist for further evaluation, unless the physician has good reason to believe that the referral is unnecessary. (See appendix C of this subpart for examples of conditions in which referrals may be unnecessary.)

(3) The hematologist or internist must be provided with the information provided to the physician in compliance with paragraph (f) of this section and with the medical record in compliance with § 197.570(b).

(4) If the hematologist or internist determines that additional tests are needed, the employer shall ensure that these additional tests are provided. These test must be completed in thirty days, whether or not the employee continues to perform benzene operations.

(e) *Emergency medical examinations.* (1) Whenever an employee is exposed to benzene resulting from an emergency, a sample of that employee's urine must be taken at the end of the employee's shift and a urinary phenol test must be performed on the sample within 72 hours. Where due to unavoidable circumstances the sample can not be tested by a laboratory within 72 hours of exposure, the sample shall be frozen until it can be delivered to the laboratory. The specific gravity of the urine must be corrected to 1.024. Since certain foods and medications can result in elevated phenol levels, the employee must provide the physician with a dietary and medication history.

(2) If the result of the urinary phenol test is below 75 mg phenol/l of urine, no further testing is required.

(3) If the result of the urinary phenol test is equal to or greater than 75 mg phenol/l of urine, the employee's complete blood count including an erythrocyte count, a leukocyte count with differential, and a thrombocyte count must be taken at monthly intervals for a duration of three months following the emergency.

(4) If any of the conditions specified in paragraph (d)(1) of this section exists, the additional examinations and referrals specified in paragraph (d) of this section must be performed and the employee must be provided with periodic medical examinations, if any are recommended by the examining physician.

(f) *Information provided to the physician.* The following information must be provided to the examining physician:

(1) A copy of this subpart and its appendices.

(2) A description of the affected employee's duties as they relate to the employee's exposure.

(3) The employee's actual or representative exposure level.

(4) A description of the respirator and personal protective clothing and equipment used or to be used, if any.

(5) Records of all previous employment-related medical examinations of the affected employee which were conducted while in the employ of the current employer and which have not been provided to the examining physician.

(g) *Physician's written opinion.* (1) The employer shall ensure that, within 45 days of each examination required by this section, the employer and the employee must be provided with a copy of the examining physician's written opinion of the examination.

(2) The written opinion must contain at least the following information:

(i) The occupationally pertinent results of the medical examination and tests.

(ii) All medical conditions, if any, of the employee which the examining physician believes would subject the employee to a greater than normal risk of material impairment of health if the employee is exposed again to benzene.

(iii) The examining physician's recommended limitations, if any, upon the employee's future exposure to benzene or use of respirators or other personal protective clothing or equipment.

(iv) A statement that the employee has been informed by the physician of the results of the medical examination and of all medical conditions of the employee resulting from benzene exposure which require further explanation or treatment.

(3) The physician's written opinion must not reveal specific records, findings, or diagnoses that have no bearing on the employee's ability to work in a benzene-exposed workplace, ability to use a respirator, or ability to use personal protective clothing or equipment.

(h) *Removal from exposure.* (1) From the time an employee is referred to a hematologist or internist in compliance with paragraph (d)(2) of this section, the employee must not be permitted to enter areas where personal exposure may exceed the action level until the physician determines in compliance with paragraph (h)(2) of this section that the employee again may enter those areas.

(2) After examination by and consultation with the hematologist or internist, the examining physician decides whether or not to permit the employee to enter areas where personal exposure may exceed the action level. The employee must provide the employer with a written copy of the physician's decision signed by the physician. If the decision recommends that the employee not be permitted to enter those areas, the decision must include the examining physician's opinion as to when the employee may be permitted to reenter those areas and the requirements for future medical examinations to review the decision.

(3) Within six months of the date a decision in compliance with paragraph (h)(2) of this section not to permit reentry is made, the employee must be provided with a follow-up examination and a decision of the examining physician (based on the follow-up examination and consultation with a hematologist or internist) as to whether reentry should be permitted and, if so, when, or whether it should be permanently prohibited.

[CGD 88–040, 56 FR 52135, Oct. 17, 1991; 56 FR 65006, Dec. 13, 1991]

§ 197.565 Notifying personnel of benzene hazards.

(a) *Material safety data sheet.* A material safety data sheet (MSDS) addressing benzene must be made available to all persons involved in the benzene operation. The MSDS must describe the physical and chemical characteristics, physical and health hazards, permissible exposure limits, precautions for safe handling and use, control measures such as personal protection equipment, and first aid procedures for benzene. A copy of appendices A and B of this subpart or a MSDS on benzene meeting the requirements of 29 CFR 1910.1200(g) is sufficient.

(b) *Training.* (1) All employees must be provided with training at the time of their initial assignment to a work area where benzene is present and, if exposures are above the action level, at least once a year thereafter. Employees transferring to a new work area must be provided with training specific to that new work area.

(2) The training must provide information on—

(i) Which operations on the vessel involve or may involve exposure to benzene;

(ii) The methods and observations that may be used to detect the presence or release of benzene;

(iii) The physical and health hazards associated with exposure to benzene;

(iv) The measures that may be taken and the equipment that may be used to protect persons from the hazards of benzene exposure;

(v) The proper selection, fitting, fit testing, and use of personal protective equipment in emergency situations;

(vi) The meaning of a regulated area and the means specified in § 197.535(c) to indicate a regulated area;

(vii) The contents of this subpart and of appendices A through E of this subpart and on where copies of this material are available; and

(viii) The medical surveillance program specified in § 197.560.

§ 197.570 Recordkeeping.

(a) *Record of personal exposure monitoring.* (1) The employer shall maintain an accurate record of all monitoring conducted in compliances with § 197.540 for three years.

(2) The record must include—

(i) The dates, number, duration, and results of each sample taken, and a description of the procedure used to determine representative personal exposures;

(ii) A description of the sampling and analytical methods used;

(iii) A description of the type of respirator and personal protective clothing and equipment worn, if any; and

(iv) The name, social security number, and job classification of each person monitored and of all other persons whose exposure the monitoring is intended to represent; and

(v) The exposure levels to which monitored persons were subjected, even if this level is below the PEL.

(b) *Medical record.* (1) The employer shall maintain an accurate medical record for each employee subjected to medical surveillance specified in § 197.560 for three years after the employee's employment is terminated.

(2) The record must include—

(i) The name and social security number of the employee;

(ii) The physician's written opinion on the initial, periodic, and special examinations of the employee, including the results of medical examinations and tests and all opinions and recommendations;

(iii) A list of medical complaints, if any, by the employee related to exposure to benzene;

(iv) A copy of the information provided to the physician required in § 197.560(f)(2) through (f)(5); and

(v) A copy of the employee's medical and work history related to exposure to benzene or other hematologic toxin.

(c) *Availability of records.* (1) All records required to be maintained by this section must be made available upon request to the Coast Guard.

(2) Records of personal exposure monitoring in compliance with (a) of this section must be provided upon request to persons involved in the operation.

(3) A copy of each item entered into the medical record in compliance with paragraph (b) of this section for a particular employee must be given to that employee at the time the item is entered into the medical record.

(4) Medical records required by paragraph (b) of this section must be provided to persons upon the written request of the subject employee.

(d) *Transfer of records.* (1) If the employer ceases to do business and there is no successor to receive and retain the records for the prescribed period, the employer shall make the best effort to transfer all records required in paragraphs (a) and (b) of this section relating to the affected employees to those employees for their disposition. Before transferring medical records to former employees, the employer shall determine whether any forwarding address provided by the employee is still valid and whether the employee desires the records. If a current or former employee refuses to accept the records or does not respond to notification of their availability, the records shall be destroyed.

(2) If the employer ceases to engage in operations involving benzene, the employer shall retain the records for inspection unless the employee requests them as provided in § 197.570(c).

(e) *Confidentiality of records.* Except as specifically required by this Subpart, the employer shall keep confidential all records required to be maintained by this Subpart.

§ 197.575 Observation of monitoring.

(a) Persons involved in benzene operations or their representatives must be provided with an opportunity to observe all monitoring in compliance with § 197.540. Coast Guard officials may also observe all monitoring in compliance with § 197.540.

(b) When observation of monitoring requires entry into regulated areas, the observers shall use respirator and personal protective clothing and equipment approved in compliance with this subpart and comply with § 197.530.

§ 197.580 Appendices.

(a) Appendices A through D and F of this subpart contain technical information on benzene and its effects and provide guidance for medical surveillance, monitoring, and measuring. The appendices are informational and advisory and do not create mandatory requirements.

(b) Appendix E of this subpart contains tests and procedures for fitting respirators. As required by §197.550(d)(1), compliance with appendix E of this subpart is mandatory.

APPENDIX A TO SUBPART C OF PART 197—SAMPLE SUBSTANCE SAFETY DATA SHEET, BENZENE

I. Substance Identification

(a) *Substance:* Benzene.

(b) *Performance standard exposure limits:*

(1) Airborne: The maximum time-weighted average (TWA) exposure limit is one part of benzene vapor per million parts of air (one ppm) for an eight-hour workday and the maximum short-term exposure limit (STEL) is five ppm for any 15-minute period.

(2) Dermal: Eye contact must be prevented and skin contact with liquid benzene must be limited.

(c) *Appearance and odor:* Benzene is a clear, colorless liquid with a pleasant, sweet odor. The odor of benzene does not provide adequate warning of its hazard.

II. Health Hazard Data

(a) *Ways in which benzene affects your health.* Benzene can affect your health if you inhale it or if it comes in contact with your skin or eyes. Benzene is also harmful if you swallow it.

(b) *Effects of overexposure.* (1) Short-term (acute) overexposure: If you are overexposed to high concentrations of benzene, well above the levels where its odor is first recognizable, you may feel breathless, irritable, euphoric, or giddy and you may experience irritation in your eyes, nose, and respiratory tract. You may develop a headache, feel dizzy, nauseated, or intoxicated. Severe exposures may lead to convulsions and loss of consciousness.

(2) Long-term (chronic) exposure: Repeated or prolonged exposure to benzene, even at relatively low concentrations, may result in various blood disorders ranging from anemia to leukemia, an irreversible, fatal disease. Many blood disorders associated with benzene exposure may occur without symptoms.

III. Protective Clothing and Equipment

(a) *Respirators.* Respirators are required for those operations in which engineering controls or work practice controls are not feasible for reducing exposure to the permissible level or are not chosen as the method of complying with the performance standard. If respirators are worn, they must have joint Mine Safety and Health Administration and the National Institute for Occupational Safety and Health (NIOSH) seal of approval. Cartridges or canisters must be replaced before the end of their service life, or the end of the shift, whichever occurs first. If you experience difficulty breathing while wearing a respirator, you may request a positive pressure respirator from your employer. You must be thoroughly trained to use the assigned respirator, and the training will be provided by your employer.

(b) *Protective clothing.* You must wear appropriate protective clothing (such as boots, gloves, sleeves, and aprons) over any parts of your body that could be exposed to liquid benzene.

(c) *Eye and face protection.* You must wear splash-proof safety goggles if it is possible that benzene may get into your eyes. In addition, you must wear a face shield if your face could be splashed with benzene liquid.

IV. Emergency and First Aid Procedures

(a) *Eye and face exposure.* If benzene is splashed in your eyes, wash it out immediately with large amounts of water. If irritation persists or vision appears to be affected, see a doctor as soon as possible.

(b) *Skin exposure.* If benzene is spilled on your clothing or skin, remove the contaminated clothing and wash the exposed skin with large amounts of water and soap immediately. Wash contaminated clothing before you wear it again.

(c) *Breathing.* If you or any other person breathes in large amounts of benzene, get the exposed person to fresh air at once. Apply artificial respiration if breathing has stopped. Call for medical assistance or a doctor as soon as possible. Never enter any vessel or confined space where the benzene concentration might be high without proper safety equipment and with at least one other person present who will stay outside. A life line should be used.

(d) *Swallowing.* If benzene has been swallowed and the subject is conscious, do not induce vomiting. Call for medical assistance or a doctor immediately.

V. Medical Requirements

If you will be exposed to benzene at a concentration at or above 0.5 ppm as an eight-hour time-weighted average or have been exposed at or above 10 ppm in the past while employed by your current employer, your employer may be required by 46 CFR 197.560 to provide a medical examination and history and laboratory tests. These tests must be provided without cost to you. In addition, if you are accidentally exposed to benzene (either by ingestion, inhalation, or skin/eye contact) under emergency conditions known or suspected to constitute a toxic exposure to benzene, your employer is required to make special laboratory tests available to you.

VI. Observation of Monitoring

The employer is required to conduct monitoring that is representative of your exposure to benzene, and you or your designated representative are entitled to observe the monitoring procedure. You are entitled to observe the steps taken in the measurement procedure and to record the results obtained. When the monitoring procedure is taking place in an area where respirators or personal protective clothing and equipment are required to be worn, you or your representative must wear the protective clothing and equipment (See 46 CFR 197.575.)

VII. Access to Records

You or your representative may see the records of monitoring of your exposure to benzene upon written request to your employer. Your medical examination records may be furnished to you, your physician, or a representative designated by you. (See 46 CFR 197.570(c).)

VIII. Precautions for Safe Use, Handling, and Storage

Benzene liquid is highly flammable. Benzene vapor may form explosive mixtures in air. All sources of ignition must be controlled. Use non-sparking tools when opening or closing benzene containers. Fire extinguishers, where required, must be readily available. Know where they are located and how to operate them. Smoking is prohibited in areas where benzene is used or stored.

APPENDIX B TO SUBPART C OF PART 197—SUBSTANCE TECHNICAL GUIDELINES, BENZENE

I. Physical and Chemical Data

(a) *Substance identification.* (1) Synonyms: Benzol, benzole, coal naphtha, cyclohexatriene, phene, phenyl hydride, pyrobenzol. (Benzin, petroleum benzin, and benzine do not contain benzene).

(2) Formula: $C_6 H_6$ (CAS Registry Number: 71-43-2).

(b) *Physical data.* (1) Boiling point (760 mm Hg): 80.1 °C (176 °F).

(2) Specific gravity (water = 1): 0.879.

(3) Vapor density (air = 1): 2.7.

(4) Melting point: 5.5 °C (42 °F).

(5) Vapor pressure at 20 °C (68 °F): 75 mm Hg.

(6) Solubility in water: .06%.

(7) Evaporation rate (ether = 1): 2.8.

(8) Appearance and odor: Clear, colorless liquid with a distinctive sweet odor.

II. Fire, Explosion, and Reactivity Hazard Data

(a) *Fire.* (1) Flash point (closed cup): −11 °C (12 °F).

(2) Autoignition temperature: 580 °C (1076 °F).

(3) Flammable limits in air, % by volume: Lower: 1.3%, Upper: 7.5%.

(4) Extinguishing media: Carbon dioxide, dry chemical, or foam.

(5) Special fire fighting procedures: Do not use a solid stream of water, because it will scatter and spread the fire. Fine water spray may be used to keep fire-exposed containers cool.

(6) Unusual fire and explosion hazards: Benzene is a flammable liquid. Its vapors can form explosive mixtures. All ignition sources must be controlled when benzene is used, handled, or stored. Areas where liquid or vapor may be released are considered hazardous locations. Benzene vapors are heavier than air. Thus, benzene vapors may travel along the deck and ground and be ignited by open flames or sparks at locations remote from the site at which benzene is handled.

(7) Benzene is classified as a flammable liquid for the purpose of conforming to the requirements of 49 CFR 172.101 concerning the designation of materials as hazardous materials. Locations where benzene may be present in quantities sufficient to produce explosive or ignitable mixtures are considered Class I Group D locations for the purposes of conforming to the requirements of 46 CFR parts 30 through 40, 151, and 153 when determining the requirements for electrical equipment as specified in Subchapter J (Electrical engineering).

(b) *Reactivity.* (1) Conditions contributing to instability: Heat.

(2) Incompatibility: Heat and oxidizing materials.

(3) Hazardous decomposition products: Toxic gases and vapors (such as carbon monoxide).

III. Spill and Leak Procedures

(a) *Steps to be taken if the material is released or spilled.* As much benzene as possible should be absorbed with suitable materials, such as dry sand or earth. That remaining must be flushed with large amounts of water. Do not flush benzene into a confined space, such as a sewer, because of explosion danger. Remove all ignition sources. Ventilate enclosed places.

(b) *Waste disposal method.* Disposal methods must conform to state and local regulations. If allowed, benzene may be disposed of (a) by absorbing it in dry sand or earth and disposing in a sanitary landfill, (b), if in small quantities, by removing it to a safe location away from buildings or other combustible sources or by pouring onto dry sand or earth and cautiously igniting it, and (c), if in large

Appendix C to Subpart C of Part 197—Medical Surveillance Guidelines for Benzene

I. Route of Entry

Inhalation; skin absorption.

II. Toxicology

Benzene is primarily an inhalation hazard. Systemic absorption may cause depression of the hematopoietic system, pancytopenia, aplastic anemia, and leukemia. Inhalation of high concentrations may affect the functioning of the central nervous system. Aspiration of small amounts of liquid benzene immediately causes pulmonary edema and hemorrhage of pulmonary tissue. There is some absorption through the skin. Absorption may be more rapid in the case of abraded skin or if it is present in a mixture or as a contaminant in solvents which are readily absorbed. The defatting action of benzene may produce primary irritation due to repeated or prolonged contact with the skin. High concentrations are irritating to the eyes and the mucous membranes of the nose and respiratory tract.

III. Signs and Symptoms

Direct skin contact with benzene may cause erythema. Repeated or prolonged contact may result in drying, scaling dermatitis or development of secondary skin infections. In addition, benzene is absorbed through the skin. Local effects of benzene vapor or liquid on the eye are slight. Only at very high concentrations is there any smarting sensation in the eye. Inhalation of high concentrations of benzene may have an initial stimulatory effect on the central nervous system characterized by exhilaration, nervous excitation, or giddiness, followed by a period of depression, drowsiness, or fatigue. A sensation of tightness in the chest accompanied by breathlessness may occur and ultimately the victim may lose consciousness. Tremors, convulsions, and death may follow from respiratory paralysis or circulatory collapse in a few minutes to several hours following severe exposures.

The detrimental effect on the blood-forming system of prolonged exposure to small quantities of benzene vapor is of extreme importance. The hematopoietic system is the chief target for benzene's toxic effects which are manifested by alterations in the levels of formed elements in the peripheral blood. These effects may occur at concentrations of benzene which may not cause irritation of mucous membranes or any unpleasant sensory effects. Early signs and symptoms of benzene morbidity are varied. Often, they are not readily noticed and are non-specific. Complaints of headache, dizziness, and loss of appetite may precede or follow clinical signs. Rapid pulse and low blood pressure, in addition to a physical appearance of anemia, may accompany a complaint of shortness of breath and excessive tiredness. Bleeding from the nose, gums, or mucous membranes and the development of purpuric spots (small bruises) may occur as the condition progresses. Clinical evidence of leukopenia, anemia, and thrombocytopenia, singly or in combination, may be among the first signs.

Bone marrow may appear normal, aplastic, or hyperplastic and may not, in all situations, correlate with peripheral blood forming tissues. Because of variations in the susceptibility to benzene morbidity, there is no "typical" blood picture. The onset of effects of prolonged benzene exposure may be delayed for many months or years after the actual exposure has ceased. Identification or correlation with benzene exposure must be sought out in the occupational history.

IV. Treatment of Acute Toxic Effects

Remove from exposure immediately. Make sure you are adequately protected and do not risk being overcome by fumes. Give oxygen or artificial resuscitation, if indicated. Flush eyes, wash skin if contaminated, and remove all contaminated clothing. Symptoms of intoxication may persist following severe exposures. Recovery from mild exposures is usually rapid and complete.

V. Surveillance and Preventive Considerations

(a) *General.* The principal effects of benzene exposure addressed in 46 CFR part 197, subpart C, appendix A, are pathological changes in the hematopoietic system, reflected by changes in the peripheral blood and manifested clinically as pancytopenia, aplastic anemia, or leukemia. Consequently, the medical surveillance program specified in 46 CFR 197.560 is designed to observe, on a regular basis, blood indices for early signs of these effects. Although early signs of leukemia are not usually available, emerging diagnostic technology and innovative regimes are making consistent surveillance for leukemia, as well as other hematopoietic effects, more and more beneficial.

Initial and periodic medical examinations must be provided as required in 46 CFR 197.560. There are special provisions for medical tests in the event of hematologic abnormalities or emergencies.

The blood values which require referral to a hematologist or internist are noted in 46 CFR 197.560(d) (i), (ii), and (iii). That section specifies that, if blood abnormalities persist, the employee must be referred unless the physician has good reason to believe that the referral is unnecessary. Examples of conditions that might make a referral unnecessary despite abnormal blood limits are iron or folate deficiency, menorrhagia, or blood loss due to some unrelated medical abnormality.

Symptoms and signs of benzene toxicity can be non-specific. Only a detailed history and appropriate investigative procedures will enable a physician to rule out or confirm conditions that place the employee at increased risk. To assist the examining physician with regard to which laboratory tests are necessary and when to refer an employee to the specialist, the following guidelines have been established.

(b) *Hematology Guidelines.* A minimum battery of tests is to be performed by strictly standardized methods.

(1) Red cell, white cell, platelet counts, white blood cell differential, hematocrit, and red cell indices must be performed by an accredited laboratory. The normal ranges for the red cell and white cell counts are influenced by altitude, race, and sex and, therefore, should be determined by an accredited laboratory in the specific area where the tests are performed.

Either a decline from an absolute normal or from an individual's base line to a subnormal value or a rise to a supra-normal value are indicative of potential toxicity, particularly if all blood parameters decline. The normal total white blood count is approximately 7,200/mm^3 plus or minus 3,000. For cigarette smokers, the white count may be higher and the upper range may be 2,000 cells higher than normal for the laboratory. In addition, infection, allergies, and some drugs may raise the white cell count. The normal platelet count is approximately 250,000 with a range of 140,000 to 400,000. Counts outside this range should be regarded as possible evidence of benzene toxicity.

Certain abnormalities found through routine screening are of greater significance in the benzene-exposed worker and require prompt consultation with a specialist, namely:

(i) Thrombocytopenia.

(ii) A trend of decreasing white cell, red cell, or platelet indices in an individual over time is more worrisome than an isolated abnormal finding at one test time. The importance of a trend highlights the need to compare an individual's test results to baseline, to previous periodic tests, or to both.

(iii) A constellation or pattern of abnormalities in the different blood indices is of more significance than a single abnormality. A low white count not associated with any abnormalities in other cell indices may be a normal statistical variation. Whereas, if the low white count is accompanied by decreases in the platelet and/or red cell indices, such a pattern is more likely to be associated with benzene toxicity and merits thorough investigation.

Anemia, leukopenia, macrocytosis, or an abnormal differential white blood cell count should alert the physician to investigate further and to refer the patient if repeat tests confirm the abnormalities. If routine screening detects an abnormality, the follow-up tests which may be helpful in establishing the etiology of the abnormality are the peripheral blood smear and the reticulocyte count.

The extreme range of normal for reticulocytes is 0.4 to 2.5 percent of the red cells. The usual range is 0.5 to 1.2 percent of the red cells. A decline in reticulocytes to levels of less than 0.4 percent is to be regarded as possible evidence of benzene toxicity requiring accelerated surveillance (unless another specific cause is found). An increase in reticulocyte levels to above 2.5 percent also may be consistent with, but not characteristic of, benzene toxicity.

(2) A careful examination of the peripheral blood smear is an important diagnostic test. As with the reticulocyte count, the smear should be with fresh uncoagulated blood obtained from a needle tip following venipuncture or from a drop of earlobe blood (capillary blood). If necessary, the smear may, under certain limited conditions, be made from a blood sample anticoagulated with EDTA (but never with oxalate or heparin). When the smear is to be prepared from a specimen of venous blood which has been collected by a commercial Vacutainer® type tube containing neutral EDTA, the smear should be made as soon as possible after the venesection. A delay of up to 12 hours is permissible between the drawing of the blood specimen into EDTA and the preparation of the smear if the blood is stored at refrigerator (not freezing) temperature.

(3) The minimum mandatory observations to be made from the smear are as follows:

(i) The differential white blood cell count.

(ii) Description of abnormalities in the appearance of red cells.

(iii) Description of any abnormalities in the platelets.

(iv) A careful search must be made of every blood smear for immature white cells such as band forms (in more than normal proportion, i.e., over ten percent of the total differential count), any number of metamyelocytes, myelocytes, or myeloblasts. Any nucleate or multinucleated red blood cells should be reported. Large "giant" platelets or fragments of megakaryocytes must be recognized.

An increase in the proportion of band forms among the neutrophilic granulocytes is an abnormality deserving special mention. Such an increase may represent a change which should be considered as an early warning of benzene toxicity in the absence of other causative factors (most commonly infection). Likewise, the appearance of metamyelocytes, in the absence of another probable cause, is to be considered a possible indication of benzene-induced toxicity.

An upward trend in the number of basophils, which normally do not exceed about 2.0 percent of the total white cells, is to be regarded as possible evidence of benzene toxicity. A rise in the eosinophil count is less specific but may indicate toxicity if the rise is above 6.0 percent of the total white count.

The normal range of monocytes is from 2.0 to 8.0 percent of the total white count with an average of about 5.0 percent. About 20 percent of individuals reported to have mild but persisting abnormalities caused by exposure to benzene show a persistent monocytosis. The findings of a monocyte count which persists at more than ten to 12 percent of the normal white cell count (when the total count is normal) or persistence of an absolute monocyte count in excess of 800/mm^3 should be regarded as a possible sign of benzene-induced toxicity.

A less frequent but more serious indication of benzene toxicity is the finding in the peripheral blood of the so-called "pseudo" (or acquired) Pelger-Huet anomaly. In this anomaly, many, or sometimes the majority, of the neutrophilic granulocytes possess two round nuclear segments, or, less often, one or three round segments, rather than three normally elongated segments. When this anomaly is not hereditary, it is often, but not invariably, predictive of subsequent leukemia. However, only about two percent of patients who ultimately develop acute myelogenous leukemia show the acquired Pelger-Huet anomaly. Other tests that can be administered to investigate blood abnormalities are discussed below. However, these tests should be undertaken by the hematologist.

An uncommon sign, which cannot be detected from the smear but can be elicited by a "sucrose water test" of peripheral blood, is transient paroxysmal nocturnal hemoglobinuria (PNH). This sign may first occur insidiously during a period of established aplastic anemia and may be followed within one to a few years by the appearance of rapidly fatal, acute myelogenous leukemia. Clinical detection of PNH, which occurs in only one or two percent of those destined to have acute myelogenous leukemia, may be difficult. If the "sucrose water test" is positive, the somewhat more definitive Ham test, also known as the acid-serum hemolysis test, may provide confirmation.

(v) Individuals documented to have developed acute myelogenous leukemia years after initial exposure to benzene may have progressed through a preliminary phase of hematologic abnormality. In some instances, pancytopenia (i.e., a lowering in the counts of all circulating blood cells of bone marrow origin, but not to the extent implied by the term "aplastic anemia") preceded leukemia for many years. Depression of a single blood cell type or platelets may represent a harbinger of aplasia or leukemia. The finding of two or more cytopenias or pancytopenia in a benzene-exposed individual must be regarded as highly suspicious of more advanced, although still reversible, toxicity. Pancytopenia coupled with the appearance of immature cells (myelocytes, myeloblasts, erythroblasts, etc.) with abnormal cells (pseudo Pelger-Huet anomaly, atypical nuclear heterochromatin, etc.) or of unexplained elevations of white blood cells must be regarded as evidence of benzene overexposure, unless proved otherwise. Many severely aplastic patients manifested the ominous finding of five to ten percent myeloblasts in the marrow, occasional myeloblasts and myelocytes in the blood, and 20 to 30 percent monocytes. It is evident that isolated cytopenias, pancytopenias, and even aplastic anemias induced by benzene may be reversible and complete recovery has been reported on cessation of exposure. However, because any of these abnormalities is serious, the employee must immediately be removed from any possible exposure to benzene vapor. Certain tests may substantiate the employee's prospects for progression or regression. One such test would be an examination of the bone marrow, but the decision to perform a bone marrow aspiration or needle biopsy must be made by the hematologist.

The findings of basophilic stippling in circulating red blood cells (usually found in one to five percent of red cells following marrow injury) and detection in the bone marrow of what are termed "ringed sideroblasts" must be taken seriously, as they have been noted in recent years to be premonitory signs of subsequent leukemia.

Recently peroxidase-staining of circulating or marrow neutrophil granulocytes, employing benzidine dihydrochloride, have revealed the disappearance of, or diminution in, peroxidase in a sizable proportion of the granulocytes. This has been reported as an early sign of leukemia. However, relatively few patients have been studied to date. Granulocyte granules are normally strongly peroxidase positive. A steady decline in leukocyte alkaline phosphatase has also been reported as suggestive of early acute leukemia. Exposure to benzene may cause an early rise in serum iron, often but not always associated with a fall in the reticulocyte count. Thus, serial measurements of serum iron levels may provide a means of determining whether or not there is a trend representing sustained suppression of erythropoiesis.

Measurement of serum iron and determination of peroxidase and of alkaline phosphatase activity in peripheral granulocytes can be performed in most pathology laboratories. Peroxidase and alkaline phosphatase staining are usually undertaken when the index of suspicion for leukemia is high.

Appendix D to Subpart C of Part 197—Sampling and Analytical Methods for Benzene Monitoring—Measurement Procedures

Measurements taken for the purpose of determining employee exposure to benzene are best taken so that the representative average eight-hour exposure may be determined from a single eight-hour sample or two four-hour samples. Short-time interval samples (or grab samples) may also be used to determine average exposure level if a minimum of five measurements are taken in a random manner over the eight-hour work shift. In random sampling, any portion of the work shift has the same chance of being sampled as any other. The arithmetic average of all random samples taken on one work shift is an estimate of an employee's average level of exposure for that work shift. Air samples should be taken in the employee's breathing zone (i.e., air that would most nearly represent that inhaled by the employee). Sampling and analysis must be performed with procedures meeting the requirements of 46 CFR part 197, subpart C.

There are a number of methods available for monitoring employee exposures to benzene. The sampling and analysis may be performed by collection of the benzene vapor on charcoal adsorption tubes, with subsequent chemical analysis by gas chromatography. Sampling and analysis also may be performed by portable direct reading instruments, real-time continuous monitoring systems, passive dosimeters, or other suitable methods. The employer is required to select a monitoring method which meets the accuracy and precision requirements of 46 CFR 197.540(a)(6) for the weather conditions expected. Section 197.540(a)(6) requires that monitoring must have an accuracy, to a 95 percent confidence level, of not less than plus or minus 25 percent for concentrations of benzene greater than or equal to 0.5 ppm.

In developing the following analytical procedures, the OSHA Laboratory modified NIOSH Method S311 and evaluated it at a benzene air concentration of one ppm. A procedure for determining the benzene concentration in bulk material samples was also evaluated. This work, as reported in OSHA Laboratory Method No. 12, includes the following two analytical procedures:

I. OSHA Method 12 for Air Samples

Analyte: Benzene.
Matrix: Air.
Procedure: Adsorption on charcoal, desorption with carbon disulfide, analysis by gas chromatograph.
Detection limit: 0.04 ppm.
Recommended air volume and sampling rate: 10 liter at 0.2 liter/min.

1. Principle of the method

1.1. A known volume of air is drawn through a charcoal tube to trap the organic vapors present.
1.2. The charcoal in the tube is transferred to a small, stoppered vial and the analyte is desorbed with carbon disulfide.
1.3. An aliquot of the desorbed sample is injected into a gas chromatograph.
1.4. The area of the resulting peak is determined and compared with areas obtained from standards.

2. Advantages and disadvantages of the method

2.1. The sampling device is small, portable, and involves no liquids. Interferences are minimal and most of those which do occur can be eliminated by altering chromatographic conditions. The samples are analyzed by means of a quick, instrumental method.
2.2. The amount of sample which can be taken is limited by the number of milligrams that the tube will hold before overloading. When the sample value obtained for the backup section of the charcoal tube exceeds 25 percent of that found on the front section, the possibility of sample loss exists.

3. Apparatus

3.1. A calibrated personal sampling pump having a flow that can be determined within ±five percent at the recommended flow rate.
3.2. Charcoal tubes: Glass with both ends flame sealed, seven cm long with a six mm O.D. and a four mm I.D., containing two sections of 20/40 mesh activated charcoal separated by a two mm portion of urethane foam. The activated charcoal is prepared from coconut shells and is fired at 600 °C before packing. The adsorbing section contains 100 mg of charcoal and the back-up section 50 mg. A three mm portion of urethane foam is placed between the outlet end of the tube and the back-up section. A plug of silanized glass wool is placed in front of the adsorbing section. The pressure drop across the tube must be less than one inch of mercury at a flow rate of one liter per minute.
3.3. Gas chromatograph equipped with a flame ionization detector.
3.4. Column (10 ft.×1/8 in. stainless steel) packed with 80/100 Supelcoport coated with 20 percent SP 2100 and 0.1 percent CW 1500.
3.5. An electronic integrator or some other suitable method for measuring peak area.
3.6. Two-milliliter sample vials with Teflon-lined caps.
3.7. Microliter syringes: ten microliter (ten µl) syringe, and other convenient sizes for making standards. One µl syringe for sample injections.
3.8. Pipets: 1.0 ml delivery pipets.
3.9. Volumetric flasks: convenient sizes for making standard solutions.

4. Reagents

4.1. Chromatographic quality carbon disulfide (CS₂). Most commercially available carbon disulfide contains a trace of benzene which must be removed. It can be removed with the following procedure. Heat, under reflux for two to three hours, 500 ml of carbon disulfide, ten ml concentrated sulfuric acid, and five drops of concentrated nitric acid. The benzene is converted to nitrobenzene. The carbon disulfide layer is removed, dried with anhydrous sodium sulfate, and distilled. The recovered carbon disulfide should be benzene free. (It has recently been determined that benzene can also be removed by passing the carbon disulfide through a 13x molecular sieve).

4.2. Benzene, reagent grade.

4.3. p-Cymene, reagent grade, (internal standard).

4.4. Desorbing reagent. The desorbing reagent is prepared by adding 0.05 ml of p-cymene per milliliter of carbon disulfide. (The internal standard offers a convenient means correcting analytical response for slight inconsistencies in the size of sample injections. If the external standard technique is preferred, the internal standard can be eliminated.)

4.5. Purified GC grade helium, hydrogen, and air.

5. Procedure

5.1. Cleaning of equipment. All glassware used for the laboratory analysis should be properly cleaned and free of organics which could interfere in the analysis.

5.2. Calibration of personal pumps. Each pump must be calibrated with a representative charcoal tube in the line.

5.3. Collection and shipping of samples.

5.3.1. Immediately before sampling, break the ends of the tube to provide an opening at least one-half the internal diameter of the tube (two mm).

5.3.2. The smaller section of the charcoal is used as the backup and should be placed nearest the sampling pump.

5.3.3. The charcoal tube should be placed in a vertical position during sampling to minimize channeling through the charcoal.

5.3.4. Air being sampled should not be passed through any hose or tubing before entering the charcoal tube.

5.3.5. A sample size of 10 liters is recommended. Sample at a flow rate of approximately 0.2 liters per minute. The flow rate should be known with an accuracy of at least ±five percent.

5.3.6. The charcoal tubes should be capped with the supplied plastic caps immediately after sampling.

5.3.7. Submit at least one blank tube (a charcoal tube subjected to the same handling procedures, without having any air drawn through it) with each set of samples.

5.3.8. Take necessary shipping and packing precautions to minimize breakage of samples.

5.4. Analysis of samples.

5.4.1. Preparation of samples. In preparation for analysis, each charcoal tube is scored with a file in front of the first section of charcoal and broken open. The glass wool is removed and discarded. The charcoal in the first (larger) section is transferred to a two ml vial. The separating section of foam is removed and discarded and the second section is transferred to another capped vial. These two sections are analyzed separately.

5.4.2. Desorption of samples. Before analysis, 1.0 ml of desorbing solution is pipetted into each sample container. The desorbing solution consists of 0.05 µl internal standard per milliliter of carbon disulfide. The sample vials are capped as soon as the solvent is added. Desorption should be done for 30 minutes with occasional shaking.

5.4.3. GC conditions. Typical operating conditions for the gas chromatograph are as follows:

1. 30 ml/min (60 psig) helium carrier gas flow.
2. 30 ml/min (40 psig) hydrogen gas flow to detector.
3. 240 ml/min (40 psig) air flow to detector.
4. 150 °C injector temperature.
5. 250 °C detector temperature.
6. 100 °C column temperature.

5.4.4. Injection size. One µl.

5.4.5. Measurement of area. The peak areas are measured by an electronic integrator or some other suitable form of area measurement.

5.4.6. An internal standard procedure is used. The integrator is calibrated to report results in ppm for a 10 liter air sample after correction for desorption efficiency.

5.5. Determination of desorption efficiency.

5.5.1. Importance of determination. The desorption efficiency of a particular compound may vary from one laboratory to another and from one lot of chemical to another. Thus, it is necessary to determine, at least once, the percentage of the specific compound that is removed in the desorption process, provided the same batch of charcoal is used.

5.5.2. Procedure for determining desorption efficiency. The reference portion of the charcoal tube is removed. To the remaining portion, amounts representing 0.5X, 1X, and 2X (X represents target concentration) based on a 10 liter air sample, are injected into several tubes at each level. Dilutions of benzene with carbon disulfide are made to allow injection of measurable quantities. These tubes are then allowed to equilibrate at least overnight. Following equilibration, they are analyzed following the same procedure as the samples. Desorption efficiency is determined by dividing the amount of benzene found by amount spiked on the tube.

Pt. 197, Subpt. C, App. D

6. Calibration and standards

A series of standards varying in concentration over the range of interest is prepared and analyzed under the same GC conditions that will be used on the samples. A calibration curve is prepared by plotting concentration (μg/ml) versus peak area.

7. Calculations

Benzene air concentration can be calculated from the following equation:

$mg/m^3 = (A)(B)/(C)(D)$

Where:

A = μg/ml benzene, obtained from the calibration curve; B = desorption volume (one ml); C = liters of air sampled; and D = desorption efficiency.

The concentration in mg/m³ can be converted to ppm (at 25° and 760 mm) with following equation:

$ppm = (mg/m^3)(24.46)/(78.11)$

Where:

24.46 = molar volume of an ideal gas 25 °C and 760 mm; and 78.11 = molecular weight of benzene.

8. Backup data

8.1 Detection limit—Air Samples. The detection limit for the analytical procedure is 1.28 ng with a coefficient of variation of 0.023 at this level. This would be equivalent to an air concentration of 0.04 ppm for a 10 liter air sample. This amount provided a chromatographic peak that could be identifiable in the presence of possible interferences. The detection limit data were obtained by making one μl injections of a 1.283 μg/ml standard.

Injection	Area count	
1	655.4	
2	617.5	
3	662.0	X=640.2
4	641.1	SD=14.9
5	636.4	CV=0.023
6	629.2	

8.2 Pooled coefficient of variation—Air Samples. The pooled coefficient of variation for the analytical procedure was determined by one μl replicate injections of analytical standards. The standards were 16.04, 32.08, and 64.16 μg/ml, which are equivalent to 0.5, 1.0, and 2.0 ppm for a 10 liter air sample respectively.

8.3 Storage data—Air Samples. Samples were generated at 1.03 ppm benzene at 80% relative humidity, 22 °C, and 643 mm. All samples were taken for 50 minutes at 0.2 liters/min. Six samples were analyzed immediately and the rest of the samples were divided into two groups by fifteen samples each. One group was stored at refrigerated temperature of −25 °C and the other group was stored at ambient temperature (approximately 23 °C). These samples were analyzed over a period of fifteen days. The results are tabulated below.

Injection	Area counts		
	0.5 ppm	1.0 ppm	2.0 ppm
1	3996.5	8130.2	16481
2	4059.4	8235.6	16493
3	4052.0	8307.9	16535
4	4027.2	8263.2	16609
5	4046.8	8291.1	16552
6	4137.9	8288.8	16618
X=	4053.3	8254.0	16548.3
SD=	47.2	62.5	57.1
CV=	0.0116	0.0076	0.0034
CV=0.008.			

PERCENT RECOVERY

Day analyzed	Refrigerated			Ambient		
0	97.4	98.7	98.9	97.4	98.7	98.9
0	97.1	100.6	100.9	97.1	100.6	100.9
2	95.8	96.4	95.4	95.4	96.6	96.9
5	93.9	93.7	92.4	92.4	94.3	94.1
9	93.6	95.5	94.6	95.2	94.7	96.6
13	94.3	95.3	93.7	91.0	95.0	94.6
15	96.8	95.8	94.2	92.9	96.3	95.9

8.4 Desorption data. Samples were prepared by injecting liquid benzene onto the A section of charcoal tubes. Samples were prepared that would be equivalent to 0.5, 1.0, and 2.0 ppm for a 10 liter air sample.

PERCENT RECOVERY

Sample	0.5 ppm	1.0 ppm	2.0 ppm
1	99.4	98.8	99.5
2	99.5	98.7	99.7
3	99.2	98.6	99.8
4	99.4	99.1	100.0
5	99.2	99.0	99.7
6	99.8	99.1	99.9

Coast Guard, DHS

Pt. 197, Subpt. C, App. D

Percent Recovery—Continued

Sample	0.5 ppm	1.0 ppm	2.0 ppm
X=	99.4	98.9	99.8
SD=	0.22	0.21	0.18
CV=	0.0022	0.0021	0.0018
X=99.4.			

8.5 Carbon disulfide. Carbon disulfide from a number of sources was analyzed for benzene contamination. The results are given in the following table. The benzene contaminant can be removed with the procedures given in section I.4.1.

Sample	μg Benzene/ml	ppm equivalent (for 10 liter air sample)
ALDRICH Lot 83017	4.20	0.13
BAKER Lot 720364	1.01	0.03
BAKER Lot 822351	1.01	0.03
Malinkrodt Lot WEMP	1.74	0.05
Malinkrodt Lot WDSJ	5.65	0.18
Malinkrodt Lot WHGA	2.90	0.09
Treated CS_2		

II. OSHA Laboratory Method No. 12 for Bulk Samples

Analyte: Benzene.
Matrix: Bulk Samples.
Procedure: Bulk samples are analyzed directly by high performance liquid chromatography (HPLC).
Detection limits: 0.01% by volume.

1. Principle of the method

1.1. An aliquot of the bulk sample to be analyzed is injected into a liquid chromatograph.
1.2. The peak area for benzene is determined and compared to areas obtained from standards.

2. Advantages and disadvantages of the method

2.1. The analytical procedure is quick, sensitive, and reproducible.
2.2. Reanalysis of samples is possible.
2.3. Interferences can be circumvented by proper selection of HPLC parameters.
2.4. Samples must be free of any particulates that may clog the capillary tubing in the liquid chromatograph. This may require distilling the sample or clarifying with a clarification kit.

3. Apparatus

3.1. Liquid chromatograph equipped with a UV detector.
3.2. HPLC Column that will separate benzene from other components in the bulk sample being analyzed. The column used for validation studies was a Waters uBondapack C18, 30 cm×3.9 mm.
3.3. A clarification kit to remove any particulates in the bulk if necessary.

3.4. A micro-distillation apparatus to distill any samples if necessary.
3.5. An electronic integrator or some other suitable method of measuring peak areas.
3.6. Microliter syringes—ten μl syringe and other convenient sizes for making standards. 10 μl syringe for sample injections.
3.7. Volumetric flasks, five ml and other convenient sizes for preparing standards and making dilutions.

4. Reagents

4.1. Benzene, reagent grade.
4.2. HPLC grade water, methyl alcohol, and isopropyl alcohol.

5. Collection and shipment of samples

5.1. Samples should be transported in glass containers with Teflon-lined caps.
5.2. Samples should not be put in the same container used for air samples

6. Analysis of samples

6.1. Sample preparation. If necessary, the samples are distilled or clarified. Samples are analyzed undiluted. If the benzene concentration is out of the working range, suitable dilutions are made with isopropyl alcohol.
6.2. HPLC conditions. The typical operating conditions for the high performance liquid chromatograph are:
6.2.1. Mobile phase—Methyl alcohol/water, 50/50.
6.2.2. Analytical wavelength—254 nm.
6.2.3. Injection size—10 μl.
6.3. Measurement of peak area and calibration. Peak areas are measured by an integrator or other suitable means. The integrator is calibrated to report results in % benzene by volume.

7. Calculations

Because the integrator is programmed to report results in % benzene by volume in an undiluted sample, the following equation is used: % Benzene by Volume=A×B.
Where: A=% by volume on report. B=Dilution Factor. (B=one for undiluted sample).

8. Backup data

8.1. Detection limit—Bulk Samples. The detection limit for the analytical procedure for bulk samples is 0.88 μg, with a coefficient of variation of 0.019 at this level. This amount provided a chromatographic peak that could be identifiable in the presence of possible interferences. The detection limit date were obtained by making ten μl injections of a 0.10% by volume standard.

Injection	Area Count
1	45386
2	44214

Pt. 197, Subpt. C, App. E

Injection	Area Count	
3	43822	X=44040.1
4	44062	SD=852.5
6	42724	CV=0.019

8.2. Pooled coefficient of variation—Bulk Samples. The pooled coefficient of variation for the analytical procedure was determined by 50 μl replicate injections of analytical standards. The standards were 0.01, 0.02, 0.04, 0.10, 1.0, and 2.0% benzene by volume.

AREA COUNT (PERCENT)

Injection #	0.01	0.02	0.04	0.10	1.0	2.0
1	45386	84737	166097	448497	4395380	9339150
2	44241	84300	170832	441299	4590800	9484900
3	43822	83835	164160	443719	4593200	9557580
4	44062	84381	164445	444842	4642350	9677060
5	44006	83012	168398	442564	4646430	9766240
6	42724	81957	173002	443975	4646260	
X=	44040.1	83703.6	167872	444149	4585767	9564986
SD=	852.5	1042.2	3589.8	2459.1	96839.3	166233
CV=	0.0194	0.0125	0.0213	0.0055	0.0211	0.0174
CV=0.017.						

APPENDIX E TO SUBPART C OF PART 197—RESPIRATOR FIT TESTS

PROCEDURES

This appendix contains the procedures for properly fitting a respirator to employees who may be exposed to benzene and includes the Initial Fit Tests (IFT), the Qualitative Fit Tests (QLFT), and the Quantitative Fit Test (QNFT).

Note that respirators (negative pressure or positive pressure) must not be worn when conditions prevent a tight seal between the faceplate and the skin or the proper functioning of the inhalation or exhalation valves. In order for a respirator to protect the wearer, the facepiece must make a proper seal against the wearer's face. Several factors can negatively affect the respirator to face seal and reduce the level of protection afforded by the respirator. Among these are facial shape, temple pieces of eyeglasses, facial abnormalities (e.g., scars and indentations) absence of dentures, hair style or length of hair, specific skin conditions, and facial hair. Therefore, nothing can come between or otherwise interfere with the sealing surface of the respirator and the face or interfere with the function of the inhalation or exhalation valves.

I. Initial Fit Tests (IFT)

(a) The test subject must be allowed to select the most comfortable respirator from a selection of respirators of various sizes. The selection must include at least three sizes of elastomeric facepieces for the type of respirator that is to be tested (i.e., three sizes of half mask or three sizes of full facepiece).

(b) Before the selection process, the test subject must be shown how to put on a respirator, how it should be positioned on the face, how to set strap tension, and how to determine a comfortable fit. A mirror must be available to assist the subject in evaluating the fit and positioning the respirator. This instruction is only a preliminary review and must not constitute the subject's formal training on respirator use.

(c) The test subject must be informed that he or she is being asked to select the respirator which provides the most comfortable fit. Each respirator represents a different size and shape and, if fitted and used properly, should provide adequate protection.

(d) The test subject must be instructed to hold each facepiece up to the face and eliminate those facepieces which obviously do not give a comfortable fit.

(e) The more comfortable facepieces must be noted and the most comfortable mask donned and worn at least five minutes to assess comfort. Assistance in assessing comfort may be given by discussing the points in section I(f) of this appendix. If the test subject is not familiar with using a particular respirator, the test subject must be directed to don the mask several times and to adjust the straps each time to become adept at setting proper tension on the straps.

(f) Assessment of comfort must include reviewing the following points with the test subject and allowing the test subject adequate time to determine the comfort of the respirator:

(1) Position of the mask on the nose.
(2) Room for eye protection.
(3) Room to talk.
(4) Position of mask on face and cheeks.

(g) The following criteria must be used to help determine the adequacy of the respirator fit:

(1) Chin properly placed.
(2) Adequate strap tension, not overly tightened.
(3) Fit across nose bridge.
(4) Respirator of proper size to span distance from nose to chin.
(5) Tendency of respirator to slip.

Coast Guard, DHS

Pt. 197, Subpt. C, App. E

(6) Self-observation in mirror to evaluate fit and respirator position.

(h) The following negative and positive pressure fit tests must be conducted. Before conducting a negative or positive pressure fit test, the subject must be told to seat the mask on the face by moving the head from side-to-side and up and down slowly while taking in a few slow deep breaths Another facepiece must be selected and retested if the test subject fails the fit check tests.

(1) *Positive pressure fit test.* The exhalation valve must be closed off and the subject must exhale gently onto the facepiece. The face fit is considered satisfactory if a slight positive pressure can be built up inside the facepiece without any evidence of outward leakage of air at the seal. For most respirators this method of leak testing requires the wearer to first remove the exhalation valve cover before closing off the exhalation valve and then carefully replacing it after the test.

(2) *Negative pressure fit test.* The inlet opening of the canister or cartridge(s) must be closed off by covering with the palm of the hand(s) or by replacing the filter seal(s). The subject must inhale gently so that the facepiece collapses slightly and hold his or her breath for ten seconds. If the facepiece remains in its slightly collapsed condition and no inward leakage of air is detected, the tightness of the respirator is considered satisfactory.

(i) The test must not be conducted if the subject has any hair growth between the skin and the facepiece sealing surface, such as stubble beard growth, beard, or long sideburns which cross the respirator sealing surface. Any type of apparel, such as a skull cap or the temple bars of eye glasses, which projects under the facepiece or otherwise interferes with a satisfactory fit must be altered or removed.

(j) If the test subject exhibits difficulty in breathing during the tests, the subject must be referred to a physician trained in respiratory disease or pulmonary medicine to determine whether the test subject can wear a respirator while performing his or her duties.

(k) The test subject must be given the opportunity to wear the successfully fitted respirator for a period of two weeks. If at any time during this period the respirator becomes uncomfortable, the test subject must be given the opportunity to select a different facepiece and to be retested.

(l) Exercise regimen. Before beginning the fit test, the test subject must be given a description of the fit test and of the test subject's responsibilities during the test procedure. The description of the process must include a description of the test exercises that the subject must perform. The respirator to be tested must be worn for at least five minutes before the start of the fit test.

(m) Test Exercises. The test subject must perform the following exercises in the test environment:

(1) Normal breathing. In a normal standing position, without talking, the subject must breathe normally.

(2) Deep breathing. In a normal standing position, the subject must breathe slowly and deeply, taking caution so as to not hyperventilate.

(3) Turning head side to side. Standing in place, the subject must slowly turn his or her head from side to side between the extreme positions on each side. The subject must hold his or her head at each extreme momentarily and inhale.

(4) Moving head up and down. Standing in place, the subject must slowly move his or her head up and down. The subject must be instructed to inhale in the up position (i.e., when looking toward the ceiling).

(5) Talking. The subject must talk slowly and loudly enough so as to be heard clearly by the test conductor. The subject must count backward from 100, recite a memorized poem or song, or read the following passage:

RAINBOW PASSAGE

When the sunlight strikes raindrops in the air, they act like a prism and form a rainbow. The rainbow is a division of white light into many beautiful colors. These take the shape of a long round arch, with its path high above, and its two ends apparently beyond the horizon. There is, according to legend, a boiling pot of gold at one end. People look, but no one ever finds it. When a man looks for something beyond reach, his friends say he is looking for the pot of gold at the end of the rainbow.

(6) Grimace. The test subject must grimace by smiling or frowning.

(7) Bending over. The test subject must bend at the waist as if to touch the toes or, for test environments such as shroud type QNFT units which prohibit bending at the waist, the subject must jog in place.

(8) Normal breathing. Same as exercise 1.

Each test exercise must be performed for one minute, except for the grimace exercise which must be performed for 15 seconds. The test subject must be questioned by the test conductor regarding the comfort of the respirator upon completion of test exercises. If it has become uncomfortable, another respirator must be tried and the subject retested.

(n) The employer shall certify that a successful fit test has been administered to the test subject. The certification must include the following information:

(1) Name of employee.

(2) Type, brand, and size of respirator.

(3) Date of test.

Where QNFT is used, the fit factor, strip chart, or other recording of the results of the

Pt. 197, Subpt. C, App. E

test must be retained with the certification. The certification must be maintained until the next fit test is administered.

II. Qualitative Fit Tests (QLFT)

(a) *General.* (1) The employer shall designate specific individuals to administer the respirator qualitative fit test program. The employer may contract for these services.

(2) The employer shall ensure that persons administering QLFT are able to properly prepare test solutions, calibrate equipment, perform tests, recognize invalid tests, and determine whether the test equipment is in proper working order.

(3) The employer shall ensure that QLFT equipment is kept clean and maintained so as to operate at the parameters for which it was designed.

(b) *Isoamyl acetate tests.* (1) Odor threshold screening test. The odor threshold screening test, performed without wearing a respirator, is intended to determine if the test subject can detect the odor of isoamyl acetate.

(i) Three one-liter glass jars with metal lids must be used.

(ii) Odor free water (e.g. distilled or spring water) at approximately 25 degrees C must be used for the solutions.

(iii) An isoamyl acetate (IAA) (also known at isopentyl acetate) stock solution must be prepared by adding one cc of pure IAA to 800 cc of odor free water in a one liter jar and by shaking the jar for 30 seconds. A new solution must be prepared at least weekly.

(iv) The screening test must be conducted in a room separate from the room used for actual fit testing. The two rooms must be well ventilated but not connected to the same recirculating ventilation system.

(v) An odor test solution must be prepared in a second one-liter jar by placing 0.4 cc of the stock solution into 500 cc of odor free water using a clean dropper or pipette. The solution must be shaken for 30 seconds and allowed to stand for two to three minutes so that the IAA concentration above the liquid may reach equilibrium. This solution must be used for only one day.

(vi) A test blank must be prepared in a third one-liter jar by adding 500 cc of odor free water.

(vii) The odor test jar and the test blank jar must be labeled "1" and "2" for identification. The labels must be placed on the jar lids so that the labels can be periodically peeled off dried, and switched to maintain the integrity of the test.

(viii) The following instruction must be typed on a card and placed on a table in front of the odor test jar and the test blank jar:

The purpose of this test is to determine if you can smell banana oil at a low concentration. The two bottles in front of you contain water. One of these bottles also contains a small amount of banana oil. Be sure the covers are on tight, then shake each bottle for two seconds. Unscrew the lid of each bottle, one at a time, and sniff at the mouth of the bottle. Indicate to the test conductor which bottle contains banana oil.

(ix) The mixtures in the jars used in the IAA odor threshold screening must be prepared in an area separate from the test area, in order to prevent olfactory fatigue in the test subject.

(x) If the test subject is unable to correctly identify the jar containing the odor test solution, the IAA qualitative fit test must not be performed.

(xi) If the test subject correctly identifies the jar containing the odor test solution, the test subject may proceed to respirator selection and fit testing.

(2) Isoamyl acetate fit test. (i) The fit test chamber must be a clear 55-gallon drum liner or similar device suspended inverted over a two foot diameter frame so that the top of the chamber is about six inches above the test subject's head. The inside top center of the chamber must have a small hook attached.

(ii) Each respirator used for the fitting and fit testing must be equipped with organic vapor cartridges or offer protection against organic vapors. The cartridges or masks must be changed at least weekly.

(iii) After selecting, donning, and properly adjusting a respirator, the test subject must wear the respirator to the fit testing room. This room must be separate from the room used for odor threshold screening and respirator selection and must be well ventilated by an exhaust fan, lab hood, or other device to prevent general room contamination.

(iv) A copy of the test exercises and any prepared text from which the subject is to read must be taped to the inside of the test chamber.

(v) Upon entering the test chamber, the test subject must be given a six inch by five inch piece of paper towel or other porous, absorbent, single-ply material, folded in half and wetted with 0.75 cc of pure IAA. The test subject must hang the wet towel on the hook at the top of the chamber.

(vi) Two minutes must be allowed for the IAA test concentration to stabilize before starting the fit test exercises. This would be an appropriate time to talk with the test subject, to explain the fit test, the importance of the subject's cooperation, and the purpose for the head exercises, or to demonstrate some of the exercises.

(vii) The test subject must be instructed to perform the exercises described in section I(n) of this appendix. If at any time during the test the subject detects the banana like odor of IAA, the test is failed. The subject must be removed quickly from the test

460

chamber and the test area to avoid olfactory fatigue.

(viii) If the test is failed, the subject must return to the selection room, remove the respirator, repeat the odor sensitivity test, select and don another respirator, return to the test chamber, and again take the IAA fit test. The process must continue until a respirator that fits well is found. If the odor sensitivity test is failed, the subject must wait at least five minutes before retesting to allow odor sensitivity to return.

(ix) When a respirator is found that passes the test, the subject must demonstrate the efficiency of the respirator by breaking the face seal and taking a breath before exiting the chamber. If the subject cannot detect the odor of IAA, the test is deemed inconclusive and must be rerun.

(x) When the test subject leaves the chamber, the subject must remove the saturated towel and return it to the person conducting the test. To keep the test area from becoming contaminated, the used towel must be kept in a self-sealing bag to avoid significant IAA concentration build-up in the test chamber for subsequent tests.

(c) *Saccharin solution aerosol test.* The saccharin solution aerosol test is an alternative qualitative test. Although it is the only validated test currently available for use with particulate disposable dust respirators not equipped with high-efficiency filters, it may also be used for testing other respirators. The entire screening and testing procedure must be explained to the test subject before the conduct of the saccharin test threshold screening test.

(1) Saccharin taste threshold screening test. The test, performed without wearing a respirator, is intended to determine whether the test subject can detect the taste of saccharin.

(i) The subject must wear an enclosure about the head and shoulders that is approximately 12 inches in diameter by 14 inches tall with at least the front portion clear. If the enclosure is also used for the saccharin solution aerosol fit test in compliance with section II(c)(2) of this appendix, the enclosure must allow free movements of the head when a respirator is worn. An enclosure substantially similar to the Minnesota, Mining and Manufacturing (3M) hood assembly, parts No. FT 14 and No. FT 15 combined, is adequate.

(ii) The test enclosure must have a ¾ inch hole in front of the test subject's nose and mouth area to accommodate the nebulizer nozzle.

(iii) The test subject must don the test enclosure. Throughout the threshold screening test, the test subject must breathe with mouth wide open and tongue extended.

(iv) Using a DeVilbiss Model 40 Inhalation Medication Nebulizer, the test conductor must spray the threshold check solution in accordance with II(c)(1)(v) of this appendix into the enclosure. The nebulizer must be clearly marked to distinguish it from the fit test solution nebulizer.

(v) The threshold check solution consists of 0.83 grams of sodium saccharin USP in one cc of warm water. It may be prepared by putting one cc of the fit test solution (see section II(c)(2)(iv) of this appendix) in 100 cc of distilled water.

(vi) To produce the aerosol, the nebulizer bulb must be firmly squeezed so that it collapses completely. Then, the bulb must be released and allowed to expand fully.

(vii) The bulb must be squeezed rapidly ten times and the test subject must be asked whether he or she tastes the saccharin.

(viii) If the first response is negative, the ten rapid squeezes must be repeated and the test subject is again asked whether he or she tastes the saccharin.

(ix) If the second response is negative, ten more squeezes are repeated rapidly and the test subject again asked whether the saccharin is tasted.

(x) The test conductor must take note of the number of squeezes required to solicit a taste response.

(xi) If the saccharin is not tasted after 30 squeezes, the test subject may not perform the saccharin fit test.

(xii) If a taste response is elicited, the test subject must be asked to take note of the taste for reference in the fit test.

(xiii) Correct use of the nebulizer means that approximately one cc of liquid is used at a time in the nebulizer body.

(xiv) The nebulizer must be thoroughly rinsed in water, shaken dry, and refilled at least each morning and afternoon or at least every four-hours.

(2) Saccharin solution aerosol fit test. (i) The test subject may not eat, drink (except plain water), or chew gum for 15 minutes before the test.

(ii) The fit test must be conducted with the same type of enclosure used for the saccharin taste threshold screening test in accordance with section II(c)(1) of this appendix.

(iii) The test subject must don the enclosure while wearing the respirator selected in the saccharin taste threshold screening test. The respirator must be properly adjusted and equipped with a particulate filter(s).

(iv) A second DeVilbiss Model 40 Inhalation Medication Nebulizer must be used to spray the fit test solution into the enclosure. This nebulizer must be clearly marked to distinguish it from the nebulizer used for the threshold check solution in accordance with section II(c)(1)(iv) of this appendix.

(v) The fit test solution must be prepared by adding 83 grams of sodium saccharin to 100 cc of warm water.

(vi) The test subject must breathe with mouth wide open and tongue extended.

Pt. 197, Subpt. C, App. E

(vii) The nebulizer must be inserted into the hole in the front of the enclosure and the fit test solution must be sprayed into the enclosure using the same number of squeezes required to elicit a taste response in the screening test in accordance with sections II(c)(1)(vi) through II(c)(1)(xi) of this appendix.

(viii) After generating the aerosol, the test subject must be instructed to perform the exercises in section I(n) of this appendix.

(ix) Every 30 seconds, the aerosol concentration must be replenished using one half the number of squeezes used initially.

(x) The test subject must indicate to the test conductor if, at any time during the fit test, the taste of saccharin is detected.

(xi) If the taste of saccharin is detected, the fit must be deemed unsatisfactory and a different respirator must be tried.

(d) *Irritant fume test.* The irritant fume test is an alternative qualitative fit test.

(1) The respirator to be tested must be equipped with high-efficiency particulate air (HEPA) filters.

(2) The test subject must be allowed to smell a weak concentration of the irritant smoke before the respirator is donned to become familiar with the smoke's characteristic odor.

(3) Both ends of a ventilation smoke tube containing stannic oxychloride, such as the Marine Safety Appliance part No. 5645 or equivalent, must be broken. One end of the smoke tube must be attached to a low flow air pump set to deliver 200 milliliters per minute.

(4) The test subject must be advised that the smoke may be irritating to the eyes and that the subject must keep his or her eyes closed while the test is performed.

(5) The test conductor must direct the stream of irritant smoke from the smoke tube towards the face seal area of the test subject. The test must be started with the smoke tube at least 12 inches from the facepiece, moved gradually to within one inch, and moved around the whole perimeter of the mask

(6) Each test subject who passes the smoke test without evidence of a response must be given a sensitivity check of the smoke from the same tube once the respirator has been removed. This check is necessary to determine whether the test subject reacts to the smoke. Failure to evoke a response voids the fit test.

(7) The fit test must be performed in a location with exhaust ventilation sufficient to prevent general contamination of the testing area by the irritant smoke.

III. Quantitative Fit Tests (ONFT)

(a) *General.* (1) The employer shall designate specific individuals to administer the respirator quantitative fit test program.

46 CFR Ch. I (10–1–04 Edition)

(2) The employer shall ensure that persons administering QNFT are able to properly calibrate equipment, perform tests, recognize invalid tests, calculate fit factors, and determine whether the test equipment is in proper working order.

(3) The employer shall ensure that QNFT equipment is kept clean and maintained so as to operate at the parameters for which it was designed.

(b) *Definitions.* (1) *Quantitative fit test* means a test which is performed in a test chamber and in which the normal air-purifying element of the respirator is replaced with a high-efficiency particulate air (HEPA) filter, in the case of particulate QNFT aerosols, or with a sorbent offering contaminant penetration protection equivalent to high-efficiency filters, if the QNFT test agent is a gas or vapor.

(2) *Challenge agent* means the aerosol, gas, or vapor introduced into a test chamber so that its concentration inside and outside of the respirator may be measured.

(3) *Test subject* means the person wearing the respirator for quantitative fit testing.

(4) *Normal standing position* means an erect and straight stance with arms down along the sides and eyes looking straight ahead.

(5) *Maximum peak penetration method* means the method of determining test agent penetration in the respirator as determined by strip chart recordings of the test. The highest peak penetration for a given exercise is taken to be representative of average penetration into the respirator for that exercise.

(6) *Average peak penetration method* means the method of determining test agent penetration into the respirator by using a strip chart recorder, integrator, or computer. The agent penetration is determined by an average of the peak heights on the graph, or by computer integration, for each exercise except the grimace exercise. Integrators or computers which calculate the actual test agent penetration into the respirator for each exercise also may be used in accordance with this method.

(7) *Fit factor* means the ratio of challenge agent concentration outside with respect to the inside of a respirator inlet covering (facepiece or enclosure).

(c) *Apparatus.* (1) Instrumentation. Aerosol generation, dilution, and measurement systems using corn oil or sodium chloride as test aerosols must be used for quantitative fit testing.

(2) Test chamber. The test chamber must be large enough to permit all test subjects to perform freely all required exercises without disturbing the challenge agent concentration or the measurement apparatus. The test chamber must be equipped and constructed so that the challenge agent is effectively isolated from the ambient air, yet is uniform in concentration throughout the chamber.

Coast Guard, DHS   Pt. 197, Subpt. C, App. E

(3) When testing air-purifying respirators, the normal filter or cartridge element must be replaced with a high-efficiency particulate filter supplied by the same manufacturer.

(4) The sampling instrument must be selected so that a strip chart record may be made of the test showing the rise and fall of the challenge agent concentration with each inspiration and expiration at fit factors of at least 2,000. Integrators or computers which integrate the amount of test agent penetration leakage into the respirator for each exercise may be used if a record of the readings is made.

(5) The combination of substitute air-purifying elements, challenge agent, and challenge agent concentration in the test chamber must be such that the test subject is not exposed to a concentration of the challenge agent in excess of the established exposure limit for the challenge agent at any time during the testing process.

(6) The sampling port on the test specimen respirator must be placed and constructed so that no leakage occurs around the port (e.g. where the respirator is probed), so that a free air flow is allowed into the sampling line at all times, and so that there is no interference with the fit or performance of the respirator.

(7) The test chamber and test set up must permit the person administering the test to observe the test subject inside the chamber during the test.

(8) The equipment generating the challenge atmosphere must maintain a constant concentration of challenge agent inside the test chamber to within a ten percent variation for the duration of the test.

(9) The time lag (i.e. the interval between an event and the recording of the event on the strip chart, computer, or integrator) must be kept to a minimum. There must be a clear association between the occurrence of an event inside the test chamber and the recording of that event.

(10) The sampling line tubing for the test chamber atmosphere and for the respirator sampling port must be of equal diameter and of the same material. The length of the two lines must be equal.

(11) The exhaust flow from the test chamber must pass through a high-efficiency filter before release.

(12) When sodium chloride aerosol is used, the relative humidity inside the test chamber must not exceed 50 percent.

(13) The limitations of instrument detection must be taken into account when determining the fit factor.

(14) Test respirators must be maintained in proper working order and inspected for deficiencies, such as cracks, missing valves, and gaskets.

(d) *Procedural requirements.* (1) When performing the initial positive or negative pressure test, the sampling line must be crimped closed in order to avoid air pressure leakage during either of these tests.

(2) In order to reduce the amount of QNFT time, an abbreviated screening isoamyl acetate test or irritant fume test may be used in order to quickly identify poor fitting respirators which passed the positive or negative pressure test. When performing a screening isoamyl acetate test, combination high-efficiency organic vapor cartridges or canisters must be used.

(3) A reasonably stable challenge agent concentration must be measured in the test chamber before testing. For canopy or shower curtain type of test units, the determination of the challenge agent stability may be established after the test subject has entered the test environment.

(4) Immediately after the subject enters the test chamber, the challenge agent concentration inside the respirator must be measured to ensure that the peak penetration does not exceed five percent for a half mask or one percent for a full facepiece respirator.

(5) A stable challenge concentration must be obtained before the actual start of testing.

(6) Respirator restraining straps must not be overtightened for testing. The straps must be adjusted by the wearer without assistance from other persons to give a fit reasonably comfortable for normal use.

(7) After obtaining a stable challenge concentration, the test subject must be instructed to perform the exercises described in section I(n) of this appendix. The test must be terminated whenever any single peak penetration exceeds five percent for half masks and one percent for full facepiece respirators. The test subject must be refitted and retested. If two of the three required tests are terminated, the fit is deemed inadequate.

(8) In order to successfully complete a QNFT, three successful fit tests must be conducted. The results of each of the three independent fit tests must exceed the minimum fit factor needed for the class of respirator (e.g., half mask respirator, full facepiece respirator).

(9) Calculation of fit factors. (i) The fit factor must be determined for the quantitative fit test by taking the ratio of the average chamber concentration to the concentration inside the respirator.

(ii) The average test chamber concentration is the arithmetic average of the test chamber concentration at the beginning and of the end of the test.

(iii) The concentration of the challenge agent inside the respirator must be determined by one of the following methods:

(A) Average peak concentration.

(B) Maximum peak concentration.

463

(C) Integration by calculation of the area under the individual peak for each exercise. This includes computerized integration.

(10) Interpretation of test results. The fit factor established by the quantitative fit testing must be the lowest of the three fit factor values calculated from the three required fit tests.

(11) The test subject must not be permitted to wear a half mask or a full facepiece respirator unless a minimum fit factor equivalent to at least ten times the hazardous exposure level is obtained.

(12) Filters used for quantitative fit testing must be replaced at least weekly, whenever increased breathing resistance is encountered, or whenever the test agent has altered the integrity of the filter media. When used, organic vapor cartridges and canisters must be replaced daily or whenever there is an indication of a breakthrough by a test agent.

APPENDIX F TO SUBPART C OF PART 197—SAMPLE WORKER CERTIFICATION FORM

BENZENE WORKER'S CERTIFICATION

I, _____ (Name of worker), certify in accordance with 46 CFR 197.530—

(1) That I have had, within the previous twelve months, at least one medical examination in compliance with 46 CFR 197.560 or 29 CFR 1910.1028;

(2) That the physician conducting the latest medical examination in compliance with paragraph (1) of this certification did not recommend that I be excluded from areas where personal exposure may exceed the action level as defined in 46 CFR 197.505;

(3) That all respirators and personal protective clothing and equipment that I will use while on the vessel meet the requirements of 46 CFR 197.550(b) and 197.555(c) or of 29 CFR 1910.1028; and

(4) That all respirators that I will use while on the vessel have been fitted and fit tested in accordance with 46 CFR 197.550 (c) and (d) or with 29 CFR 1910.1028.

_____
(signature of worker)

_____
(printed name of worker)

_____
(date signed by worker)

APPENDIX A TO PART 197—AIR NO-DECOMPRESSION LIMITS

The following table gives the depth versus bottom time limits for single, no-decompression, air dives made within any 12-hour period. The limit is the maximum bottom time in minutes that a diver can spend at that depth without requiring decompression beyond that provided by a normal ascent rate of 60 fsw per minute. (Although bottom time is concluded when ascent begins, a slower ascent rate would increase the bottom time thereby requiring decompression.) An amount of nitrogen remains in the tissues of a diver after any air dive, regardless of whether the dive was a decompression or no-decompression dive. Whenever another dive is made within a 12-hour period, the nitrogen remaining in the blood and body tissues of the diver must be considered when calculating his decompression.

AIR NO-DECOMPRESSION LIMITS

Depth (feet):	No-decompression limits (minutes)
35	310
40	200
50	100
60	60
70	50
80	40
90	30
100	25
110	20
120	15
130	10

(Source: U.S. Navy Diving Manual, 1 September 1973.)

PART 198 [RESERVED]

INDEX

SUBCHAPTER V—MARINE OCCUPATIONAL SAFETY AND HEALTH STANDARDS

EDITORIAL NOTE: This listing is provided for informational purposes only. It is compiled and kept current by the U.S. Coast Guard, Department of Homeland Security. This index is updated as of October 1, 2003.

Part, subpart, or section

A

Access to Records	197.580, Appendix A(VII)
ACFM	197.204
Action level	197.505
Additional examinations and referrals	197.560(d)
Additional exposure monitoring	197.540(c)
Air compressor output	197.450(a)
Air compressor system	197.310
Air diving, surface supplied	197.432
Air No-decompression limits	197.346(e), 197.482(a)(9), 197.580, Appendix A
Air purifying element	197.550(f)(3)
American Red Cross Standard First Aid handbook	197.314(a)(2)
Analysis of samples	197.580, Appendix D (II)(6)
ANSI address	197.205(b)(1), 197.510(a)
ANSI Code	197.204, 197.336(a)
Apparatus	197.580, Appendix D(I)(3), 197.580, Appendix D(II)(3), 197.580, Appendix D(III)(c)
Appeal, right of	197.203
Appendices	197.580

Appendix A - Sample Substance Safety Data Sheet, Benzene
Appendix B - Substance Technical Guidelines, Benzene
Appendix C - Medical Surveillance Guidelines for Benzene
Appendix D - Sampling and Analytical Methods for Benzene Monitoring-Measurement Procedures
Appendix E - Respirator Fit Tests

Applicability, benzene	197.501
Applicability, equipment	197.300
Applicability, general	197.200
Applicability, operations	197.400
ASME address	197.205(b)(2)
ASME Code	197.204
ATA	197.204
Authorized person	197.505
Availability of records	197.570(c)
Availability of standards	197.205

B

Backup data	197.580, Appendix D(I)(8), 197.580, Appendix D(II)(8)
Bell	197.204, 197.432(e)(3), 197.434(c), 197.434(d)
Bell, open diving	197.334
Benzene	197.505

46 CFR Ch. I (10–1–04 Edition)

Benzene Worker's Certification .... 197.580, Appendix F
Bottom time .... 197.204, 197.410(a)(4)
Breathing gas/breathing mixture .... 197.204, 197.410(a)(8), 197.410(a)(9)(i)(B)
Breathing gas supply .... 197.340, 197.410(a)(2)
Breathing gas tests 197.450
Breathing supply hoses 197.312, 197.456
Breathing supply system .... 197.450(c)
Breathing zone 197.505
Bunks .... 197.332(f)
Buoyancy-changing devices 197.342
Bursting pressure .... 197.204, 197.312(a)(2)

C

Casualty 197.484, 197.486, 197.488
Chamber, decompression 197.204, 197.332
Check valve .... 197.310(a)(i)
Closed bell .... 197.434(d), 197.434(h)
Coast Guard .... 197.200, 197.202(a), 197.203, 197.206(a), 197.328, 197.488(c), 197.501(a),
197.510(a), 197.545(e), 197.575(a)
Commandant .... 197.206(b)
Commercial diver 197.204
Commercial diving operations 197.200, 197.204
Communications .... 197.322(a)(3), 197.346(b)(3), 197.402(b)(1), 197.410(a)(5), 197.410(a)(6)
Compressed gas cylinders 197.338
Confidentiality of records .... 197.570(e)
Corrosion-resistant material .... 197.320(a)(5)
Cylinder 197.204

D

Decompression chamber .... 197.204, 197.314(c)(1)
Decompression sickness .... 197.204, 197.314(c)(3)
Decompression table .... 197.204, 197.314(c)(2)
Deepwater port .... 197.202(a)
Deepwater port safety zone .... 197.202(a)
Definitions 197.204, 197.505
Depth 197.204
Depth gage .... 197.346(a)(B)(8), 197.458
Designation in writing .... 197.208(a), 197.210(a)
Designation of diving supervisor 197.210
Designation of person-in-charge 197.208
Determination of personal exposure 197.540
Dive location .... 197.204, 197.314(a)
Dive procedures 197.410
Dive team 197.204
Diver 197.204
Diver-carried reserve breathing gas 197.204, 197.340
Diver's equipment 197.346
Diver's safety harness 197.324
Diving equipment 197.346, 197.460
Diving installation 197.204
Diving ladder and stage 197.320
Diving mode 197.204
Diving operations .... 197.202(b)
Diving stage 197.204
Diving supervisor 197.204, 197.404
Diving, SCUBA 197.430
Drain valve .... 197.310(a)(1)(iv)

466

Subchapter V Index

Dry suit .... 197.342(a)

E

Electrical systems .... 197.328(d)(18)
Electrically powered respiratory protective equipment .... 197.550(b)(3)
Emergency 197.505
Emergency locating device .... 197.330(a)(6)
Emergency medical examination .... 197.560(e)
Employee 197.505
Employer 197.505
Engineering controls .... 197.545(b)(1)
Environmental monitoring .... 197.535(a)
Equipment, diver's 197.346, 197.460
Equipment, first aid 197.314
Exhaust valve .... 197.322(a)(2)

F

Face mask .... 197.346(a)(B)(2)
Facility 197.204
Federal Register .... 197.510(a)
Filtration system .... 197.310(c)
Fins .... 197.346(a)(B)(6)
First aid and treatment equipment 197.314, 197.454
Fit tests, respirator .... 197.580 Appendix E
Fsw 197.204

G

Gages and timekeeping devices 197.318
Gas diving, mixed surface supplied 197.434
Gas embolism 197.204

H

Heavy-weight diving outfit .... 197.204, 197.346(b)
Helmet cushion .... 197.346(b)(4)
Hydrostatic test .... 197.328(c)(2)(iii)
Hyperbaric conditions 197.204

I

Illumination .... 197.328(d)(10), 197.332(e)
Incorporation by reference 197.510
Inflatable flotation devices .... 197.344, 197.346(a)(B)(3)
Information provided to the physician .... 197.560(f)
Initial exposure monitoring .... 197.540(b)
Injurious corrosion 197.204
Intakes .... 197.310(b)
Inwater decompression .... 197.436(c)(6)

J

J-valve .... 197.346(a)(A)

K

Kink resistant .... 197.312(a)(4)(i)
Knife .... 197.346(a)(B)(5)

467

L

Lifting equipment .... 197.330(a)(3), 197.334(b)
Liveboating... 197.204, 197.436
Logbooks 197.480, 197.482
Logbook entries 197.482

M

Manually activated inflation device... 197.344(b)
Manually operated exhaust valve .... 197.344(e)
Marine scientific research and development purposes by educational institutions .... 197.202(a)(1)
Master... 197.208
Material Safety Data Sheets (MSDS) .... 197.565(a)
Maximum allowable working pressure .... 197.310(d)
Maximum working pressure .... 197.204, 197.312(a)(1), (i), (iii)
Medical kit .... 197.314(a)(1), 197.314(c)(4), 197.454
Medical examination, initial .... 197.560(b)
Medical record .... 197.570(b)
Medical requirements .... 197.580, Appendix A(V)
Medical surveillance 197.560
Mine Safety and Health Administration (MSHA)................................... 197.550(b)
Mixed gas diving, surface supplied... 197.434
Mobile Offshore Drilling Unit... 197.202(a)

N

National Institute for Occupational Safety and Health (NIOSH) .... 197.580, Appendix A(III)
No-decompression limits 197.204
Non-return valve... 197.322(a)(1)
Notice of casualty... 197.484
Notification of exposure monitoring results .... 197.540(e)
Notifying personnel of benzene hazards 197.565

O

Observation of monitoring... 197.575
Officer-in-Charge, Marine Inspection .... 197.462, 197.484(a), 197.486, 197.488
Open diving bells... 197.324
Operations involving benzene 197.505
Operations manual (contents) 197.420
Oral inflation device .... 197.344(c)
Outer Continental Shelf .... 197.202(a)
Over-pressure relief device .... 197.344(d)
Oxygen cleaning 197.452
Oxygen safety 197.326

P

Performance standard.. 197.505, 197.520
Periodic exposure monitoring... 197.540(c)
Periodic medical examinations .... 197.560(c)
Permissible exposure limits (PELs) .... 197.505, 197.515, 197.530(a)
Person-in-charge 197.402, 197.505, 197.525
Personal exposure 197.505, 197.540
Personal protective clothing and equipment 197.555
Persons other than employees 197.530
Physician's written opinion .... 197.560(g)

Subchapter V Index

Platform, open grating .... 197.320(b)(2)
Pneumatic test .... 197.328(2)(iii)(B), 197.462(d)(2)(3)
Pneumofathometer .... 197.346(b)(3)
Pressure gage .... 197.310(a)(1)(ii)
Pressure piping 197.336, 197.462
Pressure vessel 197.204, 197.462
Pressure vessel, repairs and modifications .... 197.300(c)(d)
Program to reduce personal exposure 197.545
Propellers, vessel .... 197.436(a)(3)
Psi(g) 197.204
Purpose of subpart 197.200
PVHO 197.204, 197.328, 197.330, 197.332, 197.462

R

Radiographic .... 197.328(c)(ii)
Record keeping 197.570
Record of personal exposure monitoring .... 197.570(a)
Regulated area 197.505, 197.535
Relief valve .... 197.310(a)(1)(iii)
Removal from exposure .... 197.560(h)
Repetitive dive .... 197.482(b)(5)
Research and development for the advancement of diving equipment and
     technology .... 197.202(a)(2)
Respirators .... 197.530(a)(3)
Respirator selection .... 197.550(b)
Respirator fit tests .... 197.580, Appendix E, 197.550(c), 197.550(d)
Respirator inspection .... 197.550(f)
Respirator maintenance .... 197.550(g)
Respirator storage .... 197.550(h)
Respirator use .... 197.550(e)
Respiratory protection 197.550
Responsibilities of the diving supervisor 197.404
Responsibilities of the person-in-charge 197.402, 197.525
Restricted visibility .... 197.436(b)
Resuscitator .... 197.314(a)(3)
Retention of records after casualty 197.488
Revised work practices .... 197.545(b)(2)
Right of appeal 197.203

S

Safety, oxygen 197.326
Saturation diving 197.204
SCUBA diving 197.430
Search and rescue .... 197.202(a)(3)
Short-term exposure limit (STEL) .... 197.505, 197.515(b)
Shut-off valves .... 197.310(d)
Sound-powered headset .... 197.332(m)
Speech unscrambler .... 197.328(d)(17)
Standby diver 197.204, 197.340
Substitutes 197.206
Surface supplied air diving 197.204, 197.432
Surface-supplied helmets and masks 197.322
Surface-supplied mixed-gas diving 197.204
Swim fins .... 197.346(a)(B)(6)

469

T

Timekeeping device 197.204, 197.458
Time-weighted average exposure limit (TWA) .... 197.505, 197.515(a)
Toxicology .... 197.580, Appendix C(II)
Training... 197.565(b)
Transfer of records .... 197.570(d)
Treatment table.. 197.204
Two-way communications............. 197.314(b), 197.322(a)(3), 197.328(d)(5), 197.328(d)(6), 197.410(a)(5), 197.410(a)(6)

U

Umbilical.. 197.204, 197.312(b), 197.322(a)(1), 197.330

V

Valves .... 197.310.(a)(i), 197.310(a)(1)(iii), 197.310(a)(1)(iv), 197.310(d), 197.322(a)(1), 197.310(a)(2)
Vessel.. 197.204
Vessel propellers .... 197.436(a)(3)
Visibility, restricted.. 197.436(b)
Volume tank .... 197.204, 197.310(a)

W

Weight belt .... 197.346(a)(B)(4)
Weighted shoes .... 197.346(b)(4)
Welded joints .... 197.328(c)(ii)
Working pressure... 197.204
Wristwatch, diver's .... 197.346(a)(B)(7)
Written report of casualty 197.486

SUBCHAPTER W—LIFESAVING APPLIANCES AND ARRANGEMENTS

PART 199—LIFESAVING SYSTEMS FOR CERTAIN INSPECTED VESSELS

Subpart A—General

Sec.
199.01　Purpose.
199.03　Relationship to international standards.
199.05　Incorporation by reference.
199.07　Additional equipment and requirements.
199.09　Equivalents.
199.10　Applicability.
199.20　Exemptions.
199.30　Definitions.
199.40　Evaluation, testing and approval of lifesaving appliances and arrangements.
199.45　Tests and inspections of lifesaving equipment and arrangements.

Subpart B—Requirements for All Vessels

199.60　Communications.
199.70　Personal lifesaving appliances.
199.80　Muster list and emergency instructions.
199.90　Operating instructions.
199.100　Manning of survival craft and supervision.
199.110　Survival craft muster and embarkation arrangements.
199.120　Launching stations.
199.130　Stowage of survival craft.
199.140　Stowage of rescue boats.
199.145　Marine evacuation system launching arrangements.
199.150　Survival craft launching and recovery arrangements; general.
199.153　Survival craft launching and recovery arrangements using falls and a winch.
199.155　Lifeboat launching and recovery arrangements.
199.157　Free-fall lifeboat launching and recovery arrangements.
199.160　Rescue boat embarkation, launching and recovery arrangements.
199.170　Line-throwing appliance.
199.175　Survival craft and rescue boat equipment.
199.176　Markings on lifesaving appliances.
199.178　Marking of stowage locations.
199.180　Training and drills.
199.190　Operational readiness, maintenance, and inspection of lifesaving equipment.

Subpart C—Additional Requirements for Passenger Vessels

199.200　General.
199.201　Survival craft.
199.202　Rescue boats.
199.203　Marshalling of liferafts.
199.211　Lifebuoys.
199.212　Lifejackets.
199.214　Immersion suits and thermal protective aids.
199.217　Muster list and emergency instructions.
199.220　Survival craft and rescue boat embarkation arrangements.
199.230　Stowage of survival craft.
199.240　Muster stations.
199.245　Survival craft embarkation and launching arrangements.
199.250　Drills.

Subpart D—Additional Requirements for Cargo Vessels

199.260　General.
199.261　Survival craft.
199.262　Rescue boats.
199.271　Lifebuoys.
199.273　Immersion suits.
199.280　Survival craft embarkation and launching arrangements.
199.290　Stowage of survival craft.

Subpart E—Additional Requirements for Vessels Not Subject to SOLAS

199.500　General.
199.510　EPIRB requirements.
199.520　Lifeboat requirements.

Subpart F—Exemptions and Alternatives for Vessels Not Subject to SOLAS

199.600　General.
199.610　Exemptions for vessels in specified services.
199.620　Alternatives for all vessels in a specified service.
199.630　Alternatives for passenger vessels in a specified service.
199.640　Alternatives for cargo vessels in a specified service.

AUTHORITY: 46 U.S.C. 3306, 3703; Pub. L 103–206, 107 Stat. 2439; Department of Homeland Security Delegation No. 0170.1.

SOURCE: CGD 84–069, 61 FR 25313, May 20, 1996, unless otherwise noted.

Subpart A—General

§ 199.01 Purpose.

(a) This part sets out the requirements for lifesaving appliances and arrangements for all inspected U.S. vessels except for—

(1) Offshore supply vessels, which are covered by subchapter L of this chapter;

(2) Mobile Offshore Drilling Units (MODU), which are covered by subchapter I-A of this chapter;

(3) Small passenger vessels, which are covered by subchapters K and T of this chapter; and

(4) Sailing school vessels, which are covered by part 169 of this chapter.

(b) This subpart and subparts B, C, and D of this part set out the requirements for vessels on international voyages that are subject to the International Convention for the Safety of Life at Sea, 1974, and its Protocol of 1978, as amended (SOLAS).

(c) Subparts E and F of this part set out additional requirements, alternatives, and exemptions for vessels that are not subject to SOLAS.

§ 199.03 Relationship to international standards.

(a) This subpart and subparts B, C, and D of this part are based on Chapter III, SOLAS. Section numbers in this subpart and subparts B, C, and D of this part are generally related to the regulation numbers in Chapter III, SOLAS, but paragraph designations are not related to the numbering in Chapter III, SOLAS. To find the corresponding Chapter III, SOLAS regulation for this subpart and subparts B, C, and D of this part, beginning with § 199.10, divide the section number following the decimal point by 10.

(b) For purposes of this part, any vessel carrying a valid Passenger Ship Safety Certificate supplemented by a Record of Equipment, or a valid Cargo Ship Safety Equipment Certificate supplemented by a Record of Equipment, is considered to have met the requirements of this part if the equipment meets § 199.40 and if, in addition to the requirements of SOLAS Chapter III, the vessel meets the following requirements:

(1) Each new lifeboat and launching appliance on a tank vessel may be of aluminum construction only if its stowage location is protected with a water spray system in accordance with § 199.290(b).

(2) Each child-size lifejacket and immersion suit must be appropriately marked and stowed separately from adult or extended-size devices as required in § 199.70(b)(2).

(3) Each lifejacket and immersion suit must be marked with the vessel's name in accordance with §§ 199.70 (b)(3) and (c)(3).

(4) Inflatable lifejackets, if carried, must be of the same or similar design as required by § 199.70(b).

(5) Containers for lifejackets, immersion suits, and anti-exposure suits must be marked as specified in § 199.70(d).

(6) Instructions for passengers must include illustrated instructions on the method of donning lifejackets as required in § 199.80(c)(5).

(7) Each liferaft must be arranged to permit it to drop into the water from the deck on which it is stowed as required in § 199.130(c)(3).

(8) Lifeboats and rescue boats must be arranged to allow safe disembarkation onto the vessel after a drill in accordance with § 199.110(h).

(9) The requirements for guarding of falls in § 199.153 (e) and (g) must be met.

(10) The winch drum requirements described in § 199.153(f) must be met for all survival craft winches, including multiple drum winches.

(11) The maximum lowering speed requirements for launching arrangements using falls and a winch in §§ 199.153 (i) and (j) must be met.

(12) An auxiliary line must be kept with each line-throwing appliance in accordance with § 199.170(c)(2).

(13) Immersion suits must be carried on all cargo vessels except those operating between the 32 degrees north and 32 degrees south latitude in accordance with § 199.273.

(14) Vessels carrying immersion suits must conduct drills in accordance with §§ 199.180 (d)(11) and (d)(12).

(c) The certificates in paragraph (b) of this section will be accepted as proof of compliance with the requirements in this part unless the Officer in Charge,

Coast Guard, DHS § 199.07

Marine Inspection (OCMI), determines that—

(1) The condition of the vessel or of its equipment does not correspond substantially with the particulars of its certificates; or

(2) The vessel and its equipment have not been maintained in conformance with the provisions of the regulations in this part.

[CGD 84–069, 61 FR 25313, May 20, 1996, as amended at 63 FR 52816, Oct. 1, 1998; USCG–1999–6216, 64 FR 53229, Oct. 1, 1999]

§ 199.05 Incorporation by reference.

(a) Certain material is incorporated by reference into this part with the approval of the Director of the Federal Register under 5 U.S.C. 552(a) and 1 CFR part 51. To enforce any edition other than that specified in paragraph (b) of this section, the Coast Guard must publish notice of change in the FEDERAL REGISTER; and the material must be available to the public. All approved material is available for inspection at the U.S. Coast Guard, Lifesaving and Fire Safety Standards Division (G–MSE–4), 2100 Second Street SW., Washington, DC 20593–0001, and at the National Archives and Records Administration (NARA). For information on the availability of this material at NARA, call 202–741–6030, or go to: *http://www.archives.gov/federal_register/code_of_federal_regulations/ibr_locations.html*. All approved material is available from the sources indicated in paragraph (b) of this section.

(b) The material approved for incorporation by reference in this part and the sections affected are as follows:

AMERICAN SOCIETY FOR TESTING AND MATERIALS (ASTM)

100 Barr Harbor Drive, West Conshohocken, PA 19428–2959

ASTM D 93–97, Standard Test Methods for Flash Point by Pensky-Martens Closed Cup Tester.	199.261; 199.290
ASTM F 1003–86 (1992), Standard Specification for Searchlights on Motor Lifeboats.	199.175
ASTM F 1014-92, Standard Specification for Flashlights on Vessels.	199.175

INTERNATIONAL MARITIME ORGANIZATION (IMO)

Publications Section, 4 Albert Embankment, London, SE1 7SR, United Kingdom

MSC Circular 699, Revised Guidelines for Passenger Safety Instructions, 17 July 1995.	199.217
Resolution A.520(13), Code of Practice for the Evaluation, Testing and Acceptance of Prototype Novel Life-saving Appliances and Arrangements, 17 November 1983.	199.40
Resolution A.657(16), Instructions for Action in Survival Craft, 19 November 1989.	199.175
Resolution A.658(16), Use and Fitting of Retro-reflective Materials on Life-saving Appliances, 20 November 1989.	199.70; 199.176
Resolution A.760(18), Symbols Related to Life-saving Appliances and Arrangements, 17 November 1993.	199.70; 199.90
Resolution MSC.4(48), International Code for the Construction and Equipment of Ships carrying Dangerous Chemicals in Bulk (IBC Code), 1994.	199.30; 199.280
Resolution MSC.5(48), International Code for the Construction and Equipment of Ships carrying Liquefied Gases in Bulk, (IGC Code), 1993.	199.30; 199.280

[CGD 84–069, 61 FR 25313, May 20, 1996; 61 FR 40281, Aug. 1, 1996, as amended by CGD 96–041, 61 FR 50735, Sept. 27, 1996; CGD 97–057, 62 FR 51051, Sept. 30, 1997; USCG–1999–6216, 64 FR 53229, Oct. 1, 1999; USCG–1999–5151, 64 FR 67187, Dec. 1, 1999; 69 FR 18803, Apr. 9, 2004; USCG–2004–18884, 69 FR 58352, Sept. 30, 2004]

§ 199.07 Additional equipment and requirements.

The OCMI may require a vessel to carry specialized or additional lifesaving equipment other than as required in this part if the OCMI determines that the conditions of a voyage

§ 199.09

present uniquely hazardous circumstances that are not adequately addressed by existing requirements.

§ 199.09 Equivalents.

When this part requires a particular fitting, material, or lifesaving appliance or arrangement, the Commandant (G-MSE) may accept any other fitting, material, or lifesaving appliance or arrangement that is at least as effective as that required by this part. The Commandant may require engineering evaluations and tests to determine the equivalent effectiveness of the substitute fitting, material, or lifesaving appliance or arrangement.

§ 199.10 Applicability.

(a) *General.* Unless expressly provided otherwise in this Chapter, this part applies to all vessels inspected under U.S. law as set out in Table 199.10(a).

TABLE 199.10(a)—LIFESAVING REQUIREMENTS FOR INSPECTED VESSELS.

46 CFR Subchapter	Vessel Type	Vessel Service	Subchapter W Subparts applicable [1]					Other [2]
			A	B	C	D	E	F	
D	Tank ≥ 500 tons	International voyage [3]	X	X		X			
D	Tank < 500 tons	International voyage [3]	X	X		X	X	X	
D	Tank	All other services	X	X		X	X	X	
H	Passenger	International voyage [3]	X	X	X				
H	Passenger	Short Inter'l voyage [3]	X	X	X				
H	Passenger	All other services	X	X	X		X	X	
I	Cargo ≥ 500 tons	International voyage [3]	X	X		X			
I	Cargo < 500 tons	International voyage [3]	X	X		X	X	X	
I	Cargo	All other services	X	X		X	X	X	
I-A	MODU	All							46 CFR 108
K	Small Passenger	International voyage [3]	X	X	X				
K	Small Passenger	Short Inter'l voyage [3]	X	X	X				
K	Small Passenger	All other services							46 CFR 117
L	Offshore Supply	All			X [4]	X [5]			46 CFR 133
R—Part 167	Public Nautical School	International voyage [3]	X	X	X [4]	X [5]			
R—Part 167	Public Nautical School	All other services	X	X	X [4]	X [5]	X	X	
R—Part 168	Civilian Nautical School	International voyage [3]	X	X	X [4]	X [5]			
R—Part 168	Civilian Nautical School	All other services	X	X	X [4]	X [5]	X	X	
R—Part 169	Sailing School	All services							46 CFR 169.500
T	Small Passenger	International voyage [3]	X	X	X				
T	Small Passenger	Short Int'l voyage [3]	X	X	X				
T	Small Passenger	All other services							46 CFR 180
U	Oceanographic Res.	International voyage [3]	X	X	X [4]	X [5]			
U	Oceanographic Res.	All other services	X	X	X [4]	X [5]	X	X	

Notes:
[1] Subchapter W does not apply to inspected nonself-propelled vessels without accommodations or work stations on board.
[2] Indicates section where primary lifesaving system requirements are located. Other regulations may also apply.
[3] Not including vessels solely navigating the Great Lakes of North America and the River Saint Lawrence as far east as a straight line drawn from Cap des Rosiers to West Point, Anticosti Island and, on the north side Anticosti Island, the 63rd meridian.
[4] Applies to vessels carrying more than 50 special personnel, or vessels carrying not more than 50 special personnel if the vessels meet the structural fire protection requirements in subchapter H of this chapter for passenger vessels of the same size.
[5] Applies to vessels carrying not more than 50 special personnel that do not meet the structural fire protection requirements in subchapter H of this chapter for passenger vessels of the same size.

(b) *Inspected vessels not covered under this subchapter.* This part does not apply to non-self-propelled vessels without accommodations or work stations on board. Unless otherwise required by this chapter, it does not apply to offshore supply vessels; mobile offshore drilling units; small passenger vessels; and sailing school vessels.

(c) *Conversion of cargo vessel to passenger vessel.* For purposes of the application of this part, a cargo vessel, whenever constructed, which is converted to a passenger vessel is deemed to be a passenger vessel that is constructed on the date on which the conversion commences.

(d) *Vessels on international voyages.* This subpart and subparts B, C, and D of this part apply to vessels engaged on international voyages, except—

(1) Cargo vessels of less than 500 tons gross tonnage;

(2) Vessels not propelled by mechanical means;

Coast Guard, DHS § 199.10

(3) Wooden vessels of primitive build; and

(4) Vessels solely navigating the Great Lakes of North America and the River Saint Lawrence as far east as a straight line drawn from Cap des Rosiers to West Point, Anticosti Island, and on the north side Anticosti Island, the 63rd meridian.

(5) Tank vessels constructed before October 1, 1996 engaged in voyages between the continental United States and Alaska or Hawaii, and all other vessels engaged on international voyages which were constructed before July 1, 1986, must meet the requirements of §§ 199.70(b)(4)(i), 199.80, 199.90, 199.100, 199.180, 199.190 (paragraph (b) applies as much as practicable), 199.214, 199.217, 199.250, 199.261 (b)(2) and (e), and 199.273, and must fit retro-reflective material on all floating appliances, lifejackets and immersion suits. Except for the requirements of §§ 199.261 (b)(2) and (e), vessels may retain the number, type, and arrangement of lifesaving appliances previously required and approved for the vessel as long as the arrangement or appliance is maintained in good condition to the satisfaction of the OCMI.

(e) *Passenger vessels.* For the purposes of this part, the following vessels must meet the requirements for passenger vessels:

(1) Passenger vessels.

(2) Special purpose vessels carrying more than 50 special personnel.

(3) Special purpose vessels carrying not more than 50 special personnel if the vessels meet the structural fire protection requirements in subchapter H of this chapter for passenger vessels of the same size.

(f) *Cargo vessels.* For the purposes of this part, the following vessels must meet the requirements for cargo vessels:

(1) Cargo vessels.

(2) Tank vessels.

(3) Special purpose vessels carrying not more than 50 special personnel that do not meet the structural fire protection requirements in subchapter H of this chapter for passenger vessels of the same size.

(g) *Subparts applying to vessels on international and short international voyages.* (1) Passenger vessels on international voyages must meet the requirements of this subpart and subparts B and C of this part.

(2) Cargo vessels on international voyages must meet the requirements of this subpart and subparts B and D of this part.

(3) The provisions for passenger vessels on short international voyages in this subpart and subparts B and C of this part do not apply to special purpose vessels described in paragraphs (e)(2) and (3) of this section.

(h) *Vessels not subject to SOLAS.* Vessels not on international voyages and vessels listed in paragraph (d) of this section must meet the requirements of this subpart and subparts B, C, D, and E of this part unless otherwise exempted or permitted by subpart F of this part.

(1) Vessels on other than international voyages and vessels listed in paragraph (d) of this section which were constructed prior to October 1, 1996, must—

(i) By October 1, 1999, meet the requirements of §§ 199.70(b)(4)(i), 199.80, 199.90, 199.100, 199.180, 199.190 (paragraph (b) applies as much as practicable), 199.217, 199.250, 199.273, and 199.510, and fit retroreflective material on all floating appliances, lifejackets, and immersion suits;

(ii) By October 1, 2003, passenger vessels must carry the number and type of survival craft specified in table 199.630 of this part and cargo vessels in oceans and coastwise service must carry the number and type of survival craft specified in § 199.261(b)(2) and (e);

(iii) By October 1, 2003, passenger vessels must carry the immersion suits and thermal protective aids specified in § 199.214; and

(iv) Except for the requirements in paragraphs (h)(1)(ii) and (h)(1)(iii) of this section, vessels may retain the number, type, and arrangement of lifesaving equipment, including lifeboats, lifeboat davits, winches, inflatable liferafts, liferaft launching equipment, rescue boats, lifefloats, and buoyant apparatus previously required and approved for the vessel as long as the arrangement or appliance is maintained in good condition to the satisfaction of the OCMI.

475

§ 199.20

(2) This paragraph does not apply to public vessels.

(i) *New lifesaving appliances or arrangements.* When any lifesaving appliance or arrangement on a vessel subject to this part is replaced, or when the vessel undergoes repairs, alterations, or modifications of a major character involving replacement of, or any addition to, the existing lifesaving appliance or arrangements, each new lifesaving appliance and arrangement must meet the requirements of this part, unless the OCMI determines that the vessel cannot accommodate the new appliance or arrangement, except that—

(1) A survival craft is not required to meet the requirements of this part if it is replaced without replacing its davit and winch; and

(2) A davit and its winch are not required to meet the requirements of this part if one or both are replaced without replacing the survival craft.

(j) *Repairs and alterations to lifesaving appliances.* No extensive repairs or alterations, except in an emergency, may be made to a lifesaving appliance without advance notification to the OCMI. Insofar as possible, each repair or alteration must be made with material, and tested in the manner, specified in this subchapter and applicable to the new construction requirements in subchapter Q of this chapter. Emergency repairs or alterations must be reported as soon as practicable to the OCMI responsible for the port or location where the vessel may call after such repairs are made. Lifeboats, rescue boats, or rigid liferafts may not be reconditioned for use on a vessel other than the one they were originally built for, unless specifically accepted by the OCMI.

(k) *Vessels reflagged under Sec. 1137, Coast Guard Authorization Act of 1996.* Vessels that qualify for a certificate of inspection under the provisions of section 1137, Coast Guard Authorization Act of 1996, Public Law 104–324, 110 Stat. 3988 (46 U.S.C.A. app. 1187, Note), are not subject to the requirements of this part if such vessels meet lifesaving equipment standards required under section 1137 as determined by the Commandant.

[CGD 84–069, 63 FR 52817, Oct. 1, 1998; 63 FR 56066, Oct. 20, 1998; 63 FR 63798, Nov. 17, 1998; USCG–1999–6216, 64 FR 53229, Oct. 1, 1999]

§ 199.20 Exemptions.

(a) *Vessels engaged on international voyages.* (1) The following types of vessels engaged on international voyages may request an exemption from Commandant (G–MOC) from requirements of this part:

(i) A vessel for which the sheltered nature and conditions of an international voyage would render the application of any specific requirements of this part unreasonable or unnecessary and which in the course of the voyage does not proceed more than 20 miles from the nearest land.

(ii) A vessel embodying features of a novel kind to which the application of any provision of this part would seriously impede research into the development of such features and their incorporation on vessels engaged on international voyages.

(2) A written request for exemption under this section must be submitted to the cognizant OCMI for review and forwarding to Commandant (G–MOC).

(b) *Single voyage exemption from SOLAS requirements.* A vessel that is not normally engaged on international voyages, but which, under exceptional circumstances, is required to undertake a single international voyage, may be exempted from the applicable requirements in this subpart and subparts B, C, and D of this part by the Commandant (G–MOC). A written request for exemption under this paragraph must be submitted to the cognizant OCMI for review and forwarding to Commandant (G–MOC).

(c) *Exemption Certificates.* When Commandant (G–MOC) grants an exemption under paragraph (a) or (b) of this section, an Exemption Certificate describing the exemption will be issued by the appropriate OCMI. The Exemption Certificate must be carried on board the vessel at all times and must be available to Coast Guard personnel upon request.

(d) *Vessels not engaged on international voyages.* (1) If a District Commander

Coast Guard, DHS § 199.30

determines that the overall safety of the persons on board a vessel will not be significantly reduced, the District Commander may grant an exemption from compliance with a provision of this part to a specific vessel for a specified geographic area within the boundaries of the Coast Guard District. This exemption may be limited to certain periods of the year.

(2) Requests for exemption under this paragraph must be made in writing to the OCMI for transmission to the District Commander for the area in which the vessel is in service or will be in service.

(3) If the exemption is granted by the District Commander, the OCMI will endorse the vessel's Certificate of Inspection with a statement describing the exemption.

[CGD 84–069, 61 FR 25313, May 20, 1996, as amended by CGD 96–041, 61 FR 50735, Sept. 27, 1996; USCG–1999–6216, 64 FR 53229, Oct. 1, 1999]

§ 199.30 Definitions.

The following definitions apply to this part:

Accommodation means a cabin, or other covered or enclosed place, intended to be occupied by persons. Each place in which passengers and special personnel is carried is considered an accommodation, whether or not it is covered or enclosed. Accommodations include, but are not limited to halls, dining rooms, mess rooms, lounges, corridors, lavatories, cabins, offices, hospitals, cinemas, game and hobby rooms, and other similar places open to persons on board.

Anti-exposure suit means a protective suit designed for use by rescue boat crews and marine evacuation system parties.

Approval series means the first six digits of a number assigned by the Coast Guard to approved equipment. Where approval is based on a subpart of subchapter Q of this chapter, the approval series corresponds to the number of the subpart. A listing of current and formerly approved equipment and materials may be found on the Internet at: *http://cgmix.uscg.mil/equipment.* Each OCMI may be contacted for information concerning approved equipment.

Approved lifesaving appliance means carrying an approval granted by the Commandant under subchapter Q of this chapter.

Cargo vessel means any vessel that is not a passenger vessel.

Certificated person means a person holding a U.S. merchant mariner's document with an endorsement as a lifeboatman or another inclusive rating under part 12 of this chapter.

Child, for the purpose of determining the number of lifejackets required under this part, means a person less than 41 kilograms (90 pounds) in mass.

Civilian nautical school means any school or branch thereof operated and conducted in the United States, except State nautical schools and schools operated by the United States or any agency thereof, which offers instruction for the primary purpose of training for service in the merchant marine.

Coastwise voyage means a voyage on the waters of any ocean or the Gulf of Mexico no more than 20 nautical miles offshore.

Commandant means the Commandant of the U.S. Coast Guard.

Crew means all persons carried on board the vessel to provide navigation and maintenance of the vessel, its machinery, systems, and arrangements essential for propulsion and safe navigation or to provide services for other persons on board.

District Commander means an officer of the U.S. Coast Guard designated by the Commandant to command all Coast Guard activities within a Coast Guard District. Coast Guard Districts are described in 33 CFR part 2.

Detection means the determination of the location of survivors or survival craft.

Embarkation ladder means the ladder provided at survival craft embarkation stations to permit safe access to survival craft after launching.

Embarkation station means the place where a survival craft is boarded.

Extended-size lifejacket means a lifejacket that is approved for use by adults as well as by some larger children.

Ferry means a vessel as described in § 70.10–1 of this chapter.

Float-free launching means that method of launching a survival craft or lifesaving appliance whereby the craft or appliance is automatically released from a sinking vessel and is ready for use.

Free-fall launching means that method of launching a survival craft whereby the craft, with its full complement of persons and equipment on board, is released and allowed to fall into the sea without any restraining apparatus.

Immersion suit means a protective suit that reduces loss of body heat of a person wearing it in cold water.

Inflatable appliance means an appliance that depends upon nonrigid, gas-filled chambers for buoyancy and that is normally kept uninflated until ready for use.

Inflated appliance means an appliance that depends upon nonrigid, gas-filled chambers for buoyancy and that is kept inflated and ready for use at all times.

International voyage means a voyage from the United States to a port outside the United States or conversely; or, a voyage originating and terminating at ports outside the United States. Voyages between the continental United States and Hawaii or Alaska, and voyages between Hawaii and Alaska, shall be considered international voyages for the purposes of this part.

Lakes, bays, and sounds means the waters of any lakes, bays, or sounds other than the waters of the Great Lakes.

Launching appliance or *launching arrangement* means the method or devices designed to transfer a survival craft or rescue boat from its stowed position to the water. For a launching arrangement using a davit, the term includes the davit, winch, and falls.

Length of vessel, means the load-line length defined in § 42.13–15(a) of this chapter.

Lifejacket means a flotation device approved as a life preserver or lifejacket.

Major character means any repair, alteration or modification to a vessel that is a major conversion as decided by the Commandant (G–MOC).

Major conversion means a conversion of a vessel that—

(a) Substantially changes the dimensions or carrying capacity of the vessel;

(b) Changes the type of the vessel;

(c) Substantially prolongs the life of the vessel; or

(d) Otherwise so changes the vessel that it is essentially a new vessel.

Marine evacuation system means an appliance designed to rapidly transfer large numbers of persons from an embarkation station by means of a passage to a floating platform for subsequent embarkation into associated survival craft, or directly into associated survival craft.

Mobile offshore drilling unit (MODU) means a vessel capable of engaging in drilling operations for the exploration or exploitation of subsea resources.

Muster station means the place where persons on board assemble before boarding a survival craft.

Nautical school vessel means a vessel operated by or in connection with a nautical school or an educational institution under Section 13 of the Coast Guard Authorization Act of 1986.

Novel lifesaving appliance or arrangement means a lifesaving appliance or arrangement that has new features not fully covered by the provisions of this part but that provides an equal or higher standard of safety.

Ocean means the waters of any ocean or the Gulf of Mexico more than 20 nautical miles offshore.

Oceanographic research vessel means a vessel that the Secretary finds is being employed only in instruction in oceanography or limnology, or both, or only in oceanographic or limnological research, including those studies about the sea such as seismic, gravity meter, and magnetic exploration and other marine geophysical or geological surveys, atmospheric research, and biological research.

Officer in Charge, Marine Inspection (OCMI), means a Coast Guard Officer responsible for marine inspection functions in a Marine Inspection Zone. Marine Inspection Zones are described in 33 CFR part 2.

Passenger means—

(a) On an international voyage, every person other than—

(1) The master and the members of the crew or other persons employed or engaged in any capacity on board a vessel on the business of that vessel; and

(2) A child under 1 year of age.

(b) On other than an international voyage, an individual carried on the vessel, except—

(1) The owner or an individual representative of the owner or, in the case of a vessel under charter, an individual charterer or individual representative of the charterer;

(2) The master; or

(3) A member of the crew engaged in the business of the vessel who has not contributed consideration for carriage and who is paid for onboard services.

Passenger for hire means a passenger for whom consideration is contributed as a condition of carriage on the vessel, whether directly or indirectly flowing to the owner, charterer, operator, agent, or any other person having an interest in the vessel.

Passenger vessel means—

(1) On an international voyage, a vessel of at least 100 tons gross tonnage carrying more than 12 passengers; and

(2) On other than an international voyage, a vessel of at least 100 tons gross tonnage—

(i) Carrying more than 12 passengers, including at least one passenger-for-hire; or

(ii) That is chartered and carrying more than 12 passengers; or

(iii) That is a submersible vessel carrying at least one passenger-for-hire.

Public vessel means a vessel that—

(a) Is owned, or demise chartered, and operated by the U.S. Government or a government of a foreign country including a vessel operated by the Coast Guard or Saint Lawrence Seaway Development Corporation, but not a vessel owned or operated by the Department of Transportation or any corporation organized or controlled by the Department; and

(b) Is not engaged in commercial service.

Rescue boat means a boat designed to rescue persons in distress and to marshal survival craft.

Retrieval means the safe recovery of survivors.

Rivers, in relation to vessel service, means operating exclusively in the waters of rivers and/or canals.

Scientific personnel means individuals on board an oceanographic research vessel only to engage in scientific research, or to instruct or receive instruction in oceanography or limnology.

Seagoing condition means the operating condition of the vessel with the personnel, equipment, fluids, and ballast necessary for safe operation on the waters where the vessel operates.

Similar stage of construction means the stage at which—

(a) Construction identifiable with a specific vessel begins; and

(b) Assembly of that vessel has commenced comprising at least 50 metric tons (55.1 U.S. tons) or 1 percent of the estimated mass of all structural material, whichever is less.

Short international voyage is an international voyage in the course of which a vessel is not more than 200 miles from a port or place in which the passengers and crew could be placed in safety. Neither the distance between the last port of call in the country in which the voyage begins and the final port of destination, nor the return voyage, may exceed 600 miles. The final port of destination is the last port of call in the scheduled voyage at which the vessel commences its return voyage to the country in which the voyage began.

Special personnel means all persons who are not passengers or members of the crew and who are carried on board a special purpose vessel in connection with the special purpose of that vessel or because of special work being carried out aboard that vessel. Special personnel include—

(a) On oceanographic research vessels, scientific personnel; and

(b) On nautical school vessels, students, cadets, and instructors who are not members of the crew.

Special purpose vessel means a mechanically self-propelled vessel which by reason of its function carries on board more than 12 special personnel including passengers. Special purpose vessels include oceanographic research vessels and nautical school vessels.

Survival craft means a craft capable of sustaining the lives of persons in distress from the time of abandoning the vessel on which the persons were originally carried. The term includes lifeboats, liferafts, buoyant apparatus, and lifefloats, but does not include rescue boats.

§ 199.40

Tank vessel means a vessel that is constructed or adapted to carry, or that carries, oil or hazardous material in bulk as cargo or cargo residue, and that—

(a) Is a vessel of the United States;

(b) Operates on the navigable waters of the United States; or

(c) Transfers oil or hazardous material in a port or place subject to the jurisdiction of the United States.

Toxic vapor or gas means a product for which emergency escape respiratory protection is required under Subchapter 17 of the International Code for the Construction and Equipment of Ships carrying Dangerous Chemicals in Bulk (IBC Code) and under Subchapter 19 of the International Code for the Construction and Equipment of Ships carrying Liquefied Gases in Bulk (IGC Code).

Vessel constructed means a vessel, the keel of which is laid or which is at a similar stage of construction.

Warm water means water where the monthly mean low water temperature is normally more than 15 °C (59 °F).

[CGD 84–069, 61 FR 25313, May 20, 1996, as amended by USCG–1999–6216, 64 FR 53229, Oct. 1, 1999; USCG–1999–5040, 67 FR 34807, May 15, 2002; USCG–2004–18884, 69 FR 58352, Sept. 30, 2004]

§ 199.40 Evaluation, testing and approval of lifesaving appliances and arrangements.

(a) Each item of lifesaving equipment required by this part to be carried on board the vessel must be approved.

(b) Each item of lifesaving equipment carried on board the vessel in addition to those required by this part must—

(1) Be approved; or

(2) Be accepted by the cognizant OCMI for use on the vessel.

(c) The Commandant (G–MSE) may accept a novel lifesaving appliance or arrangement if it provides a level of safety equivalent to the requirements of this part and the appliance or arrangement—

(1) Is evaluated and tested in accordance with IMO Resolution A.520(13), Code of Practice for the Evaluation, Testing and Acceptance of Prototype Novel Life-saving Appliances and Arrangements; or

(2) Has successfully undergone evaluation and tests that are substantially equivalent to those recommendations.

(d) During the vessel's construction and when any modification to the lifesaving arrangement is done after construction, a vessel owner must obtain acceptance of lifesaving arrangements from the Commandant (G–MSC).

(e) The OCMI may accept substitute lifesaving appliances other than those required by this part except for—

(1) Survival craft and rescue boats; and

(2) Survival craft and rescue boat launching and embarkation appliances.

(f) Acceptance of lifesaving appliances and arrangements will remain in effect unless—

(1) The OCMI deems their condition to be unsatisfactory or unfit for the service intended; or

(2) The OCMI deems the crew's ability to use and assist others in the use of the lifesaving appliances or arrangements to be inadequate.

§ 199.45 Tests and inspections of lifesaving equipment and arrangements.

(a) *Initial inspection.* The initial inspection of lifesaving appliances and arrangements for certification includes a demonstration of—

(1) The proper condition and operation of the survival craft and rescue boat launching appliances at loads ranging from light load to 10 percent overload;

(2) The proper condition and operation of lifeboats and rescue boats, including engines and release mechanisms;

(3) The proper condition of flotation equipment such as lifebuoys, lifejackets, immersion suits, work vests, lifefloats, buoyant apparatus, and associated equipment;

(4) The proper condition of distress signaling equipment, including emergency position indicating radiobeacons (EPIRB), search and rescue transponders (SART), and pyrotechnic signaling devices;

(5) The proper condition of line-throwing appliances;

Coast Guard, DHS § 199.70

(6) The proper condition and operation of embarkation appliances, including embarkation ladders and marine evacuation systems;

(7) The ability of the crew to effectively carry out abandon-ship and fire-fighting procedures; and

(8) The ability to meet the egress and survival craft launching requirements of this part.

(b) *Reinspections.* Tests and inspections of the lifesaving equipment shall be carried out during each inspection for renewal of certification and periodic inspection, and shall include, as applicable, a demonstration of—

(1) The proper condition and operation of the survival craft and rescue boat launching appliances at loads ranging from light load to full load, except that any portion of the load test conducted in connection with replacement or end-for-ending of a fall since the vessel's last inspection or reinspection, need not be repeated;

(2) The proper condition and operation of lifeboats and rescue boats, including engines and release mechanisms;

(3) The proper condition of flotation equipment such as lifebuoys, lifejackets, immersion suits, work vests, lifefloats, buoyant apparatus, and associated equipment;

(4) The proper servicing of each inflatable liferaft and inflatable lifejacket has been serviced as required under this chapter;

(5) The proper servicing of each hydrostatic release unit, other than a disposable hydrostatic release unit, as required under this chapter; and

(6) The ability of crew to effectively carry out abandon-ship and fire-fighting procedures.

(c) *Other inspections.* (1) Lifesaving appliances and arrangements are subject to tests and inspections described in paragraph (a) of this section whenever a new lifesaving appliance is installed on the vessel. The test in paragraph (a)(1) of this section must be carried out whenever a wire fall for a launching appliance is replaced or turned end-for-end.

(2) Lifesaving appliances and arrangements are subject to tests and inspections described in paragraph (b) of this section during vessel boardings to ensure that the appliances and arrangements comply with applicable requirements, are in satisfactory condition, and remain fit for the service.

[CGD 84–069, 61 FR 25313, May 20, 1996, as amended by USCG–1999–4976, 65 FR 6510, Feb. 9, 2000]

Subpart B—Requirements for All Vessels

§ 199.60 Communications.

(a) *Radio lifesaving appliances.* Radio lifesaving appliance installations and arrangements must meet the requirements of 47 CFR part 80.

(b) *Emergency position indicating radiobeacons (EPIRB) and search and rescue transponders (SART).* Each EPIRB and SART should have the name of the vessel plainly marked or painted on its label, except for EPIRBs or SARTs in an inflatable liferaft or permanently installed in a survival craft.

(c) *Distress signals.* Each vessel must—

(1) Carry not less than 12 rocket parachute flares approved under approval series 160.136; and

(2) Stow the flares on or near the vessel's navigating bridge.

(d) *Onboard communications and alarm systems.* Each vessel must meet the requirements for onboard communications between emergency control stations, muster and embarkation stations, and strategic positions on board. Each vessel must also meet the emergency alarm system requirements in subchapter J of this chapter, which must be supplemented by either a public address system or other suitable means of communication.

§ 199.70 Personal lifesaving appliances.

(a) *Lifebuoys.* Each vessel must carry lifebuoys approved under approval series 160.150 as follows:

(1) *Stowage.* Lifebuoys must be stowed as follows:

(i) Each lifebuoy must be capable of being rapidly cast loose.

(ii) No lifebuoy may be permanently secured to the vessel in any way.

(iii) Each lifebuoy stowage position must be marked with either the words "LIFEBUOY" or "LIFE BUOY", or

§ 199.70

with the appropriate symbol from IMO Resolution A.760(18).

(iv) Lifebuoys must be so distributed as to be readily available on each side of the vessel and, as far as practicable, on each open deck extending to the side of the vessel. At least one lifebuoy must be located near the stern of the vessel. The lifebuoys with attached self-igniting lights must be equally distributed on both sides of the vessel.

(v) At least two lifebuoys, each with attached self-activating smoke signals, must be stowed where they can be quickly released from the navigating bridge and should, when released, fall directly into the water without striking any part of the vessel.

(2) *Markings.* Each lifebuoy must be marked in block capital letters with the name of the vessel and the name of the port required to be marked on the stern of the vessel under § 67.123 of part 67 of this chapter.

(3) *Attachments and fittings.* Lifebuoys must have the following attachments and fittings:

(i) At least one lifebuoy on each side of the vessel fitted with a buoyant lifeline that is—

(A) At least as long as twice the height where it is stowed above the waterline with the vessel in its lightest seagoing condition, or 30 meters (100 feet) in length, whichever is the greater;

(B) Non-kinking;

(C) Not less than 8 millimeters inch) in diameter;

(D) Of a breaking strength which is not less than 5 kiloNewtons (1,124 pounds-force); and

(E) Is, if synthetic, a dark color or certified by the manufacturer to be resistant to deterioration from ultraviolet light.

(ii) At least one-half the total number of lifebuoys on the vessel must each be fitted with a self-igniting light approved under approval series 161.010. The self-igniting light may not be attached to the lifebuoys required by this section to be fitted with lifelines.

(iii) At least two lifebuoys on the vessel must be fitted with a self-activating smoke signal approved under approval series 160.157. Lifebuoys fitted with smoke signals must also be fitted with lights.

46 CFR Ch. I (10–1–04 Edition)

(b) *Lifejackets.* Each vessel must carry lifejackets approved under approval series 160.155, 160.176 or 160.177. If the vessel carries inflatable lifejackets, they must be of the same or similar design and have the same method of operation.

(1) *General.* Each vessel must carry a lifejacket for each person on board, and in addition—

(i) A number of lifejackets suitable for children equal to at least 10 percent of the total number of passengers on board must be provided, or such greater number as may be required to provide a lifejacket of suitable size for each person smaller than the lower size limit of the adult-size lifejacket; and

(ii) A sufficient number of lifejackets must be carried for persons on watch and for use at remotely located survival craft stations.

(2) *Stowage.* Lifejackets must be stowed as follows:

(i) The lifejackets must be readily accessible.

(ii) [Reserved]

(iii) The lifejackets stowage positions must be marked with the words "LIFEJACKETS" or "CHILD LIFEJACKETS" as appropriate, or with the appropriate symbol from IMO Resolution A.760(18).

(iv) The additional lifejackets for persons on watch required by paragraph (b)(1)(ii) of this section must be stowed on the bridge, in the engine control room, and at other manned watch stations.

(v) Where, due to the particular arrangements of the vessel, the lifejackets required by paragraph (b) of this section may become inaccessible, alternative provisions must be made to the satisfaction of the OCMI that may include an increase in the number of lifejackets to be carried.

(3) *Markings.* Each lifejacket must be marked—

(i) In block capital letters with the name of the vessel; and

(ii) With Type I retro-reflective material approved under approval series 164.018. The arrangement of the retro-reflective material must meet IMO Resolution A.658(16).

(4) *Attachments and fittings.* Lifejackets must have the following attachments and fittings:

482

(i) Each lifejacket must have a lifejacket light approved under approval series 161.112 securely attached to the front shoulder area of the lifejacket.

(ii) Each lifejacket must have a whistle firmly secured by a cord to the lifejacket.

(c) *Rescue boat and marine evacuation system immersion suits or anti-exposure suits*—(1) *General.* Each vessel, except vessels operating on routes between 32 degrees north latitude and 32 degrees south latitude, must carry immersion suits approved under approval series 160.171 or anti-exposure suits approved under approval series 160.153 of suitable size for each person assigned to the rescue boat crew and each person assigned to a marine evacuation system crew.

(2) *Stowage.* Immersion suits or anti-exposure suits must be stowed so they are readily accessible. The stowage positions must be marked with either the words "IMMERSION SUITS" or "ANTI-EXPOSURE SUITS" as appropriate, or with the appropriate symbol from IMO Resolution A.760(18).

(3) *Markings.* Each immersion suit or anti-exposure suit must be marked in such a way as to identify the person or vessel to which it belongs.

(4) *Attachments and fittings.* Immersion suits or anti-exposure suits must have the following attachments and fittings:

(i) Each immersion suit or anti-exposure suit must have a lifejacket light approved under approval series 161.112 securely attached to the front shoulder area of the immersion suit or anti-exposure suit.

(ii) Each immersion suit or anti-exposure suit must have a whistle firmly secured by a cord to the immersion suit or anti-exposure suit.

(d) *Lifejacket, immersion suit, and anti-exposure suit containers.* Each lifejacket, immersion suit, and anti-exposure suit container must be marked in block capital letters and numbers with the quantity, identity, and size of the equipment stowed inside the container. The equipment may be identified in words or with the appropriate symbol from IMO Resolution A.760(18).

[CGD 84–069, 61 FR 25313, May 20, 1996, as amended at 63 FR 52818, Oct. 1, 1998; 63 FR 56066, Oct. 20, 1998; 64 FR 53229, Oct. 1, 1999]

§ 199.80 Muster list and emergency instructions.

(a) *General.* Clear instructions must be provided on the vessel that detail the actions each person on board should follow in the event of an emergency.

(b) *Muster list.* Copies of the muster list must be posted in conspicuous places throughout the vessel including on the navigating bridge, in the engine room, and in crew accommodation spaces. The muster list must be posted before the vessel begins its voyage. After the muster list has been prepared, if any change takes place that necessitates an alteration in the muster list, the master must either revise the existing muster list or prepare a new one. Each muster lists must at least specify—

(1) The instructions for operating the general emergency alarm system and public address system;

(2) The emergency signals;

(3) The actions to be taken by the persons on board when each signal is sounded;

(4) How the order to abandon the vessel will be given.

(5) The officers that are assigned to make sure that lifesaving and firefighting appliances are maintained in good condition and ready for immediate use;

(6) The duties assigned to the different members of the crew. Duties to be specified include—

(i) Closing the watertight doors, fire doors, valves, scuppers, sidescuttles, skylights, portholes, and other similar openings in the vessel's hull;

(ii) Equipping the survival craft and other lifesaving appliances;

(iii) Preparing and launching the survival craft;

(iv) Preparing other lifesaving appliances;

(v) Mustering the passengers and other persons on board;

(vi) Using communication equipment;

(vii) Manning the emergency squad assigned to deal with fires and other emergencies; and

(viii) Using firefighting equipment and installations.

(7) The duties assigned to members of the crew in relation to passengers and

§ 199.90

other persons on board in case of an emergency. Assigned duties to be specified include—

(i) Warning the passengers and other persons on board;

(ii) Seeing that passengers and other persons on board are suitably dressed and have donned their lifejackets or immersion suits correctly;

(iii) Assembling passengers and other persons on board at muster stations;

(iv) Keeping order in the passageways and on the stairways and generally controlling the movements of the passengers and other persons on board; and

(v) Making sure that a supply of blankets is taken to the survival craft; and

(8) The substitutes for key persons if they are disabled, taking into account that different emergencies require different actions.

(c) *Emergency instructions.* Illustrations and instructions in English, and any other appropriate language as determined by the OCMI, must be posted in each passenger cabin and in spaces occupied by persons other than crew, and must be conspicuously displayed at each muster station. The illustrations and instructions must include information on—

(1) The fire and emergency signal;

(2) Their muster station;

(3) The essential actions they must take in an emergency;

(4) The location of lifejackets, including child-size lifejackets; and

(5) The method of donning lifejackets.

[CGD 84–069, 61 FR 25313, May 20, 1996, as amended at 63 FR 52818, Oct. 1, 1998]

§ 199.90 Operating instructions.

Each vessel must have posters or signs displayed in the vicinity of each survival craft and the survival craft's launching controls that—

(a) Illustrate the purpose of controls;

(b) Illustrate the procedures for operating the launching device;

(c) Give relevant instructions or warnings;

(d) Can be easily seen under emergency lighting conditions; and

(e) Display symbols in accordance with IMO Resolution A.760(18).

§ 199.100 Manning of survival craft and supervision.

(a) There must be a sufficient number of trained persons on board the vessel for mustering and assisting untrained persons.

(b) There must be a sufficient number of deck officers, able seamen, or certificated persons on board the vessel to operate the survival craft and launching arrangements required for abandonment by the total number of persons on board.

(c) There must be one person placed in charge of each survival craft to be used. The person in charge must—

(1) Be a deck officer, able seaman, or certificated person. The OCMI, considering the nature of the voyage, the number of persons permitted on board, and the characteristics of the vessel, may permit persons practiced in the handling and operation of liferafts or inflatable buoyant apparatus to be placed in charge of liferafts or inflatable buoyant apparatus; and

(2) Have a list of the survival craft crew and ensure that the crewmembers are acquainted with their duties.

(d) There must be a second-in-command designated for each lifeboat. This person should be a deck officer, able seaman, or certificated person. The second-in-command of a lifeboat must also have a list of the lifeboat crew.

(e) There must be a person assigned to each motorized survival craft who is capable of operating the engine and carrying out minor adjustments.

(f) The master must make sure that the persons required under paragraphs (a), (b), (c), and (d) of this section are equitably distributed among the vessel's survival craft.

[CGD 84–069, 61 FR 25313, May 20, 1996, as amended at 63 FR 52819, Oct. 1, 1998]

§ 199.110 Survival craft muster and embarkation arrangements.

(a) Each muster station must have sufficient space to accommodate all persons assigned to muster at that station. One or more muster stations must be close to each embarkation station.

(b) Each muster station and embarkation station must be readily accessible to accommodation and work areas.

Coast Guard, DHS § 199.130

(c) Each muster station and embarkation station must be adequately illuminated by lighting with power supplied from the vessel's emergency source of electrical power.

(d) Each alleyway, stairway, and exit giving access to a muster and embarkation station must be adequately illuminated by lighting that is capable of having its power supplied by the vessel's emergency source of electrical power.

(e) Each davit-launched and free-fall survival craft muster station and embarkation station must be arranged to enable stretcher cases to be placed in the survival craft.

(f) Each launching station, or each two adjacent launching stations, must have an embarkation ladder as follows:

(1) Each embarkation ladder must be approved under approval series 160.117 or be a rope ladder approved under approval series 160.017.

(2) Each embarkation ladder must extend in a single length from the deck to the waterline with the vessel in its lightest seagoing condition under unfavorable conditions of trim and with the vessel listed not less than 15 degrees either way.

(3) Provided that there is at least one embarkation ladder on each side of the vessel, the OCMI may permit additional embarkation ladders to be other approved devices that provide safe and rapid access to survival craft in the water.

(4) The OCMI may accept other safe and effective means of embarkation for use with a liferaft required under § 199.261(e).

(g) If a davit-launched survival craft is embarked over the edge of the deck, the craft must be provided with a means for bringing it against the side of the vessel and holding it alongside the vessel to allow persons to safely embark.

(h) If a davit-launched survival craft is not intended to be moved to the stowed position with persons on board, the craft must be provided with a means for bringing it against the side of the vessel and holding it alongside the vessel to allow persons to safely disembark after a drill.

[CGD 84–069, 61 FR 25313, May 20, 1996, as amended by USCG–1998–4442, 63 FR 52192, Sept. 30, 1998; 63 FR 52819, Oct. 1, 1998]

§ 199.120 Launching stations.

(a) Each launching station must be positioned to ensure safe launching with clearance from the propeller and from the steeply overhanging portions of the hull.

(b) Each survival craft must be launched down the straight side of the vessel, except for free-fall launched survival craft.

(c) Each launching station in the forward part of the vessel must—

(1) Be in a sheltered position that is located aft of the collision bulkhead; and

(2) Have a launching appliance approved with an endorsement as being of sufficient strength for forward installation.

§ 199.130 Stowage of survival craft.

(a) *General.* Each survival craft must be stowed—

(1) As close to the accommodation and service spaces as possible;

(2) So that neither the survival craft nor its stowage arrangements will interfere with the embarkation and operation of any other survival craft or rescue boat at any other launching station;

(3) As near the water surface as is safe and practicable;

(4) Except for liferafts intended for throw-overboard launching, not less than 2 meters above the waterline with the vessel—

(i) In the fully loaded condition;

(ii) Under unfavorable conditions of trim; and

(iii) Listed up to 20 degrees either way, or to the angle at which the vessel's weatherdeck edge becomes submerged, whichever is less.

(5) Sufficiently ready for use so that two crew members can complete preparations for embarkation and launching in less than 5 minutes;

(6) In a secure and sheltered position and protected from damage by fire and explosion, as far as practicable; and

§ 199.140

(7) So as not to require lifting from its stowed position in order to launch, except that—

(i) A davit-launched liferaft may be lifted by a manually powered winch from its stowed position to its embarkation position; or

(ii) A survival craft that weights 185 kilograms (407.8 pounds) or less may be lifted not more than 300 millimeters (1 foot) in order to launch.

(b) *Additional lifeboat stowage requirements.* In addition to the requirements of paragraph (a) of this section, each lifeboat must be stowed as follows:

(1) Each lifeboat for lowering down the side of the vessel must be stowed as far forward of the vessel's propeller as practicable. Each lifeboat, in its stowed position, must be protected from damage by heavy seas.

(2) Each lifeboat must be stowed attached to its launching appliance.

(3) Each lifeboat must have a means for recharging the lifeboat batteries from the vessel's power supply at a supply voltage not exceeding 50 volts.

(c) *Additional liferaft stowage requirements.* In addition to the requirements of paragraph (a) of this section, each liferaft must be stowed as follows:

(1) Each liferaft must be stowed to permit manual release from its securing arrangements.

(2) Each liferaft must be stowed at a height above the waterline not greater than the maximum stowage height indicated on the liferaft container with the vessel in its lightest seagoing condition. Each liferaft without an indicated maximum stowage height must be stowed not more than 18 meters (59 feet) above the waterline with the vessel in its lightest seagoing condition.

(3) Each liferaft must be arranged to permit it to drop into the water from the deck on which it is stowed. A liferaft stowage arrangements meets this requirement if it—

(i) Is outboard of the rail or bulwark;

(ii) Is on stanchions or on a platform adjacent to the rail or bulwark; or

(iii) Has a gate or other suitable opening large enough to allow the liferaft to be pushed directly overboard and, if the liferaft is intended to be available for use on either side of the vessel, such gate or opening is provided on each side of the vessel.

(4) Each davit-launched liferaft must be stowed within reach of its lifting hook, unless some means of transfer is provided that is not rendered inoperable—

(i) Within the limits of trim and list specified in paragraph (a)(4) of this section;

(ii) By vessel motion; or

(iii) By power failure.

(5) Each rigid container for an inflatable liferaft to be launched by a launching appliance must be secured so that the container or parts of it do not fall into the water during and after inflation and launching of the contained liferaft.

(6) Each liferaft must have a painter system providing a connection between the vessel and the liferaft.

(7) Each liferaft or group of liferafts must be arranged for float-free launching. The arrangement must ensure that the liferaft or liferafts, when released and inflated, are not dragged under by the sinking vessel. A hydrostatic release unit used in a float-free arrangement must be approved under approval series 160.162.

§ 199.140 Stowage of rescue boats.

(a) *General.* Rescue boats must be stowed—

(1) To be ready for launching in not more than 5 minutes.

(2) In a position suitable for launching and recovery;

(3) In a way that neither the rescue boat nor its stowage arrangements will interfere with the operation of any survival craft at any other launching station; and

(4) If it is also a lifeboat, in compliance with the requirements of § 199.130.

(b) Each rescue boat must have a means provided for recharging the rescue boat batteries from the vessel's power supply at a supply voltage not exceeding 50 volts.

(c) Each inflated rescue boat must be kept fully inflated at all times.

[CGD 84–069, 61 FR 25313, May 20, 1996, as amended at 63 FR 52819, Oct. 1, 1998]

§ 199.145 Marine evacuation system launching arrangements.

(a) *Arrangements.* Each marine evacuation system must—

Coast Guard, DHS

§ 199.150

(1) Be capable of being deployed by one person;

(2) Enable the total number of persons for which it is designed, to be transferred from the vessel into the inflated liferafts within a period of 30 minutes in the case of a passenger vessel and 10 minutes in the case of a cargo vessel from the time an abandonship signal is given;

(3) Be arranged so that liferafts may be securely attached to and released from the marine evacuation system platform by a person either in the liferaft or on the platform;

(4) Be capable of being deployed from the vessel under unfavorable conditions of trim of up to 10 degrees either way and of list of up to 20 degrees either way;

(5) If the marine evacuation system has an inclined slide, it must—

(i) Be arranged so the angle of the slide from horizontal is within a range of 30 to 35 degrees when the vessel is upright and in its lightest seagoing condition; and

(ii) If the vessel is a passenger vessel, be arranged so the angle of the slide from horizontal is no more than 55 degrees in the final stage of flooding as described in subchapter S of this chapter; and

(6) Be capable of being restrained by a bowsing line or other positioning system that is designed to deploy automatically and if necessary, is capable of being adjusted to the position required for evacuation.

(b) *Stowage.* Each marine evacuation system must be stowed as follows:

(1) There must not be any openings between the marine evacuation system's embarkation station and the vessel's side at the waterline with the vessel in its lightest seagoing condition.

(2) The marine evacuation system's launching positions must be arranged, as far as practicable, to be straight down the vessel's side and to safely clear the propeller and any steeply overhanging positions of the hull.

(3) The marine evacuation system must be protected from any projections of the vessel's structure or equipment.

(4) The marine evacuation system's passage and platform, when deployed; its stowage container; and its operational arrangement must not interfere with the operation of any other lifesaving appliance at any other launching station.

(5) The marine evacuation system's stowage area must be protected from damage by heavy seas.

(c) *Stowage of associated liferafts.* Inflatable liferafts used in conjunction with the marine evacuation system must be stowed—

(1) Close to the system container, but capable of dropping clear of the deployed chute and boarding platform;

(2) So it is capable of individual release from its stowage rack;

(3) In accordance with the requirements of § 199.130; and

(4) With pre-connected or easily connected retrieving lines to the platform.

§ 199.150 Survival craft launching and recovery arrangements; general.

(a)(1) Each launching appliance for a lifeboat must be approved under approval series 160.132 with a winch approved under approval series 160.115.

(2) Each launching appliance for a davit-launched liferaft must be approved under approval series 160.163 with an automatic disengaging apparatus approved under approval series 160.170.

(b) Unless expressly provided otherwise in this part, each survival craft must be provided with a launching appliance or marine evacuation system, except those survival craft that—

(1) Can be boarded from a position on deck less than 4.5 meters (14.75 feet) above the waterline with the vessel in its lightest seagoing condition and that are stowed for launching directly from the stowed position under unfavorable conditions of trim of 10 degrees and list of 20 degrees either way;

(2) [Reserved]

(3) Are carried in excess of the survival craft for 200 percent of the total number of persons on board the vessel, and that have a mass of not more than 185 kilograms (407 pounds);

(4) Are carried in excess of the survival craft for 200 percent of the total number of persons on board the vessel and that are stowed for launching directly from the stowed position under unfavorable conditions or trim of 10 degrees and list of 20 degrees either way; or

§ 199.153

(5) Are provided for use in conjunction with a marine evacuation system and that are stowed for launching directly from the stowed position under unfavorable conditions of trim of 10 degrees and list of 20 degrees either way.

(c) With the exception of the secondary means of launching for free-fall lifeboats, each launching appliance must be arranged so that the fully equipped survival craft it serves can be safely launched against unfavorable conditions of trim of up to 10 degrees either way and of list of up to 20 degrees either way—

(1) When the survival craft is loaded with its full complement of persons; and

(2) When not more than the required operating crew is on board.

(d) A launching appliance must not depend on any means other than gravity or stored mechanical power, independent of the vessel's power supplies, to launch the survival craft it serves in both the fully loaded and equipped condition and in the light condition.

(e) Each launching appliance's structural attachment to the vessel must be designed, based on the ultimate strength of the construction material, to be at least 4.5 times the load imparted on the attachment by the launching appliance and its fully loaded survival craft under the most adverse combination of list and trim under paragraph (c) of this section.

(f) Each launching appliance must be arranged so that—

(1) All parts requiring regular maintenance by the vessel's crew are readily accessible and easily maintained;

(2) The launching appliance remains effective under conditions of icing;

(3) The same type of release mechanism is used for each similar survival craft carried on board the vessel;

(4) The preparation and handling of each survival craft at any one launching station does not interfere with the prompt preparation and handling of any other survival craft at any other station;

(5) The persons on board the vessel can safely and rapidly board the survival craft; and

(6) During preparation and launching, the survival craft, its launching appliance, and the area of water into which it is to be launched are illuminated by lighting supplied from the vessel's emergency source of electrical power.

(g) Each launching and recovery arrangement must allow the operator on the deck to observe the survival craft at all times during launching.

(h) Means must be provided outside the machinery space to prevent any discharge of water onto survival craft during launching.

(i) If there is a danger of the survival craft being damaged by the vessel's stabilizer wings, the stabilizer wings must be able to be brought inboard using power from the emergency source of electrical power. Indicators operated by the vessel's emergency power system must be provided on the navigating bridge to show the position of the stabilizer wings.

§ 199.153 Survival craft launching and recovery arrangements using falls and a winch.

Survival craft launching and recovery arrangements, in addition to meeting the requirements in § 199.150, must meet the following requirements:

(a) Each launching mechanism must be arranged so it may be actuated by one person from a position on the vessel's deck, and except for secondary launching appliances for free-fall launching arrangements, from a position within the survival craft.

(b) Each fall wire must be of rotation-resistant and corrosion-resistant steel wire rope.

(c) The breaking strength of each fall wire and each attachment used on the fall must be at least six times the load imparted on the fall by the fully-loaded survival craft.

(d) Each fall must be long enough for the survival craft to reach the water with the vessel in its lightest seagoing condition, under unfavorable conditions of trim, and with the vessel listed not less than 20 degrees either way.

(e) Each unguarded fall must not pass near any operating position of the winch, such as hand cranks, pay out wheels, and brake levers.

(f) Each winch drum must be arranged so the fall wire winds onto the drum in one or more level wraps. A multiple drum winch must be arranged so that the falls wind off at the same rate when lowering and onto the drums at the same rate when hoisting.

(g) Each fall, where exposed to damage or fouling, must have guards or equivalent protection. Each fall that leads along a deck must be covered with a guard that is not more than 300 millimeters (1 foot) above the deck.

(h) The lowering speed for a fully loaded survival craft must be not less than the speed obtained from one of the following formulas:

(1) $S=0.4+(0.02\ H)$, where S the lowering speed in meters per second and H is the lowering height in meters from the davit head to the waterline with the vessel in its lightest seagoing condition, with H not greater than 30 regardless of the actual lowering height.

(2) $S=79+(1.2\ H)$, where S is the lowering speed in feet per minute and H is the lowering height in feet from the davit head to the waterline with the vessel in its lightest seagoing condition, with H not greater than 99 regardless of the actual lowering height.

(i) The lowering speed for a survival craft loaded with all of its equipment must be not less than 70 percent of the speed required under paragraph (h) of this section.

(j) The lowering speed for a fully loaded survival craft must be not more than 1.3 meters per second (256 feet per minute).

(k) If a survival craft is recovered by electric power, the electrical installation, including the electric power-operated boat winch, must meet the requirements in subchapter J of this chapter. If a survival craft is recovered by any means using power, including a portable power source, safety devices must be provided that automatically cut off the power before the davit arms or falls reach the stops in order to avoid overstressing the falls or davits, unless the motor is designed to prevent such overstressing.

(l) Each launching appliance must be fitted with brakes that meet the following requirements:

(1) The brakes must be capable of stopping the descent of the survival craft or rescue boat and holding the survival craft or rescue boat securely when loaded with its full complement of persons and equipment.

(2) The brake pads must, where necessary, be protected from water and oil.

(3) Manual brakes must be arranged so that the brake is always applied unless the operator, or a mechanism activated by the operator, holds the brake control in the off position.

[CGD 84–069, 61 FR 25313, May 20, 1996, as amended at 63 FR 52819, Oct. 1, 1998]

§ 199.155 Lifeboat launching and recovery arrangements.

Lifeboat launching and recovery arrangements, in addition to meeting the requirements in §§ 199.150 and 199.153, must meet the following requirements:

(a) Each lifeboat must be provided with a launching appliance. The launching appliance must be capable of launching and recovering the lifeboat with its crew.

(b) Each launching appliance arrangement must allow the operator on the vessel to observe the lifeboat at all times during recovery.

(c) Each launching appliance arrangement must be designed to ensure persons can safely disembark from the survival craft prior to its stowage.

(d) Each lifeboat, other than a totally enclosed lifeboat, must be provided with a davit span with not less than two lifelines of sufficient length to reach the water with the vessel in its lightest seagoing condition, under unfavorable conditions of trim, and with the vessel listed up to 20 degrees either way.

§ 199.157 Free-fall lifeboat launching and recovery arrangements.

(a) The launching appliance for a free-fall lifeboat must be designed and installed so that the launching appliance and the lifeboat it serves operate as a system to protect the occupants from harmful acceleration forces and to effectively clear the vessel.

(b) The launching appliance must be designed and arranged so that, in its ready to launch position, the distance from the lowest point on the lifeboat it serves to the water surface with the vessel in its lightest seagoing condition does not exceed the lifeboat's certificated free-fall height.

(c) The launching appliance must be arranged to preclude accidental release

§ 199.160

of the lifeboat in its unattended stowed position. If the means provided to secure the lifeboat cannot be released from inside the lifeboat, the means to secure the lifeboat must be arranged to preclude boarding the lifeboat without first releasing it.

(d) Each free-fall launching arrangement must be provided with a secondary means to launch the lifeboat by falls. Such means must comply with the requirements of §§ 199.150, 199.153, and 199.155. Notwithstanding § 199.150(c), the secondary launching appliance must be capable of launching the lifeboat against unfavorable conditions of trim of 2 degrees either way and of list of 5 degrees either way. The secondary launching appliance need not comply with the speed requirements of §§ 199.153 (g), (h), and (i). If the secondary launching appliance is not dependent on gravity, stored mechanical power, or other manual means, the launching arrangement must be connected both to the vessel's main and emergency power supplies.

§ 199.160 Rescue boat embarkation, launching and recovery arrangements.

(a) Each rescue boat must be capable of being launched with the vessel making headway of 5 knots in calm water. A painter may be used to meet this requirement.

(b) Each rescue boat embarkation and launching arrangement must permit the rescue boat to be boarded and launched in the shortest possible time.

(c) The rescue boat must meet the embarkation and launching arrangement requirements of §§ 199.110 (e) and (g), 199.150, 199.155, and if the launching arrangement uses falls and a winch, § 199.153.

(d) If the rescue boat is one of the vessel's survival craft, the rescue boat must also meet the following requirements:

(1) The rescue boat must meet the muster and embarkation arrangement requirements of § 199.110 and the launching station requirements of § 199.120.

(2) If the launching arrangement uses a single fall, the rescue boat may have an automatic disengaging apparatus approved under approval series 160.170 instead of a lifeboat release mechanism.

(e) Rapid recovery of the rescue boat must be possible when loaded with its full complement of persons and equipment. If the rescue boat is also a lifeboat, rapid recovery must be possible when loaded with its lifeboat equipment and an approved rescue boat complement of at least six persons.

(f) Each rescue boat launching appliance must be fitted with a powered winch motor.

(g) Each rescue boat launching appliance must be capable of hoisting the rescue boat when loaded with its full rescue boat complement of persons and equipment at a rate of not less than 0.3 meters per second (59 feet per minute).

§ 199.170 Line-throwing appliance.

(a) *General.* Each vessel must have a line-throwing appliance approved under approval series 160.040.

(b) *Stowage.* The line-throwing appliance and its equipment must be readily accessible for use.

(c) *Additional equipment.* Each vessel must carry the following equipment for the line-throwing appliance—

(1) The equipment on the list provided by the manufacturer with the approved appliance; and

(2) An auxiliary line that—

(i) Is at least 450 meters (1,500 feet) long;

(ii) Has a breaking strength of at least 40 kiloNewtons (9,000 pounds-force); and

(iii) Is, if synthetic, of a dark color or certified by the manufacturer to be resistant to deterioration from ultraviolet light.

§ 199.175 Survival craft and rescue boat equipment.

(a) All lifeboat and rescue boat equipment—

(1) Must be secured within the boat by lashings, by storage in lockers or compartments, by storage in brackets or similar mounting arrangements, or by other suitable means;

(2) Must be secured in such a manner as not to interfere with any abandonment procedures or reduce seating capacity;

(3) Must be as small and of as little mass as possible;

Coast Guard, DHS § 199.175

(4) Must be packed in a suitable and compact form; and

(5) Should be stowed so the items do not—

(i) Reduce the seating capacity;

(ii) Adversely affect the seaworthiness of the survival craft or rescue boat; or

(iii) Overload the launching appliance.

(b) Each lifeboat, rigid liferaft, and rescue boat, unless otherwise stated in this paragraph, must carry the equipment listed in this paragraph and specified for it in table 199.175 of this section under the vessel's category of service. A lifeboat that is also a rescue boat must carry the equipment in the table column marked for a lifeboat.

(1) *Bailer.* The bailer must be buoyant.

(2) *Bilge pump.* The bilge pump must be approved under approval series 160.044 and must be installed in a ready-to-use condition as follows:

(i) The bilge pump for a lifeboat approved for less than 70 persons must be either size 2 or size 3.

(ii) The bilge pump for a lifeboat approved for 70 persons or more must be size 3.

(3) *Boathook.* In the case of a boat launched by falls, the boathook must be kept free for fending-off purposes. For inflated rescue boats and for rigid-inflated rescue boats, each boathook must be designed to minimize the possibility of damage to the inflated portions of the hull.

(4) *Bucket.* The bucket must be made of corrosion-resistant material and should either be buoyant or have an attached lanyard at least 1.8 meters (6 feet) long.

(5) *Can opener.* A can opener may be in a jackknife approved under approval series 160.043.

(6) *Compass.* The compass and its mounting arrangement must be approved under approval series 160.014. In a totally enclosed lifeboat, the compass must be permanently fitted at the steering position; in any other boat it must be provided with a binnacle, if necessary to protect it from the weather, and with suitable mounting arrangements.

(7) *Dipper.* The dipper must be rustproof and attached to a lanyard that should be at least 0.9 meters (3 feet) long.

(8) *Drinking cup.* The drinking cup must be graduated and rustproof. The cup should also be of a breakage-resistant material.

(9) *Fire extinguisher.* The fire extinguisher must be approved under approval series 162.028. The fire extinguisher must be type B–C, size II, or larger. Two type B–C, size I fire extinguishers may be carried in place of a type B–C, size II fire extinguisher.

(10) *First aid kit.* The first aid kit in a lifeboat and in a rescue boat must be approved under approval series 160.041. The first aid kit in a rigid liferaft must be approved under approval series 160.054.

(11) *Fishing kit.* The fishing kit must be approved under approval series 160.061.

(12) *Flashlight.* The flashlight must be a type I or type III that is constructed and marked in accordance with the American Society of Testing and Materials (ASTM) F 1014 (incorporated by reference, see § 199.05). One spare set of batteries and one spare bulb, stored in a watertight container, must be provided for each flashlight.

(13) *Hatchet.* The hatchet must be approved under approval series 160.013. The hatchet should be stowed in brackets near the release mechanism and, if more than one hatchet is carried, the hatchets should be stowed at opposite ends of the boat.

(14) *Heaving line.* The heaving line must be buoyant, must be at least 30 meters (99 feet) long, must have a buoyant rescue quoit attached to one end, and should be at least 8 millimeters (5/16 inches) in diameter.

(15) *Instruction card.* The instruction card must be waterproof and contain the information required by IMO Resolution A.657(16). The instruction card should be located so that it can be easily seen upon entering the liferaft.

(16) *Jackknife.* The jackknife must be approved under approval series 160.043 and must be attached to the boat by its lanyard.

(17) *Knife.* The knife must be of the non-folding type with a buoyant handle as follows:

(i) The knife for a rigid liferaft must be secured to the raft by a lanyard and

491

§ 199.175

stowed in a pocket on the exterior of the canopy near the point where the painter is attached to the liferaft. If an approved jackknife is substituted for the second knife required on a liferaft equipped for 13 or more persons, the jackknife must also be secured to the liferaft by a lanyard.

(ii) The knife in an inflated or rigid-inflated rescue boat must be of a type designed to minimize the possibility of damage to the fabric portions of the hull.

(18) *Ladder.* The boarding ladder must be capable of being used at each entrance on either side or at the stern of the boat to enable persons in the water to board the boat. The lowest step of the ladder must be not less than 0.4 meters (15.75 inches) below the boat's light waterline.

(19) *Mirror.* The signalling mirror must be approved under approval series 160.020.

(20) *Oars and paddles.* Each lifeboat and rescue boat must have buoyant oars or paddles of the number, size, and type specified by the manufacturer of the boat. An oarlock or equivalent device, either permanently installed or attached to the boat by a lanyard or chain, must be provided for each oar. Each oar should have the vessel's name marked on it in block letters.

(21) *Painter.* (i) One painter on a lifeboat and the painter on a rescue boat must be attached by a painter release device at the forward end of the lifeboat. The second painter on a lifeboat must be secured at or near the bow of the lifeboat, ready for use. On lifeboats to be launched by free-fall launching, both painters must be stowed near the bow ready for use.

(A) If the painter is of synthetic material, the painter must be of a dark color or certified by the manufacturer to be resistant to deterioration from ultraviolet light.

(B) The painter for a lifeboat and each painter for a rescue boat must be of a length that is at least twice the distance from the stowage position of the boat to the waterline with the vessel in its lightest seagoing condition, or must be 15 meters (50 feet) long, whichever is the greater.

(C) The painter must have a breaking strength of at least 34 kiloNewtons (7,700 pounds-force).

(ii) The painter for a rigid liferaft must be of a length that is at least 20 meters (66 feet) plus the distance from the liferaft's stowed position to the waterline with the vessel in its lightest seagoing condition, or must be 15 meters (50 feet) long, whichever is the greater.

(A) If the painter is of synthetic material, the painter must be of a dark color or certified by the manufacturer to be resistant to deterioration from ultraviolet light.

(B) The painter must have a breaking strength of at least 15 kiloNewtons (3,370 pounds-force) for liferafts approved for more than 25 persons, of at least 20 kiloNewtons (2,250 pounds-force) for liferafts approved for 9 to 25 persons, and of at least 7.5 kiloNewtons (1,687 pounds-force) for any other liferaft.

(C) The painter must have a float-free link meeting the requirements of part 160, subpart 160.073 of this chapter secured to the end of the painter that is attached to the vessel. The float-free link arrangement must break under a load of 2.2±0.4 kiloNewtons (400 to 536 pounds-force).

(22) *Provisions.* Each unit of provisions must be approved under approval series 160.046 and must provide at least 10,000 kiloJoules (2,390 calories). Individual provision packages may provide less than 10,000 kiloJoules, as long as the total quantity of provisions on board provides for at least 10,000 kiloJoules per person.

(23) *Pump.* The pump or bellows must be manually operated and should be arranged so it is capable of inflating any part of the inflatable structure of the rescue boat.

(24) *Radar reflector.* The radar reflector must be capable of detection at a distance of 4 nautical miles and must have a mounting arrangements to install it on the boat in its proper orientation. A 9-GigaHertz radar transponder may be substituted for the radar reflector if the transponder is accepted by the Federal Communications Commission as meeting the requirements of 47 CFR part 80 and is stowed in the boat or raft.

Coast Guard, DHS §199.175

(25) *Rainwater collection device.* The rainwater collection device must be arranged to collect falling rain and direct it into the water tanks in the lifeboat. If the lifeboat carries a manually-powered, reverse osmosis desalinator approved under approval series 160.058, a rainwater collection device is not required.

(26) *Repair kit.* The repair kit for an inflated and a rigid-inflated rescue boat must be packed in a suitable container and include at least—

(i) Six sealing clamps;

(ii) Five 50-millimeter (2-inch) diameter tube patches;

(iii) A roughing tool; and

(iv) A container of cement compatible with the tube fabric. The cement must have an expiration date on its container that is not more than 24 months after the date of manufacture of the cement.

(27) *Sea anchor.* (i) The sea anchor for a lifeboat must be approved under approval series 160.019.

(ii) Each sea anchor for a rigid liferaft must be of the type specified by the liferaft manufacturer and must be fitted with a shock resistant hawser. It may also be fitted with a tripping line. One sea anchor must be permanently attached to the liferaft in such a way that, when the liferaft is waterborne, it will cause the liferaft to lie oriented to the wind in the most stable manner. The second sea anchor must be stowed in the liferaft as a spare. A davit-launched liferaft and a liferaft on a passenger vessel must have the permanently attached sea anchor arranged to deploy automatically when the liferaft floats free.

(iii) The sea anchor for a rescue boat must be of the type specified by the rescue boat manufacturer, and must have a hawser of adequate strength that is at least 10 meters (33 feet) long.

(28) *Searchlight.* (i) The searchlight must be of the type originally provided with the approved lifeboat or rescue boat, or must be certified by the searchlight manufacturer to meet ASTM F 1003 (incorporated by reference, see §199.05). The boat must carry two spare bulbs.

(ii) The searchlight must be permanently mounted on the canopy or must have a stanchion-type or collapsible-type, portable mounting on the canopy. The mounting must be located to enable operation of the searchlight by the boat operator.

(iii) The searchlights power source must be capable of operating the light without charging or recharging for not less than—

(A) Three hours of continuous operation; or

(B) Six hours total operation when it is operated in cycles of 15 minutes on and 5 minutes off.

(iv) If the searchlight's power source is an engine starting battery, there must be sufficient battery capacity to start the engine at the end of either operating period specified in paragraph (b)(28)(iii) of this section.

(v) The searchlight's power source must be connected to the searchlight using watertight electrical fittings.

(29) *Seasickness kit.* The seasickness kit must be in a waterproof package and must include one waterproof seasickness bag, anti-seasickness medication sufficient for one person for 48 hours, and instructions for using the medication. Each seasickness kit should be stowed within reach of the seat for which it is intended.

(30) *Signal, smoke.* The smoke signal must be approved under approval series 160.122.

(31) *Signal, hand flare.* The hand flare must be approved under approval series 160.121.

(32) *Signal, rocket parachute flare.* The rocket parachute flare must be approved under approval series 160.136.

(33) *Skates and fenders.* The skates and fenders must be as specified by the lifeboat or rescue boat manufacturer to facilitate launching and prevent damage to a lifeboat intended for launching down the side of a vessel.

(34) *Sponge.* The sponge must be suitable for soaking up water.

(35) *Survival instructions.* The survival instructions must be as described in IMO Resolution A.657(16), Annex I for liferafts and Annex II for lifeboats.

(36) *Table of lifesaving signals.* The table of lifesaving signals must be as described in Annex IV to the International Regulations for Preventing Collisions at Sea 1972, as amended, and must be printed on a waterproof card or stored in a waterproof container.

§ 199.175

(37) *Thermal protective aid.* The thermal protective aid must be approved under approval series 160.174.

(38) *Tool kit.* The tool kit must contain sufficient tools for minor adjustments to the engine and its accessories.

(39) *Towline.* The towline must be buoyant and at least 50 meters (164 feet) long. The towline must have a breaking strength of not less than 13.3 kiloNewtons (3,000 pounds-force) or be of sufficient strength to tow the largest liferaft carried on the vessel when loaded with its full complement of persons and equipment at a speed of at least 2 knots.

(40) *Water.* The water must be emergency drinking water approved under approval series 160.026.

(i) The requirement for up to one-third of the emergency drinking water may be met by a desalting apparatus approved under approval series 160.058 that is capable of producing the substituted amount of water in 2 days.

(ii) The requirement for up to two-thirds of the emergency drinking water may be met by a manually-powered, reverse osmosis desalinator approved under approval series 160.058 and that is capable of producing the substituted amount of water in 2 days.

(41) *Whistle.* The whistle must be corrosion-resistant, and should be a ball-type or multi-tone whistle that is attached to a lanyard.

TABLE 199.175—SURVIVAL CRAFT EQUIPMENT

Item No.	Item	International voyage Lifeboat	International voyage Rigid liferaft (SOLAS A pack)	International voyage Rescue boat	Short international voyage Lifeboat	Short international voyage Rigid liferaft (SOLAS B pack)	Short international voyage Rescue boat
1	Bailer[1]	1	1	1	1	1	1
2	Bilge pump[2]	1			1		
3	Boathook	2		1	2		1
4	Bucket[3]	2		1	2		1
5	Can opener	3	3		3		
6	Compass	1		1	1		1
7	Dipper	1			1		
8	Drinking cup	1	1		1		
9	Fire extinguisher	1		1	1		1
10	First aid kit	1	1	1	1	1	1
11	Fishing kit	1	1				
12	Flashlight	1	1	1	1	1	1
13	Hatchet	2			2		
14	Heaving line	2	1	2	2	1	2
15	Instruction card		1			1	
16	Jackknife	1			1		
17	Knife[1][4]		1	1		1	1
18	Ladder	1			1		
19	Mirror, signalling	1	1		1	1	
20	Oars, units[5][6]	1		1	1		1
	Paddles		2			2	
21	Painter	2	1	1	2	1	1
22	Provisions (units per person)	1	1				
23	Pump[7]			1			1
24	Radar reflector	1	1	1	1	1	1
25	Rainwater collection device	1			1		
26	Repair kit[7]			1			1
27	Sea anchor	1	2	1	1	2	1
28	Searchlight	1		1	1		1
29	Seasickness kit (units per person)	1	1		1	1	
30	Signal, smoke	2	2		2	1	
31	Signal, hand flare	6	6		6	3	
32	Signal, parachute flare	4	4		4	2	
33	Skates and fenders[8]	1		1	1		1
34	Sponge[7]		2	2		2	2
35	Survival instructions	1	1		1	1	
36	Table of lifesaving signals	1	1		1	1	
37	Thermal protective aids[9]	10%	10%	10%	10%	10%	10%
38	Tool kit	1			1		
39	Towline[10]	1		1	1		1
40	Water (liters per person)	3	1.5		3		

Coast Guard, DHS § 199.178

TABLE 199.175—SURVIVAL CRAFT EQUIPMENT—Continued

Item No.	Item	International voyage			Short international voyage		
		Lifeboat	Rigid liferaft (SOLAS A pack)	Rescue boat	Lifeboat	Rigid liferaft (SOLAS B pack)	Rescue boat
41	Whistle	1	1	1	1	1	1

Notes:
[1] Each liferaft equipped for 13 persons or more must carry two of these items.
[2] Not required for boats of self-bailing design.
[3] Not required for inflated or rigid-inflated rescue boats.
[4] A hatchet counts towards this requirement in rigid rescue boats.
[5] Oars are not required on a free-fall lifeboat; a unit of oars means the number of oars specified by the boat manufacturer.
[6] Rescue boats may substitute buoyant paddles for oars, as specified by the manufacturer.
[7] Not required for a rigid rescue boat.
[8] Required if specified by the boat manufacturer.
[9] Sufficient thermal protective aids are required for at least 10% of the persons the survival craft is equipped to carry, but not less than two.
[10] Required only if the lifeboat is also the rescue boat.

[CGD 84–069, 61 FR 25313, May 20, 1996; 61 FR 40281, Aug. 1, 1996; 63 FR 52819, Oct. 1, 1998; USCG–1999–6216, 64 FR 53229, Oct. 1, 1999; USCG–2000–7790, 65 FR 58465, Sept. 29, 2000; USCG–2004–18884, 69 FR 58352, Sept. 30, 2004]

§ 199.176 Markings on lifesaving appliances.

(a) *Lifeboats and rescue boats.* Each lifeboat and rescue boat must be plainly marked as follows:

(1) Each side of each lifeboat and rescue boat bow must be marked in block capital letters and numbers with—

(i) The name of the vessel; and

(ii) The name of the port required to be marked on the stern of the vessel to meet the requirements of subpart 67.123 of this chapter.

(2) The number of persons for which the boast is equipped must be clearly marked, preferably on the bow, in permanent characters. The number of persons for which the boat is equipped must not exceed the number of persons shown on its nameplate.

(3) The number of the boat and a means of identifying the vessel to which the boat belongs, such as the vessel's name, must be plainly marked or painted so that the markings are visible from above the boat.

(4) The Type II retro-reflective material approved under approval series 164.018 must be placed on the boat to meet the arrangement requirements in IMO Resolution A.658(16).

(b) *Rigid liferafts.* Each rigid liferaft must be marked as follows:

(1) The name of the vessel must be marked on each rigid liferaft.

(2) The name of the port required to be marked on the stern of the vessel to meet the requirements of § 67.123 of this chapter must be marked on each rigid liferaft.

(3) The rigid liferaft must be marked with the words "SOLAS A pack" or "SOLAS B pack", to reflect the pack inside.

(4) The length of the painter must be marked on each rigid liferaft.

(5) At each entrance of each rigid liferaft, the number of persons for which the rigid liferaft is equipped must be marked in letters and numbers at least 100 millimeters (4 inches) high and in a color contrasting to that of the liferaft. The number of persons for which the liferaft is equipped must not exceed the number of persons shown on its nameplate.

[CGD 84–69, 61 FR 52313, May 20, 1996, as amended at 63 FR 52819, Oct. 1, 1998]

§ 199.178 Marking of stowage locations.

(a) Containers, brackets, racks, and other similar stowage locations for lifesaving equipment must be marked with symbols in accordance with IMO Resolution A.760(18) indicating the device stowed in that location.

(b) If more than one device is stowed in a location, the number of devices stowed must be indicated.

(c) Survival craft should be numbered consecutively starting from the vessel's bow. Survival craft on the starboard side should be numbered with

§ 199.180

odd numerals and survival craft on the port side should be numbered with even numerals.

(d) Each liferaft stowage location should be marked with the capacity of the liferaft stowed there.

§ 199.180 **Training and drills.**

(a) *Training materials.* Training material must be on board each vessel and must consist of a manual of one or more volumes written in easily understood terms and illustrated wherever possible, or of audiovisual training aids, or of both as follows:

(1) If a training manual is used, a copy must be in each crew messroom and recreation room or in each crew cabin. If audiovisual training aids are used, they must be incorporated into the onboard training sessions described in paragraph (g) of this section.

(2) The training material must explain in detail—

(i) The procedure for donning lifejackets, immersion suits, and anti-exposure suits carried on board;

(ii) The procedure for mustering at the assigned stations;

(iii) The procedure for boarding, launching, and clearing the survival craft and rescue boats;

(iv) The method of launching from within the survival craft;

(v) The procedure for releasing survival craft from launching appliances;

(vi) The method and use of water spray systems in launching areas when such systems are required for the protection of aluminum survival craft or launching appliances;

(vii) The illumination in the launching areas;

(viii) The use of all survival equipment;

(ix) The use of all detection equipment for the location of survivors or survival craft;

(x) With the assistance of illustrations, the use of radio lifesaving appliances;

(xi) The use of sea anchors;

(xii) The use of the survival craft engine and accessories;

(xiii) The recovery of survival craft and rescue boats, including stowage and securing;

(xiv) The hazards of exposure and the need for warm clothing;

(xv) The best use of the survival craft for survival;

(xvi) The methods of retrieval, including the use of helicopter rescue gear such as slings, baskets, and stretchers; the use of breeches-buoy and shore lifesaving apparatus; and the use of the vessel's line-throwing apparatus;

(xvii) All other functions contained in the muster list and emergency instructions; and

(xviii) The instructions for emergency repair of the lifesaving appliances.

(b) *Familiarity with emergency procedures.* (1) Every crewmember with emergency duties assigned on the muster list must be familiar with their assigned duties before the voyage begins.

(2) On a vessel engaged on voyage when the passengers or special personnel are scheduled to be on board for more than 24 hours, musters of the passengers and special personnel must take place within 24 hours after their embarkation. Passengers and special personnel must be instructed in the use of the lifejackets and the action to take in an emergency.

(3) Whenever new passengers or special personnel embark, a safety briefing must be given immediately before sailing or immediately after sailing. The briefing must include the instructions required by § 199.80 and must be made by means of an announcement in one or more languages likely to be understood by the passengers and special personnel. The announcement must be made on the vessel's public address system or by other equivalent means likely to be heard by the passengers and special personnel who have not yet heard it during the voyage. The briefing may be included in the muster required by paragraph (b)(2) of this section if the muster is held immediately upon departure. Information cards or posters, or video programs displayed on the vessel video displays, may be used to supplement the briefing, but may not be used to replace the announcement.

(c) *Drills—general.* (1) Drills must, as far as practicable, be conducted as if there were an actual emergency.

(2) Every crewmember must participate in at least one abandon-ship drill

Coast Guard, DHS § 199.180

and one fire drill every month. The drills of the crew must take place within 24 hours of the vessel leaving a port if more than 25 percent of the crew have not participated in abandon-ship and fire drills on board that particular vessel in the previous month.

(3) Drills must be held before sailing when a vessel enters service for the first time, after modification of a major character, or when a new crew is engaged.

(4) The OCMI may accept other equivalent drill arrangements for those classes of vessels for which compliance with this paragraph is impracticable.

(d) *Abandon-ship drills.* (1) Abandon-ship drills must include—

(i) Summoning persons on board to muster stations with the general alarm followed by drill announcements on the public address or other communication system and ensuring that the persons on board are made aware of the order to abandon ship;

(ii) Reporting to stations and preparing for the duties described in the muster list;

(iii) Checking that persons on board are suitably dressed;

(iv) Checking that lifejackets or immersion suits are correctly donned;

(v) Lowering of at least one lifeboat after any necessary preparation for launching;

(vi) Starting and operating the lifeboat engine; and

(vii) Operating davits used for launching the liferafts.

(2) Abandon-ship drills should also include conducting a mock search and rescue of passengers or special personnel trapped in their staterooms, and giving instructions in the use of radio lifesaving appliances.

(3) Different lifeboats must, as far as practicable, be lowered to comply with the requirements of paragraph (d)(1)(v) of this section at successive drills.

(4) Except as provided in paragraphs (d)(5) and (d)(6) of this section, each lifeboat must be launched with its assigned operating crew aboard and maneuvered in the water at least once every 3 months during an abandon-ship drill.

(5) Lowering into the water, rather than launching of a lifeboat arranged for free-fall launching, is acceptable when free-fall launching is impracticable, provided that the lifeboat is free-fall launched with its assigned operating crew aboard and is maneuvered in the water at least once every 6 months. However, when compliance with the 6-month requirement is impracticable, the OCMI may extend this period to 12 months, provided that arrangements are made for simulated launching at intervals of not more than 6 months.

(6) The OCMI may exempt a vessel operating on short international voyages from the requirement to launch the lifeboats on both sides of the vessel if berthing arrangements in port and operations do not permit launching of lifeboats on one side. However, all lifeboats on the vessel must be lowered at least once every 3 months and launched at least annually.

(7) As far as is reasonable and practicable, rescue boats, other than lifeboats which are also rescue boats, must be launched with their assigned crew aboard and maneuvered in the water each month. Such launching and maneuvering must occur at least once every 3 months.

(8) If lifeboat and rescue boat launching drills are carried out with the vessel making headway, such drills must, because of the dangers involved, be practiced in sheltered waters only and be under the supervision of an officer experienced in such drills.

(9) If a vessel is fitted with marine evacuation systems, drills must include an exercising of the procedures required for the deployment of such a system up to the point immediately preceding actual deployment of the system. This aspect of drills should be augmented by regular instruction using the on board training aids. Additionally, every crewmember assigned to duties involving the marine evacuation system must, as far as practicable, participate in a full deployment of a similar system into water, either on board a vessel or ashore, every 2 years but not longer than every 3 years. This training may be associated with the deployments required by § 199.190(k).

(10) Emergency lighting for mustering and abandonment must be tested at each abandon-ship drill.

(11) If a vessel carries immersion suits or anti-exposure suits, the suits must be worn by crewmembers in at least one abandon ship drill in any three-month period. If wearing the suits is impracticable due to warm weather, the crewmembers must be instructed on their donning and use.

(12) If a vessel carries immersion suits for persons other than the crew, the abandon-ship drill must include instruction to these persons on the stowage, donning, and use of the suits.

(e) *Line-throwing appliance.* A drill must be conducted on the use of the line-throwing appliance at least once every 3 months. The actual firing of the appliance is at the discretion of the master.

(f) *Fire drills.* (1) Fire drills must, as far as practicable, be planned with due consideration given to the various emergencies that may occur for that type of vessel and its cargo.

(2) Each fire drill must include—

(i) Reporting to stations and preparing for the duties described in the muster list for the particular fire emergency being simulated;

(ii) Starting of fire pumps and the use of two jets of water to determine that the system is in proper working order;

(iii) Checking the firemen's outfits and other personal rescue equipment;

(iv) Checking the relevant communications equipment;

(v) Checking the operation of watertight doors, fire doors, and fire dampers and main inlets and outlets of ventilation systems in the drill area; and

(vi) Checking the necessary arrangements for subsequent abandonment of the vessel.

(3) The equipment used during drills must immediately be brought back to its fully operational condition. Any faults and defects discovered during the drills must be remedied as soon as possible.

(g) *Onboard training and instruction.* (1) Onboard training in the use of the vessel's lifesaving appliances, including survival craft equipment, and in the use of the vessel's fire-extinguishing appliances must be given as soon as possible but not later than 2 weeks after a crewmember joins the vessel.

(2) If the crewmember is on a regularly scheduled rotating assignment to the vessel, the training required in paragraph (g)(1) of this section need be given only within 2 weeks of the time the crewmember first joins the vessel.

(3) The crew must be instructed in the use of the vessel's fire-extinguishing and lifesaving appliances and in survival at sea at the same interval as the drills. Individual units of instruction may cover different parts of the vessel's lifesaving and fire-extinguishing appliances, but all the vessel's lifesaving and fire-extinguishing appliances must be covered within any period of 2 months.

(4) Every crewmember must be given instructions that include, but are not limited to—

(i) The operation and use of the vessel's inflatable liferafts;

(ii) The problems of hypothermia, first aid treatment for hypothermia, and other appropriate first aid procedures;

(iii) Any special instructions necessary for use of the vessel's lifesaving appliances in severe weather and severe sea conditions; and

(iv) The operation and use of fire-extinguishing appliances.

(5) Onboard training in the use of davit-launched liferafts must take place at intervals of not more than 4 months on each vessel with davit-launched liferafts. Whenever practicable, this training must include the inflation and lowering of a liferaft. If this liferaft is a special liferaft intended for training purposes only and is not part of the vessel's lifesaving equipment, this liferaft must be conspicuously marked.

(h) *Records.* (1) When musters are held, details of abandon-ship drills, fire drills, drills of other lifesaving appliances, and onboard training must be recorded in the vessel's official logbook. Logbook entries must include—

(i) The date and time of the drill, muster, or training session;

(ii) The survival craft and fire-extinguishing equipment used in the drills;

(iii) Identification of inoperative or malfunctioning equipment and the corrective action taken;

Coast Guard, DHS § 199.190

(iv) Identification of crewmembers participating in drills or training sessions; and

(v) The subject of the onboard training session.

(2) If a full muster, drill, or training session is not held at the appointed time, an entry must be made in the logbook stating the circumstances and the extent of the muster, drill, or training session held.

[CGD 84–69, 61 FR 25313, May 20, 1996, as amended at 63 FR 52819, Oct. 1, 1998]

§ 199.190 **Operational readiness, maintenance, and inspection of lifesaving equipment.**

(a) *Operational readiness.* Before the vessel leaves port and at all times during the voyage, each lifesaving appliance must be in working order and ready for immediate use.

(b) *Maintenance.* (1) The manufacturer's instructions for onboard maintenance of lifesaving appliances must be on board the vessel. The following must be provided for each appliance.

(i) Checklists for use when carrying out the inspections required under paragraph (e) of this section.

(ii) Maintenance and repair instructions.

(iii) A schedule of periodic maintenance.

(iv) A diagram of lubrication points with the recommended lubricants.

(v) A list of replaceable parts.

(vi) A list of sources of spare parts.

(vii) A log for records of inspections and maintenance.

(2) In lieu of compliance with paragraph (b)(1) of this section, the OCMI may accept a shipboard planned maintenance program that includes the items listed in that paragraph.

(c) *Spare parts and repair equipment.* Spare parts and repair equipment must be provided for each lifesaving appliance and component that is subject to excessive wear or consumption and that needs to be replaced regularly.

(d) *Weekly inspections and tests.* (1) Each survival craft, rescue boat, and launching appliance must be visually inspected to ensure its readiness for use.

(2) Each lifeboat engine and rescue boat engine must be run ahead and astern for a total of not less than 3 minutes unless the ambient temperature is below the minimum temperature required for starting the engine. During this time, demonstrations should indicate that the gear box and gear box train are engaging satisfactorily. If the special characteristics of an outboard motor fitted to a rescue boat would not allow the outboard motor to be run other than with its propeller submerged for a period of 3 minutes, the outboard motor should be run for such period as prescribed in the manufacturer's handbook.

(3) The general alarm system must be tested.

(e) *Monthly inspections.* (1) Each lifesaving appliance, including lifeboat equipment, must be inspected monthly using the checklists required under paragraph (b)(1)(i) of this section to make sure the appliance and the equipment are complete and in good working order. A report of the inspection, including a statement as to the condition of the equipment, must be recorded in the vessel's official logbook.

(2) Each EPIRB and each SART, other than an EPIRB or SART in an inflatable liferaft, must be tested monthly. The EPIRB must be tested using the integrated test circuit and output indicator to determine that it is operative.

(f) *Annual inspections.* Annual inspections must include the following:

(1) Each survival craft, except for inflatable craft, must be stripped, cleaned, and thoroughly inspected and repaired, as needed, at least once each year and each fuel tank must be emptied, cleaned, and refilled with fresh fuel.

(2) Each davit, winch, fall, and other launching appliance must be thoroughly inspected and repaired, as needed, once each year.

(3) Each item of survival equipment with an expiration date must be replaced during the annual inspection if the expiration date has passed.

(4) Each battery clearly marked with an expiration date and used in an item of survival equipment must be replaced during the annual inspection if the expiration date has passed.

(5) Except for a storage battery used in a lifeboat or rescue boat, each battery without an expiration date that is

§ 199.190

used in an item of survival equipment must be replaced during the annual inspection.

(g) *Servicing of inflatable lifesaving appliances, inflated rescue boats, and marine evacuation systems.* (1) Each inflatable lifesaving appliance and marine evacuation system must be serviced—

(i) Within 12 months of its initial packing; and

(ii) Within 12 months of each subsequent servicing, except when servicing is delayed until the next scheduled inspection of the vessel, provided the delay does not exceed 5 months.

(2) Each inflatable lifejacket must be serviced in accordance with servicing procedures meeting the requirements of part 160, subpart 160.176 of this chapter. Each hybrid inflatable lifejacket must be serviced in accordance with the owners manual and meet the requirements of part 160, subpart 160.077 of this chapter.

(3) An inflatable liferaft or inflatable buoyant apparatus must be serviced at a facility specifically approved by the Commandant for the particular brand, and in accordance with servicing procedures meeting the requirements of part 160, subpart 160.151, of this chapter—

(i) No later than the month and year on its servicing sticker affixed under 46 CFR 160.151-57(n), except that servicing may be delayed until the next scheduled inspection of the vessel, provided that the delay does not exceed 5 months; and

(ii) Whenever the container is damaged or the container straps or seals are broken.

(4) Each inflated rescue boat must be repaired and maintained in accordance with the manufacturer's instructions. All repairs to inflated chambers must be made at a servicing facility approved by the Commandant, except for emergency repairs carried out on board the vessel.

(h) *Periodic servicing of hydrostatic release units.* Each hydrostatic release unit, other than a disposable hydrostatic release unit, must be serviced in accordance with repair and testing procedures meeting the requirements of part 160, subpart 160.062 of this chapter—

(1) Within 12 months of its manufacture; and

46 CFR Ch. I (10–1–04 Edition)

(2) Within 12 months of each subsequent servicing, except when servicing is delayed until the next scheduled inspection of the vessel, provided the delay does not exceed 5 months.

(i) *Periodic servicing of launching appliances and release gear.* (1) Launching appliances must be serviced at the intervals recommended in the manufacturer's instructions or as set out in the shipboard planned maintenance program.

(2) Launching appliances must be thoroughly examined at intervals not exceeding 5 years and, upon completion of the examination, the launching appliance must be subjected to a dynamic test of the winch brake.

(3) Lifeboat and rescue boat release gear must be serviced at the intervals recommended in the manufacturer's instructions, or as set out in the shipboard-planned-maintenance program.

(4) Lifeboat and rescue boat release gear must be subjected to a thorough examination by properly trained personnel familiar with the system at each inspection for certification.

(5) Lifeboat and rescue boat release gear must be operationally tested under a load of 1.1 times the total mass of the lifeboat when loaded with its full complement of persons and equipment whenever overhauled or at least once every 5 years.

(j) *Maintenance of falls.* (1) Each fall used in a launching appliance must—

(i) Be turned end-for-end at intervals of not more than 30 months; and

(ii) Be renewed when necessary due to deterioration or at intervals of not more than 5 years, whichever is earlier.

(2) As an alternative to paragraph (j)(1) of this section, each fall may—

(i) Be inspected annually; and

(ii) Be renewed whenever necessary due to deterioration or at intervals of not more than 4 years, whichever is earlier.

(k) *Rotational deployment of marine evacuation systems.* In addition, to or in conjunction with, the servicing intervals of marine evacuation systems required by paragraph (g)(1) of this section, each marine evacuation system must be deployed from the vessel on a

Coast Guard, DHS

§ 199.201

rotational basis. Each marine evacuation system must be deployed at least once every 6 years.

[CGD 84–069, 61 FR 25313, May 20, 1996; 61 FR 40281, Aug. 1, 1996, as amended by CGD 85–205, 62 FR 25557, May 9, 1997; CGD 84–069, 63 FR 52819, Oct. 1, 1998; USCG–2001–11118, 67 FR 58542, Sept. 17, 2002]

Subpart C—Additional Requirements for Passenger Vessels

§ 199.200 General.

Passenger vessels and special purpose vessels described in § 199.10(e), must meet the requirements in this subpart in addition to the requirements in subparts A and B of this part.

[CGD 84–069, 61 FR 25313, May 20, 1996, as amended by USCG–1999–6216, 64 FR 53229, Oct. 1, 1999]

§ 199.201 Survival craft.

(a) Each survival craft must be approved and equipped as follows:

(1) Each lifeboat must be approved under approval series 160.135 and equipped as specified in table 199.175 of this part.

(2) Each inflatable liferaft must be approved under approval series 160.151 and equipped with—

(i) A SOLAS A pack; or

(ii) For a passenger vessel on a short international voyage, a SOLAS B pack.

(3) Each rigid liferaft must be approved under approval series 160.118 and equipped as specified in table 199.175 of this part.

(4) Each marine evacuation system must be approved under approval series 160.175.

(5) Each liferaft must have a capacity of six persons or more.

(b) Each passenger vessel must carry the following:

(1) A combination of lifeboats and liferafts that have an aggregate capacity sufficient to accommodate the total number of persons on board, provided that—

(i) On each side of the vessel, lifeboats with an aggregate capacity sufficient to accommodate at least 37.5 percent of the total number of persons on board are carried; and

(ii) Any liferafts that are provided in combination with the lifeboats are served by launching appliances or marine evacuation systems equally distributed on each side of the vessel.

(2) In addition to the survival craft required in paragraph (b)(1) of this section, additional liferafts must be provided that have a aggregate capacity sufficient to accommodate at least 25 percent of the total number of persons on board. The additional liferafts—

(i) Must be served by at least one launching appliance or marine evacuation system on each side of the vessel. These launching appliances or marine evacuation systems must be those described under paragraph (b)(1)(ii) of this section or be equivalent approved appliances capable of being used on both sides of the vessel; and

(ii) Are not required to be stowed in accordance with § 199.130(c)(4).

(c) Each passenger vessel engaged on a short international voyage that also complies with the standards of subdivision requirements for vessels on short international voyages as described in subchapter S of this chapter may, as an alternative to the lifeboat requirements in paragraph (b)(1)(i) of this section, carry lifeboats with an aggregate capacity sufficient to accommodate at least 30 percent of the total number of persons on board. These lifeboats must be equally distributed, as far as practicable, on each side of the vessel.

(d) Each passenger vessel that is less than 500 tons gross tonnage and is certificated to permit less than 200 persons on board is not required to meet the requirements of paragraphs (b) or (c) of this section if it meets the following:

(1) On each side of the vessel—

(i) Liferafts are carried with an aggregate capacity sufficient to accommodate the total number of persons on board and are stowed in a position providing for easy side-to-side transfer at a single open deck level; or

(ii) Liferafts are carried with an aggregate capacity sufficient to accommodate 150 percent of the total number of persons on board. If the rescue boat required under § 199.202 is also a lifeboat, its capacity may be included to meet the aggregate capacity requirement.

§ 199.202

(2) If the largest survival craft on either side of the vessel is lost or rendered unserviceable, there must be survival craft available for use on each side of the vessel, including those which are stowed in a position providing for side-to-side transfer at a single open deck level, with a capacity sufficient to accommodate the total number of persons on board.

§ 199.202 Rescue boats.

(a) Each passenger vessel of 500 tons gross tonnage and over must carry on each side of the vessel at least one rescue boat approved under approval series 160.156 that is equipped as specified in table 199.175 of this part.

(b) Each passenger vessel of less than 500 tons gross tonnage must carry at least one rescue boat approved under approval series 160.156 that is equipped as specified in table 199.175 of this part.

(c) A lifeboat is accepted as a rescue boat if, in addition to being approved under approval series 160.135, it is also approved under approval series 160.156.

§ 199.203 Marshalling of liferafts.

(a) Each passenger vessel must have a lifeboat or rescue boat for each six liferafts when—

(1) Each lifeboat and rescue boat is loaded with its full complement of persons; and

(2) The minimum number of liferafts necessary to accommodate the remainder of the persons on board have been launched.

(b) A passenger vessel engaged on a short international voyage that also complies with the standards of subdivision requirements for vessels on short international voyages as described in subchapter S of this chapter may have a lifeboat or rescue boat for each nine liferafts when—

(1) Each lifeboat and rescue boat is loaded with its full complement of persons; and

(2) The minimum number of liferafts necessary to accommodate the remainder of the persons on board have been launched.

§ 199.211 Lifebuoys.

(a) Each passenger vessel must carry the number of lifebuoys prescribed in table 199.211 of this section.

TABLE 199.211—REQUIREMENTS FOR LIFEBUOYS FOR PASSENGER VESSELS

Length of vessel in meters (feet)	Minimum number of lifebuoys
Under 60 (196)	8
60(196) and under 120(393)	12
120(393) and under 180 (590)	18
180 (590) and under 240 (787)	24
240 (787) and over	30

(b) Notwithstanding § 199.70(a)(3)(ii), each passenger vessel under 60 meters (196 feet) in length must carry at least six lifebuoys with self-igniting lights.

[CGD 84–069, 61 FR 25313, May 20, 1996; 61 FR 40281, Aug. 1, 1996]

§ 199.212 Lifejackets.

(a) In addition to the lifejackets required under § 199.70(b), each passenger vessel must carry lifejackets for at least 5 percent of the total number of persons on board. These lifejackets must be stowed in conspicuous places on deck or at muster stations.

(b) Where lifejackets for persons other than the crew are stowed in staterooms located remotely from direct routes between public spaces and muster stations, any additional lifejackets required by § 199.70(b)(2)(v) for these persons must be stowed in the public spaces, near muster stations, or on direct routes between them. These lifejackets must be stowed so that their distribution and donning does not impede orderly movement to muster stations and survival craft embarkation stations.

Coast Guard, DHS § 199.245

§ 199.214 Immersion suits and thermal protective aids.

(a) Each passenger vessel must carry at least three immersion suits approved under approval series 160.171 for each lifeboat on the vessel.

(b) In addition to the requirements in paragraph (a) of this section, each passenger vessel must carry a thermal protective aid approved under approval series 160.174 for each person not provided with an immersion suit.

(c) The immersion suits and thermal protective aids required under paragraphs (a) and (b) of this section are not required if the passenger vessel operates only on routes between 32 degrees north and 32 degrees south latitude.

§ 199.217 Muster list and emergency instructions.

(a) The format of each passenger vessel muster list required under § 199.80 must be approved by the OCMI.

(b) The passenger vessel muster list or emergency instructions must include procedures for locating and rescuing persons other than the crew who may be trapped in their staterooms.

(c) As an alternative to the requirements in § 199.80(c), the passenger vessel emergency instructions may meet the requirements of MSC Circular 699 (Guidelines for Passenger Safety Instructions).

§ 199.220 Survival craft and rescue boat embarkation arrangements.

(a) Survival craft embarkation arrangements must be designed for—

(1) Each lifeboat to be boarded and launched either directly from the stowed position or from an embarkation deck, but not both; and

(2) Davit-launched liferafts to be boarded and launched from a position immediately adjacent to the stowed positions or from a position where, as described under § 199.130(c)(4), the liferaft is transferred before launching.

(b) Each rescue boat must be able to be boarded and launched directly from the stowed position with the number of persons assigned to crew the rescue boat on board. Notwithstanding paragraph (a)(1) of this section, if the rescue boat is also a lifeboat and the other lifeboats are boarded and launched from an embarkation deck, the arrangements must be such that the rescue boat can also be boarded and launched from the embarkation deck.

[CGD 84–069, 61 FR 25313, May 20, 1996, as amended by USCG–1999–6216, 64 FR 53229, Oct. 1, 1999]

§ 199.230 Stowage of survival craft.

(a) To meet the requirements of § 199.130(b)(1), each lifeboat on a passenger vessel of 80 meters (262 feet) in length and upwards must be stowed where the after-end of the lifeboat is at least 1.5 times the length of the lifeboat forward of the vessel's propeller.

(b) The stowage height of a survival craft must take into account the vessel's escape provisions, the vessel's size, and the weather conditions likely to be encountered in the vessel's intended area of operation.

(c) The height of the davit head of each davit when it is in position to launch the survival craft should, as far as practicable, not exceed 15 meters (49 feet) to the waterline when the vessel is in its lightest seagoing condition.

§ 199.240 Muster stations.

Each passenger vessel must, in addition to meeting the requirements of § 199.110, have muster stations that—

(a) Are near the embarkation stations, unless a muster station is also an embarkation station;

(b) Permit ready access to the embarkation station, unless a muster station is also an embarkation station; and

(c) Have sufficient room to marshal and instruct passengers and special personnel.

§ 199.245 Survival craft embarkation and launching arrangements.

(a) Each davit-launched liferaft must be arranged to be rapidly boarded by its full complement of persons.

(b) All survival craft required for abandonment by the total number of persons on board must be capable of being launched with the survival crafts' full complement of persons and equipment within a period of 30 minutes from the time the abandon-ship signal is given.

§ 199.250 Drills.

(a) An abandon-ship drill and a fire drill, as described in § 199.180, must be conducted on each passenger vessel at least weekly.

(b) The entire crew does not have to be involved in every drill, but each crewmember must participate in an abandon-ship drill and a fire drill each month.

(c) Passengers and special personnel must be strongly encouraged to attend abandon-ship and fire drills.

Subpart D—Additional Requirements for Cargo Vessels

§ 199.260 General.

Cargo vessels and special purpose vessels, as described in § 199.10(f), must meet the requirements in this subpart in addition to the requirements in subparts A and B of this part.

[CGD 84–069, 61 FR 25313, May 20, 1996, as amended by USCG–1999–6216, 64 FR 53229, Oct. 1, 1999]

§ 199.261 Survival craft.

(a) Each survival craft must be approved and equipped as follows:

(1) Each lifeboat must be a totally enclosed lifeboat approved under approval series 160.135 and equipped as specified in table 199.175 of this part.

(2) Each inflatable liferaft must be approved under approval series 160.151 and be equipped with a SOLAS A pack.

(3) Each rigid liferaft must be approved under approval series 160.118 and be equipped as specified in table 199.175 of this part.

(4) Each liferaft must have a capacity of six persons or more.

(5) Each marine evacuation system must be approved under approval series 160.175.

(b) Each cargo vessel must carry—

(1) On each side of the vessel, lifeboats with an aggregate capacity sufficient to accommodate the total number of persons on board; and

(2) Liferafts—

(i) With an aggregate capacity sufficient to accommodate the total number of persons on board and that are stowed in a position providing for easy side-to-side transfer at a single open deck level; or

(ii) With an aggregate capacity on each side sufficient to accommodate the total number of persons on board.

(c) A cargo vessel is not required to meet the requirements of paragraph (b) of this section if it carries—

(1) Lifeboats capable of being free-fall launched over the stern of the vessel that have an aggregate capacity sufficient to accommodate the total number of persons on board; and

(2) On each side of the vessel, liferafts with an aggregate capacity sufficient to accommodate the total number of persons on board with the liferafts on at least one side of the vessel being served by launching appliances or marine evacuation systems.

(d) Cargo vessels less than 85 meters (278 feet) in length, with the exception of tank vessels, are not required to meet paragraphs (b) or (c) of this section if they meet the following:

(1) On each side of the vessel—

(i) Liferafts are carried with an aggregate capacity sufficient to accommodate the total number of persons on board and are stowed in a position providing for easy side-to-side transfer at a single open deck level; or

(ii) Liferafts are carried with an aggregate capacity sufficient to accommodate 150 percent of the total number of persons on board. If the rescue boat required under § 199.262 is also a lifeboat, its capacity may be included to meet the aggregate capacity requirement.

(2) In the event the largest survival craft on either side of the vessel is lost or rendered unserviceable, there must be survival craft available for use on each side of the vessel, including those which are stowed in a position providing for side-to-side transfer at a single open deck level, with a capacity sufficient to accommodate the total number of persons on board.

(e) Each cargo vessel on which the horizontal distance from the extreme end of the stem or stern of the vessel to the nearest end of the closest survival craft is more than 100 meters (328 feet) must carry, in addition to the liferafts required by paragraphs (b)(2) and (c)(2) of this section, a liferaft stowed as far forward or aft, or one as far forward and another as far aft, as is reasonable and practicable. The requirement for the liferaft to float free under § 199.130(c)(7) does not apply to a liferaft under this paragraph, provided it is arranged for quick manual release.

(f) Each lifeboat on a tank vessel certificated to carry cargos that emit toxic vapors or gases must be approved as a lifeboat with a self-contained air support system or a fire-protected lifeboat.

(g) Each lifeboat must be approved as a fire-protected lifeboat if it is carried on a tank vessel certificated to carry cargos that have a flashpoint less than 60 °C as determined under ASTM D 93 (incorporated by reference, see § 199.05).

[CGD 84–069, 61 FR 25313, May 20, 1996, as amended by USCG–1999–5151, 64 FR 67187, Dec. 1, 1999]

§ 199.262 Rescue boats.

(a) Each cargo vessel must carry at least one rescue boat. Each rescue boat must be approved under approval series 160.156 and be equipped as specified in table 199.175 of this part.

(b) A lifeboat is accepted as a rescue boat if, in addition to being approved under approval series 160.135, it also is approved under approval series 160.156.

§ 199.271 Lifebuoys.

Each cargo vessel must carry the number of lifebuoys prescribed in table 199.271 of this section.

TABLE 199.271—REQUIREMENTS FOR LIFEBUOYS ON CARGO VESSELS

Length of vessel in meters (feet)	Minimum number of lifebuoys
Under 100 (328)	8
100 (328) and under 150 (492)	10
150 (492) and under 200 (656)	12
200 (656) and over	14

§ 199.273 Immersion suits.

(a) Each cargo vessel must carry an immersion suit approved under approval series 160.171 of an appropriate size for each person on board.

(b) If watch stations, work stations, or work sites are remote from cabins, staterooms, or berthing areas and the immersion suits stowed in those locations, there must be, in addition to the immersion suits required under paragraph (a) of this section, enough immersion suits stowed at the watch stations, work stations, or work sites to equal the number of persons normally on watch in, or assigned to, those locations at any time.

(c) The immersion suits required under paragraphs (a) and (b) of this section are not required if the cargo vessel operates only on routes between 32 degrees north and 32 degrees south latitude.

(d) The immersion suits required under this section can be included to meet the requirements of § 199.70(c).

[CGD 84–069, 61 FR 25313, May 20, 1996; 61 FR 40281, Aug. 1, 1996]

§ 199.280 Survival craft embarkation and launching arrangements.

(a) Each lifeboat must be arranged to be boarded and launched directly from the stowed position.

(b) Each davit-launched liferaft must be arranged to be boarded and launched from a position immediately adjacent to the stowed position or from a position where, under § 199.130(c)(4), the liferaft is transferred before launching.

(c) Cargo vessels of 20,000 tons gross tonnage or more must carry lifeboats that are capable of being launched, using painters if necessary, with the vessel making headway at speeds up to 5 knots in clam water.

(d) All survival craft required for abandonment by the total number of persons on board must be capable of

§ 199.290

being launched with their full complement of persons and equipment within 10 minutes from the time the abandon-ship signal is given.

(e) On a tank vessel carrying crude oil, product, chemicals, or liquefied gases, notwithstanding the requirements of § 199.150(c), each launching appliance, together with its lowering and recovery gear, must be arranged so that the fully equipped survival craft the launching appliance serves can be safely lowered on the lower side of the vessel at the angle of heel after damage calculated in accordance with—

(1) The International Convention for the Prevention of Pollution from Ships, 1973, as amended by the Protocol of 1978 (MARPOL 73/78), in the case of an oil tanker;

(2) The International Code for the Construction and Equipment of Ships carrying Dangerous Chemicals in Bulk, in the case of a chemical tanker; or

(3) The International Code for the Construction and Equipment of Ships carrying Liquefied Gases in Bulk, in the case of a gas carrier.

[CGD 84–069, 61 FR 25313, May 20, 1996, as amended by USCG–1999–6216, 64 FR 53229, Oct. 1, 1999]

§ 199.290 Stowage of survival craft.

(a) To meet the requirements of § 199.130(b)(1), each lifeboat—

(1) On a cargo vessel 80 meters (262 feet) or more in length but less than 120 meters (393 feet) in length, must be stowed with the after-end of the lifeboat at a distance not less than one length of the lifeboat forward of the vessel's propeller; and

(2) On a cargo vessel 120 meters (393 feet) or more in length, must be stowed with the after end of the lifeboat not less than 1.5 times the length of the lifeboat forward of the vessel's propeller.

(b) On a tank vessel certificated to carry cargos that have a flashpoint less than 60 °C as determined under ASTM D 93 (incorporated by reference, see § 199.05), each lifeboat or launching appliance of aluminum construction must be protected by a water spray system meeting the requirements of part 34, subpart 34.25 of this chapter.

(c) Other than the stowage position for the liferaft required under

46 CFR Ch. I (10–1–04 Edition)

§ 199.261(e), no stowage position or muster and embarkation station for a survival craft on a tank vessel may be located on or above a cargo tank, slop tank, or other tank containing explosives or hazardous liquids.

(d) Each lifeboat and davit-launched liferaft must be arranged to be boarded by its full complement of persons within 3 minutes from the time the instruction to board is given.

[CGD 84–069, 61 FR 25313, May 20, 1996, as amended by USCG–1999–5151, 64 FR 67187, Dec. 1, 1999]

Subpart E—Additional Requirements for Vessels Not Subject to SOLAS

§ 199.500 General.

This subpart sets out requirements in addition to the requirements in subparts A, B, C, and D of this part applicable to vessels not subject to SOLAS.

§ 199.510 EPIRB requirements.

(a) Each vessel must carry a category 1 406 MHz satellite EPIRB meeting the requirements of 47 CFR part 80.

(b) When the vessel is underway, the EPIRB must be stowed in its float-free bracket with the controls set for automatic activation and be mounted in a manner so that it will float free if the vessel sinks.

§ 199.520 Lifeboat requirements.

When the vessel's lifeboats are used to carry persons to and from the vessel in a harbor or at an anchorage, the survival craft remaining on the vessel must have an aggregate capacity sufficient to accommodate all persons remaining on board.

Subpart F—Exemptions and Alternatives for Vessels Not Subject to SOLAS

§ 199.600 General.

This subpart sets out specific exemptions and alternatives to requirements in subparts A, B, C, D, and E of this part for vessels not subject to SOLAS.

§ 199.610 Exemptions for vessels in specified services.

(a) *All vessels.* Vessels operating in coastwise, Great Lakes, lakes, bays and sounds, and rivers services are exempt from requirements in subparts A through E of this part as specified in table 199.610(a) of this section.

§ 199.610

TABLE 199.610(a)—EXEMPTIONS FOR ALL VESSELS IN SPECIFIED SERVICES

Section or paragraph in this part	Service			
	Coastwise	Great Lakes	Lakes, bays, and sounds	Rivers
199.60(c): Distress signals	(1)	(1)	Exempt	Exempt.
199.70(a)(3)(iii): Lifebuoys fitted with smoke signals	Exempt	Exempt	Exempt	Exempt.
199.70(b)(1)(i): Carriage of additional child-size lifejackets	(2)	(2)	(2)	(2)
199.70(b)(4)(i): Lifejacket lights (for lifejackets)	(3)	(3)	Exempt	Exempt.
199.70(c)(4)(i): Lifejacket lights (for immersion suits)	(3)	(3)	Exempt	Exempt.
199.70(b)(4)(ii): Lifejacket whistles	Exempt	Exempt	Exempt	Exempt.
199.70(c): Immersion suits for rescue boat crew members	Not Exempt	Not Exempt	Exempt	Exempt.
199.70(c)(4)(ii): Immersion suit whistles	Exempt	Exempt	Exempt	Exempt.
199.100(c)(1): Requirements for person-in-charge of survival craft	Not Exempt	Not Exempt	Not Exempt	Exempt.
199.100(d): Designation of second-in-command of lifeboat	(4)	(4)	(4)	(4)
199.110(f): Embarkation ladders at launching stations	(5)	(5)	(5)	Exempt.
199.130(a)(4): Survival craft stowage position	Not Exempt	Not Exempt	Exempt	Exempt.
199.170: Line-throwing appliance	Not Exempt	Exempt	Exempt	Exempt.
199.175(b)(21)(i)(G) or 199.640(j)(4)(iii)(E): Float-free link	(6)	(6)	(6)	(6)
199.190(j): Renewal of survival craft falls	Not Exempt	(7)	(7)	(7)
199.202 or 199.262 Rescue boats	(8)	(8)	(8)	(8)
199.510: EPIRB requirement	(8 9)	(8 10)	Exempt	Exempt.

Notes:
[1] Exempt if the vessel operates on a route with a duration of 30 minutes or less.
[2] Exempt if the vessel does not carry persons smaller than the lower size limit of the lifejackets carried.
[3] Exempt if the vessel is a ferry or has no overnight accommodations.
[4] Exempt if the lifeboat has a carrying capacity of less than 40 persons.
[5] Exempt if the distance is less than 3 meters (10 feet) from the embarkation deck to the water with the vessel in its lightest seagoing operating condition.
[6] Exempt if the vessel operates on a route on which the water depth is never more than the length of the painter.
[7] Exempt if the vessel operates on a fresh water route and inspection shows that the falls are not damaged by corrosion.
[8] Exempt if the vessel is non-self propelled and in tow, moored to or alongside a MODU or a self-propelled vessel, or moored to shore.
[9] Exempt if the vessel is a cargo vessel under 300 tons gross tonnage and operates on a route no more than 3 nautical miles from shore.
[10] Exempt if the vessel operates on a route no more than 3 nautical miles from shore.

Coast Guard, DHS § 199.620

(b) *Passenger vessels.* In addition to the exemptions in paragraph (a) of this section, passenger vessels operating in coastwise; Great Lakes; lakes, bays, and sounds; and rivers service are exempt from requirements in subparts A through E of this part as specified in table 199.610(b) of this section.

TABLE 199.610(b)—EXEMPTIONS FOR PASSENGER VESSELS IN SPECIFIED SERVICES

Section or paragraph in this part	Service			
	Coastwise	Great Lakes	Lakes, bays, and sounds	Rivers
199.203: Marshalling of liferafts	Not Exempt	Exempt	Exempt	Exempt.
199.211(b): Lights on lifebuoys	(1)	(1)	(1)	(1)
199.212(a): Carriage of additional five percent lifejackets.	Exempt	Exempt	Exempt	Exempt.
199.214: Immersion suits and thermal protective aids in lifeboats.	Not Exempt	Not Exempt	Exempt	Exempt.

Note:
[1] Exempt if the length of vessel is under 60 meters (197 feet) and there are self-igniting lights attached to at least one-half the required lifebuoys.

(c) *Cargo vessels.* In addition to the exemptions in paragraph (a) of this section, cargo vessels are exempt from requirements in subparts A through E of this part as specified in table 199.610(c) of this section.

TABLE 199.610(c)—EXEMPTIONS FOR CARGO VESSELS IN SPECIFIED SERVICES

Section or paragraph in this part	Service				
	Oceans	Coastwise	Great Lakes	Lakes, Bays, and Sounds	Rivers
199.70(a)(3)(ii): Lights on lifebuoys	Not exempt	(1)	(1)	(1)	(1)
199.80(b): Muster list	(2)	(2)	(2)	(2)	(2)
199.262(a): Rescue boats	(2 and 3)	(3)	(3)	(3)	(3)
199.273: Immersion suits	Not exempt	Not exempt	Not exempt	Exempt	Exempt

Notes:
[1] Exempt if the length of vessel is under 30 meters (99 feet).
[2] Exempt if the vessel is under 500 tons gross tonnage.
[3] Exempt if—(i) the OCMI determines the vessel is arranged to allow a helpless person to be recovered from the water.
A(ii) recovery of the helpless person can be observed from the navigating bridge; and
A(iii) the vessel does not regularly engage in operations that restrict its maneuverability.

[CGD 84–069, 61 FR 25313, May 20, 1996, as amended at 63 FR 52819, Oct. 1, 1998; USCG–1999–6216, 64 FR 53229, Oct. 1, 1999; USCG–2000–7790, 65 FR 58465, Sept. 29, 2000]

§ 199.620 Alternatives for all vessels in a specified service.

(a) *General.* Vessels operating in oceans; coastwise; Great Lakes; lakes, bays, and sounds; and rivers service may comply with alternative requirements to subparts A through E of this part as described in this section for the services specified in table 199.620(a) of this section.

§ 199.620

46 CFR Ch. I (10-1-04 Edition)

TABLE 199.620(a)—ALTERNATIVE REQUIREMENTS FOR ALL VESSELS IN A SPECIFIED SERVICE

Section or paragraph in this part:	Service and reference to alternative requirement section or paragraph			
	Oceans	Coastwise	Great Lakes	Lakes, bays and sounds	Rivers
199.70(a): Lifebuoy approval series	199.620(b)[1]	199.620(b)[1]	199.620(b)	199.620(b)	199.620(b)
199.70(b): Lifejacket approval series	199.620(c)[2]	199.620(c)[2]	199.620(c)	199.620(c)	199.620(c)
199.70(b)(1): Number of lifejackets carried	No Alternative	199.620(d)	199.620(d)	199.620(d)	199.620(d)
199.70(b)(4)(i): Lifejacket light approval series	No Alternative	199.620(e)	199.620(e)	Not Applicable	Not Applicable
199.100(b): Manning of survival craft	No Alternative	No Alternative	No Alternative	No Alternative	199.620(o)
199.110(f): Embarkation ladder	199.620(f)	199.620(f)	199.620(f)	199.620(f)	199.620(f)
199.130(b): Survival craft stowage position	No Alternative	No Alternative	199.620(g)	199.620(g)	199.620(g)
199.170: Line-throwing appliance approval series	199.620(h)[3]	199.620(h)[3]	Not Applicable	Not Applicable	Not Applicable
199.175: Lifeboat, rescue boat, and rigid liferaft equipment	199.620(i)[4]	199.620(i)	199.620(i)	199.620(i)	199.620(i)
199.180 Training and drills	199.620(p)	199.620(p)	199.620(p)	199.620(p)	199.620(p)
199.190: Spares and repair equipment	199.620(n)	199.620(n)	199.620(n)	199.620(n)	199.620(n)
199.190(g)(3): Service Intervals for Inflatable liferaft or inflatable buoyant apparatus.	199.620(q)	199.620(q)	199.620(q)	199.620(q)	199.620(q)
199.201(a)(2) or 199.261: Inflatable liferaft equipment	199.620(l)[4]	199.620(l)	199.620(l)	199.620(l)	199.620(l)
199.201(a)(2) or 199.261: Liferaft approval series	No Alternative	199.620(k)	199.620(k)	199.620(k)	199.620(k)

[1] Alternative applies if lifebuoy is orange.
[2] Alternative applies only to cargo vessels that are less than 500 tons gross tonnage.
[3] Alternative applies to cargo vessels that are less than 500 tons gross tonnage and to all passenger vessels.
[4] Alternative applies to passenger vessels limited to operating no more than 50 nautical miles from shore.

Coast Guard, DHS

§ 199.620

(b) *Lifebuoy approval series.* As an alternative to a lifebuoy approved under approval series 160.150, vessels may carry a lifebuoy approved under approval series 160.050.

(c) *Lifejackets approval series.* As an alternative to a lifejacket meeting the approval requirements in § 199.70, vessels may carry a lifejacket approved under approval series 160.002, 160.005, 160.055, or 160.077.

(d) *Lifejacket quantity.* Vessels may carry lifejackets as follows:

(1) If lifejackets are stowed in cabins, staterooms, or berthing areas that are readily accessible to each watch or work station, the requirement in § 199.70(b)(2)(iv) to have lifejackets at each watch or work station need not be met.

(2) If the vessel carries lifejackets that are designated extended-size, then the number of child-size lifejackets carried to meet § 199.70(b)(1)(i) may be reduced. To take the reduction in child-size lifejackets, extended-size lifejackets having the same lower size limit must be substituted for all of the required adult lifejackets. The number of child-size lifejackets required depends on the lower size limit of the extended-size lifejackets and is calculated by any one of the following formulas where PC is the number of child-size lifejackets expressed as a percentage of the number of lifejackets required under § 199.70(b)(1):

(i) PC=LS÷4.1, where LS equals the lower size limit expressed in kilograms.

(ii) PC=LS÷9, where LS equals the lower size limit expressed in pounds.

(iii) PC=(LS−81)÷7.6, where LS equals the lower size limit expressed in centimeters.

(iv) PC=(LS−32)÷3, where LS equals the lower size limit expressed in inches.

(e) *Lifejacket light approval series.* As an alternative to lights approved under approval series 161.112, vessels may use lights for lifejackets and immersions suits approved under series 161.012. However, lifejacket lights bearing Coast Guard approval number 161.012/2/1 are not permitted on vessels certificated to operate on waters where water temperature may drop below 10° C (50° F).

(f) *Embarkation ladder.* An embarkation ladder may be a chain ladder approved under approval series 160.017.

(g) *Survival craft stowage positions.* Vessels having widely separated accommodation and service spaces may have, as an alternative to the requirements of § 199.130(b), all required lifeboats and 50 percent of the required liferafts stowed as close as possible to the accommodation and service space that normally holds the greatest number of persons, with the remainder of the liferafts stowed as close as possible to each other accommodation and service space.

(h) *Line-throwing appliance approval series.* As an alternative to a line-throwing appliance that meets the requirements in § 199.170, vessels may carry a line-throwing appliance approved under approval series 160.031, which may have an auxiliary line that is at least 150 meters (500 feet).

(i) *Lifeboat, rescue boat, and rigid liferaft equipment; oceans and coastwise.* Lifeboats, rescue boats, and rigid liferafts may carry the equipment specified in table 199.175 of this part for vessels on a short international voyage.

(j) *Lifeboat, rescue boat, and rigid liferaft equipment; other services.* As an alternative to meeting the survival craft equipment requirements of § 199.175, a vessel may carry the equipment specified in table 199.620(j) of this section under the vessel's category of service. Each item in the table has the same description as in § 199.175.

TABLE 199.620(j)—SURVIVAL CRAFT EQUIPMENT

Item No.	Item	Great Lakes			Lakes, bays and sounds			Rivers		
		Life-boat	Rigid liferaft	Rescue boat	Life-boat	Rigid liferaft	Rescue boat	Life-boat	Rigid liferaft	Rescue boat
1	Bailer[1]	1	1	1	1	1	1	....	....	....
2	Bilge pump[2]	1	....	....	1	....	....	....	....	....
3	Boathook	1	....	1	1	....	1	1	....	1

511

§ 199.630

TABLE 199.620(j)—SURVIVAL CRAFT EQUIPMENT—Continued

Item No.	Item	Great Lakes Lifeboat	Great Lakes Rigid liferaft	Great Lakes Rescue boat	Lakes, bays and sounds Lifeboat	Lakes, bays and sounds Rigid liferaft	Lakes, bays and sounds Rescue boat	Rivers Lifeboat	Rivers Rigid liferaft	Rivers Rescue boat
4	Bucket[3]	1	.....	1	1	.....	.....	1	.....	.....
9	Fire extinguisher	1	.....	1	1	.....	1	1	.....	1
12	Flashlight	1	1	1	.....	.....	.....	.....	.....	.....
13	Hatchet	2	.....	.....	1	.....	.....	1	.....	.....
15	Instruction card	.....	1	.....	.....	1	.....	.....	1	.....
18	Ladder	1	.....	1	.....	.....	.....	.....	.....	.....
20	Oars, units[4][5]	1	.....	1	1	.....	1	1	.....	1
	Paddles	.....	2	.....	.....	2	.....	.....	2	.....
21	Painter	2	1	1	1	1	1	1	1	1
23	Pump[6]	.....	.....	1	.....	.....	1	.....	.....	1
26	Repair kit[6]	.....	.....	1	.....	.....	1	.....	.....	1
27	Sea anchor	1	2	1	.....	.....	.....	.....	.....	.....
28	Searchlight	1	.....	1	.....	.....	.....	.....	.....	.....
31	Signal, hand flare	6	6	.....	6	6	.....	.....	.....	.....
32	Signal, parachute flare	4	4	.....	.....	.....	.....	.....	.....	.....
33	Skates and fenders[7]	1	.....	1	1	.....	1	1	.....	1
34	Sponge[6]	.....	2	2	.....	2	2	.....	.....	.....
35	Survival instructions	1	1	.....	1	1	.....	1	.....	.....
38	Tool kit	1	.....	.....	1	.....	.....	1	.....	.....
39	Towline[8]	1	.....	1	1	.....	1	1	.....	1

Notes:
[1] Each liferaft approved for 13 persons or more must carry two of these items.
[2] Not required for boats of self-bailing design.
[3] Not required for inflated or rigid-inflated rescue boats.
[4] Oars not required on a free-fall lifeboat; a unit of oars means the number of oars specified by the boat manufacturer.
[5] Rescue boats may substitute buoyant paddles for oars, as specified by the manufacturer.
[6] Not required for a rigid rescue boat.
[7] Required if specified by the manufacturer.
[8] Required only if the lifeboat is also the rescue boat.

(k) *Liferaft approval series.* As an alternative to liferafts that meet the requirements in §§ 199.201(a) and 199.261(a), vessels may—

(1) Carry inflatable liferafts approved under approval series 160.051; and

(2) Have liferafts with a capacity less than six persons.

(l) *Inflatable liferaft equipment.* As an alternative to the SOLAS A Pack, vessels may have a SOLAS B Pack for each inflatable liferaft.

(m) [Reserved]

(n) *Spare parts and repair equipment.* As an alternative to carrying spare parts and repair equipment as required in § 199.190(c), a vessel need not carry spare parts and repair equipment if it operates daily out of a shore base where spare parts and repair equipment are available.

(o) Deckhands may be used to operate the survival craft and launching arrangements.

(p) Training and drill subjects required under § 199.180 may be omitted if the vessel is not fitted with the relevant equipment, installation or system.

(q) For a new liferaft or inflatable buoyant apparatus, the first annual servicing may be deferred to two years after initial packing if so indicated on the servicing sticker.

[CGD 84–069, 61 FR 25313, May 20, 1996; 61 FR 40281, Aug. 1, 1996, as amended at 63 FR 52820, Oct. 1, 1998; 63 FR 56066, Oct. 20, 1998; USCG–2001–10224, 66 FR 48621, Sept. 21, 2001; USCG–2001–11118, 67 FR 58542, Sept. 17, 2002]

§ 199.630 Alternatives for passenger vessels in a specified service.

(a) In addition to the alternatives for certain requirements in § 199.620, passenger vessels operating in oceans; coastwise; Great Lakes; lakes, bays, and sounds; and rivers service may comply with alternative requirements to subparts A through C of this part as described in this section for the services specified in table 199.630(a) of this section.

TABLE 199.630(a)—ALTERNATIVE REQUIREMENTS FOR PASSENGER VESSELS IN A SPECIFIED SERVICE

Section or paragraph in this part	Service and reference to alternative requirement section or paragraph				
	Oceans	Coastwise	Great Lakes	Lakes, bays, and sounds	Rivers
199.60(c): Distress signals	No Alternative	No Alternative	199.630(b)	Not Applicable	Not Applicable.
199.100(c): Person in charge of survival craft	No Alternative	199.630(l)	199.630(l)	199.630(l)	199.630(l)
199.100(d): Lifeboat second-in-command	No Alternative	No Alternative	199.630(m)	199.630(m)	Not Applicable.
199.201(b): Number and type of survival craft carried.	199.630(c)[1]	199.630(c) or 199.630(d)[2].	199.630(c) or 199.630(d)[2] or 199.630(e) or 199.630(f)[2] or 199.630(g)[2] [3] or 199.630(h)[4].	199.630(c) or 199.630(d) or 199.630(e) or 199.630(f)[2] or 199.630(g) or 199.630(h)[4].	199.630(c) or 199.630(e) or 199.630(f) or 199.630(g) or 199.630(h)[4].
199.202: Rescue boat approval series	No Alternative	No Alternative	No Alternative	199.630(j)[5]	199.630(j).
199.203: Marshaling of liferafts	No Alternative	199.630(j)	Not Applicable	Not Applicable	Not Applicable.
199.211(a): Quantity of lifebuoys	No Alternative	199.630(k)	199.630(k)	199.630(k)	199.630(k).

Notes:
[1] Alternative applies if the vessel operates on a route no more than 50 nautical miles from shore.
[2] Alternative applies if the vessel is a ferry or has no overnight accommodations for passengers.
[3] Alternative applies during periods of the year the vessel operates in warm water.
[4] Alternative applies if the vessel operates in shallow water not more than 3 miles from shore where the vessel cannot sink deep enough to submerge the topmost deck.
[5] Alternative applies if the vessel operates on sheltered lakes or harbors.

§ 199.630

(b) As an alternative to distress signals that meet the requirements of § 199.60, vessels may carry at least 12 hand red flare distress signals approved under approval series 160.021 or 160.121.

(c) As an alternative to the lifeboat capacity requirements of § 199.201(b)(1)(i), vessels may carry lifeboats with an aggregate capacity sufficient to accommodate not less than 30 percent of the total number of persons on board. These lifeboats must be equally distributed, as far as practicable, on each side of the vessel. Liferafts on these vessels may be either SOLAS A or SOLAS B liferafts.

(d) As an alternative to the survival craft requirements of § 199.201(b), vessels may carry inflatable buoyant apparatus having an aggregate capacity, together with the capacities of any lifeboats, rescue boats, and liferafts carried on board sufficient to, accommodate the total number of persons on board. These inflatable buoyant apparatus must—

(1) Be served by launching appliances or marine evacuation systems evenly distributed on each side of the vessel if the embarkation deck is more than 3 meters (10 feet) above—

(i) The waterline under normal operating conditions; or

(ii) The equilibrium waterline after the vessel is subjected to the assumed damage and subdivision requirements in part 171 of this chapter;

(2) Be stowed in accordance with the requirements of §§ 199.130(a), 199.130(c), and 199.178; and

(3) Be equipped in accordance with the requirements in table 199.640(j) of this part.

(e) As an alternative to the survival craft requirements of § 199.201(b), vessels may carry—

(1) Liferafts having an aggregate capacity, together with the capacities of any lifeboats carried on board, sufficient to accommodate the total number of persons on board that are served by launching appliances or marine evacuation systems evenly distributed on each side of the vessel; and

(2) In addition to the liferafts required in paragraph (e)(1) of this section, additional liferafts that have an aggregate capacity sufficient to accommodate at least 10 percent of the total number of persons, or equal to the capacity of the largest single survival craft on the vessel, whichever is the greater. The additional liferafts are not required to be stowed in accordance with § 199.130(c), but they must be served by at least one launching appliance or marine evacuation system on each side of the vessel.

(f) As an alternative to the survival craft requirements of § 199.201(b), vessels may have a safety assessment approved by the local OCMI that addresses the following:

(1) The navigation and vessel safety conditions within the vessel's planned operating area including—

(i) The scope and degree of the risks or hazards to which the vessel will be subject during normal operations;

(ii) The existing vessel traffic characteristics and trends, including traffic volume; the sizes and types of vessels involved; potential interference with the flow of commercial traffic; the presence of any unusual cargoes; and other similar factors;

(iii) The port and waterway configuration and variations in local conditions of geography, climate, and other similar factors; and

(iv) Environmental factors.

(2) A comprehensive shipboard safety management and contingency plan that is tailored to the particular vessel, is easy to use, is understood by vessel management personnel both on board and ashore, is updated regularly, and includes—

(i) Guidance to assist the vessel's crew in meeting the demand of catastrophic vessel damage;

(ii) Procedures to mobilize emergency response teams;

(iii) Procedures for moving passengers from the vessel's spaces to areas protected from fire and smoke, to embarkation areas, and off the vessel. The procedures must address provisions for passengers with physical or mental impairments;

(iv) Lists of external organizations that the vessel's operator would call for assistance in the event of an incident;

(v) Procedures for establishing and maintaining communications on board the vessel and with shoreside contacts; and

(vi) Guidance on theoretical, practical, and actual simulation training that includes the personnel or organizations identified in the plan so they can practice their roles in the event of an incident.

(g) As an alternative to the survival craft requirements of §199.201(b), vessels may carry inflatable buoyant apparatus having an aggregate capacity sufficient to accommodate 67 percent of the total number of persons on board, minus the capacities of any lifeboats, rescue boats and liferafts carried on board. These inflatable buoyant apparatus must meet the arrangement requirements of §199.630 (d)(1) through (d)(3). The number of persons accommodated in an inflatable buoyant apparatus may not exceed 150% of its rated capacity.

(h) A vessel need not comply with the requirements for survival craft in §199.201(b) if the vessel operates—

(1) On a route that is in shallow water not more than 3 miles from shore and the vessel cannot sink deep enough to submerge the topmost deck; or

(2) Where the cognizant OCMI determines that survivors can wade ashore.

(i) As an alternative to the rescue boat required in §199.202, vessels may carry a rescue boat meeting the requirements of part 160, subpart 160.056 of this chapter if it is equipped with a motor and meets the following:

(1) The towline for the rescue boat must be at least the same size and length as the rescue boat painter.

(2) The rescue boat must meet the embarkation, launching, and recovery arrangement requirements in §§199.160 (b) through (f). The OCMI may allow deviations from the rescue boat launching requirements based on the characteristics of the boat and the conditions of the vessel's route.

(j) As an alternative to the requirements of §199.203(a), a vessel that meets the subdivision requirements in §171.068 of this chapter may meet the requirements of §199.203(b).

(k) Vessels carrying lifebuoys may carry—

(1) The number of lifebuoys specified in table 199.630(k) of this section instead of the number required in §199.211; and

(2) If the vessel carries less than four lifebuoys, at least two with a self-igniting light attached to the lifebuoy. A buoyant lifeline may be fitted to one of the lifebuoys with a self-igniting light.

TABLE 199.630(k)—REQUIREMENTS FOR LIFEBUOYS

Length of vessel in meters (feet)	Minimum number of lifebuoys
Under 30 (98)	3
30 (98) and under 60 (196)	4
60 (196) and under 90 (297)	5
90 (297) and under 120 (393)	12
120 (393) and under 180 (590)	18
180 (590) and under 240 (787)	24
240 (787) and over	30

(l) A deck officer, able seaman, certificated person, or person practiced in the handling of liferafts or inflatable buoyant apparatus is not required to be placed in charge of each inflatable buoyant apparatus, provided that there are a sufficient number of such persons on board to launch the inflatable buoyant apparatus and supervise the embarkation of the passengers. The number of persons on board for the purpose of launching and operating inflatable buoyant apparatus may be reduced during any voyage where the vessel is carrying less than the number of passengers permitted on board, and the number of such persons is sufficient to launch and operate the number of survival craft required to accommodate everyone on board.

(m) The person designated second-in-command of survival craft is not required to be a certificated person if the person is practiced in the handling and operation of survival craft.

[CGD 84–069, 61 FR 25313, May 20, 1996; 61 FR 40281, Aug. 1, 1996, as amended at 63 FR 52821, Oct. 1, 1998; 63 FR 56067, Oct. 20, 1998; 63 FR 63798, Nov. 17, 1998]

§ 199.640 Alternatives for cargo vessels in a specified service.

(a) In addition to the alternatives for certain requirements in §199.620, cargo vessels operating in oceans; coastwise; Great Lakes; lakes, bays, and sounds; and rivers service may comply with alternative requirements to subparts A, B, and D of this part as described in this section for the services specified in table 199.640(a) of this section.

§ 199.640

TABLE 199.640(a)—ALTERNATIVE REQUIREMENTS FOR CARGO VESSELS IN A SPECIFIED SERVICE

Section or paragraph in this part	Service or reference to alternative requirement section				
	Oceans	Coastwise	Great Lakes	Lakes, bays, and sounds	Rivers
199.60(c): Distress signals	199.640(b)[1] ...	199.640(b)[1] ...	199.640(b)[1] or 199.630(b).	Not Applicable ..	Not Applicable.
199.261: Number and type of survival craft carried.	199.640(c)[6] ...	199.640(c)[6] ...	199.640(c)[2] or 199.640(d) or 199.640(e)[3] or 199.640(f)[4].	199.640(c)[2] or 199.640(d) or 199.640(e)[3] or 199.640(f)[4].	199.640(c) or 199.640(d) or 199.640(e)[3] or 199.640(f)[4].
199.262: Rescue boat substitution ..	No Alternative	199.640(g)	199.640(g)	199.640(g) or 199.640(h)[5].	199.640(g) or 199.640(h).
199.271: Lifebuoy quantity	No Alternative	199.640(i)	199.640(i)	199.640(i)	199.640(i).

Notes:
[1] Alternative applies to vessels less than 150 tons gross tonnage that do not carry passengers or persons in addition to the crew.
[2] Alternative applies to cargo vessels less than 85 meters in length, tank vessels less than 500 tons gross tonnage, and nonself-propelled vessels.
[3] Alternative applies during periods of the year that the vessel operates in warm water.
[4] Alternative applies if the vessel operates in shallow water not more than 3 miles from shore where the vessel cannot sink deep enough to submerge the topmost deck.
[5] Alternative applies if the vessel operates on sheltered lakes or harbors.
[6] Alternative applies to vessels less than 500 tons gross tonnage.

(b) Vessels of less than 150 tons gross tonnage that do not carry persons other than the crew, may carry, as an alternative to distress signals that meet the requirements of § 199.60, six hand red flare distress signals approved under approval series 160.021 and six hand orange smoke distress signals approved under approval series 160.037.

(c) As an alternative to the survival craft requirements of §§ 199.261(b), (c), or (d), vessels may carry one or more liferafts with an aggregate capacity sufficient to accommodate the total number of persons on board. The liferafts must be—

(1) Readily transferable for launching on either side of the vessel; or

(2) Supplemented with additional liferafts to bring the total capacity of the liferafts available on each side of the vessel to at least 100 percent of the total number of persons on board. If additional liferafts are provided and the rescue boat required under § 199.262 is also a lifeboat, its capacity may be included in meeting the aggregate capacity requirement.

(d) As an alternative to the survival craft requirements in §§ 199.261 (b), (c), or (d), vessels may carry one or more totally enclosed lifeboats with an aggregate capacity sufficient to accommodate the total number of persons on board and one or more liferafts with an aggregate capacity sufficient to accommodate the total number of persons on board. This combination of survival craft must meet the following:

(1) The aggregate capacity of the lifeboats and liferafts on each side of the vessel must be sufficient to accommodate the total number of persons on board.

(2) If the survival craft are stowed more than 100 meters (328 feet from either the stem or the stern of the vessel, an additional liferaft must be carried and stowed as far forward or aft as is reasonable and practicable. The requirement for the liferaft to float free under § 199.290(b) does not apply to a liferaft under this paragraph, provided the liferaft is arranged for quick manual release.

(e) As an alternative to the survival craft requirements in §§ 199.261 (b), (c), or (d), during periods of the year the vessel operates in warm water, a vessel may carry lifefloats with an aggregate capacity sufficient to accommodate the total number of people on board. The lifefloat launching arrangement, stowage, and equipment must meet the requirements in § 199.640(j).

(f) A vessel need not comply with the requirements for survival craft in §§ 199.261 (b), (c), or (d) if the vessel operates—

(1) On a route that is in shallow water not more than 3 miles from shore and where the vessel cannot sink deep enough to submerge the topmost deck; or

Coast Guard, DHS § 199.640

(2) Where the cognizant OCMI determines that survivors can wade ashore.

(g) As an alternative to the rescue boat requirement in § 199.262(a), vessels may carry a motor-propelled workboat or a launch that meets all the embarkation, launching, and recovery arrangement requirements in §§ 199.160 (b) through (f). The OCMI may allow deviations from the rescue boat launching requirements based on the characteristics of the boat and the conditions of the vessel's route.

(h) An an alternative to the rescue boat requirement in § 199.262, vessels may carry a rescue boat meeting the requirements of part 160, subpart 160.056 of this chapter if the rescue boat is equipped with a motor and meets the following:

(1) The towline for the rescue boat must be at least the same size and length as the rescue boat painter.

(2) The rescue boat must meet the embarkation, launching, and recovery arrangement requirements in § 199.160(b). A manually-powered winch may be used if personnel embark and disembark the rescue boat only when it is in the water. If the rescue boat is launched or recovered with personnel on board, the embarkation, launching, and recovery arrangements must also meet § 199.160 (c) through (f). The OCMI may allow deviations from the rescue boat launching requirements based on the characteristics of the boat and the conditions of the vessel's route.

(i) As an alternative to the number of lifebuoys required in § 199.271, vessels may carry—

(1) If the vessel is self-propelled, the number of lifebuoys specified in table 199.640(i) of this section; or

(2) If the vessel is non self-propelled, one lifebuoy on each end of the vessel.

TABLE 199.640(i)—REQUIREMENTS FOR LIFEBUOYS

Length of vessel in meters (feet)	Minimum No. of Lifebuoys
Under 30 (98)	3
30 (98) and under 60 (196)	4
60 (196) and under 100 (328)	6
100 (328) and under 150 (492)	10
150 (492) and under 200 (656)	12
200 (656) and over	14

(j) *Vessels carrying buoyant apparatus, inflatable buoyant apparatus, or lifefloats.* Vessels carrying buoyant apparatus, inflatable buoyant apparatus, or lifefloats must meet the following:

(1) *General.* Each buoyant apparatus and inflatable buoyant apparatus must be approved under approval series 160.010. Each lifefloat must be approved under approval series 160.027.

(2) *Stowage.* Each buoyant apparatus, inflatable buoyant apparatus, or lifefloat must, in addition to meeting the general stowage requirements of § 199.130(a), be stowed as follows:

(i) Each inflatable buoyant apparatus must meet the liferaft stowage requirements in § 199.130(c).

(ii) Each buoyant apparatus and lifefloat must—

(A) Meet the liferaft stowage requirements in §§ 199.130(c) (1), (2), (3), (6), and (7); or

(B) Meet the liferaft stowage requirements in §§ 199.130(c) (1), (2), (3), and (6), and have lashings that can be easily released.

(iii) A painter must be secured to the buoyant apparatus or lifefloat by—

(A) The attachment fitting provided by the manufacturer; or

(B) A wire or line that encircles the body of the buoyant apparatus or lifefloat, that will not slip off, and that meets the requirements of paragraph (4)(iii) of this section.

(iv) If buoyant apparatus or lifefloats are arranged in groups with each group secured by a single painter—

(A) The combined mass of each group must not exceed 185 kilograms (407.8 pounds);

(B) Each buoyant apparatus or lifefloat must be individually attached to the group's single painter by its own painter, which must be long enough to allow the buoyant apparatus or lifefloat to float without contacting any other buoyant apparatus or lifefloat in the group;

(C) The strength of the float-free link and the strength of the group's single painter must be appropriate for the combined capacity of the group of buoyant apparatus or lifefloats;

(D) The group of buoyant apparatus or lifefloats must not be stowed in more than four tiers and, when stowed

§ 199.640

in tiers, the separate units must be kept apart by spacers; and

(E) The group of buoyant apparatus or lifefloats must be stowed to prevent shifting with easily detached lashings.

(3) *Marking.* Each buoyant apparatus or lifefloat must be marked plainly in block capital letters and numbers with the name of the vessel and the number of persons approved to use the device as shown on its nameplate.

(4) *Equipment.* Unless otherwise stated in this paragraph, each buoyant apparatus and lifefloat must carry the equipment listed in this paragraph and specified for it in table 199.640(j) of this section under the vessel's category of service.

(i) *Boathook.*

(ii) *Paddle.* Each paddle must be at least 1.2 meters (4 feet) long and buoyant.

(iii) *Painter.* The painter must—

(A) Be at least 30 meters (100 feet) long, but not less than three times the distance from the deck where the buoyant apparatus, inflatable buoyant apparatus, or lifefloats are stowed to the vessel's waterline with the vessel in its lightest seagoing condition;

(B) Have a breaking strength of at least 6.7 kiloNewtons (1,500 pounds-force), or if the capacity of the buoyant apparatus or lifefloat is 50 persons or more, have a breaking strength of at least 13.4 kiloNewtons (3,000 pounds-force);

(C) If made of a synthetic material, be of a dark color or be certified by the manufacturer to be resistant to deterioration from ultraviolet light;

(D) Be stowed in such a way that it runs out freely when the buoyant apparatus or lifefloat floats away from the sinking vessel; and

(E) Have a float-free link meeting the requirements of part 160, subpart 160.073 of this chapter secured to the end of the painter that is attached to the vessel, that is of the proper strength for the size and number of the buoyant apparatus or lifefloats attached to the float-free link.

(iv) *Self-igniting light.* The self-igniting light must be approved under approval series 161.010 and must be attached to the buoyant apparatus or lifefloat by a 12-thread manila or equivalent lanyard that is at least 5.5 meters (18 feet) long.

TABLE 199.640(j)—BUOYANT APPARATUS AND LIFEFLOAT EQUIPMENT

Item No.	Item	Oceans, coastwise, and Great Lakes	Lakes, bays, sounds, and rivers
i	Boathook[1]	1	1
ii	Paddles[1]	2	2
iii	Painter	1	1
iv	Self-igniting light[2]	1	

Notes:
[1] Not required to be carried on buoyant apparatus.
[2] Not required to be carried on buoyant apparatus or lifefloats with a capacity of 24 persons or less.

[CGD 84–069, 61 FR 25313, May 20, 1996, as amended at 63 FR 52821, Oct. 1, 1998]

INDEX

SUBCHAPTER W—LIFESAVING APPLIANCES AND ARRANGEMENTS

EDITORIAL NOTE: This listing is provided for informational purposes only. It is compiled and kept up-to-date by the Coast Guard, Department of Homeland Security. This index is updated as of October 1, 2003.

Part, Subpart, or Section

A

Accommodation, definition 199.30
Accommodations, crew and passenger 199.30
Additional equipment and requirements 199.07
Alternative requirements for all vessels in a specified service, table .... 199.620(a)
Alternative requirements for cargo vessels in a specified service, table .... 199.640(a)
Alternative requirements for passenger vessels in a specified service, table .... 199.630(a)
Alternatives for all vessels in a specified service: .... 199.620(a)
    Embarkation ladder .... 199.620(f)
    EPIRB requirements .... 199.620(m)
    General .... 199.620(a)
    Inflatable liferaft equipment .... 199.620(l)
    Lifeboat, rescue boat, and rigid liferaft equipment (oceans/coastwise) .... 199.620(i)
    Lifeboat, rescue boat, and rigid liferaft equipment (other services) .... 199.620(j)
    Lifebuoy approval series .... 199.620(b)
    Lifejacket approval series .... 199.620(c)
    Lifejacket light approval series .... 199.620(e)
    Lifejacket quantity .... 199.620(d)
    Liferaft approval series .... 199.620(k)
    Line-throwing appliance approval series .... 199.620(h)
    Spare parts and repair equipment .... 199.620(n)
    Survival craft stowage positions .... 199.620(g)
Alternatives for cargo vessels in a specified service 199.640
Alternatives for passenger vessels in a specified service 199.630
Alternatives for vessels not subject to SOLAS, general 199.500
Anti-exposure suit, definition 199.30
Applicability of part 199.10
Approval series, definition 199.30
Approved, definition 199.30
Associated liferafts .... 199.145(c)
Auxiliary line .... 199.03(b)(12), 199.170(c)(2), 199.620(h)

B

Bailer .... 199.175(b)(1)
Batteries (less than 50 volts) .... 199.140(b)
    Flashlight .... 199.175(b)(12)
    Replacement .... 199.190(F)(4), 199.190(F)(5)
    Searchlight .... 199.175(b)(29)(iv)
Bilge pump .... 199.130(b)(3), 199.175(b)(2)

519

Boathook .... 199.175(b)(3), 199.640(j)(4)
Bucket 199.175
Buoyant apparatus and lifefloat equipment, table .... 199.640(j)
Buoyant apparatus, equipment for .... 199.640(j)(4)

C

Can opener .... 199.175(b)(5)
Cargo Ship Safety Equipment Certificate .... 199.03(b)
Cargo vessel, definition 199.30
Cargo vessel, requirements .... Part D
Certificated person, definition 199.30
Cargo vessel and special purpose vessel, general 199.260
Child, definition 199.30
Child-size lifejacket 199.03
Civilian nautical school, definition 199.30
Coastwise voyage, definition 199.30
Commandant, definition 199.30
Communications: 199.60
  Distress signals .... 199.60(c)
  Emergency position indicating radiobeacons (EPIRB) .... 199.60(b)
  Onboard communications and alarm systems .... 199.60(d)
  Radio lifesaving appliances .... 199.60(a)
  Search and rescue transponders (SART) .... 199.60(b)
Compass .... 199.175(b)(6)
Crew, definition 199.30

D

Definitions: 199.30
  Accommodation 199.30
  Anti-exposure suit 199.30
  Approval series 199.30
  Approved 199.30
  Cargo vessel 199.30
  Certificated person 199.30
  Child 199.30
  Civilian nautical school 199.30
  Coastwise voyage 199.30
  Commandant 199.30
  Crew 199.30
  District Commander 199.30
  Detection 199.30
  Embarkation ladder 199.30
  Embarkation station 199.30
  Extended-size lifejacket 199.30
  Ferry 199.30
  Float-free launching 199.30
  Free-fall launching 199.30
  Immersion suit 199.30
  Inflatable appliance 199.30
  Inflated appliance 199.30
  International voyage 199.30
  Lakes, bays, and sounds 199.30
  Launching appliance or launching arrangement 199.30
  Length of vessel 199.30
  Lifejacket 199.30
  Major character 199.30
  Major conversion 199.30

Subchapter W Index

Marine evacuation system 199.30
Mobile offshore drilling unit (MODU) 199.30
Muster station 199.30
Nautical school vessel 199.30
Novel lifesaving appliance or arrangement 199.30
Ocean 199.30
Oceanographic research vessel 199.30
Officer in Charge, Marine Inspection (OCMI) 199.30
Passenger 199.30
Passenger for hire 199.30
Passenger vessel 199.30
Public nautical school 199.30
Public vessel 199.30
Rescue boat 199.30
Retrieval 199.30
Rivers 199.30
Seagoing condition 199.30
Scientific personnel 199.30
Similar stage of construction 199.30
Short international voyage 199.30
Special personnel 199.30
Special purpose vessel 199.30
Survival craft 199.30
Tank vessel 199.30
Toxic vapor or gas 199.30
Vessel constructed 199.30
Warm water 199.30
Dipper 199.30
Drills: .... 199.180(c), 199.250
Abandon-ship .... 199.180(d)
Fire .... 199.180(f)
General .... 199.180(c)
On use of line-throwing appliance .... 199.180(e)
Records .... 199.180(h)
Drinking cup .... 199.175(b)(8)

E

Embarkation and launching arrangements: survival craft 199.245, 199.280
Embarkation ladder, definition 199.30
Embarkation station, definition 199.30
Emergency procedures .... 199.180(b)
EPIRB requirements 199.510
Equivalents: 199.09
For fitting 199.09
For lifesaving appliances or arrangement 199.09
For material 199.09
Evaluation, testing and approval of lifesaving appliances and arrangements 199.40
Exemptions: 199.20
Exemption Certificates .... 199.20(c)
Single voyage exemption from SOLAS requirements .... 199.20(b)
Vessels engaged on international voyages .... 199.20(a)
Vessels not engaged on international voyages .... 199.20(d)
Exemptions and alternatives for vessels not subject to SOLAS .... subpart F, part 199
Exemptions for all vessels in specified services, table .... 199.610(a)
Exemptions for cargo vessels in specified services, table .... 199.610(c)

Exemptions for passenger vessels in specified services, table	199.610(b)
Exemptions for vessels in specified services:	199.610
All vessels	199.610(a)
Cargo vessels	199.610(c)
Non-self propelled vessels	199.610(a)(1)
Passenger vessels	199.610(b)
Vessels operating in fresh water	199.610(a)(4)
Vessels operating in shallow water	199.610(a)(3)
Vessels operating on short runs	199.610(a)(2)
Extended-size lifejacket, definition	199.30

F

Ferry, definition	199.30
Fire extinguisher	199.175(b)(9)
First aid kit	199.175(b)(10)
Flashlight	199.175(b)(12)
Float-free launching, definition	199.30
Free-fall launching, definition	199.30
Free fall lifeboat launching and recovery arrangements	199.157

H

Hatchet	199.175(b)(13)
Heaving line	199.175(b)(14)

I

Immersion suit:	199.273
Definition	199.30
Immersion suits and thermal protective aids	199.214
Incorporation by reference	199.05
Inflatable appliance, definition	199.30
Inflated appliance, definition	199.30
Instruction card	199.175(b)(15)
International voyage, definition	199.30

J

Jackknife	199.175(b)(16)

K

Knife	199.175(b)(17)

L

Ladder	199.175(b)(18)
Lakes, bays, and sounds, definition	199.30
Launching appliance, definition	199.30
Launching arrangement, definition	199.30
Launching stations	199.120
Length of vessel, definition	199.30
Lifeboat:	199.30
Cargo Vessels	199.30, 199.260
Free-fall launching and recovery arrangements	199.157
Passenger Vessels	199.30
Requirements	199.520
Lifeboat launching and recovery arrangements	199.155
Lifebuoys:	199.70(a), 199.211, 199.271

Subchapter W Index

Attachments and fittings	199.70(a)(3)
Markings	199.70(a)(2)
Stowage	199.70(a)(1)
Lifejacket:	199.70(b), 199.212
Attachments and fittings	199.70(b)(4)
Definition	199.30
General	199.70(b)(1)
Markings	199.70(b)(3)
Stowage	199.70(b)(2)
Lifejacket, immersion suit, and anti-exposure suite containers	199.70(d)
Liferafts, cargo and passenger vessels	199.30
Lifesaving systems for certain inspected vessels	part 199
General	subpart A, part 199
Line-throwing appliance	199.170
Additional equipment	199.170(c)
General	199.170(a)
Stowage	199.170(b)

M

Major character, definition	199.30
Major conversion, definition	199.30
Manning of survival craft and supervision	199.100
Marine evacuation system, definition:	199.30
Marking of stowage locations	199.178
Marine evacuation system launching arrangements	199.145
Arrangements	199.145(a)
Stowage	199.145(b)
Stowage of associated liferafts	199.145(c)
Markings on lifesaving appliances	199.176
Lifeboats and rescue boats	199.176(a)
Rigid liferafts	199.176(b)
Marshalling of liferafts	199.203
Mirror	199.175(b)(19)
Mobile offshore drilling unit (MODU), definition	199.30
Muster list and emergency instructions	199.80, 199.217
Emergency instructions	199.80(c)
General	199.80(a)
Muster list	199.80(b)
Muster station, definition	199.30
Muster stations	199.240

N

Nautical school vessel, definition	199.30
Novel lifesaving appliances or arrangements, definition	199.30

O

Oars and paddles	199.175(b)(20)
Ocean, definition	199.30
Oceanographic research vessel, definition	199.30
Operating instructions	199.90
Operational readiness, maintenance and inspection of lifesaving equipment:	199.190
Annual inspections	199.190(f)
Maintenance	199.190(b)
Maintenance of falls	199.190(j)
Monthly inspections	199.190(e)

Operational readiness .... 199.190(a)
Periodic servicing of hydrostatic release units .... 199.190(h)
Periodic servicing of launching appliances and release gear .... 199.190(i)
Servicing of inflatable lifesaving appliances, inflated rescue boats and
    marine evacuation systems .... 199.190(g)
Spare-parts and repair equipment .... 199.190(c)
Weekly inspections and tests .... 199.190(d)

P

Painter .... 199.175(b)(21)
Passenger, definition 199.30
Passenger vessels additional requirements .... Subpart C
Passenger for hire, definition 199.30
Passenger vessel, definition 199.30
Personal lifesaving appliances 199.70
Public nautical school, definition 199.30
Public vessel, definition 199.30
Purpose of part 199.01

R

Radar reflector .... 199.175(b)(24)
Rainwater collection device .... 199.175(b)(25)
Relationship to international standards 199.03
Rescue boat: 199.202, 199.262
    Embarkation, launching and recovery arrangements 199.160
Rescue boat and marine evacuation system immersion suits or anti-ex-
    posure suits .... 199.70(c)
    Attachments and fittings .... 199.70(c)(4)
    General .... 199.70(c))(1)
    Markings .... 199.70(c)(3)
    Stowage .... 199.70(c)(2)
Rescue boat embarkation, launching and recovery arrangements 199.160
Requirements for all vessels .... subpart B, part 199
Requirements for lifebuoys, table .... 199.630(k), 199.640(i)
Requirements for lifebuoys for passenger vessels, table 199.211
Requirements for lifebuoys on cargo vessels, table 199.271
Retrieval, definition 199.30
Rivers, definition 199.30

S

Scientific personnel, definition 199.30
Seagoing condition, definition 199.30
Similar stage of construction, definition 199.30
Short international voyage, definition 199.30
Special personnel, definition 199.30
Special purpose vessel, definition 199.30
Stowage of survival crafts: 199.130
Stowage of rescue boats: 199.140
    Inflated rescue boats .... 199.140(c)
    General .... 199.140(a)
    Rescue .... 199.140(b)
Stowage of survival craft: 199.130, 199.230, 199.290
    Additional lifeboat stowage requirements .... 199.130(b)
    Additional liferaft stowage requirements .... 199.130(c)
    General .... 199.130(a)
Survival craft: 199.201, 199.261

Subchapter W Index

Definition	199.30
Embarkation and launching arrangements	199.280
Launching and recovery arrangements, general	199.150
Launching and recovery arrangements, with falls and a winch	199.153
Stowage	199.130, 199.230
Survival craft and rescue boat equipment:	199.175
Bailer	199.175(b)(1)
Bilge pump	199.175(b)(2)
Boathook	199.175(b)(3)
Bucket	199.175(b)(4)
Can opener	199.175(b)(5)
Compass	199.175(b)(6)
Dipper	199.175(b)(7)
Drinking cup	199.175(b)(8)
Fire extinguisher	199.175(b)(9)
First aid kit	199.175(b)(10)
Fishing kit	199.175(b)(11)
Flashlight	199.175(b)(12)
Hatchet	199.175(b)(13)
Heaving line	199.175(b)(14)
Instruction card	199.175(b)(15)
Jackknife	199.175(b)(16)
Knife	199.175(b)(17)
Ladder	199.175(b)(18)
Mirror	199.175(b)(19)
Oars and paddles	199.175(b)(20)
Painter	199.175(b)(21)
Provisions	199.175(b)(22)
Pump	199.175(b)(23)
Radar reflector	199.175(b)(24)
Rainwater collection device	199.175(b)(25)
Repair kit	199.175(b)(26)
Sea anchor	199.175(b)(27)
Searchlight	199.175(b)(28)
Seasickness kit	199.175(b)(29)
Signal, handflare	199.175(b)(31)
Signal, rocket parachute flare	199.175(b)(32)
Signal, smoke	199.175(b)(30)
Skates and fenders	199.175(b)(33)
Sponge	199.175(b)(34)
Survival instructions	199.175(b)(35)
Table of lifesaving signals	199.175(b)(36)
Thermal protective aid	199.175(b)(37)
Tool kit	199.175(b)(38)
Towline	199.175(b)(39)
Water	199.175(b)(40)
Whistle	199.175(b)(41)
Survival craft embarkation and launching arrangements	199.245
Survival craft equipment, table	199.175, 199.620(j)
Survival craft launching and recovery arrangements, general	199.150
Survival craft launching and recovery arrangements, using falls and a winch	199.153
Survival craft muster and embarkation arrangements	199.110
Survival craft and rescue boat embarkation arrangements	199.220

T

Tables:	part 199

Alternative requirements for all vessels in a specified service .... 199.620(a)
Alternative requirements for cargo vessels in a specified service .... 199.640(a)
Alternative requirements for passenger vessels in a specified service .... 199.630(a)
Buoyant apparatus and lifefloat equipment .... 199.640(j)
Exemptions for all vessels in specified services .... 199.610(a)
Exemptions for cargo vessels in specified services .... 199.610(c)
Exemptions for passenger vessels in specified services .... 199.610(b)
Requirements for lifebuoys .... 199.630(k), 199.640(i)
Requirements for lifebuoys for passenger vessels 199.211
Requirements for lifebuoys on cargo vessels 199.271
Survival craft equipment .... 199.175, 199.620(j)
Tank vessel, definition 199.30
Tests and inspections of lifesaving equipment and arrangements: 199.45
   Initial inspection .... 199.45(a)
   Other inspections .... 199.45(c)
   Reinspections .... 199.45(b)
Toxic vapor or gas, definition 199.30
Training and drills 199.180
   Abandon-ship drills .... 199.180(d)
   Drills, general .... 199.180(c)
   Familiarity with emergency procedures .... 199.180(b)
   Fire drills .... 199.180(f)
   Line-throwing appliance .... 199.180(e)
   Onboard training and instruction .... 199.180(g)
   Records .... 199.180(h)
   Training materials .... 199.180(a)

V

Vessel constructed, definition 199.30
Vessels carrying buoyant apparatus, inflatable buoyant apparatus, or lifefloats: .... 199.640(j)
   Equipment .... 199.640(j)(4)
   General .... 199.640(j)(1)
   Marking .... 199.640(j)(3)
   Stowage .... 199.640(j)(2)

W

Warm water, definition 199.30

FINDING AIDS

A list of CFR titles, subtitles, chapters, subchapters and parts and an alphabetical list of agencies publishing in the CFR are included in the CFR Index and Finding Aids volume to the Code of Federal Regulations which is published separately and revised annually.

Material Approved for Incorporation by Reference
Table of CFR Titles and Chapters
Alphabetical List of Agencies Appearing in the CFR
List of CFR Sections Affected

FINDING AIDS

Material Approved for Incorporation by Reference

(Revised as of October 1, 2004)

The Director of the Federal Register has approved under 5 U.S.C. 552(a) and 1 CFR part 51 the incorporation by reference of the following publications. This list contains only those incorporations by reference effective as of the revision date of this volume. Incorporations by reference found within a regulation are effective upon the effective date of that regulation. For more information on incorporation by reference, see the preliminary pages of this volume.

46 CFR (PARTS 166–199)
COAST GUARD, DEPARTMENT OF HOMELAND SECURITY

	46 CFR
American Boat and Yacht Council 3069 Solomon's Island Road, Edgewater, MD 21037	
P–1–73—Safe Installation of Exhaust Systems for Propulsion and Auxiliary Engines, 1973.	169.115; 169.609; 169.703
H–24.9 (g) and (h)—Fuel Strainers and Fuel Filters, 1975	169.115; 169.629
H–2.5—Ventilation of Boats Using Gasoline—Design and Construction, 1981.	169.115; 169.629
A–1–78—Marine LPG—Liquefied Petroleum Gas Systems, 1978	169.115; 169.703
A–3–70—Recommended Practices and Standards Covering Galley Stoves, 1970.	169.115; 169.703
A–22–78—Marine CHG—Compressed Natural Gas Systems, 1978	169.115; 169.703
A–1–78 Marine LPG-Liquefied Petroleum Gas Systems, December 15, 1978.	184.05–1
A–1–93—Marine Liquefied Petroleum Gas (LPG) Systems	184.240
A–3–93—Galley Stoves	184.200
A–7–70—Boat Heating Systems	184.200
A–16–89—Electric Navigation Lights	183.130
A–22–78 Marine CNG-Compressed Natural Gas Systems, December 15, 1978.	184.05–1
A–22–93—Marine Compressed Natural Gas (CNG) Systems	184.240
E–8–94—Alternating Current (AC) Electrical Systems on Boats	183.130
E–9–90—Direct Current (DC) Electrical Systems on Boats	183.130
H–2–89—Ventilation of Boats Using Gasoline	182.130; 182.460
H–22–86—DC Electric Bilge Pumps Operating Under 50 Volts	182.130; 182.500
H–24–93—Gasoline Fuel Systems	182.130; 182.440; 182.445; 182.450; 182.455
H–25–94—Portable Gasoline Fuel Systems	182.130; 182.458
H–32–87—Ventilation of Boats Using Diesel Fuel	182.130; 182.465; 182.470
H–33–89—Diesel Fuel Sysems	182.130; 182.440; 182.445; 182.450; 182.455
P–1—Safe Installation of Exhaust Systems for Propulsion and Auxiliary Machinery, 1973.	182.15–15; 182.15–20

Title 46–Shipping

46 CFR (PARTS 166–199)—Continued
COAST GUARD, DEPARTMENT OF HOMELAND SECURITY—Continued

	46 CFR
P–1–93—Installation of Exhaust Systems for Propulsion and Auxiliary Engines.	177.405; 177.410; 182.130; 182.425; 182.430
P–4–89—Marine Inboard Engines	182.130; 182.420

American Bureau of Shipping
Publications Department, 16855 Northchase Drive, Houston, Texas 77060

Rules for Building and Classing Steel Vessels, 1981	167.15–27; 167.20–1
Guide for Building and Classing High-Speed Craft, February, 1997	175.600; 177.300
Rules for Building and Classing Aluminum Vessels, 1975	177.300
Rules for Building and Classing Reinforced Plastic Vessels, 1978	177.300
Rules for Building and Classing Steel Vessels, 1995	182.410; 183.360
Rules for Building and Classing Steel Vessels Under 61 Meters (200 Feet) in Length, 1983.	177.300
Rules for Building and Classing Steel Vessels for Service on Rivers and Intracoastal Waterways, 1995.	177.300
Rules for Building and Classing Steel Vessels, 1981	188.35–1; 189.15–1; 190.01–10; 190.01–15; 195.01–5

American National Standards Institute (ANSI)
25 West 43rd Street, Fourth floor, New York, NY 10036 Telephone: (212) 642–4900

A 17.1–1984, including supplements A17.1a–1985 and A17.1b–1985—Safety Code for Elevators and Escalators.	183.540
B 31.1–1986—Code for Pressure Piping, Power Piping	182.710
Z 26.1–1977, including 1980 supplement—Safety Glazing Materials For Glazing Motor Vehicles Operating on Land Highways.	177.1030
ANSI B31.1–80 Power Piping	197.204; 197.205; 197.336
ANSI/ASME PVHO 1 Safety Standard for Pressure Vessels for Human Occupancy, 1981.	197.204; 197.205; 197.300; 197.328
ANSI Z 88.2–80 Practices for Respiratory Protection	197.550

American Society of Mechanical Engineers
Three Park Avenue, New York, NY 10016–5990; Telephone: (800) THE–ASME

Boiler and Pressure Vessel Code, Section VIII, 1980	197.204; 197.205; 197.300; 197.310; 197.328
ASME/ANSI B31.3 Process Piping, 1996, including 1996 Addenda	Appendix A to part 193

American Society for Testing and Materials
100 Barr Harbor Drive, West Conshohocken, PA, 19428-2959, Telephone (610) 832-9585, FAX (610) 832-9555

ASTM A 53–96 Standard Specification for Pipe, Steel, Black and Hot-Dipped, Zinc-Coated Welded and Seamless.	Appendix A to part 192; 195.3
ASTM A 106–95 Standard Specification for Seamless Carbon Steel Pipe for High-Temperature Service.	Appendix A to part 192; 195.3
ASTM B 96-93, Standard Specification for Copper-Silicon Alloy Plate, Sheet, Strip, and Rolled Bar for General Purposes and Pressure Vessels.	175.600; 182.440
ASTM B 97–77 Copper-Silicon Alloy Plate, Sheet, Strip and Rolled Bar for General Purposes.	182.15–25

Material Approved for Incorporation by Reference

46 CFR (PARTS 166–199)—Continued
COAST GUARD, DEPARTMENT OF HOMELAND SECURITY—Continued

	46 CFR
ASTM B 117–73 (Reapproved 1979)—Method of Salt Spray (Fog) Testing.	175.400
ASTM B 117-97, Standard Practice for Operating Salt Spray (Fog) Apparatus.	175.400; 175.600
ASTM B 122–79 Copper-Nickel Zinc Alloy (Nickel Silver) and Copper-Nickel Alloy Plate, Strip, and Rolled Bar.	182.15–25
ASTM B 122/B 122 M-95, Standard Specification for Copper-Nickel-Tin Alloy, Copper-Nickel-Zinc Alloy (Nickel Silver), and Copper-Nickel Alloy Plate, Sheet, Strip, and Rolled Bar.	175.600; 182.440
ASTM B 127–80a Nickel-Copper Alloy (UNS NO4400) Plate, Sheet and Strip.	182.15–25; 182.20–25
ASTM B 127-98, Standard Specification for Nickel-Copper Alloy (UNS NO4400) Plate, Sheet, and Strip.	175.600; 182.440
ASTM B 152–79 Copper, Sheet, Strip, Plate and Rolled Bar	182.15–25
ASTM B 152-97a, Standard Specification for Copper Sheet, Strip, Plate, and Rolled Bar.	175.600; 182.440
ASTM B 209–81 Aluminum Alloy Sheet and Plate	182.15–25; 182.20–25
ASTM B 209-96, Standard Specification for Aluminum and Aluminum-Alloy Sheet and Plate.	175.600; 182.440
ASTM D 93–80 Test for Flash Point by Pennsky-Martens Closed Tester.	182.15–1; 182.20–1
ASTM D 93–94, Flash Point by Pensky-Martens Closed Cup Tester	175.400; 199.05; 199.261; 199.290
ASTM D 93–97, Standard Test Methods for Flash Point by Pensky-Martens Closed Cup Tester.	175.400; 175.600; 199.05; 199.261; 199.290
ASTM D 323–79 Test for Vapor Pressure of Petroleum Products (Reid Method).	188.10–21
ASTM D 635–91 Rate of Burning and/or Extent and Time of Burning of Self-Supporting Plastics in a Horizontal Position.	182.440
ASTM D 635–97, Standard Test Method for Rate of Burning and/or Extent and Time of Burning of Plastics in a Horizontal Position.	175.600; 182.440
ASTM D 638–96 Standard Test Method for Tensile Properties of Plastics.	Appendix A to part 192
ASTM D 2513–96a Standard Specification for Thermoplastic Gas Pressure Pipe, Tubing, and Fittings.	Appendix A to part 192
ASTM D 2863-95, Standard Test Method for Measuring the Minimum Oxygen Concentration to Support Candle-like Combustion of Plastics (Oxygen Index).	175.600; 182.440
ASTM D 2863–91 Measuring the Minimum Oxygen Concentration to Support Candle-like Combustion of Plastics (Oxygen Index).	182.440
ASTM E 84–94 Surface Burning Characteristics of Building Materials	177.410
ASTM E 84-98, Standard Test Method for Surface Burning Characteristics of Building Materials.	175.600; 177.410
ASTM F 1003, Standard Specification for Searchlights on Motor Lifeboats, 1986 (Reapproved 1992).	199.05; 199.175
ASTM F 1003-86 (1992), Standard Specification for Searchlights on Motor Lifeboats.	199.05; 199.175
ASTM F 1014–86 Standard Specification for Flashlights on Vessels	192.20–15(j); 195.35–5(c)(2); 199.05; 199.175

Title 46–Shipping

46 CFR (PARTS 166–199)—Continued
COAST GUARD, DEPARTMENT OF HOMELAND SECURITY—Continued

	46 CFR
ASTM F 1014-92, Standard Specification for Flashlights on Vessels	195.01-3; 195.35-5; 199.05; 199.175
ASTM F 1121-87 (1993), Standard Specification for International Shore Connections for Marine Fire Applications.	193.01-3; 193.10-10
ASTM F 1121–87 International Shore Connections for Marine Fire Applications.	193.10
ASTM F 1196–89, Sliding Watertight Door Assemblies	170.270; 174.100; 190.01
ASTM F 1196-94, Standard Specification for Sliding Watertight Door Assemblies.	170.015; 170.270; 174.007; 174.100
ASTM F 1197-89 (1994), Standard Specification for Sliding Watertight Door Control Systems.	170.015; 170.270; 174.007; 174.100
ASTM F 1197–89 Sliding Watertight Door Control Systems	190.01
ASTM F 1546–94 Standard Specification for Fire Hose Nozzles	167.027–3

Coast Guard
Commandant [G–MVI], 2100 2nd St. SW., Washington, DC 20593

160.014 "Compass and Mounting dated Dec. 14, 1944" (Specification for Compasses: Magnetic, Liquid-filled, Mariners, Compensating, for Lifeboats (with mounting) for Merchant Vessels),1944.	192.20–15

Department of Defense
DODSSP Standarization Document Order Desk, 700 Robbins Ave., Bldg. 4D, Philadelphia, PA 19111-5098

Federal specifications:

ZZ–H–451 Hose, Fire, Woven-Jacketed Rubber or Cambric-lined, with Couplings, F	167.45–5; 169.115; 169.563; 181.15–10; 193.10–10
NAVSEA Cable Comparison Guide, 1975	183.10–20
BB–N–411 Nitrogen, Technical, C	197.340
BB–O–925 Oxygen, Technical, Gas and Liquid, A	197.340

Military Specifications:

MIL–P–21929B; Plastic Material, Cellular Polyurethane, Foam in Place, Rigid (1970)	170.245
MIL–R–21607E (SH); Resins, Polyester, Low Pressure Laminating, Fire-Retardant, May 25, 1990	175.600; 177.410
MIL–P–21929B (1970)—Plastic Material, Cellular Polyurethane, Foam-in-Place, Rigid (2 and 4 pounds per cubic foot)	179.240
MIL–P–21929C; Plastic Material, Cellular Polyurethane, Foam in Place, Rigid (1991) (including Amendment 1, dated May 27, 1994)	175.600; 179.240

Institute of Electrical and Electronic Engineers (formerly American Institute of Electrical Engineers)
Service Center, 445 Hoes Lane, Piscataway, NJ 08855 Telephone: (800) 678–4333

45—Recommended Practice for Electrical Installations on Shipboard, 1977.	167.25–1; 167.40–1; 183.01–15; 183.05–45; 183.10–10; 183.340

International Maritime Organization
4 Albert Embankment, London SE1 7SR, England Telephone: 0171-587 3210; FAX: 0171-587 3210; Telex: 23588. Purchase from: IMO Sales, New York Nautical Instrument and Service Corp., 140 W. Broadway, New York, NY 10013. Telephone: (212) 962-4522; FAX: (212) 406-8420

Material Approved for Incorporation by Reference

46 CFR (PARTS 166–199)—Continued
COAST GUARD, DEPARTMENT OF HOMELAND SECURITY—Continued

	46 CFR
IMO "International Maritime Dangerous Goods (IMDG) Code, 1994 Consolidated Edition, as amended by Amendment 28 (1996) (English edition)".	171.12; 172.401; 172.407
Resolution A.264(VIII) Amendment to Chapter VI of the International Convention for the Safety of Life at Sea, 1960, November 20, 1973.	172.015; 172.020
Resolution A.265 (VIII)	170.135, 171.075, 171.082
Resolution MSC.23 (59) Publication No. 240-E, International Code for the Safe Carriage of Grain in Bulk, 1991.	172.015; 172.020
Resolution A.520(13), Code of Practice for the Evaluation, Testing and Acceptance of Prototype Novel Life-Saving Appliances and Arrangements, dated November 17, 1983.	175.540
Resolution A.649(16), Code for the Construction and Equipment of Mobile Offshore Drilling Units (MODU Code), October 19, 1989 with Amendments of June, 1991.	181.108; 181.503
Resolution A.658(16), Use and Fitting of Retro-Reflective Materials on Life-Saving Appliances, dated November 20, 1989.	185.604
Resolution A.688(17), Fire Test Procedures For Ignitability of Bedding Components, dated November 6, 1991.	177.405
Resolution A.760(18), Symbols Related to Life-Saving Appliances and Arrangements, dated November 17, 1993.	185.604(g)
MSC Circular 699, Revised Guidelines for Passenger Safety Instructions, 17 July, 1995.	199.05; 199.217
Resolution A.520(13), Code of Practice for the Evaluation, Testing, and Acceptance of Prototype Novel Life-Saving Appliances and Arrangements, 19 November, 1983.	199.05; 199.40
Resolution A.657(16), Instructions for Action in Survival Craft, 19 October, 1989.	199.05; 199.175
Resolution A.658(16), Use and Fitting of Retro-reflective Materials on Life-Saving Appliances, 20 November, 1989.	199.05; 199.70; 199.176
Resolution A.760(18), Symbols Related to Life-Saving Appliances and Arrangements, 17 November, 1993.	199.05; 199.70; 199.90
Resolution MSC.4(48), International Code for the Construction and Equipment of Ships Carrying Dangerous Chemicals in Bulk (IBC Code), 1994.	199.05; 199.30; 199.280
Resolution MSC.5(48), International Code for the Construction and Equipment of Ships Carrying Liquified Gases in Bulk (ICG Code), 1993.	199.05; 199.30; 199.280

Lloyd's Register of Shipping
17 Battery Place, Suite 1013, New York, NY 10004

Rules and Regulations for the Classification of Yachts and Small Craft, as amended through 1983.	177.300

Manufacturers Standardization Society of the Valve and Fittings Industry, Inc.
127 Park Street NW., Vienna, VA 22180

MSS SP44–96 Steel Pipe Line Flanges	Appendix A to part 192

National Fire Protection Association
1 Batterymarch Park, Quincy, MA 02269–9101, Telephone: (800) 344-3555

70—National Electrical Code, 1980	169.115; 169.672
302—Pleasure and Commercial Motor Craft Chapter 6, 1980	169.115; 169.703
306—Control of Gas Hazards on Vessels, 1980	167.30–1; 169.115; 169.236

Title 46–Shipping

46 CFR (PARTS 166–199)—Continued
COAST GUARD, DEPARTMENT OF HOMELAND SECURITY—Continued

	46 CFR
NFPA 10–1994—Portable Fire Extinguishers	176.810
NFPA 17–1994—Dry Chemical Extinguishing Systems	181.425
NFPA 17A–1994—Wet Chemical Extinguishing Systems	181.425
NFPA 70—National Electrical Code, 1980	183.01–10; 183.05–45; 183.05–50; 183.10–20
NFPA 70–1993—National Electrical Code (NEC)	183.370
Section 250–95	183.370
Section 310–13	183.340
Section Section 310–15	183.340
Article 430	183.320
Article 445	183.320
NFPA 302—Pleasure and Commercial Motor Craft, 1989	184.05–1
NFPA 302–1994—Pleasure and Commercial Motor Craft, Chapter 6	184.200; 184.200
NFPA 306–1993—Control of Gas Hazards on Vessels	176.710
NFPA 1963–1989—Fire Hose Connections	181.320
NFPA 30 Flammable and Combustible Liquids Code, 1996	Appendixes A to part 192 and 193
NFPA306—Control of Gas Hazards on Vessels (Formerly "Control of Gas Hazards on Vessels to be Repaired"), 1975.	189.50–1

National Institute of Standards and Technology (formerly National Bureau of Standards)
c/o Superintendent of Documents, U.S. Government Printing Office, Washington, DC 20402, Telephone 202–512–1800

Special Pub. 440 (SD Cat. No. C13, 10.490) Color: Universal Language and Dictionary of Names, 1976.	169.115

Society of Automotive Engineers (SAE)
400 Commonwealth Dr., Warrendale, PA 15096–0001, Telephone: (412) 776–4841

SAE J–1475—Hydraulic Hose Fittings For Marine Applications, 1984	182.720
SAE J–1928—Devices Providing Backfire Flame Control for Gasoline Engines in Marine Applications, August 1989.	182.415
SAE J–1942—Hose and Hose Assemblies for Marine Applications, 1992.	182.720

Underwriters Laboratories, Inc.
Available from: Global Engineering Documents, 15 Inverness Way East, Englewood, CO 80112, Telephone (800) 854–7179 or
Global Engineering Documents, 7730 Carondelet Ave., Suite 470, Clayton, MO 63105, Telephone (800) 854–7179

UL 19–78 Woven-jacketed Rubber Lined Fire Hose	167.45–5; 169.115; 169.563
UL 19–78 Woven-Jacketed, Rubber Lined Fire Hose	181.15–10
UL 19–1992—Lined Fire Hose and Hose Assemblies	181.320
UL 174–1989, as amended through June 23, 1994—Household Electric Storage Tank Water Heaters.	182.320
UL 197–78 (Revisions through 1979) Commercial Electric Cooking Appliances.	183.01–15; 183.10–45
UL 217–1993—Single and Multiple Station Smoke Detectors	181.450
UL 486A–1992—Wire Connectors and Soldering Lugs For Use With Copper Conductors.	183.340
UL 489–1995—Molded—Case Circuit Breakers and Circuit Breaker Enclosures.	183.380

Material Approved for Incorporation by Reference

46 CFR (PARTS 166–199)—Continued
COAST GUARD, DEPARTMENT OF HOMELAND SECURITY—Continued

	46 CFR
UL 595–74 (Revisions through 1980) Marine Type Electric Lighting Fixtures	183.01–15
UL 595–1991—Marine Type Electric Lighting Fixtures	183.410
UL 710–1990, as amended through Sept. 16, 1993—Exhaust Hoods for Commercial Cooking Equipment.	181.425
UL 1058–1989, as amended through April 19, 1994—Halogenated Agent Extinguishing System Units.	181.410
UL 1102–80 Non Integral Marine Fuel Tanks	182.15–25
UL 1102–1992—Non integral Marine Fuel Tanks	182.440
UL 1110–1988, as amended through May 16, 1994—Marine Combustible Gas Indicators.	182.480
UL 1111–1988—Marine Carburetor Flame Arresters	182.415
UL 1453–1988, as amended through June 7, 1994—Electric Booster and Commercial Storage Tank Water Heaters.	182.320
UL 1570–1995—Fluorescent Lighting Fixtures	183.410
UL 1571–1995—Incandescent Lighting Fixtures	183.410
UL 1572–1995—High Intensity Discharge Lighting Fixtures	183.410
UL 1573–1995—Stage and Studio Discharge Lighting Units	183.410
UL 1574–1995—Track Lighting Systems	183.410(c)
UL 19–71 Woven Jacketed, Rubber Lined Fire Hose	193.10–10

Table of CFR Titles and Chapters
(Revised as of October 1, 2004)

Title 1—General Provisions

I   Administrative Committee of the Federal Register (Parts 1—49)
II Office of the Federal Register (Parts 50—299)
IV Miscellaneous Agencies (Parts 400—500)

Title 2—Grants and Agreements

SUBTITLE A—OFFICE OF MANAGEMENT AND BUDGET GUIDANCE FOR GRANTS AND AGREEMENTS

I   [Reserved]
II Office of Management and Budget Circulars and Guidance [Reserved]

SUBTITLE B—FEDERAL AGENCY REGULATIONS FOR GRANTS AND AGREEMENTS [RESERVED]

Title 3—The President

I   Executive Office of the President (Parts 100—199)

Title 4—Accounts

I   General Accounting Office (Parts 1—99)

Title 5—Administrative Personnel

I   Office of Personnel Management (Parts 1—1199)
II   Merit Systems Protection Board (Parts 1200—1299)
III   Office of Management and Budget (Parts 1300—1399)
V   The International Organizations Employees Loyalty Board (Parts 1500—1599)
VI   Federal Retirement Thrift Investment Board (Parts 1600—1699)
VIII Office of Special Counsel (Parts 1800—1899)
IX   Appalachian Regional Commission (Parts 1900—1999)
XI   Armed Forces Retirement Home (Part 2100)
XIV   Federal Labor Relations Authority, General Counsel of the Federal Labor Relations Authority and Federal Service Impasses Panel (Parts 2400—2499)

537

Title 5—Administrative Personnel—Continued

Chap.	
XV	Office of Administration, Executive Office of the President (Parts 2500—2599)
XVI	Office of Government Ethics (Parts 2600—2699)
XXI	Department of the Treasury (Parts 3100—3199)
XXII	Federal Deposit Insurance Corporation (Part 3201)
XXIII	Department of Energy (Part 3301)
XXIV	Federal Energy Regulatory Commission (Part 3401)
XXV	Department of the Interior (Part 3501)
XXVI	Department of Defense (Part 3601)
XXVIII	Department of Justice (Part 3801)
XXIX	Federal Communications Commission (Parts 3900—3999)
XXX	Farm Credit System Insurance Corporation (Parts 4000—4099)
XXXI	Farm Credit Administration (Parts 4100—4199)
XXXIII	Overseas Private Investment Corporation (Part 4301)
XXXV	Office of Personnel Management (Part 4501)
XL	Interstate Commerce Commission (Part 5001)
XLI	Commodity Futures Trading Commission (Part 5101)
XLII	Department of Labor (Part 5201)
XLIII	National Science Foundation (Part 5301)
XLV	Department of Health and Human Services (Part 5501)
XLVI	Postal Rate Commission (Part 5601)
XLVII	Federal Trade Commission (Part 5701)
XLVIII	Nuclear Regulatory Commission (Part 5801)
L	Department of Transportation (Part 6001)
LII	Export-Import Bank of the United States (Part 6201)
LIII	Department of Education (Parts 6300—6399)
LIV	Environmental Protection Agency (Part 6401)
LV	National Endowment for the Arts (Part 6501)
LVI	National Endowment for the Humanities (Part 6601)
LVII	General Services Administration (Part 6701)
LVIII	Board of Governors of the Federal Reserve System (Part 6801)
LIX	National Aeronautics and Space Administration (Part 6901)
LX	United States Postal Service (Part 7001)
LXI	National Labor Relations Board (Part 7101)
LXII	Equal Employment Opportunity Commission (Part 7201)
LXIII	Inter-American Foundation (Part 7301)
LXV	Department of Housing and Urban Development (Part 7501)
LXVI	National Archives and Records Administration (Part 7601)
LXVII	Institute of Museum and Library Services (Part 7701)
LXIX	Tennessee Valley Authority (Part 7901)
LXXI	Consumer Product Safety Commission (Part 8101)
LXXIII	Department of Agriculture (Part 8301)
LXXIV	Federal Mine Safety and Health Review Commission (Part 8401)

Title 5—Administrative Personnel—Continued

Chap.	
LXXVI	Federal Retirement Thrift Investment Board (Part 8601)
LXXVII	Office of Management and Budget (Part 8701)

Title 6—Homeland Security

I	Department of Homeland Security, Office of the Secretary (Parts 0—99)

Title 7—Agriculture

SUBTITLE A—OFFICE OF THE SECRETARY OF AGRICULTURE (PARTS 0—26)

SUBTITLE B—REGULATIONS OF THE DEPARTMENT OF AGRICULTURE

I	Agricultural Marketing Service (Standards, Inspections, Marketing Practices), Department of Agriculture (Parts 27—209)
II	Food and Nutrition Service, Department of Agriculture (Parts 210—299)
III	Animal and Plant Health Inspection Service, Department of Agriculture (Parts 300—399)
IV	Federal Crop Insurance Corporation, Department of Agriculture (Parts 400—499)
V	Agricultural Research Service, Department of Agriculture (Parts 500—599)
VI	Natural Resources Conservation Service, Department of Agriculture (Parts 600—699)
VII	Farm Service Agency, Department of Agriculture (Parts 700—799)
VIII	Grain Inspection, Packers and Stockyards Administration (Federal Grain Inspection Service), Department of Agriculture (Parts 800—899)
IX	Agricultural Marketing Service (Marketing Agreements and Orders; Fruits, Vegetables, Nuts), Department of Agriculture (Parts 900—999)
X	Agricultural Marketing Service (Marketing Agreements and Orders; Milk), Department of Agriculture (Parts 1000—1199)
XI	Agricultural Marketing Service (Marketing Agreements and Orders; Miscellaneous Commodities), Department of Agriculture (Parts 1200—1299)
XIV	Commodity Credit Corporation, Department of Agriculture (Parts 1400—1499)
XV	Foreign Agricultural Service, Department of Agriculture (Parts 1500—1599)
XVI	Rural Telephone Bank, Department of Agriculture (Parts 1600—1699)
XVII	Rural Utilities Service, Department of Agriculture (Parts 1700—1799)
XVIII	Rural Housing Service, Rural Business-Cooperative Service, Rural Utilities Service, and Farm Service Agency, Department of Agriculture (Parts 1800—2099)
XX	Local Television Loan Guarantee Board (Parts 2200—2299)

Title 7—Agriculture—Continued

Chap.	
XXVI	Office of Inspector General, Department of Agriculture (Parts 2600—2699)
XXVII	Office of Information Resources Management, Department of Agriculture (Parts 2700—2799)
XXVIII	Office of Operations, Department of Agriculture (Parts 2800—2899)
XXIX	Office of Energy, Department of Agriculture (Parts 2900—2999)
XXX	Office of the Chief Financial Officer, Department of Agriculture (Parts 3000—3099)
XXXI	Office of Environmental Quality, Department of Agriculture (Parts 3100—3199)
XXXII	Office of Procurement and Property Management, Department of Agriculture (Parts 3200—3299)
XXXIII	Office of Transportation, Department of Agriculture (Parts 3300—3399)
XXXIV	Cooperative State Research, Education, and Extension Service, Department of Agriculture (Parts 3400—3499)
XXXV	Rural Housing Service, Department of Agriculture (Parts 3500—3599)
XXXVI	National Agricultural Statistics Service, Department of Agriculture (Parts 3600—3699)
XXXVII	Economic Research Service, Department of Agriculture (Parts 3700—3799)
XXXVIII	World Agricultural Outlook Board, Department of Agriculture (Parts 3800—3899)
XLI	[Reserved]
XLII	Rural Business-Cooperative Service and Rural Utilities Service, Department of Agriculture (Parts 4200—4299)

Title 8—Aliens and Nationality

I	Department of Homeland Security (Immigration and Naturalization) (Parts 1—499)
V	Executive Office for Immigration Review, Department of Justice (Parts 1000—1399)

Title 9—Animals and Animal Products

I	Animal and Plant Health Inspection Service, Department of Agriculture (Parts 1—199)
II	Grain Inspection, Packers and Stockyards Administration (Packers and Stockyards Programs), Department of Agriculture (Parts 200—299)
III	Food Safety and Inspection Service, Department of Agriculture (Parts 300—599)

Title 10—Energy

I	Nuclear Regulatory Commission (Parts 0—199)
II	Department of Energy (Parts 200—699)

Title 10—Energy—Continued

Chap.
III Department of Energy (Parts 700—999)
X Department of Energy (General Provisions) (Parts 1000—1099)
XVII Defense Nuclear Facilities Safety Board (Parts 1700—1799)
XVIII Northeast Interstate Low-Level Radioactive Waste Commission (Part 1800)

Title 11—Federal Elections

I Federal Election Commission (Parts 1—9099)

Title 12—Banks and Banking

I Comptroller of the Currency, Department of the Treasury (Parts 1—199)
II Federal Reserve System (Parts 200—299)
III Federal Deposit Insurance Corporation (Parts 300—399)
IV Export-Import Bank of the United States (Parts 400—499)
V Office of Thrift Supervision, Department of the Treasury (Parts 500—599)
VI Farm Credit Administration (Parts 600—699)
VII National Credit Union Administration (Parts 700—799)
VIII Federal Financing Bank (Parts 800—899)
IX Federal Housing Finance Board (Parts 900—999)
XI Federal Financial Institutions Examination Council (Parts 1100—1199)
XIV Farm Credit System Insurance Corporation (Parts 1400—1499)
XV Department of the Treasury (Parts 1500—1599)
XVII Office of Federal Housing Enterprise Oversight, Department of Housing and Urban Development (Parts 1700—1799)
XVIII Community Development Financial Institutions Fund, Department of the Treasury (Parts 1800—1899)

Title 13—Business Credit and Assistance

I Small Business Administration (Parts 1—199)
III Economic Development Administration, Department of Commerce (Parts 300—399)
IV Emergency Steel Guarantee Loan Board, Department of Commerce (Parts 400—499)
V Emergency Oil and Gas Guaranteed Loan Board, Department of Commerce (Parts 500—599)

Title 14—Aeronautics and Space

I Federal Aviation Administration, Department of Transportation (Parts 1—199)
II Office of the Secretary, Department of Transportation (Aviation Proceedings) (Parts 200—399)

Title 14—Aeronautics and Space—Continued

Chap.

- III Commercial Space Transportation, Federal Aviation Administration, Department of Transportation (Parts 400—499)
- V National Aeronautics and Space Administration (Parts 1200—1299)
- VI Air Transportation System Stabilization (Parts 1300—1399)

Title 15—Commerce and Foreign Trade

SUBTITLE A—OFFICE OF THE SECRETARY OF COMMERCE (PARTS 0—29)

SUBTITLE B—REGULATIONS RELATING TO COMMERCE AND FOREIGN TRADE

- I Bureau of the Census, Department of Commerce (Parts 30—199)
- II National Institute of Standards and Technology, Department of Commerce (Parts 200—299)
- III International Trade Administration, Department of Commerce (Parts 300—399)
- IV Foreign-Trade Zones Board, Department of Commerce (Parts 400—499)
- VII Bureau of Industry and Security, Department of Commerce (Parts 700—799)
- VIII Bureau of Economic Analysis, Department of Commerce (Parts 800—899)
- IX National Oceanic and Atmospheric Administration, Department of Commerce (Parts 900—999)
- XI Technology Administration, Department of Commerce (Parts 1100—1199)
- XIII East-West Foreign Trade Board (Parts 1300—1399)
- XIV Minority Business Development Agency (Parts 1400—1499)

SUBTITLE C—REGULATIONS RELATING TO FOREIGN TRADE AGREEMENTS

- XX Office of the United States Trade Representative (Parts 2000—2099)

SUBTITLE D—REGULATIONS RELATING TO TELECOMMUNICATIONS AND INFORMATION

- XXIII National Telecommunications and Information Administration, Department of Commerce (Parts 2300—2399)

Title 16—Commercial Practices

- I Federal Trade Commission (Parts 0—999)
- II Consumer Product Safety Commission (Parts 1000—1799)

Title 17—Commodity and Securities Exchanges

- I Commodity Futures Trading Commission (Parts 1—199)
- II Securities and Exchange Commission (Parts 200—399)
- IV Department of the Treasury (Parts 400—499)

Title 18—Conservation of Power and Water Resources

Chap.
- I Federal Energy Regulatory Commission, Department of Energy (Parts 1—399)
- III Delaware River Basin Commission (Parts 400—499)
- VI Water Resources Council (Parts 700—799)
- VIII Susquehanna River Basin Commission (Parts 800—899)
- XIII Tennessee Valley Authority (Parts 1300—1399)

Title 19—Customs Duties

- I Bureau of Customs and Border Protection, Department of Homeland Security; Department of the Treasury (Parts 0—199)
- II United States International Trade Commission (Parts 200—299)
- III International Trade Administration, Department of Commerce (Parts 300—399)
- IV Bureau of Immigration and Customs Enforcement, Department of Homeland Security (Parts 400—599)

Title 20—Employees' Benefits

- I Office of Workers' Compensation Programs, Department of Labor (Parts 1—199)
- II Railroad Retirement Board (Parts 200—399)
- III Social Security Administration (Parts 400—499)
- IV Employees Compensation Appeals Board, Department of Labor (Parts 500—599)
- V Employment and Training Administration, Department of Labor (Parts 600—699)
- VI Employment Standards Administration, Department of Labor (Parts 700—799)
- VII Benefits Review Board, Department of Labor (Parts 800—899)
- VIII Joint Board for the Enrollment of Actuaries (Parts 900—999)
- IX Office of the Assistant Secretary for Veterans' Employment and Training, Department of Labor (Parts 1000—1099)

Title 21—Food and Drugs

- I Food and Drug Administration, Department of Health and Human Services (Parts 1—1299)
- II Drug Enforcement Administration, Department of Justice (Parts 1300—1399)
- III Office of National Drug Control Policy (Parts 1400—1499)

Title 22—Foreign Relations

- I Department of State (Parts 1—199)
- II Agency for International Development (Parts 200—299)
- III Peace Corps (Parts 300—399)

Title 22—Foreign Relations—Continued

Chap.

IV International Joint Commission, United States and Canada (Parts 400—499)
V Broadcasting Board of Governors (Parts 500—599)
VII Overseas Private Investment Corporation (Parts 700—799)
IX Foreign Service Grievance Board Regulations (Parts 900—999)
X Inter-American Foundation (Parts 1000—1099)
XI International Boundary and Water Commission, United States and Mexico, United States Section (Parts 1100—1199)
XII United States International Development Cooperation Agency (Parts 1200—1299)
XIV Foreign Service Labor Relations Board; Federal Labor Relations Authority; General Counsel of the Federal Labor Relations Authority; and the Foreign Service Impasse Disputes Panel (Parts 1400—1499)
XV African Development Foundation (Parts 1500—1599)
XVI Japan-United States Friendship Commission (Parts 1600—1699)
XVII United States Institute of Peace (Parts 1700—1799)

Title 23—Highways

I Federal Highway Administration, Department of Transportation (Parts 1—999)
II National Highway Traffic Safety Administration and Federal Highway Administration, Department of Transportation (Parts 1200—1299)
III National Highway Traffic Safety Administration, Department of Transportation (Parts 1300—1399)

Title 24—Housing and Urban Development

SUBTITLE A—OFFICE OF THE SECRETARY, DEPARTMENT OF HOUSING AND URBAN DEVELOPMENT (PARTS 0—99)

SUBTITLE B—REGULATIONS RELATING TO HOUSING AND URBAN DEVELOPMENT

I Office of Assistant Secretary for Equal Opportunity, Department of Housing and Urban Development (Parts 100—199)
II Office of Assistant Secretary for Housing-Federal Housing Commissioner, Department of Housing and Urban Development (Parts 200—299)
III Government National Mortgage Association, Department of Housing and Urban Development (Parts 300—399)
IV Office of Housing and Office of Multifamily Housing Assistance Restructuring, Department of Housing and Urban Development (Parts 400—499)
V Office of Assistant Secretary for Community Planning and Development, Department of Housing and Urban Development (Parts 500—599)
VI Office of Assistant Secretary for Community Planning and Development, Department of Housing and Urban Development (Parts 600—699) [Reserved]

Title 24—Housing and Urban Development—Continued

Chap.

VII Office of the Secretary, Department of Housing and Urban Development (Housing Assistance Programs and Public and Indian Housing Programs) (Parts 700—799)

VIII Office of the Assistant Secretary for Housing—Federal Housing Commissioner, Department of Housing and Urban Development (Section 8 Housing Assistance Programs, Section 202 Direct Loan Program, Section 202 Supportive Housing for the Elderly Program and Section 811 Supportive Housing for Persons With Disabilities Program) (Parts 800—899)

IX Office of Assistant Secretary for Public and Indian Housing, Department of Housing and Urban Development (Parts 900—1699)

X Office of Assistant Secretary for Housing—Federal Housing Commissioner, Department of Housing and Urban Development (Interstate Land Sales Registration Program) (Parts 1700—1799)

XII Office of Inspector General, Department of Housing and Urban Development (Parts 2000—2099)

XX Office of Assistant Secretary for Housing—Federal Housing Commissioner, Department of Housing and Urban Development (Parts 3200—3899)

XXV Neighborhood Reinvestment Corporation (Parts 4100—4199)

Title 25—Indians

I Bureau of Indian Affairs, Department of the Interior (Parts 1—299)

II Indian Arts and Crafts Board, Department of the Interior (Parts 300—399)

III National Indian Gaming Commission, Department of the Interior (Parts 500—599)

IV Office of Navajo and Hopi Indian Relocation (Parts 700—799)

V Bureau of Indian Affairs, Department of the Interior, and Indian Health Service, Department of Health and Human Services (Part 900)

VI Office of the Assistant Secretary-Indian Affairs, Department of the Interior (Parts 1000—1199)

VII Office of the Special Trustee for American Indians, Department of the Interior (Part 1200)

Title 26—Internal Revenue

I Internal Revenue Service, Department of the Treasury (Parts 1—899)

Title 27—Alcohol, Tobacco Products and Firearms

I Alcohol and Tobacco Tax and Trade Bureau, Department of the Treasury (Parts 1—399)

II Bureau of Alcohol, Tobacco, Firearms, and Explosives, Department of Justice (Parts 400—699)

Title 28—Judicial Administration

Chap.
- I   Department of Justice (Parts 0—299)
- III Federal Prison Industries, Inc., Department of Justice (Parts 300—399)
- V   Bureau of Prisons, Department of Justice (Parts 500—599)
- VI Offices of Independent Counsel, Department of Justice (Parts 600—699)
- VII Office of Independent Counsel (Parts 700—799)
- VIII Court Services and Offender Supervision Agency for the District of Columbia (Parts 800—899)
- IX National Crime Prevention and Privacy Compact Council (Parts 900—999)
- XI Department of Justice and Department of State (Parts 1100—1199)

Title 29—Labor

SUBTITLE A—OFFICE OF THE SECRETARY OF LABOR (PARTS 0—99)
SUBTITLE B—REGULATIONS RELATING TO LABOR

- I   National Labor Relations Board (Parts 100—199)
- II Office of Labor-Management Standards, Department of Labor (Parts 200—299)
- III National Railroad Adjustment Board (Parts 300—399)
- IV Office of Labor-Management Standards, Department of Labor (Parts 400—499)
- V   Wage and Hour Division, Department of Labor (Parts 500—899)
- IX Construction Industry Collective Bargaining Commission (Parts 900—999)
- X   National Mediation Board (Parts 1200—1299)
- XII Federal Mediation and Conciliation Service (Parts 1400—1499)
- XIV Equal Employment Opportunity Commission (Parts 1600—1699)
- XVII Occupational Safety and Health Administration, Department of Labor (Parts 1900—1999)
- XX Occupational Safety and Health Review Commission (Parts 2200—2499)
- XXV Employee Benefits Security Administration, Department of Labor (Parts 2500—2599)
- XXVII Federal Mine Safety and Health Review Commission (Parts 2700—2799)
- XL Pension Benefit Guaranty Corporation (Parts 4000—4999)

Title 30—Mineral Resources

- I   Mine Safety and Health Administration, Department of Labor (Parts 1—199)
- II Minerals Management Service, Department of the Interior (Parts 200—299)
- III Board of Surface Mining and Reclamation Appeals, Department of the Interior (Parts 300—399)

Title 30—Mineral Resources—Continued

Chap.
IV   Geological Survey, Department of the Interior (Parts 400—499)
VII Office of Surface Mining Reclamation and Enforcement, Department of the Interior (Parts 700—999)

Title 31—Money and Finance: Treasury

SUBTITLE A—OFFICE OF THE SECRETARY OF THE TREASURY (PARTS 0—50)

SUBTITLE B—REGULATIONS RELATING TO MONEY AND FINANCE
I   Monetary Offices, Department of the Treasury (Parts 51—199)
II   Fiscal Service, Department of the Treasury (Parts 200—399)
IV   Secret Service, Department of the Treasury (Parts 400—499)
V   Office of Foreign Assets Control, Department of the Treasury (Parts 500—599)
VI   Bureau of Engraving and Printing, Department of the Treasury (Parts 600—699)
VII   Federal Law Enforcement Training Center, Department of the Treasury (Parts 700—799)
VIII Office of International Investment, Department of the Treasury (Parts 800—899)
IX   Federal Claims Collection Standards (Department of the Treasury—Department of Justice) (Parts 900—999)

Title 32—National Defense

SUBTITLE A—DEPARTMENT OF DEFENSE
I   Office of the Secretary of Defense (Parts 1—399)
V   Department of the Army (Parts 400—699)
VI   Department of the Navy (Parts 700—799)
VII   Department of the Air Force (Parts 800—1099)

SUBTITLE B—OTHER REGULATIONS RELATING TO NATIONAL DEFENSE
XII   Defense Logistics Agency (Parts 1200—1299)
XVI   Selective Service System (Parts 1600—1699)
XVIII   National Counterintelligence Center (Parts 1800—1899)
XIX   Central Intelligence Agency (Parts 1900—1999)
XX   Information Security Oversight Office, National Archives and Records Administration (Parts 2000—2099)
XXI   National Security Council (Parts 2100—2199)
XXIV   Office of Science and Technology Policy (Parts 2400—2499)
XXVII   Office for Micronesian Status Negotiations (Parts 2700—2799)
XXVIII Office of the Vice President of the United States (Parts 2800—2899)

Title 33—Navigation and Navigable Waters

I   Coast Guard, Department of Homeland Security (Parts 1—199)
II Corps of Engineers, Department of the Army (Parts 200—399)

Title 33—Navigation and Navigable Waters—Continued

Chap.

IV   Saint Lawrence Seaway Development Corporation, Department of Transportation (Parts 400—499)

Title 34—Education

SUBTITLE A—OFFICE OF THE SECRETARY, DEPARTMENT OF EDUCATION (PARTS 1—99)

SUBTITLE B—REGULATIONS OF THE OFFICES OF THE DEPARTMENT OF EDUCATION

I   Office for Civil Rights, Department of Education (Parts 100—199)

II   Office of Elementary and Secondary Education, Department of Education (Parts 200—299)

III   Office of Special Education and Rehabilitative Services, Department of Education (Parts 300—399)

IV   Office of Vocational and Adult Education, Department of Education (Parts 400—499)

V   Office of Bilingual Education and Minority Languages Affairs, Department of Education (Parts 500—599)

VI   Office of Postsecondary Education, Department of Education (Parts 600—699)

XI   National Institute for Literacy (Parts 1100—1199)

SUBTITLE C—REGULATIONS RELATING TO EDUCATION

XII   National Council on Disability (Parts 1200—1299)

Title 35—Panama Canal

I   Panama Canal Regulations (Parts 1—299)

Title 36—Parks, Forests, and Public Property

I   National Park Service, Department of the Interior (Parts 1—199)

II   Forest Service, Department of Agriculture (Parts 200—299)

III   Corps of Engineers, Department of the Army (Parts 300—399)

IV   American Battle Monuments Commission (Parts 400—499)

V   Smithsonian Institution (Parts 500—599)

VII   Library of Congress (Parts 700—799)

VIII   Advisory Council on Historic Preservation (Parts 800—899)

IX   Pennsylvania Avenue Development Corporation (Parts 900—999)

X   Presidio Trust (Parts 1000—1099)

XI   Architectural and Transportation Barriers Compliance Board (Parts 1100—1199)

XII   National Archives and Records Administration (Parts 1200—1299)

XV   Oklahoma City National Memorial Trust (Part 1501)

XVI   Morris K. Udall Scholarship and Excellence in National Environmental Policy Foundation (Parts 1600—1699)

Chap.

Title 37—Patents, Trademarks, and Copyrights

I United States Patent and Trademark Office, Department of Commerce (Parts 1—199)
II Copyright Office, Library of Congress (Parts 200—299)
IV Assistant Secretary for Technology Policy, Department of Commerce (Parts 400—499)
V Under Secretary for Technology, Department of Commerce (Parts 500—599)

Title 38—Pensions, Bonuses, and Veterans' Relief

I Department of Veterans Affairs (Parts 0—99)

Title 39—Postal Service

I United States Postal Service (Parts 1—999)
III Postal Rate Commission (Parts 3000—3099)

Title 40—Protection of Environment

I Environmental Protection Agency (Parts 1—1099)
IV Environmental Protection Agency and Department of Justice (Parts 1400—1499)
V Council on Environmental Quality (Parts 1500—1599)
VI Chemical Safety and Hazard Investigation Board (Parts 1600—1699)
VII Environmental Protection Agency and Department of Defense; Uniform National Discharge Standards for Vessels of the Armed Forces (Parts 1700—1799)

Title 41—Public Contracts and Property Management

SUBTITLE B—OTHER PROVISIONS RELATING TO PUBLIC CONTRACTS
50 Public Contracts, Department of Labor (Parts 50-1—50-999)
51 Committee for Purchase From People Who Are Blind or Severely Disabled (Parts 51-1—51-99)
60 Office of Federal Contract Compliance Programs, Equal Employment Opportunity, Department of Labor (Parts 60-1—60-999)
61 Office of the Assistant Secretary for Veterans' Employment and Training Service, Department of Labor (Parts 61-1—61-999)
SUBTITLE C—FEDERAL PROPERTY MANAGEMENT REGULATIONS SYSTEM
101 Federal Property Management Regulations (Parts 101-1—101-99)
102 Federal Management Regulation (Parts 102-1—102-299)
105 General Services Administration (Parts 105-1—105-999)
109 Department of Energy Property Management Regulations (Parts 109-1—109-99)
114 Department of the Interior (Parts 114-1—114-99)
115 Environmental Protection Agency (Parts 115-1—115-99)

Title 41—Public Contracts and Property Management—Continued

Chap.

128 Department of Justice (Parts 128-1—128-99)

SUBTITLE D—OTHER PROVISIONS RELATING TO PROPERTY MANAGEMENT [RESERVED]

SUBTITLE E—FEDERAL INFORMATION RESOURCES MANAGEMENT REGULATIONS SYSTEM

201 Federal Information Resources Management Regulation (Parts 201-1—201-99) [Reserved]

SUBTITLE F—FEDERAL TRAVEL REGULATION SYSTEM

300 General (Parts 300-1—300-99)
301 Temporary Duty (TDY) Travel Allowances (Parts 301-1—301-99)
302 Relocation Allowances (Parts 302-1—302-99)
303 Payment of Expenses Connected with the Death of Certain Employees (Part 303-70)
304 Payment of Travel Expenses from a Non-Federal Source (Parts 304-1—304-99)

Title 42—Public Health

I Public Health Service, Department of Health and Human Services (Parts 1—199)
IV Centers for Medicare & Medicaid Services, Department of Health and Human Services (Parts 400—499)
V Office of Inspector General-Health Care, Department of Health and Human Services (Parts 1000—1999)

Title 43—Public Lands: Interior

SUBTITLE A—OFFICE OF THE SECRETARY OF THE INTERIOR (PARTS 1—199)

SUBTITLE B—REGULATIONS RELATING TO PUBLIC LANDS

I Bureau of Reclamation, Department of the Interior (Parts 200—499)
II Bureau of Land Management, Department of the Interior (Parts 1000—9999)
III Utah Reclamation Mitigation and Conservation Commission (Parts 10000—10010)

Title 44—Emergency Management and Assistance

I Federal Emergency Management Agency, Department of Homeland Security (Parts 0—399)
IV Department of Commerce and Department of Transportation (Parts 400—499)

Title 45—Public Welfare

SUBTITLE A—DEPARTMENT OF HEALTH AND HUMAN SERVICES (PARTS 1—199)

SUBTITLE B—REGULATIONS RELATING TO PUBLIC WELFARE

Title 45—Public Welfare—Continued

Chap.	
II	Office of Family Assistance (Assistance Programs), Administration for Children and Families, Department of Health and Human Services (Parts 200—299)
III	Office of Child Support Enforcement (Child Support Enforcement Program), Administration for Children and Families, Department of Health and Human Services (Parts 300—399)
IV	Office of Refugee Resettlement, Administration for Children and Families, Department of Health and Human Services (Parts 400—499)
V	Foreign Claims Settlement Commission of the United States, Department of Justice (Parts 500—599)
VI	National Science Foundation (Parts 600—699)
VII	Commission on Civil Rights (Parts 700—799)
VIII	Office of Personnel Management (Parts 800—899)
X	Office of Community Services, Administration for Children and Families, Department of Health and Human Services (Parts 1000—1099)
XI	National Foundation on the Arts and the Humanities (Parts 1100—1199)
XII	Corporation for National and Community Service (Parts 1200—1299)
XIII	Office of Human Development Services, Department of Health and Human Services (Parts 1300—1399)
XVI	Legal Services Corporation (Parts 1600—1699)
XVII	National Commission on Libraries and Information Science (Parts 1700—1799)
XVIII	Harry S. Truman Scholarship Foundation (Parts 1800—1899)
XXI	Commission on Fine Arts (Parts 2100—2199)
XXIII	Arctic Research Commission (Part 2301)
XXIV	James Madison Memorial Fellowship Foundation (Parts 2400—2499)
XXV	Corporation for National and Community Service (Parts 2500—2599)

Title 46—Shipping

I	Coast Guard, Department of Homeland Security (Parts 1—199)
II	Maritime Administration, Department of Transportation (Parts 200—399)
III	Coast Guard (Great Lakes Pilotage), Department of Homeland Security (Parts 400—499)
IV	Federal Maritime Commission (Parts 500—599)

Title 47—Telecommunication

I	Federal Communications Commission (Parts 0—199)
II	Office of Science and Technology Policy and National Security Council (Parts 200—299)

Chap.
Title 47—Telecommunication—Continued

III National Telecommunications and Information Administration, Department of Commerce (Parts 300—399)

Title 48—Federal Acquisition Regulations System

1 Federal Acquisition Regulation (Parts 1—99)
2 Department of Defense (Parts 200—299)
3 Department of Health and Human Services (Parts 300—399)
4 Department of Agriculture (Parts 400—499)
5 General Services Administration (Parts 500—599)
6 Department of State (Parts 600—699)
7 United States Agency for International Development (Parts 700—799)
8 Department of Veterans Affairs (Parts 800—899)
9 Department of Energy (Parts 900—999)
10 Department of the Treasury (Parts 1000—1099)
12 Department of Transportation (Parts 1200—1299)
13 Department of Commerce (Parts 1300—1399)
14 Department of the Interior (Parts 1400—1499)
15 Environmental Protection Agency (Parts 1500—1599)
16 Office of Personnel Management, Federal Employees Health Benefits Acquisition Regulation (Parts 1600—1699)
17 Office of Personnel Management (Parts 1700—1799)
18 National Aeronautics and Space Administration (Parts 1800—1899)
19 Broadcasting Board of Governors (Parts 1900—1999)
20 Nuclear Regulatory Commission (Parts 2000—2099)
21 Office of Personnel Management, Federal Employees Group Life Insurance Federal Acquisition Regulation (Parts 2100—2199)
23 Social Security Administration (Parts 2300—2399)
24 Department of Housing and Urban Development (Parts 2400—2499)
25 National Science Foundation (Parts 2500—2599)
28 Department of Justice (Parts 2800—2899)
29 Department of Labor (Parts 2900—2999)
30 Department of Homeland Security, Homeland Security Acquisition Regulation (HSAR) (Parts 3000—3099)
34 Department of Education Acquisition Regulation (Parts 3400—3499)
35 Panama Canal Commission (Parts 3500—3599)
44 Federal Emergency Management Agency (Parts 4400—4499)
51 Department of the Army Acquisition Regulations (Parts 5100—5199)
52 Department of the Navy Acquisition Regulations (Parts 5200—5299)
53 Department of the Air Force Federal Acquisition Regulation Supplement (Parts 5300—5399)

Title 48—Federal Acquisition Regulations System—Continued

Chap.

54	Defense Logistics Agency, Department of Defense (Parts 5400—5499)
57	African Development Foundation (Parts 5700—5799)
61	General Services Administration Board of Contract Appeals (Parts 6100—6199)
63	Department of Transportation Board of Contract Appeals (Parts 6300—6399)
99	Cost Accounting Standards Board, Office of Federal Procurement Policy, Office of Management and Budget (Parts 9900—9999)

Title 49—Transportation

SUBTITLE A—OFFICE OF THE SECRETARY OF TRANSPORTATION (PARTS 1—99)

SUBTITLE B—OTHER REGULATIONS RELATING TO TRANSPORTATION

I	Research and Special Programs Administration, Department of Transportation (Parts 100—199)
II	Federal Railroad Administration, Department of Transportation (Parts 200—299)
III	Federal Motor Carrier Safety Administration, Department of Transportation (Parts 300—399)
IV	Coast Guard, Department of Homeland Security (Parts 400—499)
V	National Highway Traffic Safety Administration, Department of Transportation (Parts 500—599)
VI	Federal Transit Administration, Department of Transportation (Parts 600—699)
VII	National Railroad Passenger Corporation (AMTRAK) (Parts 700—799)
VIII	National Transportation Safety Board (Parts 800—999)
X	Surface Transportation Board, Department of Transportation (Parts 1000—1399)
XI	Bureau of Transportation Statistics, Department of Transportation (Parts 1400—1499)
XII	Transportation Security Administration, Department of Homeland Security (Parts 1500—1699)

Title 50—Wildlife and Fisheries

I	United States Fish and Wildlife Service, Department of the Interior (Parts 1—199)
II	National Marine Fisheries Service, National Oceanic and Atmospheric Administration, Department of Commerce (Parts 200—299)
III	International Fishing and Related Activities (Parts 300—399)
IV	Joint Regulations (United States Fish and Wildlife Service, Department of the Interior and National Marine Fisheries Service, National Oceanic and Atmospheric Administration, Department of Commerce); Endangered Species Committee Regulations (Parts 400—499)

Title 50—Wildlife and Fisheries—Continued

Chap.
V   Marine Mammal Commission (Parts 500—599)
VI Fishery Conservation and Management, National Oceanic and Atmospheric Administration, Department of Commerce (Parts 600—699)

CFR Index and Finding Aids

Subject/Agency Index
List of Agency Prepared Indexes
Parallel Tables of Statutory Authorities and Rules
List of CFR Titles, Chapters, Subchapters, and Parts
Alphabetical List of Agencies Appearing in the CFR

Alphabetical List of Agencies Appearing in the CFR
(Revised as of October 1, 2004)

Agency	CFR Title, Subtitle or Chapter
Administrative Committee of the Federal Register	1, I
Advanced Research Projects Agency	32, I
Advisory Council on Historic Preservation	36, VIII
African Development Foundation	22, XV
Federal Acquisition Regulation	48, 57
Agency for International Development, United States	22, II
Federal Acquisition Regulation	48, 7
Agricultural Marketing Service	7, I, IX, X, XI
Agricultural Research Service	7, V
Agriculture Department	5, LXXIII
Agricultural Marketing Service	7, I, IX, X, XI
Agricultural Research Service	7, V
Animal and Plant Health Inspection Service	7, III; 9, I
Chief Financial Officer, Office of	7, XXX
Commodity Credit Corporation	7, XIV
Cooperative State Research, Education, and Extension Service	7, XXXIV
Economic Research Service	7, XXXVII
Energy, Office of	7, XXIX
Environmental Quality, Office of	7, XXXI
Farm Service Agency	7, VII, XVIII
Federal Acquisition Regulation	48, 4
Federal Crop Insurance Corporation	7, IV
Food and Nutrition Service	7, II
Food Safety and Inspection Service	9, III
Foreign Agricultural Service	7, XV
Forest Service	36, II
Grain Inspection, Packers and Stockyards Administration	7, VIII; 9, II
Information Resources Management, Office of	7, XXVII
Inspector General, Office of	7, XXVI
National Agricultural Library	7, XLI
National Agricultural Statistics Service	7, XXXVI
Natural Resources Conservation Service	7, VI
Operations, Office of	7, XXVIII
Procurement and Property Management, Office of	7, XXXII
Rural Business-Cooperative Service	7, XVIII, XLII
Rural Development Administration	7, XLII
Rural Housing Service	7, XVIII, XXXV
Rural Telephone Bank	7, XVI
Rural Utilities Service	7, XVII, XVIII, XLII
Secretary of Agriculture, Office of	7, Subtitle A
Transportation, Office of	7, XXXIII
World Agricultural Outlook Board	7, XXXVIII
Air Force Department	32, VII
Federal Acquisition Regulation Supplement	48, 53
Air Transportation Stabilization Board	14, VI
Alcohol and Tobacco Tax and Trade Bureau	27, I
Alcohol, Tobacco, Firearms, and Explosives, Bureau of	27, II
AMTRAK	49, VII
American Battle Monuments Commission	36, IV
American Indians, Office of the Special Trustee	25, VII
Animal and Plant Health Inspection Service	7, III; 9, I
Appalachian Regional Commission	5, IX

Agency	CFR Title, Subtitle or Chapter
Architectural and Transportation Barriers Compliance Board	36, XI
Arctic Research Commission	45, XXIII
Armed Forces Retirement Home	5, XI
Army Department	32, V
Engineers, Corps of	33, II; 36, III
Federal Acquisition Regulation	48, 51
Benefits Review Board	20, VII
Bilingual Education and Minority Languages Affairs, Office of	34, V
Blind or Severely Disabled, Committee for Purchase From People Who Are	41, 51
Broadcasting Board of Governors	22, V
Federal Acquisition Regulation	48, 19
Census Bureau	15, I
Centers for Medicare & Medicaid Services	42, IV
Central Intelligence Agency	32, XIX
Chief Financial Officer, Office of	7, XXX
Child Support Enforcement, Office of	45, III
Children and Families, Administration for	45, II, III, IV, X
Civil Rights, Commission on	45, VII
Civil Rights, Office for	34, I
Coast Guard	33, I; 46, I; 49, IV
Coast Guard (Great Lakes Pilotage)	46, III
Commerce Department	44, IV
Census Bureau	15, I
Economic Affairs, Under Secretary	37, V
Economic Analysis, Bureau of	15, VIII
Economic Development Administration	13, III
Emergency Management and Assistance	44, IV
Federal Acquisition Regulation	48, 13
Fishery Conservation and Management	50, VI
Foreign-Trade Zones Board	15, IV
Industry and Security, Bureau of	15, VII
International Trade Administration	15, III; 19, III
National Institute of Standards and Technology	15, II
National Marine Fisheries Service	50, II, IV, VI
National Oceanic and Atmospheric Administration	15, IX; 50, II, III, IV, VI
National Telecommunications and Information Administration	15, XXIII; 47, III
National Weather Service	15, IX
Patent and Trademark Office, United States	37, I
Productivity, Technology and Innovation, Assistant Secretary for	37, IV
Secretary of Commerce, Office of	15, Subtitle A
Technology, Under Secretary for	37, V
Technology Administration	15, XI
Technology Policy, Assistant Secretary for	37, IV
Commercial Space Transportation	14, III
Commodity Credit Corporation	7, XIV
Commodity Futures Trading Commission	5, XLI; 17, I
Community Planning and Development, Office of Assistant Secretary for	24, V, VI
Community Services, Office of	45, X
Comptroller of the Currency	12, I
Construction Industry Collective Bargaining Commission	29, IX
Consumer Product Safety Commission	5, LXXI; 16, II
Cooperative State Research, Education, and Extension Service	7, XXXIV
Copyright Office	37, II
Corporation for National and Community Service	45, XII, XXV
Cost Accounting Standards Board	48, 99
Council on Environmental Quality	40, V
Court Services and Offender Supervision Agency for the District of Columbia	28, VIII
Customs and Border Protection Bureau	19, I
Defense Contract Audit Agency	32, I
Defense Department	5, XXVI; 32, Subtitle A; 40, VII

Agency	CFR Title, Subtitle or Chapter
Advanced Research Projects Agency	32, I
Air Force Department	32, VII
Army Department	32, V; 33, II; 36, III; 48, 51
Defense Intelligence Agency	32, I
Defense Logistics Agency	32, I, XII; 48, 54
Engineers, Corps of	33, II; 36, III
Federal Acquisition Regulation	48, 2
National Imagery and Mapping Agency	32, I
Navy Department	32, VI; 48, 52
Secretary of Defense, Office of	32, I
Defense Contract Audit Agency	32, I
Defense Intelligence Agency	32, I
Defense Logistics Agency	32, XII; 48, 54
Defense Nuclear Facilities Safety Board	10, XVII
Delaware River Basin Commission	18, III
District of Columbia, Court Services and Offender Supervision Agency for the	28, VIII
Drug Enforcement Administration	21, II
East-West Foreign Trade Board	15, XIII
Economic Affairs, Under Secretary	37, V
Economic Analysis, Bureau of	15, VIII
Economic Development Administration	13, III
Economic Research Service	7, XXXVII
Education, Department of	5, LIII
Bilingual Education and Minority Languages Affairs, Office of	34, V
Civil Rights, Office for	34, I
Educational Research and Improvement, Office of	34, VII
Elementary and Secondary Education, Office of	34, II
Federal Acquisition Regulation	48, 34
Postsecondary Education, Office of	34, VI
Secretary of Education, Office of	34, Subtitle A
Special Education and Rehabilitative Services, Office of	34, III
Vocational and Adult Education, Office of	34, IV
Educational Research and Improvement, Office of	34, VII
Elementary and Secondary Education, Office of	34, II
Emergency Oil and Gas Guaranteed Loan Board	13, V
Emergency Steel Guarantee Loan Board	13, IV
Employee Benefits Security Administration	29, XXV
Employees' Compensation Appeals Board	20, IV
Employees Loyalty Board	5, V
Employment and Training Administration	20, V
Employment Standards Administration	20, VI
Endangered Species Committee	50, IV
Energy, Department of	5, XXIII; 10, II, III, X; 48, 9
Federal Acquisition Regulation	48, 9
Federal Energy Regulatory Commission	5, XXIV; 18, I
Property Management Regulations	41, 109
Energy, Office of	7, XXIX
Engineers, Corps of	33, II; 36, III
Engraving and Printing, Bureau of	31, VI
Environmental Protection Agency	5, LIV; 40, I, IV, VII
Federal Acquisition Regulation	48, 15
Property Management Regulations	41, 115
Environmental Quality, Office of	7, XXXI
Equal Employment Opportunity Commission	5, LXII; 29, XIV
Equal Opportunity, Office of Assistant Secretary for	24, I
Executive Office of the President	3, I
Administration, Office of	5, XV
Environmental Quality, Council on	40, V
Management and Budget, Office of	5, III, LXXVII; 14, VI; 48, 99
National Drug Control Policy, Office of	21, III
National Security Council	32, XXI; 47, 2
Presidential Documents	3
Science and Technology Policy, Office of	32, XXIV; 47, II

Agency	CFR Title, Subtitle or Chapter
Trade Representative, Office of the United States	15, XX
Export-Import Bank of the United States	5, LII; 12, IV
Family Assistance, Office of	45, II
Farm Credit Administration	5, XXXI; 12, VI
Farm Credit System Insurance Corporation	5, XXX; 12, XIV
Farm Service Agency	7, VII, XVIII
Federal Acquisition Regulation	48, 1
Federal Aviation Administration	14, I
Commercial Space Transportation	14, III
Federal Claims Collection Standards	31, IX
Federal Communications Commission	5, XXIX; 47, I
Federal Contract Compliance Programs, Office of	41, 60
Federal Crop Insurance Corporation	7, IV
Federal Deposit Insurance Corporation	5, XXII; 12, III
Federal Election Commission	11, I
Federal Emergency Management Agency	44, I
Federal Acquisition Regulation	48, 44
Federal Employees Group Life Insurance Federal Acquisition Regulation	48, 21
Federal Employees Health Benefits Acquisition Regulation	48, 16
Federal Energy Regulatory Commission	5, XXIV; 18, I
Federal Financial Institutions Examination Council	12, XI
Federal Financing Bank	12, VIII
Federal Highway Administration	23, I, II
Federal Home Loan Mortgage Corporation	1, IV
Federal Housing Enterprise Oversight Office	12, XVII
Federal Housing Finance Board	12, IX
Federal Labor Relations Authority, and General Counsel of the Federal Labor Relations Authority	5, XIV; 22, XIV
Federal Law Enforcement Training Center	31, VII
Federal Management Regulation	41, 102
Federal Maritime Commission	46, IV
Federal Mediation and Conciliation Service	29, XII
Federal Mine Safety and Health Review Commission	5, LXXIV; 29, XXVII
Federal Motor Carrier Safety Administration	49, III
Federal Prison Industries, Inc.	28, III
Federal Procurement Policy Office	48, 99
Federal Property Management Regulations	41, 101
Federal Railroad Administration	49, II
Federal Register, Administrative Committee of	1, I
Federal Register, Office of	1, II
Federal Reserve System	12, II
Board of Governors	5, LVIII
Federal Retirement Thrift Investment Board	5, VI, LXXVI
Federal Service Impasses Panel	5, XIV
Federal Trade Commission	5, XLVII; 16, I
Federal Transit Administration	49, VI
Federal Travel Regulation System	41, Subtitle F
Fine Arts, Commission on	45, XXI
Fiscal Service	31, II
Fish and Wildlife Service, United States	50, I, IV
Fishery Conservation and Management	50, VI
Food and Drug Administration	21, I
Food and Nutrition Service	7, II
Food Safety and Inspection Service	9, III
Foreign Agricultural Service	7, XV
Foreign Assets Control, Office of	31, V
Foreign Claims Settlement Commission of the United States	45, V
Foreign Service Grievance Board	22, IX
Foreign Service Impasse Disputes Panel	22, XIV
Foreign Service Labor Relations Board	22, XIV
Foreign-Trade Zones Board	15, IV
Forest Service	36, II
General Accounting Office	4, I
General Services Administration	5, LVII; 41, 105
Contract Appeals, Board of	48, 61
Federal Acquisition Regulation	48, 5

Agency	CFR Title, Subtitle or Chapter
Federal Management Regulation	41, 102
Federal Property Management Regulations	41, 101
Federal Travel Regulation System	41, Subtitle F
General	41, 300
Payment From a Non-Federal Source for Travel Expenses	41, 304
Payment of Expenses Connected With the Death of Certain Employees	41, 303
Relocation Allowances	41, 302
Temporary Duty (TDY) Travel Allowances	41, 301
Geological Survey	30, IV
Government Ethics, Office of	5, XVI
Government National Mortgage Association	24, III
Grain Inspection, Packers and Stockyards Administration	7, VIII; 9, II
Harry S. Truman Scholarship Foundation	45, XVIII
Health and Human Services, Department of	5, XLV; 45, Subtitle A
Centers for Medicare & Medicaid Services	42, IV
Child Support Enforcement, Office of	45, III
Children and Families, Administration for	45, II, III, IV, X
Community Services, Office of	45, X
Family Assistance, Office of	45, II
Federal Acquisition Regulation	48, 3
Food and Drug Administration	21, I
Human Development Services, Office of	45, XIII
Indian Health Service	25, V; 42, I
Inspector General (Health Care), Office of	42, V
Public Health Service	42, I
Refugee Resettlement, Office of	45, IV
Homeland Security, Department of	6, I
Coast Guard	33, I; 46, I; 49, IV
Coast Guard (Great Lakes Pilotage)	46, III
Customs and Border Protection Bureau	19, I
Federal Emergency Management Agency	44, I
Immigration and Customs Enforcement Bureau	19, IV
Immigration and Naturalization	8, I
Transportation Security Administration	49, XII
Housing and Urban Development, Department of	5, LXV; 24, Subtitle B
Community Planning and Development, Office of Assistant Secretary for	24, V, VI
Equal Opportunity, Office of Assistant Secretary for	24, I
Federal Acquisition Regulation	48, 24
Federal Housing Enterprise Oversight, Office of	12, XVII
Government National Mortgage Association	24, III
Housing—Federal Housing Commissioner, Office of Assistant Secretary for	24, II, VIII, X, XX
Housing, Office of, and Multifamily Housing Assistance Restructuring, Office of	24, IV
Inspector General, Office of	24, XII
Public and Indian Housing, Office of Assistant Secretary for	24, IX
Secretary, Office of	24, Subtitle A, VII
Housing—Federal Housing Commissioner, Office of Assistant Secretary for	24, II, VIII, X, XX
Housing, Office of, and Multifamily Housing Assistance Restructuring, Office of	24, IV
Human Development Services, Office of	45, XIII
Immigration and Customs Enforcement Bureau	19, IV
Immigration and Naturalization	8, I
Immigration Review, Executive Office for	8, V
Independent Counsel, Office of	28, VII
Indian Affairs, Bureau of	25, I, V
Indian Affairs, Office of the Assistant Secretary	25, VI
Indian Arts and Crafts Board	25, II
Indian Health Service	25, V; 42, I
Industry and Security, Bureau of	15, VII
Information Resources Management, Office of	7, XXVII
Information Security Oversight Office, National Archives and Records Administration	32, XX
Inspector General	

Agency	CFR Title, Subtitle or Chapter
Agriculture Department	7, XXVI
Health and Human Services Department	42, V
Housing and Urban Development Department	24, XII
Institute of Peace, United States	22, XVII
Inter-American Foundation	5, LXIII; 22, X
Interior Department	
American Indians, Office of the Special Trustee	25, VII
Endangered Species Committee	50, IV
Federal Acquisition Regulation	48, 14
Federal Property Management Regulations System	41, 114
Fish and Wildlife Service, United States	50, I, IV
Geological Survey	30, IV
Indian Affairs, Bureau of	25, I, V
Indian Affairs, Office of the Assistant Secretary	25, VI
Indian Arts and Crafts Board	25, II
Land Management, Bureau of	43, II
Minerals Management Service	30, II
National Indian Gaming Commission	25, III
National Park Service	36, I
Reclamation, Bureau of	43, I
Secretary of the Interior, Office of	43, Subtitle A
Surface Mining and Reclamation Appeals, Board of	30, III
Surface Mining Reclamation and Enforcement, Office of	30, VII
Internal Revenue Service	26, I
International Boundary and Water Commission, United States and Mexico, United States Section	22, XI
International Development, United States Agency for	22, II
Federal Acquisition Regulation	48, 7
International Development Cooperation Agency, United States	22, XII
International Fishing and Related Activities	50, III
International Investment, Office of	31, VIII
International Joint Commission, United States and Canada	22, IV
International Organizations Employees Loyalty Board	5, V
International Trade Administration	15, III; 19, III
International Trade Commission, United States	19, II
Interstate Commerce Commission	5, XL
James Madison Memorial Fellowship Foundation	45, XXIV
Japan–United States Friendship Commission	22, XVI
Joint Board for the Enrollment of Actuaries	20, VIII
Justice Department	5, XXVIII; 28, I, XI; 40, IV
Alcohol, Tobacco, Firearms, and Explosives, Bureau of	27, II
Drug Enforcement Administration	21, II
Federal Acquisition Regulation	48, 28
Federal Claims Collection Standards	31, IX
Federal Prison Industries, Inc.	28, III
Foreign Claims Settlement Commission of the United States	45, V
Immigration Review, Executive Office for	8, V
Offices of Independent Counsel	28, VI
Prisons, Bureau of	28, V
Property Management Regulations	41, 128
Labor Department	5, XLII
Benefits Review Board	20, VII
Employee Benefits Security Administration	29, XXV
Employees' Compensation Appeals Board	20, IV
Employment and Training Administration	20, V
Employment Standards Administration	20, VI
Federal Acquisition Regulation	48, 29
Federal Contract Compliance Programs, Office of	41, 60
Federal Procurement Regulations System	41, 50
Labor-Management Standards, Office of	29, II, IV
Mine Safety and Health Administration	30, I
Occupational Safety and Health Administration	29, XVII
Public Contracts	41, 50
Secretary of Labor, Office of	29, Subtitle A

Agency	CFR Title, Subtitle or Chapter
Veterans' Employment and Training Service, Office of the Assistant Secretary for	41, 61; 20, IX
Wage and Hour Division	29, V
Workers' Compensation Programs, Office of	20, I
Labor-Management Standards, Office of	29, II, IV
Land Management, Bureau of	43, II
Legal Services Corporation	45, XVI
Library of Congress	36, VII
Copyright Office	37, II
Local Television Loan Guarantee Board	7, XX
Management and Budget, Office of	5, III, LXXVII; 14, VI; 48, 99
Marine Mammal Commission	50, V
Maritime Administration	46, II
Merit Systems Protection Board	5, II
Micronesian Status Negotiations, Office for	32, XXVII
Mine Safety and Health Administration	30, I
Minerals Management Service	30, II
Minority Business Development Agency	15, XIV
Miscellaneous Agencies	1, IV
Monetary Offices	31, I
Morris K. Udall Scholarship and Excellence in National Environmental Policy Foundation	36, XVI
National Aeronautics and Space Administration	5, LIX; 14, V
Federal Acquisition Regulation	48, 18
National Agricultural Library	7, XLI
National Agricultural Statistics Service	7, XXXVI
National and Community Service, Corporation for	45, XII, XXV
National Archives and Records Administration	5, LXVI; 36, XII
Information Security Oversight Office	32, XX
National Bureau of Standards	15, II
National Capital Planning Commission	1, IV
National Commission for Employment Policy	1, IV
National Commission on Libraries and Information Science	45, XVII
National Council on Disability	34, XII
National Counterintelligence Center	32, XVIII
National Credit Union Administration	12, VII
National Crime Prevention and Privacy Compact Council	28, IX
National Drug Control Policy, Office of	21, III
National Foundation on the Arts and the Humanities	45, XI
National Highway Traffic Safety Administration	23, II, III; 49, V
National Imagery and Mapping Agency	32, I
National Indian Gaming Commission	25, III
National Institute for Literacy	34, XI
National Institute of Standards and Technology	15, II
National Labor Relations Board	5, LXI; 29, I
National Marine Fisheries Service	50, II, IV, VI
National Mediation Board	29, X
National Oceanic and Atmospheric Administration	15, IX; 50, II, III, IV, VI
National Park Service	36, I
National Railroad Adjustment Board	29, III
National Railroad Passenger Corporation (AMTRAK)	49, VII
National Science Foundation	5, XLIII; 45, VI
Federal Acquisition Regulation	48, 25
National Security Council	32, XXI
National Security Council and Office of Science and Technology Policy	47, II
National Telecommunications and Information Administration	15, XXIII; 47, III
National Transportation Safety Board	49, VIII
National Weather Service	15, IX
Natural Resources Conservation Service	7, VI
Navajo and Hopi Indian Relocation, Office of	25, IV
Navy Department	32, VI
Federal Acquisition Regulation	48, 52
Neighborhood Reinvestment Corporation	24, XXV
Northeast Interstate Low-Level Radioactive Waste Commission	10, XVIII

Agency	CFR Title, Subtitle or Chapter
Nuclear Regulatory Commission	5, XLVIII; 10, I
Federal Acquisition Regulation	48, 20
Occupational Safety and Health Administration	29, XVII
Occupational Safety and Health Review Commission	29, XX
Offices of Independent Counsel	28, VI
Oklahoma City National Memorial Trust	36, XV
Operations Office	7, XXVIII
Overseas Private Investment Corporation	5, XXXIII; 22, VII
Panama Canal Commission	48, 35
Panama Canal Regulations	35, I
Patent and Trademark Office, United States	37, I
Payment From a Non-Federal Source for Travel Expenses	41, 304
Payment of Expenses Connected With the Death of Certain Employees	41, 303
Peace Corps	22, III
Pennsylvania Avenue Development Corporation	36, IX
Pension Benefit Guaranty Corporation	29, XL
Personnel Management, Office of	5, I, XXXV; 45, VIII
Federal Acquisition Regulation	48, 17
Federal Employees Group Life Insurance Federal Acquisition Regulation	48, 21
Federal Employees Health Benefits Acquisition Regulation	48, 16
Postal Rate Commission	5, XLVI; 39, III
Postal Service, United States	5, LX; 39, I
Postsecondary Education, Office of	34, VI
President's Commission on White House Fellowships	1, IV
Presidential Documents	3
Presidio Trust	36, X
Prisons, Bureau of	28, V
Procurement and Property Management, Office of	7, XXXII
Productivity, Technology and Innovation, Assistant Secretary	37, IV
Public Contracts, Department of Labor	41, 50
Public and Indian Housing, Office of Assistant Secretary for	24, IX
Public Health Service	42, I
Railroad Retirement Board	20, II
Reclamation, Bureau of	43, I
Refugee Resettlement, Office of	45, IV
Regional Action Planning Commissions	13, V
Relocation Allowances	41, 302
Research and Special Programs Administration	49, I
Rural Business-Cooperative Service	7, XVIII, XLII
Rural Development Administration	7, XLII
Rural Housing Service	7, XVIII, XXXV
Rural Telephone Bank	7, XVI
Rural Utilities Service	7, XVII, XVIII, XLII
Saint Lawrence Seaway Development Corporation	33, IV
Science and Technology Policy, Office of	32, XXIV
Science and Technology Policy, Office of, and National Security Council	47, II
Secret Service	31, IV
Securities and Exchange Commission	17, II
Selective Service System	32, XVI
Small Business Administration	13, I
Smithsonian Institution	36, V
Social Security Administration	20, III; 48, 23
Soldiers' and Airmen's Home, United States	5, XI
Special Counsel, Office of	5, VIII
Special Education and Rehabilitative Services, Office of	34, III
State Department	22, I; 28, XI
Federal Acquisition Regulation	48, 6
Surface Mining and Reclamation Appeals, Board of	30, III
Surface Mining Reclamation and Enforcement, Office of	30, VII
Surface Transportation Board	49, X
Susquehanna River Basin Commission	18, VIII
Technology Administration	15, XI
Technology Policy, Assistant Secretary for	37, IV

Agency	CFR Title, Subtitle or Chapter
Technology, Under Secretary for	37, V
Tennessee Valley Authority	5, LXIX; 18, XIII
Thrift Supervision Office, Department of the Treasury	12, V
Trade Representative, United States, Office of	15, XX
Transportation, Department of	5, L
Commercial Space Transportation	14, III
Contract Appeals, Board of	48, 63
Emergency Management and Assistance	44, IV
Federal Acquisition Regulation	48, 12
Federal Aviation Administration	14, I
Federal Highway Administration	23, I, II
Federal Motor Carrier Safety Administration	49, III
Federal Railroad Administration	49, II
Federal Transit Administration	49, VI
Maritime Administration	46, II
National Highway Traffic Safety Administration	23, II, III; 49, V
Research and Special Programs Administration	49, I
Saint Lawrence Seaway Development Corporation	33, IV
Secretary of Transportation, Office of	14, II; 49, Subtitle A
Surface Transportation Board	49, X
Transportation Statistics Bureau	49, XI
Transportation, Office of	7, XXXIII
Transportation Security Administration	49, XII
Transportation Statistics Bureau	49, XI
Travel Allowances, Temporary Duty (TDY)	41, 301
Treasury Department	5, XXI; 12, XV; 17, IV; 31, IX
Alcohol and Tobacco Tax and Trade Bureau	27, I
Community Development Financial Institutions Fund	12, XVIII
Comptroller of the Currency	12, I
Customs and Border Protection Bureau	19, I
Engraving and Printing, Bureau of	31, VI
Federal Acquisition Regulation	48, 10
Federal Law Enforcement Training Center	31, VII
Fiscal Service	31, II
Foreign Assets Control, Office of	31, V
Internal Revenue Service	26, I
International Investment, Office of	31, VIII
Monetary Offices	31, I
Secret Service	31, IV
Secretary of the Treasury, Office of	31, Subtitle A
Thrift Supervision, Office of	12, V
Truman, Harry S. Scholarship Foundation	45, XVIII
United States and Canada, International Joint Commission	22, IV
United States and Mexico, International Boundary and Water Commission, United States Section	22, XI
Utah Reclamation Mitigation and Conservation Commission	43, III
Veterans Affairs Department	38, I
Federal Acquisition Regulation	48, 8
Veterans' Employment and Training Service, Office of the Assistant Secretary for	41, 61; 20, IX
Vice President of the United States, Office of	32, XXVIII
Vocational and Adult Education, Office of	34, IV
Wage and Hour Division	29, V
Water Resources Council	18, VI
Workers' Compensation Programs, Office of	20, I
World Agricultural Outlook Board	7, XXXVIII

List of CFR Sections Affected

All changes in this volume of the Code of Federal Regulations that were made by documents published in the FEDERAL REGISTER since January 1, 2001, are enumerated in the following list. Entries indicate the nature of the changes effected. Page numbers refer to FEDERAL REGISTER pages. The user should consult the entries for chapters and parts as well as sections for revisions.

For the period before January 1, 2001, see the "List of CFR Sections Affected, 1949–1963, 1964–1972, 1973–1985, and 1986–2000" published in 11 volumes.

2001

46 CFR
66 FR Page

Chapter I
167.65–45 (a) and (c) amended 48621
172.048 Added 55574
172.065 Tables (a) and (b) amended 55574
172.070 Added 55575
182.455 (c) amended 48621
196.05–1 (a) and (c) amended 48621
199.620 (a) table amended; (m) removed 48621

2002

46 CFR
67 FR Page

Chapter I
167.05–40 Added; interim 21082
167.15–30 Heading, (a)(1) and (2) revised; interim 21082
167.15–33 Added; interim 21083
 OMB number 55162
 OMB number correctly added 64315
167.15–35 (b) and (c) amended; interim 21083
169 Authority citation revised 34799
169.103 (a) and (b) revised 34799
169.107 (a) through (f) and (h) through (z) paragraph designations and (g) removed; amended 34799
169.229 Heading, (a)(1) and (2) revised; interim 21083
169.230 Added; interim 21083
 OMB number 55162
 OMB number correctly added 64315

46 CFR—Continued
67 FR Page

Chapter I—Continued
169.231 (b) redesignated as (c); new (b) added; interim 21084
169.513 (b) revised 58541
169.531 Removed 58541
169.837 (b)(4) revised 58541
175 Authority citation revised 34799
175.118 Added 34799
175.400 Amended; interim 21084
 Amended 34800
176.600 Heading, (a) and (c) introductory text revised; (b) amended; (e) added 21084
176.612 Redesignated as 176.665; interim 21084
176.615 Added; interim 21084
 OMB number 55162
176.620 Added; interim 21085
176.625 Added; interim 21085
176.630 Redesignated as 176.670; interim 21084
 Added; interim 21085
 OMB number 55162
176.635 Added; interim 21085
176.640 Added; interim 21086
 OMB number 55162
176.645 Added; interim 21086
176.650 Added; interim 21086
176.655 Added; interim 21086
 OMB number 55162
176.660 Added; interim 21086
 OMB number 55162
176.665 Redesignated from 176.612; interim 21084
 (a) and (c) amended; interim 21087
176.670 Redesignated as 176.675; new 176.670 redesignated from 176.630; interim 21084

565

46 CFR—Continued

67 FR Page

Chapter I—Continued
176.675 Redesignated from 176.670; interim.................................21084
  Amended; interim........................21087
183.380 (f) amended...........................61279
185.730 (a) and (b) revised................58542
188 Authority citation revised......34800
188.05–1 (a) introductory text and table revised;............................34800
189.55–15 (a)(2) amended; (a)(3) removed; (a)(4) redesignated as (a)(3)...61279
199 Authority citation revised......34807
199.30 Amended.............................34807
199.190 (g)(3) revised......................58542
199.620 (a) table revised; (q) added..58542

2003

46 CFR

68 FR Page

Chapter I
Chapter I Heading revised..............16953
176 Authority citation revised......39315
  Authority citation correctly revised...41916
176.404 (a) revised; interim............39315
  Regulation at 68 FR 39315 confirmed.......................................60512
188.10–45 Second section removed; CFR correction.............45785
189.25–5 Second section removed; CFR correction........................45785

2004

(Regulations published from January 1, 2004 through October 1, 2004)

46 CFR

69 FR Page

Chapter I
166 Authority citation revised......58350
167 Authority citation revised......58350
167.01–20 (b) amended....................58350
167.05–40 Regulation at 67 FR 21082 confirmed.........................47382
167.15–30 Regulation at 67 FR 21082 confirmed.........................47382
167.15–33 Regulation at 67 FR 21083 confirmed.........................47382
167.15–35 Regulation at 67 FR 21083 confirmed.........................47382
168 Authority citation revised......58350
169 Authority citation revised......58350
169.117 (b) amended........................58350

46 CFR—Continued

69 FR Page

Chapter I—Continued
169.229 Regulation at 67 FR 21083 confirmed.................................47382
169.230 Regulation at 67 FR 21083 confirmed.................................47382
169.231 Regulation at 67 FR 21084 confirmed.................................47382
170 Authority citation revised......58350
170.015 Nomenclature change........18803
170.020 (b) amended.......................58350
171 Authority citation revised......58350
172 Authority citation revised......58350
172.020 Nomenclature change........18803
173 Authority citation revised......58350
174 Authority citation revised......58350
174.007 Nomenclature change........18803
175 Authority citation revised......47384, 58351
175.400 Regulation at 67 FR 21084 confirmed.................................47382
  Amended 47384, 58351
175.600 Nomenclature change........18803
175.900 (b) amended........................58351
176 Authority citation revised......47384
176.600 Regulation at 67 FR 21084 confirmed.................................47382
176.612 Regulation at 67 FR 21084 confirmed.................................47382
176.615 Regulation at 67 FR 21084 confirmed.................................47382
176.620 Regulation at 67 FR 21085 confirmed.................................47382
  Revised...47384
176.625 Regulation at 67 FR 21085 confirmed.................................47382
176.630 Regulations at 67 FR 21084 and 21085 confirmed 47382
  (d) amended 47384
176.635 Regulation at 67 FR 21085 confirmed.................................47382
176.640 Regulation at 67 FR 21086 confirmed.................................47382
  (c) added 47384
176.645 Regulation at 67 FR 21086 confirmed.................................47382
  (a)(3) amended 47384
176.650 (a)(2) revised......................47384
176.655 Regulation at 67 FR 21086 confirmed.................................47382
  (a) revised; (d) added.....................47384
176.660 Regulation at 67 FR 21086 confirmed.................................47382
  (a) and (d)(1) revised 47384
176.665 Regulations at 67 FR 21084 and 21087 confirmed 47382
176.670 Regulation at 67 FR 21084 confirmed.................................47382

List of CFR Sections Affected

46 CFR—Continued

69 FR Page

Chapter I—Continued
176.675 Regulations at 67 FR 21084
  and 21087 confirmed 47382
177 Authority citation revised 58351
177.202 (d) amended 58351
178 Authority citation revised 58351
179 Authority citation revised 58351
180 Authority citation revised 58351
181 Authority citation revised 58351
182 Authority citation revised 58351
182.455 (a)(1) amended 58351
183 Authority citation revised 58351
184 Authority citation revised 58351
185 Authority citation revised 58351
188 Authority citation revised 58351
188.01-15 (b) amended 58351

46 CFR—Continued

69 FR Page

Chapter I—Continued
189 Authority citation revised 58351
190 Authority citation revised 58351
193 Authority citation revised 58351
193.01-3 Nomenclature change 18803
194 Authority citation revised 58351
195 Authority citation revised 58351
196 Authority citation revised 58352
197 Authority citation revised 58352
197.510 Nomenclature change 18803
199 Authority citation revised 58352
199.05 Nomenclature change 18803
  (a) amended 58352
199.30 Amended............................. 58352
199.175 (b)(21)(ii)(B) amended 58352